Age	Physical Developments	Neurological Developments	Cognitive Developments	Language Developments	Emotional Developments	Social Developments	Self/Gender/Identity Developments	Moral Developments
18–30 months	Toddler can walk up steps. Artwork consists of scribbles.	Number of synapses increases. Myelination of frontal lobes occurs; this development may underlie self-awareness. Unneeded synapses are pruned.	Toddler uses mental representations and symbols. Object permanency is achieved. Toddler can form concepts and categories. Episodic memory emerges. Preoperational stage begins.	Naming explosion takes place. First sentences are often telegraphic. Child begins to engage in conversations. Child overregularizes language rules.	Self-evaluative emotions (embarrassment, envy, empathy) have emerged, as well as precursors of shame and guilt. Negativism begins. Self-evaluative emotions emerge.	Urge for autonomy is developing. Conflicts with older siblings increase. Play with others is mostly parallel.	Child recognizes self in a mirror. Use of first-person pronouns shows self-awareness. Gender awareness emerges.	Child may show prosocial behavior. Guilt, shame, and empathy promote moral development. Aggression occurs in conflicts over toys and space.
30–36 months	Child has full set of primary teeth. Child can jump in place.	Neurons continue to undergo integration and differentiation.	Child can count. Child knows basic color words. Child understands analogies about familiar items. Child can explain familiar causal relations.	Child learns new words almost daily. Child combines three or more words, and can say up to 1,000 words. Child uses past tense.	Child shows growing ability to "read" others' emotions, mental states, and intentions.	Child shows increasing interest in other people, especially children.	Child applies descriptive terms to self.	Aggression becomes less physical, more verbal.
3–4 years	Child can copy shapes and draws designs. Child can pour liquids, eat with silverware, and use toilet alone. Child dresses self with help.	Brain is about 90 percent adult weight. Handedness is apparent. Myelination of pathways related to hearing is complete.	Child understands symbols. Autographical memory may begin. Child engages in pretend play. Child can do pictorial calculations involving whole numbers. Child understands fractional qualities.	Vocabulary, grammar, and syntax are improving and more complex. Emergent literacy skills are developing. Private speech increases.	Negativism peaks; temper tantrums are common. Little explicit awareness of pride and shame.	Child shows increasing interest in other people. Pretend play has sociodramatic themes. Sibling conflicts over property are common.	Children play with others of same sex, reinforcing gender-typed behavior. Self-definition focuses on external traits. Thinking about the self is all-or-none.	Altruism and other prosocial behavior become more common; motive is to earn praise and avoid disapproval. Guilt and concern about wrongdoing peaks. Moral reasoning is rigid.
5–6 years	Child can descend stairway unaided, hop, jump, and change directions. Child dresses self without help. Primary teeth begin to fall out, replaced by permanent teeth.	Brain is almost adult size, but not fully developed. Cortical regions connected with language are maturing.	Theory of mind matures: child can distinguish between fantasy and reality. Encoding, generalization, and strategy construction begin to become more efficient.	Speech is almost adultlike, and spoken vocabulary is about 2,600 words. Child understands about 20,000 words. Child can retell plots.	Negativism declines. Child recognizes pride and shame in others, but not in self.	Patterns of bullying and victimization may be established.	Sense of competence is developing. Self-concept links various aspects of the self, mostly in positive terms. Gender constancy is achieved.	Moral reasoning is becoming less inflexible.

(Continued inside back cover)

Human Development

Human Development

Eleventh Edition

Diane E. Papalia

Sally Wendkos Olds

Ruth Duskin Feldman

Boston   Burr Ridge, IL   Dubuque, IA   New York   San Francisco   St. Louis
Bangkok   Bogotá   Caracas   Kuala Lumpur   Lisbon   London   Madrid   Mexico City
Milan   Montreal   New Delhi   Santiago   Seoul   Singapore   Sydney   Taipei   Toronto

Mc Graw Hill **Higher Education**

Published by McGraw-Hill, an imprint of The McGraw-Hill Companies, Inc., 1221 Avenue of the Americas, New York, NY 10020. Copyright © 2009, 2007, 2004, 2001, 1998, 1995, 1992, 1989, 1986, 1981, 1978. All rights reserved. No part of this publication may be reproduced or distributed in any form or by any means, or stored in a database or retrieval system, without the prior written consent of The McGraw-Hill Companies, Inc., including, but not limited to, in any network or other electronic storage or transmission, or broadcast for distance learning.

This book is printed on acid-free paper.

3 4 5 6 7 8 9 0 DOW/DOW 0 9

ISBN: 978-0-07-337016-3
MHID: 0-07-337016-9

Editor in Chief: *Michael Ryan*
Publisher: *Beth Mejia*
Executive Editor: *Mike Sugarman*
Executive Marketing Manager: *James Headley*
Director of Development: *Dawn Groundwater*
Developmental Editor: *Joanne Butler*
Supplements Editor: *Emily Pecora*
Production Editor: *Holly Paulsen*
Manuscript Editor: *Jan McDearmon*
Art Director: *Preston Thomas*
Design Manager: *Margarite Reynolds*
Text Designer: *Kay Lieberherr, Linda Robertson*
Cover Designer: *Hiroko Chastain*
Illustrator: *Dartmouth Publishing, Inc.*
Senior Photo Research Coordinator: *Nora Agbayani*
Photo Research: *Toni Michaels*
Permissions Editor: *Marty Moga*
Media Project Manager: *Thomas Brierly*
Production Supervisor: *Tandra Jorgensen*
Composition: *10.5/13 Times by Aptara, Inc.*
Printing: *45# New Era Matt Plus,* RR Donnelley
Cover: *Hans Neleman/Getty Images*

Credits: The credits section for this book begins on page C-1 and is considered an extension of the copyright page.

Library of Congress Cataloging-in-Publication Data has been applied for.

www.mhhe.com

About the Authors

As a professor, **Diane E. Papalia** taught thousands of undergraduates at the University of Wisconsin–Madison. She received her bachelor's degree in psychology from Vassar College and both her master's degree in child development and family relations and her Ph.D. in life-span developmental psychology from West Virginia University. She has published numerous articles in such professional journals as *Human Development, International Journal of Aging and Human Development, Sex Roles, Journal of Experimental Child Psychology,* and *Journal of Gerontology.* Most of these papers have dealt with her major research focus, cognitive development from childhood through old age. She is especially interested in intelligence in old age and factors that contribute to the maintenance of intellectual functioning in late adulthood. She is a Fellow in the Gerontological Society of America. She is the coauthor of *A Child's World,* now in its eleventh edition, with Sally Wendkos Olds and Ruth Duskin Feldman; of *Adult Development and Aging,* now in its third edition, with Harvey L. Sterns, Ruth Duskin Feldman, and Cameron J. Camp; of *Psychology* with Sally Wendkos Olds; and of *Child Development: A Topical Approach* with Dana Gross and Ruth Duskin Feldman.

Sally Wendkos Olds is an award-winning professional writer who has written more than 200 articles in leading magazines and is the author or coauthor of seven books addressed to general readers, in addition to the three textbooks she has coauthored with Diane E. Papalia, two of them with Ruth Duskin Feldman. Her newest book, *Super Granny: Cool Projects, Activities, and Other Great Stuff to Do with Your Grandkids,* is addressed to contemporary grandmothers. She is currently revising her classic guide *The Complete Book of Breastfeeding* for its fourth edition. She is also the author of *A Balcony in Nepal: Glimpses of a Himalayan Village, The Working Parents' Survival Guide,* and *The Eternal Garden: Seasons of Our Sexuality,* and the coauthor of *Raising a Hyperactive Child* (winner of the Family Service Association of America National Media Award) and *Helping Your Child Find Values to Live By.* She has spoken widely on the topics of her books and articles to both professional and lay audiences, in person and on television and radio. She received her bachelor's degree from the University of Pennsylvania, where she majored in English literature and minored in psychology. She was elected to Phi Beta Kappa and was graduated summa cum laude.

Ruth Duskin Feldman is an award-winning writer and educator. With Diane E. Papalia and Sally Wendkos Olds, she has coauthored four editions of *A Child's World* and six editions of *Human Development,* including this one. She also is coauthor of *Adult Development and Aging* and of *Child Development: A Topical Approach.* A former teacher, she has developed educational materials for all levels from elementary school through college and has prepared ancillaries to accompany the Papalia-Olds books. She is author or coauthor of four books addressed to general readers, including *Whatever Happened to the Quiz Kids? Perils and Profits of Growing Up Gifted,* republished in 2000 as an Authors Guild Back-in-Print edition of iUniverse. She has written for numerous newspapers and magazines and has lectured extensively and made national and local media appearances throughout the United States on education and gifted children. She received her bachelor's degree from Northwestern University, where she was graduated with highest distinction and was elected to Phi Beta Kappa.

To our husbands,

David Mark Olds and Gilbert Feldman,

loving partners in growth and development.

And to Diane's best friend,

the late Jeffrey L. Claflin,

who was a constant source of companionship,

comfort, and fun.

And to our grown children,

Anna Victoria,

Nancy, Jennifer, and Dorri,

Steven, Laurie, and Heidi,

who have taught us much about

child and adult development.

Brief Contents

Contents

PART **3**

Early Childhood

PART 4
Middle Childhood

PART 5
Adolescence

PART 6
Emerging and Young Adulthood

PART 7
Middle Adulthood

PART **8**

Late Adulthood

PART 9

The End of Life

Preface

Human development is a journey. From the moment of conception, human beings set out on a course of new experiences that will continue throughout their lifetime. Though each journey is unique, there are familiar landmarks: Babies grow into children, who grow into adults. The study of human development sheds light on both the unique and the shared experiences along this journey through life.

OUR AIMS FOR THIS EDITION

This most recent edition of *Human Development* represents a painstaking effort to substantially streamline the text. We know what a challenge it is to cover the depth and breadth of human development in a single term and have worked hard to provide a text that is comprehensive yet concise. In this eleventh edition, therefore, our primary aim was to **significantly shorten the text** while providing the most current information available and maintaining the engaging tone and accessible style that have been the hallmarks of this book. As always, we seek to emphasize the continuity of development and its contrasts across cultures, to highlight interrelationships among the physical, cognitive, and psychosocial domains, and to integrate theoretical, research-related, and practical concerns.

Cutting-Edge Research

We have sifted through the plethora of literature published each year to select cutting-edge theory and research that will add significantly to students' understanding. We have broadened the research base of each chapter and have added recent references throughout, as well as the most current statistics available.

An important theme of the eleventh edition is an enhanced emphasis on **evolutionary theory** as it affects the study of child development. Beginning with expanded material in Chapter 2, several chapters discuss evolutionary interpretations of topics ranging from early cognitive abilities (Chapter 5) to gender (Chapter 8).

With the growing importance of cognitive neuroscience, we now present sections on **brain development** in early and middle childhood (Chapters 7 and 9) as well as in the fetus and infant (Chapter 4) and the adolescent (Chapter 11). We include various studies throughout the text that shed light on the role of the brain in cognition and emotions. Also new to this edition are the concept of **epigenesis** (Chapter 3) and extended discussions of Esther Thelen's **dynamic systems theory** of infant development (Chapters 4 and 5). Another important change is a greatly expanded discussion of **emerging adulthood** (Chapters 13 and 14). In addition, we have added new sections on **mental health** to Chapters 13 and 15 and have significantly updated our treatment of **Alzheimer's disease** in Chapter 17.

Content Changes

Following is a chapter-by-chapter list of topics that are new to this edition or have been substantially revised and/or updated.

Chapter 1: Domains of development and Baltes' life-span approach

Chapter 2: The concept of reciprocal determinism, evolutionary theory, and longitudinal research

Chapter 3: Multiple births, sex determination, epigenesis, genetic/chromosomal abnormalities, environmental prenatal hazards, prenatal care, preconception care, and signs and symptoms of pregnancy

Chapter 4: How childbirth has changed, medicated/unmedicated delivery, low birthweight, postmaturity, stillbirth, SIDS, immunization, nutritional issues, benefits of breastfeeding, brain development, birth complications, Thelen's dynamic systems theory, and autism

Chapter 5: Infant imitative abilities, dynamic systems theory, interpretation of infant object search, symbolic development, pictorial competence, categorization, gestures, language and brain development, and evolutionary interpretation of infant memory ability

Chapter 6: Three temperamental types, Kagan's research on shyness, gender, long-term effects of attachment patterns, early child care, maltreatment, and postpartum depression

Chapter 7: Healthy eating and sleeping habits, brain development, sleep disturbances, artistic development, obesity, SES, ethnicity, homelessness, smoking, air pollution, pesticides and lead, memory, language delay, and private speech

Chapter 8: Play, evolutionary approach to gender roles, gender differences in play, aggression, sibling relations, and only children

Chapter 9: Brain development and IQ, stuttering, asthma, executive function, influence of race/ethnicity and SES on IQ, second language education, and ADHD

Chapter 10: Cultural factors and parenting practices, family structure, different family types, prejudice, bullying, and mental health

Chapter 11: Globalization of adolescence, brain development, eating disorders, drug abuse, depression, and dropouts

Chapter 12: Identity formation, sexual orientation, sexual behavior, HIV/AIDS, teen pregnancy, individuation and family conflict, family structure, antisocial behavior, and youth violence epidemic

Chapter 13: Health issues, mental health, sexual behavior, STDs, college experiences, and entering the world of work

Chapter 14: Recentering, failure to launch, adult friendships, gay relationships, fictive kin, marital relationships, becoming parents, and cohabitation.

Chapter 15: Menopause, osteoporosis, breast cancer, hormone therapy, retirement, and literacy

Chapter 16: Generativity, marriage and health, childlessness, aging parents, and caregiving

Chapter 17: Population statistics, life expectancy including racial and gender issues, caloric restriction effects, the aging brain, sexual functioning, and Alzheimer's disease

Chapter 18: Work and retirement trends, living arrangements, relationships, cohabitation, and mistreatment of the elderly

Chapter 19: Near death experiences, surviving a spouse, losing a child, suicide, and coping with loss

Cultural Influences

This edition continues our emphasis on cultural and historical influences on development. Reviewers have praised our focus on culture as a particular strength of this book. Cross-cultural research is fully integrated throughout the text as well as highlighted in Window on the World boxes, reflecting the diversity of the population in the United States and in other societies.

Pedagogical Features

We are gratified by the overwhelmingly favorable response to the pedagogy we have developed for *Human Development,* which includes the following features.

A new feature, Did You Know . . ., introduces each chapter by highlighting interesting and enlightening findings mentioned in the chapter.

Two types of boxes enhance the chapters by highlighting topics related to the main text. Each box contains a Check It Out section referring the student to relevant Internet links where further information can be found.

- *Research in Action* boxes provide an in-depth examination of research topics briefly mentioned in the text. Research in Action boxes include "The Autism 'Epidemic'" (Chapter 4), "Does Play Have an Evolutionary Basis?" (Chapter 8), "Do Barbie Dolls Affect Girls' Body Image?" (Chapter 9), "Intimate Partner Violence" (Chapter 14), and "Centenarians" (Chapter 17).

Did You **Know...**

- In some societies there is no concept of adolescence or middle age?
- Many scholars maintain that races are *not* physically distinguishable categories of people?
- Within the next 50 years, it has been estimated that about half the U.S. population will be Hispanic, black, or Asian?
- More than 36 million people in the United States live in poverty?
- According to some research, children who have been exposed to television and computers from an early age develop differently than children who grow up without them?
- Memory, strength, and endurance can be improved with training and practice, even in late life?

These are just a few of the interesting and important topics we will cover in this chapter as you begin your study of human development. In this introductory chapter, we describe how the field of human development has itself developed. We present the goals and basic concepts of the field today. We identify aspects of human development and show how they interrelate. Next, we summarize major developments during each period of life. Finally, we look at influences on development and the contexts in which it occurs.

BOX 9-1 Research *in Action*

Do Barbie Dolls Affect Girls' Body Image?

"I looked at a Barbie doll when I was 6 and said, 'This is what I want to look like,'" the model Cindy Jackson said on CBS News (2004). "I think a lot of little 6-year-old girls or younger even now are looking at that doll and thinking, 'I want to be her.'" It took 31 operations, 14 years, and $100,000, but Jackson's obsession with Barbie got her a new look and an entry in the *Guinness Book of World Records.*

Barbie is the best-selling fashion doll around the world. In the United States, 99 percent of 3- to 10-year-old girls own at least one Barbie doll, and the average girl owns eight. Though she is sold as "every girl," Barbie is far from average. Her body proportions are "unrealistic, unattainable, and unhealthy" (Dittmar, Halliwell, & Ive, 2006, p. 284). "If she were alive, Barbie would be a woman standing 7 feet tall with a waistline of 18 inches and a bust-line of 38 to 40 inches," writes the psychotherapist Abigail Natenshon (2006), a specialist in eating disorders. In fact, Barbie's waist, as compared to her bust size, is 39 percent smaller than that of a woman with the eating disorder anorexia (see Chapter 11). Fewer than 1 in 100,000 women actually have Barbie's body proportions.

According to Bandura's social-cognitive theory, Barbie dolls are role models for young girls, transmitting a cultural ideal of beauty. The media reinforce this ideal. Girls who do not measure up may experience *body dissatisfaction*—negative thoughts about their bodies, leading to low self-esteem. By age 6, studies show, many girls wish to be thinner than they are.

To test Barbie's effect on young girls' body image, researchers read picture books to English girls, ages 5½ to 8½. One group saw picture stories about Barbie; control groups saw stories about a full-figured fashion doll called Emme or about no doll (Dittmar et al., 2006). Afterward, the girls completed questionnaires in which they were asked to agree or disagree with such statements as "I'm pretty happy about the way I look" and "I really like what I weigh."

The findings were striking. Among the youngest girls (ages 5½ to 6½), a single exposure to the Barbie picture book significantly lowered body esteem and increased the discrepancy between actual and ideal body size. This did not happen with the girls in the two control groups. The effect of Barbie on body image was even stronger in 6½- to 7½-year-olds. However, the findings for the oldest group, ages 7½ to 8½, were completely different: Pictures of Barbie had no direct effect on body image at this age.

What accounts for this difference? Girls up to age 7 may be in a sensitive period in which they acquire idealized images of beauty. As girls grow older, they may internalize the ideal of thinness as part of their emerging identity. Once the ideal is internalized, its power no longer depends on direct exposure to the original role model (Dittmar et al., 2006).

Or, it may be that girls simply outgrow Barbie. In another study (Kuther & McDonald, 2004), sixth- through eighth-grade girls were asked about their childhood experiences with Barbie. All the girls had owned at least two Barbie dolls but said they no longer played with them. Looking back, some of the girls saw Barbie as a positive influence: "She is like the perfect person . . . that everyone wants to be like." But most of the girls saw Barbie as an unrealistic role model: "Barbie dolls provide a false stereotype . . . as it is physically impossible to attain the same body size. . . . There wouldn't be enough room for organs and other necessary things. . . . Barbie has this perfect body and now every girl is trying to have her body because they are so unhappy with themselves."

Barbie now has a major competitor: Bratz, an ultrathin doll with a large round face, sassy mouth, and heavy makeup. Longitudinal research will help determine whether fashion dolls such as Barbie and Bratz have a lasting impact on body image.

What's Your View?

If you had (or have) a young daughter, would you allow her to play with Barbie or Bratz dolls? Why or why not?

Check It Out

For more information on this topic, go to www.bam.gov/ teachers/body_image_dolls.html. This site describes a classroom activity in which students take measurements of toy action figures and fashion dolls and figure out how they would look if they were the height of a normal adult man or woman.

- *Window on the World* boxes explore the way an issue in the chapter is treated or experienced in one or more foreign cultures, or in a United States minority group. Window on the World boxes include "Surviving the First Five Years of Life" (Chapter 7), "The Globalization of Adolescence" (Chapter 11), and "Cultural Differences in Women's Experience of Menopause" (Chapter 15).

BOX 7-1 Window *on the World*

Surviving the First Five Years of Life

The chances of a child's living to his or her fifth birthday have doubled during the past four decades, but prospects for survival depend to a great extent on where the child lives. Worldwide, more than 17 million children under 5 died in 1970. In 2007, the number of deaths in this age group dropped below 10 million for the first time in modern history (Bryce et al., 2005; UNICEF Press Centre, 2007; WHO, 2003)—but this is still far too many, and the gains have not benefited all children equally.

International efforts to improve child health focus on the first five years because nearly 9 out of 10 deaths of children under age 15 occur during those years. Fully 98 percent of child deaths occur in poor, rural regions of developing countries; 42 percent of these deaths occur in sub-Saharan Africa and 29 percent in Southeast Asia (Bryce et al., 2005; WHO, 2003; see figure). A baby born in Sierra Leone on Africa's west coast is three and a half times more likely to die before age 5 than a child born in India and more than 100 times more likely to die than a child born in Iceland, which has the world's lowest child mortality rate (WHO, 2003).

Worldwide, four major causes of death, accounting for 54 percent of deaths in children younger than 5, are communicable

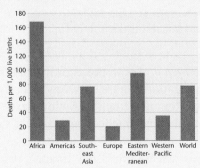

Comparative child mortality in six regions of the world, 2002.
(Source: WHO, 2003.)

Our comprehensive learning system is a unique, coordinated set of elements that work together to foster active learning. The names of the pedagogical features—Guideposts, Checkpoints, and What's Your View? (critical thinking questions)—are designed to reinforce our central theme of a journey through life.

- *Guideposts for Study:* This list of questions at the beginning of each chapter highlights the key concepts to learn. Each Guidepost appears again to introduce the related text section.

- *Checkpoints:* These questions, in the margins throughout each chapter, help students assess how well they grasp the concepts in the preceding text sections.

Guideposts *for Study*

1. How does conception normally occur, and what causes multiple births?
2. How does heredity operate in determining sex and transmitting normal and abnormal traits?
3. How do scientists study the relative influences of heredity and environment, and how do heredity and environment work together?
4. What roles do heredity and environment play in physical health, intelligence, and personality?

- *What's Your View?* These critical thinking questions, in the margins throughout each chapter and in the boxes, encourage students to examine their thoughts about a topic or to apply the information presented in the text.

- *Summary and Key Terms:* Concluding each chapter, these resources, organized under each Guidepost and including key terms, guide students as they review the chapter and check their learning.

Summary and Key Terms

Basic Theoretical Issues

Guidepost 1: *What purposes do theories serve, and what are two basic theoretical issues on which developmental scientists differ?*

- A theory is used to organize and explain data and generate hypotheses that can be tested by research.
- Developmental theories differ on two basic issues: the active or reactive character of development and the existence of continuity or discontinuity in development.
- Two contrasting models of human development are the mechanistic model and the organismic model.

theory (22)
hypotheses (22)
mechanistic model (23)

stage theory, Vygotsky's sociocultural theory, and the information-processing approach. Neo-Piagetian theorists blend Piagetian principles with insights gained from information-processing research.

cognitive perspective (30)
cognitive-stage theory (31)
organization (31)
schemes (31)
adaptation (31)
assimilation (31)
accommodation (31)
equilibration (31)
sociocultural theory (32)
zone of proximal development (ZPD) (32)

Supplementary Materials

Human Development, eleventh edition, is accompanied by a complete learning and teaching package. Each component of this package has been thoroughly revised and expanded to include important new course material.

For the Student

Online Learning Center for Students The official website for the text (www.mhhe.com/papaliahd11e) provides students with access to a variety of learning tools, including chapter outlines, key terms flashcards, student self-quizzes, web links to relevant psychology sites, and video segments available through McGraw-Hill's exclusive Discovery Channel licensing arrangement, chosen to illustrate key concepts in human development.

Student Study Guide Peggy Skinner, South Plains College
This comprehensive study guide (ISBN 0077234936) is organized by chapter and integrates the Guideposts for Study found in the main text. It is designed to help students make the most of their time when reviewing the material in the text and when studying for exams. The study guide includes a variety of self-tests, including true/false, multiple-choice, and essay questions.

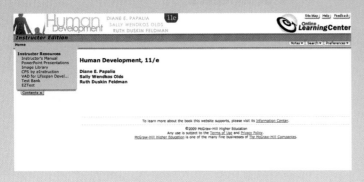

For the Instructor

Online Learning Center for Instructors The password-protected instructor side of the Online Learning Center (www.mhhe.com/papaliahd11e) contains the Instructor's Manual, Test Bank, PowerPoint slides, CPS Questions, Image Gallery, and other valuable material to help you design and enhance your course. See more information about specific assets below. Ask your local McGraw-Hill representative for password information.

- **Instructor's Manual,** authored by Tammy Lochridge, Itawamba Community College. Designed specifically for the eleventh edition, this manual contains valuable resources for both new and experienced teachers. Organized around the Guideposts for Study in the textbook, the Instructor's Manual offers Total Teaching Package outlines, suggested lecture openers, critical thinking exercises, essay questions, ideas for independent study, video and multimedia resources, suggested readings, and web resources for each chapter.

- **Test Bank,** authored by Ann Mullis, Florida State University. This comprehensive test bank offers more than 2,000 multiple-choice and essay questions. Organized by chapter, the questions are designed to test factual, applied, and conceptual understanding. Consistent with the integrative nature of our supplements package, all test bank questions are keyed to the Guideposts for Study in the text, and are compatible with EZ Test, McGraw-Hill's computerized test bank program.

  McGraw-Hill's EZ Test is a flexible and easy-to-use electronic testing program that allows instructors to create tests from book-specific items. It accommodates a wide range of question types, and allows instructors to edit existing questions or create new ones. Multiple versions of the test can be created, and any test can be exported for use with course management systems such as WebCT or Blackboard. EZ Test Online is a new service that gives you a place to easily administer your EZ Test–created exams and quizzes online. The program is available for Windows and Macintosh environments.

- **PowerPoint Slides**, authored by Wanda Clark, South Plains College. These presentations cover the key points of each chapter and include charts and graphs from the text. They can be used as is, or you may modify them to meet your specific needs.

- **Classroom Performance System (CPS) by eInstruction.** These questions, formatted for use with the interactive Classroom Performance System, are organized by chapter and designed to test factual, applied, and conceptual understanding. These test questions are also compatible with EZTest, McGraw-Hill's computerized test bank program.

- **Image Gallery.** These files include all of the figures, tables, and photos from this textbook (more than 150 images in all) for which McGraw-Hill holds copyright.

McGraw-Hill's Visual Asset Database for Lifespan Development (VAD) McGraw-Hill's Visual Assets Database for Lifespan Development (VAD 2.0) (www.mhhe.com/vad) is an online database of videos for use in the developmental psychology classroom, created specifically for instructors. You can customize classroom presentations by downloading the videos to your computer and showing the videos on their own or insert them into your course cartridge or PowerPoint presentations. All of the videos are available with or without captions. Ask your McGraw-Hill representative for access information.

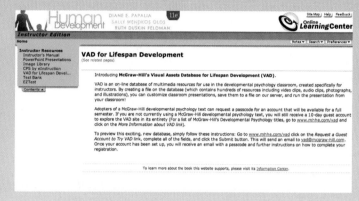

Multimedia Courseware for Child Development
Charlotte J. Patterson, University of Virginia
This video-based set of two CD-ROMs covers classic and contemporary experiments in child development. Respected researcher Charlotte J. Patterson selected the content and wrote accompanying modules that can be assigned to students. These modules include suggestions for additional projects as well as a testing component. Multimedia Courseware can be packaged with the text at a discount.

McGraw-Hill Contemporary Learning Series

- *Annual Editions: Human Development.* This reader is a collection of articles on topics related to the latest research and thinking in human development. Annual Editions are updated regularly and include useful features such as a topic guide, an annotated table of contents, unit overviews, and a topical index.

- *Taking Sides: Clashing Views on Controversial Issues in Life-Span Development.* Current controversial issues are presented in a debate-style format designed to stimulate student interest and develop critical thinking skills. Each issue is thoughtfully framed with an issue summary, an issue introduction, and a postscript.

- *Notable Selections in Human Development.* This book is a collection of articles, book excerpts, and research studies that have shaped the study of human development and our contemporary understanding of it. The selections are organized topically around major areas of study within human development. Each selection is preceded by a headnote that established the relevance of the article or study and provides biographical information on the author.

ACKNOWLEDGMENTS

We would like to express our gratitude to the many friends and colleagues who, through their work and their interest, helped us clarify our thinking about human development. Their thoughtful suggestions and recommendations have influenced the content of this and previous editions of *Human Development*. This book is their book, too. We especially appreciate the assistance of the following individuals:

Mike Arpin, *Coffeyville Community College*

Renée L. Babcock, *Central Michigan University*

Alan Bates, *Snead State Community College*

Dan Bellack, *Trident Technical College*

Deneen Brackett, *Prairie State College*

Gregory S. Braswell, *Illinois State University*

Joy Brown, *University of North Alabama*

Amy Carrigan, *University of St. Francis*

Evelyn Chiang, *University of Florida*

Perle Slavic Cowen, *College of Nursing, University of Iowa*

Pam Deyell-Gingold, *Merced College*

Elaina Frieda, *Auburn University*

Nicole Gendler, *University of New Mexico*

Arthur Gonchar, *University of La Verne*

Lori Harris, *Murray State University*

Jutta Heckhausen, *University of California, Irvine*

Henrietta Hestick, *Baltimore County Community College*

Debra Hollister, *Valencia Community College*

Heather Holmes-Lonergan, *Metro State College of Denver*

Suzy Horton, *Mesa Community College*

John Hotz, *St. Cloud State University*

Robyn Inmon, *South Plains College*

Kelly Jarvis, *University of California, Irvine*

Jyotsna Kalavar, *Pennsylvania State University New Kensington*

Bruce Kozak, *Daytona Beach Community College*

Deborah Laible, *Southern Methodist University*

Sonya Leathers, *University of Illinois at Chicago*

Tammy B. Lochridge, *Itawamba Community College*

Karla Miley, *Black Hawk College*

Veronica F. Ogata, *Kapi'olani Community College*

Kaelin Olsen, *Utah State University*

Randall Osborne, *Texas State University–San Marcos*

Lori K. Perez, *California State University, Fresno*

Diane Powers, *Iowa Central Community College, Catonsville*

Thomas Rabak, *Central Washington University*

Jennifer Redlin, *Minnesota State Community and Technical College*

Teresa Roberts, *California State University, Sacramento*

Stephanie J. Rowley, *University of Michigan*

Pamela Schuetze, *Buffalo State College*

Peter Segal, *York College of the City University of New York*

Jack Shilkret, *Anne Arundel Community College*

Peggy Skinner, *South Plains College*

J. Blake Snider, *East Tennessee State University*

Mary-Ellen Sollinger, *Delaware Technical and Community College*

Kevin Sumrall, *Montgomery College*

Rachelle Tannenbaum, *Anne Arundel Community College*

Monique L. Ward, *University of Michigan*

Kristin Webb, *Alamance Community College*

Colin William, *Columbus State Community College*

Lois Willoughby, *Miami-Dade College, Kendall*

We appreciate the strong support we have had from our publisher. We would like to express our special thanks to Mike Sugarman, executive editor; Dawn Groundwater, director of development; Joanne Butler, freelance developmental editor, whose dedicated oversight benefited this project in innumerable ways; Carol Mulligan, who took great care in preparing the bibliography; Holly Paulsen, production editor; Margarite Reynolds, design manager; Toni Michaels, photo researcher; and Emily Pecora, supplements editor.

As always, we welcome and appreciate comments from readers, which help us continue to improve *Human Development*

Diane E. Papalia
Sally Wendkos Olds
Ruth Duskin Feldman

There is nothing permanent except change.

—Heraclitus, fragment (sixth century B.C.)

Did You **Know...**

- In some societies there is no concept of adolescence or middle age?
- Many scholars maintain that races are *not* physically distinguishable categories of people?
- Within the next 50 years, it has been estimated that about half the U.S. population will be Hispanic, black, or Asian?
- More than 36 million people in the United States live in poverty?
- According to some research, children who have been exposed to television and computers from an early age develop differently than children who grow up without them?
- Memory, strength, and endurance can be improved with training and practice, even in late life?

These are just a few of the interesting and important topics we will cover in this chapter as you begin your study of human development. In this introductory chapter, we describe how the field of human development has itself developed. We present the goals and basic concepts of the field today. We identify aspects of human development and show how they interrelate. Next, we summarize major developments during each period of life. Finally, we look at influences on development and the contexts in which it occurs.

After you have studied this chapter, you should be able to answer each of the Guidepost questions on the following page. Look for them again in the margins throughout the chapter, where they point to important concepts. To check your understanding of these Guideposts, review the end-of-chapter Summary. Checkpoints throughout the chapter will help you verify your understanding of what you have read.

Guideposts *for Study*

1. What is human development, and how has its study evolved?
2. What do developmental scientists study?
3. What kinds of influences make one person different from another?
4. What are seven principles of the life-span developmental approach?

Human Development: An Ever-Evolving Field

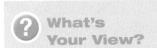
Guidepost 1

What is human development, and how has its study evolved?

human development Scientific study of processes of change and stability throughout the human life span.

From the moment of conception, human beings begin a process of change that will continue throughout their lives. A single cell becomes a living, breathing, walking, talking person. And though this single cell develops into a unique individual, the changes human beings experience during their lifetimes have certain common patterns. Babies grow and become children, who grow and become adults. Similarly, some human characteristics have common patterns. Children who are shy are likely to remain shy as adults.

Human development is the scientific study of these patterns of change and stability. Development is *systematic:* It is coherent and organized. It is *adaptive:* It is aimed at dealing with internal and external conditions of existence. Development may take varied routes and may or may not have a definite goal, but there is some connection between the often-imperceptible changes of which it is composed. Which characteristics are most likely to endure? Which are likely to change, and why? These are among the questions that the study of human development seeks to answer.

The professionals who study the science of human development are called *developmental scientists.* Their work can have a dramatic impact on human lives. Research findings often have direct application to child rearing, education, health, and social policy.

For example, researchers in Boston found that public school students who went to school hungry or lacked essential nutrients in their diet had poorer grades and more emotional and behavioral problems than their classmates. After the schools started a free breakfast program, participating students improved their math grades, were absent and tardy less often, and had fewer emotional and behavioral problems (Kleinman et al., 2002; Murphy et al., 1998). Research showing that the adolescent brain is still immature has prompted suggestions that adolescents accused of crimes be exempt from the death penalty. An understanding of adult development can help people understand and deal with life transitions: a woman returning to work after maternity leave, a person making a career change or about to retire, a widow or widower dealing with loss, someone coping with a terminal illness.

Studying the Life Span

life-span development Concept of human development as a lifelong process, which can be studied scientifically.

Developmental scientists have come to recognize human development as a lifelong process—a concept known as **life-span development.** Early studies such as the Stanford Studies of Gifted Children, which traced through old age the development of people who had been identified as unusually intelligent in childhood, the

Berkeley Growth and Guidance Studies, and the Oakland (Adolescent) Growth Study have given us much information on long-term development. More recently, Paul B. Baltes's life-span developmental approach, discussed at the end of this chapter, has provided a comprehensive conceptual framework for the study of life-span development.

Human Development Today

As the field of human development became a scientific discipline, its goals evolved to include *description, explanation, prediction,* and *intervention.* For example, to *describe* when most children say their first word or how large their vocabulary typically is at a certain age, developmental scientists observe large groups of children and establish norms, or averages, for behavior at various ages. They then attempt to *explain* how children acquire language and why some children learn to speak later than usual. This knowledge may make it possible to *predict* future behavior, such as the likelihood that a child will have serious speech problems. Finally, an understanding of how language develops may be used to *intervene* in development, for example, by giving a child speech therapy.

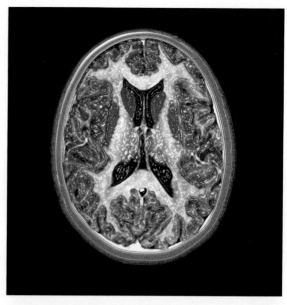

Brain imaging techniques, such as functional magnetic resonance imaging (fMRI), positron emission tomography (PET), and electroencephalogram (EEG), are used to map out where certain thought processes take place within the structure of the brain.

The scientific study of human development is ever evolving. The questions that developmental scientists seek to answer, the methods they use, and the explanations they propose are more sophisticated and more varied than they were even twenty-five years ago. These shifts reflect progress in understanding as new investigations build on or challenge those that went before. They also reflect advances in technology. Sensitive instruments that measure eye movements, heart rate, blood pressure, muscle tension, and the like are turning up intriguing connections between biological functions and childhood intelligence. Digital technology and computers allow investigators to scan infants' facial expressions for early signs of emotions and to analyze how mothers and babies communicate. Advances in brain imaging make it possible to probe the mysteries of temperament, to pinpoint the sources of logical thought, and to compare a normally aging brain with the brain of a person with dementia.

Almost from the start, developmental science has been interdisciplinary. Today students of human development draw collaboratively from a wide range of disciplines, including psychology, psychiatry, sociology, anthropology, biology, genetics (the study of inherited characteristics), family science (the interdisciplinary study of family relations), education, history, and medicine. This book includes findings from research in all these fields.

Checkpoint

Can you . . .

♦ Give examples of practical applications of research on human development?

♦ Identify four goals of the scientific study of human development?

♦ Name at least six disciplines involved in the study of human development?

The Study of Human Development: Basic Concepts

Developmental scientists study processes of change and stability in all *domains,* or aspects, of development and throughout all periods of the life span.

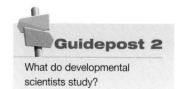

Guidepost 2

What do developmental scientists study?

Domains of Development

Developmental scientists study three major domains: physical, cognitive, and psychosocial. Growth of the body and brain, sensory capacities, motor skills, and health are parts of **physical development.** Learning, attention, memory, language,

physical development Growth of body and brain, including patterns of change in sensory capacities, motor skills, and health.

These children examining snails on a sand table are engaging in all three domains of development: sensory perception (physical development), learning (cognitive development), and social relationships building (psychosocial development).

cognitive development Pattern of change in mental abilities, such as learning, attention, memory, language, thinking, reasoning, and creativity.

psychosocial development Pattern of change in emotions, personality, and social relationships.

thinking, reasoning, and creativity make up **cognitive development.** Emotions, personality, and social relationships are aspects of **psychosocial development.**

Although we talk separately about physical, cognitive, and psychosocial development, these domains are interrelated: Each aspect of development affects the others. As one researcher points out, "Our brains work better, our thinking is sharper, our mood brighter, and our vulnerability to disease diminished if we are physically fit" (Diamond, 2007, p. 153). For example, a child with frequent ear infections may develop language more slowly than a child without this physical problem. During puberty, dramatic physical and hormonal changes affect the developing sense of self. In contrast, physical changes in the brains of some older adults may lead to intellectual and personality deterioration.

Cognitive advances and declines are closely related to physical, emotional, and social factors. A child who is precocious in language development may evoke positive reactions in others and gain in self-worth. Memory development reflects gains or losses in physical connections in the brain. An adult who has trouble remembering people's names may feel awkward and reticent in social situations.

Psychosocial development can affect cognitive and physical functioning. Indeed, without meaningful social connections, physical and mental health can suffer. Motivation and self-confidence are important contributors to school success, whereas negative emotions such as sadness, anger, fear, or anxiety about taking a test can impair performance. Researchers even have identified possible links between personality and length of life. Conversely, physical and cognitive capacities can affect psychosocial development. They contribute greatly to self-esteem and can affect social acceptance and choice of occupation.

Thus, although for simplicity's sake we look separately at physical, cognitive, and psychosocial development, development is a unified process. Throughout the text, we will highlight links among the three major domains of development.

Periods of the Life Span

social construction A concept or practice that may appear natural and obvious to those who accept it, but that in reality is an invention of a particular culture or society.

Division of the life span into periods is a **social construction:** a concept or practice that may appear natural and obvious to those who accept it, but in reality is an invention of a particular culture or society. There is no objectively definable moment when a child becomes an adult or a young person becomes old. In fact, the concept of childhood itself can be viewed as a social construction. Some evidence indicates that children in earlier times were regarded and treated much like small adults. However, this suggestion has been disputed (Ariès, 1962; Elkind, 1986; Pollock, 1983). Archaeological finds from ancient Greece show that children played with clay dolls and dice made of bones of sheep and goats. Pottery and tombstones depict children sitting on high chairs and riding goat-pulled carts (Mulrine, 2004).

The concept of *adolescence* as a period of development in industrial societies is quite recent. Until the early twentieth century, young people in the United States were considered children until they left school, married or got a job, and entered the adult world. By the 1920s, with the establishment of comprehensive high schools to meet the needs of a growing economy and with more families able to support extended formal education for their children, the teenage years became a distinct period of development (Keller, 1999). In some preindustrial societies, such as the Chippewa Indians, the concept of adolescence still does not exist. The Chippewa have only two periods of childhood: from birth until the child walks, and from walking to puberty. What we call adolescence is part of adulthood (Broude, 1995). As we discuss in Chapter 16, the Gusii of Kenya have no concept of middle age.

In this book, we follow a sequence of eight periods generally accepted in Western industrial societies. After describing the crucial changes that occur in the first period, before birth, we trace all three domains of development through infancy and toddlerhood, early childhood, middle childhood, adolescence, young adulthood, middle adulthood, and late adulthood (Table 1-1). For each period after infancy and toddlerhood (when change is most dramatic), we have combined physical and cognitive development into a single chapter.

The age divisions shown in Table 1-1 are approximate and somewhat arbitrary. This is especially true of adulthood, when there are no clear-cut social or physical landmarks, such as starting school or entering puberty, to signal a shift from one period to another. Individual differences exist in the way people deal with the characteristic events and issues of each period.

Despite these differences, certain basic developmental needs must be met and certain developmental tasks mastered during each period for normal development to occur. A new baby, for example, is dependent on adults to meet his or her basic needs for food, clothing, and shelter as well as for human contact and affection. Babies form attachments to parents or caregivers, who also become attached to them. As babies learn to walk and talk, they become toddlers. Though more self-reliant and able to assert their autonomy, they also need parents or caregivers to provide a safe environment in which to do so. During early childhood, children develop more self-control and more interest in other children. Control over behavior gradually shifts from parent to child during middle childhood, when the peer group becomes increasingly important. A main developmental task of adolescence is the search for identity—personal, sexual, and occupational. As adolescents become physically mature, they must deal with sometimes conflicting needs and emotions as they prepare to leave the parental nest.

During emerging adulthood, an exploratory period in the early to midtwenties, many people are not yet ready to settle down to the typical tasks of young adulthood: establishing independent lifestyles, occupations, and usually, families. By the thirties, most adults have successfully fulfilled those tasks. During middle adulthood, some decline in physical capabilities is likely. At the same time, many middle-aged people find excitement and challenge in life changes—launching new careers and adult children—while some face the need to care for elderly parents. In late adulthood, people need to cope with losses in their faculties, the loss of loved ones, and preparations for death. If they retire, they must deal with the loss of work-based

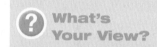

What's Your View?

• Why do you think various societies divide the periods of development differently?

Checkpoint

Can you . . .

♦ Identify the three domains of development and give examples of how they are interrelated?

♦ Name eight periods of human development (as defined in this book) and list several key issues or tasks of each period?

Age Period	Physical Developments	Cognitive Developments	Psychosocial Developments
Prenatal Period (conception to birth)	Conception occurs by normal fertilization or other means. The genetic endowment interacts with environmental influences from the start. Basic body structures and organs form; brain growth spurt begins. Physical growth is the most rapid in the life span. Vulnerability to environmental influences is great.	Abilities to learn and remember and to respond to sensory stimuli are developing.	Fetus responds to mother's voice and develops a preference for it.
Infancy and Toddlerhood (birth to age 3)	All senses and body systems operate at birth to varying degrees. The brain grows in complexity and is highly sensitive to environmental influence. Physical growth and development of motor skills are rapid.	Abilities to learn and remember are present, even in early weeks. Use of symbols and ability to solve problems develop by end of second year. Comprehension and use of language develop rapidly.	Attachments to parents and others form. Self-awareness develops. Shift from dependence toward autonomy occurs. Interest in other children increases.
Early Childhood (ages 3 to 6)	Growth is steady; appearance becomes more slender and proportions more adultlike. Appetite diminishes, and sleep problems are common. Handedness appears; fine and gross motor skills and strength improve.	Thinking is somewhat egocentric, but understanding of other people's perspectives grows. Cognitive immaturity results in some illogical ideas about the world. Memory and language improve. Intelligence becomes more predictable. Preschool experience is common, and kindergarten experience is more so.	Self-concept and understanding of emotions become more complex; self-esteem is global. Independence, initiative, and self-control increase. Gender identity develops. Play becomes more imaginative, more elaborate, and usually more social. Altruism, aggression, and fearfulness are common. Family is still the focus of social life, but other children become more important.
Middle Childhood (ages 6 to 11)	Growth slows. Strength and athletic skills improve. Respiratory illnesses are common, but health is generally better than at any other time in the life span.	Egocentrism diminishes. Children begin to think logically but concretely. Memory and language skills increase. Cognitive gains permit children to benefit from formal schooling. Some children show special educational needs and strengths.	Self-concept becomes more complex, affecting self-esteem. Coregulation reflects gradual shift in control from parents to child. Peers assume central importance.

relationships but may get increased pleasure out of friendships, family, volunteer work, and the opportunity to explore previously neglected interests. Many older people become more introspective, searching out the meaning of their lives.

Guidepost 3

What kinds of influences make one person different from another?

Influences on Development

What makes each person unique? Although students of development look at the universal processes of development experienced by all normal human beings, they must also consider **individual differences** in characteristics, influences, and

Age Period	Physical Developments	Cognitive Developments	Psychosocial Developments
Adolescence (ages 11 to about 20)	Physical growth and other changes are rapid and profound. Reproductive maturity occurs. Major health risks arise from behavioral issues, such as eating disorders and drug abuse.	Ability to think abstractly and use scientific reasoning develops. Immature thinking persists in some attitudes and behaviors. Education focuses on preparation for college or vocation.	Search for identity including sexual identity, becomes central. Relationships with parents are generally good. Peer group may exert a positive or negative influence.
Emerging and Young Adulthood (ages 20 to 40)	Physical condition peaks, then declines slightly. Lifestyle choices influence health.	Thought and moral judgments become more complex. Educational and occupational choices are made, sometimes after period of exploration.	Personality traits and styles become relatively stable, but changes in personality may be influenced by life stages and events. Intimate relationships and personal lifestyles are established but may not be lasting. Most people marry, and most become parents.
Middle Adulthood (ages 40 to 65)	Slow deterioration of sensory abilities, health, stamina, and strength may begin, but individual differences are wide. Women experience menopause.	Mental abilities peak; expertise and practical problem-solving skills are high. Creative output may decline but improve in quality. For some, career success and earning powers peak; for others, burnout or career change may occur.	Sense of identity continues to develop; midlife transition may occur. Dual responsibilities of caring for children and parents may cause stress. Launching of children leaves empty nest.
Late Adulthood (age 65 and over)	Most people are healthy and active, although health and physical abilities generally decline. Slowing of reaction time affects some aspects of functioning.	Most people are mentally alert. Although intelligence and memory may deteriorate in some areas, most people find ways to compensate.	Retirement from workforce may occur and may offer new options for use of time. People develop more flexible strategies to cope with personal losses and impending death. Relationships with family and close friends can provide important support. Search for meaning in life assumes central importance.

developmental outcomes. People differ in gender, height, weight, and body build; in health and energy level; in intelligence; and in temperament, personality, and emotional reactions. The contexts of their lives differ too: the homes, communities, and societies they live in, the relationships they have, the schools they go to (or whether they go to school at all), and how they spend their free time.

Heredity, Environment, and Maturation

Some influences on development originate primarily with **heredity:** inborn traits or characteristics inherited from the biological parents. Other influences come

individual differences Differences in characteristics, influences, or developmental outcomes.

heredity Inborn traits or characteristics inherited from the biological parents.

environment Totality of nonhereditary, or experiential, influences on development.

largely from the outer and inner **environments:** the world outside the self beginning in the womb, and the learning that comes from experience. Which of these two factors has more impact on development? The issue of the relative importance of *nature* (heredity) and *nurture* (environmental influences both before and after birth) historically generated intense debate.

Today scientists have found ways to measure more precisely the roles of heredity and environment in the development of specific traits within a population. When we look at a particular person, however, research with regard to almost all characteristics points to a blend of inheritance and experience. Thus, even though intelligence is strongly influenced by heredity, parental stimulation, education, peer influence, and other variables also affect it. Although there still is considerable dispute about the relative importance of nature and nurture, contemporary theorists and researchers are more interested in finding ways to explain how they work together rather than arguing about which factor is more important.

maturation Unfolding of a natural sequence of physical and behavioral changes.

Many typical changes of infancy and early childhood, such as the abilities to walk and talk, are tied to **maturation** of the body and brain—the unfolding of a natural sequence of physical changes and behavior patterns. As children grow into adolescents and then into adults, individual differences in innate characteristics and life experience play a greater role. Throughout life, however, maturation continues to influence certain biological processes, such as brain development.

Even in processes that all people undergo, rates and timing of development vary. Throughout this book, we talk about average ages for the occurrence of certain events: the first word, the first step, the first menstruation or nocturnal emission, the development of logical thought, and menopause. But these ages are *merely* averages. Each individual's actual age of occurrence for these events will vary. Only when deviation from the average is extreme should we consider development exceptionally advanced or delayed.

In trying to understand human development, then, we need to consider how heredity and environment interact. We need to understand which developments are primarily maturational and which are not. We need to look at influences that affect many or most people at a certain age or a certain time in history and also at those that affect only certain individuals. Finally, we need to see how timing can accentuate the impact of certain influences. All these issues will be discussed throughout this text.

Contexts of Development

Human beings are social beings. Right from the start, they develop within a social and historical context. For an infant, the immediate context normally is the family, but the family in turn is subject to the wider and ever-changing influences of neighborhood, community, and society.

nuclear family Two-generational kinship, economic, and household unit consisting of one or two parents and their biological children, adopted children, or stepchildren.

Family The **nuclear family** is a household unit consisting of one or two parents and their children, whether biological, adopted, or stepchildren. Historically, the two-parent nuclear family has been the dominant family unit in the United States and other Western societies. However, the nuclear family today is different from what it used to be. Instead of the large, rural family in which parents and children worked side by side on the family farm, we now see smaller, urban families in which both parents work outside the home and children spend much of their time in school or child care. The increased incidence of divorce also has impacted the nuclear family. Children of divorced parents may live with one or the other parent or may move back and forth between them. The household may include a stepparent and stepsiblings or a parent's live-in partner. There are increasing numbers of single and childless adults, unmarried parents, and gay and lesbian households (Hernandez, 1997, 2004; Teachman, Tedrow, & Crowder, 2000).

In many societies in Asia, Africa, and Latin America and among some U.S. families that trace their lineage to those countries, the **extended family**—a multigenerational network of grandparents, aunts, uncles, cousins, and more distant relatives—is the traditional family form. Many or most people live in *extended-family households*, where they have daily contact with kin. Adults often share breadwinning and child-raising responsibilities, and older children are responsible for younger brothers and sisters. Often these households are headed by women (Aaron, Parker, Ortega, & Calhoun, 1999; Johnson et al., 2003). Today the extended-family household is becoming slightly less typical in some developing countries due to industrialization and migration to urban centers (Brown, 1990; Gorman, 1993; Kinsella & Phillips, 2005). At the same time, with the aging of the population, multigenerational family bonds may be increasingly important in Western societies (Bengtson, 2001).

Socioeconomic Status and Neighborhood A family's **socioeconomic status (SES)** is based on family income and the educational and occupational levels of the adults in the household. Throughout this book, we examine many studies that relate SES to developmental processes (such as mothers' verbal interactions with their children) and to developmental outcomes (such as health and cognitive performance; Table 1-2). SES affects these processes and

In the United States, unmarried or divorced parents, stepfamilies, and gay and lesbian households have increased over the past 150 years, requiring adjustments to our understanding of the concept of family.

Table 1-2	Poverty Hurts Children	
Outcomes		**Low-Income Children's Higher Risk**
Health		
Death, in infancy		1.6 times more likely
Premature birth (*under 37 weeks*)		1.8 times more likely
Low birth weight		1.9 times more likely
Inadequate prenatal care		2.8 times more likely
No regular source of health care		2.7 times more likely
Having too little food sometime in the past 4 months		8.0 times more likely
Education		
Lower math scores at ages 7 to 8		5 test points lower
Lower reading scores at ages 7 to 8		4 test points lower
Repeating a grade		2.0 times more likely
Being expelled from school		3.4 times more likely
Being a dropout at ages 16 to 24		3.5 times more likely
Finishing a four-year college		50 percent as likely

Source: Children's Defense Fund, 2004.

extended family Multigenerational kinship network of parents, children, and other relatives, sometimes living together in an extended-family household.

socioeconomic status (SES) Combination of economic and social factors describing an individual or family, including income, education, and occupation.

outcomes indirectly, through such associated factors as the kinds of homes and neighborhoods people live in and the quality of nutrition, medical care, and schooling available to them.

More than half of the world's population (53 percent) live on less than the international poverty standard of $2 a day (Population Reference Bureau, 2006). In the United States, where poverty thresholds vary with family size and composition, about 36.5 million people, or 12.3 percent of the population, had incomes below poverty level in 2006 (DeNavas-Walt, Proctor, & Smith, 2005).

Poverty, especially if it is long-lasting, is harmful to the physical, cognitive, and psychosocial well-being of children and families. Poor children are more likely than other children to have emotional or behavioral problems, and their cognitive potential and school performance suffer more (Evans, 2004). The harm done by poverty may be indirect, through its impact on parents' emotional state and parenting practices and on the home environment they create (see Chapter 10). Threats to well-being multiply if, as often happens, several **risk factors**—conditions that increase the likelihood of a negative outcome—are present.

Affluence doesn't necessarily protect children from risk. Some children in affluent families face pressure to achieve and are often left on their own by busy parents. Such children have high rates of substance abuse, anxiety, and depression (Luthar & Latendresse, 2005).

The composition of a neighborhood affects children as well. Living in a poor neighborhood with large numbers of unemployed people makes it less likely that effective social support will be available (Black & Krishnakumar, 1998). Still, positive development can occur despite serious risk factors. Consider the television star Oprah Winfrey, the country singer Shania Twain, and the former U.S. president Abraham Lincoln, all of whom grew up in poverty (Kim-Cohen, Moffitt, Caspi, & Taylor, 2004).

Culture and Race/Ethnicity **Culture** refers to a society's or group's total way of life, including customs, traditions, laws, knowledge, beliefs, values, language, and physical products, from tools to artworks—all of the behavior and attitudes that are learned, shared, and transmitted among members of a social group. Culture is constantly changing, often through contact with other cultures. For example, Europeans arriving on American shores learned how to grow corn from the native Indians. Cultural contact today has been enhanced by computers and telecommunications. E-mail and instant messaging offer almost instantaneous communication across the globe, and digital services such as iTunes give people around the world easy access to one another's music and movies.

An **ethnic group** consists of people united by a distinctive culture, ancestry, religion, language, and/or national origin, all of which contribute to a sense of shared identity and shared attitudes, beliefs, and values. Most ethnic groups trace their roots to a country of origin, where they or their forebears shared a common culture that continues to influence their way of life. Ethnic and cultural patterns affect development by their influence on the composition of a household, its economic and social resources, the way its members act toward one another, the foods they eat, the games children play, the way they learn, how well they do in school, the occupations adults engage in, and the way family members think and perceive the world (Parke, 2004). For example, children of immigrants in the United States are nearly twice as likely as native-born children to live with extended families and are less likely to have mothers who work outside the home (Hernandez, 2004; Shields & Behrman, 2004).

The United States has always been a nation of immigrants and ethnic groups, but the primary ethnic origins of the immigrant population have shifted from

risk factors Conditions that increase the likelihood of a negative developmental outcome.

culture A society's or group's total way of life, including customs, traditions, beliefs, values, language, and physical products— all learned behavior, passed on from parents to children.

ethnic group A group united by ancestry, race, religion, language, and/or national origins, which contribute to a sense of shared identity.

What's Your View?

• How might you be different if you had grown up in a culture other than your own?

Figure 1-1

Past and projected percentages of U.S. children in specified racial/ethnic groups. (Source: Hernandez, 2004, p. 18, Fig. 1. Data from Population Projections Program, Population Division, U.S. Census Bureau, issued January 13, 2000.)

KEY:

■ Asian/Pacific Islander, non-Hispanic

■ American Indian, non-Hispanic

■ Black, non-Hispanic

■ Hispanic

■ White, non-Hispanic

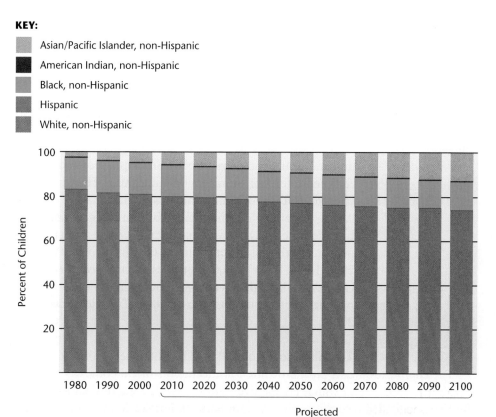

Europe and Canada to Asia and Latin America (Hernandez, 2004). In 2007, more than 20 percent of the population were immigrants or children of immigrants. More immigrants came from Mexico, 40 percent, than from any other country, and the remaining 60 percent came from nations in the Caribbean, East and West Asia, Australia, Central and South America, Indochina, the former Soviet Union, and Africa. By 2040 the minority population is projected to rise to 50 percent (Hernandez, Denton, & Macartney, 2007; Figure 1-1).

Wide diversity exists within broad ethnic groups. The European-descended "white majority" consists of many distinct ethnicities—German, Belgian, Irish, French, Italian, and so on. Cuban Americans, Puerto Ricans, and Mexican Americans—all Hispanic Americans—have different histories and cultures and may be of African, European, Native American, or mixed descent (Johnson et al., 2003; Sternberg, Grigorenko, & Kidd, 2005). African Americans from the rural South differ from those of Caribbean ancestry. Asian Americans hail from a variety of countries with distinct cultures, from modern, industrial Japan to communist China to the remote mountains of Nepal, where many people still practice their ancient way of life. Native Americans consist of hundreds of recognized nations, tribes, bands, and villages (Lin & Kelsey, 2000).

Many scholars now agree that the term *race,* historically and popularly viewed as an identifiable biological category, is a social construct. There is no clear scientific consensus on its definition, and it is impossible to measure reliably (Bonham, Warshauer-Baker, & Collins, 2005; Helms, Jernigan, & Mascher, 2005; Smedley & Smedley, 2005; Sternberg et al., 2005). Human genetic variation occurs along a broad continuum, and 90 percent of such variation occurs *within* rather than among socially defined races (Bonham et al., 2005; Ossorio & Duster, 2005). Nevertheless, race as a social category remains a factor in research because it makes a difference in "how individuals are treated, where they live, their employment opportunities, the quality of their health care, and

Golf legend Tiger Woods is one of many Americans with dual or multiple ethnic backgrounds.

whether [they] can fully participate" in their society (Smedley & Smedley, 2005, p. 23).

Categories of culture, race, and ethnicity are fluid (Bonham et al., 2005; Sternberg et al., 2005), "continuously shaped and redefined by social and political forces" (Fisher et al., 2002, p. 1026). Geographic dispersion and intermarriage together with adaptation to varying local conditions have produced a great heterogeneity of physical and cultural characteristics within populations (Smedley & Smedley, 2005; Sternberg et al., 2005). Thus, the golf champion Tiger Woods, who has a black father and an Asian American mother, may fall into more than one racial/ethnic category and may identify more strongly with one or another at different times (Hitlin, Brown, & Elder, 2006; Lin & Kelsey, 2000). A term such as *black* or *Hispanic* can be an **ethnic gloss**—an overgeneralization that obscures or blurs such variations (Parke, 2004; Trimble & Dickson, 2005).

The Historical Context   At one time developmental scientists paid little attention to the historical context—the time in which people live. Then, as early longitudinal studies of childhood extended into the adult years, investigators began to focus on how certain experiences, tied to time and place, affect the course of people's lives. Today, as we will discuss in the next section, the historical context is an important part of the study of development.

ethnic gloss Overgeneralization about an ethnic or cultural group that obscures differences within the group.

Checkpoint

Can you . . .

◆ Give examples of the influences of family and neighborhood composition, socioeconomic status, culture, race/ethnicity, and historical context?

normative Characteristic of an event that occurs in a similar way for most people in a group.

cohort A group of people born at about the same time.

historical generation A group of people strongly influenced by a major historical event during their formative period.

What's Your View?

• Can you think of a historical event that has molded your life? If so, in what ways?

Normative and Nonnormative Influences

To understand similarities and differences in development, we need to look at two types of **normative** influences—biological or environmental events that affect many or most people in a society in similar ways—and also at events that touch only certain individuals (Baltes & Smith, 2004).*

Normative age-graded influences are highly similar for people in a particular age group. The timing of biological events is fairly predictable within a normal range. For example, people don't experience puberty at age 35 or menopause at 12.

Normative history-graded influences are significant environmental events that shape the behavior and attitudes of an age **cohort,** a group of people born at about the same time, or a **historical generation,** a group of people who experience the same life-changing event at a formative time in their lives. A historical generation may contain more than one cohort, but not all cohorts are part of historical generations. Depending on when and where they live, cohorts or generations may feel the impact of famines, wars, or major epidemics and of such societal and technological developments as the changing roles of women and the impact of television and computers. For example, the generations that came of age during the Great Depression and World War II tend to show a strong sense of social interdependence and trust that is not as evident among more recent generations (Rogler, 2002). The strength of a history-graded influence may depend on the type of event, the age of the person, and the short-term and long-term personal and social effects of the event.

*Unless otherwise noted, this section is based largely on Baltes & Smith, 2004.

Widespread use of computers is a normative history-graded influence on children's development, which did not exist in earlier generations.

Nonnormative influences are unusual events that have a major impact on *individual* lives because they disturb the expected sequence of the life cycle. They are either typical events that happen at an atypical time of life (such as the death of a parent when a child is young) or atypical events (such as winning the lottery). Some of these influences are largely beyond a person's control and may present rare opportunities or severe challenges that the person perceives as turning points. On the other hand, people sometimes help create their own nonnormative life events—say, by deciding to have a baby in their midfifties or taking up a risky hobby such as skydiving—and thus participate actively in their own development. Taken together, normative and nonnormative influences contribute to the unpredictability of human development as well as to the challenges people experience in trying to build their lives.

nonnormative Characteristic of an unusual event that happens to a particular person or a typical event that happens at an unusual time of life.

Checkpoint

Can you . . .

♦ Give examples of normative age-graded, normative history-graded, and nonnormative influences?

Timing of Influences: Critical or Sensitive Periods

In a well-known study, Konrad Lorenz (1957), an Austrian zoologist, waddled, honked, and flapped his arms—and got newborn ducklings to follow him as they would the mother duck. Lorenz showed that newly hatched ducklings will instinctively follow the first moving object they see, whether or not it is a member of their species. This phenomenon is called **imprinting,** and Lorenz believed that it was automatic and irreversible. Usually, this instinctive bond is with the mother; but, if the natural course of events is disturbed, other attachments, such as the one to Lorenz, can form. Imprinting, said Lorenz, is the result of a *predisposition toward learning:* the readiness of an organism's nervous system to acquire certain information during a brief *critical period* in early life.

imprinting Instinctive form of learning in which, during a critical period in early development, a young animal forms an attachment to the first moving object it sees, usually the mother.

BOX 1-1 **Research** *in Action*

Is There a Critical Period for Language Acquisition?

In 1967 Eric Lenneberg (1967, 1969) proposed a critical period for language acquisition beginning in early infancy and ending around puberty. Lenneberg argued that it would be difficult, if not impossible, for a child who had not yet acquired language by the onset of puberty to do so after that age.

In 1970, a 13-year-old girl called Genie (not her real name) offered the opportunity for a test of Lenneberg's hypothesis. Genie was discovered in a suburb of Los Angeles (Curtiss, 1977; Fromkin, Krashen, Curtiss, Rigler, & Rigler, 1974; Pines, 1981; Rymer, 1993). The victim of an abusive father, she had been confined for nearly 12 years to a small room in her parents' home, tied to a potty chair and cut off from normal human contact. When found, she recognized only her name and the word *sorry*. Could Genie be taught to speak, or was it too late? The National Institutes of Mental Health (NIMH) funded a study to provide intensive testing and language training for Genie.

Genie's progress during the study both supported and challenged the idea of a critical period for language acquisition. She learned some simple words and could string them together into primitive sentences. She also learned the fundamentals of sign language. But "her speech remained, for the most part, like a somewhat garbled telegram" (Pines, 1981, p. 29). Her mother regained custody, cut her off from the NIMH researchers, and then eventually sent her into the foster care system. A series of abusive foster homes rendered Genie silent once more.

What explains Genie's initial progress and her inability to sustain it? Her understanding of her name and the single word *sorry* may mean that her language-learning mechanisms had been triggered early in the critical period, allowing later learning to occur. The timing of the NIMH language training and her ability to learn some simple words at age 13 may indicate that she was still in the critical period, though near its end. On the other hand, her extreme abuse and neglect may have retarded her so much that she could not be considered a true test of the critical period concept (Curtiss, 1977).

Genie's case dramatizes the difficulty of acquiring language after the early years of life, but, because of the complicating factors, it does not permit conclusive judgments about whether such

acquisition is possible. Some researchers consider the prepubertal years a sensitive rather than critical period for learning language (Newport, Bavelier, & Neville, 2001; Schumann, 1997). Brain imaging research has found that even if the parts of the brain best suited to language processing are damaged early in childhood, nearly normal language development can continue as other parts of the brain take over (Boatman et al., 1999; Hertz-Pannier et al., 2002; M. H. Johnson, 1998). In fact, shifts in brain organization and utilization occur throughout the course of normal language learning (M. H. Johnson, 1998; Neville & Bavelier, 1998).

If either a critical or a sensitive period for language learning exists, what explains it? Do the brain's mechanisms for acquiring language decay as the brain matures? That would seem strange, as other cognitive abilities improve. An alternative hypothesis is that this very increase in cognitive sophistication interferes with an adolescent's or adult's ability to learn a language. Young children acquire language in small chunks that can be digested readily. Older learners, when they first begin learning a language, tend to absorb a great deal at once and then may have trouble analyzing and interpreting it (Newport, 1991).

What's Your View?

Have you had difficulty learning a new language as an adult? If so, does this box help you understand why?

Check It Out

For more information on language learning go to www.facstaff.bucknell.edu/rbeard/acquisition.html. This website was developed by Professor Robert Beard of the Linguistics Program at Bucknell University. The page cited gives a brief, accurate overview of the nature-nurture question as it concerns language acquisition. Links to other related sites of interest are given.

critical period Specific time when a given event or its absence has a specific impact on development.

A **critical period** is a specific time when a given event, or its absence, has a specific impact on development. Critical periods are not absolutely fixed; if ducklings' rearing conditions are varied to slow their growth, the usual critical period for imprinting can be lengthened, and imprinting itself may even be reversed. The window of opportunity, some scientists now believe, may never completely shut (Bruer, 2001).

Do human beings experience critical periods, as ducklings do? If a woman receives X-rays, takes certain drugs, or contracts certain diseases at certain times during pregnancy, the fetus may show specific ill effects, depending on the nature of the shock and on its timing. If a muscle problem interfering with the ability

Newly hatched ducklings followed and became attached to the first moving object they saw, which just happened to be ethologist Konrad Lorenz. Lorenz called this behavior imprinting.

to focus both eyes on the same object is not corrected within a critical period early in childhood, depth perception probably will not develop (Bushnell & Boudreau, 1993).

However, the concept of critical periods in humans is controversial. Because many aspects of development, even in the physical domain, have been found to show **plasticity,** or modifiability of performance, it may be more useful to think about **sensitive periods,** when a developing person is especially responsive to certain kinds of experiences (Bruer, 2001). Further research is needed to discover "which aspects of behavior are likely to be altered by environmental events at specific points in development and which aspects remain more plastic and open to influence across wide spans of development" (Parke, 2004, p. 8). Box 1-1 discusses how the concepts of critical and sensitive periods apply to language development.

plasticity Range of modifiability of performance.

sensitive periods Times in development when a person is particularly open to certain kinds of experiences.

Checkpoint

Can you . . .

◆ Contrast critical and sensitive periods and give examples?

Paul B. Baltes's Life-Span Developmental Approach

Paul B. Baltes (1936–2006) and his colleagues (1987; Baltes & Smith, 2004; Baltes, Lindenberger, & Staudinger, 1998; Staudinger & Bluck, 2001) have identified seven key principles of a life-span developmental approach that sum up many of the concepts discussed in this chapter. Together these principles serve as a widely accepted conceptual framework for the study of life-span development:

1. *Development is lifelong.* Development is a lifelong process of change. Each period of the life span is affected by what happened before and will affect what is to come. Each period has unique characteristics and value; no period is more or less important than any other.

2. *Development is multidimensional.* It occurs along multiple interacting dimensions—biological, psychological, and social—each of which may develop at varying rates.

3. *Development is multidirectional.* As people gain in one area, they may lose in another, sometimes at the same time. Children grow mostly in one direction— up—both in size and in abilities. Then the balance gradually shifts. Adolescents typically gain in physical abilities, but their facility in learning a new language typically declines. Some abilities, such as vocabulary, typically continue to increase throughout most of adulthood; others, such as the ability to solve unfamiliar problems, may diminish; but some new attributes, such as expertise, may increase with age. People seek to maximize gains by concentrating

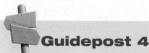

Guidepost 4

What are seven principles of the life-span developmental approach?

on doing things they do well and to minimize losses by learning to manage or compensate for them—for example, by writing "to-do" lists when memory flags.

4. *Relative influences of biology and culture shift over the life span.* The process of development is influenced by both biology and culture, but the balance between these influences changes. Biological abilities, such as sensory acuity and muscular strength and coordination, weaken with age, but cultural supports, such as education, relationships, and technologically age-friendly environments, may help compensate.

5. *Development involves changing resource allocations.* Individuals choose to invest their resources of time, energy, talent, money, and social support in varying ways. Resources may be used for growth (for example, learning to play an instrument or improving one's skill), for maintenance or recovery (practicing to maintain or regain proficiency), or for dealing with loss when maintenance and recovery are not possible. The allocation of resources to these three functions changes throughout life as the total available pool of resources decreases. In childhood and young adulthood, the bulk of resources typically goes to growth; in old age, to regulation of loss. In midlife, the allocation is more evenly balanced among the three functions.

6. *Development shows plasticity.* Many abilities, such as memory, strength, and endurance, can be improved significantly with training and practice, even late in life. However, even in children, plasticity has limits that depend in part on the various influences on development. One of the tasks of developmental research is to discover to what extent particular kinds of development can be modified at various ages.

7. *Development is influenced by the historical and cultural context.* Each person develops within multiple contexts—circumstances or conditions defined in part by maturation and in part by time and place. Human beings not only influence but also are influenced by their historical-cultural context. As we will discuss throughout this book, developmental scientists have found significant cohort differences, for example, in intellectual functioning, in women's midlife emotional development, and in the flexibility of personality in old age.

✓ Checkpoint

Can you . . .

♦ Summarize the seven principles of Baltes's life-span developmental approach?

Now that you have had a brief introduction to the field of human development and some of its basic concepts, it's time to look more closely at the issues developmental scientists think about and how they do their work. In Chapter 2, we discuss some influential theories of how development takes place and the methods investigators commonly use to study it.

Summary and Key Terms

Human Development: An Ever-Evolving Field

Guidepost 1: *What is human development, and how has its study evolved?*

- Human development is the scientific study of processes of change and stability.

- Developmental research has important applications in various fields.

- As researchers have become interested in following development through adulthood, life-span development has become a field of study.

- The study of human development seeks to describe, explain, predict, and, when appropriate, intervene in development.

- Students of human development draw on such disciplines as psychology, psychiatry, sociology, anthropology, biology, genetics, family science, education, history, philosophy, and medicine.
- Methods of studying human development are still evolving, making use of advanced technologies.

human development (4)

life-span development (4)

The Study of Human Development: Basic Concepts

Guidepost 2: *What do developmental scientists study?*

- Developmental scientists study change and stability in all domains of development throughout the life span.
- The three major domains of development are physical, cognitive, and psychosocial. Each affects the others.
- The concept of periods of development is a social construction. In this book, the life span is divided into eight periods: prenatal, infancy and toddlerhood, early childhood, middle childhood, adolescence, emerging and young adulthood, middle adulthood, and late adulthood. In each period, people have characteristic developmental needs and tasks.

physical development (5)

cognitive development (6)

psychosocial development (6)

social construction (6)

Influences on Development

Guidepost 3: *What kinds of influences make one person different from another?*

- Influences on development come from both heredity and environment. Many typical changes during childhood are related to maturation. Individual differences tend to increase with age.
- In some societies, the nuclear family predominates; in others, the extended family.
- Socioeconomic status (SES) affects developmental processes and outcomes through the quality of home and neighborhood environments, nutrition, medical care, and schooling. Multiple risk factors increase the likelihood of poor outcomes.

- Important environmental influences stem from culture, race/ethnicity, and historical context. Race is viewed by most scholars as a social construction.
- Influences may be normative (age-graded or history-graded) or nonnormative.
- There is evidence of critical or sensitive periods for certain kinds of early development.

individual differences (9)

heredity (9)

environment (10)

maturation (10)

nuclear family (10)

extended family (11)

socioeconomic status (SES) (11)

risk factors (12)

culture (12)

ethnic group (12)

ethnic gloss (14)

normative (14)

cohort (14)

historical generation (14)

nonnormative (15)

imprinting (15)

critical period (16)

plasticity (17)

sensitive periods (17)

Paul B. Baltes's Life-Span Developmental Approach

Guidepost 4: *What are seven principles of the life-span developmental approach?*

- The principles of Baltes's life-span developmental approach include the propositions that (1) development is lifelong, (2) development is multidimensional, (3) development is multidirectional, (4) the relative influences of biology and culture shift over the life span, (5) development involves changing resource allocations, (6) development shows plasticity, and (7) development is influenced by the historical and cultural context.

There is one thing even more vital to science than intelligent methods; and that is, the sincere desire to find out the truth, whatever it may be.

—Charles Sanders Peirce, *Collected Papers,* vol. 5, 1934

Did You **Know...**

- Theories are never set in stone; they are always open to change as a result of new findings?
- People shape their world as it shapes them?
- Cross-cultural research enables us to learn which aspects of development are universal and which are culturally influenced?
- An experiment is the *only* way to demonstrate that one event causes another?
- The results of laboratory experiments may be less applicable to real life than experiments carried out in a home, school, or public setting?

These are just a few of the interesting and important topics we will cover in this chapter. Here, we present an overview both of major theories of human development and of research methods used to study it. In the first part of the chapter, we explore major issues and theoretical perspectives that underlie much research in human development. In the remainder of the chapter, we look at how researchers gather and assess information so that, as you read further in this book, you will be better able to judge whether research findings and conclusions rest on solid ground. After you have studied this chapter, you should be able to answer each of the Guidepost questions on the following page.

Guideposts *for Study*

1. What purposes do theories serve, and what are two basic theoretical issues on which developmental scientists differ?

2. What are five theoretical perspectives on human development, and what are some theories representative of each?

3. How do developmental scientists study people, and what are some advantages and disadvantages of each research method?

4. What ethical problems may arise in research on humans?

Guidepost 1

What purposes do theories serve, and what are two basic theoretical issues on which developmental scientists differ?

theory Coherent set of logically related concepts that seeks to organize, explain, and predict data.

hypotheses Possible explanations for phenomena, used to predict the outcome of research.

Basic Theoretical Issues

When Ahmed earned an engineering degree from M.I.T. with honors, his father, an award-winning engineer, beamed. "The apple doesn't fall far from the tree," he said.

Statements like that one, which abound in everyday life, are informal, or intuitive, theories about why people develop as they do. Scientists have formal theories about human development. Like laypeople's informal theories, scientific theories are not dry, abstract, or esoteric. They deal with the substance of real life.

A scientific **theory** is a set of logically related concepts or statements that seek, in this field, to describe and explain development and to predict what kinds of behavior might occur under certain conditions. Theories organize and explain *data,* the information gathered by research. As painstaking research adds, bit by bit, to the body of knowledge, theoretical concepts, such as the idea of an *identity crisis,* discussed later in this chapter, help us make sense of, and see connections between, isolated pieces of data.

Theory and research are interwoven strands in the seamless fabric of scientific study. Theories inspire further research and predict its results. They do this by generating **hypotheses,** tentative explanations or predictions that can be tested by further research. Research can indicate whether a theory is accurate in its predictions but cannot conclusively show a theory to be true.

Theories change to incorporate new findings. Sometimes research supports a hypothesis and the theory on which it was based. At other times, scientists must modify their theories to account for unexpected data. Research findings often suggest additional hypotheses to be examined and provide direction for dealing with practical issues.

A theory is based on certain assumptions, which may or may not turn out to be true. A theorist's assumptions may be influenced by his culture and time in history. For example, Charles Darwin's theory of evolution, which preceded modern cell biology, assumed that all life forms evolved from a single ancestor. This assumption has been challenged by newer evolutionary research. One such model suggests that a loose grouping of cells eventually split into three primary lines of descent (Liu, 2006; Woese, 1998).

Developmental science cannot be completely objective. Theories and research about human behavior are products of very human individuals, whose inquiries and interpretations are inevitably influenced by their own values and experience. In striving for greater objectivity, researchers must scrutinize how they and their colleagues conduct their work, the assumptions on which it is based, and how they arrive at their conclusions.

Throughout this book, we examine many, often conflicting, theories. In assessing them, it is important to keep in mind that they reflect the outlooks of the human beings who originated them. The way theorists explain development depends in part on their assumptions about two basic issues: (1) whether people are active or reactive in their own development, and (2) whether development is continuous or occurs in stages. A third issue, whether development is more influenced by heredity or by environment, was introduced in Chapter 1 and will be discussed more fully in Chapter 3.

✓ **Checkpoint**

Can you . . .

◆ Explain the relationships among theories, hypotheses, and research?

Issue 1: Is Development Active or Reactive?

Are people active in their own development? This controversy goes back to the eighteenth century. The English philosopher John Locke held that a young child is a *tabula rasa*—a "blank slate"—on which society "writes." In contrast, the French philosopher Jean Jacques Rousseau believed that children are born "noble savages" who develop according to their own positive natural tendencies if not corrupted by society. We now know that both views are too simplistic. Children have internal drives and needs that influence development, but children also are social animals who cannot develop optimally in isolation.

Mechanistic Model   The debate over Locke's and Rousseau's philosophies led to two contrasting models, or images, of development: *mechanistic* and *organismic.* Locke's view was the forerunner of the **mechanistic model.** In this model, people are like machines that react to environmental input (Pepper, 1942, 1961). A machine is the sum of its parts. To understand it, we can break it down into its smallest components and then reassemble it.

Machines do not operate of their own volition; they react automatically to physical forces or inputs. Fill a car with gas, turn the ignition key, press the accelerator, and the vehicle will move. In the mechanistic view, human behavior is much the same: It results from the operation of biological parts in response to external or internal stimuli. If we know enough about how the human "machine" is put together and about the forces acting on it, we can predict what the person will do.

Mechanistic research seeks to identify the factors that make people behave as they do. For example, in seeking to explain why some college students drink too much alcohol, a mechanistic theorist might look for environmental influences, such as advertising and whether the student's friends are heavy drinkers.

Organismic Model   Rousseau was the precursor of the **organismic model.** This model sees people as active, growing organisms that set their own development in motion (Pepper, 1942, 1961). They initiate events; they do not just react. Thus, the driving force for change is internal. Environmental influences do not *cause* development, though they can speed or slow it.

Because human behavior is viewed as an organic whole, it cannot be predicted by breaking it down into simple responses to environmental stimulation. The meaning of a family relationship, for example, goes beyond what can be learned from studying its individual members and their day-to-day interactions. An organismic theorist, in studying why some students drink too much, would be likely to look at what kinds of situations they choose to participate in, and with whom. Do they choose friends who prefer to party or to study?

mechanistic model Model that views human development as a series of predictable responses to stimuli.

organismic model Model that views human development as internally initiated by an active organism and as occurring in a sequence of qualitatively different stages.

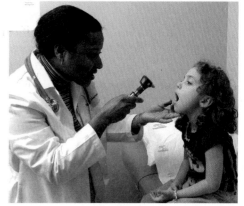

Are more women becoming doctors today because of inner motivation or environmental influences? Mechanistic and organismic theorists might give different answers to that question.

Table 2-1	Five Perspectives on Human Development	

Perspective	Important Theories	Basic Propositions
Psychoanalytic	Freud's psychosexual theory	Behavior is controlled by powerful unconscious urges.
	Erikson's psychosocial theory	Personality is influenced by society and develops through a series of crises.
Learning	Behaviorism, or traditional learning theory (Pavlov, Skinner, Watson)	People are responders; the environment controls behavior.
	Social learning (social cognitive) theory (Bandura)	Children learn in a social context by observing and imitating models. Children are active contributors to learning.
Cognitive	Piaget's cognitive-stage theory	Qualitative changes in thought occur between infancy and adolescence. Children are active initiators of development.
	Vygotsky's sociocultural theory	Social interaction is central to cognitive development.
	Information-processing theory	Human beings are processors of symbols.
Contextual	Bronfenbrenner's bioecological theory	Development occurs through interaction between a developing person and five surrounding, interlocking contextual systems of influences, from microsystem to chronosystem.
Evolutionary/ sociobiological	Bowlby's attachment theory	Human beings have the adaptive mechanisms to survive; critical or sensitive periods are stressed; evolutionary and biological bases for behavior and predisposition toward learning are important.

For organicists, development has an underlying, orderly structure, though it may not be obvious from moment to moment. As a fertilized egg cell develops into an embryo and then into a fetus, it goes through a series of qualitative changes not overtly predictable from what came before. Swellings on the head become eyes, ears, mouth, and nose. The brain begins to coordinate breathing, digestion, and elimination. Sex organs form. Similarly, organicists describe development after birth as a progressive sequence of stages, moving toward full maturation.

Issue 2: Is Development Continuous or Discontinuous?

The mechanistic and organismic models also differ on the second issue: Is development *continuous,* that is, gradual and incremental, or *discontinuous,* that is, abrupt or uneven?

Mechanistic theorists see development as continuous, like walking or crawling up a ramp. Development, in mechanistic models, is always governed by the same processes, allowing prediction of earlier behaviors from later ones.

Mechanistic theorists deal with **quantitative change**—changes in number or amount, such as in height, weight, size of vocabulary, or frequency of communication. A baby who gains three pounds in his first three months of life experiences a quantitative change. Quantitative researchers may measure how much a person can remember, rather than what memory is or how it operates. Quantitative changes are largely continuous and unidirectional.

Organismic theorists emphasize **qualitative change**—changes in kind, structure, or organization. Qualitative change is *discontinuous:* It is marked by the emergence of new phenomena that cannot be anticipated easily on the basis of earlier functioning. The change from a nonverbal child to one who understands words and can communicate verbally is a qualitative change.

quantitative change Change in number or amount, such as in height, weight, or the size of vocabulary.

qualitative change Change in kind, structure, or organization, such as the change from nonverbal to verbal communication.

Technique Used	Stage-Oriented	Causal Emphasis	Active or Reactive Individual
Clinical observation	Yes	Innate factors modified by experience	Reactive
Clinical observation	Yes	Interaction of innate and experiential factors	Active
Rigorous scientific (experimental) procedures	No	Experience	Reactive
Rigorous scientific (experimental) procedures	No	Experience modified by innate factors	Active and reactive
Flexible interviews; meticulous observation	Yes	Interaction of innate and experiential factors	Active
Cross-cultural research; observation of child interacting with more competent person	No	Experience	Active
Laboratory research; technological monitoring of physiologic responses	No	Interaction of innate and experiential factors	Active
Naturalistic observation and analysis	No	Interaction of innate and experiential factors	Active
Naturalistic and laboratory observation	No	Interaction of innate and experiential factors	Active and reactive (theorists vary)

Organismic theorists see development as occurring in a series of distinct stages, like stair steps. At each stage, people cope with different kinds of problems and develop different kinds of abilities. Each stage builds on the previous one and prepares the way for the next. Organicists see this unfolding structure of development as universal: Everyone goes through the same stages in the same order, though the precise timing varies.

Theoretical Perspectives

Theories generally fall within broad perspectives that emphasize different kinds of developmental processes and take different positions on the issues described in the previous section. These perspectives influence the questions researchers ask, the methods they use, and the ways they interpret data. Therefore, to evaluate and interpret research, it is important to recognize the theoretical perspective on which it is based.

Five major perspectives underlie much influential theory and research on human development: (1) *psychoanalytic,* (2) *learning,* (3) *cognitive,* (4) *contextual,* and (5) *evolutionary/sociobiological.* Here is a general overview of the central focus, main propositions, methods, and causal emphasis of each of these perspectives and some leading theorists within each perspective. These are summarized in Table 2-1 and will be referred to throughout this book.

Perspective 1: Psychoanalytic

Sigmund Freud (1856–1939), a Viennese physician, originated the **psychoanalytic perspective,** which views development as shaped by unconscious forces that motivate human behavior. *Psychoanalysis,* the therapeutic approach Freud developed, seeks to give patients insight into unconscious emotional conflicts by asking

Checkpoint

Can you . . .

♦ Discuss two issues regarding human development?

♦ Contrast the mechanistic and organismic models?

♦ Compare quantitative and qualitative change?

Guidepost 2

What are five theoretical perspectives on human development, and what are some theories representative of each?

psychoanalytic perspective View of human development as being shaped by unconscious forces.

Sigmund Freud developed an original theory of psychosexual development. His daughter, Anna, shown here, followed in his footsteps and constructed her own theories of personality development.

psychosexual development In Freudian theory, an unvarying sequence of stages of childhood personality development in which gratification shifts from the mouth to the anus and then to the genitals.

questions designed to summon up long-buried memories. Following is a summary of Freud's theory of psychosexual development. Other theorists and practitioners, including Erik H. Erikson, whom we discuss next, have expanded and modified Freud's theory.

Sigmund Freud: Psychosexual Development   Freud (1953, 1964a, 1964b) believed that people are born with biological drives that must be redirected to make it possible to live in society. He proposed three hypothetical parts of the personality: the *id,* the *ego,* and the *superego.* Newborns are governed by the *id,* which operates under the *pleasure principle*—the drive to seek immediate satisfaction of their needs and desires. When gratification is delayed, as it is when infants have to wait to be fed, they begin to see themselves as separate from the outside world. The *ego,* which represents reason, develops gradually during the first year or so of life and operates under the *reality principle.* The ego's aim is to find realistic ways to gratify the id that are acceptable to the *superego,* which develops at about age 5 or 6. The *superego* includes the conscience and incorporates socially approved "shoulds" and "should nots" into the child's value system. The superego is highly demanding; if its standards are not met, a child may feel guilty and anxious. The ego mediates between the impulses of the id and the demands of the superego.

Freud proposed that personality forms through unconscious childhood conflicts between the inborn urges of the id and the requirements of civilized life. These conflicts occur in an unvarying sequence of five maturationally based stages of **psychosexual development** (Table 2-2), in which sensual pleasure shifts from one body zone to another—from the mouth to the anus and then to the genitals. At each stage, the behavior that is the chief source of gratification (or frustration) changes—from feeding to elimination and eventually to sexual activity.

Freud considered the first three stages—those of the first few years of life—to be crucial for personality development. According to Freud, if children receive too little or too much gratification in any of these stages, they are at risk of *fixation*—an arrest in development that can show up in adult personality. Babies whose needs are not met during the *oral stage,* when feeding is the main source of sensual pleasure, may grow up to become nail-biters or smokers or to develop "bitingly" critical personalities. A person who, as a toddler, had too-strict toilet training may be fixated at the *anal stage,* when the chief source of pleasure was moving the bowels. Such a person may become obsessively clean, rigidly tied to schedules and routines, or defiantly messy.

According to Freud, a key event in psychosexual development occurs in the *phallic stage* of early childhood. Boys develop sexual attachment to their mothers, and girls to their fathers, and they have aggressive urges toward the same-sex parent, whom they regard as a rival. Freud called these developments the *Oedipus* and *Electra complexes.*

Children eventually resolve their anxiety over these feelings by identifying with the same-sex parent and move into the *latency stage* of middle childhood, a period of relative emotional calm and intellectual and social exploration. They redirect their sexual energies into other pursuits, such as schoolwork, relationships, and hobbies.

The *genital stage,* the final stage, lasts throughout adulthood. The sexual urges repressed during latency now resurface to flow in socially approved channels, which Freud defined as heterosexual relations with persons outside the family of origin.

Freud's theory made historic contributions and inspired a whole generation of followers, some of whom took psychoanalytic theory in new directions. Some of Freud's ideas, such as his notion of the Oedipus crisis, now are widely considered obsolete. Others, such as the concepts of the id and superego, cannot be

Psychosexual Stages (Freud)	Psychosocial Stages (Erikson)	Cognitive Stages (Piaget)
Oral (birth to 12–18 months). Baby's chief source of pleasure involves mouth-oriented activities (sucking and feeding).	*Basic trust versus mistrust (birth to 12–18 months)*. Baby develops sense of whether world is a good and safe place. Virtue: hope.	*Sensorimotor (birth to 2 years)*. Infant gradually becomes able to organize activities in relation to the environment through sensory and motor activity.
Anal (12–18 months to 3 years). Child derives sensual gratification from withholding and expelling feces. Zone of gratification is anal region, and toilet training is important activity.	*Autonomy versus shame and doubt (12–18 months to 3 years)*. Child develops a balance of independence and self-sufficiency over shame and doubt. Virtue: will.	*Preoperational (2 to 7 years)*. Child develops a representational system and uses symbols to represent people, places, and events. Language and imaginative play are important manifestations of this stage. Thinking is still not logical.
Phallic (3 to 6 years). Child becomes attached to parent of the other sex and later identifies with same-sex parent. Superego develops. Zone of gratification shifts to genital region.	*Initiative versus guilt (3 to 6 years)*. Child develops initiative when trying out new activities and is not overwhelmed by guilt. Virtue: purpose.	
Latency (6 years to puberty). Time of relative calm between more turbulent stages.	*Industry versus inferiority (6 years to puberty)*. Child must learn skills of the culture or face feelings of incompetence. Virtue: skill.	*Concrete operations (7 to 11 years)*. Child can solve problems logically if they are focused on the here and now but cannot think abstractly.
Genital (puberty through adulthood). Reemergence of sexual impulses of phallic stage, channeled into mature adult sexuality.	*Identity versus identity confusion (puberty to young adulthood)*. Adolescent must determine own sense of self ("Who am I?") or experience confusion about roles. Virtue: fidelity.	*Formal operations (11 years through adulthood)*. Person can think abstractly, deal with hypothetical situations, and think about possibilities.
	Intimacy versus isolation (young adulthood). Person seeks to make commitments to others; if unsuccessful, may suffer from isolation and self-absorption. Virtue: love.	
	Generativity versus stagnation (middle adulthood). Mature adult is concerned with establishing and guiding the next generation or else feels personal impoverishment. Virtue: care.	
	Integrity versus despair (late adulthood). Older adult achieves acceptance of own life, allowing acceptance of death, or else despairs over inability to relive life. Virtue: wisdom.	

Note: All ages are approximate.

scientifically tested. Although Freud opened our eyes to the importance of early sexual urges, many psychoanalysts today reject his narrow emphasis on sexual and aggressive drives to the exclusion of other motives. Nevertheless, several of his central themes have "stood the test of time" (Westen, 1998, p. 334). Freud made us aware of the importance of unconscious thoughts, feelings, and motivations; the role of childhood experiences in forming personality; the ambivalence of emotional responses, especially responses to parents; the role of mental representations of the self and others in the establishment of intimate relationships; and the path of normal development from an immature, dependent state to a mature, interdependent state. In all these ways, Freud left an indelible mark on psychoanalysis and developmental psychology (Westen, 1998).

We need to remember that Freud's theory grew out of his place in history and in society. Freud based his theories about normal development, not on a population of average children, but on a clientele of upper-middle-class adults, mostly

Checkpoint

Can you . . .

◆ Identify the chief focus of the psychoanalytic perspective?

◆ Name Freud's five stages of development and three parts of the personality?

The psychoanalyst Erik H. Erikson emphasized societal influences on personality.

psychosocial development In Erikson's eight-stage theory, the socially and culturally influenced process of development of the ego, or self.

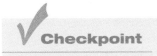

Checkpoint

Can you . . .

♦ Tell two ways in which Erikson's theory differs from Freud's?

learning perspective View of human development which holds that changes in behavior result from experience or from adaptation to the environment.

behaviorism Learning theory that emphasizes the predictable role of environment in causing observable behavior.

women, in therapy. His concentration on the influences of sexual urges and early experience did not take into account other, and later, influences on personality—including the influences of society and culture, which many heirs to the Freudian tradition, such as Erik Erikson, stress.

Erik Erikson: Psychosocial Development   Erik Erikson (1902–1994), a German-born psychoanalyst who originally was part of Freud's circle in Vienna, modified and extended Freudian theory by emphasizing the influence of society on the developing personality. Erikson also was a pioneer in taking a life-span perspective. Whereas Freud maintained that early childhood experiences permanently shape personality, Erikson contended that ego development is lifelong.

Erikson's (1950, 1982; Erikson, Erikson, & Kivnick, 1986) theory of **psychosocial development** covers eight stages across the life span (refer to Table 2-2), which we will discuss in the appropriate chapters throughout this book. Each stage involves what Erikson originally called a *crisis* in personality—a major psychosocial theme that is particularly important at that time and will remain an issue to some degree throughout the rest of life. These issues, which emerge according to a maturational timetable, must be satisfactorily resolved for healthy ego development.*

Each stage requires the balancing of a positive tendency and a corresponding negative one. The positive tendency should predominate, but some degree of the negative is needed as well. The critical theme of infancy, for example, is *basic trust versus basic mistrust.* People need to trust the world and the people in it. However, they also need a reasonable amount of mistrust to protect themselves from danger. The successful outcome of each stage is the development of a particular *virtue,* or strength—in this case, the virtue of *hope.* The resolution of later crises or conflicts depends on the resolution reached in previous stages.

Erikson's theory is important because of its emphasis on social and cultural influences and on development beyond adolescence. He is perhaps most widely known for his concept of the *identity crisis* (discussed in Chapter 12), which has generated considerable research and public discussion.

Perspective 2: Learning

The **learning perspective** maintains that development results from *learning,* a long-lasting change in behavior based on experience or adaptation to the environment. Learning theorists seek to discover objective laws that govern changes in observable behavior. They see development as continuous (not occurring in stages) and emphasize quantitative change.

Learning theorists have helped to make the study of human development more scientific. Their terms are defined precisely, and their theories can be tested in the laboratory. Two important learning theories are *behaviorism* and *social learning theory.*

Behaviorism   Behaviorism is a mechanistic theory, which describes observed behavior as a predictable response to experience. Although biology sets limits on what people do, behaviorists view the environment as much more influential. They hold that human beings at all ages learn about the world the same way other organisms do: by reacting to conditions, or aspects of their environment, that they find pleasing, painful, or threatening. Behavioral research focuses on *associative learning,* in which a mental link is formed between two events. Two kinds of associative learning are *classical conditioning* and *operant conditioning.*

*Erikson later broadened the concept of "crisis" and referred instead to conflicting or competing tendencies.

Classical Conditioning   The Russian physiologist Ivan Pavlov (1849–1936) devised experiments in which dogs learned to salivate at the sound of a bell that rang at feeding time. These experiments were the foundation for **classical conditioning,** in which a response (in this case, salivation) to a stimulus (the bell) is evoked after repeated association with a stimulus that normally elicits the response (food).

The American behaviorist John B. Watson (1878–1958) applied such stimulus-response theories to children, claiming that he could mold any infant in any way he chose. His writings influenced a generation of parents to apply principles of learning theory to child raising. In one of the earliest and most famous demonstrations of classical conditioning in human beings (Watson & Rayner, 1920), he taught an 11-month-old baby known as "Little Albert" to fear furry white objects.

In this study, Albert was exposed to a loud noise just as he was about to stroke a furry white rat. The noise frightened him, and he began to cry. After repeated pairings of the rat with the loud noise, Albert whimpered with fear whenever he saw the rat. Although such research would be considered unethical today, the study showed that a baby could be conditioned to fear things he or she had not been afraid of before.

Classical conditioning occurs throughout life. Food likes and dislikes may be a result of conditioned learning. Fear of drowning or of heights may arise from having fallen off a diving board or from the top of a slide.

Operant Conditioning   Baby Angel lies in his crib. When he starts to babble ("ma-ma-ma"), his mother smiles and repeats the syllables. Angel learns that his behavior (babbling) can produce a desirable consequence (loving attention from a parent); and so he keeps babbling to attract his mother's attention. An originally accidental behavior (babbling) has become a conditioned response

This kind of learning is called **operant conditioning** because the individual learns from the consequences of "operating" on the environment. Like classical conditioning, operant conditioning involves associative learning, but in operant conditioning the association is between a behavior and its consequences. Also, unlike classical conditioning, operant conditioning involves voluntary behavior, such as Angel's babbling.

The American psychologist B. F. Skinner (1904–1990), who formulated the principles of operant conditioning, worked primarily with rats and pigeons, but Skinner (1938) maintained that these principles apply to human beings as well. He found that an organism will tend to repeat a response that has been reinforced by desirable consequences and will suppress a response that has been punished. Thus, **reinforcement** is the process by which a behavior is strengthened, *increasing* the likelihood that the behavior will be repeated. In Angel's case, his mother's attention reinforces his babbling. **Punishment** is the process by which a behavior is weakened, *decreasing* the likelihood of repetition. If Angel's mother frowned when he babbled, he would be less likely to babble again. Whether a consequence is reinforcing or punishing depends on the person. What is reinforcing for one person may be punishing for another. For a child who likes being alone, being sent to his or her room could be reinforcing rather than punishing.

classical conditioning Learning based on association of a stimulus that does not ordinarily elicit a particular response with another stimulus that does elicit the response.

operant conditioning Learning based on association of behavior with its consequences.

reinforcement In operant conditioning, a process that strengthens and encourages repetition of a desired behavior.

punishment In operant conditioning, a process that weakens and discourages repetition of a behavior.

According to Skinner's principles, a punishment, such as this child's time-out, reduces the likelihood that a behavior will be repeated

Reinforcement is most effective when it immediately follows a behavior. If a response is no longer reinforced, it will eventually be *extinguished,* that is, return to its original (baseline) level. If, after a while, no one repeats Angel's babbling, he may babble less often than if his babbles still brought reinforcement.

Behavior modification, or behavior therapy, is a form of operant conditioning used to gradually eliminate undesirable behavior or to instill positive behavior. It is particularly effective among people with special needs, mental or emotional disabilities, or eating disorders. However, Skinnerian psychology is limited in application because, in its focus on broad principles of development, it does not adequately address individual differences in behavior and social and cultural influences.

Social Learning (Social Cognitive) Theory   The American psychologist Albert Bandura (b. 1925) developed many of the principles of **social learning theory.** Whereas behaviorists see the environment, acting on the person, as the chief impetus for development, Bandura (1977, 1989; Bandura & Walters, 1963) suggests that the impetus for development is bidirectional. Bandura called this concept **reciprocal determinism**—the person acts on the world as the world acts on the person.

Classic social learning theory maintains that people learn appropriate social behavior chiefly by observing and imitating models—that is, by watching other people, such as parents, teachers, or sports heroes. This process is called **observational learning,** or *modeling.* The choice of a model depends on the *consequences* of the model's behavior; people tend to choose models who are prestigious, who control resources, or who are rewarded for what they do—in other words, whose behavior is perceived as valued in their culture. Imitation of models is an important element in how children learn a language, deal with aggression, develop a moral sense, and learn gender-appropriate behaviors. Adults learn by observation and imitation of coaches, mentors, and colleagues. Observational learning can occur even if a person does not imitate the observed behavior.

Bandura's (1989) updated version of social learning theory is *social cognitive theory.* The change of name reflects a greater emphasis on cognitive processes as central to development. Cognitive processes are at work as people observe models, learn *chunks* of behavior, and mentally put the chunks together into complex new behavior patterns. Rita, for example, imitates the toes-out walk of her dance teacher but models her dance steps after those of Carmen, a slightly more advanced student. Even so, she develops her own style of dancing by putting her observations together into a new pattern.

Through feedback on their behavior, children gradually form standards for judging their actions and become more selective in choosing models who exemplify those standards. They also begin to develop a sense of **self-efficacy,** the confidence that they have what it takes to succeed.

Perspective 3: Cognitive

The **cognitive perspective** focuses on thought processes and the behavior that reflects those processes. This perspective encompasses both organismic and mechanistically influenced theories. It includes the cognitive-stage theory of Piaget and Vygotsky's sociocultural theory of cognitive development. It also includes the information-processing approach and neo-Piagetian theories, which combine elements of information-processing theory and Piagetian theory.

Jean Piaget's Cognitive-Stage Theory   Our understanding of how children think owes a great deal to the work of the Swiss theoretician Jean Piaget (1896–1980).

social learning theory Theory that behaviors are learned by observing and imitating models. Also called *social cognitive theory.*

reciprocal determinism Bandura's term for bidirectional forces that affect development.

observational learning Learning through watching the behavior of others.

self-efficacy Sense of one's capability to master challenges and achieve goals.

Checkpoint

Can you . . .

- ◆ Identify the chief concerns of the learning perspective?

- ◆ Tell how classical conditioning and operant conditioning differ?

- ◆ Contrast reinforcement and punishment?

- ◆ Compare behaviorism and social learning theory?

cognitive perspective View that thought processes are central to development.

Piaget's **cognitive-stage theory** was the forerunner of today's "cognitive revolution" with its emphasis on mental processes. Piaget, who was a biologist and philosopher by training, viewed development organismically, as the product of children's efforts to understand and act on their world.

Piaget's *clinical method* combined observation with flexible questioning. To find out how children think, Piaget followed up their answers with more questions. In this way, he discovered that a typical 4-year-old believed that pennies or flowers were more numerous when arranged in a line than when heaped or piled up. From his observations of his own and other children, Piaget created a comprehensive theory of cognitive development.

Piaget suggested that cognitive development begins with an inborn ability to adapt to the environment. By rooting for a nipple, feeling a pebble, or exploring the boundaries of a room, young children develop a more accurate picture of their surroundings and greater competence in dealing with them. This cognitive growth occurs through three interrelated processes: *organization, adaptation,* and *equilibration.*

Organization is the tendency to create categories, such as birds, by observing the characteristics that individual members of a category, such as sparrows and cardinals, have in common. According to Piaget, people create increasingly complex cognitive structures called **schemes,** ways of organizing information about the world that govern the way the child thinks and behaves in a particular situation. As children acquire more information, their schemes become more and more complex. Take sucking, for example. A newborn infant has a simple scheme for sucking but soon develops varied schemes for how to suck at the breast, a bottle, or a thumb.

Adaptation is Piaget's term for how children handle new information in light of what they already know. Adaptation occurs through two complementary processes: (1) **assimilation,** taking in new information and incorporating it into existing cognitive structures, and (2) **accommodation,** adjusting one's cognitive structures to fit the new information. Take sucking, again. A breast- or bottle-fed baby who begins to suck on the spout of a sippy cup is showing assimilation— using an old scheme to deal with a new situation. When the infant discovers that sipping from a cup requires different tongue and mouth movements from those used to suck on a breast or bottle, she accommodates by modifying the old scheme. She has adapted her original sucking scheme to deal with a new experience: the cup.

Equilibration—a constant striving for a stable balance, or equilibrium—dictates the shift from assimilation to accommodation. When children cannot handle new experiences within their existing cognitive structures, they experience an uncomfortable state of disequilibrium, as the baby does in trying to suck on the sippy cup in the same way as on a breast or bottle. By organizing new mental and behavioral patterns that integrate the new experience (in this case, the cup), the child restores equilibrium. Thus, assimilation and accommodation work together to produce equilibrium. Throughout life, the quest for equilibrium is the driving force behind cognitive growth.

Piaget described cognitive development as occurring in four universal, qualitatively different stages (listed in Table 2-2 and discussed in detail in later

Jean Piaget studied children's cognitive development by observing and talking with them in many settings, asking questions to find out how their minds worked.

cognitive-stage theory Piaget's theory that children's cognitive development advances in a series of four stages involving qualitatively distinct types of mental operations.

organization Piaget's term for the creation of categories or systems of knowledge.

schemes Piaget's term for organized patterns of thought and behavior used in particular situations.

adaptation Piaget's term for adjustment to new information about the environment, achieved through processes of assimilation and accommodation.

assimilation Piaget's term for incorporation of new information into an existing cognitive structure.

accommodation Piaget's term for changes in a cognitive structure to include new information.

equilibration Piaget's term for the tendency to seek a stable balance among cognitive elements; achieved through a balance between assimilation and accommodation.

chapters). Each stage emerges at a time of disequilibrium, to which the child's mind adapts by learning to think in a new or modified way. From infancy through adolescence, mental operations evolve from learning based on simple sensory and motor activity to logical, abstract thought.

Piaget's observations have yielded much information and some surprising insights. Who, for example, would have thought that most children younger than about age 7 do not realize that a ball of clay that has been rolled into a worm shape before their eyes still contains the same amount of clay? Or that an infant might think that a person who has moved out of sight no longer exists? Piaget has shown us that children's minds are not miniature adult minds. Knowing how children think makes it easier for parents and teachers to understand and teach them. Piaget's theory has provided rough benchmarks for what to expect of children at various ages and has helped educators design curricula appropriate to varying levels of development.

Yet, Piaget seems to have seriously underestimated the abilities of infants and young children. Some contemporary psychologists question his distinct stages, pointing instead to evidence that cognitive development is more gradual and continuous (Courage & Howe, 2002). Research beginning in the late 1960s has challenged Piaget's idea that thinking develops in a single, universal progression of stages leading to formal thought. Instead, children's cognitive processes seem closely tied to specific content (what they are thinking *about*) as well as to the context of a problem and the kinds of information and thought a culture considers important (Case & Okamoto, 1996). Further, research on adults suggests that Piaget's focus on formal logic as the climax of cognitive development is too narrow. It does not account for the emergence of such mature abilities as practical problem solving, wisdom, and the capacity to deal with ambiguous situations and competing truths.

Lev Vygotsky's Sociocultural Theory The Russian psychologist Lev Semenovich Vygotsky (1896–1934) focused on the social and cultural processes that guide children's cognitive development. Vygotsky's (1978) **sociocultural theory,** like Piaget's theory, stresses children's active engagement with their environment; but, whereas Piaget described the solo mind taking in and interpreting information about the world, Vygotsky saw cognitive growth as a *collaborative* process. Children, said Vygotsky, learn through social interaction. They acquire cognitive skills as part of their induction into a way of life. Shared activities help children internalize their society's modes of thinking and behaving and make those folkways their own. Vygotsky placed special emphasis on *language*—not merely as an expression of knowledge and thought but as an essential *means* to learning and thinking about the world.

According to Vygotsky, adults or more advanced peers must help direct and organize a child's learning before the child can master and internalize it. This guidance is most effective in helping children cross the **zone of proximal development (ZPD),** the gap between what they are already able to do and what they are not quite ready to accomplish by themselves. (*Proximal* means "nearby.") Children in the ZPD for a particular task can almost, but not quite, perform the task on their own. With the right kind of guidance, however, they can do it successfully. Responsibility for directing and monitoring learning gradually shifts to the child—much as, when an adult teaches a child to float, the adult first supports the child in the water and then lets go gradually as the child's body relaxes into a horizontal position.

Some followers of Vygotsky (Wood, 1980; Wood, Bruner, & Ross, 1976) have applied the metaphor of *scaffolds*—the temporary platforms on which construction

Checkpoint

Can you . . .

◆ List three interrelated principles that bring about cognitive growth, according to Piaget, and give an example of each?

According to Lev Vygotsky, children learn through social interaction

sociocultural theory Vygotsky's theory of how contextual factors affect children's development.

zone of proximal development (ZPD) Vygotsky's term for the difference between what a child can do alone and what the child can do with help.

workers stand—to this way of teaching. **Scaffolding** is the temporary support that parents, teachers, or others give a child in doing a task until the child can do it alone. For example, when a child is learning to float, a parent or teacher supports a child's back, first with a hand, then with only a finger, until the child can float without support.

Vygotsky's theory has important implications for education and for cognitive testing. Tests that focus on a child's potential for learning provide a valuable alternative to standard intelligence tests that assess what the child has already learned; and many children may benefit from the sort of expert guidance Vygotsky prescribes. (The ZPD and scaffolding are discussed further in Chapters 7 and 9.)

The Information-Processing Approach   The **information-processing approach** seeks to explain cognitive development by analyzing the processes involved in making sense of incoming information and performing tasks effectively: such processes as attention, memory, planning strategies, decision making, and goal setting. The information-processing approach is not a single theory but a framework that supports a wide range of theories and research.

Some information-processing theorists compare the brain to a computer. Sensory impressions go in; behavior comes out. But what happens in between? How does the brain use sensations and perceptions, say, of an unfamiliar word, to recognize that word again? Information-processing researchers *infer* what goes on between a stimulus and a response. For example, they may ask a person to recall a list of words and then observe any difference in performance if the person repeats the list over and over before being asked to recall the words. Through such studies, some information-processing researchers have developed *computational models* or flowcharts that analyze the specific steps people go through in gathering, storing, retrieving, and using information.

Information-processing theorists, like Piaget, see people as active thinkers about their world. Unlike Piaget, they generally do *not* propose stages of development. Instead, they view development as continuous. They note age-related increases in the speed, complexity, and efficiency of mental processing and in the amount and variety of material that can be stored in memory. Brain imaging research, discussed later in this chapter, supports important aspects of information-processing models, such as the existence of separate physical structures to handle conscious and unconscious memory (Schacter, 1999; Yingling, 2001).

The information-processing approach has practical applications. It enables researchers to estimate an infant's later intelligence from the efficiency of sensory perception and processing. It enables parents and teachers to help children learn by making them more aware of their mental processes and of strategies to enhance them. Psychologists use information-processing models to test, diagnose, and treat learning problems.

Neo-Piagetian Theories   In response to criticisms of Piaget's theory, some developmental psychologists have sought to integrate elements of his theory with the information-processing approach. Instead of describing a single, general system of increasingly logical mental operations, these neo-Piagetians focus on *specific* concepts, strategies, and skills, such as number concepts and comparisons of "more" and "less." They suggest that children develop cognitively by becoming more efficient at processing information. Because of this emphasis on efficiency of processing, the neo-Piagetian approach helps account for individual differences in cognitive ability and for uneven development in various domains.

scaffolding Temporary support to help a child master a task.

information-processing approach Approach to the study of cognitive development by observing and analyzing the mental processes involved in perceiving and handling information.

Checkpoint

Can you . . .

◆ Explain how Vygotsky's theory differs from Piaget's and how it applies to educational teaching and testing?

◆ Describe what information-processing researchers do, and tell three ways in which such research can be applied?

◆ Tell how neo-Piagetian theory draws from both Piaget and the information-processing approach?

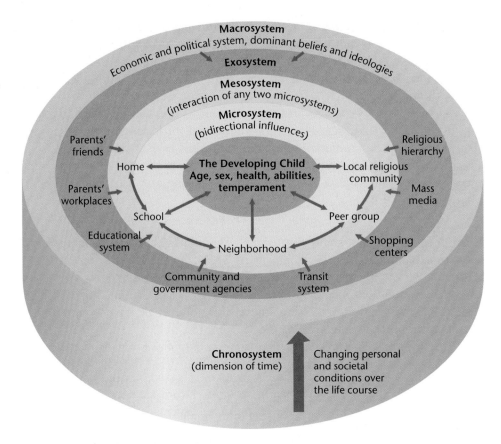

Perspective 4: Contextual

According to the **contextual perspective**, development can be understood only in
its social context. Contextualists see the individual, not as a separate entity interacting with the environment, but as an inseparable part of it. (Vygotsky's sociocultural theory, which we discussed as part of the cognitive perspective, also can
be classified as contextual.)

The American psychologist Urie Bronfenbrenner's (1917–2005) **bioecological
theory** (1979, 1986, 1994; Bronfenbrenner & Morris, 1998) identifies five levels of
environmental influence, ranging from very intimate to very broad: *microsystem,
mesosystem, exosystem, macrosystem,* and *chronosystem* (Figure 2-1). To understand the complexity of influences on development, we must see a person within
the context of these multiple environments.

A *microsystem* is the everyday environment of home, school, work, or neighborhood, including face-to-face relationships with spouse, children, parents, friends,
classmates, teachers, employers, or colleagues. How does a new baby affect the parents' lives? How do male professors' attitudes affect a young woman's performance
in college?

The *mesosystem* is the interlocking of various microsystems—linkages
between home and school, work and neighborhood. How does a bitterly con-
tested divorce affect a person's performance at work? How does unhappiness on
the job affect a parent-child relationship?

The *exosystem* consists of linkages between a microsystem and outside
systems or institutions that affect a person indirectly. How does a community's
transit system affect job opportunities? Does television programming that may encourage criminal behavior make people less secure in their homes?

The *macrosystem* consists of overarching cultural patterns, such as dominant
beliefs, ideologies, and economic and political systems. How is an individual affected by living in a capitalist or socialist society?

Finally, the *chronosystem* adds the dimension of time: change or constancy in the person and the environment. This can include changes in family structure, place of residence, or employment, as well as larger cultural changes such as wars and economic cycles.

According to Bronfenbrenner, a person is not merely an outcome of development, but is also a shaper of it. People effect their development through their biological and psychological characteristics, talents and skills, disabilities, and temperament.

By looking at systems that affect individuals in and beyond the family, this bioecological approach helps us to see the variety of influences on development. The contextual perspective also reminds us that findings about the development of people in one culture or in one group within a culture (such as white, middle-class Americans) may not apply equally to people in other societies or cultural groups.

✔ **Checkpoint**

Can you . . .

♦ State the chief assumptions of the contextual perspective?

♦ Differentiate Bronfenbrenner's five systems of contextual influence?

Perspective 5: Evolutionary/Sociobiological

The **evolutionary/sociobiological perspective** proposed by E. O. Wilson (1975) focuses on evolutionary and biological bases of behavior. Influenced by Darwin's theory of evolution, it draws on findings of anthropology, ecology, genetics, ethology, and evolutionary psychology to explain the adaptive, or survival, value of behavior for an individual or species. The evolutionary/sociobiological approach is not necessarily a separate theoretical perspective; it both borrows from and predicts findings of, for example, social learning theory, cognitive-developmental theory, and contextualism (MacDonald, 1988, 1998)

According to Darwin, species have developed through the related processes of *survival of the fittest* and *natural selection*. Species with traits better adapted, or fitted, to their environments survive and reproduce; those less adapted, or less fitted, do not. Thus, through reproduction, more adaptive characteristics are *selected* to be passed on to future generations, and less adaptive characteristics die out.

Evolved mechanisms are behaviors that developed to solve problems in adapting to an earlier environment. For example, sudden aversion to certain foods during pregnancy may originally have evolved to protect the vulnerable fetus from toxic substances. Such evolved mechanisms may survive even though they no longer serve a useful purpose (Bjorklund & Pellegrini, 2000, 2002), or they may evolve further in response to changing environmental conditions. Although most evolved mechanisms are tailored to a specific problem, others, such as human intelligence, are viewed as having evolved to help people face a wide range of problems (MacDonald, 1998).

Ethology is the study of the distinctive adaptive behaviors of animal species. Ethologists suggest that, for each species, certain innate behaviors, such as squirrels' burying of nuts in the fall and spiders' spinning of webs, have evolved to increase the odds of survival. Lorenz's newborn ducklings' instinct to follow their mother, discussed in Chapter 1, is another example. By observing animals, usually in their natural surroundings, ethologists seek to identify which behaviors are universal and which are specific to a particular species or are modified by culture. The British psychologist John Bowlby (1969) applied ethological principles to aspects of human development. For example, he viewed infants' attachment to a caregiver as a mechanism that evolved to protect the infants from predators. (Attachment is discussed more fully in Chapter 6.)

Evolutionary psychology applies Darwinian principles to individual behavior. According to this theory, people unconsciously strive, not only for personal survival, but also to perpetuate their genetic legacy. They do so by seeking to maximize their chances of having offspring who will inherit their characteristics and

evolutionary/sociobiological perspective View of human development that focuses on evolutionary and biological bases of behavior.

ethology Study of distinctive adaptive behaviors of species of animals that have evolved to increase survival of the species.

evolutionary psychology Application of Darwinian principles of natural selection and survival of the fittest to individual behavior.

survive to reproduce. However, an evolutionary perspective does *not* necessarily reduce human behavior entirely to the effects of genes seeking to reproduce themselves. It also places great weight on the environment to which a person must adapt. A *developmental systems approach* views human development as the outcome of a dynamic process of bidirectional interaction between person and environment (Bjorklund & Pellegrini, 2000; Lickliter & Honeycutt, 2003; Nelson, 2005). An example, discussed in Chapter 4, is Esther Thelen's theory and research on how infants learn to walk.

Evolutionary *developmental* psychologists apply evolutionary principles to child development. They study such topics as parenting strategies, gender differences in play, and peer relations, and they identify behaviors that are adaptive at different ages. For example, as we discuss in Box 8-1, the extended period of immaturity and dependency during infancy and childhood allows children to spend much of their time in play; and, as Piaget maintained, it is largely through play that cognitive development occurs. Play also enables children to develop motor skills and, through pretending, to experiment with social roles.

A Shifting Balance

No one theory of human development is universally accepted, and no one theoretical perspective explains all facets of development. As the study of human development has evolved, the mechanistic and organismic models have shifted in influence. Most of the early pioneers in the field, including Freud, Erikson, and Piaget, favored organismic or stage approaches. The mechanistic view gained support during the 1960s with the popularity of learning theories.

Today much attention is focused on the biological and evolutionary bases of behavior. Instead of looking for broad stages, developmental scientists seek to discover what specific kinds of behavior show continuity and what processes are involved in each. Rather than abrupt changes, a close examination of Piaget's stages of cognitive development, for example, reveals gradual, sometimes almost imperceptible, advances that add up to a qualitative shift. Similarly, most infants do not learn to walk overnight, but rather by a series of tentative movements that gradually become more self-assured. Even when observable behavior seems to change suddenly, the biological or neurological processes that underlie that behavioral change may be continuous (Courage & Howe, 2002).

Instead of debating active versus reactive development, investigators often find that influences are *bidirectional:* People change their world even as it changes them. A baby girl born with a cheerful disposition is likely to get positive responses from adults, which strengthen her trust that her smiles will be rewarded and motivate her to smile more. A manager who offers constructive criticism and emotional support to her subordinates is likely to elicit greater efforts to produce. Improved productivity, in turn, is likely to encourage her to keep using this managerial style.

Theories of human development grow out of, and are tested by, research. Although most researchers draw from a variety of theoretical perspectives, research questions and methods often reflect a researcher's particular theoretical orientation. For example, in trying to understand how a child develops a sense of right and wrong, a behaviorist would examine the way the parents respond to the child's behavior: what kinds of behavior they punish or praise. A social learning theorist would focus on imitation of moral examples, possibly in stories or in movies. An information-processing researcher might do a task analysis to identify the steps a child goes through in determining the range of moral options available and then in deciding which option to pursue.

With the vital connection between theory and research in mind, let's look at the methods developmental researchers use.

Research Methods

Guidepost 3

How do developmental scientists study people, and what are some advantages and disadvantages of each research method?

Researchers in human development work within two methodological traditions: *quantitative* and *qualitative.* **Quantitative research** deals with measurable data. Quantitative researchers might study, for example, how much fear or anxiety patients feel before surgery as measured by standardized tests, physiological changes, or statistical analysis. **Qualitative research** involves the interpretation of nonnumerical data, such as the nature or quality of participants' subjective experiences, feelings, or beliefs. Qualitative researchers might study how patients describe their emotions before surgery or how girls describe their experience of puberty.

Quantitative research is based on the **scientific method,** which generally characterizes scientific inquiry in any field. Its usual steps are (1) *identifying a problem* to be studied, often on the basis of a theory or of previous research; (2) *formulating hypotheses* to be tested by research; (3) *collecting data;* (4) *analyzing the data* to determine whether they support the hypothesis; (5) *forming tentative conclusions;* and (6) *disseminating findings* so that other observers can check, learn from, analyze, repeat, and build on the results.

Qualitative research is more open-ended and exploratory. Qualitative researchers gather and examine data to see what hypotheses may emerge. Qualitative research cannot yield general conclusions, but it can be a rich source of insights into individual attitudes and behavior.

The selection of quantitative or qualitative methods depends on the topic for study, how much is already known about it, the researcher's expertise and theoretical orientation, and the setting. Quantitative research is often done in laboratory settings under controlled conditions. Qualitative research is usually conducted in everyday settings to investigate topics about which little is known.

quantitative research Research that deals with objectively measurable data.

qualitative research Research that focuses on nonnumerical data, such as subjective experiences, feelings, or beliefs.

scientific method System of established principles and processes of scientific inquiry, which includes identifying a problem to be studied, formulating a hypothesis to be tested by research, collecting data, analyzing the data, forming tentative conclusions, and disseminating findings.

Sampling

To be sure that the results of their research are true generally and not just for specific participants, quantitative researchers need to control who gets into the study. Because studying an entire *population* (a group to whom the findings may apply) may be too costly and time-consuming, investigators select a **sample,** a smaller group within the population. The sample should adequately represent the target population; that is, it should show relevant characteristics in the same proportions as in the entire population. Otherwise the results cannot properly be *generalized,* or applied to the population as a whole. To judge how generalizable the findings are likely to be, researchers need to compare the characteristics of the people in the sample with those of the population as a whole.

Often researchers seek to achieve representativeness through **random selection,** in which each person in a population has an equal and independent chance of being chosen. The result of random selection is a *random sample.* If we wanted to study the effects of an educational program, for example, one way to select a random sample of students in a human development class would be to put all of their names into a large bowl, stir it, and then draw out a certain number of names. A random sample, especially a large one, is likely to represent the population well. Unfortunately, a random sample of a large population is often difficult to obtain. Instead, many studies use samples selected for convenience or accessibility (for example, children born in a particular hospital or

sample Group of participants chosen to represent the entire population under study.

random selection Selection of a sample in such a way that each person in a population has an equal and independent chance of being chosen.

Table 2-3	Characteristics of Major Methods of Data Collection		
Type	**Main Characteristics**	**Advantages**	**Disadvantages**
Self-report: diary, interview, or questionnaire	Participants are asked about some aspect of their lives; questioning may be highly structured or more flexible.	Can provide firsthand information about a person's life, attitudes, or opinions.	Participant may not remember information accurately or may distort responses in a socially desirable way; how question is asked or by whom may affect answer.
Naturalistic observation	People are observed in their normal setting, with no attempt to manipulate behavior.	Provides good description of behavior; does not subject people to unnatural settings that may distort behavior.	Lack of control; observer bias.
Laboratory observation	Participants are observed in the laboratory, with no attempt to manipulate behavior.	Provides good descriptions; offers greater control than naturalistic observation, since all participants are observed under same controlled conditions.	Observer bias; controlled situation can be artificial.
Behavioral and performance measures	Participants are tested on abilities, skills, knowledge, competencies, or physical responses.	Provides objectively measurable information; avoids subjective distortions.	Cannot measure attitudes or other nonbehavioral phenomena; results may be affected by extraneous factors.

Checkpoint

Can you . . .

♦ Compare quantitative and qualitative research, and give an example of each?

♦ Summarize the six steps in the scientific method, and tell why each is important?

♦ Explain the purpose of random selection and tell how it can be achieved?

patients in a particular nursing home). The findings of such studies may not apply to the population as a whole.

In qualitative research, samples tend to be small and need not be random. Participants in this kind of research may be chosen for their ability to communicate the nature of a certain experience, such as how it feels to go through puberty or to undergo a particular type of surgery.

Forms of Data Collection

Common ways of gathering data (Table 2-3) include *self-reports* (verbal reports by study participants), *observation* of participants in laboratory or natural settings, and *behavioral or performance measures.* Depending in part on time and financial constraints, researchers may use one or more of these data collection techniques in any research design. Qualitative research tends to depend heavily on interviews and on observation in natural settings, whereas quantitative research makes use of more structured methods. Currently there is a trend toward increased use of self-reports and observation in combination with more objective measures.

Self-Reports: Diaries, Interviews, Questionnaires The simplest form of self-report is a *diary* or log. Participants may be asked, for example, to record what they eat each day or the times when they feel depressed. In studying young children, *parental self-reports*—diaries, journals, interviews, or questionnaires—are commonly used, often together with other methods such as video or audio recording. Parents may be recorded playing with their babies and then may be shown the recording and asked to explain why they reacted as they did.

In an *interview,* researchers ask questions about attitudes, opinions, or behavior. To reach more people and protect their privacy, researchers sometimes distribute a printed or online *questionnaire,* which participants fill out and return.

By questioning a large number of people, investigators can get a broad picture—at least of what the respondents *say* they believe or do or have done.

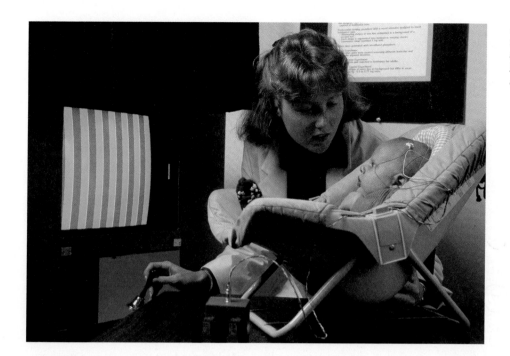

A baby under laboratory observation may or may not behave the same way as in a naturalistic setting, such as at home, but both kinds of observation can provide valuable information.

However, people willing to participate in interviews or fill out questionnaires may not accurately represent the population as a whole. Furthermore, heavy reliance on self-reports may be unwise because people may not have thought about what they feel and think or honestly may not know. People may forget when and how events actually took place or may consciously or unconsciously distort their replies to fit what is considered socially desirable.

How a question is asked, and by whom, can affect the answer. When questioned about potentially risky or socially disapproved behavior, such as sexual habits and drug use, respondents may be more candid in responding to a computerized survey than to a paper-and-pencil survey (Turner et al., 1998).

Naturalistic and Laboratory Observation   Observation takes two forms: *naturalistic observation* and *laboratory observation*. In **naturalistic observation,** researchers look at people in real-life settings. The researchers do not try to alter behavior or the environment; they simply record what they see. In **laboratory observation,** researchers observe and record behavior in a controlled environment, such as a laboratory. By observing all participants under the same conditions, investigators can more clearly identify any differences in behavior not attributable to the environment.

naturalistic observation Research method in which behavior is studied in natural settings without intervention or manipulation.

laboratory observation Research method in which all participants are observed under the same controlled conditions.

Both kinds of observation can provide valuable descriptions of behavior, but they have limitations. For one, they do not explain *why* people behave as they do, though the observers may suggest interpretations. Then, too, an observer's presence can alter behavior. When people know they are being watched, they may act differently. Finally, there is a risk of *observer bias:* the researcher's tendency to interpret data to fit expectations or to emphasize some aspects and minimize others.

During the 1960s, laboratory observation was used most commonly to achieve more rigorous control. Now digital recorders and computers enable researchers to analyze moment-by-moment changes in behavior, for example, in interactions between spouses (Gottman & Notarius, 2000). Such methods make naturalistic observation more accurate and objective than it otherwise would be.

Behavioral and Performance Measures   For many kinds of research, investigators use more objective measures of behavior or performance instead of, or in

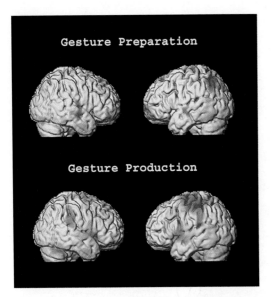

Researchers can analyze an fMRI (functional magnetic resonance imaging) brain scan taken during an activity or task to observe the link between cognitive activity and what happens in the brain. The regions shown in red are activated when thinking about making a gesture (preparation) and then in performing it (production).

operational definition Definition stated solely in terms of the operations or procedures used to produce or measure a phenomenon.

cognitive neuroscience Study of links between neural processes and cognitive abilities.

case study Study of a single subject, such as an individual or family.

addition to, self-reports or observation. Tests and other behavioral and neuropsychological measures may be used to assess abilities, skills, knowledge, competencies, or physiological responses, such as heart rate and brain activity. Although these measures are less subjective than self-reports or personal observation, such factors as fatigue and self-confidence can affect results.

Some written tests, such as intelligence tests, compare performance with that of other test-takers. Such tests can be meaningful and useful only if they are both *valid* (that is, the tests measure the abilities they claim to measure) and *reliable* (that is, the results are reasonably consistent from one time to another). (The validity of intelligence tests is in question, as we discuss in Chapter 9.) To avoid bias, tests must be *standardized,* that is, given and scored by the same methods and criteria for all test-takers.

When measuring a characteristic such as intelligence, it is important to define exactly what is to be measured in a way that other researchers will understand so that they can repeat the experiment and/or comment on the results. For this purpose, researchers use an **operational definition**—a definition stated solely in terms of the operations or procedures used to produce or measure a phenomenon. Intelligence, for example, can be defined as the ability to achieve a certain score on a test covering logical relationships, memory, and vocabulary recognition. Some people may disagree with this definition, but no one can reasonably claim that it is not clear.

For most of the history of psychology, theorists and researchers studied cognitive processes apart from the physical structures of the brain in which these processes occur. Now, sophisticated imaging instruments, such as functional magnetic resonance imaging (fMRI) and positron emission tomography (PET), make it possible to see the brain in action, and the new field of **cognitive neuroscience** is linking our understanding of cognitive functioning with what happens in the brain.

Basic Research Designs

A research design is a plan for conducting a scientific investigation: what questions are to be answered, how participants are to be selected, how data are to be collected and interpreted, and how valid conclusions can be drawn. Four basic designs used in developmental research are *case studies, ethnographic studies, correlational studies,* and *experiments.* The first two designs are qualitative; the last two are quantitative. Each design has advantages and drawbacks, and each is appropriate for certain kinds of research problems (Table 2-4).

Case Studies A **case study** is a study of an individual, such as the research done with Genie, the 13-year-old girl who had been confined to a small room and never learned to talk (described in Box 1-1). Some theories, such as Freud's, have grown out of clinical case studies, which include careful observation and interpretation of what patients say and do. Case studies also may use behavioral or physiological measures and biographical, autobiographical, or documentary materials.

Case studies offer useful, in-depth information. They can explore sources of behavior and can test treatments, and they can suggest directions for further research. A related advantage is flexibility: The researcher is free to explore avenues of inquiry that arise during the course of the study. However, case studies, being qualitative in design, have shortcomings. From studying Genie, for instance, we learn much about the development of a single child, but not how the information applies to children in general. Furthermore, case studies cannot explain behavior

Type	Main Characteristics	Advantages	Disadvantages
Case study	In-depth study of single individual.	Flexibility; provides detailed picture of one person's behavior and development; can generate hypotheses.	May not generalize to others; conclusions not directly testable; cannot establish cause and effect.
Ethnographic study	In-depth study of a culture or subculture.	Can help overcome culturally based biases in theory and research; can test universality of developmental phenomena.	Subject to observer bias.
Correlational study	Attempt to find positive or negative relationship between variables.	Enables prediction of one variable on basis of another; can suggest hypotheses about causal relationships.	Cannot establish cause and effect.
Experiment	Controlled procedure in which an experimenter controls the independent variable to determine its effect on the dependent variable; may be conducted in the laboratory or field.	Establishes cause-and-effect relationships; is highly controlled and can be repeated by another investigator; degree of control greatest in the laboratory experiment.	Findings, especially when derived from laboratory experiments, may not generalize to situations outside the laboratory.

Table 2-4 Basic Research Designs

with certainty because there is no way to test their conclusions. Even though it seems reasonable that Genie's severely deprived environment contributed to or even caused her language deficiency, it may be that she had cognitive disabilities even before she was abused.

Ethnographic Studies An **ethnographic study** seeks to describe the pattern of relationships, customs, beliefs, technology, arts, and traditions that make up a society's way of life. Ethnographic research can be qualitative, quantitative, or both. It uses a combination of methods, including **participant observation**, a form of naturalistic observation in which researchers live or participate in the societies or smaller groups they observe, often for long periods of time.

Because of ethnographers' involvement in the events or societies they are observing, their findings are especially open to observer bias. On the positive side, ethnographic research can help overcome cultural biases in theory and research (Box 2-1). Ethnography demonstrates the error of assuming that principles developed from research in Western cultures are universally applicable.

Correlational Studies A **correlational study** seeks to determine whether a *correlation,* or statistical relationship, exists between *variables,* phenomena that change or vary among people or can be varied for purposes of research. Correlations are expressed in terms of direction (positive or negative) and magnitude (degree). Two variables that are correlated *positively* increase or decrease together. In Chapter 10, we describe studies that show a positive, or direct, correlation between televised violence and aggression. That is, children who watch more violent television tend to fight more than children who watch less violent television. Two variables have a *negative,* or inverse, correlation if, as one increases, the other decreases. Studies show a negative correlation between amount of schooling and the risk of developing dementia (mental deterioration) due to Alzheimer's disease in old age. In other words, the less education, the more dementia (Katzman, 1993).

Correlations are reported as numbers ranging from −1.0 (a perfect negative relationship) to +1.0 (a perfect positive relationship). Perfect correlations are

ethnographic study In-depth study of a culture, which uses a combination of methods including participant observation.

participant observation Research method in which the observer lives with the people or participates in the activity being observed.

correlational study Research design intended to discover whether a statistical relationship between variables exists.

BOX **2-1** **Window** *on the* **World**

Purposes of Cross-Cultural Research

When David, a European American child, was asked to identify the missing detail in a picture of a face with no mouth, he said, "The mouth." But Ari, an Asian immigrant child in Israel, said that the *body* was missing. Since art in his culture does not present a head as a complete picture, he thought the absence of a body was more important than the omission of "a mere detail like the mouth" (Anastasi, 1988, p. 360).

By looking at children from different cultural groups, researchers can learn in what ways development is universal (and thus intrinsic to the human condition) and in what ways it is culturally determined. For example, children everywhere learn to speak in the same sequence, advancing from cooing and babbling to single words and then to simple combinations of words. The words vary from culture to culture, but toddlers around the world put them together to form sentences. Such findings suggest that the capacity for learning language is universal and inborn.

On the other hand, culture can exert a surprisingly large influence on early motor development. African babies, whose parents often prop them in a sitting position and bounce them on their feet, tend to sit and walk earlier than U.S. babies (Rogoff & Morelli, 1989). The society in which children grow up

also influences the skills they learn. In the United States, children learn to read, write, and, increasingly, to operate computers. In rural Nepal, they learn how to drive water buffalo and find their way along mountain paths.

One important reason to conduct research among different cultural groups is to recognize biases in traditional Western theories and research that often go unquestioned until they are shown to be a product of cultural influences. Because so much research in child development has focused on Western industrialized societies, typical development in these societies may be seen as the norm, or standard of behavior. Measuring against this "norm" leads to narrow—and often wrong—ideas about development. Pushed to its extreme, this belief can cause the development of children in other ethnic and cultural groups to be seen as deviant (Rogoff & Morelli, 1989).

Barriers exist to our understanding of cultural differences, particularly those involving minority subcultures. As with David and Ari in our opening example, a question or task may have different conceptual meanings for different cultural groups. Sometimes the barriers are linguistic. In a study of children's understanding of kinship relations among the Zinacanta

---

rare. The closer a correlation comes to $+1.0$ or -1.0, the stronger the relationship, either positive or negative. A correlation of zero means that the variables have no relationship.

Correlations enable us to predict one variable in relation to another. On the basis of the positive correlation between watching televised violence and aggression, we can predict that children who watch violent shows are more likely to get into fights than children who do *not* watch such shows. The greater the magnitude of the correlation between the two variables, the greater the ability to predict one from the other.

Although strong correlations suggest possible cause-and-effect relationships, these are merely hypotheses and need to be examined and tested critically. We cannot be sure from a positive correlation between televised violence and aggressiveness that watching televised violence *causes* aggression; we can conclude only that the two variables are related. It is possible that the causation goes the other way: aggressive behavior may lead children to watch more violent programs. Or a third variable—perhaps an inborn predisposition toward aggressiveness or a violent living environment—may cause a child *both* to watch violent programs and to act aggressively. Similarly, we cannot be sure that schooling protects against dementia; it may be that another variable, such as socioeconomic status, might explain both lower levels of schooling and higher levels of dementia. The only way to show with certainty that one variable causes another is through experimentation—a method that, when studying human beings, is not always possible for practical or ethical reasons.

Experiments   An **experiment** is a controlled procedure in which the experimenter manipulates variables to learn how one affects another. Scientific experiments must

② **experiment** Rigorously controlled, replicable procedure in which the researcher manipulates variables to assess the effect of one on the other.

people of Chiapas, Mexico (Greenfield & Childs, 1978), instead of asking "How many brothers do you have?" the researchers—knowing that the Zinacantas have separate terms for older and younger siblings—asked, "What is the name of your older brother?" Using the same question across cultures might have obscured, rather than revealed, cultural differences and similarities (Parke, 2004).

Results of observational studies of ethnic or cultural groups may be affected by the ethnicity of the researchers. For example, in one study European American observers noted more conflict and restrictiveness in African American mother-daughter relationships than African American observers noted (Gonzales, Cauce, & Mason, 1996).

In this book we discuss several influential theories developed from research in Western societies that do not hold up when tested on people from other cultures—theories about gender roles, abstract thinking, moral reasoning, and other aspects of human development. Throughout this book, we consistently look at children in cultures and subcultures other than the dominant one in the United States to show how closely development is tied to society and culture and to add to our understanding of

normal development in many settings. In so doing, however, we need to keep in mind the pitfalls involved in cross-cultural comparisons.

What's Your View?

Can you think of a situation in which you made an incorrect assumption about a person because you were unfamiliar with her or his cultural background?

Check It Out

For more information on this topic, go to http://psychology.ucsc.edu. This is the website for the Department of Psychology at the University of California, Santa Cruz. Select the *Get to Know Our Faculty* link and read about the work of faculty members who conduct cross-cultural research in human development: Barbara Rogoff and David Harrington.

be conducted and reported in such a way that another experimenter can *replicate* them, that is, repeat them in exactly the same way with different participants to verify the results and conclusions.

Groups and Variables   A common way to conduct an experiment is to divide the participants into two kinds of groups. An **experimental group** consists of people who are to be exposed to the experimental manipulation or *treatment*—the phenomenon the researcher wants to study. Afterward, the effect of the treatment will be measured one or more times to find out what changes, if any, it caused. A **control group** consists of people who are similar to the experimental group but do not receive the experimental treatment or may receive a different treatment. An experiment may include one or more of each type of group. If the experimenter wants to compare the effects of different treatments (say, of two methods of teaching), the overall sample may be divided into *treatment groups,* each of which receives one of the treatments under study. To ensure objectivity, some experiments, particularly in medical research, use *double-blind* procedures, in which neither participants nor experimenters know who is receiving the treatment and who is instead receiving an inert *placebo.*

One team of researchers (Whitehurst et al., 1988) wanted to find out what effect a special method of reading picture books to very young children might have on their language and vocabulary skills. The researchers compared two groups of middle-class children ages 21 to 35 months. In the *experimental group,* the parents adopted the new read-aloud method (the *treatment*), which consisted of encouraging children's active participation and giving frequent, age-based feedback. In the *control group,* parents simply read aloud as they usually did.

experimental group In an experiment, the group receiving the treatment under study.

control group In an experiment, a group of people, similar to those in the experimental group, who do not receive the treatment under study.

After 1 month, the children in the experimental group were 8.5 months ahead of the control group in level of speech and 6 months ahead in vocabulary; 9 months later, the experimental group was still 6 months ahead of the control group. It is reasonable to conclude, then, that this read-aloud method improved the children's language and vocabulary skills.

In this experiment, the type of reading approach was the *independent variable,* and the children's language skills were the *dependent variable.* An **independent variable** is something over which the experimenter has direct control. A **dependent variable** is something that may or may not change as a result of changes in the independent variable; in other words, it *depends* on the independent variable. In an experiment, a researcher manipulates the independent variable to see how changes in it will affect the dependent variable.

Random Assignment If an experiment finds a significant difference in the performance of the experimental and control groups, how do we know that the cause was the independent variable, in other words, that the conclusion is valid? For example, in the read-aloud experiment, how can we be sure that the reading method and not some other factor (such as intelligence) caused the difference in language development of the two groups? The best way to control for effects of such extraneous factors is **random assignment:** assigning the participants to groups in such a way that each person has an equal chance of being placed in any group. (Random assignment differs from random selection, which determines who gets into the full sample.)

If assignment is random and the sample is large enough, differences in such factors as age, gender, and ethnicity will be evenly distributed so that the groups initially are as alike as possible in every respect except for the variable to be tested. Otherwise, unintended differences between the groups might *confound,* or contaminate, the results, and any conclusions drawn from the experiment would have to be viewed with suspicion. To control for confounds, the experimenter must make sure that everything except the independent variable is held constant during the course of the experiment. For example, in the read-aloud study, parents of the experimental and control groups must spend the same amount of time reading to their children. When participants in an experiment are randomly assigned to treatment groups and conditions other than the independent variable are carefully controlled, the experimenter can be reasonably confident that a causal relationship has (or has not) been established—that any differences between the reading skills of the two groups are due to the reading method and not some other factor.

Of course, with respect to some variables we might want to study, such as age, gender, and race/ethnicity, random assignment is not possible. We cannot assign Terry to be 5 years old and Brett to be 10, or one to be a boy and the other a girl, or one to be African American and the other Asian American. When studying such a variable—for example, whether boys or girls are stronger in certain abilities—researchers can strengthen the validity of their conclusions by randomly selecting participants and by trying to make sure that they are statistically equivalent in other ways that might make a difference in the study.

Laboratory, Field, and Natural Experiments The control necessary for establishing cause and effect is most easily achieved in *laboratory experiments.* In this type of experiment the participants are brought to a laboratory, where they are subject to conditions manipulated by the experimenter. The experimenter records the participants' reactions to these conditions, perhaps comparing them with their own or other participants' behavior under different conditions.

independent variable In an experiment, the condition over which the experimenter has direct control.

dependent variable In an experiment, the condition that may or may not change as a result of changes in the independent variable.

random assignment Assignment of participants in an experiment to groups in such a way that each person has an equal chance of being placed in any group.

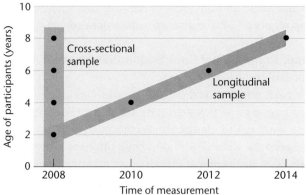

Figure 2-2

Developmental research designs. In the cross-sectional study, groups of 2-, 4-, 6-, and 8-year-olds were tested in 2008 to obtain data about age-related differences. In the longitudinal study, a sample of children were first measured in 2008, when they were 2 years old; follow-up testing is done when the children are 4, 6, and 8, to measure age-related changes. *Note:* Dots indicate times of measurement.

However, not all experiments can be readily done in the laboratory. A *field experiment* is a controlled study conducted in an everyday setting, such as home or school. The reading experiment described earlier (Whitehurst et al., 1988) was a field experiment.

Laboratory and field experiments differ in two important respects. One is the *degree of control* exerted by the experimenter; the other is the degree to which findings can be *generalized* beyond the study setting. Laboratory experiments can be more rigidly controlled and thus are easier to replicate; however, the results may be less generalizable to real life. Because of the artificiality of the laboratory situation, participants may not act as they normally would. Thus, if children who watch violent television shows in the laboratory become more aggressive in that setting, we cannot be sure that children who watch violent shows at home hit their little brothers or sisters more often than children who do not watch such shows or watch fewer of them.

When, for practical or ethical reasons, it is impossible to conduct a true experiment, a *natural experiment* may provide a way of studying certain events. A natural experiment compares people who have been accidentally assigned to separate groups by circumstances of life—one group who were exposed, say, to famine or AIDS or a birth defect or superior education, and another group who were not. A natural experiment, despite its name, is actually a correlational study because controlled manipulation of variables and random assignment to treatment groups are not possible.

One natural experiment looked at what happened when a casino opened on an Indian reservation in North Carolina, raising the income of tribal members (Costello, Compton, Keeler, & Angold, 2003). The study found a decline in behavioral disorders among children in these families as compared with children in the same area whose families did not receive increased income. Still, because it was correlational, the study could not prove that the increased income actually *caused* improvements in mental health.

Experiments have two important advantages over other research designs: They can establish cause-and-effect relationships, and they permit replication. However, experiments can be too artificial and too narrowly focused. In recent decades, therefore, many researchers have concentrated less on laboratory experimentation or have supplemented it with a wider array of methods.

Developmental Research Designs

The two most common research strategies used to study development are *cross-sectional* and *longitudinal* studies (Figure 2-2). Cross-sectional studies show similarities and differences among age groups; longitudinal studies reveal how people

Checkpoint

Can you . . .

♦ Compare the uses and drawbacks of case studies, ethnographic studies, correlational studies, and experiments?

♦ Explain why only a controlled experiment can establish causal relationships?

♦ Distinguish among laboratory, field, and natural experiments, and tell what kinds of research seem most suitable to each?

♦ Compare the advantages and disadvantages of various forms of data collection?

cross-sectional study Study designed to assess age-related differences, in which people of different ages are assessed on one occasion.

longitudinal study Study designed to assess age changes in a sample over time.

change or stay the same as they grow older. Because each of these designs has drawbacks, researchers also have devised *sequential* designs.

Cross-Sectional, Longitudinal, and Sequential Studies In a **cross-sectional study,** people of different ages are assessed at one point in time. In one cross-sectional study, researchers asked 3-, 4-, 6-, and 7-year-olds questions about a picture of a woman who appeared to be thinking, These researchers found a striking increase with age in children's awareness of thinking as mental activity (J. H. Flavell, Green, & Flavell, 1995). These findings strongly suggest that, as children become older, their understanding of mental processes improves. However, we cannot draw such a conclusion with certainty. We don't know whether the 7-year-olds' awareness of mental activity when they were 3 years old was the same as that of the current 3-year-olds in the study. The only way to see whether actual *change* occurs with age is to conduct a longitudinal study of a particular person or group.

In a **longitudinal study,** researchers study the same person or group of people more than once, sometimes years apart. They may measure a single characteristic, such as vocabulary size, intelligence, height, or aggressiveness, or they may look at several aspects of development to find relationships among them.

In 1962, Glen H. Elder Jr. worked on the Oakland Growth Study, a longitudinal study of 167 urban children born around 1920. The study began at the outset of the Great Depression of the 1930s, when the participants, who had spent their childhoods in the boom years of the Roaring Twenties, were entering adolescence. Elder (1974) observed how societal disruption alters family processes and children's development. Many fathers, preoccupied with job losses and irritable about their loss of status within the family, drank heavily. Mothers found jobs and took on more parental authority. Parents argued more. Adolescents tended to show developmental difficulties. However, boys who obtained jobs to help out became more independent and were better able to escape the stressful family atmosphere than were girls, who helped at home. As adults, these men were strongly work oriented but also valued family activities and cultivated dependability in their children.

Both cross-sectional and longitudinal designs have strengths and weaknesses (Table 2-5). Advantages of cross-sectional research include speed and economy; data can be gathered relatively quickly from large numbers of people. And, because participants are assessed only once, there is no problem of either attrition (participants dropping out) or repeated testing, as is the case with longitudinal research. One drawback of cross-sectional studies is that they may obscure individual differences by focusing on group averages alone. Their major disadvantage, however, is that the results may be affected by cohort differences—the differing experiences of people born at different times, for example, before and after the advent of the Internet. Cross-sectional studies are sometimes interpreted as yielding information about developmental changes, but such information is often misleading. Thus, the proportion of research devoted to longitudinal studies, especially short-term studies, is increasing (Parke et al., 1994).

Longitudinal research, in repeatedly studying the same people, can track individual patterns of continuity and change. However, a longitudinal study of one cohort may not apply to another. Thus, the results of a study of children born in the 1920s, such as the Oakland Growth Study, may not apply to children born in the 1990s. Furthermore, longitudinal studies generally are more time-consuming and expensive than cross-sectional studies; it may be hard to keep track of a large group of participants over the years, to keep records, and to keep the study going despite possible turnover in research personnel. Then there is the problem of attrition: Participants may die, move away, or drop out. Longitudinal studies also tend

Table 2-5

Table 2-5	Cross-Sectional, Longitudinal, and Sequential Research: Pros and Cons		
Type of Study	**Procedure**	**Advantages**	**Disadvantages**
Cross-sectional	Data are collected on people of different ages at the same time.	Can show similarities and differences among age groups; speedy, economical; presents no problem of attrition or repeated testing.	Cannot establish age effects; masks individual differences; can be confounded by cohort effects.
Longitudinal	Data are collected on same person or persons over a period of time.	Can show age-related change or continuity; avoids confounding age with cohort effects.	Is time-consuming, expensive; presents problems of attrition, bias in sample, and effects of repeated testing; results may be valid only for cohort tested or sample studied.
Sequential	Data are collected on successive cross-sectional or longitudinal samples.	Can avoid drawbacks of both cross-sectional and longitudinal designs.	Requires large amount of time and effort and analysis of very complex data.

to be biased in that participants who stay with the study tend to be above average in intelligence and socioeconomic status. Finally, results can be affected by repeated testing. Participants may do better on later tests because of familiarity with test procedures.

A current trend is toward large, multicentered longitudinal studies with government or larger institution support, which can trace development within a population on a very broad scale. For example, a 21-year National Children's Study (2004) under the auspices of the U.S. Department of Health and Human Services and other government agencies is to follow some 100,000 U.S. children across the country from conception to adulthood. The study is *prospective:* it will include couples of childbearing age who are not yet expecting a child. By following these families, researchers hope to measure how biology and environmental factors interact in influencing children's health.

A **sequential study**—a sequence of cross-sectional and/or longitudinal studies— is a complex strategy designed to overcome the drawbacks of both cross-sectional and longitudinal research (see Table 2-5). Researchers may assess a cross-sectional sample on two or more occasions (that is, in sequence) to find out how members of each age cohort have changed. This procedure permits researchers to separate age-related changes from cohort effects. Another sequential design consists of a sequence of longitudinal studies, running concurrently but starting one after another. This design enables researchers to compare individual differences in the

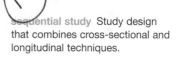

sequential study Study design that combines cross-sectional and longitudinal techniques.

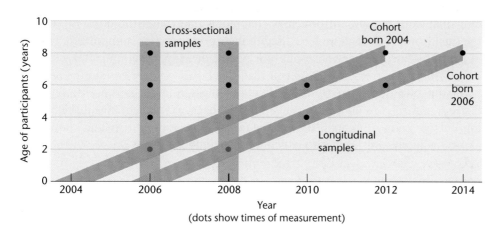

Figure 2-3

A sequential design. Two successive cross-sectional groups of 2-, 4-, 6-, and 8-year-olds were tested in 2006 and 2008. Also, a longitudinal study of a group of children first measured in 2006, when they were 2 years old, is followed by a similar longitudinal study of another group of children who were 2 years old in 2008.

✓ Checkpoint

Can you . . .

◆ List advantages and disadvantages of longitudinal, cross-sectional, and sequential research?

Guidepost 4

What ethical problems may arise in research on humans?

✓ Checkpoint

Can you . . .

◆ List at least three ethical issues affecting rights of research participants?

◆ Identify three principles that should govern inclusion of participants in research?

course of developmental change. A combination of cross-sectional and longitudinal sequences (Figure 2-3) can provide a more complete picture of development than would be possible with longitudinal or cross-sectional research alone. The major drawbacks of sequential studies relate to time, effort, and complexity. Sequential designs require large numbers of participants and the collection and analysis of huge amounts of data over a period of years. Interpreting their findings and conclusions can demand a high degree of sophistication.

Ethics of Research

Should research that might harm its participants ever be undertaken? How can we balance the possible benefits against the risk of mental, emotional, or physical injury to individuals?

Objections to the study of "Little Albert" (described earlier in this chapter) as well as several other early studies gave rise to today's more stringent ethical standards. Institutional review boards at colleges, universities, and other institutions review proposed research from an ethical standpoint. Guidelines of the American Psychological Association (APA, 2002) cover such issues as *informed consent* (consent freely given with full knowledge of what the research entails), *avoidance of deception,* protection of participants from *harm and loss of dignity,* guarantees of *privacy and confidentiality,* the *right to decline or withdraw* from an experiment at any time, and the responsibility of investigators to *correct any undesirable effects,* such as anxiety or shame.

In resolving ethical dilemmas, researchers are expected to be guided by three principles: (1) *beneficence,* the obligation to maximize potential benefits to participants and minimize possible harm; (2) *respect* for participants' autonomy and protection of those who are unable to exercise their own judgment; and (3) *justice,* inclusion of diverse groups together with sensitivity to any special impact the research may have on them. In evaluating risks and benefits, researchers should consider participants' developmental needs (Thompson, 1990) and be sensitive to cultural issues and values (Fisher et al., 2002).

The Society for Research in Child Development (2007) has developed standards for age-appropriate treatment of children in research, covering such principles as avoidance of physical or psychological harm, obtaining the child's assent as well as a parent's or guardian's informed consent, and responsibility to follow up on any information that could jeopardize the child's well-being. For example, infants' and very young children's ability to cope with the stress of the research situation may hinge on the presence of a parent or trusted caregiver, a familiar setting and procedure, and familiar objects.

Our final word in these introductory chapters is that this entire book is far from the final word. Although we have tried to incorporate the most important and the most up-to-date information about how people develop, developmental scientists are constantly learning more. As you read this book, you are certain to come up with your own questions. By thinking about them, and perhaps eventually conducting research to find answers, it is possible that you yourself, now just embarking on the study of human development, will someday add to our knowledge about the interesting species to which we all belong.

Summary and Key Terms

Basic Theoretical Issues

Guidepost 1: *What purposes do theories serve, and what are two basic theoretical issues on which developmental scientists differ?*

- A theory is used to organize and explain data and generate hypotheses that can be tested by research.
- Developmental theories differ on two basic issues: the active or reactive character of development and the existence of continuity or discontinuity in development.
- Two contrasting models of human development are the mechanistic model and the organismic model.

theory (22)

hypotheses (22)

mechanistic model (23)

organismic model (23)

quantitative change (24)

qualitative change (24)

Theoretical Perspectives

Guidepost 2: *What are five theoretical perspectives on human development, and what are some theories representative of each?*

- The psychoanalytic perspective sees development as motivated by unconscious emotional drives or conflicts. Leading examples are Freud's and Erikson's theories.

psychoanalytic perspective (25)

psychosexual development (26)

psychosocial development (28)

- The learning perspective views development as a result of learning based on experience. Leading examples are Watson's and Skinner's behaviorism and Bandura's social learning (social cognitive) theory.

learning perspective (28)

behaviorism (28)

classical conditioning (29)

operant conditioning (29)

reinforcement (29)

punishment (29)

social learning theory (30)

reciprocal determinism (30)

observational learning (30)

self-efficacy (30)

- The cognitive perspective is concerned with thought processes. Leading examples are Piaget's cognitive-stage theory, Vygotsky's sociocultural theory, and the information-processing approach. Neo-Piagetian theorists blend Piagetian principles with insights gained from information-processing research.

cognitive perspective (30)

cognitive-stage theory (31)

organization (31)

schemes (31)

adaptation (31)

assimilation (31)

accommodation (31)

equilibration (31)

sociocultural theory (32)

zone of proximal development (ZPD) (32)

scaffolding (33)

information-processing approach (33)

- The contextual perspective focuses on the individual in a social context. A leading example is Bronfenbrenner's bioecological theory.

contextual perspective (34)

bioecological theory (34)

- The evolutionary/sociobiological perspective, represented by E. O. Wilson and influenced by Darwin's theory of evolution, focuses on the adaptiveness, or survival value, of behavior. A leading example is Bowlby's attachment theory.

evolutionary/sociobiological perspective (35)

ethology (35)

evolutionary psychology (35)

Research Methods

Guidepost 3: *How do developmental scientists study people, and what are some advantages and disadvantages of each research method?*

- Research can be either quantitative or qualitative, or both.
- To arrive at sound conclusions, quantitative researchers use the scientific method.
- Random selection of a research sample can ensure generalizability.
- Three forms of data collection are self-reports, observation, and behavioral and performance measures.

quantitative research (37)

qualitative research (37)

scientific method (37)

sample (37)

random selection (37)

naturalistic observation (39)

laboratory observation (39)

operational definitions (40)

cognitive neuroscience (40)

case study (40)

ethnographic study (41)

participant observation (41)

correlational study (41)

experiment (42)

experimental group (43)

control group (43)

independent variable (44)

dependent variable (44)

random assignment (44)

cross-sectional study (46)

longitudinal study (46)

sequential study (47)

- A design is a plan for conducting research. Two qualitative designs used in developmental research are the case study and the ethnographic study. Cross-cultural research can indicate whether certain aspects of development are universal or culturally influenced.

- Two quantitative designs are the correlational study and the experiment. Only experiments can firmly establish causal relationships.

- Experiments must be rigorously controlled so as to be valid and replicable. Random assignment of participants can ensure validity.

- Laboratory experiments are easiest to control and replicate, but findings of field experiments may be more generalizable. Natural experiments may be useful in situations in which true experiments would be impractical or unethical.

- The two most common designs used to study age-related development are cross-sectional and longitudinal. Cross-sectional studies assess age differences; longitudinal studies describe continuity or change in the same participants. The sequential study is intended to overcome the weaknesses of the other two designs.

Ethics of Research

Guidepost 4: *What ethical problems may arise in research on humans?*

- Researchers seek to resolve ethical issues on the basis of principles of beneficence, respect, and justice.

- Ethical issues in research include the rights of participants to informed consent, avoidance of deception, protection from harm and loss of dignity and self-esteem, and guarantees of privacy and confidentiality.

- Standards for protection of children used in research cover such principles as parental informed consent and protection from harm or jeopardy to the child's well-being.

3 Forming a New Life

If I could have watched you grow

as a magical mother might,

if I could have seen through my magical transparent belly,

there would have been such ripening within. . . .

—Anne Sexton, 1966

Did You **Know...**

- "Identical twins" may not be exactly identical?
- All but 300 human genes have counterparts in mice?
- "Birth defects" do not always appear at birth?
- Fetuses can learn and remember while in the womb, and they respond to their mother's voice?
- Drinking or smoking during pregnancy can do permanent damage to an unborn child?
- Prenatal care should begin *before* conception?

These are just a few of the interesting and important topics we will cover in this chapter. Prospective parents have an awesome responsibility for the development of the new life they have set in motion. First, parents provide the basic genetic material that makes each person unique. Second, they are sources of environmental influence—both the mother and father affect the health of their unborn child by what they do and what they are exposed to. Environmental influences also include the social and cultural environment parents provide their growing child.

In this chapter, we describe how conception normally occurs, how the mechanisms of heredity operate, and how biological inheritance interacts with environmental influences within and outside the womb. We trace the course of prenatal development, describe influences on it, and discuss ways to monitor it. After you have studied this chapter, you should be able to answer each of the Guidepost questions on the following page.

Guideposts *for Study*

1. How does conception normally occur, and what causes multiple births?

2. How does heredity operate in determining sex and transmitting normal and abnormal traits?

3. How do scientists study the relative influences of heredity and environment, and how do heredity and environment work together?

4. What roles do heredity and environment play in physical health, intelligence, and personality?

5. What are the three stages of prenatal development, and what happens during each stage?

6. What environmental influences can affect prenatal development?

7. What techniques can assess a fetus's health, and why is prenatal care important?

Guidepost 1

How does conception normally occur, and what causes multiple births?

Conceiving New Life

Tania wanted to have a baby. She carefully watched the calendar, counting the days after each menstrual period so as to take advantage of her *fertile window.* What Tania didn't realize is that, although a woman is usually fertile between the 6th and 21st days of the menstrual cycle, the timing of the fertile window can be highly unpredictable (Wilcox, Dunson, & Baird, 2000). This means that she may be able to conceive at any time during the month.

How Fertilization Takes Place

fertilization Union of sperm and ovum to produce a zygote; also called *conception.*

zygote One-celled organism resulting from fertilization.

Fertilization, or *conception,* is the process by which sperm and ovum—the male and female *gametes,* or sex cells—combine to create a single cell called a **zygote,** which then duplicates itself again and again by cell division to produce all the cells that make up a baby. But conception is not as simple as it sounds. Several independent events need to coincide to conceive a child. And, as we will discuss later in this chapter, not all conceptions end in birth.

At birth, a girl is believed to have about 2 million immature ova in her two ovaries, each ovum in its own *follicle,* or small sac. In a sexually mature woman, *ovulation*—rupture of a mature follicle in either ovary and expulsion of its ovum—occurs about once every 28 days until menopause. The ovum is swept along through one of the fallopian tubes by the *cilia,* tiny hair cells, toward the uterus, or womb.

Sperm are produced in the testicles (testes), or reproductive glands, of a mature male at a rate of several hundred million a day and are ejaculated in the semen at sexual climax. Deposited in the vagina, they try to swim through the *cervix,* the opening of the uterus, and into the fallopian tubes; but only a tiny fraction make it that far. As we will see, which sperm meets which ovum has tremendous implications for the new person.

Fertilization normally occurs while the ovum is passing through the fallopian tube. If fertilization does not occur, the ovum and any sperm cells in the woman's body die. The sperm are absorbed by the woman's white blood cells, and the ovum passes through the uterus and exits through the vagina. (In Chapter 13, we discuss techniques of artificially assisted reproduction often used when one or both prospective parents are infertile.)

What Causes Multiple Births?

In August 2007, Karen Jepp of Calgary, Alberta, Canada, gave birth to identical quadruplets—a 1 in 13 million event. The quads, who had been conceived without fertility drugs, were born about two months early by cesarean delivery and, at last report, were doing fine (Cates, 2007).

Multiple births happen in two ways. Most commonly, the mother's body releases two ova within a short time (or sometimes a single unfertilized ovum splits) and then both are fertilized. The resulting babies are **dizygotic twins** (*di* means "two"), commonly called *fraternal twins*. The second way is for a single *fertilized* ovum to split into two. The babies that result from this cell division are **monozygotic twins** (*mono* means "one"), commonly called *identical twins*. Triplets, quadruplets, and other multiple births can result from either of these processes or a combination of both.

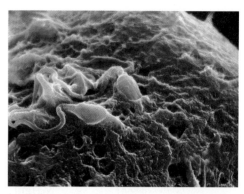

This color-enhanced scanning electron micrograph (SEM) shows two sperm (orange) *attracted to an ovum's furry surface* (blue). *A sperm's long tail enables it to swim through the cervix and up the fallopian tube. The sperm's rounded head releases enzymes that help it penetrate the ovum's thick surface and fertilize the ovum by fusing with its nucleus. Only one sperm can penetrate the ovum; immediately afterward, the ovum's membrane thickens, forming a barrier to competing sperm.*

The many cases of mistaken identity among identical twins attest to their photocopy-like physical appearance. But although monozygotic twins typically have much the same hereditary makeup and are the same sex, they can differ in some respects. They may not be identical in temperament. In some physical characteristics, such as cowlicks, dental patterns, and handedness, they may be mirror images of each other; one may be left-handed and the other right-handed. Indeed, recent research has found differences in genetic makeup in some monozygotic twins (Bruder et al., 2008). Furthermore, through a process called *epigenesis* (discussed later in this chapter), differences between monozygotic twins tend to magnify as twins grow older, especially if they live apart (Fraga et al., 2005).

Dizygotic twins, who are created from different sperm cells and usually from different ova, are no more alike in hereditary makeup than any other siblings and may be the same sex or of different sexes. Dizygotic twins tend to run in families and so may have a genetic basis, whereas monozygotic twins usually occur purely by chance (Martin & Montgomery, 2002; National Center for Health Statistics [NCHS], 1999). A tendency toward twinning seems to be inherited from a woman's mother; thus, when dizygotic twins skip a generation, it is normally because a mother of dizygotic twins has only sons, to whom she cannot pass on the tendency (NCHS, 1999).

dizygotic twins Twins conceived by the union of two different ova (or a single ovum that has split) with two different sperm cells; also called *fraternal twins;* they are no more alike genetically than any other siblings.

monozygotic twins Twins resulting from the division of a single zygote after fertilization; also called *identical twins;* they are genetically similar.

Doctors recently identified a rare third type of twins, called *semi-identical*—the result of two sperm cells fusing with a single ovum. Semi-identical twins are more genetically similar than dizygotic twins but less similar than monozygotic twins (Souter et al., 2007).

The rate of monozygotic twins (about 4 per 1,000 live births) appears to be constant at all times and places, but the rate of dizygotic twins, the more common type, varies (Martin & Montgomery, 2002; NCHS, 1999). For example, West African and African American women are more likely to have dizygotic twins than Caucasian women, who, in turn, are more likely to have them than Chinese or Japanese women (Martin & Montgomery, 2002).

The incidence of dizygotic twins and higher multiple births in the United States has grown rapidly. Between 1980 and 2005, the twin birthrate increased by 70 percent, from 19 to 32.2 twins per 1,000 live births. Twins, triplets, and higher multiples accounted for 3.4 percent of all births in 2005 (Martin, Hamilton, et al.,

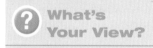

? What's Your View?

- Would you want to have twins or higher multiples?

- If you are a twin or higher multiple, how does that experience affect you?

2007). Two related factors in the rise in multiple births are (1) the trend toward delayed childbearing and (2) the increased use of fertility drugs, which stimulate ovulation, and of assisted reproductive techniques such as in vitro fertilization, which tend to be used more by older women (Hoyert, Mathews, et al., 2006; Martin et al., 2007).

The explosion of multiple births, especially triplets and higher multiples, is of concern because such births, which often result from assisted reproduction, are associated with increased risks: pregnancy complications, premature delivery, low-birth-weight infants, and disability or death of the infant (Hoyert, Mathews, et al., 2006; Jain, Missmer, & Hornstein, 2004; Martin, Hamilton, et al., 2007; Wright, Schieve, Reynolds, & Jeng, 2003). Perhaps because of such concerns, the proportion of assisted reproduction procedures involving three or more embryos has declined and the birthrate for triplets and higher multiples, which had quadrupled during the 1980s and 1990s, has since taken a downturn (Martin, Hamilton, et al., 2007).

Mechanisms of Heredity

The science of genetics is the study of *heredity*—the inborn factors, inherited from one's biological parents, that affect development. When ovum and sperm unite, they endow the baby-to-be with a genetic makeup that influences a wide range of characteristics from color of eyes and hair to health, intellect, and personality.

The Genetic Code

The basis of heredity is a chemical called **deoxyribonucleic acid (DNA).** The double-helix structure of a DNA molecule resembles a long, spiraling ladder whose steps are made of pairs of chemical units called *bases* (Figure 3-1). The bases—adenine (A), thymine (T), cytosine (C), and guanine (G)—are the "letters" of the **genetic code,** which cellular machinery "reads."

Chromosomes are coils of DNA that consist of smaller segments called **genes,** the functional units of heredity. Each gene is located in a definite position on its chromosome and contains thousands of bases. The sequence of bases in a gene tells the cell how to make the proteins that enable it to carry out specific functions. The complete sequence of genes in the human body constitutes the **human genome.**

Every cell in the normal human body except the sex cells (sperm and ova) has 23 pairs of chromosomes—46 in all. Through a type of cell division called *meiosis,* which the sex cells undergo when they are developing, each sex cell ends up with only 23 chromosomes—

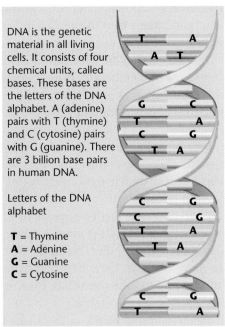

DNA is the genetic material in all living cells. It consists of four chemical units, called bases. These bases are the letters of the DNA alphabet. A (adenine) pairs with T (thymine) and C (cytosine) pairs with G (guanine). There are 3 billion base pairs in human DNA.

Letters of the DNA alphabet

T = Thymine
A = Adenine
G = Guanine
C = Cytosine

Figure 3-1
DNA: The genetic code. (Source: Ritter, 1999.)

Guidepost 2

How does heredity operate in determining sex and transmitting normal and abnormal traits?

deoxyribonucleic acid (DNA) Chemical that carries inherited instructions for the development of all cellular forms of life.

genetic code Sequence of bases within the DNA molecule; governs the formation of proteins that determine the structure and functions of living cells.

chromosomes Coils of DNA that consist of genes.

genes Small segments of DNA located in definite positions on particular chromosomes; functional units of heredity.

human genome Complete sequence of genes in the human body.

one from each pair. Thus, when sperm and ovum fuse at conception, they produce a zygote with 46 chromosomes, 23 from the father and 23 from the mother (Figure 3-2).

At conception, then, the single-celled zygote has all the biological information needed to guide its development into a human baby. Through *mitosis,* a process by which the non-sex cells divide in half over and over again, the DNA replicates itself, so that each newly formed cell has the same DNA structure as all the others. Thus, each cell division creates a genetic duplicate of the original cell, with the same hereditary information. When development is normal, each cell (except the sex cells) continues to have 46 chromosomes identical to those in the original zygote. As the cells divide, they differentiate, specializing in a variety of complex bodily functions that enable the child to grow and develop.

Genes spring into action when conditions call for the information they can provide. Genetic action that triggers the growth of body and brain is often regulated by hormonal levels—both in the mother and in the developing baby—that are affected by such environmental conditions as nutrition and stress. Thus, from the start, heredity and environment are interrelated.

What Determines Sex?

In many villages in Nepal, it is common for a man whose wife has borne no male babies to take a second wife. In some societies, a woman's failure to produce sons is justification for divorce. The irony of these customs is that it is the father's sperm that genetically determines a child's sex.

At the moment of conception, the 23 chromosomes from the sperm and the 23 from the ovum form 23 pairs. Twenty-two pairs are **autosomes,** chromosomes that are not related to sexual expression. The twenty-third pair are **sex chromosomes**—one from the father and one from the mother—that govern the baby's sex.

Sex chromosomes are either *X chromosomes* or *Y chromosomes.* The sex chromosome of every ovum is an X chromosome, but the sperm may contain either an X or a Y chromosome. The Y chromosome contains the gene for maleness, called the *SRY* gene. When an ovum (X) is fertilized by an X-carrying sperm, the zygote formed is XX, a genetic female. When an ovum (X) is fertilized by a Y-carrying sperm, the resulting zygote is XY, a genetic male (Figure 3-3).

Initially, the embryo's rudimentary reproductive system is almost identical in males and in females. Six to eight weeks after conception, male embryos normally start producing the male hormone testosterone, which ordinarily results in the development of a male body with male sexual organs. However, the process is not automatic. Research with mice has found that hormones must first signal the *SRY* gene, which then triggers cell differentiation and formation of the testes. Without this signaling, a genetically male mouse will develop female instead of male genitals (Hughes, 2004; Meeks, Weiss, & Jameson, 2003; Nef et al., 2003). It is likely that a similar mechanism occurs in human males. Conversely, the development of the female reproductive system is controlled by a signaling molecule called *Wnt-4,* a variant form of which can masculinize a genetically female fetus (Biason-Lauber, Konrad, Navratil, & Schoenle, 2004; Hughes, 2004; Vainio, Heikkiia, Kispert, Chin, & McMahon, 1999). Thus, sexual differentiation appears to be a more complex process than simple genetic determination.

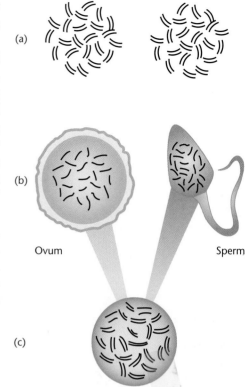

(a)

(b)

Ovum   Sperm

(c)

Zygote

Figure 3-2 Hereditary composition of the zygote. (a) Body cells of women and men contain 23 pairs of chromosomes, which carry the genes, the basic units of inheritance. (b) Each sex cell (ovum and sperm) has only 23 single chromosomes because of a special kind of cell division (meiosis). (c) At fertilization, the 23 chromosomes from the sperm join the 23 from the ovum so that the zygote receives 46 chromosomes, or 23 pairs.

autosomes In humans, the 22 pairs of chromosomes not related to sexual expression.

sex chromosomes Pair of chromosomes that determines sex: XX in the normal human female, XY in the normal human male.

Figure 3-3

Genetic determination of sex. Because all babies receive an X chromosome from the mother, sex is determined by whether an X or a Y chromosome is received from the father.

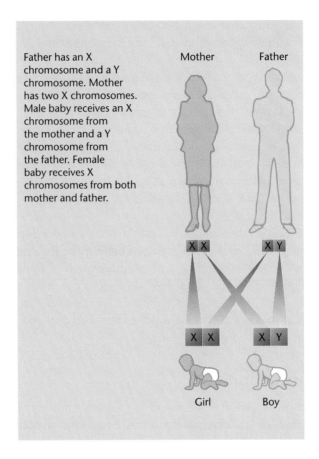

Father has an X chromosome and a Y chromosome. Mother has two X chromosomes. Male baby receives an X chromosome from the mother and a Y chromosome from the father. Female baby receives X chromosomes from both mother and father.

Mother   Father

X X   X Y

X X   X Y

Girl   Boy

Checkpoint

Can you . . .

♦ Describe the structure of DNA and its role in the inheritance of characteristics?

♦ Distinguish between meiosis and mitosis?

♦ Explain why it is the sperm that normally determines a baby's sex and discuss possible complicating factors?

Further complexities arise from the fact that women have two X chromosomes, whereas men have only one. For many years researchers believed that the duplicate genes on one of a woman's two X chromosomes are inactive, or turned off. Recently, however, researchers discovered that only 75 percent of the genes on the extra X chromosome are inactive. About 15 percent remain active, and 10 percent are active in some women but not in others (Carrel & Willard, 2005). This variability in gene activity could help explain gender differences both in normal traits and in disorders linked to the X chromosome, which are discussed later in this chapter. The extra X chromosome also may help explain why women are generally healthier and longer-lived than men: harmful changes in a gene on one X chromosome may be offset by a backup copy on the other X chromosome (Migeon, 2006).

Patterns of Genetic Transmission

During the 1860s, Gregor Mendel, an Austrian monk, laid the foundation for our understanding of patterns of inheritance by crossbreeding pea plants that produced only yellow seeds with pea plants that produced only green seeds. The resulting hybrid plants produced only yellow seeds, meaning, he said, that yellow was *dominant* over green. Yet when he bred the yellow-seeded hybrids with each other, only 75 percent of their offspring had yellow seeds, and the other 25 percent had green seeds. This showed that a hereditary characteristic (in this case, the color green) can be *recessive,* that is, carried by an organism that does not express, or show, it.

Today we know that the genetic picture in humans is far more complex than Mendel imagined. Most human traits fall along a continuous spectrum (for example, from light skin to dark). One normal trait that people inherit through simple dominant transmission is the ability to curl the tongue lengthwise.

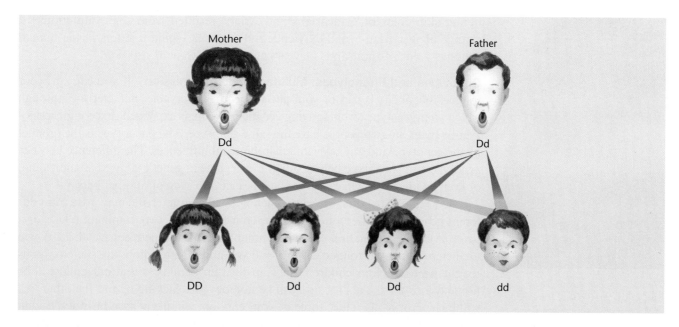

Figure 3-4

Because of dominant inheritance, the same observable phenotype (in this case, tongue curling) can result from two genotypes (DD and Dd). A phenotype expressing a recessive characteristic (inability to curl) must have a homozygous genotype (dd).

Dominant and Recessive Inheritance Can you curl your tongue? If so, you inherited this ability through *dominant inheritance*. If your parents can curl their tongues but you cannot, *recessive inheritance* occurred. How do these two types of inheritance work?

Genes that can produce alternative expressions of a characteristic are called **alleles.** Every person receives a pair of alleles for a given characteristic, one from each parent. When both alleles are the same, the person is **homozygous** for the characteristic; when they are different, the person is **heterozygous.** In **dominant inheritance,** when a person is heterozygous for a particular trait, the dominant allele governs. In other words, when an offspring receives contradictory alleles for a trait, only one of them, the dominant one, will be expressed. **Recessive inheritance,** the expression of a recessive trait, occurs only when a person receives two recessive alleles, one from each parent.

If you inherited one allele for tongue-curling ability from each parent (Figure 3-4), you are homozygous for tongue curling and can curl your tongue. If, say, your mother passed on an allele for the ability and your father passed on an allele lacking it, you are heterozygous. Because the ability is dominant (D) and its lack is recessive (d), you, again, can curl your tongue. But if you received the recessive allele from both parents, you cannot curl your tongue.

Most traits result from **polygenic inheritance,** the interaction of several genes. Skin color is the result of three or more sets of genes on three different chromosomes. These genes work together to produce different amounts of brown pigment, resulting in hundreds of shades of skin color. Intelligence may be affected by fifty or more genes. Indeed, whereas more than a thousand rare genes individually determine abnormal traits, there is no known single gene that, by itself, significantly accounts for individual differences in any complex normal behavior. Instead, such behaviors are likely to be influenced by many genes with small but sometimes identifiable effects.

Traits may be affected by **mutations:** permanent alterations in genetic material. A study comparing genomes of four racial/ethnic groups found that the

alleles Two or more alternative forms of a gene that occupy the same position on paired chromosomes and affect the same trait.

homozygous Possessing two identical alleles for a trait.

heterozygous Possessing differing alleles for a trait.

dominant inheritance Pattern of inheritance in which, when a child receives different alleles, only the dominant one is expressed.

recessive inheritance Pattern of inheritance in which a child receives identical recessive alleles, resulting in expression of a nondominant trait.

polygenic inheritance Pattern of inheritance in which multiple genes at different sites on chromosomes affect a complex trait.

mutations Permanent alterations in genes or chromosomes that may produce harmful characteristics.

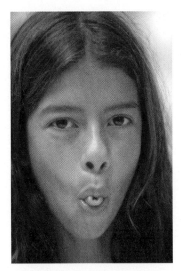

The ability to curl the tongue lengthwise, as this girl is doing, is unusual in that it is inherited through simple dominant transmission. Most normal traits are influenced by multiple genes, often in combination with environmental factors.

phenotype Observable characteristics of a person.

genotype Genetic makeup of a person, containing both expressed and unexpressed characteristics.

multifactorial transmission Combination of genetic and environmental factors to produce certain complex traits.

lighter skin color of Caucasians and Asians resulted from slight mutations—a change of just 1 letter of DNA code out of the 3.1 billion letters in the human genome—tens of thousands of years ago (Lamason et al., 2005).

Genotypes and Phenotypes: Multifactorial Transmission If you can curl your tongue, that ability is part of your **phenotype,** the observable characteristics through which your **genotype,** or underlying genetic makeup, is expressed. Except for monozygotic twins, no two people have the same genotype. The phenotype is the product of the genotype and any relevant environmental influences. The difference between genotype and phenotype helps explain why a clone (a genetic copy of an individual) or even an identical twin can never be an exact duplicate of another person.

As Figure 3-4 shows, the same phenotypical characteristic may arise from different genotypes: either a homozygous combination of two dominant alleles or a heterozygous combination of one dominant allele and one recessive allele. If you are heterozygous for tongue curling, and you and a mate who is also heterozygous for the trait have four children, the statistical probability is that one child will be homozygous for the ability, one will be homozygous lacking it, and the other two will be heterozygous. Thus, three of your children will likely have phenotypes that include tongue curling, but this ability will arise from two different genotypical patterns (homozygous and heterozygous).

Tongue curling has a strong genetic base; but, for most traits, experience modifies the expression of the genotype—a phenomenon called **multifactorial transmission.** Imagine that Steven has inherited musical talent. If he takes music lessons and practices regularly, he may delight his family with his performances. If his family likes and encourages classical music, he may play Bach preludes; if the other children on his block influence him to prefer popular music, he may eventually form a rock group. However, if from early childhood he is not encouraged and not motivated to play music, and if he has no access to a musical instrument or to music lessons, his genotype for musical ability may not be expressed (or may be expressed to a lesser extent) in his phenotype. Some physical characteristics (including height and weight) and most psychological characteristics (such as intelligence and personality traits, as well as musical ability) are products of multifactorial transmission. Many disorders arise when an inherited predisposition (an abnormal variant of a normal gene) interacts with an environmental factor, either before or after birth. Attention-deficit/hyperactivity disorder (ADHD), discussed in Chapter 9, is one of several behavioral disorders thought to be transmitted multifactorially (Price, Simonoff, Waldman, Asherson, & Plomin, 2001).

Later in this chapter we discuss in more detail how environmental influences work together with the genetic endowment to influence development.

epigenesis Mechanism that turns genes on or off and determines functions of body cells.

Epigenesis: Environmental Influence on Gene Expression Until recently, most scientists believed that the genes a child inherits were firmly established during fetal development, though their effects on behavior could be modified by experience. Now, mounting evidence suggests that gene expression itself is controlled by a third component, a mechanism that governs the functioning of genes without affecting the DNA structure. This phenomenon is called **epigenesis.** Furthermore, far from being fixed once and for all, epigenesis is affected by continuing bidirectional interplay with nongenetic influences (Gottlieb, 2007; Rutter, 2007).

Epigenesis (meaning "on the genes"), or the *epigenetic framework,* refers to chemical molecules attached to a gene, which alter the way a cell reads the gene's DNA. The epigenetic framework can be visualized as "a code written in pencil in the margins around the DNA" (Gosden & Feinberg, 2007, p. 731). Because every cell in the body inherits the same DNA sequence, the function of epigenetic markers is to differentiate various types of body cells. They do so by switching particular genes on or off during embryonic formation. Sometimes errors arise in the process, which may lead to birth defects or disease (Gosden & Feinberg, 2007).

Epigenetic markers may contribute to such common ailments as cancer, diabetes, and heart disease. Epigenesis also may explain why one monozygotic twin is susceptible to a disease such as schizophrenia whereas the other twin is not, and why some twins get the same disease but at different ages (Fraga et al., 2005; Wong, Gottesman, & Petronis, 2005).

Epigenetic changes can occur throughout life in response to environmental factors such as nutrition and stress (Rakyan & Beck, 2006). In one twin study, blood analysis showed epigenetic differences in 35 percent of the sample, and these differences were associated with age and lifestyle factors such as diet, physical activity, and smoking (Fraga et al., 2005).

Epigenetic modifications, especially those that occur early in life, may even be heritable. Studies of human sperm cells found age-related epigenetic variations capable of being passed on to future generations (Rakyan & Beck, 2006).

One example of epigenesis is *genome,* or *genetic, imprinting.* Imprinting is the differential expression of certain genetic traits, depending on whether the trait has been inherited from the mother or the father. In imprinted gene pairs, genetic information inherited from the parent of one sex is activated, but genetic information from the other parent is not. Imprinted genes play an important role in regulating fetal growth and development. When a normal pattern of imprinting is disrupted, abnormal fetal growth or congenital growth disorders may result (Hitchins & Moore, 2002).

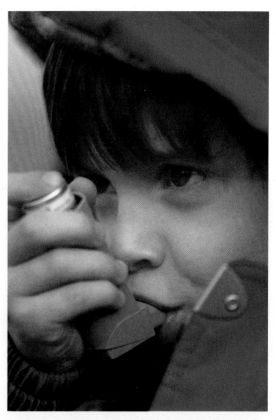

Problems in genome imprinting may explain why a child with an asthmatic mother is more likely to develop asthma than a child with an asthmatic father.

Problems in genome imprinting may explain why the child of a diabetic father but not of a diabetic mother is likely to develop diabetes and why the opposite is true for asthma (Day, 1993). Imprinting problems also may explain why children who inherit the Huntington's gene from their fathers are far more likely to be affected at an early age than children who inherit the Huntington's gene from their mothers (Sapienza, 1990) and why children who receive a certain allele from their mothers are more likely to have autism than those who receive that allele from their fathers (Ingram et al., 2000).

Genetic and Chromosomal Abnormalities

Babies born with serious birth defects are at high risk of dying at or shortly after birth or during infancy or childhood. Most birth disorders are fairly rare (Table 3-1), affecting only about 3 percent of live births (Waknine, 2006). Nevertheless, they are the leading cause of infant death in the United States, accounting for 19.5 percent of all deaths in the first year in 2005 (Kung, Hoyert, Xu, & Murphy, 2008). The most prevalent defects are cleft lip or cleft palate, followed by Down syndrome. Other serious malformations involve the eye, the face, the mouth, or the circulatory, gastronomical, or musculoskeletal systems (Centers for Disease Control and Prevention [CDC], 2006b).

Not all genetic or chromosomal abnormalities are apparent at birth. Symptoms of Tay-Sachs disease (a fatal degenerative disease of the central nervous system that at one time occurred mostly among Jews of eastern European ancestry) and sickle-cell anemia (a blood disorder most common among African Americans) may not appear until at least age 6 months; cystic fibrosis (a condition, especially

✔ **Checkpoint**

Can you . . .

♦ Tell how dominant inheritance and recessive inheritance work, and why most normal traits are *not* the products of simple dominant or recessive transmission?

♦ Explain how epigenesis and genome imprinting occur, and give examples?

Table 3 -1   Some Birth Defects

Problem	Characteristics of Condition	Who Is at Risk	What Can Be Done
Alpha₁ antitrypsin deficiency	Enzyme deficiency that can lead to cirrhosis of the liver in early infancy and emphysema and degenerative lung disease in middle age.	1 in 1,000 white births	No treatment.
Alpha thalassemia	Severe anemia that reduces ability of the blood to carry oxygen; nearly all affected infants are stillborn or die soon after birth.	Primarily families of Malaysian, African, and Southeast Asian descent	Frequent blood transfusions.
Beta thalassemia (Cooley's anemia)	Severe anemia resulting in weakness, fatigue, and frequent illness; usually fatal in adolescence or young adulthood.	Primarily families of Mediterranean descent	Frequent blood transfusions.
Cystic fibrosis	Overproduction of mucus, which collects in the lung and digestive tract; children do not grow normally and usually do not live beyond age 30; the most common inherited *lethal* defect among white people.	1 in 2,000 white births	Daily physical therapy to loosen mucus; antibiotics for lung infections; enzymes to improve digestion; gene therapy (in experimental stage).
Duchenne muscular dystrophy	Fatal disease usually found in males, marked by muscle weakness; minor mental retardation is common; respiratory failure and death usually occur in young adulthood.	1 in 3,000 to 5,000 male births	No treatment.
Hemophilia	Excessive bleeding, usually affecting males; in its most severe form, can lead to crippling arthritis in adulthood.	1 in 10,000 families with a history of hemophilia	Frequent transfusions of blood with clotting factors.
Neural-tube defects: Anencephaly	Absence of brain tissues; infants are stillborn or die soon after birth.	1 in 1,000	No treatment.
Spina bifida	Incompletely closed spinal canal, resulting in muscle weakness or paralysis and loss of bladder and bowel control; often accompanied by hydrocephalus, an accumulation of spinal fluid in the brain, which can lead to mental retardation.	1 in 1,000	Surgery to close spinal canal prevents further injury; shunt placed in brain drains excess fluid and prevents mental retardation.
Phenylketonuria (PKU)	Metabolic disorder resulting in mental retardation.	1 in 15,000 births	Special diet begun in first few weeks of life can prevent mental retardation.
Polycystic kidney disease	*Infantile form:* enlarged kidneys, leading to respiratory problems and congestive heart failure. *Adult form:* kidney pain, kidney stones, and hypertension resulting in chronic kidney failure.	1 in 1,000	Kidney transplants.
Sickle-cell anemia	Deformed, fragile red blood cells that can clog the blood vessels, depriving the body of oxygen; symptoms include severe pain, stunted growth, frequent infections, leg ulcers, gallstones, susceptibility to pneumonia, and stroke.	1 in 500 African Americans	Painkillers, transfusions for anemia and to prevent stroke, antibiotics for infections.
Tay-Sachs disease	Degenerative disease of the brain and nerve cells, resulting in death before age 5.	Historically found mainly in eastern European Jews	No treatment.

Source: Adapted from AAP Committee on Genetics, 1996; NIH Consensus Development Panel, 2001; Tisdale, 1988, pp. 68–69.

common in children of northern European descent, in which excess mucus accumulates in the lungs and digestive tract), not until age 4; and glaucoma (a disease in which fluid pressure builds up in the eye) and Huntington's disease (a progressive degeneration of the nervous system), usually not until middle age.

It is in genetic defects and diseases that we see most clearly the operation of dominant and recessive transmission, and also of a variation, *sex-linked inheritance*, discussed in a subsequent section.

Dominant or Recessive Inheritance of Defects   Most of the time, normal genes are dominant over those carrying abnormal traits, but sometimes the gene for an abnormal trait is dominant. When one parent has a dominant abnormal gene and one recessive normal gene and the other parent has two recessive normal genes, each of their children has a 50-50 chance of inheriting the dominant abnormal gene. Among the 1,800 disorders known to be transmitted by dominant inheritance are achondroplasia (a type of dwarfism) and Huntington's disease.

Recessive defects are expressed only if a child receives the same recessive gene from each biological parent. Some defects transmitted recessively, such as sickle-cell anemia, are more common among certain ethnic groups that, through marriage and reproduction within the group, have passed down recessive characteristics.

Defects transmitted by recessive inheritance are more likely to be lethal at an early age than those transmitted by dominant inheritance. If a dominantly transmitted defect killed before the age of reproduction, it could not be passed on to the next generation and therefore would soon disappear. A recessive defect can be transmitted by carriers who do not have the disorder and thus may live to reproduce.

Some traits are only partly dominant or partly recessive. In **incomplete dominance** a trait is not fully expressed. For example, people with only one sickle-cell allele and one normal allele do not have sickle-cell anemia but do show some manifestations of the condition, such as shortness of breath at high altitudes.

incomplete dominance Pattern of inheritance in which a child receives two different alleles, resulting in partial expression of a trait.

Sex-Linked Inheritance of Defects   In **sex-linked inheritance** (Figure 3-5) certain recessive disorders linked to genes on the sex chromosomes affect male and female children differently. Red-green color blindness is one of these sex-linked conditions. Another is hemophilia, a disorder in which blood does not clot when it should.

Sex-linked recessive traits are carried on one of the X chromosomes of an unaffected mother. The mother is a *carrier;* she does not have the disorder but can pass on the gene for it to her children. Sex-linked disorders almost always appear only in male children; in females, a normal dominant gene on the X chromosome from the father generally overrides the defective gene on the X chromosome from the mother. Boys are more vulnerable to these disorders because there is no opposite dominant gene on the shorter Y chromosome from the father to override a defect on the X chromosome from the mother.

sex-linked inheritance Pattern of inheritance in which certain characteristics carried on the X chromosome inherited from the mother are transmitted differently to her male and female offspring.

Occasionally, however, a female does inherit a sex-linked condition. For example, if her father is a hemophiliac and her mother happens to be a carrier for the disorder, the daughter has a 50 percent chance of receiving the abnormal X chromosome from each parent and having the disease.

Chromosomal Abnormalities   Chromosomal abnormalities typically occur because of errors in cell division, resulting in an extra or missing chromosome. Some of these errors happen in the sex cells during meiosis. For example, Klinefelter syndrome is caused by an extra female sex chromosome (shown by the pattern XXY). Turner syndrome results from a missing sex chromosome (XO). The likelihood of errors in meiosis may increase in offspring of women age 35 or older. Characteristics of the most common sex chromosome disorders are shown in Table 3-2.

Figure 3-5

Sex-linked inheritance.

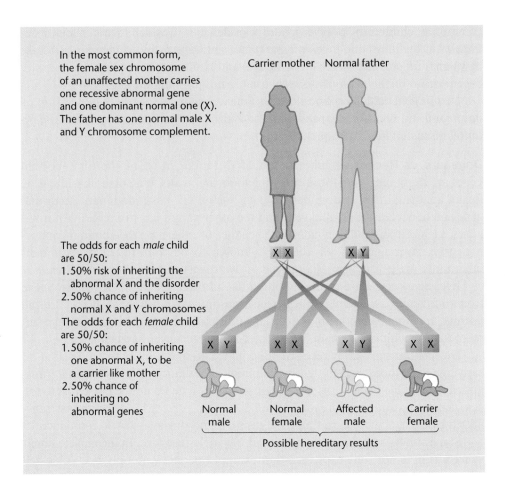

In the most common form, the female sex chromosome of an unaffected mother carries one recessive abnormal gene and one dominant normal one (X). The father has one normal male X and Y chromosome complement.

Carrier mother   Normal father

The odds for each *male* child are 50/50:
1. 50% risk of inheriting the abnormal X and the disorder
2. 50% chance of inheriting normal X and Y chromosomes

The odds for each *female* child are 50/50:
1. 50% chance of inheriting one abnormal X, to be a carrier like mother
2. 50% chance of inheriting no abnormal genes

Normal male   Normal female   Affected male   Carrier female

Possible hereditary results

Table 3-2	Sex Chromosome Abnormalities		
Pattern/Name	**Typical Characteristics***	**Incidence**	**Treatment**
XYY	Male; tall stature; tendency to low IQ, especially verbal.	1 in 1,000 male births	No special treatment
XXX (triple X)	Female; normal appearance, menstrual irregularities, learning disorders, mental retardation.	1 in 1,000 female births	Special education
XXY (Kleinfelter)	Male; sterility, underdeveloped secondary sex characteristics, small testes, learning disorders.	1 in 1,000 male births	Hormone therapy, special education
XO (Turner)	Female; short stature, webbed neck, impaired spatial abilities, no menstruation, infertility, underdeveloped sex organs, incomplete development of secondary sex characteristics.	1 in 1,500 to 2,500 female births	Hormone therapy, special education
Fragile X	Minor-to-severe mental retardation; symptoms, which are more severe in males, include delayed speech and motor development, speech impairments, and hyperactivity; the most common *inherited* form of mental retardation.	1 in 1,200 male births; 1 in 2,000 female births	Educational and behavioral therapies when needed

*Not every affected person has every characteristic.

Other chromosomal abnormalities occur in the autosomes during cell division. **Down syndrome,** the most common, accounts for about 40 percent of all cases of moderate-to-severe mental retardation (Pennington, Moon, Edgin, Stedron, & Nadel, 2003). The condition is also called *trisomy-21*, because it is usually caused by an extra 21st chromosome or the translocation of part of the 21st chromosome onto another chromosome. The most obvious physical characteristic associated with the disorder is a downward-sloping skin fold at the inner corners of the eyes.

Approximately 1 in every 700 babies born alive has Down syndrome. About 94 percent of these babies are born to normal parents (Pennington et al., 2003). The risk is greatest with older parents; when the mother is under age 35, the disorder is more likely to be hereditary. In 95 percent of cases the extra chromosome appears to come from the mother's ovum (Antonarakis & Down Syndrome Collaborative Group, 1991); the other 5 percent seem to be related to the father.

The brains of these children appear normal at birth but shrink in volume by young adulthood, particularly in the hippocampal area, resulting in cognitive dysfunction (Pennington et al., 2003). Yet, as adults, many live in group homes and are able to support themselves. More than 70 percent of people with Down syndrome live into their sixties, but they are at elevated risk of early death from various causes, including leukemia, cancer, Alzheimer's disease, and cardiovascular disease (Hayes & Batshaw, 1993; Hill et al., 2003).

Alvaro Trejo paints at the Mexican School of Down Art in Mexico City. The school, where all students have Down syndrome, is working to combat preconceptions about what people with mental disabilities can do.

Genetic Counseling and Testing

When Alicia became pregnant after five years of marriage, she and her husband, Eduardo, were overjoyed. They turned their study into a nursery and eagerly looked forward to bringing the baby home. But the baby never entered that brightly decorated nursery. She was born dead, a victim of *anencephaly*, a birth defect in which much of the baby's brain is missing and some of the internal organs are malformed. The heartbroken couple were afraid to try again. They still wanted a baby but feared that they might not be able to conceive a normal child.

Genetic counseling can help prospective parents like Alicia and Eduardo assess their risk of bearing children with genetic or chromosomal defects. People who have already had a child with a genetic defect, who have a family history of hereditary illness, who suffer from conditions known or suspected to be inherited, or who come from ethnic groups at higher-than-average risk of passing on genes for certain diseases can get information about their likelihood of producing affected children.

Geneticists have made great contributions to avoidance of birth defects. For example, genetic testing has virtually eliminated Tay-Sachs disease in the Jewish population (Kolata, 2003). Similarly, screening and counseling of women of childbearing age from Mediterranean countries, where beta thalassemia (refer back to Table 3-1) is common, has brought a decline in births of affected babies and greater knowledge of the risks of being a carrier (Cao, Saba, Galanello, & Rosatelli, 1997).

Down syndrome Chromosomal disorder characterized by moderate-to-severe mental retardation and by such physical signs as a downward-sloping skin fold at the inner corners of the eyes.

genetic counseling Clinical service that advises prospective parents of their probable risk of having children with hereditary defects.

Figure 3-6

A karyotype is a photograph that shows the chromosomes when they are separated and aligned for cell division. We know that this is a karyotype of a person with Down syndrome because there are three copies of chromosome 21 instead of the usual two. Because pair 23 consists of two X's, we know that this is the karyotype of a female. (Source: Babu & Hirschhorn, 1992; March of Dimes, 1987.)

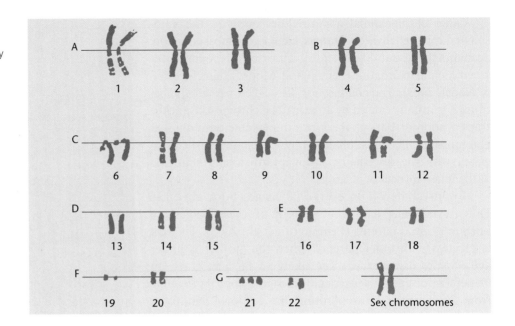

Checkpoint

Can you . . .

◆ Explain the operation of dominant inheritance, recessive inheritance, incomplete dominance, sex-linked inheritance, and mutations in transmission of birth defects?

◆ Tell three ways chromosomal disorders occur?

◆ Explain the purposes of genetic counseling?

A genetic counselor takes a family history and gives the prospective parents and any biological children physical examinations. Laboratory investigations of blood, skin, urine, or fingerprints may be performed. Chromosomes from body tissues may be analyzed and photographed, and the photographs enlarged and arranged according to size and structure on a chart called a *karyotype*. This chart can show chromosomal abnormalities and can indicate whether a person who appears normal might transmit genetic defects to a child (Figure 3-6). The counselor tries to help clients understand the mathematical risk of a particular condition, explains its implications, and presents information about alternative courses of action.

Today, researchers are rapidly identifying genes that contribute to many serious diseases and disorders, as well as those that influence normal traits. Their work is likely to lead to widespread genetic testing to reveal genetic profiles—a prospect that involves dangers as well as benefits (Box 3-1).

Guidepost 3

How do scientists study the relative influences of heredity and environment, and how do heredity and environment work together?

Nature and Nurture: Influences of Heredity and Environment

The relative importance of heredity and environment was a major issue among early psychologists and the general public. Today it has become clear that, although certain rare physical disorders are virtually 100 percent inherited, phenotypes for most normal traits, such as those having to do with intelligence and personality, are subject to a complex array of hereditary and environmental forces. Let's see how scientists study and explain the influences of heredity and environment and how these two forces work together.

Studying Heredity and Environment

behavioral genetics Quantitative study of relative hereditary and environmental influences on behavior.

One approach to the study of heredity and environment is quantitative: It seeks to measure *how much* heredity and environment influence particular traits. This is the traditional goal of the science of **behavioral genetics**.

BOX 3-1 Research *in Action*

Genetic Testing and Genetic Engineering

Scientists have now completed the mapping of the human genome, which is estimated to contain between 20,000 and 25,000 genes (International Human Genome Sequencing Consortium, 2004). Among the interesting findings are that all but 300 human genes have counterparts in mice (Wade, 2001), and the genomes of humans and chimpanzees are nearly 99 percent alike (Clark et al., 2003).

The mapping of the human genome has greatly advanced our ability to identify which genes control specific traits or behaviors and the developmental unfolding of these traits (Parke, 2004). A new field of science, *genomics,* the study of the functions and interactions of the various genes, will have untold implications for *medical genetics,* the application of genetic information to therapeutic purposes (McKusick, 2001; Patenaude, Guttmacher, & Collins, 2002). As efforts shift from finding genes to understanding how they affect behavior, scientists will be able to identify genes that cause, trigger, or increase susceptibility to particular disorders so as to screen at-risk population groups.

The genetic information gained from such research could increase our ability to predict, prevent, control, treat, and cure disease—even to pinpoint specific drug treatments to specific individuals. Already, genetic screening of newborns is saving lives and preventing mental retardation by permitting identification and treatment of infants with such disorders as sickle-cell anemia and phenylketonuria (PKU) (Holtzman, Murphy, Watson, & Barr, 1997; Khoury et al., 2003). Genetic screening for breast cancer probably would identify 88 percent of high-risk persons, significantly more than are identified by currently used risk factors (Pharaoh et al., 2002).

Gene therapy is an experimental technique for repairing or replacing defective genes. Between 1999 and 2002, French researchers reversed severe combined immunodeficiency, a serious immune disease, in seven out of ten affected babies under 1 year old by taking bone marrow cells from the babies, genetically altering the cells, and then injecting them into the babies. At follow-up 3 months and again 7½ years later, the patients remained healthy (Cavazzana-Calvo & Fischer, 2007). However, after three recipients of gene therapy developed leukemia and two died, in 2005, the U.S. Food and Drug Administration suspended three such experiments in the United States (Harris, 2005). In 2007, another patient died in a gene therapy treatment for arthritis (Weiss, 2007); but in that same year, gene therapy was used successfully in the United Kingdom to treat a rare type of inherited blindness (Bainbridge et al., 2008).

Genetic testing itself involves such ethical and political issues as privacy and fair use of genetic information. Although medical data are supposed to be confidential, it is almost impossible to keep such information private. Some courts have ruled that blood relatives have a legitimate claim to information about a patient's genetic health risks that may affect them, even though such disclosures violate confidentiality (Clayton, 2003).

A major concern is *genetic determinism:* the misconception that a person with a gene for a disease is bound to get the disease. All genetic testing can tell us is the *likelihood* that a person will get a disease. Most diseases involve a complex combination of genes or depend in part on lifestyle or other environmental factors. Job and insurance discrimination on the basis of genetic information has occurred—even though tests may be imprecise and unreliable and people deemed at risk of a disease may never develop it (Clayton, 2003; Khoury et al., 2003; Lapham, Kozma, & Weiss, 1996). Federal and state antidiscrimination laws provide some protection, but it is not consistent or comprehensive. Policies protecting confidentiality of research also are needed.

The psychological impact of test results is another concern. Predictions are imperfect; a false positive result may cause needless anxiety, and a false negative result may lull a person into complacency. And what if a genetic condition is incurable? Is there any point in knowing you have the gene for a potentially debilitating condition if you cannot do anything about it? A panel of experts has recommended against genetic testing for diseases for which there is no known cure (Institute of Medicine [IOM], 1993).

Additional concerns involve the testing of children. Should a child be tested to benefit a sibling or someone else? How will a child be affected by learning that he or she is likely to develop a disease 20, 30, or 50 years later? The American Academy of Pediatrics Committee on Bioethics (2001) recommends against genetic testing of children for conditions that cannot be treated in childhood.

Particularly chilling is the prospect that genetic testing could be misused to justify sterilization of people with "undesirable" genes or abortion of a normal fetus with the "wrong" genetic makeup (Plomin & Rutter, 1998). Gene therapy has the potential for similar abuse. Should it be used to make a short child taller or a chubby child thinner? To improve an unborn baby's appearance or intelligence? The path from therapeutic correction of defects to genetic engineering for cosmetic or functional purposes may well be a slippery slope, leading to a society in which some parents could afford to provide the "best" genes for their children and others could not (Rifkin, 1998).

Genetic testing "will almost certainly revolutionize the practice of medicine" (Anderson, 1998, p. 30). It is not yet clear whether the benefits will outweigh the risks.

What's Your View?

Would you want to know that you had a gene predisposing you to lung cancer? To Alzheimer's disease? Would you want your child to be tested for these genes?

Check It Out

For more information on this topic, go to www.ornl.gov/sci/techresources/Human_Genome/medicine/medicine.shtml. This is the Human Genome Project website. Information about disease diagnosis and prediction, disease intervention, genetic counseling, and ethical, legal, and social issues is presented.

Monozygotic twins separated at birth are sought after by researchers who want to study the impact of genes on personality. These twins, separated at birth and adopted by different families, were reunited at age 31. Both had become firefighters. Was this a coincidence or did it reflect the influence of heredity?

heritability Statistical estimate of contribution of heredity to individual differences in a specific trait within a given population.

What's Your View?

• In what ways are you like your mother and in what ways like your father? How are you similar and dissimilar to your siblings? Which differences would you guess come chiefly from heredity and which from environment? Can you see possible effects of both?

concordant Term describing tendency of twins to share the same trait or disorder.

Measuring Heritability **Heritability** is a statistical estimate of the contribution heredity makes toward individual differences in complex traits *within a given population*. Heritability does *not* refer to the relative influence of heredity and environment between populations or in a particular individual; those influences may be virtually impossible to separate. Nor does heritability tell us how traits develop or to what extent they can be modified. It merely indicates the statistical extent to which genes contribute to individual differences in a trait in a certain population.

Heritability is expressed as a number ranging from 0.0 to 1.0; the greater the number, the greater the heritability of a trait, with 1.0 meaning that genes are 100 percent responsible for differences in the trait. Because heritability cannot be measured directly, researchers in behavioral genetics rely chiefly on three types of correlational research: *family, adoption,* and *twin studies.*

In *family studies,* researchers measure the degree to which biological relatives share certain traits and whether the closeness of the familial relationship is associated with the degree of similarity. If the correlation is strong, the researchers infer a genetic influence. However, family studies cannot rule out environmental influences. A family study alone cannot tell us whether obese children of obese parents inherited the tendency or whether they are fat because their diet is like that of their parents. For that reason, researchers do adoption studies, which can separate the effects of heredity from those of a shared environment.

Adoption studies look at similarities between adopted children and their adoptive families and also between adopted children and their biological families. When adopted children are more like their biological parents and siblings in a particular trait (say, obesity), we see the influence of heredity. When they are more like their adoptive families, we see the influence of environment.

Studies of twins compare pairs of monozygotic twins with same-sex dizygotic twins. (Same-sex twins are used to avoid any confounding effects of gender.) Monozygotic twins are twice as genetically similar, on average, as dizygotic twins, who are no more genetically similar than other same-sex siblings. When monozygotic twins are more **concordant** (that is, have a statistically greater tendency to show the same trait) than dizygotic twins, we see the likely effects of heredity. Concordance rates, which may range from 0.0 to 1.0, estimate the probability that a pair of twins in a sample will be concordant for a trait present in one of them.

When monozygotic twins show higher concordance for a trait than do dizygotic twins, the likelihood of a genetic factor can be studied further through adoption studies. Studies of monozygotic twins separated in infancy and reared apart have found strong resemblances between the twins. Twin and adoption studies support a moderate to high hereditary basis for many normal and abnormal characteristics (McGuffin et al., 2001).

Behavioral geneticists recognize that the effects of genetic influences, especially on behavioral traits, are rarely inevitable: Even in a trait strongly influenced by heredity, the environment can have substantial impact (Rutter, 2002). In fact, environmental interventions sometimes can overcome genetically "determined" conditions. For example, a special diet begun soon after birth often can prevent mental retardation in children with the genetic disease phenylketonuria (PKU) (refer back to Table 3-1).

Checkpoint

Can you . . .

♦ State the basic assumption underlying studies of behavioral genetics and how it applies to family studies, twin studies, and adoption studies?

How Heredity and Environment Work Together

Today many developmental scientists have come to regard a solely quantitative approach to the study of heredity and environment as simplistic. They see these two forces as fundamentally intertwined. Instead of looking at genes and experience as operating directly on an organism, they see both as part of a complex *developmental system* (Gottlieb, 1991, 1997; Lickliter & Honeycutt, 2003). From conception on, throughout life, a combination of constitutional factors (related to biological and psychological makeup) and social, economic, and cultural factors help shape development. The more advantageous these circumstances and the experiences to which they give rise, the greater is the likelihood of optimum development.

Let's consider several ways in which inheritance and experience work together.

Reaction Range Many characteristics vary, within limits, under varying hereditary or environmental conditions. The concept of *reaction range* can help us visualize how this happens.

Reaction range refers to a range of potential expressions of a hereditary trait. Body size, for example, depends largely on biological processes, which are genetically regulated. Even so, a range of sizes is possible, depending on environmental opportunities and constraints and a person's behavior. In societies in which nutrition has dramatically improved, an entire generation has grown up to tower over the generation before. The better-fed children share their parents' genes but have responded to a healthier world. Once a society's average diet becomes adequate for more than one generation, however, children tend to grow to heights similar to their parents'. Ultimately, height has genetic limits: We don't see people who are only 1 foot tall or are 10 feet tall.

Heredity can influence whether a reaction range is wide or narrow. For example, a child born with a defect producing mild cognitive limitations is more able to respond to a favorable environment than a child born with more severe limitations. Likewise, a child with greater native intelligence is likely to benefit more from an enriched home and school environment than a child with normal intelligence (Figure 3-7).

Instead of a reaction range, advocates of a developmental system model prefer to talk about a *norm of reaction*. Although they recognize that heredity does set some limits, they argue that, because development is so complex and the effects of differing environments so variable, these limits are unknowable and their effects unpredictable. Thus, knowing how a child performs in a cognitively impoverished environment does not enable us to predict the child's performance in a more stimulating environment (Gottlieb, 1991, 1997).

reaction range Potential variability, depending on environmental conditions, in the expression of a hereditary trait.

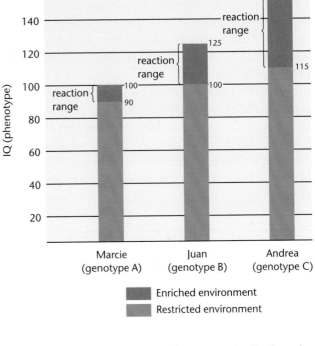

Figure 3-7

Intelligence and reaction range. Children with different genotypes for intelligence will show varying reaction ranges when exposed to a restricted or enriched environment.

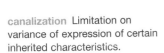
canalization Limitation on variance of expression of certain inherited characteristics.

Canalization Certain behaviors develop along genetically dug channels; it takes an extreme change in environment to alter their course. This phenomenon is called **canalization.** Behaviors that depend largely on maturation appear only when a child is ready. One example is motor development. Normal babies follow a typical sequence of motor development: crawling, walking, and running, in that order, at certain approximate ages. However, even motor development can be influenced by environmental experience, such as cultural child-rearing practices that affect its pace and timing (see Chapter 4).

Cognition and personality are more subject to variations in experience, such as the kinds of families children grow up in, the schools they attend, and the people they encounter. Consider language. Before children can talk, they must reach a certain level of neurological and muscular maturation. No 6-month-old could speak this sentence, no matter how enriched the infant's home life might be. Yet, environment does play a large part in language development, as we discuss in Chapter 5. If parents encourage babies' first sounds by talking back to them, children are likely to start to speak earlier than if their early vocalizing is ignored.

Recently scientists have begun to recognize that a usual or typical *experience* can dig channels for development (Gottlieb, 1991). For example, infants who hear only the sounds peculiar to their native language soon lose the ability to perceive sounds characteristic of other languages. Throughout this book you will find many examples of how socioeconomic status, neighborhood conditions, and educational opportunity can powerfully shape developmental outcomes, from the pace and complexity of language development to the likelihood of early sexual activity and antisocial behavior.

Genotype-Environment Interaction Another way that genes and environment work together is through **genotype-environment interaction**—the effects of similar environmental conditions on genetically different individuals. To take a familiar example, many people are exposed to pollen and dust, but people with a genetic predisposition are more likely to develop allergic reactions. In a longitudinal study of about 1,000 people ages 3 to 26 in Dunedin, New Zealand, adults with the short form of the *MAOA* gene tended to show antisocial personalities *if* they had

genotype-environment interaction The portion of phenotypic variation that results from the reactions of genetically different individuals to similar environmental conditions.

been severely maltreated as children. Having the long form of the same gene *reduced* the likelihood of antisocial behavior even after severe maltreatment (Caspi et al., 2002). Other research based on the same data found gene-environment interactions affecting depression (Caspi et al., 2003) and schizophrenia (Caspi et al., 2005).

Genotype-Environment Correlation Because genes influence a person's exposure to particular environments, the environment often reinforces genetic differences (Rutter, 2007). That is, certain genetic and environmental influences tend to act in the same direction. This is called **genotype-environment correlation,** or *genotype-environment covariance,* and it works in three ways to strengthen the phenotypic expression of a genotypic tendency (Bergeman & Plomin, 1989; Scarr, 1992; Scarr & McCartney, 1983). The first two ways are common among younger children, the third among older children, adolescents, and adults.

Adolescents with musical abilities usually seek out musical friends and might even start up their own band as these young people have done. This is an example of niche-picking.

- *Passive correlations:* Parents, who provide the genes that predispose a child toward a trait, also tend to provide an environment that encourages the development of that trait. For example, a musical parent is likely to create a home environment in which music is heard regularly, to give a child music lessons, and to take the child to musical events. If the child inherited the parent's musical talent, the child's musicality will reflect a combination of genetic and environmental influences. This type of correlation is called *passive* because the child has no control over it. It is most applicable to young children, whose parents, the source of their genetic legacy, also have a great deal of control over their early experiences.

- *Reactive, or evocative, correlations:* Children with differing genetic makeups evoke different reactions from adults. Thus, parents who are not musically inclined may make a special effort to provide musical experiences for a child who shows interest and ability in music. This response, in turn, strengthens the child's genetic inclination toward music. This type of correlation is called *reactive* because the parents react to the child's genetic makeup.

- *Active correlations:* As children get older and have more freedom to choose their own activities and environments, they *actively* select or create experiences consistent with their genetic tendencies. A shy child is more likely than an outgoing child to spend time in solitary pursuits. An adolescent with a talent for music will probably seek out musical friends, take music classes, and go to concerts if such opportunities are available. This tendency to seek out environments compatible with one's genotype is called **niche-picking;** it helps explain why identical twins reared apart tend to have similar characteristics and lifestyles.

What Makes Siblings So Different? The Nonshared Environment Although two children in the same family may bear a striking physical resemblance, siblings can differ greatly in intellect and especially in personality (Plomin, 1989).

genotype-environment correlation Tendency of certain genetic and environmental influences to reinforce each other; may be passive, reactive (evocative), or active. Also called *genotype-environment covariance.*

niche-picking Tendency of a person, especially after early childhood, to seek out environments compatible with his or her genotype.

One reason may be genetic differences, which lead children to need different kinds of stimulation or to respond differently to a similar home environment. For example, one child may be more affected by family discord than another (Rutter, 2002). In addition, studies in behavioral genetics suggest that many of the experiences that strongly affect development vary for different children in a family (McGuffin et al., 2001; Plomin & Daniels, 1987; Plomin & DeFries, 1999).

These **nonshared environmental effects** result from the unique environment in which each child in a family grows up. Children in a family have a shared environment—the home they live in, the people in it, and the activities a family jointly engage in—but they also, even if they are twins, have experiences that are not shared by their brothers and sisters. Parents and siblings may treat each child differently. Certain events, such as illnesses and accidents, and experiences outside the home affect one child and not another. Indeed, some behavioral geneticists have concluded that although heredity accounts for most of the similarity between siblings, the nonshared environment accounts for most of the difference (McClearn et al., 1997; Plomin, 1996; Plomin & Daniels, 1987; Plomin & DeFries, 1999; Plomin, Owen, & McGuffin, 1994). However, methodological challenges and additional empirical evidence point to the more moderate conclusion that nonshared environmental effects do not greatly outweigh shared ones; rather, there seems to be a balance between the two (Rutter, 2002).

Genotype-environment correlations may play an important role in the nonshared environment. Children's genetic differences may lead parents and siblings to react to them differently and treat them differently, and genes may influence how children perceive and respond to that treatment and what its outcome will be. Children also mold their environments by the choices they make—what they do and with whom—and their genetic makeup influences these choices. A child who has inherited artistic talent may spend a great deal of time creating "masterpieces" in solitude, while a sibling who is athletically inclined spends more time playing ball with others. Thus, not only will the children's abilities (in, say, painting or soccer) develop differently, but their social lives will be different as well. These differences tend to be accentuated as children grow older and have more experiences outside the family (Bergeman & Plomin, 1989; Bouchard, 1994; Plomin, 1990, 1996; Plomin et al., 1994; Scarr, 1992; Scarr & McCartney, 1983).

The old nature-nurture puzzle is far from resolved; we know now that the problem is more complex than previously thought. A variety of research designs can continue to augment and refine our understanding of the forces affecting development.

Some Characteristics Influenced by Heredity and Environment

Keeping in mind the complexity of unraveling the influences of heredity and environment, let's look at what is known about their roles in producing certain characteristics.

Physical and Physiological Traits Not only do monozygotic twins generally look alike, but they also are more concordant than dizygotic twins in their risk for such medical disorders as high blood pressure, heart disease, stroke, rheumatoid arthritis, peptic ulcers, and epilepsy (Brass, Isaacsohn, Merikangas, & Robinette, 1992; Plomin et al., 1994). Life span, too, seems to be influenced by genes (Sorensen, Nielsen, Andersen, & Teasdale, 1988).

---

nonshared environmental effects The unique environment in which each child grows up, consisting of distinctive influences or influences that affect one child differently than another.

Checkpoint

Can you . . .

♦ Explain and give at least one example of reaction range or norm of reaction, canalization, and genotype-environment interaction?

♦ Differentiate the three types of genotype-environment correlation?

♦ List three kinds of influences that contribute to nonshared environmental effects?

Guidepost 4

What roles do heredity and environment play in physical health, intelligence, and personality?

Obesity (sometimes called *overweight*) is measured by body mass index, or BMI (comparison of weight to height). A child who is at or above the 95th percentile for his or her age and sex is considered obese. Another criterion, used primarily for adults, is percentage of body fat: 25 percent or more for men and 30 percent or more for women. Obesity is a multifactorial condition; twin studies, adoption studies, and other research suggest that 40 to 70 percent of the risk is genetic, but environmental influences also contribute to it (Chen et al., 2004). At least 250 genes or chromosome regions are associated with obesity (Pérusse, Chagnon, Weisnagel, & Bouchard, 1999). One key gene on chromosome 10 normally controls appetite, but an abnormal version of this gene can stimulate hunger and overeating (Boutin et al., 2003).

obesity Extreme overweight in relation to age, sex, height, and body type.

The kind and amount of food eaten in a particular home or in a particular social or ethnic group and the amount of exercise that is encouraged can increase or decrease the likelihood that a person will become overweight. The rise in the prevalence of obesity in Western countries seems to result from the interaction of a genetic predisposition with overeating, supersized portions, and inadequate exercise (Leibel, 1997; see Chapters 7, 9, 11, and 13). In addition, some research suggests that obesity spreads through social ties. If one sibling is obese, the other sibling is likely to become obese as well. The same is true of spouses and friends, but not of neighbors (Christakis & Fowler, 2007).

Intelligence Heredity exerts a strong influence on general intelligence (as measured by intelligence tests) and, to a lesser extent, on specific abilities such as memory, verbal ability, and spatial ability (McClearn et al., 1997; Petrill et al., 2004; Plomin et al., 1994; Plomin & DeFries, 1999; Plomin & Spinath, 2004). Several genes have been tentatively associated with intelligence, but only one of these associations has been replicated so far (Dick et al., 2007; Posthuma & de Geus, 2006). Intelligence also depends in part on brain size and structure, which are under strong genetic control (Toga & Thompson, 2005). Experience counts, too; as Figure 3-7 shows, an enriched or impoverished environment can substantially affect the development and expression of innate ability (Neisser et al., 1996). Environmental influence is greater, and heritability lower, among poor families than among more economically privileged families. Parents' educational levels have a similar effect (Posthuma & de Geus, 2006; Toga & Thompson, 2005).

Indirect evidence of the role of heredity in intelligence comes from adoption and twin studies. Adopted children's IQs are consistently closer to the IQs of their biological mothers than to those of their adoptive parents and siblings, and monozygotic twins are more alike in intelligence than dizygotic twins (Petrill et al., 2004; Plomin & DeFries, 1999).

The genetic influence, which is primarily responsible for stability in cognitive performance, increases with age. This increase probably is a result of niche-picking. The shared family environment seems to have a dominant influence on young children but almost no influence on adolescents, who are more apt to find their own niche by actively selecting environments compatible with their hereditary abilities and related interests. The *non*shared environment, in contrast, is influential throughout life and is primarily responsible for changes in cognitive performance (Bouchard, 2004; Petrill et al., 2004; Toga & Thompson, 2005).

Personality and Psychopathology Scientists have identified genes directly linked with specific aspects of personality such as a trait called neuroticism, which may contribute to depression and anxiety (Lesch et al.,

This 2½-year-old-girl clinging to her mother may be "just in a phase," or maybe her shyness is an inborn aspect of her temperament.

temperament Characteristic disposition, or style of approaching and reacting to situations.

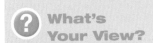

What's Your View?

- What practical difference does it make whether a trait such as obesity, intelligence, or shyness is influenced more by heredity or by environment, given that heritability can be measured only for a population, not for an individual?

schizophrenia Mental disorder marked by loss of contact with reality; symptoms include hallucinations and delusions.

Checkpoint

Can you . . .

♦ Assess the evidence for genetic and environmental influences on physical and physiological traits, intelligence, temperament, and schizophrenia?

Guidepost 5

What are the three stages of prenatal development, and what happens during each stage?

gestation Period of development between conception and birth.

1996). Heritability of personality traits appears to be between 40 and 50 percent, and there is little evidence of shared environmental influence (Bouchard, 2004).

Temperament, an aspect of personality, is a person's characteristic way of approaching and reacting to situations. It appears to be largely inborn and is often consistent over the years, though it may respond to special experiences or parental handling (A. Thomas & Chess, 1984; A. Thomas, Chess, & Birch, 1968). Siblings—both twins and nontwins—tend to be similar in temperament, though parents often see them as more different than they actually are (Saudino, Wertz, Gagne, & Chawla, 2004). An observational study of 100 pairs of 7-year-old siblings (50 pairs of adoptive siblings and 50 pairs of siblings by birth) found significant genetic influences on the temperamental characteristics of activity, sociability, and emotionality (Schmitz, Saudino, Plomin, Fulker, & DeFries, 1996).

There is evidence for a strong hereditary influence on such mental disorders as schizophrenia, autism, alcoholism, and depression. All tend to run in families and to show greater concordance between monozygotic twins than between dizygotic twins. However, heredity alone does not produce such disorders; an inherited tendency can be triggered by environmental factors.

Schizophrenia is a neurological disorder characterized by loss of contact with reality and by such symptoms as hallucinations and delusions (Berry, Jobanputra, & Pal, 2003; Tuulio-Henriksson et al., 2002; Vaswani & Kapur, 2001). Estimates of heritability are as high as 80 to 85 percent (McGuffin, Owen, & Farmer, 1995; Picker, 2005). However, monozygotic twins are not always concordant for schizophrenia, perhaps due to epigenesis (Fraga et al., 2005; Wong et al., 2005).

Research has identified several genes that increase susceptibility to schizophrenia (Xu et al., 2005; Cannon et al., 2005; Egan et al., 2004). A postmortem examination suggests that the disorder may originate in a lack of a chemical called *reelin*, which helps position nerve cells in the developing brain (Impagnatiello et al., 1998).

Researchers have also looked at possible nongenetic influences. Schizophrenia may stem from a series of neurological insults in fetal life (Picker, 2005; Rapoport, Addington, & Frangou, 2005), such as exposure to influenza in the first trimester of pregnancy (Brown, Begg, et al., 2004) or to maternal rubella and respiratory infections in the second and third trimesters. Infants born in urban areas or in late winter or early spring appear to be at increased risk, as are those whose mothers experienced obstetric complications or who were poor or severely deprived as a result of war or famine (Picker, 2005). A link between fetal malnutrition and schizophrenia has been demonstrated in studies in the Netherlands (Susser & Lin, 1992), Finland (Wahlbeck, Forsen, Osmond, Barker, & Eriksson, 2001), and China (St. Clair et al., 2005).

Advanced paternal age is a risk factor for schizophrenia. In several large population-based studies, the risk of the disorder was heightened when the father was age 30 or older (Byrne, Agerbo, Ewald, Eaton, & Mortenson, 2003; Malaspina et al., 2001; Sipos et al., 2004). (Autism, depression, and alcoholism are discussed later in this book.)

Prenatal Development

If you had been born in China, you would probably celebrate your birthday on your estimated date of conception rather than your date of birth. This Chinese custom recognizes the importance of **gestation,** the approximately 38-week period of development between conception and birth. The normal range of gestation is between 38 and 42 weeks.

Table 3-3   Early Signs and Symptoms of Pregnancy

Physical Change	Causes and Timing
Tender, swollen breasts or nipples	Increased production of the female hormones estrogen and progesterone stimulates breast growth to prepare for producing milk (most noticeable in a first pregnancy).
Fatigue; need to take extra naps	Woman's heart is pumping harder and faster to produce extra blood to carry nutrients to the fetus. Stepped-up production of hormones takes extra effort. Progesterone depresses central nervous system and may cause sleepiness. Concerns about pregnancy may sap energy.
Slight bleeding or cramping	*Implantation bleeding* may occur about 10 to 14 days after fertilization when fertilized ovum attaches to lining of uterus. Many women also have cramps (similar to menstrual cramps) as the uterus begins to enlarge.
Food cravings	Hormonal changes may alter food preferences, especially during first trimester, when hormones have greatest impact.
Nausea with or without vomiting	Rising levels of estrogen produced by placenta and fetus cause stomach to empty more slowly. Also, heightened sense of smell may trigger nausea in response to certain odors, such as coffee, meat, dairy products, or spicy foods. *Morning sickness* may begin as early as 2 weeks after conception, but usually around 4 to 8 weeks, and may occur at any time of day.
Frequent urination	Enlarging uterus during first trimester exerts pressure on the bladder.
Frequent, mild headaches	Increased blood circulation caused by hormonal changes may bring these on.
Constipation	Increase in progesterone may slow digestion, so food passes more slowly through intestinal tract.
Mood swings	Flood of hormones early in pregnancy can produce emotional highs and lows.
Faintness and dizziness	Lightheaded feeling may be triggered by blood vessel dilation and low blood pressure or by low blood sugar.
Raised basal body temperature	Basal body temperature (taken first thing in the morning) normally rises soon after ovulation each month and then drops during menstruation. When menstruation ceases, temperature remains elevated.

Source: Mayo Clinic, 2005.

Gestational age is usually dated from the first day of an expectant mother's last menstrual cycle. For many women, the first clear sign of pregnancy is a missed menstrual period. But even before that first missed period, a pregnant woman's body undergoes subtle changes (Table 3-3). Although these signs are not unique to pregnancy, a woman who experiences one or more may take a home pregnancy test or seek medical confirmation that she is pregnant or not.

In this section we trace the course of gestation, or prenatal development and discuss environmental factors that can affect the developing person-to-be. In the next section, we assess techniques for determining whether development is proceeding normally and explain the importance of prenatal care.

gestational age Age of an unborn baby, usually dated from the first day of an expectant mother's last menstrual cycle.

Stages of Prenatal Development

Prenatal development takes place in three stages: *germinal, embryonic,* and *fetal.* (Table 3-4 gives a month-by-month description.) During these three stages of gestation, the original single-celled zygote grows into an *embryo* and then a *fetus.*

Both before and after birth, development proceeds according to two fundamental principles: Growth and motor development occur from top down and from the center of the body outward. The embryo's head and trunk develop before the limbs, and the arms and legs before the fingers and toes.

 Germinal Stage (Fertilization to 2 Weeks)   During the **germinal stage,** from fertilization to about 2 weeks of gestational age, the zygote divides, becomes more complex, and is implanted in the wall of the uterus (Figure 3-8).

germinal stage First 2 weeks of prenatal development, characterized by rapid cell division, blastocyst formation, and implantation in the wall of the uterus.

Table 3-4 Prenatal Development

Month	Description
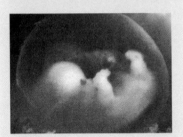 *1 month*	During the first month, growth is more rapid than at any other time during prenatal or postnatal life; the embryo reaches a size 10,000 times greater than the zygote. By the end of the first month, it measures about ½ inch in length. Blood flows through its veins and arteries, which are very small. It has a minuscule heart, beating 65 times a minute. It already has the beginning of a brain, kidneys, liver, and digestive tract. The umbilical cord, its lifeline to the mother, is working. By looking very closely through a microscope, it is possible to see the swellings on the head that will eventually become eyes, ears, mouth, and nose. Its sex cannot yet be detected.
 *7 weeks*	By the end of the second month, the embryo becomes a fetus. It is less than 1 inch long and weighs only ⅓ ounce. Its head is half its total body length. Facial parts are clearly developed, with tongue and teeth buds. The arms have hands, fingers, and thumbs, and the legs have knees, ankles, feet, and toes. The fetus has a thin covering of skin and can make handprints and footprints. Bone cells appear at about 8 weeks. Brain impulses coordinate the function of the organ system. Sex organs are developing; the heartbeat is steady. The stomach produces digestive juices; the liver, blood cells. The kidneys remove uric acid from the blood. The skin is now sensitive enough to react to tactile stimulation.
 *3 months*	By the end of the third month, the fetus weighs about 1 ounce and measures about 3 inches in length. It has fingernails, toenails, eyelids (still closed), vocal cords, lips, and a prominent nose. Its head is still large—about one-third its total length—and its forehead is high. Sex can easily be detected. The organ systems are functioning, and so the fetus may now breathe, swallow amniotic fluid into the lungs and expel it, and occasionally urinate. Its ribs and vertebrae have turned into cartilage. The fetus can now make a variety of specialized responses: it can move its legs, feet, thumbs, and head; its mouth can open and close and swallow. If its eyelids are touched, it squints; if its palm is touched, it makes a partial fist; if its lip is touched, it will suck; and if the sole of the foot is stroked, the toes will fan out. These reflexes will be present at birth but will disappear during the first months of life.
 *4 months*	The body is catching up to the head, which is now only one-fourth the total body length, the same proportion it will be at birth. The fetus now measures 8 to 10 inches and weighs about 6 ounces. The umbilical cord is as long as the fetus and will continue to grow with it. The placenta is now fully developed. The mother may be able to feel the fetus kicking, a movement known as *quickening,* which some societies and religious groups consider the beginning of human life. The reflex activities that appeared in the third month are now brisker because of increased muscular development.
5 months	The fetus, now weighing about 12 ounces to 1 pound and measuring about 1 foot, begins to show signs of an individual personality. It has definite sleep-wake patterns, has a favorite position in the uterus (called its *lie*), and becomes more active—kicking, stretching, squirming, and even hiccuping. By putting an ear to the mother's abdomen, it is possible to hear the fetal heartbeat. The sweat and sebaceous glands are functioning. The respiratory system is not yet adequate to sustain life outside the womb; a baby born at this time does not usually survive. Coarse hair has begun to grow for eyebrows and eyelashes, fine hair is on the head, and a woolly hair called *lanugo* covers the body.

Month	Description
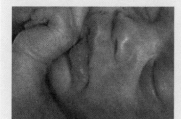 *6 months*	The rate of fetal growth has slowed a little—by the end of the sixth month, the fetus is about 14 inches long and weighs 1¼ pounds. It has fat pads under the skin; the eyes are complete, opening, closing, and looking in all directions. It can hear, and it can make a fist with a strong grip. A fetus born early in the sixth month has only a slight chance of survival, because the breathing apparatus has not matured. However, medical advances have made survival increasingly likely if birth occurs near the end of the sixth month.
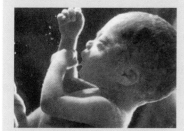 *7 months*	By the end of the seventh month, the fetus, about 16 inches long and weighing 3 to 5 pounds, now has fully developed reflex patterns. It cries, breathes, and swallows, and it may suck its thumb. The lanugo may disappear at about this time, or it may remain until shortly after birth. Head hair may continue to grow. The chances that a fetus weighing at least 3½ pounds will survive are fairly good, provided it receives intensive medical attention. It will probably need to be kept in an isolette until a weight of 5 pounds is attained.
 *8 months*	The 8-month-old fetus is 18 to 20 inches long and weighs between 5 and 7 pounds. Its living quarters are becoming cramped, and so its movements are curtailed. During this month and the next, a layer of fat is developing over the fetus's entire body, which will enable it to adjust to varying temperatures outside the womb.
9 months–newborn	About a week before birth, the fetus stops growing, having reached an average weight of about 7½ pounds and a length of about 20 inches, with boys tending to be a little longer and heavier than girls. Fat pads continue to form, the organ systems are operating more efficiently, the heart rate increases, and more wastes are expelled through the umbilical cord. The reddish color of the skin is fading. At birth, the fetus will have been in the womb for about 266 days, though gestational age is usually estimated at 280 days because most doctors date the pregnancy from the mother's last menstrual period.

Note: Even in these early stages, individuals differ. The figures and descriptions given here represent averages.

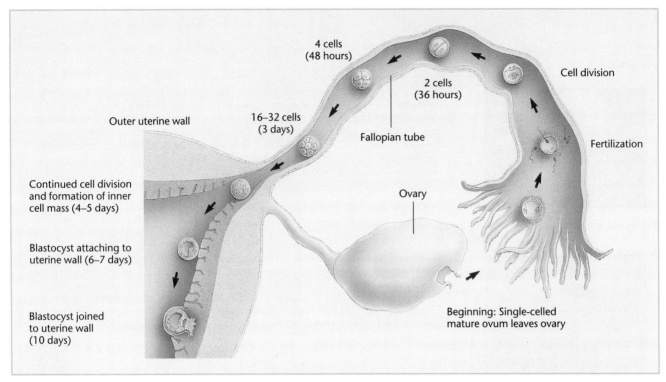

Figure 3-8

Early development of a human embryo. This simplified diagram shows the progress of the ovum as it leaves the ovary, is fertilized in the fallopian tube, and then divides while traveling to the lining of the uterus. Now a blastocyst, it is implanted in the uterus and becomes an embryo. It will continue to grow larger and more complex until it is ready to be born.

Within 36 hours after fertilization, the zygote enters a period of rapid cell division and duplication (mitosis). Seventy-two hours after fertilization, it has divided first into 16 and then into 32 cells; a day later it has 64 cells. This division will continue until the original single cell has developed into the 800 billion or more specialized cells that make up the human body—a process that continues well after birth.

While the fertilized ovum is dividing, it is also making its way through the fallopian tube to the uterus, a journey of 3 or 4 days. Its form changes into a *blastocyst,* a fluid-filled sphere, which floats freely in the uterus until the sixth day after fertilization, when it begins to implant itself in the uterine wall. Only about 10 to 20 percent of fertilized ova complete the task of implantation and continue to develop.

Before implantation, as cell differentiation begins, some cells around the edge of the blastocyst cluster on one side to form the *embryonic disk,* a thickened cell mass from which the embryo begins to develop. This mass will differentiate into three layers. The *ectoderm,* the upper layer, will become the outer layer of skin, the nails, hair, teeth, sensory organs, and the nervous system, including the brain and spinal cord. The *endoderm,* the lower layer, will become the digestive system, liver, pancreas, salivary glands, and respiratory system. The *mesoderm,* the middle layer, will develop and differentiate into the inner layer of skin, muscles, skeleton, and excretory and circulatory systems.

Other parts of the blastocyst begin to develop into organs that will nurture and protect development in the womb: the *amniotic cavity,* or *amniotic sac,* with its outer layers, the *amnion* and *chorion;* the *placenta;* and the *umbilical cord* (Figure 3-9). The *amniotic sac* is a fluid-filled membrane that encases the developing embryo, protecting it and giving it room to move and grow. The *placenta*

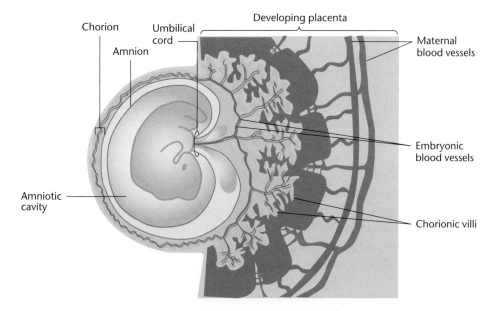

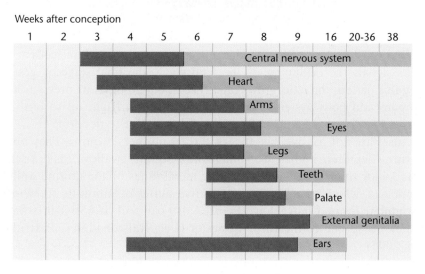

Figure 3-9
The developing embryo (approximately 6 weeks gestational age). Throughout its development, the embryo is enclosed and cushioned by the expandable, fluid-filled amniotic cavity. The umbilical cord develops to contain the embryonic blood vessels that carry blood to and from the placenta. Diffusion across the chorionic villi removes wastes from the embryonic blood and adds nutrients and oxygen without commingling of maternal and embryonic blood.

Figure 3-10
When birth defects occur. Body parts and systems are most vulnerable to damage during critical periods when they are developing most rapidly (darkly shaded areas), generally within the first trimester of pregnancy. (Source: J. E. Brody, 1995; data from March of Dimes.) Note: Intervals of time are not all equal.

allows oxygen, nourishment, and wastes to pass between mother and embryo. It is connected to the embryo by the *umbilical cord.* Nutrients from the mother pass from her blood to the embryonic blood vessels, which carry them, via the umbilical cord, to the embryo. In turn, embryonic blood vessels in the umbilical cord carry embryonic wastes to the placenta, where they can be eliminated by maternal blood vessels. The mother's and embryo's circulatory systems are not directly linked; instead, this exchange occurs by diffusion across the blood vessel walls. The placenta also helps to combat internal infection and gives the unborn child immunity to various diseases. It produces the hormones that support pregnancy, prepare the mother's breasts for lactation, and eventually stimulate the uterine contractions that will expel the baby from the mother's body.

Embryonic Stage (2 to 8 Weeks) During the **embryonic stage,** the second stage of gestation, from about 2 to 8 weeks, the organs and major body systems—respiratory, digestive, and nervous—develop rapidly. This is a critical period, when the embryo is most vulnerable to destructive influences in the prenatal environment (Figure 3-10). An organ system or structure that is still developing at the time of exposure is most likely to be affected. Defects that occur later in pregnancy are likely to be less serious.

embryonic stage Second stage of gestation (2 to 8 weeks), characterized by rapid growth and development of major body systems and organs.

spontaneous abortion Natural expulsion from the uterus of an embryo that cannot survive outside the womb; also called *miscarriage.*

Checkpoint

Can you . . .

♦ Describe how a zygote becomes an embryo, and explain why defects and miscarriages most often occur during the embryonic stage?

fetal stage Final stage of gestation (from 8 weeks to birth), characterized by increased differentiation of body parts and greatly enlarged body size.

ultrasound Prenatal medical procedure using high-frequency sound waves to detect the outline of a fetus and its movements, so as to determine whether a pregnancy is progressing normally.

The most severely defective embryos usually do not survive beyond the first *trimester,* or three-month period, of pregnancy. A **spontaneous abortion,** commonly called a *miscarriage,* is the expulsion from the uterus of an embryo or fetus that is unable to survive outside the womb. As many as 1 in 4 recognized pregnancies end in miscarriage, and the actual figure may be as high as 1 in 2 because many spontaneous abortions take place before the woman realizes she is pregnant. About 3 out of 4 miscarriages occur during the first trimester (Neville, undated). Most miscarriages result from abnormal pregnancies; about 50 to 70 percent involve chromosomal abnormalities (Hogge, 2003). Smoking, drinking alcohol, and drug use increase the risks of miscarriage (American College of Obstetricians and Gynecologists, 2002).

Males are more likely than females to be spontaneously aborted or to be *stillborn* (dead at or after the 20th week of gestation). Thus, although about 125 males are conceived for every 100 females—a fact that has been attributed to the greater mobility of sperm carrying the smaller Y chromosome—only about 105 boys are born for every 100 girls. Males' greater vulnerability continues after birth: More die early in life, and at every age they are more susceptible to many disorders. As a result, there are only about 96 males for every 100 females in the United States (Martin, Hamilton, et al., 2007; Spraggins, 2003).

Fetal Stage (8 Weeks to Birth)   The appearance of the first bone cells at about 8 weeks signals the beginning of the **fetal stage,** the final stage of gestation. During this period, the fetus grows rapidly to about 20 times its previous length, and organs and body systems become more complex. Right up to birth, final details such as fingernails, toenails, and eyelids continue to develop.

Fetuses are not passive passengers in their mothers' wombs. They breathe, kick, turn, flex their bodies, do somersaults, squint, swallow, make fists, hiccup, and suck their thumbs. The flexible membranes of the uterine walls and amniotic sac, which surround the protective buffer of amniotic fluid, permit and stimulate limited movement. Fetuses also can feel pain, but it is unlikely that they do so before the third trimester (Lee, Ralston, Drey, Partridge, & Rosen, 2005).

Scientists can observe fetal movement through **ultrasound,** the use of high-frequency sound waves to detect the outline of the fetus. Other instruments can monitor heart rate, changes in activity level, states of sleep and wakefulness, and cardiac reactivity.

The movements and activity level of fetuses show marked individual differences, and their heart rates vary in regularity and speed. Male fetuses, regardless of size, are more active and tend to move more vigorously than female fetuses throughout gestation. Thus, infant boys' tendency to be more active than girls may be at least partly inborn (DiPietro, Hodgson, Costigan, Hilton, & Johnson, 1996).

Beginning at about the 12th week of gestation, the fetus swallows and inhales some of the amniotic fluid in which it floats. The amniotic fluid contains substances that cross the placenta from the mother's bloodstream and enter the fetus's bloodstream. Partaking of these substances may stimulate the budding senses of taste and smell and may contribute to the development of organs needed for breathing and digestion (Mennella & Beauchamp, 1996a; Ronca & Alberts, 1995; Smotherman & Robinson, 1995, 1996). Mature taste cells appear at about 14 weeks of gestation. The olfactory system, which controls the sense of smell, also is well developed before birth (Bartoshuk & Beauchamp, 1994; Mennella & Beauchamp, 1996a).

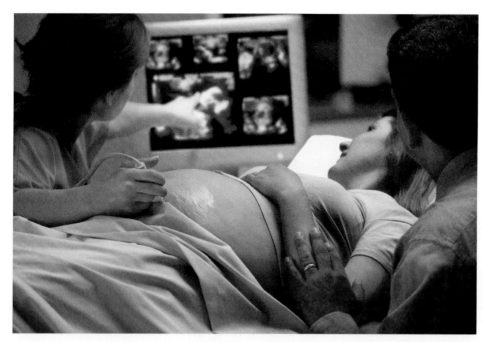

Ultrasound, the procedure this woman is undergoing, is a diagnostic tool that presents an immediate image of the fetus in the womb. High-frequency sound waves directed at the woman's abdomen reveal the fetus's outline and movements. Ultrasound is widely used to monitor fetal development and detect abnormalities.

Fetuses respond to the mother's voice and heartbeat and the vibrations of her body, suggesting that they can hear and feel. Hungry infants, no matter on which side they are held, turn toward the breast in the direction from which they hear the mother's voice (Noirot & Algeria, 1983, cited in Rovee-Collier, 1996). Thus familiarity with the mother's voice may have an evolutionary survival function: to help newborns locate the source of food. Responses to sound and vibration seem to begin at 26 weeks of gestation, increase, and then reach a plateau at about 32 weeks (Kisilevsky, Muir, & Low, 1992).

Fetuses seem to learn and remember. In one experiment, 3-day-old infants sucked more on a nipple that activated a recording of a story their mother had frequently read aloud during the last six weeks of pregnancy than they did on nipples that activated recordings of two other stories. Apparently, the infants recognized the pattern of sound they had heard in the womb. A control group, whose mothers had not recited a story before birth, responded equally to all three recordings (DeCasper & Spence, 1986). Similar experiments have found that newborns age 2 to 4 days prefer musical and speech sequences heard before birth. They also prefer their mother's voice to those of other women, female voices to male voices, and their mother's native language to another language (DeCasper & Fifer, 1980; DeCasper & Spence, 1986; Fifer & Moon, 1995; Lecanuet, Granier-Deferre, & Busnel, 1995; Moon, Cooper, & Fifer, 1993).

How do we know that these preferences develop before rather than after birth? When 60 fetuses heard a female voice reading, their heart rate increased if the voice was their mothers' and decreased if it was a stranger's (Kisilevsky et al., 2003). In another study, newborns were given the choice of sucking to turn on a recording of the mother's voice or a filtered version of her voice as it might sound in the womb. The newborns sucked more often to turn on the filtered version, suggesting that fetuses develop a preference for the kinds of sounds they hear before birth (Fifer & Moon, 1995; Moon & Fifer, 1990).

✔ **Checkpoint**

Can you . . .

♦ List several changes that occur during the fetal stage?

♦ Discuss findings about fetal activity, sensory development, and memory?

Guidepost 6

What environmental influences can affect prenatal development?

teratogenic Capable of causing birth defects.

Environmental Influences: Maternal Factors

Because the prenatal environment is the mother's body, virtually everything that impinges on her well-being, from her diet to her moods, may alter her unborn child's environment and affect its growth.

Not all environmental hazards are equally risky for all fetuses. Some factors that are **teratogenic** (birth defect–producing) in some cases have little or no effect in others. The timing of exposure (refer back to Figure 3-10), the dose, duration, and interaction with other teratogenic factors may make a difference. Sometimes vulnerability may depend on a gene either in the fetus or in the mother. For example, fetuses with a particular variant of a growth gene, called *transforming growth factor alpha,* have six times more risk than other fetuses of developing a cleft palate if the mother smokes while pregnant (Hwang et al., 1995).

Nutrition and Maternal Weight   Because she is "eating for two," it is important for an expectant mother to take in enough nutrients to adequately feed herself and her fetus. Pregnant women typically need 300 to 500 additional calories a day, including extra protein. Women of normal weight and body build who gain 16 to 40 pounds are less likely to have birth complications or to bear babies whose weight at birth is dangerously low or overly high. However, desirable weight gain also depends on body mass index (BMI) before pregnancy. Studies show that about one-third of U.S. mothers gain more or less than the recommended amount (Martin, Hamilton, et al., 2007).

Either too much or too little weight gain can be risky. A woman who gains too much risks having a large baby who needs to be delivered by cesarean section. If a woman does not gain enough, her baby is likely to suffer growth retardation in the womb, to be born prematurely or very small, or to die at or near birth (Martin, Hamilton, et al., 2006).

A mother's weight *before* pregnancy matters too. Obese women risk having children with birth defects (Watkins, Rasmussen, Honein, Botto, & Moore, 2003). Obesity also increases the risk of other complications of pregnancy, including miscarriage, difficulty inducing labor, and a greater likelihood of cesarean delivery (Brousseau, 2006; Cnattingius, Bergstrom, Lipworth, & Kramer, 1998).

What an expectant mother eats is also important. For example, newborns whose mothers ate fish high in DHA, an omega-3 fatty acid found in certain fish, such as Atlantic salmon and tuna, showed more mature sleep patterns (a sign of advanced brain development) than infants whose mothers' blood had lower levels of DHA (Cheruku, Montgomery-Downs, Farkas, Thoman, & Lammi-Keefe, 2002; Colombo et al., 2004).

Folic acid, or folate (a B vitamin), is critical in a pregnant woman's diet. For some time, China had the highest incidence in the world of babies born with anencephaly and spina bifida (refer back to Table 3-1). In the 1980s researchers linked this high incidence with the timing of the babies' conception. Traditionally, Chinese couples marry in January or February and try to conceive as soon as possible. Thus, their pregnancies often begin in the winter, when rural women have little access to fresh fruits and vegetables, important sources of folic acid.

After medical detective work established the lack of folic acid as a cause of anencephaly and spina bifida, China embarked on a massive program to give folic acid supplements to prospective mothers. The result was a large reduction in the prevalence of these defects (Berry et al., 1999). Addition of folic acid to enriched grain products has been mandatory in the United States since 1998, reducing the incidence of these defects (Honein, Paulozzi, Mathews, Erickson, & Wong, 2001). It is estimated that if all women took 5 milligrams of folic acid each day before pregnancy and during the first trimester, an estimated 85 percent of neural-tube defects could be prevented (Wald, 2004).

Malnutrition Prenatal malnutrition may have long-range effects. In rural Gambia, in western Africa, people born during the *hungry season,* when foods from the previous harvest are depleted, are ten times more likely to die in early adulthood than people born during other parts of the year (Moore et al., 1997). Children in the United Kingdom whose mothers had low vitamin D levels late in pregnancy had low bone mineral content at age 9, potentially increasing their risk of osteoporosis in later life (Javaid et al., 2006). And, as we reported earlier, several studies have revealed a link between fetal undernutrition and schizophrenia.

It is important to identify malnutrition early in pregnancy so that it can be treated. Malnourished women who take dietary supplements while pregnant tend to have bigger, healthier, more active, and more visually alert infants (J. L. Brown, 1987; Vuori et al., 1979); and women with low zinc levels who take daily zinc supplements are less likely to have babies with low birth weight and small head circumference (Goldenberg et al., 1995). In a large-scale randomized study of low-income households in 347 Mexican communities, women who took nutrient-fortified dietary supplements while pregnant or lactating tended to have infants who grew more rapidly and were less likely to be anemic (Rivera, Sotres-Alvarez, Habicht, Shamah, & Villalpando, 2004).

Drug Intake Practically everything an expectant mother takes in makes its way to the uterus. Drugs may cross the placenta, just as oxygen, carbon dioxide, and water do. Vulnerability is greatest in the first few months of gestation, when development is most rapid.

What are the effects of the use of specific drugs during pregnancy? Let's look first at medical drugs; then at alcohol, nicotine, and caffeine; and finally at three illegal drugs: marijuana, cocaine, and methamphetamine.

Medical Drugs Among the medical drugs that may be harmful during pregnancy are the antibiotic tetracycline; certain barbiturates, opiates, and other central nervous system depressants; several hormones, including diethylstilbestrol (DES) and androgens; certain anticancer drugs, such as methotrexate; and Accutane, a drug often prescribed for severe acne (Koren, Pastuszak, & Ito, 1998). Angiotensin-converting enzyme (ACE) inhibitors and nonsteroidal anti-inflammatory drugs (NSAIDs), such as naproxen and ibuprofen, have been linked to birth defects when taken anytime from the first trimester on (Ofori, Oraichi, Blais, Rey, & Berard, 2006; Cooper et al., 2006). In addition, certain antipsychotic drugs used to manage severe psychiatric disorders may have serious potential effects on the fetus, including withdrawal symptoms at birth (AAP Committee on Drugs, 2000). The American Academy of Pediatrics (AAP) Committee on Drugs (1994) recommends that *no* medication be taken by a pregnant or breast-feeding woman unless it is essential for her health or her child's (Koren et al., 1998).

Alcohol Prenatal alcohol exposure is the most common cause of mental retardation and the leading preventable cause of birth defects in the United States. **Fetal alcohol syndrome (FAS)** is characterized by a combination of retarded growth, face and body malformations, and disorders of the central nervous system. FAS and other, less severe, alcohol-related conditions are estimated to occur in nearly 1 in every 100 births (Sokol, Delaney-Black, & Nordstrom, 2003).

What's Your View?

• Once banned for causing birth defects, thalidomide has since been found to be effective in many illnesses, from mouth ulcers to brain cancer. Should its use for these purposes be permitted even though there is a risk that pregnant women might take it? If so, what safeguards should be required?

fetal alcohol syndrome (FAS) Combination of mental, motor, and developmental abnormalities affecting the offspring of some women who drink heavily during pregnancy.

A mother who drinks during pregnancy risks having a child born with fetal alcohol syndrome, as this 4-year-old boy was.

Even small amounts of social drinking may harm a fetus (Sokol et al., 2003), and the more the mother drinks, the greater the effect. Moderate or heavy drinking during pregnancy seems to disturb an infant's neurological and behavioral functioning, and this may affect early social interaction with the mother, which is vital to emotional development (Nugent, Lester, Greene, Wieczorek-Deering, & Mahony, 1996). Heavy drinkers who continue to drink after becoming pregnant are likely to have babies with reduced skull and brain growth as compared with babies of nondrinking women or expectant mothers who stop drinking (Handmaker et al., 2006).

FAS-related problems can include, in infancy, reduced responsiveness to stimuli, slow reaction time, and reduced visual acuity (sharpness of vision) (Carter et al., 2005; Sokol et al., 2003) and, throughout childhood, short attention span, distractibility, restlessness, hyperactivity, learning disabilities, memory deficits, and mood disorders (Sokol et al., 2003) as well as aggressiveness and problem behavior (Sood et al., 2001). Prenatal alcohol exposure is a risk factor for development of drinking problems and alcohol disorders in young adulthood (Alati et al., 2006; Baer, Sampson, Barr, Connor, & Streissguth, 2003).

Some FAS effects, such as retardation, behavioral and learning problems, and hyperactivity, tend to persist (Kerns, Don, Mateer, & Streissguth, 1997; Spohr, Willms, & Steinhausen, 1993; Streissguth et al., 1991; Strömland & Hellström, 1996). However, affected children may be less likely to develop behavioral and mental health problems if they are diagnosed early and are reared in stable, nurturing environments (Streissguth et al., 2004). Because there is no known safe level of drinking during pregnancy, it is best to avoid alcohol from the time a woman begins *thinking* about becoming pregnant until she stops breast-feeding (AAP Committee on Substance Abuse and Committee on Children with Disabilities, 1993; Sokol et al., 2003).

Nicotine Maternal smoking has been identified as the single most important factor in low birth weight in developed countries (DiFranza, Aligne, & Weitzman, 2004). Women who smoke during pregnancy are more than one and a half times as likely as nonsmokers to bear low-birth-weight babies (weighing less than 5½ pounds at birth). Even light smoking (fewer than five cigarettes a day) is associated with a greater risk of low birth weight (Martin, Hamilton, et al., 2005; Shankaran et al., 2004; Hoyert, Mathews, Menacker, Strobino, & Guyer, 2006).

Tobacco use during pregnancy also brings increased risks of miscarriage, growth retardation, stillbirth, small head circumference, sudden infant death, colic (uncontrollable, extended crying for no apparent reason) in early infancy, hyperkinetic disorder (excessive movement), and long-term respiratory, neurological, cognitive, and behavioral problems (AAP Committee on Substance Abuse, 2001; DiFranza et al., 2004; Hoyert, Mathews, et al., 2006; Linnet et al., 2005; Martin, Hamilton, et al., 2007; Shankaran et al., 2004; Smith et al., 2006; Sondergaard, Henriksen, Obel, & Wisborg, 2001; Shah, Sullivan, & Carter, 2006). The effects of prenatal exposure to secondhand smoke on cognitive development tend to be worse when the child also experiences socioeconomic hardships, such as substandard housing, malnutrition, and inadequate clothing during the first two years of life (Rauh et al., 2004).

Caffeine Can the caffeine a pregnant woman consumes in coffee, tea, cola, or chocolate cause trouble for her fetus? For the most part, results have been mixed. It does seem clear that caffeine is *not* a teratogen for human babies (Christian &

Brent, 2001). A controlled study of 1,205 new mothers and their babies showed no effect of reported caffeine use on low birth weight, premature birth, or retarded fetal growth (Santos, Victora, Huttly, & Carvalhal, 1998). On the other hand, in a controlled study of 1,063 pregnant women, those who consumed at least two cups of regular coffee or five cans of caffeinated soda daily had twice the risk of miscarriage as those who consumed no caffeine (Weng, Odouli, & Li, 2008). Four or more cups of coffee a day during pregnancy may dramatically increase the risk of sudden death in infancy (Ford et al., 1998).

Marijuana, Cocaine, and Methamphetamine   Studies of marijuana use by pregnant women are sparse. However, some evidence suggests that heavy marijuana use can lead to birth defects, low birth weight, withdrawal-like symptoms (excessive crying and tremors) at birth, and increased risk of attention disorders and learning problems later in life (March of Dimes Birth Defects Foundation, 2004b). In two longitudinal studies, prenatal use of marijuana was associated with impaired attention, impulsivity, and difficulty in use of visual and perceptual skills after age 3, suggesting that the drug may affect functioning of the brain's frontal lobes (Fried & Smith, 2001).

Cocaine use during pregnancy has been associated with spontaneous abortion, delayed growth, premature labor, low birth weight, small head size, birth defects, and impaired neurological development (Bunikowski et al., 1998; Chiriboga, Brust, Bateman, & Hauser, 1999; Macmillan et al., 2001; March of Dimes Birth Defects Foundation, 2004a; Scher, Richardson, & Day, 2000; Shankaran et al., 2004). In some studies, cocaine-exposed newborns show acute withdrawal symptoms and sleep disturbances (O'Brien & Jeffery, 2002). In a more recent study, high prenatal cocaine exposure was associated with childhood behavior problems, independent of the effects of alcohol and tobacco exposure (Bada et al., 2007). So great has been the concern about prenatal cocaine exposure that some states have taken criminal action against expectant mothers suspected of using cocaine. Other studies, however, have found no specific connection between prenatal cocaine exposure and physical, motor, cognitive, emotional, or behavioral deficits that could not also be attributed to other risk factors, such as low birth weight; exposure to tobacco, alcohol, or marijuana; or a poor home environment (Frank, Augustyn, Knight, Pell, & Zuckerman, 2001; Messinger et al., 2004; Singer et al., 2004).

Methamphetamine use among pregnant women is an increasing concern in the United States. In a study of 1,618 infants, 84 were found to have been exposed to methamphetamine. The methamphetamine-exposed infants were more likely to have low birth weight and to be small for their gestational age than the remainder of the sample. This finding suggests that prenatal methamphetamine exposure is associated with fetal growth restriction (Smith et al., 2006).

Maternal Illnesses   Both prospective parents should try to prevent all infections—common colds, flu, urinary tract and vaginal infections, as well as sexually transmitted diseases. If the mother does contract an infection, she should have it treated promptly.

Acquired immune deficiency syndrome (AIDS) is a disease caused by the human immunodeficiency virus (HIV), which undermines functioning of the immune system. If an expectant mother has the virus in her blood, *perinatal transmission* may occur: The virus may cross over to the fetus's bloodstream through the placenta during pregnancy, labor, or delivery or, after birth, through breast milk.

The biggest risk factor for perinatal HIV transmission is a mother who is unaware she has HIV. In the United States, new pediatric AIDS cases have

What's Your View?

• Does society's interest in protecting an unborn child justify coercive measures against pregnant women who ingest harmful substances?

acquired immune deficiency syndrome (AIDS) Viral disease that undermines effective functioning of the immune system.

declined steadily since 1992 due to routine testing and treatment of pregnant women and newborn babies and to advances in the prevention, detection, and treatment of HIV infection in infants. As a result, the estimated rate of perinatal HIV infection is now less than 2 percent. The risk of transmission also can be reduced by choosing cesarean delivery, especially when a woman has not received antiretroviral therapy, and by promotion of alternatives to breast-feeding among high-risk women (CDC, 2006a).

Rubella (German measles), if contracted by a woman before her eleventh week of pregnancy, is almost certain to cause deafness and heart defects in her baby. Chances of catching rubella during pregnancy have been greatly reduced in Europe and the United States since the late 1960s, when a vaccine was developed that is now routinely administered to infants and children. However, rubella is still a serious problem in developing countries where immunizations are not routine (Plotkin, Katz, & Cordero, 1999).

An infection called *toxoplasmosis,* caused by a parasite harbored in the bodies of cattle, sheep, and pigs and in the intestinal tracts of cats, typically produces either no symptoms or symptoms like those of the common cold. In an expectant woman, however, especially in the second and third trimesters of pregnancy, it can cause fetal brain damage, severely impaired eyesight or blindness, seizures, miscarriage, stillbirth, or death of the baby. If the baby survives, there may be later problems, including eye infections, hearing loss, and learning disabilities. Treatment with antiparasitic drugs during the first year of life can reduce brain and eye damage (McLeod et al., 2006). To avoid infection, expectant mothers should not eat raw or very rare meat, should wash hands and all work surfaces after touching raw meat, should peel or thoroughly wash raw fruits and vegetables, and should not dig in a garden where cat feces may be buried. Women who have a cat should have it checked for the disease, should not feed it raw meat, and, if possible, should have someone else empty the litter box (March of Dimes, 2002).

Offspring of mothers with diabetes are two to five times more likely to develop birth defects, especially of the heart and of the spinal cord (neural-tube defects), than offspring of other women. Research on mice suggests why: High blood glucose levels, typical in diabetics, deprive an embryo of oxygen, with resultant cell damage, during the first eight weeks of pregnancy, when its organs are forming. Women with diabetes need to be sure their blood glucose levels are under control *before* becoming pregnant (Li, Chase, Jung, Smith, & Loeken, 2005). Use of multivitamin supplements during the three months before conception and the first three months of pregnancy can help reduce the risk of diabetes-associated birth defects (Correa, Botto, Lin, Mulinare, & Erickson, 2003).

Maternal Anxiety and Stress Some tension and worry during pregnancy are normal and do not necessarily increase risks of birth complications, such as low birth weight (Littleton, Breitkopf, & Berenson, 2006). Moderate maternal anxiety may even spur organization of the developing brain. In a series of studies, 2-year-olds whose mothers had shown moderate anxiety midway through pregnancy scored higher on measures of motor and mental development than did age-mates whose mothers had not shown anxiety during pregnancy (DiPietro, 2004; DiPietro, Novak, Costigan, Atella, & Reusing, 2006).

On the other hand, a mother's self-reported anxiety during pregnancy has been associated with an 8-month-old's inattentiveness during a developmental assessment (Huizink, Robles de Medina, Mulder, Visser, & Buitelaar, 2002) and a preschooler's negative emotionality or behavioral disorders in early childhood

(Martin, Noyes, Wisenbaker, & Huttunen, 2000; O'Connor, Heron, Golding, Beveridge, & Glover, 2002).

Unusual maternal **stress** during pregnancy may negatively affect the offspring (Dingfelder, 2004; Huizink, Mulder, & Buitelaar, 2004). In one study, pregnant women whose partners or children died or were hospitalized for cancer or heart attacks were at elevated risk of giving birth to children with malformations, such as cleft lip, cleft palate, and heart malformations (Hansen, Lou, & Olsen, 2000). Also, major stress during the 24th to 28th weeks of pregnancy may produce autism by deforming the developing brain (Beversdorf et al., 2001).

Maternal Age   On December 30, 2006, in Barcelona, Spain, a 67-year-old woman became the oldest woman on record to give birth. She had become pregnant after in vitro fertilization and had twins by cesarean section.

Births to U.S. women in their thirties and forties—and, to a lesser extent, even in their fifties and sixties—have nearly doubled since 1980, from 19 percent to more than 37 percent of all births (Martin, Hamilton, et al., 2006), demonstrating a history-graded influence. How does delayed childbearing affect the risks to mother and baby?

Although most risks to the infant's health are not much greater than for babies born to younger mothers, the chance of miscarriage or stillbirth rises with maternal age. In fact, the risk of miscarriage reaches 90 percent for women age 45 or older (Heffner, 2004). Women over 30 to 35 are more likely to suffer complications due to diabetes, high blood pressure, or severe bleeding. There is also higher risk of premature delivery, retarded fetal growth, birth defects, and chromosomal abnormalities, such as Down syndrome. However, due to widespread screening among older expectant mothers, fewer malformed babies are born nowadays (Berkowitz, Skovron, Lapinski, & Berkowitz, 1990; P. Brown, 1993; Cunningham & Leveno, 1995; Heffner, 2004).

Adolescent mothers tend to have premature or underweight babies—perhaps because a young girl's still-growing body consumes vital nutrients the fetus needs (Fraser, Brockert, & Ward, 1995; Martin, Hamilton, et al., 2007). These newborns are at heightened risk of death in the first month, disabilities, or health problems. Risks of teenage pregnancy are discussed further in Chapter 12.

Outside Environmental Hazards   Air pollution, chemicals, radiation, extremes of heat and humidity, and other environmental hazards can affect prenatal development. Pregnant women who regularly breathe air that contains high levels of fine combustion-related particles are more likely to bear infants who are premature or undersized (Parker, Woodruff, Basu, & Schoendorf, 2005) or have chromosomal abnormalities (Bocskay et al., 2005). Exposure to high concentrations of disinfection by-products is associated with low birth weight and slowed fetal growth (Hinckley, Bachand, & Reif, 2005). Women who work with chemicals used in manufacturing semiconductor chips have about twice the rate of miscarriage as other female workers (Markoff, 1992), and women exposed to DDT tend to have more preterm births (Longnecker, Klebanoff, Zhou, & Brock, 2001). Two insecticides, chlorpyrifos and diazinon, apparently cause stunting of prenatal growth (Whyatt et al., 2004). Research in the United Kingdom found a 33 percent increase in risk of nongenetic birth

This pregnant woman shopping for fruits and vegetables at an open-air market on a busy street is probably unaware of the potential danger to her fetus from traffic-related air pollution.

defects among families who were living within two miles of hazardous waste sites (Vrijheld et al., 2002).

Fetal exposure to low levels of environmental toxins, such as lead, mercury, and dioxin, as well as nicotine and ethanol, may help explain the sharp rise in asthma, allergies, and autoimmune disorders such as lupus (Dietert, 2005). Childhood cancers, including leukemia, have been linked to pregnant mothers' drinking chemically contaminated groundwater (Boyles, 2002) and use of home pesticides (Menegaux et al., 2006). Infants exposed prenatally even to low levels of lead, especially during the third trimester, tend to show IQ deficits at ages 6 to 10 (Schnaas et al., 2006).

Women who have routine dental X-rays during pregnancy triple their risk of having full-term, low-birth-weight babies (Hujoel, Bollen, Noonan, & del Aguila, 2004). In utero exposure to radiation 8 through 15 weeks after fertilization has been linked to mental retardation, small head size, chromosomal malformations, Down syndrome, seizures, and poor performance on IQ tests and in school (Yamazaki & Schull, 1990).

Environmental Influences: Paternal Factors

A man's exposure to lead, marijuana or tobacco smoke, large amounts of alcohol or radiation, DES, pesticides, or high ozone levels may result in abnormal or poor-quality sperm (Sokol et al., 2006; Swan et al., 2003). Offspring of male workers at a British nuclear processing plant were at elevated risk of being born dead (Parker, Pearce, Dickinson, Aitkin, & Craft, 1999). Babies whose fathers had diagnostic X-rays within the year prior to conception or had high lead exposure at work tended to have low birth weight and slowed fetal growth (Lin, Hwang, Marshall, & Marion, 1998; Shea, Little, & the ALSPAC Study Team, 1997). Among nearly 238,000 infants born in Singapore over a four-year period, birth defects were more strongly linked to fathers' occupations—especially such jobs as plant and machine operation and assembly—than to mothers' occupations (Chia et al., 2004).

Men who smoke have an increased likelihood of transmitting genetic abnormalities (AAP Committee on Substance Abuse, 2001). A pregnant woman's exposure to the father's secondhand smoke has been linked with low birth weight, infant respiratory infections, sudden infant death, and cancer in childhood and adulthood (Ji et al., 1997; D. H. Rubin, Krasilnikoff, Leventhal, Weile, & Berget, 1986; Sandler, Everson, Wilcox, & Browder, 1985; Wakefield, Reid, Roberts, Mullins, & Gillies, 1998). In a study of 214 nonsmoking mothers in New York City, exposure to *both* paternal smoking and urban air pollution resulted in a 7 percent reduction in birth weight and a 3 percent reduction in head circumference (Perera, Rauh, et al., 2004).

Older fathers may be a significant source of birth defects due to damaged or deteriorated sperm. In 2004 about 10 percent of fathers of new babies were ages 35 to 55 and over (Martin, Hamilton, et al., 2006). Advancing paternal age is associated with increases in the risk of several rare conditions, including dwarfism (Wyrobek et al., 2006); it also may be a factor in a disproportionate number of cases of schizophrenia (Byrne et al., 2003; Malaspina et al., 2001) and of autism and related disorders (Reichenberg et al., 2006). On the other hand, in a study of more than 2.6 million U.S. births, infants with teenage fathers had a greater risk of premature birth, of low birth weight, and of being small for their gestational age than infants of fathers age 40 or older (Weng et al., 2008).

What's Your View?

• Should men of childbearing age be forced to abstain from cocaine, marijuana, tobacco, and other substances that can produce genetic abnormalities in sperm? How could such a prohibition be enforced?

Checkpoint

Can you . . .

◆ Summarize recommendations for an expectant mother's diet?

◆ Discuss effects on the developing fetus of an expectant mother's use of medical drugs, alcohol, tobacco, caffeine, marijuana, cocaine, and methamphetamine?

◆ Assess the risks of maternal illnesses, anxiety, stress, advanced age, and exposure to environmental hazards during pregnancy?

◆ Identify at least three ways in which the father can influence environmentally caused defects?

Table 3-5 Prenatal Assessment Techniques

Technique	Description	Uses and Advantages	Risks and Notes
Ultrasound (sonogram), sonoembryology	High-frequency sound waves directed at the mother's abdomen produce a picture of fetus in uterus. Sonoembryology uses high-frequency transvaginal probes and digital image processing to produce a picture of embryo in uterus.	Monitor fetal growth, movement, position, and form; assess amniotic fluid volume; judge gestational age; detect multiple pregnancies. Detect major structural abnormalities or death of a fetus. Guide amniocentesis and chorionic villus sampling. Help diagnose sex-linked disorders. Sonoembryology can detect unusual defects during embryonic stage.	Done routinely in many places. Can be used for sex-screening of unborn babies.
Embryoscopy, fetoscopy	Tiny viewing scope is inserted in woman's abdomen to view embryo or fetus. Can assist in diagnosis of nonchromosomal genetic disorders.	Can guide fetal blood transfusions and bone marrow transplants.	Riskier than other prenatal diagnostic procedures.
Amniocentesis	Sample of amniotic fluid is withdrawn under guidance of ultrasound and analyzed. Most commonly used procedure to obtain fetal cells for testing.	Can detect chromosomal disorders and certain genetic or multifactorial defects; more than 99 percent accuracy rate. Usually performed in women ages 35 and over; recommended if prospective parents are known carriers of Tay-Sachs disease or sickle-cell anemia or have family history of Down syndrome, spina bifida, or muscular dystrophy. Can help diagnose sex-linked disorders.	Normally not performed before 15 weeks' gestation. Results usually take 1 to 2 weeks. Small (0.5% to 1%) added risk of fetal loss or injury; early amniocentesis (at 11 to 13 weeks' gestation) is riskier and not recommended. Can be used for sex-screening of unborn babies.
Chorionic villus sampling (CVS)	Tissues from hairlike chorionic villi (projections of membrane surrounding fetus) are removed from placenta and analyzed.	Early diagnosis of birth defects and disorders. Can be performed between 10 and 12 weeks' gestation; yields highly accurate results within a week.	Should not be performed before 10 weeks' gestation. Some studies suggest 1% to 4% more risk of fetal loss than with amniocentesis.
Preimplantation genetic diagnosis	After in vitro fertilization, a sample cell is removed from the blastocyst and analyzed.	Can avoid transmission of genetic defects or predispositions known to run in the family; a defective blastocyst is *not* implanted in uterus.	No known risks.
Umbilical cord sampling (cordocentesis, or fetal blood sampling)	Needle guided by ultrasound is inserted into blood vessels of umbilical cord.	Allows direct access to fetal DNA for diagnostic measures, including assessment of blood disorders and infections, and therapeutic measures such as blood transfusions.	Fetal loss or miscarriage is reported in 1% to 2% of cases; increases risk of bleeding from umbilical cord and fetal distress.
Maternal blood test	A sample of the prospective mother's blood is tested for alpha fetoprotein.	May indicate defects in formation of brain or spinal cord (anencephaly or spina bifida); also can predict Down syndrome and other abnormalities. Permits monitoring of pregnancies at risk for low birth weight or stillbirth.	No known risks, but false negatives are possible. Ultrasound and/or amniocentesis needed to confirm suspected conditions.

Sources: Chodirker et al., 2001; Cicero, Curcio, Papageorghiou, Sonek, & Nicolaides, 2001; Cunniff & the Committee on Genetics, 2004; Kurjak, Kupesic, Matijevic, Kos, & Marton, 1999; Verlinsky et al., 2002.

Monitoring and Promoting Prenatal Development

Guidepost 7

What techniques can assess a fetus's health, and why is prenatal care important?

Not long ago, almost the only decision parents had to make about their babies before birth was the decision to conceive; most of what happened in the intervening months was beyond their control. Now scientists have developed an array of tools to assess an unborn baby's progress and well-being and even to intervene to correct some abnormal conditions (Table 3-5).

Progress is being made in the use of noninvasive procedures, such as ultrasound and blood tests, to detect chromosomal abnormalities. In one study, a combination of three noninvasive tests conducted at 11 weeks of gestation predicted the presence of Down syndrome with 87 percent accuracy. When the 11-week tests were followed by further noninvasive testing early in the second trimester, accuracy reached 96 percent (Malone et al., 2005). Contrary to previous findings, amniocentesis and chorionic villus sampling, which can be used earlier in pregnancy, carry only a slightly higher miscarriage risk than these noninvasive procedures (Caughey, Hopkins, & Norton, 2006; Eddleman et al., 2006).

Screening for defects and diseases is only one reason for the importance of early prenatal care. Early, high-quality prenatal care, which includes educational, social, and nutritional services, can help prevent maternal or infant death and other birth complications. It can provide first-time mothers with information about pregnancy, childbirth, and infant care. Poor women who get prenatal care benefit by being put in touch with other needed services, and they are more likely to get medical care for their infants after birth (Shiono & Behrman, 1995).

Disparities in Prenatal Care

In the United States prenatal care is widespread, but not universal as in many European countries, and it lacks uniform national standards and guaranteed financial coverage. Use of early prenatal care (during the first three months of pregnancy) has risen since 1990 from 75.8 percent to 83.9 percent of pregnant women in 43 reporting areas.* Still, in 2005, 3.5 percent of expectant mothers received no care until the last trimester or no care at all (Martin, Hamilton, et al., 2007). Furthermore, rates of low birth weight and premature birth continue to rise (see Chapter 5). Why?

One answer is the increasing number of multiple births, which require especially close prenatal attention. These pregnancies often end in early births, low birth weight, and a heightened risk of death within the first year (Martin, Hamilton, et al., 2006).

A second answer is that the benefits of prenatal care are not evenly distributed. Although use of prenatal care has grown, especially among ethnic groups that tend *not* to receive early care, the women most at risk of bearing low-birth-weight babies—teenage and unmarried women, those with little education, and black and non-Hispanic white women—are still least likely to receive it (Martin, Hamilton, et al., 2005, 2006, 2007; National Center for Health Statistics [NCHS], 2005; USDDHS, 1996a). Figure 3-11 shows percentages of various ethnic groups that receive late or no prenatal care.

A related concern is an ethnic disparity in fetal and postbirth mortality. After adjusting for such risk factors as SES, overweight, smoking, hypertension, and diabetes, the chances of perinatal death (death between 20 weeks' gestation and one week after birth) remain 3.4 times higher for blacks, 1.5 times higher for Hispanics, and 1.9 times higher for other minorities than for whites (Healy et al., 2006).

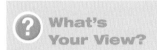

What's Your View?

• Can you suggest ways to induce more pregnant women to seek early prenatal or preconception care?

---

*The reporting instrument for prenatal care utilization in the United States was revised in 2003, but only 13 out of 56 reporting areas had adopted the new instrument as of 2005. Results for areas using the new instrument were substantially worse than those reported above: 70.2 percent of mothers began prenatal care in the first trimester, and 7.7 percent received late or no prenatal care.

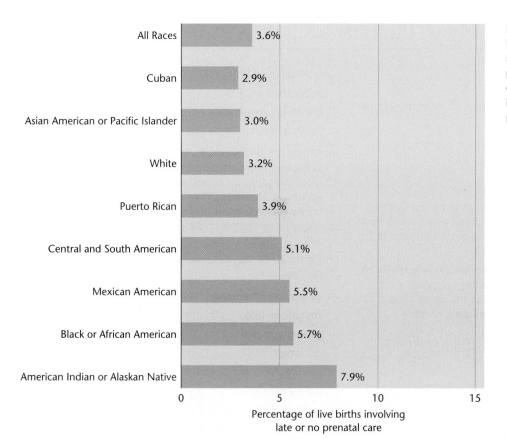

The Need for Preconception Care

A more fundamental answer is that even early prenatal care is insufficient. Care should begin *before* pregnancy to identify preventable risks. The CDC (2006c) has issued comprehensive, research-based guidelines for *preconception care* for all women of childbearing age. Such care should include the following:

- *Physical examinations* and the taking of medical and family histories
- *Vaccinations* for rubella and hepatitis B
- *Risk screening* for genetic disorders and infectious diseases such as STDs
- *Counseling* women to avoid smoking and alcohol, maintain a healthy body weight, and take folic acid supplements

Interventions should be provided where risks are indicated and also between pregnancies for women who have had poor pregnancy outcomes in the past.

The CDC (2006c) urges all adults to create a reproductive life plan so as to focus attention on reproductive health, avoid unintended pregnancies, and improve pregnancy outcomes. The CDC also calls for increased health insurance for low-income women to make sure they have access to preventive care.

Good preconception and prenatal care can give every child the best possible chance for entering the world in good condition to meet the challenges of life outside the womb—challenges we discuss in the next three chapters.

Checkpoint

Can you . . .

- Describe seven techniques for identifying defects or disorders prenatally?
- Discuss possible reasons for disparities in utilization of prenatal care?
- Tell why early, high-quality prenatal care is important and why preconception care is needed?

Summary and Key Terms

Conceiving New Life

Guidepost 1: *How does conception normally occur, and what causes multiple births?*

- Fertilization, the union of an ovum and a sperm, results in the formation of a one-celled zygote, which then duplicates itself by cell division.
- Multiple births can occur either by the fertilization of two ova (or one ovum that has split) or by the splitting of one fertilized ovum. Higher multiple births result from either one of these processes or a combination of the two.
- Dizygotic (fraternal) twins have different genetic makeups and may be of different sexes. Although monozygotic (identical) twins typically have much the same genetic makeup, they may differ in temperament or other respects.

fertilization (54)

zygote (54)

dizygotic twins (55)

monozygotic twins (55)

Mechanisms of Heredity

Guidepost 2: *How does heredity operate in determining sex and transmitting normal and abnormal traits?*

- The basic functional units of heredity are the genes, which are made of deoxyribonucleic acid (DNA). DNA carries the biochemical instructions, or genetic code, that governs the development of cell functions. Each gene is located by function in a definite position on a particular chromosome. The complete sequence of genes in the human body is called the *human genome*.

deoxyribonucleic acid (DNA) (56)

genetic code (56)

chromosomes (56)

genes (56)

human genome (56)

- At conception, each normal human being receives 23 chromosomes from the mother and 23 from the father. These form 23 pairs of chromosomes—22 pairs of autosomes and 1 pair of sex chromosomes. A child who receives an X chromosome from each parent is genetically female. A child who receives a Y chromosome from the father is genetically male.
- The simplest patterns of genetic transmission are dominant and recessive inheritance. When a pair of alleles are the same, a person is homozygous for the trait; when they are different, the person is heterozygous.

autosomes (57)

sex chromosomes (57)

alleles (59)

homozygous (59)

heterozygous (59)

dominant inheritance (59)

recessive inheritance (59)

- Most normal human characteristics are the result of polygenic or multifactorial transmission. Except for most monozygotic twins, each child inherits a unique genotype. Dominant inheritance and multifactorial transmission explain why a person's phenotype does not always express the underlying genotype.
- The epigenetic framework controls the functions of particular genes; it can be affected by environmental factors.

polygenic inheritance (59)

mutations (59)

phenotype (60)

genotype (60)

multifactorial transmission (60)

epigenesis (60)

- Birth defects and diseases may result from simple dominant, recessive, or sex-linked inheritance, from mutations, or from genome imprinting. Chromosomal abnormalities also can cause birth defects.
- Through genetic counseling, prospective parents can receive information about the mathematical odds of bearing children with certain defects.
- Genetic testing involves risks as well as benefits.

incomplete dominance (63)

sex-linked inheritance (63)

Down syndrome (65)

genetic counseling (65)

Nature and Nurture: Influences of Heredity and Environment

Guidepost 3: *How do scientists study the relative influences of heredity and environment, and how do heredity and environment work together?*

- Research in behavioral genetics is based on the assumption that the relative influences of heredity and environment within a population can be measured statistically. If heredity is an important influence on a trait, genetically closer persons will be more similar in that trait. Family studies, adoption studies, and studies of twins enable researchers to measure the heritability of specific traits.
- The concepts of reaction range, canalization, genotype-environment interaction, genotype-environment correlation (or covariance), and niche-picking describe ways in which heredity and environment work together.

- Siblings tend to be more different than alike in intelligence and personality. According to some behavioral geneticists, heredity accounts for most of the similarity, and nonshared environmental effects account for most of the difference.

behavioral genetics (66)

heritability (68)

concordant (68)

reaction range (69)

canalization (70)

genotype-environment interaction (70)

genotype-environment correlation (71)

niche-picking (71)

nonshared environmental effects (72)

Guidepost 4: *What roles do heredity and environment play in physical health, intelligence, and personality?*

- Obesity, longevity, intelligence, temperament, and other aspects of personality are influenced by both heredity and environment.
- Schizophrenia is a highly heritable neurological disorder that also is environmentally influenced.

obesity (73)

temperament (74)

schizophrenia (74)

Prenatal Development

Guidepost 5: *What are the three stages of prenatal development, and what happens during each stage?*

- Prenatal development occurs in three stages of gestation: the germinal, embryonic, and fetal stages.
- Severely defective embryos often are spontaneously aborted during the first trimester of pregnancy.
- As fetuses grow, they move less, but more vigorously. Swallowing amniotic fluid, which contains substances from the mother's body, stimulates taste and smell. Fetuses seem able to hear, exercise sensory discrimination, learn, and remember.

gestation (74)

gestational age (75)

germinal stage (75)

embryonic stage (79)

spontaneous abortion (80)

fetal stage (80)

ultrasound (80)

Guidepost 6: *What environmental influences can affect prenatal development?*

- The developing organism can be greatly affected by its prenatal environment. The likelihood of a birth defect may depend on the timing and intensity of an environmental event and its interaction with genetic factors.
- Important environmental influences involving the mother include nutrition, smoking, intake of alcohol or other drugs, transmission of maternal illnesses or infections, maternal stress, maternal age, and external environmental hazards, such as chemicals and radiation. External influences also may affect the father's sperm.

teratogenic (82)

fetal alcohol syndrome (FAS) (83)

acquired immune deficiency syndrome (AIDS) (85)

stress (87)

Guidepost 7: *What techniques can assess a fetus's health, and why is prenatal care important?*

- Ultrasound, sonoembryology amniocentesis, chorionic villus sampling, fetoscopy, preimplantation genetic diagnosis, umbilical cord sampling, and maternal blood tests can be used to determine whether an unborn baby is developing normally.
- Early, high-quality prenatal care is essential for healthy development. It can lead to detection of defects and disorders and, especially if begun early and targeted to the needs of at-risk women, may help reduce maternal and infant death, low birth weight, and other birth complications.
- Racial/ethnic disparities in prenatal care may be a factor in disparities in low birth weight and perinatal death.
- Preconception care for every woman of childbearing age would reduce unintended pregnancies and increase the chances of good pregnancy outcomes.

The experiences of the first three years of life are almost entirely lost to us, and when we attempt to enter into a small child's world, we come as foreigners who have forgotten the landscape and no longer speak the native tongue.

—Selma Fraiberg, *The Magic Years,* 1959

Did You Know...

- In 1900, only 5 percent of expectant mothers in the United States gave birth in hospitals, as compared with 99 percent today?

- Baby boys' deliveries are more likely to involve complications than baby girls'?

- At about 30 percent of all births, the cesarean rate in the United States is among the highest in the world?

- In the industrialized world, smoking during pregnancy is the leading factor in low birth weight?

- Worldwide, about 8 million infants die before their first birthday each year?

- Cultural practices, such as how much freedom babies have to move about, can affect the age at which they begin to walk?

These are just a few of the interesting and important topics we will cover in this chapter. In it, we describe how babies come into the world, how newborn babies look, and how their body systems work. We discuss ways to safeguard their life and health. We observe how sensory perception goes hand in hand with an infant's growing motor skills and helps shape the astoundingly rapid development of the brain. We see how infants become busy, active toddlers and how parents and other caregivers can foster healthy growth and development. After you have read and studied this chapter, you should be able to answer each of the Guidepost questions on the following page.

Guideposts *for Study*

1. How has childbirth changed in developed countries?

2. How does labor begin, what happens during each of the three stages of childbirth, and what alternative methods of delivery are available?

3. How do newborn infants adjust to life outside the womb, and how can we tell whether a new baby is healthy and is developing normally?

4. What complications of childbirth can endanger newborn babies, and what are the prospects for infants with complicated births?

5. What factors affect infants' chances for survival and health?

6. What influences growth, and how do the brain and the senses develop?

7. What are the early milestones in motor development, and what are some influences on it?

Guidepost 1

How has childbirth changed in developed countries?

Childbirth and Culture: How Birthing Has Changed

Before the twentieth century, childbirth in Europe and in the United States, as in most developing countries, was a female social ritual.* The woman, surrounded by female relatives and neighbors, sat up in her bed or perhaps in the stable, modestly draped in a sheet; if she wished, she might stand, walk around, or squat over a birth stool.

The midwife who presided over the event had no formal training; she offered "advice, massages, potions, irrigations, and talismans" (Fontanel & d'Harcourt, 1997, p. 28). After the baby emerged, the midwife cut and tied the umbilical cord and cleaned and examined the newborn. Within a few hours or days, a peasant mother would be back at work in the fields; a more affluent woman could rest for several weeks.

Childbirth in those times was "a struggle with death" for both mother and baby (Fontanel & d'Harcourt, 1997, p. 34). In seventeenth- and eighteenth-century France, a woman had a 1 in 10 chance of dying while or shortly after giving birth. Thousands of babies were stillborn, and 1 out of 4 who were born alive died during their first year.

Not much about childbirth has changed in some developing countries in sub-Saharan Africa and South Asia. There, 60 million women deliver at home each year without the benefit of skilled care, and more than 500,000 women and 4 million newborns die in or shortly after childbirth (Sines, Syed, Wall, & Worley, 2007).

In the Western world, in contrast, the development of the science of obstetrics early in the nineteenth century and of maternity hospitals after the turn of the twentieth century revolutionized childbirth. In 1900, only 5 percent of U.S. deliveries occurred in hospitals; by 1920, in some cities, 65 percent did (Scholten, 1985). A similar trend took place in Europe. In the United States in 2005, 99 percent of

*This discussion is based largely on Eccles (1982); Fontanel & d'Harcourt (1997); Gélis (1991); and Scholten (1985).

babies were born in hospitals, and 91.6 percent of births were attended by physicians. Nearly 8 percent were attended by midwives, usually certified nurse-midwives (Martin, Hamilton, et al., 2007).

The dramatic reductions in risks surrounding pregnancy and childbirth in industrialized countries, particularly during the past 50 years, are largely due to the availability of antibiotics, blood transfusions, safe anesthesia, improved hygiene, and drugs for inducing labor. In addition, improvements in prenatal assessment and care make it far more likely that a baby will be born healthy.

However, the "medicalization" of childbirth has had social and emotional costs, according to some critics (Fontanel & d'Harcourt, 1997). Today a small but growing percentage of women in developed countries are going back to the intimate, personal experience of home birth, which can involve the whole family. Home births usually are attended by a trained nurse-midwife, with the resources of medical science close at hand. Arrangements may be made with a physician and a nearby hospital in case an emergency arises.

Freestanding, homelike birth centers are another option. Studies suggest that births in both of these settings can be as safe and much less expensive than those in hospitals when deliveries are low-risk and are attended by skilled practitioners (Anderson & Anderson, 1999; Durand, 1992; Guyer, Strobino, Ventura, & Singh, 1995; Korte & Scaer, 1984).

Hospitals, too, are finding ways to humanize childbirth. Labor and delivery may take place in a comfortable birthing room, under soft lights, with the father or partner present as a coach and older siblings invited to visit after the birth. Rooming-in policies allow a baby to stay in the mother's room much or all of the time so that mothers can feed their newborns when they are hungry rather than when an arbitrary schedule allows. By "demedicalizing the experience of childbirth, some hospitals and birthing centers are seeking to establish—or reestablish—an environment in which tenderness, security, and emotion carry as much weight as medical techniques" (Fontanel & d'Harcourt, 1997, p. 57).

In 2005 nearly 25,000 U.S. babies were born at home (Martin, Hamilton, et al., 2007).

 Checkpoint

Can you . . .

♦ Identify two ways childbirth has changed in developed countries and tell why it is less risky than it once was?

♦ Compare advantages of various settings for childbirth?

The Birth Process

Emily woke up with some strange sensations in her belly. She had felt the baby, her first, moving all through her second and third trimesters, but this felt different. Her due date was still two weeks off. Could she finally be feeling the birth contractions she had heard and read so much about. Was she in labor?

Labor is an apt term for the process of giving birth. Birth is hard work for both mother and baby. What brings on labor is a series of uterine, cervical, and other changes called **parturition.** Parturition typically begins about two weeks before delivery, when sharply rising estrogen levels stimulate the uterus to contract and the cervix to become more flexible.

The uterine contractions that expel the fetus begin—typically, about 266 days after conception—as tightenings of the uterus. A woman may have felt false

Guidepost 2

How does labor begin, what happens during each of the three stages of childbirth, and what alternative methods of delivery are available?

parturition Process of uterine, cervical, and other changes, usually lasting about two weeks, preceding childbirth.

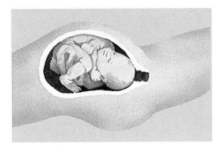

(a) First stage

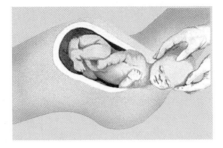

(b) Second stage

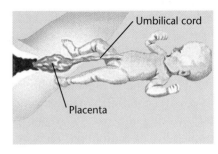

Umbilical cord

Placenta

(c) Third stage

Figure 4-1

The three stages of childbirth. (a) During the first stage of labor, a series of stronger and stronger contractions dilates the cervix, the opening to the mother's womb. (b) During the second stage, the baby's head moves down the birth canal and emerges from the vagina. (c) During the brief third stage, the placenta and umbilical cord are expelled from the womb. Then the cord is cut. (Source: Adapted from Lagercrantz & Slotkin, 1986.)

contractions (known as *Braxton-Hicks contractions*) at times during the final months of pregnancy, or even as early as the second trimester, when the muscles of the uterus tighten for up to two minutes. In comparison with the relatively mild and irregular Braxton-Hicks contractions, real labor contractions are more frequent, rhythmic, and painful, and they increase in frequency and intensity.

Stages of Childbirth

Labor takes place in three overlapping stages (Figure 4-1). The *first stage,* the longest, typically lasts 12 to 14 hours for a woman having her first child; it tends to be shorter for children that follow. During this stage, regular and increasingly frequent uterine contractions cause the cervix to dilate, or widen, in preparation for delivery.

During the *second stage,* which typically lasts up to an hour or two, the contractions become stronger and closer together. The second stage begins when the baby's head begins to move through the cervix into the vaginal canal, and it ends when the baby emerges completely from the mother's body. If this stage lasts longer than two hours, signaling that the baby needs help, a doctor may grasp the baby's head with forceps or, more often, use vacuum extraction with a suction cup to pull it out of the mother's body. At the end of this stage, the baby is born; but it is still attached to the placenta in the mother's body by the umbilical cord, which must be cut and clamped. During the *third stage,* which lasts about 10 to 60 minutes, the placenta and the remainder of the umbilical cord are expelled from the mother.

Electronic Fetal Monitoring

electronic fetal monitoring
Mechanical monitoring of fetal heartbeat during labor and delivery.

Electronic fetal monitoring can be used to track the fetus's heartbeat during labor and delivery and to indicate how the fetal heart is responding to the stress of uterine contractions. Monitoring can detect any serious problems and alert the attending physician or midwife that a fetus needs help. The procedure was used in 85.4 percent of live births in the United States in 2003 (Martin, Hamilton, et al., 2005).

Electronic fetal monitoring can provide valuable information in high-risk deliveries, including those in which the fetus is very small, is premature, is in a breech position (feet or buttocks down), or seems to be in distress, or in which labor is induced through administration of drugs. However, monitoring can have drawbacks if it is used routinely in low-risk pregnancies. It is costly; it restricts the mother's movements during labor; and, most important, it has an extremely high false-positive rate, suggesting that fetuses are in trouble when they are not. Such warnings may prompt doctors to deliver by the riskier cesarean method rather than vaginally (Nelson, Dambrosia, Ting, & Grether, 1996).

Vaginal versus Cesarean Delivery

The usual method of childbirth, previously described, is *vaginal delivery*. Alternatively, **cesarean delivery** can be used to surgically remove the baby from the uterus through an incision in the mother's abdomen. In 2005, a record-high 30.3 percent of U.S. births were by cesarean delivery, a 46 percent increase since 1996 (Martin, Hamilton, et al., 2007). Use of this procedure also increased in European countries during the 1990s, but cesarean birthrates in the United States are among the highest in the world (International Cesarean Awareness Network, 2003).

cesarean delivery Delivery of a baby by surgical removal from the uterus.

The operation is commonly performed when labor progresses too slowly, when the fetus seems to be in trouble, or when the mother is bleeding vaginally. Often a cesarean is needed when the fetus is in the breech position (feet or buttocks first) or in the transverse position (lying crosswise in the uterus) or when the head is too big to pass through the mother's pelvis.

The increase in cesarean rates has been attributed primarily to rising proportions of heavy, premature, and low-birth-weight babies, multiple births, and older first-time mothers. However, cesarean rates for women at no indicated risk and without previous cesarean deliveries more than doubled between 1991 and 2003. This trend suggests that physicians' fear of malpractice suits or women's preferences may play a part in choosing cesarean deliveries (Ecker & Frigoletto, 2007; Martin, Hamilton, et al., 2006, 2007).

Cesarean deliveries carry risks of serious complications for the mother, such as bleeding, infection, damage to pelvic organs, and postoperative pain, and heighten risks of problems in future pregnancies (Ecker & Frigoletto, 2007). They also deprive the baby of important benefits of normal birth: the surge of hormones that clear the lungs of excess fluid, mobilize stored fuel to nourish cells, and send blood to the heart and brain (Lagercrantz & Slotkin, 1986).

Despite these risks, most physicians warn that a vaginal birth after cesarean (VBAC) should be attempted only with caution. VBACs have been associated with greater (though still low) risks of uterine rupture and brain damage (Landon et al., 2004) as well as infant death (Smith, Pell, Cameron, & Dobbie, 2002). As the risks of such deliveries have become widely known, the rate of VBACs among U.S. women has fallen by 67 percent since 1996 (Hoyert, Mathews, et al., 2006). Today, if a woman has had a cesarean delivery, chances are about 90 percent that any subsequent deliveries will be by cesarean (Martin, Hamilton, et al., 2007).

Medicated versus Nonmedicated Delivery

For centuries, pain was considered an unavoidable part of giving birth. In the mid-nineteenth century, England's Queen Victoria was among the first women to use anesthesia during childbirth when she gave birth to her eighth child. Sedation with ether or chloroform became common practice as more births took place in hospitals (Fontanel & d'Harcourt, 1997).

During the twentieth century, several alternative methods of **natural childbirth** or **prepared childbirth** were developed. These methods minimize or eliminate the use of drugs that may pose risks for babies and enable both parents to participate fully in a natural, empowering experience. In 1914 Dr. Grantly Dick-Read, an English gynecologist, suggested that pain in childbirth was caused mostly by fear of the unknown and the resulting muscular tension. His "Childbirth without

natural childbirth Method of childbirth that seeks to prevent pain by eliminating the mother's fear through education about the physiology of reproduction and training in breathing and relaxation during delivery.

prepared childbirth Method of childbirth that uses instruction, breathing exercises, and social support to induce controlled physical responses to uterine contractions and reduce fear and pain.

In Rajasthan, India, as in many other traditional societies, a doula, or experienced helper, stays at a woman's bedside throughout labor and provides emotional support. Research has found that women attended by doulas tend to have shorter labor and easier deliveries.

? What's Your View?

- If you or your partner were expecting a baby, and the pregnancy seemed to be going smoothly, would you prefer (a) hospital, birth center, or home birth, (b) attendance by a physician or midwife, and (c) medicated or nonmedicated delivery? Give reasons.

- If you are a man, would you choose to be present at the birth?

- If you are a woman, would you want your partner present?

Fear" method educates expectant mothers about the physiology of reproduction and trains them in physical fitness and in breathing and relaxation during labor and delivery.

The Lamaze method, introduced by the French obstetrician Fernand Lamaze in the late 1950s, teaches expectant mothers to work actively with their bodies through controlled breathing. The woman is trained to pant or breathe rapidly in sync with the increasing intensity of her contractions and to concentrate on other sensations to ease the perception of pain. She learns to relax her muscles as a conditioned response to the voice of her coach (usually the prospective father or a friend), who attends classes with her, takes part in the delivery, and helps with the exercises. Using the LeBoyer method, introduced in the 1970s, a woman gives birth in a quiet room under low lights, to reduce stress, and the newborn is gently massaged to ease crying. Another technique, developed by the French physician Michael Odent, is submersion of the laboring mother in a soothing pool of water. Other methods use mental imagery, massage, gentle pushing, and deep breathing. Perhaps most extreme is the Bradley Method, which rejects all obstetrical procedures and other medical interventions.

Today, improvements in medicated delivery have led many mothers to choose pain relief, sometimes along with natural methods. General anesthesia, which renders the woman completely unconscious and greatly increases the risks to mother and baby, is rarely used, even in cesarean births (Eltzschig et al., 2003). A woman may be given local (vaginal) anesthesia, also called a *pedunal block,* if she wants and needs it, usually during the second stage of labor or if forceps are used. Or she can receive an *analgesic* (painkiller), which reduces the perception of pain by depressing the activity of the central nervous system. However, analgesics may slow labor, cause maternal complications, and make the baby less alert after birth.

Approximately 60 percent of women in labor have regional (*epidural or spinal*) injections (Eltzschig et al., 2003). Regional anesthesia, which is injected into a space in the spinal cord between the vertebrae in the lumbar (lower) region, blocks the nerve pathways that would carry the sensation of pain to the brain.

Epidurals given early can shorten labor with no added risk of needing cesarean delivery (Wong et al., 2005).

With any of these forms of anesthesia, a woman can see and participate in the birth process and can hold her newborn immediately afterward. All of these drugs, however, pass through the placenta and enter the fetal blood supply and tissues and thus may pose some danger to the baby.

Pain relief should not be the only consideration in a decision about whether a woman should have anesthesia. More important to her satisfaction with the childbirth experience may be her involvement in decision making, her relationship with the professionals caring for her, and her expectations about labor. Social and cultural attitudes and customs may play a part (Eltzschig et al., 2003). A woman and her doctor should discuss the various options early in pregnancy, but her choices may change once labor is under way.

In many traditional cultures, childbearing women are attended by a *doula,* an experienced mentor, coach, and helper who can furnish emotional support and information and can stay at a woman's bedside throughout labor. In eleven randomized, controlled studies, women attended by doulas had shorter labor, less anesthesia, and fewer forceps and cesarean deliveries than women not attended by doulas (Klaus & Kennell, 1997).

Checkpoint

Can you . . .

♦ Describe the three stages of vaginal childbirth?

♦ Discuss reasons for the sharp increase in cesarean births?

♦ Compare medicated delivery with alternative methods of childbirth?

The Newborn Baby

The **neonatal period,** the first four weeks of life, is a time of transition from the uterus, where a fetus is supported entirely by the mother, to an independent existence. What are the physical characteristics of newborn babies, and how are they equipped for this crucial transition?

Guidepost 3

How do newborn infants adjust to life outside the womb, and how can we tell whether a new baby is healthy and is developing normally?

Size and Appearance

An average **neonate,** or newborn, in the United States is about 20 inches long and weighs about 7½ pounds. At birth, 95 percent of full-term babies weigh between 5½ and 10 pounds and are between 18 and 22 inches long. Boys tend to be slightly longer and heavier than girls, and a firstborn child is likely to weigh less at birth than laterborns. In their first few days, neonates lose as much as 10 percent of their body weight, primarily because of a loss of fluids. They begin to gain weight again at about the fifth day and are generally back to birth weight by the tenth to the fourteenth day.

neonatal period First four weeks of life, a time of transition from intrauterine dependency to independent existence.

neonate Newborn baby, up to 4 weeks old.

New babies have distinctive features, including a large head (one-fourth the body length) and a receding chin (which makes it easier to nurse). At first, a neonate's head may be long and misshapen because of the molding that eased its passage through the mother's pelvis. This temporary molding occurs because an infant's skull bones are not yet fused; they will not be completely joined for 18 months. The places on the head where the bones have not yet grown together—the *fontanels,* or soft spots—are covered by a tough membrane.

Many newborns have a pinkish cast; their skin is so thin that it barely covers the capillaries through which blood flows. During the first few days, some neonates are very hairy because some of the *lanugo,* a fuzzy prenatal hair, has not yet fallen off. Almost all new babies are covered with *vernix caseosa* ("cheesy varnish"), an oily protection against infection that dries within the first few days.

"Witch's milk," a secretion that sometimes leaks from the swollen breasts of newborn boys and girls around the third day of life, was believed during the Middle Ages to have special healing powers. Like the whitish or blood-tinged vaginal discharge of some newborn girls, this fluid emission results from high levels of the hormone estrogen, which is secreted by the placenta just before birth and goes away within a few days or weeks. A newborn, especially if premature, also may have swollen genitals.

Body Systems

Before birth, blood circulation, respiration, nourishment, elimination of waste, and temperature regulation are accomplished through the mother's body. After birth, all of the baby's systems and functions must operate on their own. Most of the work of this transition occurs during the first four to six hours after delivery (Ferber & Makhoul, 2004).

The fetus and mother have separate circulatory systems and separate heartbeats; the fetus's blood is cleansed through the umbilical cord, which carries used blood to the placenta and returns a fresh supply. A neonate's blood circulates wholly within the baby's body. The heartbeat at first is fast and irregular, and blood pressure does not stabilize until about ten days after birth.

The fetus gets oxygen through the umbilical cord, which also carries away carbon dioxide. A newborn needs much more oxygen than before and now must get it alone. Most babies start to breathe as soon as they are exposed to air. If breathing has not begun within about five minutes, the baby may suffer permanent brain injury caused by **anoxia,** lack of oxygen, or *hypoxia,* a reduced oxygen supply. Because infants' lungs have only one-tenth as many air sacs as adults' do, infants (especially those born prematurely) are susceptible to respiratory problems. Anoxia or hypoxia may occur during delivery (though rarely so) as a result of repeated compression of the placenta and umbilical cord with each contraction. This form of *birth trauma* can leave permanent brain damage, causing mental retardation, behavior problems, or even death.

In the uterus, the fetus relies on the umbilical cord to bring food from the mother and to carry fetal body wastes away. At birth, babies instinctively suck to take in milk, and their own gastrointestinal secretions digest it. During the first few days infants secrete *meconium,* a stringy, greenish-black waste matter formed in the fetal intestinal tract. When the bowels and bladder are full, the sphincter muscles open automatically; a baby will not be able to control these muscles for many months.

The layers of fat that develop during the last two months of fetal life enable healthy full-term infants to keep their body temperature constant after birth despite changes in air temperature. Newborn babies also maintain body temperature by increasing their activity when air temperature drops.

Three or four days after birth, about half of all babies (and a larger proportion of babies born prematurely) develop **neonatal jaundice:** their skin and eyeballs look yellow. This kind of jaundice is caused by the immaturity of the liver. Usually it is not serious, does not need treatment, and has no long-term effects. However, because healthy U.S. newborns usually go home from the hospital within 48 hours or less, jaundice may go unnoticed and may lead to complications (AAP Committee on Quality Improvement, 2002). Severe jaundice that is not monitored and treated promptly may result in brain damage.

Medical and Behavioral Assessment

The first few minutes, days, and weeks after birth are crucial for development. It is important to know as soon as possible whether a baby has any problem that needs special care.

anoxia Lack of oxygen, which may cause brain damage.

neonatal jaundice Condition, in many newborn babies, caused by immaturity of liver and evidenced by yellowish appearance; can cause brain damage if not treated promptly.

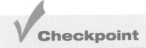

Checkpoint

Can you . . .

◆ Describe the normal size and appearance of a newborn, and list several changes that occur within the first few days?

◆ Compare five fetal and neonatal body systems?

◆ Identify two dangerous conditions that can appear soon after birth?

Table 4-1	Apgar Scale			
Sign*	0	1	2	
Appearance (color)	Blue, pale	Body pink, extremities blue	Entirely pink	
Pulse (heart rate)	Absent	Slow (below 100)	Rapid (over 100)	
Grimace (reflex irritability)	No response	Grimace	Coughing, sneezing, crying	
Activity (muscle tone)	Limp	Weak, inactive	Strong, active	
Respiration (breathing)	Absent	Irregular, slow	Good, crying	

*Each sign is rated in terms of absence or presence from 0 to 2; highest overall score is 10.

Source: Adapted from Apgar, 1953.

The Apgar Scale One minute after delivery, and then again five minutes after birth, most babies are assessed using the **Apgar scale** (Table 4-1). Its name, after its developer, Dr. Virginia Apgar (1953), helps us remember its five subtests: *a*ppearance (color), *p*ulse (heart rate), *g*rimace (reflex irritability), *a*ctivity (muscle tone), and *r*espiration (breathing). The newborn is rated 0, 1, or 2 on each measure, for a maximum score of 10. A 5-minute score of 7 to 10—achieved by 98.5 percent of babies born in the United States—indicates that the baby is in good to excellent condition (Martin, Hamilton, et al., 2007). A score below 7 means the baby needs help to establish breathing; a score below 4 means the baby needs immediate life-saving treatment. If resuscitation is successful, bringing the baby's score to 4 or more at 10 minutes, no long-term damage is likely to result (AAP Committee on Fetus and Newborn & American College of Obstetricians and Gynecologists Committee on Obstetric Practice, 1996). In general, Apgar scores reliably predict survival during the first month of life (Casey, McIntire, & Leveno, 2001).

Assessing Neurological Status: The Brazelton Scale The **Brazelton Neonatal Behavioral Assessment Scale (NBAS)** is used to help parents, health care providers, and researchers assess neonates' responsiveness to their physical and social environment, to identify strengths and possible vulnerabilities in neurological functioning, and to predict future development. The test, suitable for infants up to 2 months old, is named for its designer, Dr. T. Berry Brazelton (1973, 1984; Brazelton & Nugent, 1995). It assesses *motor organization,* as shown by such behaviors as activity level and the ability to bring a hand to the mouth; *reflexes; state changes,* such as irritability, excitability, and ability to quiet down after being upset; *attention and interactive capacities,* as shown by general alertness and response to visual and auditory stimuli; and indications of *central nervous system instability,* such as tremors and changes in skin color. The NBAS takes about 30 minutes, and scores are based on a baby's best performance.

Neonatal Screening for Medical Conditions As we mentioned in Chapter 3, children who inherit the enzyme disorder phenylketonuria, or PKU will become mentally retarded unless they are fed a special diet beginning in the first three to six weeks of life (National Institutes of Health [NIH] Consensus Development Panel, 2001). Screening tests administered soon after birth often can discover this and other correctable defects.

Apgar scale Standard measurement of a newborn's condition; it assesses appearance, pulse, grimace, activity, and respiration.

Brazelton Neonatal Behavioral Assessment Scale (NBAS) Neurological and behavioral test to measure neonate's responses to the environment.

Table 4-2 States of Arousal in Infancy

State	Eyes	Breathing	Movements	Responsiveness
Regular sleep	Closed; no eye movement	Regular and slow	None, except for sudden, generalized startles	Cannot be aroused by mild stimuli.
Irregular sleep	Closed; occasional rapid eye movements	Irregular	Muscles twitch, but no major movements	Sounds or light bring smiles or grimaces in sleep.
Drowsiness	Open or closed	Irregular	Somewhat active	May smile, startle, suck, or have erections in response to stimuli.
Alert inactivity	Open	Even	Quiet; may move head, limbs, and trunk while looking around	An interesting environment (with people or things to watch) may initiate or maintain this state.
Waking activity and crying	Open	Irregular	Much activity	External stimuli (such as hunger, cold, pain, being restrained, or being laid down) bring about more activity, perhaps starting with soft whimpering and gentle movements and turning into a rhythmic crescendo of crying or kicking, or perhaps beginning and enduring as uncoordinated thrashing and spasmodic screeching.

Source: Adapted from information in Prechtl & Beintema, 1964; P. H. Wolff, 1966.

Checkpoint

Can you . . .

♦ Discuss the uses of the Apgar test and the Brazelton scale?

♦ Weigh arguments for and against routine screening for rare disorders?

Routine screening of all newborn babies for such rare conditions as PKU (1 case in 15,000 births), congenital hypothyroidism (1 in 3,600 to 5,000), galactosemia (1 in 60,000 to 80,000), and other, even rarer, disorders is expensive. Yet the cost of testing thousands of newborns to detect one case of a rare disease may be less than the cost of caring for one mentally retarded person for a lifetime. Now, with more sophisticated blood tests, a single blood specimen can be screened for 20 or more disorders, so about half of all states as well as many developed countries have expanded their mandatory screening programs (Howell, 2006). In a study of newborns in several New England states, infants identified by screening were less likely to become retarded or to need hospitalization than those identified by clinical diagnosis. However, the tests can generate false-positive results, suggesting that a problem exists when it does not, and may trigger anxiety and costly, unnecessary treatment (Waisbren et al., 2003).

States of Arousal

Babies have an internal clock that regulates their daily cycles of eating, sleeping, and elimination and perhaps even their moods. These periodic cycles of wakefulness, sleep, and activity, which govern an infant's **state of arousal,** or degree of alertness (Table 4-2), seem to be inborn and highly individual. Changes in state are coordinated by multiple areas of the brain and are accompanied by changes in the functioning of virtually all body systems (Ingersoll & Thoman, 1999).

Most new babies sleep about 75 percent of their time—up to 18 hours a day—but wake up every 3 to 4 hours, day and night, for feeding (Ferber & Makhoul, 2004; Hoban, 2004). Newborns' sleep alternates between quiet (regular) and active (irregular) sleep. Active sleep is probably the equivalent of rapid eye movement (REM) sleep, which in adults is associated with dreaming. Active sleep appears rhythmically in cycles of about 1 hour and accounts for up to 50 percent of a newborn's total sleep time. The amount of REM sleep declines to less than

state of arousal An infant's physiological and behavioral status at a given moment in the periodic daily cycle of wakefulness, sleep, and activity.

30 percent of daily sleep time by age 3 and continues to decrease steadily throughout life (Hoban, 2004).

Beginning in their first month, nighttime sleep periods gradually lengthen as babies grow more wakeful in the daytime and need less sleep overall. Some infants begin to sleep through the night as early as 3 months. By 6 months, an infant typically sleeps for 6 hours straight at night, but brief nighttime waking is normal even during late infancy and toddlerhood. A 2-year-old typically sleeps about 13 hours a day, including a single nap, usually in the afternoon (Hoban, 2004).

Babies' sleep rhythms and schedules vary across cultures. Among the Micronesian Truk and the Canadian Hare peoples, babies and children have no regular sleep schedules; they fall asleep whenever they feel tired. Some U.S. parents try to time the evening feeding to encourage nighttime sleep. Mothers in rural Kenya allow their babies to nurse as they please, and their 4-month-olds continue to sleep only 4 hours at a stretch (Broude, 1995).

Complications of Childbirth

"It must be a boy," say some mothers whose labor and delivery prove long and difficult. This old wives' tale is grounded in some truth: Boys' deliveries are more likely to involve complications than girls', in part because boy babies tend to be larger (Bekedam, Engelsbel, Mol, Buitendijk, & van der Pal-de Bruin, 2002; Eogan, Geary, O'Connell, & Keane, 2003).

Although the great majority of births result in normal, healthy babies, some, sadly, do not. Some are born prematurely or very small, some remain in the womb too long, and some are born dead or die soon after birth. Let's look at these potential complications of birth and how they can be avoided or treated so as to maximize the chances of favorable outcomes.

Low Birth Weight

About 2 out of 3 babies with low birth weight are **preterm (premature) infants,** born before completing the 37th week of gestation (Martin, Hamilton, et al., 2007). **Small-for-date (small-for-gestational-age) infants,** who may or may not be preterm, weigh less than 90 percent of babies of the same gestational age. Their small size is generally a result of inadequate prenatal nutrition, which slows fetal growth.

Prematurity and low birth weight together constitute the second leading cause of death in infancy in the United States after birth defects and the leading cause during the neonatal period (Kung et al., 2008; Hoyert, Heron, et al., 2006). Preventing or treating these conditions can greatly increase the number of babies who survive the first year of life.

How Many Babies Are Preterm, and Why? In 2005, 12.7 percent of U.S. infants were born preterm, 25 percent more than in 1990 and 33 percent more than in 1981. This trend may in part reflect the rise in multiple births and induced and cesarean deliveries (Martin, Hamilton, et al., 2007).

Preterm birth is involved in nearly half of neurological birth defects, such as cerebral palsy, and more than one-third of infant deaths. More than 70 percent of preterm births are late preterm, delivered between 34 and 36 weeks' gestation; these babies tend to weigh more and to be at lower risk than those born earlier in gestation (Martin, Hamilton, et al., 2006, 2007).

✓ **Checkpoint**

Can you . . .

◆ Explain how states of arousal reflect neurological status, and discuss variations in newborns' states?

◆ Tell how sleep patterns change, and how cultural practices can affect these patterns?

Guidepost 4

What complications of childbirth can endanger newborn babies, and what are the prospects for infants with complicated births?

preterm (premature) infants Infants born before completing the 37th week of gestation.

small-for-date (small-for-gestational-age) infants Infants whose birth weight is less than that of 90 percent of babies of the same gestational age, as a result of slow fetal growth.

Such measures as enhanced prenatal care, nutritional interventions, home monitoring of uterine activity, and administration of drugs, bed rest, and hydration for women who go into labor early have failed to stem the tide of premature births (Goldenberg & Rouse, 1998; Lockwood, 2002). One promising treatment is a form of the hormone progesterone called *hydroxyprogesterone caproate,* or *17P.* In a two-and-a-half-year trial at 13 major medical research centers, giving 17P to women who had borne premature babies reduced repeat preterm births by as much as one-third (Meis et al., 2003).

How Many Babies Are Low Birth Weight, and Why?   In 2005, 8.2 percent of babies born in the United States had **low birth weight,** weighing less than 2,500 grams (5½ pounds) at birth—the highest rate of low birth weight since 1968. *Very-low-birth-weight* babies, who weigh less than 1,500 grams (about 2 to 3½ pounds), accounted for nearly 1.5 percent of births (Martin, Hamilton, et al., 2007). Very-low-birth-weight babies are nearly 100 times more likely to die during their first year of life than babies of normal birth weight, and *moderately-low-birth-weight* babies who weigh between 1,500 and 2,499 grams at birth (3½ to 5 pounds) are more than 5 times more likely to die. Much of the increase in low birth weight, like the rise in premature births, is probably due to increased use of induced and cesarean deliveries, delayed childbearing, fertility drugs, and multiple births; but low birth weight also is increasing among single births (Martin, Hamilton, et al., 2007).

The United States is more successful than any other country in the world in saving low-birth-weight babies, but the rate of such births to U.S. women remains higher than in many European and Asian nations. Overall, 15.5 percent of all births, or more than 20 million infants, worldwide—more than 95 percent of them in developing countries—have low birth weight. (The true extent of low birth weight may be much higher because as many as 3 out of 4 newborns in the developing world are not weighed.) Low birth weight in developing regions stems primarily from the mother's poor health and nutrition. In a double-blind study of 8,468 pregnant women in Tanzania, daily multivitamin supplements reduced the incidence of low birth weight (Fawzi et al., 2007). In the industrialized world, smoking during pregnancy is the leading factor in low birth weight (United Nations Children's Fund [UNICEF] and World Health Organization, [WHO] 2004).

Who Is Likely to Have a Low-Birth-Weight Baby?   Factors increasing the likelihood that a woman will have an underweight baby include (1) *demographic and socioeconomic factors,* such as being African American, under age 17 or over 40, poor, unmarried, or undereducated, and being born in certain regions, such as the southern and plains states (Thompson, Goodman, Chang, & Stukel, 2005); (2) *medical factors predating the pregnancy,* such as having no children or more than four, being short or thin, having had previous low-birth-weight infants or multiple miscarriages, having had low birth weight oneself, or having genital or urinary abnormalities or chronic hypertension; (3) *prenatal behavioral and environmental factors,* such as poor nutrition, inadequate prenatal care, smoking, use of alcohol or other drugs, or exposure to stress, high altitude, or toxic substances; and (4) *medical conditions associated with the pregnancy,* such as vaginal bleeding, infections, high or low blood pressure, anemia, depression, and too little weight gain (Arias, MacDorman, Strobino, & Guyer, 2003; Chomitz, Cheung, & Lieberman, 1995; Nathanielsz, 1995; Shiono & Behrman, 1995; Yonkers, quoted in Bernstein, 2003) and having last given birth fewer

low birth weight Weight of less than 5½ pounds (2,500 grams) at birth because of prematurity or being small for date.

A girl under age 17 who smokes while pregnant has two risk factors for bearing a low-birth-weight baby.

than six months or more than five years before (Conde-Agudelo, Rosas-Bermúdez, Kafury-Goeta, 2006).

The high proportion (14 percent) of low-birth-weight babies in the African American population—about twice as high as that of white and Hispanic babies—is the major factor in the high mortality rates of black babies (Hoyert, Mathews, et al., 2006; Martin, Hamilton, et al., 2007). Researchers have identified a genetic variant that may account for the high rates of premature delivery among African American women (Wang et al., 2006). Other suggested reasons for the greater prevalence of low birth weight, preterm births, and infant mortality among African American babies include (1) health behaviors and SES; (2) higher levels of stress in African American women; (3) greater susceptibility to stress; (4) the impact of racism, which may contribute to or exacerbate stress; and (5) ethnic differences in stress-related body processes, such as blood pressure and immune reactions (Giscombé & Lobel, 2005).

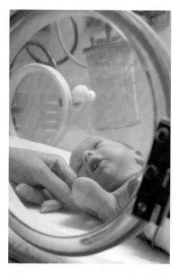

The antiseptic, temperature-controlled crib, or isolette, in which this premature baby lies has holes through which the infant can be examined, touched, and massaged. Frequent human contact helps low-birth-weight infants thrive.

Immediate Treatment and Outcomes The most pressing fear regarding very small babies is that they will die in infancy. Because their immune systems are not fully developed, they are especially vulnerable to infection, which has been linked to slowed growth and developmental delays (Stoll et al., 2004). Also, these infants' nervous systems may be too immature for them to perform functions basic to survival, such as sucking, so they may need to be fed intravenously (through the veins). Feeding them breast milk can help prevent infection (AAP Section on Breastfeeding, 2005; Furman, Taylor, Minich, & Hack, 2003). Because they do not have enough fat to insulate them and to generate heat, it is hard for them to stay warm. Low Apgar scores in a preterm newborn are a strong indication of the need for intensive care (Weinberger et al., 2000).

A low-birth-weight or at-risk preterm baby is placed in an *isolette* (an antiseptic, temperature-controlled crib) and fed through tubes. To counteract the sensory impoverishment of life in an isolette, hospital workers and parents are encouraged to give these small babies special handling. Gentle massage seems to foster growth, weight gain, motor activity, alertness, and behavioral organization, as assessed by the Brazelton NBAS (T. Field, 1998b; T. Field, Diego, & Hernandez-Reif, 2007).

Kangaroo care, a method of skin-to-skin contact in which a newborn is laid face down between the mother's breasts for an hour or so at a time after birth, can help preemies—and full-term infants—make the adjustment from fetal life to the jumble of sensory stimuli in the outside world. This soothing maternal contact seems to reduce stress on the central nervous system and help with self-regulation of sleep and activity (Ferber & Makhoul, 2004).

kangaroo care Method of skin-to-skin contact in which a newborn is laid face down between the mother's breasts for an hour or so at a time after birth.

Respiratory distress syndrome is common in preterm babies who lack an adequate amount of an essential lung-coating substance called *surfactant,* which keeps air sacs from collapsing. These babies may breathe irregularly or stop breathing altogether. Administering surfactant to high-risk preterm newborns has dramatically increased survival rates since 1994 (Corbet et al., 1995; Goldenberg & Rouse, 1998; Horbar et al., 1993; Martin, Hamilton, et al., 2005; Msall, 2004; Stoelhorst et al., 2005) as well as neurological and developmental status at 18 to 22 months (Vohr, Wright, Poole, & McDonald for the NICHD Neonatal Research Network Follow-up Study, 2005). Since 2000 the percentage of *extremely-low-birth-weight* infants (about 1 to 2 pounds at birth) who survived without neurological impairment has increased further (Wilson-Costello et al., 2007).

Long-Term Outcomes Even if low-birth-weight babies survive the dangerous early days, there is concern for their future. For example, both preterm and small-for-gestational-age infants may be at increased risk of adult-onset diabetes, and small-for-gestational-age infants appear to be at increased risk of cardiovascular disease (Hofman et al., 2004; Sperling, 2004).

In longitudinal studies of extremely-low-birth-weight infants and those born before 26 weeks of gestation, the survivors tend to be smaller than full-term children and more likely to have neurological, sensory, cognitive, educational, and behavioral problems (Anderson, Doyle, and the Victorian Infant Collaborative Study Group, 2003; Marlow, Wolke, Bracewell, & Samara for the EPICure Study Group, 2005; Mikkola et al., 2005; Saigal, Stoskopf, Streiner, & Burrows, 2001). Among a cohort of extremely-low-birth-weight infants in Finland, only 26 percent showed normal development at age 5 (Mikkola et al., 2005).

The less low-birth-weight children weigh at birth, the lower their IQs and achievement test scores tend to be and the more likely they are to require special education or to repeat a grade (Saigal, Hoult, Streiner, Stoskopf, & Rosenbaum, 2000). Cognitive deficits, especially in memory and processing speed, have been noted among very-low-birth-weight babies (2 to 3½ pounds at birth) by age 5 or 6 months, continuing through childhood (Rose & Feldman, 2000; Rose, Feldman, & Jankowski, 2002) and into adulthood (Fearon et al., 2004; Greene, 2002; Hack et al., 2002; Hardy, Kuh, Langenberg, & Wadsworth, 2003). Very-low-birth-weight children and adolescents also tend to have more behavioral and mental health problems than those born at normal weight (Hack et al., 2004).

On the other hand, in a longitudinal study of 296 infants who weighed, on average, just over 2 pounds at birth and were considered borderline retarded, most showed cognitive improvement in early childhood and intelligence in the normal range by age 8. Children in two-parent families, those whose mothers were highly educated, those who had not suffered significant brain damage, and those who did not need special help did best (Ment et al., 2003). And, in a prospective longitudinal study of 166 extremely-low-birth-weight babies in Ontario, Canada, where health care is universal, a significant majority overcame earlier difficulties to become functioning young adults—finishing high school, working, and living independently, and many of them pursuing postsecondary education. These children were predominantly white and in two-parent families, about half of them of high SES (Saigal et al., 2006). Birth weight alone, then, does not necessarily determine the outcome. Environmental factors make a difference, as we discuss in a subsequent section.

Postmaturity

Nearly 6 percent of pregnant women in the United States have not gone into labor after 42 or more weeks' gestation (Martin, Hamilton, et al., 2007). At that point, a baby is considered **postmature.** Postmature babies tend to be long and thin, because they have kept growing in the womb but have had an insufficient blood supply toward the end of gestation. Possibly because the placenta has aged and become less efficient, it may provide less oxygen. The baby's greater size also complicates labor; the mother has to deliver a baby the size of a normal 1-month-old.

Because postmature fetuses are at risk of brain damage or even death, doctors sometimes induce labor or perform cesarean deliveries. The increasing use of both of these techniques probably explains a decline in postterm births in recent years (Martin, Hamilton, et al., 2006).

Stillbirth

Stillbirth, the death of a fetus at or after the 20th week of gestation, is a tragic union of opposites—birth and death. Sometimes fetal death is diagnosed

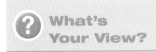

What's Your View?

- In view of the long-term outlook for very-low-birth-weight babies and the expense involved in helping them survive, how much of society's resources should be put into rescuing these babies?

postmature Referring to a fetus not yet born as of 2 weeks after the due date or 42 weeks after the mother's last menstrual period.

stillbirth Death of a fetus at or after the 20th week of gestation.

prenatally; in other cases, the baby's death is discovered during labor or delivery. Boys are more likely to be stillborn than girls (Bekedam, Engelsbel, Mol, Buitendijk, & van der Pal-de Bruin, 2002; Eogan, Geary, O'Connell, & Keane, 2003). Although the cause of stillbirth is not clearly understood, many stillborn infants are small for their gestational age, indicating malnourishment in the womb (Surkan et al., 2004).

The incidence of stillbirth in the United States has dropped steadily since 1985, mainly due to a decline in third-trimester deaths. However, fetal deaths remain more common than in many other developed countries (MacDorman, Hoyert, Martin, Munson, & Hamilton, 2007). In 2004 there were 6.2 stillbirths for every 1,000 live births plus fetal deaths (MacDorman, Munson, & Kirmeyer, 2007). The reduction in stillbirths may be due to electronic fetal monitoring, ultrasound, and other measures to identify fetuses at risk for restricted growth. Fetuses believed to have problems can be delivered prematurely (Goldenberg & Rouse, 1998).

Checkpoint

Can you . . .

◆ Discuss the risk factors, treatment, and outcomes for low-birth-weight babies?

◆ Explain the risks attending postmaturity?

◆ Discuss trends and risk factors for stillbirth?

Can a Supportive Environment Overcome Effects of Birth Complications?

From an evolutionary standpoint, people—like other organisms—thrive, reproduce, and survive in environments suitable to their needs and expectations. Thus, appropriate environmental characteristics can help an infant develop optimally. Furthermore, human beings are adaptable, especially during the early years. A major longitudinal study suggests that, given a supportive environment, resilience can occur even in the face of a difficult start in life.

For nearly five decades, Emmy E. Werner (1987, 1995; Werner & Smith, 2001) and a team of pediatricians, psychologists, public health workers, and social workers have followed 698 children, born in 1955 on the Hawaiian island of Kauai, from gestation to middle adulthood. The researchers interviewed the mothers-to-be, monitored their pregnancies, and interviewed them again when the children were ages 1, 2, and 10. They observed the children at home, gave them aptitude, achievement, and personality tests in elementary and high school, and obtained progress reports from their teachers. The young people themselves were interviewed periodically after they reached adulthood.

The physical and psychological development of children who had suffered low birth weight or other birth complications were seriously impaired *only* when the children grew up in persistently poor environmental circumstances. Unless the early damage was so serious as to require institutionalization, those children who had a stable and enriching environment did well (E. E. Werner, 1985, 1987). In fact, they had fewer language, perceptual, emotional, and school problems than did children who had *not* experienced unusual stress at birth but who had received little intellectual stimulation or emotional support at home (E. E. Werner, 1989; E. E. Werner et al., 1968). The children who had been exposed to *both* birth-related problems and later stressful experiences had the worst health and the most delayed development (E. E. Werner, 1987).

Most remarkable is the resilience of children who escaped damage despite *multiple* sources of stress. Even when birth complications were combined with chronic poverty, family discord, divorce, or parents who were mentally ill, many children came through relatively unscathed. Of the 276 children who at age 2 had been identified as having four or more risk factors, two-thirds developed serious learning or behavior problems by age 10 or, by age 18, had become pregnant, gotten in trouble with the law, or become emotionally disturbed. Yet by age 30, one-third of these highly at-risk children had managed to become "competent,

Thanks to their own resilience, fully a third of the at-risk children studied by Emmy Werner and her colleagues developed into self-confident, successful adults. These children had a positive and active approach to problem solving, the abilities to see some useful aspects of even painful experiences and to attract responses from other people, and faith in an optimistic vision of a fulfilling life.

confident, and caring adults" (E. E. Werner, 1995, p. 82). Of the full sample, about half of those on whom the researchers were able to obtain follow-up data successfully weathered the age-30 and age-40 transitions. Women tended to be better adapted than men (E. Werner & Smith, 2001).

Protective factors, which tended to reduce the impact of early stress, fell into three categories: (1) individual attributes, such as energy, sociability, and intelligence; (2) affectionate ties with at least one supportive family member; and (3) rewards at school, work, or place of worship that provide a sense of meaning and control over one's life (E. E. Werner, 1987). Although the home environment seemed to have the most marked effect in childhood, in adulthood the individuals' own qualities made a greater difference (E. E. Werner, 1995).

This study underlines the need to look at development in context. It shows how biological and environmental influences interact, making resiliency possible even in babies born with serious complications. (Characteristics of resilient children are further discussed in Chapter 10.)

Survival and Health

Infancy and toddlerhood are risky times of life. How many babies die during the first year, and why? What can be done to prevent dangerous or debilitating childhood diseases? How can we ensure that infants and toddlers live, grow, and develop as they should?

Death during Infancy

Great strides have been made in protecting the lives of new babies, but these advances are not evenly distributed. Worldwide, about 8 million infants—more than 1 in 20 born alive—die each year before their first birthday (Population Reference Bureau, 2005; UNICEF, 2002). The vast majority of these deaths are in developing countries, especially in South Asia and sub-Saharan Africa. Nearly half—almost 4 million—occur during the neonatal period, two-thirds in the first week of life, and as many as one-half in the first 24 hours. Similarly, about two-thirds of maternal deaths from complications of childbirth occur during the immediate postnatal period (Sines et al., 2007).

The primary causes of neonatal death worldwide are preterm delivery (28 percent), sepsis or pneumonia (26 percent), and asphyxiation at birth (23 percent) (Bryce, Boschi-Pinto, Shibuya, & the WHO Child Health Epidemiology Reference Group, 2005). Many of these deaths are preventable, resulting from a combination of poverty, poor maternal health and nutrition, infection, and poor medical care (Lawn et al., 2005; UNICEF, 2003). Community-based postnatal care for mothers and babies in the first few days after birth might save many of these lives. One such program, Saving Newborn Lives, currently operates in 19 countries, offering home visits by trained community health workers who teach new mothers how to care for their babies (Sines et al., 2007).

In the United States, the **infant mortality rate**—the proportion of babies who die within the first year—has fallen almost every year since 1980. In 2005, 6.87 infants died for every 1,000 live births (Kung et al., 2008). Mortality rates for twins and triplets have diminished along with rates for single births (Luke & Brown, 2006). More than half of infant deaths take place in the first week of life, and two-thirds occur during the neonatal period (Hoyert, Heron, Murphy, & Kung, 2006; Kochanek, Murphy, Anderson, & Scott, 2004; Martin, Hamilton, et al., 2007).

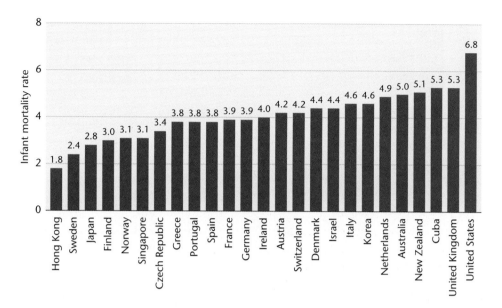

Figure 4-2

Infant mortality rates in industrialized countries. Despite dramatic improvements, the United States has a higher infant mortality rate than 24 other industrialized nations, largely because of its diverse population, health disparities for disadvantaged groups, and its high percentage of low-birth-weight infants, especially among African American infants. (Source: United Nations Statistics Division, 2007.)

Birth defects (congenital malformations) are the leading cause of infant deaths in the United States, followed by disorders related to prematurity or low birth weight, sudden infant death syndrome (SIDS), maternal complications of pregnancy, and complications of the placenta, umbilical cord, and membranes. These five causes together account for more than half of infant deaths (Kung et al., 2008).

The improvement in U.S. infant mortality rates since 1990, even at a time when more babies were born perilously small, is attributable largely to prevention of SIDS (discussed in the next section) as well as to effective treatment for respiratory distress and medical advances in keeping very small babies alive (Arias et al., 2003). Another factor is a striking reduction in air pollution in some cities due to permanent losses of manufacturing (Greenstone & Chay, 2003). Still, mainly because of the prevalence of low birth weight, U.S. babies have a poorer chance of reaching their first birthday than do babies in many other developed countries (Arias et al., 2003; Hamilton et al., 2007; Figure 4-2). Indeed, nearly half (49 percent) of infant deaths in the United States in 2003 were among the 0.8 percent of infants whose birth weight was less than 1,000 grams (about 2 pounds) (Mathews & MacDorman, 2006).

Racial/Ethnic Disparities in Infant Mortality Although infant mortality has declined for all races and ethnic groups in the United States, large disparities remain (Figure 4-3). Black babies are more than twice as likely to die in their first year as white and Hispanic babies (Kung et al., 2008; Mathews & MacDorman, 2007). This disparity largely reflects the greater prevalence of low birth weight and SIDS among African Americans (Kochanek & Smith, 2004; Kochanek et al., 2004). Infant mortality among American Indians and Alaska Natives is about one and a half times that among white babies, mainly due to SIDS and fetal alcohol syndrome (American Public Health Association, 2004; NCHS, 2006).

Intragroup variations are often overlooked. Within the Hispanic population, Puerto Rican infants are more than twice as likely to die as Cuban infants (Kung et al., 2008). Asian Americans, overall, are least likely to die in infancy, but Hawaiian infants are more than three times as likely to die as Chinese American babies (NCHS, 2006).

Figure 4-3

Infant mortality rates by race/ethnicity of mother, 1995 and 2004. Despite some decline, non-Hispanic blacks continue to have the highest infant mortality rates. (Source: Mathews & MacDorman, 2007.)

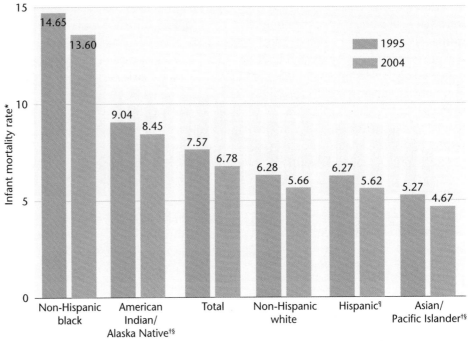

* Deaths of infants age < 1 year per 1,000 live births
† Includes persons of Hispanic and non-Hispanic origin
§ Difference not significant at $p < 0.05$ (z test)
¶ Persons of Hispanic origin might be of any race

Racial or ethnic disparities in access to and quality of health care for minority children (Flores, Olson, & Tomany-Korman, 2005) may help account for differences in infant mortality, but behavioral factors such as obesity, smoking, and alcohol consumption also play a part. Because causes and risk factors for infant mortality vary among ethnic groups, efforts to further reduce infant deaths need to focus on factors specific to each ethnic group (Hesso & Fuentes, 2005).

Sudden Infant Death Syndrome (SIDS)   Sudden infant death syndrome (SIDS), sometimes called *crib death*, is the sudden death of an infant under age 1 in which the cause of death remains unexplained after a thorough investigation that includes an autopsy. SIDS is the leading cause of postneonatal infant death in the United States (Anderson & Smith, 2005). It peaks between 2 and 3 months and is most common among African American and American Indian/Alaska Native babies; boy babies; those born preterm; and those whose mothers are young and received late or no prenatal care (AAP Task Force on Sudden Infant Death Syndrome, 2005).

SIDS most likely results from a combination of factors. An underlying biological defect may make some infants vulnerable during a critical period to certain contributing or triggering experiences, such as prenatal exposure to smoke—an identified risk factor.

At least six gene mutations affecting the heart have been linked to SIDS cases (Ackerman et al., 2001; Cronk et al., 2006; Tester et al., 2006). Nearly 10 percent of victims have mutations or variations in genes associated with irregular heart rhythms (arrhythmias), according to a survey of 201 SIDS deaths in a single cohort in Norway (Arnestad et al., 2007; Wang et al., 2007). A gene variant that appears in 1 out of 9 African Americans may help explain the greater incidence of SIDS among black babies (Plant et al., 2006; Weese-Mayer et al., 2004).

sudden infant death syndrome (SIDS) Sudden and unexplained death of an apparently healthy infant.

An important clue has emerged from the discovery of defects in the brain stem, which regulates breathing, heartbeat, body temperature, and arousal (Paterson et al., 2006). These defects may prevent SIDS babies who are sleeping face down or on their sides from waking or turning their heads when they breathe stale air containing carbon dioxide trapped under their blankets (AAP Task Force on Infant Sleep Position and Sudden Infant Death Syndrome, 2000; Panigrahy et al., 2000). Even in normal infants, sleeping on the stomach inhibits the swallowing reflex, a natural protection against choking (Jeffery, Megevand, & Page, 1999).

Research strongly supports a relationship between SIDS and sleeping on the stomach. SIDS rates declined in the United States by 53 percent between 1992 and 2001 (AAP Task Force on Sudden Infant Death Syndrome, 2005) and in some other countries by as much as 70 percent following recommendations that healthy babies be laid down to sleep on their backs (Dwyer, Ponsonby, Blizzard, Newman, & Cochrane, 1995; Hunt, 1996; Skadberg et al., 1998; Willinger, Hoffman, & Hartford, 1994).

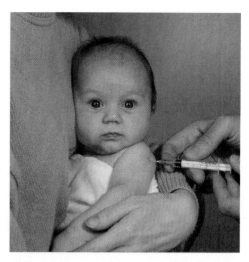

The rates of infectious diseases have plummeted in the United States thanks to widespread immunization. Many children, however, in low-income urban areas are not properly immunized.

Doctors recommend that infants *not* sleep on soft surfaces, such as pillows, quilts, or sheepskin, or under loose covers, which, especially when the infant is face down, may increase the risk of overheating or rebreathing (breathing the infant's own exhaled carbon dioxide) (AAP Task Force on Sudden Infant Death Syndrome, 2005). The risk of SIDS is increased twentyfold when infants sleep in adult beds, sofas, or chairs, or on other surfaces not designed for infants (Scheers, Rutherford, & Kemp, 2003). Studies associate use of pacifiers with lower risk of SIDS. Contrary to popular reports, studies show no connection between immunizations and SIDS (AAP Task Force on Sudden Infant Death Syndrome, 2005; Hauck et al., 2003, 2005; Mitchell, Blair, & L'Hoir, 2006).

Deaths from Injuries Unintentional injuries are the sixth leading cause of death in infancy in the United States (Kung et al., 2008) and the third leading cause of death after the first four weeks of life, following SIDS and birth defects (Anderson & Smith, 2005). For children older than 1 year, unintentional injury is the leading cause of death (Bernard, Paulozzi, & Wallace, 2007). Despite declining injury rates in all racial/ethnic groups, black and American Indian/Alaska Native infants and toddlers are approximately twice as likely to die of injuries as white or Hispanic ones (Pressley, Barlow, Kendig, & Paneth-Pollak, 2007). Black infants are more than three times as likely as white infants to be victims of homicide (Tomashek, Hsia, & Iyasu, 2003).

About 90 percent of all injury deaths in infancy are due to one of four causes: suffocation, motor vehicle traffic, drowning, and residential fires or burns (Pressley et al., 2007). Many of these accidental injuries occur at home. Some injuries reported as accidental may actually be inflicted by caregivers unable to cope with a crying baby (see discussion of maltreatment in Chapter 6).

Immunization for Better Health

Childhood illnesses such as measles, pertussis (whooping cough), and polio, once common, are now largely preventable, thanks to the development of vaccines that mobilize the body's natural defenses. Unfortunately, many children still are not adequately protected.

In 2002, nearly 2 million (76 percent) of the 2.5 million vaccine-preventable deaths among children less than age 5 were in Africa and Southeast Asia. An

Checkpoint

Can you . . .

◆ Summarize trends in infant mortality and injury deaths, and give reasons for racial/ethnic disparities?

◆ Discuss risk factors for, causes of, and prevention of sudden infant death syndrome?

What's Your View?

• Should parents have the right to refuse to immunize their children? If not, how can they be compelled to do so?

Checkpoint

Can you . . .

♦ Explain why full immunization of all infants and preschoolers is important?

Guidepost 6

What influences growth, and how do the brain and the senses develop?

cephalocaudal principle Principle that development proceeds in a head-to-tail direction, that is, that upper parts of the body develop before lower parts of the trunk.

proximodistal principle Principle that development proceeds from within to without, that is, that parts of the body near the center develop before the extremities.

estimated 70 to 78 percent of children ages 12 to 23 months worldwide had full routine vaccination coverage between 1990 and 2004. At least 90 percent of European, Western Pacific, and American children were fully covered, compared with only 69 percent of Southeast Asian children and 66 percent of African children. A Global Immunization Vision Strategy for 2006–2015 seeks to extend routine vaccinations to every eligible person (Department of Immunization, Vaccines, and Biologicals, WHO; UNICEF; Global Immunization Division, National Center for Immunization and Respiratory Diseases; & McMorrow, 2006).

In the United States, thanks to a nationwide immunization initiative, vaccine-preventable infectious diseases have dropped to an all-time low, falling as much as 99 percent (Roush, Murphy, & the Vaccine-Preventable Disease Table Working Group, 2007). Still, many children lack one or more of the required shots, and there is substantial regional variation in coverage (CDC, 2006c).

Some parents hesitate to immunize their children because of speculation that certain vaccines—particularly the diphtheria-pertussis-tetanus (DPT) and measles-mumps-rubella (MMR) vaccines—may cause autism or other neurodevelopmental disorders, but the preponderance of evidence suggests no reason for this concern (see Box 4-1, on page 122). Some parents worry that infants receive too many vaccines for their immune system to handle safely. (Today's children routinely receive 11 vaccines and as many as 20 shots by age 2.) Actually, the opposite is true. Multiple vaccines fortify the immune system against a variety of bacteria and viruses and reduce related infections (Offit et al., 2002).

Early Physical Development

Fortunately, most infants survive, develop normally, and grow up healthy. What principles govern their development? What are the typical growth patterns of body and brain? How do babies' needs for nourishment and sleep change? How do their sensory and motor abilities develop?

Principles of Development

As before birth, physical growth and development follow the *cephalocaudal principle* and *proximodistal principle.*

According to the **cephalocaudal principle,** growth occurs from the top down. Because the brain grows rapidly before birth, a newborn baby's head is disproportionately large. The head becomes proportionately smaller as the child grows in height and the lower parts of the body develop (Figure 4-4). Sensory and motor development proceed according to the same principle: Infants learn to use the upper parts of the body before the lower parts. They see objects before they can control their trunk, and they learn to do many things with their hands long before they can crawl or walk.

According to the **proximodistal principle** (inner to outer), growth and motor development proceed from the center of the body outward. In the womb, the head and trunk develop before the arms and legs, then the hands and feet, and then the fingers and toes. During infancy and early childhood, the limbs continue to grow faster than the hands and feet. Similarly, children first develop the ability to use their upper arms and upper legs (which are closest to the center of the body), then their forearms and forelegs, then hands and feet, and finally, fingers and toes.

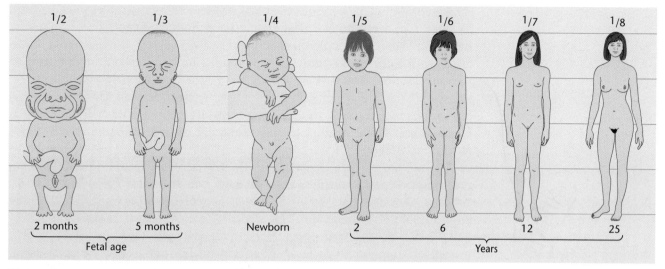

Figure 4-4

Changes in proportions of the human body during growth. The most striking change is that the head becomes smaller relative to the rest of the body. The fractions indicate head size as a proportion of total body length at several ages. More subtle is the stability of the trunk proportion (from neck to crotch). The increasing leg proportion is almost exactly the reverse of the decreasing head proportion.

Patterns of Growth

Children grow faster during the first three years, especially during the first few months, than ever again. At 5 months, the average baby boy's birth weight has doubled to 16 pounds, and, by 1 year, it has nearly tripled to 23 pounds. This rapid growth rate tapers off during the second and third years (Figure 4-5). A boy typically gains about 5 pounds by his second birthday and 3½ pounds by his third, when he weighs 31½ pounds. A boy's height typically increases by 10 inches during the first year, by almost 5 inches during the second year, and by a little more than 3 inches during the third year, to reach about 37 inches. Girls follow a parallel pattern but are slightly smaller. At 3 years, the average girl weighs 30½ pounds and is half an inch shorter than the average boy (Kuczmarski et al., 2000). Of course, individual growth rates vary greatly. As a baby grows, body shape and proportions change too; a 3-year-old typically is slender compared with a chubby, potbellied 1-year-old.

Teething usually begins around age 3 or 4 months, when infants begin grabbing almost everything in sight to put into their mouths; but the first tooth may not actually arrive until sometime between ages 5 and 9 months, or even later. By the first birthday, babies generally have six to eight teeth. By age 3, all twenty primary, or deciduous, teeth are in place, and children can chew any food they want to.

The genes an infant inherits have a strong influence on whether the child will be tall or short, thin or stocky, or somewhere in between. This genetic influence interacts with such environmental influences as nutrition and living conditions. For example, Japanese American children are taller and weigh more than children the same age in Japan, probably because of dietary differences (Broude, 1995). Today, children in the Netherlands and many other developed countries are growing taller and maturing sexually at an earlier age than children did a century ago, probably because of better nutrition, improved sanitation and medical care, and the decrease in child labor.

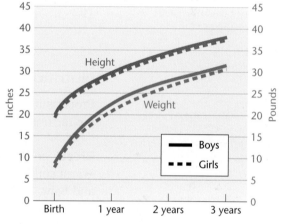

Figure 4-5

Growth in height and weight during infancy and toddlerhood. Babies grow most rapidly in both height and weight during the first few months of life, then taper off somewhat by age 3. Baby boys are slightly larger, on average, than baby girls. *Note:* Curves are for the 50th percentile for each sex. (Source: Kuczmarski et al., 2000.)

Checkpoint

Can you . . .

- Summarize typical patterns of physical growth and change during the first three years?

- Identify factors that affect growth?

Table 4-3	Benefits of Breast-Feeding over Formula-Feeding

Breast-fed babies . . .

- Are less likely to contract infectious illnesses such as diarrhea, respiratory infections, otitis media (an infection of the middle ear), and staphylococcal, bacterial, and urinary tract infections.
- Have a lower risk of SIDS and of postneonatal death.
- Have less risk of inflammatory bowel disease.
- Have better visual acuity, neurological development, and long-term cardiovascular health, including cholesterol levels.
- Are less likely to develop obesity, asthma, eczema, diabetes, lymphoma, childhood leukemia, and Hodgkin's disease.
- Are less likely to show language and motor delays.
- Score higher on cognitive tests at school age and into young adulthood.
- Have fewer cavities and are less likely to need braces.

Breast-feeding mothers . . .

- Enjoy quicker recovery from childbirth with less risk of postpartum bleeding.
- Are more likely to return to their prepregnancy weight and less likely to develop long-term obesity.
- Have reduced risk of anemia and almost no risk of repeat pregnancy while breast-feeding.
- Report feeling more confident and less anxious.
- Are less likely to develop osteoporosis or ovarian and premenopausal breast cancer.

Sources: AAP Section on Breastfeeding, 2005; Black, Morris, & Bryce, 2003; Chen & Rogan, 2004; Dee, Li, Lee, & Grummer-Strawn, 2007; Kramer et al., 2008; Lanting, Fidler, Huisman, Touwen, & Boersma, 1994; Mortensen, Michaelson, Sanders, & Reinisch, 2002; Owen, Whincup, Odoki, Gilg, & Cook, 2002; Singhal, Cole, Fewtrell, & Lucas, 2004; United States Breastfeeding Committee, 2002.

Nutrition

Proper nutrition is essential to healthy growth. Feeding needs change rapidly during the first three years of life.

Breast or Bottle?   Feeding a baby is an emotional as well as a physical act. Warm contact with the mother's body fosters emotional linkage between mother and baby. Such bonding can take place through either breast-feeding or bottle-feeding and through many other caregiving activities, most of which can be performed by fathers as well as mothers. The quality of the relationship between parent and child and the provision of abundant affection and cuddling may be at least as important as the feeding method.

Nutritionally speaking, however, breast-feeding is almost always best for infants—and mothers (Table 4-3). The American Academy of Pediatrics Section on Breastfeeding (2005) recommends that babies be *exclusively* breast-fed for six months. Breast-feeding should begin immediately after birth and should continue for at least one year, longer if mother and baby wish. The only acceptable alternative to breast milk is an iron-fortified formula that is based on either cow's milk or soy protein and contains supplemental vitamins and minerals. Infants weaned during the first year should receive iron-fortified formula. At 1 year, babies can switch to cow's milk (AAP Section on Breastfeeding, 2005).

Nursing mothers need to be as careful as when they were pregnant about what they take into their bodies. Breast-feeding is inadvisable if a mother is infected with the AIDS virus or any other infectious illness, if she has untreated active tuberculosis, if she has been exposed to radiation, or if she is taking any drug that would not be safe for the baby (AAP Section on Breastfeeding, 2005). The risk of transmitting HIV infection to an infant continues as long as an infected mother breast-feeds (Breastfeeding and HIV International Transmission Study Group, 2004).

Encouraging Breast-Feeding   Since 1971, when only 25 percent of U.S. mothers even tried to nurse (Ryan, 1997), recognition of the benefits of breast milk has brought about a striking reversal of this pattern. According to a large national random survey, 77 percent of infants born in 2005–2006 were breast-fed (McDowell, Wang, & Kennedy-Stephenson, 2008). However, only about 38 percent of infants are still breast-fed at 6 months, and only 16 percent at 12 months. Breast-feeding rates vary among ethnic groups, with higher rates among immigrant women in each group, presumably reflecting customs in their countries of origin. For example, only 48 percent of U.S.-born African American mothers breast-feed, whereas 88 percent of immigrant black women do so (Singh, Kogan, & Dee, 2007).

Increases in breast-feeding in the United States are most notable in socioeconomic groups that historically have been less likely to breast-feed: black women, teenage women, poor women, working women, and women with no more than a high school education. However, many of these women do not continue breast-feeding. Flexible scheduling and privacy for nursing mothers at work and at school as well as education about the benefits of breast-feeding and availability of breast pumping facilities might increase its prevalence in these groups (Ryan et al., 2002; Taveras et al., 2003).

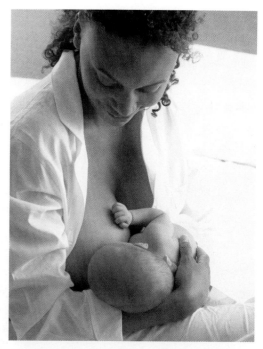

Breast milk has been called the "ultimate health food" because it offers so many benefits to babies—physical, cognitive, and emotional.

Worldwide, only about one-half of infants are ever breast-fed (UNICEF, 2002). Since 1991, 16,000 hospitals and birthing centers worldwide and at least 32 U.S. hospitals have been designated as "Baby-Friendly" under a United Nations initiative for encouraging institutional support of breast-feeding. These institutions offer new mothers rooming-in, tell them of the benefits of breast-feeding, help them start nursing within one hour of birth, show them how to maintain lactation, encourage on-demand feeding, give infants nothing but breast milk unless medically necessary, and establish ongoing breast-feeding support groups. Breast-feeding in U.S. hospitals greatly increased after the program went into effect, and mothers were more likely to continue nursing (Merewood, Mehta, Chamberlain, Philipp, & Bauchner, 2005). In studies in France and Belarus (in the former Soviet Union), mothers trained to support breast-feeding were more likely to breast-feed exclusively, were less likely to report difficulties with breast-feeding, and tended to continue longer (Kramer et al., 2001; Labarere et al., 2005).

What's Your View?

• "Every mother who is physically able should breast-feed." Do you agree or disagree? Give reasons.

Other Nutritional Concerns   Pediatric experts recommend that iron-enriched solid foods—usually beginning with cereals—be introduced gradually during the second half of the first year. At this time, too, fruit juice may be introduced (AAP Section on Breastfeeding, 2005). Unfortunately, many parents do not follow these guidelines. According to random telephone interviews with parents and caregivers of more than 3,000 U.S. infants and toddlers, 29 percent of infants are given solid food before 4 months, 17 percent drink juice before 6 months, and 20 percent drink cow's milk before 12 months. Furthermore, like older children and adults, many infants and toddlers eat too much and eat the wrong kinds of food. From 7 to 24 months, the median food intake is 20 to 30 percent above normal daily requirements (Fox, Pac, Devaney, & Jankowski, 2004). By 19 to 24 months, french fries become the most commonly consumed vegetable. More than 30 percent of children this age eat no fruit, but 60 percent eat baked desserts, 20 percent candy, and 44 percent sweetened beverages each day (American Heart Association [AHA] et al., 2006).

A child under age 3 with an obese parent is likely to become obese as an adult, regardless of the child's own weight.

✔ Checkpoint

Can you ...

♦ Summarize pediatric recommendations regarding early feeding and the introduction of cow's milk, solid foods, and fruit juices?

♦ Discuss the dangers of early malnutrition?

♦ Cite factors that contribute to obesity in later life?

central nervous system Brain and spinal cord.

In many low-income communities around the world, malnutrition in early life is widespread—and often fatal. Malnutrition is implicated in more than half of deaths of children globally, and many children are irreversibly damaged by age 2 (World Bank, 2006). Undernourished children who survive their first five years are at high risk for stunted growth and poor health and functioning throughout life. In a longitudinal study of a large-scale government-sponsored nutritional program in 347 poor rural communities of Mexico, infants who received fortified nutrition supplements—along with nutrition education, health care, and financial assistance for the family—showed better growth and lower rates of anemia than a control group of infants not yet assigned to the program (Rivera, Sotres-Alvarez, Habicht, Shamah, & Villalpando, 2004).

Being overweight has increased in infancy as in all age groups in the United States. In 2000–2001, 5.9 percent of U.S. infants up to 6 months old were classified as overweight, meaning that their weight for height was in the 95th percentile for age and gender, up from 3.4 percent in 1980. An additional 11.1 percent were at risk for overweight (in the 85th percentile), up from 7 percent in 1980 (Kim et al., 2006). Rapid weight gain during the first four to six months is associated with future risk of overweight (AHA et al., 2006).

Two factors seem to influence most strongly the chances that an overweight child will become an obese adult: whether the child has an obese parent and the age of the child. Before age 3, parental obesity is a stronger predictor of a child's obesity as an adult than is the child's own weight. Having one obese parent increases the odds of obesity in adulthood by 3 to 1, and if both parents are obese, the odds increase to more than 10 to 1 (AAP Committee on Nutrition, 2003). Among 70 children followed from age 3 months to 6 years, little difference in weight and body composition appeared by age 2 between children with overweight mothers and children with lean mothers. However, by age 4, those with overweight mothers tended to weigh more and, by age 6, also had more body fat than those with lean mothers (Berkowitz, Stallings, Maislin, & Stunkard, 2005). Thus, a 1- or 2-year-old who has an obese parent—or especially two obese parents—may be a candidate for preventive efforts.

The Brain and Reflex Behavior

What makes newborns respond to a nipple? What tells them to start the sucking movements that allow them to control their intake of fluids? These are functions of the **central nervous system**—the brain and *spinal cord* (a bundle of nerves running through the backbone)—and of a growing peripheral network of nerves extending to every part of the body (Figure 4-6). Through this network, sensory messages travel to the brain, and motor commands travel back.

Building the Brain   The growth of the brain is a lifelong process fundamental to physical, cognitive, and emotional development. Through various brain imaging tools, researchers are gaining a clearer picture of how brain growth occurs (Toga, Thompson, & Sowell, 2006).

The brain at birth is only about one-fourth to one-third of its eventual adult volume (Toga et al., 2006). By age 6, it is almost adult size; but specific parts of the brain continue to grow and develop functionally into adulthood (Gabbard, 1996).*

*Unless otherwise referenced, the discussion in this section is largely based on Gabbard (1996), Society for Neuroscience (2005), and Toga et al. (2006).

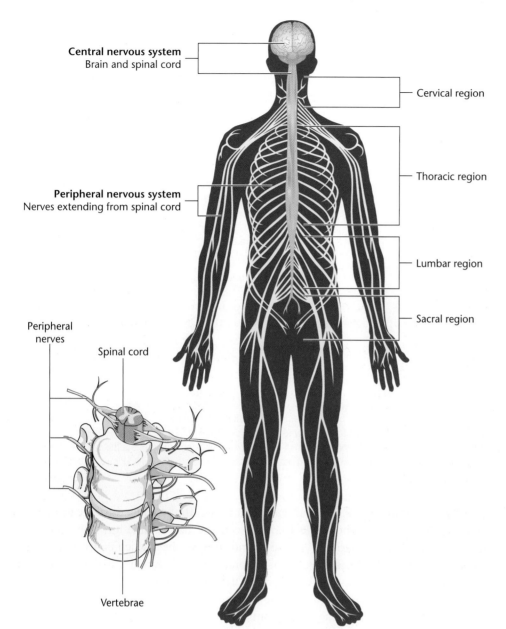

Central nervous system
Brain and spinal cord

Cervical region

Thoracic region

Peripheral nervous system
Nerves extending from spinal cord

Lumbar region

Sacral region

Peripheral nerves

Spinal cord

Vertebrae

Figure 4-6

The human nervous system. The central nervous system consists of the brain and spinal cord. The brain sends nerve signals to specific parts of the body through peripheral nerves; these are known as the peripheral nervous system. Peripheral nerves connect skeletal muscles with cells specialized to respond to sensations such as touch and pain. Peripheral nerves in the cervical region serve the neck and arms; those in the thoracic region serve the trunk, or main part of the body; those in the lumbar region serve the legs; and those in the sacral region serve the bowels and bladder. (Source: Adapted from Society for Neuroscience, 2005.)

The brain's growth occurs in fits and starts called *brain growth spurts.* Different parts of the brain grow more rapidly at different times.

Major Parts of the Brain Beginning about three weeks after conception, the brain gradually develops from a long hollow tube into a spherical mass of cells (Figure 4-7). By birth, the growth spurt of the spinal cord and *brain stem* (the part of the brain responsible for such basic bodily functions as breathing, heart rate, body temperature, and the sleep-wake cycle) has nearly run its course. The *cerebellum* (the part of the brain that maintains balance and motor coordination) grows fastest during the first year of life (Casaer, 1993).

The *cerebrum,* the largest part of the brain, is divided into right and left halves, or hemispheres, each with specialized functions. This specialization of the hemispheres is called **lateralization.** The left hemisphere is mainly concerned with language and logical thinking, the right hemisphere with visual and spatial functions such as map reading and drawing. Joining the two hemispheres is a tough band of tissue called the *corpus callosum,* which allows them to share information and

lateralization Tendency of each of the brain's hemispheres to have specialized functions.

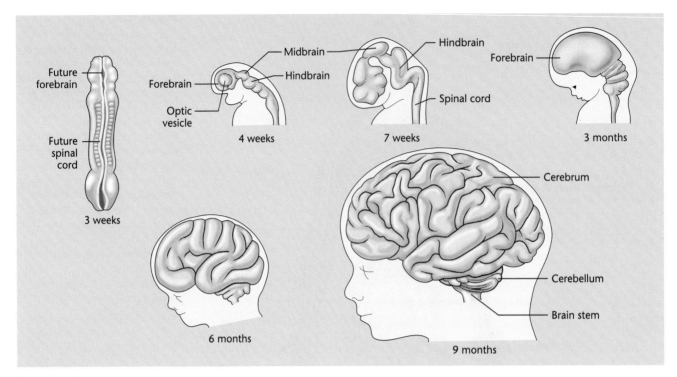

Figure 4-7

Brain development during gestation. Fetal nervous system development begins at about 3 weeks with the closing of the neural tube (left), from which will develop the brain and the spinal cord. By 4 weeks, major regions of the brain appear in primitive form: the forebrain, midbrain, hindbrain, and optic vesicle, from which the eye develops, As the brain grows, the front part expands greatly to form the cerebrum, the large, convoluted upper mass that will be the seat of conscious brain activity. The brain stem, an extension of the spinal cord, is almost fully developed at birth, but the cerebellum (above the brain stem) grows most rapidly during the first year. (Source: Society for Neuroscience, 2005.)

coordinate commands. The corpus callosum grows dramatically during childhood, reaching adult size by about age 10. Each cerebral hemisphere has four lobes, or sections: the *occipital, parietal, temporal,* and *frontal* lobes, which control different functions (Figure 4-8) and develop at different rates. The regions of the *cerebral cortex* (the outer surface of the cerebrum) that govern vision, hearing, and other sensory information grow rapidly in the first few months after birth and are mature by age 6 months, but the areas of the frontal cortex responsible for abstract thought, mental associations, remembering, and deliberate motor responses grow very little during this period and remain immature for several years (Gilmore et al., 2007).

The brain growth spurt that begins at about the third trimester of gestation and continues until at least the fourth year of life is important to the development of neurological functioning. Smiling, babbling, crawling, walking, and talking— all the major sensory, motor, and cognitive milestones of infancy and toddlerhood— reflect the rapid development of the brain, particularly the cerebral cortex. (Box 4-1 discusses autism, a disorder related to abnormal brain growth.)

neurons Nerve cells.

Brain Cells   The brain is composed of *neurons* and *glial cells.* **Neurons,** or nerve cells, send and receive information. *Glia,* or glial cells, nourish and protect the neurons.

Beginning in the second month of gestation, an estimated 250,000 immature neurons are produced every minute through cell division (mitosis). At birth, most of the more than 100 billion neurons in a mature brain are already formed but are not yet fully developed. The number of neurons increases most rapidly between the 25th week of gestation and the first few months after birth. This cell proliferation is accompanied by a dramatic growth in cell size.

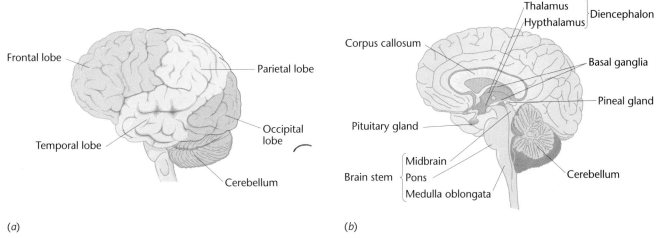

Figure 4-8

Parts of the brain. The brain consists of three main parts: the *brain stem,* the *cerebellum,* and the *cerebrum.* The brain stem, an extension of the spinal cord, is one of the regions of the brain most completely developed at birth. It controls such basic body functions as breathing, circulation, and reflex behavior. The cerebellum, at birth, begins to control balance and muscle tone; it later coordinates sensory and motor activity. The cerebrum constitutes almost 70 percent of the weight of the nervous system and handles thought, memory, language, and emotion, as well as sensory input and conscious motor control. (a) *Exterior view of the left side of the brain.* The cerebrum is divided into two halves or hemispheres, each of which has four sections or lobes: the *occipital lobe,* which processes visual information; the *temporal lobe,* which helps with hearing and language; the *parietal lobe,* which receives touch sensations and spatial information and facilitates eye-hand coordination; and the *frontal lobe,* which develops gradually during the first year and permits such higher-level functions as speech and reasoning. The cerebral cortex, the outer surface of the cerebrum, consists of gray matter; it is the seat of thought processes and mental activity. (b) *Interior view of right hemisphere (left hemisphere removed).* Several important structures deep within the cerebrum—the thalamus, hippocampus (not shown), and basal ganglia, all of which affect control of basic movements and functions—are largely developed at birth.

Originally the neurons are simply cell bodies with a nucleus, or center, composed of deoxyribonucleic acid (DNA), which contains the cell's genetic programming. As the brain grows, these rudimentary cells migrate to various parts of it (Bystron, Rakic, Molnar, & Blakemore, 2006). Most of the neurons in the cortex are in place by 20 weeks of gestation, and its structure becomes fairly well-defined during the next 12 weeks.

Once in place, the neurons sprout *axons* and *dendrites*—narrow, branching, fiberlike extensions. Axons send signals to other neurons, and dendrites receive incoming messages from them, through *synapses,* the nervous system's communication links. The synapses are tiny gaps, which are bridged with the help of chemicals called *neurotransmitters* that are released by the neurons. Eventually, a particular neuron may have anywhere from 5,000 to 100,000 synaptic connections to and from the body's sensory receptors, its muscles, and other neurons within the central nervous system.

The multiplication of dendrites and synaptic connections, especially during the last two and one-half months of gestation and the first six months to two years of life (Figure 4-9, on page 124), accounts for much of the brain's growth and permits the emergence of new perceptual, cognitive, and motor abilities. As the neurons multiply, migrate to their assigned locations, and develop connections, they undergo the complementary processes of *integration* and *differentiation.* Through **integration,** the neurons that control various groups of muscles coordinate their activities. Through **differentiation,** each neuron takes on a specific, specialized structure and function.

At first, the brain produces more neurons and synapses than it needs. Those that are not used or do not function well die out. This process of **cell death,** or pruning of excess cells, begins during the prenatal period and continues after birth (Figure 4-10, on page 125), helping to create an efficient nervous system.

integration Process by which neurons coordinate the activities of muscle groups.

differentiation Process by which cells acquire specialized structures and functions.

cell death In brain development, normal elimination of excess brain cells to achieve more efficient functioning.

BOX 4-1 Research *in Action*

The Autism "Epidemic"

Autism is a severe disorder of brain functioning characterized by lack of normal social interaction, impaired communication, repetitive movements, and a highly restricted range of activities and interests. (See table for a list of typical behaviors.) Diagnosis is typically confirmed by brain imaging (Center for Autism Research, undated).

POSSIBLE SIGNS OF AUTISM

Children with autism may show the following characteristics in varying combinations and degrees of severity.

Inappropriate laughing or giggling
Lack of fear of danger
Apparent insensitivity to pain
Rejection of cuddling
Sustained unusual or repetitive play
Uneven physical or verbal skills
Avoidance of eye contact
Preferring to be alone
Difficulty expressing needs except through gestures
Inappropriate attachment to objects
Insistence on sameness
Echoing words or phrases
Inappropriate response to sound
Spinning objects or self
Difficulty interacting with others

SOURCE: Autism Society of America, 2008.

Autism seems to involve a lack of coordination between different regions of the brain needed for complex tasks (Just, Cherkassky, Keller, Kana, & Minshew, 2007; Williams, Goldstein, & Minshew, 2006). Postmortem studies have found fewer neurons in the amygdala in the brains of people who had autism (Schumann & Amaral, 2006). People with autism also show deficits in executive function and theory of mind, discussed in Chapter 7 (Zelazo & Müller, 2002).

Asperger syndrome is a related but less severe disorder. Children with Asperger syndrome usually function at a higher level than children with autism. They typically have an obsessive interest in a single topic to the exclusion of all others, and they talk about it to anyone who will listen. They have large vocabularies and stilted speech patterns and are often awkward and poorly coordinated. Their odd or eccentric behavior makes social contacts difficult (National Institute of Neurological Disorders and Stroke, 2007).

Perhaps due to increased awareness and more accurate diagnosis, the reported prevalence of these conditions has increased markedly since the mid-1970s. Approximately 1 in 150 children are diagnosed with autism and related disorders annually, and 4 out of 5 are boys (Markel, 2007; Myers, Johnson, & Council on Children with Disabilities, 2007; Newschaffer, Falb, & Gurney, 2005; Schieve et al., 2006). The greater prevalence of autism in boys has been attributed to a number of factors, among them (1) boys' larger brain size and the larger-than-average brains of autistic children (Gilmore et al., 2007) and (2) boys' natural strength in systematizing and the propensity of autistic children to systematize (Baron-Cohen, 2005). These findings support the idea of autism as an extreme version of the normal male brain.

Autism and related disorders run in families and have a strong genetic basis (Constantino, 2003; Ramoz et al., 2004; Rodier, 2000). An international team of researchers has identified at least one gene and pinpointed the location of another that may contribute to autism (Szatmari et al., 2007). Deletions and duplications of gene copies at chromosome 16 may account for a small number of cases (Eichler & Zimmerman, 2008; Weiss et al., 2008). Other research associated high levels of fetal testosterone in amniotic fluid with poorer-quality social relationships and more restricted interests at age 4, suggesting that higher fetal testosterone levels may be involved in the male vulnerability to autism (Knickmeyer, Baron-Cohen, Raggatt, & Taylor, 2005).

Only about half the neurons originally produced survive and function in adulthood (Society for Neuroscience, 2005). Yet, even as unneeded neurons die out, others may continue to form during adult life (Eriksson et al., 1998; Gould, Reeves, Graziano, & Gross, 1999). Meanwhile, connections among cortical cells continue to strengthen and to become more reliable and precise, enabling more flexible and more advanced motor and cognitive functioning (Society for Neuroscience, 2005).

myelination Process of coating neural pathways with a fatty substance myelin, that enables faster communication between cells.

Myelination   Much of the credit for efficiency of neural communication goes to the glial cells, which coat the neural pathways with a fatty substance called *myelin*. This process of **myelination** enables signals to travel faster and more smoothly, permitting the achievement of mature functioning.

Myelination begins about halfway through gestation in some parts of the brain and continues into adulthood in others. The pathways related to the sense of

Environmental factors, such as exposure to certain viruses or chemicals, may trigger an inherited tendency toward autism (Rodier, 2000). Many parents have blamed thimerosal, a preservative used in vaccines, for the increased incidence of autism. The prevalence of the disorder did decline when the U.S. Public Health service recommended the use of thimerosal-free vaccines (Geier & Geier, 2006), but the Centers for Disease Control and Prevention (2004), on the basis of multiple studies on thimerosal and its effects, has found no conclusive link between the preservative and autism. Later research also has failed to find a relationship between childhood vaccination and autism (Baird et al., 2008; Thompson et al., 2007). Other factors, such as certain complications of pregnancy, advanced parental age, first births, threatened fetal loss, epidural anesthesia, induced labor, and cesarean delivery have been associated with higher incidence of autism. (Juul-Dam, Townsend, & Courchesne, 2001; Glasson et al., 2004; Reichenberg et al., 2006).

Studies of younger siblings of affected children found that those who did not respond to their names by age 12 months or who showed deficits in communicative and cognitive skills at 16 months were likely to develop an autism-related disorder or developmental delay (Nadig et al., 2007; Stone, McMahon, Yoder, & Walden, 2007). Studies like these offer promise for early detection and treatment at a time when the brain is most plastic and systems related to communication are beginning to develop (Dawson, 2007).

Very early signs of possible autism or related disorders include the following (Johnson, Myers, & the Council on Children with Disabilities, 2007):

- No joyful gazing at a parent or caregiver
- No back-and-forth babbling between infant and parent (beginning about age 5 months)
- Not recognizing a parent's voice

- Failure to make eye contact
- Delayed onset of babbling (past 9 months)
- No or few gestures, such as waving or pointing
- Repetitive movements with objects

Later, as speech develops, these are important signs:

- No single words by 16 months
- No babbling, pointing, or other communicative gestures by 1 year
- No two-word phrases by 2 years
- Loss of language skills at any age

Though no known cure is available, substantial improvement may occur with highly structured early educational interventions that help the child develop independence and personal responsibility; speech and language therapy; and instruction in social skills, along with medical management as necessary (Myers, Johnson, & Council on Children with Disabilities, 2007).

What's Your View?

Have you ever known anyone with autism? If so, in what ways did that person's behavior seem unusual?

Check It Out

For an inside view of autism, go to www.autism.org/temple/inside.html. Temple Grandin, assistant professor of animal science at Colorado State University, describes her experiences as an autistic child and the methods that enabled her to direct her energies into constructive activities and a successful career.

touch—the first sense to develop—are myelinated by birth. Myelination of visual pathways, which are slower to mature, begins at birth and continues during the first five months of life. Pathways related to hearing may begin to be myelinated as early as the fifth month of gestation, but the process is not complete until about age 4. The parts of the cortex that control attention and memory are not fully myelinated until young adulthood. Myelination of the *hippocampus,* a structure deep in the temporal lobe that plays a key role in memory, continues to increase until at least age 70 (Benes, Turtle, Khan, & Farol, 1994).

Myelination of sensory and motor pathways before birth in the spinal cord and after birth in the cerebral cortex may account for the appearance and disappearance of early reflexes.

Early Reflexes When you blink at a bright light, your eyelids are acting involuntarily. Such an automatic, innate response to stimulation is called a

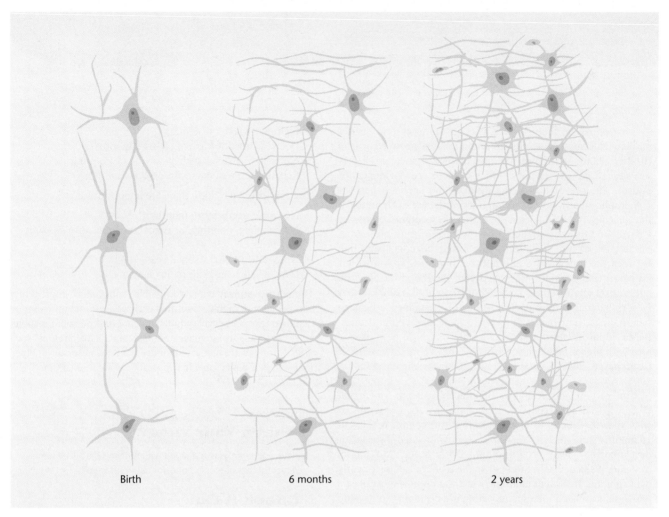

Birth

6 months

2 years

Figure 4-9

Growth of neural connections during first two years of life. The rapid increase in the brain's density and weight is due largely to the formation of dendrites, extension of nerve cell bodies, and the synapses that link them. This mushrooming communications network sprouts in response to environmental stimulation and makes possible impressive growth in every domain of development. (Source: Conel, 1959.) Reprinted by permission of the publisher from *The Postnatal Development of the Human Cerebral Cortex,* Vols. I-VIII by Jesse LeRoy Conel, Cambridge, Mass: Harvard University Press. Copyright © 1939, 1975 by the President and Fellows of Harvard College.

reflex behaviors Automatic, involuntary, innate responses to stimulation.

reflex behavior. Reflex behaviors are controlled by the lower brain centers that govern other involuntary processes, such as breathing and heart rate.

Human infants have an estimated 27 major reflexes, many of which are present at birth or soon after (Gabbard, 1996) (Table 4-4). *Primitive reflexes,* such as sucking, rooting for the nipple, and the Moro reflex (a response to being startled or beginning to fall), are related to instinctive needs for survival and protection or may support the early connection to the caregiver. Some primitive reflexes may be part of humanity's evolutionary legacy; one example is the grasping reflex, which enables infant monkeys to hold on to their mothers' fur.

As the higher brain centers become active during the first two to four months, infants begin to show *postural reflexes*: reactions to changes in position or balance. For example, infants who are tilted downward extend their arms in the parachute reflex, an instinctive attempt to break a fall. *Locomotor reflexes,* such as the walking and swimming reflexes, resemble voluntary movements that do not appear until months after the reflexes have disappeared.

Most of the early reflexes disappear during the first six to twelve months. Reflexes that continue to serve protective functions—such as blinking, yawning,

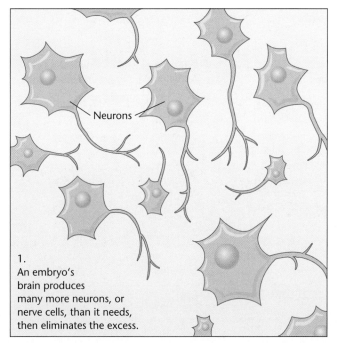

1.
An embryo's brain produces many more neurons, or nerve cells, than it needs, then eliminates the excess.

Neurons

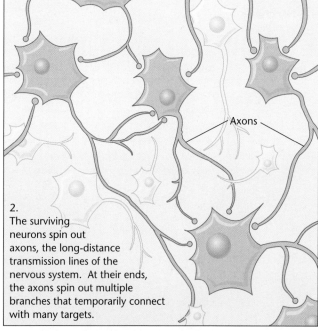

2.
The surviving neurons spin out axons, the long-distance transmission lines of the nervous system. At their ends, the axons spin out multiple branches that temporarily connect with many targets.

Axons

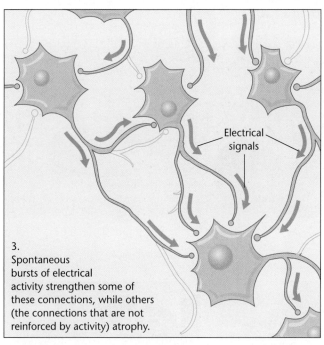

3.
Spontaneous bursts of electrical activity strengthen some of these connections, while others (the connections that are not reinforced by activity) atrophy.

Electrical signals

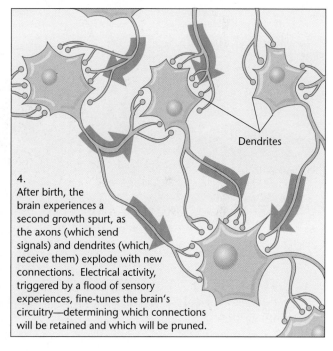

4.
After birth, the brain experiences a second growth spurt, as the axons (which send signals) and dendrites (which receive them) explode with new connections. Electrical activity, triggered by a flood of sensory experiences, fine-tunes the brain's circuitry—determining which connections will be retained and which will be pruned.

Dendrites

Figure 4-10

Wiring the brain: development of neural connections before and after birth. (Source: Nash, 1997, p. 51.)

coughing, gagging, sneezing, shivering, and dilation of the pupils in the dark—remain. Disappearance of unneeded reflexes on schedule is a sign that motor pathways in the cortex have been partially myelinated, enabling a shift to voluntary behavior. Thus, we can evaluate a baby's neurological development by seeing whether certain reflexes are present or absent.

Molding the Brain: The Role of Experience   Although the brain's early development is genetically directed, it is continually modified both positively and negatively by environmental experience. The technical term for this malleability,

Checkpoint

Can you . . .

♦ Describe early brain development?

♦ Explain the functions of reflex behaviors and why some drop out?

Table 4-4   Early Human Reflexes

Reflex	Stimulation	Baby's Behavior	Typical Age of Appearance	Typical Age of Disappearance
Moro	Baby is dropped or hears loud noise.	Extends legs, arms, and fingers, arches back, draws back head.	7th month of gestation	3 months
Darwinian (grasping)	Palm of baby's hand is stroked.	Makes strong fist; can be raised to standing position if both fists are closed around a stick.	7th month of gestation	4 months
Tonic neck	Baby is laid down on back.	Turns head to one side, assumes fencer position, extends arm and leg on preferred side, flexes opposite limbs.	7th month of gestation	5 months
Babkin	Both of baby's palms are stroked at once.	Mouth opens, eyes close, neck flexes, head tilts forward.	Birth	3 months
Babinski	Sole of baby's foot is stroked.	Toes fan out; foot twists in.	Birth	4 months
Rooting	Baby's cheek or lower lip is stroked with finger or nipple.	Head turns; mouth opens; sucking movements begin.	Birth	9 months
Walking	Baby is held under arms, with bare feet touching flat surface.	Makes steplike motions that look like well-coordinated walking.	1 month	4 months
Swimming	Baby is put into water face down.	Makes well-coordinated swimming movements.	1 month	4 months

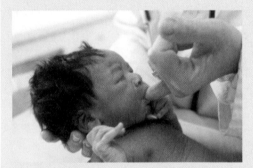

Rooting reflex

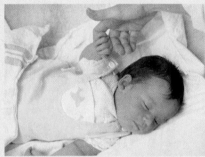

Darwinian reflex

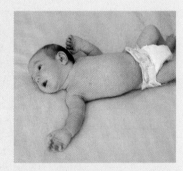

Tonic neck reflex

Moro reflex

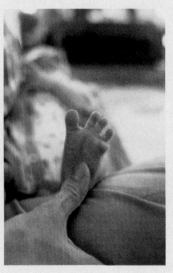

Babinski reflex

Walking reflex

or modifiability, of the brain is **plasticity.** Plasticity may be an evolutionary mechanism to enable adaptation to environmental change (Pascual-Leone, Amedi, Fregni, & Merabet, 2005; Toga et al., 2006).

plasticity Modifiability, or "molding," of the brain through experience.

Plasticity enables learning (Pascual-Leone et al., 2005). Individual differences in intelligence may reflect differences in the brain's ability to develop neural connections in response to experience (Garlick, 2003). Early experience can have lasting effects on the capacity of the central nervous system to learn and store information (Society for Neuroscience, 2005).

During this formative period, the brain is especially vulnerable. Exposure to hazardous drugs, environmental toxins, or maternal stress before or after birth can threaten the developing brain, and malnutrition can interfere with normal cognitive growth (Rose, 1994; Thompson, 2001). So, too, early abuse or sensory impoverishment may leave an imprint on the brain (J. E. Black, 1998). In one study, a monkey raised until 6 months old with one eyelid closed became permanently blind in that eye, apparently through loss of working connections between that eye and the visual cortex (Society for Neuroscience, 2005); Thus, if certain cortical connections are not made early in life, these circuits may shut down forever.

By the same token, enriched experience can spur brain development (Society for Neuroscience, 2005) and even make up for past deprivation (J. E. Black, 1998). Animals raised in toy-filled cages sprout more axons, dendrites, and synapses than animals raised in bare cages (Society for Neuroscience, 2005). Plasticity continues throughout life as neurons change in size and shape in response to environmental experience (Rutter, 2002). Such findings have sparked successful efforts to stimulate the brain development of premature infants (Als et al., 2004) and children with Down syndrome and to help victims of brain damage recover function.

Ethical constraints prevent controlled experiments on the effects of environmental deprivation on human infants. However, the discovery of thousands of infants and young children who had spent virtually their entire lives in overcrowded Romanian orphanages offered a natural experiment (Ames, 1997). Found after the fall of the dictator Nicolae Ceausescu in December 1989, these abandoned children appeared to be starving, passive, and emotionless. They had spent much of their time lying quietly in their cribs or beds with nothing to look at. They had had little contact with one another or with their caregivers and had heard little conversation or even noise. Most of the 2- and 3-year-olds did not walk or talk, and the older children played aimlessly. PET scans of their brains showed extreme inactivity in the temporal lobes, which regulate emotion and receive sensory input.

Many of these orphans were placed in adoptive homes in the United Kingdom (Rutter & the English and Romanian Adoptees [ERA] Study Team, 1998; Rutter, O'Connor, & the ERA Study Team, 2004) or in foster care in Romania (Fox, Nelson, Zeanah, & Johnson, 2006). In both cases, age of adoption and length of previous institutionalization were key factors in the children's prospects for cognitive improvement. In the English study, for example, Romanian children who had been removed from institutions before age 6 months showed no associated cognitive impairment by age 11 as compared with a control group of English children adopted within the United Kingdom, but the average IQs of Romanian children adopted into English families after age 6 months were 15 points lower. At ages 6 and 11, the latest-placed adoptees were the most cognitively impaired, though this group did show modest progress (Beckett et al., 2006). Apparently, then, it may take very early environmental stimulation to fully overcome the effects of extreme deprivation.

What's Your View?

• In view of what is now known about the plasticity of the infant brain, how can we make sure that every baby has access to an appropriately stimulating environment?

Can you . . .

♦ Discuss how early experience can affect brain growth and development both positively and negatively, and give examples?

Another study looked at social and emotional development in Romanian infants adopted into Wisconsin families. Three and a half years after adoption, these children produced low levels of two hormones, oxytocin and vasopressin, which are critical to the development of social bonds, such as the bond between mother and child (Fries, Ziegler, Kurian, Jacoris, & Pollak, 2005). It may be that there is a critical or sensitive period early in life for this biological mechanism to be established.

Early Sensory Capacities

The rearward regions of the developing brain, which control sensory information, grow rapidly during the first few months of life, enabling newborn infants to make fairly good sense of what they touch, see, smell, taste, and hear (Gilmore et al., 2007).

Touch and Pain   Touch is the first sense to develop, and for the first several months it is the most mature sensory system. When a newborn's cheek is stroked near the mouth, the baby responds by trying to find a nipple, probably an evolved survival mechanism (Rakison, 2005). Early signs of this rooting reflex (refer back to Table 4-4) appear in the womb, two months after conception. By 32 weeks of gestation, all body parts are sensitive to touch, and this sensitivity increases during the first five days of life (Haith, 1986).

In the past, physicians performing surgery (such as circumcision) on newborn babies often used no anesthesia because of a mistaken belief that neonates cannot feel pain or feel it only briefly. Actually, there is evidence that the capacity for pain perception may emerge by the third trimester of pregnancy (Lee et al., 2005). Newborns can and do feel pain; and they become more sensitive to it during the next few days. The American Academy of Pediatrics and Canadian Paediatric Society (2000) now maintain that prolonged or severe pain can do long-term harm to newborns and that pain relief during surgery is essential.

Smell and Taste   The senses of smell and taste also begin to develop in the womb. The flavors and odors of foods an expectant mother consumes may be transmitted to the fetus through the amniotic fluid. After birth, a similar transmission occurs through breast milk (Mennella & Beauchamp, 1996b).

A preference for pleasant odors seems to be learned in utero and during the first few days after birth, and the odors transmitted through the mother's breast milk may further contribute to this learning (Bartoshuk & Beauchamp, 1994). This attraction to the fragrance of the mother's milk may be another evolutionary survival mechanism (Rakison, 2005). In a study of French 3- and 4-day-olds, both those who were being breast-fed and those who were being formula-fed showed a preference for the odor of human milk (Marlier & Schaal, 2005).

Certain taste preferences seem to be largely innate (Bartoshuk & Beauchamp, 1994). Newborns prefer sweet tastes to sour, bitter, or salty tastes (Haith, 1986). Sweetened water calms crying newborns, whether full term or two to three weeks premature—evidence that not only the taste buds themselves (which seem to be fairly well developed by 20 weeks of gestation), but also the mechanisms that produce this calming effect are functional before normal term (B. A. Smith & Blass, 1996). An inborn sweet tooth may help a baby adapt to life outside the womb, as breast milk is quite sweet (Harris, 1997). Newborns' rejection of bitter tastes is probably another survival mechanism, as many bitter substances are toxic (Bartoshuk & Beauchamp, 1994).

Taste preferences developed in infancy may last into early childhood. In one study, 4- and 5-year-olds who, as infants, had been fed different types of formula had differing food preferences (Mennella & Beauchamp, 2002). Exposure to the flavors of healthy foods through breast-feeding may improve acceptance of healthy foods after weaning and later in life (American Heart Association et al., 2006).

Hearing Hearing, too, is functional before birth; fetuses respond to sounds and seem to learn to recognize them. From an evolutionary perspective, early recognition of voices and language heard in the womb may lay the foundation for the relationship with the mother, which is critical to early survival (Rakison, 2005).

Auditory discrimination develops rapidly after birth. Three-day-old infants can tell new speech sounds from those they have heard before (L. R. Brody, Zelazo, & Chaika, 1984). At 1 month, babies can distinguish sounds as close as *ba* and *pa* (Eimas, Siqueland, Jusczyk, & Vigorito, 1971).

Because hearing is a key to language development, hearing impairments should be identified as early as possible. Hearing loss occurs in 1 to 3 of 1,000 live births and, if left undetected, can lead to developmental delays (Gaffney et al., 2003). Early hearing detection and intervention programs have been established in all 50 states and are mandated in 39 of them, as well as in several European countries.

Sight Vision is the least developed sense at birth, perhaps because there is so little to see in the womb. From an evolutionary developmental perspective, the other senses, as we have pointed out, are more directly related to a newborn's survival. Visual perception and the ability to use visual information—identifying caregivers, finding food, and avoiding dangers—become more important as infants become more alert and active (Rakison, 2005).

The eyes of newborns are smaller than those of adults, the retinal structures are incomplete, and the optic nerve is underdeveloped. A neonate's eyes focus best from about 1 foot away—just about the typical distance from the face of a person holding a newborn. This focusing distance may have evolved to promote mother-infant bonding. There is some evidence that the ability to recognize faces—specifically, a caregiver's face—may be an innate survival mechanism (Rakison, 2005).

Newborns blink at bright lights. Their field of peripheral vision is very narrow; it more than doubles between 2 and 10 weeks and is well developed by 3 months (Maurer & Lewis, 1979; E. Tronick, 1972). The ability to follow a moving target also develops rapidly in the first months, as does color perception (Haith, 1986). Four-month-old babies can discriminate among red, green, blue, and yellow (M. Bornstein, Kessen, & Weiskopf, 1976; Teller & Bornstein, 1987).

Visual acuity at birth is approximately 20/400 but improves rapidly, reaching the 20/20 level by about 8 months (Kellman & Arterberry, 1998; Kellman & Banks, 1998). (This measure of vision means that a person can read letters on a specified line on a standard eye chart from 20 feet away.) *Binocular vision*—the use of both eyes to focus, enabling perception of depth and distance—usually does not develop until 4 or 5 months (Bushnell & Boudreau, 1993). Early screening is essential to detect any problems that may interfere with vision (AAP Committee on Practice and Ambulatory Medicine and Section on Opthalmology, 1996, 2002).

Motor Development

Babies do not have to be taught such basic motor skills as grasping, crawling, and walking. They just need room to move and freedom to see what they can do. When the central nervous system, muscles, and bones are ready and the environment offers the right opportunities for exploration and practice, babies keep surprising the adults around them with new abilities.

Checkpoint

Can you . . .

◆ Give evidence for early development of the senses?

◆ Tell how breast-feeding plays a part in the development of smell and taste?

◆ List three ways in which newborns' vision is underdeveloped?

Guidepost 7

What are the early milestones in motor development, and what are some influences on it?

Lifting and holding up the head from a prone position, crawling along the floor to reach something enticing, such as a furry cat's tail, and walking well enough to push a wagon full of blocks are important early milestones of motor development.

Milestones of Motor Development

Motor development is marked by a series of milestones: achievements that develop systematically, each newly mastered ability preparing a baby to tackle the next. Babies first learn simple skills and then combine them into increasingly complex **systems of action,** which permit a wider or more precise range of movement and more effective control of the environment. In developing the precision grip, for example, an infant first tries to pick things up with the whole hand, fingers closing against the palm. Later the baby masters the *pincer grasp,* in which thumb and index finger meet at the tips to form a circle, making it possible to pick up tiny objects. In learning to walk, an infant gains control of separate movements of the arms, legs, and feet before putting these movements together to take that momentous first step.

The **Denver Developmental Screening Test** (Frankenburg, Dodds, Fandal, Kazuk, & Cohrs, 1975) is used to chart progress between ages 1 month and 6 years and to identify children who are not developing normally. The test measures **gross motor skills** (those using large muscles), such as rolling over and catching a ball, and **fine motor skills** (using small muscles), such as grasping a rattle and copying a circle. It also assesses language development (for example, knowing the definitions of words) and personality and social development (such as smiling spontaneously and dressing without help). The newest edition, the Denver II Scale (Frankenburg et al., 1992), includes revised norms (Table 4-5 gives examples).

When we talk about what the "average" baby can do, we refer to the 50 percent Denver norms. Actually, normality covers a wide range; but about half of babies master these skills before the ages given, and about half afterward. Also, the Denver norms were developed with reference to a Western population and are not necessarily valid in assessing children from other cultures.

As we trace typical progress in head control, hand control, and locomotion, notice how these developments follow the *cephalocaudal* (head to tail) and *proximodistal* (inner to outer) principles outlined earlier. Note, too, that although boy babies tend to be a little bigger and more active than girl babies, there are no gender differences in infants' motor development (Mondschein, Adolph, & Tamis-LeMonda, 2000).

systems of action Increasingly complex combinations of motor skills, which permit a wider or more precise range of movement and more control of the environment.

Denver Developmental Screening Test Screening test given to children 1 month to 6 years old to determine whether they are developing normally.

gross motor skills Physical skills that involve the large muscles.

fine motor skills Physical skills that involve the small muscles and eye-hand coordination.

Table 4-5	Milestones of Motor Development	
Skill	**50 Percent**	**90 Percent**
Rolling over	3.2 months	5.4 months
Grasping rattle	3.3 months	3.9 months
Sitting without support	5.9 months	6.8 months
Standing while holding on	7.2 months	8.5 months
Grasping with thumb and finger	8.2 months	10.2 months
Standing alone well	11.5 months	13.7 months
Walking well	12.3 months	14.9 months
Building tower of two cubes	14.8 months	20.6 months
Walking up steps	16.6 months	21.6 months
Jumping in place	23.8 months	2.4 years
Copying circle	3.4 years	4.0 years

Note: This table shows the approximate ages when 50 percent and 90 percent of children can perform each skill, according to the Denver Training Manual II.

Source: Adapted from Frankenburg et al., 1992.

Head Control At birth, most infants can turn their heads from side to side while lying on their backs. While lying chest down, many can lift their heads enough to turn them. Within the first two to three months, they lift their heads higher and higher—sometimes to the point where they lose their balance and roll over on their backs. By 4 months, almost all infants can keep their heads erect while being held or supported in a sitting position.

Hand Control Babies are born with a grasping reflex. If the palm of an infant's hand is stroked, the hand closes tightly. At about 3½ months, most infants can grasp an object of moderate size, such as a rattle, but have trouble holding a small object. Next, they begin to grasp objects with one hand and transfer them to the other, and then to hold (but not pick up) small objects. Some time between 7 and 11 months, their hands become coordinated enough to pick up a tiny object, such as a pea, using the pincer grasp. By 15 months, the average baby can build a tower of two cubes. A few months after the third birthday, the average toddler can copy a circle fairly well.

Locomotion After three months, the average infant begins to roll over deliberately (rather than accidentally, as before)—first from front to back and then from back to front. The average baby can sit without support by 6 months and can assume a sitting position without help by about 8½ months.

Between 6 and 10 months, most babies begin to get around under their own power by means of creeping or crawling. This new achievement of *self-locomotion* has striking cognitive and psychosocial ramifications (Bertenthal & Campos, 1987; Bertenthal, Campos, & Barrett, 1984; Bertenthal, Campos, & Kermoian, 1994; J. Campos, Bertenthal, & Benson, 1980). Crawling infants become more sensitive to where objects are, how big they are, whether they can be moved, and how they look. Crawling helps babies learn to judge distances and perceive depth. They learn to look to caregivers for clues as to whether a situation is secure or frightening—a skill known as *social referencing* (Hertenstein & Campos, 2004; see Chapter 6).

By holding on to a helping hand or a piece of furniture, the average baby can stand at a little past age 7 months. A little more than four months later, most babies let go and stand alone. The average baby can stand well about two weeks before the first birthday.

All these developments lead up to the major motor achievement of infancy: walking. Humans begin to walk later than other species, possibly because babies' heavy heads and short legs make balance difficult. For some months before they can stand without support, babies practice cruising while holding on to furniture. Soon after they can stand alone well, at about 11½ months, most infants take their first unaided steps. Within a few weeks, shortly after the first birthday, the average child is walking fairly well and thus achieves the status of toddler.

During the second year, children begin to climb stairs one at a time, putting one foot after another on the same step; later they will alternate feet. Walking down stairs comes later. Also in their second year, toddlers run and jump. By age 3½, most children can balance briefly on one foot and begin to hop.

Motor Development and Perception

Sensory perception enables infants to learn about themselves and their environment so they can make better judgments about how to navigate in it. Motor experience, together with awareness of their changing bodies, sharpens and modifies their perceptual understanding of what is likely to happen if they move in a certain way. This bidirectional connection between perception and action, mediated by the developing brain, gives infants much useful information about themselves and their world (Adolph & Eppler, 2002).

Sensory and motor activity seem fairly well coordinated from birth (Bertenthal & Clifton, 1998). Infants begin reaching for and grasping objects at about 4 to 5 months; by 5½ months, they can adapt their reach to moving or spinning objects (Wentworth, Benson, & Haith, 2000). Piaget and other researchers long maintained that reaching depended on **visual guidance:** the use of the eyes to guide the movement of the hands (or other parts of the body). Now, research has found that infants in that age group can use other sensory cues to reach for an object. They can locate an unseen rattle by its sound, and they can reach for a glowing object in the dark, even though they cannot see their hands (Clifton, Muir, Ashmead, & Clarkson, 1993). They even can reach for an object based only on their memory of its location (McCarty, Clifton, Ashmead, Lee, & Goubet, 2001). Slightly older infants, ages 5 to 7½ months, can grasp a moving, fluorescent object in the dark—a feat that requires awareness, not only of how their own hands move, but also of the object's path and speed, so as to anticipate the likely point of contact (Robin, Berthier, & Clifton, 1996).

Depth perception, the ability to perceive objects and surfaces in three dimensions, depends on several kinds of cues that affect the image of an object on the retina of the eye. These cues involve not only binocular coordination, but also motor control (Bushnell & Boudreau, 1993). *Kinetic cues* are produced by movement of the object or the observer, or both. To find out whether an object is moving, a baby might hold his or her head still for a moment, an ability that is well established by about 3 months.

Sometime between 5 and 7 months, after babies can reach for and grasp objects, they develop **haptic perception,** the ability to acquire information by handling objects rather than by simply looking at them. Haptic perception enables babies to respond to such cues as relative size and differences in texture and shading (Bushnell & Boudreau, 1993).

Eleanor and James Gibson's Ecological Theory of Perception

In a classic experiment by Richard Walk and Eleanor Gibson (1961), 6-month-old babies were placed on a plexiglass tabletop laid over a checkerboard pattern that

visual guidance Use of the eyes to guide movements of the hands or other parts of the body.

depth perception Ability to perceive objects and surfaces three-dimensionally.

haptic perception Ability to acquire information about properties of objects, such as size, weight, and texture, by handling them.

created the illusion of a vertical drop in the center of the table—a **visual cliff**. Would the infants perceive this illusion of depth? The babies did see a difference between the "ledge" and the "cliff." They crawled freely on the ledge but avoided the cliff, even when they saw their mothers beckoning from the far side of the table.

How do babies decide whether to move across a ledge or down a hill? According to Eleanor Gibson's and James J. Gibson's **ecological theory of perception** (E. J. Gibson, 1969; J. J. Gibson, 1979; Gibson & Pick, 2000), locomotor development depends on increasing sensitivity to physical attributes of the surrounding environment and is an outcome of both perception and action (Adolph & Eppler, 2002). With experience, babies become better able to gauge the environment in which they move and to act accordingly (Adolph, 1997, 2000; Adolph et al., 2003; Adolph & Eppler, 2002). In visual cliff experiments, infants who have been crawling for some time are more likely than novices to avoid the cliff. Similarly, when faced with actual downward slopes of increasing steepness, infants' judgments become more accurate and their explorations more efficient as they gain practice in crawling. They apparently learn from experience how far they can push their limits without losing their balance (Adolph & Eppler, 2002).

No matter how enticing a mother's arms are, this baby is staying away from them. As young as she is, she can perceive depth and wants to avoid falling off what looks like a cliff.

visual cliff Apparatus designed to give an illusion of depth and used to assess depth perception in infants.

ecological theory of perception Theory developed by Eleanor and James Gibson, which describes developing motor and perceptual abilities as interdependent parts of a functional system that guides behavior in varying contexts.

How Motor Development Occurs: Thelen's Dynamic Systems Theory

The typical sequence of motor development was traditionally thought to be genetically programmed—a largely automatic, preordained series of steps directed by the maturing brain. Today, many developmental scientists consider this view too simplistic. Instead, according to Esther Thelen (1995; Smith & Thelen, 2003), motor development is a continuous process of interaction between baby and environment.

Thelen pointed to the *walking reflex:* stepping movements a neonate makes when held upright with the feet touching a surface. This behavior usually disappears by the fourth month. Not until the latter part of the first year, when a baby is getting ready to walk, do such movements appear again. The usual explanation is a shift to cortical control: Thus, an older baby's deliberate walking is a new skill masterminded by the developing brain. But, Thelen observed, a newborn's stepping involves the same kinds of movements the neonate makes while lying down and kicking. Why would stepping stop, only to reappear months later, whereas kicking continues? The answer, she suggested, might be that babies' legs become thicker and heavier during the early months but not yet strong enough to carry the baby's increased weight (Thelen & Fisher, 1982, 1983). In fact, when infants who had stopped stepping were held in warm water, which helps support their legs, stepping reappeared. Their ability to produce the movement had not changed—only the physical and environmental conditions that inhibited or promoted it.

Maturation alone cannot explain such an observation, said Thelen. Development does not have a single, simple cause. Infant and environment form an interconnected, dynamic system, which includes the infant's motivation as well as his muscular strength and position in the environment at a particular moment in time (for example, lying in a crib or being held in a pool). Similarly, when an infant tries to reach for a rattle or mobile, opportunities and constraints presented by the infant's physical characteristics, the intensity of her desire, her energy level, the speed and direction of her arm, and the changing positions of her arm and

dynamic systems theory (DST) Esther Thelen's theory, which holds that motor development is a dynamic process of active coordination of multiple systems within the infant in relation to the environment.

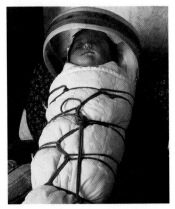

Some observers have suggested that babies from the Yucatan develop motor skills later than American babies because they are swaddled. However, Navajo babies, like this one, are also swaddled for most of the day, and they begin to walk at about the same time as other American babies, suggesting a hereditary explanation.

Checkpoint

Can you . . .

- Trace a typical infant's progress in head control, hand control, and loco-motion, according to the Denver norms?
- Discuss how maturation, perception, and cultural influences relate to early motor development?
- Compare the Gibsons' ecological theory of perception and Thelen's dynamic systems theory?

hand at each point in the process affect whether and how she can achieve the goal. Ultimately, a solution emerges as the baby explores various combinations of movements and selects those that most efficiently contribute to that end. Rather than being solely in charge of this process, the maturing brain is only one part of it.

According to Thelen's **dynamic systems theory (DST),** *"behavior emerges in the moment from the self-organization of multiple components"* (Spencer et al., 2006, p. 1523). DST emphasizes four principles: (1) the element of time—not only in the moment a behavior occurs, but in the effects of behavioral decisions that accumulate over time; (2) the interaction of multiple causes or subsystems; (3) the integration of perception and cognition with action; and (4) the differing developmental pathways of individual children (Smith & Thelen, 2003; Spencer et al., 2006). According to Thelen, normal babies develop the same skills in the same order because they are built approximately the same way and have similar physical challenges and needs. Thus, they eventually discover that walking is more efficient than crawling in most situations. However, this discovery arises from each particular baby's physical characteristics and experience in a particular context. That this is so may explain why some babies learn to walk earlier and differently than others.

Thelen believed that the principles of DST apply in all realms of development. Like jazz musicians, infants improvise personal solutions to problems by selecting and integrating multiple patterns or strands of behavior (Spencer et al., 2006).

Cultural Influences on Motor Development

Dynamic systems theory includes an emphasis on the context in which development occurs. Thus, although motor development follows a virtually universal sequence, its *pace* does respond to certain cultural factors. A normal rate of development in one culture may be quite different in another.

According to some research, African babies tend to be more advanced than U.S. and European infants in sitting, walking, and running. In Uganda, for example, babies typically walk at 10 months, as compared with 12 months in the United States and 15 months in France. Asian babies tend to develop these skills even later. Such differences may in part be related to ethnic differences in temperament (H. Kaplan & Dove, 1987; see Chapter 6) or may reflect a culture's child-rearing practices (Gardiner & Kosmitzki, 2005).

Some cultures actively encourage early development of motor skills. In many African and West Indian cultures in which infants show advanced motor development, adults use special handling routines, such as bouncing and stepping exercises, to strengthen babies' muscles. In one study, Jamaican infants, whose mothers used such handling routines daily, sat, crawled, and walked earlier than English infants, whose mothers gave them no such special handling (Hopkins & Westra, 1988, 1990).

On the other hand, some cultures discourage early motor development. Children of the Ache in eastern Paraguay do not begin to walk until age 18 to 20 months (H. Kaplan & Dove, 1987). Ache mothers pull their babies back to their laps when the infants begin to crawl away. The Ache mothers closely supervise their babies to protect them from the hazards of nomadic life. Yet, as 8- to 10-year-olds, Ache children climb tall trees, chop branches, and play in ways that enhance their motor skills (H. Kaplan & Dove, 1987). Normal development, then, need not follow the same timetable to reach the same destination.

By the time small children can run, jump, and play with toys requiring fairly sophisticated coordination, they are very different from the neonates described at the beginning of this chapter. The cognitive changes that have taken place are equally dramatic, as we discuss in Chapter 5.

SUMMARY AND KEY TERMS

Childbirth and Culture: How Birthing Has Changed

Guidepost 1: *How has childbirth changed in developed countries?*

- In Europe and the United States, childbirth before the twentieth century was not much different from childbirth in some developing countries today. Birth was a female ritual that occurred at home and was attended by a midwife. Pain relief was minimal, and risks for mother and baby were high.

- The development of the science of obstetrics professionalized childbirth. Births took place in hospitals and were attended by physicians. Medical advances dramatically improved safety.

- Today, delivery at home or in birth centers attended by midwives can be a relatively safe alternative to physician-attended hospital delivery for women with normal, low-risk pregnancies.

The Birth Process

Guidepost 2: *How does labor begin, what happens during each of the three stages of childbirth, and what alternative methods of delivery are available?*

- Birth normally occurs after a preparatory period of parturition.

- The birth process consists of three stages: (1) dilation of the cervix; (2) descent and emergence of the baby; and (3) expulsion of the umbilical cord and the placenta.

- Electronic fetal monitoring can detect signs of fetal distress, especially in high-risk births.

- About 30 percent of births in the United States are by cesarean delivery.

- Alternative methods of childbirth can minimize the need for painkilling drugs and maximize parents' active involvement.

- Modern epidurals can give effective pain relief with smaller doses of medication than in the past.

- The presence of a doula can provide physical benefits as well as emotional support.

parturition (97)

electronic fetal monitoring (98)

cesarean delivery (99)

natural childbirth (99)

prepared childbirth (99)

The Newborn Baby

Guidepost 3: *How do newborn infants adjust to life outside the womb, and how can we tell whether a new baby is healthy and is developing normally?*

- The neonatal period is a time of transition from intrauterine to extrauterine life.

- At birth, the circulatory, respiratory, digestive, elimination, and temperature regulation systems become independent of the mother's. If a newborn cannot start breathing within about 5 minutes, brain injury may occur.

- Newborns have a strong sucking reflex and secrete meconium from the intestinal tract. They are commonly subject to neonatal jaundice due to immaturity of the liver.

- At 1 minute and 5 minutes after birth, a neonate's Apgar score can indicate how well he or she is adjusting to extrauterine life. The Brazelton Neonatal Behavioral Assessment Scale can assess responses to the environment and predict future development.

- Neonatal screening is done for certain rare conditions, such as PKU and congenital hypothyroidism.

- A newborn's state of arousal is governed by periodic cycles of wakefulness, sleep, and activity. Sleep takes up the major, but a diminishing, amount of a neonate's time. By about six months babies do most of their sleeping at night.

- Cultural customs affect sleep patterns.

neonatal period (101)

neonate (101)

anoxia (102)

neonatal jaundice (102)

Apgar scale (103)

Brazelton Neonatal Behavioral Assessment Scale (NBAS) (103)

state of arousal (104)

Complications of Childbirth

Guidepost 4: *What complications of childbirth can endanger newborn babies, and what are the prospects for infants with complicated births?*

- Complications of childbirth include low birth weight, postmature birth, and stillbirth.

- Low-birth-weight babies may be either preterm (premature) or small for gestational age. Low birth weight is a major factor in infant mortality and can cause long-term physical and cognitive problems. Very-low-birth-weight babies have a less promising prognosis than those who weigh more.

- A supportive postnatal environment and other protective factors often can improve the outcome for babies suffering from birth complications.

preterm (premature) infants (105)

small-for-date (small-for-gestational-age) infants (105)

low birth weight (106)

kangaroo care (107)

postmature (108)

stillbirth (108)

protective factors (110)

Survival and Health

Guidepost 5: *What factors affect infants' chances for survival and health?*

- The vast majority of infant deaths occur in developing countries. Postnatal care can reduce infant mortality.

- Although infant mortality has diminished in the United States, it is still disturbingly high, especially among African American babies. Birth defects are the leading cause of death in infancy, followed by disorders related to prematurity and low birth weight, sudden infant death syndrome (SIDS), maternal complications of pregnancy, and complications of the placenta, umbilical cord, and membranes.

- Sudden infant death syndrome (SIDS) is the leading cause of postneonatal death in the United States. SIDS rates have declined markedly following recommendations to lay babies on their backs to sleep.

- Vaccine-preventable diseases have declined as rates of immunization have improved, but many preschoolers are not fully protected.

infant mortality rate (110)

sudden infant death syndrome (SIDS) (112)

Early Physical Development

Guidepost 6: *What influences growth, and how do the brain and the senses develop?*

- Normal physical growth and sensory and motor development proceed according to the cephalocaudal and proximodistal principles.

- A child's body grows most dramatically during the first year of life; growth proceeds at a rapid but diminishing rate throughout the first three years.

- Breast-feeding offers many health advantages and sensory and cognitive benefits and, if possible, should be done exclusively for at least the first six months.

- Overweight babies are not at special risk of becoming obese adults unless they have obese parents.

- The central nervous system controls sensorimotor activity. Lateralization enables each hemisphere of the brain to specialize in different functions.

- The brain grows most rapidly during the months before and immediately after birth as neurons migrate to their assigned locations, form synaptic connections, and undergo integration and differentiation. Cell death and myelination improve the efficiency of the nervous system.

- Reflex behaviors—primitive, locomotor, and postural— are indications of neurological status. Most early reflexes drop out during the first year as voluntary, cortical control develops.

- Especially during the early period of rapid growth, environmental experience can influence brain development positively or negatively.

- Sensory capacities, present from birth and even in the womb, develop rapidly in the first months of life. Very young infants show pronounced abilities to discriminate between stimuli.

- Touch is the first sense to develop and mature. Newborns are sensitive to pain. Smell, taste, and hearing also begin to develop in the womb.

- Vision is the least well developed sense at birth. Peripheral vision, color perception, acuteness of focus, binocular vision, and the ability to follow a moving object with the eyes all develop within the first few months.

cephalocaudal principle (114)

proximodistal principle (114)

central nervous system (118)

lateralization (119)

neurons (120)

integration (121)

differentiation (121)

cell death (121)

myelination (122)

reflex behaviors (124)

plasticity (127)

Motor Development

Guidepost 7: *What are the early milestones in motor development, and what are some influences on it?*

- Motor skills develop in a certain sequence, which may depend largely on maturation but also on context, experience, and motivation. Simple skills combine into increasingly complex systems.

- Self-locomotion brings about changes in all domains of development.

- Perception is intimately related to motor development. Depth perception and haptic perception develop in the first half of the first year.

- According to Gibson's ecological theory, sensory perception and motor activity are coordinated from birth, helping infants figure out how to navigate in their environment.

- Thelen's dynamic systems theory holds that infants develop motor skills, not by maturation alone, but by active coordination of multiple systems of action within a changing environment.

- Cultural practices may influence the pace of early motor development.

systems of action (130)

Denver Developmental Screening Test (130)

gross motor skills (130)

fine motor skills (130)

visual guidance (132)

depth perception (132)

haptic perception (132)

visual cliff (133)

ecological theory of perception (133)

dynamic systems theory (DST) (134)

5 Cognitive Development during the First Three Years

So runs my dream; but what am I?

An infant crying in the night;

An infant crying for the light,

And with no language but a cry.

—Alfred, Lord Tennyson, *In Memoriam,* Canto 54, 1850

Did You **Know...**

- Parental responsiveness to a child's needs can affect the child's intelligence?
- Early intervention can boost IQs of at-risk children?
- Newborns as young as 2 days prefer new sights to familiar sights?
- Brain growth spurts coincide with changes in cognitive behavior?
- Use of gestures helps babies learn to talk?
- Infants and toddlers who are read to frequently learn to read earlier?

These are just a few of the interesting and important topics we will cover in this chapter. In it we look at infants' and toddlers' cognitive abilities from a variety of perspectives—behaviorist, psychometric, Piagetian, information processing, cognitive neuroscientific, and social-contextual. We trace the early development of language and discuss how it comes about. After you have studied this chapter, you should be able to answer each of the Guidepost questions on the following page.

139

Guideposts *for Study*

1. What are six approaches to the study of cognitive development?
2. How do infants learn, and how long can they remember?
3. Can infants' and toddlers' intelligence be measured, and how can it be improved?
4. How did Piaget explain early cognitive development?
5. How can we measure infants' ability to process information, and when do infants begin to understand characteristics of the physical world?
6. What can brain research reveal about the development of cognitive skills?
7. How does social interaction with adults advance cognitive competence?
8. How do babies develop language, and what influences contribute to linguistic progress?

Guidepost 1

What are six approaches to the study of cognitive development?

behaviorist approach Approach to the study of cognitive development that is concerned with basic mechanics of learning.

psychometric approach Approach to the study of cognitive development that seeks to measure intelligence quantitatively.

Piagetian approach Approach to the study of cognitive development that describes qualitative stages in cognitive functioning.

information-processing approach Approach to the study of cognitive development that analyzes processes involved in perceiving and handling information.

cognitive neuroscience approach Approach to the study of cognitive development that links brain processes with cognitive ones.

social-contextual approach Approach to the study of cognitive development that focuses on environmental influences, particularly parents and other caregivers.

Studying Cognitive Development: Six Approaches

How do babies learn to solve problems? When does memory develop? What accounts for individual differences in cognitive abilities? Can we measure a baby's intelligence or predict how smart that baby will be in the future? These questions have long intrigued developmental scientists, many of whom have taken one of six approaches to their study:

- The **behaviorist approach** studies the basic *mechanics* of learning, which fall in the domain of cognitive development. Behaviorists are concerned with how behavior changes in response to experience.

- The **psychometric approach** measures *quantitative differences* in abilities that make up intelligence by using tests that indicate or predict these abilities.

- The **Piagetian approach** looks at changes, or stages, in the *quality* of cognitive functioning. It is concerned with how the mind structures its activities and adapts to the environment.

- The **information-processing approach** focuses on perception, learning, memory, and problem solving. It aims to discover how children process information from the time they encounter it until they use it.

- The **cognitive neuroscience approach** examines the hardware of the central nervous system. It seeks to identify what brain structures are involved in specific aspects of cognition.

- The **social-contextual approach** examines the effects of environmental aspects of the learning process, particularly the role of parents and other caregivers.

Behaviorist Approach: Basic Mechanics of Learning

Guidepost 2

How do infants learn, and how long can they remember?

Babies are born with the ability to learn from what they see, hear, smell, taste, and touch, and they have some ability to remember what they learn. Although learning theorists recognize maturation as a limiting factor, their main interest is in mechanisms of learning. Let's look first at two learning processes that behaviorists study: *classical conditioning* and *operant conditioning*. Later we will consider *habituation,* a form of learning that information-processing researchers study.

Classical and Operant Conditioning

Eager to capture Anna's memorable moments, her father took pictures of the infant smiling, crawling, and showing off her other achievements. Whenever the flash went off, Anna blinked. One evening when Anna was 11 months old, she saw her father hold the camera up to his eye—and she blinked *before* the flash. She had learned to associate the camera with the bright light, so that the sight of the camera alone caused her to blink.

Anna's blinking at the sight of the camera is an example of **classical conditioning,** in which a person learns to make a reflex, or involuntary, response (in this case, blinking) to a stimulus (the camera) that originally did not bring about the response (Figure 5-1). Classical conditioning enables infants to anticipate an event before it happens by forming associations between stimuli, such as the camera and the flash, that regularly occur together. Classically conditioned learning will become *extinct,* or fade, if it is not reinforced by repeated association. Thus, if Anna frequently saw the camera without the flash, she eventually would stop blinking at the sight of the camera alone.

In classical conditioning, the learner is passive, absorbing and automatically reacting to stimuli. In contrast, in **operant conditioning**—as when a baby learns that babbling brings loving attention—the learner acts, or operates, on the environment. The infant learns to make a certain response to an environmental stimulus (babbling at the sight of her or his parents) in order to produce a particular effect (parental attention). Researchers often use operant conditioning to study other phenomena, such as memory.

classical conditioning Learning based on associating a stimulus that does not ordinarily elicit a response with another stimulus that does elicit the response.

operant conditioning Learning based on reinforcement or punishment.

Infant Memory

Can you remember anything that happened to you before you were about 2 years old? Chances are you can't. This inability to remember early events is called *infantile amnesia.* Developmental scientists have proposed various explanations for this common phenomenon. One explanation, held by Piaget (1969) and others, is that early events are not retained in memory because the brain is not yet developed enough to store them. Freud, in contrast, believed that early memories are stored but are repressed because they are emotionally troubling. Other researchers suggest that children cannot store events in memory until they can talk about them (Nelson, 1992).

Today, research using operant conditioning with nonverbal, age-appropriate tasks suggests that infants' memory processes may not differ fundamentally from

An Indian snake charmer's son plays with a snake his father has trained, showing that fear of snakes is a learned, not instinctive, response. Children can be conditioned to fear animals that are associated with unpleasant or frightening experiences.

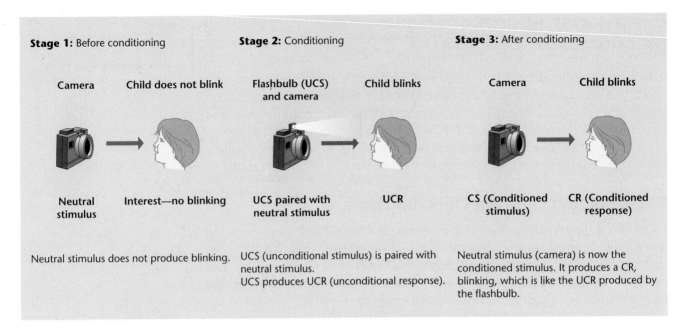

Stage 1: Before conditioning | **Stage 2:** Conditioning | **Stage 3:** After conditioning

Camera | Child does not blink | Flashbulb (UCS) and camera | Child blinks | Camera | Child blinks

Neutral stimulus | Interest—no blinking | UCS paired with neutral stimulus | UCR | CS (Conditioned stimulus) | CR (Conditioned response)

Neutral stimulus does not produce blinking. | UCS (unconditional stimulus) is paired with neutral stimulus. UCS produces UCR (unconditional response). | Neutral stimulus (camera) is now the conditioned stimulus. It produces a CR, blinking, which is like the UCR produced by the flashbulb.

Figure 5-1

Three steps in classical conditioning.

those of older children and adults except that infants' retention time is shorter. These studies have found that babies will repeat an action days or weeks later—*if* they are periodically reminded of the situation in which they learned it (Rovee-Collier, 1999).

In a series of experiments by Carolyn Rovee-Collier (1996, 1999) and her associates, infants were operantly conditioned to kick in order to activate a mobile attached to one ankle by a ribbon. Babies 2 to 6 months old, when shown the same mobiles days or weeks later, repeated the kicking, even though their ankles were no longer attached to the mobiles. When the infants saw these mobiles, they kicked more than before the conditioning, showing that recognition of the mobiles triggered a memory of their initial experience with them.

In a similar task, older infants and toddlers were conditioned to press a lever to make a miniature train go around a track. The length of time a conditioned response could be retained increased with age, from two days for 2-month-olds to 13 weeks for 18-month-olds (Hartshorn et al., 1998; Rovee-Collier, 1996, 1999).

Young infants' memory of a behavior seems to be linked specifically to the original cue. Two- to 6-month-olds repeated the learned behavior *only* when they saw the original mobile or train. In contrast, 9- to 12-month-olds would try out the behavior on a different train if no more than two weeks had gone by since the training (Rovee-Collier, 1999).

A familiar context can improve recollection when a memory has weakened. Three-, 9-, and 12-month-olds initially could recognize the mobile or train in a different setting from the one in which they were trained, but not after long delays. Periodic nonverbal reminders through brief exposure to the original stimulus can sustain a memory from early infancy through 1 to 2 years old (Rovee-Collier, 1999).

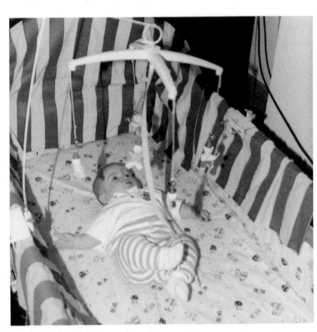

In this photo from a classic experiment, babies 2 to 6 months old who learn that their kicking activates a mobile remember this skill even if the mobile is removed for up to two weeks. When the mobile is returned, the baby starts kicking as soon as he sees it. Brightly striped cloth around the crib helps him remember the original context.

At least one prominent memory researcher disputes the claim that such conditioned memories are qualitatively the same as the memories of older children and adults. From an evolutionary developmental perspective, abilities develop as they can fulfill useful functions in adapting to the environment. The early procedural and perceptual knowledge demonstrated by infants kicking a mobile to activate it is not the same as an older child's or adult's explicit memory of specific events. Infancy is a time of great change, and retention of specific experiences is unlikely to be useful for long. This may be one reason that adults do not remember events that occurred when they were infants (Nelson, 2005). Later in this chapter we will discuss brain research that sheds more light on the development of memory in infancy.

Psychometric Approach: Developmental and Intelligence Testing

Although there is no clear scientific consensus on a definition of intelligence (Sternberg et al., 2005), most professionals agree that **intelligent behavior** is *goal oriented* and *adaptive:* directed at adjusting to the circumstances and conditions of life. Intelligence, as ordinarily understood, enables people to acquire, remember, and use knowledge; to understand concepts and relationships; and to solve everyday problems.

The precise nature of intelligence has been debated for many years, and so has the best way to measure it. The modern intelligence testing movement began in the early twentieth century, when school administrators in Paris asked the psychologist Alfred Binet to devise a way to identify children who could not handle academic work and needed special instruction. The test that Binet and his colleague, Theodore Simon, developed was the forerunner of psychometric tests that score intelligence by numbers.

The goals of psychometric testing are to measure quantitatively the factors that are thought to make up intelligence (such as comprehension and reasoning) and, from the results of that measurement, to predict future performance (such as school achievement). **IQ (intelligence quotient) tests** consist of questions or tasks that are supposed to show how much of the measured abilities a person has, by comparing that person's performance with norms established by a large group of test-takers who were in the standardization sample.

For school-age children, intelligence test scores can predict academic performance fairly accurately and reliably, as we discuss in Chapter 9. Testing infants and toddlers is another matter. Because babies cannot tell us what they know and how they think, the most obvious way to gauge their intelligence is by assessing what they can do. But if they do not grasp a rattle, it is hard to tell whether they do not know how, do not feel like doing it, do not realize what is expected of them, or have simply lost interest.

Testing Infants and Toddlers

Although it is virtually impossible to measure infants' intelligence, it *is* possible to test their cognitive development. **Developmental tests** compare a baby's performance on a series of tasks with norms established on the basis of observation of what large numbers of infants and toddlers can do at particular ages.

The **Bayley Scales of Infant and Toddler Development** (Bayley, 1969, 1993, 2005) is a widely used developmental test designed to assess children from 1 month to 3½ years. Scores on the Bayley-III indicate a child's strengths, weaknesses, and competencies in each of five developmental areas: *cognitive, language,*

✔ Checkpoint

Can you . . .

◆ Compare six important approaches to the study of cognitive development and identify their goals?

◆ Give examples of classical and operant conditioning, and discuss what operant conditioning studies have found about infant memory?

Guidepost 3

Can infants' and toddlers' intelligence be measured, and how can it be improved?

intelligent behavior Behavior that is goal oriented and adaptive to circumstances and conditions of life.

IQ (intelligence quotient) tests Psychometric tests that seek to measure intelligence by comparing a test-taker's performance with standardized norms.

developmental tests Psychometric tests that compare a baby's performance on a series of tasks with standardized norms for particular ages.

Bayley Scales of Infant and Toddler Development Standardized test of infants' and toddlers' mental and motor development.

motor, *social-emotional,* and *adaptive behavior.* An optional *behavior rating scale* can be completed by the examiner, in part on the basis of information from the child's caregiver. Separate scores, called *developmental quotients* (DQs), are calculated for each scale. DQs are most useful for early detection of emotional disturbances and sensory, neurological, and environmental deficits and can help parents and professionals plan for a child's needs.

Assessing the Impact of the Early Home Environment

Intelligence was once thought to be fixed at birth, but we now know that it is influenced by both inheritance and experience. As discussed in Chapter 4, early brain stimulation is a key to future cognitive development. What characteristics of the early home environment may influence measured intelligence and other measures of cognitive development?

Home Observation for Measurement of the Environment (HOME) Instrument to measure the influence of the home environment on children's cognitive growth.

Using the **Home Observation for Measurement of the Environment (HOME)** (R. H. Bradley, 1989; Caldwell & Bradley, 1984), trained observers interview the primary caregiver and rate on a yes-or-no checklist the intellectual stimulation and support observed in a child's home. HOME scores are significantly correlated with measures of cognitive development (Totsika & Sylva, 2004).

One important factor that HOME assesses is parental responsiveness. HOME gives credit to the parent of an infant or toddler for caressing or kissing the child during an examiner's visit. A longitudinal study found positive correlations between parents' responsiveness to their 6-month-olds and the children's IQ, achievement test scores, and teacher-rated classroom behavior through age 13 (Bradley, Corwyn, Burchinal, et al., 2001).

HOME also assesses the number of books in the home, the presence of playthings that encourage the development of concepts, and parents' involvement in children's play. In an analysis of HOME assessments of 29,264 U.S. children, learning stimulation was consistently associated with kindergarten achievement scores, as well as with language competence and motor and social development (Bradley, Corwyn, Burchinal, et al., 2001).

Of course, some HOME items may be less culturally relevant in non-Western than in Western families (Bradley, Corwyn, McAdoo, et al., 2001). Also, we cannot be sure on the basis of correlational findings that parental responsiveness or an enriched home environment actually increases a child's intelligence. All we can say is that these factors are associated with high intelligence. Intelligent, well-educated parents may be more likely to provide a positive, stimulating home environment; and because they also pass their genes on to their children, there may be a genetic influence as well.

The Home Observation for Measurement of the Environment gives positive ratings to parents who praise their children and are attentive to their questions.

Other research has identified seven aspects of the early home environment that enable cognitive and psychosocial development and help prepare children for school. These seven conditions are (1) encouraging exploration of the environment; (2) mentoring in basic cognitive and social skills; (3) celebrating developmental advances; (4) guidance in practicing and extending skills; (5) protection from inappropriate disapproval, teasing, and punishment; (6) communicating richly and responsively; and (7) guiding and limiting behavior. The consistent presence of all seven conditions early in life is "causally linked to many areas of brain functioning and cognitive development" (C. T. Ramey & S. L. Ramey, 2003, p. 4). Table 5-1 lists specific suggestions to help babies develop cognitive competence.

Table 5-1 Fostering Competence

Findings from studies using the HOME scales and from neurological studies and other research suggest the following guidelines for fostering infants' and toddlers' cognitive development:

1. In the early months, *provide sensory stimulation* but avoid overstimulation and distracting noises.
2. As babies grow older, *create an environment that fosters learning*—one that includes books, interesting objects (which do not have to be expensive toys), and a place to play.
3. *Respond to babies' signals.* This establishes a sense of trust that the world is a friendly place and gives babies a sense of control over their lives.
4. *Give babies the power to effect changes,* through toys that can be shaken, molded, or moved. Help a baby discover that turning a doorknob opens a door, flicking a light switch turns on a light, and opening a faucet produces running water for a bath.
5. *Give babies freedom to explore.* Do not confine them regularly during the day in a crib, jump seat, or small room and only for short periods in a playpen. Baby-proof the environment and let them go!
6. *Talk to babies.* They will not pick up language from listening to the radio or television; they need interaction with adults.
7. In talking to or playing with babies, *enter into whatever they are interested in* at the moment instead of trying to redirect their attention to something else.
8. *Arrange opportunities to learn basic skills,* such as labeling, comparing, and sorting objects (say, by size or color), putting items in sequence, and observing the consequences of actions.
9. *Applaud new skills and help babies practice and expand them.* Stay nearby but do not hover.
10. *Read to babies in a warm, caring atmosphere from an early age.* Reading aloud and talking about the stories develop preliteracy skills.
11. *Use punishment sparingly.* Do not punish or ridicule results of normal trial-and-error exploration.

Sources: R. R. Bradley & Caldwell, 1982; R. R. Bradley, Caldwell, & Rock, 1988; R. H. Bradley et al., 1989; C. T. Ramey & Ramey, 1998a, 1998b; S. L. Ramey & Ramey, 1992; Staso, quoted in Blakeslee, 1997; J. H. Stevens & Bakeman, 1985; B. L. White, 1971; B. L. White, Kaban, & Attanucci, 1979.

Early Intervention

Early intervention, as defined under the Individuals with Disabilities Education Act, is a systematic process of planning and providing therapeutic and educational services for families that need help in meeting infants', toddlers', and preschool children's developmental needs. Two randomly assigned, controlled studies, among others, have tested the effectiveness of early intervention (C. T. Ramey & S. L. Ramey, 1998b, 2003).

Project CARE (Wasik, Ramey, Bryant, & Sparling, 1990) and the Abecedarian Project (C. T. Ramey & Campbell, 1991) involved a total of 174 North Carolina babies from at-risk homes. In each project, from age 6 weeks until kindergarten, an experimental group was enrolled in Partners for Learning, a full-day, year-round early childhood education program at a university child development center. The program had a low child-teacher ratio and used learning games to foster specific cognitive, linguistic, perceptual-motor, and social skills. Control groups received pediatric and social work services, formula, and home visits, as the experimental groups did, but were not enrolled in Partners for Learning (C. T. Ramey & S. L., Ramey, 2003).

In both projects, the children who received the early intervention showed a widening advantage over the control groups in developmental test scores during the first 18 months. By age 3, the average IQ of the Abecedarian children was 101 and of CARE children, 105—equal to or better than average for the general population—as compared with only 84 and 93 for the control groups (C. T. Ramey & S. L. Ramey, 1998b).

early intervention Systematic process of providing services to help families meet young children's developmental needs.

What's Your View?

- On the basis of the seven essential aspects of the early home environment listed in the text, can you suggest specific ways to help infants and toddlers get ready for schooling?

Studies have shown that early educational intervention can help offset environmental risks.

As often happens with early intervention programs, these early gains were not fully maintained. Still, scores tended to remain higher and more stable among children who had been in Partners for Learning than in the control groups (Burchinal et al., 1997). Both the experimental and control groups' IQs and math scores increasingly fell below national norms while reading scores held steady but below average. However, the children in the Abecedarian Project who had been enrolled in Partners for Learning continued to outdo the control group on all measures and were less likely to repeat a grade or to be placed in special education (Campbell, Pungello, Miller-Johnson, Burchinal, & Ramey, 2001; C. T. Ramey et al., 2000; C. T. Ramey & S. L. Ramey, 2003). At 21, 70 percent of the Abecedarian experimental group were in skilled jobs or higher education, in contrast with only 40 percent of the control group. The experimental group were three times more likely to attend a four-year college and were less likely to experience teen pregnancy, to smoke, or to use drugs (C. T. Ramey & S. L. Ramey, 2003). These findings and others like them show that early educational intervention can help offset environmental risks (Brooks-Gunn, 2003).

The most effective early interventions are those that (1) start early and continue throughout the preschool years; (2) are highly time-intensive (that is, occupy more hours in a day or more days in a week, month, or year); (3) provide direct educational experiences, not just parental training; (4) include health, family counseling, and social services; and (5) are tailored to individual differences and needs. As in the two North Carolina projects, initial gains tend to diminish unless there is enough ongoing environmental support for further progress (Brooks-Gunn, 2003; C. T. Ramey & S. L. Ramey, 1996, 1998a).

Piagetian Approach: The Sensorimotor Stage

The first of Piaget's four stages of cognitive development is the **sensorimotor stage.** During this stage (birth to approximately age 2), infants learn about themselves and their world through their developing sensory and motor activity. Babies change from creatures who respond primarily through reflexes and random behavior into goal-oriented toddlers.

Checkpoint

Can you . . .

♦ Tell why developmental tests are sometimes given to infants and toddlers?

♦ Identify aspects of the early home environment that may influence cognitive development?

♦ Discuss the value of early intervention?

Guidepost 4

How did Piaget explain early cognitive development?

sensorimotor stage Piaget's first stage in cognitive development, in which infants learn through senses and motor activity.

Table 5-2	Six Substages of Piaget's Sensorimotor Stage of Cognitive Development*

Substage	Ages	Description	Behavior
1. Use of reflexes	Birth to 1 month	Infants exercise their inborn reflexes and gain some control over them. They do not coordinate information from their senses. They do not grasp an object they are looking at.	Dorri begins sucking when her mother's breast is in her mouth.
2. Primary circular reactions	1 to 4 months	Infants repeat pleasurable behaviors that first occur by chance (such as thumb sucking). Activities focus on the infant's body rather than the effects of the behavior on the environment. Infants make first acquired adaptations; that is, they suck different objects differently. They begin to coordinate sensory information and grasp objects.	When given a bottle, Dylan, who is usually breast-fed, is able to adjust his sucking to the rubber nipple.
3. Secondary circular reactions	4 to 8 months	Infants become more interested in the environment; they repeat actions that bring interesting results (such as shaking a rattle) and prolong interesting experiences. Actions are intentional but not initially goal directed.	Alejandro pushes pieces of dry cereal over the edge of his high chair tray one at a time and watches each piece as it falls to the floor.
4. Coordination of secondary schemes	8 to 12 months	Behavior is more deliberate and purposeful (intentional) as infants coordinate previously learned schemes (such as looking at and grasping a rattle) and use previously learned behaviors to attain their goals (such as crawling across the room to get a desired toy). They can anticipate events.	Anica pushes the button on her musical nursery rhyme book, and "Twinkle, Twinkle, Little Star" plays. She pushes this button over and over again, choosing it instead of the buttons for the other songs.
5. Tertiary circular reactions	12 to 18 months	Toddlers show curiosity and experimentation; they purposefully vary their actions to see results (for example, by shaking different rattles to hear their sounds). They actively explore their world to determine what is novel about an object, event, or situation. They try out new activities and use trial and error in solving problems.	When Bjorn's big sister holds his favorite board book up to his crib bars, he reaches for it. His first efforts to bring the book into his crib fail because the book is too wide. Soon, Bjorn turns the book sideways, pulls it in, and hugs it, delighted with his success.
6. Mental combinations	18 to 24 months	Now that toddlers can mentally represent events, they are no longer confined to trial and error to solve problems. Symbolic thought enables toddlers to begin to think about events and anticipate their consequences without always resorting to action. Toddlers begin to demonstrate insight. They can use symbols, such as gestures and words, and can pretend.	Jenny plays with her shape box, searching carefully for the right hole for each shape before trying—and succeeding.

* Infants show enormous cognitive growth during Piaget's sensorimotor stage, as they learn about the world through their senses and their motor activities. Note their progress in problem solving and the coordination of sensory information. All ages are approximate.

Substages of the Sensorimotor Stage

The sensorimotor stage consists of six substages (Table 5-2), which flow from one to another as a baby's **schemes,** organized patterns of thought and behavior, become more elaborate. During the first five substages, babies learn to coordinate input from their senses and organize their activities in relation to their environment. During the sixth and last substage, they progress from trial-and-error learning to using symbols and concepts to solve simple problems.

Much of this early cognitive growth comes about through **circular reactions,** in which an infant learns to reproduce pleasurable or interesting events originally discovered by chance. Initially, an activity such as sucking produces a sensation so enjoyable that the baby wants to repeat it. The repetition again produces pleasure, which motivates the baby to do it yet again (Figure 5-2). The originally chance behavior has been consolidated into a new scheme.

schemes Piaget's term for organized patterns of thought and behavior used in particular situations.

circular reactions Piaget's term for processes by which an infant learns to reproduce desired occurrences originally discovered by chance.

Figure 5-2
Primary, secondary, and tertiary circular reactions.

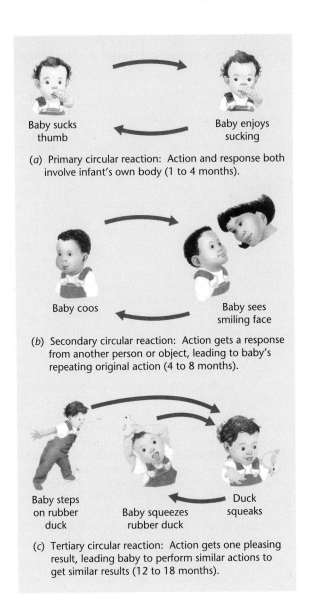

(*a*) Primary circular reaction: Action and response both involve infant's own body (1 to 4 months).

(*b*) Secondary circular reaction: Action gets a response from another person or object, leading to baby's repeating original action (4 to 8 months).

(*c*) Tertiary circular reaction: Action gets one pleasing result, leading baby to perform similar actions to get similar results (12 to 18 months).

In the *first substage* (birth to about 1 month), neonates begin to exercise some control over their inborn reflexes, engaging in a behavior even when its normal stimulus is not present. For example, newborns suck reflexively when their lips are touched. But they soon learn to find the nipple even when they are not touched, and they suck at times when they are not hungry. These newer behaviors illustrate how infants modify and extend the scheme for sucking.

In the *second substage* (about 1 to 4 months), babies learn to repeat purposely a pleasant bodily sensation first achieved by chance (say, sucking their thumbs, as in Figure 5-2a). Also, they begin to turn toward sounds, showing the ability to coordinate different kinds of sensory information (vision and hearing).

The *third substage* (about 4 to 8 months) coincides with a new interest in manipulating objects and learning about their properties. Babies intentionally repeat an action not merely for its own sake, as in the second substage, but to get results *beyond the infant's own body*. For example, a baby this age will repeatedly shake a rattle to hear its noise or (as in Figure 5-2b) coo when a friendly face appears, so as to make the face stay longer.

By the time infants reach the *fourth substage* (about 8 to 12 months), they have learned to generalize from past experience to solve new problems. They will crawl to get something they want, grab it, or push away a barrier to it (such as

Table 5-3	Key Developments of the Sensorimotor Stage	
Concept or Skill	**Piaget's View**	**More Recent Findings**
Imitation	Invisible imitation develops around 9 months; deferred imitation begins after development of mental representations in the sixth substage (18–24 months).	Controversial studies have found invisible imitation of facial expressions in newborns and deferred imitation as early as 6 weeks, Deferred imitation of complex activities seems to exist as early as 6 months.
Object permanence	Develops gradually between the third and sixth substage.	Infants as young as 3½ months (second substage) seem to show object knowledge, though interpretation of findings is in dispute.
Symbolic development	Depends on representational thinking, which develops in the sixth substage (18–24 months).	Understanding that pictures stand for something else occurs at about 19 months. Children under 3 tend to have difficulty interpreting scale models.
Categorization	Depends on representational thinking, which develops during the sixth substage (18–24 months).	Infants as young as 3 months seem to recognize perceptual categories; by the end of the first year they can categorize by function.
Causality	Develops slowly between 4–6 months and 1 year, based on an infant's discovery, first of effects of own actions and then of effects of outside forces.	Some evidence suggests early awareness of specific causal events in the physical world, but general understanding of causality may be slower to develop.
Number	Depends on use of symbols, which begins in the sixth substage (18–24 months)	Infants as young as 5 months may recognize and mentally manipulate small numbers, but interpretation of findings is in dispute.

someone else's hand). They modify and coordinate previous schemes, such as the schemes for crawling, pushing, and grabbing, to find one that works. This substage marks the development of complex, goal-directed behavior.

In the *fifth substage* (about 12 to 18 months), babies will *vary* an action to get a similar result. For example, a toddler may squeeze a rubber duck that squeaked when stepped on, to see whether it will squeak again (as in Figure 5-2c). For the first time, children show originality in problem solving. By trial and error, they try out new behaviors until they find the best way to attain a goal.

The *sixth substage* (about 18 months to 2 years) is a great breakthrough—a transition to the preoperational stage of early childhood. **Representational ability**—the ability to mentally represent objects and actions in memory, largely through symbols such as words, numbers, and mental pictures—frees toddlers from immediate experience. They can pretend, and their representational ability affects the sophistication of their pretending (Bornstein, Haynes, O'Reilly, & Painter, 1996). They can think about actions before taking them. They no longer have to go through laborious trial and error to solve problems—they can try out solutions in their minds.

During these six substages, infants develop the abilities to think and remember. They also develop knowledge about aspects of the physical world, such as objects and spatial relationships. Researchers inspired by Piaget have found that some of these developments conform fairly closely to his observations, but other developments, including representational ability, may occur earlier than Piaget claimed. (Table 5-3 compares Piaget's views on these and other topics with more current findings; refer to this table as you read on.)

representational ability Piaget's term for capacity to store mental images or symbols of objects and events.

Checkpoint

Can you . . .

- Summarize major developments during the six substages of the sensorimotor stage?

- Explain how primary, secondary, and tertiary circular reactions work?

- Tell why the development of representational ability is important?

Do Imitative Abilities Develop
Earlier than Piaget Thought?

Imitation is an important way of learning; it becomes especially valuable toward the end of the first year, as babies try out new skills (Nelson, 2005). Piaget maintained that **invisible imitation**—imitation using parts of the body that a baby cannot see, such as the mouth—develops at about 9 months, after **visible imitation,** the use of hands or feet, for example, which babies can see. Yet in a series of studies by Andrew Meltzoff and M. Keith Moore (1983, 1989), babies less than 72 hours old appeared to imitate adults by opening their mouths and sticking out their tongues—a response that other research has found to disappear by about 2 months (Bjorklund & Pellegrini, 2000). According to Meltzoff and Gopnik (1993), this early imitative behavior is the result of an evolved "like me" mechanism; the infant seeks to imitate faces that have the same properties (tongues that can stick out) as his or her own. This "like me" mechanism may be the basis for *social cognition*—the ability to understand the goals, actions, and feelings of others (Meltzoff, 2007; see Chapter 6). Meltzoff and Moore (1994) further suggest that infants have an inborn predisposition to imitate human faces that may serve the evolutionary (survival) purpose of communication with a caregiver (Rakison, 2005).

Other researchers have suggested that the tongue thrust may simply be exploratory behavior aroused by the sight of an adult tongue (Bjorklund, 1997; S. S. Jones, 1996). In any event, imitation appears to serve a different adaptive purpose for a young infant than for an older infant (Bjorklund & Pellegrini, 2000).

Piaget also held that children under 18 months cannot engage in **deferred imitation** of an act they saw some time before because they are not yet able to retain mental representations. However, Piaget may have underestimated infants' and toddlers' representational ability because of their limited ability to express what they remember. Babies as young as 6 weeks have imitated an adult's facial movements after a 24-hour delay, in the presence of the same adult, who this time was expressionless. This observation suggests that very young babies *can* retain a mental representation of a simple event (Meltzoff & Moore, 1994, 1998). Deferred imitation of novel or complex events seems to begin by 6 to 9 months (Meltzoff & Moore, 1998; Bauer, 2002). Thus, the findings on deferred imitation agree with those on operant conditioning (Rovee-Collier, 1999): Infants do seem capable of remembering after a delay.

In **elicited imitation,** researchers induce infants and toddlers to imitate a specific series of actions they have seen but not necessarily done before. The initial demonstration may be accompanied by a simple verbal explanation (Bauer, 1996, 2002; Bauer, Wenner, Dropik, & Wewerka, 2000; Bauer, Wiebe, Carver, Waters, & Nelson, 2003). After a one-month delay, with no further demonstration or explanation, about 45 percent of 9-month-olds can reproduce a simple two-step procedure, such as dropping a toy car down a chute and then pushing the car to make it roll to the end of a track and turn on a light (Bauer, 2002; Bauer et al., 2003). Elicited imitation becomes more reliable between 12 and 24 months (Bauer et al., 2000).

One study predicted individual differences in performance of this task from scans of the infants' brains as they looked at photos of the same procedure a week after first seeing it. The memory traces of infants who could not repeat the procedure in the right order were less robust, indicating that they had failed to consolidate the memory for long-term storage (Bauer et al., 2003). Four factors seem to determine young children's long-term recall: (1) the number of times a sequence of events has been experienced, (2) whether the child actively participates or merely observes, (3) whether the child is given verbal reminders of the experience, and (4) whether the sequence of events occurs in a logical, causal order (Bauer et al., 2000).

Development of Knowledge about Objects and Space

The ability to perceive the size and shape of objects and to discern their movements may be an early evolved mechanism for avoidance of predators (Rakison, 2005). The *object concept*—the idea that objects have their own independent existence, characteristics, and locations in space—is a later *cognitive* development fundamental to an orderly view of physical reality. The object concept is the basis for children's awareness that they themselves exist apart from objects and other people. It is essential to understanding a world full of objects and events.

When Does Object Permanence Develop?   One aspect of the object concept is **object permanence,** the realization that an object or person continues to exist when out of sight. The development of this concept in many cultures can be seen in the game of peekaboo (Box 5-1).

Object permanence develops gradually during the sensorimotor stage. At first, infants have no such concept. By the third substage, from about 4 to 8 months, they will look for something they have dropped; but, if they cannot see it, they act as if it no longer exists. In the fourth substage, about 8 to 12 months, they will look for an object in a place where they first found it after seeing it hidden, even if they later saw it being moved to another place. In the fifth substage, 12 to 18 months, they no longer make this error, according to Piaget; they will search for an object in the *last* place they saw it hidden. However, they will not search for it in a place where they did *not* see it hidden. By the sixth substage, 18 to 24 months, object permanence is fully achieved; toddlers will look for an object even if they did not see it hidden.

Esther Thelen's dynamic systems theory proposes that the decision where to search for a hidden object is not about what babies *know,* but about what they *do,* and why. One factor is how much time has elapsed between the infant's seeing the object hidden in a new place and the infant's reaching for it. If the elapsed time is brief, the infant is more likely to reach for the object in the new location. When the time interval is longer, however, the memory of having previously found the object in the old place inclines the infant to search there again, and that inclination grows stronger the more times the infant has found it there (Smith & Thelen, 2003; Spencer, Smith, & Thelen, 2001; Spencer et al., 2006).

Other research suggests that babies may fail to search for hidden objects because they cannot yet carry out a two-step or two-handed sequence of actions, such as moving a cushion or lifting the cover of a box before grasping the object. When given repeated opportunities, during a period of one to three months, to explore, manipulate, and learn about such a task, infants at 6 to 12 months can succeed (Bojczyk & Corbetta, 2004).

When object permanence is tested by hiding the object only by darkness, making it retrieveable in one motion, infants in the third substage (4 to 8 months) perform surprisingly well. In one

object permanence Piaget's term for the understanding that a person or object still exists when out of sight.

This little girl seems to be showing some concept of object permanence by searching for an object that is partially hidden. The age when object permanence begins to develop is in dispute.

BOX **5-1** **Window** *on the World*

Playing Peekaboo

In rural South Africa, a Bantu mother smiles at her 9-month-old son, covers her eyes, and asks, "Uphi?" (where?). Seconds later, the mother says, "Hapa!" (here) and uncovers her eyes to the baby's delight. A Japanese mother plays the same game with her 12-month-old daughter, to the same joyous response. When a U.S. grandfather visits his 15-month-old grandson, the boy raises his shirt to cover his eyes, picking up the game his grandfather started on his last visit—two months earlier.

Peekaboo is played across diverse cultures (Fernald & O'Neill, 1993). The moment the caregiver reappears, marked by exaggerated gestures and voice tones, is exhilarating for the child, no matter the culture. The excitement of the game is heightened by infants' fascination with faces and voices, especially the high-pitched tones an adult uses when playing the game.

Peekaboo serves several important purposes. Psychoanalysts say it helps babies learn to overcome anxiety when their mothers disappear. Cognitive psychologists maintain that it helps babies develop ideas about object permanence. It also may help babies learn rules that govern social routines such as taking turns in conversation. Further, peekaboo requires paying attention, a prerequisite for learning.

As babies develop the cognitive competency to predict future events, the game takes on new dimensions. Between 3 and 5 months, the baby's smiles and laughter as the adult's face moves in and out of view signal the infant's developing expectation of what will happen next. At 5 to 8 months, the baby shows anticipation—looking and smiling as the adult's voice signals the adult's imminent reappearance. By 1 year, babies start to initiate the game, actively engaging adults in play. Now it is the adult who generally responds to the baby's physical or vocal cues.

Parents often use scaffolding to teach infants peekaboo and other games. In one study mothers showed their babies how to play peekaboo with a doll (Rome-Flanders, Cronk, & Gourde, 1995). The amount and type of scaffolding varied with the infant's age and skill. The need to attract a child's attention to begin the game declined as time went on. Also, as babies became more able to understand spoken language, the need for modeling decreased as direct verbal instruction ("Cover the doll") increased. Indirect verbal instruction ("Where is the doll?"), used to focus attention on the next step in the game, remained constant throughout the entire age range. Reinforcement (saying "Peekaboo!" when the infant uncovered the doll) was fairly constant from 9 months on. By 24 months most babies had mastered the game and the overall amount of scaffolding dropped substantially.

What's Your View?

Have you ever played peekaboo consistently with the same infant over time? If so, did you notice changes with age in the child's participation?

Check It Out

For more information on this topic, go to http://vapt.cisat.jmu .edu/newsletters/volume3number2.pdf (an article by Steve Harvey, Ph.D., from *Zero to Three*, "Dynamic Play Therapy: Integrated Expressive Arts Approach to the Family Treatment of Infants and Toddlers").

study, 6½-month-olds saw a ball drop down a chute and land in one of two spots, each identifiable by a distinctive sound. When the light was turned off and the procedure was repeated, the babies reached for the ball in the appropriate location, guided only by the sound (Goubet & Clifton, 1998). This showed that they knew the ball continued to exist and could tell where it had gone.

Methods based only on infants' looking behavior eliminate the need for any motor activity and thus can be used at very early ages. As we discuss in the next major section of this chapter, research using information-processing methodology suggests that infants as young as 3 or 4 months seem not only to have a sense of object permanence but also to understand causality and categorization, to have a rudimentary concept of number, and to know other principles governing the physical world.

Symbolic Development, Pictorial Competence, and Understanding of Scale Much of the knowledge people acquire about their world is gained, not through direct observation or experience, but through *symbols,* intentional representations of reality. Learning to interpret symbols is, then, an essential task of childhood. First, however, children must become *symbol-minded:* attentive to symbols and their relationships to the things they represent (DeLoache, 2004). One aspect of symbolic development, studied by Judy DeLoache and her colleagues, is the growth of *pictorial competence,* the ability to understand the nature of pictures (DeLoache, Pierroutsakos, & Uttal, 2003).

In studies carried out in both the United States and Africa's Ivory Coast, infants were observed using their hands to explore pictures as if they were objects—rubbing, patting, or attempting to lift a depicted object off the page. This manual exploration of pictures diminishes by 15 months. However, it is not until about 19 months that children are able to point at a picture of a bear or telephone while saying its name ("beh" or "teltone"), demonstrating an understanding that a picture is a symbol of something else (DeLoache et al., 2003; DeLoache, Pierroutsakos, Uttal, Rosengren, & Gottlieb, 1998; Pierroutsakos & DeLoache, 2003). By age 2, children understand that a picture is *both* an object and a symbol (Preissler & Bloom, 2007).

Although toddlers may spend a good deal of time watching television, they at first seem unaware that what they are seeing is a representation of reality (Troseth, Saylor, & Archer, 2006). In one series of experiments, 2- and 2½-year-olds watched via a video monitor as an adult hid an object in an adjoining room. When taken to the room, the 2½-year-olds found the hidden object easily, but 2-year-olds could not. Yet the younger children did find the object if they had watched through a window as it was being hidden (Troseth & DeLoache, 1998). Apparently, what the 2-year-olds lacked was representational understanding of screen images. In a follow-up experiment, 2-year-olds who were told face-to-face where to find a hidden toy were able to do so, whereas age-mates who were told the same information from a person on video did not (Troseth, Saylor, & Archer, 2006).

Toddlers often make *scale errors*—momentary misperceptions of the relative sizes of symbolic and real objects. In one study, 18- to 36-month-olds were recorded trying to slide down tiny slides, sit in dollhouse chairs, and squeeze into miniature cars after similar, child-sized objects were removed from their playroom. Such scale errors are clearly distinguishable from pretend play (DeLoache, Uttal, & Rosengren, 2004) and may in part result from lack of impulse control. In addition, the researchers suggested that two different brain systems normally work together during interactions with familiar objects. One system enables the child to recognize and categorize an object ("That's a buggy") and plan what to do with it ("I'm going to lie in it"). A separate system may be involved in perceiving the size of the object and using this information to control actions pertaining to it. Faulty teamwork between these immature brain systems is a possible reason for young children's frequent scale errors (DeLoache, 2006).

According to the **dual representation hypothesis,** it is difficult for toddlers to mentally represent both a symbol and the object it represents at the same time, and so they may confuse the two (DeLoache, 2006; DeLoache et al., 2003). This may be why 2-year-olds tend to have problems interpreting scale models. They can use representational thinking to guide them to the actual location of something shown in a photograph (Suddendorf, 2003), but apparently they think of the model as an object in itself, rather than a representation of something else (DeLoache, 2000).

In one experiment, 2½-year-olds who were told that a "shrinking machine" had shrunk a room to the size of a miniature model were more successful in finding

Eighteen- to 36-month-olds were observed trying to slide down tiny slides, sit in dollhouse chairs, and squeeze into miniature cars after similar, but child-sized objects were removed from their playroom.

dual representation hypothesis Proposal that children under age 3 have difficulty grasping spatial relationships because of the need to keep more than one mental representation in mind at the same time.

a toy hidden in the room on the basis of its position in the model than were children the same age who were told that the "little room" was just like the "big room." What seems to make the second task harder is that it requires a child to mentally represent both the symbol (the "little room") and its relationship to the thing it stands for (the "big room") at the same time. With the "shrinking machine," children do not have to perform this dual operation, because they are told that the room and the model are one and the same. Three-year-olds do not seem to have this problem with models (DeLoache, Miller, & Rosengren, 1997).

Evaluating Piaget's Sensorimotor Stage

According to Piaget, the journey from reflex behavior to the beginnings of thought is long and slow. For eighteen months or so, babies learn only from their senses and movements; not until 18 to 24 months do they make the breakthrough to conceptual thought. Now, as we have seen, research using simplified tasks and modern tools suggests that certain limitations Piaget saw in infants' early cognitive abilities may instead have reflected immature linguistic and motor skills.

In some ways, then, infants and toddlers seem to be more cognitively competent than Piaget imagined. This does not mean that infants come into the world with minds fully formed. As Piaget observed, immature forms of cognition precede more mature forms. We can see this, for example, in the errors young infants make in searching for hidden objects. However, Piaget may have been mistaken in his emphasis on motor experience as the primary engine of cognitive growth. Infants' perceptions are far ahead of their motor abilities, and today's methods enable researchers to make observations and inferences about those perceptions. The relationship between perception and cognition is a major area of investigation, as we will discuss in the next section.

Checkpoint

Can you . . .

◆ Explain why Piaget may have underestimated some of infants' cognitive abilities, and discuss the implications of more recent research?

Guidepost 5

How can we measure infants' ability to process information, and when do infants begin to understand characteristics of the physical world?

Information-Processing Approach: Perceptions and Representations

Information-processing researchers analyze the separate parts of a complex task, such as Piaget's object search tasks, to figure out what abilities are necessary for each part of the task and at what age these abilities develop. Information-processing researchers also measure, and draw inferences from, what infants pay attention to, and for how long.

Habituation

At about 6 weeks, Stefan lies peacefully in his crib near a window, sucking a pacifier. It is a cloudy day, but suddenly the sun breaks through, and an angular shaft of light appears on the end of the crib. Stefan stops sucking for a few moments, staring at the pattern of light and shade. Then he looks away and starts sucking again.

We don't know what was going on in Stefan's mind when he saw the shaft of light, but we can tell by his sucking and looking behavior at what point he began paying attention and when he stopped. Much information-processing research with infants is based on **habituation,** a type of learning in which repeated or continuous exposure to a stimulus, such as the shaft of light, reduces attention to that stimulus. In other words, familiarity breeds loss of interest.

Researchers study habituation in newborns by repeatedly presenting a stimulus (usually a sound or visual pattern) and then monitoring such responses as heart rate, sucking, eye movements, and brain activity. A baby who has been sucking typically stops or sucks less vigorously when the stimulus is first presented and

habituation Type of learning in which familiarity with a stimulus reduces, slows, or stops a response.

BOX 5-2 **Research** *in Action*

Do Infants and Toddlers Watch Too Much Television?

Six-month-old Caitlin bounces up and down, claps, and laughs out loud as the bright images of her Baby Einstein DVD flash across the screen. Caitlin has been watching Baby Einstein since she was 5 weeks old. She is neither precocious nor unusual. According to a random survey of 1,000 parents of preschoolers (Zimmerman, Christakis, & Meltzoff, 2007), by 3 months of age, 40 percent of U.S. infants watch an hour of television, DVDs, or videos every day. By age 2, 90 percent of U.S. children watch television an average of one and a half hours a day. Another national survey (Vandewater et al., 2007) found that 68 percent of children age 2 and under watched television daily, and almost one-fifth of these children had television sets in their bedrooms. Many of these very young children watch alone despite evidence that parental involvement and participation increase the positive impact of educational shows.

The top reasons parents gave in the Zimmerman survey for exposing their young children to various types of media were (1) belief that the media are educational, (2) belief that viewing is enjoyable or relaxing for the child, and (3) use of the media as an electronic babysitter. In the Vandewater survey, the two most common reasons for putting a TV in a young child's bedroom were (1) to free the family television for other family members and (2) to keep the child occupied.

During the past ten years an avalanche of media geared to infants and toddlers has been made available. Television shows now aim at children as young as 12 months; computer games have been developed with special keyboards for infants as young as 9 months; and educational DVDs target 1-month-old infants.

This increased screen time flies in the face of recommendations by the American Academy of Pediatrics Committee on Public Education (2001) that children under 2 be discouraged from watching television at all. Instead, the committee recommends they engage in activities that promote brain development, such as talking, playing, singing, and reading with parents. In one survey (Rideout, Vandewater, & Wartella, 2003), children under 2 spent more than twice as much time watching TV as they spent being read to (see figure). "Heavy watchers" were less likely to learn to read by age 6.

What impact does constant media use have on neurological and cognitive development? Does it stimulate aggressive behavior? Does having a TV in the bedroom interfere with sleep? Do video and computer games help visual and spatial skills or risk eyestrain and ergonomic problems? There is already evidence that background media interfere with toddlers' concentration on

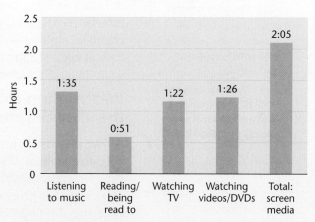

Average amount of time children under 2 spend on media and other activities in a typical day, according to mothers' reports.
Note: These data include only children who participate in these activities. (Source: Rideout et al., 2003.)

play (Anderson & Pempek, 2005), but further study is needed to determine how heavy exposure to television affects infants' and toddlers' development. One thing is clear: Time spent on media takes away time from exploratory play and from interaction with family members, both of which are developmentally important activities.

Source: Unless otherwise referenced, this box is based on Rideout, Vandewater, & Wartella (2003); Vandewater et al. (2007); and Zimmerman et al. (2007).

What's Your View?

At what age would you let a baby watch television or play a computer game, and what restrictions, if any, would you place on such activities?

Check It Out

For more information on this topic, go to www.pbs.org/parents/childrenandmedia/article-faq.html for research-based answers to questions about children's television use.

infant expects the next picture to appear (visual anticipation). These measurements are thought to indicate attentiveness and processing speed, as well as the tendency to form expectations on the basis of experience. In a longitudinal study, visual reaction time and visual anticipation at 3½ months correlated with IQ at age 4 (Dougherty & Haith, 1997).

✔ **Checkpoint**

Can you . . .

♦ Summarize the information-processing approach to the study of cognitive development?

♦ Explain how habituation measures the efficiency of infants' information processing?

♦ Identify several early perceptual and processing abilities that serve as predictors of intelligence?

All in all, there is much evidence that the abilities infants use to process sensory information are related to the cognitive abilities intelligence tests measure. Still, we need to be cautious in interpreting these findings. Most of the studies used small samples. Also, the predictability of childhood IQ from measures of habituation and recognition memory is only modest. Furthermore, predictions based on information-processing measures alone do not take into account the influence of environmental factors. For example, maternal responsiveness in early infancy seems to play a part in the link between early attentional abilities and cognitive abilities later in childhood (Bornstein & Tamis-LeMonda, 1994) and even at age 18 (Sigman, Cohen, & Beckwith, 1997).

Information Processing and the Development of Piagetian Abilities

As we discussed in a previous section, evidence suggests that several of the cognitive abilities Piaget described as developing toward the end of the sensorimotor stage actually arise much earlier. Research based on infants' visual processing has given developmental scientists a window into the timing of such cognitive developments as categorization, causality, object permanence, and number, all of which depend on formation of mental representations (refer back to Table 5-3).

Categorization   Dividing the world into meaningful categories is vital to thinking about objects or concepts and their relationships. It is the foundation of language, reasoning, problem solving, and memory; without it, the world would seem chaotic and meaningless (Rakison, 2005).

According to Piaget, the ability to classify, or group things into categories, does not appear until the sixth sensorimotor substage, around 18 months. Yet, by looking longer at items in a new category, even 3-month-olds seem to know, for example, that a dog is not a cat (Quinn, Eimas, & Rosenkrantz, 1993). Indeed, brain imaging has found that basic components of the neural structures needed to support categorization are functional within the first six months of life (Quinn, Westerlund, & Nelson, 2006). From an evolutionary perspective, infants may be born with a rudimentary ability to discern certain limited categories (such as snakes and spiders) that are dangerous to humans (Rakison, 2005).

For the most part, infants at first seem to categorize on the basis of *perceptual* features, such as shape, color, and pattern. By 12 to 14 months their categories become broadly *conceptual,* based on real-world knowledge, particularly of function (Mandler, 1998, 2007; Mandler & McDonough, 1993, 1996, 1998; Oakes, Coppage, & Dingel, 1997). In one series of experiments, 10- and 11-month-olds recognized that chairs with zebra-striped upholstery belong in the category of furniture, not animals (Pauen, 2002). When infants were allowed to handle tiny models, even 7-month-olds could tell that animals are different from vehicles or furniture. As time goes on, these broad concepts become more specific. For example, 2-year-olds recognize particular categories, such as "car" and "airplane," within the overall category of "vehicles" (Mandler, 2007).

In the second year, language becomes a factor. Hearing an experimenter name an object and/or point out its function can help 14- to 18-month-olds with category formation (Booth & Waxman, 2002). In one study, 14-month-olds who understood more words were more flexible in their categorizing than those with smaller understood vocabularies; they categorized objects by more than one criterion, such as material as well as shape (Ellis & Oakes, 2006).

Causality An understanding of *causality,* the principle that events have identifiable causes, is important because it "allows people to predict and control their world" (L. B. Cohen, Rundell, Spellman, & Cashon, 1999). Piaget maintained that this understanding develops slowly during infants' first year. At about 4 to 6 months, as infants become able to grasp objects, they begin to recognize that they can act on their environment. Thus, said Piaget, the concept of causality is rooted in a dawning awareness of the power of one's own intentions. However, according to Piaget, infants do not yet know that causes must come before effects; and not until close to 1 year do they realize that forces outside of themselves can make things happen.

Some information-processing research suggests that a mechanism for recognizing causality may exist much earlier (Mandler, 1998), possibly even at birth. Infants 6½ months old have shown by habituation and dishabituation that they seem to see a difference between events that are the immediate cause of other events (such as a brick striking a second brick, which is then pushed out of position) and events that occur with no apparent cause (such as a brick moving away from another brick without having been struck by it) (Leslie, 1982, 1984).

Other researchers have replicated these findings with 6-month-olds but not with younger infants (L. B. Cohen & Amsel, 1998). These investigators attribute the growth of causal understanding to a gradual improvement in information-processing skills. As infants accumulate more information about how objects behave, they are better able to see causality as a general principle operating in a variety of situations (L. B. Cohen & Amsel, 1998; L. B. Cohen & Oakes, 1993; L. B. Cohen et al., 1999; Oakes, 1994).

One research team set up a "blicket detector," rigged to light up and play music only when certain objects (called "blickets") were placed on it. Children as young as 2 years were able to decide, by watching the device operate, which objects were blickets (because they activated the blicket detector) and which were not (Gopnik, Sobel, Schulz, & Glymour, 2001). In a follow-up study, 2-year-olds correctly placed the blicket on the detector even when the decision depended on making inferences from ambiguous information, as when two different objects, one a blicket and one not, had been placed on the detector at the same time (Sobel, Tenenbaum, & Gopnik, 2004). Finally, in another study that did not depend on motor activity, 8-month-olds showed by anticipatory eye movements that they could make similar inferences (Sobel & Kirkham, 2006). Apparently, infants' understanding of familiar events in the physical world enables them to think logically about causation.

Research has also explored infants' expectations about hidden causes. In one experiment, 10- to 12-month-olds looked longer when a human hand emerged from the opposite side of a lighted stage onto which a beanbag had been thrown than when the hand emerged from the same side as the beanbag, suggesting that the infants understood that the hand probably had thrown the beanbag. The infants did *not* have the same reaction when a toy train rather than a hand appeared or when the thrown object was a self-propelled puppet (Saxe, Tenenbaum, & Carey, 2005). In another set of experiments, infants as young as 7 months used the motion of a beanbag to infer the position of a hand, but not of a toy block (Saxe, Tzelnic, & Carey, 2007). Thus 7-month-olds appear to know that (1) an object incapable of self-motion must have a causal agent to set it in motion, (2) a hand is a more likely causal agent than a toy train or block, and (3) the existence and position of an unseen causal agent can be inferred from the motion of an inanimate object.

Seven-month-old babies appear to understand that an object incapable of self-motion, such as a beanbag, must be set in motion by a causal agent, such as a hand.

Figure 5-3

How early do infants show object permanence? In this experiment, 3½-month-olds watched a short carrot and then a tall carrot slide along a track, disappear behind a screen, and then reappear. After they became accustomed to seeing these events, the opaque screen was replaced by a screen with a large notch at the top. The short carrot did not appear in the notch when passing behind the screen; the tall carrot, which should have appeared in the notch, also did not. The babies looked longer at the tall than at the short carrot event, suggesting that they were surprised that the tall carrot did not appear in the notch. (*Source:* Baillargeon & DeVos, 1991.)

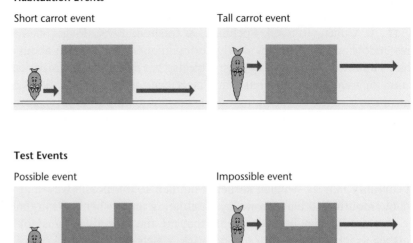

Habituation Events

Short carrot event

Tall carrot event

Test Events

Possible event

Impossible event

violation-of-expectations
Research method in which dishabituation to a stimulus that conflicts with experience is taken as evidence that an infant recognizes the new stimulus as surprising.

Object Permanence   **Violation-of-expectations** research begins with a familiarization phase, in which infants see an event or series of events happen normally. After the infant is habituated to this procedure, the event is changed in a way that conflicts with (violates) normal expectations. An infant's tendency to look longer at the changed event is interpreted as evidence that the infant recognizes it as surprising.

Using the violation-of-expectations method, Renée Baillargeon (Baillargeon & DeVos, 1991) found evidence of object permanence in infants as young as 3½ months. The babies watched as a tall carrot disappeared behind a screen of the same height but failed to appear in a large notch in the upper part of the screen before reappearing again on the other side. The infants showed surprise by looking longer at this "impossible event" than at a "possible event" involving a short carrot, as shown in Figure 5-3.

Such studies suggest that at least rudimentary forms of object permanence may be present in the early months of life. One proposal is that infants are born with reasoning abilities—*innate learning mechanisms* that help them make sense of the information they encounter—or that they acquire these abilities very early (Baillargeon, 1994). Some investigators go further, suggesting that infants at birth may already have intuitive *core knowledge* of basic physical principles in the form of specialized brain modules that help infants organize their perceptions and experience (Spelke, 1994, 1998).

However, these interpretations are controversial. Does an infant's visual interest in an impossible condition reveal a *conceptual* understanding of the way things work or merely a *perceptual* awareness that something unusual has happened? The fact that an infant looks longer at one scene than at another may show only that the infant can see a difference between the two. It does not tell us what the infant knows about the difference or even that the infant is actually surprised. The "mental representation" the infant refers to may be no more than a brief sensory memory of something just seen. It's also possible that an infant, in becoming accustomed to the habituation event, develops the expectations that are then violated by the surprising event and did not have such knowledge or expectations before (Goubet & Clifton, 1998; Haith, 1998; Haith & Benson, 1998; Mandler, 1998; Munakata, 2001; Munakata, McClelland, Johnson, & Siegler, 1997).

Defenders of this research insist that a conceptual interpretation best accounts for the findings (Baillargeon, 1999; Spelke, 1998), although a variation on one of Baillargeon's experiments suggests otherwise. In her original research, Baillargeon

(1994) showed infants of various ages a "drawbridge" rotating 180 degrees. When the infants became habituated to the rotation, a barrier was introduced in the form of a box. At 4½ months, infants seemed to show (by looking longer) that they understood that the drawbridge could not move through the entire box, but not until 6½ months did infants recognize that the drawbridge cannot pass through 80 percent of the box. Later investigators replicated the experiment but eliminated the box. At 5 -months, infants still looked longer at the 180-degree rotation than at a lesser degree of rotation, even though no barrier was present—suggesting that they simply were demonstrating a preference for greater movement (Rivera, Wakeley, & Langer, 1999). Still other researchers, using dynamic field theory, showed that the "drawbridge effect" could result simply from the mechanics of habituation and dishabituation (Schöner & Thelen, 2006). Thus, critics say, we must be careful about overestimating infants' cognitive abilities from data that may have simpler explanations or may represent only partial achievement of mature abilities (Haith, 1998).

Cognitive Neuroscience Approach: The Brain's Cognitive Structures

Piaget's claim that neurological maturation is a major factor in cognitive development is borne out by modern research, which reveals that brain growth spurts (periods of rapid growth and development) coincide with changes in cognitive behavior (Fischer & Rose, 1994, 1995).

Memory Systems

Some researchers have used brain scans to determine which brain structures affect which cognitive functions and to chart developmental changes. Brain scans provide physical evidence of the location of two separate long-term memory systems—*implicit* and *explicit*—that acquire and store different kinds of information (Squire, 1992; Vargha-Khadem et al., 1997). **Implicit memory,** which develops early in infancy, pertains to habits and skills that occur without effort, such as knowing how to throw a ball or an infant's kicking on seeing a familiar mobile (Nelson, 2005). **Explicit memory** is conscious or intentional recollection, usually of facts, names, events, or other information that can be stated or declared. Delayed imitation of complex behaviors is evidence that explicit memory is developing in late infancy and toddlerhood.

In early infancy, when the structures responsible for memory storage are not fully formed, memories are relatively fleeting (Serres, 2001). The maturing of the hippocampal system makes longer-lasting memories possible (Bauer, 2002; Bauer et al., 2000, 2003).

The large portion of the frontal lobe directly behind the forehead, the prefrontal cortex, is thought to control many aspects of cognition. This part of the brain develops more slowly than any other (M. H. Johnson, 1998). During the second half of the first year, the prefrontal cortex and associated circuitry develop the capacity for **working memory**—short-term storage of information the brain is actively processing, or working on. It is in working memory that mental representations are prepared for, or recalled from, storage.

The relatively late appearance of working memory may be largely responsible for the slow development of object permanence, which seems to occur in a rearward portion of the prefrontal cortex (Nelson, 1995). By 12 months, this region may be developed enough to permit an infant to avoid search errors by controlling the impulse to search in a place where an object previously was found (Bell & Fox, 1992; Diamond, 1991).

Checkpoint

Can you . . .

◆ Discuss three areas in which information-processing research challenges Piaget's account of development?

◆ Describe the violation-of-expectations research method, tell how and why it is used, and list some criticisms of it?

Guidepost 6

What can brain research reveal about the development of cognitive skills?

implicit memory Unconscious recall, generally of habits and skills; sometimes called *procedural memory.*

explicit memory Intentional and conscious memory, generally of facts, names, and events.

working memory Short-term storage of information being actively processed.

Understanding of Number

Brain research has clarified a dispute about infants' understanding of simple numerical relationships. Some violation-of-expectations research suggested that an understanding of number may begin long before Piaget's sixth substage, when he claimed children first begin to use symbols. Karen Wynn (1992) tested whether 5-month-old babies can add and subtract small numbers of objects. The infants watched as Mickey Mouse dolls were placed behind a screen, and a doll was either added or taken away. The screen then was lifted to reveal either the expected number or a different number of dolls. In a series of experiments, the babies looked longer at surprising "wrong" answers than at expected "right" ones, suggesting (according to Wynn) that they had mentally "computed" the right answers.

According to Wynn, this research suggests that numerical concepts are inborn—that when parents teach their babies numbers, they may only be teaching them the names ("one, two, three") for *concepts* the babies already know. However, this is mere speculation, as the infants in these studies were already 5 months old. Furthermore, critics claimed, infants might simply be responding *perceptually* to the puzzling presence of a doll they saw removed from behind the screen or the absence of a doll they saw placed there (Haith, 1998; Haith & Benson, 1998). Other studies suggest that, although infants do seem to discriminate visually between sets of, say, two and three objects, they merely notice differences in the overall contours, area, or collective mass of the sets of objects rather than compare the number of objects in the sets (Clearfield & Mix, 1999; Mix, Huttenlocher, & Levine, 2002).

In response to that criticism, McCrink and Wynn (2004) designed an experiment to show that 9-month-olds can add and subtract numbers too large for mere perceptual discrimination. The infants saw five abstract objects go behind an opaque square. Five more objects then appeared and went behind the square. The infants looked longer when the screen dropped to reveal five objects than when it revealed ten. Similarly, when ten objects went behind the square and five emerged and went away, the infants looked longer when the screen dropped to reveal ten objects than when it revealed five. The authors concluded that "humans possess an early system that supports numerical combination and manipulation" (p. 780). This experiment does not, however, shed light on whether that system is inborn.

Researchers in Israel then replicated Wynn's original findings, this time with 6- to 9-month-old infants who wore brain-monitoring netting. The infants' brain activity indicated that they were actually detecting the numerical errors in the same way, but more slowly, than adults did. The authors concluded that the basic brain circuitry involved in numerical error detection is working by the second half of the first year (Berger, Tzur, & Posner, 2007).

Although memory systems continue to develop beyond infancy, the emergence of the brain's memory structures during that period underlines the importance of environmental stimulation during the early months of life. Social-contextual theorists and researchers pay particular attention to the impact of environmental influences.

Social-Contextual Approach: Learning from Interactions with Caregivers

Researchers influenced by Vygotsky's sociocultural theory study how the cultural context affects early social interactions that may promote cognitive competence. **Guided participation** refers to mutual interactions with adults that help structure children's activities and bridge the gap between a child's understanding and an adult's. This concept was inspired by Vygotsky's view of learning as a collaborative

Checkpoint

Can you . . .

◆ Identify the brain structures apparently involved in explicit, implicit, and working memory, and mention a task made possible by each?

◆ Tell how brain research clarifies a controversy over infants' numerical abilities?

Guidepost 7

How does social interaction with adults advance cognitive competence?

guided participation Adult's participation in a child's activity that helps to structure it and bring the child's understanding of it closer to the adult's.

process. Guided participation often occurs in shared play and in ordinary, every-day activities in which children learn informally the skills, knowledge, and values important in their culture.

In one cross-cultural study (Rogoff, Mistry, Göncü, & Mosier, 1993), researchers visited the homes of 14 one- to two-year-olds in each of four places: a Mayan town in Guatemala, a tribal village in India, and middle-class urban neighborhoods in Salt Lake City and Turkey. The investigators interviewed caregivers about their child-rearing practices and watched them help the toddlers learn to dress themselves and to play with unfamiliar toys.

Cultural differences affected the types of guided participation the researchers observed. In the Guatemalan town, where toddlers normally saw their mothers sewing and weaving at home to help support the family, and in the Indian village, where they accompanied their mothers at work in the fields, the children customarily played alone or with older siblings while the mother worked nearby. After initial demonstration and instruction, mostly nonverbal, in, for example, how to tie shoes, the children took over, while the parent or other caregiver remained available to help. The U.S. toddlers, who had full-time homemaker mothers or were in day care, interacted with their parents in the context of the child's play rather than in the parents' work or social worlds. Caregivers spoke with the children as peers and managed and motivated their learning with praise and excitement. Turkish families, who were in transition from a rural to an urban way of life, showed a pattern somewhere between the other two.

The cultural context, then, influences the way caregivers contribute to cognitive development. Direct adult involvement in children's play and learning may be better adapted to a middle-class urban community, in which parents or caregivers have more time, greater verbal skills, and possibly more interest in children's play and learning, than to a rural community in a developing country, in which children frequently observe and participate in adults' work activities (Rogoff et al., 1993).

✓ Checkpoint

Can you . . .

◆ Give an example of how cultural patterns affect caregivers' contributions to toddlers' learning?

Language Development

Language is a communication system based on words and grammar. Once children know words, they can use them to represent objects and actions. They can reflect on people, places, and things; and they can communicate their needs, feelings, and ideas in order to exert more control over their lives.

The growth of language illustrates the interaction of all aspects of development. As the physical structures needed to produce sounds mature and the neuronal connections necessary to associate sound and meaning become activated, social interaction with adults introduces babies to the communicative nature of speech. Let's look at a typical sequence of milestones in language development* (Table 5-4) and at some characteristics of early speech. Then we'll consider how babies acquire language, how brain growth is linked to language development, and how parents and other caregivers contribute to it.

◆ Guidepost 8

How do babies develop language, and what influences contribute to linguistic progress?

language Communication system based on words and grammar.

Sequence of Early Language Development

Before babies can use words, they make their needs and feelings known through sounds that progress from crying to cooing and babbling, then to accidental imitation, and then to deliberate imitation. These sounds are known as **prelinguistic speech.** Infants also grow in the ability to recognize and understand speech

prelinguistic speech Forerunner of linguistic speech; utterance of sounds that are not words. Includes crying, cooing, babbling, and accidental and deliberate imitation of sounds without understanding their meaning.

*This sequence is typical among Western, middle-class children, who have been studied the most.

Table 5-4	Language Milestones from Birth to 3 Years

Age in Months	Development
Birth	Can perceive speech, cry, make some response to sound.
1½ to 3	Coos and laughs.
3	Plays with speech sounds.
5 to 6	Recognizes frequently heard sound patterns.
6 to 7	Recognizes all phonernes of native language.
6 to 10	Babbles in strings of consonants and vowels.
9	Uses gestures to communicate and plays gesture games.
9 to 10	Intentionally imitates sounds.
9 to 12	Uses a few social gestures.
10 to 12	No longer can discriminate sounds not in own language.
10 to 14	Says first word (usually a label for something).
10 to 18	Says single words.
12 to 13	Understands symbolic function of naming; passive vocabulary grows.
13	Uses more elaborate gestures.
14	Uses symbolic gesturing.
16 to 24	Learns many new words, expanding expressive vocabulary rapidly from about 50 words to as many as 400; uses verbs and adjectives.
18 to 24	Says first sentence (2 words).
20	Uses fewer gestures; names more things.
20 to 22	Has comprehension spurt.
24	Uses many two-word phrases; no longer babbles; wants to talk.
30	Learns new words almost every day; speaks in combinations of three or more words; makes grammatical mistakes.
36	Says up to 1,000 words, 80 percent intelligible; makes some mistakes in syntax.

Source: Bates, O'Connell, & Shore, 1987; Capute, Shapiro, & Palmer, 1987; Kuhl, 2004; Lalonde & Werker, 1995; Lenneberg, 1969. Newman, 2005.

sounds and to use meaningful gestures. Babies typically say their first word around the end of the first year, and toddlers begin speaking in sentences about eight months to a year later.

Early Vocalization *Crying* is a newborn's only means of communication. Different pitches, patterns, and intensities signal hunger, sleepiness, or anger (Lester & Boukydis, 1985). Between 6 weeks and 3 months, babies start *cooing* when they are happy—squealing, gurgling, and making vowel sounds like "ahhh." At about 3 to 6 months, babies begin to play with speech sounds, matching the sounds they hear from people around them.

Babbling—repeating consonant-vowel strings, such as "ma-ma-ma-ma"—occurs between ages 6 and 10 months. Although it is often mistaken for a baby's first words, babbling is not real language because it does not hold meaning for the baby.

Imitation is a key to early language development. First, infants *accidentally* imitate language sounds and then imitate themselves making these sounds. Then, at about 9 to 10 months, infants *deliberately* imitate sounds without understanding them. Once they have a repertoire of sounds, they string them together in patterns that sound like language but seem to have no meaning. Finally, after infants become familiar with the sounds of words and phrases, they begin to attach meanings to them (Fernald, Perfors, & Marchman, 2006; Jusczyk & Hohne, 1997).

Perceiving Language Sounds and Structure   Imitation of language sounds requires the ability to perceive subtle differences between sounds, and infants can do this from or even before birth. Their brains seem to be preset to discriminate basic linguistic units, perceive linguistic patterns, and categorize them as similar or different (Kuhl, 2004).

This process of sound discrimination apparently begins in the womb. In one experiment, the heart rates of fetuses in the 35th week of gestation slowed when a tape recording of a rhyme the mother had spoken frequently was played near her abdomen. The fetal heart rate did *not* slow for a different rhyme another pregnant woman had spoken. Because the voice on the tape was not the mother's, the fetuses apparently were responding to the linguistic sounds they had heard the mother use. This finding suggests that hearing the "mother tongue" before birth may pretune an infant's ears to pick up its sounds (DeCasper, Lecanuet, Busnel, Granier-Deferre, & Maugeais, 1994).

At first, infants can discriminate the sounds of any language. In time, however, the ongoing process of pattern perception and categorization commits the brain's neural networks to further learning of the patterns of the infant's native language and constrains future learning of nonnative language patterns (Kuhl, 2004; Kuhl, Conboy, Padden, Nelson, & Pruitt, 2005).

By 6 to 7 months, hearing babies have learned to recognize the approximately 40 *phonemes,* or basic sounds, of their native language and to adjust to slight differences in the way different speakers form those sounds (Kuhl, Williams, Lacerda, Stevens, & Lindblom, 1992). The ability to discriminate native-language sounds at this age predicts individual differences in language abilities during the second year (Tsao, Liu, & Kuhl, 2004), whereas nonnative sound discrimination does not (Kuhl et al., 2005).

By 10 to 12 months, babies lose their sensitivity to sounds that are not part of the language or languages they usually hear spoken. For example, Japanese infants no longer make a distinction between "ra" and "la," a distinction that does not exist in Japanese. Although the ability to perceive nonnative sounds is not entirely lost, the brain no longer routinely discriminates them (Bates, O'Connell, & Shore, 1987; Lalonde & Werker, 1995; Werker, 1989). How does this change occur? One hypothesis, supported by behavioral studies and brain imaging, is that infants mentally "compute" the relative frequency of particular phonetic sequences in their language and learn to ignore sequences they infrequently hear (Kuhl, 2004).

During the second half of the first year, babies begin to become aware of the phonological rules of their language—how sounds are arranged in speech. In one series of experiments, 7-month-olds listened longer to sentences containing a different order of nonsense sounds (such as "wo fe wo," or ABA) from the order to which the infants had been habituated (such as "ga ti ti," or ABB). The sounds used in the test were different from those used in the habituation phase, so the infants' discrimination must have been based on the patterns of repetition alone. This finding suggests that infants may have a mechanism for discerning abstract rules of sentence structure (Marcus, Vijayan, Rao, & Vishton, 1999).

Gestures   Before babies can speak, they point. At 11 months, Maika pointed to her cup to show that she wanted it. She also pointed to a dog chasing his tail, using the gesture to communicate with her mother about an interesting sight. At 12 months, she pointed at a pen her brother had dropped and was looking for. This use of pointing to provide information showed that she understood something about another person's state of mind and wanted to help—an early indication

This toddler is communicating with his father by pointing at something that catches his eye. Gesturing seems to come naturally to young children and may be an important part of language learning.

of *social cognition* (discussed in Chapter 7) (Liszkowski, Carpenter, Striano, & Tomasello, 2006; Tomasello, Carpenter, & Liszkowski, 2007).

By 12 months, Maika learned some *conventional social gestures:* waving bye-bye, nodding her head to mean *yes,* and shaking her head to signify *no.* By about 13 months, she used more elaborate *representational gestures;* for example, she would hold an empty cup to her mouth to show that she wanted a drink or hold up her arms to show that she wanted to be picked up.

Symbolic gestures, such as blowing to mean *hot* or sniffing to mean *flower,* often emerge around the same time as babies say their first words, and they function much like words. Both hearing and deaf babies use such gestures in much the same ways (Goldin-Meadow, 2007). By using them, babies show an understanding that symbols can refer to specific objects, events, desires, and conditions. Gestures usually appear before children have a vocabulary of 25 words and drop out when children learn the word for the idea they were gesturing and can say it instead (Lock, Young, Service, & Chandler, 1990).

Learning gestures seems to help babies learn to talk. Early gestures are a good predictor of later vocabulary size (Goldin-Meadow, 2007). In one experiment (Goodwyn & Acredolo, 1998), 11-month-olds learned gestures by watching their parents perform them while saying the corresponding words. Between 15 and 36 months, when tested on vocal language development, these children outperformed two other groups—one whose parents had only said words and another who had received neither vocal nor gestural training.

Toddlers often combine gestures with words. Gesture-word combinations serve as a signal that a child is about to begin using multi-word sentences (Goldin-Meadow, 2007).

First Words The average baby says a first word sometime between 10 and 14 months, initiating **linguistic speech**—verbal expression that conveys meaning. At first, an infant's total verbal repertoire is likely to be "mama" or "dada." Or it may be a simple syllable that has more than one meaning depending on the context in which the child utters it. "Da" may mean "I want that," "I want to go out," or "Where's Daddy?" Such a word, which expresses a complete thought, is called a **holophrase**.

Babies understand many words before they can use them. Long before infants can connect sounds to meanings, they learn to recognize sound patterns they hear frequently, such as their names. Infants 5 months old listen longer to their own names than to other names (Newman, 2005). Six-month-olds look longer at a video of their mothers when they hear the word *mommy* and of their fathers when they hear *daddy,* suggesting that they are beginning to associate sound with meaning—at least with regard to special people (Tincoff & Jusczyk, 1999). By 13 months, most children understand that a word stands for a specific thing or event, and they can quickly learn the meaning of a new word (Woodward, Markman, & Fitzsimmons, 1994).

Between 10 months and 2 years, the process by which babies learn words gradually changes from simple association to following social cues. At 10 months, infants associate a name they hear with an object they find interesting, such as a sparkling wand, whether or not the name is the correct one for that object. At 12 months, they begin to pay attention to cues from adults, such as looking or

linguistic speech Verbal expression designed to convey meaning.

holophrase Single word that conveys a complete thought.

pointing at an object while saying its name. However, they still learn names only for interesting objects and ignore uninteresting ones, such as a cabinet latch. By 18 to 24 months, children follow social cues in learning names, regardless of the intrinsic interest of the objects (Golinkoff & Hirsh-Pasek, 2006; Pruden, Hirsh-Pasek, Golinkoff, & Hennon, 2006). At 24 months, children quickly recognize names of familiar objects in the absence of visual cues (Swingley & Fernald, 2002).

Passive (receptive, or understood) *vocabulary* continues to grow as verbal comprehension gradually becomes faster and more accurate and efficient (Fernald, Perfors, & Marchman, 2006). By 18 months, 3 out of 4 children can understand 150 words and can say 50 of them (Kuhl, 2004). Children with larger vocabularies and quicker reaction times can recognize spoken words from just the first part of the word. For example, when they hear "daw" or "ki," they will point to a picture of a dog or kitten (Fernald, Swingley, & Pinto, 2001).

Addition of new words to the *expressive* (spoken) *vocabulary* is slower at first. Then, sometime between 16 and 24 months, a "naming explosion" may occur, though this phenomenon is not universal (Ganger & Brent, 2004). Within a few months, a toddler may go from saying about 50 words to saying several hundred (Courage & Howe, 2002). Rapid gains in spoken vocabulary reflect increases in speed and accuracy of word recognition during the second year (Fernald, Pinto, Swingley, Weinberg, & McRoberts, 1998; Fernald et al., 2006) as well as an understanding that things belong in categories (Courage & Howe, 2002).

Nouns seem to be the easiest type of word to learn. In a cross-cultural study, Spanish, Dutch, French, Hebrew, Italian, Korean, and U.S. parents all reported that their 20-month-old children knew more nouns than any other class of words (Bornstein & Cote et al., 2004). At 24 to 36 months, children can figure out the meaning of unfamiliar adjectives from context or from the nouns they modify (Mintz, 2005).

First Sentences The next important linguistic breakthrough comes when a toddler puts two words together to express one idea ("Dolly fall"). Generally, children do this between 18 and 24 months. However, this age range varies greatly. Although prelinguistic speech is fairly closely tied to chronological age, linguistic speech is not. Most children who begin talking fairly late catch up eventually—and many make up for lost time by talking nonstop to anyone who will listen! (True delayed language development is discussed in Chapter 7.)

A child's first sentences typically deal with everyday events, things, people, or activities (Braine, 1976; Rice, 1989; Slobin, 1973). At first children typically use **telegraphic speech,** consisting of only a few essential words. When Rita says, "Damma deep," she seems to mean, "Grandma is sweeping the floor." Children's use of telegraphic speech, and the form it takes, varies, depending on the language being learned (Braine, 1976; Slobin, 1983). Word order generally conforms to what a child hears; Rita does not say, "Deep Damma," when she sees her grandmother sweeping.

telegraphic speech Early form of sentence use consisting of only a few essential words.

Does the omission of functional words such as *is* and *the* mean that a child does not know these words? Not necessarily; the child may merely find them hard to reproduce. Even infants are sensitive to the presence of functional words; at 10½ months, they can tell a normal passage from one in which the functional words have been replaced by similar-sounding nonsense words (Jusczyk, 2003).

Sometime between 20 and 30 months, children show increasing competence in **syntax,** the rules for putting sentences together in their language. They become somewhat more comfortable with articles (*a, the*), prepositions (*in, on*), conjunctions (*and, but*), plurals, verb endings, past tense, and forms of the verb *to be* (*am, are, is*). They also become increasingly aware of the communicative purpose of

syntax Rules for forming sentences in a particular language.

speech and of whether their words are being understood (Shwe & Markman, 1997)—a sign of growing sensitivity to the mental lives of others. By age 3, speech is fluent, longer, and more complex. Although children often omit parts of speech, they get their meaning across well.

Characteristics of Early Speech

Early speech has a character all its own, no matter what language a child is speaking (Slobin, 1971).

As we have seen, young children *simplify*. They use telegraphic speech to say just enough to get their meaning across ("No drink milk!").

Young children *understand grammatical relationships they cannot yet express*. At first, Nina may understand that a dog is chasing a cat, but she cannot string together enough words to express the complete action. Her sentence comes out as "Puppy chase" rather than "Puppy chase kitty."

Young children *underextend word meanings*. Lisa's uncle gave her a toy car, which the 13-month-old called her "koo-ka." Then her father came home with a gift, saying, "Look, Lisa, here's a little car for you." Lisa shook her head. "Koo-ka," she said, and ran and got the one from her uncle. To her, *that* car—and *only* that car—was a little car, and it took some time before she called any other toy cars by the same name. Lisa was underextending the word *car* by restricting it to a single object.

Young children also *overextend word meanings*. At 14 months, Amir jumped in excitement at the sight of a gray-haired man on the television screen and shouted, "Gampa!" Amir was overgeneralizing, or overextending, a word; he thought that because his grandfather had gray hair, all gray-haired men could be called "Grandpa." As children develop a larger vocabulary and get feedback from adults on the appropriateness of what they say, they overextend less. ("No, honey, that man looks a little like Grandpa, but he's somebody else's grandpa, not yours.")

Young children *overregularize rules*. They apply rules rigidly, not knowing that some rules have exceptions. When Delilah, looking out the window with her father on a gloomy day, repeats after him, "windy… cloudy… rainy…," and then adds, "coldy," this represents progress. When children first learn the rules for, in this instance, forming adjectives from nouns, they apply them universally. The next step is to learn the exceptions to the rules, which they generally do by early school age.

Classic Theories of Language Acquisition: The Nature-Nurture Debate

Is linguistic ability learned or inborn? In the 1950s, a debate raged between two schools of thought: one led by B. F. Skinner, the foremost proponent of learning theory, the other by the linguist Noam Chomsky.

Skinner (1957) maintained that language learning, like other learning, is based on experience and that children learn language through operant conditioning. Word learning depends on selective reinforcement; the word *kitty* is reinforced only when the family cat appears. As this process continues, children are reinforced for speech that is more and more adultlike.

Observation, imitation, and reinforcement do contribute to language development, but, as Chomsky (1957) persuasively argued, they cannot fully explain it (Flavell, Miller, & Miller, 1993; Owens, 1996). For one thing, word combinations and nuances are so many and so complex that they cannot all be acquired by specific imitation and reinforcement. Then, caregivers often reinforce utterances that are not strictly grammatical, as long as they make sense. ("Gampa go bye-bye.") Adult speech itself is an unreliable model to imitate, as it is often ungrammatical

Checkpoint

Can you . . .

◆ Trace a typical sequence of milestones in early language development?

◆ Describe five ways in which early speech differs from adult speech?

and contains false starts, unfinished sentences, and slips of the tongue. Also, learning theory does not account for children's imaginative ways of saying things they have never heard—as when 2-year-old Anna described a sprained ankle as a "sprangle" and said she didn't want to go to sleep yet because she wasn't "yawny."

Chomsky's view is called **nativism.** Unlike Skinner's learning theory, nativism emphasizes the active role of the learner. Because language is universal among human beings, Chomsky (1957, 1972, 1995) proposed that the human brain has an innate capacity for acquiring language; babies learn to talk as naturally as they learn to walk. He suggested that an inborn **language acquisition device (LAD)** programs children's brains to analyze the language they hear and to figure out its rules.

Is linguistic ability learned or inborn? Though inborn language capacity may underlie this baby's ability to speak, when this father repeats the sounds his baby makes he is reinforcing the likelihood the baby will repeat those sounds—highlighting the influences of both nature and nurture.

Support for the nativist position comes from newborns' ability to differentiate similar sounds, suggesting that they are born with perceptual "tuning rods" that pick up characteristics of speech. Nativists point out that almost all children master their native language in the same age-related sequence without formal teaching. Furthermore, the brains of human beings, the only animals with fully developed language, contain a structure that is larger on one side than on the other, suggesting that an inborn mechanism for sound and language processing may be localized in the larger hemisphere—the left for most people (Gannon, Holloway, Broadfield, & Braun, 1998). Still, the nativist approach does not explain precisely how such a mechanism operates. It does not tell us why some children acquire language more rapidly and efficiently than others, why children differ in linguistic skill and fluency, or why (as we'll see) speech development appears to depend on having someone to talk with, not merely on hearing spoken language.

Aspects of both learning theory and nativism have been used to explain how deaf babies learn sign language, which is structured much like spoken language and is acquired in the same sequence. Deaf babies of deaf parents seem to copy the sign language they see their parents using, just as hearing babies copy vocal utterances. Using hand motions more systematic and deliberate than those of hearing babies, deaf babies first string together meaningless motions and repeat them over and over in what has been called *hand-babbling* (Petitto & Marentette, 1991). As parents reinforce these gestures, the babies attach meaning to them.

However, deaf children of hearing parents make up their own sign language when they do not have models to follow—evidence that imitation and reinforcement alone cannot explain the emergence of linguistic expression (Goldin-Meadow & Mylander, 1998; Hoff, 2006). Since the 1970s, successive waves of Nicaraguan deaf schoolchildren who were being taught only lip-reading in Spanish have developed a true sign language, which has gradually evolved from simple gestures into words and sentences that follow linguistic rules (Senghas & Coppola, 2001; Senghas, Kita, & Ozyürek, 2004). Likewise, Al-Sayyid Bedouin Sign Language, which evolved spontaneously in an isolated village in Israel's Negev desert, has a distinct, systematic grammatical structure unlike that of

nativism Theory that human beings have an inborn capacity for language acquisition.

language acquisition device (LAD) In Chomsky's terminology, an inborn mechanism that enables children to infer linguistic rules from the language they hear.

Israeli Sign Language or of the Arabic dialect spoken by hearing members of the community (Sandler, Meir, Padden, & Aronoff, 2005).

Furthermore, learning theory does not explain the correspondence between the ages at which linguistic advances in both hearing and nonhearing babies typically occur (Padden, 1996; Petitto, Katerelos, et al., 2001; Petitto & Kovelman, 2003). Deaf babies begin hand-babbling between ages 7 and 10 months, about the age when hearing infants begin voice-babbling (Petitto, Holowka, et al., 2001; Petitto & Marentette, 1991). Deaf babies also begin to use sentences in sign language at about the same time that hearing babies begin to speak in sentences (Meier, 1991; Newport & Meier, 1985). These observations suggest that an inborn language capacity may underlie the acquisition of both spoken and signed language and that advances in both kinds of language are tied to brain maturation.

Most developmental scientists today maintain that language acquisition, like most other aspects of development, depends on an intertwining of nature and nurture. Children, whether hearing or deaf, probably have an inborn capacity to acquire language, which may be activated or constrained by experience.

Influences on Early Language Development

What determines how quickly and how well children learn to understand and use language? Research has focused on both neurological and environmental influences.

Brain Development   The tremendous brain growth during the early months and years is closely linked with language development. A newborn's cries are controlled by the *brain stem* and *pons,* the most primitive parts of the brain and the earliest to develop (refer back to Figure 4-8). Repetitive babbling may emerge with the maturation of parts of the *motor cortex,* which control movements of the face and larynx. A brain imaging study points to the emergence of a link between the brain's phonetic perception and motor systems as early as 6 months—a connection that strengthens by 6 to 12 months (Imada et al., 2006). The development of language actively affects brain networks, committing them to the recognition of native language sounds only (Kuhl, 2004; Kuhl et al., 2005). Cortical regions associated with language continue to develop until at least the late preschool years or beyond—some, even until adulthood.

In about 98 percent of people, the left hemisphere is dominant for language, though the right hemisphere participates as well (Nobre & Plunkett, 1997; Owens, 1996). Studies of babbling babies show that the mouth opens more on the right side than on the left. Since the left hemisphere of the brain controls activity on the right side of the body, lateralization of linguistic functions apparently takes place very early in life (Holowka & Petitto, 2002). Language lateralization increases into young adulthood, enabling continued growth in language skills (Szaflarski, Holland, Schmithorst, & Weber-Byars, 2004).

Social Interaction: The Role of Parents and Caregivers   Language is a social act. It takes not only the necessary biological machinery and cognitive capacity but also interaction with a communicative partner. Children who grow up without normal social contact do not develop language normally. Neither do children who are exposed to language only through television. Parents or other caregivers play an important role at each stage of language development. They do so (1) by providing *opportunities for communicative experience,* which motivate babies to learn language, and (2) by providing *models of language use* (Hoff, 2006).

✔ **Checkpoint**

Can you . . .

◆ Summarize how learning theory and nativism seek to explain language acquisition, and point out strengths and weaknesses of each theory?

◆ Discuss implications of how deaf babies acquire language?

As Bronfenbrenner's bioecological model would predict, the age of parents or caregivers, the way they interact with and talk with an infant, the child's birth order, child care experience, and, later, schooling, peers, and television exposure all affect the pace and course of language acquisition. So does the wider culture. The milestones of language development described in this chapter are typical of Western, middle-class children who are spoken to directly. They are not necessarily typical in all cultures, nor at all socioeconomic levels (Hoff, 2006).

Prelinguistic Period At the babbling stage, adults help an infant advance toward true speech by repeating the sounds the baby makes. The baby soon joins in the game and repeats the sounds back. Parents' imitation of babies' sounds affects the amount of infant vocalization (Goldstein, King, & West, 2003) and the pace of language learning (Hardy-Brown & Plomin, 1985; Hardy-Brown, Plomin, & DeFries, 1981). It also helps babies experience the social aspect of speech (Kuhl, 2004). As early as 4 months, babies in a game of peekaboo show sensitivity to the structure of social exchange with an adult (Rochat, Querido, & Striano, 1999; refer back to Box 5-1).

Vocabulary Development When babies begin to talk, parents or caregivers can boost vocabulary development by repeating their first words and pronouncing them correctly. Joint attention, discussed earlier in this chapter, leads to more rapid vocabulary development (Hoff, 2006). In one

Bilingual children often use elements of both languages, but this doesn't mean they confuse the two languages.

longitudinal study, mothers' responsiveness to 9-month-olds' and, even more so, to 13-month-olds' vocalization and play predicted the timing of language milestones, such as first spoken words and sentences (Tamis-LeMonda, Bornstein, & Baumwell, 2001).

A strong relationship exists between the frequency of specific words in mothers' speech and the order in which children learn these words (Huttenlocher, Haight, Bryk, Seltzer, & Lyons, 1991) as well as between mothers' talkativeness and the size of toddlers' vocabularies (Huttenlocher, 1998). Mothers with higher socioeconomic status tend to use richer vocabularies and longer utterances, and their 2-year-olds have larger spoken vocabularies—as much as eight times as large as those of low-SES children the same age (Hoff, 2003; C. T. Ramey & Ramey, 2003). By age 3, vocabularies of low-income children vary greatly, depending in large part on the diversity of word types they have heard their mothers use (Pan, Rowe, Singer, & Snow, 2005).

Parental sensitivity and responsiveness may count even more than the number of words a mother uses. In a yearlong study of 290 low-income families of 2-year-olds, both parents' sensitivity, positive regard for the child, and the cognitive stimulation they provided during play predicted the child's receptive vocabulary and cognitive development at ages 2 and 3 (Tamis-LeMonda et al., 2004).

In households where more than one language is spoken, babies achieve similar milestones in each language on the same schedule as children who hear only one language (Petitto, Katerelos, et al., 2001; Petitto & Kovelman, 2003). However, children learning two languages tend to have smaller vocabularies in each language than children learning only one language (Hoff, 2006). Bilingual children often use elements of both languages, sometimes in the same utterance—a phenomenon called **code mixing** (Petitto, Katerelos, et al., 2001; Petitto & Kovelman, 2003). In Montreal, children as young as 2 in dual-language households differentiate between the two languages, using French with a predominantly French-speaking father and English with a predominantly English-speaking mother (Genesee, Nicoladis, & Paradis, 1995). This ability to shift from one language to another is called **code switching**.

Child-Directed Speech You do not have to be a parent to speak *parentese*. If, when you talk to an infant or toddler, you speak slowly in a high-pitched voice with exaggerated ups and downs, simplify your speech, exaggerate vowel sounds, and use short words and sentences and much repetition, you are engaging in **child-directed speech (CDS),** sometimes called *parentese* or *motherese*. Most adults and even children do it naturally. Such baby talk has been documented in many languages and cultures. In one observational study, mothers in the United States, Russia, and Sweden were taped speaking to their 2- to 5-month-old infants. Whether the mothers were speaking English, Russian, or Swedish, they produced more exaggerated vowel sounds when talking to the infants than when talking to other adults. At 20 weeks, the babies' babbling contained distinct vowels that reflected phonetic differences in their mothers' speech (Kuhl et al., 1997).

By reading aloud to his young daughter and asking questions about the pictures in the book, this father is helping her build language skills and learn how letters look and sound.

code mixing Use of elements of two languages, sometimes in the same utterance, by young children in households where both languages are spoken.

code switching Changing one's speech to match the situation, as in people who are bilingual.

child-directed speech (CDS) Form of speech often used in talking to babies or toddlers; includes slow, simplified speech, a high-pitched tone, exaggerated vowel sounds, short words and sentences, and much repetition; also called *parentese* or *motherese*.

literacy Ability to read and write.

Many researchers believe that CDS helps infants learn their native language or at least pick it up faster by exaggerating and directing attention to the distinguishing features of speech sounds (Kuhl et al., 2005). Other investigators challenge the value of CDS. They contend that babies speak sooner and better if they hear and can respond to more complex adult speech. In fact, some researchers say, children discover the rules of language faster when they hear complex sentences that use these rules more often and in more ways (Oshima-Takane, Goodz, & Derevensky, 1996). Nonetheless, infants themselves prefer to hear simplified speech. This preference is clear before 1 month and it does not seem to depend on any specific experience (Cooper & Aslin, 1990; Kuhl et al., 1997; Werker, Pegg, & McLeod, 1994).

Preparing for Literacy: The Benefits of Reading Aloud

Most babies love to be read to. The frequency with which caregivers read to them can influence how well children speak and eventually how well and how soon they develop **literacy**—the ability to read and write. In a study of 2,581 low-income families, about half of the mothers reported reading daily to their preschool children between 14 months and 3 years. Children who had been read to daily had better cognitive and language skills at age 3 (Raikes et al., 2006).

The way parents or caregivers read to children makes a difference. Adults tend to have one of three styles of reading to children: the *describer style, comprehender style*, and *performance-oriented style*. A *describer* focuses on describing what is going on in the pictures and inviting the child to do so ("What are the Mom and Dad having for breakfast?"). A *comprehender* encourages the child to look more deeply at the meaning of a story and to make inferences and predictions ("What do you think the lion will do now?"). A *performance-oriented* reader reads the story straight through, introducing the main themes beforehand and asking questions afterward. An adult's read-aloud style is best tailored to the needs and skills of the child. In an experimental study of 50 four-year-olds in Dunedin, New Zealand, the describer style resulted in the greatest overall benefits for vocabulary and print skills, but the performance-oriented style was more beneficial for children who started out with large vocabularies (Reese & Cox, 1999).

One promising technique is *dialogic, or shared, reading*. In this method (Whitehurst & Lonigan, 1998) parents ask challenging, open-ended questions rather than those calling for a simple yes or no ("What is the cat doing?" instead of "Is the cat asleep?"). They follow up the child's answers with more questions, repeat and expand on what the child says, correct wrong answers and give alternative possibilities, help the child as needed, and give praise and encouragement. They encourage the child to relate a story to the child's own experience ("Have you ever seen a duck swimming? What did it look like?").

Children who are read to often, especially in this way, when they are 1 to 3 years old, show better language skills at ages 2 to 5 and better reading comprehension at age 7 than do their peers (Crain-Thoreson & Dale, 1992; Wells, 1985). However, dialogic reading does not come naturally to most parents, according to a study of 120 rural families with 2- and 3-year-olds. Small-group instruction increased parents' use of the method more than fourfold and had significant positive effects on children's vocabulary and language use (Huebner & Meltzoff, 2005).

Social interaction in reading aloud, play, and other daily activities is a key to much of childhood development. Children call forth responses from the people around them and, in turn, react to those responses. In Chapter 6, we look more closely at these bidirectional influences as we explore early psychosocial development.

Checkpoint

Can you . . .

- Name areas of the brain involved in early language development, and tell the function of each?

- Give evidence of plasticity in the brain's linguistic areas?

- Explain the importance of social interaction, and give at least three examples of how parents or caregivers help babies learn to talk?

- Assess the arguments for and against the value of child-directed speech (CDS)?

- Tell why reading aloud to children at an early age is beneficial, and describe an effective way of doing so?

Summary and Key Terms

Studying Cognitive Development: Six Approaches

Guidepost 1: *What are six approaches to the study of cognitive development?*

- Six approaches to the study of cognitive development are behaviorist, psychometric, Piagetian, information processing, cognitive neuroscience, and social-contextual.

- All of these approaches can shed light on how early cognition develops.

    behaviorist approach (140)

    psychometric approach (140)

    Piagetian approach (140)

    information-processing approach (140)

    cognitive neuroscience approach (140)

    social-contextual approach (140)

Behaviorist Approach: Basic Mechanics of Learning

Guidepost 2: *How do infants learn, and how long can they remember?*

- Two simple types of learning that behaviorists study are classical conditioning and operant conditioning.

- Rovee-Collier's research suggests that infants' memory processes are much like those of adults, though this conclusion has been questioned. Infants' memories can be jogged by periodic reminders.

classical conditioning (141)

operant conditioning (141)

Psychometric Approach: Developmental and Intelligence Testing

Guidepost 3: *Can infants' and toddlers' intelligence be measured, and how can it be improved?*

- Psychometric tests measure factors presumed to make up intelligence.
- Developmental tests, such as the Bayley Scales of Infant and Toddler Development, can indicate current functioning but are generally poor predictors of later intelligence.
- The home environment may affect measured intelligence.
- If the home environment does not provide the necessary conditions that pave the way for cognitive competence, early intervention may be needed.

intelligent behavior (143)

IQ (intelligence quotient) tests (143)

developmental tests (143)

Bayley Scales of Infant and Toddler Development (143)

Home Observation for Measurement of the Environment (HOME) (144)

early intervention (145)

Piagetian Approach: The Sensorimotor Stage

Guidepost 4: *How did Piaget explain early cognitive development?*

- During Piaget's sensorimotor stage, infants' schemes become more elaborate. They progress from primary to secondary to tertiary circular reactions and finally to the development of representational ability, which makes possible deferred imitation, pretending, and problem solving.
- Object permanence develops gradually, according to Piaget, and is not fully operational until 18 to 24 months.
- Research suggests that a number of abilities, including imitation and object permanence, develop earlier than Piaget described.

sensorimotor stage (146)

schemes (147)

circular reactions (147)

representational ability (149)

invisible imitation (150)

visible imitation (150)

deferred imitation (150)

elicited imitation (150)

object permanence (151)

dual representation hypothesis (153)

Information-Processing Approach; Perceptions and Representations

Guidepost 5: *How can we measure infants' ability to process information, and when do infants begin to understand characteristics of the physical world?*

- Information-processing researchers measure mental processes through habituation and other signs of visual and perceptual abilities. Contrary to Piaget's ideas, such research suggests that representational ability is present virtually from birth.
- Indicators of the efficiency of infants' information processing, such as speed of habituation, tend to predict later intelligence.
- Such information-processing research techniques as habituation, novelty preference, and the violation-of-expectations method have yielded evidence that infants as young as 3 to 6 months may have a rudimentary grasp of such Piagetian abilities as categorization, causality, object permanence, a sense of number, and an ability to reason about characteristics of the physical world. Some researchers suggest that infants may have innate learning mechanisms for acquiring such knowledge. However, the meaning of these findings is in dispute.

habituation (154)

dishabituation (155)

visual preference (155)

visual recognition memory (155)

cross-modal transfer (156)

violation-of-expectations (160)

Cognitive Neuroscience Approach: The Brain's Cognitive Structures

Guidepost 6: *What can brain research reveal about the development of cognitive skills?*

- Explicit memory and implicit memory are located in different brain structures.
- Working memory emerges between 6 and 12 months of age.
- Neurological developments help explain the emergence of Piagetian skills and memory abilities.

implicit memory (161)

explicit memory (161)

working memory (161)

Social-Contextual Approach: Learning from Interactions with Caregivers

Guidepost 7: *How does social interaction with adults advance cognitive competence?*

- Social interactions with adults contribute to cognitive competence through shared activities that help children learn skills, knowledge, and values important in their culture.

guided participation (162)

Language Development

Guidepost 8: *How do babies develop language, and what influences contribute to linguistic progress?*

- The acquisition of language is an important aspect of cognitive development.

- Prelinguistic speech includes crying, cooing, babbling, and imitating language sounds. By 6 months, babies have learned the basic sounds of their language and have begun to link sound with meaning. Perception of categories of sounds in the native language may commit the neural circuitry to further learning in that language only.

- Before they say their first word, babies use gestures.

- The first word typically comes sometime between 10 and 14 months, initiating linguistic speech. For many toddlers, a naming explosion occurs sometime between 16 and 24 months.

- The first brief sentences generally come between 18 and 24 months. By age 3, syntax and communicative abilities are fairly well developed.

- Early speech is characterized by oversimplification, underextending and overextending word meanings, and overregularizing rules.

- Two classic theoretical views about how children acquire language are learning theory and nativism. Today, most developmental scientists hold that an inborn capacity to learn language may be activated or constrained by experience.

- Influences on language development include neural maturation and social interaction.

- Family characteristics, such as socioeconomic status, adult language use, and maternal responsiveness, affect a child's vocabulary development.

- Children who hear two languages at home generally learn both at the same rate as children who hear only one language, and they can use each language in appropriate circumstances.

- Child-directed speech (CDS) seems to have cognitive, emotional, and social benefits, and infants show a preference for it. However, some researchers dispute its value.

- Reading aloud to a child from an early age helps pave the way for literacy.

language (163)

prelinguistic speech (163)

linguistic speech (166)

holophrase (166)

telegraphic speech (167)

syntax (167)

nativism (169)

language acquisition device (LAD) (169)

code mixing (172)

code switching (172)

child-directed speech (CDS) (172)

literacy (172)

I'm like a child

trying to do everything

say everything

and be everything

all at once

—John Hartford, "Life Prayer," 1971

Did You **Know...**

- Pride, shame, and guilt are among the last emotions to develop?

- Altruistic behavior is fairly common among toddlers?

- In certain cultures infants typically receive care from five or more people in a given hour and are routinely breast-fed by women other than the mother?

- The "terrible twos" does not exist as a stage of development in some cultures?

- Conflict with siblings or playmates can help toddlers learn to negotiate and resolve disputes?

- The impact of parental employment and early child care is much less than that of family characteristics, such as a mother's sensitivity to her child?

These are just a few of the interesting and important topics we will cover in this chapter. In it, we trace the shift from the dependence of infancy to the independence of childhood. We first examine foundations of psychosocial development: emotions, temperament, gender, and early experiences with parents. We consider Erikson's views about the development of trust and autonomy. We look at relationships with caregivers, at the emerging sense of self, and at the foundations of conscience. We explore relationships with siblings and other children. Then, we consider the increasingly widespread impact of parental employment and early child care. Finally, we discuss child abuse and neglect, which are most common in infancy and toddlerhood, and what can be done to protect children from harm. After you have studied this chapter, you should be able to answer each of the Guidepost questions on the following page.

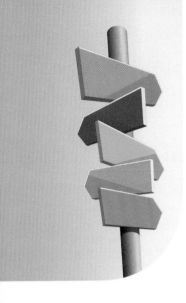

Guideposts *for Study*

1. When and how do emotions develop, and how do babies show them?

2. How do infants show temperamental differences, and how enduring are those differences?

3. What roles do mothers and fathers play in early personality development?

4. When and how do gender differences appear?

5. How do infants gain trust in their world and form attachments, and how do infants and caregivers read each other's nonverbal signals?

6. When and how does the sense of self arise, and how do toddlers exercise autonomy and develop standards for socially acceptable behavior?

7. How do infants and toddlers interact with siblings and other children?

8. How do parental employment and early child care affect infants' and toddlers' development?

9. What are the causes and consequences of child abuse and neglect, and what can be done about them?

Guidepost 1

When and how do emotions develop, and how do babies show them?

personality The relatively consistent blend of emotions, temperament, thought, and behavior that makes a person unique.

emotions Subjective reactions to experience that are associated with physiological and behavioral changes.

Foundations of Psychosocial Development

Although babies share common patterns of development, each, from the start, shows a distinct **personality:** the relatively consistent blend of emotions, temperament, thought, and behavior that makes each person unique (Eisenberg, Fabes, Guthrie, & Reiser, 2000). One baby may usually be cheerful; another easily upset. One toddler plays happily with other children; another prefers to play alone. Such characteristic ways of feeling, thinking, and acting, which reflect both inborn and environmental influences, affect the way children respond to others and adapt to their world. From infancy on, personality development is intertwined with social relationships (Table 6-1); and this combination is called *psychosocial development.*

In our exploration of psychosocial development we'll first look at emotions, the building blocks of personality; then at temperament, or disposition; and then at an infant's earliest social experiences in the family. Then, we'll discuss how parents shape behavioral differences between boys and girls.

Emotions

Emotions, such as sadness, joy, and fear, are subjective reactions to experience that are associated with physiological and behavioral changes (Sroufe, 1997). People differ in how often they feel a particular emotion, in the kinds of events that may produce it, in the physical manifestations they show, and in how they act as a result. Culture influences the way people feel about a situation and the way they show their emotions. For example, some Asian cultures, which stress social harmony, discourage expression of anger but place much importance on shame. The opposite is often true in American culture, which stresses self-expression, self-assertion, and self-esteem (Cole, Bruschi, & Tamang, 2002).

Table 6-1	Highlights of Infants' and Toddlers' Psychosocial Development, Birth to 36 Months

Approximate Age, Months	Characteristics
0–3	Infants are open to stimulation. They begin to show interest and curiosity, and they smile readily at people.
3–6	Infants can anticipate what is about to happen and experience disappointment when it does not. They show this by becoming angry or acting warily. They smile, coo, and laugh often. This is a time of social awakening and early reciprocal exchanges between the baby and the caregiver.
6–9	Infants play social games and try to get responses from people. They talk to, touch, and cajole other babies to get them to respond. They express more differentiated emotions, showing joy, fear, anger, and surprise.
9–12	Infants are intensely preoccupied with their principal caregiver, may become afraid of strangers, and act subdued in new situations. By 1 year, they communicate emotions more clearly, showing moods, ambivalence, and gradations of feeling.
12–18	Toddlers explore their environment, using the people they are most attached to as a secure base. As they master the environment, they become more confident and more eager to assert themselves.
18–36	Toddlers sometimes become anxious because they now realize how much they are separating from their caregivers. They work out their awareness of their limitations in fantasy and in play and by identifying with adults.

Source: Adapted from Sroufe, 1979.

First Signs of Emotion   There is no mistaking when a newborn is unhappy—she lets out piercing cries, flails her arms and legs, and stiffens her body. It is harder to tell when she is happy. During the first month, newborns typically become quiet at the sound of a human voice or when they are picked up. They may smile when their hands are moved together to play pat-a-cake. As time goes by, infants respond more to people—smiling, cooing, reaching out, and eventually going to them.

These early signals or clues to babies' feelings are important indicators of development. When babies want or need something, they cry; when they feel sociable, they smile or laugh. When their messages bring a response, their sense of connection with other people grows. Their sense of control over their world grows, too, as they see that their cries bring help and comfort and that their smiles and laughter elicit smiles and laughter in return. They become more able to participate actively in regulating their states of arousal and their emotional life.

Crying   Crying is the most powerful way—and sometimes the only way—infants can communicate their needs. Some research has distinguished four patterns of crying (Wolff, 1969): the basic *hunger cry* (a rhythmic cry, which is not always associated with hunger); the *angry cry* (a variation of the rhythmic cry, in which excess air is forced through the vocal cords); the *pain cry* (a sudden onset of loud crying without preliminary moaning, sometimes followed by holding the breath); and the *frustration cry* (two or three drawn-out cries, with no prolonged breath-holding) (Wood & Gustafson, 2001).

Some parents worry that constantly picking up a crying baby will spoil the infant. In one study, delays in responding to fussing did seem to reduce fussing during the first six months, perhaps because the babies learned to deal with minor irritations on their own (Hubbard & van IJzendoorn, 1991). However, if parents wait until cries of distress escalate to shrieks of rage, it may become more difficult

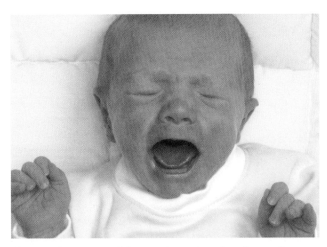

Crying is the most powerful way, and sometimes the only way, that babies can communicate their needs. Parents may soon learn to recognize whether their baby is crying because of hunger, anger, frustration, or pain.

to soothe the baby; and such a pattern, if experienced repeatedly, may interfere with an infant's developing ability to regulate, or manage, his or her own emotional state (R. A. Thompson, 1991). Ideally, the most developmentally sound approach may be to *prevent* distress, making soothing unnecessary.

Smiling and Laughing   The earliest faint smiles occur spontaneously soon after birth, apparently as a result of subcortical nervous system activity. These involuntary smiles frequently appear during periods of REM sleep (refer back to Chapter 4). They become less frequent during the first three months as the cortex matures (Sroufe, 1997).

The earliest *waking* smiles may be elicited by mild sensations, such as gentle jiggling or blowing on the infant's skin. In the second week, a baby may smile drowsily after a feeding. By the third week, most infants begin to smile when they are alert and paying attention to a caregiver's nodding head and voice. At about 1 month, smiles generally become more frequent and more social. During the second month, as visual recognition develops, babies smile more at visual stimuli, such as faces they know (Sroufe, 1997; Wolff, 1963).

By the fourth month, infants laugh out loud when kissed on the stomach or tickled. As babies grow older, they become more actively engaged in joyful exchanges. A 6-month-old may giggle in response to the mother making unusual sounds or appearing with a towel over her face; a 10-month-old may laughingly try to put the towel back on her face when it falls off. This change reflects cognitive development: By laughing at the unexpected, babies show that they know what to expect. By turning the tables, they show awareness that they can make things happen. Laughter also helps babies release tension, such as fear of a threatening object (Sroufe, 1997).

When Do Emotions Appear?   Emotional development is an orderly process in which complex emotions unfold from simpler ones. According to one widely used model of emotional development (Lewis, 1997; Figure 6-1), soon after birth babies show signs of contentment, interest, and distress. These are diffuse, reflexive, mostly physiological responses to sensory stimulation or internal processes. During the next six months or so, these early emotional states differentiate into true emotions: joy, surprise, sadness, disgust, and then anger and fear—reactions to events that have meaning for the infant. As we discuss in a subsequent section, the emergence of these basic, or primary, emotions is related to the biological clock of neurological maturation.

Self-conscious emotions, such as embarrassment, empathy, and envy, arise only after children have developed **self-awareness:** the cognitive understanding that they have a recognizable identity, separate and different from the rest of their world. This consciousness of self seems to emerge between 15 and 24 months. Self-awareness is necessary before children can be aware of being the focus of attention, identify with what other "selves" are feeling, or wish they had what someone else has.

By about age 3, having acquired self-awareness plus a good deal of knowledge about their society's accepted standards, rules, and goals, children become better able to evaluate their own thoughts, plans, desires, and behavior against what is considered socially appropriate. Only then can they demonstrate the **self-evaluative emotions** of pride, guilt, and shame (Lewis, 1995, 1997, 1998).

✔ **Checkpoint**

Can you . . .

◆ Explain the significance of patterns of crying, smiling, and laughing?

self-conscious emotions Emotions, such as embarrassment, empathy, and envy, that depend on self-awareness.

self-awareness Realization that one's existence and functioning are separate from those of other people and things.

self-evaluative emotions Emotions, such as pride, shame, and guilt, that depend on both self-awareness and knowledge of socially accepted standards of behavior.

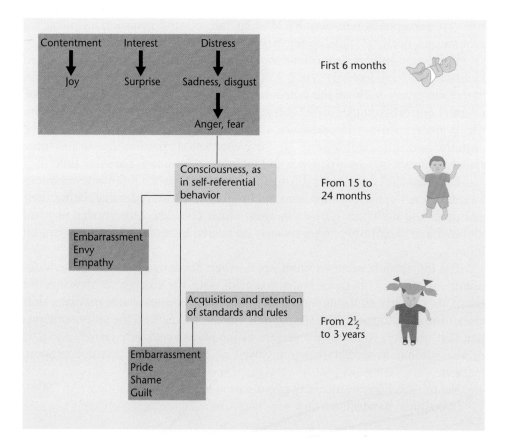

Contentment | Interest | Distress
Joy | Surprise | Sadness, disgust

Anger, fear

First 6 months

Consciousness, as in self-referential behavior

From 15 to 24 months

Embarrassment
Envy
Empathy

Acquisition and retention of standards and rules

From 2½ to 3 years

Embarrassment
Pride
Shame
Guilt

FIGURE 6-1

Differentiation of emotions during the first three years. The primary, or basic, emotions emerge during the first six months or so; the self-conscious emotions develop beginning in the second year, as a result of the emergence of self-awareness together with accumulation of knowledge about societal standards. *Note:* There are two kind of embarrassment. The earlier kind does not involve evaluation of behavior and may simply be a response to being singled out as the object of attention. The second kind, evaluative embarrassment, which emerges during the third year, is a mild form of shame. (Source: Adapted from Lewis, 1997.)

Empathy and Altruistic Helping A guest of 18-month-old Alex's father, whom Alex has never seen before, dropped his pen on the floor, and it rolled under a cabinet, where he couldn't quite reach it. Alex, being small enough, crawled under the cabinet, retrieved the pen, and gave it to the guest. By acting out of concern for a stranger with no expectation of reward, Alex showed *altruistic behavior* (Warneken & Tomasello, 2006).

Altruistic behavior like Alex's is fairly common. In one experiment, 18-month-old toddlers helped in 6 out of 10 situations in which the experimenter was having trouble reaching a goal, but did not help in similar situations in which the experimenter did *not* seem to be having trouble—for example, when he had dropped a pen deliberately. Such behaviors may reflect **empathy,** a growing ability to imagine how another person might feel in a particular situation (Zahn-Waxler, Radke-Yarrow, Wagner, & Chapman, 1992). This ability to "put oneself in another person's place" seems to arise during the second year and increases with age (Eisenberg, 2000; Eisenberg & Fabes, 1998).

empathy Ability to put oneself in another person's place and feel what the other person feels.

Brain Growth and Emotional Development The development of the brain after birth is closely connected with changes in emotional life: Emotional experiences not only are affected by brain development but also can have long-lasting effects on the structure of the brain (Mlot, 1998; Sroufe, 1997).

Four major shifts in brain organization roughly correspond to changes in emotional processing (Schore, 1994; Sroufe, 1997; refer back to Figure 4-8). During the first three months, differentiation of basic emotions begins as the *cerebral cortex* becomes functional, bringing

Children who do not live up to behavioral standards may feel guilty and try to make amends by cleaning up after they've spilled. Guilt is thought to develop between ages 2½ and 3.

cognitive perceptions into play. REM sleep and reflexive behavior, including the spontaneous neonatal smile, diminish.

The second shift occurs around 9 or 10 months, when the *frontal lobes* begin to interact with the *limbic system,* a seat of emotional reactions. At the same time, limbic structures such as the *hippocampus* become larger and more adultlike. Connections between the frontal cortex and the *hypothalamus* and limbic system, which process sensory information, may facilitate the relationship between the cognitive and emotional spheres. As these connections become denser and more elaborate, an infant can experience and interpret emotions at the same time.

The third shift takes place during the second year, when infants develop self-awareness, self-conscious emotions, and a greater capacity for regulating their emotions and activities. These changes, which coincide with greater physical mobility and exploratory behavior, may be related to myelination of the frontal lobes.

The fourth shift occurs around age 3, when hormonal changes in the autonomic (involuntary) nervous system coincide with the emergence of evaluative emotions. Underlying the development of such emotions as shame may be a shift away from dominance by the *sympathetic system,* the part of the autonomic system that prepares the body for action, as the *parasympathetic system,* the part of the autonomic system that is involved in excretion and sexual excitation, matures.

Neurological factors also may play a part in temperamental differences (Mlot, 1998), the topic to which we turn next.

Temperament

Temperament is sometimes defined as a person's characteristic, biologically based way of approaching and reacting to people and situations. Temperament has been described as the *how* of behavior: not *what* people do, but *how* they go about doing it (Thomas & Chess, 1977). Two toddlers, for example, may be equally able to dress themselves and may be equally motivated, but one may do it more quickly than the other, be more willing to put on a new outfit, and be less distracted if the cat jumps on the bed. Some researchers look at temperament more broadly. A child may not act the same way in all situations. Also, temperament may affect not only the way children approach and react to the outside world, but the way they regulate their mental, emotional, and behavioral functioning (Rothbart, Ahadi, & Evans, 2000).

Temperament has an emotional dimension; but, unlike emotions such as fear, excitement, and boredom, which come and go, temperament is relatively consistent and enduring. Individual differences in temperament, which are thought to derive from a person's basic biological makeup, form the core of the developing personality.

Studying Temperamental Patterns: The New York Longitudinal Study To better appreciate how temperament affects behavior, let's look at three sisters. Amy, the eldest, was a cheerful, calm baby who ate, slept, and eliminated at regular times. She greeted each day and most people with a smile, and the only sign that she was awake during the night was the tinkle of the musical toy in her crib. When Brooke, the middle sister, woke up, she would open her mouth to cry before she even opened her eyes. She slept and ate little and irregularly; she laughed and cried loudly, often bursting into tantrums; and she had to be convinced that new people and new experiences were not threatening before she would have anything to do with them. The youngest sister, Christina, was mild in her responses, both

Checkpoint

Can you . . .

♦ Trace a typical sequence of emergence of the basic, self-conscious, and evaluative emotions, and explain its connection with cognitive and neurological development?

Guidepost 2

How do infants show temperamental differences, and how enduring are those differences?

temperament Characteristic disposition, or style of approaching and reacting to situations.

Table 6-2	Three Temperamental Patterns (according to the New York Longitudinal Study)		
"Easy" Child	**"Difficult" Child**	**"Slow-to-Warm-Up" Child**
Has moods of mild to moderate intensity, usually positive.	Displays intense and frequently negative moods; cries often and loudly; also laughs loudly.	Has mildly intense reactions, both positive and negative.
Responds well to novelty and change.	Responds poorly to novelty and change.	Responds slowly to novelty and change.
Quickly develops regular sleep and feeding schedules.	Sleeps and eats irregularly.	Sleeps and eats more regularly than the difficult child, less regularly than the easy child.
Takes to new foods easily.	Accepts new foods slowly.	Shows mildly negative initial response to new stimuli (a first encounter with a new food, person, place, or situation).
Smiles at strangers.	Is suspicious of strangers.	
Adapts easily to new situations.	Adapts slowly to new situations.	
Accepts most frustrations with little fuss.	Reacts to frustration with tantrums.	
Adapts quickly to new routines and rules of new games.	Adjusts slowly to new routines.	Gradually develops liking for new stimuli after repeated, unpressured exposures.

Source: Adapted from Thomas, A. and S. Chess, "Genesis and evolution of behavioral disorders: From infancy to early adult life." *American Journal of Psychiatry,* 141 (1) 1984, pp. 1–9. Copyright (c) 1984 by the American Psychiatric Association. Reproduced with permission.

positive and negative. She did not like most new situations, but if allowed to proceed at her own slow pace, she would eventually become interested and involved.

Amy, Brooke, and Christina exemplify the three main types of temperament found by the New York Longitudinal Study (NYLS). In this pioneering study on temperament, researchers followed 133 infants into adulthood. The researchers looked at how active the children were; how regular their hunger, sleep, and bowel habits were; how readily they accepted new people and situations; how they adapted to changes in routine; how sensitive they were to noise, bright lights, and other sensory stimuli; how intensely they responded; whether their mood tended to be pleasant, joyful, and friendly or unpleasant, unhappy, and unfriendly; and whether they persisted at tasks or were easily distracted (A. Thomas, Chess, & Birch, 1968).

The researchers were able to place most of the children in the study into one of three categories (Table 6-2).

- Forty percent were **"easy" children** like Amy: generally happy, rhythmic in biological functioning, and accepting of new experiences.

- Ten percent were what the researchers called **"difficult" children** like Brooke: more irritable and harder to please, irregular in biological rhythms, and more intense in expressing emotion.

- Fifteen percent were **"slow-to-warm-up" children** like Christina: mild but slow to adapt to new people and situations (A. Thomas & Chess, 1977, 1984).

Many children (including 35 percent of the NYLS sample) do not fit neatly into any of these three categories. A baby may eat and sleep regularly but be afraid of strangers. A child may be easy most of the time, but not always. Another child may warm up slowly to new foods but adapt quickly to new babysitters (A. Thomas & Chess, 1984). A child may laugh intensely but not show intense frustration, and a child with rhythmic toilet habits may show irregular sleeping patterns (Rothbart et al., 2000). All these variations are normal.

"easy" children Children with a generally happy temperament, regular biological rhythms, and a readiness to accept new experiences.

"difficult" children Children with irritable temperament, irregular biological rhythms, and intense emotional responses.

"slow-to-warm-up" children Children whose temperament is generally mild but who are hesitant about accepting new experiences.

Tyrell's ready smile and excitement about new experiences, such as walking, are signs of an easy temperament.

goodness of fit Appropriateness of environmental demands and constraints to a child's temperament.

How Stable Is Temperament? Temperament appears to be largely inborn, probably hereditary (Braungart, Plomin, DeFries, & Fulker, 1992; Emde et al., 1992; Schmitz et al., 1996; A. Thomas & Chess, 1977, 1984), and fairly stable. Newborn babies show different patterns of sleeping, fussing, and activity, and these differences tend to persist to some degree (Korner, 1996; Korner et al., 1985). In fact, researchers using temperamental types similar to those of the NYLS have found that temperament at age 3 closely predicts personality at ages 18 and 21 (Caspi, 2000; Caspi & Silva, 1995; Newman, Caspi, Moffitt, & Silva, 1997).

That does not mean, however, that temperament is fully formed at birth. Temperament develops as various emotions and self-regulatory capacities appear (Rothbart et al., 2000) and can change in response to parental treatment and other life experiences (Belsky, Fish, & Isabella, 1991; Kagan & Snidman, 2004). Temperament also may be affected by culturally influenced child-raising practices. Infants in Malaysia tend to be less adaptable, more wary of new experiences, and more readily responsive to stimuli than U.S. babies. This may be because Malay parents do not often expose young children to situations that require adaptability, and they encourage infants to be acutely aware of sensations, such as the need for a diaper change (Banks, 1989).

Temperament and Adjustment: Goodness of Fit According to the NYLS, the key to healthy adjustment is **goodness of fit**—the match between a child's temperament and the environmental demands and constraints the child must deal with. If a very active child is expected to sit still for long periods, if a slow-to-warm-up child is constantly pushed into new situations, or if a persistent child is constantly taken away from absorbing projects, trouble may occur.

Parents who recognize that a child acts in a certain way because of inborn tendencies, not out of willfulness, laziness, or stupidity, may be less likely to feel guilty, anxious, or hostile, to feel a loss of control, or to be rigid or impatient. They can anticipate a child's reactions and help the child adapt—for example, by gradually introducing a child to new situations or by giving early warnings of the need to stop an activity.

Shyness and Boldness: Influences of Biology and Culture As we have mentioned, temperament seems to have a biological basis. In longitudinal research with about 500 children starting in infancy, Jerome Kagan and his colleagues have studied an aspect of temperament called *inhibition to the unfamiliar,* or shyness, which has to do with how boldly or cautiously the child approaches unfamiliar objects and situations.

When presented at 4 months with a series of new stimuli, about 20 percent of the infants cried, pumped their arms and legs, and sometimes arched their backs; this group were called inhibited or "high-reactive." About 40 percent showed little distress or motor activity and were more likely to smile spontaneously; they were labeled as uninhibited or "low-reactive ." The researchers suggested that inhibited children may be born with an unusually excitable amygdala, a part of the brain that detects and reacts to unfamiliar events and is involved in emotional responses (Kagan & Snidman, 2004).

Infants who had been identified as inhibited or uninhibited seemed to maintain these patterns to some degree during childhood (Kagan, 1997; Kagan & Snidman,

1991a, 1991b, 2004), along with specific differences in physiological characteristics. Inhibited children were more likely to have a thin body build, narrow face, and blue eyes, whereas uninhibited children were taller, heavier, and more often brown-eyed. In addition, inhibited children showed higher and less variable heart rates than uninhibited children, and the pupils of their eyes dilated more (Arcus & Kagan, 1995). It may be that the genes that contribute to reactivity and inhibited or uninhibited behavior also influence these physiological traits (Kagan & Snidman, 2004).

Behavioral differences between these two types of children tended to smoothe out by early adolescence, though the physiological distinctions remained. However, less than 5 percent of each group developed the behavioral features of the other type. For example, some high-reactive children no longer seemed extremely shy, but they still did not show the relaxed spontaneity characteristic of low-reactives (Kagan & Snidman, 2004). At age 15, there was a stronger disconnect between behavior and biology than at earlier ages. Still, more high-than low-reactives were subdued in unfamiliar situations and reported anxiety about the future (Kagan, Snidman, Kahn, & Towsley, 2007).

These findings suggest, again, that experience can moderate or accentuate early tendencies. Male toddlers who were inclined to be fearful and shy were more likely to remain so at age 3 if their parents were highly accepting of the child's reactions. If parents encouraged their sons to venture into new situations, the boys tended to become less inhibited (Park, Belsky, Putnam, & Crnic, 1997). In other research, when mothers responded insensitively to infants who were behaviorally inhibited, the inhibition tended to remain stable or increase. These authors suggested that insensitive caregiving behavior may alter the neural systems that underlie reactions to stress and novelty (Fox, Hane, & Pine, 2007). Other environmental influences, such as birth order, race/ethnicity, culture, relationships with teachers and peers, and unpredictable events also can reinforce or soften a child's original temperamental bias (Kagan & Snidman, 2004).

Earliest Social Experiences: The Infant in the Family

Infant care practices and patterns of interaction vary greatly around the world, depending on the culture's view of infants' nature and needs. In Bali, infants are believed to be ancestors reborn or gods brought to life in human form and thus must be treated with utmost dignity and respect. The Beng of West Africa think that young babies can understand all languages, whereas people in the Micronesian atoll of Ifaluk believe that babies cannot understand language at all, and therefore adults do not speak to them (DeLoache & Gottlieb, 2000).

In some societies, infants have multiple caregivers. Among the Efe people of central Africa, infants typically receive care from five or more people in a given hour and are routinely breast-fed by other women besides the mother (Tronick, Morelli, & Ivey, 1992). Among the Gusii in western Kenya, where infant mortality is high, parents keep their infants close to them, respond quickly when they cry, and feed them on demand (LeVine, 1974, 1989, 1994). The same is true of Aka foragers (hunter-gatherers) in central Africa, who move around frequently in small, tightly knit groups marked by extensive sharing, cooperation, and concern about danger. However, Ngandu farmers in the same region, who tend to live farther apart and to stay in one place for long periods of time, are more likely to leave their infants alone and to let them fuss or cry, smile, vocalize, or play (Hewlett, Lamb, Shannon, Leyendecker, & Schölmerich, 1998).

As we discuss patterns of adult-infant interaction we need to keep in mind that many of these patterns are culture-based. With that caution in mind, let's

What's Your View?

- In the United States, many people consider shyness undesirable. How should a parent handle a shy child? Do you think it is best to accept the child's temperament or try to change it?

Checkpoint

Can you . . .

- Describe the three patterns of temperament identified by the New York Longitudinal Study?
- Assess evidence for the stability of temperament?
- Explain the importance of goodness of fit?
- Discuss evidence of biological influences on shyness and boldness?

Guidepost 3

What roles do mothers and fathers play in early personality development?

When infant monkeys could choose whether to go to a wire "mother" or a warm, soft, terry-cloth "mother," they spent more time clinging to the cloth mother, even if their food came from the wire mother.

• "Despite the increasingly active role many of today's fathers play in child raising, a mother will always be more important to babies and young children than a father." Do you agree or disagree?

look first at the roles of the mother and father—how they care for and play with their babies, and how their influence begins to shape personality differences between boys and girls. Later in this chapter, we will look more deeply at relationships with parents and then at interactions with siblings. In Chapter 10 we examine such nontraditional families as those headed by single parents and those formed by gay and lesbian couples.

The Mother's Role In a series of pioneering experiments by Harry Harlow and his colleagues, rhesus monkeys were separated from their mothers six to twelve hours after birth and raised in a laboratory. The infant monkeys were put into cages with one of two kinds of surrogate "mothers": a plain cylindrical wire-mesh form or a form covered with terry cloth. Some monkeys were fed from bottles connected to the wire mothers; others were fed by the warm, cuddly cloth mothers. When the monkeys were allowed to spend time with either kind of mother, they all spent more time clinging to the cloth surrogates, even if they were being fed only by the wire surrogates. In an unfamiliar room, the babies "raised" by cloth surrogates showed more natural interest in exploring than those "raised" by wire surrogates, even when the appropriate mothers were there.

Apparently, the monkeys also remembered the cloth surrogates better. After a year's separation, the "cloth-raised" monkeys eagerly ran to embrace the terry-cloth forms, whereas the "wire-raised" monkeys showed no interest in the wire forms (Harlow & Zimmerman, 1959). None of the monkeys in either group grew up normally, however (Harlow & Harlow, 1962), and none were able to nurture their own offspring (Suomi & Harlow, 1972).

It is hardly surprising that a dummy mother would not provide the same kinds of stimulation and opportunities for positive development as a live mother. These experiments show that feeding is not the only, or even the most important, thing babies get from their mothers. Mothering includes the comfort of close bodily contact and, at least in monkeys, the satisfaction of an innate need to cling.

Human infants also have needs that must be satisfied if they are to grow up normally. One of these needs is for a mother who responds warmly and promptly to the infant. The importance of maternal (and paternal) responsiveness has been supported by many studies. In one study, 264 infants and their mothers were videotaped at home four times over the infants' 6th to 12th month. Half of the mothers received instruction in responsiveness behaviors, such as maintaining a positive attitude and speaking encouragingly. By 13 months, babies whose mothers had learned the responsiveness behaviors showed greater increases in social, emotional, communicative, and cognitive competence than those whose mothers had not received the instruction (Landry, Smith, & Swank, 2006). Later in this chapter we will discuss how responsiveness contributes to the mutual attachment between infants and mothers that develops during infancy, with far-reaching effects on psychosocial and cognitive development.

The Father's Role The fathering role is essentially a social construction (Doherty, Kouneski, & Erickson, 1998), having different meanings in different cultures. The role may be taken or shared by someone other than the biological father: the mother's brother, as in Botswana, or a grandfather, as in Vietnam (Engle & Breaux, 1998; Richardson, 1995; Townsend, 1997). In some societies, fathers are more involved in their young children's lives—economically, emotionally, and in time spent—than in other cultures. In many parts of the world, what it means to be a father has changed dramatically and continues to change (Engle & Breaux, 1998).

Among the Huhot of Inner Mongolia, a province of China, fathers traditionally are responsible for economic support and discipline and mothers for nurturing (Jankowiak, 1992). Men almost never hold infants. Fathers interact more with toddlers but perform child care duties only if the mother is absent. However, urbanization and maternal employment are changing these attitudes. Fathers—especially college-educated fathers—now seek more intimate relationships with children, especially sons (Engle & Breaux, 1998).

Among the Aka of central Africa, in contrast with the Huhot, "fathers provide more direct infant care than fathers in any other known society" (Hewlett, 1992, p. 169). In Aka families, husbands and wives frequently cooperate in subsistence tasks and other activities (Hewlett, 1992). Thus, the father's involvement in child care is part and parcel of his overall role in the family.

In the United States, fathers' involvement in caregiving has greatly increased as more mothers have begun to work outside the home and concepts of fathering have changed (Cabrera et al., 2000; Casper, 1997; Pleck, 1997). A father's frequent and positive involvement with his child, from infancy on, is directly related to the child's well-being and physical, cognitive, and social development (Cabrera et al., 2000; Kelley, Smith, Green, Berndt, & Rogers, 1998; Shannon, Tamis-LeMonda, London, & Cabrera, 2002).

As more mothers work outside the home, fathers in the United States are taking on more child care responsibilities and in some cases are the primary caregivers.

Gender: How Different Are Baby Boys and Girls?

Being male or female affects how people look, how they move, how they work, and how they play. It influences what they think about themselves and what others think of them. All these characteristics—and more—are included in the word **gender:** what it means to be male or female.

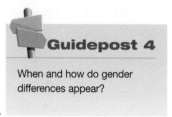

Guidepost 4

When and how do gender differences appear?

Gender Differences in Infants and Toddlers Measurable differences between baby boys and baby girls are few, at least in U.S. samples. Boys are a bit longer and heavier and may be slightly stronger, but, as we mentioned in Chapter 3, they are physically more vulnerable from conception on. Girls are less reactive to stress and more likely to survive infancy (Davis & Emory, 1995; Keenan & Shaw, 1997). Boys' brains at birth are about 10 percent larger than girls' brains, a difference that continues into adulthood (Gilmore et al., 2007). On the other hand, the two sexes are equally sensitive to touch and tend to teethe, sit up, and walk at about the same ages (Maccoby, 1980). They also achieve other motor milestones of infancy at about the same times.

gender Significance of being male or female.

One of the earliest *behavioral* differences between boys and girls, appearing between ages 1 and 2, is in preferences for toys and play activities and for playmates of the same sex (Campbell, Shirley, Heywood, & Crook, 2000; Serbin et al., 2001; Turner & Gervai, 1995). Boys as young as 17 months tend to play more aggressively than girls (Baillargeon et al., 2007). Between ages 2 and 3, boys and girls tend to say more words pertaining to their own sex (such as "tractor" versus "necklace") than to the other sex (Stennes, Burch, Sen, & Bauer, 2005).

By using age-appropriate tasks, cognitive psychologists have found evidence that infants begin to perceive differences between males and females long before their behavior is gender-differentiated and even before they can talk. Habituation studies have found that 6-month-olds respond differently to male and female voices. By 9 to 12 months, infants can tell the difference between male and female faces, apparently on the basis of hair and clothing. During the second year infants begin to associate gender-typical toys, such as dolls, with a face of the correct gender (Martin, Ruble, & Szkrybalo, 2002). In elicited imitation studies (refer back to Chapter 5), 25-month-old boys spend more time imitating "boy" tasks, such as shaving a teddy bear, whereas girls spend about the same amount of time imitating activities associated with each sex (Bauer, 1993).

How Parents Shape Gender Differences   Parents in the United States tend to *think* baby boys and girls are more different than they actually are. In a study of 11-month-old infants who had recently begun crawling, mothers consistently had higher expectations for their sons' success in crawling down steep and narrow slopes than for their daughters'. Yet, when tested on the slopes, the baby girls and boys showed identical levels of performance (Mondschein, Adolph, & Tamis-LeMonda, 2000).

U.S. parents begin to influence boys' and girls' personalities very early. Fathers, especially, promote **gender-typing,** the process by which children learn behavior that their culture considers appropriate for each sex (Bronstein, 1988). Fathers treat boys and girls more differently than mothers do, even during the first year (M. E. Snow, Jacklin, & Maccoby, 1983). During the second year, fathers talk more and spend more time with sons than with daughters (Lamb, 1981). Mothers talk more, and more supportively, to daughters than to sons (Leaper, Anderson, & Sanders, 1998), and girls at this age tend to be more talkative than boys (Leaper & Smith, 2004). Fathers of toddlers play more roughly with sons and show more sensitivity to daughters (Kelley et al., 1998).

However, a highly physical style of play, characteristic of many fathers in the United States, is not typical of fathers in all cultures. Swedish and German fathers usually do not play with their babies this way (Lamb, Frodi, Frodi, & Hwang, 1982; Parke, Grossman, & Tinsley, 1981). African Aka fathers (Hewlett, 1987) and those in New Delhi, India, also tend to play gently with small children (Roopnarine, Hooper, Ahmeduzzaman, & Pollack, 1993; Roopnarine, Talokder, Jain, Josh, & Srivastav, 1992). Such cross-cultural variations suggest that rough play is *not* a function of male biology, but instead is culturally influenced.

We discuss gender-typing and gender differences in more depth in Chapter 8.

Developmental Issues in Infancy

How does a dependent newborn, with a limited emotional repertoire and pressing physical needs, become a child with complex feelings and the abilities to understand and control them? Much of this development revolves around relationships with caregivers.

Developing Trust

Human babies are dependent on others for food, for protection, and for their very lives for a far longer period than any other mammals. How do they come to trust that their needs will be met? According to Erikson (1950), early experiences are the key.

As we discussed in Chapter 2, the first of Erikson's eight stages in psychosocial development is **basic trust versus basic mistrust.** This stage begins in infancy and continues until about 18 months. In these early months, babies develop a sense of the reliability of the people and objects in their world. They need to develop a balance between trust (which lets them form intimate relationships) and mistrust (which enables them to protect themselves). If trust predominates, as it should,

gender-typing Socialization process by which children, at an early age, learn appropriate gender roles.

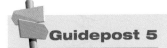

Checkpoint

Can you . . .

◆ Give examples of cultural differences in infant care?

◆ Compare the roles of fathers and mothers in meeting infants' needs?

◆ Discuss gender differences in infants and toddlers and how parents influence gender-typing?

Guidepost 5

How do infants gain trust in their world and form attachments, and how do infants and caregivers read each other's nonverbal signals?

basic trust versus basic mistrust Erikson's first stage in psychosocial development, in which infants develop a sense of the reliability of people and objects.

children develop the virtue of *hope:* the belief that they can fulfill their needs and obtain their desires (Erikson, 1982). If mistrust predominates, children will view the world as unfriendly and unpredictable and will have trouble forming relationships.

The critical element in developing trust is sensitive, responsive, consistent caregiving. Erikson saw the feeding situation as the setting for establishing the right mix of trust and mistrust. Can the baby count on being fed when hungry, and can the baby therefore trust the mother as a representative of the world? Trust enables an infant to let the mother out of sight "because she has become an inner certainty as well as an outer predictability" (Erikson, 1950, p. 247).

✓ **Checkpoint**

Can you . . .

◆ Explain the importance of basic trust and identify the critical element in its development?

Developing Attachments

When Ahmed's mother is near, he looks at her, smiles at her, babbles to her, and crawls after her. When she leaves, he cries; when she comes back, he squeals with joy. When he is frightened or unhappy, he clings to her. Ahmed has formed his first attachment to another person.

Attachment is a reciprocal, enduring emotional tie between an infant and a caregiver, each of whom contributes to the quality of the relationship. From an evolutionary point of view, attachments have adaptive value for babies, ensuring that their psychosocial as well as physical needs will be met (MacDonald, 1998). According to ethological theory, infants and parents are biologically predisposed to become attached to each other, and attachment promotes a baby's survival.

attachment Reciprocal, enduring tie between two people—especially between infant and caregiver—each of whom contributes to the quality of the relationship.

Studying Patterns of Attachment   The study of attachment owes much to the ethologist John Bowlby (1951), a pioneer in the study of bonding in animals. From his animal studies and from observations of disturbed children in a London psychoanalytic clinic, Bowlby became convinced of the importance of the mother-baby bond and warned against separating mother and baby without providing good substitute care. Mary Ainsworth, a student of Bowlby's in the early 1950s, went on to study attachment in African babies in Uganda through naturalistic observation in their homes (Ainsworth, 1967). Ainsworth later de-

Strange Situation Laboratory technique used to study infant attachment.

vised the **Strange Situation,** a now-classic, laboratory-based technique designed to assess attachment patterns between an infant and an adult. Typically, the adult is the mother (though other adults have taken part as well), and the infant is 10 to 24 months old.

The Strange Situation consists of a sequence of episodes and takes less than half an hour. During that time, the mother twice leaves the baby in an unfamiliar room, the first time with a stranger. The second time she leaves the baby alone, and the stranger comes back before the mother does. The mother then encourages the baby to explore and play again and gives comfort if the baby seems to need it (Ainsworth, Blehar, Waters, & Wall, 1978). Of particular concern is the baby's response each time the mother returns.

When Ainsworth and her colleagues observed 1-year-olds in the Strange Situation

Both Anna and Diane contribute to the attachment betwen them by the way they act toward each other. The way the baby molds herself to her mother's body shows her trust and reinforces Diane's feelings for her child, which she displays through sensitivity to Anna's needs.

Chapter 6   Psychosocial Development during the First Three Years   **189**

and at home, they found three main patterns of attachment. These are *secure attachment* (the most common category, into which about 60 to 75 percent of low-risk North American babies fall) and two forms of anxious, or insecure, attachment: *avoidant* (15 to 25 percent) and *ambivalent, or resistant* (10 to 15 percent) (Vondra & Barnett, 1999).

Babies with **secure attachment** cry or protest when the mother leaves and greet her happily when she returns. They use her as a secure base, leaving her to go off and explore but returning occasionally for reassurance. They are usually cooperative and relatively free of anger. Babies with **avoidant attachment** rarely cry when the mother leaves but avoid her on her return. They tend to be angry and do not reach out in time of need. They dislike being held but dislike being put down even more. Babies with **ambivalent (resistant) attachment** become anxious even before the mother leaves and are very upset when she goes out. When she returns, they show their ambivalence by seeking contact with her while at the same time resisting it by kicking or squirming. Resistant babies do little exploration and are hard to comfort.

These three attachment patterns are universal in all cultures in which they have been studied—cultures as different as those in Africa, China, and Israel—though the percentage of infants in each category varies (True, Pisani, & Oumar, 2001; van IJzendoorn & Kroonenberg, 1988; van IJzendoorn & Sagi, 1999). Attachment *behaviors,* however, vary across cultures. Among the Gusii of east Africa, on the western edge of Kenya, infants are greeted with handshakes, and Gusii infants reach out for a parent's hand much as Western infants cuddle up for a hug (van IJzendoorn & Sagi, 1999). Contrary to Ainsworth's original findings, babies seem to develop attachments to both parents at about the same time, and security of attachment to father and mother is usually quite similar (Fox, Kimmerly, & Schafer, 1991).

Other research (Main & Solomon, 1986) has identified a fourth attachment pattern, **disorganized-disoriented attachment.** Babies with the disorganized pattern seem to lack an organized strategy to deal with the stress of the Strange Situation. Instead, they show contradictory, repetitive, or misdirected behaviors (seeking closeness to the stranger instead of the mother). They may greet the mother brightly when she returns but then turn away or approach without looking at her. They seem confused and afraid. This may be the least secure pattern. It is most likely to occur in babies whose mothers are insensitive, intrusive, or abusive or have suffered unresolved loss. The child's temperament does not seem to be a factor (Carlson, 1998; van IJzendoorn, Schuengel, & Bakermans-Kranenburg, 1999).

Disorganized attachment is thought to occur in at least 10 percent of low-risk infants but in much higher proportions in certain at-risk populations, such as premature children, those with autism or Down syndrome, and those whose mothers abuse alcohol or drugs (Vondra & Barnett, 1999). This attachment pattern tends to remain fairly stable and seems to be a risk factor for later behavioral problems, especially aggressive conduct (van IJzendoorn et al., 1999). (Table 6-3 describes how babies with each of the four patterns of attachment react to the Strange Situation.)

How Attachment Is Established   On the basis of a baby's interactions with the mother, proposed Ainsworth and Bowlby, the baby builds a "working model" of what can be expected from her. As long as the mother continues to act the same way, the model holds up. If her behavior changes—not just once or twice but consistently—the baby may revise the model, and security of attachment may change.

secure attachment Pattern in which an infant cries or protests when the primary caregiver leaves and actively seeks out the caregiver on his or her return.

avoidant attachment Pattern in which an infant rarely cries when separated from the primary caregiver and avoids contact on his or her return.

ambivalent (resistant) attachment Pattern in which an infant becomes anxious before the primary caregiver leaves, is extremely upset during his or her absence, and both seeks and resists contact on his or her return.

disorganized-disoriented attachment Pattern in which an infant, after separation from the primary caregiver, shows contradictory repetitious, or misdirected behaviors on his or her return.

Table 6-3	Attachment Behaviors in the Strange Situation

Attachment Classification	Behavior
Secure	Gloria plays and explores freely when her mother is nearby. She responds enthusiastically when her mother returns.
Avoidant	When Sam's mother returns, Sam does not make eye contact or greet her. It is almost as if he has not noticed her return.
Ambivalent (Resistant)	James hovers close to his mother during much of the Strange Situation, but he does not greet her positively or enthusiastically during the reunion episode. Instead, he is angry and upset.
Disorganized/Disoriented	Erica responds to the Strange Situation with inconsistent, contradictory behavior. She seems to fall apart, overwhelmed by the stress.

Source: Based on Thompson, 1998, pp. 37–39.

A baby's working model of attachment is related to Erikson's concept of basic trust. Secure attachment reflects trust; insecure attachment, mistrust. Securely attached babies have learned to trust not only their caregivers but their own ability to get what they need. Thus, babies who cry a lot and whose mothers respond sensitively and soothingly tend to be securely attached (Del Carmen, Pedersen, Huffman, & Bryan, 1993; McElwain & Booth-LaForce, 2006). Equally important are mutual interaction, stimulation, a positive attitude, warmth and acceptance, and emotional support (De Wolff & van IJzendoorn, 1997; Lundy, 2003).

In a prospective longitudinal study of South African infants, mothers whose infants were insecurely attached at 18 months tended to have been remote (detached) and intrusive when the infants were 2 months old and continued to be so. Despite the extreme poverty in which these families lived and the legacy of the apartheid system, an official policy of racial segregation that lasted until the early 1990s, nearly 62 percent of the infants were judged secure, a tribute to the power of positive parenting even amid environmental adversity (Tomlinson, Cooper, & Murray, 2005). In contrast, among institutionalized infants and toddlers in Bucharest, Romania, more than 65 percent were classified as disorganized and only about 19 percent as secure (Zeanah, Smyke, Koga, & Carlson, 2005).

Alternative Methods of Attachment Study Although much research on attachment has been based on the Strange Situation, some investigators have questioned its validity. The Strange Situation *is* strange; it is also artificial. It asks mothers not to initiate interaction, exposes babies to repeated comings and goings of adults, and expects the infants to pay attention to them. Also, the Strange Situation may be less valid in some non-Western cultures. Research on Japanese infants, who are less commonly separated from their mothers than U.S. babies, showed high rates of resistant attachment, which may reflect the extreme stressfulness of the Strange Situation for these babies (Miyake, Chen, & Campos, 1985).

Because attachment influences a wider range of behaviors than are seen in the Strange Situation, other researchers have devised methods to study children in natural settings. The Waters and Deane (1985) Attachment Q-set (AQS) has mothers or other home observers sort a set of descriptive words or phrases ("cries a lot"; "tends to cling") into categories ranging from most to least characteristic of the child and then compare these descriptions with expert descriptions of the prototypical secure child.

In a study using the AQS, mothers in China, Colombia, Germany, Israel, Japan, Norway, and the United States described their children as behaving more like than unlike the "most secure child." Furthermore, the mothers' descriptions of "secure-base" behavior were about as similar across cultures as within a culture. These findings suggest that the tendency to use the mother as a secure base is universal, though it may take somewhat varied forms (Posada et al., 1995).

Functional MRIs of Japanese mothers found a neural basis for attachment. Certain areas of a mother's brain were activated at the sight of her own infant smiling or crying but not at the sight of other infants showing those behaviors (Noriuchi, Kikuchi, & Senoo, 2008.)

The Role of Temperament How much does temperament influence attachment and in what ways? Findings vary (Susman-Stillman, Kalkoske, Egeland, & Waldman, 1996; Vaughn et al., 1992). In a study of 6- to 12-month-olds and their families, both a mother's sensitivity and her baby's temperament influenced attachment patterns (Seifer, Schiller, Sameroff, Resnick, & Riordan, 1996). Neurological or physiological conditions may underlie temperamental differences in attachment. For example, variability in an infant's heart rate is associated with irritability, and heart rate seems to vary more in insecurely attached infants (Izard, Porges, Simons, Haynes, & Cohen, 1991).

A baby's temperament may have not only a direct impact on attachment but also an indirect impact through its effect on the parents. In a series of studies in the Netherlands (van den Boom, 1989, 1994), 15-day-old infants classified as irritable were much more likely than nonirritable infants to be insecurely (usually avoidantly) attached at 1 year. However, irritable infants whose mothers received home visits with instruction on how to soothe their babies were as likely to be rated as securely attached as the nonirritable infants. Thus, irritability on an infant's part may prevent the development of secure attachment but not if the mother has the skills to cope with the baby's temperament (Rothbart et al., 2000). Goodness of fit between parent and child may well be a key to understanding security of attachment.

Stranger Anxiety and Separation Anxiety Chloe used to be a friendly baby, smiling at strangers and going to them, continuing to coo happily as long as someone—anyone—was around. Now, at 8 months, she turns away when a new person approaches and howls when her parents try to leave her with a babysitter. Chloe is experiencing both **stranger anxiety,** wariness of a person she does not know, and **separation anxiety,** distress when a familiar caregiver leaves her.

Stranger anxiety and separation anxiety used to be considered emotional and cognitive milestones of the second half of infancy, reflecting attachment to the mother. However, newer research suggests that, although stranger anxiety and separation anxiety are fairly typical, they are not universal. Whether a baby cries when someone new approaches or when a parent leaves may say more about the baby's temperament or life circumstances than about security of attachment (R. J. Davidson & Fox, 1989).

Babies rarely react negatively to strangers before age 6 months but commonly do so by 8 or 9 months (Sroufe, 1997). This change may reflect cognitive development. Chloe's stranger anxiety involves memory for faces, the ability to compare the stranger's appearance with her mother's, and perhaps the recollection

stranger anxiety Wariness of strange people and places, shown by some infants during the second half of the first year.

separation anxiety Distress shown by someone, typically an infant, when a familiar caregiver leaves.

of situations in which she has been left with a stranger. If Chloe is allowed to get used to the stranger gradually in a familiar setting, she may react more positively (Lewis, 1997; Sroufe, 1997).

Separation anxiety may be due not so much to the separation itself as to the quality of substitute care. When substitute caregivers are warm and responsive and play with 9-month-olds *before* they cry, the babies cry less than when they are with less responsive caregivers (Gunnar, Larson, Hertsgaard, Harris, & Brodersen, 1992).

Stability of care is also important. Pioneering work by René Spitz (1945, 1946) on institutionalized children emphasizes the need for substitute care to be as close as possible to good mothering. Research has underlined the value of continuity and consistency in caregiving, so children can form early emotional bonds with their caregivers. Bonds can be formed with multiple caregivers, as long as the caregiving situation is stable.

Today, neither intense fear of strangers nor intense protest when the mother leaves is considered to be a sign of secure attachment. Researchers measure attachment more by what happens when the mother returns than by how many tears the baby sheds at her departure.

Little Maria is showing separation anxiety about her parents' leaving her with a babysitter. Separation anxiety is common among 6-to 12-month-old babies.

Long-Term Effects of Attachment   As attachment theory proposes, security of attachment seems to affect emotional, social, and cognitive competence (van IJzendoorn & Sagi, 1997). The more secure a child's attachment to a nurturing adult, the more likely that the child will develop good relationships with others.

If children, as infants, had a secure base and could count on parents' or caregivers' responsiveness, they are apt to feel confident enough to be actively engaged in their world (Jacobsen & Hofmann, 1997). In a study of 70 fifteen-month-olds, those who were securely attached to their mothers, as measured by the Strange Situation, showed less stress in adapting to child care than did insecurely attached toddlers (Ahnert, Gunnar, Lamb, & Barthel, 2004).

Securely attached toddlers tend to have larger, more varied vocabularies than those who are insecurely attached (Meins, 1998). They have more positive interactions with peers, and their friendly overtures are more likely to be accepted (Fagot, 1997). Insecurely attached toddlers tend to show more negative emotions (fear, distress, and anger), whereas securely attached children are more joyful (Kochanska, 2001).

Between ages 3 and 5, securely attached children are likely to be more curious, competent, empathic, resilient, and self-confident, to get along better with other children, and to form closer friendships than children who were insecurely attached as infants (Arend, Gove, & Sroufe, 1979; Elicker et al., 1992; J. L. Jacobson & Wille, 1986; Waters, Wippman, & Sroufe, 1979; Youngblade & Belsky, 1992). They interact more positively with parents, preschool teachers, and peers; are better able to resolve conflicts; and tend to have a more positive self-image (Elicker et al., 1992; Verschueren, Marcoen, & Schoefs, 1996).

Secure attachment seems to prepare children for the intimacy of friendship (Carlson, Sroufe, & Egeland, 2004). In middle childhood and adolescence, securely attached children (at least in Western cultures, where most studies have been done) tend to have the closest, most stable friendships (Schneider, Atkinson, & Tardif, 2001; Sroufe, Carlson, & Shulman, 1993) and to be socially well-adjusted (Jaffari-Bimmel, Juffer, van IJzendoorn, Bakermans-Kranenberg, & Mooijaart, 2006). Secure attachment in infancy also influences the quality of attachment to a romantic partner in young adulthood (Simpson, Collins, Tran, & Haydon, 2007).

Insecurely attached children, in contrast, often have inhibitions and negative emotions in toddlerhood, hostility toward other children at age 5, and dependency during the school years (Calkins & Fox, 1992; Kochanska, 2001; Lyons-Ruth, Alpern, & Repacholi, 1993; Sroufe, Carlson, Shulman, 1993). Those with disorganized attachment tend to have behavior problems at all levels of schooling and psychiatric disorders at age 17 (Carlson, 1998).

In a longitudinal study of 1,364 families with 1-month-old infants, children who were avoidantly attached at 15 months tended to be rated by their mothers as less socially competent than securely attached children and by their teachers as more aggressive or anxious during the preschool and school-age years. However, effects of parenting on the children's behavior during these years were more important than early attachment. Insecure or disorganized children whose parenting had improved were less aggressive in school than those whose parenting had not improved or had gotten worse. Secure children, on the other hand, were relatively immune to parenting that became less sensitive, perhaps because their early working models buoyed them up even under changed conditions. This study suggests that the continuity generally found between attachment and later behavior might be explained by continuity in the home environment (NICHD Early Child Care Research Network, 2006).

Intergenerational Transmission of Attachment Patterns The *Adult Attachment Interview (AAI)* (George, Kaplan, & Main, 1985; Main, 1995; Main, Kaplan, & Cassidy, 1985) asks adults to recall and interpret feelings and experiences related to their childhood attachments. Studies using the AAI have found that the way adults recall early experiences with parents or caregivers affects their emotional well-being and may influence the way they respond to their own children (Adam, Gunnar, & Tanaka, 2004; Dozier, Stovall, Albus, & Bates, 2001; Pesonen, Raïkkönen, Keltikangas-Järvinen, Strandberg, & Järvenpää, 2003; Slade, Belsky, Aber, & Phelps, 1999). A mother who was securely attached to *her* mother or who understands why she was insecurely attached can accurately recognize the baby's attachment behaviors, respond encouragingly, and help the baby form a secure attachment to her (Bretherton, 1990). Mothers who are preoccupied with their past attachment relationships tend to show anger and intrusiveness in interactions with their children. Depressed mothers who dismiss memories of their past attachments tend to be cold and unresponsive to their children (Adam et al., 2004). Parents' attachment history also influences their perceptions of their baby's temperament, and those perceptions may affect the parent-child relationship (Pesonen et al., 2003).

A cycle of insecure attachment can be broken. In one study, 54 first-time Dutch mothers who were classified by the AAI as insecurely attached received home visits in which they either were given feedback to enhance sensitive parenting or participated in discussions of their childhood experiences in relation to their current caregiving. After the interventions, these mothers were more sensitive than a control group who had not received the visits. Maternal gains in sensitivity to children's needs most strongly affected the security of infants with highly reactive (negatively emotional) temperaments (Klein-Velderman, Bakermans-Kranenburg, Juffer, & van IJzendoorn, 2006).

Checkpoint

Can you . . .

♦ Describe four patterns of attachment?

♦ Discuss how attachment is established, including the role of the baby's temperament?

♦ Discuss factors affecting stranger anxiety and separation anxiety?

♦ Describe long-term behavioral influences of attachment patterns and intergenerational transmission of attachment?

Emotional Communication with Caregivers: Mutual Regulation

At 1 month, Max gazes attentively at his mother's face. At 2 months, when his mother smiles at him and rubs his tummy, he smiles back. By 3 months, Max smiles first, inviting his mother to play (Lavelli & Fogel, 2005).

Infants are communicating beings; they have a strong drive to interact with others (Striano, 2004). The ability of both infant and caregiver to respond appropriately and sensitively to each other's mental and emotional states is known as **mutual regulation.** Infants take an active part in mutual regulation by sending behavioral signals, like Max's smiles, that influence the way caregivers behave toward them.

Healthy interaction occurs when a caregiver reads a baby's signals accurately and responds appropriately. When a baby's goals are met, the baby is joyful or at least interested (E. Z. Tronick, 1989). If a caregiver ignores an invitation to play or insists on playing when the baby has signaled "I don't feel like it" by turning away, the baby may feel frustrated or sad. When babies do not achieve desired results, they keep trying to repair the interaction. Normally, interaction moves back and forth between well-regulated and poorly regulated states, and babies learn from these shifts how to send signals and what to do when their initial signals do not result in the desired effect. Mutual regulation helps babies learn to read others' behavior and to develop expectations about it. Even very young infants can perceive emotions expressed by others and can adjust their behavior accordingly (Legerstee & Varghese, 2001; Montague & Walker-Andrews, 2001; Termine & Izard, 1988), but they are disturbed when someone—whether the mother or a stranger, and regardless of the reason—breaks off interpersonal contact (Striano, 2004). (Box 6-1 discusses how a mother's depression may contribute to developmental problems in her baby.)

mutual regulation Process by which infant and caregiver communicate emotional states to each other and respond appropriately.

Social Referencing

When babies look at their caregivers on encountering a new person or toy, they are engaging in **social referencing,** seeking emotional information to guide behavior (Hertenstein & Campos, 2004). In social referencing, one person forms an understanding of how to act in an ambiguous, confusing, or unfamiliar situation by seeking and interpreting another person's perception of it.

social referencing Understanding an ambiguous situation by seeking another person's perception of it.

Research provides experimental evidence of social referencing at 12 months (Moses, Baldwin, Rosicky, & Tidball, 2001). When exposed to jiggling or vibrating toys fastened to the floor or ceiling, both 12- and 18-month-olds moved closer to or farther from the toys depending on the experimenters' expressed emotional reactions ("Yecch!" or "Nice!"). In a pair of studies, 12-month-olds (but not 10-month-olds) adjusted their behavior toward certain unfamiliar objects according to nonvocal emotional signals given by an actress on a television screen (Mumme & Fernald, 2003). In another pair of experiments (Hertenstein & Campos, 2004), whether 14-month-olds touched plastic creatures that dropped within their reach was related to the positive or negative emotions they had seen an adult express about the same objects an hour before. However, 11-month-olds responded to such emotional cues only if the delay was very brief (3 minutes).

Social referencing—and the ability to retain information gained from it—may play a role in such key developments of toddlerhood as the rise of self-conscious emotions (embarrassment and pride), the development of a sense of self, and the processes of *socialization* and *internalization,* to which we turn in the next section of this chapter.

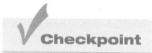

✓ Checkpoint

Can you . . .

♦ Describe how mutual regulation works and explain its importance?

♦ Give examples of how infants seem to use social referencing?

BOX 6-1 **Research** *in Action*

How Postpartum Depression Affects Early Development

Reading emotional signals lets mothers assess and meet babies' needs and helps babies respond to the mother's behavior toward them. What happens when that communication system seriously breaks down, and can anything be done about it?

Much media attention has been focused on the issue of postpartum depression. Such celebrities as Brooke Shields and Marie Osmond have shared stories of their personal battles with this distressing condition. And far too often we read tragic stories about women such as Andrea Yates, who killed her five children while under the grip of severe postpartum depression.

Postpartum depression—major or minor depression occurring within four weeks of giving birth—affects about 14.5 percent of new mothers (Wisner, Chambers, & Sit, 2006). A dramatic drop in estrogen and progesterone following childbirth may trigger depression. Depression also may be brought on by the significant emotional and lifestyle changes new mothers face. First-time mothers are at especially high risk (Munk-Olsen, Laursen, Pedersen, Mors, & Mortensen, 2006).

Unless treated promptly, postpartum depression may impact the way a mother interacts with her baby, with detrimental effects on the child's cognitive and emotional development (Gjerdingen, 2003). Depressed mothers are less sensitive to their infants than nondepressed mothers, and their interactions with their babies are generally less positive (NICHD Early Child Care Research Network, 1999b). Depressed mothers are less likely to interpret and respond to an infant's cries (Donovan, Leavitt, & Walsh, 1998).

Babies of depressed mothers may give up on sending emotional signals and learn that they have no power to draw responses from other people, that their mothers are unreliable, and that the world is untrustworthy. They also may become depressed themselves (Ashman & Dawson, 2002; Gelfand & Teti, 1995; Teti et al., 1995), whether due to a failure of mutual regulation, an inherited predisposition to depression, or exposure to hormonal or other biochemical influences in the prenatal environment. It may be that a combination of genetic, prenatal, and environmental factors puts infants of depressed mothers at risk. A bidirectional influence may be at work; an infant who does not respond normally may further depress the mother, and her unresponsiveness may in turn further depress the infant (T. Field, 1995, 1998a, 1998c; Lundy et al., 1999). Depressed mothers who are able to maintain good interactions with their infants tend to nurture better emotional regulation in their children than do other depressed mothers (Field, Diego, Hernandez-Reif, Schanberg, & Kuhn, 2003). Interactions with a nondepressed adult can help infants compensate for the effects of depressed mothering (T. Field, 1995, 1998a, 1998c).

Infants of depressed mothers tend to show unusual patterns of brain activity, similar to the mothers' patterns. Within 24 hours of birth, they show relatively less activity in the left frontal region of the brain, which seems to be specialized for approach emotions such as joy and anger, and more activity in the right frontal region, which controls *withdrawal* emotions, such as distress and disgust (G. Dawson et al., 1992, 1999; T. Field, 1998a, 1998c;

T. Field, Fox, Pickens, Nawrocki, & Soutollo, 1995; N. A. Jones, Field, Fox, Lundy, & Davalos, 1997). Newborns of depressed mothers also tend to have higher levels of stress hormones (Lundy et al., 1999), lower scores on the Brazelton Neonatal Behavior Assessment Scale, and lower vagal tone, which is associated with attention and learning (T. Field, 1998a, 1998c; N. A. Jones et al., 1998). These findings suggest that a woman's depression during pregnancy may contribute to her newborn's neurological and behavioral functioning.

Children with depressed mothers tend to be insecurely attached (Gelfand & Teti, 1995; Teti et al., 1995). They are likely to grow poorly, to perform poorly on cognitive and linguistic measures, and to have behavior problems (T. Field, 1998a, 1998c; T. M. Field et al., 1985; Gelfand & Teti, 1995; NICHD Early Child Care Research Network, 1999b; Zuckerman & Beardslee, 1987). As toddlers these children tend to have trouble suppressing frustration and tension (Cole, Barrett, & Zahn-Waxler, 1992; Seiner & Gelfand, 1995), and in early adolescence they are at risk for violent behavior (Hay, 2003).

Antidepressant drugs such as Zoloft (a selective serotonin reuptake inhibitor) and nortriptyline (a tricyclic) appear to be safe and effective for treating postpartum depression (Wisner et al., 2006). Other techniques that may help improve a depressed mother's mood include listening to music, visual imagery, aerobics, yoga, relaxation, and massage therapy (T. Field, 1995, 1998a, 1998c). Massage also can help depressed babies (T. Field, 1998a, 1998b; T. Field et al., 1996), possibly through effects on neurological activity (N. A. Jones et al., 1997). In one study, such mood-brightening measures—plus social, educational, and vocational rehabilitation for the mother and day care for the infant—improved their interaction behavior. The infants showed faster growth and had fewer pediatric problems, more normal biochemical values, and better developmental test scores than a control group (T. Field, 1998a, 1998b).

What's your view

Can you suggest ways to help depressed mothers and babies, other than those mentioned here?

Check It Out

For further information on this topic, go to www.nimh .nih.gov/health/publications/depression-what-every-woman-should-know/summary.shtml (a National Institute of Mental Health resource called "Women and Depression: Discovering Hope") or www.nimh.nih.gov/publications/depression/ summary.shtml (a general summary depression, also on the Web site of the National Institute of Mental Health).

Developmental Issues in Toddlerhood

Guidepost 6

When and how does the sense of self arise, and how do toddlers exercise autonomy and develop standards for socially acceptable behavior?

About halfway between their first and second birthdays, babies become toddlers. This transformation can be seen not only in such physical and cognitive skills as walking and talking, but in the ways children express their personalities and interact with others. A toddler becomes a more active, intentional partner in interactions and sometimes initiates them. Caregivers can now more clearly read the child's signals. Such in-sync interactions help toddlers gain communicative skills and social competence and motivate compliance with a parent's wishes (Harrist & Waugh, 2002).

Let's look at three psychological issues that toddlers—and their caregivers—have to deal with: the emerging *sense of self;* the growth of *autonomy,* or self-determination; and *socialization,* or *internalization of behavioral standards.*

The Emerging Sense of Self

The **self-concept** is our image of ourselves—our total picture of our abilities and traits. It describes what we know and feel about ourselves and guides our actions (Harter, 1996). Children incorporate into their self-image the picture that others reflect back to them.

self-concept Sense of self; descriptive and evaluative mental picture of one's abilities and traits.

When and how does the self-concept develop?* From a jumble of seemingly isolated experiences (say, from one breast-feeding session to another), infants begin to extract consistent patterns that form rudimentary concepts of self and other. Depending on what kind of care the infant receives and how she or he responds, pleasant or unpleasant emotions become connected with sensorimotor experiences (such as sucking) that play an important part in the growing organization of the self (Harter, 1998).

Between 4 and 10 months, when infants learn to reach, grasp, and make things happen, they experience a sense of personal *agency,* the realization that they can control external events. At about this time infants develop *self-coherence,* the sense of being a physical whole with boundaries separate from the rest of the world. These developments occur in interaction with caregivers in games such as peek-a-boo, in which the infant becomes increasingly aware of the difference between self and other.

The emergence of *self-awareness*—conscious knowledge of the self as a distinct, identifiable being—builds on this dawning of perceptual distinction between self and others. By at least 3 months infants pay attention to their mirror image (Courage & Howe, 2002); 4- to 9-month-olds show more interest in images of others than of themselves (Rochat & Striano, 2002). This early *perceptual* discrimination may be the foundation of the *conceptual* self-awareness that develops between 15 and 18 months.

Self-awareness can be tested by studying whether an infant recognizes his or her own image. In a classic line of research, investigators dabbed rouge on the noses of 6- to 24-month-olds and sat them in front of a mirror. Three-fourths of 18-month-olds and all 24-month-olds touched their red noses more often than before, whereas babies younger than 15 months never did. This behavior suggests that older toddlers knew they did not normally have red noses and still recognized the image in the mirror as their own (Lewis, 1997; Lewis &

Four- to nine-month-olds show more interest in images of others than in images of themselves.

*The discussion in this section is indebted to Harter, 1998.

What's Your View?

- What kinds of caregiving practices do you think would help a toddler develop a healthy sense of self?

autonomy versus shame and doubt Erikson's second stage in psychosocial development, in which children achieve a balance between self-determination and control by others.

Brooks, 1974). In a later study, 18- and 24-month-olds seated in a chair with a tray that blocked their view of themselves from the waist down were about as likely to touch a sticker on their legs, which was visible only in a mirror, as on their faces (Nielsen, Suddendorf, & Slaughter, 2006). Once children can recognize themselves, they show a preference for looking at their own video image over an image of another child the same age (Nielsen, Dissanayake, & Kashima, 2003).

By 20 to 24 months, toddlers begin to use first-person pronouns, another sign of self-awareness (Lewis, 1997). Between 19 and 30 months, they begin to apply descriptive terms ("big" or "little"; "straight hair" or "curly hair") and evaluative terms ("good," "pretty," or "strong") to themselves. The rapid development of language enables children to think and talk about the self and to incorporate parents' verbal descriptions ("You're so smart!" "What a big boy!") into their emerging self-image (Stipek, Gralinski, & Kopp, 1990).

Development of Autonomy

As children mature—physically, cognitively, and emotionally—they are driven to seek independence from the very adults to whom they are attached. "Me do!" is the byword as toddlers use their developing muscles and minds to try to do everything on their own—not only to walk, but to feed and dress themselves and to explore their world.

Erikson (1950) identified the period from about 18 months to 3 years as the second stage in personality development, **autonomy versus shame and doubt**, which is marked by a shift from external control to self-control. Having come through infancy with a sense of basic trust in the world and an awakening self-awareness, toddlers begin to substitute their own judgment for their caregivers'. The virtue that emerges during this stage is *will*. Toilet training is an important step toward autonomy and self-control. So is language; as children are better able to make their wishes known, they become more powerful. Because unlimited freedom is neither safe nor healthy, said Erikson, shame and doubt have a necessary place. Toddlers need adults to set appropriate limits, and shame and doubt help them recognize the need for those limits.

In the United States, the "terrible twos" are a normal sign of the drive for autonomy. Toddlers have to test the notions that they are individuals, that they have some control over their world, and that they have new, exciting powers. They are driven to try out their own ideas, exercise their own preferences, and make their own decisions. This drive typically shows itself in the form of *negativism,* the tendency to shout, "No!" just for the sake of resisting authority. Almost all U.S. children show negativism to some degree; it usually begins before age 2, tends to peak at about 3½ to 4, and declines by age 6. Caregivers who view children's expressions of self-will as a normal, healthy striving for independence, not as stubbornness, can help them learn self-control, contribute to their sense of competence, and avoid excessive conflict. (Table 6-4 gives specific, research-based suggestions for dealing with the terrible twos.)

Many U.S. parents might be surprised to hear that the terrible twos are not universal. In some developing countries, the transition from infancy to early childhood is relatively smooth and harmonious (Mosier & Rogoff, 2003; Box 6-2).

According to Erikson, toilet training is an important step toward autonomy and self-control.

Table 6-4	Dealing with the Terrible Twos

Table 6-4 — Dealing with the Terrible Twos

The following research-based guidelines can help parents of toddlers discourage negativism and encourage socially acceptable behavior.

- *Be flexible.* Learn the child's natural rhythms and special likes and dislikes.
- *Think of yourself as a safe harbor,* with safe limits, from which a child can set out and discover the world and to which the child can keep coming back for support.
- *Make your home child-friendly.* Fill it with unbreakable objects that are safe to explore.
- *Avoid physical punishment.* It is often ineffective and may even lead a toddler to do more damage.
- *Offer a choice*—even a limited one—to give the child some control. ("Would you like to have your bath now or after we read a book?")
- *Be consistent* in enforcing necessary requests.
- *Don't interrupt an activity unless absolutely necessary.* Try to wait until the child's attention has shifted.
- *If you must interrupt, give warning.* ("We have to leave the playground soon.")
- *Suggest alternative activities* when behavior becomes objectionable. (When Ashley is throwing sand in Keiko's face, say, "Oh, look! Nobody's on the swings now. Let's go over and I'll give you a good push!")
- *Suggest; don't command.* Accompany requests with smiles or hugs, not criticism, threats, or physical restraint.
- *Link requests with pleasurable activities.* ("It's time to stop playing so that you can go to the store with me.")
- *Remind the child of what you expect:* "When we go to this playground, we *never* go outside the gate."
- *Wait a few moments before repeating a request* when a child doesn't comply immediately.
- *Use a "time-out" to end conflicts.* In a nonpunitive way, remove either yourself or the child from a situation.
- *Expect less self-control during times of stress* (illness, divorce, the birth of a sibling, or a move to a new home).
- *Expect it to be harder for toddlers to comply with "dos" than with "don'ts."* "Clean up your room" takes more effort than "Don't write on the furniture."
- *Keep the atmosphere as positive as possible.* Make your child *want* to cooperate.

Sources: Haswell, Hock, & Wenar, 1981; Kochanska & Aksan, 1995; Kopp, 1982; Kuczynski & Kochanska, 1995; Power & Chapieski, 1986.

Checkpoint

Can you . . .

- Trace the early development of the self-concept?
- Describe the conflict of autonomy versus shame and doubt and explain why the terrible twos is considered a normal phenomenon?

The Roots of Moral Development: Socialization and Internalization

Socialization is the process by which children develop habits, skills, values, and motives that make them responsible, productive members of society. Compliance with parental expectations can be seen as a first step toward compliance with societal standards of behavior. Socialization rests on **internalization** of these standards. Children who are successfully socialized no longer obey rules or commands merely to get rewards or avoid punishment; they have made society's standards their own (Grusec & Goodnow, 1994; Kochanska & Aksan, 1995; Kochanska, Tjebkes, & Forman, 1998).

socialization Development of habits, skills, values, and motives shared by responsible, productive members of a society.

internalization During socialization, process by which children accept societal standards of conduct as their own.

Developing Self-Regulation   Laticia, age 2, is about to poke her finger into an electric outlet. In her child-proofed apartment, the sockets are covered, but not here in her grandmother's home. When Laticia hears her father shout, "No!" the toddler pulls her arm back. The next time she goes near an outlet, she starts to poke her finger, hesitates, and then says, "No." She has stopped herself from doing something she remembers she is not supposed to do. She is beginning to show **self-regulation:** control of her behavior to conform to a caregiver's demands or expectations of her, even when the caregiver is not present.

self-regulation A child's independent control of behavior to conform to understood social expectations.

BOX 6-2 **Window** *on the World*

Are Struggles with Toddlers Necessary?

Are the terrible twos a normal phase in child development? Many Western parents and psychologists think so. Actually, though, the terrible twos do not appear to be universal.

In Zinacantan, Mexico, toddlers do not typically become demanding and resistant to parental control. Instead, toddlerhood in Zinacantan is a time when children move from being mama's babies toward being "mother's helpers," responsible children who tend a new baby and help with household tasks (Edwards, 1994). A similar developmental pattern seems to occur in Mazahua families in Mexico and among Mayan families in San Pedro, Guatemala. San Pedro parents "do not report a particular age when they expect children to become especially contrary or negative" (Mosier & Rogoff, 2003, p. 1058).

One arena in which issues of autonomy and control appear in Western cultures is in sibling conflicts over toys and the way children respond to parental handling of these conflicts. To explore these issues, a cross-cultural study compared 16 San Pedro families with 16 middle-class European American families in Salt Lake City. All of the families had toddlers 14 to 20 months old and older siblings 3 to 5 years old. The researchers interviewed each mother about her child-raising practices. They then handed the mother a series of attractive objects (such as dolls and puppets) and, in the presence of the older sibling, asked the mother to help the toddler operate them, with no instructions about the older child. Researchers found striking differences in the way siblings interacted in the two cultures and in the way the mothers viewed and handled sibling conflict.

Whereas older siblings in Salt Lake City often tried to take and play with the objects, this did not generally happen in San Pedro. Instead, the older San Pedro children would offer to help their younger siblings, or the two children would play with the toys together. When there was a conflict over possession of the toys, the San Pedro mothers favored the toddlers 94 percent of the time, even taking an object away from the older child if the younger child wanted it; and the older siblings tended to go along, willingly handing the objects to the toddlers or letting them have the objects from the start. In contrast, in more than one-third of the interactions in Salt Lake City, the mothers tried to treat both children equally, negotiating with them or suggesting that they take turns or share. These observations were consistent with reports of mothers in both cultures as to how they handled such issues at home. San Pedro children are given a privileged position until age 3; then they are expected to willingly cooperate with social expectations.

What explains these cultural contrasts? A clue emerged when the mothers were asked at what age children can be held responsible for their actions. Most of the Salt Lake mothers maintained that their toddlers understood the consequences of touching prohibited objects; several said this understanding arises as early as 7 months. Yet all but one of the San Pedro mothers placed the age of understanding social consequences of actions much later—between 2 and 3 years. The Salt Lake mothers regarded their toddlers as capable of intentional misbehavior and punished their toddlers for it; most San Pedro mothers did not. All of the Salt Lake preschoolers (toddlers and their siblings) were under direct caregiver supervision; 11 of the 16 San Pedro preschoolers were on their own much of the time and had more mature household responsibilities.

The researchers suggest that the terrible twos may be a phase specific to societies that place individual freedom before the needs of the group. Ethnographic research suggests that, in societies that place higher value on group needs, freedom of choice does exist, but it goes hand in hand with interdependence, responsibility, and expectations of cooperation. Salt Lake parents seem to believe that responsible behavior develops gradually from engaging in fair competition and negotiations. San Pedro parents seem to believe that responsible behavior develops rapidly when children are old enough to understand the need to respect others' desires as well as their own.

What's Your View?

From your experience or observation of toddlers, which of the two ways of handling sibling conflict would you expect to be more effective?

Check It Out

For more information on this topic, go to www.zerotothree.org. Here you will find links to a survey of 3,000 parents and other adults about commonly asked questions regarding the handling of young children and a downloadable article on "Cultural Models for Early Caregiving."

Self-regulation is the foundation of socialization, and it links all domains of development—physical, cognitive, emotional, and social. Until Laticia was physically able to get around on her own, electric outlets posed no hazard. To stop herself from poking her finger into an outlet requires that she consciously remember and understand what her father told her. Cognitive awareness, however, is not enough; restraining herself also requires emotional control. By reading their parents' emotional responses to their behavior, children continually absorb information about what conduct their parents approve of. As children process, store, and act on this information, their strong desire to please their parents leads them to do as they know their parents want them to, whether or not the parents are there to see.

Before they can control their own behavior, children may need to be able to regulate, or control, their *attentional processes* and to modulate negative emotions (Eisenberg, 2000). Attentional regulation enables children to develop willpower and cope with frustration (Sethi, Mischel, Aber, Shoda, & Rodriguez, 2000).

The growth of self-regulation parallels the development of the self-conscious and evaluative emotions, such as empathy, shame, and guilt (Lewis, 1995, 1997, 1998). It requires the ability to wait for gratification. It is correlated with measures of conscience development, such as resisting temptation and making amends for wrongdoing (Eisenberg, 2000). In most children, the development of self-regulation is not complete until age 3 (Kopp, 1982).

Origins of Conscience: Committed Compliance **Conscience** includes both emotional discomfort about doing something wrong and the ability to refrain from doing it. Before children can develop a conscience, they need to have internalized moral standards. Conscience depends on willingness to do the right thing because a child believes it is right, not (as in self-regulation) just because someone else said so.

Grazyna Kochanska (1993, 1995, 1997a, 1997b) and her colleagues have looked for the origins of conscience in a longitudinal study of a group of toddlers and mothers in Iowa. Researchers studied 103 children ages 26 to 41 months and their mothers playing together with toys for two to three hours, both at home and in a homelike laboratory setting (Kochanska & Aksan, 1995). After a free-play period, a mother would give her child 15 minutes to put away the toys. The laboratory had a special shelf with other, unusually attractive toys, such as a bubble gum machine, a walkie-talkie, and a music box. The child was told not to touch anything on the shelf. After about an hour, the experimenter asked the mother to go into an adjoining room, leaving the child alone with the toys. A few minutes later, a woman entered, played with several of the forbidden toys, and then left the child alone again for 8 minutes.

Children were judged to show **committed compliance** if they willingly followed the orders to clean up and not to touch the special toys, without reminders or lapses. Children showed **situational compliance** if they needed prompting; their compliance depended on ongoing parental control. Committed compliance is related to internalization of parental values and rules (Kochanska, Coy, & Murray, 2001).

The roots of committed compliance go back to infancy. Committed compliers, most typically girls, tend to be those who, at 8 to 10 months, could refrain from touching when told, "No!" Committed compliance tends to increase with age, whereas situational compliance decreases (Kochanska, Tjebkes, & Forman, 1998). Mothers of committed compliers, as contrasted with mothers of situational compliers, tend to rely on gentle guidance rather than force, threats, or other forms of negative control (Eisenberg, 2000; Kochanska & Aksan, 1995; Kochanska et al., 2004).

Receptive cooperation goes beyond committed compliance. It is a child's eager willingness to cooperate harmoniously with a parent, not only in disciplinary situations, but in a variety of daily interactions, including routines, chores, hygiene, and play. Receptive cooperation enables a child to be an active partner in

conscience Internal standards of behavior, which usually control one's conduct and produce emotional discomfort when violated.

committed compliance Kochanska's term for wholehearted obedience of a parent's orders without reminders or lapses.

situational compliance Kochanska's term for obedience of a parent's orders only in the presence of signs of ongoing parental control.

receptive cooperation Kochanska's term for eager willingness to cooperate harmoniously with a parent in daily interactions, including routines, chores, hygiene, and play.

What's Your View?

- In view of Kochanska's research on the roots of conscience, what questions would you ask about the early socialization of antisocial adolescents and adults?

Checkpoint

Can you . . .

- Tell when and how self-regulation develops and how it contributes to socialization?

- Distinguish among committed compliance, situational compliance, and receptive cooperation?

- Discuss how temperament, attachment, and parenting practices affect socialization?

Guidepost 7

How do infants and toddlers interact with siblings and other children?

socialization. In a longitudinal study of 101 7-month-olds, those who were prone to anger, who received unresponsive parenting, or who were insecurely attached at 15 months tended to be low in receptive cooperation at that age. Children who were securely attached and whose mothers had been responsive to the child during infancy tended to be high in receptive cooperation (Kochanska, Aksan, & Carlson, 2005).

Factors in the Success of Socialization   The way parents go about the job of socializing a child together with a child's temperament and the quality of the parent-child relationship may help predict how hard or easy socialization will be (Kochanska, 1993, 1995, 1997a, 1997b, 2002). Factors in the success of socialization may include security of attachment, observational learning from parents' behavior, and the mutual responsiveness of parent and child (Kochanska, Aksan, Knaack, & Rhines, 2004; Maccoby, 1992). All these as well as socioeconomic and cultural factors (Harwood, Schoelmerich, Ventura-Cook, Schulze, & Wilson, 1996) may play a part in motivation to comply. However, not all children respond to socialization in the same way. For example, a temperamentally fearful toddler may respond better to gentle reminders than to strong admonitions (Kochanska, Aksan, & Joy, 2007).

Secure attachment and a warm, mutually responsive, parent-child relationship seem to foster committed compliance and conscience development. From the child's second year until early school age, researchers observed more than 200 mothers and children in lengthy, naturalistic interactions: caregiving routines, preparing and eating meals, playing, relaxing, and doing household chores. Children who were judged to have mutually responsive relationships with their mothers tended to show *moral emotions* such as guilt and empathy; *moral conduct* in the face of strong temptation to break rules or violate standards of behavior; and *moral cognition,* as judged by their response to hypothetical, age-appropriate moral dilemmas (Kochanska, 2002).

Constructive conflict over a child's misbehavior—conflict that involves negotiation, reasoning, and resolution—can help children develop moral understanding by enabling them to see another point of view. In one observational study, 2½-year-olds whose mothers gave clear explanations for their requests, compromised, or bargained with the child were better able to resist temptation at age 3 than children whose mothers had threatened, teased, insisted, or given in. Discussion of emotions in conflict situations ("How would you feel if . . .") also led to conscience development, probably by fostering the development of moral emotions (Laible & Thompson, 2002).

Contact with Other Children

Although parents exert a major influence on children's lives, relationships with other children—both in the home and out of it—are also important from infancy on.

Siblings

Sibling relationships play a distinct role in socialization (Vandell, 2000). Sibling conflicts can become a vehicle for understanding social relationships (Dunn & Munn, 1985; Ram & Ross, 2001). Lessons and skills learned from interactions with siblings carry over to relationships outside the home (Brody, 1998).

Babies usually become attached to their older brothers and sisters. Although rivalry may be present, so is affection. The more securely attached siblings are to their parents, the better they get along with each other (Teti & Ablard, 1989).

Nevertheless, as babies begin to move around and become more assertive, they inevitably come into conflict with siblings—at least in U.S. culture. Sibling conflict increases dramatically after the younger child reaches 18 months (Vandell & Bailey, 1992). During the next few months, younger siblings begin to participate more fully in family interactions and become more involved in family disputes. As they do, they become more aware of others' intentions and feelings. They begin to recognize what kind of behavior will upset or annoy an older brother or sister and what behavior is considered "naughty" or "good" (Dunn & Munn, 1985).

As this cognitive and social understanding grows, sibling conflict tends to become more constructive, and the younger sibling participates in attempts to reconcile. As with parent-child conflict, constructive conflict with siblings helps children recognize each other's needs, wishes, and point of view, and it helps them learn how to fight, disagree, and compromise within the context of a safe, stable relationship (Vandell & Bailey, 1992).

In many non-Western cultures, it is common to see older siblings caring for younger siblings, as these Chinese children are doing.

Sociability with Nonsiblings

Infants and—even more so—toddlers show interest in people outside the home, particularly people their own size. During the first few months, they look, smile, and coo at other babies (T. M. Field, 1978). From about 6 to 12 months, they increasingly smile at, touch, and babble to them (Hay, Pedersen, & Nash, 1982). At about 1 year, when the biggest items on their agenda are learning to walk and to manipulate objects, babies pay less attention to other people (T. M. Field & Roopnarine, 1982). This stage does not last long, though. From about 1½ years to almost 3, children show growing interest in what other children do and an increasing understanding of how to deal with them (Eckerman, Davis, & Didow, 1989; Eckerman & Stein, 1982).

Toddlers learn by imitating one another. Games such as follow-the-leader help toddlers connect with other children and pave the way for more complex games during the preschool years (Eckerman et al., 1989). Imitation of each other's actions leads to more frequent verbal communication (such as "You go in playhouse," "Don't do it!" or "Look at me"), which helps peers coordinate joint activity (Eckerman & Didow, 1996). Cooperative activity develops during the second and third years as social understanding grows (Brownell, Ramani, & Zerwas, 2006). As with siblings, conflict too can have a purpose: helping children learn how to negotiate and resolve disputes (Caplan, Vespo, Pedersen, & Hay, 1991).

Some children, of course, are more sociable than others, reflecting such temperamental traits as their usual mood, readiness to accept new people, and ability to adapt to change. Sociability is also influenced by experience; babies who spend time with other babies, as in child care, become sociable earlier than those who spend almost all their time at home.

✔ **Checkpoint**

Can you . . .

♦ Explain how sibling relationships play a part in socialization?

♦ Describe changes in sibling interactions during toddlerhood?

♦ Trace changes in sociability during the first three years, and state two influences on it?

These children in a high-quality group day care program are likely to do at least as well cognitively and socially as children cared for full-time at home. The most important element of day care is the caregiver or teacher, who exerts a strong influence on the children in her care.

Guidepost 8

How do parental employment and early child care affect infants' and toddlers' development?

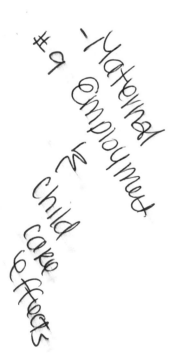

Children of Working Parents

Parents' work determines more than the family's financial resources. Much of adults' time, effort, and emotional involvement goes into their occupations. How do their work and their child care arrangements affect infants and toddlers? Most research on this subject pertains to mothers' work. More than half (52.9 percent) of mothers of infants under 1 year and 57.5 percent of women with children under 3 were in the labor force in 2004 (Bureau of Labor Statistics, 2005).

Effects of Maternal Employment

Longitudinal data on 900 European American children from the National Institute of Child Health and Human Development (NICHD) Study of Early Child Care, discussed in the next section, showed negative effects on cognitive development at 15 months to 3 years when mothers worked 30 or more hours a week by a child's 9th month. Maternal sensitivity, a high-quality home environment, and high-quality child care lessened but did not eliminate these negative effects (Brooks-Gunn, Han, & Waldfogel, 2002).

Similarly, among 6,114 children from the National Longitudinal Survey of Youth (NLSY), those whose mothers worked full-time in the first year after giving birth were more likely to show negative cognitive and behavioral outcomes at ages 3 to 8 than children whose mothers worked part-time or not at all during their first year. However, children in disadvantaged families showed less negative cognitive effects than children in more advantaged families (Hill, Waldfogel, Brooks-Gunn, & Han, 2005).

On the other hand, a longitudinal study of an ethnically, socioeconomically, and geographically diverse sample of 1,364 children during their first 3 years suggests that the economic and social benefits of maternal employment may outweigh any disadvantages resulting from reduced time with a child. Mothers who worked outside the home compensated for some of their work time by reducing time spent on non–child care activities. Differences in time spent with infants were modestly related to maternal sensitivity but did not seem to affect social or cognitive outcomes. Infants whose mothers spent more time with them did have more stimulating home environments, but so did infants whose mothers spent more time at work. It seems, then, that mothers who are temperamentally prone to be sensitive and to provide stimulating, warm home environments may find ways to do so whether or not they are employed (Huston & Aronson, 2005).

Early Child Care

One factor in the impact of a mother's working outside the home is the type of substitute care a child receives. In 2005, about 60 percent of U.S. children not yet in kindergarten were in some type of regular child care (Iruka & Carver, 2006.) More than 50 percent of the 11.3 million whose mothers were employed received care from relatives—30 percent from grandparents, 25 percent from their fathers, 3 percent from siblings, and 8 percent from other relatives. More than 30 percent were in organized day care or preschools. With nonrelative care averaging $129 a week (U.S. Census Bureau, 2008b), affordability and quality of care are pressing issues.

Factors in Impact of Child Care The impact of early child care may depend on the type, amount, quality, and stability of care as well as the family's income and the age at which children start receiving nonmaternal care. By 9 months, about 50 percent of U.S. infants are in some kind of regular nonparental child care arrangement, and 86 percent of these infants enter child care before they reach 6 months. More than 50 percent of these babies are in child care more than 30 hours a week (NCES, 2005a).

Temperament and gender may make a difference (Crockenberg, 2003). Shy children in child care experience greater stress, as shown by cortisol levels, than sociable children (Watamura, Donzella, Alwin, & Gunnar, 2003), and insecurely attached children undergo greater stress than securely attached children when introduced to full-time child care (Ahnert et al., 2004). Boys are more vulnerable to stress, in child care and elsewhere, than are girls (Crockenberg, 2003).

Quality of care contributes to cognitive and psychosocial competence (Marshall, 2004; de Schipper, Riksen-Walraven, & Geurts, 2006). Quality of care can be measured by *structural characteristics,* such as staff training and the ratio of children to caregivers; and by *process characteristics,* such as the warmth, sensitivity, and responsiveness of caregivers and the developmental appropriateness of activities. Structural quality and process quality may be related; in one study, well-trained caregivers and low child-staff ratios were associated with higher process quality, which, in turn, was associated with better cognitive and social outcomes (Marshall, 2004).

The most important element in quality of care is the caregiver; stimulating interactions with responsive adults are crucial to early cognitive, linguistic, and psychosocial development. Low staff turnover is important; infants need consistent caregiving in order to develop trust and secure attachments (Burchinal, Roberts, Nabors, & Bryant, 1996; Shonkoff & Phillips, 2000). Stability of care facilitates coordination between parents and child care providers, which may help protect against any negative effects of long hours of care (Ahnert & Lamb, 2003). Unfortunately, most child care centers do not meet all recommended guidelines for quality care (Bergen, Reid, & Torelli, 2000; NICHD Early Child Care Research Network, 1998c, 1999a; Table 6-5).

Table 6-5	Checklist for Choosing a Good Child Care Facility

- Is the facility licensed? Does it meet minimum state standards for health, fire, and safety? (Many centers and home care facilities are not licensed or regulated.)
- Is the facility clean and safe? Does it have adequate indoor and outdoor space?
- Does the facility have small groups, a high adult-to-child ratio, and a stable, competent, highly involved staff?
- Are caregivers trained in child development?
- Are caregivers warm, affectionate, accepting, responsive, and sensitive? Are they authoritative but not too restrictive, and neither too controlling nor merely custodial?
- Does the program promote good health habits?
- Does it provide a balance between structured activities and free play? Are activities age appropriate?
- Do the children have access to educational toys and materials, which stimulate mastery of cognitive and communicative skills at a child's own pace?
- Does the program nurture self-confidence, curiosity, creativity, and self-discipline?
- Does it encourage children to ask questions, solve problems, express feelings and opinions, and make decisions?
- Does it foster self-esteem, respect for others, and social skills?
- Does it help parents improve their child-rearing skills?
- Does it promote cooperation with public and private schools and the community?

Sources: American Academy of Pediatrics (AAP), 1986; Belsky, 1984; Clarke-Stewart, 1987; NICHD Early Child Care Research Network, 1996; Olds, 1989; Scarr, 1998.

The NICHD Study: Isolating Child Care Effects   Because child care is an integral part of what Bronfenbrenner calls a child's bioecological system (refer back to Chapter 2), it is difficult to measure its influence alone. The most comprehensive attempt to separate child care effects from such other factors as family characteristics, the child's characteristics, and the care the child receives at home is an ongoing study sponsored by the National Institute of Child Health and Human Development (NICHD).

This longitudinal study of 1,364 children and their families began in 1991 in 10 university centers across the United States, shortly after the children's birth. The sample was diverse socioeconomically, educationally, and ethnically; nearly 35 percent of the families were poor or near poor. Most infants entered nonmaternal care before 4 months and received, on average, 33 hours of care each week. Child care arrangements varied widely in type and quality. Researchers measured the children's social, emotional, cognitive, and physical development at frequent intervals from age 1 month through the first seven years of life.

The study showed that the amount and quality of care children received as well as the type and stability of care influenced specific aspects of development. For example, the more time a child spent in child care up to age 4½, the more likely that child was to be seen by adults as aggressive, disobedient, and hard to get along with, then and in kindergarten and on into sixth grade—though this effect was limited in size. Long days in child care have been associated with stress for 3- and 4-year-olds (Belsky et al., 2007; NICHD Early Child Care Research Network, 2003).

On the other hand, children in child care centers with low child-staff ratios, small group sizes, and trained, sensitive, responsive caregivers who provided positive interactions and language stimulation scored higher on tests of language comprehension, cognition, and readiness for school than did children in lower-quality care. Their mothers also reported fewer behavior problems (NICHD Early Child Care Research Network, 1999a, 2000, 2002). In a follow-up study, children who had received higher-quality care before entering kindergarten had better

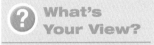
What's Your View?

- In the light of findings about effects of early child care, what advice would you give a new mother about the timing of her return to work and the selection of child care?

vocabulary scores in fifth grade than children who had received lower-quality care (Belsky et al., 2007).

However, factors related to child care were less influential than family characteristics, such as income, the home environment, the amount of mental stimulation the mother provides, and the mother's sensitivity to her child. These characteristics strongly predict developmental outcomes, regardless of how much time children spend in outside care (Belsky et al., 2007; Marshall, 2004; NICHD Early Child Care Research Network, 1998a, 1998b, 2000, 2003).

Child care had no direct effect on attachment, no matter how early infants entered care or how many hours they spent in it. Neither did the stability and quality of care affect attachment in and of themselves. However, when unstable, poor-quality, or more-than-minimal amounts of child care (10 or more hours a week) were combined with insensitive, unresponsive mothering, insecure attachment was more likely. On the other hand, high-quality care seemed to help offset insensitive mothering (NICHD Early Child Care Research Network, 1997, 2001b).

It should not be surprising that what look like effects of child care often may be related to family characteristics. After all, stable families with favorable home environments are more able and therefore more likely to place their children in high-quality care.

One area in which the NICHD study did find independent effects of child care was in interactions with peers. Between ages 2 and 3, children whose caregivers were sensitive and responsive tended to become more positive and competent in play with other children (NICHD Early Child Care Research Network, 2001a).

To sum up, the NICHD findings give high-quality child care good marks overall, especially for its impact on cognitive development and interaction with peers. Some observers say that the areas of concern the study pinpointed—stress levels in infants and toddlers and possible behavior problems related to amounts of care—might be counteracted by activities that enhance children's attachment to caregivers and peers, emphasize child-initiated learning and internalized motivation, and focus on group social development (Maccoby & Lewis, 2003).

Maltreatment: Abuse and Neglect

Although most parents are loving and nurturing, some cannot or will not take proper care of their children, and some deliberately harm them. *Maltreatment,* whether perpetrated by parents or others, is deliberate or avoidable endangerment of a child.

Maltreatment: Facts and Figures

Maltreatment takes several specific forms, and the same child can be a victim of more than one type (USDHHS, Administration on Children, Youth, and Families, 2006):

- **Physical abuse,** injury to the body through punching, beating, kicking, shaking or burning

- **Neglect,** failure to meet a child's basic needs, such as food, clothing, medical care, protection, and supervision

- **Sexual abuse,** any sexual activity involving a child and an older person

- **Emotional maltreatment,** including rejection, terrorization, isolation, exploitation, degradation, ridicule, or failure to provide emotional support, love, and affection

Checkpoint

Can you . . .

- Evaluate the impact of a mother's employment on her baby's well-being?
- List at least five criteria for good child care?
- Compare the impact of child care and of family characteristics on emotional, social, and cognitive development?

Guidepost 9

What are the causes and consequences of child abuse and neglect, and what can be done about them?

physical abuse Action taken deliberately to endanger another person, involving potential bodily injury.

neglect Failure to meet a dependent's basic needs.

sexual abuse Physically or psychologically harmful sexual activity or any sexual activity involving a child and an older person.

emotional maltreatment Rejection, terrorization, isolation, exploitation, degradation, ridicule, or failure to provide emotional support, love, and affection; or other action or inaction that may cause behavioral, cognitive, emotional, or mental disorders.

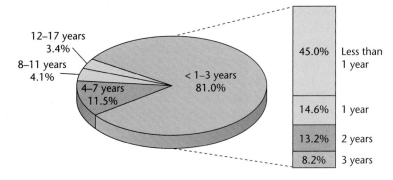

Figure 6-2

Deaths from maltreatment by age, 2004. More than three-quarters (81 percent) of fatalities are of children younger than 4, and 45 percent are of infants younger than 1 year. (Source: USDHHS, Administration on Children, Youth, and Families, 2006.)

failure to thrive An apparently healthy, well-fed baby's failure to grow, often as a result of emotional neglect.

shaken baby syndrome (SBS) Form of maltreatment in which shaking an infant or toddler can cause brain damage, paralysis, or death.

The rate of child abuse and neglect per 1,000 in the U.S. population has dropped from 13.4 children in 1990 to 11.9 in 2004. Still, state and local child protective services agencies investigated and confirmed some 872,000 cases in 2004 (USDHHS, Administration on Children, Youth, and Families, 2006), and the actual number may have been considerably higher (Theodore et al., 2005). More than 60 percent of children identified as maltreated are neglected. About 18 percent are physically abused, 10 percent are sexually abused, and 7 percent emotionally maltreated. An estimated 1,490 U.S. children died of abuse or neglect in 2004. More than one-third of child fatalities were attributed to neglect (USDHHS, Administration on Children, Youth, and Families, 2006).

Children are abused and neglected at all ages and across socioeconomic lines, but the highest rates of victimization and of death from maltreatment are for ages 3 and younger (USDHHS, Administration on Children, Youth, and Families, 2006; Figure 6-2). Some infants die of **failure to thrive**, often due to neglect. Failure to thrive can result from a combination of inadequate nutrition, disturbed interactions with parents, and other factors, such as disease, difficulties in breast-feeding, and improper formula preparation or feeding techniques. Poverty is the greatest single risk factor for failure to thrive worldwide (Block, Krebs, Committee on Child Abuse and Neglect, & Committee on Nutrition, 2005).

Shaken baby syndrome (SBS) is a form of maltreatment found mainly in children under 2 years, most often in infants. A caregiver who is frustrated or angered by an infant's crying, and who is unable to handle stress or has unrealistic expectations for infant behavior, may lose control and shake a crying baby in a desperate attempt to quiet the child. Because a baby has weak neck muscles and a large, heavy head, shaking makes the fragile brain bounce back and forth inside the skull. This causes bruising, bleeding, and swelling and can lead to permanent, severe brain damage, paralysis, or death (AAP, 2000; NINDS, 2006). Head trauma is the leading cause of death in child abuse cases in the United States (Dowshen et al., 2004). About 20 percent of shaken babies die within a few days. Survivors may be left with a range of disabilities, from learning and behavioral disorders to neurological injuries, retardation, paralysis, or blindness, or in a permanent vegetative state (King et al., 2003; National Center on Shaken Baby Syndrome, 2000; NINDS, 2006).

Contributing Factors: An Ecological View

As Bronfenbrenner's bioecological theory would suggest, abuse and neglect reflect the interplay of multiple layers of contributing factors involving the family, the community, and the larger society.

Characteristics of Abusive and Neglectful Parents and Families In nearly 8 out of 10 cases of maltreatment the perpetrators are the child's parents, usually the mother; and 63 percent of these cases involve neglect. Seven percent of perpetrators are other relatives, and 4 percent are unmarried partners of parents. Three out of four perpetrators who are family friends and neighbors commit sexual abuse (USDHHS, Administration on Children, Youth, and Families, 2006).

Maltreatment by parents is a symptom of extreme disturbance in child rearing, usually aggravated by other family problems, such as poverty, lack of education, alcoholism, depression, or antisocial behavior. A disproportionate number of abused and neglected children are in large, poor, or single-parent families, which tend to be under stress and to have trouble meeting children's needs (Sedlak & Broadhurst, 1996; USDHHS, 2004). Yet what pushes one parent over the edge, another may take in stride. Although most neglect cases occur in very poor families, most low-income parents do not neglect their children.

The likelihood that a child will be physically abused has little to do with the child's own characteristics and more to do with the household environment (Jaffee et al., 2004). Abuse may begin when a parent who is already anxious, depressed, or hostile tries to control a child physically but loses self-control and ends up shaking or beating the child. Parents who abuse children tend to have marital problems and to fight physically. Their households are often disorganized, and they experience more stressful events than other families.

Parents who are neglectful distance themselves from their children. Many of the mothers were neglected themselves as children and are depressed or feel hopeless. Many of the fathers have deserted or do not give enough financial or emotional support (Dubowitz, 1999).

Abuse and neglect sometimes occur in the same families (USDHHS, Administration on Children, Youth, and Families, 2006). Such families tend to have no one to turn to in times of stress and no one to see what is happening (Dubowitz, 1999). Substance abuse is a factor in at least one-third of cases of abuse and neglect (USDHHS, 1999a). Sexual abuse often occurs along with other family disturbances such as physical abuse, emotional maltreatment, substance abuse, and family violence (Kellogg & the Committee on Child Abuse and Neglect, 2005).

Community Characteristics and Cultural Values   What makes one low-income neighborhood a place where children are highly likely to be maltreated and another, matched for ethnic population and income levels, safer? In one inner-city Chicago neighborhood, the proportion of children who died from maltreatment (1 death for every 2,541 children) was about twice the proportion in another inner-city neighborhood. In the high-abuse community, criminal activity was rampant, and facilities for community programs were dreary. In the low-abuse neighborhood, people described their community as a poor but decent place to live. They painted a picture of a neighborhood with robust social support networks, well-known community services, and strong political leadership. In a community like this, maltreatment is less likely to occur (Garbarino & Kostelny, 1993).

Two cultural factors associated with child abuse are societal violence and physical punishment of children. In countries where violent crime is infrequent and children are rarely spanked, such as Japan, China, and Tahiti, child abuse is rare (Celis, 1990). In the United States, homicide, domestic violence, and rape are common, and many states still permit corporal punishment in schools. According to a representative sampling, more than 9 out of 10 parents of preschoolers and about half of parents of school-age children report using physical punishment at home (Straus & Stewart, 1999; see chapter 8).

Helping Families in Trouble

State and local child protective services agencies investigate reports of maltreatment. After making a determination of maltreatment, they determine what steps, if any, need to be taken and marshal community resources to help. Agency staff may try to help the family resolve their problems or arrange for alternative care for children who cannot safely remain at home. In 2004, approximately 60 percent of victims received such services (USDHHS, Administration on Children, Youth, and Families, 2006).

Services for children who have been abused and their parents include shelters, education in parenting skills, and therapy. However, availability of services is often limited. In a nationally representative survey, nearly half (47.9 percent) of 2- to 14-year-olds investigated by child welfare agencies after reported maltreatment had clinically significant emotional or behavioral problems, but only one-fourth of those with such problems received mental health care (Burns et al., 2004).

When authorities remove children from their homes, the usual alternative is foster care. In 2004, about 19 percent of victims of maltreatment were placed in foster homes (USDHHS, Administration on Children, Youth, and Families, 2006). Foster care removes a child from immediate danger, but it is often unstable, further alienates the child from the family, and may turn out to be another abusive situation. Often a child's basic health and educational needs are not met (David and Lucile Packard Foundation, 2004; NRC, 1993b).

In part because of a scarcity of traditional foster homes and an increasing caseload, a growing proportion of placements (31 percent) are in kinship foster care, under the care of grandparents or other family members (Berrick, 1998; Geen, 2004). Although most foster children who leave the system are reunited with their families, about 28 percent reenter foster care within the next 10 years (Wulczyn, 2004). Children who have been in foster care are more likely than other children to become homeless, to commit crimes, and to become teenage mothers (David and Lucile Packard Foundation, 2004).

Long-Term Effects of Maltreatment

Consequences of maltreatment may be physical, emotional, cognitive, and social, and these types of consequences are often interrelated. A physical blow to a child's head can cause brain damage resulting in cognitive delays and emotional and social problems. Similarly, severe neglect or unloving parents can have traumatic effects on the developing brain (Fries et al., 2005). In one study, neglected children were more likely than either abused or non-maltreated children to misread emotional signals on faces (Sullivan, Bennett, Carpenter, & Lewis, 2007).

Long-term consequences of maltreatment may include poor physical, mental, and emotional health; impaired brain development (Glaser, 2000); cognitive, language, and academic difficulties; problems in attachment and social relationships (NCCANI, 2004); memory problems (Brunson et al., 2005), and, in adolescence, heightened risks of poor academic achievement, delinquency, teenage pregnancy, alcohol and drug use, and suicide (Dube et al., 2003; Dube et al., 2001; Lansford et al., 2002; NCCANI, 2004). An estimated one-third of adults who were abused and neglected in childhood victimize their own children (NCCANI, 2004).

In a study that followed 68 sexually abused children for five years, these children showed more disturbed behavior, had lower self-esteem, and were more depressed, anxious, or unhappy than a control group (Swanston, Tebbutt, O'Toole, & Oates, 1997). Sexually abused children may become sexually active at an early age (Fiscella, Kitzman, Cole, Sidora, & Olds, 1998). Adults who were sexually abused as children tend to be anxious, depressed, angry, or hostile; to mistrust people; to feel isolated and stigmatized; to be sexually maladjusted (Browne & Finkelhor, 1986); and to abuse alcohol or drugs (NRC, 1993b; USDHHS, 1999a).

Why do some abused children grow up to become antisocial or abusive, while others do not? One possible difference is genetic; some genotypes may be more resistant to trauma than others (Caspi et al., 2002; Jaffee et al., 2005). Research with rhesus monkeys suggests another answer. When baby monkeys endured high rates of maternal rejection and abuse in the first month of life, their brains produced less

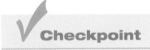

Checkpoint

Can you . . .

- Define four types of child abuse and neglect?

- Discuss the incidence of maltreatment and explain why it is hard to measure?

- Identify contributing factors having to do with the family, the community, and the culture?

- Cite ways to prevent or stop maltreatment and help its victims?

- Give examples of long-term effects of child abuse and neglect and factors that promote resilience?

serotonin, a brain chemical. Low levels of serotonin are associated with anxiety, depression, and impulsive aggression in humans as well as in monkeys. Abused female monkeys who became abusive mothers had less serotonin in their brains than abused females who did not become abusive mothers. This finding suggests that treatment with drugs that increase serotonin levels early in life may prevent an abused child from growing up to abuse her own children (Maestripieri et al., 2006).

Many maltreated children show remarkable resilience. Optimism, self-esteem, intelligence, creativity, humor, and independence are protective factors, as is the social support of a caring adult (NCCANI, 2004). In Chapter 10 we further discuss factors that affect resilience.

The experiences of the first three years lay the foundation for future development. In Part 4, we'll see how young children build on that foundation.

Summary and Key Terms

Foundations of Psychosocial Development

Guidepost 1: *When and how do emotions develop, and how do babies show them?*

- Emotional development is orderly; complex emotions seem to develop from earlier, simpler ones.
- Crying, smiling, and laughing are early signs of emotion. Other indices are facial expressions, motor activity, body language, and physiological changes.
- Brain development is closely linked with emotional development.
- Self-conscious and self-evaluative emotions arise after the development of self-awareness.

   personality (178)

   emotions (178)

   self-conscious emotions (180)

   self-awareness (180)

   self-evaluative emotions (180)

   empathy (181)

Guidepost 2: *How do infants show temperamental differences, and how enduring are those differences?*

- Many children seem to fall into one of three categories of temperament: "easy," "difficult," and "slow-to-warm-up."
- Temperamental patterns appear to be largely inborn and to have a biological basis. They are generally stable but can be modified by experience.
- Goodness of fit between a child's temperament and environmental demands aids adjustment.
- Cross-cultural differences in temperament may reflect child-raising practices.

   temperament (182)

   "easy" children (183)

   "difficult" children (183)

   "slow-to-warm-up" children (183)

   goodness of fit (184)

Guidepost 3: *What roles do mothers and fathers play in early personality development?*

- Child-raising practices and caregiving roles vary around the world.
- Infants have strong needs for maternal closeness, warmth, and responsiveness as well as physical care.
- Fatherhood is a social construction. Fathering roles differ in various cultures.

Guidepost 4: *When and how do gender differences appear?*

- Although significant gender differences typically do not appear until after infancy, U.S. fathers, especially, promote early gender-typing.

   gender (187)

   gender-typing (188)

Developmental Issues in Infancy

Guidepost 5: *How do infants gain trust in their world and form attachments, and how do infants and caregivers read each other's nonverbal signals?*

- According to Erikson, infants in the first 18 months are in the first stage of personality development, basic trust versus basic mistrust. Sensitive, responsive, consistent caregiving is the key to successful resolution of this conflict.
- Research based on the Strange Situation has found four patterns of attachment: secure, avoidant, ambivalent (resistant), and disorganized-disoriented.
- Newer instruments measure attachment in natural settings and in cross-cultural research.
- Attachment patterns may depend on a baby's temperament as well as on the quality of parenting and may have long-term implications for development.
- Stranger anxiety and separation anxiety may arise during the second half of the first year and appear to be related to temperament and circumstances.

- A parent's memories of childhood attachment can influence his or her own child's attachment.
- Mutual regulation enables babies to play an active part in regulating their emotional states.
- A mother's depression, especially if severe or chronic, may have serious consequences for her infant's development.
- Social referencing has been observed by 12 months.

basic trust versus basic mistrust (188)

attachment (189)

Strange Situation (189)

secure attachment (190)

avoidant attachment (190)

ambivalent (resistant) attachment (190)

disorganized-disoriented attachment (190)

stranger anxiety (192)

separation anxiety (192)

mutual regulation (195)

social referencing (195)

Developmental Issues in Toddlerhood

Guidepost 6: *When and how does the sense of self arise, and how do toddlers exercise autonomy and develop standards for socially acceptable behavior?*

- The sense of self arises between 4 and 10 months, as infants begin to perceive a difference between self and others and to experience a sense of agency and self-coherence.
- The self-concept builds on this perceptual sense of self and develops between 15 and 24 months with the emergence of self-awareness and self-recognition.
- Erikson's second stage concerns autonomy versus shame and doubt. In U.S. culture, negativism is a normal manifestation of the shift from external control to self-control.
- Socialization, which rests on internalization of societally approved standards, begins with the development of self-regulation.
- A precursor of conscience is committed compliance to a caregiver's demands; toddlers who show committed compliance tend to internalize adult rules more readily than those who show situational compliance. Children who show receptive cooperation can be active partners in their socialization.
- Parenting practices, a child's temperament, the quality of the parent-child relationship, and cultural and socio-economic factors may affect the ease and success of socialization.

self-concept (197)

autonomy versus shame and doubt (198)

socialization (199)

internalization (199)

self-regulation (199)

conscience (201)

committed compliance (201)

situational compliance (201)

receptive cooperation (202)

Contact with Other Children

Guidepost 7: *How do infants and toddlers interact with siblings and other children?*

- Sibling relationships play a distinct role in socialization; what children learn from relations with siblings carries over to relationships outside the home.
- Between ages 1½ and 3 years, children tend to show more interest in other children and increasing understanding of how to deal with them.

Children of Working Parents

Guidepost 8: *How do parental employment and early child care affect infants' and toddlers' development?*

- In general, mothers' workforce participation during a child's first three years seems to have little impact on development, but cognitive development may suffer when a mother works 30 or more hours a week by her child's ninth month.
- Substitute child care varies in quality. The most important element in quality of care is the caregiver.
- Although quality, quantity, stability, and type of care influence psychosocial and cognitive development, the influence of family characteristics seems greater overall.

Maltreatment: Abuse and Neglect

Guidepost 9: *What are the causes and consequences of child abuse and neglect, and what can be done about them?*

- Forms of maltreatment are physical abuse, neglect, sexual abuse, and emotional maltreatment.
- Most victims of maltreatment are infants and toddlers. Some die due to failure to thrive. Others are victims of shaken baby syndrome.
- Characteristics of the abuser or neglecter, the family, the community, and the larger culture all contribute to child abuse and neglect.
- Maltreatment can interfere with physical, cognitive, emotional, and social development, and its effects can continue into adulthood. Still, many maltreated children show remarkable resilience.
- Preventing or stopping maltreatment may require multifaceted, coordinated community efforts.

physical abuse (207)

neglect (207)

sexual abuse (207)

emotional maltreatment (207)

failure to thrive (208)

shaken baby syndrome (SBS) (208)

7 | Physical and Cognitive Development in Early Childhood

Children live in a world of imagination and feeling. . . .
They invest the most insignificant object with any form
they please, and see in it whatever they wish to see.

—Adam G. Oehlenschlager, 1857

Did You **Know...**

- Sleepwalking and sleeptalking are common in early childhood?
- The leading cause of death in early childhood in the United States is accidents, and most of them occur in the home?
- Poor and minority children are more likely than other children to have health problems and to lack medical insurance and access to care?
- Until age 3, most children don't understand the relationship between pictures and the objects they represent?
- The way parents talk with a child about a shared memory can affect how well the child will remember it?
- When children talk to themselves, they may be trying to solve a problem by thinking out loud?

These are just a few of the interesting and important topics we will cover in this chapter. In it, we look at physical and cognitive development during the years from 3 to 6. Children grow more slowly than before, but still at a fast pace; and they make so much progress in muscle development and coordination that they can do much more. Children also make enormous advances in the abilities to think, speak, and remember. We trace all these developing capabilities and consider several health concerns. We also discuss an experience increasingly common in many places: early childhood education. After you have read and studied this chapter, you should be able to answer each of the Guidepost questions on the following page.

Guideposts *for Study*

1. How do children's bodies and brains change between ages 3 and 6, and what sleep problems and motor achievements are common?

2. What are the major health and safety risks for young children?

3. What are typical cognitive advances and immature aspects of preschool children's thinking?

4. What memory abilities expand in early childhood?

5. How is preschoolers' intelligence measured, and what are some influences on it?

6. How does language improve during early childhood, and what happens when its development is delayed?

7. What purposes does early childhood education serve, and how do children make the transition to kindergarten?

Guidepost 1

How do children's bodies and brains change between ages 3 and 6, and what sleep problems and motor achievements are common?

PHYSICAL DEVELOPMENT

Aspects of Physical Development

In early childhood, children slim down and shoot up. They need less sleep than before and are more likely to develop sleep problems. They improve in running, hopping, skipping, jumping, and throwing balls. They also become better at tying shoelaces, drawing with crayons, and pouring cereal; and they begin to show a preference for using either the right or left hand.

Bodily Growth and Change

Children grow rapidly between ages 3 and 6, but less quickly than before. At about 3, children normally begin to lose their babyish roundness and take on the slender, athletic appearance of childhood. As abdominal muscles develop, the toddler potbelly tightens. The trunk, arms, and legs grow longer. The head is still relatively large, but the other parts of the body continue to catch up as body proportions steadily become more adultlike.

The pencil mark on the wall that shows Eve's height is 37 inches from the floor, and this "average" 3-year-old now weighs about 30 pounds. Her twin brother Isaac, like most boys this age, is a little taller and heavier and has more muscle per pound of body weight, whereas Eve, like most girls, has more fatty tissue. Both boys and girls typically grow 2 to 3 inches a year during early childhood and gain 4 to 6 pounds annually (Table 7-1). Boys' slight edge in height and weight continues until the growth spurt of puberty.

Muscular and skeletal growth progresses, making children stronger. Cartilage turns to bone at a faster rate than before, and bones become harder, giving the child a firmer shape and protecting the internal organs. These changes, coordinated by the still-maturing brain and nervous system, promote the development of a wide range of motor skills. The increased capacities of the respiratory and circulatory systems build physical stamina and, along with the developing immune system, keep children healthier.

Checkpoint

Can you . . .

♦ Describe typical physical changes between ages 3 and 6, and compare boys' and girls' growth patterns?

Table 7-1	Physical Growth, Ages 3 to 6 (50th percentile)*				
	HEIGHT, INCHES			**WEIGHT, POUNDS**	
Age	Boys	Girls		Boys	Girls
3	37½	37		32	30
3½	39	38½		34	32½
4	40½	39½		36	35
4½	41½	41		38	37
5	43	42½		40	40
5½	44½	44		43	42
6	45½	45½		46	45

* Fifty percent of children in each category are above this height or weight level, and 50 percent are below it.

Source: Kuczmarski et al., 2000.

Table 7-2	Encouraging Healthy Eating Habits

- Parents, not children, should choose mealtimes.
- If the child is not overweight, allow him or her to decide how much to eat. Don't pressure the child to clean the plate.
- Serve portions appropriate to the child's size and age.
- Serve simple, easily identifiable foods. Preschoolers often balk at mixed dishes such as casseroles.
- Serve finger foods as often as possible.
- Introduce only one new food at a time, along with a familiar food the child likes. Offer small servings of new or disliked foods; give second helpings if wanted.
- After a reasonable time, remove the food and do not serve more until the next meal. A healthy child will not suffer from missing a meal, and children need to learn that certain times are appropriate for eating.
- Give the child a choice of foods containing similar nutrients: rye or whole wheat bread, a peach or an apple, yogurt or milk.
- Serve nonfat or lowfat dairy products as sources of calcium and protein.
- Encourage a child to help prepare food; a child can help make sandwiches or mix and spoon out cookie dough.
- Limit snacking while watching television or videos. Discourage nutrient-poor foods such as salty snacks, fried foods, ice cream, cookies, and sweetened beverages, and instead suggest nutritious snack foods, such as fruits and raw vegetables.
- Turn childish delights to advantage. Serve food in appealing dishes; dress it up with garnishes or little toys; make a party out of a meal.
- Don't fight rituals, in which a child eats foods one at a time, in a certain order.
- Have regular family meals. Make mealtimes pleasant with conversation on interesting topics, keeping talk about eating itself to a minimum.

Sources: American Heart Association et al., 2006; Rolls, Engell, & Birch, 2000; Williams & Caliendo, 1984.

Good nutrition is necessary to support growth and muscle development; Table 7-2 lists some suggestions to help children eat well.

Sleep Patterns and Problems

Sleep patterns change throughout the growing-up years (Figure 7-1), and early childhood has its own distinct rhythms. Most U.S. children average about 11 hours of sleep at night by age 5 and give up daytime naps (Hoban, 2004). In some

Figure 7-1

Typical sleep requirements in childhood. Unlike infants, who sleep about as long day and night, preschoolers get all or almost all their sleep in one long nighttime period. The number of hours of sleep steadily decreases throughout childhood, but individual children may need more or fewer hours than shown here. (Source: Ferber, 1985; similar data in Iglowstein et al., 2003.)

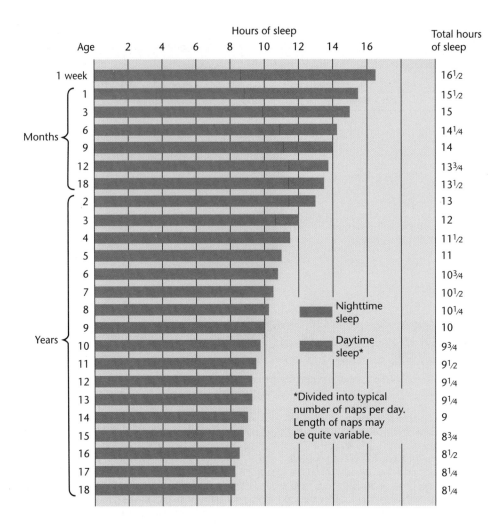

#1 — Sleeping Patterns

other cultures the timing of sleep may vary. Among the Gusii of Kenya, the Javanese in Indonesia, and the Zuni in New Mexico, young children have no regular bedtime and are allowed to stay up until they are sleepy. Among the Canadian Hare, 3-year-olds don't take naps but are put to sleep right after dinner and sleep as long as they wish in the morning (Broude, 1995).

About 1 in 10 U.S. parents or caregivers of preschoolers say their child has a sleep problem, such as frequent night waking or talking while asleep (National Sleep Foundation, 2004). Sleep disturbances may be caused by accidental activation of the brain's motor control system (Hobson & Silvestri, 1999) or by incomplete arousal from a deep sleep (Hoban, 2004) or may be triggered by disordered breathing or restless leg movements (Guilleminault, Palombini, Pelayo, & Chervin, 2003). These disturbances tend to run in families (AACAP, 1997; Hobson & Silvestri, 1999; Hoban, 2004) and are often associated with separation anxiety (Petit, Touchette, Tremblay, Boivin, & Montplaisir, 2007).

In most cases sleep disturbances are only occasional and usually are outgrown. (Table 7-3 gives suggestions for helping children go—or go back—to sleep.) Persistent sleep problems may indicate an emotional, physiological, or neurological condition that needs to be examined.

A child who experiences a *sleep (or night) terror* appears to awaken abruptly early in the night from a deep sleep in a state of agitation. The child may scream and sit up in bed, breathing rapidly and staring or thrashing about. Yet he is not really awake, quiets down quickly, and the next morning remembers nothing

Table 7-3	Encouraging Good Sleep Habits

Helping Children Go to Sleep
- Establish a regular, unrushed bedtime routine—about 20 minutes of quiet activities, such as reading a story, singing lullabies, or having quiet conversation.
- Allow no scary or loud television shows.
- Avoid highly stimulating, active play before bedtime.
- Keep a small night-light on if it makes the child feel more comfortable.
- Don't feed or rock a child at bedtime.
- Stay calm but don't yield to requests for "just one more" story, one more drink of water, or one more bathroom trip.
- Offer rewards for good bedtime behavior, such as stickers on a chart or simple praise.
- Try sending the child to bed a little later. Sending a child to bed too early is a common reason for sleep problems.

Helping Children Go Back to Sleep
- If a child gets up during the night, take him or her back to bed. Speak calmly, but be pleasantly firm and consistent.
- After a nightmare, reassure a frightened child and occasionally check in on the child. If frightening dreams persist for more than six weeks, consult a doctor.
- After night terrors, do not wake the child. If the child wakes, don't ask any questions. Just let the child go back to sleep.
- Help the child get enough sleep on a regular schedule; overtired or stressed children are more prone to night terrors.
- Walk or carry a sleepwalking child back to bed. Childproof your home with gates at the top of stairs and at windows and with bells on the child's bedroom door, so as to know when she or he is out of bed.

Sources: American Academy of Child and Adolescent Psychiatry (ACAP), 1997; American Academy of Pediatrics (AAP), 1992; L. A. Adams & Rickert, 1989; Graziano & Mooney, 1982.

about the episode. Sleep terrors are quite common (Petit et al., 2007). They occur mostly between ages 3 and 13 (Laberge, Tremblay, Vitaro, & Montplaisir, 2000) and affect boys more often than girls (AACAP, 1997; Hobson & Silvestri, 1999).

Walking and, especially, talking during sleep are fairly typical in early childhood (Petit et al., 2007). Although sleepwalking itself is harmless, sleepwalkers may be in danger of hurting themselves (AACAP, 1997; Hoban, 2004; Vgontzas & Kales, 1999). Still, it is best not to interrupt sleepwalking or night terrors, as interruptions may confuse and further frighten the child (Hoban, 2004; Vgontzas & Kales, 1999).

Nightmares are also common. They are often brought on by staying up too late, eating a heavy meal close to bedtime, or overexcitement, perhaps from watching an overstimulating television program, seeing a terrifying movie, or hearing a frightening bedtime story (Vgontzas & Kales, 1999). An occasional bad dream is no cause for alarm, but frequent or persistent nightmares may signal excessive stress (Hoban, 2004).

Most children stay dry, day and night, by ages 3 to 5; but **enuresis**—repeated, involuntary urination at night by children old enough to be expected to have bladder control—is not unusual. About 10 to 15 percent of 5-year-olds, more commonly boys, wet the bed regularly, perhaps while sleeping deeply. More than half outgrow the condition by age 8 without special help (Community Paediatrics Committee, 2005).

Children (and their parents) need to be reassured that enuresis is common and not serious. The child is not to blame and should not be punished.

Sleepwalking is common among young children. It is best to try not to wake a sleepwalking child but rather to gently guide the child back to bed.

enuresis Repeated urination in clothing or in bed.

Table 7-4	Gross Motor Skills in Early Childhood	
3-Year-Olds	**4-Year-Olds**	**5-Year-Olds**
Cannot turn or stop suddenly or quickly	Have more effective control of stopping, starting, and turning	Can start, turn, and stop effectively in games
Can jump a distance of 15 to 24 inches	Can jump a distance of 24 to 33 inches	Can make a running jump of 28 to 36 inches
Can ascend a stairway unaided, alternating feet	Can descend a long stairway alternating feet, if supported	Can descend a long stairway unaided, alternating feet
Can hop, using largely an irregular series of jumps with some variations added	Can hop four to six steps on one foot	Can easily hop a distance of 16 feet

Source: Corbin, 1973.

Checkpoint

Can you . . .

♦ Identify five common sleep problems and give recommendations for handling them?

Generally, parents need not do anything unless children themselves are distressed by bed-wetting. Enuresis that persists beyond ages 8 to 10 may be a sign of poor self-concept or other psychological problems (Community Paediatrics Committee, 2005).

Brain Development

Brain development during early childhood is less dramatic than during infancy, but a brain growth spurt continues until at least age 3, when the brain is approximately 90 percent of adult weight (Gabbard, 1996). The density of synapses in the prefrontal cortex peaks at age 4 (Lenroot & Giedd, 2006). Myelination of pathways for hearing is also complete around that age (Benes, Turtle, Khan, & Farol, 1994). By age 6, the brain has attained about 95 percent of its peak volume. However, wide individual differences exist. Two healthy, normally functioning children of the same age could have as much as a 50 percent difference in brain volume (Lenroot & Giedd, 2006).

A gradual change occurs in the corpus callosum, which links the left and right hemispheres. Progressive myelination of fibers in the corpus callosum permits more rapid transmission of information and better integration between them (Toga et al., 2006). This development, which continues until age 15, improves such functions as coordination of the senses, memory processes, attention and arousal, and speech and hearing (Lenroot & Giedd, 2006). From ages 3 to 6, the most rapid growth occurs in the frontal areas that regulate the planning and organizing of actions. From ages 6 to 11, the most rapid growth is in an area that primarily supports associative thinking, language, and spatial relations (Thompson et al., 2000).

Brain development affects other aspects of development. One of them is growth in motor skills.

Motor Skills

Development of the sensory and motor areas of the cerebral cortex permits better coordination between what children want to do and what they can do. Preschool children make great advances in **gross motor skills,** such as running and jumping, which involve the large muscles (Table 7-4). Because their bones and muscles are stronger and their lung capacity is greater, they can run, jump, and climb farther and faster.

gross motor skills Physical skills that involve the large muscles.

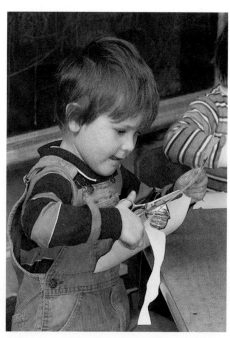

Children make significant advances in motor skills during the preschool years. As they develop physically, they are better able to make their bodies do what they want. Large-muscle development lets them ride a tricycle or kick a ball; increasing eye-hand coordination helps them use scissors or chopsticks. Children with disabilities can do many normal activities with the aid of special devices.

Children vary in adeptness, depending on their genetic endowment and their opportunities to learn and practice motor skills. Only 20 percent of 4-year-olds can throw a ball well, and only 30 percent can catch well (AAP Committee on Sports Medicine and Fitness, 1992). Most children under age 6 are *not* ready to take part in any organized sport. Physical development flourishes best in active, unstructured free play.

Fine motor skills, such as buttoning shirts and drawing pictures, involve eye-hand and small-muscle coordination. Gains in these skills allow young children to take more responsibility for their personal care.

As they develop motor skills, preschoolers continually merge abilities they already have with those they are acquiring, to produce more complex capabilities. Such combinations of skills are known as **systems of action.**

Handedness **Handedness,** the preference for using one hand over the other, is usually evident by about age 3. Because the left hemisphere of the brain, which controls the right side of the body, is usually dominant, most people favor their right side. In people whose brains are more functionally symmetrical, the right hemisphere tends to dominate, making them left-handed. Handedness is not always clear-cut; not everybody prefers one hand for every task. Boys are more likely to be left-handed than are girls.

Is handedness genetic? One theory proposes the existence of a single gene for right-handedness. According to this theory, people who inherit this gene from either or both parents—about 82 percent of the population—are right-handed. Those who do *not* inherit the gene still have a 50-50 chance of being right-handed; otherwise they will be left-handed or ambidextrous. Random determination of handedness among those who do *not* receive the gene could explain why some monozygotic twins have differing hand preferences as well as why 8 percent of the offspring of two right-handed parents are left-handed (Klar, 1996).

fine motor skills Physical skills that involve the small muscles and eye-hand coordination.

systems of action Increasingly complex combinations of skills, which permit a wider or more precise range of movement and more control of the environment.

handedness Preference for using a particular hand.

Figure 7-2

Artistic development in early childhood. There is a great difference between the very simple shapes shown in (a) and the detailed pictorial drawings in (e). (Source: Kellogg, 1970.)

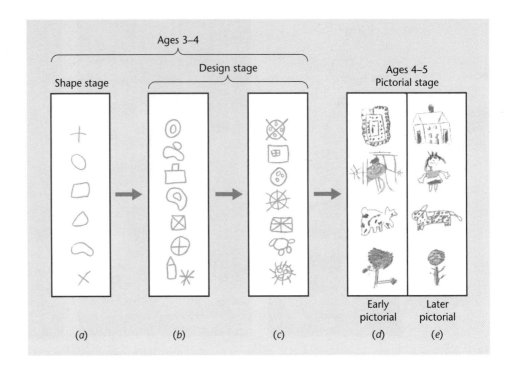

- Drawings from children's early pictorial stage show energy and freedom, according to Kellogg; those from the later pictorial stage show care and accuracy. Why do you think these changes occur?

Checkpoint

Can you . . .

- Summarize changes in the brain during childhood and discuss their possible effects?
- Distinguish between gross motor skills and fine motor skills, and give examples of each type that improve during early childhood?
- Tell how brain functioning is related to motor skills and handedness?
- Evaluate Kellogg's findings on young children's drawing skills in light of other research?

Artistic Development   In a landmark study of children's art, Rhoda Kellogg (1970) examined more than 1 million drawings by children, half of them under age 6. She discovered what she believed to be a universal progression of changes, reflecting maturation of the brain as well as of the muscles (Figure 7-2). She found that 2-year-olds *scribble*—not randomly but in patterns, such as vertical and zigzag lines. By age 3, children draw *shapes*—circles, squares, rectangles, triangles, crosses, and Xs—and then begin combining the shapes into more complex *designs*. The *pictorial* stage typically begins between ages 4 and 5. The switch from abstract form and design to depicting real objects marks a fundamental change in the purpose of children's drawing, reflecting the cognitive development of representational ability.

In Kellogg's view, this developmental sequence occurs by processes internal to the child; the less adult involvement the better. By asking children what their drawings are meant to represent, Kellogg warned, adults may encourage greater pictorial accuracy but stifle the energy and freedom children typically show in their early efforts.

This individualistic model is dominant in the United States, but it is not the only model. Vygotsky, for example, saw the development of drawing skills as occurring in the context of social interactions (Braswell, 2006). Children pick up the features of adult drawing that are within their zone of proximal development (ZPD; see page 241). Four- and five-year-olds who are already drawing simple figures may imitate the way their mother draws a hand, for example, whereas children who are still in the scribbling stage do not (Braswell & Callanan, 2003). Children also learn by looking at and talking about each other's drawings (Braswell, 2006).

Furthermore, the patterns Kellogg discerned in children's drawings are not universal. Many cross-cultural variations exist in, for example, the way children make a person or an animal. Finally, Kellogg's view that adult intervention has a negative influence on children's drawing, although widely shared by many U.S. educators, is also culture-bound. Chinese parents, for example, provide art instruction or models for their children; and Chinese children tend to be more advanced artistically than U.S. children (Braswell, 2006).

Health and Safety

Because of widespread immunization, many of what once were the major diseases of childhood are much less common in Western industrialized countries. In the developing world, however, such vaccine-preventable diseases as measles, pertussis (whooping cough), and tetanus still take a large toll. Even in technologically advanced societies, this is a less healthy time for some children than for others.

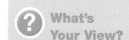
Guidepost 2

What are the major health and safety risks for young children?

Preventing Obesity

Obesity (sometimes called *overweight*) is a serious problem among U.S. preschoolers. In 2003–2006, more than 12 percent of 2- to 5-year-olds had a body mass index (BMI) at or above the 95th percentile for their age, and about 12 percent more were at or above the 85th percentile (Ogden, Carroll, & Flegal, 2008). The greatest increase in prevalence of overweight is among children in low-income families (Ritchie et al., 2001), cutting across all ethnic groups (AAP Committee on Nutrition, 2003; Center for Weight and Health, 2001).

Worldwide, an estimated 22 million children under age 5 are obese (Belizzi, 2002). As junk food spreads through the developing world, as many as 20 to 25 percent of 4-year-olds in some countries, such as Egypt, Morocco, and Zambia, are obese—a larger proportion than are malnourished.

A tendency toward obesity can be hereditary, but the main factors driving the obesity epidemic are environmental (AAP, 2004). Excessive weight gain hinges on caloric intake and lack of exercise (AAP Committee on Nutrition, 2003). As growth slows, preschoolers need fewer calories in proportion to their weight than they did before.

What's Your View?

• Much television advertising aimed at young children fosters poor nutrition and weight gain by promoting fats and sugars rather than proteins and vitamins. How might parents counteract these pressures?

Prevention of obesity in the early years is critical (AAP Committee on Nutrition, 2003; Quattrin, Liu, Shaw, Shine, & Chiang, 2005). Overweight children tend to become obese adults (AAP Committee on Nutrition, 2003; Whitaker et al., 1997), and excess body mass is a threat to health. Thus early childhood is a good time to treat overweight, when a child's diet is still subject to parental influence or control (Quattrin et al., 2005; Whitaker et al., 1997).

A key to preventing obesity may be to make sure older preschoolers are served appropriate portions—and not to force them to clean their plates (Rolls et al., 2000; refer to Table 7-2). Too little physical activity is an important factor in obesity as well. In a longitudinal study of 8,158 U.S. children, each additional hour of TV watching above two hours increased the likelihood of obesity at age 30 by 7 percent (Viner & Cole, 2005).

Undernutrition

Nearly half (46 percent) of young children in south Asia, 30 percent in sub-Saharan Africa, 8 percent in Latin America and the Caribbean, and 27 percent worldwide are moderately or

An obese child might have trouble keeping up with peers—physically and socially. Obesity among young children has increased.

severely underweight (UNICEF, 2002). Undernutrition is an underlying cause in more than half of all deaths before age 5 (Bryce, Boschi-Pinto, Shibuya, Black, & WHO Child Health Epidemiology Reference Group, 2005). Even in the United States, 17 percent of children under 18 lived in food-insecure households in 2005 (Federal Interagency Forum on Child and Family Statistics, 2007).

Because undernourished children usually live in extremely deprived circumstances, the specific effects of poor nutrition may be hard to determine. However, taken together, these deprivations may negatively affect not only growth and physical well-being but cognitive and psychosocial development as well (Alaimo, Olson, & Frongillo, 2001). Moreover, effects of undernutrition may be long lasting. Among 1,559 children born on the island of Mauritius in a single year, those who were undernourished at age 3 had poorer verbal and spatial abilities, reading skills, scholastic ability, and neuropsychological performance than their peers at age 11 (Liu, Raine, Venables, Dalais, & Mednick, 2003).

Effects of undernutrition on growth can be largely reversed with improved diet (Lewit & Kerrebrock, 1997), but the most effective treatments go beyond physical care. A longitudinal study (Grantham-McGregor, Powell, Walker, Chang, & Fletcher, 1994) followed two groups of Jamaican children with low developmental levels who had been hospitalized for severe undernourishment in infancy or toddlerhood and who came from extremely poor, often unstable homes. Health care paraprofessionals played with an experimental group in the hospital and, after discharge, visited them at home every week for three years, showing the mothers how to make toys and encouraging them to interact with their children. Three years after the program stopped, the experimental group's IQs were well above those of a control group who had received only standard medical care (though not as high as those of a third, well-nourished group). Furthermore, the IQs of the experimental group remained higher than those of the control group as much as 14 years after leaving the hospital.

Early education may help counter the effects of undernourishment. In another Mauritian study, 3- to 5-year-olds received nutritional supplements and medical examinations and were placed in special preschools with small classes. At age 17, these children had lower rates of antisocial behavior and mental health problems than a control group (Raine et al., 2003).

Deaths and Accidental Injuries

More than 7 out of 10 deaths of children under age 5 occur in poor, rural regions of sub-Saharan Africa and south Asia, where nutrition is inadequate, water is unsafe, and sanitary facilities are lacking (Black et al., 2003; Bryce et al,. 2005). Box 7-1 discusses children's chances of surviving the first five years of life the world over.

In the United States, deaths in childhood are relatively few compared with deaths in adulthood, and most are caused by injury rather than illness (Hoyert et al., 2007). Most deaths from injuries among preschoolers occur in the home—often from fires, drowning in bathtubs, suffocation, poisoning, or falls (Nagaraja et al., 2005). Everyday medications, such as aspirin, acetaminophen, and cough medicines, and even vitamins can be dangerous to inquisitive young children. During 2001–2003, an estimated 53,000 children ages 4 and under were treated in U.S. hospital emergency departments for unintentional ingestion of prescription and over-the-counter medicines (Burt, Annest, Ballesteros, & Budnitz, 2006).

U.S. laws requiring mandating the use of car seats, childproof caps on medicine bottles and other dangerous household products, regulation of product

? What's Your View?

• In view of childhood undernutrition's apparent long-term effects on physical, social, and cognitive development, what can and should be done to combat it?

✓ Checkpoint

Can you . . .

♦ Summarize obesity trends among preschoolers, and explain why overweight is a concern in early childhood?

♦ Identify effects related to undernutrition and factors that may influence the long-term outcome?

♦ Compare the health status of young children in developed and developing countries?

♦ Tell where and how young children are most likely to be injured?

safety, mandatory helmets for bicycle riders, and safe storage of firearms and of medicines have improved child safety. Making playgrounds safer would be another valuable measure.

Health in Context: Environmental Influences

Why do some children have more illnesses or injuries than others? Some children seem genetically predisposed toward certain medical conditions. In addition, environmental factors play major roles.

Socioeconomic Status and Race/Ethnicity The lower a family's SES, the greater a child's risks of illness, injury, and death (Chen, Matthews, & Boyce, 2002). Poor children—who represent 1 in 5 U.S. children under age 6 and are disproportionately minority children—are more likely than other children to have chronic conditions and activity limitations, to lack health insurance, and to have unmet medical and dental needs. However, the general health of poor children has been improving; between 1984 and 2003, the percentage of poor children in very good or excellent health rose from 62 percent to 71 percent, as compared with 86 to 89 percent for nonpoor children (Federal Interagency Forum on Child and Family Statistics, 2005, 2007).

Access to quality health care is a particular problem among black and Latino children, especially those who are poor or near poor (Flores et al., 2005). Even though poverty rates for black and Latino families have dropped dramatically, they remain much higher than for white families (Hernandez & Macartney, 2008). In 2005, 21 percent of Hispanic American children and 12 percent of black children lacked health insurance (Federal Interagency Forum on Child and Family Statistics, 2007). In 2004, more than 7 percent of Hispanic children under 6 years old had no usual source of health care (NCHS, 2006).

Medicaid, a government program that provides medical assistance to eligible low-income persons and families, has been a safety net for many poor children since 1965. However, it has not reached millions of children whose families earn too much to qualify but too little to afford private insurance. The federal government in 1997 authorized the State Children's Health Insurance Program (SCHIP) to help states extend health care coverage to uninsured children in poor and near-poor families. At the end of 2004, 3.9 million children were enrolled (Smith & Rousseau, 2005). Still, 11 percent of all children had no health coverage in 2005, and 5 percent had no usual source of health care (Federal Interagency Forum on Child and Family Statistics, 2007). In October 2007, President George W. Bush, citing financial and other reasons, twice vetoed a bill to reauthorize and expand SCHIP for five years (Iglehart, 2007). Instead, the program was extended temporarily through 2009.

More than a million children in the United States are homeless, putting them at heightened risk for disease, depression, and academic and behavioral problems.

Homelessness Homelessness has increased dramatically in the United States since 1980 (National Coalition for the Homeless, 2006b, 2006c, 2006e). An estimated 1.35 million children—2 percent of all children and 10 percent of all poor children—are homeless each year, but the true number is most likely higher (National Coalition for the Homeless, 2006a; National Law Center on Homelessness and Poverty, 2004). Many homeless families are headed by single mothers in their twenties, often

BOX **7-1** Window *on the World*

Surviving the First Five Years of Life

The chances of a child's living to his or her fifth birthday have doubled during the past four decades, but prospects for survival depend to a great extent on where the child lives. Worldwide, more than 17 million children under 5 died in 1970. In 2007, the number of deaths in this age group dropped below 10 million for the first time in modern history (Bryce et al., 2005; UNICEF Press Centre, 2007; WHO, 2003)—but this is still far too many, and the gains have not benefited all children equally.

International efforts to improve child health focus on the first five years because nearly 9 out of 10 deaths of children under age 15 occur during those years. Fully 98 percent of child deaths occur in poor, rural regions of developing countries; 42 percent of these deaths occur in sub-Saharan Africa and 29 percent in Southeast Asia (Bryce et al., 2005; WHO, 2003; see figure). A baby born in Sierra Leone on Africa's west coast is three and a half times more likely to die before age 5 than a child born in India and more than 100 times more likely to die than a child born in Iceland, which has the world's lowest child mortality rate (WHO, 2003).

Worldwide, four major causes of death, accounting for 54 percent of deaths in children younger than 5, are communicable diseases: pneumonia, diarrhea, malaria, and neonatal sepsis (see figure). In more than half of these deaths, undernutrition is an underlying cause (Bryce et al., 2005).

More advanced developing countries of the Eastern Mediterrean region, Latin America, and Asia are experiencing a shift toward the pattern in developed countries, where child deaths are most likely to be caused by complications of birth. At least 169 countries have shown declines in child mortality in the past three decades. The most striking reduction was in Oman, on the southern end of the Arabian peninsula, from

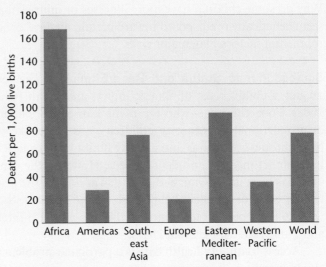

Comparative child mortality in six regions of the world, 2002.
(Source: WHO, 2003.)

242 child deaths per 1,000 live births in 1970 to only 15 per 1,000 in 2002. India and China also have achieved impressive declines. In general, however, the strongest improvement has occurred in rich industrialized nations and in those developing countries where child mortality was already relatively low. Thus, although the mortality gap between the developed and developing worlds has narrowed, disparities among developing regions have widened (WHO, 2003).

In some African countries, HIV/AIDS is responsible for as many as 6 out of 10 child deaths, often in children who lose their

fleeing domestic violence (Buckner, Bassuk, Weinreb, & Brooks, 1999; National Coalition for the Homeless, 2006d).

Many homeless children spend their early years in unstable, insecure, and often unsanitary environments. They may be cut off from ready access to medical care and schooling. These children suffer more physical health problems than poor children who have homes, and they are more likely to die in infancy. Homeless children also tend to suffer from depression and anxiety and to have academic and behavior problems (CDF, 2004; National Coalition for the Homeless, 2006a; Weinreb et al., 2002). In large cities that have provided safe housing for poor and homeless families in stable neighborhoods, the children's behavior and school performance improved greatly (CDF, 2004).

Exposure to Smoking, Air Pollution, Pesticides, and Lead   Parental smoking, both at home and in the family car, is a preventable cause of childhood illness and death. The potential damage caused by exposure to tobacco is greatest during the early years of life (DiFranza, Aligne, & Weitzman, 2004), when children's bodies are still developing. Children exposed to parental smoke are at increased risk of

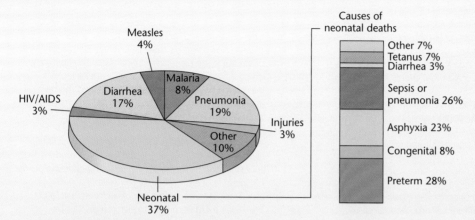

Major causes of death in children younger than 5 and in neonates (yearly average, 2000–2003).
(Source: Bryce et al., 2005.)

Children in poor countries and children of the poor in rich countries are most likely to die young. Survival gains have been slower in rural than in urban areas and, in some countries, such as the United States, have disproportionately benefited those with higher incomes. But even poor U.S. children are less likely to die young than better-off children in Africa (WHO, 2003).

mothers to the disease. Fourteen African countries, after achieving significant reductions in child mortality during the 1970s and 1980s, actually saw *more* young children die in 2002 than in 1990. On the other hand, eight countries in the region have reduced child mortality by more than 50 percent since 1970 (WHO, 2003).

In Latin America, the most dramatic reductions in child mortality have taken place in Chile, Costa Rica, and Cuba, where child deaths have dropped more than 80 percent since 1970. In contrast, Haitian children still die at a rate of 133 per 1,000, almost double the rate in Bolivia, which has the next worst mortality record in the Americas (WHO, 2003).

What's Your View?

What might be done to produce more rapid and more evenly distributed improvements in child mortality throughout the world?

Check It Out

For more information on this topic, go to www.who.int/whr/2003/chapter1/en/index2.html. This is the website for the WHO report discussed in this box.

respiratory infections such as bronchitis and pneumonia, ear problems, worsened asthma, and slowed lung growth (Office on Smoking and Health, 2006).

Air pollution is associated with increased risks of death and of chronic respiratory disease. Environmental contaminants also may play a role in certain childhood cancers, neurological disorders, attention-deficit/hyperactivity disorder, and mental retardation (Goldman et al., 2004; Woodruff et al., 2004). In 2005, 60 percent of U.S. children up to age 17 lived in counties that failed to meet one or more national air quality standards (Federal Interagency Forum for Child and Family Statistics, 2007).

Children are more vulnerable than adults to chronic pesticide damage (Goldman et al., 2004). There is some, though not definitive, evidence that low-dose pesticide exposure may affect the developing brain (Weiss et al., 2004). Pesticide exposure is greater among children in agricultural and inner-city families (Dilworth-Bart & Moore, 2006).

Children can get elevated concentrations of lead from contaminated food or water, from airborne industrial wastes, from putting contaminated fingers in their mouths, or from inhaling dust or playing with paint chips in places where there is

Advance	Significance	Example
Table 7-5 Cognitive Advances during Early Childhood		
Use of symbols	Children do not need to be in sensorimotor contact with an object, person, or event in order to think about it.	Simon asks his mother about the elephants they saw on their trip to the circus several months earlier.
	Children can imagine that objects or people have properties other than those they actually have.	Rolf pretends that a slice of apple is a vacuum cleaner "vrooming" across the kitchen table.
Understanding of identities	Children are aware that superficial alterations do not change the nature of things.	Antonio knows that his teacher is dressed up as a pirate but is still his teacher underneath the costume.
Understanding of cause and effect	Children realize that events have causes.	Seeing a ball roll from behind a wall, Aneko looks behind the wall for the person who kicked the ball.
Ability to classify	Children organize objects, people, and events into meaningful categories.	Rosa sorts the pinecones she collected on a nature walk into two piles: "big" and "little."
Understanding of number	Children can count and deal with quantities.	Lindsay shares some candy with her friends, counting to make sure that each girl gets the same amount.
Empathy	Children become more able to imagine how others might feel.	Emilio tries to comfort his friend when he sees that his friend is upset.
Theory of mind	Children become more aware of mental activity and the functioning of the mind.	Blanca wants to save some cookies for herself, so she hides them from her brother in a pasta box. She knows her cookies will be safe there because her brother will not look in a place where he doesn't expect to find cookies.

peeling lead-based paint. Lead poisoning can interfere with cognitive development and can lead to irreversible neurological and behavioral problems (AAP Committee on Environmental Health, 2005; Bellinger, 2004; Federal Interagency Forum for Child and Family Statistics, 2007). Very high levels of blood lead concentration may cause headaches, abdominal pain, loss of appetite, agitation, or lethargy and eventually vomiting, stupor, and convulsions (AAP Committee on Environmental Health, 2005). Yet all these effects are completely preventable.

Children's median blood lead levels have dropped by 89 percent in the United States since 1976–1980 due to laws mandating removal of lead from gasoline and paints and reducing smokestack emissions (Federal Interagency Forum for Child and Family Statistics, 2005). Still, about 25 percent of U.S. children live in households with deteriorating lead paint (AAP Committee on Environmental Health, 2005).

Checkpoint

Can you . . .

♦ Discuss environmental influences that endanger children's health and development?

COGNITIVE DEVELOPMENT

Piagetian Approach: The Preoperational Child

Guidepost 3

What are typical cognitive advances and immature aspects of preschool children's thinking?

preoperational stage In Piaget's theory, the second major stage of cognitive development, in which symbolic thought expends but children can not yet use logic.

Jean Piaget called early childhood the **preoperational stage** of cognitive development because children this age are not yet ready to engage in logical mental operations, as they will be in the stage of concrete operations in middle childhood (discussed in Chapter 9). However, the preoperational stage, which lasts from approximately ages 2 to 7, is characterized by a great expansion in the use of symbolic thought, or representational ability, which first emerged during the sensorimotor stage. Let's look at some aspects of preoperational thought (Table 7-5 and 7-6) and at recent research, some of which challenges Piaget's conclusions.

Table 7-6	Immature Aspects of Preoperational Thought (according to Piaget)	

Limitation	Description	Example
Centration: inability to decenter	Children focus on one aspect of a situation and neglect others.	Jacob teases his younger sister that he has more juice than she does because his juice box has been poured into a tall, skinny glass, but hers has been poured into a short, wide glass.
Irreversibility	Children fail to understand that some operations or actions can be reversed, restoring the original situation.	Jacob does not realize that the juice in each glass can be poured back into the juice box from which it came, contradicting his claim that he has more than his sister.
Focus on states rather than transformations	Children fail to understand the significance of the transformation between states.	In the conservation task, Jacob does not understand that transforming the shape of a liquid (pouring it from one container into another) does not change the amount.
Transductive reasoning	Children do not use deductive or inductive reasoning; instead they jump from one particular to another and see cause where none exists.	Luis was mean to his sister. Then she got sick. Luis concludes that he made his sister sick.
Egocentrism	Children assume everyone else thinks, perceives, and feels as they do.	Kara doesn't realize that she needs to turn a book around so that her father can see the picture she is asking him to explain to her. Instead, she holds the book directly in front of her, where only she can see it.
Animism	Children attribute life to objects not alive.	Amanda says that spring is trying to come but winter is saying, "I won't go! I won't go!"
Inability to distinguish appearance from reality	Children confuse what is real with outward appearance.	Courtney is confused by a sponge made to look like a rock. She states that it looks like a rock and it really is a rock.

Advances of Preoperational Thought

Advances in symbolic thought are accompanied by a growing understanding of space, causality, identities, categorization, and number. Some of these understandings have roots in infancy and toddlerhood; others begin to develop in early childhood but are not fully achieved until middle childhood.

The Symbolic Function   "I want ice cream!" announces Juanita, age 4, trudging indoors from the hot, dusty backyard. She has not seen anything that triggered this desire—no open freezer door, no television commercial. She no longer needs this kind of sensory cue to think about something. She remembers ice cream, its coldness and taste, and she purposefully seeks it out. This absence of sensory or motor cues characterizes the **symbolic function:** the ability to use symbols, or mental representations—words, numbers, or images to which a person has attached meaning. The use of symbols is a universal mark of human culture. Without symbols, people could not communicate verbally, make change, read maps, or treasure photos of distant loved ones. Symbols help children to remember and think about things that are not physically present.

Preschool children show the symbolic function through the growth of deferred imitation, pretend play, and language. *Deferred imitation,* which becomes more robust after 18 months, is based on a mental representation of a previously observed event. In **pretend play,** also called *fantasy play, dramatic play,* or *imaginative play,* children may make an object, such as a doll, represent, or symbolize, something else, such as a person. *Language* uses a system of symbols (words) to communicate.

symbolic function   Piaget's term for ability to use mental representations (words, numbers, or images) to which a child has attached meaning.

pretend play   Play involving imaginary people and situations; also called *fantasy play, dramatic play,* or *imaginative play.*

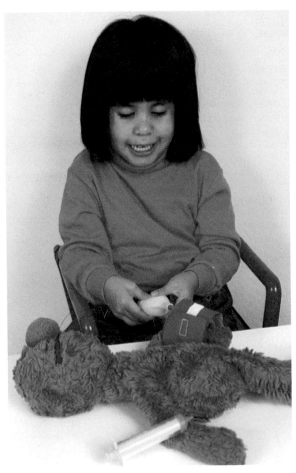

As Anna pretends to take Grover's blood pressure, she is showing a major cognitive achievement: deferred imitation, the ability to act out a behavior she observed some time before.

Understanding of Objects in Space   As we reported in Chapter 5, it is not until at least age 3 that most children reliably grasp the relationships between pictures, maps, or scale models and the objects or spaces they represent. Older preschoolers can use simple maps, and they can transfer the spatial understanding gained from working with models to maps and vice versa (DeLoache, Miller, & Pierroutsakos, 1998). In a series of experiments, preschoolers were asked to use a simple map to find or place an object at the corresponding location in a similarly shaped but much larger space. Ninety percent of 5-year-olds but only 60 percent of 4-year-olds were able to do so (Vasilyeva & Huttenlocher, 2004).

Understanding of Causality   Piaget maintained that preoperational children cannot yet reason logically about cause and effect. Instead, he said, they reason by **transduction.** They mentally link two events, especially events close in time, whether or not there is logically a causal relationship. For example, Luis may think that his "bad" thoughts or behavior caused his own or his sister's illness or his parents' divorce.

transduction   Piaget's term for a preoperational child's tendency to mentally link particular phenomena, whether or not there is logically a causal relationship.

Yet, as we saw in Chapter 5, 2-year-olds and even infants, when tested with age-appropriate methods, do seem to grasp cause and effect; and, by early childhood, children can talk about causal relationships. In naturalistic observations of 2½- to 5-year-olds' everyday conversations with their parents, children showed flexible causal reasoning, appropriate to the subject. Types of explanations ranged from physical ("The scissors have to be clean so I can cut better") to social-conventional ("I have to stop now because you said to") (Hickling & Wellman, 2001). However, preschoolers seem to view all causal relationships as equally and absolutely predictable. In one series of experiments, 3- to 5-year-olds, unlike adults, were just as sure that a person who does not wash his or her hands before eating will get sick as they were that a person who jumps up will come down (Kalish, 1998).

Understanding of Identities and Categorization   The world becomes more orderly and predictable as preschool children develop a better understanding of *identities:* the concept that people and many things are basically the same even if they change in form, size, or appearance. This understanding underlies the emerging self-concept (see Chapter 8).

Categorization, or classification, requires a child to identify similarities and differences. By age 4, many children can classify by two criteria, such as color and shape. Children use this ability to order many aspects of their lives, categorizing people as "good," "bad," "nice," "mean," and so forth.

One type of categorization is the ability to distinguish living from nonliving things. When Piaget asked young children whether the wind and the clouds were alive, their answers led him to think they were confused about what is alive and what is not. The tendency to attribute life to objects that are not alive is called **animism.** However, when later researchers questioned 3- and 4-year-olds about something more familiar to them—differences between a rock, a person, and a doll—the children showed they understood that people are alive and rocks and dolls are not (Gelman, Spelke, & Meck, 1983).

animism   Tendency to attribute life to objects that are not alive.

Understanding of Number As we discussed in Chapter 5, research by Karen Wynn suggests that infants as young as 4½ months have a rudimentary concept of number. They seem to know that if one doll is added to another doll, there should be two dolls, not just one. Other research has found that *ordinality*—the concept of comparing quantities (*more or less, bigger or smaller*)—seems to begin at around 12 to 18 months and at first is limited to comparisons of very few objects (Siegler, 1998). By age 4, most children have words for comparing quantities. They can say that one tree is *bigger* than another or one cup holds *more* juice than another. They know that if they have one cookie and then get another cookie, they have more cookies than they had before and that if they give one cookie to another child, they have fewer cookies. They also can solve simple numerical ordinality problems ("Megan picked six apples, and Joshua picked four apples; which child picked more?") with up to nine objects (Byrnes & Fox, 1998).

Not until age 3½ or older do most children consistently apply the *cardinality* principle in counting (Wynn, 1990). That is, when asked to count six items, children younger than 3½ tend to recite the number-names (one through six) but not to say how many items there are altogether (six). However, there is some evidence that children as young as 2½ use cardinality in practical situations, such as checking to make sure which plate has more cookies on it (Gelman, 2006). By age 5, most children can count to 20 or more and know the relative sizes of the numbers 1 through 10 (Siegler, 1998). Children intuitively devise strategies for adding by counting on their fingers or by using other objects (Naito & Miura, 2001).

By the time they enter elementary school, most children have developed basic *number sense* (Jordan, Kaplan, Oláh, & Locuniak, 2006). This basic level of number skills includes *counting, number knowledge* (ordinality), *number transformations* (simple addition and subtraction), *estimation* ("Is this group of dots more or less than 5?"), and recognition of *number patterns* (2 plus 2 equals 4, and so does 3 plus 1).

SES and preschool experience affect how rapidly children advance in math. By age 4, children from middle-income families have markedly better number skills than low-SES children, and their initial advantage tends to continue. Children whose preschool teachers do a lot of "math talk" (such as asking children to help count days on a calendar) tend to make greater gains (Klibanoff, Levine, Huttenlocher, Vasilyeva, & Hedges, 2006).

Immature Aspects of Preoperational Thought

One of the main characteristics of preoperational thought is **centration**: the tendency to focus on one aspect of a situation and neglect others. According to Piaget, preschoolers come to illogical conclusions because they cannot **decenter**—think about several aspects of a situation at one time. Centration can limit young children's thinking about social as well as physical relationships.

Egocentrism **Egocentrism** is a form of centration. According to Piaget, young children center so much on their own point of view that they cannot take in another's. Three-year-olds are not as egocentric as newborn babies; but, said Piaget, they still think the universe centers on them. Egocentrism may help explain why young children sometimes have trouble separating reality from what goes on inside their own heads and why they may show confusion about what causes what. When Luis believes that his "bad thoughts" have made his sister sick, or that he caused his parents' marital troubles, he is thinking egocentrically.

✔ Checkpoint

Can you . . .

◆ Summarize findings about preschool children's understanding of symbols, space, causality, identities, categorization, and number?

centration In Piaget's theory, the tendency of preoperational children to focus on one aspect of a situation and neglect others.

decenter In Piaget's terminology, to think simultaneously about several aspects of a situation.

egocentrism Piaget's term for inability to consider another person's point of view; a characteristic of young children's thought.

Figure 7-3

Piaget's three-mountain task. A preoperational child is unable to describe the mountains from the doll's point of view—an indication of egocentrism, according to Piaget.

To study egocentrism, Piaget designed the *three-mountain task* (Figure 7-3). A child sits facing a table that holds three large mounds. A doll is placed on a chair at the opposite side of the table. The investigator asks the child how the "mountains" would look to the doll. Piaget found that young children usually could not answer the question correctly; instead, they described the mountains from their own perspective. Piaget saw this as evidence that preoperational children cannot imagine a different point of view (Piaget & Inhelder, 1967).

However, another experimenter who posed a similar problem in a different way got different results (Hughes, 1975). A child sat in front of a square board divided by "walls" into four sections. A toy police officer stood at the edge of the board; a doll was moved from one section to another. After each move the child was asked, "Can the police officer see the doll?" Then another toy police officer was brought into the action, and the child was told to hide the doll from both officers. Thirty children between ages 3½ and 5 were correct 9 out of 10 times.

Why were these children able to take another person's point of view (the police officer's) when those doing the mountain task were not? It may be because the police officer task calls for thinking in more familiar, less abstract ways. Most children do not look at mountains and do not think about what other people might see when looking at one, but most 3-year-olds know about dolls and police officers and hiding. Thus, young children may show egocentrism primarily in situations beyond their immediate experience.

conservation Piaget's term for awareness that two objects that are equal according to a certain measure remain equal in the face of perceptual alteration so long as nothing has been added to or taken away from either object.

Conservation Another classic example of centration is the failure to understand **conservation,** the fact that two things that are equal remain so if their appearance is altered, as long as nothing is added or taken away. Piaget found that children do not fully grasp this principle until the stage of concrete operations and that they develop different kinds of conservation at different ages. Table 7-7 shows how various dimensions of conservation have been tested.

In the conservation of liquid test, 5-year-old Jacob is shown two identical clear glasses, each short and wide and each holding the same amount of water. Jacob is asked, "Is the amount of water in the two glasses equal?" When he agrees, the researcher pours the water from one glass into a third glass, a tall, thin one. Jacob is now asked, "Do both glasses contain the same amount of water? Or does one contain more? Why?" In early childhood—after watching the water being poured out of one of the short, wide glasses into a tall, thin glass or even after pouring it himself—Jacob will say that either the taller glass or the wider glass contains more water. When asked why, he says, "This one is bigger this way," stretching his arms to show the height or width. Preoperational children cannot consider height *and* width at the same time. Because they center on one aspect, they cannot think logically, said Piaget.

irreversibility Piaget's term for a preoperational child's failure to understand that an operation can go in two or more directions.

The ability to conserve is also limited by **irreversibility:** failure to understand that an operation or action can go two or more ways. Once Jacob can imagine restoring the original state of the water by pouring it back into the other glass, he will realize that the amount of water in both glasses is the same.

Preoperational children commonly think as if they were watching a slide show with a series of static frames: they *focus on successive states,* said Piaget, and do not recognize transformations from one state to another. In the conservation experiment, they focus on the water as it stands in each glass rather than on the water being poured from one glass to another, and so they fail to realize that the amount of water is the same.

Checkpoint

Can you . . .

♦ Tell how centration limits preoperational thought?

♦ Discuss research that challenges Piaget's views on egocentrism in early childhood?

♦ Give several reasons preoperational children have difficulty with conservation?

Table 7-7	Tests of Various Kinds of Conservation			
Conservation Task	What Child Is Shown*	Transformation	Question for Child	Preoperational Child's Usual Answers
Number	Two equal, parallel rows of candies	Space the candies in one row farther apart.	"Are there the same number of candies in each row or does one row have more?"	"The longer one has more."
Length	Two parallel sticks of the same length	Move one stick to the right.	"Are both sticks the same size or is one longer?"	"The one on the right (or left) is longer."
Liquid	Two identical glasses holding equal amounts of liquid	Pour liquid from one glass into a taller, narrower glass.	"Do both glasses have the same amount of liquid or does one have more?"	"The taller one has more."
Matter (mass)	Two balls of clay of the same size	Roll one ball into a sausage shape.	"Do both pieces have the same amount of clay or does one have more?"	"The sausage has more."
Weight	Two balls of clay of the same weight	Roll one ball into a sausage shape.	"Do both weigh the same or does one weigh more?"	"The sausage weighs more."
Area	Two toy rabbits, two pieces of cardboard (representing grassy fields), with blocks or toys (representing barns on the fields); same number of "barns" on each board	Rearrange the blocks on one piece of board.	"Does each rabbit have the same amount of grass to eat or does one have more?"	"The one with the blocks close together has more to eat."
Volume	Two glasses of water with two equal-sized balls of clay in them	Roll one ball into a sausage shape.	"If we put the sausage back in the glass, will the water be the same height in each glass, or will one be higher?"	"The water in the glass with the sausage will be higher."

* Child then acknowledges that both items are equal.

Do Young Children Have Theories of Mind?

Piaget (1929) was the first scholar to investigate children's **theory of mind,** their emerging awareness of their own mental processes and those of other people. He asked children such questions as "Where do dreams come from?" and "What do you think with?" On the basis of the answers, he concluded that children younger than 6 cannot distinguish between thoughts or dreams and real physical entities and have no theory of mind. However, more recent research indicates that between ages 2 and 5, children's knowledge about mental processes grows dramatically (Astington, 1993; Bower, 1993; Flavell et al., 1995; Wellman, Cross, & Watson, 2001).

theory of mind Awareness and understanding of mental processes.

Again, methodology seems to have made the difference. Piaget's questions were abstract, and he expected children to be able to put their understanding into words. Contemporary researchers observe children in everyday activities or give them concrete examples. In this way, we have learned, for example, that 3-year-olds can tell the difference between a boy who has a cookie and a boy who is thinking about a cookie, and they know which boy can touch, share, and eat it (Astington, 1993). Let's look at several aspects of theory of mind.

Knowledge about Thinking and Mental States   Between ages 3 and 5, children come to understand that thinking goes on inside the mind; that it can deal with either real or imaginary things; that someone can be thinking of one thing while doing or looking at something else; that a person whose eyes and ears are covered can think about objects; that someone who looks pensive is probably thinking; and that thinking is different from seeing, talking, touching, and knowing (Flavell et al., 1995).

However, preschoolers generally believe that mental activity starts and stops. Not until middle childhood do children know that the mind is continuously active (Flavell, 1993; Flavell et al., 1995). Preschoolers also have little or no awareness that they or other people think in words, or "talk to themselves in their heads," or that they think while they are looking, listening, reading, or talking (Flavell, Green, Flavell, & Grossman, 1997). Preschoolers typically believe they can dream about anything they wish. Five-year-olds recognize that experiences, emotions, knowledge, and thoughts can affect the content of dreams. Not until age 11, however, do children fully realize that they cannot control their dreams (Woolley & Boerger, 2002).

Social cognition, the recognition that others have mental states (Povinelli & Giambrone, 2001; refer back to Chapter 6), accompanies the decline of egocentrism and the development of empathy. By age 3, children realize that a person who does not immediately find what she wants will keep looking. They know that if someone gets what he wants he will be happy, and if not, he will be sad (Wellman & Woolley, 1990). Four-year-olds begin to understand that people have differing beliefs about the world—true or mistaken—and that these beliefs affect their actions.

False Beliefs and Deception   The understanding that people can hold false beliefs flows from the realization that people hold mental representations of reality, which can sometimes be wrong. Three-year-olds appear to lack such an understanding (Flavell et al., 1995). An analysis of 178 studies in various countries, using a number of variations on false belief tasks, found this consistent developmental pattern (Wellman & Cross, 2001; Wellman, Cross, & Watson, 2001). However, when preschoolers were told to respond with gestures rather than with words, children near their fourth birthday did better in recognizing false beliefs (Carlson, Wong, Lemke, & Cosser, 2005).

Three-year-olds' failure to recognize false beliefs may stem from egocentric thinking. At that age, children tend to believe that everyone else knows what they know and believes what they do, and they have trouble understanding that their own beliefs can be false (Lillard & Curenton, 1999). Four-year-olds understand that people who see or hear different versions of the same event may come away with different beliefs. Not until about age 6, however, do children realize that two people who see or hear the *same* thing may interpret it differently (Pillow & Henrichon, 1996).

Because deception is an effort to plant a false belief in someone else's mind, it requires a child to suppress the impulse to be truthful. Some studies have found that children become capable of deception as early as age 2 or 3; others, at 4 or 5. The difference may have to do with the means of deception children are expected to use. In a series of experiments, 3-year-olds were asked whether they would like to play a trick on an experimenter by giving a false clue about which of two boxes a ball had been hidden in. The children were better able to carry out the deception when asked to put a picture of the ball on the wrong box, or to point to that box with an arrow, than when they pointed with their fingers, which children this age are accustomed to doing truthfully (Carlson, Moses, & Hix, 1998).

Piaget maintained that young children regard all falsehoods—intentional or not—as lies. However, when 3- to 6-year-olds were told a story about the danger of eating contaminated food and were given a choice between interpreting a character's action as a lie or a mistake, about three-fourths of the children in all age groups characterized it accurately (Siegal & Peterson, 1998). Apparently, then, even 3-year-olds have some understanding of the role of intent in deception.

Distinguishing between Appearance and Reality According to Piaget, only at age 5 or 6 do children begin to understand the distinction between what *seems* to be and what *is*. Much research bears him out, though some studies have found this ability beginning to emerge before age 4 (Friend & Davis, 1993; C. Rice, Koinis, Sullivan, Tager-Flusberg, & Winner, 1997).

In one classic series of experiments (Flavell, Green, & Flavell, 1986), 3-year-olds seemed to confuse appearance and reality in a variety of tests. For example, when the children put on special sunglasses that made milk look green, they said the milk *was* green, even though they had just seen white milk. However, 3-year-olds' difficulty in distinguishing appearance from reality may itself be more apparent than real. When children were asked questions about the uses of such objects as a candle wrapped like a crayon, only 3 out of 10 answered correctly. But when asked to respond with actions rather than words ("I want a candle to put on a birthday cake"), 9 out of 10 handed the experimenter the crayonlike candle (Sapp, Lee, & Muir, 2000).

Distinguishing between Fantasy and Reality Sometime between 18 months and 3 years, children learn to distinguish between real and imagined events. Three-year-olds know the difference between a real dog and a dog in a dream, and between something invisible (such as air) and something imaginary. They can pretend and can tell when someone else is pretending (Flavell et al., 1995). By 3, and, in some cases, by age 2, they know that pretense is intentional; they can tell the difference between trying to do something and pretending to do the same thing (Rakoczy, Tomasello, & Striano, 2004).

Still, the line between fantasy and reality may seem to blur at times. In one study (Harris, Brown, Marriott, Whittall, & Harmer, 1991), 4- to 6-year-olds, left alone in a room, preferred to touch a box holding an imaginary bunny rather than a box holding an imaginary monster, even though most of the children claimed they were just pretending. However, in a partial replication of the study, in which the experimenter stayed in the room and clearly ended the pretense, only about 10 percent of the children touched or looked in either of the boxes, and almost all showed a clear understanding that the creatures were imaginary (Golomb & Galasso, 1995). Thus it is difficult to know, when questioning children about pretend objects, whether children are giving serious answers or are keeping up the pretense (M. Taylor, 1997).

Magical thinking in children ages 3 and older does *not* seem to stem from confusion between fantasy and reality. Often magical thinking is a way to explain events that do not seem to have obvious realistic explanations (usually because children lack knowledge about them), or simply to indulge in the pleasures of pretending—as with a belief in imaginary companions. Children, like adults, generally are aware of the magical nature of fantasy figures but are more willing to entertain the possibility that they may be real (Woolley, 1997). Magical thinking tends to decline near the end of the preschool period (Woolley, Phelps, Davis, & Mandell, 1999).

All in all, then, research on various aspects of theory of mind suggests that young children may have a clearer picture of reality than Piaget believed.

Is it really Minnie Mouse? These children aren't quite sure. The ability to distinguish fantasy from reality develops by age 3, but 4-to-6-year-olds may imagine that a fantasy figure is real.

Influences on Individual Differences in Theory-of-Mind Development Some children develop theory-of-mind abilities earlier than others. To some degree, this development reflects brain maturation and general improvements in cognition. What other influences explain these individual differences?

Social competence and language development contribute to an understanding of thoughts and emotions (Cassidy, Werner, Rourke, Zubernis, & Balaraman, 2003). Children whose teachers and peers rate them high on social skills are better able to recognize false beliefs, to distinguish between real and feigned emotion, and to take another person's point of view; and these children also tend to have strong language skills (Cassidy et al., 2003; Watson, Nixon, Wilson, & Capage, 1999).

The kind of talk a young child hears at home may make a difference. Three-year-olds whose mothers talk with them about others' mental states tend to show better theory-of-mind skills (Ruffman, Slade, & Crowe, 2002).

Families that encourage pretend play stimulate the development of theory-of-mind skills. As children play roles, they try to assume others' perspectives. Talking with children about how the characters in a story feel helps them develop social understanding (Lillard & Curenton, 1999). Empathy usually arises earlier in children whose families talk frequently about feelings and causality (Dunn, Brown, Slomkowski, Tesla, & Youngblade, 1991; Dunn, 1991).

Bilingual children, who speak and hear more than one language at home, do somewhat better than children with only one language on certain theory-of-mind tasks (Bialystok & Senman, 2004; Goetz, 2003). Bilingual children know that an object or idea can be represented linguistically in more than one way, and this knowledge may help them see that different people may have different perspectives. Bilingual children also recognize the need to match their language to that of their partner, and this recognition may make them more aware of others' mental states. Finally, bilingual children tend to have better attentional control, which may enable them to focus on what is true or real rather than on what only seems to be so (Bialystok & Senman, 2004; Goetz, 2003).

Checkpoint

Can you . . .

◆ Give examples of research that challenges Piaget's views on young children's cognitive limitations?

◆ Describe changes between ages 3 and 6 in children's knowledge about the way their minds work, and identify influences on that development?

Guidepost 4

What memory abilities expand in early childhood?

Information-Processing Approach: Memory Development

During early childhood, children improve in attention and in the speed and efficiency with which they process information; and they begin to form long-lasting memories. Still, young children do not remember as well as older ones. For one thing, young children tend to focus on exact details of an event, which are easily forgotten, whereas older children and adults generally concentrate on the gist of what happened. Also, young children, because of their lesser knowledge of the world, may fail to notice important aspects of a situation, such as when and where it occurred, which could help jog their memory.

Basic Processes and Capacities

Information-processing theorists think of memory as a filing system that has three steps, or processes: *encoding, storage,* and *retrieval.* **Encoding** is like putting information in a folder to be filed in memory; it attaches a code, or label, to the information so that it will be easier to find when needed. Events are encoded along with information about the context in which they are encountered. **Storage** is putting the folder away in the filing cabinet. **Retrieval** occurs when the information is needed; the child then searches for the file and takes it out. Difficulties in any of these processes can interfere with efficiency.

The way the brain stores information is believed to be universal, though the efficiency of the system varies (Siegler, 1998). Information-processing models

encoding Process by which information is prepared for long-term storage and later retrieval.

storage Retention of information in memory for future use.

retrieval Process by which information is accessed or recalled from memory storage.

depict the brain as containing three "storehouses": *sensory memory, working memory,* and *long-term memory.*

Sensory memory is a temporary holding tank for incoming sensory information. Sensory memory shows little change from infancy on (Siegler, 1998). However, without processing (encoding), sensory memories fade quickly.

Information being encoded or retrieved is kept in **working memory,** sometimes called *short-term memory*—a short-term storehouse for information a person is actively working on: trying to understand, remember, or think about. Brain imaging studies have found that working memory is located partly in the *prefrontal cortex,* the large portion of the frontal lobe directly behind the forehead (Nelson et al., 2000).

The efficiency of working memory is limited by its capacity. Researchers may assess the capacity of working memory by asking children to recall a series of scrambled digits (for example, 2-8-3-7-5-1 if they heard 1-5-7-3-8-2). The capacity of working memory—the number of digits a child can recall—increases rapidly. At age 4, children usually remember only two digits; at 12 they typically remember six (Zelazo, Müller, Frye, & Marcovitch, 2003).

The growth of working memory permits the development of **executive function,** the conscious control of thoughts, emotions, and actions to accomplish goals or solve problems. Executive function enables children to plan and carry out goal-directed mental activity. It is thought to emerge around the end of an infant's first year and develops in spurts with age. Changes in executive function between ages 2 and 5 enable children to make up and use complex rules for solving problems (Zelazo et al., 2003; Zelazo & Müller, 2002).

According to a widely used model, a **central executive** controls processing operations in working memory (Baddeley, 1981, 1986, 1992, 1996, 1998). The central executive orders information encoded for transfer to **long-term memory,** a storehouse of virtually unlimited capacity that holds information for long periods of time. The central executive also retrieves information from long-term memory for further processing. The central executive can temporarily expand the capacity of working memory by moving information into two separate subsidiary systems while the central executive is occupied with other tasks. One of these subsidiary systems holds verbal information (as in the digit task) and the other, visual/spatial images.

Recognition and Recall

Recognition and *recall* are types of retrieval. **Recognition** is the ability to identify something encountered before (for example, to pick out a missing mitten from a lost-and-found box). **Recall** is the ability to reproduce knowledge from memory. Preschool children, like all age groups, do better on recognition than on recall, but both abilities improve with age. The more familiar children are with an item, the better they can recall it (Lange, MacKinnon, & Nida, 1989).

Young children often fail to use strategies for remembering—even strategies they already know—unless reminded (Flavell, 1970). This tendency not to generate efficient strategies may reflect lack of awareness of how a strategy would be useful (Sophian, Wood, & Vong, 1995). Older children tend to become more efficient in the spontaneous use of memory strategies (see Chapter 9).

Forming and Retaining Childhood Memories

Memory of experiences in early childhood is rarely deliberate: Young children simply remember events that made a strong impression. Most of these early conscious memories seem to be short-lived. One investigator has distinguished three

sensory memory Initial, brief, temporary storage of sensory information.

working memory Short-term storage of information being actively processed.

executive function Conscious control of thoughts, emotions, and actions to accomplish goals or solve problems.

central executive In Baddeley's model, element of working memory that controls the processing of information.

long-term memory Storage of virtually unlimited capacity that holds information for long periods.

recognition Ability to identify a previously encountered stimulus.

recall Ability to reproduce material from memory.

✓ Checkpoint

Can you . . .

♦ Identify three processes and three storehouses of memory?

♦ Compare recognition and recall?

types of childhood memory that serve different functions: *generic, episodic,* and *autobiographical* (Nelson, 1993).

Generic memory, which begins at about age 2, produces a **script,** or general outline of a familiar, repeated event, such as riding the bus to preschool or having lunch at Grandma's house. It helps a child know what to expect and how to act.

Episodic memory refers to awareness of having experienced a particular event or episode at a specific time and place. Young children remember more clearly events that are new to them. Given a young child's limited memory capacity, episodic memories are temporary. Unless they recur several times (in which case they are transferred to generic memory), they last for a few weeks or months and then fade (Nelson, 2005).

Autobiographical memory, a type of episodic memory, refers to memories of distinctive experiences that form a person's life history. Not everything in episodic memory becomes part of autobiographical memory—only those memories that have a special, personal meaning to the child (Fivush & Nelson, 2004). Autobiographical memory generally emerges between ages 3 and 4 (Howe, 2003; Fivush & Nelson, 2004; Nelson, 2005; Nelson & Fivush, 2004).

A suggested explanation for the relatively slow arrival of autobiographical memory is that children cannot store in memory events pertaining to their own lives until they develop a concept of self (Howe, 2003; Howe & Courage, 1993, 1997; Nelson & Fivush, 2004). Also critical is the emergence of language, which enables children to share memories and organize them into personal narratives (Fivush & Nelson, 2004; Nelson & Fivush, 2004; Nelson, 2005).

Influences on Memory Retention   Why do some early memories last longer and more clearly than others? One factor is the uniqueness of the event; another factor is its emotional impact. Young children are apt to err in recalling precise details of a frequently repeated event (Powell & Thomson, 1996). They tend to confuse a particular event, such as a trip to the supermarket, with other, similar events.

Still another factor is children's active participation, either in the event itself or in its retelling or reenactment. Preschoolers tend to remember things they *did* better than things they merely *saw* (Murachver, Pipe, Gordon, Owens, & Fivush, 1996). Still another factor is self-awareness. In one experiment, children who, at 2½, had shown higher levels of self-awareness retold their memories more accurately at 3½ (Reese & Newcombe, 2007).

Finally, and most important, the way adults talk with a child about shared experiences strongly affects autobiographical memory as well as other cognitive and linguistic skills (Cleveland & Reese, 2005; Fivush & Haden, 2006; Nelson & Fivush, 2004; McGuigan & Salmon, 2004). Investigators influenced by Vygotsky's sociocultural theory support a **social interaction model,** which holds that children collaboratively construct autobiographical memories with parents or other adults as they talk about shared events. Adults initiate and guide these conversations, which show children how memories are organized in narrative form in their culture and place past events in a coherent, meaningful framework (Fivush & Haden, 2006).

Parents tend to have consistent styles of talking with children about shared experiences (Fivush & Haden, 2006). When a child gets stuck, adults with a *low elaborative* style repeat their own previous statements or questions. Such a parent might ask, "Do you remember how we traveled to Florida?" and then, receiving no answer, ask, "How did we get there? We went in the _____." A parent with a *high elaborative* style would ask a question that elicits more information: "Did we go by car or by plane?" In one study, children at ages 2½ and 3½ whose mothers

generic memory   Memory that produces scripts of familiar routines to guide behavior.

script   General remembered outline of a familiar, repeated event, used to guide behavior.

episodic memory   Long-term memory of specific experiences or events, linked to time and place.

autobiographical memory   Memory of specific events in one's life.

social interaction model   Model, based on Vygotsky's sociocultural theory, which proposes that children construct autobiographical memories through conversation with adults about shared events.

had been trained to use highly elaborative techniques in talking with their children recalled richer memories than children of untrained mothers (Reese & Newcombe, 2007). Mothers tend to talk more elaboratively with girls than with boys. This finding may explain why women tend to have detailed, vivid recollections of childhood experiences from an earlier age than men do (Fivush & Haden, 2006; Nelson & Fivush, 2004).

How does elaborative talk promote autobiographical memory? It does so by providing verbal labels for aspects of an event and giving it an orderly, comprehensible structure (Nelson & Fivush, 2004). In reminiscing about past events, children learn to interpret those events and the thoughts and emotions connected with them. They build a sense of self as continuous in time, and they learn that their own perspective on an experience may differ from another person's perspective on the same experience (Fivush & Haden, 2006).

"Remember when we went to the zoo?" Young children are most likely to remember unique events and may recall details from a special trip for a year or longer.

Influence of Culture The relationship between elaborative, parent-guided reminiscing and children's autobiographical memory has been replicated widely across cultures (Fivush & Haden, 2006). However, mothers in middle-class Western cultures tend to be more elaborative than mothers in non-Western cultures (Fivush & Haden, 2006). In reminiscing with 3-year-olds, U.S. mothers might say, "Do you remember when you went swimming at Nana's? What did you do that was really neat?" Chinese mothers tend to ask leading questions, leaving little for the child to add ("What did you play at the place of skiing? Sat on the ice ship, right?") (Nelson & Fivush, 2004).

Checkpoint

Can you . . .

◆ Identify three types of early memories and four factors that affect retention?

◆ Discuss how social interaction and culture influence memory?

Intelligence: Psychometric and Vygotskian Approaches

One factor that may affect the strength of early cognitive skills is intelligence. Let's look at two ways intelligence is measured—through traditional psychometric tests and through newer tests of cognitive potential.

Guidepost 5

How is preschoolers' intelligence measured, and what are some influences on it?

Traditional Psychometric Measures

Although preschool children are easier to test than infants and toddlers, they still need to be tested individually. Because 3- to 5-year-olds are more proficient with language than younger children, intelligence tests for this age group can include more verbal items; and these tests, beginning at age 5, tend to be fairly reliable in predicting measured intelligence and school success later in childhood (Bornstein & Sigman, 1986; Neisser et al., 1996). The two most commonly used individual tests for preschoolers are the Stanford-Binet Intelligence Scales and the Wechsler Preschool and Primary Scale of Intelligence.

The **Stanford-Binet Intelligence Scales** are used for ages 2 and up and take 45 to 60 minutes. The child is asked to define words, string beads, build with blocks, identify the missing parts of a picture, trace mazes, and show an understanding of numbers. The child's score is supposed to measure fluid reasoning (the ability to solve abstract or novel problems), knowledge, quantitative reasoning, visual-spatial processing, and working memory. The fifth edition, revised in 2003, includes nonverbal methods of testing all five of these dimensions of cognition and permits comparisons of verbal and nonverbal performance. In addition to providing a full-scale IQ, the Stanford-Binet yields separate measures of verbal and nonverbal IQ plus composite scores spanning the five cognitive dimensions.

The **Wechsler Preschool and Primary Scale of Intelligence, Revised (WPPSI-III)** is an individual test taking 30 to 60 minutes. It has separate levels for ages 2½ to 4 and 4 to 7 and yields separate verbal and performance scores as well as a combined score. The 2002 revision includes new subtests designed to measure both verbal and nonverbal fluid reasoning, receptive versus expressive vocabulary, and processing speed. Both the Stanford-Binet and the WPPSI-III have been restandardized on samples of children representing the population of preschool-age children in the United States. The WPPSI-III also has been validated for special populations, such as children with intellectual disabilities, developmental delays, language disorders, and autistic disorders.

Influences on Measured Intelligence

A common misconception is that IQ scores represent a fixed quantity of inborn intelligence. In reality, an IQ score is simply a measure of how well a child can do certain tasks at a certain time in comparison with others of the same age. Indeed, test scores of children in many industrialized countries have risen steadily since testing began, forcing test developers to raise standardized norms (Flynn, 1984, 1987). This trend was thought to reflect exposure to educational television, preschools, better-educated parents, smaller families in which each child receives more attention, and a wide variety of mentally demanding games, as well as changes in the tests themselves. However, in tests of Norwegian and Danish army recruits, the trend has slowed and even reversed since the 1970s and 1980s, perhaps because such influences have reached a saturation point (Sundet et al., 2004; Teasdale & Owen, 2008).

The degree to which family environment influences a child's intelligence is in question. We do not know how much of parents' influence on intelligence comes from their genetic contribution and how much from the fact that they provide a child's earliest environment for learning. Twin and adoption studies suggest that family life has its strongest influence in early childhood, and this influence diminishes greatly by adolescence (McGue, 1997; Neisser et al., 1996). However, these studies have been done largely with white, middle-class samples; their results may not apply to low-income and nonwhite families (Neisser et al., 1996). In a longitudinal study of low-income African American children, the influence of the home environment remained substantial—at least as strong as that of the mother's IQ (Burchinal et al., 1997).

The correlation between socioeconomic status and IQ is well documented (Neisser et al., 1996). Family income is associated with cognitive development and achievement in the preschool years and beyond. Family economic circumstances can exert a powerful influence, not so much in themselves as in the way they affect other factors such as health, stress, parenting practices, and the atmosphere in the home (Brooks-Gunn, 2003; Evans, 2004; McLoyd, 1990, 1998; NICHD Early Child Care Research Network, 2005a; Rouse, Brooks-Gunn, & McLanahan, 2005).

Pragmatics and Social Speech

As children learn vocabulary, grammar, and syntax, they become more competent in **pragmatics**—the practical knowledge of how to use language to communicate. This includes knowing how to ask for things, how to tell a story or joke, how to begin and continue a conversation, and how to adjust comments to the listener's perspective. These are all aspects of **social speech:** speech intended to be understood by a listener.

With improved pronunciation and grammar, it becomes easier for others to understand what children say. Most 3-year-olds are quite talkative, and they pay attention to the effect of their speech on others. If people cannot understand them, they try to explain themselves more clearly. Four-year-olds, especially girls, simplify their language and use a higher register when speaking to 2-year-olds (Owens, 1996; Shatz & Gelman, 1973).

Most 5-year-olds can adapt what they say to what the listener knows. They can now use words to resolve disputes, and they use more polite language and fewer direct commands in talking to adults than to other children. Almost half of 5-year-olds can stick to a conversational topic for about a dozen turns—if they are comfortable with their partner and if the topic is one they know and care about.

Private Speech

Anna, age 4, was alone in her room painting. When she finished, she was overheard saying aloud, "Now I have to put the pictures somewhere to dry. I'll put them by the window. They need to get dry now."

Private speech—talking aloud to oneself with no intent to communicate with others—is normal and common in childhood, accounting for up to half of what 4- to 10-year-old children say (Berk, 1986a). Piaget (1962/1923) saw private speech as a sign of cognitive immaturity. Because young children are egocentric, he suggested, they are unable to recognize others' viewpoints and therefore are unable to communicate meaningfully. Instead, they simply vocalize whatever is on their minds.

Vygotsky (1962/1934) did not look upon private speech as egocentric. He saw it as a special form of communication: conversation with the self. Research generally supports Vygotsky. In a study of 3-to-5-year-olds, 86 percent of the children's remarks were *not* egocentric (Berk, 1986a). The most sociable children and those who engage in the most social speech tend to use the most private speech as well, supporting Vygotsky's view that private speech is stimulated by social experience (Berk, 1986a, 1986b, 1992; Berk & Garvin, 1984; Kohlberg, Yaeger, & Hjertholm, 1968). There also is evidence for the role of private speech in self-regulation, as Anna was doing ("Now I have to put the pictures somewhere to dry"). (Berk & Garvin, 1984; Furrow, 1984). Private speech tends to increase when children are trying to solve problems or perform difficult tasks, especially without adult supervision (Berk, 1992; Berk & Garvin, 1984).

Vygotsky proposed that private speech increases during the preschool years and then fades away during the early part of middle childhood as children become more able to guide and master their actions. However, the pattern now appears to be more complex. Whereas Vygotsky considered the need for private speech a universal stage of cognitive development, studies have found a wide range of individual differences, with some children using it very little or not at all (Berk, 1992).

Delayed Language Development

The fact that Albert Einstein did not start to use words until he was between 2 and 3 years old (Isaacson, 2007) may encourage parents of other children whose

pragmatics The practical knowledge needed to use language for communicative purposes.

social speech Speech intended to be understood by a listener.

private speech Talking aloud to oneself with no intent to communicate with others.

speech develops later than usual. About 5 to 8 percent of preschool children show speech and language delays (U.S. Preventive Services Task Force, 2006).

It is unclear why some children speak late. They do not necessarily lack linguistic input at home. Hearing problems and head and facial abnormalities may be associated with speech and language delays, as are premature birth, family history, socioeconomic factors, and other developmental delays (Dale et al., 1998; U.S. Preventive Services Task Force, 2006). Heredity seems to play a role (Kovas et al., 2005; Lyytinen, Poikkeus, Laakso, Eklund, & Lyytinen, 2001; Spinath, Price, Dale, & Plomin, 2004). Boys are more likely than girls to be late talkers (Dale et al., 1998; U.S. Preventive Services Task Force, 2006). Children with language delays may have problems in fast mapping; they may need to hear a new word more often than other children do before they can incorporate it into their vocabularies (M. Rice, Oetting, Marquis, Bode, & Pae, 1994).

Like Albert Einstein, many children who speak late—especially those whose comprehension is normal—eventually catch up (Dale, Price, Bishop, & Plomin, 2003; Thal, Tobias, & Morrison, 1991). However, some 40 to 60 percent of children with early language delays, if left untreated, may experience far-reaching cognitive, social, and emotional consequences (U.S. Preventive Services Task Force, 2006).

It is not always easy to predict whether a late talker will need help. In longitudinal, community-based studies of 8,386 two-year-old twins born in England and Wales in 1994 and 1995, only about 40 percent of those reported to have early language delays continued to show language problems at ages 3 and 4 (Dale et al., 2003). Speech and language therapy sometimes can be effective, but samples studied are generally small and findings vary (U.S. Preventive Services Task Force, 2006).

Preparation for Literacy

To understand what is on the printed page, children first need to master certain prereading skills (Lonigan, Burgess, & Anthony, 2000; Muter, Hulme, Snowling, & Stevenson, 2004). **Emergent literacy** refers to the development of these skills.

emergent literacy Preschoolers' development of skills, knowledge, and attitudes that underlie reading and writing.

Prereading skills can be divided into two types: (1) oral language skills, such as vocabulary, syntax, narrative structure, and the understanding that language is used to communicate; and (2) specific phonological skills (linking letters with sounds) that help in decoding the printed word. Each of these types of skills seems to have its own independent effect (NICHD Early Child Care Research Network, 2005b; Lonigan et al., 2000; Whitehurst & Lonigan, 1998). In a two-year longitudinal study of 90 British schoolchildren, the development of word recognition appeared critically dependent on phonological skills, whereas oral language skills such as vocabulary and grammatical skills were more important predictors of reading comprehension (Muter et al., 2004).

Social interaction is an important factor in literacy development. Children are more likely to become good readers and writers if, during the preschool years, parents provide conversational challenges the children are ready for—if they use a rich vocabulary and center dinner-table talk on the day's activities, on mutually remembered past events, or on questions about why people do things and how things work (Reese, 1995; Snow, 1990, 1993).

Toys and games that familiarize children with the alphabet and the sounds the letters make can give them a head start in learning to read.

As children learn the skills they will need to translate the written word into speech, they also learn that writing can express ideas, thoughts, and feelings. Preschool children in the United States pretend to write by scribbling, lining up their marks from left to right (Brenneman, Massey, Machado, & Gelman, 1996). Later they begin using letters, numbers, and letterlike shapes to represent words, syllables, or phonemes. Often their spelling is so inventive that they cannot read it themselves (Whitehurst & Lonigan, 1998)!

Reading to children is one of the most effective paths to literacy. According to a U.S. government report, 86 percent of girls and 82 percent of boys are read to at home at least three times a week (Freeman, 2004). Children who are read to from an early age learn that reading and writing in English move from left to right and from top to bottom and that words are separated by spaces. They also are motivated to learn to read (Siegler, 1998; Whitehurst & Lonigan, 1998).

Moderate exposure to educational television can help prepare children for literacy, especially if parents talk with children about what they see. In one study, the more time 3- to 5-year-olds spent watching *Sesame Street,* the more their vocabulary improved (M. L. Rice, Huston, Truglio, & Wright, 1990). In a longitudinal study, the content of television programs viewed at ages 2 and 4 predicted academic skills three years later (Wright et al., 2001).

Early Childhood Education

Going to preschool is an important step, widening a child's physical, cognitive, and social environment. The transition to kindergarten, the beginning of "real school," is another momentous step. The number of 3- and 4-year-olds enrolled in preschool has steadily increased during the past 30 years, from about 18 percent in 1973 to about 54 percent in 2002 (NCES, 2004a).

Goals and Types of Preschools

In some countries, such as China, preschools are expected to provide academic preparation for schooling. In contrast, many preschools in the United States and many other Western countries traditionally have followed a *child-centered* philosophy stressing social and emotional growth in line with young children's developmental needs—though some, such as those based on the theories of Piaget or the Italian educator Maria Montessori, have a stronger cognitive emphasis.

As part of a debate over how to improve education, pressures have grown to offer instruction in basic academic skills in U.S. preschools. Defenders of the developmental approach maintain that academically oriented programs neglect young children's needs for exploration and free play and that too much teacher-initiated instruction may interfere with self-initiated learning (Elkind, 1986; Zigler, 1987).

What type of preschool is best for children? Studies in the United States support the child-centered, developmental approach. One field study (Marcon, 1999) compared 721 four- and five-year-olds from three types of preschool classrooms in Washington, D.C.: *child-initiated, academically directed,* and *middle-of-the-road* (a blend of the other two approaches). Children from child-initiated programs, in which they actively directed their own learning experiences, excelled in basic academic skills. They also had more advanced motor skills than the other two groups and scored higher than the middle-of-the-road group in behavioral and communicative skills. These findings suggest that a single, coherent philosophy of education may work better than an attempt to blend diverse approaches and that a child-centered approach seems more effective than an academic approach.

✓ **Checkpoint**

Can you . . .

◆ Trace normal progress in 3- to 6-year-olds' vocabulary, grammar, syntax, and conversational abilities?

◆ Give reasons why children use private speech?

◆ Discuss possible causes, consequences, and treatment of delayed language development?

◆ Identify factors that promote preparation for literacy?

Guidepost 7

What purposes does early childhood education serve, and how do children make the transition to kindergarten?

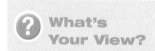
What's Your View?

• Should the primary purpose of preschool be to provide a strong academic foundation or to foster social and emotional development?

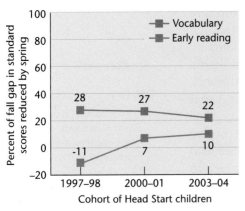

Figure 7-4

Reduction of the gap between 4-year-old Head Start children and national norms from fall to spring of 1997, 2000, and 2003. *Note:* Vocabulary and early reading scores for this analysis are reported for children age 4 or older who were assessed in English in both fall and spring.
(Source: Administration for Children and Families, 2006a.)

Compensatory Preschool Programs

An estimated 2 out of 3 children in poor urban areas enter school poorly prepared to learn (Zigler, 1998). Since the 1960s, large-scale programs have been developed to better prepare these children for school.

The best-known compensatory preschool program for children of low-income families in the United States is Project Head Start, a federally funded program launched in 1965. Consistent with its whole child approach, its goals are not only to enhance cognitive skills, but also to improve physical health and to foster self-confidence and social skills. The program provides medical, dental, and mental health care, social services, and at least one hot meal a day. Currently about 1 out of 3 Head Start children are from non-English-speaking homes (predominantly Hispanic), and a majority live in single-mother homes (Administration for Children and Families (ACF), 2006a).

Has Head Start lived up to its name? Data support its effectiveness in improving school readiness, and teacher and program quality continues to improve (ACF, 2006a, 2006b; USDHHS, 2003b). Similarly, children who attend the newer state-sponsored programs tend to show better cognitive and language skills and do better in school than children who do not attend (USDHHS, 2003a).

Head Start children make gains in vocabulary, letter recognition, early writing, early mathematics, and social skills; and, as shown in Figure 7-4, the gap between their vocabulary and early reading scores and national norms has narrowed significantly since the late 1990s (ACF, 2006a). Furthermore, their skills continue to progress in kindergarten. Gains are closely related to parental involvement (ACF, 2006b).

An analysis of long-term effects of Head Start suggests that the benefits outweigh the costs (Ludwig & Phillips, 2007). Children from Head Start and other compensatory programs are less likely to be placed in special education or to repeat a grade and are more likely to finish high school than low-income children who did not attend such programs (Neisser et al., 1996). "Graduates" of one such program, the Perry Preschool Project, were much less likely to become juvenile delinquents or to become pregnant in their teens (Berrueta-Clement, Schweinhart, Barnett, Epstein, & Weikart, 1985; Schweinhart, Barnes, & Weikart, 1993; see Chapter 17). Outcomes are best with earlier and longer-lasting intervention through high-quality, center-based programs (Brooks-Gunn, 2003; Reynolds & Temple, 1998; Zigler & Styfco, 1993, 1994, 2001).

In 1995, Early Head Start began to offer child and family development services to low-income families with infants and toddlers. At ages 2 and 3, according to randomized studies, participants scored higher on standardized developmental and vocabulary tests and were at less risk of slow development than children not in the program. At age 3, they were less aggressive, more absorbed in play, and more positively engaged with their parents. Early Head Start parents were more emotionally supportive, provided more learning and language stimulation, read to their children more, and spanked less. Programs that offered a mix of center-based services and home visits showed better results than those that concentrated on one setting or the other (Commissioner's Office of Research and Evaluation and Head Start Bureau, 2001; Love et al., 2002, 2005).

The Child in Kindergarten

Originally a year of transition between the relative freedom of home and the structure of "real school," kindergarten in the United States today has become more like first grade. Children spend less time on self-chosen activities and more time on worksheets and preparing to read.

Although some states do not require kindergarten programs or kindergarten attendance, most 5-year-olds attend kindergarten. Since the late 1970s, an increasing number of kindergarteners spend a full day in school, rather than the traditional half day (National Center for Education Statistics [NCES], 2004a). A practical impetus for this trend is the growing number of single-parent and dual-earner households. In addition, large numbers of children already have experienced preschool, prekindergarten programs, or full-time child care and are ready for a more rigorous kindergarten curriculum (Walston & West, 2004).

Do children learn more in full-day kindergarten? According to longitudinal research, public school children in full-day kindergarten are more likely than half-day students to receive daily instruction in prereading skills, math skills, social studies, and science (Walston & West, 2004) and tend to do better by the end of kindergarten and in the primary grades (Vecchiotti, 2003; Walston & West, 2004). However, by the end of third grade, children who went to full-day and half-day kindergarten are substantially equal in reading, math, and science achievement (Rathbun, West, & Germino-Hausken, 2004).

Several factors affect a child's readiness for kindergarten. One is the preparation the child receives beforehand. Children who come to kindergarten from advantaged home environments tend to do better in reading and math, and the achievement gap between advantaged and disadvantaged children often widens during the first four years of school (Denton, West, & Walston, 2003; Rathbun et al., 2004). Analysis of six large longitudinal studies found strong correlations between math test scores in kindergarten and academic success in fifth grade. Reading scores were less strongly correlated (Duncan et al., 2007).

Emotional and social adjustment also affect readiness for kindergarten and strongly predict school success. More important than knowing the alphabet or being able to count to 20, kindergarten teachers say, are the abilities to sit still, follow directions, wait one's turn, and regulate one's own learning (Blair, 2002; Brooks-Gunn, 2003; Raver, 2002). However, the analysis of longitudinal studies found little correlation between behavior problems in kindergarten and later school success (Duncan et al., 2007). Adjustment to kindergarten can be eased by enabling preschoolers and parents to visit before the start of kindergarten, shortening school days early in the school year, having teachers make home visits, holding parent orientation sessions, and keeping parents informed about what is going on in school (Schulting, Malone, & Dodge, 2005).

The blossoming physical and cognitive skills of early childhood affect children's self-image, their emotional adjustment, and how well they get along at home and with schoolmates, as we'll see in Chapter 8.

Checkpoint

Can you . . .

♦ Compare goals and effectiveness of varying types of preschool programs?

♦ Assess the benefits of compensatory preschool education?

♦ Discuss factors that affect adjustment to kindergarten?

Summary and Key Terms

PHYSICAL DEVELOPMENT

Aspects of Physical Development

Guidepost 1: *How do children's bodies and brains change between ages 3 and 6, and what sleep problems and motor achievements are common?*

• Physical growth continues during the years from 3 to 6, but more slowly than during infancy and toddlerhood.

Boys are on average slightly taller, heavier, and more muscular than girls. Internal body systems are maturing.

• Sleep patterns change during early childhood, as throughout life, and are affected by cultural expectations. Occasional sleepwalking, sleep terrors, and nightmares are common, but persistent sleep problems may indicate emotional disturbances.

• Bed-wetting is usually outgrown without special help.

- Brain development continues steadily throughout childhood and affects motor development.
- Children progress rapidly in gross and fine motor skills, developing more complex systems of action.
- Handedness is usually evident by age 3, reflecting dominance by one hemisphere of the brain.
- According to Kellogg's research, stages of art production, which reflect brain development and fine motor coordination, are the scribbling stage, shape stage, design stage, and pictorial stage.

enuresis (219)

gross motor skills (220)

fine motor skills (221)

systems of action (221)

handedness (221)

Health and Safety

Guidepost 2: *What are the major health and safety risks for young children?*

- Although major contagious illnesses are rare today in industrialized countries due to widespread immunization, preventable disease continues to be a major problem in the developing world.
- The prevalence of obesity among preschoolers has increased.
- Undernutrition can affect all aspects of development.
- Accidents, most frequently in the home, are the leading cause of death in childhood in the United States.
- Environmental factors such as exposure to poverty, homelessness, smoking, air pollution, and pesticides increase the risks of illness or injury. Lead poisoning can have serious physical, cognitive, and behavioral effects.

COGNITIVE DEVELOPMENT

Piagetian Approach: The Preoperational Child

Guidepost 3: *What are typical cognitive advances and immature aspects of preschool children's thinking?*

- Children in the preoperational stage show several important advances, as well as some immature aspects of thought.
- The symbolic function enables children to reflect on people, objects, and events that are not physically present. It is shown in deferred imitation, pretend play, and language.
- Symbolic development helps preoperational children make more accurate judgments of spatial relationships. They can link cause and effect with regard to familiar situations, understand the concept of identity, categorize, compare quantities, and understand principles of counting.

- Preoperational children appear to be less egocentric than Piaget thought.
- Centration keeps preoperational children from understanding principles of conservation. Their logic also is limited by irreversibility and a focus on states rather than transformations.
- The theory of mind, which develops markedly between ages 3 and 5, includes awareness of a child's own thought processes, social cognition, understanding that people can hold false beliefs, ability to deceive, ability to distinguish appearance from reality, and ability to distinguish fantasy from reality.
- Maturational and environmental influences affect individual differences in theory-of-mind development.

preoperational stage (228)

symbolic function (229)

pretend play (229)

transduction (230)

animism (230)

centration (231)

decenter (231)

egocentrism (231)

conservation (232)

irreversibility (232)

theory of mind (233)

Information-Processing Approach: Memory Development

Guidepost 4: *What memory abilities expand in early childhood?*

- Information-processing models describe three steps in memory: encoding, storage, and retrieval.
- Although sensory memory shows little change with age, the capacity of working memory increases greatly. The central executive controls the flow of information to and from long-term memory.
- At all ages, recognition is better than recall, but both increase during early childhood.
- Early episodic memory is only temporary; it fades or is transferred to generic memory.
- Autobiographical memory typically begins at about age 3 or 4; it may be related to self-recognition and language development.
- According to the social interaction model, children and adults co-construct autobiographical memories by talking about shared experiences.
- Children are more likely to remember unusual activities that they actively participate in. The way adults talk with children about events influences memory formation.

encoding (236)

storage (236)

retrieval (236)

sensory memory (237)

working memory (237)

executive function (237)

central executive (237)

long-term memory (237)

recognition (237)

recall (237)

generic memory (238)

script (238)

episodic memory (238)

autobiographical memory (238)

social interaction model (238)

Intelligence: Psychometric and Vygotskian Approaches

Guidepost 5: *How is preschoolers' intelligence measured, and what are some influences on it?*

- The two most commonly used psychometric intelligence tests for young children are the Stanford-Binet Intelligence Scales and the Wechsler Preschool and Primary Scale of Intelligence, Revised (WPPSI-III).
- Intelligence test scores have risen in industrialized countries.
- Intelligence test scores may be influenced by a number of factors, including the home environment and SES.
- Newer tests based on Vygotsky's concept of the zone of proximal development (ZPD) indicate immediate potential for achievement. Such tests, combined with scaffolding, can help parents and teachers guide children's progress.

Stanford-Binet Intelligence Scales (240)

Wechsler Preschool and Primary Scale of Intelligence, Revised (WPPSI-III) (240)

zone of proximal development (ZPD) (241)

scaffolding (241)

Language Development

Guidepost 6: *How does language improve during early childhood, and what happens when its development is delayed?*

- During early childhood, vocabulary increases greatly, and grammar and syntax become fairly sophisticated. Children become more competent in pragmatics.
- Private speech is normal and common; it may aid in the shift to self-regulation.
- Causes of delayed language development are unclear. If untreated, language delays may have serious cognitive, social, and emotional consequences.
- Interaction with adults can promote emergent literacy.

fast mapping (241)

pragmatics (243)

social speech (243)

private speech (243)

emergent literacy (244)

Early Childhood Education

Guidepost 7: *What purposes does early childhood education serve, and how do children make the transition to kindergarten?*

- Goals of preschool education vary across cultures.
- The academic content of early childhood education programs in the United States has increased, but studies support a child-centered approach.
- Compensatory preschool programs have had positive outcomes, and participants' performance is approaching national norms. Compensatory programs that start early may have better results.
- Many children today attend full-day kindergarten. Success in kindergarten depends largely on emotional and social adjustment and prekindergarten preparation.

Play gives children a chance to practice what they are learning. . . . They have to play with what they know to be true in order to find out more, and then they can use what they learn in new forms of play.

—Fred Rogers, *Mister Rogers Talks with Parents* (1983)

Did You Know...

- Young children find it hard to understand that they can have conflicting emotions?

- Gender preferences in toys and playmates appear as early as 12 to 24 months, but boys and girls on average are more alike than different?

- Children who play alone are not necessarily less mature than children who play with others?

- Imaginary friends are most common among firstborn and only children?

- The most effective type of parenting is warm and accepting but firm in maintaining standards?

- Sibling rivalry is *not* the main pattern of behavior between brothers and sisters early in life?

These are just a few of the interesting and important topics we will cover in this chapter. The years from ages 3 to 6 are pivotal in children's psychosocial development. Emotional development and sense of self are rooted in the experiences of those years. Yet the story of the self is not completed in early childhood; we continue to write it even as adults.

In this chapter we discuss preschool children's understanding of themselves and their feelings. We see how their sense of male or female identity arises and how it affects their behavior. We describe the activity on which children, at least in industrialized countries, typically spend most of their time: play. We consider the influence, for good or ill, of what parents do. Finally, we discuss relationships with siblings and other children. After you have read and studied this chapter, you should be able to answer each of the Guidepost questions on the following page.

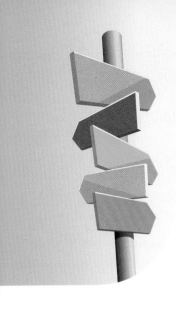

Guideposts *for Study*

1. How does the self-concept develop during early childhood, and how do children show self-esteem, emotional growth, and initiative?

2. How do boys and girls become aware of the meaning of gender, and what explains differences in behavior between the sexes?

3. How do preschoolers play, and how does play contribute to and reflect development?

4. How do parenting practices influence development?

5. Why do young children help or hurt others, and why do they develop fears?

6. How do young children get along with—or without—siblings, playmates, and friends?

Guidepost 1

How does the self-concept develop during early childhood, and how do children show self-esteem, emotional growth, and initiative?

self-concept Sense of self; descriptive and evaluative mental picture of one's abilities and traits.

The Developing Self

"Who in the world am I? Ah, *that's* the great puzzle," said Alice in Wonderland, after her size had abruptly changed—again. Solving Alice's "puzzle" is a lifelong process of getting to know one's self.

The Self-Concept and Cognitive Development

The **self-concept** is our total picture of our abilities and traits. It is "a *cognitive construction* . . . a system of descriptive and evaluative representations about the self," that determines how we feel about ourselves and guides our actions (Harter, 1996, p. 207).* The sense of self also has a social aspect: Children incorporate into their self-image their growing understanding of how others see them.

The self-concept begins to come into focus in toddlerhood, as children develop self-awareness. It becomes clearer as a person gains in cognitive abilities and deals with the developmental tasks of childhood, of adolescence, and then of adulthood.

self-definition Cluster of characteristics used to describe oneself.

Changes in Self-Definition: The 5 to 7 Shift   Children's **self-definition**—the way they describe themselves—typically changes between about ages 5 and 7, reflecting self-concept development. At age 4, Jason says,

> My name is Jason and I live in a big house with my mother and father and sister, Lisa. I have a kitty that's orange and a television set in my own room. . . . I like pizza and I have a nice teacher. I can count up to 100, want to hear me? I love my dog, Skipper. I can climb to the top of the jungle gym, I'm not scared! Just happy. You can't be happy *and* scared, no way! I have brown hair, and I go to preschool. I'm really strong. I can lift this chair, watch me! (Harter, 1996, p. 208)

The way Jason describes himself is typical of U.S. children his age. He talks mostly about concrete, observable behaviors; external characteristics, such as physical features; preferences; possessions; and members of his household. He mentions particular skills (running and climbing) rather than general abilities (being athletic). His self-descriptions are unrealistically positive. Not until around age 7 will he

---

* This discussion of children's developing understanding of themselves from age 4 on, including their understanding of their emotions, is indebted to Susan Harter (1990, 1993, 1996, 1998).

describe himself in terms of generalized traits, such as *popular, smart,* or *dumb;* recognize that he can have conflicting emotions; and be self-critical while holding a positive overall self-concept.

What specific changes make up this *age 5 to 7 shift?* A neo-Piagetian analysis (Case, 1985, 1992; Fischer, 1980) describes the 5 to 7 shift as occurring in three steps. At 4, Jason is at the first step, **single representations.** His statements about himself are one-dimensional ("I like pizza. . . . I'm really strong"). His thinking jumps from particular to particular, without logical connections. At this stage he cannot imagine having two emotions at once ("You can't be happy *and* scared") because he cannot consider different aspects of himself at the same time. His thinking about himself is all-or-nothing. He cannot acknowledge that his **real self,** the person he actually is, is not the same as his **ideal self,** the person he would like to be. So he describes himself as a paragon of virtue and ability.

At about age 5 or 6, Jason moves up to the second step, **representational mappings.** He begins to make logical connections between one aspect of himself and another: "I can run fast, and I can climb high. I'm also strong. I can throw a ball real far, I'm going to be on a team some day!" (Harter, 1996, p. 215). However, his image of himself is still expressed in completely positive, all-or-nothing terms. He cannot see how he might be good at some things and not at others.

The third step, *representational systems,* takes place in middle childhood (see Chapter 10), when children begin to integrate specific features of the self into a general, multidimensional concept. As all-or-nothing thinking declines, Jason's self-descriptions will become more balanced and realistic ("I'm good at hockey but bad at arithmetic").

Cultural Differences in Self-Definition Parents transmit, often through everyday conversations, cultural ideas and beliefs about how to define the self. For example, Chinese parents tend to encourage *interdependent* aspects of the self: compliance with authority, appropriate conduct, humility, and a sense of belonging to the community. European American parents are more apt to encourage *independent* aspects of the self: individuality, self-expression, and self-esteem.

A comparative study of 180 European American and Chinese preschoolers, kindergartners, and second graders (Wang, 2004) found that children absorb differing cultural styles of self-definition as early as age 3 or 4, and these differences increase with age. European American children tend to describe themselves in terms of personal attributes and beliefs ("I am big"), whereas Chinese children talk more about social categories and relationships ("I have a sister"). European American children more often describe themselves in terms of personality traits and tendencies ("I'm good at sports"), whereas Chinese children describe specific, overt behaviors ("I play Snowmoon with my neighbor"). European American children tend to put themselves in an unqualifiedly positive light ("I am smart"), whereas Chinese children, and adults, describe themselves more neutrally ("I sometimes forget my manners"). Thus, differing cultural values influence the way children in each culture perceive and define themselves.

Self-Esteem

Self-esteem is the self-evaluative part of the self-concept, the judgment children make about their overall worth. Self-esteem is based on children's growing cognitive ability to describe and define themselves.

Jason describes himself in terms of his appearance (brown hair) and his possessions (his dog, Skipper).

single representations In neo-Piagetian terminology, first stage in development of self-definition, in which children describe themselves in terms of individual, unconnected characteristics and in all-or-nothing terms.

real self The self one actually is.

ideal self The self one would like to be.

representational mappings In neo-Piagetian terminology, second stage in development of self-definition, in which a child makes logical connections between aspects of the self but still sees these characteristics in all-or-nothing terms.

self-esteem The judgment a person makes about his or her self-worth.

This mother's approval of her 3-year-old son's artwork is an important contributor to his self-esteem. Not until middle childhood do children develop strong internal standards of self-worth.

Developmental Changes in Self-Esteem   Although children do not generally talk about a concept of self-worth until about age 8, younger children show by their behavior that they have one. In a longitudinal study in Belgium (Verschueren, Buyck, & Marcoen, 2001), researchers measured various aspects of 5-year-olds' self-perceptions, such as physical appearance, scholastic and athletic competence, social acceptance, and behavioral conduct. Children's positive or negative self-perceptions at age 5 tended to predict their self-perceptions and socioemotional functioning at age 8.

Still, before the 5 to 7 shift, children's self-esteem is not necessarily based on reality. They tend to accept the judgments of adults, who often give positive, uncritical feedback and, thus, may overrate their abilities (Harter, 1990, 1993, 1996, 1998). Like the overall self-concept, self-esteem in early childhood tends to be all-or-none: "I am good" or "I am bad" (Harter, 1996, 1998). Not until middle childhood does it become more realistic, as personal evaluations of competence based on internalization of parental and societal standards begin to shape and maintain self-worth (Harter, 1990, 1996, 1998).

Contingent Self-Esteem: The "Helpless" Pattern   When self-esteem is high, a child is motivated to achieve. However, if self-esteem is *contingent* on success, children may view failure or criticism as an indictment of their worth and may feel helpless to do better. About one-third to one-half of preschoolers, kindergartners, and first graders show elements of this *helpless pattern* (Burhans & Dweck, 1995; Ruble & Dweck, 1995).

Instead of trying a different way to complete a puzzle, as a child with unconditional self-esteem might do, helpless children feel ashamed and give up. They do not expect to succeed, and so they do not try. Whereas older children who fail may conclude that they are "dumb," preschoolers interpret failure as a sign of being "bad." This sense of being a bad person may persist into adulthood.

Children whose self-esteem is contingent on success tend to become demoralized when they fail. Often these children attribute poor performance or social

? **What's Your View?**

• Can you think of ways in which your parents or other adults helped you develop self-esteem?

rejection to their personality deficiencies, which they believe they are helpless to change. Rather than try new ways to gain approval, they repeat unsuccessful strategies or just give up. Children with noncontingent self-esteem, in contrast, tend to attribute failure or disappointment to factors outside themselves or to the need to try harder. If initially unsuccessful or rejected, they persevere, trying new strategies until they find one that works (Erdley, Cain, Loomis, Dumas-Hines, & Dweck, 1997; Harter, 1998; Pomerantz & Saxon, 2001). Children with high self-esteem tend to have parents and teachers who give specific, focused feedback rather than criticize the child as a person ("Look, the tag on your shirt is showing in front," not "Can't you see your shirt is on backward? When are you going to learn to dress yourself?").

Understanding and Regulating Emotions

"I hate you!" Maya, age 5, shouts to her mother. "You're a mean mommy!" Angry because her mother sent her to her room for pinching her baby brother, Maya cannot imagine ever loving her mother again. "Aren't you ashamed of yourself for making the baby cry?" her father asks Maya a little later. Maya nods, but only because she knows what response he wants. In truth, she feels a jumble of emotions—not the least of which is feeling sorry for herself.

The ability to understand and regulate, or control, one's feelings is one of the key advances of early childhood (Dennis, 2006). Children who can understand their emotions are better able to control the way they show them and to be sensitive to how others feel (Garner & Power, 1996). Emotional self-regulation helps children guide their behavior (Laible & Thompson, 1998) and contributes to their ability to get along with others (Denham et al., 2003).

Preschoolers can talk about their feelings and often can discern the feelings of others, and they understand that emotions are connected with experiences and desires (Saarni, Mumme, & Campos, 1998). They understand that someone who gets what he wants will be happy, and someone who does not get what she wants will be sad (Lagattuta, 2005).

Emotional understanding becomes more complex with age. In one study, 32 four- to eight-year-olds and 32 adults were asked to imagine how a young boy would feel if his ball rolled into the street and he either retrieved or refrained from retrieving it. The results revealed a 5 to 7 shift in emotional understanding much like that found for self-concept development. The 4- and 5-year-olds tended to believe that the boy would be happy if he got the ball— even though he would be breaking a rule—and unhappy if he didn't. The older children, like the adults, were more inclined to believe that obedience to a rule would make the boy feel good and disobedience would make him feel bad (Lagattuta, 2005).

Understanding Conflicting Emotions One reason for younger children's confusion about their feelings is that they do not understand that they can experience contrary emotional reactions at the same time. Individual differences in understanding conflicting emotions are evident by age 3. In one longitudinal study, 3-year-olds who could identify whether a face looked happy or sad and who could tell how a puppet felt when enacting a situation involving happiness, sadness, anger, or fear were better able at the end of kindergarten to explain a story character's conflicting emotions. These children tended to come from families that often discussed why people behave as they do (J. R. Brown & Dunn, 1996). Most children acquire a more sophisticated understanding of conflicting emotions during middle childhood (Harter, 1996; see Chapter 10).

Checkpoint

Can You . . .

- Trace early self-concept development and discuss cultural influences on it?

- Explain the significance of the 5 to 7 shift?

- Tell how young children's self-esteem differs from older children's and how the *helpless pattern* arises?

Understanding Emotions Directed toward the Self   Emotions directed toward the self, such as guilt, shame, and pride, typically develop by the end of the third year, after children gain self-awareness and accept the standards of behavior their parents have set. However, even children a few years older often lack the cognitive sophistication to *recognize* these emotions and what brings them on (Kestenbaum & Gelman, 1995).

In one study (Harter, 1993), 4- to 8-year-olds were told two stories. In the first story, a child takes a few coins from a jar after being told not to do so; in the second story, a child performs a difficult gymnastic feat—a flip on the bars. Each story was presented in two versions: one in which a parent sees the child doing the act and another in which no one sees the child. The children were asked how they and the parent would feel in each circumstance.

Again, the answers revealed a gradual progression in understanding of feelings about the self, reflecting the 5 to 7 shift (Harter, 1996). At ages 4 to 5, children did not say that either they or their parents would feel pride or shame. Instead they used such terms as "worried" or "scared" (for the money jar incident) and "excited" or "happy" (about the gymnastic accomplishment). At 5 to 6, children said their parents would be ashamed or proud of them but did not acknowledge feeling these emotions themselves. At 6 to 7, children said they would feel proud or ashamed, but only if they were observed. Not until ages 7 to 8 did children say that they would feel ashamed or proud of themselves even if no one saw them.

Checkpoint

Can You . . .

- Trace two typical developments in understanding of emotions?
- Explain the significance of Erikson's third stage of personality development?

Guidepost 2

How do boys and girls become aware of the meaning of gender, and what explains differences in behavior between the sexes?

Erikson: Initiative versus Guilt

The need to deal with conflicting feelings about the self is at the heart of the third stage of personality development identified by Erik Erikson (1950): **initiative versus guilt.** The conflict arises from the growing desire to plan and carry out activities and the growing pangs of conscience the child may have about such plans.

Preschool children can do—and want to do—more and more. At the same time, they are learning that some of the things they want to do meet social approval, whereas others do not. How do children reconcile their desire to *do* with their desire for approval?

This conflict marks a split between two parts of the personality: the part that remains a child, full of exuberance and a desire to try new things and test new powers, and the part that is becoming an adult, constantly examining the propriety of motives and actions. Children who learn how to regulate these opposing drives develop the virtue of *purpose,* the courage to envision and pursue goals without being unduly inhibited by guilt or fear of punishment (Erikson, 1982).

Gender

Gender identity, awareness of one's femaleness or maleness and all it implies in one's society of origin, is an important aspect of the developing self-concept. How different are young boys and girls? What causes those differences? How do children develop gender identity, and how does it affect their attitudes and behavior?

Gender Differences

Gender differences are psychological or behavioral differences between males and females. As we discussed in Chapter 6, measurable differences between baby boys and girls are few. Although some gender differences become more pronounced after age 3, boys and girls on average remain more alike than different. Extensive evidence from many studies supports this *gender similarities hypothesis*. Fully 78 percent of gender differences are small to negligible, and some differences, such as in self-esteem, change with age.

Among the larger differences are boys' superior motor performance, especially after puberty, and their moderately greater propensity for physical aggression (Hyde, 2005) beginning by age 2 (Archer, 2004; Baillargeon et al., 2007; Pellegrini & Archer, 2005). (Aggression is discussed later in this chapter.) Temperamentally, from infancy on girls are better able to pay attention and to inhibit inappropriate behavior. Boys are more active and take more intense pleasure in physical activity (Else-Quest, Hyde, Goldsmith, & Van Hulle, 2006).

Cognitive gender differences are few and small (Spelke, 2005). Overall, intelligence test scores show no gender differences (Keenan & Shaw, 1997), perhaps because the most widely used tests are designed to eliminate gender bias (Neisser et al., 1996). Boys and girls do equally well on tasks involving basic mathematical skills and are equally capable of learning math. However, there are small differences in specific abilities. Girls tend to perform better on tests of verbal fluency, mathematical computation, and memory for locations of objects. Boys tend to perform better in verbal analogies, mathematical word problems, and memory for spatial configurations. In most studies, these differences do not emerge until elementary school or later (Spelke, 2005). Also, boys' mathematical abilities vary more than girl's, with more boys at both the highest and lowest ends of the ability range (Halpern et al., 2007.) In early childhood and again during preadolescence and adolescence, girls tend to use more responsive language, such as praise, agreement, acknowledgment, and elaboration on what someone else has said (Leaper & Smith, 2004).

We need to remember, of course, that gender differences are valid for large groups of boys and girls but not necessarily for individuals. By knowing a child's sex, we cannot predict whether that *particular* boy or girl will be faster, stronger, smarter, more obedient, or more assertive than another child.

This preschool boy dressed as a cowboy has developed a strong sense of gender roles. The clearest behavioral difference between young boys and young girls is boys' greater aggressiveness.

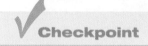

Checkpoint

Can You . . .

♦ Summarize the main behavioral and cognitive differences between boys and girls?

Perspectives on Gender Development

What accounts for gender differences, and why do some of them emerge with age? The most influential explanations, until recently, centered on the differing experiences and social expectations that boys and girls meet almost from birth (Halpern, 1997; Neisser et al., 1996). These experiences and expectations concern three related aspects of gender identity: *gender roles, gender-typing,* and *gender stereotypes.*

Gender roles are the behaviors, interests, attitudes, skills, and personality traits that a culture considers appropriate for males or females. All societies have gender roles. Historically, in most cultures, women have been expected to devote most of their time to caring for the household and children, while men were providers and protectors. Women were expected to be compliant and nurturing; men, to be active, aggressive, and competitive. Today, gender roles, especially in Western cultures, have become more diverse and more flexible.

Gender-typing, the acquisition of a gender role (refer back to Chapter 6), takes place early in childhood, but children vary greatly in the degree to which they become gender-typed (Iervolino, Hines, Golombok, Rust, & Plomin, 2005).

gender roles   Behaviors, interests, attitudes, skills, and traits that a culture considers appropriate for each sex; differ for males and females.

gender-typing   Socialization process whereby children, at an early age, learn appropriate gender roles.

Table 8-1   Five Perspectives on Gender Development

Theories	Major Theorists	Key Processes	Basic Beliefs
Biological Approach		Genetic, neurological, and hormonal activity	Many or most behavioral differences between the sexes can be traced to biological differences.
Evolutionary Approach	Charles Darwin	Natural sexual selection	Children develop gender roles in preparation for adult mating and reproductive behavior.
Psychoanalytic Approach	Sigmund Freud	Resolution of unconscious emotional conflict	Gender identity occurs when child identifies with same-sex parent.
Cognitive Approach Cognitive-developmental theory	Lawrence Kohlberg	Self-categorization	Once a child learns she is a girl or he is a boy, child sorts information about behavior by gender and acts accordingly.
Gender-schema theory	Sandra Bem, Carol Lynn Martin, & Charles F. Halverson	Self-categorization based on processing of cultural information	Child organizes information about what is considered appropriate for a boy or a girl on the basis of what a particular culture dictates and behaves accordingly. Child sorts by gender because the culture dictates that gender is an important schema.
Social Learning Approach Social cognitive theory	Albert Bandura	Observation of models, reinforcement	Child mentally combines observations of gendered behavior and creates own behavioral variations.

gender stereotypes
Preconceived generalizations about male or female role behavior.

Gender stereotypes are preconceived generalizations about male or female behavior ("All females are passive and dependent; all males are aggressive and independent"). Gender stereotypes pervade many cultures. They appear to some degree in children as young as 2 or 3, increase during the preschool years, and reach a peak at age 5 (Campbell, Shirley, & Candy, 2004; Ruble & Martin, 1998).

How do children acquire gender roles, and why do they adopt gender stereotypes? Are these purely social constructs, or do they reflect innate differences between males and females? Let's look at five theoretical perspectives on gender development (summarized in Table 8-1): *biological, evolutionary, psychoanalytic, cognitive,* and *social learning.* Each of these perspectives can contribute to our understanding, but none fully explains why boys and girls differ in some respects not in others.

Biological Approach   The existence of similar gender roles in many cultures suggests that some gender differences may be biologically based. Investigators are uncovering evidence of genetic, hormonal, and neurological explanations for some gender differences.

Scientists have identified more than 50 genes that may explain differences in anatomy and function between the brains of male and female mice. If similar genetic differences exist in humans, then sexual identity may be hardwired into the brain even before sexual organs form and hormonal activity begins (Dewing, Shi, Horvath, & Vilain, 2003). By age 5, when the brain reaches approximate adult size, boys' brains are about 10 percent larger than girls' brains, and girls have a lower proportion of gray matter, or neuronal cells (Halpern et al., 2007; Reiss, Abrams, Singer, Ross, & Denckla, 1996).

Hormones in the bloodstream before or about the time of birth may affect the developing brain. The male hormone testosterone is related to aggressiveness in adult animals, but the relationship in humans is less clear (Simpson, 2001).

For one thing, hormonal influences are hard to disentangle from genetic or later environmental influences (Iervolino et al., 2005). In any event, testosterone levels do not appear to be related to aggressiveness in children (Constantino et al., 1993).

Some research focuses on children with unusual prenatal hormonal histories. Girls with a disorder called *congenital adrenal hyperplasia (CAH)* have high prenatal levels of *androgens* (male sex hormones). Although raised as girls, they tend to develop into tomboys, showing preferences for boys' toys, rough play, and male playmates, as well as strong spatial skills. *Estrogens* (female sex hormones), on the other hand, seem to have less influence on boys' gender-typed behavior. However, these studies are natural experiments and cannot establish cause and effect. Other factors than hormonal differences may play a role (Ruble & Martin, 1998).

Perhaps the most dramatic examples of biologically based research have to do with infants born with ambiguous sexual structures that appear to be part male and part female. John Money and his colleagues (Money, Hampson, & Hampson, 1955) developed guidelines for infants born with such disorders. He recommended that the child be assigned as early as possible to the gender that holds the potential for the most nearly normal functioning and for stable gender identity.

However, studies demonstrate the difficulty of predicting the outcome of sex assignment at birth. In one study, 14 genetically male children born without normal penises but with testes were legally and surgically assigned to female sex during the first month of life and were raised as girls. Between ages 5 and 16, eight declared themselves male (though two were living ambiguously). Five declared unwavering female identity but expressed difficulty fitting in with other girls; and one, after learning that she had been born male, refused to discuss the subject with anyone. Meanwhile, two boys whose parents had refused the initial sexual assignment remained male (Reiner & Gearhart, 2004). In another study, 25 of 27 genetically male children born without penises were raised as girls but considered themselves boys and, as children, engaged in rough play (Reiner, 2000). These cases suggest that gender identity may be rooted in chromosomal structure and cannot easily be changed (Diamond & Sigmundson, 1997).

Evolutionary Approach   The evolutionary approach sees gendered behavior as biologically based—with a purpose. From this controversial perspective, children's gender roles underlie the evolved mating and child-rearing strategies of adult males and females.

According to Darwin's (1871) **theory of sexual selection,** the selection of sexual partners is a response to the differing reproductive pressures that early men and women confronted in the struggle for survival of the species (Wood & Eagly, 2002). The more widely a man can spread his seed, the greater his chances to pass on his genetic inheritance. Thus, men tend to seek as many partners as possible. They value physical prowess because it enables them to compete for mates and for control of resources and social status, which women value. Because a woman invests more time and energy in pregnancy and can bear only a limited number of children, each child's survival is of utmost importance to her; so she looks for a mate who will remain with her and support their offspring. The need to raise each child to reproductive maturity also explains why women tend to be more caring and nurturant than men (Bjorklund & Pellegrini, 2000; Wood & Eagly, 2002).

According to evolutionary theory, male competitiveness and aggressiveness and female nurturance develop during childhood as preparation for these adult roles (Pellegrini & Archer, 2005). Boys play at fighting; girls play at parenting. In caring for children, women often must put a child's needs and feelings ahead

theory of sexual selection Darwin's theory that gender roles developed in response to men's and women's differing reproductive needs.

of their own. Thus, young girls tend to be better able than young boys to control and inhibit their emotions and to refrain from impulsive behavior (Bjorklund & Pellegrini, 2000).

If this theory is correct, gender roles should be universal and resistant to change. Evidence in support of the theory is that in all cultures, women tend to be children's primary caregivers, though in some societies this responsibility is shared with the father or others (Wood & Eagly, 2002). Evidence for men's increasing involvement in child care are the 160,000 stay-at-home dads in the United States and the 189,000 children they care for (Fields, 2003, 2004).

Critics of evolutionary theory suggest that society and culture are as important as biology in determining gender roles. Evolutionary theory claims that men's primary role is to provide for subsistence while women's primary role is child care, but in some nonindustrial societies women are the main or equal providers. In an analysis of mating preferences in 37 cultures, women in traditional societies did tend to prefer older men with financial resources, and men to prefer younger women with homemaking skills; but these preferences were less pronounced in more egalitarian societies where women had reproductive freedom and educational opportunities (Wood & Eagly, 2002).

Some evolutionary theorists, therefore, see the evolution of gender roles as a dynamic process. They acknowledge that gender roles (such as men's involvement in child rearing) may change in an environment different from that in which these roles initially evolved (Crawford, 1998).

Psychoanalytic Approach   "Daddy, where will you live when I grow up and marry Mommy?" asks Mario, age 4. From the psychoanalytic perspective, Mario's question is part of his acquisition of gender identity. That process, according to Freud, is one of **identification,** the adoption of characteristics, beliefs, attitudes, values, and behaviors of the parent of the same sex. Freud considered identification an important personality development of early childhood. Some social learning theorists also have used the term.

> **identification**   In Freudian theory, the process by which a young child adopts characteristics, beliefs, attitudes, values, and behaviors of the parent of the same sex.

According to Freud, identification will occur for Mario when he represses or gives up the wish to possess the parent of the other sex (his mother) and identifies with the parent of the same sex (his father). Although this explanation for gender development has been influential, it has been difficult to test and has little research support (Maccoby, 1992). Despite some evidence that preschoolers tend to act more affectionately toward the opposite-sex parent and more aggressively toward the same-sex parent (Westen, 1998), most developmental psychologists today favor other explanations.

Cognitive Approach   Sarah figures out she is a girl because people call her a girl. As she continues to observe and think about her world, she concludes that she will always be female. She comes to understand gender by actively thinking about and constructing her own gender-typing. This is the heart of Lawrence Kohlberg's (1966) cognitive-developmental theory.

Kohlberg's Cognitive-Developmental Theory   In Kohlberg's theory, *gender knowledge precedes gendered behavior* ("I am a boy, so I like to do boy things"). Children actively search for cues about gender in their social world. As they come to realize which gender they belong to, they adopt behaviors they perceive as consistent with being male or female. Thus, 3-year-old Sarah prefers dolls to trucks because she sees girls playing with dolls and therefore views playing with dolls as consistent with her being a girl. And she plays mostly with other girls, whom she assumes will share her interests (Ruble & Martin, 1998; Martin & Ruble, 2004).

The acquisition of gender roles, said Kohlberg, hinges on **gender constancy,** also called *sex-category constancy*—a child's realization that his or her gender will always be the same. Once children achieve this realization, they are motivated to adopt behaviors appropriate to their gender. Gender constancy seems to develop in three stages: *gender identity, gender stability,* and *gender consistency* (Martin et al., 2002; Ruble & Martin, 1998; Szkrybalo & Ruble, 1999). *Gender identity* (awareness of one's own gender and that of others) typically occurs between ages 2 and 3. *Gender stability* comes when a girl realizes that she will grow up to be a woman, and a boy that he will grow up to be a man—in other words, that gender does not change. However, children at this stage may base judgments about gender on superficial appearances (clothing or hairstyle) and stereotyped behaviors. Finally—sometime between ages 3 and 7, or even later—comes *gender consistency:* the realization that a girl remains a girl even if she has a short haircut and plays with trucks, and a boy remains a boy even if he has long hair and earrings. Once children realize that their behavior or dress will not affect their gender, they may become less rigid in their adherence to gender norms (Martin et al., 2002).

Much research challenges Kohlberg's view that gender-typing depends on gender constancy. Long before children attain the final stage of gender constancy, they show gender-typed preferences (Bussey & Bandura, 1992; Martin & Ruble, 2004; Ruble & Martin, 1998). For example, gender preferences in toys and playmates appear as early as 12 to 24 months. However, these findings do not challenge Kohlberg's basic insight: that gender concepts influence behavior (Martin et al., 2002).

Today, cognitive-developmental theorists no longer claim that gender constancy must precede gender-typing (Martin et al., 2002). Instead, they suggest, gender-typing may be heightened by the more sophisticated understanding that gender constancy brings (Martin & Ruble, 2004). Each stage of gender constancy increases children's receptivity to gender-relevant information. The achievement of gender identity may motivate children to learn more about gender; gender stability and gender consistency may motivate them to be sure they are acting "like a boy" or "like a girl." Studies have found significant linkage between levels of gender constancy and various aspects of gender development (Martin et al., 2002).

Gender-Schema Theory   Another cognitive approach, which combines elements of cognitive-developmental and social learning theory, is **gender-schema theory.** It seeks to describe a cognitive mechanism through which gender learning and gender-typing occur. Among its leading proponents is Sandra Bem (1983, 1985, 1993); others are Carol Lynn Martin and Charles F. Halverson (1981). A *schema* (much like Piaget's *schemes*) is a mentally organized network of information that influences a wide variety of behaviors. According to gender-schema theory, children begin (very likely in infancy) to categorize events and people, organizing their observations around the schema, or category, of gender. They organize information on this basis because they see that their society classifies people that way: Males and females wear different clothes, play with different toys, and use separate bathrooms. Once children know what gender they are, they take on gender roles by developing a concept of what it means to be male or female in their culture. Children then match their behavior to their culture's gender schema—what boys and girls are "supposed" to be and do.

According to this theory, gender schemas promote gender stereotypes by influencing judgments about behavior. When a new boy his age moves in next door, 4-year-old Brandon knocks on his door, carrying a toy truck—apparently assuming that the new boy will like the same toys he likes. Bem suggests that children who show such stereotypical behavior may be experiencing pressure for gender conformity that

gender constancy Awareness that one will always be male or female; also called *sex-category constancy*.

gender-schema theory Theory, proposed by Bem, that children socialize themselves in their gender roles by developing a mentally organized network of information about what it means to be male or female in a particular culture.

inhibits healthy self-exploration. However, there is little evidence that gender schemas are at the root of stereotyped behavior or that children who are highly gender-typed necessarily feel pressure to conform (Yunger, Carver, & Perry, 2004).

Another problem with both gender-schema theory and Kohlberg's theory is that gender-stereotyping does not always become stronger with increased gender knowledge; in fact, the opposite is often true (Bussey & Bandura, 1999). Another view, which has research support, is that gender-stereotyping rises and then falls in a developmental pattern (Ruble & Martin, 1998; Welch-Ross & Schmidt, 1996). Around ages 4 to 6, when, according to gender-schema theory, children are constructing and then consolidating their gender schemas, they notice and remember only information consistent with these schemas and even exaggerate it. In fact, they tend to *mis*remember information that challenges gender stereotypes, such as photos of a girl sawing wood or a boy cooking, and to insist that the genders in the photos were the other way around. Young children are quick to accept gender labels; when told that an unfamiliar toy is for the other sex, they will drop it like a hot potato, and they expect others to do the same (C. L. Martin, Eisenbud, & Rose, 1995; Martin & Ruble, 2004; Ruble & Martin, 1998).

By ages 5 and 6, children develop a repertoire of rigid stereotypes about gender that they apply to themselves and others. A boy will pay more attention to what he considers boys' toys and a girl to girls' toys. A boy will expect to do better at boy things than at girl things, and if he does try, say, to dress a doll, he will be all thumbs. Then, around age 7 or 8, schemas become more complex as children begin to take in and integrate contradictory information, such as the fact that many girls have short hair. Children develop more complex beliefs about gender and become more flexible in their views about gender roles (Martin & Ruble, 2004; Ruble & Martin, 1998; M. G. Taylor, 1996; Trautner et al., 2005).

Cognitive approaches to gender development have made an important contribution by exploring how children think about gender and what they know about it at various ages. However, these approaches may not fully explain the link between knowledge and conduct. There is disagreement about precisely what mechanism prompts children to act out gender roles and why some children become more strongly gender-typed than others (Bussey & Bandura, 1992, 1999; Martin & Ruble, 2004; Ruble & Martin, 1998). Some investigators point to socialization.

Social Learning Approach   In traditional social learning theory, children acquire gender roles by observing models. Children generally choose models they see as powerful or nurturing. Typically, one model is a parent, often of the same sex, but children also pattern their behavior after other adults or after peers. Behavioral feedback together with direct teaching by parents, teachers, and other adults reinforces gender-typing. A boy who models his behavior after his father or male peers is commended for acting "like a boy." A girl gets compliments on a pretty dress or hairstyle. In this model, gendered behavior precedes gender knowledge. ("I am rewarded for doing boy things, so I must be a boy.")

social cognitive theory Albert Bandura's expansion of social learning theory; holds that children learn gender roles through socialization.

According to **social cognitive theory,** an expansion of social learning theory, observation enables children to learn much about gender-typed behaviors before performing them. They can mentally combine observations of multiple models and can generate their own behavioral variations. Instead of viewing the environment as a given, social cognitive theory recognizes that children select or even create their environments through their choice of playmates and activities. However, critics say that social cognitive theory does not explain how children differentiate between boys and girls before they have a concept of gender, or what initially motivates children to acquire gender knowledge, or how gender norms become internalized—questions that other cognitive theories attempt to answer (Martin et al., 2002).

For social cognitive theorists, socialization—the way a child interprets and internalizes experiences with parents, teachers, peers, and cultural institutions—plays a central part in gender development. Socialization begins in infancy, long before a conscious understanding of gender begins to form. Gradually, as children begin to regulate their activities, standards of behavior become internalized. A child no longer needs praise, rebukes, or a model's presence to act in socially appropriate ways. Children feel good about themselves when they live up to their internal standards and feel bad when they do not. A substantial part of the shift from socially guided control to self-regulation of gender-related behavior may take place between ages 3 and 4 (Bussey & Bandura, 1992). How do parents, peers, and the media influence this development?

Family Influences   When Louisiana governor Kathleen Blanco's 4-year-old grandson David was asked what he wanted to be when he grew up, he wasn't sure. He shrugged off all his mother's suggestions—firefighter, soldier, policeman, airplane pilot. Finally, she asked whether he'd like to be governor. "Mom," he replied, "I'm a boy!" (Associated Press, 2004).

David's response illustrates how strong family influences may be, even fostering counterstereotypical preferences. Usually, though, experience in the family seems to reinforce gender-typical preferences and attitudes. We say "seems" because it is difficult to separate parents' genetic influence from the influence of the environment they create. Also, parents may be responding to rather than encouraging children's gender-typed behavior (Iervolino et al., 2005).

Boys tend to be more strongly gender-socialized concerning play preferences than girls. Parents, especially fathers, generally show more discomfort if a boy plays with a doll than if a girl plays with a truck (Lytton & Romney, 1991; Ruble & Martin, 1998; Sandnabba & Ahlberg, 1999). Girls have more freedom than boys in their clothes, games, and choice of playmates (Miedzian, 1991).

In egalitarian households, the father's role in gender socialization seems especially important (Fagot & Leinbach, 1995). In an observational study of 4-year-olds in British and Hungarian cities, boys and girls whose fathers did more housework and child care were less aware of gender stereotypes and engaged in less gender-typed play than peers in more gender-typical families (Turner & Gervai, 1995).

Siblings also influence gender development, according to a three-year longitudinal study of 198 first- and secondborn siblings and their parents. Secondborns tend to become more like their older siblings in attitudes, personality, and leisure activities, whereas firstborns are more influenced by their parents and less by their younger siblings (McHale, Updegraff, Helms-Erikson, & Crouter, 2001). Young children with an older sibling of the same sex tend to be more gender-typed than those whose older sibling is of the other sex (Iervolino et al., 2005).

Peer Influences   Anna, at age 5, insisted on dressing in a new way. She wanted to wear leggings with a skirt over them, and boots—indoors and out. When her mother asked her why, Anna replied, "Because Katie dresses like this—and Katie's the king of the girls!"

Even in early childhood, the peer group is a major influence on gender-typing. By age 3, preschoolers generally play in sex-segregated groups that reinforce gender-typed behavior, and the influence of the peer group increases with age (Martin et al., 2002; Ruble & Martin, 1998). Children who play in same-sex groups tend to be more gender-typed than children who do not (Maccoby, 2002; Martin & Fabes, 2001). Peer groups show more disapproval of boys who act like girls than of girls who are tomboys (Ruble & Martin, 1998). Indeed, play choices

What's Your View?

- Where would you place your views on the continuum between the following extremes? Explain.

- Family A thinks girls should wear only ruffly dresses and boys should never wash dishes or cry.

- Family Z treats sons and daughters exactly alike, without making any references to the children's sex.

at this age may be more strongly influenced by peers and the media than by the models children see at home (Turner & Gervai, 1995). Generally, however, peer and parental attitudes reinforce each other (Bussey & Bandura, 1999).

Cultural Influences   When a young girl in Nepal touched the plow that her brother was using, she was scolded. In this way she learned that as a female she must refrain from acts her brother was expected to perform (D. Skinner, 1989).

In the United States, television is a major format for the transmission of cultural attitudes toward gender. Although women in television programs and commercials are now more likely to be working outside the home and men are sometimes shown caring for children or cooking, for the most part life as portrayed on television continues to be more stereotyped than life in the real world (Coltrane & Adams, 1997; Ruble & Martin, 1998).

Social learning theory predicts that children who watch a lot of television will become more gender-typed by imitating the models they see on the screen. Dramatic supporting evidence emerged from a natural experiment in several Canadian towns with access to television transmission for the first time. Children who had had relatively unstereotyped attitudes showed marked increases in traditional views two years later (Kimball, 1986).

Children's books, especially illustrated ones, have long been a source of gender stereotypes. Today, the proportion of women as main characters has greatly increased, and children are shown more frequently in nongender-typed activities (girls dressing up as pilots or ambulance drivers, boys attending tea parties or helping with laundry). However, even in the finest picture books, women are still shown mostly in traditional domestic roles, whereas men are seldom seen caring for children or doing housework (Gooden, 2001). Fathers, in fact, are largely absent, and when they do appear, they are shown as withdrawn and ineffectual (Anderson & Hamilton, 2005).

Major strengths of the socialization approach include the breadth and multiplicity of processes it examines and the scope for individual differences it reveals. But this very complexity makes it difficult to establish clear causal connections between the way children are raised and the way they think and act. Just what aspects of the home environment and the peer culture promote gender-typing? Do parents and peers treat boys and girls differently because they *are* different or because the culture says they *should be* different? Does differential treatment *produce* or *reflect* gender differences? Or, as social cognitive theory suggests, is there a bidirectional relationship? Further research may help us see how socializing agents mesh with children's biological tendencies and cognitive understandings with regard to gender-related attitudes and behavior.

Checkpoint

Can You . . .

♦ Compare five approaches to the study of gender development?

♦ Assess evidence for biological explanations of gender differences?

♦ Discuss how various theories explain the acquisition of gender roles, and assess the support for each theory?

Guidepost 3

How do preschoolers play, and how does play contribute to and reflect development?

Play: The Business of Early Childhood

Carmen, age 3, pretends that the pieces of cereal floating in her bowl are "fishies" swimming in the milk, and she "fishes," spoonful by spoonful. After breakfast, she puts on her mother's hat, picks up a briefcase, and is a "mommy" going to work. She rides her tricycle through the puddles, comes in for an imaginary phone call, turns a wooden block into a truck and says, "Vroom, vroom!" Carmen's day is one round of play after another.

It would be a mistake to dismiss Carmen's activities as "just fun." Although play may not seem to serve any obvious purpose, it has important current and long-term functions (Bjorklund & Pellegrini, 2002; P. K. Smith, 2005b). Play is important to healthy development of body and brain. It enables children to engage with the world around them; to use their imagination; to discover flexible ways to use objects and solve problems; and to prepare for adult roles.

Play contributes to all domains of development. Through play, children stimulate the senses, exercise their muscles, coordinate sight with movement, gain mastery over their bodies, make decisions, and acquire new skills. As they sort blocks of different shapes, count how many they can pile on each other, or announce that "my tower is bigger than yours," they lay the foundation for mathematical concepts. As they cooperate to build sandcastles or tunnels on the beach, they learn skills of negotiation and conflict resolution (Ginsburg & Committee on Communications and Committee on Psychosocial Aspects of Child and Family Health, 2007). Indeed, play is so important to children's development that the United Nations High Commissioner for Human Rights (1989) has recognized it as a right of every child. According to evolutionary theory, any activity that serves so many vital functions at a certain phase of life must have an evolutionary basis (Box 8-1).

Children need plenty of time for free exploratory play. Today, many parents expose young children to enrichment videos and academically oriented playthings. These activities may—or may not—be valuable in themselves, but not if they interfere with child-directed play (Ginsburg et al., 2007).

Children of differing ages have differing styles of play, play at different things, and spend different amounts of time in various types of play (Bjorklund & Pellegrini, 2002). Physical play, for example, begins in infancy with apparently aimless rhythmic movements. As gross motor skills improve, preschoolers exercise their muscles by running, jumping, skipping, hopping, and throwing. Toward the end of this period and into middle childhood, *rough-and-tumble play* involving wrestling, kicking, and chasing becomes more common, especially among boys (see Chapter 9).

Researchers categorize children's play in varying ways. One common classification system is by *cognitive complexity*. Another classification is based on the *social dimension* of play.

functional play Play involving repetitive large muscular movements.

constructive play Play involving use of objects or materials to make something.

dramatic play Play involving imaginary people or situations; also called *pretend play, fantasy play,* or *imaginative play.*

Cognitive Levels of Play

Courtney, at 3, talked for a doll, using a deeper voice than her own. Miguel, at 4, wore a kitchen towel as a cape and flew around as Batman. These children were engaged in play involving make-believe people or situations—one of four categories of play Smilansky (1968) identified as showing increasing levels of cognitive complexity. The categories are *functional play, constructive play, dramatic play,* and *games with rules.*

The simplest category, which begins during infancy, is **functional play** (sometimes called *locomotor play*), consisting of repeated practice in large muscular movements, such as rolling a ball (Bjorklund & Pellegrini, 2002).

The second category, **constructive play** (also called *object play*), is the use of objects or materials to make something, such as a house of blocks or a crayon drawing. Children spend an estimated 10 to 15 percent of their time playing with objects (Bjorklund & Pellegrini, 2002).

The third category, **dramatic play** (also called *pretend play, fantasy play,* or *imaginative play*), involves imaginary objects, actions, or roles; it rests on the symbolic function, which emerges during the last part of the second year (Piaget,

These young "veterinarians" examining their "patient" are participating in dramatic play based on the ability to use symbols to stand for people or things.

BOX **8-1** **Research** *in Action*

Does Play Have an Evolutionary Basis?

Children play for the pure pleasure it brings. Yet, from an evolutionary standpoint, play serves a greater purpose. This activity that (1) takes up considerable time and energy, (2) shows a characteristic age progression, peaking in childhood and declining with sexual maturity, (3) is encouraged by parents, and (4) occurs in all cultures seems to have been naturally selected for its significant benefits for children (Bjorklund & Pellegrini, 2000; P. K. Smith, 2005b).

Many psychologists and educators see play as an adaptive activity characteristic of the long period of immaturity and dependence during which children gain the physical attributes and cognitive and social learning necessary for adult life. Play aids bone and muscle development and gives children a chance to master activities and develop a sense of their capabilities (Bjorklund & Pellegrini, 2000). Through play, children practice, in a risk-free environment, behaviors and skills they will need as adults (Hawes, 1996). Animal studies suggest that the evolution of play may be linked to the evolution of intelligence. The most intelligent animals—birds and mammals—play, whereas less intelligent species—fish, reptiles, and amphibians—do not, as far as we can tell (Hawes, 1996).

Parents, according to evolutionary theory, encourage play because the future benefits of children's skill acquisition outweigh any benefits of current productive activity in which children, at their relatively low skill levels, might engage (P. K. Smith, 2005b). Gender differences in children's play enable boys and girls to practice adult behaviors important for reproduction and survival (Bjorklund & Pellegrini, 2002; Geary, 1999).

Different types of play serve different adaptive functions. Early *locomotor play* is common among all mammals and may support brain development. Later, *exercise play* may help develop muscle strength, endurance, physical skills, and efficiency of movement (P. K. Smith, 2005b). *Play with objects* is found mainly among primates: humans, monkeys, and apes. Object play may have served an evolutionary purpose in the development of tools, by enabling people to learn the properties of objects and what can be done with them (Bjorklund & Pellegrini, 2002). In premodern societies, object play tends to focus on developing useful skills, such as making baskets and pounding

grain (P. K. Smith, 2005b). Young mammals, like human children, engage in *social play,* such as wrestling and chasing each other, which strengthens social bonds, facilitates cooperation, and lessens aggression (Hawes, 1996).

Dramatic play seems to be an almost exclusively human activity. It appears to be universal but is less frequent in societies in which children are expected to participate in adult work (P. K. Smith, 2005a). In traditional hunter-gatherer societies, children imitate adult subsistence activities such as hunting, fishing, and preparing food. These highly repetitive routines seem to serve primarily as practice for adult activities (P. K. Smith, 2005b). As humans began to settle in permanent communities, dramatic play may have evolved so as to practice the changing skills needed for new ways of life. In modern urban industrial societies, themes of dramatic play are highly influenced by the mass media. At least in higher-SES families, dramatic play is encouraged by an abundance of toys, the absence of demands on children to help in subsistence activities, heavy parental involvement in play, and play-based preschool curricula (P. K. Smith, 2005a).

Investigators still have much to learn about the functions and benefits of play, but one thing seems clear: the time children spend playing is time well spent.

What's Your View?

From your observations of children's play, what immediate and long-range purposes does it appear to serve?

Check It Out

For more information on this topic, go to http://nationalzoo .si.edu/Publications/ZooGoer/1996/1/junglegyms.cfm. This is the website for *Zoogoer,* a newsletter of the Smithsonian National Zoological Park. It features an article on the evolution of play in animals and humans.

1962). Although functional play and constructive play precede dramatic play in Smilanksy's hierarchy, these three types of play often occur at the same ages (Bjorklund & Pellegrini, 2002; Smith, 2005a).

Dramatic play peaks during the preschool years, increasing in frequency and complexity (Bjorklund & Pellegrini, 2002; Smith, 2005a), and then declines as school-age children become more involved in **formal games with rules**—organized games with known procedures and penalties, such as hopscotch and marbles. However, many children continue to engage in pretending well beyond the elementary school years. An estimated 12 to 15 percent of preschoolers' time is spent

formal games with rules
Organized games with known procedures and penalties.

in pretend play (Bjorklund & Pellegrini, 2002), but the trend toward academically oriented kindergarten programs may limit the amount of time children can spend in such play (Bergen, 2002; Ginsburg et al., 2007).

Dramatic play at age 2 is largely imitative, often initiated by an adult caregiver, and follows familiar scripts such as feeding a baby doll or taking a stuffed animal's temperature. By age 3 or 4, pretense becomes more imaginative and self-initiated. Children may use a block to represent a cup or just imagine the cup (P. K. Smith, 2005a).

Dramatic play involves a combination of cognition, emotion, language, and sensorimotor behavior. It may strengthen the development of dense connections in the brain and strengthen the later capacity for abstract thought. Studies have found the quality of dramatic play to be associated with social and linguistic competence (Bergen, 2002). By making tickets for an imaginary train trip or pretending to read eye charts in a doctor's office, children build emergent literacy skills (Christie, 1991, 1998). Pretend play also may further the development of theory-of-mind skills (refer to Chapter 7). The peak period for pretend play, early childhood, is also the peak period for acquisition of such skills as recognizing false beliefs (P. K. Smith, 2005b).

The Social Dimension of Play

In a classic study done in the 1920s, Mildred B. Parten (1932) identified six types of play ranging from the least to the most social (Table 8-2). She found that as children get older, their play tends to become more social—that is, more interactive and more cooperative. At first children play alone, then alongside other children, and finally together. Today, however, many researchers view Parten's characterization of children's play development as too simplistic. Children of all ages engage in all of Parten's categories of play (K. H. Rubin, Bukowski, & Parker, 1998).

Parten apparently regarded nonsocial play as less mature than social play. She suggested that young children who continue to play alone may develop social, psychological, or educational problems. Yet, certain types of nonsocial play, particularly parallel play and solitary independent play, may consist of activities that *foster* cognitive, physical, and social development. In one study of 4-year-olds, *parallel constructive play* (for example, working on puzzles near another child who is also doing so) was most common among children who were good problem solvers, were popular with other children, and were seen by teachers as socially skilled (K. Rubin, 1982).

Researchers now look not only at *whether* a child plays alone but at *why.* Among 567 kindergartners, teachers, observers, and classmates rated almost 2 out of 3 children who played alone as socially and cognitively competent; they simply preferred to play that way (Harrist, Zain, Bates, Dodge, & Pettit, 1997). On the other hand, solitary play sometimes can be a sign of shyness, anxiety, fearfulness, or social rejection (Coplan et al., 2004; Henderson, Marshall, Fox, & Rubin, 2004; Spinrad et al., 2004).

Reticent play, a combination of Parten's unoccupied and onlooker categories, is often a manifestation of shyness (Coplan et al., 2004). However, such reticent behaviors as playing near other children, watching what they do, or wandering aimlessly may sometimes be a prelude to joining in others' play (K. H. Rubin et al., 1998; Spinrad et al., 2004). In a short-term longitudinal study, reticent children were well-liked and showed few problem behaviors (Spinrad et al., 2004). Nonsocial play, then, seems to be far more complex than Parten imagined.

Table 8-2	Parten's Categories of Social and Nonsocial Play

Category	Description
Unoccupied behavior	The child does not seem to be playing but watches anything of momentary interest.
Onlooker behavior	The child spends most of the time watching other children play. The onlooker talks to them, asking questions or making suggestions, but does not enter into the play. The onlooker is definitely observing particular groups of children rather than anything that happens to be exciting.
Solitary independent play	The child plays alone with toys that are different from those used by nearby children and makes no effort to get close to them.
Parallel play	The child plays independently but among the other children, playing with toys like those used by the other children but not necessarily playing with them in the same way. Playing *beside* rather than *with* the others, the parallel player does not try to influence the other children's play.
Associative play	The child plays with other children. They talk about their play, borrow and lend toys, follow one another, and try to control who may play in the group. All the children play similarly if not identically; there is no division of labor and no organization around any goal. Each child acts as she or he wishes and is interested more in being with the other children than in the activity itself.
Cooperative or organized supplementary play	The child plays in a group organized for some goal—to make something, play a formal game, or dramatize a situation. One or two children control who belongs to the group and direct activities. By a division of labor, children take on different roles and supplement each other's efforts.

Source: Adapted from Parten, 1932, pp. 249–251.

One kind of play that becomes more social during the preschool years is dramatic play (K. H. Rubin et al., 1998; D. G. Singer & J. L. Singer, 1990). Children typically engage in more dramatic play when playing with someone else than when playing alone (Bjorklund & Pellegrini, 2002). As dramatic play becomes more collaborative, story lines become more complex and innovative, offering rich opportunities to practice interpersonal and language skills and to explore social conventions and roles. In pretending together, children develop joint problem-solving, planning, and goal-seeking skills; gain understanding of other people's perspectives; and construct an image of the social world (Bergen, 2002; Bodrova & Leong, 1998; Bjorklund & Pellegrini, 2002; J. I. F. Davidson, 1998; J. E. Johnson, 1998; Nourot, 1998; P. K. Smith, 2005a).

A common type of dramatic play involves imaginary companions. This normal phenomenon of childhood is seen most often in firstborn and only children, who lack the close company of siblings. Girls are more likely than boys to have imaginary friends, or at least to acknowledge them; boys are more likely to impersonate imaginary characters (Carlson & Taylor, 2005).

Children who have imaginary companions can distinguish fantasy from reality (M. Taylor, Cartwright, & Carlson, 1993). They play more imaginatively than other children and are more cooperative (D. G. Singer & J. L. Singer, 1990; J. L. Singer & D. G. Singer, 1981); and they do not lack for friends (Gleason et al., 2000). In one study of 152 preschoolers, 4-year-olds who reported having imaginary companions did better on theory-of-mind tasks (such as differentiating

What's Your View?

• How do you think the growing use of computers for both games and educational activities might affect preschool children's social and cognitive development?

appearance and reality and recognizing false beliefs) than children who did not create such companions (M. Taylor & Carlson, 1997), and these children showed greater emotional understanding three years later.

How Gender Influences Play

As we have mentioned, sex segregation is common among preschoolers and becomes more prevalent in middle childhood. This tendency seems to be universal across cultures (P. K. Smith, 2005a). Although biology (sex hormones), gender identification, and adult reinforcement all seem to influence gender differences in play, the influence of the peer group may be more powerful (Smith, 2005a). Boys of all ages engage in more physical play than girls do (Bjorklund & Pellegrini, 2002; P. K. Smith, 2005b). Boys

Preschool girls and boys do not typically play together. When they do, they usually play with "masculine" toys such as cars and trucks or blocks.

and girls are equally likely to play with objects, but boys do so more vigorously (Smith, 2005b). Boys tend to like active, outdoor physical play in large mixed-age groups; girls prefer quiet, harmonious play with one playmate. Boys play spontaneously on sidewalks, streets, or empty lots; girls tend to choose more structured, adult-supervised activities (Benenson, 1993; Bjorklund & Pellegrini, 2002; Fabes, Martin, & Hanish, 2003; Serbin, Moller, Gulko, Powlishta, & Colburne, 1994; P. K. Smith, 2005a).

Girls engage in more dramatic play than boys. Boys' pretend play often involves danger or discord and competitive, dominant roles, as in mock battles. Girls' pretend stories generally focus on social relationships and nurturing, domestic roles, as in playing house (Bjorklund & Pellegrini, 2002; Pellegrini & Archer, 2005; P. K. Smith, 2005a). However, boys' play is more strongly gender-stereotyped than girls' (Bjorklund & Pellegrini, 2002). Thus, in mixed-sex groups, play tends to revolve around traditionally masculine activities (Fabes et al., 2003).

How Culture Influences Play

Cultural values affect the play environments adults set up for children, and these environments in turn affect the frequency of specific forms of play across cultures (Bodrova & Leong, 1998). One observational study compared 48 middle-class Korean American and 48 middle-class Anglo-American children in separate preschools (Farver, Kim, & Lee, 1995). The three Anglo-American preschools, in keeping with normative U.S. values, encouraged independent thinking and active involvement in learning by letting children select from a wide range of activities. The Korean American preschool, in keeping with traditional Korean values, emphasized development of academic skills and completion of tasks. The Anglo-American preschools encouraged social interchange among children and collaborative activities with teachers. In the Korean American preschool, children were allowed to talk and play only during outdoor recess.

Not surprisingly, the Anglo-American children engaged in more social play, whereas the Korean Americans engaged in more unoccupied or parallel play. At the same time, Korean American children played more cooperatively, often offering toys to other children—very likely a reflection of their culture's emphasis on group harmony. Anglo-American children were more aggressive and often responded negatively to other children's suggestions, reflecting the competitiveness of American culture.

 **Checkpoint**

Can You . . .

- Identify four cognitive levels of play and six categories of social and nonsocial play?

- Explain how cognitive and social dimensions of play may be connected?

- Tell how gender and culture influence the way children play, and give examples?

Parenting

As children gradually become their own persons, their upbringing can be a complex challenge. Parents must deal with small people who have independent minds and wills, but who still have a lot to learn about what kinds of behavior work well in society.

Forms of Discipline

discipline Methods of molding children's character and of teaching them to exercise self-control and engage in acceptable behavior.

The word *discipline* means "instruction" or "training." In the field of human development, **discipline** refers to methods of molding character and of teaching self-control and acceptable behavior. It can be a powerful tool for socialization with the goal of developing self-discipline. What forms of discipline work best? Researchers have looked at a wide range of techniques.

Reinforcement and Punishment "You're such a wonderful helper, Nick! "Thank you so much for putting away your toys." Nick's mother smiles warmly at her son as he plops his dump truck into the toy box. Her words and actions provide gentle discipline for her son and teach him that putting away his toys is a positive behavior that should be repeated.

Parents sometimes punish children to stop undesirable behavior, but children usually learn more from being reinforced for good behavior. *External* reinforcements may be tangible (treats, more playtime) or intangible (a smile, a word of praise, a hug, extra attention, or a special privilege). Whatever the reinforcement, the child must see it as rewarding and must receive it fairly consistently after showing the desired behavior. Eventually, the behavior should provide an *internal* reinforcement: a sense of pleasure or accomplishment.

Although positive reinforcement is usually most effective, there are times when punishment, such as isolation or denial of privileges, is necessary. Sometimes a child is willfully defiant. In such situations, punishment, if consistent, immediate, and clearly tied to the offense, may be effective. It should be administered calmly, in private, and aimed at eliciting compliance, not guilt. It is most effective when accompanied by a short, simple explanation (AAP Committee on Psychosocial Aspects of Child and Family Health, 1998; Baumrind, 1996a, 1996b).

Too harsh punishment, on the other hand, can be harmful. Children who are punished harshly and frequently may have trouble interpreting other people's actions and words; they may attribute hostile intentions where none exist (B. Weiss, Dodge, Bates, & Pettit, 1992). Young children who have been punished harshly may act aggressively (Nix et al., 1999) or may become passive because they feel helpless. Children may become frightened if parents lose control and may eventually try to avoid a punitive parent, undermining the parent's ability to influence behavior (Grusec & Goodnow, 1994).

corporal punishment Use of physical force with the intention of causing pain but not injury so as to correct or control behavior.

Corporal punishment, used by as many as 94 percent of U.S. parents of 3- and 4-year-olds (Straus & Stewart, 1999), has been defined as "the use of physical force with the intention of causing a child to experience pain, but not injury, for the purpose of correction or control of the child's behavior" (Straus, 1994a, p. 4). It can include spanking, hitting, slapping, pinching, shaking (which can be fatal to infants), and other physical acts. Corporal punishment is popularly believed to be more effective than other methods, to instill respect for parental authority, and to be harmless if done in moderation by loving parents (Kazdin & Benjet, 2003; McLoyd & Smith, 2002). However, a growing body of evidence from cross-sectional and longitudinal studies suggests that it is often counterproductive and should be avoided (Straus, 1999; Straus & Stewart, 1999). On the other hand, a

6-year study of 1,990 European American, African American, and Hispanic children found that spanking does *not* lead to problem behavior *if* it is done in the context of strong emotional support (McLoyd & Smith, 2002) or if it is done in cultures where spanking is seen as normal and common, such as Kenya (Lansford et al., 2005).

Still, most research strongly suggests that frequent or severe corporal punishment is potentially harmful to children. Apart from the risk of injury, children who experience corporal punishment may fail to internalize moral messages, develop poor parent-child relationships, and show increased physical aggressiveness or antisocial behavior (Gershoff, 2002; MacMillan et al., 1999; Strassberg, Dodge, Pettit, & Bates, 1994), even in adulthood (Straus & Stewart, 1999). Furthermore, there is no clear line between mild and harsh spanking, and one often leads to the other (Kazdin & Benjet, 2003). Thus, even though no harm from very mild spanking has been established (Larzalere, 2000), it seems prudent to choose other, less risky means of discipline (Kazdin & Benjet, 2003). The American Academy of Pediatrics Committee on Psychosocial Aspects of Child and Family Health (1998) recommends positive reinforcement to encourage desired behaviors and verbal reprimands, time-outs (brief isolation to give the child a chance to cool down), or removal of privileges to discourage undesired behaviors—all within a positive, supportive, loving parent-child relationship.

The line between some forms of punishment and physical or emotional abuse is not always easy to draw, but discipline clearly becomes abusive when it results in injury to a child. **Psychological aggression** refers to verbal attacks that may result in psychological harm, such as (1) yelling or screaming, (2) threatening to spank or hit the child, (3) swearing or cursing at the child, (4) threatening to send the child away or kick the child out of the house, and (5) calling the child dumb or lazy. Some psychologists equate the last three categories with emotional abuse. Psychological aggression, like physical aggression (spanking), is almost universal among U.S. parents. In a nationally representative sampling of 991 parents, 98 percent reported using some form of psychological aggression by the time a child was 5, and about 90 percent thereafter (Straus & Field, 2003).

psychological aggression Verbal attacks on a child by a parent that may result in psychological harm.

Inductive Reasoning, Power Assertion, and Withdrawal of Love When Sara took candy from a store, her father did not lecture her on honesty, spank her, or tell her what a bad girl she had been. Instead, he explained how the owner of the store would be harmed by her failure to pay for the candy, asked her how she thought the store owner might feel, and then took her back to the store to return the candy.

Inductive techniques, such as those Sara's father used, are designed to encourage desirable behavior or discourage undesirable behavior by reasoning with a child. They include setting limits, demonstrating logical consequences of an action, explaining, discussing, negotiating, and getting ideas from the child about what is fair. Inductive techniques are usually the most effective method of getting children to accept parental standards (M. L. Hoffman, 1970a, 1970b; Jagers, Bingham, & Hans, 1996; McCord, 1996).

inductive techniques Disciplinary techniques designed to induce desirable behavior by appealing to a child's sense of reason and fairness.

Inductive reasoning tends to arouse empathy for the victim of wrongdoing as well as guilt on the part of the wrongdoer (Krevans & Gibbs, 1996). Kindergartners whose mothers reported using reasoning were more likely to see the moral wrongness of behavior that hurts other people (as opposed to merely breaking rules) than children whose mothers took away privileges (Jagers et al., 1996).

Two other broad categories of discipline are *power assertion* and *temporary withdrawal of love*. **Power assertion** is intended to stop or discourage undesirable behavior through physical or verbal enforcement of parental control; it includes demands, threats, withdrawal of privileges, spanking, and other types of punishment. **Withdrawal of love** may include ignoring, isolating, or showing

power assertion Disciplinary strategy designed to discourage undesirable behavior through physical or verbal enforcement of parental control.

withdrawal of love Disciplinary strategy that involves ignoring, isolating, or showing dislike for a child.

What's Your View?

• As a parent, what form of discipline would you favor if your 3-year-old took a cookie from the cookie jar? Refused to nap? Hit his little sister? Tell why.

Checkpoint

Can You . . .

◆ Compare five forms of discipline, and discuss their effectiveness?

dislike for a child. Neither of these is as effective as inductive reasoning in most circumstances, and both may be harmful (M. L. Hoffman, 1970a, 1970b; Jagers et al., 1996; McCord, 1996).

The effectiveness of parental discipline may hinge on how well the child understands and accepts the parent's message, both cognitively and emotionally (Grusec & Goodnow, 1994). For the child to accept the message, the child has to recognize it as appropriate; so parents need to be fair and accurate as well as clear and consistent about their expectations. They need to fit the discipline to the misdeed and to the child's temperament and cognitive and emotional level. A child may be more motivated to accept the message if the parents are normally warm and responsive and if they arouse the child's empathy for someone the child has harmed (Grusec & Goodnow, 1994). How well children accept a disciplinary method also may depend on whether the type of discipline used is accepted in the family's culture (Lansford et al., 2005).

One point on which many experts agree is that a child interprets and responds to discipline in the context of an ongoing relationship with a parent. Some researchers therefore look beyond specific parental practices to overall styles, or patterns, of parenting.

Parenting Styles

Why does Stacy sit quietly on the rug and listen to a story while Cameron fidgets and pokes his classmates? Why does Consuelo work on a puzzle for 20 minutes while David throws the pieces of his puzzle across the room when he can't fit them? Why are children so different in their responses to the same situation? Temperament is a major factor, of course; but some research suggests that styles of parenting may affect children's competence in dealing with their world.

Diana Baumrind and the Effectiveness of Authoritative Parenting   In pioneering research, Diana Baumrind (1971, 1996b; Baumrind & Black, 1967) studied 103 preschool children from 95 families. Through interviews, testing, and home studies, she measured how the children were functioning, identified three parenting styles, and described typical behavior patterns of children raised according to each. Baumrind's work and the large body of research it inspired have established strong associations between each parenting style and a particular set of child behaviors (Baumrind, 1989; Darling & Steinberg, 1993; Pettit, Bates, & Dodge, 1997).

Authoritarian parenting, according to Baumrind, emphasizes control and unquestioning obedience. Authoritarian parents try to make children conform to a set standard of conduct and punish them arbitrarily and forcefully for violating it. They are more detached and less warm than other parents. Their children tend to be more discontented, withdrawn, and distrustful.

Permissive parenting emphasizes self-expression and self-regulation. Permissive parents make few demands and allow children to monitor their own activities as much as possible. When they do have to make rules, they explain the reasons for them. They consult with children about policy decisions and rarely punish. They are warm, noncontrolling, and undemanding. Their preschool children tend to be immature—the least self-controlled and the least exploratory.

Authoritative parenting emphasizes a child's individuality but also stresses social constraints. Authoritative parents have confidence in their ability to guide children, but they also respect children's independent decisions, interests, opinions, and personalities. They are loving and accepting but also demand good behavior and are firm in maintaining standards. They impose limited, judicious punishment when necessary, within the context of a warm, supportive relationship. They

authoritarian parenting   In Baumrind's terminology, parenting style emphasizing control and obedience.

permissive parenting   In Baumrind's terminology, parenting style emphasizing self-expression and self-regulation.

authoritative parenting   In Baumrind's terminology, parenting style blending respect for a child's individuality with an effort to instill social values.

favor inductive discipline, explaining the reasoning behind their stands and encouraging verbal give-and-take. Their children apparently feel secure in knowing both that they are loved and what is expected of them. Preschoolers with authoritative parents tend to be the most self-reliant, self-controlled, self-assertive, exploratory, and content.

Eleanor Maccoby and John Martin (1983) added a fourth parenting style—*neglectful,* or *uninvolved*—to describe parents who, sometimes because of stress or depression, focus on their needs rather than on those of the child. Neglectful parenting has been linked with a variety of behavioral disorders in childhood and adolescence (Baumrind, 1991; Parke & Buriel, 1998; R. A. Thompson, 1998).

Why does authoritative parenting seem to enhance children's social competence? It may be because authoritative parents set sensible expectations and realistic standards. By making clear, consistent rules, they let children know what is expected of them. In authoritarian homes, children are so strictly controlled that often they cannot make independent choices about their own behavior. In permissive homes, children receive so little guidance that they may become uncertain and anxious about whether they are doing the right thing. In authoritative homes, children know when they are meeting expectations and can decide whether it is worth risking parental displeasure to pursue a goal. These children are expected to perform well, fulfill commitments, and participate actively in family duties as well as family fun. They know the satisfaction of accepting responsibilities and achieving success. Parents who make reasonable demands show that they believe their children can meet them—and that the parents care enough to insist that they do.

When conflict arises, an authoritative parent can teach the child positive ways to communicate his or her point of view and negotiate acceptable alternatives. ("If you don't want to throw away those rocks you found, where do you think we should keep them?") Internalization of this broader set of skills, not just of specific behavioral demands, may well be a key to the success of authoritative parenting (Grusec & Goodnow, 1994).

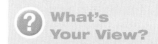

What's Your View?

- If you have or were to have children, to what extent would you want them to adopt your values and behavioral standards? Give examples.

Support and Criticisms of Baumrind's Model In research based on Baumrind's work, the superiority of authoritative parenting (or similar conceptions of parenting style) has repeatedly been supported (Baumrind, 1989; Darling & Steinberg, 1993). For example, a longitudinal study of 585 ethnically and socioeconomically diverse families in Tennessee and Indiana with children from prekindergarten through grade 6 found that four aspects of early supportive parenting—warmth, use of inductive discipline, interest and involvement in children's contacts with peers, and proactive teaching of social skills—predicted children's later behavioral, social, and academic outcomes (Pettit, Bates, & Dodge, 1997).

Still, Baumrind's model has provoked controversy because it seems to suggest that there is one "right" way to raise children. Also, because Baumrind's findings are correlational, they merely establish associations between each parenting style and a particular set of child behaviors. They do not show that different styles of child rearing *cause* children to be more or less competent. It is also impossible to know whether the children Baumrind studied were, in fact, raised in a particular style. It may be that some of the better-adjusted children were raised inconsistently, but by the time of the study their parents had adopted the authoritative pattern (Holden & Miller, 1999). In addition, Baumrind did not consider innate factors, such as temperament, that might have affected children's competence and exerted an influence on the parents.

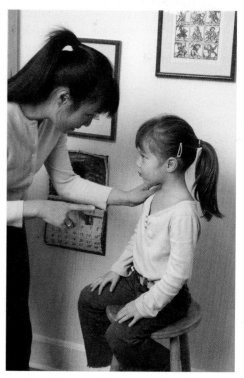

Traditional Chinese culture stresses adults' responsibility to maintain the social order by teaching children socially proper behavior.

Cultural Differences in Parenting Styles   Another concern is that Baumrind's categories reflect the dominant North American view of child development and may not apply to some cultures or socioeconomic groups. Among Asian Americans, obedience and strictness are not associated with harshness and domination but instead with caring, concern, and involvement and with maintaining family harmony. Traditional Chinese culture, with its emphasis on respect for elders, stresses adults' responsibility to maintain the social order by teaching children socially proper behavior. This obligation is carried out through firm and just control and governance of the child and even by physical punishment if necessary (Zhao, 2002). Although Asian American parenting is frequently described as authoritarian, the warmth and supportiveness that characterize Chinese American family relationships may more closely resemble Baumrind's authoritative parenting but without the emphasis on the European American values of individuality, choice, and freedom (Chao, 1994) and with stricter parental control (Chao, 2001).

Indeed, a dichotomy between the individualistic values of Western parenting and the collectivist values of Asian parenting may be overly simplistic. In interviews with 64 Japanese mothers of 3- to 6-year-olds (Yamada, 2004), the mothers' descriptions of their parenting practices reflected the search for a balance between granting appropriate autonomy and exercising disciplinary control. The mothers let children make their own decisions within what they saw as the child's personal domain, such as play activities, playmates, and clothing, and this domain enlarged with the child's age. When health, safety, moral issues, or conventional social rules were involved, the mothers set limits or exercised control. When conflicts arose, the mothers used reasoning rather than power-assertive methods or sometimes gave in to the child, apparently on the theory that the issue wasn't worth struggling over—or that the child might be right after all.

Special Behavioral Concerns

Three issues of special concern to parents, caregivers, and teachers of preschool children are how to promote altruism, curb aggression, and deal with fears that often arise at this age.

Prosocial Behavior   Alex, at 3½, responded to two fellow preschoolers' complaints that they did not have enough modeling clay, his favorite plaything, by giving them half of his. By acting out of concern for others with no expectation of reward, Alex was showing **altruism.** Altruistic acts like Alex's often entail cost, self-sacrifice, or risk. Altruism is at the heart of **prosocial behavior,** voluntary activity intended to benefit another.

Even before their second birthday, children often help others, share belongings and food, and offer comfort. Such behaviors may reflect a growing ability to imagine how another person might feel (Zahn-Waxler, Radke-Yarrow, Wagner, & Chapman, 1992). Girls tend to be more prosocial than boys, but the differences are small (Eisenberg & Fabes, 1998).

Genes and environment each contribute to individual differences in prosocial behavior. This finding comes from a study of 9,319 twin pairs whose prosocial behavior was rated by parents and teachers at ages 3, 4, and 7. Parents who showed affection and followed positive disciplinary strategies tended to encourage their children's natural tendency to prosocial behavior (Knafo & Plomin, 2006).

Parents of prosocial children typically are prosocial themselves. They point out models of prosocial behavior and steer children toward stories, films, and television programs that depict cooperation, sharing, and empathy and encourage sympathy, generosity, and helpfulness (J. L. Singer & D. G. Singer, 1998). Relationships with

Checkpoint

Can You . . .

◆ Summarize Baumrind's model of parenting styles?

◆ Explain how parents' way of resolving conflicts with young children can contribute to the success of authoritative child rearing?

◆ Discuss criticisms of Baumrind's model and cultural variations in parenting styles?

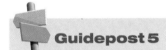

Guidepost 5

Why do young children help or hurt others, and why do they develop fears?

altruism   Behavior intended to help others out of inner concern and without expectation of external reward; may involve self-denial or self-sacrifice.

prosocial behavior   Any voluntary behavior intended to help others.

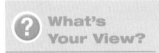

What's Your View?

• In a increasingly suspicious society concerned about "stranger danger," is it wise to encourage children to offer help to strangers?

siblings provide an important scenario for trying out caring behavior and learning to see another person's point of view. Peers and teachers also can model and reinforce prosocial behavior (Eisenberg, 1992; Eisenberg & Fabes, 1998).

Cultures vary in the degree to which they foster prosocial behavior. Traditional cultures in which people live in extended family groups and share work seem to instill prosocial values more than cultures that stress individual achievement (Eisenberg & Fabes, 1998).

The kind of aggression involved in fighting over a toy, without intention to hurt or dominate the other child, is instrumental aggression. It surfaces mostly during social play and normally declines as children learn to ask for what they want.

Aggression When Noah roughly snatches a ball away from Jake, he is interested only in getting the ball, not in hurting or dominating Jake. This is **instrumental aggression,** or aggression used as an instrument to reach a goal—the most common type of aggression in early childhood. Between ages 2½ and 5, children frequently struggle over toys and control of space. Aggression surfaces mostly during social play; children who fight the most also tend to be the most sociable and competent. In fact, the ability to show some instrumental aggression may be a necessary step in social development.

instrumental aggression Aggressive behavior used as a means of achieving a goal.

As children develop more self-control and become better able to express themselves verbally, they typically shift from showing aggression with blows to doing it with words (Coie & Dodge, 1998). However, individual differences remain. In a longitudinal study of 383 preschoolers, 11 percent of the girls and 9 percent of the boys showed high levels of aggression between ages 2 and 5. Boys and girls who were inattentive at age 2, and girls who showed poor emotion regulation at that age, tended to have conduct problems at age 5 (Hill, Degnan, Calkins, & Keane, 2006). Children who, as preschoolers, often engage in violent fantasy play may, at age 6, be prone to violent displays of anger (Dunn & Hughes, 2001).

Gender Differences in Aggression Aggression is an exception to the generalization that boys and girls are more similar than different (Hyde, 2005). In all cultures studied, as among most mammals, boys are more physically and verbally aggressive than girls. This gender difference is apparent by age 2 (Archer, 2004; Baillargeon et al., 2007; Pellegrini & Archer, 2005). Research with genetically engineered mice suggests that the SRY gene on the Y chromosome may play a role (Gatewood et al., 2006).

However, girls may be more aggressive than they seem (McNeilly-Choque, Hart, Robinson, Nelson, & Olsen, 1996; Putallaz & Bierman, 2004). Whereas boys engage in more **overt aggression**—physical or verbal aggression openly directed at its target—girls, especially as they grow older, are more likely to practice **relational (social) aggression.** This more subtle kind of aggression consists of damaging or interfering with relationships, reputation, or psychological well-being, often through teasing, manipulation, ostracism, or bids for control. It may include spreading rumors, name-calling, put-downs, or excluding someone from a group. It can be either overt or *covert (indirect)*—for example, making mean faces or ignoring someone. Among preschoolers, it tends to be direct and face-to-face ("You can't come to my party if you don't give me that toy") (Archer, 2004; Brendgen et al., 2005; Crick, Casas, & Nelson, 2002).

overt aggression Aggression that is openly directed at its target.

relational (social) aggression Aggression aimed at damaging or interfering with another person's relationships, reputation, or psychological well-being.

Influences on Aggression Why are some children more aggressive than others? Temperament may play a part. Children who are intensely emotional and low in self-control tend to express anger aggressively (Eisenberg, Fabes, Nyman, Bernzweig, & Pinuelas, 1994).

Both physical and social aggression have genetic and environmental sources, but their relative influence differs. Among 234 six-year-old twins, physical aggression was 50 to 60 percent heritable; the remainder of the variance was attributable to nonshared environmental influences (unique experiences). Social aggression was much more environmentally influenced; the variance was only 20 percent genetic, 20 percent explained by shared environmental influences, and 60 percent by nonshared experiences (Brendgen et al., 2005).

Parental behaviors strongly influence aggressiveness. In one study, 5-year-old boys who had been exposed prenatally to cocaine and who lived in poor, unstable, or stressful environments with single mothers tended to be high in aggressive behavior, such as fighting and bullying (Bendersky, Bennett, & Lewis, 2006). In several longitudinal studies, insecure attachment and lack of maternal warmth and affection in infancy predicted aggressiveness in early childhood (Coie & Dodge, 1998; MacKinnon-Lewis, Starnes, Volling, & Johnson, 1997). Manipulative behaviors such as withdrawal of love and making a child feel guilty or ashamed may foster social aggression (Brendgen et al., 2005).

Aggressiveness may result from a combination of a stressful and unstimulating home atmosphere, harsh discipline, lack of maternal warmth and social support, exposure to aggressive adults and neighborhood violence, and transient peer groups, which prevent stable friendships (Dodge, Pettit, & Bates, 1994; Grusec & Goodnow, 1994). In a study of 431 Head Start participants in an inner-city neighborhood, parents reported that more than half had witnessed gang activity, drug trafficking, police pursuits and arrests, or people carrying weapons, and some of the children and families had been victimized themselves. These children showed symptoms of distress at home and aggressive behavior at school (Farver, Xu, Eppe, Fernandez, & Schwartz, 2005).

Why does witnessing violence lead to aggression? In a classic social learning experiment (Bandura, Ross, & Ross, 1961), 3- to 6-year-olds individually watched adult models play with toys. Children in one experimental group saw the adult model play quietly. The model for the other experimental group spent most of the 10-minute session punching, throwing, and kicking a life-size inflated doll. A control group did not see any model. After the sessions, the children, who were mildly frustrated by seeing toys they were not allowed to play with, went into another playroom. The children who had seen the aggressive model acted much more aggressively than those in the other groups, imitating many of the same things they had seen the model say and do. The children who had seen the quiet model were less aggressive than the control group. This finding suggests that parents may be able to moderate the effects of frustration by modeling nonaggressive behavior.

Television has enormous power for modeling either prosocial behavior or aggression. In Chapter 10 we discuss the influence of televised violence on aggressive behavior.

Culture and Aggression   Culture can influence how much aggressive behavior a child shows. For example, in Japan, anger and aggression contradict the cultural emphasis on harmony. Japanese mothers are more likely than U.S. mothers to use inductive discipline, pointing out how aggressive behavior hurts others. Japanese mothers also show strong disappointment when children fail to meet behavioral standards (Zahn-Waxler et al., 1996).

Fearfulness   Passing fears are common in early childhood. Many 2- to 4-year-olds are afraid of animals, especially dogs. By age 6, children are more likely to be

What's Your View?

• Are there situations in which a child should be encouraged to be aggressive?

afraid of the dark. Other common fears are of thunderstorms, doctors, and imaginary creatures (DuPont, 1983; Stevenson-Hinde & Shouldice, 1996). Most of these disappear as children grow older and lose their sense of powerlessness.

Young children's fears stem largely from their intense fantasy life and their tendency to confuse appearance with reality. Sometimes their imaginations get carried away, making them worry about being attacked by a lion or being abandoned. Young children are more likely to be frightened by something that looks scary, such as a cartoon monster, than by something capable of doing great harm, such as a nuclear explosion (Cantor, 1994). For the most part, older children's fears are more realistic and self-evaluative (for example, fear of failing a test), because they know they are being evaluated by others (Stevenson-Hinde & Shouldice, 1996).

Fears may come from personal experience or from hearing about other people's experiences (Muris, Merckelbach, & Collaris, 1997). A preschooler whose mother is sick in bed may become upset by a story about a mother's death, even if it is an animal mother. Often fears come from appraisals of danger, such as the likelihood of being bitten by a dog, or are triggered by events, such as a child who was hit by a car becoming afraid to cross the street. Children who have lived through an earthquake, kidnapping, war, or some other frightening event may fear that it will happen again (Kolbert, 1994).

Parents can help prevent children's fears by instilling a sense of trust and normal caution without being too protective, and also by overcoming their own unrealistic fears. They can help a fearful child by reassurance and by encouraging open expression of feelings ("I know it is scary, but the thunder can't hurt you"). Ridicule ("Don't be such a baby!"), coercion ("Pat the nice doggie—it won't hurt you"), and logical persuasion ("The closest bear is 20 miles away, locked in a zoo!") are not helpful. Not until elementary school can children tell themselves that what they fear is not real (Cantor, 1994).

A young girl gets up the courage to touch a tarantula as her nervous cousin looks on. Systematic desensitization can help children overcome fears.

Checkpoint

Can You . . .

♦ Discuss influences on altruism, aggression, and fearfulness?

Relationships with Other Children

Although the most important people in young children's world are the adults who take care of them, relationships with siblings and playmates become more important in early childhood. Virtually every characteristic activity and personality issue of this age, from gender development to prosocial or aggressive behavior, involves other children. Let's look first at sibling relationships and then at children who have no siblings. Then, we will explore relationships with peers and friends.

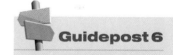

Guidepost 6

How do young children get along with—or without—siblings, playmates, and friends?

Sibling Relationships

"It's mine!"

"No, it's mine!"

"Well, I was playing with it first!"

The earliest, most frequent, and most intense disputes among siblings are over property rights—who owns a toy or who is entitled to play with it. Although exasperated adults may not always see it that way, sibling disputes and their settlement can be viewed as socialization opportunities, in which children learn to stand up for principles and negotiate disagreements (Ross, 1996). Another arena for socialization is joint dramatic play. Siblings who frequently play "let's pretend" develop a history of shared understandings that allow them to more easily resolve issues and build on each other's ideas (Howe et al., 2005).

Despite the frequency of conflict, sibling rivalry is *not* the main pattern between brothers and sisters early in life. Affection, interest, companionship, and influence are also prevalent in sibling relationships. Observations spanning three and a half years that began when younger siblings were about 1½ and the older siblings ranged from 3 to 4½ found prosocial and play-oriented behaviors to be more common than rivalry, hostility, and competition (Abramovitch, Corter, & Lando, 1979; Abramovitch, Corter, Pepler, & Stanhope, 1986; Abramovitch, Pepler, & Corter, 1982). Older siblings initiated more behavior, both friendly and unfriendly; younger siblings tended to imitate the older ones. As the younger children reached age 5, the siblings became less physical and more verbal in showing both aggression and care and affection.

At least one finding of this research has been replicated in many studies: same-sex siblings, particularly girls, are closer and play together more peaceably than boy-girl pairs (Kier & Lewis, 1998). Because older siblings tend to dominate younger ones, the quality of the relationship is more affected by the emotional and social adjustment of the older child than of the younger (Pike, Coldwell, & Dunn, 2005).

The quality of sibling relationships tends to carry over to relationships with other children. A child who is aggressive with siblings is likely to be aggressive with friends as well (Abramovitch et al., 1986). Siblings who frequently play amicably together tend to develop prosocial behaviors (Pike et al., 2005).

Likewise, friendships can influence sibling relationships. Older siblings who have experienced a good relationship with a friend before the birth of a sibling are likely to treat their younger siblings better and are less likely to develop antisocial behavior in adolescence (Kramer & Kowal, 2005). For a young child at risk for behavioral problems, a positive relationship with *either* a sibling or a friend can buffer the effects of a negative relationship with the other (McElwain & Volling, 2005).

The Only Child

In the United States, 21 percent of children under 18 have no siblings in the home (Kreider & Fields, 2005). Are only children spoiled, selfish, lonely, or maladjusted? An analysis of 115 studies belies that stereotype. In occupational and educational achievement and verbal intelligence, only children perform slightly better than children with siblings. Only children tend to be more motivated to achieve and to have slightly higher self-esteem; and they do not differ in emotional adjustment, sociability, or popularity. Perhaps these children do better because, consistent with evolutionary theory, parents who have limited time and resources to spend focus more attention on only children, talk to them more, do more with them, and expect more of them than do parents with more than one child (Falbo, 2006; Falbo & Polit, 1986; Polit & Falbo, 1987). And, because most children today spend considerable time in play groups, child care, and preschool, only children do not lack opportunities for social interaction with peers (Falbo, 2006).

Research in China also has produced largely encouraging findings about only children. In 1979, to control an exploding population, the People's Republic of China established an official policy of limiting families to one child each. Although the policy has since been relaxed somewhat, most urban families now have only one child, and most rural families no more than two (Hesketh, Lu, & Xing, 2005). Thus, in many Chinese cities, schoolrooms are almost completely filled with children who have no brothers or sisters. This situation offered researchers a natural experiment: an opportunity to study the adjustment of large numbers of only children.

A review of the literature found no significant differences in behavioral problems (Tao, 1998). Indeed, only children seemed to be at a distinct psychological advantage in a society that favors and rewards such a child. Among 731 urban children and adolescents, those with siblings reported higher levels of fear, anxiety, and depression than only children, regardless of sex or age (Yang, Ollendick, Dong, Xia, & Lin, 1995).

Among 4,000 third and sixth graders, personality differences between only children and those with siblings—as rated by parents, teachers, peers, and the children themselves—were few. Only children's academic achievement and physical growth were about the same as, or better than, children with siblings (Falbo & Poston, 1993). In a randomized study in Beijing first-grade classrooms (Jiao, Ji, & Jing, 1996), only children outperformed classmates with siblings in memory, language, and mathematics skills. This finding may reflect the greater attention, stimulation, hopes, and expectations that parents shower on a baby they know will be their first and last.

Young children learn the importance of being a friend to have a friend. This sighted girl (right) *is being a friend by helping her blind playmate enjoy the beach.*

Most of the studies used urban samples. Further research may reveal whether the findings hold up in rural areas and small towns, where children with siblings are more numerous, and whether only children maintain their cognitive superiority as they move through school.

Playmates and Friends

Friendships develop as people develop. Toddlers play alongside or near each other, but not until about age 3 do children begin to have friends. Through friendships and interactions with casual playmates, young children learn how to get along with others. They learn that being a friend is the way to have a friend. They learn how to solve problems in relationships and how to put themselves in another person's place, and they see models of various kinds of behavior. They learn moral values and gender-role norms, and they practice adult roles.

Preschoolers usually like to play with children of the same age and sex. Children who have frequent positive experiences with each other are most likely to become friends (Rubin et al., 1998; Snyder et al., 1996). About 3 out of 4 preschoolers have such mutual friendships (Hartup & Stevens, 1999).

The traits that young children look for in a playmate are similar to the traits they look for in a friend (C. H. Hart, DeWolf, Wozniak, & Burts, 1992). In one study, 4- to 7-year-olds rated the most important features of friendships as doing things together, liking and caring for each other, sharing and helping one another, and to a lesser degree, living nearby or going to the same school. Younger children rated physical traits, such as appearance and size, higher than older children did and rated affection and support lower (Furman & Bierman, 1983). Preschool children prefer prosocial playmates (C. H. Hart et al., 1992). They reject disruptive, demanding, intrusive, or aggressive children (Ramsey & Lasquade, 1996; Roopnarine & Honig, 1985).

Well-liked preschoolers and kindergartners and those who are rated by parents and teachers as socially competent generally cope well with anger. They avoid

✔ **Checkpoint**

Can You . . .

◆ Explain how the resolution of sibling disputes contributes to socialization?

◆ Tell how birth order and gender affect typical patterns of sibling interaction?

◆ Compare the development of only children with that of children with siblings?

◆ Discuss how preschoolers choose playmates and friends, how they behave with friends, and how they benefit from friendships?

insults and threats. Instead, they respond directly, in ways that minimize further conflict and keep relationships going. Less well-liked children tend to hit back or tattle (Fabes & Eisenberg, 1992).

Peer relationships become even more important during middle childhood, which we examine in Chapters 9 and 10.

Summary and Key Terms

The Developing Self

Guidepost 1: *How does the self-concept develop during early childhood, and how do children show self-esteem, emotional growth, and initiative?*

- The self-concept undergoes major change in early childhood. According to a neo-Piagetian model, self-definition shifts from single representations to representational mappings. Young children do not see the difference between the real self and the ideal self.
- Culture affects the self-definition.
- Self-esteem in early childhood tends to be global and unrealistic, reflecting adult approval.
- Understanding of emotions directed toward the self and of simultaneous emotions develops gradually.
- According to Erikson, the developmental conflict of early childhood is initiative versus guilt. Successful resolution of this conflict results in the virtue of *purpose*.

self-concept (252)
self-definition (252)
single representations (253)
real self (253)
ideal self (253)
representational mappings (253)
self-esteem (253)
initiative versus guilt (256)

Gender

Guidepost 2: *How do boys and girls become aware of the meaning of gender, and what explains differences in behavior between the sexes?*

- Gender identity is an aspect of the developing self-concept.
- The main gender difference in early childhood is boys' greater aggressiveness. Girls tend to be more empathic and prosocial and less prone to problem behavior. Some cognitive differences appear early, others not until preadolescence or later.
- Children learn gender roles at an early age through gender-typing. Gender stereotypes peak during the preschool years.

- Five major perspectives on gender development are biological, evolutionary, psychoanalytic, cognitive, and social learning.
- Evidence suggests that some gender differences may be biologically based.
- Evolutionary theory sees children's gender roles as preparation for adult mating behavior.
- In Freudian theory, a child identifies with the same-sex parent after giving up the wish to possess the other parent.
- Cognitive-developmental theory maintains that gender identity develops from thinking about one's gender. According to Kohlberg, gender constancy leads to acquisition of gender roles. Gender-schema theory holds that children categorize gender-related information by observing what males and females do in their culture.
- According to social cognitive theory, children learn gender roles through socialization. Parents, peers, the media, and culture influence gender-typing.

gender identity (256)
gender roles (257)
gender-typing (257)
gender stereotypes (258)
theory of sexual selection (259)
identification (260)
gender constancy (261)
gender-schema theory (261)
social cognitive theory (262)

Play: The Business of Early Childhood

Guidepost 3: *How do preschoolers play, and how does play contribute to and reflect development?*

- Play has physical, cognitive, and psychosocial benefits. Changes in the types of play children engage in reflect cognitive and social development.
- According to Smilansky, children progress cognitively from functional play to constructive play, dramatic play, and then formal games with rules. Dramatic play becomes increasingly common during early childhood and helps children develop social and cognitive skills. Rough-and-tumble play also begins during early childhood.

- According to Parten, play becomes more social during early childhood. However, later research has found that nonsocial play is not necessarily immature.
- Children prefer to play with (and play more socially with) others of their sex.
- Cognitive and social aspects of play are influenced by the culturally approved environments adults create for children.

functional play (265)

constructive play (265)

dramatic play (265)

formal games with rules (266)

Parenting

Guidepost 4: *How do parenting practices influence development?*

- Discipline can be a powerful tool for socialization.
- Both positive reinforcement and prudently administered punishment can be appropriate tools of discipline within the context of a positive parent-child relationship.
- Power assertion, inductive techniques, and withdrawal of love are three categories of discipline. Reasoning is generally the most effective and power assertion the least effective in promoting internalization of parental standards. Spanking and other forms of corporal punishment can have negative consequences.
- Baumrind identified three parenting styles: authoritarian, permissive, and authoritative. A fourth style, neglectful or uninvolved, was identified later. Authoritative parents tend to raise more competent children. However, Baumrind's findings may be misleading when applied to some cultures.

discipline (270)

corporal punishment (270)

psychological aggression (271)

inductive techniques (271)

power assertion (271)

withdrawal of love (271)

authoritarian parenting (272)

permissive parenting (272)

authoritative parenting (272)

Guidepost 5: *Why do young children help or hurt others, and why do they develop fears?*

- The roots of altruism and prosocial behavior appear early. This may be an inborn disposition, which can be cultivated by parental modeling and encouragement.
- Instrumental aggression—first physical, then verbal—is most common in early childhood.
- Boys tend to practice overt aggression, whereas girls often engage in relational aggression.
- Preschool children show temporary fears of real and imaginary objects and events; older children's fears tend to be more realistic.

altruism (274)

prosocial behavior (274)

instrumental aggression (275)

overt (direct) aggression (275)

relational (social) aggression (275)

Relationships with Other Children

Guidepost 6: *How do young children get along with—or without—siblings, playmates, and friends?*

- Most sibling interactions are positive. Older siblings tend to initiate activities, and younger siblings to imitate. Same-sex siblings, especially girls, get along best.
- Siblings tend to resolve disputes on the basis of moral principles.
- The kind of relationship children have with siblings often carries over into other peer relationships.
- Only children seem to develop at least as well as children with siblings.
- Preschoolers choose playmates and friends who are like them and with whom they have positive experiences.
- Aggressive children are less popular than prosocial children.

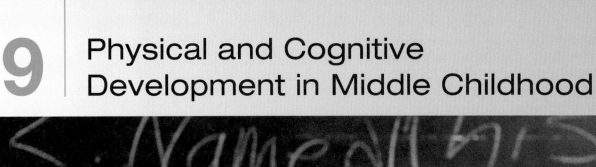

9 | Physical and Cognitive Development in Middle Childhood

> What we must remember above all in the education of our children is that their love of life should never weaken.
>
> —Natalia Ginzburg, *The Little Virtues*, 1985

Did You **Know...**

- If current trends continue, nearly 50 percent of the children in North America and South America, 39 percent in Europe, and 20 percent in China will be overweight in 2010?
- The incidence of asthma has been increasing worldwide?
- Research suggests that playing with Barbie dolls can make girls feel bad about the way they look?
- According to the neuropsychologist Howard Gardner, there are eight separate types of intelligence, and only three of them are measured by IQ tests?
- Children who believe they can master schoolwork are more likely to do so?
- Studies support the value of high-quality bilingual education?

These are just a few of the interesting and important topics we will cover in this chapter. Although motor abilities improve less dramatically in middle childhood than before, these years are an important time for the development of strength, stamina, endurance, and motor proficiency. In this chapter we look at these and other physical developments. Cognitively, we see how attainment of Piaget's stage of concrete operations enables children to think logically and to make more mature judgments. We see how children improve in memory and problem solving, how their intelligence is tested, and how the abilities to read and write open the door to participation in a wider world. We look at factors affecting school achievement, and we examine the controversies over IQ testing, methods of teaching reading, and second-language education. Finally, we see how schools educate children with exceptional needs. After you have read and studied this chapter, you should be able to answer each of the Guidepost questions on the following page.

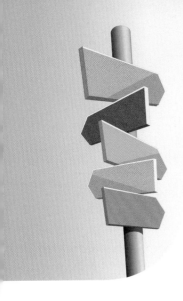

Guideposts *for Study*

1. What gains in growth, brain development, and motor development occur in school-age children, and what are their nutritional and sleep needs?

2. What are the principal health and fitness concerns for school-age children, and what can be done to make these years healthier and safer?

3. How do school-age children's thinking and moral reasoning differ from those of younger children?

4. What advances in memory and other information-processing skills occur during middle childhood?

5. How accurately can schoolchildren's intelligence be measured?

6. How do communicative abilities expand during middle childhood, and how do children best learn a second language?

7. How do children adjust to school, and what influences school achievement?

8. How do schools meet special needs?

PHYSICAL DEVELOPMENT

Aspects of Physical Development

Guidepost 1

What gains in growth, brain development, and motor development occur in school-age children, and what are their nutritional and sleep needs?

If we were to walk by a typical elementary school just after the three o'clock bell, we would see a virtual explosion of children of all shapes and sizes. Tall ones, short ones, husky ones, and slender ones would be bursting out of the school doors into the open air. We would see that school-age children look very different from children a few years younger. They are taller, and most are fairly wiry; but more are likely to be overweight than in past decades.

Height and Weight

Growth during middle childhood slows considerably. Still, although day-by-day changes may not be obvious, they add up to a startling difference between 6-year-olds, who are still small children, and 11-year-olds, many of whom are now beginning to resemble adults.

Children grow about 2 to 3 inches each year between ages 6 and 11 and approximately double their weight during that period (Ogden, Fryar, Carroll, & Flegal, 2004). Girls retain somewhat more fatty tissue than boys, a characteristic that will persist through adulthood. The average 10-year-old weighs about 11 pounds more than those of 40 years ago—nearly 85 pounds for a boy and 88 pounds for a girl (Ogden et al., 2004). African American boys and girls tend to grow faster than white boys and girls. By about age 6, African American girls have more muscle and bone mass than European American (white) or Mexican American girls, and Mexican American girls have a higher percentage of body fat than white girls the same size (Ellis, Abrams, & Wong, 1997).

Nutrition and Sleep

To support their steady growth and constant exertion, schoolchildren need, on average, 2,400 calories every day—more for older children and less for younger ones. Nutritionists recommend a varied diet including plenty of grains, fruits, and vegetables and high levels of complex carbohydrates, found in potatoes, pasta, bread, and cereals.

Sleep needs decline from about 11 hours a day at age 5 to a little more than 10 hours at age 9 and about 9 hours at age 13. Healthy school-age children should be highly alert in the daytime. However, sleep problems, such as resistance to going to bed, insomnia, and daytime sleepiness are common in the United States during these years, in part because many children, as they grow older, are allowed to set their own bedtimes (Hoban, 2004) and to have television sets in their bedrooms (National Sleep Foundation, 2004).

Brain Development

Changes in the brain's structure and functioning support the cognitive advances we discuss later in this chapter. Maturation and learning in middle childhood and beyond depend on fine-tuning of the brain's connections, along with more efficient selection of the regions of the brain appropriate for particular tasks. Together, these changes increase the speed and efficiency of brain processes and enhance the ability to filter out irrelevant information (Amso & Casey, 2006).

The study of the brain's structure is complex. At any particular moment, it is the product of the interaction between genetic, epigenetic, and environmental factors. Magnetic resonance imaging (MRI) enables researchers to observe, with no health risk to the children under study, how the brain changes over time and how these changes vary from one child to another (Blakemore & Choudhury, 2006; Kuhn, 2006; Lenroot & Giedd, 2006).

One important maturational change clearly seen in brain imaging studies is a *loss in the density of gray matter* (closely packed neuronal bodies) in certain regions of the cerebral cortex (Figure 9-1). This process reflects pruning of unused dendrites. The volume of gray matter in the cortex forms an inverted "U," peaking at different times in different lobes. Gray matter in the parietal lobes, which deal with spatial understanding, reaches, on average, its maximum volume at about age 10 in girls and 11½ in boys; in the frontal lobes, which handle higher-order functions such as thinking, at age 11 in girls and age 12 in boys; and in the temporal lobes, which help with language, at about age 16 in both girls and boys. Beneath the cortex, gray matter volume in the caudate—a part of the basal ganglia, which are involved in control of movement and muscle tone and in mediating higher cognitive functions, attention, and emotional states—peaks at age 7½ in girls and age 10 in boys (Lenroot & Giedd, 2006).

This loss in density of gray matter is balanced by a steady *increase in white matter,* axons or nerve fibers that transmit information between neurons to distant regions of the brain. These connections thicken and myelinate, beginning with the frontal lobes and moving toward the rear of the brain. Between ages 6 and 13, striking growth takes place in connections between the temporal and parietal lobes. White matter growth may not begin to drop off until well into adulthood (Giedd et al., 1999; Kuhn, 2006; Lenroot & Giedd, 2006; NIMH, 2001b; Paus et al., 1999).

Another way neuroscientists measure brain development is by changes in the *thickness* of the cortex. Researchers have observed cortical thickening between ages 5 and 11 in regions of the temporal and frontal lobes. At the same

Figure 9-1

Gray-matter maturation in the cerebral cortex, ages 5 to 20. Losses in gray matter density reflect maturation of various regions of the cortex, permitting more efficient functioning. Blue areas correspond to specific parts of the cortex undergoing loss of gray matter at a given age. These structures and their functional significance are described at right. (Source: Amso & Casey, 2006; adapted from Gogtay et al., 2004.)

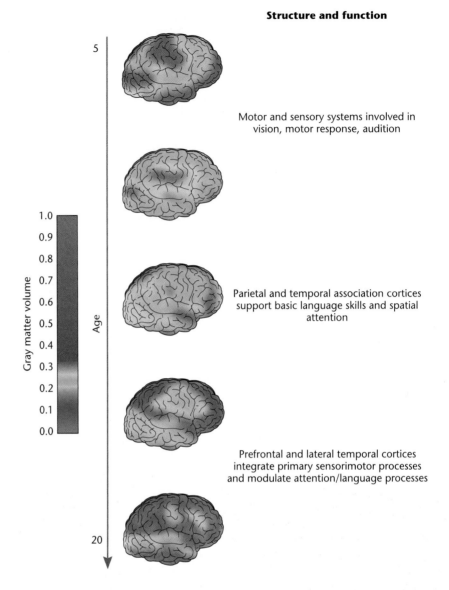

Structure and function

Motor and sensory systems involved in vision, motor response, audition

Parietal and temporal association cortices support basic language skills and spatial attention

Prefrontal and lateral temporal cortices integrate primary sensorimotor processes and modulate attention/language processes

Checkpoint

Can you . . .

♦ Summarize typical growth patterns of boys and girls in middle childhood, including ethnic variations?

♦ Summarize the nutritional and sleep needs of school-age children?

♦ Discuss changes in the brain at this age and their effects?

time, thinning occurs in the rear portion of the frontal and parietal cortex in the brain's left hemisphere. This change correlates with improved performance on the vocabulary portion of an intelligence test (Toga et al., 2006).

The amount of gray matter in the frontal cortex, which is largely genetic, is thought to be linked with differences in IQ (Thompson, Cannon, et al., 2001; Toga & Thompson, 2005). Some research suggests, however, that the key may not be *how much* gray matter a child has, but rather the *pattern of development* of the prefrontal cortex. In children of average intelligence, the prefrontal cortex is relatively thick at age 7, peaks in thickness by age 8, and then gradually thins as unneeded connections are pruned. In the most intelligent 7-year-olds, in contrast, the cortex does not peak in thickness until age 11 or 12. This prolonged thickening of the prefrontal cortex may represent an extended critical period for developing high-level thinking circuits (Shaw et al., 2006).

Motor Development and Physical Play

Motor skills continue to improve in middle childhood (Table 9-1). However, a nationally representative survey based on time-use diaries found that school-age children in the United States spend less time each week on sports and other

Table 9-1	Motor Development in Middle Childhood

Age	Selected Behaviors
6	Girls are superior in movement accuracy; boys are superior in forceful, less complex acts.
	Skipping is possible.
	Children can throw with proper weight shift and step.
7	One-footed balancing without looking becomes possible.
	Children can walk 2-inch-wide balance beams.
	Children can hop and jump accurately into small squares.
	Children can execute accurate jumping-jack exercise.
8	Children have 12-pound pressure on grip strength.
	The number of games participated in by both sexes is greatest at this age.
	Children can engage in alternate rhythmic hopping in a 2-2, 2-3, or 3-3 pattern.
	Girls can throw a small ball 40 feet.
9	Boys can run 16½ feet per second.
	Boys can throw a small ball 70 feet.
10	Children can judge and intercept pathways of small balls thrown from a distance.
	Girls can run 17 feet per second.
11	A standing broad jump of 5 feet is possible for boys and of 4½ feet for girls.

Source: From Bryant J. Cratty, *Perceptual and Motor Development in Infants and Children,* 3rd ed. Copyright (c) 1986 by Allyn & Bacon. Adapted by permission of the publisher.

outdoor activities than in the early 1980s and more hours on schooling and homework, in addition to time spent on television—an average of 12 to 14 hours a week—and on computer activities, which barely existed 20 years ago (Juster, Ono, & Stafford, 2004).

Recess-Time Play The games children play at recess tend to be informal and spontaneously organized. One child may play alone while nearby a group of classmates chase each other around the schoolyard. Boys play more physically active games, whereas girls favor games that include verbal expression or counting aloud, such as hopscotch and jump rope. Such recess-time activities promote growth in agility and social competence and foster adjustment to school (Pellegrini, Kato, Blatchford, & Baines, 2002).

About 10 percent of schoolchildren's free play in the early grades consists of **rough-and-tumble play**—wrestling, kicking, tumbling, grappling, and chasing, often accompanied by laughing and screaming (Bjorklund & Pellegrini, 2002). This kind of play may look like fighting but is done playfully among friends (P. K. Smith, 2005a).

Rough-and-tumble play peaks in middle childhood; the proportion typically drops to about 5 percent at age 11, about the same as in early childhood (Bjorklund & Pellegrini, 2002). Seemingly universal, rough-and-tumble play has been reported in such diverse places as India,

rough-and-tumble play
Vigorous play involving wrestling, hitting, and chasing, often accompanied by laughing and screaming.

Games at recess, such as jump rope, tend to be informal. They promote both agility and social competence.

Mexico, Okinawa, the Kalahari in Africa, the Philippines, Great Britain, and the United States as well as among most mammals (Bjorklund & Pellegrini, 2002; Humphreys & Smith, 1984). Boys around the world participate in rough-and-tumble play more than girls do, perhaps because of hormonal differences and socialization, and this may be one reason for sex segregation during play (Bjorklund & Pellegrini, 2002; Pellegrini et al., 2002; P. K. Smith, 2005a). From an evolutionary standpoint, rough-and-tumble play has important adaptive benefits: It hones skeletal and muscle development, offers safe practice for hunting and fighting skills, and channels aggression and competition. By age 11, it often becomes a way to establish dominance within the peer group (Bjorklund & Pellegrini, 2000, 2002; P. K. Smith, 2005b).

Sports and Other Physical Activities   In a nationally representative survey of U.S. 9- to 13-year-olds and their parents, 38.5 percent reported participation in organized athletics outside of school hours—most of them in baseball, softball, soccer, or basketball. About twice as many children (77.4 percent) participated in unorganized physical activity, such as bicycling and shooting baskets (Duke, Huhman, & Heitzler, 2003). Girls tend to spend less time than boys on sports (Juster et al., 2004).

Besides improving motor skills, regular physical activity has immediate and long-term health benefits: weight control, lower blood pressure, improved cardio-respiratory functioning, and enhanced self-esteem and well-being. Active children tend to become active adults. Thus, organized athletic programs should include as many children as possible and should focus on building skills rather than winning games (AAP Committee on Sports Medicine and Fitness, 1997; Council on Sports Medicine and Fitness & Council on School Health, 2006).

Checkpoint

Can you . . .

◆ Contrast in boys' and girls' recess-time activities?

◆ Explain the significance of rough-and-tumble play?

◆ Tell what types of physical play children engage in as they grow older?

Guidepost 2

What are the principal health and fitness concerns for school-age children, and what can be done to make these years healthier and safer?

Health, Fitness, and Safety

The development of vaccines for major childhood illnesses has made middle childhood a relatively safe time of life in most of the world. The death rate in these years is the lowest in the life span. Still, an increasing proportion of children are overweight, and some suffer from chronic medical conditions or accidental injuries or from lack of access to health care.

Obesity and Body Image

Obesity in children has become a major health issue worldwide. By 2010, if current trends continue, nearly 50 percent of the children in North and South America, 39 percent in Europe, and 20 percent in China will be overweight (Baker, Olsen, & Sorensen, 2007; Wang & Lobstein, 2006).

In the United States, 17 percent of school-age children—nearly three times as many as in 1980—had BMIs at or above the 95th percentile in 2003–2006, and another 33.3 percent were at or above the 85th percentile. Boys are more likely to have high BMIs than are girls (Ogden et al., 2008). Obesity has increased in all ethnic groups, though less so in black and Hispanic children. It remains most prevalent among Mexican American boys (more than 25 percent) and non-Hispanic black girls (26.5 percent) (Hernandez & Macartney, 2008; Ogden et al., 2006, 2008).

Unfortunately, children who try to lose weight are not always the ones who need to do so. Concern with **body image**—how one believes one looks—becomes important early in middle childhood, especially for girls, and may develop into

body image Descriptive and evaluative beliefs about one's appearance.

BOX 9-1 **Research** *in Action*

Do Barbie Dolls Affect Girls' Body Image?

"I looked at a Barbie doll when I was 6 and said, 'This is what I want to look like,'" the model Cindy Jackson said on CBS News (2004). "I think a lot of little 6-year-old girls or younger even now are looking at that doll and thinking, 'I want to be her.'" It took 31 operations, 14 years, and $100,000, but Jackson's obsession with Barbie got her a new look and an entry in the *Guinness Book of World Records.*

Barbie is the best-selling fashion doll around the world. In the United States, 99 percent of 3- to 10-year-old girls own at least one Barbie doll, and the average girl owns eight. Though she is sold as "every girl," Barbie is far from average. Her body proportions are "unrealistic, unattainable, and unhealthy" (Dittmar, Halliwell, & Ive, 2006, p. 284). "If she were alive, Barbie would be a woman standing 7 feet tall with a waistline of 18 inches and a bust-line of 38 to 40 inches," writes the psychotherapist Abigail Natenshon (2006), a specialist in eating disorders. In fact, Barbie's waist, as compared to her bust size, is 39 percent smaller than that of a woman with the eating disorder anorexia (see Chapter 11). Fewer than 1 in 100,000 women actually have Barbie's body proportions.

According to Bandura's social-cognitive theory, Barbie dolls are role models for young girls, transmitting a cultural ideal of beauty. The media reinforce this ideal. Girls who do not measure up may experience *body dissatisfaction*—negative thoughts about their bodies, leading to low self-esteem. By age 6, studies show, many girls wish to be thinner than they are.

To test Barbie's effect on young girls' body image, researchers read picture books to English girls, ages 5½ to 8½. One group saw picture stories about Barbie; control groups saw stories about a full-figured fashion doll called Emme or about no doll (Dittmar et al., 2006). Afterward, the girls completed questionnaires in which they were asked to agree or disagree with such statements as "I'm pretty happy about the way I look" and "I really like what I weigh."

The findings were striking. Among the youngest girls (ages 5½ to 6½), a single exposure to the Barbie picture book significantly lowered body esteem and increased the discrepancy between actual and ideal body size. This did not happen with the girls in the two control groups. The effect of Barbie on body image was even stronger in 6½- to 7½-year-olds. However, the findings for the oldest group, ages 7½ to 8½, were completely different: Pictures of Barbie had no direct effect on body image at this age.

What accounts for this difference? Girls up to age 7 may be in a sensitive period in which they acquire idealized images of beauty. As girls grow older, they may internalize the ideal of thinness as part of their emerging identity. Once the ideal is internalized, its power no longer depends on direct exposure to the original role model (Dittmar et al., 2006).

Or, it may be that girls simply outgrow Barbie. In another study (Kuther & McDonald, 2004), sixth- through eighth-grade girls were asked about their childhood experiences with Barbie. All the girls had owned at least two Barbie dolls but said they no longer played with them. Looking back, some of the girls saw Barbie as a positive influence: "She is like the perfect person . . . that everyone wants to be like." But most of the girls saw Barbie as an unrealistic role model: "Barbie dolls provide a false stereotype . . . as it is physically impossible to attain the same body size. . . . There wouldn't be enough room for organs and other necessary things. . . . Barbie has this perfect body and now every girl is trying to have her body because they are so unhappy with themselves."

Barbie now has a major competitor: Bratz, an ultrathin doll with a large round face, sassy mouth, and heavy makeup. Longitudinal research will help determine whether fashion dolls such as Barbie and Bratz have a lasting impact on body image.

What's Your View?

If you had (or have) a young daughter, would you allow her to play with Barbie or Bratz dolls? Why or why not?

Check It Out

For more information on this topic, go to www.bam.gov/teachers/body_image_dolls.html. This site describes a classroom activity in which students take measurements of toy action figures and fashion dolls and figure out how they would look if they were the height of a normal adult man or woman.

eating disorders in adolescence (see Chapter 11). Playing with physically unrealistic dolls, such as Barbie, may be an influence in that direction (Box 9-1).

Causes of Obesity As we reported in earlier chapters, obesity often results from an inherited tendency aggravated by too little exercise and too much or the wrong kinds of food (AAP Committee on Nutrition, 2003; Chen et al., 2004). Children are more likely to be overweight if they have overweight parents or other relatives. Poor nutrition also contributes (Council on Sports Medicine and

Promoting an active lifestyle through both informal and organized sports is an important way to combat the problem of childhood obesity.

Fitness & Council on School Health, 2006) as does excessive television viewing (Institute of Medicine, 2005). Even though the National Association of State Boards of Education (2000) recommends 150 minutes of physical education each week for elementary students, the average school offers it for only 85 to 98 minutes (National Center for Education Statistics, 2006a). Yet, an additional 60 minutes of physical education per week in kindergarten and first grade could reduce by half the number of overweight girls that age (Datar & Sturm, 2004b).

Why Is Childhood Obesity a Serious Concern? In a longitudinal study of 1,456 primary students in Victoria, Australia, children classified as overweight or obese fell behind their classmates in physical and social functioning by age 10 (Williams, Wake, Hesketh, Maher, & Waters, 2005). Overweight children often suffer emotionally and may compensate by indulging themselves with treats, making their physical and social problems even worse. These children are at risk for behavior problems, depression, and low self-esteem (AAP Committee on Nutrition, 2003; Datar & Sturm, 2004a; Mustillo et al., 2003). They commonly have medical problems, including high blood pressure, high cholesterol, and high insulin levels (AAP Committee on Nutrition, 2003; Muntner, He, Cutler, Wildman, & Whelton, 2004; NCHS, 2004; Sorof et al., 2004).

hypertension Chronically high blood pressure.

Overweight children tend to become obese adults, at risk for **hypertension** (high blood pressure), heart disease, orthopedic problems, diabetes, and other problems. Indeed, childhood obesity may be a stronger predictor of some diseases than adult obesity (AAP Committee on Nutrition, 2003; AAP, 2004; Baker et al., 2007; Li et al., 2004; Center for Weight and Health, 2001). By midcentury, obesity that starts in childhood may shorten life expectancy by two to five years (Ludwig, 2007).

Prevention and Treatment Preventing weight gain is easier, less costly, and more effective than treating obesity (Center for Weight and Health, 2001; Council on Sports Medicine and Fitness & Council on School Health, 2006). Parents should watch children's eating and activity patterns and address excessive weight gain *before* a child becomes severely overweight (AAP Committee on Nutrition, 2003).

To avoid overweight and prevent cardiac problems, children (like adults) should get only about 30 percent of their total calories from fat and less than 10 percent of the total from saturated fat (AAP Committee on Nutrition, 1992; U.S. Department of Agriculture & USDHHS, 2000). Studies have found no negative effects on height, weight, body mass, or neurological development from a moderately low-fat diet at this age (Rask-Nissilä et al., 2000; Shea et al., 1993).

Effective weight-management programs should include efforts of parents, schools, physicians, communities, and the larger culture (Krishnamoorthy, Hart, & Jelalian, 2006). Treatment should begin early and promote permanent changes in lifestyle, not weight loss alone (Kitzmann & Beech, 2006; Miller-Kovach, 2003). Less time in front of television and computers, changes in food labeling and advertising, healthier school meals, education to help children make better food choices, and more

Checkpoint

Can you . . .

◆ Discuss the extent of childhood obesity, how it can affect health, and how it can be treated?

time spent in physical education and informal exercise with family and friends, such as walking and unorganized sports, would help (AAP, 2004).

Other Medical Conditions

Illness in middle childhood tends to be brief. **Acute medical conditions**—occasional, short-term conditions, such as infections and warts—are common. Six or seven bouts a year with colds, flu, or viruses are typical as germs pass among children at school or at play (Behrman, 1992).

As children's experience with illness increases, so does their understanding of the causes of health and illness and of how people can promote their health (Crisp, Ungerer, & Goodnow, 1996). From a Piagetian perspective, children's understanding of health and illness is tied to cognitive development. As they mature, their explanations for disease change. Before middle childhood, children are egocentric; they believe that illness is magically produced by human actions, often their own ("I was a bad boy, so now I feel bad"). Later they explain all diseases—only a little less magically—as the doing of all-powerful germs. As children approach adolescence, they see that there can be multiple causes of disease, that contact with germs does not automatically lead to illness, and that people can do much to keep healthy.

According to a nationally representative survey of more than 200,000 households, an estimated 12.8 percent of U.S. children have or are at risk for **chronic medical conditions**: physical, developmental, behavioral, or emotional conditions that persist for three months or more (Kogan, Newacheck, Honberg, & Strickland, 2005). One chronic condition that has become increasingly common is asthma.

Asthma is a chronic respiratory disease, apparently allergy-based and characterized by sudden attacks of coughing, wheezing, and difficulty in breathing. Its incidence is increasing worldwide (Asher et al., 2006), although it may have leveled off in some parts of the Western world (Eder, Ege, & von Mutius, 2006). Its prevalence in the United States more than doubled between 1980 and 1995 and has since remained at this historically high level (Akinbami, 2006). Almost 13 percent of U.S. children and adolescents up to age 17 have been diagnosed with asthma at some time, and 8.9 percent currently have asthma (Federal Interagency Forum on Child and Family Statistics, 2007). It is 30 percent more likely to be diagnosed in boys than in girls and 20 percent more likely to be diagnosed in black children than in white children (McDaniel, Paxson, & Waldfogel, 2006).

The causes of the asthma explosion are uncertain, but a genetic predisposition is likely to be involved (Eder et al., 2006). Researchers have identified a gene mutation that increases the risk of developing asthma (Ober et al., 2008). Some researchers point to environmental factors: tightly insulated houses that intensify exposure to indoor air pollutants and allergens such as tobacco smoke, molds, and cockroach droppings. Allergies to household pets also have been suggested as risk factors (Bollinger, 2003; Etzel, 2003; Lanphear, Aligne, Auinger, Weitzman, & Byrd, 2001; Sly, 2000). However, findings regarding these proposed causes, except for smoke exposure, are inconclusive. Increasing evidence points to an association between obesity and asthma, perhaps because of an underlying lifestyle factor related to both conditions (Eder et al., 2006).

Accidental Injuries

As in early childhood, accidental injuries are the leading cause of death among school-age U.S. children (Federal Interagency Forum for Child and Family Statistics, 2007). In a nine-year study of 96,359 children born in Alberta, Canada,

acute medical conditions Illnesses that last a short time.

chronic medical conditions Illnesses or impairments that persist for at least three months.

asthma A chronic respiratory disease characterized by sudden attacks of coughing, wheezing, and difficulty in breathing.

21 percent suffered at least one injury each year, and 73 percent had repeat injuries during the study period. Boys were more likely to be injured than girls and to have repeat injuries (Spady, Saunders, Schopflocher, & Svenson, 2004).

An estimated 23,000 children each year suffer serious brain injuries from bicycle accidents, and as many as 88 percent of these injuries could be prevented by using helmets (AAP Committee on Injury and Poison Prevention, 2001). Protective headgear also is vital for baseball and softball, football, roller skating, in-line skating, skateboarding, scooter riding, horseback riding, hockey, speed sledding, snowmobiling, and tobogganing. For soccer, protective goggles and mouth guards may help reduce head and facial injuries. "Heading" the ball should be minimized because of the danger of brain injury (AAP Committee on Sports Medicine and Fitness, 2000, 2001). The AAP Committee on Accident and Poison Prevention (1988) recommends that children under 16 *not* use snowmobiles, and that older riders be required by law to be licensed. Also, because of the need for stringent safety precautions and constant supervision for trampoline use, the AAP Committee on Injury and Poison Prevention & Committee on Sports Medicine and Fitness (1999) recommend that parents not buy trampolines and that children not use them on playgrounds or at school.

Checkpoint

Can You . . .

♦ Distinguish between acute and chronic medical conditions?

♦ Discuss the incidence and causes of asthma?

♦ Identify factors that increase the risks of accidental injury?

COGNITIVE DEVELOPMENT

Piagetian Approach: The Concrete Operational Child

Guidepost 3

How do school-age children's thinking and moral reasoning differ from those of younger children?

concrete operations Third stage of Piagetian cognitive development (approximately ages 7 to 12), during which children develop logical but not abstract thinking.

At about age 7, according to Piaget, children enter the stage of **concrete operations** when they can use mental operations, such as reasoning, to solve concrete (actual) problems. Children can think logically because they can take multiple aspects of a situation into account. However, their thinking is still limited to real situations in the here and now.

Cognitive Advances

In the stage of concrete operations, children have a better understanding than preoperational children of spatial concepts, causality, categorization, inductive and deductive reasoning, conservation, and number (Table 9-2).

Spatial Relationships and Causality Why can many 6- or 7-year-olds find their way to and from school, whereas most younger children cannot? One reason is that children in the stage of concrete operations can better understand spatial relationships. They have a clearer idea of how far it is from one place to another and how long it will take to get there, and they can more easily remember the route and the landmarks along the way. Experience plays a role in this development: A child who walks to school becomes more familiar with the neighborhood.

Both the ability to use maps and models and the ability to communicate spatial information improve with age (Gauvain, 1993). Judgments about cause and effect also improve. When 5- to 12-year-olds were asked to predict how levers and balance scales would perform under varying conditions, the older children gave more correct answers. Children understood the influence of physical attributes (the number of objects on each side of a scale) earlier than they recognized the influence of spatial factors (the distance of objects from the center of the scale) (Amsel, Goodman, Savoie, & Clark, 1996).

| Table 9-2 | Advances in Selected Cognitive Abilities during Middle Childhood | |

Ability	Example
Spatial thinking	Danielle can use a map or model to help her search for a hidden object and can give someone else directions for finding the object. She can find her way to and from school, can estimate distances, and can judge how long it will take her to go from one place to another.
Cause and effect	Douglas knows which physical attributes of objects on each side of a balance scale will affect the result (i.e., number of objects matters but color does not). He does not yet know which spatial factors, such as position and placement of the objects, make a difference.
Categorization	Elena can sort objects into categories, such as shape, color, or both. She knows that a subclass (roses) has fewer members than the class of which it is a part (flowers).
Seriation and transitive inference	Catherine can arrange a group of sticks in order, from the shortest to the longest, and can insert an intermediate-size stick into the proper place. She knows that if one stick is longer than a second stick, and the second stick is longer than a third, then the first stick is longer than the third.
Inductive and deductive reasoning	Dominic can solve both inductive and deductive problems and knows that inductive conclusions (based on particular premises) are less certain than deductive conclusions (based on general premises).
Conservation	Felipe, at age 7, knows that if a clay ball is rolled into a sausage, it still contains the same amount of clay (conservation of substance). At age 9, he knows that the ball and the sausage weigh the same. Not until early adolescence will he understand that they displace the same amount of liquid if dropped in a glass of water.
Number and mathematics	Kevin can count in his head, can add by counting up from the smaller number, and can do simple story problems.

Categorization The ability to categorize helps children think logically. Categorization includes such relatively sophisticated abilities as *seriation, transitive inference,* and *class inclusion,* which improve gradually between early and middle childhood. Children show that they understand **seriation** when they can arrange objects in a series according to one or more dimensions, such as weight (lightest to heaviest) or color (lightest to darkest). By 7 or 8, children can grasp the relationships among a group of sticks on sight and arrange them in order of size (Piaget, 1952).

Transitive inference is the ability to infer a relationship between two objects from the relationship between each of them and a third object. Marcela is shown three sticks: a yellow one, a green one, and a blue one. She is shown that the yellow stick is longer than the green one, and the green one is longer than the blue. Without physically comparing the yellow and blue sticks, she immediately says that the yellow one is longer than the blue one (Chapman & Lindenberger, 1988; Piaget & Inhelder, 1967).

Class inclusion is the ability to see the relationship between a whole and its parts. Piaget (1964) found that when preoperational children are shown a bunch of 10 flowers—7 roses and 3 carnations—and are asked whether there are more roses or more flowers, they are likely to say there are more roses, because they are comparing the roses with the carnations rather than with the whole bunch. Not until age 7 or 8, and sometimes not even then, do children consistently reason that roses are a subclass of flowers and that, therefore, there cannot be more roses than flowers (Flavell, 1963; Flavell et al., 2002). However, even 3-year-olds show a rudimentary awareness of inclusion, depending on the type of task, the practical cues they receive, and their familiarity with the categories of objects they are tested on (Johnson, Scott, & Mervis, 1997).

seriation Ability to order items along a dimension.

transitive inference Understanding of the relationship between two objects by knowing the relationship of each to a third object.

class inclusion Understanding of the relationship between a whole and its parts.

Inductive and Deductive Reasoning According to Piaget, children in the stage of concrete operations use only **inductive reasoning.** Starting with observations about particular members of a class of people, animals, objects, or events, they draw general conclusions about the class as a whole. ("My dog barks. So does Terry's dog and Melissa's dog. So, it seems that all dogs bark.") Inductive conclusions must be tentative because it is always possible to come across new information (a dog that does not bark) that does not support the conclusion.

Deductive reasoning, which Piaget maintained does not develop until adolescence, starts with a general statement (premise) about a class and applies it to particular members of the class. If the premise is true of the whole class and the reasoning is sound, then the conclusion must be true: "All dogs bark. Spot is a dog. Spot barks."

Researchers gave 16 inductive and deductive problems to 16 kindergartners, 17 second graders, 16 fourth graders, and 17 sixth graders. The problems were designed so as *not* to call on knowledge of the real world. For example, one deductive problem was "All poggops wear blue boots. Tombor is a poggop. Does Tombor wear blue boots?" The corresponding inductive problem was "Tombor is a poggop. Tombor wears blue boots. Do all poggops wear blue boots?" Contrary to Piagetian theory, second graders (but not kindergartners) were able to answer both kinds of problems correctly (Galotti, Komatsu, & Voelz, 1997).

Conservation In solving various types of conservation problems, children in the stage of concrete operations can work out the answers in their heads; they do not have to measure or weigh the objects.

If one of two identical clay balls is rolled or kneaded into a different shape—say, a long, thin snake—Felipe, who is in the stage of concrete operations, will say that the ball and the snake still contain the same amount of clay. Stacy, who is in the preoperational stage, is deceived by appearances. She says the long, thin roll contains more clay because it looks longer.

Felipe, unlike Stacy, understands the principle of *identity:* He knows the clay is still the same clay, even though it has a different shape. He also understands the principle of *reversibility:* He knows he can change the snake back into a ball. And he can *decenter:* He can focus on both length and width. He recognizes that although the ball is shorter than the snake, it is also thicker. Stacy centers on one dimension (length) while excluding the other (thickness).

Typically, children can solve problems involving conservation of substance, like this one, by about age 7 or 8. However, in tasks involving conservation of weight—in which they are asked, for example, whether the ball and the snake weigh the same—children typically do not give correct answers until about age 9 or 10. In tasks involving conservation of volume—in which children must judge whether the snake and the ball displace an equal amount of liquid when placed in a glass of water—correct answers are rare before age 12. Children's thinking at this stage is so concrete, so closely tied to a particular situation, that

inductive reasoning Type of logical reasoning that moves from particular observations about members of a class to a general conclusion about that class.

deductive reasoning Type of logical reasoning that moves from a general premise about a class to a conclusion about a particular member or members of the class.

? What's Your View?

How can parents and teachers help children improve their reasoning ability?

Does one ball of clay displace more water than the other? A child who has achieved conservation of volume knows that the answer does not *depend on the ball's shape.*

they cannot readily transfer what they have learned about one type of conservation to another type, even though the underlying principles are the same.

Number and Mathematics By age 6 or 7, many children can count in their heads. They also learn to *count on:* to add 5 and 3, they start counting at 5 and then go on to 6, 7, and 8 to add the 3. It may take two or three more years for them to perform a comparable operation for subtraction, but by age 9 most children can either count up from the smaller number or down from the larger number to get the answer (Resnick, 1989).

Children also become more adept at solving simple story problems, such as "Pedro went to the store with $5 and spent $2 on candy. How much did he have left?" When the original amount is unknown—"Pedro went to the store, spent $2 and had $3 left. How much did he start out with?"—the problem is harder because the operation needed to solve it (addition) is not as clearly indicated. Few children can solve this kind of problem before age 8 or 9 (Resnick, 1989).

Research with minimally schooled people in developing countries suggests that the ability to add develops nearly universally and often intuitively, through concrete experience in a cultural context (Guberman, 1996; Resnick, 1989). These intuitive procedures are different from those taught in school. In a study of Brazilian street vendors ages 9 to 15, a researcher acting as a customer said, "I'll take two coconuts." Each one cost 40 cruzeiros; she paid with a 500-cruzeiros bill and asked, "What do I get back?" The child counted up from 80: "Eighty, 90, 100 . . ." and gave the customer 420 cruzeiros. However, when this same child was given a similar problem in the classroom ("What is 500 minus 80?"), he arrived at the wrong answer by incorrectly using a series of steps learned in school (Carraher, Schliemann, & Carraher, 1988). This finding suggests that teaching math through concrete applications, not only through abstract rules, may be more effective.

Some intuitive understanding of fractions seems to exist by age 4 (Mix, Levine, & Huttenlocher, 1999), as children show when they deal a deck of cards or distribute portions of pizza (Frydman & Bryant, 1988; Sophian, Garyantes, & Chang, 1997). However, children tend not to think about the quantity a fraction represents; instead, they focus on the numerals that make it up. Thus, they may say that 1/2 plus 1/3 equals 2/5. Also difficult for many children to grasp at first is the fact that 1/2 is bigger than 1/4—that the smaller fraction (1/4) has the larger denominator (Siegler, 1998; Sophian & Wood, 1997).

Influences of Neurological Development, Culture, and Schooling

Piaget maintained that the shift from the rigid, illogical thinking of younger children to the flexible, logical thinking of older children depends on both neurological development and experience in adapting to the environment. Support for a neurological influence comes from scalp measurements of brain activity during a conservation task. Children who had achieved conservation of volume had different brain wave patterns from those who had not yet achieved it, suggesting that they may have been using different brain regions for the task (Stauder, Molenaar, & Van der Molen, 1993).

Abilities such as conservation may depend in part on familiarity with the materials being manipulated; children can think more logically about things they know something about. Mexican children, who make pottery from an early age, understand that a clay ball that has been rolled into a coil still has the same amount of clay sooner than they understand other types of conservation (Broude, 1995). Thus, understanding of conservation may come, not only from new patterns of mental organization, but also from culturally defined experience with the physical world.

Today's schoolchildren may not be advancing through Piaget's stages as rapidly as their parents did. When 10,000 British 11- and 12-year-olds were tested on conservation of volume and weight, their performance was two to three years behind that of their counterparts 30 years earlier (Shayer, Ginsburg, & Coe, 2007). These results suggest that today's schoolchildren may be getting too much drilling on the three Rs and not enough hands-on experience with the way materials behave.

Moral Reasoning

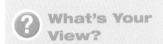

What's Your View?

• Do you think that intent is an important factor in morality? How does the criminal justice system reflect this view?

To draw out children's moral thinking, Piaget (1932) would tell them a story about two little boys: "One day Augustus noticed that his father's inkpot was empty and decided to help his father by filling it. While he was opening the bottle, he spilled a lot of ink on the tablecloth. The other boy, Julian, played with his father's inkpot and spilled a little ink on the cloth." Then Piaget would ask, "Which boy was naughtier, and why?" Children younger than 7 usually said Augustus was naughtier because he made the bigger stain. Older children recognized that Augustus meant well and made the large stain by accident, whereas Julian made a small stain while doing something he should not have been doing. Immature moral judgments, Piaget concluded, center only on the *degree* of offense; more mature judgments consider *intent.*

Piaget (1932; Piaget & Inhelder, 1969) proposed that moral reasoning develops in three stages. Children move gradually from one stage to another, at varying ages.

The first stage (approximately ages 2 to 7, corresponding with the preoperational stage) is based on *rigid obedience to authority.* Because young children are egocentric, they cannot imagine more than one way of looking at a moral issue. They believe that rules cannot be bent or changed, that behavior is either right or wrong, and that any offense (like that of Augustus) deserves punishment, regardless of intent.

Checkpoint

Can You . . .

◆ Identify six cognitive advances during middle childhood?

◆ Name three principles that help children understand conservation, and discuss influences on its mastery?

◆ Tell how Piaget's three stages of moral development reflect cognitive maturation?

The second stage (ages 7 or 8 to 10 or 11, corresponding with the stage of concrete operations) is characterized by *increasing flexibility.* As children interact with more people and come into contact with a wider range of viewpoints, they begin to discard the idea that there is a single, absolute standard of right and wrong and to develop their own sense of justice based on fairness or equal treatment for all. Because they can consider more than one aspect of a situation, they can make more subtle moral judgments.

Around age 11 or 12, when children may become capable of formal reasoning, the third stage of moral development arrives. The belief that everyone should be treated alike gives way to the ideal of *equity,* of taking specific circumstances into account. Thus, a child of this age might say that a 2-year-old who spilled ink on the tablecloth should be held to a less demanding moral standard than a 10-year-old who did the same thing.

Lawrence Kohlberg's theory of moral reasoning, which builds on Piaget's, is discussed in Chapter 11; Carol Gilligan's gender-based theory is discussed in Chapter 13.

Guidepost 4

What advances in memory and other information-processing skills occur during middle childhood?

Information-Processing Approach: Planning, Attention, and Memory

As children move through the school years, they make steady progress in the abilities to regulate and sustain attention, process and retain information, and plan and monitor their behavior. All of these interrelated developments contribute to **executive function,** the conscious control of thoughts, emotions, and actions to accomplish goals or solve problems (Luna et al., 2004; NICHD Early Child

Care Research Network, 2005c; Zelazo & Müller, 2002). As their knowledge expands, children become more aware of what kinds of information are important to pay attention to and remember. School-age children also understand more about how memory works, and this knowledge enables them to plan and use strategies, or deliberate techniques, to help them remember.

How Do Executive Skills Develop?

The gradual development of executive function from infancy through adolescence accompanies the development of the brain, in particular, the *prefrontal cortex,* the region that enables planning, judgment, and decision making (Lamm, Zelazo, & Lewis, 2006). As unneeded synapses are pruned away and pathways become myelinated, *processing speed*—usually measured by reaction time—improves dramatically, especially in girls (Camarata & Woodcock, 2006; Luna, Garver, Urban, Lazar, & Sweeney, 2004). Faster, more efficient processing increases the amount of information children can keep in working memory, enabling complex thinking and goal-directed planning (Flavell et al., 2002; Luna et al., 2004).

The home environment, too, contributes to the development of executive skills. In a longitudinal study of 700 children from infancy on, the quality of the family environment, especially between ages 4½ and 6—including such factors as available resources, cognitive stimulation, and maternal sensitivity—predicted attentional and memory performance in first grade (NICHD Early Child Care Research Network, 2005c).

School-age children develop planning skills by making decisions about their own everyday activities. Parenting practices affect the pace at which children are allowed to do this. In a three-year longitudinal study of 79 European American and 61 Latino children in a southwestern U.S. city, between second and fourth grades the responsibility for planning children's informal activities gradually shifted from parent to child, and this change was reflected in improved ability to plan classroom work (Gauvain & Perez, 2005).

Selective Attention

School-age children can concentrate longer than younger children and can focus on the information they need and want while screening out irrelevant information. For example, they can summon up from memory the appropriate meaning of a word and suppress other meanings that do not fit the context. Fifth graders are better able than first graders to keep unwanted information from reentering working memory and vying with other material for attention (Harnishfeger & Pope, 1996). This growth in *selective attention*—the ability to deliberately direct one's attention and shut out distractions—may hinge on the executive skill of *inhibitory control,* the voluntary suppression of unwanted responses (Luna et al., 2004).

The increasing capacity for selective attention is believed to be due to neurological maturation and is one of the reasons memory improves during middle childhood (Bjorklund & Harnishfeger, 1990; Harnishfeger & Bjorklund, 1993). Older children may make fewer mistakes in recall than younger children because they are better able to select what they want to remember and what they can forget (Lorsbach & Reimer, 1997).

Working Memory Span

The efficiency of working memory increases greatly in middle childhood, laying the foundation for a wide range of cognitive skills. What changes produce that vast improvement? In one study, 120 British 6- to 10-year-olds were asked to

Contestants in a spelling bee make good use of mnemonic strategies such as rehearsal, organization, and elaboration.

perform complex memory span tasks involving computerized visual and verbal images. Improvements both in processing speed and in storage capacity were found to underlie the development of working memory in this age group (Bayliss, Jarrold, Baddeley, Gunn, & Leigh, 2005).

Metamemory: Understanding Memory

metamemory Understanding of processes of memory.

Between ages 5 and 7, the brain's frontal lobes undergo significant development and reorganization. These changes may make possible improved **metamemory,** knowledge about the processes of memory (Janowsky & Carper, 1996).

From kindergarten through fifth grade, children advance steadily in understanding memory (Flavell et al., 2002; Kreutzer, Leonard, & Flavell, 1975). Kindergartners and first graders know that people remember better if they study longer, that people forget things with time, and that relearning something is easier than learning it for the first time. By third grade, children know that some people remember better than others and that some things are easier to remember than others.

Mnemonics: Strategies for Remembering

mnemonic strategies
Techniques to aid memory.

external memory aids
Mnemonic strategies using something outside the person.

rehearsal Mnemonic strategy to keep an item in working memory through conscious repetition.

organization Mnemonic strategy of categorizing material to be remembered.

elaboration Mnemonic strategy of making mental associations involving items to be remembered.

Devices to aid memory are called **mnemonic strategies.** The most common mnemonic strategy among both children and adults is use of *external memory aids.* Other common mnemonic strategies are *rehearsal, organization,* and *elaboration.*

Writing down a telephone number, making a list, setting a timer, and putting a library book by the front door are examples of **external memory aids:** prompts by something outside the person. Saying a telephone number over and over after looking it up, so as not to forget it before dialing, is a form of **rehearsal,** or conscious repetition. **Organization** is mentally placing information into categories (such as animals, furniture, vehicles, and clothing) to make it easier to recall. In **elaboration,** children associate items with something else, such as an imagined scene or story. To remember to buy lemons, ketchup, and napkins, for example, a child might visualize a ketchup bottle balanced on a lemon, with a pile of napkins handy to wipe up any spills.

Table 9-3	Four Common Memory Strategies		
Strategy	**Definition**	**Development in Middle Childhood**	**Example**
External memory aids	Prompting by something outside the person	5- and 6-year-olds can do this, but 8-year-olds are more likely to think of it.	Dana makes a list of the things she has to do today.
Rehearsal	Conscious repetition	6-year-olds can be taught to do this; 7-year-olds do it spontaneously.	Ian says the letters in his spelling words over and over until he knows them.
Organization	Grouping by categories	Most children do not do this until at least age 10, but younger children can be taught to do it.	Luis recalls the animals he saw in the zoo by thinking first of the mammals, then the reptiles, then the amphibians, then the fish, and then the birds.
Elaboration	Associating items to be remembered with something else, such as a phrase, scene, or story	Older children are more likely to do this spontaneously and remember better if they make up their own elaboration; younger children remember better if someone else makes it up.	Yolanda remembers the lines of the musical staff (E, G, B, D, F) by associating them with the phrase "*Every Good Boy Does Fine.*"

As children get older, they develop better strategies, use them more effectively, and tailor them to meet specific needs (Bjorklund, 1997; Table 9-3).

Information Processing and Piagetian Tasks

Improvements in information processing may help explain the advances Piaget described. For example, 9-year-olds may be better able than 5-year-olds to find their way to and from school because they can scan a scene, take in its important features, and remember objects in context in the order in which they were encountered (Allen & Ondracek, 1995).

Improvements in memory may contribute to the mastery of conservation tasks. Young children's working memory is so limited that they may not be able to remember all the relevant information (Siegler & Richards, 1982). They may forget, for example, that two differently shaped pieces of clay were originally identical. Gains in working memory may enable older children to solve such problems.

Robbie Case (1985, 1992), a neo-Piagetian theorist, suggested that as a child's application of a concept or scheme becomes more automatic, it frees space in working memory to deal with new information. This process may help explain why children master different types of conservation at different ages; they may need to be able to use one type of conservation without conscious thought before they can extend that scheme to other types of conservation.

Psychometric Approach: Assessment of Intelligence

Schoolchildren's intelligence may be measured by either individual or group psychometric tests. The most widely used individual test is the **Wechsler Intelligence Scale for Children (WISC-III).** This test for ages 6 through 16 measures verbal

✔ Checkpoint

Can You . . .

◆ Identify four ways in which information processing improves during middle childhood?

◆ Explain the importance of executive function, selective attention, and metamemory?

◆ Name four common mnemonic aids and discuss developmental differences in their use?

◆ Give examples of how improved information processing explains cognitive advances Piaget described?

Guidepost 5

How accurately can schoolchildren's intelligence be measured?

and performance abilities, yielding separate scores for each as well as a total score. The separate subtest scores pinpoint a child's strengths and help diagnose specific problems. For example, if a child does well on verbal tests (such as general information and basic arithmetic operations) but poorly on performance tests (such as doing a puzzle or drawing the missing part of a picture), the child may be slow in perceptual or motor development. A child who does well on performance tests but poorly on verbal tests may have a language problem. Another commonly used individual test is the Stanford-Binet Intelligence Scales, described in Chapter 7.

A popular group test, the **Otis-Lennon School Ability Test (OLSAT8),** has levels for kindergarten through twelfth grade. Children are asked to classify items, show an understanding of verbal and numerical concepts, display general information, and follow directions. Separate scores for verbal comprehension, verbal reasoning, pictorial reasoning, figural reasoning, and quantitative reasoning can identify specific strengths and weaknesses.

The IQ Controversy

The use of psychometric intelligence tests such as those just described is controversial. On the positive side, because IQ tests have been standardized and widely used, there is extensive information about their norms, validity, and reliability, as we discussed in Chapter 2. Scores on IQ tests taken during middle childhood are fairly good predictors of school achievement, especially for highly verbal children, and these scores are more reliable than during the preschool years. IQ at age 11 even has been found to predict length of life, functional independence late in life, and the presence or absence of dementia (Starr, Deary, Lemmon, & Whalley, 2000; Whalley & Deary, 2001; Whalley et al., 2000).

On the other hand, critics claim that the tests underestimate the intelligence of children who are in ill health or, for one reason or another, do not do well on tests (Anastasi, 1988; Ceci, 1991; Sternberg, 2004). Because the tests are timed, they equate intelligence with speed and penalize a child who works slowly and deliberately. Their appropriateness for diagnosing learning disabilities also has been questioned (Benson, 2003).

A more fundamental criticism is that IQ tests do not directly measure native ability; instead, they *infer* intelligence from what children already know. As we'll see, it is virtually impossible to design a test that requires no prior knowledge. Further, the tests are validated against measures of achievement, such as school performance, which are affected by such factors as schooling and culture (Sternberg, 2004, 2005). As we discuss in a later section, there is also controversy over whether intelligence is a single, general ability or whether there are types of intelligence not captured by IQ tests. For these and other reasons, strong disagreement exists over how accurately these tests assess children's intelligence.

Checkpoint

Can You . . .

♦ Name and describe two traditional intelligence tests for schoolchildren?

♦ Give arguments for and against IQ tests?

Influences on Intelligence

Both heredity and environment influence intelligence (refer to Chapter 3). Keeping in mind the controversy over whether IQ tests actually measure intelligence, let's look more closely at these influences.

Influences of Brain Development As we mentioned earlier in this chapter, the prefrontal cortex and other brain regions under strong genetic influence contribute to intelligent behavior. So does the speed and reliability of transmission of messages in the brain. Because of the brain's plasticity, environmental factors, such as the family, schooling, and culture, also affect brain structure (Toga &

Thompson, 2005). However, heritability of intelligence increases with age as children select or create environments that fit their genetic tendencies (Gray & Thompson, 2004).

Influence of Schooling Schooling seems to increase tested intelligence (Ceci & Williams, 1997; Neisser et al., 1996). Children whose school entrance was significantly delayed—as happened, for example, in the Netherlands during the Nazi occupation—lost as many as 5 IQ points each year, and some of these losses were never recovered (Ceci & Williams, 1997).

IQ scores also drop during summer vacation (Ceci & Williams, 1997). Among a national sample of 1,500 children, language, spatial, and conceptual scores improved much more between October and April, the bulk of the school year, than between April and October, which includes summer vacation and the beginning and end of the school year (Huttenlocher, Levine, & Vevea, 1998).

Influences of Race/Ethnicity and Socioeconomic Status Average test scores vary among racial/ethnic groups, inspiring claims that the tests are unfair to minorities. Historically, on average, black children scored about 15 points lower than white children and showed a comparable lag on school achievement tests (Neisser et al., 1996). These gaps have narrowed by as much as 4 to 7 points in recent years (Dickens & Flynn, 2006). Average IQ scores of Hispanic American children fall between those of black and white children, and their scores, too, tend to predict school achievement (Neisser et al., 1996).

What accounts for racial/ethnic differences in IQ? Some researchers have argued for a substantial genetic factor (Herrnstein & Murray, 1994; Jensen, 1969; Rushton & Jensen, 2005). But, although there is strong evidence of a genetic influence on *individual* differences in intelligence, there is *no direct evidence* that IQ differences among ethnic, cultural, or racial *groups* are hereditary (Gray & Thompson, 2004; Neisser et al., 1996; Sternberg et al., 2005). Instead, many studies attribute ethnic differences in IQ largely or entirely to inequalities in environment (Nisbett, 1998, 2005)—in income, nutrition, living conditions, health, parenting practices, early child care, intellectual stimulation, schooling, culture, or other circumstances such as the effects of oppression and discrimination that can affect self-esteem, motivation, and academic performance. In a longitudinal study of 500 healthy U.S. children, participants from low-income families had somewhat lower IQ and achievement test scores than those from higher-income families. However, these healthy low-income children did better than published norms for their income level, suggesting the importance of health as a factor in measured intelligence (Waber et al., 2007).

The recent narrowing of the gap in test scores parallels an improvement in the life circumstances and educational opportunities of many African American children. In addition, as we discussed in Chapter 7, some early intervention programs have had significant success in raising disadvantaged children's IQs (Nisbett, 2005).

The strength of genetic influence itself appears to vary with socioeconomic status. In a longitudinal study of 319 pairs of twins followed from birth, the genetic influence on IQ scores at age 7 among children from impoverished families was close to zero and the influence of environment was strong, whereas among children in affluent families the opposite was true. In other words, high SES strengthens genetic influence, whereas low SES tends to override it (Turkheimer, Haley, Waldron, D'Onofrio, & Gottesman, 2003).

What about Asian Americans, whose scholastic achievements consistently top those of other ethnic groups? Although there is some controversy about their

Asian American children often do well in school. The reasons seem to be cultural, not genetic.

relative performance on intelligence tests, most researchers find that these children do *not* seem to have a significant edge in IQ (Neisser et al., 1996). Instead, Asian American children's strong scholastic achievement seems to be best explained by their culture's emphasis on obedience and respect for elders, the importance Asian American parents place on education as a route to upward mobility, and the devotion of Asian American students to homework and study (Chao, 1994, 1996; Fuligni & Stevenson, 1995; Huntsinger & Jose, 1995; H. W. Stevenson, 1995; H. W. Stevenson, Chen, & Lee, 1993; H. W. Stevenson, Lee, Chen, & Lummis, 1990; H. W. Stevenson, Lee, Chen, Stigler, et al., 1990; Sue & Okazaki, 1990).

Influence of Culture   Some critics of IQ tests attribute ethnic differences in IQ to **cultural bias:** a tendency to include questions that use vocabulary or call for information or skills more familiar to some cultural groups than to others (Sternberg, 1985, 1987). These critics argue that intelligence tests are built around the dominant thinking style and language of people of European ancestry, putting minority children at a disadvantage (Heath, 1989; Helms, 1992). However, controlled studies have failed to show that cultural bias contributes substantially to overall group differences in IQ (Neisser et al., 1996).

Test developers have tried to design **culture-free tests**—tests with no culture-linked content—by posing tasks that do not require language, such as tracing mazes, putting the right shapes in the right holes, and completing pictures; but they have been unable to eliminate all cultural influences. Test designers also have found it virtually impossible to produce **culture-fair tests** consisting only of experiences common to people in various cultures.

Robert Sternberg (2004) maintains that intelligence and culture are inextricably linked. Behavior seen as intelligent in one culture may be viewed as foolish in another. For example, when given a sorting task, North Americans would be likely to place a robin under the category of birds, whereas the Kpelle people in North Africa would consider it more intelligent to place the robin in a functional category of flying things (Cole, 1998). Thus, a test of intelligence developed in one culture may not be equally valid in another. Furthermore, the schooling offered in a culture may prepare a child to do well in certain tasks and not in others, and

cultural bias   Tendency of intelligence tests to include items calling for knowledge or skills more familiar or meaningful to some cultural groups than to others.

culture-free tests   Intelligence tests that, if they were possible to design, would have no culturally linked content.

culture-fair tests   Intelligence tests that deal with experiences common to various cultures, in an attempt to avoid cultural bias.

the competencies taught and tested in school are not necessarily the same as the practical skills needed to succeed in everyday life (Sternberg, 2004, 2005).

Sternberg (2004) defines *successful intelligence* as the skills and knowledge needed for success within a particular social and cultural context. The mental processes that underlie intelligence may be the same across cultures, says Sternberg, but their products may be different—and so should be the means of assessing performance. Sternberg proposes **culture-relevant tests** that take into account the adaptive tasks that confront children in particular cultures.

Is There More Than One Intelligence?

A serious criticism of IQ tests is that they focus almost entirely on abilities that are useful in school. They do *not* assess other important aspects of intelligent behavior, such as common sense, social skills, creative insight, and self-knowledge. Yet these abilities, in which some children with modest academic skills excel, may become equally or more important in later life and may even be considered separate forms of intelligence. Two of the chief advocates of this position are Howard Gardner and Robert Sternberg.

Gardner's Theory of Multiple Intelligences   Is a child who is good at analyzing paragraphs and making analogies more intelligent than one who can play a challenging violin solo or organize a closet or pitch a curve ball at the right time? The answer is no, according to Gardner's (1993) **theory of multiple intelligences.**

Gardner, a neuropsychologist and educational researcher at Harvard University, originally identified seven distinct kinds of intelligence. According to Gardner, conventional intelligence tests tap only three intelligences: *linguistic, logical-mathematical,* and, to some extent, *spatial.* The other four, which are not reflected in IQ scores, are *musical, bodily-kinesthetic, interpersonal,* and *intrapersonal.* Gardner (1998) later added an eighth intelligence, *naturalist,* to his original list. (Table 9-4 gives definitions of each intelligence and examples of fields in which it most useful.)

High intelligence in one area does not necessarily accompany high intelligence in any of the others. A person may be extremely gifted in art (a spatial ability), precision of movement (bodily-kinesthetic), social relations (interpersonal), or self-understanding (intrapersonal), but not have a high IQ. Thus the tennis champions Venus and Serena Williams, the painter Frida Kahlo, and the cellist Yo Yo Ma could be equally intelligent, each in a different area.

Gardner (1995) would assess each intelligence directly by observing its products—how well a child can tell a story, remember a melody, or get around in a strange area—and not by standardized tests. To monitor spatial ability, for example, the examiner might hide an object from a 1-year-old, ask a 6-year-old to do a jigsaw puzzle, and give a Rubik's cube to a preadolescent. The purpose would be, not to compare individuals, but to reveal strengths and weaknesses so as to help children realize their potential.

Sternberg's Triarchic Theory of Intelligence   Sternberg's (1985, 2004) **triarchic theory of intelligence** identifies three elements, or aspects, of intelligence: *componential, experiential,* and *contextual.*

- The **componential element** is the *analytic* aspect of intelligence; it determines how efficiently people process information. It tells people how to solve problems, how to monitor solutions, and how to evaluate the results.

- The **experiential element** is *insightful* or *creative;* it determines how people approach novel or familiar tasks. It allows people to compare new information

culture-relevant tests Intelligence tests that would draw on and adjust for culturally related content.

Checkpoint

Can You . . .

♦ Assess explanations for differences in IQs of children of various racial/ethnic and cultural groups?

theory of multiple intelligences Gardner's theory that each person has several distinct forms of intelligence.

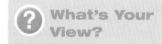

What's Your View?

- In which of Gardner's types of intelligence are you strongest?

- Did your education focus on any of these?

triarchic theory of intelligence Sternberg's theory describing three elements of intelligence: componential, experiential, and contextual.

componential element Sternberg's term for the analytic aspect of intelligence.

experiential element   Sternberg's term for the insightful or creative aspect of intelligence.

Table 9-4	Eight Intelligences, according to Gardner	
Intelligence	Definition	Fields or Occupations Where Used
Linguistic	Ability to use and understand words and nuances of meaning	Writing, editing, translating
Logical-mathematical	Ability to manipulate numbers and solve logical problems	Science, business, medicine
Spatial	Ability to find one's way around in an environment and judge relationships between objects in space	Architecture, carpentry, city planning
Musical	Ability to perceive and create patterns of pitch and rhythm	Musical composition, conducting
Bodily-kinesthetic	Ability to move with precision	Dancing, athletics, surgery
Interpersonal	Ability to understand and communicate with others	Teaching, acting, politics
Intrapersonal	Ability to understand the self	Counseling, psychiatry, spiritual leadership
Naturalist	Ability to distinguish species and their characteristics	Hunting, fishing, farming, gardening, cooking

Source: Based on Gardner, 1993, 1998.

with what they already know and to come up with new ways of putting facts together—in other words, to think originally.

contextual element Sternberg's term for the practical aspect of intelligence.

- The **contextual element** is *practical;* it determines how people deal with their environment. It is the ability to size up a situation and decide what to do: adapt to it, change it, or get out of it.

According to Sternberg, everyone has these three kinds of abilities to a greater or lesser extent. A person may be strong in one, two, or all three.

Conventional IQ tests measure mainly componential ability; and, because this ability is the kind most school tasks require in Western societies, it's not surprising that the tests are fairly good predictors of school performance. Their failure to measure experiential (insightful or creative) and contextual (practical) intelligence, says Sternberg, may explain why they are less useful in predicting success in the outside world. In studies in Usenge, Kenya, and among Yup'ik Eskimo children in southwestern Alaska, children's **tacit knowledge** of such practical matters as medicinal herbs, hunting, fishing, and preserving plants—information gleaned informally, not explicitly taught—showed no correlation with conventional measures of intelligence (Grigorenko et al., 2004; Sternberg, 2004; Sternberg et al., 2001).

tacit knowledge Sternberg's term for information that is not formally taught or openly expressed but is necessary to get ahead.

Sternberg Triarchic Abilities Test (STAT) Test that seeks to measure componential, experiential, and contextual intelligence.

The **Sternberg Triarchic Abilities Test (STAT)** (Sternberg, 1993) seeks to measure each of the three aspects of intelligence—analytic, creative, and practical—through multiple-choice and essay questions in three domains: *verbal, quantitative,* and *figural* (or spatial). For example, an analytic-figural item might be to identify the missing piece of a figure. A creative-verbal item might be to solve deductive reasoning problems that start with factually false premises (such as, "Money falls off trees"). A test of practical-quantitative intelligence might be to solve an everyday math problem involving buying tickets to a ball game or following a recipe for cookies.

Validation studies have found correlations between the STAT and several other tests of critical thinking, creativity, and practical problem solving. As predicted, the three kinds of abilities are only weakly correlated with each other (Sternberg, 1997; Sternberg & Clinkenbeard, 1995).

Other Directions in Intelligence Testing

Some other diagnostic and predictive tools are based on neurological research and information-processing theory. The second edition of the **Kaufman Assessment Battery for Children (K-ABC-II)** (Kaufman & Kaufman, 1983, 2003), an individual test for ages 3 to 18, is designed to evaluate cognitive abilities in children with diverse needs (such as autism, hearing impairments, and language disorders) and from varying cultural and linguistic backgrounds. It has subtests designed to minimize verbal instructions and responses as well as items with limited cultural content.

The Kaufman Assessment Battery for Children (K-ABC-II) is designed to evaluate cognitive abilities in children with diverse needs, such as hearing impairments and language disorders.

Dynamic tests based on Vygotsky's theories emphasize potential rather than present achievement. In contrast with traditional *static tests* that measure a child's current abilities, these tests seek to capture the dynamic nature of intelligence by measuring learning processes directly rather than through the products of past learning (Sternberg, 2004). Dynamic tests contain items up to two years above a child's current level of competence. Examiners help the child when necessary by asking leading questions, giving examples or demonstrations, and offering feedback; thus, the test itself is a learning situation. The difference between the items a child can answer alone and the items the child can answer with help is the child's zone of proximal development (ZPD).

By pointing to what a child is ready to learn, dynamic testing may give teachers more useful information than does a psychometric test and can aid in designing interventions to help children progress. It can be particularly effective with disadvantaged children (Grigorinko & Sternberg, 1998; Rutland & Campbell, 1996). However, dynamic testing is quite labor-intensive, and the ZPD may be difficult to measure precisely.

Kaufman Assessment Battery for Children (K-ABC-II) Nontraditional individual intelligence test designed to provide fair assessments of minority children and children with disabilities.

 Checkpoint

Can You . . .

- Compare Sternberg's and Gardner's theories of intelligence?
- Describe three new types of intelligence testing?

Language

Language abilities continue to grow during middle childhood. School-age children are better able to understand and interpret oral and written communication and to make themselves understood. These tasks are especially challenging for children who are not native-language speakers.

 **Guidepost 6**

How do communicative abilities expand during middle childhood, and how do children best learn a second language?

Vocabulary, Grammar, and Syntax

As vocabulary grows during the school years, children use increasingly precise verbs. They learn that a word like *run* can have more than one meaning, and they can tell from the context which meaning is intended. *Simile* and *metaphor,* figures of speech in which a word or phrase that usually designates one thing is compared or applied to another, become increasingly common (Owens, 1996; Vosniadou,

1987). Although grammar is quite complex by age 6, children during the early school years rarely use the passive voice (as in "The sidewalk is being shoveled").

Children's understanding of rules of *syntax* (how words are organized into phrases and sentences) becomes more sophisticated with age (C. S. Chomsky, 1969). For example, most children under age 5 or 6 think the sentences "John promised Bill to go shopping" and "John told Bill to go shopping" both mean that Bill is the one to go to the store. Many 6-year-olds have not yet learned how to interpret constructions such as the one in the first sentence, even though they know what a promise is and can use and understand the word correctly in other sentences. By age 8, most children can interpret the first sentence correctly, and, by age 9, virtually all children can. They now look at the meaning of a sentence as a whole instead of focusing on word order alone.

Sentence structure continues to become more elaborate. Older children use more subordinate clauses ("The boy *who delivers the newspapers* rang the doorbell"). Still, some constructions, such as clauses beginning with *however* and *although,* do not become common until early adolescence (Owens, 1996).

Pragmatics: Knowledge about Communication

The major area of linguistic growth during the school years is in **pragmatics:** the practical use of language to communicate.* Pragmatics includes both conversational and narrative skills.

Good conversationalists probe by asking questions before introducing a topic with which the other person may not be familiar. They quickly recognize a breakdown in communication and do something to repair it. There are wide individual differences in such skills; some 7-year-olds are better conversationalists than some adults (Anderson, Clark, & Mullin, 1994). There are also gender differences. In one study, 120 middle-class London fourth graders were paired up to solve a mathematical problem. When boys and girls worked together, boys tended to use more controlling statements and to utter more negative interruptions, whereas girls phrased their remarks in a more tentative, conciliatory way. Children's communication was more collaborative when working with a partner of the same sex (Leman, Ahmed, & Ozarow, 2005).

When first graders tell stories, they often relate a personal experience. Most 6-year-olds can retell the plot of a short book, movie, or television show. They are beginning to describe motives and causal links. By second grade, children's stories become longer and more complex. Fictional tales often have conventional beginnings and endings ("Once upon a time . . ." and "They lived happily ever after," or simply "The end"). Word use is more varied than before, but characters do not show growth or change, and plots are not fully developed.

Older children usually set the stage with introductory information about the setting and characters, and they clearly indicate changes of time and place during the story. They construct more complex episodes than younger children do, but with less unnecessary detail. They focus more on the characters' motives and thoughts, and they think through how to resolve problems in the plot.

Second-Language Learning

In 2005, 20 percent of U.S. children ages 5 to 17 spoke a language other than English at home. The primary language most of these children spoke was Spanish, and more than 5 percent had difficulty speaking English (Federal Interagency Forum on Child and Family Statistics, 2007). About 7 percent of the public

Checkpoint

Can You . . .

♦ Summarize improvements in language skills during middle childhood?

---

*This section is largely indebted to Owens (1996).

school population are defined as *English language learners (ELLs)* (National Center for Education Statistics, 2004a).

Some schools use an **English-immersion approach** (sometimes called ESL, or English as a second language), in which language-minority children are immersed in English from the beginning, in special classes. Other schools have adopted programs of **bilingual education,** in which children are taught in two languages, first learning in their native language with others who speak it and then switching to regular classes in English when they become more proficient in it. These programs can encourage children to become **bilingual** (fluent in two languages) and to feel pride in their cultural identity.

Advocates of early *English immersion* claim that the sooner children are exposed to English and the more time they spend speaking it, the better they learn it. Proponents of *bilingual* programs claim that children progress faster academically in their native language and later make a smoother transition to all-English classrooms (Padilla et al., 1991). Some educators maintain that the English-only approach stunts children's cognitive growth; because foreign-speaking children can understand only simple English at first, the curriculum must be watered down, and children are less prepared to handle complex material later (Collier, 1995).

Statistical analyses of multiple studies conclude that children in bilingual programs typically outperform those in all-English programs on tests of English proficiency (Crawford, 2007; Krashen & McField, 2005). Even more successful, according to some research, is a another, less common, approach: **two-way (dual-language) learning,** in which English-speaking and foreign-speaking children learn together in their own and each other's languages. This approach avoids any need to place minority children in separate classes. By valuing both languages equally, it reinforces self-esteem and improves school performance. An added advantage is that English speakers learn a foreign language at an early age, when they can acquire it most easily (Collier, 1995; W. P. Thomas & Collier, 1997, 1998). However, less than 2 percent of ELLs nationwide are enrolled in two-way programs (Crawford, 2007).

Regardless of the scientific findings, public opinion has turned against bilingual education. Enrollment in bilingual programs declined from 37 percent to 17 percent between 1992 and 2002 (Crawford, 2007). California, Arizona, and Massachusetts, which together account for one-half of the students who speak languages other than English at home, have outlawed bilingual education by referendum and have required English immersion. In 2002 the federal Bilingual Education Act was eliminated as part of No Child Left Behind. The new law includes tough accountability provisions; schools are to be assessed each year by the percentage of ELLs who have become fluent in English. This change was expected to discourage bilingual instruction (Crawford, 2002).

The Child in School

The earliest school experiences are critical in setting the stage for future success or failure. Let's look at the first-grade experience and at how children learn to read and write. Then we'll examine influences on school achievement.

Entering First Grade

Even today, when most U.S. children go to kindergarten, children often approach the start of first grade with a mixture of eagerness and anxiety. The first day of "regular" school is a milestone—a sign of the developmental advances that make this new status possible.

English-immersion approach Approach to teaching English as a second language in which instruction is presented only in English.

bilingual education System of teaching non-English-speaking children in their native language while they learn English, and later switching to all-English instruction.

bilingual Fluent in two languages.

two-way (dual-language) learning Approach to second-language education in which English speakers and non-English speakers learn together in their own and each other's languages.

Checkpoint

Can You . . .

♦ Describe and evaluate three types of second-language education?

Guidepost 7

How do children adjust to school, and what influences school achievement?

Interest, attention, and active participation all contribute to a child's academic success in school.

To make the most academic progress, a child needs to be involved in what is going on in class. Interest, attention, and active participation are positively associated with achievement test scores and, even more so, with teachers' marks from first grade through at least fourth grade (K. L. Alexander, Entwisle, & Dauber, 1993).

In a national longitudinal study, first graders at risk of school failure—either because of low SES or academic, attentional, or behavioral problems—progressed as much as their low-risk peers when teachers offered strong instructional and emotional support. Such support took the form of frequent literacy instruction, evaluative feedback, engaging students in discussions, responding to their emotional needs, encouraging responsibility, and creating a positive classroom atmosphere (Hamre & Pianta, 2005).

Becoming Literate

Learning to read and write—a major goal of the primary curriculum—frees children from the constraints of face-to-face communication, giving them access to the ideas and imagination of people in faraway lands and long-ago times. Once children can translate the marks on a page into patterns of sound and meaning, they can develop increasingly sophisticated strategies to understand what they read; and they can use written words to express ideas, thoughts, and feelings.

decoding Process of phonetic analysis by which a printed word is converted to spoken form before retrieval from long-term memory.

visually based retrieval Process of retrieving the sound of a printed word when seeing the word as a whole.

phonetic (code-emphasis) approach Approach to teaching reading that emphasizes decoding of unfamiliar words.

whole-language approach Approach to teaching reading that emphasizes visual retrieval and use of contextual clues.

Reading and Writing   Children can identify a printed word in two ways. One is called **decoding:** the child sounds out the word, translating it from print to speech before retrieving it from long-term memory. To do this, the child must master the phonetic code that matches the printed alphabet to spoken sounds (phonemes). The other method is **visually based retrieval:** the child simply looks at the word and then retrieves it. These two methods form the core of two contrasting approaches to reading instruction. The traditional approach, which emphasizes decoding, is called the **phonetic (code-emphasis) approach.** The more recent **whole-language approach** emphasizes visual retrieval and the use of contextual cues.

The whole-language approach is based on the belief that children can learn to read and write naturally, much as they learn to understand and use speech. Whole-language proponents assert that children learn to read with better comprehension and more enjoyment if they experience written language from the outset as a way to gain information and express ideas and feelings, not as a system of isolated sounds and syllables to be learned by memorization and drill. In contrast with the rigorous, teacher-directed tasks involved in phonetics instruction, whole-language programs feature real literature and open-ended, student-initiated activities.

Despite the popularity of the whole-language approach, research has found little support for its claims. A long line of research supports the view that phonemic awareness and early phonetics training are keys to reading proficiency for most children (Booth, Perfetti, & MacWhinney, 1999; Hatcher, Hulme, & Ellis, 1994; Jeynes & Littell, 2000; Liberman & Liberman, 1990; National Reading Panel, 2000; Stahl, McKenna, & Pagnucco, 1994).

Many experts recommend a blend of the best features of both approaches (National Reading Panel, 2000). Children can learn phonetic skills along with strategies to help them understand what they read. Because reading skills are the joint product of many functions in different parts of the brain, instruction solely in specific subskills—phonetics or comprehension—is less likely to succeed (Byrnes & Fox, 1998). Children who can summon both visually based and phonetic strategies, using visual retrieval for familiar words and phonetic decoding for unfamiliar words, become better, more versatile, readers (Siegler, 1998).

Metacognition, awareness of one's thinking processes, helps children monitor their understanding of what they read and enables them to develop strategies to clear up any problems—such strategies as reading slowly, rereading difficult passages, trying to visualize information, and thinking of examples. Having students recall, summarize, and ask questions about what they read can enhance comprehension (National Reading Panel, 2000).

Whatever teaching method is used, some children learn to read more easily than others. These individual differences reflect a substantial genetic influence and tend to remain stable through the elementary school years. The shared environment and the interplay between heredity and environment also play important roles (Harlaar, Dale, & Plomin, 2007).

However, children who have early reading difficulties are not necessarily condemned to reading failure. One longitudinal study followed the progress of 146 low-income children whose first grade reading scores fell below the 30th percentile. Thirty percent of the children showed steady movement toward average reading skills from second through fourth grade. The children who improved the most were those who, as kindergartners, had shown relatively strong emergent literacy skills and better classroom behavior, which permitted them to pay attention and benefit from instruction (Spira, Bracken, & Fischel, 2005).

The acquisition of writing skills goes hand in hand with the development of reading. Older preschoolers begin using letters, numbers, and letterlike shapes as symbols to represent words or parts of words (syllables or phonemes). Often their spelling is quite inventive—so much so that they may not be able to read it themselves (Whitehurst & Lonigan, 1998).

Writing is difficult for young children. Unlike conversation, which offers constant feedback, writing requires the child to judge independently whether the communicative goal has been met. The child also must keep in mind a variety of other constraints: spelling, punctuation, grammar, and capitalization, as well as the basic physical task of forming letters (Siegler, 1998).

metacognition Awareness of a person's own mental processes.

Checkpoint

Can You . . .

- Explain the impact of the first-grade experience on a child's school career, and identify factors that affect success in first grade?

- Compare the phonetic and whole-language methods of teaching reading, and discuss how comprehension improves?

- Identify factors that affect reading improvement in poor beginning readers?

- Explain why writing is hard for young children?

Influences on School Achievement

As Bronfenbrenner's bioecological theory would predict, in addition to children's own characteristics, each level of the context of their lives—from the immediate family to what goes on in the classroom to the messages children receive from peers and from the larger culture (such as "It's not cool to be smart")—influences how well they do in school. Let's look at this web of influences. (Influences of culture are discussed in Chapter 11.)

Self-Efficacy Beliefs   Students who are high in *self-efficacy*—who believe that they can master schoolwork and regulate their learning—are more likely to succeed than students who do not believe in their abilities (Bandura, Barbaranelli, Caprara, & Pastorelli, 1996; Zimmerman, Bandura, & Martinez-Pons, 1992). Self-regulated learners set challenging goals and use appropriate strategies to achieve them. They try hard, persist despite difficulties, and seek help when necessary. Students who do not believe in their ability to succeed tend to become frustrated and depressed—feelings that make success more elusive.

Gender   Girls tend to do better in school than boys; they receive higher marks, on average, in every subject (Halpern et al., 2007), are less likely to repeat grades, have fewer school problems, and outperform boys in national reading and writing assessments (Freeman, 2004). In addition, in a study of more than 8,000 males and females ranging from 2 to 90 years old, girls and women tended to do better than boys and men on timed tests (Camarata & Woodcock, 2006). On the other hand, boys do significantly better than girls on science and math tests that are not closely related to material taught in school. However, differences in mathematical abilities in elementary school, when computational facility is stressed, are small and tend to favor girls. Girls' advantage in writing and boys' advantage in science are larger and more reliable (Halpern et al., 2007). Gender differences tend to become more prominent in high school, as we discuss in Chapter 11.

A combination of several factors—early experience, biological differences (including differences in brain size and structure), and cultural expectations—may help explain these differences (Halpern et al., 2007). Boys' advantage in spatial skills may be influenced by SES, according to a study of 547 urban second and third graders. Although middle- and high-SES boys did better than girls on spatial tasks, low-SES boys did not, perhaps because they were less likely to engage in spatially-oriented activities such as building projects (Levine, Vasilyeva, Lourenco, Newcombe, & Huttenlocher, 2005).

Parenting Practices   Parents of high-achieving children create an environment for learning. They provide a place to study and to keep books and supplies; they set times for meals, sleep, and homework; they monitor how much television their children watch and what their children do after school; and they show interest in their children's lives by talking with them about school and being involved in school activities. Children whose parents are involved in their schools do better in school (Hill & Taylor, 2004).

Parenting styles may affect motivation and, thus, school success. In one study, the highest-achieving fifth graders had *authoritative* parents. These children were curious and interested in learning; they liked challenging tasks and enjoyed solving problems by themselves. *Authoritarian* parents, who kept after children to do their homework, supervised closely, and relied on extrinsic motivation, tended to have lower-achieving children. So did children of *permissive* parents, who were uninvolved and did not seem to care how well the children did in school (G. S. Ginsburg & Bronstein, 1993).

Socioeconomic Status   Socioeconomic status can be a powerful factor in educational achievement—not in and of itself, but through its influence on family atmosphere, choice of neighborhood, and parenting practices (Evans, 2004; National Research Council [NRC], 1993a; Rouse et al., 2005) and on parents' expectations for children (Davis-Kean, 2005).

In a nationally representative study of children who entered kindergarten in 1998, achievement gaps between advantaged and disadvantaged students widened during the first four years of schooling (Rathbun, West, & Germino-Hausken, 2004). Summer vacation contributes to these gaps because of differences in the typical home environment and in the summer learning experiences the children have. Low-income children do not make up for this gap, which, according to a longitudinal study of Baltimore schoolchildren, substantially accounts for differences in high school achievement and completion and college attendance (Alexander, Entwisle, & Olson, 2007).

However, SES is not the only factor in achievement. In a longitudinal study, children whose home environment at age 8 was cognitively stimulating showed higher intrinsic motivation for academic learning at ages 9, 10, and 13 than children who lived in less stimulating homes. This was true over and above effects of SES (Gottfried, Fleming, & Gottfried, 1998).

Why do some young people from disadvantaged homes and neighborhoods do well in school and improve their condition in life? What may make the difference is **social capital:** the networks of community resources children and families can draw on (Coleman, 1988). In a three-year experimental intervention in which working-poor parents received wage supplements and subsidies for child care and health insurance, their school-age children's academic achievement and behavior improved (Huston et al., 2001). Two years after the families had left the program, the impact on school achievement and motivation held steady, especially for older boys, though the effect on social and problem behavior declined (Huston et al., 2005).

Peer Acceptance Children who are liked and accepted by peers tend to do better in school. Among 248 fourth graders, those whose teachers reported that they were not liked by peers had poorer academic self-concepts and more symptoms of anxiety or depression in fifth grade and lower reading and math grades in sixth grade. Early teacher identification of children who exhibit social problems could lead to interventions that would improve such children's academic as well as emotional and social outcomes (Flook, Repetti, & Ullman, 2005).

Educational Methods The No Child Left Behind (NCLB) Act of 2001 is a sweeping educational reform emphasizing accountability, expanded parental options, local control, and flexibility. The intent is to funnel federal funding to research-based programs and practices, with special emphasis on reading and mathematics. Students in grades 3 through 8 are tested annually to see if they are meeting state-wide progress objectives. Children in schools that fail to meet state standards can transfer to another school.

Children who have a social network and who are liked and accepted by peers tend to do better in school.

social capital Family and community resources on which a person can draw.

More than 50 national education, civil rights, children's, and citizens groups have called for substantial changes in NCLB. Critics such as the National Education Association, a national teachers' organization, claim that NCLB emphasizes punishment rather than assistance for failing schools; rigid, largely unfunded, mandates rather than support for proven practices; and standardized testing rather than teacher-led, classroom-focused solutions. Research on Sternberg's triarchic theory, for example, suggests that students learn better when taught in a variety of ways, emphasizing creative and practical skills as well as memorization and critical thinking (Sternberg, Torff, & Grigorenko, 1998).

On the other hand, test scores do show improvement. In 2007, for example math scores for fourth and eighth graders on the National Assessment of Educational Progress (NAEP) rose to their highest levels since the test began in 1990. Black, white, and Hispanic students all improved (NCES, 2007b), but ethnic gaps remain (Hernandez & Macartney, 2008). Efforts to improve the teaching of reading seem to be paying off more slowly. In the NAEP in 2007, fourth graders' reading scores rose only modestly compared with those in 1990, and eighth graders' scores declined slightly but were better than in 2005 (NCES, 2007c). Meanwhile, in an international literacy test including 38 countries, U.S. fourth graders scored well above average (NCES, 2007d).

Class Size Most educators consider small class size a key factor in achievement, especially in the early grades, though findings on this point are mixed (Schneider, 2002). A longitudinal study found lasting academic benefits for students randomly assigned to classes of about 15 students in kindergarten through third grade and— especially for low-SES students—a greater likelihood of finishing high school (Finn, Gerber, & Boyd-Zaharias, 2005; Krueger, 2003; Krueger & Whitmore, 2000).

In most places, though, small classes are larger than that. In classroom observations of 890 first graders, classes with 25 students or less tended to be more social and interactive and to enable higher quality instruction and emotional support. Students in these classes tended to score higher on standardized achievement tests and beginning reading skills (NICHD Early Childhood Research Network, 2004b).

Educational Innovations When the Chicago public schools ended *social promotion,* the practice of promoting children to keep them with their age-mates even when they do not meet academic standards, many observers hailed the change. Others warned that, although retention in some cases can be a "wake-up call," more often it is the first step on a remedial track that leads to lowered expectations, poor performance, and dropping out of school (J. M. Fields & Smith, 1998; Lugaila, 2003; McCoy & Reynolds, 1999; McLeskey, Lancaster, & Grizzle, 1995; Temple, Reynolds, & Miedel, 2000). Indeed, studies found that Chicago's retention policy did *not* improve third graders' test scores, lowered sixth graders' scores, and greatly increased eighth-grade and high school dropout rates for retained students (Nagaoka & Roderick, 2004; Roderick et al., 2003).

Many educators say the only real solution to a high failure rate is to identify at-risk students early and intervene *before* they fail. In 2000–2001, 39 percent of U.S. public school districts provided alternative schools or programs for at-risk students, offering smaller classes, remedial instruction, counseling, and crisis intervention (NCES, 2003).

Some parents, unhappy with their public schools or seeking a particular style of education, are choosing charter schools or homeschooling. More than 1.2 million U.S. children now attend charter schools, some privately operated and others under charter from public school boards (Center for Education Reform, 2008). Charter schools tend to be smaller than regular public schools and tend to have a unique philosophy, curriculum, structure, or organizational style. Although parents are generally satisfied with their charter schools, studies of their effects on student outcomes have had mixed results (Braun, Jenkins, & Grigg, 2006; Bulkley & Fisler, 2002; Center for Education Reform, 2004; Detrich, Phillips, & Durett, 2002; Hoxby, 2004; National Assessment of Educational Progress, 2004; Schemo, 2004).

Homeschooling is legal in all 50 states. In 2003 some 1.1 million U.S. students representing 2.2 percent of the school-age population were homeschooled, 4 out of 5 of them full-time—a 29 percent increase from 1999. In a nationally representative government survey, the main reasons parents gave for choosing to homeschool their children were concern about a poor or unsafe learning environment in the schools and the desire to provide religious or moral instruction (Princiotta, Bielick, & Chapman, 2004).

Computer and Internet Use In 2003, about 91 percent of U.S. children and adolescents used computers at home or at school, and about 59 percent used the Internet. However, fewer African American, Hispanic American, and Native American children than white and Asian children, and fewer poor children than nonpoor children, use these technologies. Girls and boys spend about the same amount of time on computer and Internet use (Day, Janus, & Davis, 2005; DeBell & Chapman, 2006).

✓ Checkpoint

Can You . . .

◆ Discuss changes and innovations in educational philosophy and practice?

◆ Evaluate factors in school achievement?

Computer literacy and the ability to navigate the World Wide Web are opening new possibilities for individualized instruction, global communication, and early training in independent research skills. However, these tools pose dangers. First is the risk of exposure to harmful or inappropriate material. Second is the need to learn to evaluate critically information found in cyberspace and to separate facts from opinion and advertising. Third, a focus on "visual literacy" could divert financial resources from other areas of the curriculum.

✓ Checkpoint

Can You . . .

♦ Assess the value of children's computer and Internet use?

Educating Children with Special Needs

Guidepost 8

How do schools meet special needs?

Public schools have a tremendous job educating children of varying abilities from all sorts of families and cultural backgrounds. They also must educate children who have special needs: children who have learning problems and those who are gifted, talented, or creative.

Children with Learning Problems

Just as educators have become more sensitive to teaching children from varied cultural backgrounds, they also have sought to meet the needs of children with special educational needs.

Mental Retardation **Mental retardation** is significantly subnormal cognitive functioning. It is indicated by an IQ of about 70 or less, coupled with a deficiency in age-appropriate adaptive behavior (such as communication, social skills, and self-care), appearing before age 18 (Kanaya, Scullin, & Ceci, 2003). Fewer than 1 percent of U.S. children are mentally retarded (NCHS, 2004; Woodruff et al., 2004).

In 30 to 50 percent of cases the cause of mental retardation is unknown. Known causes include genetic disorders, traumatic accidents, prenatal exposure to infection or alcohol, and environmental exposure to lead or high levels of mercury (Woodruff et al., 2004). Many cases of retardation may be preventable through genetic counseling, prenatal care, amniocentesis, routine screening and health care for newborns, and nutritional services for pregnant women and infants.

Most retarded children can benefit from schooling. Intervention programs have helped many mildly or moderately retarded adults and those considered borderline (with IQs ranging from 70 up to about 85) to hold jobs, live in the community, and function in society. The profoundly retarded need constant care and supervision, usually in institutions. For some, day care centers, hostels for retarded adults, and homemaking services for caregivers can be less costly and more humane alternatives.

Learning Disabilities Nelson Rockefeller, former vice president of the United States, was one of many eminent persons with **dyslexia,** a developmental language disorder in which reading achievement is substantially below the level predicted by IQ or age. Other famous people who reportedly have dyslexia include the actors Tom Cruise, Whoopi Goldberg, and Cher; the baseball Hall-of-Famer Nolan Ryan; television host Jay Leno; and filmmaker Steven Spielberg.

Dyslexia is the most commonly diagnosed of a large number of **learning disabilities (LDs).** These are disorders that interfere with specific aspects of school achievement, such as listening, speaking, reading, writing, or mathematics, resulting in performance substantially lower than would be expected given a child's age, intelligence, and amount of schooling (APA, 1994). Mathematical disabilities, as an example, include difficulty in counting, comparing numbers,

mental retardation Significantly subnormal cognitive functioning.

dyslexia Developmental disorder in which reading achievement is substantially lower than predicted by IQ or age.

learning disabilities (LDs) Disorders that interfere with specific aspects of learning and school achievement.

calculating, and remembering basic arithmetic facts. Each of these may involve distinct disabilities. A growing percentage of U.S. children—9.7 percent in 2003—show LDs at some point in their school career (Altarac & Saroha, 2007); 5 percent are served by federally supported programs (National Center for Learning Disabilities, 2004b).

Children with LDs often have near-average to higher-than-average intelligence and normal vision and hearing, but they seem to have trouble processing sensory information. Although causes are uncertain, one factor is genetic. A review of quantitative genetic research concluded that the genes most responsible for the high heritability of the most common LDs—language impairment, reading disability, and mathematical disability—are also responsible for normal variations in learning abilities and that genes that affect one type of disability are also likely to affect other types. However, genes specific to particular learning disabilities also have been identified (Plomin & Kovas, 2005). Environmental factors may include complications of pregnancy or birth, injuries after birth, nutritional deprivation, and exposure to lead (National Center for Learning Disabilities, 2004b).

Children with LDs tend to be less task oriented and more easily distracted than other children; they are less well organized as learners and less likely to use memory strategies. Of course, not all children who have trouble with reading, arithmetic, or other specific school subjects have LDs. Some haven't been taught properly, are anxious, have trouble reading or hearing directions, lack motivation or interest in the subject, or have a developmental delay, which may eventually disappear (Geary, 1993; Ginsburg, 1997; Roush, 1995).

About 4 out of 5 children with LDs have been identified as dyslexic. Dyslexia is a chronic, persistent medical condition and tends to run in families (S. E. Shaywitz, 1998, 2003). It hinders the development of oral as well as written language skills and may cause problems with writing, spelling, grammar, and understanding speech as well as with reading (National Center for Learning Disabilities, 2004a). Reading disability is more frequent in boys than in girls (Rutter et al., 2004).

Brain imaging studies have found that dyslexia is due to a neurological defect that disrupts recognition of speech sounds (Shaywitz, Mody, & Shaywitz, 2006). Several identified genes contribute to this disruption (Meng et al., 2005; Kere et al., 2005). Many children—and even adults—with dyslexia can be taught to read through systematic phonological training, but the process does not become automatic, as it does with most readers (Eden et al., 2004; S. E. Shaywitz, 1998, 2003).

Attention-Deficit/Hyperactivity Disorder **Attention-deficit/hyperactivity disorder (ADHD)** has been called the most common mental disorder in childhood (Wolraich et al., 2005). It is a chronic condition usually marked by persistent inattention, distractibility, impulsivity, low tolerance for frustration, and a great deal of activity at the wrong time and in the wrong place, such as the classroom (APA, 1994; Woodruff et al., 2004). Among the well-known people who reportedly have had ADHD are the musician John Lennon, U.S. Senator Robert Kennedy, and the actors Robin Williams and Jim Carrey.

ADHD may affect an estimated 2 to 11 percent or more of school-age children worldwide (Zametkin & Ernst, 1999) and 3 to 7 percent in the United States (Dey et al., 2004; NCHS, 2004; Schneider & Eisenberg, 2006; Zelazo & Müller, 2002), but some research suggests that it may be underestimated (Rowland et al., 2002). On the other hand, some physicians warn that the disorder may be overdiagnosed, resulting in unnecessary overmedication of children whose parents or teachers do not know how to control them (Elliott, 2000). ADHD diagnosis rates vary greatly by gender,

attention-deficit/hyperactivity disorder (ADHD) Syndrome characterized by persistent inattention and distractibility, impulsivity, low tolerance for frustration, and inappropriate overactivity.

ethnicity, geographic area, and other contextual factors and may in part be related to pressures on children to succeed in school (Schneider & Eisenberg, 2006).

ADHD has two different but sometimes overlapping types of symptoms, making diagnosis imprecise. Some children are inattentive but not hyperactive; others show the reverse pattern (USDHHS, 1999b). However, in 85 percent of cases, the two types of symptoms go together (Barkley, 1998a). Because these characteristics appear to some degree in many normal children, some practitioners question whether ADHD is actually a distinct neurological or psychological disorder (Bjorklund & Pellegrini, 2002; Furman, 2005). However, most experts agree that there is cause for concern when the symptoms are unusually frequent and so severe as to interfere with the child's functioning in school and in daily life (AAP Committee on Children with Disabilities and Committee on Drugs, 1996; Barkley, 1998b; USDHHS, 1999b).

Imaging studies reveal that brains of children with ADHD grow in a normal pattern, with different areas thickening and then thinning at different times; but the process is delayed by about three years in certain regions of the brain, particularly the frontal cortex. These frontal regions enable a person to control movement, suppress inappropriate thoughts and actions, focus attention, remember from moment to moment, and work for rewards—all functions that are often disturbed in children with ADHD. The motor cortex is the only area that matures faster than normal, and this mismatch may account for the restlessness and fidgeting characteristic of the disorder (Shaw et al., 2007).

ADHD seems to have a substantial genetic basis with heritability approaching 80 percent (Acosta, Arcos-Burgos, & Muenke, 2004; Barkley, 1998b; Elia, Ambrosini, & Rapoport, 1999; USDHHS, 1999b; Zametkin & Ernst, 1999). Researchers have identified a variation of a gene for dopamine, a brain chemical essential for attention and cognition, low levels of which appear to be associated with ADHD (Shaw et al., 2007; Volkow et al., 2007). Birth complications that may play a part in ADHD include prematurity, the effects of a prospective mother's alcohol or tobacco use, and oxygen deprivation (Barkley, 1998b; Thapar et al., 2003; USDHHS, 1999b; Woodruff et al., 2004). Children with ADHD are more likely to show early antisocial behavior if they were of low birth weight and have a variant of a gene called COMT (Thapar et al., 2005).

Children with ADHD tend to forget responsibilities, to speak aloud rather than give themselves silent directions, to be frustrated or angered easily, and to give up when they don't see how to solve a problem. Parents and teachers may be able to help these children by breaking down tasks into small "chunks," providing frequent prompts about rules and time, and giving frequent, immediate rewards for small accomplishments (Barkley, 1998b).

ADHD is often managed with drugs, sometimes combined with behavioral therapy, counseling, training in social skills, and special classroom placement. In a 14-month randomized study of 579 children with ADHD, a carefully monitored program of Ritalin treatment, alone or in combination with behavior modification, was more effective than the behavioral therapy alone or standard community care (MTA Cooperative Group, 1999). However, the superior benefits of the program diminished during the following 10 months (MTA Cooperative Group, 2004a). A side effect of the combined treatment was slower growth in height and weight (MTA Cooperative Group, 2004b). Furthermore, long-term effects of Ritalin are unknown (Wolraich et al., 2005).

Educating Children with Disabilities In 2005–2006, 14 percent of public school students in the United States were receiving special educational services under the Individuals with Disabilities Education Act, which ensures a free,

What's Your View?

• Long-term effects of drug treatment for ADHD are unknown, but leaving the condition untreated also carries risks. If you had a child with ADHD, what would you do?

Checkpoint

Can You . . .

♦ Discuss the causes, treatments, and prognoses for three conditions that interfere with learning?

Martina is deaf but learns along with her hearing classmates with help from a special teacher who communicates via sign language.

appropriate public education for all children with disabilities. Most of these children had learning disabilities or speech or language impairments (NCES, 2007a). An individualized program must be designed for each child, with parental involvement. Children must be educated in the "least restrictive environment" appropriate to their needs—which means, whenever possible, the regular classroom.

Many of these students can be served by *inclusion programs,* in which they are integrated with nondisabled children for all or part of the day. In 2005, 52 percent of students with disabilities spent at least 80 percent of their time in regular classrooms (NCES, 2007a).

Gifted Children

The traditional criterion of giftedness is high general intelligence as shown by an IQ score of 130 or higher. This definition tends to exclude highly creative children (whose unusual answers often lower their test scores), children from minority groups (whose abilities may not be well developed, though the potential is there), and children with specific aptitudes (who may be only average or even show learning problems in other areas).

Most states and school districts have therefore adopted the broader definition in the U.S. Elementary and Secondary Education Act, which encompasses children who show high intellectual, creative, artistic, or leadership capacity or ability in specific academic fields and who need special educational services and activities in order to fully develop those capabilities. Many school districts now use multiple criteria for admission to programs for the gifted, including achievement test scores, grades, classroom performance, creative production, parent and teacher nominations, and student interviews; but IQ remains an important and sometimes the determining factor. An estimated 6 percent of the student population are considered gifted (NAGC, undated).

What's Special about Gifted Children? Psychologists who study the lives of extraordinary achievers find that high levels of performance require strong intrinsic motivation and years of rigorous training (Bloom, 1985; Csikszentmihalyi, 1996; Gardner, 1993; Gruber, 1981; Keegan, 1996). However, motivation and training will not produce giftedness unless a child is endowed with unusual ability (Winner, 2000). Conversely, children with innate gifts are unlikely to show exceptional achievement without motivation and hard work (Achter & Lubinski, 2003).

Gifted children tend to grow up in enriched family environments with much intellectual or artistic stimulation. Their parents recognize and often devote themselves to nurturing the children's gifts but also give their children an unusual degree of independence. Parents of gifted children typically have high expectations and are hard workers and high achievers themselves. But, although parenting can enhance the development of gifts, it cannot create them (Winner, 2000).

Research suggests that gifted children "are born with unusual brains that enable rapid learning in a particular domain" (Winner, 2000, p. 161). For example, children with mathematical, musical, and artistic gifts tend to have unusual activity in the right hemisphere while doing tasks normally done by the left. They are also more likely to be left-handed (Winner, 2000).

creativity Ability to see situations in a new way, to produce innovations, or to discern previously unidentified problems and find novel solutions.

Defining and Measuring Creativity One definition of **creativity** is the ability to see things in a new light—to produce something never seen before or to discern problems others fail to recognize and find new and unusual solutions. High creativity and high academic intelligence (IQ) do not necessarily go hand in hand (Anastasi & Schaefer, 1971; Getzels, 1964, 1984; Getzels & Jackson, 1962, 1963).

J. P. Guilford (1956, 1959, 1960, 1967, 1986) distinguished between two kinds of thinking: *convergent* and *divergent*. **Convergent thinking**—the kind IQ tests measure—seeks a single correct answer; **divergent thinking** comes up with a wide array of fresh possibilities. The Torrance Tests of Creative Thinking (Torrance, 1966, 1974; Torrance & Ball, 1984) call for divergent thinking; they include such tasks as listing unusual uses for a paper clip, completing a figure, and writing down what a sound brings to mind. A problem with these tests is that scores depend partly on speed, which is not a hallmark of creativity. Moreover, although the tests yield fairly reliable results, there is dispute over whether they are valid—whether they identify children who are creative in everyday life (Simonton, 1990).

Educating Gifted Children   Programs for gifted children generally stress either *enrichment* or *acceleration*. **Enrichment programs** deepen knowledge and skills through extra classroom activities, research projects, field trips, or expert coaching. **Acceleration programs**, sometimes recommended for highly gifted children, speed up their education through early school entrance, grade skipping, placement in fast-paced classes, or advanced courses. Other options include ability grouping within the classroom, which has been found to help children academically and not harm them socially (Winner, 2000), dual enrollment (for example, an eighth grader taking algebra at a nearby high school), magnet schools, and specialized schools for the gifted.

Moderate acceleration does not seem to harm social adjustment, at least in the long run (Winner, 1997). A 30-year study of 3,937 young people who took advanced placement courses in high school found that they were more satisfied with their school experience and ultimately achieved more than equally gifted young people who did not take AP courses (Bleske-Rechek, Lubinski, & Benbow, 2004).

There is no firm dividing line between being gifted and not being gifted, creative and not creative. All children benefit from being encouraged in their areas of interest and ability. What we learn about fostering intelligence and creativity in the most able youngsters may help all children make the most of their potential. The degree to which they do this will affect their self-concept and other aspects of personality, as we discuss in Chapter 10.

convergent thinking   Thinking aimed at finding the one right answer to a problem.

divergent thinking   Thinking that produces a variety of fresh, diverse possibilities.

enrichment programs   Programs for educating the gifted that broaden and deepen knowledge and skills through extra activities, projects, field trips, or mentoring.

acceleration programs   Programs for educating the gifted that move them through the curriculum at an unusually rapid pace.

Checkpoint

Can You . . .

♦ Tell how gifted children are identified?

♦ Explain why creativity is hard to measure?

♦ Compare two approaches to the education of gifted children?

Summary and Key Terms

PHYSICAL DEVELOPMENT

Aspects of Physical Development

Guidepost 1: *What gains in growth, brain development, and motor development occur in school-age children, and what are their nutritional and sleep needs?*

• Physical development is less rapid in middle childhood than in earlier years. Wide differences in height and weight exist.

• Proper nutrition and sleep are essential for normal growth and health.

• Changes in brain structure and functioning support cognitive advances.

• Because of improved motor development, boys and girls in middle childhood can engage in a wide range of motor activities.

• Informal recess-time activities help develop physical and social skills. Boys' games tend to be more physical and girls' games more verbal.

• About 10 percent of schoolchildren's play, especially among boys, is rough-and-tumble play.

• Many children, mostly boys, engage in organized, competitive sports. A sound physical education program should aim at skill development and fitness for all children.

rough-and-tumble play (287)

Health, Fitness, and Safety

Guidepost 2: *What are the principal health and fitness concerns for school-age children, and what can be done to make these years healthier and safer?*

- Middle childhood is a relatively healthy period; most children are immunized against major illnesses, and the death rate is the lowest in the life span.
- Overweight, which is increasingly common among U.S. children, entails multiple risks. It is influenced by genetic and environmental factors and is more easily prevented than treated. Many children do not get enough physical activity.
- Hypertension is becoming more common along with the rise in overweight.
- Respiratory infections and other acute medical conditions are common at this age. Chronic conditions such as asthma are most prevalent among poor and minority children.
- Accidents are the leading cause of death in middle childhood. Use of helmets and other protective devices and avoidance of trampolines, snowmobiling, and other dangerous sports can greatly reduce injuries.

body image (288)

hypertension (290)

acute medical conditions (291)

chronic medical conditions (291)

asthma (291)

COGNITIVE DEVELOPMENT

Piagetian Approach: The Concrete Operational Child

Guidepost 3: *How do school-age children's thinking and moral reasoning differ from those of younger children?*

- A child from about age 7 to age 12 is in the stage of concrete operations. Children are less egocentric than before and are more proficient at tasks requiring logical reasoning, such as spatial thinking, understanding of causality, categorization, inductive and deductive reasoning, and conservation. However, their reasoning is largely limited to the here and now.
- Neurological development, culture, and schooling seem to contribute to the rate of development of Piagetian skills.
- According to Piaget, moral development is linked with cognitive maturation and occurs in three stages as children move from rigid to more flexible thinking.

concrete operations (292)

seriation (293)

transitive inference (293)

class inclusion (293)

inductive reasoning (294)

deductive reasoning (294)

Information-Processing Approach: Planning, Attention, and Memory

Guidepost 4: *What advances in memory and other information-processing skills occur during middle childhood?*

- Executive skills, reaction time, processing speed, selective attention, metamemory, and use of mnemonic strategies improve during the school years.

executive function (297)

metamemory (298)

mnemonic strategies (298)

external memory aids (298)

rehearsal (298)

organization (298)

elaboration (298)

Psychometric Approach: Assessment of Intelligence

Guidepost 5: *How accurately can schoolchildren's intelligence be measured?*

- IQ tests are fairly good predictors of school success but may be unfair to some children.
- Differences in IQ among ethnic groups appear to result to a considerable degree from socioeconomic and other environmental differences.
- Schooling increases measured intelligence.
- Attempts to devise culture-free or culture-fair tests have been unsuccessful. Indeed, intelligence testing seems inextricably linked with culture.
- IQ tests tap only three of the intelligences in Howard Gardner's theory of multiple intelligences.
- According to Robert Sternberg's triarchic theory, IQ tests measure mainly the componential element of intelligence, not the experiential and contextual elements.
- Other directions in intelligence testing include the Sternberg Triarchic Abilities Tests (STAT), Kaufman Assessment Battery for Children (K-ABC), and dynamic tests based on Vygotsky's theory.

Wechsler Intelligence Scale for Children (WISC-III) (300)

Otis-Lennon School Ability Test (OLSAT 8) (300)

cultural bias (302)

culture-free tests (302)

culture-fair tests (302)

culture-relevant tests (303)

theory of multiple intelligences (303)

triarchic theory of intelligence (303)

componential element (303)

experiential element (303)

contextual element (304)

tacit knowledge (304)

Sternberg Triarchic Abilities Test (STAT) (304)

Kaufman Assessment Battery for Children (K-ABC-II) (305)

Language

Guidepost 6: *How do communicative abilities expand during middle childhood, and how do children best learn a second language?*

- Use of vocabulary, grammar, and syntax become increasingly sophisticated, but the major area of linguistic growth is in pragmatics.
- Methods of second-language education are controversial. Issues include speed and facility with English, long-term achievement in academic subjects, and pride in cultural identity.

pragmatics (306)

English-immersion approach (307)

bilingual education (307)

bilingual (307)

two-way (dual-language) learning (307)

The Child in School

Guidepost 7: *How do children adjust to school, and what influences school achievement?*

- Because schooling is cumulative, the foundation laid in first grade is very important.
- Despite the popularity of whole-language programs, early phonetics training is a key to reading proficiency.
- Children's self-efficacy beliefs affect school achievement.
- Girls tend to do better in school than boys.
- Parents influence children's learning by becoming involved in their schooling, motivating them to achieve, and transmitting attitudes about learning. Socioeconomic status can influence parental beliefs and practices that, in turn, influence achievement.
- Peer acceptance and class size affect learning.

- Current educational issues and innovations include social promotion, charter schools, homeschooling, and computer literacy.

decoding (308)

visually based retrieval (308)

phonetic (code-emphasis) approach (308)

whole-language approach (308)

metacognition (309)

social capital (311)

Educating Children with Special Needs

Guidepost 8: *How do schools meet special needs?*

- Three frequent sources of learning problems are mental retardation, learning disabilities (LDs), and attention-deficit/hyperactivity disorder (ADHD). Dyslexia is the most common learning disability.
- In the United States, all children with disabilities are entitled to a free, appropriate education. Children must be educated in the least restrictive environment possible, often in the regular classroom.
- An IQ of 130 or higher is a common standard for identifying gifted children.
- Creativity and IQ are *not* closely linked. Tests of creativity seek to measure divergent thinking, but their validity has been questioned.
- Special educational programs for gifted children stress enrichment or acceleration.

mental retardation (313)

dyslexia (313)

learning disabilities (LDs) (313)

attention-deficit/hyperactivity disorder (ADHD) (314)

creativity (316)

convergent thinking (317)

divergent thinking (317)

enrichment programs (317)

acceleration programs (317)

Have you ever felt like nobody?

Just a tiny speck of air.

When everyone's around you,

And you are just not there.

—Karen Crawford, age 9

Did You **Know...**

- The number of father-only families in the United States has more than quadrupled since 1970?

- Children in single-parent households do better on achievement tests in countries with supportive family policies?

- Children reared by gay or lesbian parents have been found to be as psychologically healthy as children reared by heterosexual parents?

- There are few significant differences in adjustment between adopted and nonadopted children?

- Research supports a cause-and-effect relationship between viewing media violence and aggressive behavior?

- Patterns of bullying and victimization may become established as early as kindergarten?

These are just a few of the interesting and important topics we will cover in this chapter. In it, we see how children develop a more realistic self-concept and become more self-reliant and self-controlled. Through interacting with peers they make discoveries about their own attitudes, values, and skills. Still, the family remains a vital influence. The kind of household a child lives in and the relationships in it can profoundly affect psychosocial development at a time when children are developing a stronger sense of what it means to be responsible members of a family and of society. Although most children are emotionally healthy, some have mental health problems. We look at several of these and at resilient children, who can emerge from stress healthy and strong. After you have read and studied this chapter, you should be able to answer each of the Guidepost questions on the following page.

Guideposts *for Study*

Guidepost 1

How do school-age children develop a healthy, realistic self-concept, and how do they show emotional growth?

The Developing Self

The cognitive growth that takes place during middle childhood enables children to develop more complex concepts of themselves and to gain in emotional understanding and control.

Self-Concept Development: Representational Systems

> "At school I'm feeling pretty smart in certain subjects, Language Arts and Social Studies," says 8-year-old Lisa. "I got A's in these subjects on my last report card and was really proud of myself. But I'm feeling really dumb in Arithmetic and Science, particularly when I see how well the other kids are doing. . . . I still like myself as a person, because Arithmetic and Science just aren't that important to me. How I look and how popular I am are more important." (Harter, 1996, p. 208)

Around age 7 or 8, children reach the third stage of self-concept development introduced in Chapter 8. At this time judgments about the self become more conscious, realistic, balanced, and comprehensive as children form **representational systems:** broad, inclusive self-concepts that integrate various aspects of the self (Harter, 1993, 1996, 1998).

We see these changes in Lisa's self-description. She can now focus on more than one dimension of herself. She has outgrown her earlier all-or-nothing, black-or-white self-definition. Now, she recognizes that she can be "smart" in certain subjects and "dumb" in others. She can verbalize her self-concept better, and she can weigh different aspects of it. She can compare her *real self* with her *ideal self* and can judge how well she measures up to social standards in comparison with others. All of these changes contribute to the development of self-esteem, her assessment of her *global self-worth* ("I still like myself as a person").

representational systems In neo-Piagetian terminology, the third stage in development of self-definition, characterized by breadth, balance, and the integration and assessment of various aspects of the self.

Hie takes geese to market, developing her sense of competence and building her self-esteem. By taking responsibilities that match her growing capabilities, she also learns how her Vietnamese society works, what her role is in it, and what it means to do a job well.

Self-Esteem

According to Erikson (1982), a major determinant of self-esteem is children's view of their capacity for productive work. This fourth stage of psychosocial development focuses on **industry versus inferiority.** Middle childhood is the time when children must learn skills valued in their society. Arapesh boys in New Guinea learn to make bows and arrows and to lay traps for rats; Arapesh girls learn to plant, weed, and harvest. Inuit children of Alaska learn to hunt and fish. Children in industrialized countries learn to read, write, count, and use computers.

The virtue that follows successful resolution of this stage is *competence,* a view of the self as able to master skills and complete tasks. If children feel inadequate compared with their peers, they may retreat to the protective embrace of the family. If, on the other hand, they become too industrious, they may neglect social relationships and turn into workaholics.

Parents strongly influence a child's beliefs about competence. In a longitudinal study of 514 middle-class U.S. children, parents' beliefs about their children's competence in math and sports were strongly associated with the children's beliefs (Fredricks & Eccles, 2002).

industry versus inferiority Erikson's fourth stage of psychosocial development, in which children must learn the productive skills their culture requires or else face feelings of inferiority.

Emotional Growth and Prosocial Behavior

As children grow older, they are more aware of their own and other people's feelings. They can better regulate or control their emotions and can respond to others' emotional distress (Saarni et al., 1998).

By age 7 or 8, children typically are aware of feeling shame and pride, and they have a clearer idea of the difference between guilt and shame (Harris, Olthof, Meerum Terwogt, & Hardman, 1987; Olthof, Schouten, Kuiper, Stegge, & Jennekens-Schinkel, 2000). These emotions affect their opinion of themselves (Harter, 1993, 1996). Children also understand their conflicting emotions. As Lisa says, "Most of the boys at school are pretty yucky. I don't feel that way about my little brother Jason, although he does get on my nerves. I love him but at the same time, he also does things that make me mad. But I control my temper; I'd be ashamed of myself if I didn't" (Harter, 1996, p. 208).

By middle childhood, children are aware of their culture's rules for acceptable emotional expression (Cole, Bruschi, & Tamang, 2002). Children learn what makes them angry, fearful, or sad and how other people react to displays of these emotions, and they learn to behave accordingly. When parents respond with disapproval or punishment, emotions such as anger and fear may become more intense and may impair children's social adjustment (Fabes, Leonard, Kupanoff, & Martin, 2001). Or the children may become secretive and anxious about negative feelings. As children approach early adolescence, parental intolerance of negative emotion may heighten parent-child conflict (Eisenberg, Fabes et al., 1999).

Emotional self-regulation involves effortful (voluntary) control of emotions, attention, and behavior (Eisenberg et al., 2004). Children low in effortful control tend to become visibly angry or frustrated when interrupted or prevented from doing something they want to do. Children with high effortful control can stifle the impulse to show negative emotion at inappropriate times. Effortful control may be temperamentally based but generally increases with age. Low effortful control may predict later behavior problems (Eisenberg et al., 2004).

Children tend to become more empathic and more inclined to prosocial behavior in middle childhood. Children with high self-esteem tend to be more willing to volunteer to help those who are less fortunate than they are, and volunteering, in turn, helps build self-esteem (Karafantis & Levy, 2004). Prosocial children tend to act appropriately in social situations, to be relatively free from negative emotion, and to cope with problems constructively (Eisenberg, Fabes, & Murphy, 1996). Parents who acknowledge children's feelings of distress and help them focus on solving the root problem foster empathy, prosocial development, and social skills (Bryant, 1987; Eisenberg et al., 1996).

Checkpoint

Can you . . .

♦ Discuss how the self-concept develops in middle childhood?

♦ Describe Erikson's fourth stage of psychosocial development?

♦ Identify several aspects of emotional growth in middle childhood?

Guidepost 2

How do parent-child relationships change in middle childhood, and how do family atmosphere and family structure influence children's well-being?

The Child in the Family

School-age children spend more time away from home visiting and socializing with peers than when they were younger. They also spend more time at school and on studies and less time at family meals than 20 years ago (Juster et al., 2004). Still, home and the people who live there remain an important part of most children's lives.

To understand the child in the family we need to look at the family environment—its atmosphere and structure. These in turn are affected by what goes on beyond the walls of the home. As Bronfenbrenner's theory predicts, additional layers of influence—including parents' work and socioeconomic status and societal trends such as urbanization, changes in family size, divorce, and remarriage—help shape the family environment and, thus, children's development.

Culture, too, defines the rhythms of family life and the roles of family members. Many African American families, for example, carry on extended-family traditions that include living near or with kin, a strong sense of family obligation, ethnic pride, and mutual aid (Parke & Buriel, 1998). Latino families tend to stress family commitment, respect for self and others, and moral education (Halgunseth, Ispa, & Rudy, 2006). As we look at the child in the family, then, we need to be aware of outside forces that affect it.

Family Atmosphere

The most important influences of the family environment on children's development come from the atmosphere in the home. One contributing factor to family atmosphere is whether it is supportive and loving or conflict ridden. In a study of 226 ethnically diverse families with school-age children (Kaczynski, Lindahl, Malik, & Laurenceau, 2006), marital conflict was consistently associated with ineffective parenting; and children exposed to parental discord and poor parenting tended to show high levels of both **internalizing behaviors,** such as anxiety, fearfulness, and depression, and **externalizing behaviors,** such as aggressiveness, fighting, disobedience, and hostility.

Another contributing factor to family atmosphere is how parents handle school-age children's growing need—and ability—to make their own decisions. Still another aspect is the family's economic situation. How does parents' work affect children's well-being? Does the family have enough money to provide for basic needs?

Although school-age children spend less time at home, parents continue to be important in their lives. Parents who enjoy being with their children tend to raise children who feel good about themselves—and about their parents.

internalizing behaviors Behaviors by which emotional problems are turned inward; for example, anxiety or depression.

externalizing behaviors Behaviors by which a child acts out emotional difficulties; for example, aggression or hostility.

coregulation Transitional stage in the control of behavior in which parents exercise general supervision and children exercise moment-to-moment self-regulation.

Parenting Issues: From Control to Coregulation During the course of childhood, control of behavior gradually shifts from parents to child. Middle childhood brings a transitional stage of **coregulation,** in which parent and child share power. Parents exercise oversight, but children enjoy moment-to-moment self-regulation (Maccoby, 1984). With regard to problems among peers, for example, parents now rely less on direct intervention and more on discussion with their child (Parke & Buriel, 1998). Children are more apt to follow their parents' wishes when they recognize that the parents are fair and are concerned about the child's welfare and that they may "know better" because of experience. It helps if parents try to acknowledge children's maturing judgment and take strong stands only on important issues (Maccoby, 1984).

The shift to coregulation affects the way parents handle discipline (Maccoby, 1984; Roberts, Block, & Block, 1984). Parents of school-age children are more likely to use inductive techniques. For example, 8-year-old Jared's father points out how his actions affect others: "Hitting Jermaine hurts him and makes him feel bad." In other situations, Jared's parents may appeal to his self-esteem ("What happened to the helpful boy who was here yesterday?") or moral values, ("A big, strong boy like you shouldn't sit on the train and let an old person stand"). Above all, Jared's parents let him know that he must bear the consequences of his behavior, ("No wonder you missed the school bus today—you stayed up too late last night! Now you'll have to walk to school").

The way parents and children resolve conflicts may be more important than the specific outcomes. If family conflict is constructive, it can help children see the need for rules and standards. They also learn what kinds of issues are worth arguing about and what strategies can be effective (A. R. Eisenberg, 1996). However, as children become preadolescents and their striving for autonomy becomes more insistent, the quality of family problem solving often deteriorates (Vuchinich, Angelelli, & Gatherum, 1996).

Here again, cultural differences are important. Mothers in cultures that stress family interdependence, such as in Turkey, India, and Latin America, tend to favor authoritarian parenting; but in these cultures, unlike individualistic cultures, such as the United States, this type of parenting is *not* associated with negative maternal feelings or low self-esteem in children (Rudy & Grusec, 2006). Latino

Checkpoint

Can you . . .

♦ Describe how coregulation works, and how discipline and the handling of family conflict change during middle childhood?

parents, for example, tend to exert more control and set more rules for school-age children than European American parents do. Although relatively indulgent with younger children, Latino parents may perceive 6- or 7-year-olds as mature enough to be reasonable and to meet higher behavioral expectations (Halgunseth et al., 2006). In one study, African American and Latina girls showed more respect for parental authority than did European American girls. However, when minority girls showed low respect, mothers reported more intense arguments than did European American mothers (Dixon, Graber, & Brooks-Gunn, 2008).

Effects of Parents' Work   Most studies of the impact of parents' work on children's well-being have focused on employed mothers. In 2005, 70.5 percent of U.S. mothers with children under 18 were in the workforce, and 53.8 percent of mothers with infants went to work within a year of giving birth (Bureau of Labor Statistics, 2006). Thus, many children have never known a time when their mothers were *not* working for pay.

In general, the more satisfied a mother is with her employment status, the more effective she is likely to be as a parent (Parke & Buriel, 1998). However, the impact of a mother's work depends on many other factors, including the child's age, sex, temperament, and personality; whether the mother works full-time or part-time; why she is working; whether she has a supportive or unsupportive partner, or none; the family's socioeconomic status; and the type of care the child receives before and/or after school (Parke & Buriel, 1998). Often a single mother must work to stave off economic disaster. How her working affects her children may hinge on how much time and energy she has left to spend with them and what sort of role model she is. How well parents keep track of their children may be more important than whether the mother works for pay (Crouter, MacDermid, McHale, & Perry-Jenkins, 1990). If possible, part-time work may be preferable to full-time. In an analysis of 68 studies, children did slightly better in school if their mothers worked only part-time (Goldberg, Prause, Lucas-Thompson, & Himsel, 2008).

In 2005, 57 percent of students in kindergarten through eighth grade whose mothers worked full-time and 32 percent of those whose mothers worked part-time or were looking for work were in at least one regular nonparental after-school care arrangement, most often a school- or center-based program. Some children of employed mothers, especially younger children, are supervised by relatives. Many children receive several types of out-of-school care (Carver & Iruka, 2006). Like good child care for preschoolers, good after-school programs have relatively low enrollment, low child-staff ratios, and well-educated staff. Children, especially boys, in organized after-school programs with flexible programming and a positive emotional climate tend to adjust better and do better in school (Pierce, Hamm, & Vandell, 1999; Posner & Vandell, 1999).

About 9 percent of school-age children and 23 percent of early adolescents are reported to be in *self-care,* regularly caring for themselves at home without adult supervision (Hofferth & Jankuniene, 2000; NICHD Early Childhood Research Network, 2004a). This arrangement is advisable only for older children who are mature, responsible, and resourceful and know how to get help in an emergency—and, even then, only if a parent can stay in touch by telephone.

Poverty and Parenting   In 2005, 18 percent of U.S. children up to age 17—including 35 percent of black children and 28 percent of Hispanic children—lived in poverty. Children living with single mothers were nearly five times more likely to be poor than children living with married parents—43 percent compared with 9 percent (Federal Interagency Forum on Child and Family Statistics, 2007).

What's Your View?

• If finances permit, should one parent stay home to take care of the children?

Poor children are more likely than other children to have emotional or behavioral problems, and their cognitive potential and school performance suffer even more (Brooks-Gunn, Britto, & Brady, 1998; Brooks-Gunn & Duncan, 1997; Duncan & Brooks-Gunn, 1997; McLoyd, 1998). Poverty can harm children's development through its impact on parents' emotional state and parenting practices and on the home environment they create (Brooks-Gunn & Duncan, 1997; Brooks-Gunn et al., 1998; Evans, 2004).

Vonnie McLoyd's (1990, 1998; Mistry, Vandewater, Huston, & McLoyd, 2002) analysis of the effects of poverty traces a route that leads to adult psychological distress, to effects on child rearing, and finally to emotional, behavioral, and academic problems in children. Parents who live in poverty are likely to become anxious, depressed, and irritable and thus may become less affectionate with and less responsive to their children. They may discipline inconsistently, harshly, and arbitrarily. The children tend to also become depressed, to have trouble getting along with peers, to lack self-confidence, to develop behavioral and academic problems, and to engage in antisocial acts (Brooks-Gunn et al., 1998; Evans, 2004; Evans & English, 2002; J. M. Fields & Smith, 1998; McLoyd, 1990, 1998; Mistry et al., 2002).

Fortunately, this pattern is not inevitable. Effective parenting can buffer children from the effects of low SES. Family interventions that reduce family conflict and anger and increase cohesion and warmth are especially beneficial (Repetti, Taylor, & Seeman, 2002). In a nationally representative study of 21,260 six-year-olds, it was not so much low income as material hardship—insufficient food, unstable housing, and inadequate medical care—that led to parental stress. This, in turn, affected how much time, money, and energy parents invested in their children's development and the way the parents treated their children; and these factors in turn predicted children's cognitive skills and social and emotional competence. Families that, despite poverty, managed to make ends meet did not show this pattern (Gershoff, Aber, Raver, & Lennon, 2007).

Parents who can turn to relatives or to community resources for emotional support, help with child care, and child-rearing information often can parent their children more effectively. A four-year longitudinal study of 152 single mother–headed African American families in Georgia found a pattern opposite to the one McLoyd described. Mothers who, despite economic stress, were emotionally healthy and had relatively high self-esteem tended to have academically and socially competent children who reinforced the mothers' positive parenting; and this, in turn, supported the children's continued academic success and socially desirable behavior (Brody, Kim, Murry, & Brown, 2004).

Family Structure

Family structure in the United States has changed dramatically. In earlier generations, the vast majority of children grew up in families with two married parents. Today, although about 2 out of 3 children under 18 live with two married biological, adoptive, or stepparents, that proportion represents a dramatic decline—from 77 percent in 1980 to 67 percent in 2006 (Federal Interagency Forum on Family and Child Statistics, 2007). About 10 percent of two-parent families are stepfamilies resulting from divorce and remarriage, and nearly 4 percent are cohabiting families (Kreider & Fields, 2005). Other increasingly common family types are gay and lesbian families and grandparent-headed families (discussed in chapter 16).

Other things being equal, children tend to do better in families with two continuously married parents than in cohabiting, divorced, single-parent, or stepfamilies, or when the child is born outside of marriage (S. L. Brown, 2004). The

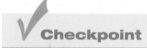

Checkpoint

Can you . . .

♦ Identify ways in which parents' work can affect children?

♦ Discuss effects of poverty on parenting?

distinction is even stronger for children growing up with two *happily* married parents. These children tend to experience a higher standard of living, more effective parenting, more cooperative co-parenting, closer relationships with both parents (especially fathers), and fewer stressful events (Amato, 2005). However, the parents' relationship, the quality of their parenting, and their ability to create a favorable family atmosphere may affect children's adjustment more than their marital status does (Amato, 2005; Bray & Hetherington, 1993; Bronstein et al., 1993; D. A. Dawson, 1991).

Family instability may be more harmful to children than the particular type of family they live in. In a study of a nationally representative sample of 5- to 14-year-olds, children who experienced several family transitions were more likely to have behavior problems and to engage in delinquent behavior than children in stable families (Fomby & Cherlin, 2007).

A father's frequent and positive involvement with his child is directly related to the child's well-being and physical, cognitive, and social development (Cabrera et al., 2000; Kelley, Smith, Green, Berndt, & Rogers, 1998; Shannon, Tamis-LeMonda, London, & Cabrera, 2002). Unfortunately, more than 23 percent of U.S. children live in households with no father (see Figure 10.1). Furthermore, about 13 percent, in one study, had never seen their fathers (NCES, 2005a).

When Parents Divorce   The United States has one of the highest divorce rates in the world. The annual *number* of divorces has tripled since 1960 (Harvey & Pauwels, 1999), though the divorce *rate* has remained stable or declined slightly since 2001 (Munson & Sutton, 2004). More than 1 million children are affected by divorce each year (Harvey & Pauwels, 1999).

Adjusting to Divorce   Divorce is stressful for children. First there is the stress of marital conflict and then of parental separation with the departure of one parent, usually the father. Children may not fully understand what is happening and why. Divorce is, of course, stressful for the parents as well and may affect their parenting. The family's standard of living is likely to drop; and, if a parent moves away, a child's relationship with the noncustodial parent may suffer (Kelly & Emery, 2003). A parent's remarriage or second divorce after remarriage can increase the stress on children, renewing feelings of loss (Ahrons & Tanner, 2003; Amato, 2003).

Children's emotional or behavioral problems also may reflect the level of parental conflict *before* the divorce (Amato, 2005). In a longitudinal study of almost 11,000 Canadian children, those whose parents later divorced showed more anxiety, depression, or antisocial behavior than those whose parents stayed married (Strohschein, 2005). If predivorce parental discord is chronic, overt, or destructive, children may be as well or better off after a divorce (Amato, 2003, 2005; Amato & Booth, 1997).

A child's adjustment to divorce may depend in part on the child's age, maturity, gender, temperament, and psychosocial adjustment before the divorce. Young children tend to be more anxious about divorce, have less realistic perceptions of what caused it, and are more likely to blame themselves, but they may adapt more quickly than older children, who better understand what is going on. School-age children are sensitive to parental pressures and loyalty conflicts and, like younger children, may fear abandonment and rejection. Boys usually find it harder to adjust than girls do and are more susceptible to social and conduct problems (Amato, 2005; Hetherington et al., 1998; Hines, 1997; Parke & Buriel, 1998).

Custody, Visitation, and Co-parenting   Children do better after divorce if the custodial parent is warm, supportive, and authoritative, monitors the child's

Children of divorce tend to be better adjusted if they have reliable, frequent contact with the noncustodial parent.

activities, and holds age-appropriate expectations; if parental conflict subsides; and if the nonresident parent maintains close contact and involvement (Ahrons & Tanner, 2003; Kelly & Emery, 2003).

In most divorces, the mother gets custody, though paternal custody is a growing trend. Children living with divorced mothers adjust better when the father pays child support, which may be a barometer of the tie between father and child and also of cooperation between the ex-spouses (Amato & Gilbreth, 1999; Kelly & Emery, 2003). Many children of divorce say that losing contact with a father is one of the most painful results of divorce (Fabricius, 2003). However, frequency of contact with the father is not as important as the quality of the father-child relationship and the level of parental conflict. Children who are close to their nonresident fathers and whose fathers are authoritative parents tend to do better in school and are less likely to have behavior problems (Amato & Gilbreth, 1999; Kelly & Emery, 2003).

In a national sample of 354 divorced families, cooperative co-parenting—active consultation between a mother and a nonresident father on parenting decisions—led to more frequent contact between father and child, and this, in turn, led to better father-child relationships and more responsive fathering (Sobolewski & King, 2005). Unfortunately, cooperative parenting is not the norm (Amato, 2005). Parent education programs that teach separated or divorced couples how to prevent or deal with conflict, keep lines of communication open, develop an effective co-parenting relationship, and help children adjust to divorce have been introduced in many courts with measurable success (Wolchik et al., 2002).

Joint custody, custody shared by both parents, can be advantageous if the parents can cooperate, as both parents can continue to be closely involved with the child. When parents have joint *legal* custody, they share the right and responsibility to make decisions regarding the child's welfare. When parents have joint *physical* custody (which is less common), the child lives part-time with each of them. An analysis of 33 studies found that children in either legal or physical joint custody were better adjusted and had higher self-esteem and better family relationships than children in sole custody. In fact, children in joint custody were as well-adjusted as children in nondivorced families (Bauserman, 2002). It is likely, though, that couples who choose joint custody are those who have less conflict.

Long-Term Effects   Most children of divorce adjust reasonably well. Still, children with divorced parents tend to have modestly lower levels of cognitive, social, and emotional well-being than children whose parents stay together (Amato, 2005). The timing of the divorce often affects the outcome. In one study, children who experienced their parents' divorce during elementary school were more likely to develop internalizing or externalizing problems, whereas children whose parents divorced later were more likely to suffer a drop in grades (Lansford et al., 2006). In another study, children who experienced parental divorce before age 16 tended to have emotional and educational problems, to initiate sexual activity early, and to be at risk for depression and suicidal thoughts (D'Onofrio et al., 2006). In adolescence, parental divorce increases the risk of antisocial behavior, difficulties with authority figures (Amato, 2003, 2005; Kelly & Emery, 2003), and dropping out of school (McLanahan & Sandefur, 1994).

The anxiety connected with parental divorce may surface as children enter adulthood and try to form intimate relationships of their own (Amato, 2003; Wallerstein, Lewis, & Blakeslee, 2000). Having experienced their parents' divorce, some young adults are afraid of making commitments that might end in disappointment (Glenn & Marquardt, 2001; Wallerstein & Corbin, 1999). According to some research, 25 percent of children of divorce reach adulthood with serious social, emotional, or psychological problems, compared with 10 percent of children whose parents stay together (Hetherington & Kelly, 2002). As adults, the children of divorce tend to have lower SES, poorer psychological well-being, and a greater chance of having a birth outside marriage. Their marriages tend to be less satisfying and are more likely to end in divorce (Amato, 2005). However, much depends on how young people resolve and interpret the experience of parental divorce. Some who saw a high degree of conflict between their parents are able to learn from that negative example and to form highly intimate relationships themselves (Shulman, Scharf, Lumer, & Maurer, 2001).

Living in a One-Parent Family   One-parent families result from divorce or separation, unwed parenthood, or death. With rising rates of divorce and of parenthood outside of marriage, the percentage of single-parent families in the United States has more than doubled since 1970 (U.S. Census Bureau, 2008a; Figure 10-1). Today about 28 percent of U.S. children live with one parent, but more than 11 percent of these households are cohabiting households that include the mother's or father's unwed partner. More than half of all black children live with a single parent, as compared with 19 percent of non-Hispanic white children and 26 percent of Hispanic children (Kreider & Fields, 2005).

Although children are far more likely to live with a single mother than with a single father, almost 5 percent of U.S. families are headed by a single father (see Figure 10-1). The number of father-only families has more than quadrupled since 1970, apparently due largely to the increase in paternal custody after divorce (Fields, 2004).

Children in single-parent families do fairly well overall but tend to lag socially and educationally behind peers in two-parent families (Amato, 2005). Children living with married parents tend to have more daily interaction with their parents, are read to more often, progress more steadily in school, and participate more in extracurricular activities than children living with a single parent (Lugaila, 2003).

However, negative outcomes for children in one-parent families are not inevitable. The child's age and level of development, the family's financial circumstances, whether there are frequent moves, and a nonresident father's involvement make a difference (Amato, 2005; Seltzer, 2000). In a longitudinal study of 1,500 white, black, and Hispanic families with 6- and 7-year-old children, the mother's educational and ability level and, to a lesser extent, family income and the quality of the home environment accounted for any negative effects of single parenting on academic performance and behavior (Ricciuti, 1999, 2004).

Because single parents often lack the resources needed for good parenting, potential risks to children in these families might be reduced or eliminated through increased access to economic, social, educational, and parenting support. In international math and science tests, the achievement gap between third and fourth graders living in single-parent households and those living with two biological parents was greater for U.S. children than for those in any other country except New Zealand. Children of single parents did better in countries with supportive family policies such as child and family allowances, tax benefits to single parents, maternity leave, and released time from work (Pong et al., 2003).

Living in a Cohabiting Family Cohabiting families are similar in many ways to married families, but the parents tend to be more disadvantaged. They have less income and education, report poorer relationships, and have more mental health problems. Thus, it is not surprising that data from a national survey of 35,938 U.S. families showed worse emotional, behavioral, and academic outcomes for 6- to 11-year-old children living with cohabiting biological parents than for those living with married biological parents. The difference in outcomes was due largely to differences in economic resources, parental well-being, and parenting effectiveness (S. L. Brown, 2004).

Furthermore, cohabiting families are more likely to break up than married families. Although about 40 percent of unwed mothers are living with the child's father at the time of birth, 25 percent of cohabiting parents are no longer together one year later, and 31 percent break up after five years (Amato, 2005).

Living in a Stepfamily Most divorced parents eventually remarry, and many unwed mothers marry men who were not the father of their children (Amato, 2005), thus forming step-, or blended, families. Fifteen percent of U.S. children live in blended families (Kreider & Fields, 2005).

Adjusting to a new stepparent may be stressful. A child's loyalties to an absent or dead parent may interfere with forming ties to a stepparent (Amato, 2005). However, some studies have found that boys—who often have more trouble than girls in adjusting to divorce and living with a single mother—benefit from a stepfather. A girl, on the other hand, may find the new man in the house a threat to her independence and to her close relationship with her mother (Bray & Hetherington, 1993; Hetherington, 1987; Hetherington et al., 1989; Hetherington

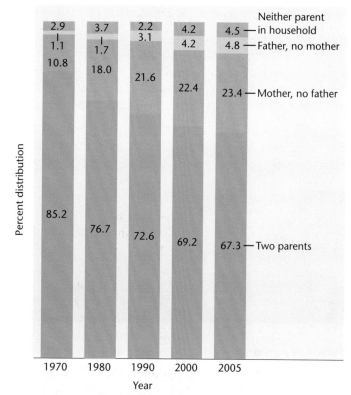

Note: Numbers may not add up to 100 percent due to rounding.

Figure 10-1

Living arrangements of children younger than 18, United States, 1970–2005. Most children live with two parents, but this proportion has dropped since 1970. Many of these two-parent families are stepfamilies.
Source: U.S. Census Bureau (2008a).

 **Checkpoint**

Can you . . .

◆ Assess the impact of parental divorce on children?

◆ Discuss how living in a single-parent or cohabiting household can affect children?

Some same-sex partners choose to adopt children. Children raised by gay or lesbian parents have been found to have no more problems than children of heterosexuals.

et al., 1998; Hines, 1997). In a longitudinal study of a nationally representative sample of U.S. adults, mothers who remarried or formed new cohabiting relationships tended to use gentler discipline than mothers who remained single, and their children reported better relationships with them. On the other hand, supervision was greater in stable single-mother families (Thomson, Mosley, Hanson, & McLanahan, 2001).

Among 173 college students of mixed ethnicity from a large midwestern U.S. city, those raised in stepfamilies tended to report lower well-being than those raised in intact families. They also were less likely to recall having been securely attached. Thus, attachment quality may help explain why people from stepfamilies tend not to fare as well emotionally, socially, and psychologically as those from intact families (Love & Murdock, 2004).

Living with Gay or Lesbian Parents   An estimated 9 million U.S. children and adolescents have at least one gay or lesbian parent. Some gays and lesbians are raising children born of previous heterosexual relationships. Others conceive by artificial means, use surrogate mothers, or adopt children (Pawelski et al., 2006; Perrin and AAP Committee on Psychosocial Aspects of Child and Family Health, 2002).

A considerable body of research has examined the development of children of gays and lesbians, including physical and emotional health, intelligence, adjustment, sense of self, moral judgment, and social and sexual functioning, and has found no special concerns (APA, 2004b). There is *no* consistent difference between homosexual and heterosexual parents in emotional health or parenting skills and attitudes; and where there are differences, they tend to favor gay and lesbian parents (Brewaeys, Ponjaert, Van Hall, & Golombok, 1997; Meezan & Rauch, 2005; Pawelski et al., 2006; Perrin and AAP Committee on Psychosocial Aspects of Child and Family Health, 2002; Wainright, Russell, & Patterson, 2004). Gay or lesbian parents usually have positive relationships with their children, and the children are no more likely than children raised by heterosexual parents to have emotional, social, academic, or psychological problems (APA, 2004b; Chan, Raboy, & Patterson, 1998; Gartrell, Deck, Rodas, Peyser, & Banks, 2005; Meezan & Rauch, 2005; Mooney-Somers & Golombok, 2000; Golombok et al., 2003; Wainright et al., 2004). Furthermore, children of gays and lesbians are no more likely to be homosexual or to be confused about their gender than are children of heterosexuals (Anderssen, Amlie, & Ytteroy, 2002; Golombok et al., 2003; Meezan & Rauch, 2005; Pawelski et al., 2006; Wainright et al., 2004).

Such findings have social policy implications for legal decisions on custody and visitation disputes, foster care, and adoptions. In the face of controversy over gay and lesbian marriages or civil unions, with its implications for the security of children, several states have considered or adopted legislation sanctioning second-parent adoption by same-sex partners. The American Academy of Pediatrics supports a right to civil marriage for gays and lesbians (Pawelski et al., 2006) and legislative and legal efforts to permit a partner in a same-sex couple to adopt the other partner's child (AAP Committee on Psychosocial Aspects of Child and Family Health, 2002).

Adoptive Families Adoption is found in all cultures throughout history. It is not only for infertile people; single people, older people, gay and lesbian couples, and people who already have biological children have become adoptive parents. In 2001, 1.4 million U.S. children under 18—about 2.5 percent—lived with at least one adoptive parent (Kreider & Fields, 2005). An estimated 60 percent of legal adoptions are by stepparents or relatives, usually grandparents (Kreider, 2003).

Adoptions usually take place through public or private agencies. Agency adoptions are supposed to be confidential, with no contact between the birth mother and the adoptive parents, and the identity of the birth mother is kept secret. However, in recent years, independent adoptions, made by direct agreement between birth parents and adoptive parents, have become more common (Brodzinsky, 1997; Goodman et al., 1998). Often these are *open adoptions,* in which both parties share information or have direct contact with the child.

Studies suggest that the presumed risks of open adoption, such as fear that a birth mother who knows her child's whereabouts will try to reclaim the child, are overstated (Grotevant, McRoy, Elde, & Fravel, 1994). In a survey of 1,059 California adoptive families, whether an adoption was open bore no relation to the children's adjustment or to the parents' satisfaction with the adoption, both of which were high (Berry, Dylla, Barth, & Needell, 1998). Likewise, in a national study, adoptive parents of adolescents reported no significant difference in their children's adjustment whether the adoption was open or confidential (Von Korff, Grotevant, & McRoy. 2006).

Adoptions of foreign-born children by U.S. families nearly quadrupled between 1978 and 2001, from 5,315 to an estimated 20,000 (Bosch et al., 2003), and 13 percent of adopted children in 2000 were foreign born. Because of the cultural preference for boys in Asian countries, more girls are available for adoption there. About 17 percent of adoptions are transracial, most often involving white parents adopting an Asian or Latin American child (Kreider, 2003).

Adopting a child carries special challenges: integrating the adopted child into the family, explaining the adoption to the child, helping the child develop a healthy sense of self, and perhaps eventually helping the child find and contact the biological parents. According to a national longitudinal study, two adoptive parents invest just as much energy and resources in their children as two biological parents do, and more than parents in other family types. And adoptive children in two-parent families do as well as biological children in two-parent families (Hamilton, Cheng, & Powell, 2007).

Few significant differences in adjustment between adopted and nonadopted children have been found (Haugaard, 1998). Children adopted in infancy are least likely to have adjustment problems (Sharma, McGue, & Benson, 1996b). Any problems that do occur may surface during middle childhood, when children become more aware of differences in the way families are formed (Freeark et al., 2005), or in adolescence (Goodman et al., 1998; Sharma, McGue, & Benson, 1996a), particularly among boys (Freeark et al., 2005).

Does foreign adoption entail special problems? Aside from the possibility of malnourishment or other serious medical conditions in children from developing countries (Bosch et al., 2003), a number of studies find no significant problems with the children's psychological adjustment, school adjustment and performance, or observed behavior at home or in the way they cope with being adopted

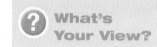

What's Your View?

- Do you think you would ever try to adopt?
- If so, would you want the adoption to be open? Why or why not?

Taksheel has an important responsibility: taking care of his younger brother. Siblings in nonindustrialized societies, such as this Surinam village, have clear culturally defined roles throughout life.

Checkpoint

Can you . . .

♦ Identify some special issues and challenges of a stepfamily?

♦ Summarize findings on outcomes of child raising by gay and lesbian parents?

♦ Discuss trends in adoption and the adjustment of adopted children?

♦ Compare sibling roles in industrialized and nonindustrialized countries?

♦ Discuss how siblings affect each other's development?

(Levy-Shiff, Zoran, & Shulman, 1997; Sharma, McGue, & Benson, 1996a). However, not all international adoptions proceed so smoothly, especially when the children have had substandard care or are older at the time of adoption. (Recall the experiences of children adopted from Romanian orphanages, discussed in Chapter 4.)

When foreign adoptees reach adolescence, they may experience feelings of loss of their native culture and growing awareness of racism and discrimination in their adopted culture. Parents with less color-blind racial attitudes are more inclined to expose their adopted children to experiences that help them identify with their native culture and to speak with their children about racism and discrimination (Lee et al., 2006).

Sibling Relationships

In remote rural areas of Asia, Africa, Oceania, and Central and South America, it is common to see older girls caring for three or four younger siblings. In such a community, older siblings have an important, culturally defined, role. Parents train children early to teach younger sisters and brothers how to gather firewood, carry water, tend animals, and grow food. Younger siblings absorb intangible values, such as respecting elders and placing the welfare of the group above that of the individual (Cicirelli, 1994). In industrialized societies such as the United States, parents generally try not to "burden" older children with the regular care of siblings (Weisner, 1993). Older siblings do teach younger siblings, but this usually happens informally and not as an established part of the social system (Cicirelli, 1994).

The number of siblings in a family and their spacing, birth order, and gender often determine roles and relationships. The larger number of siblings in nonindustrialized societies helps the family carry on its work and provide for aging members. In industrialized societies, siblings tend to be fewer and farther apart in age, enabling parents to focus more resources and attention on each child (Cicirelli, 1994).

Two longitudinal studies in England and Pennsylvania found that changes in sibling relationships were most likely to occur when one sibling was between ages 7 and 9. Both mothers and children often attributed these changes to outside friendships, which led to jealousy and competitiveness or loss of interest in and intimacy with the sibling (Dunn, 1996).

Sibling relations can be a laboratory for conflict resolution. Siblings are motivated to make up after quarrels, as they know they will see each other every day. They learn that expressing anger does not end a relationship. Children are more apt to squabble with same-sex siblings; two brothers quarrel more than any other combination (Cicirelli, 1976, 1995).

Siblings influence each other, not only *directly,* through their interactions with each other, but also *indirectly* through their impact on each other's relationship with their parents. Parents' experience with an older sibling influences their expectations and treatment of a younger one (Brody, 2004). Conversely, behavior patterns a child establishes with parents tend to spill over into the child's behavior with siblings. In a study of 101 English families, when the parent-child relationship was warm and affectionate, siblings tended to have positive relationships as well. When the parent-child relationship was conflictual, sibling conflict was more likely (Pike et al., 2005).

The Child in the Peer Group

In middle childhood the peer group comes into its own. Groups form naturally among children who live near one another or go to school together and often consist of children of the same racial or ethnic origin and similar socioeconomic status. Children who play together are usually close in age and of the same sex (Hartup, 1992; Pellegrini et al., 2002).

How does the peer group influence children? What determines their acceptance by peers and their ability to make friends?

Guidepost 3

How do relationships with peers change in middle childhood, and what influences affect popularity and choice of friends?

Positive and Negative Effects of Peer Relations

Children benefit from doing things with peers. They develop skills needed for sociability and intimacy, and they gain a sense of belonging. They are motivated to achieve, and they attain a sense of identity. They learn leadership and communication skills, cooperation, roles, and rules.

As children begin to move away from parental influence, the peer group opens new perspectives and frees them to make independent judgments. In comparing themselves with others their age, children can gauge their abilities more realistically and gain a clearer sense of self-efficacy (Bandura, 1994). The peer group helps children learn how to get along in society—how to adjust their needs and desires to those of others, when to yield, and when to stand firm. The peer group offers emotional security. It is reassuring for children to find out that they are not alone in harboring thoughts that might offend an adult.

Same-sex peer groups may help children learn gender-appropriate behaviors and incorporate gender roles into their self-concept. In a two-year study of 106 ethnically diverse but mostly middle-class third through seventh graders, a sense of being typical of one's gender and being content with that gender increased self-esteem and well-being, whereas feeling pressure—from parents, peers, or oneself—to conform to gender stereotypes lessened well-being (Yunger, Carver, & Perry, 2004).

On the negative side, peer groups may reinforce **prejudice:** unfavorable attitudes toward outsiders, especially members of certain racial or ethnic groups. Children tend to be biased toward children like themselves, but these biases, except for a preference for children of the same sex, diminish with age and cognitive development (Powlishta, Serbin, Doyle, & White, 1994). Prejudice and discrimination can do real damage. In a five-year longitudinal study of 714 African American 10- to 12-year-olds, those who saw themselves as targets of discrimination tended to show symptoms of depression or conduct problems during the next five years (Brody et al., 2006). In a study of 253 English children, prejudice against refugees was reduced by *extended contact:* reading them stories about close friendships between English children and refugee children, followed by group discussions (Cameron, Rutland, Brown, & Douch, 2006).

The peer group also can foster antisocial tendencies. Preadolescent children are especially susceptible to pressure to conform. Of course, some degree of conformity to group standards is healthy. It is unhealthy when it becomes destructive or prompts young people to act against their better judgment. It is usually in the company of peers that some children shoplift and begin to use drugs (Hartup, 1992).

prejudice Unfavorable attitude toward members of certain groups outside one's own, especially racial or ethnic groups.

What's Your View?

• How can parents and schools reduce racial, religious, and ethnic prejudice?

Popularity

Popularity becomes more important in middle childhood. Schoolchildren whose peers like them are likely to be well adjusted as adolescents. Those who are not accepted by peers or who are overly aggressive are more likely to develop psychological problems, drop out of school, or become delinquent (Hartup, 1992; Kupersmidt & Coie, 1990; Morison & Masten, 1991; Newcomb, Bukowski, & Pattee, 1993; Parker & Asher, 1987).

Popularity can be measured in two ways, and the results may differ. Researchers measure *sociometric popularity* by asking children which peers they like most and least. Such studies have identified five *peer status groups: popular* (youngsters who receive many positive nominations), *rejected* (those who receive many negative nominations), *neglected* (those who receive few nominations of either kind), *controversial* (those who receive many positive and many negative nominations), and *average* (those who do not receive an unusual number of nominations of either kind). *Perceived popularity* is measured by asking children which children are best liked by their peers.

Sociometrically popular children typically have good cognitive abilities, are high achievers, are good at solving social problems, help other children, and are assertive without being disruptive or aggressive. They are kind, trustworthy, cooperative, loyal, and self-disclosing and provide emotional support. Their superior social skills make others enjoy being with them (Cillessen & Mayeux, 2004; LaFontana & Cillessen, 2002; Masten & Coatsworth, 1998; Newcomb et al., 1993).

Children with *perceived* popularity, that is, high status, tend to be physically attractive and to have athletic and, to a lesser extent, academic ability. Whereas aggressive children are unpopular in first grade, they are increasingly accepted, and even popular, among older children (Cillessen & Mayeux, 2004; LaFontana & Cillessen, 2002; Xie, Li, Boucher, Hutchins, & Cairns, 2006).

Children can be *unpopular* (either rejected or neglected) for many reasons. Although some unpopular children are aggressive, others are hyperactive, inattentive, or withdrawn (Dodge, Coie, Pettit, & Price, 1990; Masten & Coatsworth, 1998; Newcomb et al., 1993; A. W. Pope, Bierman, & Mumma, 1991). Still others act silly and immature or anxious and uncertain. Unpopular children are often insensitive to other children's feelings and do not adapt well to new situations (Bierman, Smoot, & Aumiller, 1993). Some show undue interest in being with groups of the other sex (Sroufe, Bennett, Englund, Urban, & Shulman, 1993). Some unpopular children *expect* not to be liked, and this expectation becomes a self-fulfilling prophecy (Rabiner & Coie, 1989).

It is often in the family that children acquire behaviors that affect popularity (Masten & Coatsworth, 1998). Authoritative parents tend to have more popular children than authoritarian parents do (Dekovic & Janssens, 1992). Children of authoritarian parents who punish and threaten are likely to threaten or act mean with other children. They are less popular than children whose authoritative parents reason with them and try to help them understand how another person might feel (C. H. Hart, Ladd, & Burleson, 1990).

Culture can affect criteria for popularity. One study (Chen, Cen, Li, & He, 2005) points to effects of social change resulting from the radical restructuring of China's economic system, particularly since the late 1990s. During that time China shifted from a completely collectivist system in which the people as a whole, through their government, owned all means of production and distribution, toward a more competitive, technologically advanced, market economy with private ownership and its associated individualist values. Researchers administered sociometric measures and peer assessments of social functioning to three cohorts of third and fourth graders in Shanghai schools in 1990, 1998, and 2002. A striking change emerged with regard to shyness and sensitivity. In the 1990 cohort, shy children were accepted by peers and were high in academic achievement, leadership, and teacher-rated competence. By 2002, the results were just the reverse: Shy children tended to be rejected by peers, to be depressed, and to be rated by teachers as low in competence. In the quasi-capitalist society that China has become, social assertiveness and initiative may be more highly appreciated and encouraged than in the past, and shyness and sensitivity may lead to social and psychological difficulties for children.

✔ **Checkpoint**

Can you . . .

◆ Identify positive and negative effects of the peer group?

◆ Identify characteristics of popular and unpopular children, and discuss influences on popularity?

Friendship

Children may spend much of their free time in groups, but only as individuals do they make friends. Popularity is the peer group's opinion of a child, but friendship is a two-way street.

Children look for friends who are like them in age, sex, ethnicity, and interests. The strongest friendships involve equal commitment and mutual give-and-take. Even unpopular children can make friends; but they have fewer friends than popular children and tend to find friends among younger children, other unpopular children, or children in a different class or a different school (George & Hartmann, 1996; Hartup, 1992, 1996a, 1996b; Newcomb & Bagwell, 1995).

With their friends, children learn to communicate and cooperate. They help each other weather stressful situations, such as starting at a new school or adjusting to parents' divorce. The inevitable quarrels help children learn to resolve conflicts (Furman, 1982; Hartup, 1992, 1996a, 1996b; Hartup & Stevens, 1999; Newcomb & Bagwell, 1995). Friendship seems to help children feel good about themselves, though it's also likely that children who feel good about themselves have an easier time making friends.

Having friends is important because peer rejection and friendlessness in middle childhood may have long-term negative effects. In one longitudinal study, fifth graders who had no friends were more likely than their classmates to have low self-esteem in young adulthood and to show symptoms of depression (Bagwell, Newcomb, & Bukowski, 1998).

Children's concepts of friendship and the ways they act with their friends change with age, reflecting cognitive and emotional growth. Preschool friends play together, but friendship among school-age children is deeper and more stable. Children cannot be or have true friends until they achieve the cognitive maturity to consider other people's views and needs as well as their own (Hartup, 1992; Hartup & Stevens, 1999; Newcomb & Bagwell, 1995). On the basis of interviews with more than 250 people between ages 3 and 45, Robert Selman (1980; Selman & Selman, 1979) traced changing conceptions of friendship through five overlapping stages (Table 10-1). He found that most school-age children are in stage 2 (reciprocal friendship based on self-interest), but some older children, ages 9 and up, may be in stage 3 (intimate, mutually shared relationships).

Friends often share secrets—and laughs—as Anna and Christina are doing here. Friendships deepen and become more stable in middle childhood, reflecting cognitive and emotional growth. Girls tend to have fewer, more intimate, friends than boys.

Table 10-1	Selman's Stages of Friendship	
Stage	**Description**	**Example**
Stage 0: Momentary playmateship (ages 3 to 7)	On this *undifferentiated* level of friendship, children are egocentric and have trouble considering another person's point of view; they tend to think only about what they want from a relationship. Most very young children define their friends in terms of physical closeness and value them for material or physical attributes.	"She lives on my street" or "He has the Power Rangers."
Stage 1: One-way assistance (ages 4 to 9)	On this *unilateral* level, a "good friend" does what the child wants the friend to do.	"She's not my friend anymore, because she wouldn't go with me when I wanted her to" or "He's my friend because he always says yes when I want to borrow his eraser."
Stage 2: Two-way fair-weather cooperation (ages 6 to 12)	This *reciprocal* level overlaps stage 1. It involves give-and-take but still serves many separate self-interests, rather than the common interests of the two friends.	"We are friends; we do things for each other" or "A friend is someone who plays with you when you don't have anybody else to play with."
Stage 3: Intimate, mutually shared relationships (ages 9 to 15)	On this *mutual* level, children view a friendship as having a life of its own. It is an ongoing, systematic, committed relationship that incorporates more than doing things for each other. Friends become possessive and demand exclusivity.	"It takes a long time to make a close friend, so you really feel bad if you find out that your friend is trying to make other friends too."
Stage 4: Autonomous interdependence (beginning at age 12)	In this *interdependent stage,* children respect friends' needs for both dependency and autonomy.	"A good friendship is a real commitment, a risk you have to take; you have to support and trust and give, but you have to be able to let go too."

Sources: Selman, 1980; Selman & Selman, 1979.

Checkpoint

Can you . . .

- ◆ List characteristics children look for in friends?
- ◆ Tell how age and gender affect friendships?

School-age children distinguish among "best friends," "good friends," and "casual friends" on the basis of intimacy and time spent together (Hartup & Stevens, 1999). Children this age typically have three to five best friends but usually play with only one or two at a time (Hartup, 1992; Hartup & Stevens, 1999). School-age girls seem to care less about having many friends than about having a few close friends they can rely on. Boys have more friendships, but they tend to be less intimate and affectionate (Furman, 1982; Furman & Buhrmester, 1985; Hartup & Stevens, 1999).

Guidepost 4

What are the most common forms of aggressive behavior in middle childhood, and what influences contribute to such behavior?

Aggression and Bullying

Aggression declines and changes in form during the early school years. After age 6 or 7, most children become less aggressive as they grow less egocentric, more empathic, more cooperative, and better able to communicate. They can now put themselves in someone else's place, can understand another person's motives, and can find positive ways of asserting themselves. *Instrumental aggression,* aggression aimed at achieving an objective—the hallmark of the preschool period—becomes much less common (Coie & Dodge, 1998). However, as aggression declines overall, *hostile aggression,* aggression intended to hurt another person, proportionately increases (Coie & Dodge, 1998), often taking verbal rather than physical form (Pellegrini & Archer, 2005).

A small minority of children do not learn to control physical aggression (Coie & Dodge, 1998). These children tend to have social and psychological problems, but it is not clear whether aggression causes these problems or is a response to them, or both (Crick & Grotpeter, 1995). Highly aggressive children often egg each other on to antisocial acts. Thus, school-age boys who are physically aggressive may become juvenile delinquents in adolescence (Broidy et al., 2003).

Although aggressors tend to be personally disliked, physically aggressive boys and some relationally aggressive girls (those who, for example, talk behind another girl's back or exclude her socially) are perceived as among the most popular in the classroom (Cillessen & Mayeux, 2004; Rodkin, Farmer, Pearl, & Van Acker, 2000). In a study of peer-rejected fourth graders, aggressive boys tended to gain in social status by the end of fifth grade, suggesting that behavior shunned by younger children may be seen as cool or glamorous by preadolescents (Sandstrom & Coie, 1999). In a longitudinal study of a multiethnic group of 905 urban fifth through ninth graders, physical aggression became less disapproved as children moved into adolescence, and relational aggression was increasingly reinforced by high status among peers (Cillessen & Mayeux, 2004).

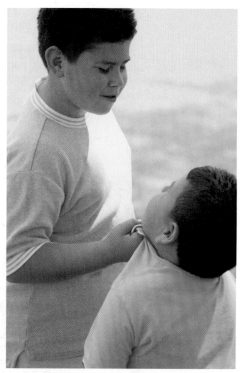

Aggressive boys tend to gain in social status by the end of fifth grade, suggesting that bullying behavior may be seen as cool or glamorous by preadolescents.

Types of Aggression and Social Information Processing What makes children act aggressively? One answer may lie in the way they process social information: what features of the social environment they pay attention to and how they interpret what they perceive (Crick & Dodge, 1994, 1996).

Instrumental, or *proactive,* aggressors view force and coercion as effective ways to get what they want. They act deliberately, not out of anger. In social learning terms, they are aggressive because they expect to be rewarded for it; and when they *are* rewarded by getting what they want, their belief in the effectiveness of aggression is reinforced (Crick & Dodge, 1996). In contrast, a child who is accidentally bumped in line may push back angrily, assuming that the other child bumped her on purpose. This is hostile, or *reactive,* aggression. Such children often have a **hostile attribution bias;** they see other children as trying to hurt them, and they strike out in retaliation or self-defense (Crick & Dodge, 1996; de Castro, Veerman, Koops, Bosch, & Monshouwer, 2002; Waldman, 1996).

Children who seek dominance and control may react aggressively to threats to their status, which they may attribute to hostility (de Castro et al., 2002; Erdley et al., 1997). Rejected children and those exposed to harsh parenting also tend to have a hostile attribution bias (Coie & Dodge, 1998; Masten & Coatsworth, 1998; Weiss, Dodge, Bates, & Pettit, 1992). Since people often *do* become hostile toward someone who acts aggressively toward them, a hostile bias may become a self-fulfilling prophecy, setting in motion a cycle of aggression (de Castro et al., 2002). Hostile attribution bias becomes more common between ages 6 and 12 (Aber, Brown, & Jones, 2003).

Aggressors need to alter the way they process social information so that they do not interpret aggression as either useful or justified. Adults can help children curb aggression by teaching them how to recognize when they are getting angry and how to control their anger. In a New York City school study, children exposed to a conflict resolution curriculum that involved discussions and group role-playing showed less hostile attribution bias, less aggression, fewer behavior problems, and more effective responses to social situations than children who did not participate in the program (Aber et al., 2003).

hostile attribution bias
Tendency to perceive others as trying to hurt one and to strike out in retaliation or self-defense.

Does Media Violence Stimulate Aggression? Children spend more time on entertainment media than on any other activity besides school and sleeping. On average, children spend about four hours a day in front of a television or computer screen—some much more than that (Anderson, Berkowitz, et al., 2003).

About 6 out of 10 U.S. television programs portray violence, usually glamorized, glorified, or trivialized (Yokota & Thompson. 2000), in addition to the constant, repetitive news coverage of natural disasters and violent acts. Among 50 major televised sporting events, such as the Super Bowl, 49 percent of commercial breaks contained at least one commercial showing unsafe behavior or violence (Tamburro, Gordon, D'Apolito, & Howard, 2004). Music videos disproportionately feature violence against women and blacks. The motion picture, music, and video game industries aggressively market violent, adult-rated products to children (AAP Committee on Public Education, 2001).

Because of the high proportion of their time that children spend with media, the images they see can become primary role models and sources of information about how people behave in the real world. The vast preponderance of experimental, longitudinal, epidemiological, and cross-cultural studies supports a causal relationship between viewing media violence and aggressive behavior in childhood, adolescence, and adulthood. In fact, the strongest single correlate of violent behavior is previous exposure to violence (AAP Committee on Public Education, 2001; Anderson, Berkowitz, et al., 2003; Anderson, Huston, Schmitt, Linebarger, & Wright, 2001; Huesmann, Moise-Titus, Podolski, & Eron, 2003).

How does media violence lead to long-term aggressiveness? It provides visceral thrills without showing the human cost and leads children to view aggression as acceptable. Children who see both heroes and villains achieving their aims through violence are likely to conclude that force is an effective way to resolve conflicts. They may learn to take violence for granted and may be less likely to intervene when they see it. The more realistically violence is portrayed, the more likely it is to be accepted (AAP Committee on Public Education, 2001; Anderson, Berkowitz, et al., 2003). Furthermore, each hour that children spend watching violent television reduces time spent with friends. Thus, violent TV fare may set off a cycle in which frequent viewers become more aggressive, and their behavior leads to social isolation and, in turn, to viewing more violent television (Bickham & Rich, 2006).

Children are more vulnerable than adults to the influence of televised violence (AAP Committee on Public Education, 2001; Coie & Dodge, 1998). Classic social learning research suggests that children imitate filmed models even more than live models (Bandura, Ross, & Ross, 1963). The influence is stronger if the child believes the violence on the screen is real, identifies with the violent character, finds that character attractive, or watches without parental supervision or intervention (Anderson, Berkowitz, et al., 2003; Coie & Dodge, 1998). Highly aggressive children are more strongly affected by media violence than are less aggressive children (Anderson, Berkowitz et al., 2003).

The long-term influence of televised violence is greater in middle childhood than at earlier ages (Eron & Huesmann, 1986). Among 427 children whose viewing habits were studied at age 8, the best predictor of aggressiveness at age 19 was the degree of violence in the shows they had watched as children (Eron, 1980, 1982). In a follow-up study, the amount of television viewed at age 8 and the preference among boys for violent shows predicted the severity of criminal offenses at age 30 (Huesmann, 1986; Huesmann & Eron, 1984).

Less research has been done on effects of newer, interactive media, such as video games and the Internet, but initial studies suggest that "effects of child-initiated virtual violence may be more profound than those of passive media, such as television." Rather than merely let a child observe rewards for violent behavior, video games "place the child in the role of the aggressor and reward him or her for successful violent behavior" (AAP Committee on Public Education, 2001, pp. 1223–1224). In experimental studies, young people, after playing video games, have shown decreases in prosocial behavior and increases in aggressive thoughts and violent retaliation to provocation (Anderson, 2000).

Media-induced aggressiveness can be minimized by cutting down on television use and by parental monitoring and guidance of the shows children watch (Anderson, Berkowitz, et al., 2003). The American Academy of Pediatrics Committee on Public Education (2001) recommends that parents limit children's media exposure to one to two hours a day. Third and fourth graders

Research shows that children who see televised violence tend to act aggresssively. When the violence is child-initiated, as in video games, the effect may be even stronger.

who participated in a six-month curriculum aimed at motivating them to monitor and reduce the time they spent on television, videotapes, and video games showed significant decreases in peer-rated aggression, as compared with a control group (Robinson, Wilde, Navacruz, Haydel, & Varady, 2001).

Bullies and Victims Aggression becomes **bullying** when it is deliberately, persistently directed against a particular target: a victim. Bullying can be physical (hitting, punching, kicking, or damaging or taking of personal belongings), verbal (name-calling or threatening), or relational or emotional (isolating and gossiping, often behind the victim's back) (Berger, 2007; Veenstra et al., 2005). Bullying can be *proactive*—done to show dominance, bolster power, or win admiration—or *reactive,* responding to a real or imagined attack. *Cyberbullying*—posting negative comments or derogatory photos of the victim on a website—has become increasingly common (Berger, 2007).

Twenty-four percent of U.S. primary schools, 42 percent of middle schools, and 21 percent of high schools report student bullying at school at least once a week (Guerino, Hurwitz, Noonan, & Kaffenberger, 2006). Bullying is a problem in other industrialized countries as well (Hara, 2002; Kanetsuna & Smith, 2002; Ruiz & Tanaka, 2001). In a survey of 50,000 children in 34 European countries, almost one-third of the children said they were bullies, victims, or both (Currie et al., 2004). In Japan and Korea, school bullying has been associated with a growing wave of student suicide and suicidal thoughts and behavior (Kim, Koh, & Leventhal, 2005; Rios-Ellis, Bellamy, & Shoji, 2000).

Bullying may reflect a genetic tendency toward aggressiveness combined with environmental influences, such as coercive parents and antisocial friends (Berger, 2007). Most bullies are boys who tend to victimize other boys; female bullies tend to target other girls (Berger, 2007; Pellegrini & Long, 2002; Veenstra et al., 2005). Male bullies tend to use overt, physical aggression; female bullies may use relational aggression (Boulton, 1995; Nansel et al., 2001). Patterns of bullying and victimization may become established as early as kindergarten; as tentative peer groups form, aggressors soon get to know which children make the easiest targets. Physical bullying declines with age, but other forms of bullying increase, especially at ages 11 to 15. Whereas younger children reject an aggressive child,

What's Your View?

• What can and should be done about children's exposure to media violence?

bullying Aggression deliberately and persistently directed against a particular target, or victim, typically one who is weak, vulnerable, and defenseless.

by early adolescence bullies are often dominant, respected, feared, and even liked (Berger, 2007).

Unlike the pattern for bullying, the likelihood of *being* bullied decreases steadily. As children get older, most of them may learn how to discourage bullying, leaving a smaller pool of available victims (Pellegrini & Long, 2002; P. K. Smith & Levan, 1995). Most victims are small, passive, weak, and submissive and may blame themselves for being bullied. Other victims are provocative; they goad their attackers, and they may even attack other children themselves (Berger, 2007; Veenstra et al., 2005).

Risk factors for victimization seem to be similar across cultures (Schwartz, Chang, & Farver, 2001). Victims do not fit in. They tend to be anxious, depressed, cautious, quiet, and submissive and to cry easily, or to be argumentative and provocative (Hodges, Boivin, Vitaro, & Bukowski, 1999; Olweus, 1995; Veenstra et al., 2005). They have few friends and may live in harsh, punitive family environments (Nansel et al., 2001; Schwartz, Dodge, Pettit, Bates, & Conduct Problems Prevention Research Group, 2000). Victims are apt to have low self-esteem, though it is not clear whether low self-esteem leads to or follows from victimization (Boulton & Smith, 1994; Olweus, 1995). In a study of 5,749 Canadian children, those who were overweight were most likely to become either victims or bullies (Janssen, Craig, Boyce, & Pickett, 2004).

Bullying, especially emotional bullying, is harmful to both bullies and victims—and can even be fatal (Berger, 2007). Bullies are at increased risk of delinquency, crime, or alcohol abuse. In the wave of school shootings since 1994, the perpetrators often had been victims of bullying (Anderson, Kaufman, et al., 2001). Victims of chronic bullying tend to develop behavior problems. They may become more aggressive themselves or may become depressed (Schwartz, McFadyen-Ketchum, Dodge, Pettit, & Bates, 1998; Veenstra et al., 2005). Furthermore, frequent bullying affects the school atmosphere, leading to widespread underachievement, alienation from school, stomachaches and headaches, reluctance to go to school, and frequent absences (Berger, 2007).

The U.S. Department of Health and Human Services has promoted Steps to Respect, a program for grades 3 to 6 that aims to (1) increase staff awareness and responsiveness to bullying, (2) teach students social and emotional skills, and (3) foster socially responsible beliefs. A randomized controlled study of 1,023 third to sixth graders found a reduction in playground bullying and argumentative behavior and an increase in harmonious interactions among children who participated in the program, as well as less bystander incitement to bullying (Frey et al., 2005). A *whole-school* approach in Norway, which involved educational leaders, teachers, and students, reduced bullying by 32 to 49 percent. However, the outcomes of most such programs in many countries have been disappointing (Berger, 2007).

Checkpoint

Can you . . .

◆ Tell how aggression changes during middle childhood, and how social information processing and media violence can contribute to it?

◆ Describe how patterns of bullying and victimization become established and change?

Guidepost 5

What emotional disorders may develop in childhood, and how are they treated?

Mental Health

The term *mental health* is a misnomer because it usually refers to emotional health. Although most children are fairly well adjusted, at least 1 in 10 children and adolescents has a diagnosed mental disturbance severe enough to cause some impairment (Leslie, Newman, Chesney, & Perrin, 2005). Diagnosis of mental disorders in children is important because these disorders can lead to psychiatric disorders in adulthood (Kim-Cohen et al., 2003). In fact, half of all mental disorders begin by age 14 (Kessler et al., 2005).

Families characterized by frequent conflict, recurrent episodes of anger and aggression, and cold, unsupportive, or neglectful parenting may leave children vulnerable to long-term physical and mental health problems, such as antisocial behavior, delinquency, anxiety, depression, and suicide. Children growing up in such families tend to be deficient in control and expression of emotions and in social competence. The cumulative risk is worsened when families live in poor, violent, or stressful neighborhoods; or when the children are genetically predisposed to overly reactive or inhibited temperaments (Repetti et al., 2002).

Let's look at several common emotional disturbances and then at types of treatment.

Common Emotional Disturbances

Children with emotional, behavioral, and developmental problems tend to be an underserved group. Compared with other children who have special health care needs, they are more likely to have conditions that affect their daily activities and cause them to miss school. They often have chronic physical conditions. Many of them lack adequate health insurance and have unmet health care needs (Bethell, Read, & Blumberg, 2005).

A reported 55.7 percent of children diagnosed with emotional, behavioral, and developmental problems have *disruptive conduct disorders:* aggression, defiance, or antisocial behavior. Almost all the rest, 43.5 percent, have *anxiety* or *mood disorders:* feeling sad, depressed, unloved, nervous, fearful, or lonely (Bethell et al., 2005).

Disruptive Conduct Disorders Temper tantrums and defiant, argumentative, hostile, or deliberately annoying behavior—common among 4- and 5-year-olds— typically are outgrown by middle childhood. When such a pattern of behavior persists until age 8, children (usually boys) may be diagnosed with **oppositional defiant disorder (ODD),** a pattern of defiance, disobedience, and hostility toward adult authority figures lasting at least six months and going beyond the bounds of normal childhood behavior. Children with ODD constantly fight, argue, lose their temper, snatch things, blame others, and are angry and resentful. They have few friends, are in constant trouble in school, and test the limits of adults' patience (APA, 2000; National Library of Medicine, 2004).

Some children with ODD also have **conduct disorder (CD),** a persistent, repetitive pattern, beginning at an early age, of aggressive, antisocial acts, such as truancy, setting fires, habitual lying, fighting, bullying, theft, vandalism, assaults, and drug and alcohol use (APA, 2000; National Library of Medicine, 2003). Between 6 and 16 percent of boys and between 2 and 9 percent of girls under age 18 in the United States have been diagnosed with clinical levels of externalizing behavior or conduct problems (Roosa et al., 2005). Some 11- to 13-year-olds progress from conduct disorder to criminal violence—mugging, rape, and break-ins—and by age 17 may be frequent, serious offenders (Coie & Dodge, 1998). Between 25 and 50 percent of these highly antisocial children become antisocial adults (USDHHS, 1999b).

What determines whether a particular child with antisocial tendencies will become severely and chronically antisocial? Neurobiological deficits, such as weak stress-regulating mechanisms, may fail to warn children to restrain themselves from dangerous or risky behavior. Such deficits may be genetically influenced or may be brought on by adverse environments such as hostile parenting or family conflict, or both (van Goozen, Fairchild, Snoek, & Harold, 2007). Also influential are stressful life events and association with deviant peers (Roosa et al., 2005).

oppositional defiant disorder (ODD) Pattern of behavior, persisting into middle childhood, marked by negativity, hostility, and defiance.

conduct disorder (CD) Repetitive, persistent pattern of aggressive, antisocial behavior violating societal norms or the rights of others.

School Phobia and Other Anxiety Disorders   Children with **school phobia** have an unrealistic fear of going to school. Some children have realistic reasons to fear going to school: a sarcastic teacher, overly demanding work, or a bully to avoid. In such cases, the environment may need changing, not the child. True school phobia may be a type of **separation anxiety disorder,** a condition involving excessive anxiety for at least four weeks concerning separation from home or from people to whom the child is attached. Although separation anxiety is normal in infancy, when it persists in older children it is cause for concern. Separation anxiety disorder affects some 4 percent of children and young adolescents and may persist through the college years. These children often come from close-knit, caring families. They may develop the disorder spontaneously or after a stressful event, such as the death of a pet, an illness, or a move to a new school (APA, 2000; Harvard Medical School, 2004a). Many children with separation anxiety also show symptoms of depression (USDHHS, 1999b).

Sometimes school phobia may be a form of **social phobia,** or *social anxiety:* extreme fear and/or avoidance of social situations such as speaking in class or meeting an acquaintance on the street. Social phobia affects about 5 percent of children; it runs in families, so there may be a genetic component. Often these phobias are triggered by traumatic experiences, such as a child's mind going blank when the child is called on in class (Beidel & Turner, 1998). Social anxiety tends to increase with age, whereas separation anxiety decreases (Costello et al., 2003).

Some children have a **generalized anxiety disorder,** not focused on any specific part of their lives. These children worry about just about everything: school grades, storms, earthquakes, and hurting themselves on the playground. They tend to be self-conscious, self-doubting, and excessively concerned with meeting the expectations of others. They seek approval and need constant reassurance, but their worry seems independent of performance or of how they are regarded by others (APA, 1994; Harvard Medical School, 2004a; USDHHS, 1999b). Far less common is **obsessive-compulsive disorder (OCD).** Children with this disorder may be obsessed by repetitive, intrusive thoughts, images, or impulses (often involving irrational fears); or may show compulsive behaviors, such as constant hand-washing; or both (APA, 2000; Harvard Medical School, 2004a; USDHHS, 1999b).

Anxiety disorders tend to run in families (Harvard Medical School, 2004a) and are twice as common among girls as among boys. The heightened female vulnerability to anxiety begins as early as age 6. Females also are more susceptible to depression, which is similar to anxiety and often goes hand in hand with it (Lewinsohn, Gotlib, Lewinsohn, Seeley, & Allen, 1998). Both anxiety and depression may be neurologically based or may stem from insecure attachment, exposure to an anxious or depressed parent, or other early experiences that make children feel a lack of control over what happens around them (Chorpita & Barlow, 1998; Harvard Medical School, 2004a). Parents who reward an anxious child with attention to the anxiety may unwittingly perpetuate it through operant conditioning (Harvard Medical School, 2004a).

Childhood Depression   **Childhood depression** is a disorder of mood that goes beyond normal, temporary sadness. Depression is estimated to occur in 2 percent of elementary school children (NCHS, 2004). Symptoms include inability to have fun or concentrate, fatigue, extreme activity or apathy, crying, sleep problems, weight change, physical complaints, feelings of worthlessness, a prolonged sense of friendlessness, or frequent thoughts about death or suicide. Childhood depression may signal the beginning of a recurrent problem that is likely to persist into adulthood (Birmaher, 1998; Birmaher et al., 1996; Cicchetti & Toth, 1998; Kye & Ryan, 1995; USDHHS, 1999b; Weissman et al., 1999).

The exact causes of childhood depression are unknown, but depressed children tend to come from families with high levels of parental depression, anxiety, substance abuse, or antisocial behavior. The atmosphere in such families may increase children's risk of depression (Cicchetti & Toth, 1998; USDHHS, 1999b).

Researchers have found several specific genes related to depression. The gene *5-HTT* helps to control the brain chemical serotonin and affects mood. In a longitudinal study of 847 people born in a single year in Dunedin, New Zealand, those who had two short versions of this gene were more likely to become depressed than those who had two long versions (Caspi et al., 2003). A short form of another gene, *SERT-s,* which also controls serotonin, is associated with enlargement of the pulvinar, a brain region involved in negative emotions (Young et al., 2007).

Children as young as 5 or 6 can accurately report depressed moods and feelings that forecast later trouble, from academic problems to major depression and ideas of suicide (Ialongo, Edelsohn, & Kellam, 2001). Depression often emerges during the transition to middle school and may be related to stiffer academic pressures (Cicchetti & Toth, 1998), weak self-efficacy beliefs, and lack of personal investment in academic success (Rudolph, Lambert, Clark, & Kurlakowsky, 2001). Depression becomes more prevalent during adolescence and is discussed further in Chapter 11.

Treatment Techniques

Psychological treatment for emotional disturbances can take several forms. In **individual psychotherapy,** a therapist sees a child one-on-one, to help the child gain insights into his or her personality and relationships and to interpret feelings and behavior. Such treatment may be helpful at a time of stress, such as the death of a parent or parental divorce, even when a child has not shown signs of disturbance. Child psychotherapy is usually more effective when combined with counseling for the parents.

In **family therapy,** the therapist sees the family together, observes how members interact, and points out both growth-producing and growth-inhibiting or destructive patterns of family functioning. Therapy can help parents confront their conflicts and begin to resolve them. This is often the first step toward resolving the child's problems as well.

Behavior therapy, or *behavior modification,* is a form of psychotherapy that uses principles of learning theory to eliminate undesirable behaviors or to develop desirable ones. A statistical analysis of many studies found that psychotherapy is generally effective with children and adolescents, but behavior therapy is more effective than nonbehavioral methods. Results are best when treatment is targeted to specific problems and desired outcomes (Weisz, Weiss, Han, Granger, & Morton, 1995). *Cognitive behavioral therapy,* which seeks to change negative thoughts through gradual exposure, modeling, rewards, or talking to oneself has proven the most effective treatment for anxiety disorders in children and adolescents (Harvard Medical School, 2004a).

When children have limited verbal and conceptual skills or have suffered emotional trauma, **art therapy** can help them describe what is troubling them without the need to put their feelings into words. The child may express deep emotions through choice of colors and subjects to depict (Kozlowska & Hanney, 1999). Observing how a family plans, carries out, and discusses an art project can reveal patterns of family interactions (Kozlowska & Hanney, 1999).

individual psychotherapy
Psychological treatment in which a therapist sees a troubled person one-on-one.

family therapy Psychological treatment in which a therapist sees the whole family together to analyze patterns of family functioning.

behavior therapy Therapeutic approach using principles of learning theory to encourage desired behaviors or eliminate undesired ones; also called *behavior modification.*

art therapy Therapeutic approach that allows a person to express troubled feelings without words, using a variety of art materials and media.

In play thereapy, the therapist observes as as a child acts out troubled feelings, often using developmentally appropriate materials such as dolls.

play therapy Therapeutic approach that uses play to help a child cope with emotional distress.

drug therapy Administration of drugs to treat emotional disorders.

Checkpoint

Can you . . .

♦ Discuss causes, symptoms, and treatments of common emotional disorders?

Guidepost 6

How do the stresses of modern life affect children, and why are some children more resilient than others?

Play therapy, in which a child plays freely while a therapist occasionally comments, asks questions, or makes suggestions, has proven effective with a variety of emotional, cognitive, and social problems, especially when consultation with parents or other close family members is part of the process (Athansiou, 2001; Bratton & Ray, 2002; Leblanc & Ritchie, 2001; Ryan & Needham, 2001; Wilson & Ryan, 2001).

The use of **drug therapy**—antidepressants, stimulants, tranquilizers, or antipsychotic medications—to treat childhood emotional disorders is controversial. During the past decade the rate at which antipsychotic medications are prescribed for children and adolescents has more than quintupled. In 2002, 1,438 in every 100,000 children and adolescents took antipsychotic drugs, compared with only 275 per 100,000 during the mid-1990s (Olfson, Blanco, Liu, Moreno, & Laje, 2006). Sufficient research on the effectiveness and safety of many of these drugs, especially for children, is lacking (Murray, de Vries, & Wong, 2004; USDHHS, 1999b; Wong, Murray, Camilleri-Novak, & Stephens, 2004; Zito et al., 2003).

The use of *selective serotonin reuptake inhibitors (SSRIs)* to treat obsessive-compulsive, depressive, and anxiety disorders increased rapidly in the 1990s (Leslie et al., 2005) but has since slipped by about 20 percent (Daly, 2005). Some studies show moderate risks of suicidal thought and behavior for children and adolescents taking antidepressants, whereas others show no significant added risk (Hammad, Laughren, & Racoosin, 2006; Simon, Savarino, Operskalski, & Wang, 2006) or lessened risk (Simon, 2006). A current analysis of 27 randomized, placebo-controlled studies found that the benefits of antidepressant use for children and adolescents outweigh the risks (Bridge et al., 2007). (Use of antidepressant drugs for adolescent depression is further discussed in Chapter 11.)

Stress and Resilience

Stressful events are part of childhood, and most young people learn to cope. Stress that becomes overwhelming, however, can lead to psychological problems. Severe stressors, such as kidnapping or child abuse, may have long-term effects on physical and psychological well-being. Yet some individuals show remarkable resilience in surmounting such ordeals.

Stresses of Modern Life   The child psychologist David Elkind (1981, 1986, 1997, 1998) has called today's child the "hurried child." He warns that the pressures of modern life are forcing children to grow up too soon and are making their childhood too stressful. Today's children are expected to succeed in school, to compete in sports, and to meet parents' emotional needs. Children are exposed to many adult problems on television and in real life before they have mastered the problems of childhood. They know about sex and violence, and they often must shoulder adult responsibilities. Many children move frequently and have to change schools and leave old friends. The tightly scheduled pace of life can be stressful. Yet children are not small adults. They feel and think like children, and they need the years of childhood for healthy development.

Given how much stress children are exposed to, it should not be surprising that anxiety in childhood has increased greatly (Twenge, 2000). Fears of

Table 10-2	Children's Age-Related Reactions to Trauma

Age	Typical Reactions
5 years or less	Fear of separation from parent Crying, whimpering, screaming, trembling Immobility or aimless motion Frightened facial expressions Excessive clinging Regressive behaviors (thumbsucking, bed-wetting, fear of dark)
6 to 11 years	Extreme withdrawal Disruptive behavior Inability to pay attention Stomachaches or other symptoms with no physical basis Declining school performance, refusal to go to school Depression, anxiety, guilt, irritability, or emotional numbing Regressive behavior (nightmares, sleep problems, irrational fears, outbursts of anger or fighting)
12 to 17 years	Flashbacks, nightmares Emotional numbing, confusion Avoidance of reminders of the traumatic event Revenge fantasies Withdrawal, isolation Substance abuse Problems with peers, antisocial behavior Physical complaints School avoidance, academic decline Sleep disturbances Depression, suicidal thoughts

Source: NIMH, 2001a.

danger and death are the most consistent fears of children at all ages (Gullone, 2000; Silverman, La Greca, & Wasserstein, 1995). This intense anxiety about safety may reflect the high rates of crime and violence in the larger society—including rare but highly publicized killings in schools (Anderson, Kaufman, et al., 2001; DeVoe et al., 2004; Garbarino, Dubrow, Kostelny, & Pardo, 1992, 1998; see Box 12-1 on page 414). In 2003–2004, 94 percent of middle schools and 74 percent of primary schools reported incidents of violent crime, such as rape, robbery, and physical attacks with or without weapons (Guerino et al., 2006).

Findings about children's fears have been corroborated in a wide range of developed and developing societies in addition to the United States. Children of low socioeconomic status—who may see their environment as threatening—tend to be more fearful than children of higher socioeconomic status (Gullone, 2000; Ollendick, Yang, King, Dong, & Akande, 1996). Children who grow up constantly surrounded by violence often have trouble concentrating and sleeping. Some become aggressive, and some come to take brutality for granted. Many do not allow themselves to become attached to other people for fear of more hurt and loss (Garbarino et al., 1992, 1998).

Children are more susceptible than adults to psychological harm from a traumatic event such as war or terrorism, and their reactions vary with age (Wexler, Branski, & Kerem, 2006; Table 10-2). Younger children, who do not understand why the event occurred, tend to focus on the consequences. Older children are more aware of, and worried about, the underlying forces that caused the event (Hagan et al., 2005).

BOX 10-1 Research *in Action*

Talking to Children about Terrorism and War

In today's world, caring adults are faced with the challenge of explaining violence, terrorism, and war to children. Although difficult, these conversations are extremely important. They give parents an opportunity to help their children feel more secure and better understand the world in which they live. Here are some pointers from the American Academy of Child & Adolescent Psychiatry:

1. *Listen to children.* Create a time and place for children to ask questions and help them express themselves. Sometimes children are more comfortable drawing pictures or playing with toys rather than talking about their feelings.
2. *Answer their questions.* When you answer tough questions about violence, be honest. Use words the child can understand, and try not to overload him or her with too much information. You may have to repeat yourself. Be consistent and reassuring.
3. *Provide support.* Children are most comfortable with structure and familiarity. Try to establish a predictable routine. Avoid exposure to violent images on TV and video games. Watch for physical signs of stress, such as trouble sleeping or separation anxiety, and seek professional help if symptoms are persistent and/or pronounced.

Many young children feel confused and anxious when faced with the realities of war and terrorism. By creating an open environment where children are free to ask questions and receive honest, consistent, and supportive messages about how to cope with violence, caring adults can reduce the likelihood of emotional difficulties.

Source: Adapted from American Academy of Child & Adolescent Psychiatry, 2003.

What's Your View?

How might you respond to a 6-year-old who asked you about what happened on September 11?

Check It Out

For more information on this topic go to www.nccev.org. The website of the National Center for Children Exposed to Violence offers many resources and numerous strategies for assisting children exposed to violence, including a page that deals with catastrophic events

The impact of a traumatic event is influenced by the type of event, how much exposure children have to it, and how much they and their families and friends are personally affected. Human-caused disasters, such as terrorism and war, are much harder on children psychologically than natural disasters, such as earthquakes and floods. Exposure to graphic news coverage can worsen the effects (Wexler et al., 2006). Most children who watched news coverage of the September 11, 2001, terrorist attacks on New York and Washington, D.C., experienced profound stress, even if they were not directly affected (Walma van der Molen, 2004).

Children's responses to a traumatic event typically occur in two stages: *first,* fright, disbelief, denial, grief, and relief if their loved ones are unharmed; *second,* several days or weeks later, developmental regression and signs of emotional distress—anxiety, fear, withdrawal, sleep disturbances, pessimism about the future, or play related to themes of the event. If symptoms last for more than a month, the child should receive counseling (Hagan et al., 2005).

Children's reactions to a traumatic event vary with age. For some, the effects may remain for years. Children may lose trust in adults' ability to protect them and may fear that the event will happen again. Children who have previously experienced trauma, such as family or community violence, are most likely to be deeply scarred (NIMH, 2001a). Parents' responses to a violent event or disaster and the way they talk with a child about it strongly influence the child's ability to recover (NIMH, 2001a). Box 10-1 gives some suggestions for talking to children about terrorism and war.

Table 10-3	Characteristics of Resilient Children and Adolescents

Source	Characteristic
Individual	Good intellectual functioning Appealing, sociable, easygoing disposition Self-efficacy, self-confidence, high self-esteem Talents Faith
Family	Close relationship to caring parent figure Authoritative parenting: warmth, structure, high expectations Socioeconomic advantages Connections to extended supportive family networks
Extrafamilial context	Bonds to prosocial adults outside the family Connections to prosocial organizations Attending effective schools

Source: Masten & Coatsworth, 1998, p. 212.

Coping with Stress: The Resilient Child   **Resilient children** are those who maintain their composure and competence under challenge or threat or who bounce back from traumatic events. These children do not possess extraordinary qualities. They simply manage, despite adverse circumstances, to derive strength from resources that promote positive development (Masten, 2001; Table 10-3).

The two most important **protective factors** that seem to help children and adolescents overcome stress and contribute to resilience are good *family relationships* and *cognitive functioning* (Masten & Coatsworth, 1998). Resilient children are likely to have good relationships and strong bonds with at least one supportive parent (Pettit et al., 1997) or caregiver or other caring, competent adult (Masten & Coatsworth, 1998). Resilient children also tend to have high IQs and to be good problem solvers, and their cognitive ability may help them cope with adversity, protect themselves, regulate their behavior, and learn from experience. They may attract the interest of teachers, who can act as guides, confidants, or mentors (Masten & Coatsworth, 1998). They may even have protective genes, which may buffer the effects of an unfavorable environment (Caspi et al., 2002; Kim-Cohen, Moffitt, Caspi, & Taylor, 2004).

Other frequently cited protective factors (Ackerman, Kogos, Youngstrom, Schoff, & Izard, 1999; Eisenberg et al., 2004; Eisenberg et al., 1997; Masten et al., 1990; Masten & Coatsworth, 1998; E. E. Werner, 1993) include the following:

- *The child's temperament or personality:* Resilient children are adaptable, friendly, well liked, independent, and sensitive to others. They are competent and have high self-esteem. They are creative, resourceful, independent, and pleasant to be with. When under stress, they can regulate their emotions by shifting attention to something else.
- *Compensating experiences:* A supportive school environment or successful experiences in studies, sports, or music or with other children or adults can help make up for a destructive home life.
- *Reduced risk:* Children who have been exposed to only one of a number of factors for psychiatric disorder (such as parental discord, low social status, a disturbed mother, a criminal father, and experience in foster care or an institution) are often better able to overcome stress than children who have been exposed to more than one risk factor.

resilient children Children who weather adverse circumstances, function well despite challenges or threats, or bounce back from traumatic events.

protective factors Influences that reduce the impact of early stress and tend to predict positive outcomes.

What's Your View?

- Do you recall an experience with a caring adult that helped you deal with adversity?

✔ **Checkpoint**

Can you . . .

♦ Explain Elkind's concept of the "hurried child"?

♦ Name the most common sources of fear, stress, and anxiety in children?

♦ Identify protective factors that contribute to resilience?

This does not mean that bad things that happen in a child's life do not matter. In general, children with unfavorable backgrounds have more adjustment problems than children with more favorable backgrounds, and even some outwardly resilient children may suffer internal distress that may have long-term consequences (Masten & Coatsworth, 1998). Still, what is heartening about these findings is that negative childhood experiences do not necessarily determine the outcome of a person's life and that many children have the strength to rise above the most difficult circumstances.

Adolescence, too, is a stressful, risk-filled time—more so than middle childhood. Yet most adolescents develop the skills and competence to deal with the challenges they face, as we'll see in Chapters 11 and 12.

Summary and Key Terms

The Developing Self

Guidepost 1: *How do school-age children develop a healthy, realistic self-concept, and how do they show emotional growth?*

- The self-concept becomes more realistic during middle childhood, when, according to a neo-Piagetian model, children form representational systems.

- According to Erikson, the chief source of self-esteem is children's view of their productive competence. This virtue develops through resolution of the fourth psychosocial conflict, industry versus inferiority.

- School-age children have internalized shame and pride and can better understand and regulate negative emotions.

- Empathy and prosocial behavior increase.

- Emotional growth is affected by parents' reactions to displays of negative emotions.

- Emotional regulation involves effortful control.

  representational systems (322)
  industry versus inferiority (323)

The Child in the Family

Guidepost 2: *Guidepost 2: How do parent-child relationships change in middle childhood, and how do family atmosphere and family structure influence children's well-being?*

- School-age children spend less time with parents and are less close to them than before; but relationships with parents continue to be important. Culture influences family relationships and roles.

- The family environment has two major components: family structure and family atmosphere.

- The emotional tone of the home, the way parents handle disciplinary issues and conflict, the effects of parents' work, and the adequacy of financial resources all contribute to family atmosphere.

- Development of coregulation may affect the way a family handles conflicts and discipline.

- The impact of mothers' employment depends on many factors concerning the child, the mother's work and her feelings about it, whether she has a supportive partner, the family's socioeconomic status, and the type of care and degree of monitoring the child receives.

- Poverty can harm children's development indirectly through its effects on parents' well-being and parenting practices.

- Many children today grow up in nontraditional family structures. Other things being equal, children tend to do better in traditional two-parent families than in cohabiting, divorced, single-parent, or stepfamilies. The structure of the family, however, is less important than its effects on family atmosphere.

- Children's adjustment to divorce depends on factors concerning the child, the parents' handling of the situation, custody and visitation arrangements, financial circumstances, contact with the noncustodial parent (usually the father), and a parent's remarriage.

- The amount of conflict in a marriage and the likelihood of its continuing after divorce may influence whether children are better off if the parents stay together.

- In most divorces the mother gets custody, though paternal custody is a growing trend. Quality of contact with a noncustodial father is more important than frequency of contact.

- Joint custody can be beneficial to children when the parents can cooperate. Joint legal custody is more common than joint physical custody.

- Although parental divorce increases the risk of long-term problems for children, most adjust reasonably well.

- Children living with only one parent are at heightened risk of behavioral and academic problems, largely related to socioeconomic status.

- Boys tend to have more trouble than girls in adjusting to divorce and single-parent living but tend to adjust better to the mother's remarriage.

- Studies have found positive developmental outcomes in children living with gay or lesbian parents.

- Adopted children are generally well adjusted, though they face special challenges.
- The roles and responsibilities of siblings in nonindustrialized societies are more structured than in industrialized societies.
- Siblings learn about conflict resolution from their relationships with each other. Relationships with parents affect sibling relationships.

internalizing behaviors (325)

externalizing behaviors (325)

coregulation (325)

The Child in the Peer Group

Guidepost 3: *How do relationships with peers change in middle childhood, and what influences affect popularity and choice of friends?*

- The peer group becomes more important in middle childhood. Peer groups generally consist of children who are similar in age, sex, ethnicity, and socioeconomic status and who live near one another or go to school together.
- The peer group helps children develop social skills, allows them to test and adopt values independent of parents, gives them a sense of belonging, and helps develop their self-concept and gender identity. It also may encourage conformity and prejudice.
- Popularity in middle childhood tends to influence future adjustment. It can be measured sociometrically or by perceived social status, and the results may differ. Popular children tend to have good cognitive abilities and social skills. Behaviors that affect popularity may be derived from family relationships and cultural values.
- Intimacy and stability of friendships increase during middle childhood. Boys tend to have more friends, whereas girls tend to have closer friends.

prejudice (335)

Guidepost 4: *What are the most common forms of aggressive behavior in middle childhood, and what influences contribute to such behavior?*

- During middle childhood, aggression typically declines. Instrumental aggression generally gives way to hostile aggression, often with a hostile bias. Highly aggressive children tend to be unpopular but may gain in status as children move into adolescence.
- Aggressiveness is promoted by exposure to media violence and can extend into adult life.
- Middle childhood is a prime time for bullying, but patterns of bullying and victimization may be established

much earlier. Victims tend to be weak and submissive or argumentative and provocative and to have low self-esteem.
- School interventions can stop or prevent bullying.

hostile attribution bias (340)

bullying (341)

Mental Health

Guidepost 5: *What emotional disorders may develop in childhood, and how are they treated?*

- Common emotional and behavioral disorders among school-age children include disruptive behavioral disorders, anxiety disorders, and childhood depression.
- Treatment techniques include individual psychotherapy, family therapy, behavior therapy, art therapy, play therapy, and drug therapy. Often therapies are used in combination.

oppositional defiant disorder (ODD) (343)

conduct disorder (CD) (343)

school phobia (344)

separation anxiety disorder (344)

social phobia (344)

generalized anxiety disorder (344)

obsessive-compulsive disorder (OCD) (344)

childhood depression (344)

individual psychotherapy (345)

family therapy (345)

behavior therapy (345)

art therapy (345)

play therapy (346)

drug therapy (346)

Guidepost 6: *How do the stresses of modern life affect children, and why are some children more resilient than others?*

- As a result of the pressures of modern life, many children experience stress. Children tend to worry about school, health, and personal safety and may be traumatized by exposure to terrorism or war.
- Resilient children are better able than others to withstand stress. Protective factors involve family relationships, cognitive ability, personality, degree of risk, and compensating experiences.

resilient children (349)

protective factors (349)

What I like in my adolescents is that they have not yet hardened. We all confuse hardening and strength. Strength we must achieve, but not callousness.

—Anaïs Nin, *The Diaries of Anaïs Nin,* Vol. IV

Did You **Know...**

- Adolescence was not recognized as a separate period of life in the Western world until the twentieth century?

- Boys and girls reach sexual maturity earlier in developed countries than in developing countries?

- Nearly half of U.S. adolescents have tried illicit drugs by the time they leave high school?

- Firearm-related deaths of 15- to 19-year-olds are far more common in the United States than in other industrialized countries?

- Adolescent girls in the United States tend to have more confidence in their academic abilities than adolescent boys do?

- Researchers disagree as to whether part-time work is beneficial or harmful to high school students?

These are just a few of the interesting and important topics we will cover in this chapter. In it, we describe the physical transformations of adolescence and how they affect young people's feelings. We look at the not-yet-mature adolescent brain, and we discuss health issues associated with this time of life. Turning to cognitive development, we examine the Piagetian stage of formal operations, which makes it possible for a young person to visualize an ideal world. We also look at changes in information-processing skills and linguistic and moral development. Finally, we explore issues of education and vocational choice. After you have read and studied this chapter, you should be able to answer each of the Guidepost questions on the following page.

Guideposts *for Study*

1. What is adolescence, when does it begin and end, and what opportunities and risks does it entail?

2. What physical changes do adolescents experience, and how do these changes affect them psychologically?

3. What brain developments occur during adolescence, and how do they affect behavior?

4. What are some common health problems in adolescence, and how can they be prevented?

5. How do adolescents' thinking and use of language differ from younger children's?

6. On what basis do adolescents make moral judgments?

7. What influences affect adolescents' school success and their educational and vocational planning and preparation?

Guidepost 1

What is adolescence, when does it begin and end, and what opportunities and risks does it entail?

adolescence Developmental transition between childhood and adulthood entailing major physical, cognitive, and psychosocial changes.

puberty Process by which a person attains sexual maturity and the ability to reproduce.

Adolescence: A Developmental Transition

Rituals to mark a child's coming of age are common in many traditional societies. For example, Apache tribes celebrate a girl's first menstruation with a four-day ritual of sunrise-to-sunset chanting. In most modern societies, the passage from childhood to adulthood is marked, not by a single event, but by a long period known as **adolescence**—a developmental transition that involves physical, cognitive, emotional, and social changes and takes varying forms in different social, cultural, and economic settings.

An important physical change is the onset of **puberty,** the process that leads to sexual maturity, or fertility—the ability to reproduce.* Traditionally, adolescence and puberty were thought to begin at the same time, around age 13, but, as we will discuss, physicians in some Western societies now see pubertal changes well before age 10. In this book, we define adolescence roughly as encompassing the years between 11 and 19 or 20.

Adolescence as a Social Construction

Adolescence is a social construction. There was no such concept in preindustrial societies; there, children were considered adults when they matured physically or began a vocational apprenticeship. Not until the twentieth century was adolescence defined as a separate stage of life in the Western world. Today, adolescence has become a global phenomenon (Box 11-1), though it may take differing forms in different cultures. In most parts of the world, entry into adulthood takes longer and is less clear-cut than in the past. Puberty begins earlier than it used to; and entrance into a vocation occurs later, often requiring longer periods of education or vocational training to prepare for adult responsibilities. Marriage with its attendant responsibilities typically comes later as well. Adolescents spend

*Some people use the term *puberty* to mean the end point of sexual maturation and refer to the process as *pubescence,* but our usage conforms to that of most psychologists today.

BOX 11-1 **Window *on the World***

The Globalization of Adolescence

Young people today live in a global neighborhood, a web of interconnections and interdependencies. Goods, information, electronic images, songs, entertainment, and fads sweep almost instantaneously around the planet. Western youth dance to Latin rhythms, and Arabic girls draw their images of romance from Indian cinema. Maori youth in New Zealand listen to African American rap music to symbolize their separation from adult society.

Adolescence is no longer solely a Western phenomenon. Globalization and modernization have set in motion societal changes the world over. Among these changes are urbanization, longer and healthier lives, reduced birth rates, and smaller families. Earlier puberty and later marriage are increasingly common. More women and fewer children work outside the home. The rapid spread of advanced technologies has made knowledge a prized resource. Young people need more schooling and skills to enter the labor force. Together these changes result in an extended transitional phase between childhood and adulthood.

Puberty in less-developed countries traditionally was marked by initiation rites such as circumcision. Today adolescents in these countries are increasingly identified by their status as students removed from the working world of adults. In this changing world, new pathways are opening up for them. They are less apt to follow in their parents' footsteps and to be guided by their advice. If they work, they are more likely to work in factories than on the family farm.

This does *not* mean that adolescence is the same the world over. The strong hand of culture shapes its meaning differently in different societies. In the United States, adolescents are spending less time with their parents and confiding in them less. In India, adolescents may wear Western clothing and use computers, but they maintain strong family ties, and their life decisions often are influenced by traditional Hindu values. In Western countries, teenage girls strive to be as thin as possible. In Niger and other African countries, obesity is considered beautiful.

In many non-Western countries, adolescent boys and girls seem to live in two separate worlds. In parts of the Middle East, Latin America, Africa, and Asia, puberty brings more restrictions on girls, whose virginity must be protected to uphold family status and ensure girls' marriageability. Boys, on the other hand, gain more freedom and mobility, and their sexual exploits are tolerated by parents and admired by peers.

Puberty heightens preparation for gender roles, which, for girls in most parts of the world, means preparation for domesticity. In Laos, a girl may spend two and a half hours a day husking, washing, and steaming rice. In Istanbul, a girl must learn the proper way to serve tea when a suitor comes to call. While boys are expected to prepare for adult work and to maintain family honor, adolescent girls in many less-developed countries, such as rural regions of China, do not go to school because the skills they would learn would be of no use after they married. Instead, they are expected to spend most of their time helping at home. As a result, girls rarely develop independent thinking and decision-making skills.

This traditional pattern is changing in some parts of the developing world, as women's employment and self-reliance become financial necessities. During the past quarter-century, the advent of public education has enabled more girls to go to school, breaking down some of the taboos and restrictions on feminine activities. Better-educated girls tend to marry later and have fewer children, enabling them to seek skilled employment in the new technological society.

Cultural change is complex; It can be both liberating and challenging. Today's adolescents are charting a new course, not always certain where it will lead. We will further discuss how globalization affects adolescents in Chapter 12.

Source: Larson & Wilson, 2004.

What's Your View?

Can you think of examples from your experience of how globalization affects adolescents?

Check It Out

For more information on the globalization of adolescence, go to www.unfpa.org/adolescents/about.htm. This page, part of the website of the United Nations Population Fund, contains an article on "Adolescent Realities in a Changing World."

much of their time in their own world, largely separate from that of adults (Larson & Wilson, 2004).

Adolescence: A Time of Opportunities and Risks

Adolescence offers opportunities for growth, not only in physical dimensions, but also in cognitive and social competence, autonomy, self-esteem, and intimacy. Young people who have supportive connections with parents, school, and

Checkpoint

Can you . . .

♦ Point out similarities and differences among adolescents in various parts of the world?

♦ Identify risky behavior patterns common during adolescence?

community tend to develop in a positive, healthful way (Youngblade et al., 2007). However, U.S. adolescents today face hazards to their physical and mental well-being, including high death rates from accidents, homicide, and suicide (Eaton et al., 2008). As we will see, risky behaviors may reflect immaturity of the adolescent brain.

However, a national survey of some 14,000 high school students reveals encouraging trends. Since the 1990s, students have become less likely to use alcohol, tobacco, or marijuana; to ride in a car without wearing a seat belt or to ride with a driver who has been drinking; to carry weapons; to have sexual intercourse or to have it without condoms; or to attempt suicide (CDC, 2006d; Eaton et al., 2008). Avoidance of such risky behaviors increases the chances that young people will come through the adolescent years in good physical and mental health.

PHYSICAL DEVELOPMENT

Puberty

Guidepost 2

What physical changes do adolescents experience, and how do these changes affect them psychologically?

The biological changes of puberty, which signal the end of childhood, include rapid growth in height and weight, changes in body proportions and form, and attainment of sexual maturity. These dramatic physical changes are part of a long, complex process of maturation that began before birth, and their psychological ramifications continue into adulthood.

How Puberty Begins: Hormonal Changes

adrenarche Maturation of adrenal glands.

gonadarche Maturation of testes or ovaries.

Puberty results from heightened production of sex-related hormones and takes place in two stages: **adrenarche,** the maturing of the adrenal glands, followed a few years later by **gonadarche,** the maturing of the sex organs.

First, sometime around age 7 or 8 (Susman & Rogol, 2004), the adrenal glands, located above the kidneys, secrete gradually increasing levels of androgens, principally *dehydroepiandrosterone (DHEA)*. DHEA plays a part in the growth of pubic, axillary (armpit), and facial hair, as well as in faster body growth, oilier skin, and the development of body odor. By age 10, levels of DHEA are 10 times what they were between ages 1 and 4 (McClintock & Herdt, 1996).

The precise time when this rush of hormonal activity begins seems to depend on reaching a critical amount of body fat necessary for successful reproduction. Thus, girls with a higher percentage of body fat in early childhood and those who experience unusual weight gain between ages 5 and 9 tend to show earlier pubertal development (Davison, Susman, & Birch, 2003; Lee et al., 2007). Studies suggest that an accumulation of leptin, a hormone in the bloodstream identified as having a role in obesity, may stimulate the hypothalamus to signal the pituitary gland, which in turn may signal the sex glands to increase their secretion of hormones (Chehab, Mounzih, Lu, & Lim, 1997; Clément et al., 1998; O'Rahilly, 1998; Strobel, Camoin, Ozata, & Strosberg, 1998; Susman & Rogol, 2004). Scientists have identified a gene, *GPR54,* on chromosome 19 that is essential for this development to occur (Seminara et al., 2003).

Some research attributes the heightened emotionality and moodiness of early adolescence to these hormonal developments. Indeed, negative emotions such as distress and hostility, as well as symptoms of depression in girls, do tend to rise as puberty progresses (Susman & Rogol, 2004). However, other influences, such as sex, age, temperament, and the timing of puberty, may moderate or even override hormonal influences (Buchanan, Eccles, & Becker, 1992).

Table 11-1   Usual Sequence of Physiological Changes in Adolescence

Female Characteristics	Age of First Appearance
Growth of breasts	6–13
Growth of pubic hair	6–14
Body growth	9.5–14.5
Menarche	10–16.5
Appearance of underarm hair	About 2 years after appearance of pubic hair
Increased output of oil- and sweat-producing glands (which may lead to acne)	About the same time as appearance of underarm hair

Male Characteristics	Age of First Appearance
Growth of testes, scrotal sac	9–13.5
Growth of pubic hair	12–16
Body growth	10.5–16
Growth of penis, prostate gland, seminal vesicles	11–14.5
Change in voice	About the same time as growth of penis
First ejaculation of semen	About 1 year after beginning of growth of penis
Appearance of facial and underarm hair	About 2 years after appearance of pubic hair
Increased output of oil- and sweat-producing glands (which may lead to acne)	About the same time as appearance of underarm hair

Table 11-2   Secondary Sex Characteristics

Girls	Boys
Breasts	Pubic hair
Pubic hair	Axillary (underarm) hair
Axillary (underarm) hair	Muscular development
Changes in voice	Facial hair
Changes in skin	Changes in voice
Increased width and depth of pelvis	Changes in skin
Muscular development	Broadening of shoulders

Timing, Signs, and Sequence of Puberty and Sexual Maturity

Changes that herald puberty now typically begin at age 8 in girls and age 9 in boys (Susman & Rogol, 2004), but a wide range of ages exists for various changes (Table 11-1). Recently, pediatricians have seen a significant number of girls with breast budding before their eighth birthdays (Slyper, 2006). The pubertal process typically takes about three to four years for both sexes. African American and Mexican American girls generally enter puberty earlier than white girls (Wu, Mendola, & Buck, 2002). Some African American girls experience pubertal changes as early as age 6 (Kaplowitz et al., 1999).

Primary and Secondary Sex Characteristics   The **primary sex characteristics** are the organs necessary for reproduction. In the female, the sex organs include the ovaries, fallopian tubes, uterus, clitoris, and vagina. In the male, they include the testes, penis, scrotum, seminal vesicles, and prostate gland. During puberty, these organs enlarge and mature.

The **secondary sex characteristics** (Table 11-2) are physiological signs of sexual maturation that do not directly involve the sex organs, for example, the breasts of

primary sex characteristics
Organs directly related to reproduction, which enlarge and mature during adolescence.

secondary sex characteristics
Physiological signs of sexual maturation (such as breast development and growth of body hair) that do not involve the sex organs.

females and the broad shoulders of males. Other secondary sex characteristics are changes in the voice and skin texture, muscular development, and the growth of pubic, facial, axillary (underarm), and body hair.

These changes unfold in a sequence that is much more consistent than their timing, though it does vary somewhat. One girl may develop breasts and body hair at about the same rate; in another girl, body hair may reach adultlike growth a year or so before breasts develop. Similar variations in pubertal status (degree of pubertal development) and timing occur among boys. Let's look more closely at these changes.

Signs of Puberty   The first external signs of puberty typically are breast tissue and pubic hair in girls and enlargement of the testes in boys (Susman & Rogol, 2004). A girl's nipples enlarge and protrude, the *areolae* (the pigmented areas surrounding the nipples) enlarge, and the breasts assume first a conical and then a rounded shape. Some adolescent boys experience temporary breast enlargement, much to their distress; this development is normal and may last up to 18 months.

Pubic hair, at first straight and silky, eventually becomes coarse, dark, and curly. It appears in different patterns in males and females. Adolescent boys are usually happy to see hair on the face and chest; but girls are generally dismayed at the appearance of even a slight amount of hair on the face or around the nipples, though this, too, is normal.

The voice deepens, especially in boys, partly in response to the growth of the larynx and partly in response to the production of male hormones. The skin becomes coarser and oilier. Increased activity of the sebaceous glands may give rise to pimples and blackheads. Acne is more common in boys and seems related to increased amounts of testosterone.

The Adolescent Growth Spurt   The **adolescent growth spurt**—a rapid increase in height, weight, and muscle and bone growth that occurs during puberty—generally begins in girls between ages 9½ and 14½ (usually at about 10) and in boys, between 10½ and 16 (usually at 12 or 13). It typically lasts about two years; soon after it ends, the young person reaches sexual maturity. Both growth hormone and the sex hormones (androgens and estrogen) contribute to this normal pubertal growth pattern (Susman & Rogol, 2004).

Because girls' growth spurt usually occurs two years earlier than that of boys, girls between ages 11 and 13 tend to be taller, heavier, and stronger than boys the same age. After their growth spurt, boys are again larger. Girls typically reach full height at age 15 and boys at age 17. The rate of muscular growth peaks at age 12½ for girls and 14½ for boys (Gans, 1990).

Boys and girls grow differently, not only in rates of growth, but also in form and shape. A boy becomes larger overall: his shoulders wider, his legs longer relative to his trunk, and his forearms longer relative to his upper arms and his height. A girl's pelvis widens to make childbearing easier, and layers of fat accumulate under her skin, giving her a more rounded appearance. Fat accumulates twice as rapidly in girls as in boys (Susman & Rogol, 2004). Because each of these changes follows its own timetable, parts of the body may be out of proportion for a while.

These striking physical changes have psychological ramifications. Most young teenagers are more concerned about their appearance than about any other aspect of themselves, and some do not like what they see in the mirror. As we will discuss in a subsequent section, these attitudes can lead to eating problems.

Signs of Sexual Maturity: Sperm Production and Menstruation   The maturation of the reproductive organs brings the beginning of menstruation in girls and the production of sperm in boys. The principal sign of sexual maturity in boys is

adolescent growth spurt Sharp increase in height and weight that precedes sexual maturity.

the production of sperm. The first ejaculation, or **spermarche,** occurs at an average age of 13. A boy may wake up to find a wet spot or a hardened, dried spot on the sheets—the result of a *nocturnal emission,* an involuntary ejaculation of semen (commonly referred to as a *wet dream*). Most adolescent boys have these emissions, sometimes in connection with an erotic dream.

The principal sign of sexual maturity in girls is *menstruation,* a monthly shedding of tissue from the lining of the womb. The first menstruation, called **menarche,** occurs fairly late in the sequence of female development; its normal timing can vary from age 10 to 16½ (refer back to Table 11-1). The average age of menarche in U.S. girls fell from greater than 14 years before 1900 to 12½ years in the 1990s. On average, black girls experience menarche six months earlier than white girls (S. E. Anderson, Dallal, & Must, 2003).

Most girls experience a growth spurt two years earlier than most boys, so between ages 11 and 13 girls tend to be taller, heavier, and stronger than boys the same age.

Influences on and Effects of Timing of Puberty On the basis of historical sources, developmental scientists have found a **secular trend**—a trend that spans several generations—in the onset of puberty: a drop in the ages when puberty begins and when young people reach adult height and sexual maturity. The trend, which also involves increases in adult height and weight, began about 100 years ago. It has occurred in such places as the United States, Western Europe, and Japan (S. E. Anderson et al., 2003).

One proposed explanation for the secular trend is a higher standard of living. Children who are healthier, better nourished, and better cared for might be expected to mature earlier and grow bigger (Slyper, 2006). Thus, the average age of sexual maturity is earlier in developed countries than in developing countries. Because of the role of body fat in triggering puberty, a contributing factor in the United States during the last part of the twentieth century may be the increase in obesity among young girls (S. E. Anderson et al., 2003; Lee et al., 2007).

A combination of genetic, physical, emotional, and contextual influences, including SES, environmental toxins, diet, exercise, prepubertal fat and body weight, and chronic illness or stress, may affect individual differences in the timing of menarche (Belsky et al., 2007; Graber, Brooks-Gunn, & Warren, 1995). Twin studies have documented the heritability of age of menarche (Mendle et al., 2006). Other research has found that the age of a girl's first menstruation tends to be similar to that of her mother *if* nutrition and standard of living remain stable from one generation to the next (Susman & Rogol, 2004). In several studies, family conflict was associated with early menarche, whereas parental warmth, harmonious family relationships, and paternal involvement in child rearing were related to later menarche (Belsky et al., 2007; Mendle et al., 2006). Girls who, as preschoolers, have had close, supportive relationships with their parents—especially with an affectionate, involved father—tend to enter puberty later than girls whose parental relationships were cold or distant or those who were raised by single mothers (Belsky et al., 2007; Ellis, McFadyen-Ketchum, Dodge, Pettit, & Bates, 1999).

spermarche Boy's first ejaculation.

menarche Girl's first menstruation.

secular trend Trend that can be seen only by observing several generations, such as the trend toward earlier attainment of adult height and sexual maturity, which began a century ago in some countries.

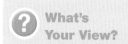

What's Your View?

- Did you mature early, late, or "on time"? How did you feel about the timing of your maturation?

Checkpoint

Can you . . .

◆ Tell how puberty begins and how its timing and length vary?

◆ Describe typical pubertal changes in boys and girls, and identify factors that affect psychological reactions to these changes?

Guidepost 3

What brain developments occur during adolescence, and how do they affect behavior?

What difference, if any, does timing of puberty make to psychological well-being? It depends on how the adolescent and others interpret the accompanying changes. Effects of early or late maturation are most likely to be negative when adolescents are much more or less developed than their peers; when they do not see the changes as advantageous; and when several stressful events, such as the advent of puberty and the transition to junior high school, occur at about the same time (Petersen, 1993; Simmons, Blyth, & McKinney, 1983). Contextual factors such as ethnicity, school, and neighborhood can make a difference. For example, early-maturing girls are more likely to show problem behavior in mixed-gender schools than in all-girl schools and in disadvantaged urban communities than in rural or middle-class urban communities (Caspi, Lynam, Moffitt, & Silva, 1993; Dick et al., 2000; Ge et al., 2002).

The Adolescent Brain

Not long ago, most scientists believed that the brain was fully mature by puberty. Now imaging studies reveal that the adolescent brain is still a work in progress. Dramatic changes in brain structures involved in emotions, judgment, organization of behavior, and self-control take place between puberty and young adulthood (Figure 11-1). The immaturity of the adolescent brain has raised questions about the extent to which adolescents can reasonably be held legally responsible for their actions (Steinberg & Scott, 2003), prompting the U.S. Supreme Court in 2005 to rule the death penalty unconstitutional for a convicted murderer who was 17 or younger when the crime was committed (Mears, 2005).

Risk taking appears to result from the interaction of two brain networks: (1) a *socioemotional network* that is sensitive to social and emotional stimuli, such as peer influence, and (2) a *cognitive-control network* that regulates responses to stimuli. The socioemotional network becomes more active at puberty, whereas the cognitive-control network matures more gradually into early adulthood. These findings may help explain teenagers' tendency toward emotional outbursts and risky behavior and why risk taking often occurs in groups (Steinberg, 2007).

Furthermore, adolescents process information about emotions differently than adults do. In one study, researchers scanned adolescents' brain activity while they identified emotions expressed by faces on a computer screen. Early adolescents (ages 11 to 13) tended to use the amygdala, a small, almond-shaped structure deep in the temporal lobe that is heavily involved in emotional and instinctual reactions. Older adolescents (ages 14 to 17) showed more adultlike patterns, using the frontal lobes, which handle planning, reasoning, judgment, emotional regulation, and impulse control and thus permit more accurate, reasoned judgments. This difference might explain early adolescents' unwise choices, such as substance abuse and sexual risk taking. Immature brain development may permit feelings to override reason and may keep some adolescents from heeding warnings that seem logical and persuasive to adults (Baird et al., 1999; Yurgelun-Todd, 2002). Underdevelopment of frontal cortical systems associated with motivation, impulsivity, and addiction may help explain why adolescents tend to seek thrills and novelty and why many of them find it hard to focus on long-term goals (Bjork et al., 2004; Chambers, Taylor, & Potenza, 2003).

To understand the immaturity of the adolescent brain, we also need to look at changes in the structure and composition of the frontal cortex. First, in adolescence, the increase in white matter typical of childhood brain development continues in the frontal lobes (ACT for Youth, 2002; Blakemore & Choudhury, 2006;

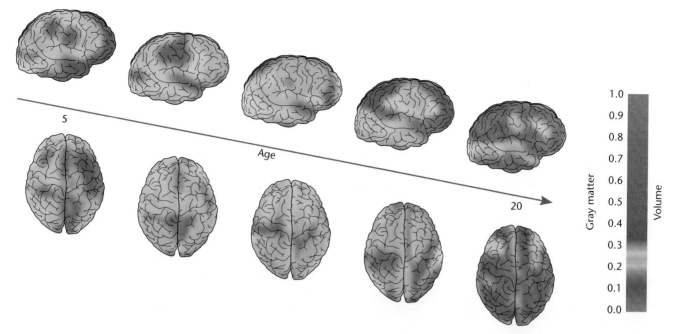

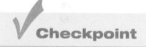

Figure 11-1

Constructed from MRI scans of healthy children and teens, these images compress 15 years of brain development (ages 5–20). Red indicates more gray matter, blue less gray matter. Gray matter wanes in a back-to-front wave as the brain matures and neural connections are pruned. (Source: Cogtay et al., 2004.)

Kuhn, 2006; NIMH, 2001b). Second, the pruning of unused dendritic connections during childhood results in a reduction in density of gray matter (nerve cells), increasing the brain's efficiency. This process begins in the rear portions of the brain and moves forward. For the most part, however, it has not yet reached the frontal lobes by adolescence.

A major spurt in production of gray matter in the frontal lobes begins around puberty. After the growth spurt, the density of gray matter declines greatly, particularly in the prefrontal cortex, as unused synapses (connections between neurons) are pruned and those that remain are strengthened (ACT for Youth, 2002; Blakemore & Choudhury, 2006; Kuhn, 2006; NIMH, 2001b). Thus, by mid- to late adolescence young people have fewer but stronger, smoother, and more effective neuronal connections, making cognitive processing more efficient (Kuhn, 2006).

Cognitive stimulation in adolescence makes a critical difference in the brain's development. The process is bidirectional: A young person's activities and experiences determine which neuronal connections will be retained and strengthened, and this development supports further cognitive growth in those areas (Kuhn, 2006). Adolescents who "exercise' their brains by learning to order their thoughts, understand abstract concepts, and control their impulses are laying the neural foundations that will serve them for the rest of their lives" (ACT for Youth, 2002, p. 1).

Physical and Mental Health

Nine out of ten 11- to 15-year-olds in Western industrialized countries consider themselves healthy, according to a survey conducted by the World Health Organization (Scheidt, Overpeck, Wyatt, & Aszmann, 2000). Still, many adolescents, especially girls, report frequent health problems, such as headache, backache, stomachache, nervousness, and feeling tired, lonely, or low. Such reports are especially common in the United States and Israel, where life tends to be fast paced and stressful (Scheidt et al., 2000).

✓ Checkpoint

Can you . . .

◆ Describe two major changes in the adolescent brain?

◆ Identify immature features of the adolescent brain, and explain how this immaturity can affect behavior?

Guidepost 4

What are some common health problems in adolescence, and how can they be prevented?

Adolescents who engage in sports tend to feel better than those who do not. And, as with their younger counterparts, safety precautions such as helmets reduce the risk of accidents and injuries.

Many health problems are preventable, stemming from lifestyle or poverty. In industrialized countries, adolescents from less affluent families tend to report poorer health and more frequent symptoms (Scheidt et al., 2000). Adolescents from more affluent families tend to have healthier diets and to be more physically active (Mullan & Currie, 2000).

Let's look at several specific health concerns: physical fitness, sleep needs, eating disorders, drug abuse, depression, and causes of death in adolescence.

Physical Activity

Exercise—or lack of it—affects both physical and mental health. The benefits of regular exercise include improved strength and endurance, healthier bones and muscles, weight control, and reduced anxiety and stress, as well as increased self-esteem, school grades, and well-being. Exercise also decreases the likelihood that an adolescent will participate in risky behavior. Even moderate physical activity has health benefits if done regularly for at least 30 minutes almost every day. A sedentary lifestyle may result in increased risk of obesity and type II diabetes, both growing problems among adolescents. It also can lead to increased likelihood of heart disease and cancer in adulthood (Carnethon, Gulati, & Greenland, 2005; Centers for Disease Control and Prevention, 2000a; Hickman, Roberts, & de Matos, 2000; NCHS, 2004; Nelson & Gordon-Larsen, 2006; Troiano, 2002).

Unfortunately, only about one-third of U.S. high school students engage in the recommended amounts of physical activity, and the proportion of young people who are inactive increases throughout the high school years (Eaton et al., 2008). U.S. adolescents exercise less frequently than in past years and than adolescents in most other industrialized countries (CDC, 2000a; Hickman et al., 2000).

Sleep Needs and Problems

Sleep deprivation among adolescents has been called an epidemic (Hansen et al., 2005). An average of 40 percent of adolescents (mostly boys) in a study of 28 industrialized countries reported morning sleepiness at least once a week, and 22 percent said they are sleepy most days (Scheidt et al., 2000).

Children generally go to sleep later and sleep less on school days the older they get. The average adolescent who slept more than ten hours at night at age 9 sleeps less than eight hours' at age 16 (Eaton et al., 2008; Hoban, 2004). Actually, adolescents need as much or more sleep than when they were younger (Hoban, 2004; Iglowstein, Jenni, Molinari, & Largo, 2003). Sleeping in on weekends does not make up for the loss of sleep on school nights (Hoban, 2004; Sadeh, Raviv, & Gruber, 2000). A pattern of late bedtimes and oversleeping in the mornings can contribute to insomnia, a problem that often begins in late childhood or adolescence (Hoban, 2004).

Sleep deprivation can sap motivation and cause irritability, and concentration and school performance can suffer. Sleepiness also can be deadly for adolescent drivers. Studies have found that young people ages 16 to 29 are most likely to be involved in crashes caused by the driver falling asleep (Millman et al., 2005).

Why do adolescents stay up late? They may need to do homework, want to talk to or text friends or surf the Web, or simply wish to act grown up. However, sleep experts now recognize that biological changes are behind adolescents' sleep problems (Sadeh et al., 2000). The timing of secretion of the hormone *melatonin* is a gauge of when the brain is ready for sleep. After puberty, this secretion takes place later at night (Carskadon, Acebo, Richardson, Tate, & Seifer, 1997). But adolescents still need just as much sleep as before; so when they go to bed later than younger children, they need to get up later as well. Yet, most secondary schools start *earlier* than elementary schools. Their schedules are out of sync with students' biological rhythms (Hoban, 2004). Teenagers tend to be least alert and most stressed early in the morning and more alert in the afternoon (Hansen et al., 2005). Starting school later, or at least offering difficult courses later in the day, would help improve students' concentration (Crouter & Larson, 1998).

Nutrition and Eating Disorders

Good nutrition is important to support the rapid growth of adolescence and to establish healthy eating habits that will last through adulthood. Unfortunately, U.S. adolescents eat fewer fruits and vegetables and consume more foods that are high in cholesterol, fat, and calories and low in nutrients than adolescents in other industrialized countries (American Heart Association et al., 2006; Vereecken & Maes, 2000). Deficiencies of calcium, zinc, and iron are common at this age (Lloyd et al., 1993; Bruner, Joffe, Duggan, Casella, & Brandt, 1996).

Worldwide, poor nutrition is most frequent in economically depressed or isolated populations but also may result from concern with body image and weight control (Vereecken & Maes, 2000). Eating disorders, including obesity, are most prevalent in industrialized societies, where food is abundant and attractiveness is equated with slimness; but these disorders appear to be increasing in non-Western countries as well (Makino, Tsuboi, & Dennerstein, 2004).

Obesity U.S. teens are about twice as likely to be overweight as their age-mates in 14 other industrialized countries, according to self-reports of height and weight from more than 29,000 boys and girls ages 13 and 15 (Lissau et al., 2004). About 34 percent of U.S. teens have a body mass index (BMI) at or above the 85th percentile for age and sex. The percentage of U.S. adolescents with BMIs at or above the 95th percentile more than tripled between 1980 and 2006, from 5 percent to nearly 18 percent (Ogden et al., 2006, 2008). Among older adolescents, obesity is 50 percent more prevalent in those from poor families (Miech et al., 2006). Mexican American girls and boys and non-Hispanic black girls, who tend to be poorer than their peers, are more likely to be overweight than non-Hispanic white adolescents (Hernandez & Macartney, 2008; NCHS, 2006; Ogden et al., 2008).

Overweight teenagers tend to be in poorer health than their peers and are more likely to have difficulty attending school, performing household chores, or engaging in strenuous activity or personal care (Swallen, Reither, Haas, & Meier, 2005). They are at heightened risk of high cholesterol, hypertension, and diabetes (NCHS, 2005). They tend to become obese adults, subject to a variety of physical, social, and psychological risks (Gortmaker, Must, Perrin, Sobol, & Dietz, 1993). Given how many adolescents are overweight today, one research team projects that by 2035 more than 100,000 additional cases of cardiovascular disease will be attributable to an increased prevalence of overweight in young and middle-aged men and women (Bibbins-Domingo, Coxson, Pletcher, Lightwood, & Goldman, 2007).

✔ Checkpoint

Can you . . .

◆ Summarize the status of adolescents' health?

◆ Explain the importance of physical activity?

◆ Tell why adolescents often get too little sleep?

Genetic and other factors, such as faulty regulation of metabolism and, at least in girls, depressive symptoms and having obese parents can increase the likelihood of teenage obesity (Morrison et al., 2005; Stice, Presnell, Shaw, & Rohde, 2005). However a study of 878 California 11- to 15-year-olds revealed that lack of exercise was the *main* risk factor for overweight in boys and girls (Patrick et al., 2004).

Programs that use behavioral modification techniques to help adolescents make changes in diet and exercise have had some success. Dieting, for adolescents, may be counterproductive, however. In a three-year study of 8,203 girls and 6,769 boys ages 9 to 14, those who dieted gained more weight than those who did *not* diet (A. E. Field et al., 2003).

Body Image and Eating Disorders   For some adolescents a determination *not* to become overweight can result in graver problems than weight gain itself. A concern with **body image**—how one believes one looks—often begins in middle childhood or earlier, intensifies in adolescence, and may lead to obsessive efforts at weight control (Davison & Birch, 2001; Schreiber et al., 1996; Vereecken & Maes, 2000). This pattern is more common and less likely to be related to actual weight problems among girls than among boys.

Because of the normal increase in girls' body fat during puberty, many girls, especially if they are advanced in pubertal development, become unhappy about their appearance, reflecting the cultural emphasis on female physical attributes (Susman & Rogol, 2004). Girls' dissatisfaction with their bodies increases during early to midadolescence, whereas boys, who are becoming more muscular, become more satisfied with their bodies (Feingold & Mazella, 1998; Rosenblum & Lewis, 1999; Swarr & Richards, 1996). By age 15, more than half the girls sampled in 16 countries were dieting or thought they should be. The United States was at the top of the list, with 47 percent of 11-year-old girls and 62 percent of 15-year-old girls concerned about their weight (Vereecken & Maes, 2000). African American girls are generally more satisfied with their bodies and less concerned about weight and dieting than are white girls (Kelly, Wall, Eisenberg, Story, & Neumark-Sztainer, 2004; Wardle et al., 2004). According to a large prospective cohort study, parental attitudes and media images play a greater part than peer influences in encouraging weight concerns (A. E. Field et al., 2001).

Excessive concern with weight control and body image may be signs of *anorexia nervosa* or *bulimia nervosa,* both of which involve abnormal patterns of food intake. These chronic disorders occur worldwide, mostly in adolescent girls and young women. However, not enough study has been done of eating disorders among men and among nonwhite ethnic groups. Furthermore, the idea that eating disorders are the result of cultural pressure to be thin is too simplistic; biological factors, including genetic factors, play an equally important role (Striegel-Moore & Bulik, 2007). Twin studies have found associations between eating disorders and the brain chemical serotonin; a variant of the protein BDNF, which influences food intake; and estrogen (Klump & Culbert, 2007).

Anorexia Nervosa   **Anorexia nervosa,** or *self-starvation,* is potentially life threatening. An estimated 0.3 to 0.5 percent of adolescent girls and young women and a smaller but growing percentage of boys and men in Western countries are known to be affected. People with anorexia have a distorted body image and, though typically severely underweight, think they are too fat. They often are good students but may be withdrawn or depressed and may engage in repetitive, perfectionist behavior. They are extremely afraid of losing control and becoming overweight (AAP Committee on Adolescence, 2003; Martínez-González et al., 2003;

body image Descriptive and evaluative beliefs about one's appearance.

anorexia nervosa Eating disorder characterized by self-starvation.

Wilson, Grilo, & Vitousek, 2007). Early warning signs include determined, secret dieting; dissatisfaction after losing weight; setting new, lower weight goals after reaching an initial desired weight; excessive exercising; and interruption of regular menstruation.

Anorexia is, paradoxically, both deliberate and involuntary: An affected person deliberately refuses food needed for sustenance, yet cannot stop doing so even when rewarded or punished. These behavior patterns have been traced back to medieval times and seem to have existed in all parts of the world. Thus, anorexia may be in part a reaction to societal pressure to be slender, but this does not seem to be the only factor or even a necessary one (Keel & Klump, 2003; Striegel-Moore & Bulik, 2007).

Bulimia Nervosa **Bulimia nervosa** affects about 1 to 2 percent of international populations (Wilson et al., 2007). A person with bulimia regularly goes on huge, short-lived eating binges (two hours or less) and then may try to purge the high caloric intake through self-induced vomiting, strict dieting or fasting, excessively vigorous exercise, or laxatives, enemas, or diuretics. These episodes occur at least twice a week for at least three months (APA, 2000). People with bulimia are usually *not* overweight, but they are obsessed with their weight and shape. They tend to have low self-esteem and may become overwhelmed with shame, self-contempt, and depression (Wilson et al., 2007).

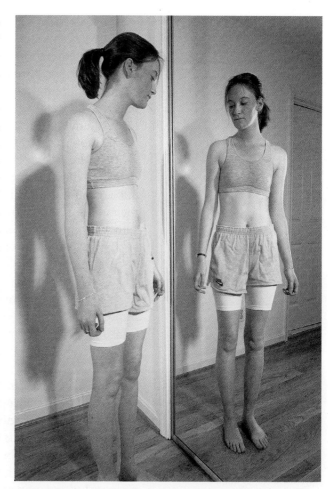

People with anorexia, such as this girl, have a distorted body image. They see themselves as fat even when they are emaciated.

A related *binge eating disorder* involves frequent binging but without subsequent fasting, exercise, or vomiting. Not surprisingly people who binge frequently tend to be overweight and to experience emotional distress and other medical and psychological disorders. An estimated 3 percent of the population are binge eaters (Wilson et al., 2007).

There is some overlap between anorexia and bulimia; some people with anorexia have bulimic episodes, and some people with bulimia lose large amounts of weight ("Eating Disorders—Part I," 1997). Unlike anorexia, there is little evidence of bulimia either historically or in cultures not subject to Western influence (Keel & Klump, 2003).

bulimia nervosa Eating disorder in which a person regularly eats huge quantities of food and then purges the body by laxatives, induced vomiting, fasting, or excessive exercise.

Treatment and Outcomes of Eating Disorders The immediate goal of treatment for anorexia is to get patients to eat and gain weight—goals that are often difficult to achieve given the strength of patients' beliefs about their bodies. One widely used treatment is a type of family therapy in which parents take control of their child's eating patterns. When the child begins to comply with parental directives, she (or he) may be given more age-appropriate autonomy (Wilson et al., 2007). Cognitive behavioral therapy, which seeks to change a distorted body image and rewards eating with such privileges as being allowed to get out of bed and leave the room, may be part of the treatment (Beumont et al., 1993; Wilson et al., 2007). Patients who show signs of severe malnutrition, are resistant to treatment, or do not make progress on an outpatient basis may be admitted to a hospital, where they can be given 24-hour nursing. Once their weight is stabilized, patients may enter less intensive daytime care (McCallum & Bruton, 2003).

Bulimia, too, is best treated with cognitive behavioral therapy (Wilson et al., 2007). Patients keep daily diaries of their eating patterns and are taught ways to avoid the temptation to binge. Individual, group, or family psychotherapy can help both anorexia and bulimia patients, usually after initial behavior therapy has brought symptoms under control. Because these patients are at risk for depression and suicide, antidepressant drugs are often combined with psychotherapy (McCallum & Bruton, 2003), but evidence of their long-term effectiveness on either anorexia or bulimia is lacking (Wilson et al., 2007).

Adolescents, with their need for autonomy, may reject family intervention and may need the structure of an institutional setting. Still, any treatment program for adolescents must involve the family. It also must provide for adolescents' developmental needs, which may be different from the needs of adult patients, and must offer the opportunity to keep up with schooling (McCallum & Bruton, 2003).

Nearly half of anorexia patients eventually make a full recovery (Steinhausen, 2002), but up to one-third drop out of treatment before achieving an appropriate weight (McCallum & Bruton, 2003). Recovery rates from bulimia average 30 to 50 percent after cognitive behavioral therapy, and many other patients show improvement (Wilson et al., 2007).

Use and Abuse of Drugs

Although the great majority of adolescents do not abuse drugs, a significant minority do. **Substance abuse** is harmful use of alcohol or other drugs. Abuse can lead to **substance dependence,** or *addiction,* which may be physiological, psychological, or both and is likely to continue into adulthood. Addictive drugs are especially dangerous for adolescents because they stimulate parts of the brain that are still developing in adolescence (Chambers et al., 2003). In 2003–2004, about 6 percent of young people ages 12 to 17 were identified as needing treatment for alcohol use and more than 5 percent as needing treatment for illicit drug use (Substance Abuse and Mental Health Services Administration [SAMHSA], 2006b).

Trends in Drug Use Nearly half (47 percent) of U.S. adolescents have tried illicit drugs by the time they leave high school. An upsurge in drug use during the early 1990s accompanied a lessening of perceptions of its dangers and a softening of peer disapproval. However, that trend has begun to reverse. Past-year use of illicit drugs is down by almost one-third among eighth graders, one-fifth among tenth graders, and one-eighth among twelfth graders since 1996 but is still well above its low point in 1991–1992 (Johnston, O'Malley, Bachman, & Schulenberg, 2008; Figure 11-2).

These findings come from the latest in a series of annual government surveys of a nationally representative sample of more than 48,000 eighth, tenth, and twelfth graders in 403 schools across the United States (Johnston et al., 2008). These surveys probably underestimate adolescent drug use because they are based on self-reports and do not reach high school dropouts, who are more likely to use drugs. Continued progress in eliminating drug abuse is slow because new drugs are constantly introduced or old drugs rediscovered by a new generation, and young people do

Checkpoint

Can you . . .

♦ Identify typical dietary deficiencies of adolescents?

♦ Discuss risk factors, effects, treatment, and prognoses for obesity, anorexia, and bulimia?

substance abuse Repeated, harmful use of a substance, usually alcohol or other drugs.

substance dependence Addiction (physical, or psychological, or both) to a harmful substance.

Figure 11-2

Trends in high school students' use of illicit druges over the previous 12 months. (Source: Johnston, O'Malley, Bachman, & Schulenberg, 2008, Fig. 1.)

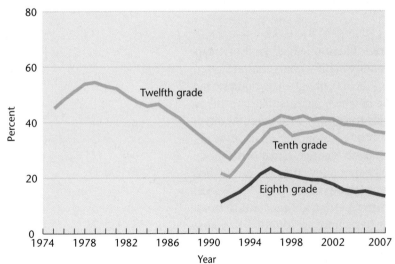

Table 11-3	Risk Factors for Teenage Drug Abuse

What is the likelihood that a particular young person will abuse drugs? Risk factors include the following:

- A "difficult" temperament
- Poor impulse control and a tendency to seek out sensation (which may have a biochemical basis)
- Family influences (such as a genetic predisposition to alcoholism, parental use or acceptance of drugs, poor or inconsistent parenting practices, family conflict, and troubled or distant family relationships)
- Early and persistent behavior problems, particularly aggression
- Academic failure and lack of commitment to education
- Peer rejection
- Associating with drug users
- Alienation and rebelliousness
- Favorable attitudes toward drug use
- Early initiation into drug use

The more risk factors that are present, the greater the chance that an adolescent will abuse drugs.

Sources: Hawkins, Catalano, & Miller, 1992; Johnson, Hoffmann, & Gerstein, 1996; Masse & Tremblay, 1997; Wong et al., 2006.

not necessarily generalize the adverse consequences of older drugs to newer drugs (Johnston et al., 2008). Table 11-3 shows risk factors for teenage drug abuse.

Although illicit drug use has declined overall, use of ecstasy (MDMA), a *club drug* popular at night clubs and raves, may be rebounding. Nonmedical use of prescription drugs, such as sedatives, tranquilizers, and narcotic pain relievers, particularly OxyContin and Vicodin, remains at high levels (Johnston et al., 2008). In fact, misuse of prescription drugs has been called the nation's second leading drug problem, after marijuana (Colliver, Kroutil, Dai, & Gfroerer, 2006).

A recent trend is the abuse of nonprescription cough and cold medications; 4 percent of eighth graders, 5 percent of tenth graders, and 6 percent of twelfth graders report taking medicines containing dextromethorphan (DXM), a cough suppressant, to get high within the past year. On the other hand, use of methamphetamine has dropped sharply since 2001; it is now used annually by less than 2 percent of eighth, tenth, and twelfth graders (Johnston et al., 2008).

Let's look more closely at alcohol, marijuana, and tobacco, the three drugs most popular with adolescents.

Alcohol, Marijuana, and Tobacco Alcohol, marijuana, and tobacco use among U.S. teenagers has followed a trend roughly parallel to that of harder drug use, with a dramatic rise during most of the 1990s followed by a smaller, gradual, decline (Johnston et al., 2008).

Alcohol is a potent, mind-altering drug with major effects on physical, emotional, and social well-being. Its use is a serious problem in many countries (Gabhainn & François, 2000). In 2006, 16 percent of U.S. eighth graders, 33 percent of tenth graders, and 44 percent of twelfth graders said they had consumed alcohol at least once during the past 30 days (Johnston et al., 2008). The majority of high school students who drink engage in *binge drinking*—consuming five or more drinks on one occasion. In a representative national study, binge drinkers were more likely than other students to report poor school performance and to engage in other risky behaviors (Miller, Naimi, Brewer, & Jones, 2007).

Marijuana is the most widely used illicit drug in the United States. Aside from its own ill effects, marijuana may lead to other addictions.

Adolescents are more vulnerable than adults to both immediate and long-term negative effects of alcohol on learning and memory (White, 2001). In one study, 15- and 16-year-old alcohol abusers who stopped drinking showed cognitive impairments weeks later in comparison with nonabusing peers (Brown, Tapert, Granholm, & Delis, 2000).

Despite the decline in *marijuana* use since 1996–1997, it is still by far the most widely used illicit drug in the United States. In 2007, about 10 percent of eighth graders, 25 percent of tenth graders, and 32 percent of twelfth graders admitted to having used it in the past year (Johnston et al., 2008).

Marijuana smoke typically contains more than 400 carcinogens, and its potency has doubled in the past 25 years (National Institute on Drug Abuse [NIDA], 2008). Heavy use can damage the brain, heart, lungs, and immune system and cause nutritional deficiencies, respiratory infections, and other physical problems. It may lessen motivation, worsen depression, interfere with daily activities, and cause family problems. Marijuana use also can impede memory, thinking speed, learning, and school performance. It can lessen perception, alertness, attention span, judgment, and the motor skills needed to drive a vehicle and thus can contribute to traffic accidents (Messinis, Krypianidou, Maletaki, & Papathanasopoulos, 2006; NIDA, 1996; SAMHSA, 2006a; Office of National Drug Control Policy, 2008; Solowij et al., 2002). Contrary to common belief, marijuana use may be addictive (Tanda, Pontieri, & DiChiara, 1997).

Adolescent *tobacco* use is a less widespread problem in the United States than in most other industrialized countries (Gabhainn & François, 2000). Smoking rates have declined by one-third to more than one-half among U.S. eighth to twelfth graders since the mid-1990s. Still, about 7 percent of eighth graders, 14 percent of tenth graders, and 22 percent of twelfth graders are current (past-month) smokers (Johnston et al., 2008). Black youth tend to smoke less but metabolize nicotine more slowly than white youth, so their bodies take longer to get rid of it and they are quicker to become dependent (Moolchan, Franken, & Jaszyna-Gasior, 2006). A randomized, controlled trial found nicotine replacement therapy plus behavioral skills training effective in helping adolescents stop smoking (Killen et al., 2004).

Substance use often begins when children enter middle school, where they become more vulnerable to peer pressure. Fourth to sixth graders may start using cigarettes, beer, and inhalants and, as they get older, move on to marijuana or harder drugs (National Parents' Resource Institute for Drug Education, 1999). The earlier young people start using a drug, the more frequently they are likely to use it and the greater their tendency to abuse it (Wong et al., 2006).

The average age for starting to drink is 13 to 14, and some children start earlier. In 2003, nearly 28 percent of underage drinkers had a drink before age 13 (Faden, 2006). Young people who begin drinking early tend to have behavior problems or to have siblings who are alcohol dependent (Kuperman et al., 2005). Those who start drinking before age 15 are more than five times more likely to become alcohol dependent or alcohol abusers than those who do not start drinking until age 21 or later (Substance Abuse and Mental Health Services Administration [SAMHSA], 2004a).

Smoking often begins in the early teenage years as a sign of toughness, rebelliousness, and passage from childhood to adulthood. This desired image enables a young initate to tolerate initial distaste for the first few puffs, after which the effects of nicotine begin to take over to sustain the habit. Within a year or two after starting to smoke, these young people inhale the same amount of nicotine as adults and experience the same cravings and withdrawal effects if they try to quit. Young adolescents attracted to smoking often come from homes, schools, and

What's Your View?

- Should marijuana be legal, like alcohol? Why or why not?
- How can adolescents be helped to avoid or curtail substance use?

neighborhoods where smoking is common. They also tend to be overweight, to have low self-esteem, and not to be succeeding at school (Jarvis, 2004).

Adolescents who begin smoking by age 11 are twice as likely as other young people to engage in risky behaviors, such as riding in a car with a drunk driver; carrying knives or guns to school; using inhalants, marijuana, or cocaine; and planning suicide. Early use of alcohol and marijuana also are associated with multiple risk behaviors (DuRant, Smith, Kreiter, & Krowchuk, 1999).

Peer influence on both smoking and drinking has been documented extensively (Center on Addiction and Substance Abuse [CASA] at Columbia University, 1996; Cleveland & Wiebe, 2003). As with hard drugs, the influence of older siblings and their friends increases the likelihood of tobacco and alcohol use (Rende, Slomkowski, Lloyd-Richardson, & Niaura, 2005).

Adolescents who believe that their parents disapprove of smoking are less likely to smoke (Sargent & Dalton, 2001). Rational discussions with parents can counteract harmful influences and discourage or limit drinking (Austin, Pinkleton, & Fujioka, 2000; Turrisi et al., 2000). However, parents also can be a negative influence. In a longitudinal study that compared 514 children of alcoholics with a matched control group, having an alcoholic parent significantly increased the risk of early alcohol use and later alcohol problems (Wong et al., 2006). The omnipresence of substance use in the media is another important influence. Movies that depict smoking increase early initiation of smoking (Charlesworth & Glantz, 2005).

Checkpoint

Can you . . .

♦ Summarize recent trends in substance use among adolescents?

♦ Discuss risk factors and influences connected with use of drugs, specifically alcohol, marijuana, and tobacco?

♦ Tell why early initiation into substance use is dangerous?

Depression

The prevalence of depression increases during adolescence. In 2004, 9 percent of young people ages 12 to 17 had experienced at least one episode of major depression, and only about 40 percent of them had been treated (SAMHSA, 2005). Depression in young people does not necessarily appear as sadness but as irritability, boredom, or inability to experience pleasure. One reason it needs to be taken seriously is the danger of suicide (Brent & Birmaher, 2002).

Adolescent girls, especially early maturing girls, are more likely to be depressed than adolescent boys (Brent & Birmaher, 2002; Ge, Conger, & Elder, 2001; SAMHSA, 2005; Stice, Presnell, & Bearman, 2001). This gender difference may be related to biological changes connected with puberty; studies show a correlation between advancing puberty status and depressive symptoms (Susman & Rogol, 2004). Other possible factors are the way girls are socialized (Birmaher et al., 1996) and their greater vulnerability to stress in social relationships (Ge et al., 2001; Hankin, Mermelstein, & Roesch, 2007).

In addition to gender, risk factors for depression include anxiety, fear of social contact, stressful life events, chronic illnesses such as diabetes or epilepsy, parent-child conflict, abuse or neglect, alcohol and drug use, sexual activity, and having a parent with a history of depression. Alcohol and drug use and sexual activity are more likely to lead to depression in girls than in boys (Brent & Birmaher, 2002; Hallfors, Waller, Bauer, Ford, & Halpern, 2005; SAMHSA, 2005; Waller et al., 2006). Body-image problems and eating disturbances can aggravate depressive symptoms (Stice & Bearman, 2001).

Depressed adolescents who do not respond to outpatient treatment or who have substance dependence or psychosis or seem suicidal may need to be hospitalized. At least 1 in 5 persons who experience bouts of depression in childhood or adolescence are at risk for bipolar disorder, in which depressive episodes ("low" periods) alternate with manic episodes ("high" periods) characterized by increased energy, euphoria, grandiosity, and risk taking (Brent & Birmaher, 2002). Even

Luis might be worried about his grades or his girlfriend—normal worries for an adolescent boy. But if sadness persists along with symptoms such as the inability to concentrate, fatigue, apathy, or feelings of worthlessness, it might indicate depression.

adolescents with symptoms not severe enough for a diagnosis of depression are at elevated risk of clinical depression and suicidal behavior by age 25 (Fergusson, Horwood, Ridder, & Beautrais, 2005).

One treatment option for adolescents with depressive symptoms is psychotherapy. An analysis of all available studies found that cognitive or noncognitive psychotherapy can be effective in the short term, but its effects last no more than a year (Weisz, McCarty, & Valeri, 2006). Selective serotonin reuptake inhibitors (SSRIs), as we mentioned in Chapter 10, are the only antidepressant medications currently approved for adolescents. Although concern about the safety of these medications has been expressed, research suggests that the benefits outweigh the risks (Bridge et al., 2007). In a major federally funded clinical trial, the most effective treatment for depressed adolescents was a combination of fluoxetine and cognitive behavioral therapy (March & the TADS Team, 2007).

Death in Adolescence

Death in adolescence is always tragic, and usually accidental (Hoyert, Heron, Murphy, & Kung, 2006), but frequently preventable. In the United States, 71 percent of deaths among 10- to 24-year-olds result from motor vehicle crashes, other unintentional injuries, homicide, and suicide (Eaton et al., 2006). The frequency of violent deaths in this age group reflects a violent culture as well as adolescents' inexperience and immaturity, which often lead to risk taking and carelessness.

Deaths from Vehicle Accidents and Firearms   Motor vehicle collisions are the leading cause of death among U.S. teenagers, accounting for 2 out of 5 deaths in adolescence. The risk of collision is greater among 16- to 19-year-olds than for any other age group and especially so among 16- and 17-year-olds who have recently started to drive (McCartt, 2001; Miniño, Anderson, Fingerhut, Boudreault, & Warner, 2006; National Center for Injury Prevention and Control [NCIPC], 2004). Collisions are more likely to be fatal when teenage passengers are in the vehicle, probably because adolescents tend to drive more recklessly in the presence of peers (Chen, Baker, Braver, & Li, 2000). The high incidence of drinking and driving among teens also contributes to these deadly statistics. In 2002, 29 percent of drivers ages 15 to 20 who died in motor crashes had been drinking alcohol, and 77 percent of those were not wearing seat belts (National Highway Traffic Safety Administration, 2003).

Firearm-related deaths of 15- to 19-year-olds (including homicide, suicide, and accidental deaths) are far more common in the United States than in other industrialized countries. They make up about one-third of all injury deaths and more than 85 percent of homicides in that age group. The chief reason for these grim statistics seems to be the ease of obtaining a gun in the United States (AAP Committee on Injury and Poison Prevention, 2000). However, youth death rates from firearms have declined since 1995 (NCHS, 2006), since police began confiscating guns on the street (T. B. Cole, 1999) and fewer young people have carried them (USDHHS, 1999b).

Suicide   Suicide is the third leading cause of death among U.S. 15- to 19-year-olds (Heron & Smith, 2007). The teenage suicide rate fell by 28 percent between 1990 and 2003, perhaps in part due to restrictions on children's access to firearms (Lubell, Swahn, Crosby, & Kegler, 2004). In 2004, however, the suicide rate shot back up by 8 percent—its highest level in 15 years, with the largest increases among teenage girls. Hanging surpassed handguns as the preferred method among girls, but boys remained more likely to use firearms (Lubell, Kegler, Crosby, & Karch, 2007).

Almost 17 percent of U.S. high school students report seriously considering suicide, and 8.4 percent report actually attempting it (NCHS, 2006). Adolescent boys are almost four times more likely than adolescent girls to succeed in taking their lives, even though girls are more likely to consider or attempt suicide (NCHS, 2004, 2005, 2006).

Although suicide occurs in all ethnic groups, Native American boys have the highest rates and African American girls the lowest. Gay, lesbian, and bisexual youths, who have high rates of depression, also have unusually high rates of suicide and attempted suicide (AAP Committee on Adolescence, 2000; Remafedi, French, Story, Resnick, & Blum, 1998).

Young people who consider or attempt suicide tend to have histories of emotional illness. They are likely to be either perpetrators or victims of violence and to have school problems, academic or behavioral. Many have suffered from maltreatment in childhood and have severe problems with relationships. They tend to think poorly of themselves, to feel hopeless, and to have poor impulse control and low tolerance for frustration and stress. These young people are often alienated from their parents and have no one outside the family to turn to. They also tend to have attempted suicide before or to have friends or family members who did so (Borowsky et al., 2001; Brent & Mann, 2006; Garland & Zigler, 1993; Johnson et al., 2002; NIMH, 1999a; "Suicide—Part I," 1996; Swedo et al., 1991). Alcohol plays a part in half of teenage suicides (AAP Committee on Adolescence, 2000). Perhaps the key factor is a tendency toward impulsive aggression. Imaging and postmortem studies of the brains of persons who have attempted or completed suicide have identified neurocognitive deficits in executive function, risk assessment, and problem solving (Brent & Mann, 2006). Protective factors that reduce the risk of suicide include a sense of connectedness to family and school, emotional well-being, and academic achievement (Borowsky et al., 2001). Suicide is further discussed in Chapter 19.

Checkpoint

Can you . . .

♦ Discuss factors affecting gender differences in adolescent depression?

♦ Name the three leading causes of death among adolescents, and identify risk factors for teenage suicide?

COGNITIVE DEVELOPMENT

Aspects of Cognitive Maturation

Most young people emerge from the teenage years with mature, healthy bodies and a zest for life. Their cognitive development has continued, too. Adolescents not only look different from younger children; they also think and talk differently. Although their thinking may remain immature in some ways, many are capable of abstract reasoning and sophisticated moral judgments and can plan more realistically for the future.

Guidepost 5

How do adolescents' thinking and use of language differ from younger children's?

Piaget's Stage of Formal Operations

Adolescents enter what Piaget called the highest level of cognitive development—**formal operations**—when they develop the capacity for abstract thought. This development, usually around age 11, gives them a new, more flexible way to manipulate information. No longer limited to the here and now, they can understand historical time and extraterrestrial space. They can use symbols to represent other symbols (for example, letting the letter X stand for an unknown numeral) and thus can learn

formal operations Piaget's final stage of cognitive development, characterized by the ability to think abstractly.

algebra and calculus. They can better appreciate metaphor and allegory and thus can find richer meanings in literature. They can think in terms of what *might be*, not just what *is*. They can imagine possibilities and can form and test hypotheses.

The ability to think abstractly has emotional implications, too. Whereas a young child could love a parent or hate a classmate, "the adolescent can love freedom or hate exploitation. . . . The possible and the ideal captivate both mind and feeling" (H. Ginsburg & Opper, 1979, p. 201).

Hypothetical-Deductive Reasoning To appreciate the difference formal reasoning makes, let's follow the progress of a typical child in dealing with a classic Piagetian problem, the pendulum problem.* The child, Adam, is shown the pendulum—an object hanging from a string. He is then shown how he can change any of four factors: the length of the string, the weight of the object, the height from which the object is released, and the amount of force he may use to push the object. He is asked to figure out which factor or combination of factors determines how fast the pendulum swings.

When Adam first sees the pendulum, he is not yet 7 years old and is in the preoperational stage. Unable to formulate a plan for attacking the problem, he tries one thing after another in a hit-or-miss manner. First he puts a light weight on a long string and pushes it; then he tries swinging a heavy weight on a short string; then he removes the weight entirely. Not only is his method random, but he also cannot understand or report what has happened.

Adam next encounters the pendulum at age 10, when he is in the stage of concrete operations. This time, he discovers that varying the length of the string and the weight of the object affects the speed of the swing. However, because he varies both factors at the same time, he cannot tell which is critical or whether both are.

Adam is confronted with the pendulum for a third time at age 15, and this time he goes at the problem systematically. He designs an experiment to test all the possible hypotheses, varying one factor at a time—first, the length of the string; next, the weight of the object; then, the height from which it is released; and finally, the amount of force used—each time holding the other three factors constant. In this way, he is able to determine that only one factor—the length of the string—determines how fast the pendulum swings.

Adam's solution of the pendulum problem shows that he has arrived at the stage of formal operations. He is now capable of **hypothetical-deductive reasoning:** He can develop a hypothesis and design an experiment to test it. He considers all the relationships he can imagine and tests them systematically, one by one, to eliminate the false and arrive at the true. Hypothetical-deductive reasoning gives him a tool to solve problems, from fixing the family car to constructing a political theory.

What brings about the shift to formal reasoning? Piaget attributed it to a combination of brain maturation and expanding environmental opportunities. Both are essential: Even if young people's neurological development has advanced enough to permit formal reasoning, they can attain it only with appropriate stimulation.

As with the development of concrete operations, schooling and culture play a role, as Piaget (1972) ultimately recognized. When adolescents in New Guinea and Rwanda were tested on the pendulum problem, none was able to solve it. On the other hand, Chinese children in Hong Kong, who had been to British schools, did at least as well as U.S. or European children. Schoolchildren in Central Java and New South Wales also showed some formal operational abilities (Gardiner &

hypothetical-deductive reasoning Ability, believed by Piaget to accompany the stage of formal operations, to develop, consider, and test hypotheses.

*This description of age-related differences in the approach to the pendulum problem is adapted from H. Ginsburg & Opper, 1979.

Kosmitzki, 2005). Apparently, formal reasoning is a learned ability that is not equally necessary or equally valued in all cultures.

Knowing what questions to ask and what strategies work are keys to hypothetical-deductive reasoning. When 30 low-performing urban sixth graders were asked to investigate factors in earthquake risk, those who received a suggestion to focus on one variable at a time made more valid inferences than those who were not given the suggestion (Kuhn & Dean, 2005). This result demonstrates that hypothetical-deductive reasoning can be taught and learned.

Evaluating Piaget's Theory   Although adolescents *do* tend to think more abstractly than younger children, there is debate about the precise age at which this advance emerges. Piaget's writings provide many examples of children displaying aspects of scientific thinking well before adolescence. At the same time, Piaget seems to have overestimated some older children's abilities. Many late adolescents and adults—perhaps one-third to one-half—seem incapable of abstract thought as Piaget defined it (Gardiner & Kosmitzki, 2005; Kohlberg & Gilligan, 1971; Papalia, 1972), and even those who are capable of this kind of thinking do not always use it.

Piaget, in most of his early writings, paid little attention to individual differences, to variations in the same child's performance on different kinds of tasks, or to social and cultural influences. In his later years, Piaget himself "came to view his earlier model of the development of children's thinking, particularly formal operations, as flawed because it failed to capture the essential *role of the situation* in influencing and constraining . . . children's thinking" (Brown, Metz, & Campione, 1996, pp. 152–153). Neo-Piagetian research suggests that children's cognitive processes are closely tied to specific content (what a child is thinking *about*) as well as to the context of a problem and the kinds of information and thought a culture considers important (Case & Okamoto, 1996; Kuhn, 2006).

Furthermore, Piaget's theory does not adequately consider such cognitive advances as gains in information-processing capacity, accumulation of knowledge and expertise in specific fields, and the role of *metacognition,* the awareness and monitoring of one's own mental processes and strategies (Flavell et al., 2002). This ability to "think about what one is thinking about" and, thus, to manage one's mental processes—in other words, enhanced executive function—may be the chief advance of adolescent thought, the result of changes occurring in the adolescent brain (Kuhn, 2006).

Changes in Information Processing

Changes in the way adolescents process information reflect the maturation of the brain's frontal lobes and may help explain the cognitive advances Piaget described. Which neural connections wither and which become strengthened is highly responsive to experience. Thus, progress in cognitive processing varies greatly among individual adolescents (Kuhn, 2006).

Information-processing researchers have identified two broad categories of measurable change in adolescent cognition: *structural change* and *functional change* (Eccles et al., 2003).* Let's look at each.

Structural Change   *Structural* changes in adolescence include (1) changes in working memory capacity and (2) the increasing amount of knowledge stored in long-term memory.

What's Your View?

• How can parents and teachers help adolescents improve their reasoning ability?

Checkpoint

Can you . . .

◆ Explain the difference between formal operational and concrete operational thinking, as exemplified by the pendulum problem?

◆ Identify factors influencing adolescents' development of formal reasoning?

◆ Evaluate strengths and weaknesses of Piaget's theory of formal operations?

---

*The discussion in the following two sections is based on Eccles et al., 2003.

The capacity of working memory, which enlarges rapidly in middle childhood, continues to increase during adolescence. The expansion of working memory may enable older adolescents to deal with complex problems or decisions involving multiple pieces of information.

Information stored in long-term memory can be *declarative, procedural,* or *conceptual.*

declarative knowledge Acquired factual knowledge stored in long-term memory.

procedural knowledge Acquired skills stored in long-term memory.

conceptual knowledge Acquired interpretive understandings stored in long-term memory.

- **Declarative knowledge** ("knowing that . . .") consists of all the factual knowledge a person has acquired (for example, knowing that 2 + 2 = 4 and that George Washington was the first U.S. president).

- **Procedural knowledge** ("knowing how to . . .") consists of all the skills a person has acquired, such as being able to multiply and divide and to drive a car.

- **Conceptual knowledge** ("knowing why") is an understanding of, for example, why an algebraic equation remains true if the same amount is added or subtracted from both sides.

Functional Change Processes for obtaining, handling, and retaining information are *functional* aspects of cognition. Among these are learning, remembering, and reasoning, all of which improve during adolescence.

Among the most important functional changes are (1) a continued increase in processing speed (Kuhn, 2006) and (2) further development of executive function, which includes such skills as selective attention, decision making, inhibitory control of impulsive responses, and management of working memory. These skills seem to develop at varying rates (Blakemore & Choudhury, 2006; Kuhn, 2006). In one laboratory study, adolescents reached adult-level performance in response inhibition at age 14, processing speed at 15, and working memory at 19 (Luna et al., 2004). However, improvements observed in laboratory situations may not necessarily reflect real life, in which behavior also depends on motivation and emotion regulation. As we discussed earlier in this chapter, adolescents' rash judgments may be related to immature brain development, which may permit feelings to override reason.

Language Development

Although individual differences are great, by ages 16 to 18 the average young person knows about 80,000 words (Owens, 1996). With the advent of formal thought, adolescents can define and discuss such abstractions as *love, justice,* and *freedom.* They more frequently use such terms as *however, otherwise, anyway, therefore, really,* and *probably* to express logical relations between clauses or sentences. They become more conscious of words as symbols that can have multiple meanings; they enjoy using irony, puns, and metaphors (Owens, 1996).

Adolescents also become more skilled in *social perspective-taking,* the ability to understand another person's point of view and level of knowledge and to speak accordingly. This ability is essential in order to persuade or just to engage in conversation. Conscious of their audience, adolescents speak a different language with peers than with adults (Owens, 1996).

The Canadian linguist Marcel Danesi (1994) argues that adolescent speech constitutes a dialect of its own: *pubilect,* "the social dialect of puberty" (p. 97). Like any other linguistic code, pubilect serves to strengthen group identity and to shut outsiders (adults) out. Teenage vocabulary is characterized by rapid change. Although some of its terms have entered common discourse, adolescents keep inventing new ones all the time.

Checkpoint

Can you . . .

- ◆ Name two major types of changes in adolescents' information-processing capabilities, and give examples of each?

- ◆ Identify characteristics of adolescents' language development that reflect cognitive advances?

- ◆ Explain the uses of pubilect?

Vocabulary may differ by gender, ethnicity, age, geographical region, neighborhood, and type of school (Labov, 1992) and varies from one clique to another. "Druggies" and "jocks" engage in different kinds of activities, which form the main subjects of their conversation. This talk, in turn, cements bonds within the clique. A study of teenage speech patterns in Naples, Italy, suggests that similar features may emerge "in any culture where teenagerhood constitutes a distinct social category" (Danesi, 1994, p. 123).

Moral Reasoning: Kohlberg's Theory

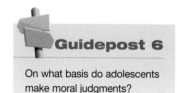

Guidepost 6

On what basis do adolescents make moral judgments?

As children attain higher cognitive levels, they become capable of more complex reasoning about moral issues. Their tendencies toward altruism and empathy increase as well. Adolescents are better able than younger children to take another person's perspective, to solve social problems, to deal with interpersonal relationships, and to see themselves as social beings. All of these tendencies foster moral development.

Let's look at Lawrence Kohlberg's groundbreaking theory of moral reasoning, at Carol Gilligan's influential work on moral development in women and girls, and at research on prosocial behavior in adolescence.

Heinz's Dilemma A woman is near death from cancer. A druggist has discovered a drug that doctors believe might save her. The druggist is charging $2,000 for a small dose—10 times what the drug costs him to make. The sick woman's husband, Heinz, borrows from everyone he knows but can scrape together only $1,000. He begs the druggist to sell him the drug for $1,000 or let him pay the rest later. The druggist refuses, saying, "I discovered the drug and I'm going to make money from it." Heinz, desperate, breaks into the man's store and steals the drug. Should Heinz have done that? Why or why not? (Kohlberg, 1969).

Heinz's problem is the most famous example of Lawrence Kohlberg's approach to studying moral development. Starting in the 1950s, Kohlberg and his colleagues posed hypothetical dilemmas like this one to 75 boys ages 10, 13, and 16 and continued to question them periodically for more than 30 years. At the heart of each dilemma was the concept of justice. By asking respondents how they arrived at their answers, Kohlberg, like Piaget, concluded that the way people look at moral issues reflects cognitive development.

Kohlberg's Levels and Stages Moral development in Kohlberg's theory bears some resemblance to Piaget's (refer back to Chapter 9), but Kohlberg's model is more complex. On the basis of thought processes shown by responses to his dilemmas, Kohlberg (1969) described three levels of moral reasoning, each divided into two stages (Table 11-4):

- *Level I:* **Preconventional morality.** People act under external controls. They obey rules to avoid punishment or reap rewards, or they act out of self-interest. This level is typical of children ages 4 to 10.

- *Level II:* **Conventional morality (or morality of conventional role conformity).** People have internalized the standards of authority figures. They are concerned about being "good," pleasing others, and maintaining the social order. This level is typically reached after age 10; many people never move beyond it, even in adulthood.

- *Level III:* **Postconventional morality (or morality of autonomous moral principles).** People recognize conflicts between moral standards and make their own judgments on the basis of principles of right, fairness, and justice. People generally do not reach this level of moral reasoning until at least early adolescence, or more commonly in young adulthood, if ever.

preconventional morality First level of Kohlberg's theory of moral reasoning in which control is external and rules are obeyed in order to gain rewards or avoid punishment or out of self-interest.

conventional morality (or morality of conventional role conformity) Second level in Kohlberg's theory of moral reasoning in which standards of authority figures are internalized.

postconventional morality (or morality of autonomous moral principles) Third level of Kohlberg's theory of moral reasoning, in which people follow internally held moral principles and can decide among conflicting moral standards.

| Table 11-4 | Kohlberg's Six Stages of Moral Reasoning |

Levels	Stages of Reasoning	Typical Answers to Heinz's Dilemma
Level I: Preconventional morality (ages 4 to 10)	*Stage 1: Orientation toward punishment and obedience.* "What will happen to me?" Children obey rules to avoid punishment. They ignore the motives of an act and focus on its physical form (such as the size of a lie) or its consequences (for example, the amount of physical damage).	*Pro:* "He should steal the drug. It isn't really bad to take it. It isn't as if he hadn't asked to pay for it first. The drug he'd take is worth only $200; he's not really taking a $2,000 drug." *Con:* "He shouldn't steal the drug. It's a big crime. He didn't get permission; he used force and broke and entered. He did a lot of damage and stole a very expensive drug."
	Stage 2: Instrumental purpose and exchange. "You scratch my back, I'll scratch yours." Children conform to rules out of self-interest and consideration for what others can do for them. They look at an act in terms of the human needs it meets and differentiate this value from the act's physical form and consequences.	*Pro:* "It's all right to steal the drug, because his wife needs it and he wants her to live. It isn't that he wants to steal, but that's what he has to do to save her." *Con:* "He shouldn't steal it. The druggist isn't wrong or bad; he just wants to make a profit. That's what you're in business for—to make money."
Level II: Conventional morality (ages 10 to 13 or beyond)	*Stage 3: Maintaining mutual relations, approval of others, the golden rule.* "Am I a good boy or girl?" Children want to please and help others, can judge the intentions of others, and develop their own ideas of what a good person is. They evaluate an act according to the motive behind it or the person performing it, and they take circumstances into account.	*Pro:* "He should steal the drug. He is only doing something that is natural for a good husband to do. You can't blame him for doing something out of love for his wife. You'd blame him if he didn't love his wife enough to save her." *Con:* "He shouldn't steal. If his wife dies, he can't be blamed. It isn't because he's heartless or that he doesn't love her enough to do everything that he legally can. The druggist is the selfish or heartless one."
	Stage 4: Social concern and conscience. "What if everybody did it?" People are concerned with doing their duty, showing respect for higher authority, and maintaining the social order. They consider an act always wrong, regardless of motive or circumstances, if it violates a rule and harms others.	*Pro:* "You should steal it. If you did nothing, you'd be letting your wife die. It's your responsibility if she dies. You have to take it with the idea of paying the druggist." *Con:* "It is a natural thing for Heinz to want to save his wife, but it's still always wrong to steal. He knows he's taking a valuable drug from the man who made it."
Level III: Postconventional morality (early adolescence, or not until young adulthood, or never)	*Stage 5: Morality of contract, of individual rights, and of democratically accepted law.* People think in rational terms, valuing the will of the majority and the welfare of society. They generally see these values as best supported by adherence to the law. While they recognize that there are times when human need and the law conflict, they believe it is better for society in the long run if they obey the law.	*Pro:* "The law wasn't set up for these circumstances. Taking the drug in this situation isn't really right, but it's justified." *Con:* "You can't completely blame someone for stealing, but extreme circumstances don't really justify taking the law into your own hands. You can't have people stealing whenever they are desperate. The end may be good, but the ends don't justify the means."
	Stage 6: Morality of universal ethical principles. People do what they as individuals think is right, regardless of legal restrictions or the opinions of others. They act in accordance with internalized standards, knowing that they would condemn themselves if they did not.	*Pro:* "This is a situation that forces him to choose between stealing and letting his wife die. In a situation where the choice must be made, it is morally right to steal. He has to act in terms of the principle of preserving and respecting life." *Con:* "Heinz is faced with the decision of whether to consider the other people who need the drug just as badly as his wife. Heinz ought to act not according to his feelings for his wife, but considering the value of all the lives involved."

Source: Adapted from Kohlberg, 1969; Lickona, 1976.

In Kohlberg's theory, it is the reasoning underlying a person's response to a moral dilemma, not the response itself, that indicates the stage of moral development. As shown in Table 11-4, two people who give opposite answers may be at the same stage if their reasoning is based on similar factors.

Some adolescents and even some adults remain at Kohlberg's level I. Like young children, they seek to avoid punishment or satisfy their needs. Most adolescents and most adults seem to be at level II, usually in stage 3. They conform to social conventions, support the status quo, and "do the right thing" to please others or to obey the law. Stage 4 reasoning (upholding social norms) is less common but increases from early adolescence into adulthood. Often adolescents show periods of apparent disequilibrium when advancing from one level to another (Eisenberg & Morris, 2004) or fall back on other ethical systems, such as religious prescriptions, rather than on Kohlberg's justice-based system (Thoma & Rest, 1999).

Kohlberg added a transitional level between levels II and III, when people no longer feel bound by society's moral standards but have not yet reasoned out their own principles of justice. Instead, they base their moral decisions on personal feelings. Before people can develop a fully principled (level III) morality, he said, they must recognize the relativity of moral standards. Many young people question their earlier moral views when they enter high school or college or the world of work and encounter people whose values, culture, and ethnic background are different from their own. Still, few people reach a level where they can choose among differing moral standards. In fact, at one point Kohlberg questioned the validity of stage 6, morality based on universal ethical principles, because so few people seem to attain it. Later, he proposed a seventh, "cosmic," stage, in which people consider the effect of their actions not only on other people but on the universe as a whole (Kohlberg, 1981; Kohlberg & Ryncarz, 1990).

Evaluating Kohlberg's Theory Kohlberg, building on Piaget, inaugurated a profound shift in the way we look at moral development. Instead of viewing morality solely as the attainment of control over self-gratifying impulses, investigators now study how children and adults base moral judgments on their growing understanding of the social world.

Initial research supported Kohlberg's theory. The American boys whom Kohlberg and his colleagues followed through adulthood progressed through Kohlberg's stages in sequence, and none skipped a stage. Their moral judgments correlated positively with age, education, IQ, and socioeconomic status (Colby, Kohlberg, Gibbs, & Lieberman, 1983). More recent research, however, has cast doubt on the delineation of some of Kohlberg's stages (Eisenberg & Morris, 2004). A study of children's judgments about laws and lawbreaking suggests that some children can reason flexibly about such issues as early as age 6 (Helwig & Jasiobedzka, 2001).

One reason the ages attached to Kohlberg's levels are so variable is that people who have achieved a high level of cognitive development do not always reach a comparably high level of moral development. A certain level of cognitive development is *necessary* but not *sufficient* for a comparable level of moral development. Thus, other processes besides cognition must be at work. Some investigators suggest that moral activity is motivated, not only by abstract considerations of justice, but also by such emotions as empathy, guilt, and distress and the internalization of prosocial norms (Eisenberg & Morris, 2004; Gibbs, 1991, 1995; Gibbs & Schnell, 1985). It also has been argued that Kohlberg's stages 5 and 6 cannot fairly be called the most mature stages of moral development because they restrict maturity to a select group of people given to philosophical reflection (Gibbs, 1995).

Furthermore, there is not always a clear relationship between moral reasoning and moral behavior. People at postconventional levels of reasoning do not necessarily act more morally than those at lower levels. Other factors, such as specific situations, conceptions of virtue, and concern for others contribute to moral behavior (Colby & Damon, 1992; Fischer & Pruyne, 2003). Generally speaking, however, adolescents who are more advanced in moral reasoning do tend to be more moral in their behavior as well as better adjusted and higher in social competence, whereas antisocial adolescents tend to use less mature moral reasoning (Eisenberg & Morris, 2004).

Influence of Parents, Peers, and Culture   Neither Piaget nor Kohlberg considered parents important to children's moral development, but more recent research emphasizes parents' contribution in both the cognitive and the emotional realms. Adolescents with supportive, authoritative parents who stimulate them to question and expand on their moral reasoning tend to reason at higher levels (Eisenberg & Morris, 2004).

Peers also affect moral reasoning by talking with each other about moral conflicts. Having more close friends, spending quality time with them, and being perceived as a leader are associated with higher moral reasoning (Eisenberg & Morris, 2004).

Kohlberg's system does not seem to represent moral reasoning in non-Western cultures as accurately as in the Western culture in which it was originally developed (Eisenberg & Morris, 2004). Older people in countries other than the United States do tend to score at higher stages than younger people. However, people in non-Western cultures rarely score above stage 4 (Edwards, 1981; Nisan & Kohlberg, 1982; Snarey, 1985), suggesting that some aspects of Kohlberg's model may not fit the cultural values of these societies.

An Ethic of Care: Gilligan's Theory

On the basis of research on women, Carol Gilligan (1982/1993) asserted that Kohlberg's theory is oriented toward values more important to men than to women. Gilligan claimed that women see morality not so much in terms of justice and fairness as of responsibility to show caring and avoid harm. They focus on not turning away from others rather than on not treating others unfairly (Eisenberg & Morris, 2004).

Research has found little support for Gilligan's claim of a male bias in Kohlberg's stages (Brabeck & Shore, 2003; Jaffee & Hyde, 2000), and she has since modified her position. However, research *has* found small gender differences in care-related moral reasoning among adolescents in some cultures (Eisenberg & Morris, 2004). For example, early adolescent girls in the United States tend to emphasize care-related concerns more than boys do, especially when tested with open-ended questions ("How important is it to keep promises to a friend?") or self-chosen moral dilemmas related to their own experience (Garmon, Basinger, Gregg, & Gibbs, 1996). The reason may be that girls generally mature earlier and have more intimate social relationships (Garmon et al., 1996; Skoe & Diessner, 1994). In an analysis of 113 studies, girls and women were more likely to think in terms of care and boys and men in terms of justice, but these differences were small (Jaffee & Hyde, 2000).

What's Your View?

• Can you think of a time when you or someone you know acted contrary to personal moral judgment? Why do you think this happened?

Prosocial Behavior and Volunteer Activity

Some researchers have studied prosocial (similar to care-oriented) moral reasoning as an alternative to Kohlberg's justice-based system. Prosocial moral reasoning is reasoning about moral dilemmas in which one person's needs or desires conflict with those of others in situations in which social rules or norms are unclear or non-existent. In a longitudinal study that followed children into early adulthood, prosocial reasoning based on personal reflection about consequences and on internalized values and norms increased with age, whereas reasoning based on such stereotypes as "it's nice to help" decreased from childhood into the late teens (Eisenberg & Morris, 2004).

Prosocial behavior, too, typically increases from childhood through adolescence (Eisenberg & Morris, 2004). Girls tend to show more prosocial behavior than boys (Eisenberg & Fabes, 1998), and this difference becomes more pronounced in adolescence (Fabes, Carlo, Kupanoff, & Laible, 1999). Girls tend to see themselves as more empathic and prosocial than boys do, and parents of girls emphasize social responsibility more than parents of boys (Eisenberg & Morris, 2004). In a large-scale study, this was true of 18-year-olds and their parents in seven countries—Australia, United States, Sweden, Hungary, Czech Republic, Bulgaria, and Russia (Flannagan, Bowes, Jonsson, Csapo, & Sheblanova, 1998). As with younger children, parents who use inductive discipline are more likely to have prosocial adolescents than parents who use power-assertive discipline.

About half of adolescents engage in some sort of community service or volunteer activity. These prosocial activities enable adolescents to become involved in adult society, to explore their potential roles as part of the community, and to link their developing sense of identity to civic involvement. Adolescent volunteers tend to have a high degree of self-understanding and commitment to others. Girls are more likely to volunteer than boys, and adolescents with high SES volunteer more than those with lower SES (Eisenberg & Morris, 2004). Students who do volunteer work outside of school tend, as adults, to be more engaged in their communities than those who do not (Eccles, 2004).

Educational and Vocational Issues

In the United States, as in all other industrialized countries and in some developing countries as well, more students finish high school than ever before, and many enroll in higher education (Eccles et al., 2003; Organisation for Economic Cooperation and Development [OECD], 2004). In 2004, nearly 87 percent of U.S. 18- to 24-year-olds not enrolled in high school had received a high school diploma or equivalent credential (Laird, DeBell, & Chapman, 2006). Among 30 member countries of the OECD (OECD, 2004), average levels of educational attainment range from only 7.4 years of schooling in Mexico to 13.8 years in Norway. The United States, with an average of 12.7 years of schooling, is on the high end of this international comparison. However, U.S. adolescents, on average, do less well on academic achievement tests than adolescents in many other countries (Baldi, Jin, Skemer, Green, & Herget, 2007, but see Gardner, 2007; Lemke et al., 2004; Snyder & Hoffman, 2001). Furthermore, although fourth- and eighth-grade student achievement, as measured by the National Assessment of Educational Progress, has improved in some areas, twelfth-grade achievement generally has not (NCES, 2003, 2005b).

Let's look at influences on school achievement and then at young people who drop out. Finally, we'll consider planning for higher education and vocations.

Checkpoint

Can You . . .

◆ List Kohlberg's levels and stages, and discuss factors that influence how rapidly children and adolescents progress through them?

◆ Evaluate Kohlberg's theory with regard to the role of emotion and socialization, parent and peer influences, and cross-cultural validity?

◆ Explain the difference between Gilligan's and Kohlberg's standards of moral reasoning, and discuss gender effects?

◆ Discuss individual differences in prosocial behavior, such as volunteering?

Guidepost 7

What influences affect adolescents' school success and their educational and vocational planning and preparation?

Influences on School Achievement

As in the elementary grades, such factors as parenting practices, socioeconomic status, and the quality of the home environment influence the course of school achievement in adolescence. Other factors include gender, ethnicity, peer influence, quality of schooling, and students' belief in themselves.

Student Motivation and Self-Efficacy   In Western countries, particularly the United States, educational practices are based on the assumption that students are, or can be, motivated to learn. Educators emphasize the value of intrinsic motivation—the student's desire to learn for the sake of learning (Larson & Wilson, 2004). Unfortunately, many U.S. students are *not* self-motivated, and motivation often declines as they enter high school (Eccles, 2004; Larson & Wilson, 2004).

In Western cultures, students high in *self-efficacy*—who believe that they can master tasks and regulate their own learning—are likely to do well in school (Zimmerman et al., 1992). In a longitudinal study of 140 eighth graders, students' self-discipline was twice as important as IQ in accounting for their grades and achievement test scores and for selection into a competitive high school program at the end of the year (Duckworth & Seligman, 2005).

In many cultures, education is based not on personal motivation but on such factors as duty (India), submission to authority (Islamic countries), and participation in the family and community (sub-Saharan Africa). In the countries of east Asia, students are expected to learn, not for the value of learning, but to meet family and societal expectations. Learning is expected to require intense effort, and students who fail or fall behind feel obligated to try again. This expectation may help explain why, in international comparisons in science and math, east Asian students substantially surpass U.S. students (Larson & Wilson, 2004). In developing countries, issues of motivation pale in the light of social and economic barriers to education: inadequate or absent schools and educational resources, the need for child labor to support the family, barriers to schooling for girls or cultural subgroups, and early marriage (Larson & Wilson, 2004). Thus, as we discuss factors in educational success, which are drawn largely from studies in the United States and other Western countries, we need to remember that they do not apply to all cultures.

Importance of SES and Related Family Characteristics   High socioeconomic status is an important predictor of academic success, according to a study of 15-year-olds' mathematical literacy in 20 relatively high-income countries (Hampden-Thompson & Johnston, 2006). In all those countries, students with at least one postsecondary-educated parent performed better than students whose parents had lower educational levels. A similar gap occurred between students whose parents had high occupational status and those whose parents were of middle or low occupational status. Having more than 200 books in the home also was associated with higher scores. All of these are indicators of socioeconomic status. Living in a two-parent family—another key predictor of math competence

Derek is taking responsibility for his own learning, doing research in the library. Responsible students like Derek are likely to do well in school.

in all 20 countries—also was related to SES. So were the disadvantages conferred by being an immigrant and speaking a nonnative language at home, which affected math achievement in most of the countries.

Gender On an international test of adolescents in 43 industrialized countries, girls in all countries were better readers than boys. Boys were ahead in mathematical literacy in about half of the countries, but these gender differences were less pronounced than in reading (OECD, 2004). In the United States, adolescent boys and girls score about the same on standardized tests in most subject-matter areas (Freeman, 2004; Sen et al., 2005). Boys have had a slight edge on standardized tests of math and science, but this gender gap appears to be shrinking as girls take equally challenging math and science courses and do as well or better in them (Spelke, 2005). Girls tend to do better than boys on assessments of reading and writing (Freeman, 2004; Sen et al., 2005).

Overall, in fact, beginning in adolescence, girls do better on verbal tasks that involve writing and language usage; boys do better in activities that involve visual and spatial functions helpful in math and science. However, boys' quantitative performance is more variable than girls': More boys score at both the lower and higher ends of the scale. Thus, girls, as a group, do better in math and science classwork, but boys (generally, a higher-end sample) score better on standardized college and graduate school admissions examinations (Halpern et al., 2007). (These differences also may be affected by the strategies boys and girls use in solving problems.)

Regardless of test scores, girls in the United States tend to have more confidence in their academic abilities than boys do. They like school a little better, earn better grades, and are more likely to graduate from high school and to plan to attend and finish college and graduate or professional schools. Boys are more likely than girls either to be underachievers, to be assigned to special or remedial education, and to be expelled or drop out of school (Eccles et al., 2003; Freeman, 2004) or to take honors courses, to apply to top colleges, and to aim for challenging careers (Eccles et al., 2003).

What causes these gender differences? The answers are complex. Research points to interacting biological and environmental explanations (Halpern et al., 2007).

Biologically, as we mentioned in Chapter 9, male and female brains are different, and they become even more different with age. Girls have more gray matter (neuronal cell bodies and nearby connections), but boys have more connective white matter (myelin) and cerebrospinal fluid, which cushion the longer paths of nerve impulses. These greater connective advantages have been linked with visual and spatial performance, which helps in math and science. Furthermore, gray matter growth peaks earlier in adolescent girls but continues to increase in adolescent boys. On the other hand, according to some studies, the corpus callosum, which connects the two brain hemispheres, is larger in girls than in boys, permitting better language processing. In addition, girls' brains are more evenly balanced across hemispheres than boys', permitting a wider range of cognitive abilities, whereas boys' brains may be more specialized. Boys' brains seem to be optimized for activity within each hemisphere, whereas girls' brains seem optimized for activity across hemispheres, permitting them to integrate verbal and analytic (left-brain) tasks with spatial and holistic (right-brain) tasks (Halpern et al., 2007).

Social and cultural forces that influence gender differences include the following (Halpern et al., 2007):

- *Home influences:* Across cultures, parents' educational level correlates with their children's math achievement. Except for highly gifted sons and daughters, the amount of parental involvement in children's education affects math performance. Parents' gender attitudes and expectations also have an effect.

- *School influences:* Subtle differences in the way teachers treat boys and girls, especially in math and science classes, have been documented.

- *Neighborhood influences:* Boys benefit more from enriched neighborhoods and are hurt more by deprived neighborhoods.

- *Women's and men's roles* in society help shape girls' and boys' choices of courses and occupations.

- *Cultural influences:* Cross-cultural studies show that the size of gender differences in math performance varies among nations and becomes greater by the end of secondary school. These differences correlate with the degree of gender equality in the society.

All in all, science is beginning to find answers to the perplexing question of why boys' and girls' abilities become more different in high school.

Parenting Styles, Ethnicity, and Peer Influence   In Western cultures, the benefits of authoritative parenting continue to affect school achievement during adolescence (Baumrind, 1991). *Authoritative parents* urge adolescents to look at both sides of issues, welcome their participation in family decisions, and admit that children sometimes know more than parents. These parents strike a balance between making demands and being responsive. Their children receive praise and privileges for good grades; poor grades bring encouragement to try harder and offers of help.

Authoritarian parents, in contrast, tell adolescents not to argue with or question adults and tell them they will "know better when they are grown up." Good grades bring admonitions to do even better; poor grades may be punished by reduced allowances or grounding. *Permissive parents* seem indifferent to grades, make no rules about watching television, do not attend school functions, and neither help with nor check their children's homework. These parents may not be neglectful or uncaring; they may, in fact, be nurturant. They may simply believe that teenagers should be responsible for their own lives.

What accounts for the academic success of authoritatively raised adolescents? Authoritative parents' greater involvement in schooling may be a factor as well as their encouragement of positive attitudes toward work. A more subtle mechanism, consistent with findings on self-efficacy, may be parents' influence on how children explain success or failure. In a study of 2,353 California and Wisconsin high school students, those who saw their parents as nonauthoritative were more likely than their peers to attribute poor grades to external causes or to low ability—forces beyond their control—rather than to their efforts. A year later, such students tended to pay less attention in class and to spend less time on homework (Glasgow et al., 1997). Thus, a sense of helplessness associated with nonauthoritative parenting may become a self-fulfilling prophecy, discouraging students from trying to succeed.

Among some ethnic groups, though, parenting styles may be less important than peer influence on academic motivation and achievement. In one study, Latino and African American adolescents, even those with authoritative parents, did less well in school than European American students, apparently because of lack of peer support for academic achievement (Steinberg, Dornbusch, & Brown, 1992). On the other hand, Asian American students, whose parents are sometimes described as authoritarian, get high grades and score better than European American students on math achievement tests, apparently because both parents *and* peers prize achievement (C. Chen & Stevenson, 1995). The strong school achievement of many young people from a variety of immigrant backgrounds reflects their families' and friends' strong emphasis on educational success (Fuligni, 1997).

The School   The quality of schooling strongly influences student achievement. A good middle or high school has an orderly, safe environment, adequate material resources, a stable teaching staff, and a positive sense of community. The school culture places a strong emphasis on academics and fosters the belief that all students can learn. It also offers opportunities for extracurricular activities, which keep students engaged and prevent them from getting into trouble after school. Teachers trust, respect, and care about students and have high expectations for them as well as confidence in their own ability to help students succeed (Eccles, 2004).

Adolescents are more satisfied with school if they are allowed to participate in making rules and feel support from teachers and other students (Samdal & Dür, 2000) and if the curriculum and instruction are meaningful and appropriately challenging and fit their interests, skill level, and needs (Eccles, 2004). In a survey of students' perceptions of their teachers, high teacher expectations were the most consistent positive predictor of students' goals and interests, and negative feedback was the most consistent negative predictor of academic performance and classroom behavior (Wentzel, 2002).

A decline in academic motivation and achievement often begins with the transition from the intimacy and familiarity of elementary school to the larger, more pressured, and less supportive environment of middle school or junior high school (Eccles, 2004). For this reason, some cities have tried eliminating the middle school transition by extending elementary school to eighth grade or have consolidated some middle schools with small high schools (Gootman, 2007). Some big-city school systems, such as New York's, Philadelphia's, and Chicago's, are experimenting with small schools in which students, teachers, and parents form a learning community united by a common vision of good education and often a special curricular focus, such as music or ethnic studies (Meier, 1995; Rossi, 1996).

Another innovation is Early College High Schools—small, personalized, high-quality schools operated in cooperation with nearby colleges. By combining a nurturing atmosphere with clear, rigorous standards, these schools enable students to complete high school requirements plus the first two years of college ("The Early College High School Initiative," n.d.).

Dropping Out of High School

Although more U.S. youths are completing high school than ever before, 3.8 percent of high school students dropped out during the 2004–2005 school year—this at a time when high school graduation is, for most purposes, a minimum requirement for labor force entry. Black and Hispanic students are more likely to drop out than white or Asian American students, and low-income students are six times more likely to drop out than high-income students (Laird, DeBell, Kienzl, & Chapman, 2007). However, the racial/ethnic gap is narrowing; between 1990 and 2005, all minority groups have shown increases in the percentage of adults age 25 or older who have finished high school (KewalRamani, Gilbertson, Fox, & Provasnik, 2007).

Why are poor and minority adolescents more likely to drop out? One reason may be ineffective schooling: low teacher expectations or differential treatment of these students; less teacher support than at the elementary level; and the perceived irrelevance of the curriculum to culturally underrepresented groups. In schools that use ability tracking, students in low-ability or noncollege tracks (where minority youth are likely to be assigned) often have inferior educational experiences. Placed

Checkpoint

Can You . . .

♦ Explain how schools in various cultures motivate students to learn?

♦ Assess the influences of personal qualities, SES, gender, ethnicity, parents, and peers on academic achievement?

♦ Give examples of educational practices that can help high school students succeed?

What's Your View?

• How can parents, educators, and societal institutions encourage young people to finish high school successfully?

with peers who are equally alienated, they may develop feelings of incompetence and negative attitudes toward school and engage in problem behaviors (Eccles, 2004).

Society suffers when young people do not finish school. Dropouts are more likely to be unemployed or to have low incomes, to end up on welfare, to become involved with drugs, crime, and delinquency, and to be in poorer health (Laird et al., 2006; NCES, 2001, 2003, 2004a).

A longitudinal study that followed 3,502 disadvantaged eighth graders into early adulthood points up the difference success in high school can make (Finn, 2006). As young adults, those who successfully completed high school were most likely to obtain postsecondary education, to have jobs, and to be consistently employed. An important factor distinguishing the successful completers was **active engagement:** the "attention, interest, investment, and effort students expend in the work of school" (Marks, 2000, p. 155). On the most basic level, active engagement means coming to class on time, being prepared, listening and responding to the teacher, and obeying school rules. A higher level of engagement consists of getting involved with the coursework—asking questions, taking the initiative to seek help when needed, or doing extra projects. Both levels of active engagement tend to pay off in positive school performance (Finn & Rock, 1997). Family encouragement, small class size, and a warm, supportive school environment promote active engagement.

Preparing for Higher Education or Vocations

How do young people develop career goals? How do they decide whether to go to college and, if not, how to enter the world of work? Many factors enter in, including individual ability and personality, education, socioeconomic and ethnic background, the advice of school counselors, life experiences, and societal values. Let's look at some influences on educational and vocational aspirations. Then we'll examine provisions for young people who do not plan to go to college. We'll also discuss the pros and cons of outside work for high school students.

Influences on Students' Aspirations Self-efficacy beliefs help shape the occupational options students consider and the way they prepare for careers (Bandura, Barbaranelli, Caprara, & Pastorelli, 2001; Bandura et al., 1996). In addition, parents' values with regard to academic achievement influence adolescents' values and occupational goals (Jodl, Michael, Malanchuk, Eccles, & Sameroff, 2001).

Despite the greater flexibility in career goals today, gender—and gender-stereotyping—still influence vocational choice (Eccles et al., 2003). Girls and boys in the United States are now equally likely to plan careers in math and science. However, boys are much more likely to earn college degrees in engineering, physics, and computer science (NCES, 2001), whereas girls are still more likely to go into nursing, social welfare professions, and teaching (Eccles et al., 2003). Much the same is true in other industrialized countries (OECD, 2004).

The educational system itself may act as a brake on vocational aspirations. Students who can memorize and analyze tend to do well in classrooms where teaching is geared to those abilities. Thus, these students are achievers in a system that stresses the abilities in which they happen to excel. Students whose strength is in creative or practical thinking—areas critical to success in certain fields—rarely get a chance to show what they can do (Sternberg, 1997). Recognition of a broader range of intelligences (refer back to Chapter 9), combined with more flexible teaching and career counseling, could allow more

active engagement Personal involvement in schooling, work, family, or other activity.

Checkpoint

Can You . . .

♦ Discuss trends in high school completion and causes and effects of dropping out?

♦ Explain the importance of active engagement in schooling?

students to meet their educational goals and enter the occupations they desire so as to make the contributions of which they are capable.

Guiding Students *Not* Bound for College   Most industrialized countries offer guidance to non-college-bound students. Germany, for example, has an apprenticeship system in which high school students go to school part-time and spend the rest of the week in paid on-the-job training supervised by an employer-mentor.

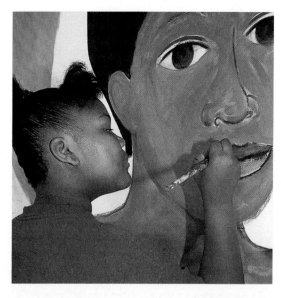

Students whose strength is in creative thinking frequently don't get a chance to show what they can do. More flexible teaching and career counseling could allow more students to make the contributions of which they are capable.

The United States lacks coordinated policies to help non-college-bound youth make a successful transition from high school to the labor market (Eccles, 2004). Vocational counseling is generally oriented toward college-bound youth. Whatever vocational training programs do exist for high school graduates who do not immediately go on to college tend to be less comprehensive than the German model and less closely tied to the needs of businesses and industries. Most of these young people must get training on the job or in community college courses. Many, ignorant about the job market, do not obtain the skills they need. Others take jobs beneath their abilities. Some do not find work at all (NRC, 1993a).

In some communities, demonstration programs help in the school-to-work transition. The most successful ones offer instruction in basic skills, counseling, peer support, mentoring, apprenticeship, and job placement (NRC, 1993a). In 1994, Congress allocated $1.1 billion to help states and local governments establish school-to-work programs in partnership with employers. Participating students improved their school performance and graduation rates and, when they entered the labor market, were more likely to find jobs and earned higher wages than students who did not participate (Hughes, Bailey, & Mechur, 2001).

Adolescents in the Workplace   In the United States, an estimated 80 to 90 percent of adolescents are employed at some time during high school, mostly in service and retail jobs (Staff, Mortimer, & Uggen, 2004). Researchers disagree over whether part-time work is beneficial to high school students (by helping them develop real-world skills and a work ethic) or detrimental (by distracting them from long-term educational and occupational goals).

Some research suggests that working students fall into two groups: those who are on an accelerated path to adulthood, and those who make a more leisurely transition, balancing schoolwork, paid jobs, and extracurricular activities. The "accelerators" work more than 20 hours a week during high school and spend little time on school-related leisure activities. Exposure to an adult world may lead them into alcohol and drug use, sexual activity, and delinquent behavior. Many of these adolescents have relatively low SES; they tend to look for full-time work right after high school and not to obtain college degrees. Intensive work experience in high school improves their prospects for work and income after high school, but not for long-term occupational attainment. The "balancers," in contrast, often come from more privileged backgrounds. For them, the effects of part-time work seem entirely benign. It helps them to gain a sense of responsibility, independence, and self-confidence and to appreciate the value of work but does not deter them from their educational paths (Staff et al., 2004).

✓ **Checkpoint**

Can You . . .

♦ Discuss influences on educational and vocational aspirations and planning?

♦ Weigh the value of part-time work for high school students?

For high school students who must or choose to work outside of school, then, the effects are more likely to be positive if they try to limit working hours and remain engaged in school activities. Cooperative educational programs that enable students to work part-time as part of their school program may be especially protective (Staff et al., 2004).

Vocational planning is one aspect of an adolescent's search for identity. The question "What shall I do?" is very close to "Who shall I be?" People who feel they are doing something worthwhile, and doing it well, feel good about themselves. Those who feel that their work does not matter—or that they are not good at it—may wonder about the meaning of their lives. A prime personality issue in adolescence, which we discuss in Chapter 12, is the effort to define the self.

Summary and Key Terms

Adolescence: A Developmental Transition

Guidepost 1: *What is adolescence, when does it begin and end, and what opportunities and risks does it entail?*

- Adolescence, in modern industrial societies, is the transition from childhood to adulthood. It lasts from about age 11 until 19 or 20.

- Early adolescence is full of opportunities for physical, cognitive, and psychosocial growth, but also of risks to healthy development. Risky behavior patterns, such as drinking alcohol, drug abuse, sexual and gang activity, and use of firearms, tend to increase throughout the teenage years; but most young people experience no major problems.

adolescence (354)

puberty (354)

PHYSICAL DEVELOPMENT

Puberty

Guidepost 2: *What physical changes do adolescents experience, and how do these changes affect them psychologically?*

- Puberty is triggered by hormonal changes. Puberty takes about four years, typically begins earlier in girls than in boys, and ends when a person can reproduce; but the timing of these events varies considerably.

- Sexual attraction seems to begin at about age 9 or 10, when the adrenal glands increase their hormonal output.

- During puberty, both boys and girls undergo an adolescent growth spurt. The reproductive organs enlarge and mature, and secondary sex characteristics appear.

- A secular trend toward earlier attainment of adult height and sexual maturity began about 100 years ago, probably because of improvements in living standards.

- The principal signs of sexual maturity are production of sperm (for males) and menstruation (for females).

adrenarche (356)

gonadarche (356)

primary sex characteristics (357)

secondary sex characteristics (357)

adolescent growth spurt (358)

spermarche (359)

menarche (359)

secular trend (359)

The Adolescent Brain

Guidepost 3: *What brain developments occur during adolescence, and how do they affect behavior?*

- The adolescent brain is not yet fully mature. It undergoes a second wave of overproduction of gray matter, especially in the frontal lobes, followed by pruning of excess nerve cells. Continuing myelination of the frontal lobes facilitates the maturation of cognitive processing.

- Adolescents process information about emotions with the amygdala, whereas adults use the frontal lobe. Thus, adolescents tend to make less accurate, less reasoned judgments.

- Underdevelopment of frontal cortical systems connected with motivation, impulsivity, and addiction may help explain adolescents' tendency toward risk taking.

Physical and Mental Health

Guidepost 4: *What are some common health problems in adolescence, and how can they be prevented?*

- For the most part, the adolescent years are relatively healthy. Health problems often are associated with poverty or lifestyle.

- Many adolescents do not engage in regular vigorous physical activity.
- Many adolescents do not get enough sleep because the high school schedule is out of sync with their natural body rhythms.
- Concern with body image, especially among girls, may lead to eating disorders.
- Three common eating disorders in adolescence are obesity, anorexia nervosa, and bulimia nervosa. All can have serious long-term effects. Anorexia and bulimia affect mostly girls and young women. Outcomes for bulimia tend to be better than for anorexia.
- Adolescent substance use has lessened in recent years; still, drug use often begins as children move into middle school.
- Marijuana, alcohol, and tobacco are the most popular drugs with adolescents. All involve serious risks. Nonmedical use of prescription and over-the-counter drugs is an increasing problem.
- The prevalence of depression increases in adolescence, especially among girls.
- Leading causes of death among adolescents include motor vehicle accidents, firearm use, and suicide.

body image (364)

anorexia nervosa (364)

bulimia nervosa (365)

substance abuse (366)

substance dependence (366)

COGNITIVE DEVELOPMENT

Aspects of Cognitive Maturation

Guidepost 5: *How do adolescents' thinking and use of language differ from younger children's?*

- Adolescents who reach Piaget's stage of formal operations can engage in hypothetical-deductive reasoning. They can think in terms of possibilities, deal flexibly with problems, and test hypotheses.
- Because environmental stimulation plays an important part in attaining this stage, not all people become capable of formal operations; and those who are capable do not always use them.
- Piaget's proposed stage of formal operations does not take into account such developments as accumulation of knowledge and expertise, gains in information processing, and the growth of metacognition. Piaget also paid little attention to individual differences, between-task variations, and the role of the situation.
- Research has found both structural and functional changes in adolescents' information processing. Structural changes include increases in declarative, procedural, and conceptual knowledge and expansion of the capacity of working memory. Functional changes include progress in deductive reasoning. However,

emotional immaturity may lead older adolescents to make poorer decisions than younger ones.
- Vocabulary and other aspects of language development, especially those related to abstract thought, such as social perspective-taking, improve in adolescence. Adolescents enjoy wordplay and create their own dialect.

formal operations (371)

hypothetical-deductive reasoning (372)

declarative knowledge (374)

procedural knowledge (374)

conceptual knowledge (374)

Guidepost 6: *On what basis do adolescents make moral judgments?*

- According to Kohlberg, moral reasoning is based on a developing sense of justice and growing cognitive abilities. Kohlberg proposed that moral development progresses from external control to internalized societal standards to personal, principled moral codes.
- Kohlberg's theory has been criticized on several grounds, including failure to credit the roles of emotion, socialization, and parental guidance. The applicability of Kohlberg's system to women and girls and to people in non-Western cultures has been questioned.

preconventional morality (375)

conventional morality (or morality of conventional role conformity) (375)

postconventional morality (or morality of autonomous moral principles) (375)

Educational and Vocational Issues

Guidepost 7: *What influences affect adolescents' school success and their educational and vocational planning and preparation?*

- Self-efficacy beliefs, parental practices, cultural and peer influences, gender, and quality of schooling affect adolescents' educational achievement.
- Although most Americans graduate from high school, the dropout rate is higher among poor, Hispanic, and African American students. However, this racial/ethnic gap is narrowing. Active engagement in studies is an important factor in keeping adolescents in school.
- Educational and vocational aspirations are influenced by several factors, including self-efficacy and parental values. Gender stereotypes have less influence than in the past.
- High school graduates who do not immediately go on to college can benefit from vocational training.
- Part-time work seems to have both positive and negative effects on educational, social, and occupational development. The long-term effects tend to be best when working hours are limited.

active engagement (384)

This face in the mirror

stares at me

demanding *Who are you? What will you become?*

And taunting, *You don't even know.*

Chastened, I cringe and agree

and then

because I'm still young,

I stick out my tongue.

—Eve Merriam, "Conversation with Myself," 1964

Did You **Know...**

- Today more teenage girls than teenage boys in the United States are sexually experienced?

- Sex education programs that encourage *both* abstinence and safe sexual practices are more effective than abstinence-only programs in delaying sexual initiation?

- More than 4 out of 10 adolescent girls in the United States have been pregnant at least once before age 20?

- Most adolescents say they have good relationships with their parents?

- The influence of peers peaks in early adolescence?

- Adolescents who participated in certain early childhood intervention programs are less likely to become juvenile delinquents than other underprivileged peers?

These are just a few of the interesting and important topics we will cover in this chapter. In Chapter 11 we looked at some physical and cognitive factors that contribute to an adolescent's sense of self, such as appearance and school achievement. In this chapter, we turn to psychosocial aspects of the quest for identity. We discuss how adolescents come to terms with their sexuality. We consider how teenagers' burgeoning individuality expresses itself in relationships with parents, siblings, and peers. We examine sources of antisocial behavior and ways of reducing the risks to adolescence so as to make it a time of positive growth and expanding possibilities. After you have read and studied this chapter, you should be able to answer each of the Guidepost questions on the following page.

Guideposts *for Study*

1. How do adolescents form an identity, and what roles do gender and ethnicity play?

2. What determines sexual orientation, what sexual practices are common among adolescents, and what leads some to engage in risky sexual behavior?

3. How do adolescents relate to parents, siblings, and peers?

4. What are the root causes of antisocial behavior and juvenile delinquency, and what can be done to reduce these risks of adolescence?

Guidepost 1

How do adolescents form an identity, and what roles do gender and ethnicity play?

identity According to Erikson, a coherent conception of the self, made up of goals, values, and beliefs to which a person is solidly committed.

identity versus identity confusion Erikson's fifth stage of psychosocial development, in which an adolescent seeks to develop a coherent sense of self, including the role she or he is to play in society. Also called *identity versus role confusion.*

The Search for Identity

The search for **identity**—which Erikson defined as a coherent conception of the self, made up of goals, values, and beliefs to which the person is solidly committed— comes into focus during the teenage years. Adolescents' cognitive development enables them to construct a "theory of the self" (Elkind, 1998). As Erikson (1950) emphasized, a teenager's effort to make sense of the self is not "a kind of maturational malaise." It is part of a healthy, vital process that builds on the achievements of earlier stages—on trust, autonomy, initiative, and industry—and lays the groundwork for coping with the challenges of adulthood. However, an identity crisis is seldom fully resolved in adolescence; issues concerning identity crop up again and again throughout adult life.

Erikson: Identity versus Identity Confusion

The chief task of adolescence, said Erikson (1968), is to confront the crisis of **identity versus identity confusion,** or *identity versus role confusion,* so as to become a unique adult with a coherent sense of self and a valued role in society. The concept of the *identity crisis* was based in part on Erikson's life experience. Growing up in Germany as the out-of-wedlock son of a Jewish woman from Denmark who had separated from her first husband, Erikson never knew his biological father. Though adopted at age 9 by his mother's second husband, a German Jewish pediatrician, he felt confusion about who he was. He floundered for some time before settling on his vocation. When he came to the United States, he needed to redefine his identity as an immigrant. All these issues found echoes in the identity crises he observed among disturbed adolescents, soldiers in combat, and members of minority groups (Erikson, 1968, 1973; L. J. Friedman, 1999).

Identity, according to Erikson, forms as young people resolve three major issues: the choice of an *occupation,* the adoption of *values* to live by, and the development of a satisfying *sexual identity.*

During middle childhood, children acquire skills needed for success in their culture. As adolescents, they need to find ways to use these skills. When young people have trouble settling on an occupational identity—or when their opportunities are artificially limited—they are at risk of behavior with serious negative consequences, such as criminal activity or early pregnancy.

According to Erikson, the *psychosocial moratorium,* the time out period that adolescence provides, allows young people to search for commitments to which they can be faithful. Many adolescents, says the psychologist David Elkind, "have a premature adulthood thrust upon them" (1998, p. 7). They lack the time or opportunity for this psychosocial moratorium—the protected period necessary to build a stable sense of self.

Adolescents who resolve the identity crisis satisfactorily develop the virtue of *fidelity:* sustained loyalty, faith, or a sense of belonging to a loved one or to friends and companions. Fidelity also can be an identification with a set of values, an ideology, a religion, a political movement, a creative pursuit, or an ethnic group (Erikson, 1982).

Fidelity is an extension of trust. In infancy, it is important for trust of others to outweigh mistrust; in adolescence, it becomes important to be trustworthy oneself. Adolescents extend their trust to mentors or loved ones. In sharing thoughts and feelings, an adolescent clarifies a tentative identity by seeing it reflected in the eyes of the beloved. However, these adolescent intimacies differ from mature intimacy, which involves greater commitment, sacrifice, and compromise.

Erikson saw the prime danger of this stage as identity or role confusion, which can greatly delay reaching psychological adulthood. (He did not resolve his identity crisis until his mid-twenties.) Some degree of identity confusion is normal. According to Erikson, it accounts for the seemingly chaotic nature of much adolescent behavior and for teenagers' painful self-consciousness. Cliquishness and intolerance of differences, both hallmarks of the adolescent social scene, are defenses against identity confusion.

Erikson's theory describes male identity development as the norm. According to Erikson, a man is not capable of real intimacy until after he has achieved a stable identity, whereas women define themselves through marriage and motherhood (something that may have been truer when Erikson developed his theory than it is today). Thus, said Erikson, women (unlike men) develop identity *through* intimacy, not *before* it. As we'll see, this male orientation of Erikson's theory has prompted criticism. Still, Erikson's concept of the identity crisis has inspired much valuable research.

Mastering the challenge of rock climbing may help this young man assess his abilities, interests, and desires. According to Erikson, this process helps adolescents resolve the crisis of identity versus identity confusion.

Marcia: Identity Status—Crisis and Commitment

Olivia, Isabella, Josh, and Jayden are about to graduate from high school. Olivia has considered her interests and her talents and plans to become an engineer. She has narrowed her college choices to three schools that offer good programs in this field.

Isabella knows exactly what she is going to do with her life. Her mother, a union leader at a plastics factory, has arranged for Isabella to enter an apprenticeship program there. Isabella has never considered doing anything else.

Josh, on the other hand, is agonizing over his future. Should he attend a community college or join the army? He cannot decide what to do now or what he wants to do eventually.

Jayden still has no idea what he wants to do, but he is not worried. He figures he can get some sort of a job and make up his mind about the future when he is ready.

These four young people are involved in identity formation. What accounts for the differences in the way they go about it, and how will these differences affect the outcome? According to research by the psychologist James E. Marcia (1966, 1980), these students are in four different **identity statuses,** states of ego (self) development.

identity statuses Marcia's term for states of ego development that depend on the presence or absence of crisis and commitment.

Table 12-1 Identity-Status Interview

Sample Questions	Typical Answers for the Four Statuses
About occupational commitment: "How willing do you think you'd be to give up going into _____ if something better came along?"	*Identity achievement.* "Well, I might, but I doubt it. I can't see what 'something better' would be for me." *Foreclosure.* "Not very willing. It's what I've always wanted to do. The folks are happy with it and so am I." *Moratorium.* "I guess if I knew for sure, I could answer that better. It would have to be something in the general area—something related . . ." *Identity diffusion.* "Oh, sure. If something better came along, I'd change just like that."
About ideological commitment: "Have you ever had any doubts about your religious beliefs?"	*Identity achievement.* "Yes, I started wondering whether there is a God. I've pretty much resolved that now. The way it seems to me is . . ." *Foreclosure.* "No, not really; our family is pretty much in agreement on these things." *Moratorium.* "Yes, I guess I'm going through that now. I just don't see how there can be a God and still so much evil in the world. . . ." *Identity diffusion.* "Oh, I don't know. I guess so. Everyone goes through some sort of stage like that. But it really doesn't bother me much. I figure that one religion is about as good as another!"

Source: Adapted from Marcia, 1966.

Through 30-minute, semistructured *identity-status interviews* (Table 12-1), Marcia distinguished four types of identity status: *identity achievement, foreclosure, moratorium,* and *identity diffusion.* The four categories differ according to the presence or absence of **crisis** and **commitment,** the two elements Erikson saw as crucial to forming identity. Marcia defined *crisis* as a period of conscious decision making and *commitment* as a personal investment in an occupation or system of beliefs (ideology). He found relationships between identity status and such characteristics as anxiety, self-esteem, moral reasoning, and patterns of behavior. Building on Marcia's theory, other researchers have identified additional personality and family variables related to identity status (Kroger, 2003; Table 12-2). Here is a more detailed sketch of young people in each identity status.

- **Identity achievement** (*crisis leading to commitment*). Olivia has resolved her identity crisis. During the crisis period, she devoted much thought and some emotional struggle to major issues in her life. She has made choices and expresses strong commitment to them. Her parents have encouraged her to make her own decisions; they have listened to her ideas and given their opinions without pressuring her to adopt them. Research in a number of cultures has found people in this category to be more mature and more socially competent than people in the other three (Kroger, 2003; Marcia, 1993).

- **Foreclosure** (*commitment without crisis*). Isabella has made commitments, not as a result of exploring possible choices, but by accepting someone else's plans for her life. She is happy and self-assured, but she becomes dogmatic when her opinions are questioned. She has close family ties, is obedient, and tends to follow a powerful leader, like her mother, who accepts no disagreement.

crisis Marcia's term for period of conscious decision making related to identity formation.

commitment Marcia's term for personal investment in an occupation or system of beliefs.

identity achievement Identity status, described by Marcia, that is characterized by commitment to choices made following a crisis, a period spent in exploring alternatives.

foreclosure Identity status, described by Marcia, in which a person who has not spent time considering alternatives (that is, has not been in crisis) is committed to other people's plans for his or her life.

Factor	Identity Achievement	Foreclosure	Moratorium	Identity Diffusion
Family	Parents encourage autonomy and connection with teachers; differences are explored within a context of mutuality.	Parents are overly involved with their children; families avoid expressing differences.	Adolescents are often involved in an ambivalent struggle with parental authority.	Parents are laissez-faire in child-rearing attitudes; are rejecting or not available to children.
Personality	High levels of ego development, moral reasoning, self-certainty, self-esteem, performance under stress, and intimacy.	Highest levels of authoritarianism and stereotypical thinking, obedience to authority, dependent relationships, low level of anxiety.	Most anxious and fearful of success; high levels of ego development, moral reasoning, and self-esteem.	Mixed results, with low levels of ego development, moral reasoning, cognitive complexity, and self-certainty; poor cooperative abilities.

*These associations have emerged from a number of separate studies. Because the studies have all been correlational, rather than longitudinal, it is impossible to say that any factor caused placement in any identity status.

Source: Kroger, 1993.

- **Moratorium** (*crisis with no commitment yet*). Josh is in crisis, struggling with decisions. He is lively, talkative, self-confident, and scrupulous but also anxious and fearful. He is close to his mother but resists her authority. He wants to have a girlfriend but has not yet developed a close relationship. He will probably come out of his crisis eventually with the ability to make commitments and achieve identity.

moratorium Identity status, described by Marcia, in which a person is currently considering alternatives (in crisis) and seems headed for commitment.

- **Identity diffusion** (*no commitment, no crisis*). Jayden has not seriously considered options and has avoided commitments. He is unsure of himself and tends to be uncooperative. His parents do not discuss his future with him; they say it's up to him. People in this category tend to be unhappy and often lonely.

identity diffusion Identity status, described by Marcia, that is characterized by absence of commitment and lack of serious consideration of alternatives.

These categories are not stages; they represent the status of identity development at a particular time, and they are likely to change in any direction as young people continue to develop (Marcia, 1979). When middle-aged people look back on their lives, they most commonly trace a path from foreclosure to moratorium to identity achievement (Kroger & Haslett, 1991). From late adolescence on, as Marcia proposed, more and more people are in moratorium or achievement: seeking or finding their own identity. About half of late adolescents remain in foreclosure or diffusion, but when development does occur, it is typically in the direction Marcia described (Kroger, 2003). Furthermore, although people in foreclosure seem to have made final decisions, that is often not so.

? What's Your View?

- Which of Marcia's identity statuses do you think you fit into as an adolescent? Has your identity status changed since then? If so, how?

Gender Differences in Identity Formation

Much research supports Erikson's view that, for women, identity and intimacy develop together. Rather than view this pattern as a departure from a male norm, however, some researchers see it as pointing to a weakness in Erikson's theory, which, they claim, is based on male-centered Western concepts of individuality, autonomy, and competitiveness. According to Carol Gilligan (1982, 1987a, 1987b; L. M. Brown & Gilligan, 1990), the female sense of self develops not so much through achieving a separate identity as through establishing relationships. Girls and women, says Gilligan, judge themselves on their handling of their responsibilities and on their ability to care for others as well as for themselves.

Some developmental scientists question how different the male and female paths to identity really are—especially today—and suggest that individual differences may be more important than gender differences (Archer, 1993; Marcia, 1993). Indeed, Marcia (1993) argues that an ongoing tension between independence and connectedness is at the heart of all of Erikson's psychosocial stages for *both* men and women. In research on Marcia's identity statuses, few gender differences have appeared (Kroger, 2003).

However, the development of self-esteem during adolescence seems to support Gilligan's view. Male self-esteem tends to be linked with striving for individual achievement, whereas female self-esteem depends more on connections with others (Thorne & Michaelieu, 1996).

The preponderance of evidence suggests that adolescent girls have lower self-esteem, on average, than adolescent boys, though this finding has been controversial. Several large, recent studies find that self-esteem drops during adolescence, more rapidly for girls than for boys, and then rises gradually into adulthood. These changes may be due in part to body image and other anxieties associated with puberty and with the transitions to junior high or middle school and high school (Robins & Trzesniewski, 2005). As we will see, the pattern seems to be different among minorities,

Ethnic Factors in Identity Formation

For many young people in minority groups, race or ethnicity is central to identity formation. Following Marcia's model, some research has identified four ethnic identity statuses (Phinney, 1998):

1. *Diffuse:* Juanita has done little or no exploration of her ethnicity and does not clearly understand the issues involved.

2. *Foreclosed:* Caleb has done little or no exploration of his ethnicity but has clear feelings about it. These feelings may be positive or negative, depending on the attitudes he absorbed at home.

3. *Moratorium:* Emiko has begun to explore her ethnicity but is confused about what it means to her.

4. *Achieved:* Diego has explored his identity and understands and accepts his ethnicity.

Table 12-3 quotes representative statements by minority young people in each status.

A study of 940 African American adolescents, college students, and adults found evidence of all four identity statuses in each age group. Only 27 percent of the adolescents were in the achieved group, as compared with 47 percent of the college students and 56 percent of the adults. Instead, adolescents were more likely to be in moratorium (42 percent), still exploring what it means to be African American. Twenty-five percent of the adolescents were in foreclosure, with feelings about African American identity based on their family upbringing. All three of these groups (achieved, in moratorium, and foreclosed) reported more positive regard for being African American than the 6 percent of adolescents who were diffused (neither committed nor exploring). Those of any age who were in the achieved status were most likely to view race as central to their identity (Yip, Seaton, & Sellers, 2006).

Another model focuses on three aspects of racial/ethnic identity: *connectedness* to one's own racial/ethnic group, *awareness of racism,* and *embedded achievement,* the belief that academic achievement is a part of group identity. A longitudinal study of low-income minority youth found that all three aspects of identity appear

Table 12-3	Representative Quotations from Each Stage of Ethnic Identity Development

Diffusion
"Why do I need to learn about who was the first black woman to do this or that? I'm just not too interested." (Black female)

Foreclosure
"I don't go looking for my culture. I just go by what my parents say and do, and what they tell me to do, the way they are." (Mexican American male)

Moratorium
"There are a lot of non-Japanese people around and it gets pretty confusing to try and decide who I am." (Asian American male)

Achieved
"People put me down because I'm Mexican, but I don't care anymore. I can accept myself more." (Mexican American female)

Source: Phinney, 1998, p. 277, Table 2.

to stabilize and even to increase slightly by midadolescence. Thus racial/ethnic identity may buffer tendencies toward a drop in grades and connection to school during the transition from middle school to high school (Altschul, Oyserman, & Bybee, 2006). On the other hand, perceived discrimination during the transition to adolescence can interfere with positive identity formation and lead to conduct problems or depression. Protective factors are nurturant, involved parenting, prosocial friends, and strong academic performance (Brody et al., 2006).

A three-year longitudinal study of 420 African American, Latino American, and European American adolescents looked at two dimensions of ethnic identity: *group esteem* (feeling good about one's ethnicity) and *exploration of the meaning of ethnicity* in one's life. Group esteem rose during both early and middle adolescence, especially for African Americans and Latinos, for whom it was lower to begin with. Exploration of the meaning of ethnicity increased only in middle adolescence, perhaps reflecting the transition from relatively homogeneous neighborhood elementary or junior high schools into more ethnically diverse high schools. Interactions with members of other ethnic groups may stimulate young peoples' curiosity about their own ethnic identity (French, Seidman, Allen, & Aber, 2006).

Contrary to the pattern among the general population, minority adolescents— both boys and girls—often gain in self-esteem with age, according to self-reports of students at a New York public high school. Family support was the strongest factor in self-esteem, followed by a positive school climate (Greene & Way, 2005).

The term **cultural socialization** refers to parental practices that teach children about their racial or ethnic heritage, promote cultural customs and traditions, and foster racial/ethnic and cultural pride. Adolescents who have experienced cultural socialization tend to have stronger and more positive ethnic identity than those who have not (Hughes et al., 2006).

Sexuality

Seeing oneself as a sexual being, recognizing one's sexual orientation, coming to terms with sexual stirrings, and forming romantic or sexual attachments all are parts of achieving *sexual identity*. Awareness of sexuality is an important aspect of identity formation, profoundly affecting self-image and relationships. Although this process is biologically driven, its expression is in part culturally defined.

cultural socialization Parental practices that teach children about their racial/ethnic heritage and promote cultural practices and cultural pride.

Checkpoint

Can you . . .

♦ List the three major issues involved in identity formation, according to Erikson?

♦ Describe four types of identity status found by Marcia?

♦ Discuss how gender and ethnicity affect identity formation?

Guidepost 2

What determines sexual orientation, what sexual practices are common among adolescents, and what leads some to engage in risky sexual behavior?

Attitudes toward sexuality have liberalizd in the United States during the past 50 years. This trend includes more open acceptance of sexual activity and a decline in the double standard by which males are freer sexually than females.

During the twentieth century a major change in sexual attitudes and behavior in the United States and other industrialized countries brought more widespread acceptance of premarital sex, homosexuality, and other previously disapproved forms of sexual activity. With widespread access to the Internet, casual sex with fleeting cyber-acquaintances who hook up through online chat rooms or singles' meeting sites has become more common. Cell phones, e-mail, and instant messaging make it easy for adolescents to arrange these hookups with disembodied strangers, insulated from adult scrutiny. All of these changes have brought increased concerns about sexual risk taking. On the other hand, the AIDS epidemic has led many young people to abstain from sexual activity outside of committed relationships or to engage in safer sexual practices.

Sexual Orientation and Identity

sexual orientation Focus of consistent sexual, romantic, and affectionate interest, either heterosexual, homosexual, or bisexual.

Although present in younger children, it is in adolescence that a person's **sexual orientation** generally becomes a pressing issue: whether that person will consistently be sexually attracted to persons of the other sex (*heterosexual*), of the same sex (*homosexual*), or of both sexes (*bisexual*). Heterosexuality predominates in nearly every known culture throughout the world. The prevalence of homosexual orientation varies widely. Depending on whether it is measured by sexual or romantic *attraction or arousal* (as in the definition we just gave) or by sexual *behavior* or sexual *identity,* the rate of homosexuality in the U.S. population ranges from 1 to 21 percent (Savin-Williams, 2006).

Many young people have one or more homosexual experiences, but isolated experiences or even occasional attractions or fantasies do not determine sexual orientation. In a national survey, 4.5 percent of 15- to 19-year-old boys and 10.6 percent of girls in that age group reported ever having had same-sex sexual contact, but only

2.4 percent of the boys and 7.7 percent of the girls reported having done so in the past year (Mosher, Chandra, & Jones, 2005). Social stigma may bias such self-reports, underestimating the prevalence of homosexuality and bisexuality.

Origins of Sexual Orientation   Much research on sexual orientation has focused on efforts to explain homosexuality. Although it once was considered a mental illness, several decades of research have found no association between homosexual orientation and emotional or social problems—apart from those apparently caused by societal treatment of homosexuals, such as a tendency to depression, (APA, n.d.; C. J. Patterson, 1992, 1995a, 1995b). These findings led the psychiatric profession in 1973 to stop classifying homosexuality as a mental disorder.

Sexual orientation seems to be at least partly genetic (Diamond & Savin-Williams, 2003). The first full genome-wide scan for male sexual orientation has identified three stretches of DNA on chromosomes 7, 8, and 10 that appear to be involved (Mustanski et al., 2005). However, because identical twins are not perfectly concordant for sexual orientation, nongenetic factors also may play a part (Diamond & Savin-Williams, 2003). Among more than 3,800 Swedish same-sex twin pairs, nonshared environmental factors accounted for about 64 percent of individual differences in sexual orientation. Genes explained about 34 percent of the variation in men and 18 percent in women. Shared family influences accounted for about 16 percent of the variation in women but had no effect in men (Långström, Rahman, Carlström, & Lichtenstein, 2008)

The more older biological brothers a man has, the more likely he is to be gay. In an analysis of 905 men and their biological, adoptive, half-, or stepsiblings, the only significant factor in sexual orientation was the number of times a man's mother had borne boys. Each older biological brother increased the chances of homosexuality in a younger brother by 33 percent. This phenomenon may be a cumulative immune-like response to the presence of successive male fetuses in the womb (Bogaert, 2006).

Imaging studies have found striking similarities of brain structure and function between homosexuals and heterosexuals of the other sex. Brains of gay men and straight women are symmetrical, whereas in lesbians and straight men the right hemisphere is slightly larger. Also, in gays and lesbians, connections in the amygdala, which is involved in emotion, are typical of the other sex (Savic & Lindström, 2008). One researcher reported a difference in the size of the hypo-thalamus, a brain structure that governs sexual activity, in heterosexual and gay men (LeVay, 1991). In brain imaging studies on pheromones, odors that attract mates, the odor of male sweat activated the hypothalamus in gay men much as it did in heterosexual women. Similarly, lesbian women, and straight men, reacted more positively to female pheromones than to male ones (Savic, Berglund, & Lindström, 2005; Savic, Berglund, & Lindström, 2006). However, these differences may be an effect of homosexuality, not a cause.

Homosexual and Bisexual Identity Development   Despite the increased acceptance of homosexuality in the United States, many adolescents who openly identify as gay, lesbian, or bisexual feel isolated in a hostile environment. They may be subject to discrimination or violence. Others may be reluctant to disclose their sexual orientation, even to their parents, for fear of strong disapproval or a rupture in the family (Hillier, 2002; C. J. Patterson, 1995b). They may find it difficult to meet and identify potential same-sex partners. (Diamond & Savin-Williams, 2003).

There is no single route to the development of gay, lesbian, or bisexual identity and behavior. Because of the lack of socially sanctioned ways to explore their sexuality, many gay and lesbian adolescents experience identity confusion (Sieving,

Checkpoint

Can you . . .

◆ Summarize research findings regarding origins of sexual orientation?

◆ Discuss homosexual identity and relationship formation?

Oliphant, & Blum, 2002). Gay, lesbian, and bisexual youth who are unable to establish peer groups that share their sexual orientation may struggle with the recognition of same-sex attractions (Bouchey & Furman, 2003; Furman & Wehner, 1997).

Sexual Behavior

According to national surveys, 77 percent of young people in the United States have had sex by age 20. This proportion has been roughly the same since the mid-1960s and the advent of the pill (Finer, 2007). The average girl has her first sexual intercourse at 17, the average boy at 16, and approximately one-fourth of boys and girls report having had intercourse by 15 (Klein & AAP Committee on Adolescence, 2005). African Americans and Latinos tend to begin sexual activity earlier than white youth (Kaiser Family Foundation, Hoff, Greene, & Davis, 2003). Though teenage boys historically have been more likely to be sexually experienced than teenage girls, trends are shifting. In 2002, 49 percent of boys and 53 percent of girls ages 15 to19 reported having had vaginal intercourse (Mosher et al., 2005).

Sexual Risk Taking   Two major concerns about adolescent sexual activity are the risks of contracting sexually transmitted diseases (STDs) and, for heterosexual activity, of pregnancy. Most at risk are young people who start sexual activity early, have multiple partners, do not use contraceptives regularly, and have inadequate information—or misinformation—about sex (Abma et al., 1997). Other risk factors are living in a socioeconomically disadvantaged community, substance use, antisocial behavior, and association with deviant peers. Parental monitoring can help reduce these risks (Baumer & South, 2001; Capaldi, Stoolmiller, Clark, & Owen, 2002).

Why do some adolescents become sexually active at an early age? Early entrance into puberty, poverty, poor school performance, lack of academic and career goals, a history of sexual abuse or parental neglect, and cultural or family patterns of early sexual experience may play a part (Klein & AAP Committee on Adolescence, 2005). The absence of a father, especially early in life, is a strong factor (Ellis et al., 2003). Teenagers who have close, warm relationships with their mothers are more likely to delay sexual activity. So are those who perceive that their mothers disapprove of such activity (Jaccard & Dittus, 2000; Sieving, McNeely, & Blum, 2000). Other reasons teenagers give for not yet having had sex are that it is against their religion or morals and that they do not want to get (or get a girl) pregnant (Abma, Martinez, Mosher, & Dawson, 2004).

One of the most powerful influences is perception of peer group norms. Young people often feel under pressure to engage in activities they do not feel ready for. In a nationally representative survey, nearly one-third of 15- to 17-year-olds, especially boys, said they had experienced pressure to have sex (Kaiser Family Foundation et al., 2003).

Among Asian American youths, heterosexual, and gay males begin sexual activity later than white, African American, and Latino males. This pattern of delayed sexual activity may reflect strong cultural pressures to save sex for marriage or adulthood and then to have children who will carry on the family name (Dubé & Savin-Williams, 1999).

As U.S. adolescents have become more aware of the risks of sexual activity, the percentage who have ever had intercourse has declined, especially among boys (Abma et al., 2004). However, noncoital forms of genital sexual activity, such as oral and anal sex and mutual masturbation, are common. Many heterosexual teens do not regard these activities as "sex" but as substitutes for, or precursors of, sex, or even as abstinence (Remez, 2000). In one national survey, just over half

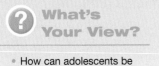

What's Your View?

• How can adolescents be helped to avoid or change risky sexual behavior?

of teenage boys and girls reported having given or received oral sex, more than had had vaginal intercourse (Mosher et al., 2005).

Use of Contraceptives   The use of contraceptives among teenagers has increased since 1990. In one survey, about 83 percent of girls and 91 percent of boys said they had used contraception the most recent time they had sex (Abma et al., 2004). Teens who, in their first relationship, delay intercourse, discuss contraception before having sex, or use more than one method of contraception are more likely to use contraceptives consistently throughout that relationship (Manlove, Ryan, & Franzetta, 2003).

The best safeguard for sexually active teens is regular use of condoms, which give some protection against STDs as well as against pregnancy. Condom use has increased in recent years, as has use of the pill and new hormonal and injectable methods of contraception or combinations of methods (Abma et al., 2004). Still, as recently as 2003, only 63 percent of sexually active high school students reported having used condoms the last time they had intercourse. Adolescents who start using prescription contraceptives often stop using condoms, not realizing that they leave themselves unprotected against STDs (Klein & AAP Committee on Adolescence, 2005).

Where Do Teenagers Get Information about Sex?   Adolescents get their information about sex primarily from friends, parents, sex education in school, and the media (Kaiser Family Foundation et al., 2003). Adolescents who can talk about sex with older siblings as well as with parents are more likely to have positive attitudes toward safer sexual practices (Kowal & Pike, 2004).

Since 1998, federal- and state-funded sex education programs stressing abstinence from sex until marriage as the best or only option have become common (Devaney, Johnson, Maynard, & Trenholm, 2002). Programs that encourage abstinence but also discuss STD prevention and safer sexual practices for the sexually active have been found to delay sexual initiation and increase contraceptive use (AAP Committee on Psychosocial Aspects of Child and Family Health and Committee on Adolescence, 2001).

However, some school programs promote abstinence as the *only* option, even though abstinence-only courses have not been shown to delay sexual activity (AAP Committee on Psychosocial Aspects of Child and Family Health and Committee on Adolescence, 2001; Satcher, 2001; Trenhom et al., 2007). Likewise, virginity pledges have only limited effectiveness (Bearman & Bruckner, 2001). Although more than 4 out of 5 teenagers report receiving formal instruction in how to say no to sex, only 2 out of 3 have been taught about birth control. Only one-half of girls and one-third of boys ages 18 and 19 say they talked with a parent about birth control before their 18th birthday (Abma et al., 2004).

Unfortunately, many teenagers get much of their sex education from the media, which associate sexual activity with fun, excitement, competition, danger, or violence and rarely show the risks of unprotected sex. In a two-year longitudinal survey of 12- to 14-year-olds, exposure to a heavy diet of sexual content in the media accelerated white students' likelihood of early intercourse. Black teens appeared to be more influenced by parental expectations and their friends' behavior (J. D. Brown et al., 2006).

Sexually Transmitted Diseases (STDs)

Sexually transmitted diseases (STDs), sometimes called *sexually transmitted infections (STIs),* are diseases spread by sexual contact. Table 12-4 summarizes some common STDs: their causes, most frequent symptoms, treatment, and consequences.

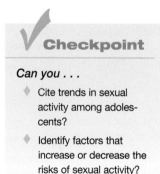

Checkpoint

Can you . . .

◆ Cite trends in sexual activity among adolescents?

◆ Identify factors that increase or decrease the risks of sexual activity?

sexually transmitted diseases (STDs)   Diseases spread by sexual contact.

Table 12-4 Common Sexually Transmitted Diseases

Disease	Cause	Symptoms: Male	Symptoms: Female	Treatment	Consequences If Untreated
Chlamydia	Bacterial infection	Pain during urination, discharge from penis	Vaginal discharge, abdominal discomfort†	Tetracycline or erythromycin	Can cause pelvic inflammatory disease or eventual sterility
Trichomoniasis	Parasitic infection, sometimes passed on in moist objects such as towels and swimsuits	Often absent	Absent or may include vaginal discharge, discomfort during intercourse, odor, painful urination	Oral antibiotic	May lead to abnormal growth of cervical cells
Gonorrhea	Bacterial infection	Discharge from penis, pain during urination*	Discomfort when urinating, vaginal discharge, abnormal menses†	Penicillin or other antibiotics	Can cause pelvic inflammatory disease or eventual sterility; also can cause arthritis, dermatitis, and meningitis
HPV (genital warts)	Human papilloma virus	Painless growths that usually appear on penis but also may appear on urethra or in rectal area*	Small, painless growths on genitals and anus; also may occur inside the vagina without external symptoms*	Removal of warts; but infection often reappears	May be associated with cervical cancer; in pregnancy, warts enlarge and may obstruct birth canal
Herpes	Herpes simplex virus	Painful blisters anywhere on the genitalia, usually on the penis*	Painful blisters on the genitalia, sometimes with fever and aching muscles; women with sores on cervix may be unaware of outbreaks*	No known cure but controlled with antiviral drug acyclovir	Possible increased risk of cervical cancer
Hepatitis B	Hepatitis B virus	Skin and eyes become yellow	Skin and eyes become yellow	No specific treatment; no alcohol	Can cause liver damage, chronic hepatitis
Syphilis	Bacterial infection	In first stage, reddish-brown sores on the mouth or genitalia or both, which may disappear, though the bacteria remain; in the second, more infectious, stage, a widespread skin rash*	In first stage, reddish-brown sores on the mouth or genitalia or both, which may disappear, though the bacteria remain; in the second, more infectious, stage, a widespread skin rash*	Penicillin or other antibiotics	Paralysis, convulsions, brain damage, and sometimes death
AIDS (acquired immune deficiency syndrome)	Human immunodeficiency virus (HIV)	Extreme fatigue, fever, swollen lymph nodes, weight loss, diarrhea, night sweats, susceptibility to other diseases*	Extreme fatigue, fever, swollen lymph nodes, weight loss, diarrhea, night sweats, susceptibility to other diseases*	No known cure; protease inhibitors and other drugs appear to extend life	Death, usually due to other diseases, such as cancer

*May be asymptomatic.
†Is often asymptomatic.

An estimated 3.2 million adolescent girls in the United States—about 1 in 4 of those ages 14 to 19—has at least one STD, according to a nationally representative study (Forhan et al., 2008). The chief reasons for the prevalence of STDs among teenagers include early sexual activity, which increases the likelihood of having multiple high-risk partners; failure to use condoms or to use them regularly and correctly; and, for women, a tendency to have sex with older partners (CDC, 2000b; Forhan et al., 2008).

STDs in adolescent girls are most likely to develop undetected. In a *single* unprotected sexual encounter with an infected partner, a girl runs a 1 percent risk of acquiring HIV, a 30 percent risk of acquiring genital herpes, and a 50 percent risk of acquiring gonorrhea (Alan Guttmacher Institute [AGI], 1999). Although teenagers tend to view oral sex as less risky than intercourse, a number of STDs, especially pharyngeal gonorrhea, can be transmitted in that way (Remez, 2000).

The most common STD, affecting 18.3 percent of 14- to 19-year-olds, is human papilloma virus (HPV), or genital warts, the leading cause of cervical cancer in women. Among girls with three or more partners, the risk jumps to 50 percent (Forhan et al., 2008).

The most common *curable* STDs are chlamydia and gonorrhea. These diseases, if undetected and untreated, can lead to severe health problems, including, in women, to pelvic inflammatory disease (PID), a serious abdominal infection. In the United States, close to 1 in 10 teenage girls and 1 in 5 boys are affected by either chlamydia or gonorrhea, or both (CDC, 2000b; Forhan et al., 2008).

Genital herpes simplex is a chronic, recurring, often painful, and highly contagious disease. It can be fatal to a person with a deficiency of the immune system or to the newborn infant of a mother who has an outbreak at the time of delivery. Its incidence has increased dramatically during the past three decades. Hepatitis B remains a prominent STD despite the availability, for more than 20 years, of a preventive vaccine. Also common among young people is trichomoniasis, a parasitic infection that may be passed along by moist towels and swimsuits (Weinstock, Berman, & Cates, 2004).

The human immunodeficiency virus (HIV), which causes AIDS, is transmitted through bodily fluids (mainly blood and semen), usually by sharing of intravenous drug needles or by sexual contact with an infected partner. The virus attacks the body's immune system, leaving a person vulnerable to a variety of fatal diseases. Symptoms of AIDS, which include extreme fatigue, fever, swollen lymph nodes, weight loss, diarrhea, and night sweats, may not appear until six months to ten or more years after initial infection.

Worldwide, of the 4.1 million new HIV infections each year, about half are in young people ages 15 to 24 (UNAIDS, 2006). In the United States, more than 1 in 4 of the estimated 1,039,000 to 1,185,000 persons living with HIV or AIDS were infected in their teens (CDC, 2007a; Kaiser Family Foundation et al., 2003). As of now, AIDS is incurable, but increasingly the related infections that kill people are being stopped with antiviral therapy, including protease inhibitors (Palella et al., 1998; Weinstock et al., 2004). A Danish study found that young patients with HIV have an estimated median survival of more than 35 years (Lohse et al., 2007). Ironically, by reducing the scare factor, this advance may be responsible for giving sexually active teens less reason to take precautions when having sex. After holding steady for three years, the estimated number of new HIV infections in U.S. 15- to 19-year-olds took a 20 percent jump to 1,213 cases in 2005 (CDC, 2007a).

Because symptoms may not appear until a disease has progressed to the point of causing serious long-term complications, early detection is important. Regular, school-based screening and treatment, together with programs that promote abstention from or postponement of sexual activity, responsible decision making, and ready availability of condoms for those who are sexually active may help control the spread of STDs (AAP Committee on Adolescence, 1994; AGI, 1994; Cohen, Nsuami, Martin, & Farley, 1999; Rotheram-Borus & Futterman, 2000).

Checkpoint

Can you . . .

- Identify and describe the most common sexually transmitted diseases?

- List risk factors for developing an STD during adolescence, and identify effective prevention methods?

There is no evidence that education about condom use and availability contributes to increased sexual activity (Klein & AAP Committee on Adolescence, 2005).

Teenage Pregnancy and Childbearing

More than 4 in 10 adolescent girls in the United States have been pregnant at least once before age 20. More than half (51 percent) of pregnant teenagers in the United States have their babies, and 35 percent choose to abort. Fourteen percent of teen pregnancies end in miscarriage or stillbirth (Klein & AAP Committee on Adolescence, 2005).

A substantial decline in teenage pregnancy has accompanied steady decreases in early intercourse and in sex with multiple partners and an increase in contraceptive use. In 2004 the teen pregnancy rate fell to 72.2 per 1,000 girls, the lowest rate reported since 1976. However, birthrates for U.S. 15- to 19-year-old girls, which had reached a record low of 40.5 live births per 1,000 girls between 1991 and 2005, rose slightly to 41.1 percent in 2006 (Ventura, Abma, Mosher, & Henshaw, 2008; Figure 12-1). All three rates have fallen more sharply among younger teens (15 to 17 years old) than among 18- and 19-year-olds.

Although declines in teenage pregnancy and childbearing have occurred among all population groups, birthrates have fallen most sharply among black teenagers—by 46 percent. Still, black and Hispanic girls are more likely to have babies than white, American Indian, or Asian American girls (Martin, Hamilton, et al., 2006). And U.S. teens are more likely to become pregnant and give birth than teenagers in most other industrialized countries (Martin, Hamilton, et al., 2005).

More than 90 percent of pregnant teenagers describe their pregnancies as unintended, and 50 percent of teen pregnancies occur within six months of sexual initiation (Klein & AAP Committee on Adolescence, 2005). Many of these girls grew up fatherless (Ellis et al., 2003). Among 9,159 women at a California primary care clinic, those who had become pregnant in adolescence were likely, as children, to have been physically, emotionally, or sexually abused and/or exposed to parental divorce or separation, domestic violence, substance abuse, or a household member who was mentally ill or engaged in criminal behavior (Hillis et al., 2004). Teenage fathers, too, tend to have limited financial resources, poor academic performance, and high dropout rates. Many teenage parents are themselves products of adolescent pregnancy (Campa & Eckenrode, 2006; Klein & AAP Committee on Adolescence, 2005; Pears, Pierce, Kim, Capaldi, & Owen, 2005).

Outcomes of Teenage Pregnancy Teenage pregnancies often have poor outcomes. Many of the mothers are impoverished and poorly educated, and some are drug users. Many do not eat properly, do not gain enough weight, and get inadequate prenatal care or none at all. Their babies are likely to be premature or dangerously small and are at heightened risk of other birth complications; late fetal, neonatal, or infant death; health and academic problems; abuse and neglect; and developmental disabilities that may continue into adolescence (AAP Committee on Adolescence, 1999; AAP Committee on Adolescence and Committee on Early Childhood, Adoption, and Dependent Care, 2001; AGI, 1999; Children's Defense Fund, 1998, 2004; Klein & AAP Committee on Adolescence, 2005; Menacker et al., 2004).

The 2007 movie Juno *portrays an adolescent dealing with an unplanned pregnancy. Unlike the movie's happy ending, teen pregnancies in real life often have poor outcomes.*

Babies of more affluent teenage mothers also may be at risk. Among more than 134,000 white, largely middle-class girls and women, 13- to 19-year-olds were more likely than 20- to 24-year-olds to have low-birth-weight babies, even when the mothers were married and well educated and had adequate prenatal care. Prenatal care apparently cannot always overcome the biological disadvantage of being born to a still-growing girl whose own body may be competing with the developing fetus for vital nutrients (Fraser et al., 1995).

Teenage unwed mothers and their families are likely to suffer financially. Child support laws are spottily enforced, court-ordered payments are often inadequate, and many young fathers cannot afford them (AAP Committee on Adolescence, 1999). Unmarried parents under age 18 are eligible for public assistance only if they live with their parents and go to school.

Teenage mothers are likely to drop out of school and to have repeated pregnancies. They and their partners may lack the maturity, skills, and social support to be good parents. Their children, in turn, tend to have developmental and academic problems, to be depressed, to engage in substance abuse and early sexual activity, to engage in gang activity, to be unemployed, and to become adolescent parents themselves (Klein & AAP Committee on Adolescence, 2005; Pogarsky, Thornberry, & Lizotte, 2006). The risks are especially great for sons of teenage mothers (Pogarsky et al., 2006). However, some of these outcomes, such as marijuana use, may be influenced by other factors, and not by early childbearing (Levine, Emery, & Pollack, 2007).

Indeed, poor outcomes of teenage parenting are far from inevitable. Several long-term studies find that, two decades after giving birth, most former adolescent mothers are not on welfare; many have finished high school and secured steady jobs, and do not have large families. Comprehensive adolescent pregnancy and home visitation programs seem to contribute to good outcomes (Klein & AAP Committee on Adolescence, 2005), as do contact with the father (Howard, Lefever, Borkowski, & Whitman, 2006) and involvement in a religious community (Carothers, Borkowski, Lefever, & Whitman, 2005).

Preventing Teenage Pregnancy   Teenage pregnancy and birthrates in the United States are many times higher than in other industrialized countries, where adolescents begin sexual activity just as early or earlier (Darroch, Singh, Frost, & the Study Team, 2001). Teenage birthrates in recent years have been nearly five times as high in the United States as in Denmark, Finland, France, Germany, Italy, the Netherlands, Spain, Sweden, and Switzerland and twelve times as high as in Japan (Ventura, Mathews, & Hamilton, 2001).

Why are U.S. rates so high? Some observers point to such factors as the reduced stigma on unwed motherhood, media glorification of sex, the lack of a clear message that sex and parenthood are for adults, the influence of childhood sexual abuse, and failure of parents to communicate with children. Comparisons with the European experience suggest the importance of other factors: U.S. girls are more likely to have multiple sex partners and less likely to use contraceptives (Darroch et al., 2001).

Europe's industrialized countries have provided universal, comprehensive sex education for a much longer time than the United States. Comprehensive programs encourage young teenagers to delay intercourse but also aim to improve

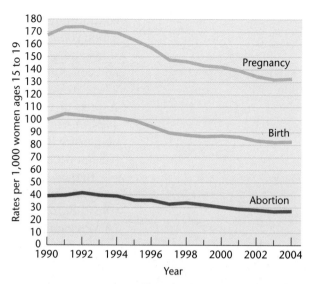

Figure 12-1

Trends in teenage pregnancy, birth, and abortion rates, by age. United States, 1990–2004. Pregnancy, birth, and induced abortion rates among 15- to 19-year-old girls have trended downward since 1990 and have reached historic lows. All three rates have fallen most sharply among younger teens. (Source: Ventura et al., 2008.)

contraceptive use among sexually active adolescents. Such programs include education about sexuality and acquisition of skills for making responsible sexual decisions and communicating with partners. They provide information about risks and consequences of teenage pregnancy, about birth control methods, and about where to get medical and contraceptive help (AAP Committee on Psychosocial Aspects of Child and Family Health and Committee on Adolescence, 2001; AGI, 1994; Kirby, 1997; I. C. Stewart, 1994). Programs aimed at adolescent boys emphasize the wisdom of delaying fatherhood and the need to take responsibility when it occurs (Children's Defense Fund, 1998).

In the United States the provision and content of sex education programs are political issues. Some critics claim that community- and school-based sex education leads to more or earlier sexual activity, even though evidence shows otherwise (AAP Committee on Adolescence, 2001; Satcher, 2001).

An important component of pregnancy prevention in European countries is access to reproductive services. Contraceptives are provided free to adolescents in Britain, France, Sweden, and, in many cases, the Netherlands. Sweden showed a fivefold reduction in the teenage birthrate following introduction of birth control education, free access to contraceptives, and free abortion on demand (Bracher & Santow, 1999). Indeed, U.S. teens who use contraception in their first sexual experience are much less likely to bear a child by age 20 (Abma et al., 2004).

The problem of teenage pregnancy requires a multifaceted solution. It must include programs and policies to encourage postponing or refraining from sexual activity, but it also must recognize that many young people do become sexually active and need education and information to prevent pregnancy and infection. It requires attention to underlying factors that put teenagers and families at risk—reducing poverty, school failure, behavioral, and family problems, and expanding employment, skills training, and family life education (AGI, 1994; Children's Defense Fund, 1998; Kirby, 1997)—and it should target those young people at highest risk (Klein & AAP Committee on Adolescence, 2005). Comprehensive early intervention programs for preschoolers and elementary school students have reduced teenage pregnancy (Lonczak et al., 2002; Hawkins et al., 1999; Schweinhart, Barnes, & Weikart, 1993).

Because adolescents with high aspirations are less likely to become pregnant, programs that motivate young people to achieve and raise their self-esteem have had some success. Teen Outreach Program (TOP), which began in 1978, helps teenagers make decisions, handle emotions, and deal with peers and adults. Among 1,600 students in TOP and 1,600 in a control group, TOP participants had about half the risk of pregnancy or school suspension and 60 percent the risk of failure of nonparticipants (Allen & Philliber, 2001).

Relationships with Family, Peers, and Adult Society

Age becomes a powerful bonding agent in adolescence. Adolescents spend more time with peers and less with family. However, most teenagers' fundamental values remain closer to their parents' than is generally realized (Offer & Church, 1991). Even as adolescents turn to peers for role models, companionship, and intimacy, they—much like toddlers beginning to explore a wider world—look to parents for a secure base from which they can try their wings. The most secure adolescents have strong, supportive relationships with parents who are attuned to the way the young people see themselves, permit and encourage their strivings for

What's Your View?

• Do you favor or oppose programs that provide contraceptives to teenagers?

Checkpoint

Can you . . .

◆ Summarize trends in teenage pregnancy and birthrates?

◆ Discuss risk factors, problems, and outcomes connected with teenage pregnancy?

◆ Describe educational programs that can prevent teenage pregnancy?

Guidepost 3

How do adolescents relate to parents, siblings, and peers?

independence, and provide a safe haven in times of emotional stress (Allen et al., 2003; Laursen, 1996).

Is Adolescent Rebellion a Myth?

The teenage years have been called a time of **adolescent rebellion,** involving emotional turmoil, conflict within the family, alienation from adult society, reckless behavior, and rejection of adult values. Yet school-based research on adolescents the world over suggests that only about 1 in 5 teenagers fits this pattern (Offer & Schonert-Reichl, 1992).

The idea of adolescent rebellion may have been born in the first formal theory of adolescence, that of the psychologist G. Stanley Hall. Hall (1904/1916) believed that young people's efforts to adjust to their changing bodies and to the imminent demands of adulthood usher in a period of *storm and stress* that produces conflict between the generations. Sigmund Freud (1935/1953) and his daughter Anna Freud (1946) described storm and stress as universal and inevitable, growing out of a resurgence of early sexual drives toward the parents.

However, the anthropologist Margaret Mead (1928, 1935), who studied growing up in Samoa and other South Pacific islands, concluded that when a culture provides a gradual, serene transition from childhood to adulthood, storm and stress is not typical. Although her research in Samoa was later challenged (Freeman, 1983), this observation was eventually supported by research in 186 preindustrial societies (Schlegel & Barry, 1991).

Full-fledged rebellion now appears to be relatively uncommon even in Western societies, at least among middle-class adolescents who are in school. Most young people feel close to and positive about their parents, share similar opinions on major issues, and value their parents' approval (Offer et al., 1989; Offer & Church, 1991; Offer, Ostrov, Howard, & Atkinson, 1988).

Furthermore, contrary to a popular belief, apparently well-adjusted adolescents are not ticking time bombs set to explode later in life. In a 34-year longitudinal study of 67 fourteen-year-old suburban boys, the vast majority adapted well to their life experiences (Offer, Offer, & Ostrov, 2004). The relatively few deeply troubled adolescents tended to come from disrupted families and, as adults, continued to have unstable family lives and to reject cultural norms. Those raised in homes with a positive family atmosphere tended to come through adolescence with no serious problems and, as adults, to have solid marriages and lead well-adjusted lives (Offer, Kaiz, Ostrov, & Albert, 2002).

Still, adolescence can be a tough time for young people and their parents. Family conflict, depression, and risky behavior are more common than during other parts of the life span (Arnett, 1999; Petersen et al., 1993). Negative emotions and mood swings are most intense during early adolescence, perhaps due to the stress connected with puberty. By late adolescence, emotionality tends to become more stable (Larson, Moneta, Richards, & Wilson, 2002).

Recognizing that adolescence may be a difficult time can help parents and teachers put trying behavior in perspective. But adults who assume that adolescent turmoil is normal and necessary may fail to heed the signals of the relatively few young persons who need special help.

Changing Time Use and Changing Relationships

One way to measure changes in adolescents' relationships with the important people in their lives is to see how they spend their discretionary time. The amount of time U.S. adolescents spend with their families declines dramatically

adolescent rebellion Pattern of emotional turmoil, characteristic of a minority of adolescents, which may involve conflict with family, alienation from adult society, reckless behavior, and rejection of adult values.

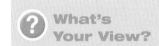
What's Your View?

• Are your values mainly similar to or different from those of your parents? If different, how did you develop these values?

Checkpoint

Can you . . .

◆ Assess the extent of storm and stress during the teenage years?

Contrary to popular belief, most adolescents are not ticking time bombs. Those raised in homes with a positive family atmosphere tend to come through adolescence with no serious problems.

during the teenage years. However, this disengagement is not a rejection of the family but a response to developmental needs. Early adolescents often retreat to their rooms; they seem to need time alone to step back from the demands of social relationships, regain emotional stability, and reflect on identity issues (Larson, 1997).

Cultural variations in time use reflect varying cultural needs, values, and practices (Verma & Larson, 2003). Young people in tribal or peasant societies spend most of their time producing bare necessities of life and have much less time for socializing than adolescents in technologically advanced societies (Larson & Verma, 1999). In some postindustrial societies such as Korea and Japan, where the pressures of schoolwork and family obligations are strong, adolescents have relatively little free time. To relieve stress, they spend their time in passive pursuits, such as watching television and "doing nothing" (Verma & Larson, 2003). In India's family-centered culture, on the other hand, middle-class urban eighth graders spend 39 percent of their waking hours with family (as compared with 23 percent for U.S. eighth graders) and report being happier when with their families than the U.S. eighth graders do. For these young people, the task of adolescence is not to separate from the family but to become more integrated with it. Similar findings have been reported in Indonesia, Bangladesh, Morocco, and Argentina (Larson & Wilson, 2004). In comparison, U.S. adolescents have a good deal of discretionary time, most of which they spend with peers, increasingly of the other sex (Juster et al., 2004; Larson & Seepersad, 2003; Verma & Larson, 2003).

Ethnicity may affect family connectedness. In some research, African American teenagers, who may look on their families as havens in a hostile world, tended to maintain more intimate family relationships and less intense peer relations than white teenagers (Giordano, Cernkovich, & DeMaris, 1993). Among 489 ninth graders, however, those with European backgrounds reported as much or more family identification and closeness as did minority students. On the other hand, those from Mexican and Chinese families, particularly immigrant families, reported a stronger sense of family obligation and assistance and spent more time on activities that carried out those obligations (Hardway & Fuligni, 2006). Still, for Chinese American youth from immigrant families, the need to adapt to U.S. society often conflicts with the pull of traditional family obligations (Fuligni, Yip, & Tseng, 2002).

With such cultural variations in mind, let's look more closely at relationships with parents, and then with siblings and peers.

Adolescents and Parents

As the English poet William Wordsworth wrote, "The child is the father of the man." This developmental pattern applies to adolescence as well. Relationships with parents during adolescence—the degree of conflict and openness of communication—are grounded largely in the emotional closeness developed in childhood; and adolescent relationships with parents, in turn, set the stage for the quality of the relationship with a partner in adulthood (Overbeek, Stattin, Vermulst, Ha, & Engels, 2007).

Most adolescents report good relations with their parents (Gutman & Eccles, 2007). Still, adolescence brings special challenges. Just as adolescents feel tension between dependency on their parents and the need to break away, parents want their children to be independent yet find it hard to let go. Parents have to walk a fine line between giving adolescents enough independence and protecting them from immature lapses in judgment. Tensions can lead to family conflict, and parenting styles can influence its shape and outcome. Effective monitoring depends on how much adolescents let parents know about their daily lives, and such disclosures may depend on the atmosphere parents have established. Also, as with younger children, adolescents' relationships with parents are affected by the parents' life situation—their work and marital and socioeconomic status.

Individuation and Family Conflict **Individuation** is an adolescent's struggle for autonomy and differentiation, or personal identity. An important aspect of individuation is carving out boundaries of control between self and parents (Nucci, Hasebe, & Lins-Dyer, 2005), and this process may entail family conflict.

In a longitudinal study, 1,357 European American and African American youth were interviewed three times between the summer before high school entry and eleventh grade. What emerged was the importance of adolescents' perceptions of family relations. Young people who saw themselves as having a great deal of autonomy over their everyday activities tended to spend more time in unsupervised socializing with peers and were at risk for problem behavior by eleventh grade. On the other hand, those who saw their parents as highly intrusive in their personal lives tended to come under negative peer influence and to join their friends in risky behaviors. Thus, parents of young adolescents must strike a delicate balance between too much freedom and too much intrusiveness (Goldstein, Davis-Kean, & Eccles, 2005).

Arguments most often concern control over everyday personal matters—chores, schoolwork, dress, money, curfews, dating, and friends—rather than issues of health and safety or right and wrong (Adams & Laursen, 2001; Steinberg, 2005). The emotional intensity of these conflicts—out of all proportion with the subject matter—may reflect the underlying individuation process. In a longitudinal study of 99 families, both individuation and family connectedness during adolescence predicted well-being in middle age (Bell & Bell, 2005).

Both family conflict and positive identification with parents are highest at age 13 and then diminish until age 17, when they stabilize or increase somewhat.

✔ **Checkpoint**

Can you . . .

◆ Identify and discuss age and cultural differences in how young people spend their time?

individuation Adolescents' struggle for autonomy and personal identity.

What's Your View?

• What issues caused the most conflict in your family when you were a teenager, and how were they resolved?

This shift reflects increased opportunities for independent adolescent decision making (Gutman & Eccles, 2007), enlarging the boundaries of what is considered the adolescent's own business (Steinberg, 2005).

Especially for girls, family relations can affect mental health. Adolescents who are given more decision-making opportunities report higher self-esteem than those who are given fewer such opportunities. In addition, negative family interactions are related to adolescent depression, whereas positive family identification is related to less depression (Gutman & Eccles, 2007).

The level of family discord may depend largely on family atmosphere. Among 335 two-parent rural midwestern families with teenagers, conflict declined during early to middle adolescence in warm, supportive families but worsened in hostile, coercive, or critical families (Rueter & Conger, 1995).

Parenting Styles and Parental Authority Authoritative parenting continues to foster healthy psychosocial development (Baumrind, 1991, 2005). Parents who show disappointment in teenagers' misbehavior are more effective in motivating responsible behavior than parents who punish harshly (Krevans & Gibbs, 1996). Overly strict, authoritarian parenting may lead an adolescent to reject parental influence and to seek peer support and approval at all costs (Fuligni & Eccles, 1993).

Authoritative parents insist on important rules, norms, and values but are willing to listen, explain, and negotiate (Lamborn, Mounts, Steinberg, & Dornbusch, 1991). They exercise appropriate control over a child's conduct (*behavioral control*) but not over the child's feelings, beliefs, and sense of self (*psychological control*) (Steinberg & Darling, 1994). Psychological control, exerted through such emotionally manipulative techniques as withdrawal of love, can harm adolescents' psychosocial development and mental health (Steinberg, 2005). Parents who are psychologically controlling tend to be unresponsive to their children's growing need for *psychological autonomy,* the right to their own thoughts and feelings (Steinberg, 2005).

Authoritative parenting seems to bolster an adolescent's self-image. A survey of 8,700 ninth to twelfth graders concluded that "the more involvement, autonomy granting, and structure that adolescents perceive from their parents, the more positively teens evaluate their own general conduct, psychosocial development, and mental health" (Gray & Steinberg, 1999, p. 584). When adolescents thought their parents were trying to dominate their psychological experience, their emotional health suffered more than when they perceived their parents as trying to control their behavior. Teens whose parents were firm in enforcing behavioral rules had more self-discipline and fewer behavior problems than those with more permissive parents. Those whose parents granted them psychological autonomy tended to become self-confident and competent in both the academic and social realms.

Problems arise when parents overstep what adolescents perceive as appropriate bounds of legitimate parental authority. The existence of a mutually agreed personal domain in which authority belongs to the adolescent has been found in various cultures and social classes from Japan to Brazil. This domain expands as parents and adolescents continually renegotiate its boundaries (Nucci et al., 2005).

Parental Monitoring and Adolescents' Self-disclosure Effective parental monitoring can help prevent adolescent problem behaviors (Barnes et al., 2006). However, young people's growing autonomy and the shrinking areas of perceived parental authority redefine the types of behavior adolescents are expected to disclose to parents (Smetana, Crean, & Campione-Barr, 2005). In a study of 276 ethnically diverse suburban ninth and twelfth graders, both adolescents and parents saw *prudential* issues, behavior related to health and safety (such as smoking, drinking, and drug use), as most subject to disclosure, followed by *moral* issues (such as lying), *conventional* issues (such as bad manners or swearing), and *multifaceted,* or borderline, issues (such as seeing an R-rated movie), which lie at the boundary between personal matters and one of the other categories. Both adolescents and parents saw *personal* issues (such as how teens spend their time and money) as least subject to disclosure. However, for each type of behavior parents were more inclined to expect disclosure than adolescents were to disclose. This discrepancy diminished between ninth and twelfth grades as parents modified their expectations to fit adolescents' growing maturity (Smetana, Metzger, Gettman, & Campione-Barr, 2006).

Among 690 Belgian adolescents, young people were more willing to disclose information about themselves when parents maintained a warm, responsive family climate in which adolescents were encouraged to speak openly and when parents provided clear expectations without being overly controlling (Soenens, Vansteenkiste, Luyckx, & Goossens, 2006)—in other words, when parenting was authoritative. Adolescents, especially girls, tend to have closer, more supportive relationships with their mothers than with their fathers, and girls confide more in their mothers (Smetana et al., 2006)

Family Structure and Family Atmosphere Adolescents, like younger children, are sensitive to the atmosphere in the family home. In a longitudinal study of 451 adolescents and their parents, changes in marital distress or marital conflict—either for better or worse—predicted corresponding changes in adolescents' adjustment (Cui, Conger, & Lorenz, 2005). In other studies, adolescent boys and girls whose parents later divorced showed more academic, psychological, and behavioral problems *before* the breakup than peers whose parents did not later divorce (Sun, 2001).

Adolescents living with their continuously married parents tend to have significantly less behavioral problems than those in other family structures (single-parent, cohabiting, or stepfamilies), according to data from a major national longitudinal study. An important factor is father involvement. High-quality involvement by a nonresident father helps a great deal, but not as much as the involvement of a father living in the home (Carlson, 2006). Although adolescents with strong ties to both parents do best, a good relationship with a nonresident father can help make up for a poor relationship with the mother (King & Sobolewski, 2006), and a committed noncustodial father-child relationship is likely to carry over to early adulthood (Aquilino, 2006b). When there is a stepfather, however, close ties to him are more influential than ties to the nonresident father (King, 2006).

Adolescents in cohabiting families, like younger children, tend to have greater behavioral and emotional problems than adolescents in married families; and, when one of the cohabiting parents is not a biological parent, school engagement suffers as well. For adolescents, unlike younger children, these effects are independent of economic resources, parental well-being, or effectiveness of parenting, suggesting that parental cohabitation itself may be more troublesome for adolescents than for younger children (S. L. Brown, 2004).

On the other hand, a multiethnic study of 12- and 13-year-old children of single mothers—first assessed when the children were 6 and 7 years old—found no negative effects of single parenting on school performance and no greater risk of problem behavior. What mattered most were the mother's educational level and ability, family income, and the quality of the home environment (Ricciuti, 2004). This finding suggests that negative effects of living in a single-parent home can be offset by positive factors.

Mothers' Employment and Economic Stress   The impact of a mother's work outside the home may depend on whether there are two parents or only one in the household. Often a single mother must work to stave off economic disaster; how her working affects her teenage children may hinge on how much time and energy she has left over to spend with them, how well she keeps track of their whereabouts, and what kind of role model she provides. A longitudinal study of 819 ten- to fourteen-year-olds from low-income urban families points up the importance of the type of care and supervision adolescents receive after school. Those who are on their own, away from home, tend to become involved in alcohol and drug use and in misconduct in school, especially if they have an early history of problem behavior. However, this is less likely to happen when parents monitor their children's activities and neighbors are actively involved (Coley, Morris, & Hernandez, 2004).

As we discussed earlier, a major problem in many single-parent families is lack of money. In a national longitudinal study, adolescent children of low-income single mothers were negatively affected by their mother's unstable employment or by her being out of work for two years. They were more likely to drop out of school and to experience declines in self-esteem and mastery (Kalil & Ziol-Guest, 2005). Furthermore, family economic hardship during adolescence can affect adult well-being. The degree of risk depends on whether parents see their situation as stressful, whether that stress interferes with family relationships, and how much it affects children's educational and occupational attainments (Sobolewski & Amato, 2005).

On the other hand, many adolescents in economically distressed families may benefit from accumulated social capital—the support of kin and community. In 51 poor, urban African American families in which teenagers were living with their mothers, grandmothers, or aunts, women who had strong kinship networks exercised firmer control and closer monitoring while granting appropriate autonomy, and their teenage charges were more self-reliant and had fewer behavior problems (R. D. Taylor & Roberts, 1995).

Adolescents and Siblings

As adolescents spend more time with peers, they have less time and less need for the emotional gratification they used to get from the sibling bond. Adolescents are less close to siblings than to either parents or friends, are less influenced by them, and become even more distant as they move through adolescence (Laursen, 1996).

Changes in sibling relationships may well precede similar changes in the relationship between adolescents and parents: more independence on the part of the younger person and less authority exerted by the older person. As children approach high school, their relationships with their siblings become progressively more equal. Older siblings exercise less power over younger ones, and younger siblings no longer need as much supervision. As relative age differences shrink, so do differences in competence and independence (Buhrmester & Furman, 1990).

Older and younger siblings tend to have different feelings about their changing relationship. As the younger sibling grows up, the older sibling may look on a newly assertive younger brother or sister as a pesky annoyance. Younger siblings still tend to look up to older siblings and try to feel more grown up by identifying with and emulating them (Buhrmester & Furman, 1990).

Checkpoint

Can you . . .

- Identify factors that affect conflict with parents and adolescents' self-disclosure?
- Discuss the impact on adolescents of parenting styles and of marital status, mothers' employment, and economic stress?

What's Your View?

- If you have one or more brothers or sisters, did your relationships with them change during adolescence?

A longitudinal study of 200 white families charted changes in sibling relations from middle childhood through adolescence (Kim, McHale, Osgood, & Crouter, 2006). As in previous research, sisters generally reported more intimacy than brothers or mixed pairs. Intimacy levels between same-sex siblings remained stable. Mixed-sex siblings, in contrast, became less intimate between middle childhood and early adolescence, but more so in middle adolescence, a time when most young people become more interested in the other sex. Sibling conflict declined across middle adolescence.

The study also found that sibling relations tend to reflect both parent-child relations and the parents' marital relationship. For example, siblings were more intimate if their mother was warm and accepting. Parent-child conflict was associated with sibling conflict. On the other hand, when fathers became less happy in their marriages, siblings became closer and quarreled less (Kim et al., 2006).

In a five-year longitudinal study of 227 Latino and African American families, sibling relationships under certain circumstances had important effects on the younger sibling. In single-mother homes, a warm and nurturing relationship with an older sister tended to prevent a younger sister from engaging in substance use and risky sexual behavior. On the other hand, having a domineering older sister tended to increase a younger sibling's high-risk sexual behavior (East & Khoo, 2005). Older siblings may influence a younger one to smoke, drink, or use drugs (Pomery et al., 2005; Rende et al., 2005). In a longitudinal study of 206 boys and their younger siblings, younger siblings hanging out with an antisocial older brother were at serious risk for adolescent antisocial behavior, drug use, sexual behavior, and violence, regardless of parental discipline (Snyder, Bank, & Burraston, 2005).

Sibling relationships become more equal as younger siblings approach or reach adolescence and the relative age difference diminishes. Even so, younger siblings still look up to their older siblings and may try to emulate them.

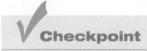

Checkpoint

Can you . . .

♦ Identify typical changes in sibling relationships during adolescence and factors that affect these relationships?

Adolescents and Peers

An important source of emotional support during the complex transition of adolescence, as well as a source of pressure for behavior that parents may deplore, is a young person's growing involvement with peers. The peer group is a source of affection, sympathy, understanding, and moral guidance; a place for experimentation; and a setting for achieving autonomy and independence from parents. It is a place to form intimate relationships that serve as rehearsals for adult intimacy.

In childhood, most peer interactions are *dyadic,* or one-to-one, though larger groupings begin to form in middle childhood. As children move into adolescence, the peer social system becomes more elaborate and diverse. Although adolescents continue to have one-to-one friendships, *cliques*—structured groups of friends who do things together—become more important. A third, and larger, type of grouping, the *crowd,* which does not normally exist before adolescence, is based not on personal interactions but on reputation, image, or identity. Crowd membership is a social construction, a set of labels by which young people divide the social map based on neighborhood, ethnicity, socioeconomic status, or other factors. All three of these levels of peer groupings may exist simultaneously, and some may overlap in membership, which may change over time. Both clique and crowd affiliations tend to become looser as adolescence progresses (B. B. Brown & Klute, 2003).

The influence of peers normally peaks at ages 12 to 13 and declines during middle and late adolescence. At age 13 or 14, popular adolescents may engage in mildly antisocial behaviors, such as trying drugs or sneaking into a movie without paying, so as to demonstrate to their peers their independence from parental

What's Your View?

• As an adolescent, were you part of a clique or crowd? If so, how did it affect your social relationships and attitudes?

The increased intimacy of adolescent friendship reflects cognitive as well as emotional development. Closer intimacy means a greater ability and desire to share emotions and feelings.

rules (Allen, Porter, McFarland, Marsh, & McElhaney, 2005). However, attachment to peers in early adolescence is not likely to forecast real trouble unless the attachment is so strong that the young person is willing to give up obeying household rules, doing schoolwork, and developing his or her own talents in order to win peer approval and popularity (Fuligni et al., 2001).

In one study of peer influence on risk taking, 306 adolescents, college-age youth, and young adults played a video game called "Chicken." For all age groups, risk taking was higher in the company of peers than alone; this was especially true of younger participants (Gardner & Steinberg, 2005).

Friendships The intensity and importance of friendships and the amount of time spent with friends are probably greater in adolescence than at any other time in the life span. Friendships tend to become more reciprocal, more equal, and more stable. Those that are less satisfying become less important or are abandoned.

Greater intimacy, loyalty, and sharing with friends mark a transition toward adultlike friendships. Adolescents begin to rely more on friends than on parents for intimacy and support, and they share confidences more than younger friends do (Berndt & Perry, 1990; Buhrmester, 1990, 1996; Hartup & Stevens, 1999; Laursen, 1996). Girls' friendships tend to be more intimate than boys', with frequent sharing of confidences (B. B. Brown & Klute, 2003). Intimacy with same-sex friends increases during early to midadolescence, after which it typically declines as intimacy with the other sex grows (Laursen, 1996).

The increased intimacy of adolescent friendship reflects cognitive as well as emotional development. Adolescents are now better able to express their private thoughts and feelings. They can more readily consider another person's point of view, and so it is easier for them to understand a friend's thoughts and feelings. Increased intimacy reflects early adolescents' concern with getting to know themselves. Confiding in a friend helps young people explore their own feelings, define their identity, and validate their self-worth (Buhrmester, 1996).

The capacity for intimacy is related to psychological adjustment and social competence. Adolescents who have close, stable, supportive friendships generally have a high opinion of themselves, do well in school, are sociable, and are unlikely to be hostile, anxious, or depressed (Berndt & Perry, 1990; Buhrmester, 1990; Hartup & Stevens, 1999). They also tend to have established strong bonds with parents (B. B. Brown & Klute, 2003). A bidirectional process seems to be at work: Good relationships foster adjustment, which in turn fosters good friendships.

Like younger children, adolescents tend to choose friends who are like them in gender, race/ethnicity, and other respects; and the qualities that lead friends to choose each other may lead them to develop in similar directions. Friends tend to have similar academic attitudes and performance and similar levels of drug use (Hamm, 2000), and they may influence each other either toward prosocial activity (Barry & Wentzel, 2006) or toward risky or problem behavior.

Parents influence adolescents' choice of friends by the neighborhoods and schools they choose for their children, by the amount and kind of supervision they exercise, and especially by the quality of their own relationships with their children (Knoester, Haynie, & Stephens, 2006).

Romantic Relationships Romantic relationships are a central part of most adolescents' social worlds. They contribute to the development of both intimacy and identity. Because they tend to involve sexual contact, they also entail risks of pregnancy, STDs, and sometimes of sexual victimization. Nearly 1 out of 11 U.S. high school students—as many boys as girls—are subjected to dating violence each year (CDC, 2006d). Breakups with romantic partners are among the strongest predictors of depression and suicide (Bouchey & Furman, 2003).

With the onset of puberty, most heterosexual boys and girls begin to think about and interact more with members of the other sex. Typically, they move from mixed groups or group dates to one-on-one romantic relationships that, unlike other-sex friendships, they describe as involving passion and a sense of commitment (Bouchey & Furman, 2003; Furman & Wehner, 1997).

Romantic relationships tend to become more intense and more intimate across adolescence. Early adolescents think primarily about how a romantic relationship may affect their status in the peer group (Bouchey & Furman, 2003). In midadolescence, most young people have at least one exclusive partner lasting for several months to about a year, and the effect of the choice of partner on peer status tends to become less important (Furman & Wehner, 1997). By age 16, adolescents interact with and think about romantic partners more than parents, friends, or siblings (Bouchey & Furman, 2003). Not until late adolescence or early adulthood, though, do romantic relationships begin to serve the full gamut of emotional needs that such relationships can serve and then only in relatively long-term relationships (Furman & Wehner, 1997).

Relationships with parents and peers may affect the quality of romantic relationships. The parent's own marriage or romantic relationship may serve as a model for their adolescent child. The peer group forms the context for most romantic relationships and may affect an adolescent's choice of a partner and the way the relationship develops (Bouchey & Furman, 2003).

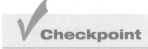

✓ Checkpoint

Can you . . .

◆ List several functions of the peer group in adolescence, and discuss the role of peer influence?

◆ Identify important features of adolescent friendships?

◆ Trace developmental changes in romantic relationships?

Antisocial Behavior and Juvenile Delinquency

What influences young people to engage in—or refrain from—violence (Box 12-1) or other antisocial acts? By what processes do antisocial tendencies develop? How do problem behaviors escalate into chronic delinquency? What determines whether a juvenile delinquent will grow up to be a hardened criminal? An interaction between environmental and genetic or biological risk factors may underlie much antisocial behavior (van Goozen, Fairchild, Snoek, & Harold, 2007).

Guidepost 4

What are the root causes of antisocial behavior and juvenile delinquency, and what can be done to reduce these risks of adolescence?

Becoming a Delinquent: Genetic and Neurological Factors

Antisocial behavior tends to run in families. Analyses of many studies have concluded that genes influence 40 to 50 percent of the variation in antisocial behavior within a population, and 60 to 65 percent of the variation in aggressive antisociality (Rhee & Waldman, 2002; Tackett, Krueger, Iacono, & McGue, 2005).

Neurobiological deficits, particularly in the portions of the brain that regulate reactions to stress, may help explain why some children become antisocial. As a result of these neurological deficits, which may result from the interaction of genetic factors or difficult temperament with adverse early environments, children may not receive or heed normal warning signals to restrain impulsive or reckless behavior (van Goozen et al., 2007).

BOX 12-1 **Research** *in Action*

The Youth Violence Epidemic

On April 20, 1999, two Columbine High School students in Littleton, Colorado, killed 12 classmates and 1 teacher before fatally shooting themselves. On April 16, 2007, a 23-year-old Virginia Tech student killed 32 people before shooting himself, making the shooting rampage the most deadly in U.S. history. During the past 10 years, school shootings have claimed the lives of 188 students and teachers worldwide and injured more than 100 people (Pearson Education, 2007).

Actually, despite all the publicity school killings receive, they are rare, representing only 1 percent of homicides among school-age youth. Most such homicides involve only a single killer and a single victim. Indeed, despite the wave of school killings since 1999, rates of school-associated homicides declined overall between 1992 and 2006 (Modzeleski et al., 2008).

Sadly, though, victims of these highly publicized cases are only a small fraction of those affected by youth violence. In 2005, more than 721,000 young people ages 10 to 24 were treated in emergency departments for injuries sustained from violence (CDC, 2007c). Persons under age 25 comprised 44.5 percent of persons arrested for violent crime and 53.9 percent of persons arrested for property crime in the United States in that year (FBI, 2007).

What causes such destructive behavior? Many influences may push young people to violent acts.

- The immature adolescent brain, particularly the prefrontal cortex, which is critical to judgment and impulse suppression.
- Ready access to guns in a culture that "romanticizes gunplay" (Weinberger, 2001, p. 2).

FIVE MYTHS ABOUT YOUTH VIOLENCE

MYTH	FACT
Most future offenders can be identified in early childhood.	Children with conduct disorders or uncontrolled behavior do not necessarily turn out to be violent adolescents.
African American and Hispanic youth are more likely than other ethnic youth to become involved in violence.	Although arrest rates differ, self-reports suggest that race and ethnicity have little effect on the overall proportion of nonfatal violent behavior.
A new breed of "super-predators," who grew to adolescence in the 1990s, threatens to make the United States an even more violent place than it is.	There is no evidence that young people involved in violence during the peak 1990s were more violent or more vicious than youths in earlier years.
Trying young offenders in tough adult criminal courts makes them less likely to commit more violent crimes.	Juveniles tried in adult courts have significantly higher rates of repeat offenses and of later felonies than young offenders tried in juvenile courts.
Most violent youths will end up being arrested for violent crimes.	Most youths involved in violent behavior will never be arrested for a violent crime.

SOURCE: Based on data from "Youth Violence," 2001.

Becoming a Delinquent: How Family, Peer, and Community Influences Interact

Researchers have identified two types of antisocial behavior: an *early-onset* type, beginning by age 11, which tends to lead to chronic juvenile delinquency in adolescence, and a milder, *late-onset* type, beginning after puberty, which tends to arise temporarily in response to the changes of adolescence: the mismatch between biological and social maturity, increased desire for autonomy, and decreased adult supervision. Late-onset adolescents tend to commit relatively minor offenses (Schulenberg & Zarrett, 2006).

The early-onset type of antisocial behavior is influenced, as Bronfenbrenner's theory would suggest, by interacting factors ranging from microsystem influences, such as parent-child hostility, poor parenting practices, and peer deviance, to macrosystem influences, such as community structure and neighborhood social support (Buehler, 2006; Tolan, Gorman-Smith, & Henry, 2003). This network of interacting influences begins to be woven early in childhood.

Late-onset antisociality typically occurs in adolescents with normal family backgrounds. Parents of children who become chronically antisocial, by contrast,

- The presence of gangs at school (NCES, 2003; "Youth Violence," 2001).
- A rejecting, coercive, or chaotic childhood home environment, which tends to produce aggressive behavior in children. The hostility they evoke in others increases their own aggression. Their negative self-image prevents them from succeeding at school or developing other, constructive, interests; and they generally associate with peers who reinforce their antisocial attitudes and behavior (Staub, 1996).
- Living in unstable, inner-city neighborhoods with low community involvement and support (Tolan et al., 2003)—though middle-class students in a suburban school are not immune.
- Having witnessed or having been victims of neighborhood violence, or having been exposed to media violence (Brookmeyer, Henrich, & Schwab-Stone, 2005; Pearce, Jones, Schwab-Stone, & Ruchkin, 2003).

Psychologists point to potential warning signs. Adolescents likely to commit violence often refuse to listen to parents and teachers, ignore the feelings and rights of others, mistreat people, rely on violence or threats to solve problems, and believe that life has treated them unfairly. They tend to do poorly in school; to cut classes or play truant; to be held back or suspended or to drop out; to be victims of bullying; to use alcohol, inhalants, and/or other drugs; to engage in early sexual activity; to join gangs; and to fight, steal, or destroy property (American Psychological Association and American Academy of Pediatrics [AAP], 1996; Resnick et al., 1997; Smith-Khuri et al., 2004; "Youth Violence," 2001).

A report by the Surgeon General of the United States challenges some myths, or stereotypes, about youth violence ("Youth Violence," 2001; see table). One of the worst myths is that nothing can be done to prevent or treat violent behavior. School-based programs for *all* children, not just those at risk, have reduced violence and aggressiveness at all grade levels. These programs are designed to prevent violent behavior by promoting social skills and emotional awareness and control (Hahn et al., 2007).

What's Your View?

What do you think is the most important factor in preventing youth violence?

Check It Out

For more information on this topic, go to www.safeyouth .org/scripts/index.asp, a website that offers recent statistics on school violence and many resources to help reduce it. Or go to www.cdc.gov/ncipc/dvp/yvguide.htm to download *Preventing Youth Violence: Program Activities Guide,* which describes the Center for Disease Control and Prevention's public health activities and research to prevent youth violence.

may have failed to reinforce good behavior in early childhood and may have been harsh or inconsistent—or both—in punishing misbehavior (Coie & Dodge, 1998; Snyder, Cramer, Afrank, & Patterson, 2005). Through the years these parents may not have been closely and positively involved in their children's lives (G. R. Patterson, DeBaryshe, & Ramsey, 1989). The children may get payoffs for antisocial behavior: When they act up, they may gain attention or get their own way. These early negative patterns pave the way for negative peer influences that promote and reinforce antisocial behavior (Collins et al., 2000; B. B. Brown, Mounts, Lamborn, & Steinberg, 1993).

By early adolescence, open hostility may exist between parent and child. When constant criticism, angry coercion, or rude, uncooperative behavior characterizes parent-child interactions, the child tends to show aggressive behavior problems, which worsen the parent-child relationship (Buehler, 2006). Ineffective parenting can leave younger siblings to the powerful influence of a deviant older brother, especially if the siblings are close in age (Snyder, Bank, & Burraston, 2005).

The choice of antisocial peers is affected mainly by environmental factors (Iervolino et al., 2002). Young people gravitate to others brought up like themselves who are similar in school achievement, adjustment, and prosocial or antisocial tendencies (Collins et al., 2000; B. B. Brown et al., 1993). As in childhood, antisocial adolescents tend to have antisocial friends, and their antisocial behavior increases when they associate with each other (Dishion, McCord, & Poulin, 1999; Hartup & Stevens, 1999; Vitaro, Tremblay, Kerr, Pagani, & Bukowski, 1997). The way antisocial teenagers talk, laugh, or smirk about rule breaking and nod knowingly among themselves seems to constitute a sort of "deviancy training" (Dishion et al., 1999). These problem children continue to elicit ineffective parenting, which predicts delinquent behavior and association with deviant peer groups or gangs (Simons, Chao, Conger, & Elder, 2001; Tolan et al., 2003).

Authoritative parenting can help young people internalize standards that may insulate them against negative peer influences and open them to positive influences (Collins et al., 2000; Mounts & Steinberg, 1995). Improved parenting during adolescence can reduce delinquency by discouraging association with deviant peers (Simons et al., 2001). Adolescents whose parents know where they are and what they are doing are less likely to engage in delinquent acts (Laird, Pettit, Bates, & Dodge, 2003) or to associate with deviant peers (Lloyd & Anthony, 2003).

Family economic circumstances may influence the development of antisocial behavior. Persistent economic deprivation can undermine sound parenting by depriving the family of social capital. Poor children are more likely than other children to commit antisocial acts, and those whose families are continuously poor tend to become more antisocial with time. Conversely, when families rise from poverty while a child is still young, the child is no more likely to develop behavior problems than a child whose family was never poor (Macmillan, McMorris, & Kruttschnitt, 2004).

Weak neighborhood social organization in a disadvantaged community can influence delinquency through its effects on parenting behavior and peer deviance (Chung & Steinberg, 2006). *Collective efficacy*—the strength of social connections within a neighborhood and the extent to which residents monitor or supervise each other's children—can influence outcomes in a positive direction (Sampson, 1997). A combination of nurturant, involved parenting and collective efficacy can discourage adolescents from association with deviant peers (Brody et al., 2001).

Long-Term Prospects

The vast majority of young people who engage in juvenile delinquency do not become adult criminals (Kosterman, Graham, Hawkins, Catalano, & Herrenkohl, 2001; Moffitt, 1993). Delinquency peaks at about age 15 and then declines as most adolescents and their families come to terms with young people's need to assert independence. However, teenagers who do not see positive alternatives or who come from dysfunctional families are more likely to adopt a permanently antisocial lifestyle (Elliott, 1993; Schulenberg & Zarrett, 2006). Those most likely to persist in violence are boys who had early antisocial influences. Least likely to persist are boys and girls who were early school achievers and girls who showed early prosocial development (Kosterman et al., 2001). Because adolescents' character is still in flux, many developmental psychologists deplore the current trend toward transferring juvenile offenders from the juvenile court system, which is aimed at rehabilitation, to criminal courts where they can be tried and sentenced as adults (Steinberg, 2000; Steinberg & Scott, 2003).

Preventing and Treating Delinquency

Because juvenile delinquency has roots early in childhood, so should preventive efforts that attack the multiple factors that can lead to delinquency. Adolescents who have taken part in certain early childhood intervention programs are less likely to get in trouble than their equally underprivileged peers (Yoshikawa, 1994; Zigler, Taussig, & Black, 1992). Effective programs are those that target high-risk urban children and last at least two years during the child's first five years. They influence children directly, through high-quality day care or education, and at the same time indirectly, by offering families assistance and support geared to their needs (Berrueta-Clement, Schweinhart, Barnett, & Epstein, 1985; Berrueta-Clement, Schweinhart, Barnett, & Weikart, 1987; Schweinhart et al., 1993; Seitz, 1990; Yoshikawa, 1994; Zigler et al., 1992).

These programs operate on Bronfenbrenner's mesosystem by affecting interactions between the home and the school or child care center. The programs also go one step further, to the exosystem, by creating supportive parent networks and linking parents with such community services as prenatal and postnatal care and educational and vocational counseling (Yoshikawa, 1994; Zigler et al., 1992). Through their multipronged approach, these interventions have an impact on several early risk factors for delinquency.

One such program is the Chicago Child-Parent Centers, a preschool program for disadvantaged children in the Chicago Public Schools that offers follow-up services through age 9. Participants studied at age 20 had better educational and social outcomes and fewer juvenile arrests than a comparison group who had received less extensive early interventions (Reynolds et al., 2001).

Once children reach adolescence, especially in poor, crime-ridden neighborhoods, interventions need to focus on spotting troubled adolescents and preventing gang recruitment (Tolan et al., 2003). Successful programs boost parenting skills through better monitoring, behavioral management, and neighborhood social support.

Programs such as teen hangouts and summer camps for behaviorally disturbed youth can be counterproductive because they bring together groups of deviant youth who tend to reinforce each other's deviancy. More effective programs—Scouts, sports, and church activities—integrate deviant youth into the nondeviant mainstream. Structured, adult-monitored or school-based activities after school, on weekend evenings, and in summer, when adolescents are most likely to be idle and to get in trouble, can reduce their exposure to settings that encourage antisocial behavior (Dodge, Dishion, & Lansford, 2006). Getting teenagers involved in constructive activities or job skills programs during their free time can pay long-range dividends. Participation in extracurricular school activities tends to cut down on dropout and criminal arrest rates among high-risk boys and girls (Mahoney, 2000).

Fortunately, the great majority of adolescents do not get into serious trouble. Those who show disturbed behavior can—and should—be helped. With love, guidance, and support, adolescents can avoid risks, build on their strengths, and explore their possibilities as they approach adult life.

The normal developmental changes in the early years of life are obvious and dramatic signs of growth. The infant lying in the crib becomes an active, exploring toddler. The young child enters and embraces the worlds of school and society. The adolescent, with a new body and new awareness, prepares to step into adulthood.

Growth and development do not come to an abrupt halt after adolescence. People change in many ways throughout early, middle, and late adulthood, as we will see in the remaining chapters of this book.

What are the chances this gang member, who has already been to prison, will become a hardened criminal? Teenagers who don't have positive alternatives are more likely to adopt antisocial lifestyles.

 **Checkpoint**

Can you . . .

♦ Explain how parental, peer, and neighborhood influences may interact to promote antisocial behavior and delinquency?

♦ Identify characteristics of programs that have been successful in preventing or stopping delinquency and other risky behavior?

Summary and Key Terms

The Search for Identity

Guidepost 1: *How do adolescents form an identity, and what roles do gender and ethnicity play?*

- A central concern during adolescence is the search for identity, which has occupational, sexual, and values components. Erik Erikson described the psychosocial conflict of adolescence as *identity versus identity confusion.* The virtue that should arise from this conflict is *fidelity.*
- James Marcia, in research based on Erikson's theory, described four identity statuses: identity achievement, foreclosure, moratorium, and identity diffusion.
- Researchers differ on whether girls and boys take different paths to identity formation. Although some research suggests that girls' self-esteem tends to fall in adolescence, later research does not support that finding.
- Ethnicity is an important part of identity. Minority adolescents seem to go through stages of ethnic identity development much like Marcia's identity statuses.

- identity (390)
- identity versus identity confusion (390)
- identity statuses (391)
- crisis (392)
- commitment (392)
- identity achievement (392)
- foreclosure (392)
- moratorium (393)
- identity diffusion (393)
- cultural socialization (395)

Sexuality

Guidepost 2: *What determines sexual orientation, what sexual practices are common among adolescents, and what leads some to engage in risky sexual behavior?*

- Sexual orientation appears to be influenced by an interaction of biological and environmental factors and to be at least partly genetic.
- Because of lack of social acceptance, the course of homosexual identity and relationship development may vary.
- Teenage sexual activity involves risks of pregnancy and sexually transmitted disease. Adolescents at greatest risk are those who begin sexual activity early, have multiple partners, do not use contraceptives, and are ill-informed about sex.
- Regular condom use is the best safeguard for sexually active teens.
- Comprehensive sex education programs delay sexual initiation and encourage contraceptive use. Abstinence-only programs have not been as effective.
- STDs are most likely to develop undetected in girls.
- Teenage pregnancy and birthrates in the United States have declined, but birthrates rose again in 2006.

- Teenage childbearing often has negative outcomes. Teenage mothers and their families tend to suffer ill health and financial hardship, and the children often suffer from ineffective parenting.

- sexual orientation (396)
- sexually transmitted diseases (STDs) (399)

Relationships with Family, Peers, and Adult Society

Guidepost 3: *How do adolescents relate to parents, siblings, and peers?*

- Although relationships between adolescents and their parents are not always easy, full-scale adolescent rebellion is unusual. For the majority of teens, adolescence is a fairly smooth transition. For the minority who seem more deeply troubled, it can predict a difficult adulthood.
- Adolescents spend an increasing amount of time with peers, but relationships with parents continue to be influential.
- Conflict with parents tends to be greatest during early adolescence. Authoritative parenting is associated with the most positive outcomes.
- Effects of family structure and maternal employment on adolescents' development may depend on such factors as economic resources, the quality of the home environment, and how closely parents monitor adolescents' whereabouts.
- Relationships with siblings tend to become more distant during adolescence, and the balance of power between older and younger siblings becomes more equal.
- The influence of the peer group is strongest in early adolescence. The structure of the peer group becomes more elaborate, involving cliques and crowds as well as friendships.
- Friendships, especially among girls, become more intimate, stable, and supportive in adolescence.
- Romantic relationships meet a variety of needs and develop with age and experience.

- adolescent rebellion (405)
- individuation (407)

Antisocial Behavior and Juvenile Delinquency

Guidepost 4: *What are the root causes of antisocial behavior and juvenile delinquency, and what can be done to reduce these risks of adolescence?*

- Chronic delinquency generally stems from early-onset antisociality. It is associated with multiple, interacting, risk factors, including ineffective parenting, school failure, peer and neighborhood influence, and low socioeconomic status. Programs that attack risk factors from an early age have had success.

If . . . happiness is the absence of fever then I will never know happiness. For I am possessed by a fever for knowledge, experience, and creation.

Diary of Anaïs Nin (1931–1934),
written when she was between 28 and 31

Did You **Know . . .**

- U.S. adults ages 20 to 40 are more likely to be poor and less likely to have health insurance than any other age group?

- Three out of four mental illnesses start by age 24?

- About 50 percent of all U.S. adults have had a sexually transmitted disease by age 24?

- The capacity for reflective thinking seems to emerge between ages 20 and 25?

- For both immediate and long-term cognitive benefits, going to college—any college—is more important than which college a person attends?

- Today many people in industrialized countries do not become fully adult until their mid- to late twenties?

These are just a few of the interesting and important topics we will cover in this chapter. Young adulthood, usually defined as approximately ages 20 to 40, typically is a can-do period: Many people at this age are on their own for the first time, setting up and running households and proving themselves in their chosen pursuits. Each day they make decisions that help determine their health, careers, and lifestyles. Increasingly, however, many young adults do not immediately settle down. For them, the early to midtwenties, or even longer, has become an exploratory period called *emerging adulthood.*

In this chapter, we look at emerging and young adults' physical functioning and identify factors that can affect health and fitness, as well as at sexual and reproductive issues. We discuss distinctive aspects of adult cognition and ways education can stimulate cognitive growth. We examine how culture and gender affect moral development. Finally, we discuss one of the most important developmental tasks of this period: entering the world of work. After you have read and studied this chapter, you should be able to answer each of the Guidepost questions on the following page.

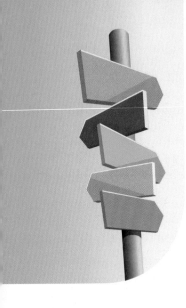

Guideposts *for Study*

1. What does it mean to be an adult, and what factors affect the timing of entrance to adulthood?
2. In what physical condition is the typical young adult, and what factors affect health and well-being?
3. What are some sexual and reproductive issues at this time of life?
4. What is distinctive about adult thought?
5. How does moral reasoning develop?
6. How do emerging adults make the transitions to higher education and work, and how do these experiences affect cognitive development?

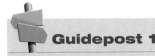

Guidepost 1

What does it mean to be an adult, and what factors affect the timing of entrance to adulthood?

Emerging Adulthood

When does a person become an adult? Contemporary U.S. society has a variety of markers. *Sexual maturity* arrives during adolescence; *cognitive* maturity may take longer. There are various definitions of *legal* adulthood: At 18, young people can vote, and, in most states, they can marry without their parents' permission; at 18 to 21 (depending on the state), they can enter into binding contracts. Using *sociological* definitions, people may be considered adults when they are self-supporting or have chosen a career, have married or formed a significant romantic partnership, or have started a family.

Psychological maturity may depend on such achievements as discovering one's identity, becoming independent of parents, developing a system of values, and forming relationships. Some psychologists suggest that the onset of adulthood is marked, not by external criteria, but by such internal indicators as a sense of autonomy, self-control, and personal responsibility—that it is more a state of mind than a discrete event (Shanahan, Porfeli, & Mortimer, 2005). From this point of view, some people never become adults, no matter what their chronological age.

For most laypeople, though, three criteria define adulthood: (1) accepting responsibility for oneself, (2), making independent decisions, and (3) becoming financially independent (Arnett, 2006). In modern industrialized countries, the achievement of these goals takes longer and follows far more varied routes than in the past. Before the mid-twentieth century, a young man just out of high school typically would seek a stable job, marry, and start a family. For a young woman, the usual route to adulthood was marriage, which occurred as soon as she found a suitable mate.

Since the 1950s, the technological revolution has made higher education or specialized training increasingly essential. The typical ages of first marriage and first childbirth have shifted sharply upward as both women and men pursue higher education or vocational opportunities (Furstenberg, Rumbaut, & Settersten, 2005; Fussell & Furstenberg, 2005). Today the road to adulthood may be marked by multiple milestones—entering college (full- or part-time), working (full- or part-time), moving away from home, getting married, and having children—and the order and timing of these transitions vary (Schulenberg, O'Malley, Bachman, & Johnston, 2005).

What's Your View?

- What criteria for adulthood do you consider most relevant?
- Do you think those criteria are influenced by the culture in which you live or grew up?

Thus, some developmental scientists suggest that, for the majority of young people in industrialized societies, the period from the late teens through the mid- to late twenties has become a distinct period of the life course, **emerging adulthood.** It is an exploratory period, a time of possibilities, an opportunity to try out new and different ways of living—a time when young people are no longer adolescents but have not yet settled into adult roles (Arnett, 2000, 2004, 2006; Furstenberg et al., 2005). We will look more closely at the varied paths of emerging adults later in this chapter and in Chapter 14.

emerging adulthood Proposed transitional period between adolescence and adulthood.

PHYSICAL DEVELOPMENT

Health and Fitness

Whether your favorite sport to watch is baseball, tennis, basketball, figure skating, or football, most of the athletes you root for are emerging and young adults, people in prime physical condition. Most people this age are at a peak of health, strength, energy, endurance, and sensory and motor functioning.

Checkpoint

Can you . . .

◆ Explain how entrance to adulthood has changed in industrialized societies?

Guidepost 2

In what physical condition is the typical young adult, and what factors affect health and well-being?

Health Status and Health Issues

During this period, the foundation for lifelong physical functioning is laid. Health may be influenced by the genes, but behavioral factors—what young adults eat, whether they get enough sleep, how physically active they are, and whether they smoke, drink, or use drugs—contribute greatly to health and well-being.

Most emerging and young adults in the United States report that they are in good to excellent health; only 5.7 percent of 18- to 44-year-olds call their health fair or poor. The most common causes of activity limitations are arthritis and other muscular and skeletal disorders (NCHS, 2006). Accidents are the leading cause of death for young Americans up to age 44 (Heron & Smith, 2007). Mortality rates for this group have been nearly cut in half during the past 50 years, and mortality rates for other age groups have dropped as well (Kochanek, Murphy, Anderson, & Scott, 2004; Pastor, Makuc, Reuben, & Xia, 2002). Still, mortality rates more than double between adolescence and young adulthood.

The health issues of these years mirror those of adolescence; however, rates of injury, homicide, and substance use peak at this time. Too many emerging and young adults are overweight and get too little exercise. In part because the institutional safety net that cushions adolescents, including the parental home and the school, is no longer there, it is easier to engage unchecked in health-threatening behaviors. Emerging and young adults have the highest poverty rate and the lowest level of health insurance of any age group, and often no regular access to health care (Callahan & Cooper, 2005; Park, Mulye, Adams, Brindis, & Irwin, 2006).

Genetic Influences on Health

The mapping of the human genome is enabling scientists to discover the genetic roots of many disorders, from obesity to certain cancers (including lung, prostate, and breast cancer) to mental health conditions (such as alcoholism and depression). For example, researchers have identified 19 different chromosomal regions linked with familial early-onset depression (Zubenko et al., 2003). Another research team has found a variant of the serotonin transporter gene that may predispose certain individuals under stress to depression (Canli et al., 2006). Scientists also have discovered a genetic component in HIV/AIDS, one of the top killers in

Playing volleyball takes strength, energy, endurance, and muscular coordination. Most young adults, like these, are in prime physical condition.

This juicy hamburger is dripping with calories and is high in animal fat, which has been linked to heart disease and some cancers.

young adults (Heron & Smith, 2007). People with more copies of a gene that helps fight HIV are less likely to become infected with the virus or to develop AIDS than people with have fewer copies of the gene (Gonzalez et al., 2005).

One risk factor for atherosclerosis (narrowing of the arteries) is cholesterol levels in the blood. Cholesterol, in combination with proteins and triglycerides (fatty acids), circulates through the bloodstream, carried by low-density lipoprotein (LDL), commonly called "bad" cholesterol. High-density lipoprotein (HDL), "good" cholesterol, flushes cholesterol out of the system. An estimated 80 percent of the variation in HDL levels within the population is due to genetic factors ("How to Raise HDL," 2001). However, behavioral habits (such as diet) also affect cholesterol levels.

Indeed, most diseases involve both heredity and environment. In one study, a person's likelihood of developing symptoms of depression was predicted by a genetic variant that is highly affected by environmental influences, such as a supportive family (S. E. Taylor, Lehman, Kiefe, & Seeman, 2006).

Behavioral Influences on Health and Fitness

The link between behavior and health illustrates the interrelationship among physical, cognitive, and emotional aspects of development. What people know about health affects what they do, and what they do affects how they feel.

By the time they reach young adulthood, a large proportion of American youth have already begun the poor practices that contribute to the three leading causes of preventable death in the United States: smoking, obesity, and alcohol abuse. A nationally representative survey of more than 14,000 young adults who had been followed since early adolescence found that diet, activity level, obesity, health care access, tobacco, alcohol, and illicit drug use, and the likelihood of acquiring an STD worsened as the young people reached adulthood (K. M. Harris, Gordon-Larsen, Chantala, & Udry, 2006).

Knowing about good (and bad) health habits is not enough. Personality, emotions, and social surroundings often outweigh what people know they should do and lead them into unhealthful behavior. Let's look at several lifestyle factors that are strongly linked with health and fitness: diet and weight control, physical activity, sleep, smoking, and alcohol and drug use. Stress, which can induce such detrimental behaviors as sleep loss, smoking, drinking, and drug use, is discussed in Chapter 15. In the next section of this chapter we consider indirect influences on health: socioeconomic status, race/ethnicity, and relationships.

Diet and Nutrition   The saying "You are what you eat" sums up the importance of nutrition for physical and mental health. What people eat affects how they look, how they feel, and how likely they are to get sick and even die. An estimated 365,000 U.S. adults die each year from causes related to poor diet and lack of physical activity (Mokdad, Marks, Stroup, & Gerberding, 2005). In a 15-year longitudinal study of 18- to 30-year-olds, those who ate plenty of fruits, vegetables, and other plant foods were less likely to develop high blood pressure, whereas those who ate a diet heavy in meat were more likely to develop it (Steffen et al., 2005).

Excess fat consumption, especially of saturated fats, increases cardiovascular risks, particularly cholesterol levels (Ervin et al., 2004), which are directly related to the risk of death from coronary heart disease (Verschuren et al., 1995). Controlling cholesterol through diet and, if necessary, medication can significantly lower this risk (Scandinavian Simvastatin Survival Study Group, 1994; Shepherd et al., 1995).

Diet also seems to protect against certain cancers, several new studies suggest. Asian American women who ate the most soy-based foods (such as tofu or miso) in childhood had a 58 percent lower risk of developing breast cancer compared with women who ate the least soy. Men who ate fish five or more times a week had a 40 percent lower risk of colorectal cancer than men who ate fish less than once a week. Prostate cancer patients with lower levels of blood cholesterol tended to develop less aggressive forms of the disease compared with patients with higher cholesterol. And smokers with vitamin E in their diet had less oxidative damage to their white blood cells than smokers low in vitamin E (Madsen et al., 2006).

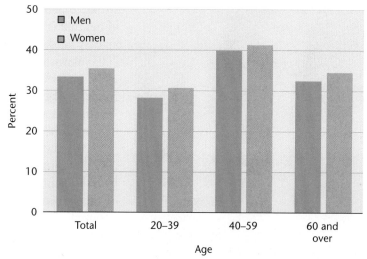

Note: Obesity is defined as body mass index ≥ 30.

Figure 13-1

Prevalence of obesity by age and sex, adults age 20 and older, United States, 2005–2006. Young adults who do not control their weight risk gaining more in middle age, when obesity is most prevalent. (Source: Ogden, Carroll, McDowell, & Flegal, 2007.)

Obesity/Overweight   The World Health Organization (WHO) has called obesity a worldwide epidemic (WHO, 1998). Obesity more than doubled in the United Kingdom between 1980 and 1994, and similar increases have been reported in Brazil, Canada, and several countries in Europe, the Western Pacific, Southeast Asia, and Africa (Taubes, 1998). Obesity rates in developing countries that have adopted Western lifestyles have tripled in the past 20 years (Hossain & Nahas, 2007).

In the United States, the average man or woman is more than 24 pounds heavier than in the early 1960s but is only about 1 inch taller. About 30 percent of 20- to 39-year-old men and women were obese in 2005–2006, a proportion that increased dramatically in middle age (Figure 13-1). The upward trend in obesity since 1980 shows no sign of reversing, despite much public attention to the problem. Two-thirds of U.S. adults say they have been told by a health practitioner that they are overweight (Ogden, Carroll, McDowell, & Flegal, 2007).

What explains the obesity epidemic? Experts point to an increase in snacking (Zizza, Siega-Riz, & Popkin, 2001), availability of inexpensive fast foods, supersized portions, high-fat diets, labor-saving technologies, and sedentary recreational pursuits, such as television and computers (Harvard Medical School, 2004c; Pereira et al., 2005; Young & Nestle, 2002). As in childhood and adolescence, an inherited tendency toward obesity may interact with such environmental and behavioral factors (Comuzzie & Allison, 1998; NCBI, 2002).

Obesity can lead to depression, and vice versa (Markowitz, Friedman, & Arent, 2008). It also carries risks of high blood pressure, heart disease, stroke, diabetes, gallstones, arthritis and other muscular and skeletal disorders, and some cancers and it diminishes quality and length of life (Gregg et al., 2005; Harvard Medical School, 2004c; Hu et al., 2001, 2004; Mokdad, Bowman, et al., 2001; Mokdad, Ford, et al., 2003; NCHS, 2004; Ogden et al., 2007; Pereira et al., 2005; Peeters et al., 2003; Sturm, 2002). Cardiovascular and mortality risks have declined in the past four decades, probably due to improved medical care, but obese adults remain at greater risk (Flegal, Graubard, Williamson, & Gail, 2005; Gregg et al., 2005). Lifestyle changes (dietary change plus exercise) or drug treatments have sustained weight-loss targets for two or more years (Powell, Calvin, and Calvin, 2007).

Physical Activity   People who are physically active reap many benefits. Aside from helping to maintain desirable body weight, physical activity builds muscles; strengthens heart and lungs; lowers blood pressure; protects against heart disease,

Checkpoint

Can you . . .

♦ Summarize the typical health status of young adults in the United States, and identify the leading cause of death in young adulthood?

♦ Tell how diet can affect the likelihood of cancer and heart disease?

♦ Give reasons for the obesity epidemic?

Incorporating more activity into daily life, say, by biking to work instead of driving, can be as effective as structured exercise.

stroke, diabetes, several cancers, and osteoporosis (a thinning of the bones that is most prevalent in middle-aged and older women); relieves anxiety and depression; and lengthens life (Barnes & Schoenborn, 2003; Bernstein et al., 2005; Boulé, Haddad, Kenny, Wells, & Sigal, 2001; NCHS, 2004; Pan, Ugnat, Mao, & Canadian Cancer Registries Epidemiology Research Group, 2005; Pratt, 1999; WHO, 2002). Inactivity is a global public health problem. A sedentary lifestyle is one of the world's 10 leading causes of death and disability (WHO, 2002).

Even moderate exercise has health benefits (NCHS, 2004; WHO, 2002). Incorporating more physical activity into daily life—for example, by walking instead of driving short distances, and climbing stairs instead of taking elevators—can be as effective as structured exercise. In a randomized trial of 201 sedentary women in a university-based weight control program, a combination of diet and exercise (primarily walking) for 12 months produced significant weight loss and improved cardiorespiratory fitness (Jakicic, Marcus, Gallagher, Napolitano, & Lang, 2003).

Sleep   The twenties and thirties are busy times, so it is not surprising that many emerging and young adults often go without adequate sleep (Monk, 2000). Among college students, family life stress, together with academic stress, is associated with high levels of insomnia (Bernert et al., 2007).

Sleep deprivation affects not only health, but cognitive, emotional, and social functioning as well. In a poll by the National Sleep Foundation (2001), respondents said they were more likely to make mistakes, become impatient or aggravated when waiting, or get upset with their children or others when they had not had enough sleep the night before. Sleep deprivation can be lethal on the road; drowsy drivers cause an estimated 1 in 25 fatal crashes (Peters et al., 1994). Lack of sleep tends to impair verbal learning (Horne, 2000), some aspects of memory (Harrison & Horne, 2000b), high-level decision making (Harrison & Horne, 2000a), and speech articulation (Harrison & Horne, 1997) and to increase distractibility (Blagrove, Alexander, & Horne, 1995). Chronic sleep deprivation (less than six hours' sleep each night for three or more nights) can seriously worsen cognitive performance (Van Dongen, Maislin, Mullington, & Dinges, 2003).

Adequate sleep improves learning of complex motor skills (Walker, Brakefield, Morgan, Hobson, & Stickgold, 2002) and consolidates previous learning. Even a short nap can prevent burnout—oversaturation of the brain's perceptual processing systems (Mednick et al., 2002).

Because smoking is addictive, it is hard to quit despite awareness of health risks. Smoking is especially harmful to African Americans, whose blood metabolizes nicotine rapidly, heightening their risk of lung cancer.

Smoking   Smoking is the leading preventable cause of death among U.S. adults, linked not only to lung cancer, but also to increased risks of heart disease, stroke, and chronic lung disease (NCHS, 2004). Exposure to passive, or secondhand, smoke has been shown to cause circulatory problems and increase the risk of cardiovascular disease (Otsuka et al., 2001) and may increase the risk of cervical cancer (Trimble et al., 2005). In 2000, smoking killed almost 5 million people worldwide, about half in developing countries and half in industrialized countries (Ezzati & Lopez, 2004).

Despite these risks, more than 23 percent of men and 18.5 percent of women over age 18 in the United States are current smokers (Substance Abuse and Mental Health Services Administration [SAMHSA], 2006c). Emerging adults are more likely to smoke than any other age group. More than 40 percent of 21- to 25-year-olds report using cigarettes SAMHSA, 2007a).

In view of the known risks, why do so many people smoke? For one thing, smoking is addictive. A tendency to addiction may be genetic, and certain genes may affect the ability to quit (Lerman et al., 1999; Pianezza et al., 1998; Sabol et al.,

1999). Many adult smokers developed the habit in their teens and cannot or will not stop. A questionnaire survey found that new or occasional smokers seem to be most influenced by the taste and sensation of smoking and by being in places where others are smoking. Experienced smokers say they are more influenced by their cravings and need, are emotionally attached to smoking, or believe that smoking enhances mental activity (Piper et al., 2004).

Giving up smoking reduces the risks of heart disease, cancer, and stroke (Kawachi et al., 1993; NIA, 1993; Wannamethee, Shaper, Whincup, & Walker, 1995). Nicotine chewing gum, nicotine patches, and nicotine nasal sprays and inhalers, especially when combined with counseling, can help addicted persons taper off gradually and safely (Cepeda-Benito, Reynoso, & Erath, 2004).

Alcohol Use The United States is a drinking society. Advertising associates liquor, beer, and wine with the good life and with being grown-up. Alcohol use peaks in emerging adulthood; about 70 percent of 21- to 25-year-olds report using alcohol in the past month, and nearly 48 percent of 21-year-olds are binge drinkers, having five or more drinks at a time (SAMHSA, 2004b).

College is a prime time and place for drinking. Although frequent drinking is common at this age, college students tend to drink more frequently and more heavily than their noncollegiate peers (SAMHSA, 2004b). In 2002 to 2005, 57.8 percent of full-time college students ages 18 to 20 had used alcohol in the past month, 17 percent heavily; and about 40 percent had engaged in binge drinking (SAMHSA, 2006c; Figure 13-2).

Light-to-moderate alcohol consumption seems to reduce the risk of fatal heart disease and stroke, and also of dementia later in life (Ruitenberg et al., 2002). However, heavy drinking over the years may lead to cirrhosis of the liver, other gastrointestinal disorders (including ulcers), pancreatic disease, certain cancers, heart failure, stroke, damage to the nervous system, psychoses, and other medical problems (AHA, 1995; Fuchs et al., 1995).

Alcohol use is associated with other risks characteristic of emerging adulthood, such as traffic accidents, crime, HIV infection (Leigh, 1999), and illicit drug and tobacco use (Hingson, Heeren, Winter, & Wechsler, 2005). In 2004–2006, an estimated 15 percent of U.S. drivers age 18 or older say they drove under the influence of alcohol, and nearly 5 percent say they drove under the influence of drugs, in the past year (SAMHSA, 2008). Alcoholism, or long-term addiction, is discussed later in this chapter under "Mental Health Problems."

Indirect Influences on Health and Fitness

Apart from the things people do, or refrain from doing, which affect their health directly, there are indirect influences on health. Among these are income, education, and race/ethnicity. Relationships also seem to make a difference, as do the paths young people take into adulthood. Binge drinking, for example, is most common among college students living away from home; and substance use declines most rapidly among young adults who are married (Schulenberg et al., 2005).

Socioeconomic Status and Race/Ethnicity The connection between socioeconomic status (SES) and health has been widely documented. Higher-income people

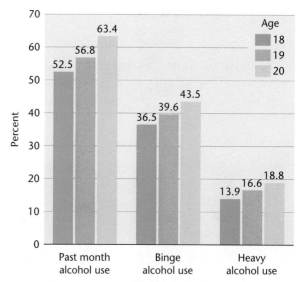

Figure 13-2

Current (past month) alcohol use, binge drinking, and heavy alcohol use among full-time college students ages 18 to 20.
(Source: SAMHSA, 2006c.)

Checkpoint

Can you . . .

- Cite benefits of exercise?
- Explain why sleep deprivation is harmful?
- Discuss trends and risks involved in smoking and alcohol use?

Living in poverty, as do this mother and her daughter who share a room in a shelter, can affect health through poor nutrition, substandard housing, and inadequate health care.

rate their health as better and live longer than lower-income people (NCHS, 2004, 2006). Education is important, too. The less schooling people have had, the greater the chance that they will develop and die from communicable diseases, injuries, or chronic ailments, or that they will become victims of homicide or suicide (NCHS, 2004; Pamuk, Makuc, Heck, Reuben, & Lochner, 1998). In particular, socioeconomic circumstances in both childhood and adulthood are important determinants of risk for cardiovascular disease, and, even more so, of stroke (Galobardes, Smith, & Lynch, 2006).

This does not mean that income and education *cause* good health; instead, they are related to environmental and lifestyle factors that tend to be causative. Better-educated and more affluent people tend to have healthier diets and better preventive health care and medical treatment. They exercise more, are less likely to be overweight, smoke less, are less likely to use illicit drugs, and are more likely to use alcohol in moderation (NCHS, 2004; Pamuk et al., 1998; SAMHSA, 2004b).

The association between SES and health sheds light on the relatively poor state of health in some minority populations (Kiefe et al., 2000). Young African American adults are 20 times more likely to have high blood pressure than young white adults (Agoda, 1995). African Americans are about twice as likely as white people to die in young adulthood, in part because young African American men are far more likely to be victims of homicide (NCHS, 2006).

However, factors associated with SES do not tell the whole story. For example, although African Americans smoke less than white Americans, they metabolize more nicotine in the blood, face higher risks of lung cancer, and have more trouble breaking the habit. Possible reasons may be genetic, biological, or behavioral (Caraballo et al., 1998; Pérez-Stable, Herrera, Jacob, & Benowitz, 1998; Sellers, 1998). A review of more than 100 studies found that racial/ethnic minorities tend to receive lower-quality health care than white people do, even when insurance status, income, age, and severity of conditions are similar (Smedley, Stith, & Nelson, 2002). We further discuss the relationship between ethnicity and health in Chapter 15.

Relationships and Health   Social relationships seem to be vital to health and well-being. Research has identified at least two interrelated aspects of the social environment that can promote health: *social integration* and *social support* (Cohen, 2004).

Social integration is active engagement in a broad range of social relationships, activities, and roles (spouse, parent, neighbor, friend, colleague, and the like). Social networks can influence emotional well-being as well as participation in healthful behaviors, such as exercising, eating nutritiously, and refraining from substance use (Cohen, 2004). Social integration has repeatedly been associated with lower mortality rates (Berkman & Glass, 2000; Rutledge et al., 2004). People with wide social networks and multiple social roles are more likely to survive heart attacks and less likely to be anxious or depressed than people with more limited social networks and roles (Cohen, Gottlieb, & Underwood, 2000) and even are less susceptible to colds (Cohen, Doyle, Skoner, Rabin, & Gwaltney, 1997).

This happily married couple is the picture of good health. Although there is a clear association between relationships and health, it's not clear which is the cause and which the effect.

Social support refers to material, informational, and psychological resources derived from the social network, on which a person can rely for help in coping with stress. In highly stressful situations, people who are in touch with others may be more likely to eat and sleep sensibly, get enough exercise, and avoid substance abuse and less likely to be distressed, anxious, or depressed or even to die (Cohen, 2004).

Because marriage offers a readily available system for both social integration and social support, it is not surprising that marriage tends to benefit health, especially for men (Wu & Hart, 2002). An interview survey of 127,545 U.S. adults found that married people, particularly in young adulthood, tend to be healthier physically and psychologically than those who are never-married, cohabiting, widowed, separated, or divorced. The sole exception is that married people, especially husbands, are more likely to be overweight or obese (Schoenborn, 2004). Dissolving a marriage, or a cohabitation, tends to have negative effects on physical or mental health or both—but so, apparently, does remaining in a bad relationship (Wu & Hart, 2002).

Mental Health Problems

For most emerging adults, mental health and well-being improve, and problem behaviors diminish. Yet, at the same time, the incidence of psychological disorders, such as major depression, schizophrenia, and bipolar disorders, increases. What explains this apparent paradox? The emerging adult transition brings an end to the relatively structured years of high school. The freedom to make life decisions and choose diverse paths is often liberating, but the responsibility to rely on oneself and to become financially self-supporting can be overwhelming (Schulenberg & Zarrett, 2006).

Nearly half of Americans (46.4 percent) have a mental illness sometime during their lifetime, and three-quarters of all mental illnesses start by age 24. Let's

Checkpoint

Can you . . .

♦ Point out differences in health and mortality that reflect income, education, and race/ethnicity?

♦ Discuss how relationships may affect physical and mental health?

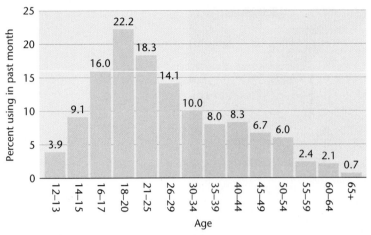

Figure 13-3

Current (past month) illicit drug use by age: 2006. Illicit drug use peaks in the emerging-adult years, when many young adults are in college or on their own for the first time. (Source: SAMHSA, 2007a, Fig. 2.3.)

alcoholism Chronic disease involving dependence on use of alcohol, causing interference with normal functioning and fulfillment of obligations.

look at some specific disorders that may develop during emerging or young adulthood.

Alcoholism Alcohol abuse and dependence are the most prevalent substance disorders, reported by 8.5 percent of the adult U.S. population. Alcohol dependence, or **alcoholism,** is a long-term physical condition characterized by compulsive drinking, which a person is unable to control (Grant et al., 2004). The heritability of a tendency to alcoholism is 50 to 60 percent (Bouchard, 2004). Alcoholism, like other addictions, such as getting hooked on smoking, seems to result from long-lasting changes in patterns of neural signal transmission in the brain. Exposure to the addictive substance (in this case, alcohol) creates a euphoric mental state accompanied by neurological changes that produce feelings of discomfort and craving when it is no longer present. From 6 to 48 hours after the last drink, alcoholics experience strong physical withdrawal symptoms (anxiety, agitation, tremors, elevated blood pressure, and sometimes seizures). Alcoholics, like drug addicts, develop a tolerance for the substance and need more and more to get the desired high (NIAAA, 1996).

Treatment for alcoholism may include detoxification (removing all alcohol from the body), hospitalization, medication, individual and group psychotherapy, and referral to a support organization, such as Alcoholics Anonymous. Although not a cure, treatment can give alcoholics new tools to cope with their addiction and lead productive lives (Friedmann, Saitz, & Samet, 1998).

Drug Use and Abuse Use of illicit drugs peaks at ages 18 to 20; more than 22 percent of this age group report indulging during the past month. As young adults settle down, get married, and take responsibility for their future, they tend to cut down on drug use. Usage rates drop sharply during the twenties, plateau in the late thirties and early forties, and then decline again into old age (SAMHSA, 2007a; Figure 13-3).

As in adolescence, marijuana is by far the most popular illicit drug among young adults. In 2006, 16.3 percent of 18- to 25-year-olds had used marijuana within the previous month compared with the 2.2 percent who had used cocaine (SAMHSA, 2007a). About 20 percent of persons with substance use disorders also have mood (depression) or anxiety disorders, and vice versa (Grant et al., 2004).

Antisocial Behavior The overall prevalence of antisocial behavior, which rises during adolescence, drops sharply during emerging adulthood. As discussed in Chapter 12, antisocial behavior follows one of two different developmental routes: early-onset and late-onset (Schulenberg & Zarrett, 2006).

Early-onset antisociality (beginning by age 11) generally has roots early in childhood. Dysfunctional family life and poor parental discipline contribute to childhood oppositional behavior, which then moves during adolescence, under the influence of deviant peers, to chronic juvenile delinquency. As adults, these young people are likely to continue an antisocial life course. In contrast, late-onset antisociality (beginning after puberty) tends to arise in young people with normal family backgrounds in response to the changes of adolescence. This group tend to commit relatively minor offenses. In emerging adulthood, with increasing opportunities to establish careers and romantic relationships, their antisocial behaviors usually stop (Schulenberg & Zarrett, 2006).

Depression Adolescence and emerging adulthood appear to be sensitive periods for the onset of depressive disorders. Between ages 15 and 22, the incidence of depression increases gradually (Schulenberg & Zarrett, 2006).

As with antisociality, childhood-or-adolescent-onset depression and adult-onset depression seem to have different origins and developmental paths. Adolescents who are depressed, and whose depression carries over into adulthood, tend to have had significant childhood risk factors, such as neurological or developmental disorders, dysfunctional or unstable families, and childhood behavioral disorders. They may have difficulty negotiating the transition to emerging adulthood. For some of them, on the other hand, emerging adulthood represents a new start, a chance to find new social roles and settings more conducive to mental health. The adult-onset group tend to have had low levels of childhood risk factors and to possess more resources to deal with the challenges of emerging adulthood; but the sudden decline in structure and support that accompanies adult life may throw them off course (Schulenberg & Zarrett, 2006).

Checkpoint

Can you . . .

♦ Discuss mental health problems common in emerging and young adulthood?

Sexual and Reproductive Issues

Sexual and reproductive activities are often a prime preoccupation of emerging and young adulthood. These natural and important functions also may involve physical concerns. Three such concerns are disorders related to menstruation, sexually transmitted diseases (STDs), and infertility.

Guidepost 3

What are some sexual and reproductive issues at this time of life?

Sexual Behavior and Attitudes

Today almost all U.S. adults have had sexual relations before marriage (Lefkowitz & Gillen, 2006). According to a nationally representative, in-person survey, 75 percent of adults have had premarital sex by age 20; 95 percent have done so by age 44. The percentages rise sharply in more recent age cohorts; among girls who turned 15 between 1964 and 1993, at least 91 percent had had premarital sex by age 30 (Finer, 2007).

Variety in sexual activity is common. Among 25- to 44-year-olds, 97 percent of men and 98 percent of women have had vaginal intercourse; 90 percent of men and 88 percent of women have had oral sex with a partner of the other sex; and 40 percent of men and 35 percent of women have had anal sex with an other-sex partner. About 6.5 percent of men and 11 percent of women have had sex with a same-sex partner (Mosher, Chandra, & Jones, 2005).

Emerging adults tend to have more sexual partners than in older age groups, but they have sex less frequently. People who become sexually active during emerging adulthood tend to engage in fewer risky behaviors—those that may lead to STDs or unplanned pregnancies—than those who began in adolescence. Condoms are the most commonly used contraceptive, though their use is inconsistent (Lefkowitz & Gillen, 2006).

Casual sex (hooking up) is fairly common, especially on college campuses. Sexual assaults on women are also a problem in this age group. Both are often associated with drinking. College students, in particular, are becoming less judgmental and more open-minded about sexual activity. However, a double standard still exists; men are expected to have more sexual freedom than women. By emerging adulthood, most lesbian, gay, bisexual, and transgendered persons are clear about their sexual identity. Many first come out to others during this period (Lefkowitz & Gillen, 2006).

Sexually Transmitted Diseases (STDs)

By far the highest rates of STDs in the United States are among emerging adults ages 18 to 25, especially among those who use alcohol and/or illicit drugs (SAMHSA, 2007b). An estimated 1 in 4 persons who have been sexually active, but nearly half of new STD cases, are in that age group, and many do not get medical diagnosis and care (Lefkowitz & Gillen, 2006).

The number of people living with HIV has risen in every region of the world since 2002, with the steepest increases in East and Central Asia and Eastern Europe. Still, sub-Saharan Africa remains by far the worst affected. A growing proportion of new infections occur in women, especially in places where hetero-sexual transmission is predominant, such as sub-Saharan Africa and the Caribbean. In the United States, most infections occur through drug abusers sharing con-taminated hypodermic needles, unprotected sex among gay or bisexual men (who may then pass on the infection to female partners), or commercial sex with prosti-tutes (UNAIDS/WHO, 2004).

With highly active antiviral therapy, death rates of persons diagnosed with HIV have dropped dramatically, and their average lifespan has increased to more than 35 years (Bhaskaran et al., 2008; Lohse et al., 2007). In the United States in 1995, AIDS was the leading cause of death for 25- to 44-year-olds; by 2003, it had fallen to ninth (Hoyert et al., 1999; NCHS, 2006). Still, in 2002 an estimated 9.9 percent of persons ages 15 to 44 had engaged in drug use or sexual behaviors that put them at height-ened risk of HIV (Anderson, Mosher, & Chandra, 2006).

Use of condoms is the most effective means of preventing STDs. A three-session intervention among U.S. Marine security guards resulted in increased perception of social support for condom use and stronger intentions to practice safer sex (Booth-Kewley, Minagawa, Shaffer, & Brodine, 2002).

Menstrual Disorders

Premenstrual syndrome (PMS) is a disorder that produces physical discomfort and emotional tension for up to the two weeks before a menstrual period. Symptoms may include fatigue, headaches, swelling and tenderness of the breasts, swollen hands or feet, abdominal bloating, nausea, cramps, constipation, food cravings, weight gain, anxiety, depression, irritability, mood swings, tearfulness, and difficulty concentrating or remembering (American College of Obstetricians & Gynecologists [ACOG], 2000; Moline & Zendell, 2000). Up to 85 percent of menstruating women may have some symptoms, but only in 5 to 10 percent do they warrant a diagnosis of PMS (ACOG, 2000).

The cause of PMS is not fully understood, but it appears to be a response to normal monthly surges of the female hormones estrogen and progesterone (Schmidt, Nieman, Danaceau, Adams, & Rubinow, 1998) as well as to levels of the male hormone testosterone and of serotonin, a brain chemical (ACOG, 2000).

The symptoms of PMS can sometimes be alleviated or minimized through aerobic exercise, eating frequent small meals, a diet high in complex carbohydrates and low in salt and caffeine, and regular sleep routines. Calcium, magnesium, and vitamin E supplements may help. Medications may relieve specific symptoms—

premenstrual syndrome (PMS) Disorder producing symptoms of physical discomfort and emotional tension for up to two weeks before a menstrual period.

for example, a diuretic for bloating and weight gain (ACOG, 2000; Moline & Zendell, 2000).

PMS can be confused with *dysmenor-rhea* (painful menstruation, or "cramps"). Cramps tend to affect adolescents and young women, whereas PMS is more typical in women in their thirties or older. Between 40 and 90 percent of women are believed to have dysmenorrhea, and in 10 to 15 percent of cases the pain is so severe as to be disabling (Newswise, 2004). Dysmenorrhea is caused by contractions of the uterus, which are set in motion by prostaglandin, a hormone-like substance; it can be treated with prostaglandin inhibitors, such as ibuprofen (Wang et al., 2004).

Infertility

An estimated 7 percent of U.S. couples experience **infertility:** inability to conceive a baby after 12 months of trying (CDC, 2005; Wright, Chang, Jeng, & Macaluso, 2006). Women's fertility begins to decline in their late twenties, with substantial decreases during their thirties. Men's fertility is less affected by age but declines significantly by their late thirties (Dunson, Colombo, & Baird, 2002). Infertility can burden a relationship emotionally, but only when infertility leads to permanent, involuntary childlessness is it associated with long-term psychological distress (McQuillan, Greil, White, & Jacob, 2003).

The most common cause of infertility in men is production of too few sperm. In some instances an ejaculatory duct may be blocked, preventing the exit of sperm, or sperm may be unable to swim well enough to reach the cervix. Some cases of male infertility seem to have a genetic basis (King, 1996; Reijo, Alagappan, Patrizio, & Page, 1996; Phillips, 1998).

In women, the cause of infertility may be the failure to produce ova or to produce normal ova; mucus in the cervix, which might prevent sperm from penetrating it; or a disease of the uterine lining, which might prevent implantation of the fertilized ovum. A major cause of declining fertility in women after age 30 is deterioration in the quality of ova (van Noord-Zaadstra et al., 1991). However, the most common cause is blockage of the fallopian tubes, preventing ova from reaching the uterus. In about half of these cases, the tubes are blocked by scar tissue from sexually transmitted diseases (King, 1996).

Sometimes hormone treatment, drug therapy, or surgery may correct the problem. However, fertility drugs increase the likelihood of multiple, high-risk births. Also, men undergoing fertility treatment are at increased risk of producing sperm with chromosomal abnormalities (Levron et al., 1998). Daily supplements of coenzyme Q10, an antioxidant, may help increase sperm motility (Balercia et al., 2004).

Unless there is a known cause for failure to conceive, the chances of success after 18 months to two years are high (Dunson, 2002). For couples struggling with infertility, science today offers several alternative ways to parenthood (Box 13-1).

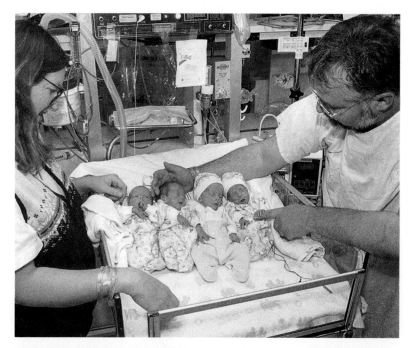

The birth of quadruplets is a less unusual occurrence than it once was. Delayed childbearing, use of fertility drugs, and assisted reproductive techniques such as in vitro fertilization increase the likelihood of multiple, usually premature, births.

infertility Inability to conceive after 12 months of trying.

Checkpoint

Can you . . .

- Summarize trends in sexual behavior and attitudes among emerging and young adults?

- Discuss the spread of STDs and ways to control it?

- Discuss the symptoms and likely causes of PMS and ways to manage it?

- Identify common causes of male and female infertility?

- Describe several means of assisted reproduction, and mention issues they raise?

BOX 13-1 **Research** *in Action*

Assisted Reproductive Technology

More than 3 million children worldwide have been conceived through *assisted reproductive technology (ART)* (Reaney, 2006; ICMART, 2006). In 2005, U.S. women delivered more than 52,000 babies with technological help, representing 1 percent of all babies born in the United States in that year (Wright, Chang, Jeng, & Macaluso, 2008).

With *in vitro fertilization (IVF)*, the most common assisted reproduction procedure, women receive fertility drugs to increase production of ova. Then ova are surgically removed, fertilized in a laboratory dish, and implanted in the woman's uterus. Because several embryos are typically transferred to the uterus to increase the chances of pregnancy, this procedure increases the likelihood of multiple, usually premature, births (Wright et al., 2006).

A newer technique, *in vitro maturation (IVM)* is performed earlier in the monthly cycle, when egg follicles are developing. Harvesting a large number of follicles before ovulation is complete and then allowing them to mature in the laboratory can make hormone injections unnecessary and thus diminish the likelihood of multiple births (Duenwald, 2003).

IVF also addresses severe male infertility. A single sperm can be injected into the ovum—a technique called *intracytoplasmic sperm injection (ICSI)*. This procedure is now used in the majority of IVF cycles (Van Voorhis, 2007).

Artificial insemination—injection of sperm into a woman's vagina, cervix, or uterus—can be used to facilitate conception if a man has a low sperm count, allowing a couple to produce their own biological offspring. If the man is infertile, a couple may choose *artificial insemination by a donor (AID)*. If the woman has no explainable cause of infertility, the chances of success can be greatly increased by stimulating her ovaries to produce excess ova and injecting semen directly into the uterus (Guzick et al., 1999).

Although success rates have improved (Duenwald, 2003), only 35 percent of women who attempted assisted reproduction in 2005 had live births (Wright et al., 2008). For one thing, the likelihood of success with IVF using a mother's own ova drops precipitously with maternal age as the quality of her ova declines (Van Voorhis, 2007).

A woman who is producing poor-quality ova or who has had her ovaries removed may try *ovum transfer*. In this procedure, an ovum, or *donor egg,* provided by a fertile younger woman is fertilized in the laboratory and implanted in the prospective mother's uterus. IVF using donor eggs tends to be highly successful (Van Voorhis, 2007). Alternatively, the ovum can be fertilized in the donor's body by artificial insemination. The embryo is retrieved from the donor and inserted into the recipient's uterus. Two other techniques with relatively higher success rates are *gamete intrafallopian transfer (GIFT)* and *zygote intrafallopian transfer (ZIFT)*, in which either the egg and sperm or the fertilized egg are inserted in the fallopian tube (CDC, 2002; Schieve et al., 2002; Society for Assisted Reproductive Technology, 1993, 2002).

In *surrogate motherhood,* a fertile woman is impregnated by the prospective father, usually by artificial insemination. She agrees to carry the baby to term and give it to the father and his partner. Courts in most states view surrogacy contracts as unenforceable, and some states have either banned the practice or placed strict conditions on it. The American Academy of Pediatrics (AAP) Committee on Bioethics (1992) recommends that surrogacy be considered a tentative, preconception adoption agreement. The committee also recommends a prebirth agreement on the period of time in which the surrogate may assert parental rights.

Assisted reproduction can result in a tangled web of legal, ethical, and psychological dilemmas (ISLAT Working Group, 1998; Schwartz, 2003). Who should have access to these methods? Should the children know about their parentage? Should genetic tests be performed on prospective donors and surrogates? When IVF results in multiple fertilized ova, should some be discarded to improve the chances of health for the survivors? What should be done with any unused embryos?

The issues multiply when a surrogate is involved (Schwartz, 2003). Who is the real parent—the surrogate or the woman whose baby she bears? What if a surrogate wants to keep the baby, as has happened in a few highly publicized cases? What if the intended parents refuse to go through with the contract? Another controversial aspect of surrogacy is the payment of money. The creation of a "breeder class" of poor and disadvantaged women who carry the babies of the well-to-do strikes many people as wrong. Similar concerns have been raised about payment for donor eggs (Gabriel, 1996). Some countries, such as France and Italy, have banned commercial surrogacy. In the United States, it is illegal in some states and legal in others, and regulations differ from state to state (Warner, 2008).

One thing seems certain: As long as there are people who want children but are unable to conceive or bear them, human ingenuity and technology will come up with ways to satisfy their desire.

What's Your View?

If you or your partner were infertile, would you seriously consider or undertake one of the methods of assisted reproduction described here? Why or why not?

Check It Out

For more information on this topic, go to www.cdc.gov/ART/index.htm. This website features research highlights about assisted reproductive technology.

COGNITIVE DEVELOPMENT

Perspectives on Adult Cognition

Guidepost 4

What is distinctive about adult thought?

Developmental theorists and researchers have studied adult cognition from a variety of perspectives. Some investigators seek to identify distinctive cognitive capacities that emerge in adulthood or distinctive ways in which adults use their cognitive abilities at successive stages of life. Other investigators focus on aspects of intelligence that exist throughout life but tend to come to the fore in adulthood. One current theory, which may apply to children as well as adults, highlights the role of emotion in intelligent behavior.

Beyond Piaget: New Ways of Thinking in Adulthood

Although Piaget described the stage of formal operations as the pinnacle of cognitive achievement, some developmental scientists maintain that changes in cognition extend beyond that stage. One line of neo-Piagetian theory and research concerns higher levels of *reflective thinking,* or abstract reasoning. Another line of investigation deals with *postformal thought,* which combines logic with emotion and practical experience in the resolution of ambiguous problems.

Reflective Thinking   **Reflective thinking** is a complex form of cognition, first defined by the American philosopher and educator John Dewey (1910/1991) as "active, persistent, and careful consideration" of information or beliefs in the light of the evidence that supports them and the conclusions to which they lead. Reflective thinkers continually question supposed facts, draw inferences, and make connections. Building on Piaget's stage of formal operations, reflective thinkers can create complex intellectual systems that reconcile apparently conflicting ideas or considerations—for example, by putting together various theories of modern physics or of human development into a single overarching theory that explains many different kinds of behavior (Fischer & Pruyne, 2003).

reflective thinking   Type of logical thinking that may emerge in adulthood, involving continuous, active evaluation of information and beliefs in the light of evidence and implications.

The capacity for reflective thinking seems to emerge between ages 20 and 25. Not until then are the cortical regions of the brain that handle higher-level thinking fully myelinated. At the same time, the brain is forming new neurons, synapses, and dendritic connections. Environmental support can stimulate the development of thicker, denser cortical connections. Although almost all adults develop the *capacity* for becoming reflective thinkers, few attain optimal proficiency in this skill, and even fewer can apply it consistently to various kinds of problems. For example, a young adult may understand the concept of justice but may have difficulty weighing it in relation to other concepts such as social welfare, law, ethics, and responsibility. This may help explain why, as we discuss later in this chapter, few adults reach Kohlberg's highest levels of moral reasoning. For many adults, college education stimulates progress toward reflective thinking (Fischer & Pruyne, 2003).

Postformal Thought   Research and theoretical work since the 1970s suggest that mature thinking is richer and more complex than Piaget described. It is characterized by the ability to deal with uncertainty, inconsistency, contradiction, imperfection, and compromise. This higher stage of adult cognition is sometimes called **postformal thought,** and it generally begins in emerging adulthood, often through exposure to higher education (Labouvie-Vief, 2006).

postformal thought   Mature type of thinking that relies on subjective experience and intuition as well as logic and is useful in dealing with ambiguity, uncertainty, inconsistency, contradiction, imperfection, and compromise.

Postformal thought is flexible, open, adaptive, and individualistic. It draws on intuition and emotion as well as on logic to help people cope with a seemingly chaotic world. It applies the fruits of experience to ambiguous situations.

Postformal thought is relativistic. Like reflective thinking, it enables adults to transcend a single logical system (such as Euclidean geometry or a particular theory of human development or an established political system) and reconcile or choose among conflicting ideas or demands (such as those of the Israelis and Palestinians or those of two romantic partners), each of which, from its perspective, may have a valid claim to truth (Labouvie-Vief, 1990a, 1990b; Sinnott, 1996, 1998, 2003). Immature thinking sees black and white (right versus wrong, intellect versus feelings, mind versus body); postformal thinking sees shades of gray. Like reflective thinking, it often develops in response to events and interactions that open up unaccustomed ways of looking at things and challenge a simple, polarized view of the world.

One prominent researcher, Jan Sinnott (1984, 1998, 2003), has proposed the following criteria of postformal thought.

- *Shifting gears*. Ability to think within at least two different logical systems and to shift back and forth between abstract reasoning and practical, real-world considerations. ("This might work on paper but not in real life.")

- *Problem definition*. Ability to define a problem as falling within a class or category of logical problems and to define its parameters. ("This is an ethical problem, not a legal one, so judicial precedents don't really help solve it.")

- *Process-product shift*. Ability to see that a problem can be solved either through a *process,* with general application to similar problems, or through a *product,* a concrete solution to the particular problem. ("I've come up against this type of problem before, and this is how I solved it" or "In this case, the best available solution would be . . .")

- *Pragmatism*. Ability to choose the best of several possible logical solutions and to recognize criteria for choosing. ("If you want the cheapest solution, do this; if you want the quickest solution, do that.")

- *Multiple solutions*. Awareness that most problems have more than one cause, that people may have differing goals, and that a variety of methods can be used to arrive at more than one solution. ("Let's try it your way; if that doesn't work, we can try my way.")

- *Awareness of paradox*. Recognition that a problem or solution involves inherent conflict. ("Doing this will give him what he wants, but it will only make him unhappy in the end.")

- *Self-referential thought*. A person's awareness that he or she must be the judge of which logic to use: in other words, that he or she is using postformal thought.

The shift to postformal thought can be emotionally unsettling. "Emerging adults may be easily swayed by their emotions to distort their thinking in self-serving and self-protective ways" (Labouvie-Vief, 2006, p. 79). Young adults over age 30 may be better able to live comfortably with complexity.

Postformal thinking often operates in a social and emotional context. Unlike the problems Piaget studied, which involve physical phenomena and require dispassionate, objective observation and analysis, social dilemmas are less clearly structured and are often fraught with emotion. It is in these kinds of situations that adults tend to call on postformal thought (Berg & Klaczynski, 1996; Sinnott, 1996, 1998, 2003).

Research has found a progression toward postformal thought throughout young and middle adulthood, especially when emotions are involved. In one study, participants were asked to judge what caused the outcomes of a series of hypothetical situations, such as a marital conflict. Adolescents and young adults tended to blame individuals, whereas middle-aged people were more likely to attribute behavior to the interplay among persons and environment. The more ambiguous the situation, the greater were the age differences in interpretation (Blanchard-Fields & Norris, 1994). We further discuss postformal thought in Chapter 15.

Schaie: A Life-Span Model of Cognitive Development

K. Warner Schaie's life-span model of cognitive development (1977–1978; Schaie & Willis, 2000) looks at the developing uses of intellect within a social context. His seven stages revolve around motivating goals that come to the fore at various stages of life. These goals shift from acquisition of information and skills (*what I need to know*) to practical integration of knowledge and skills (*how to use what I know*) to a search for meaning and purpose (*why I should know*). The seven stages are as follows:

1. *Acquisitive stage* (childhood and adolescence). Children and adolescents acquire information and skills mainly for their own sake or as preparation for participation in society.

2. *Achieving stage* (late teens or early twenties to early thirties). Young adults no longer acquire knowledge merely for its own sake; they use what they know to pursue goals, such as career and family.

3. *Responsible stage* (late thirties to early sixties). Middle-aged people use their minds to solve practical problems associated with responsibilities to others, such as family members or employees.

4. *Executive stage* (thirties or forties through middle age). People in the executive stage, which may overlap with the achieving and responsible stages, are responsible for societal systems (such as governmental or business organizations) or social movements. They deal with complex relationships on multiple levels.

5. *Reorganizational stage* (end of middle age, beginning of late adulthood). People who enter retirement reorganize their lives and intellectual energies around meaningful pursuits that take the place of paid work.

6. *Reintegrative stage* (late adulthood). Older adults may be experiencing biological and cognitive changes and tend to be more selective about what tasks they expend effort on. They focus on the purpose of what they do and concentrate on tasks that have the most meaning for them.

7. *Legacy-creating stage* (advanced old age). Near the end of life, once reintegration has been completed (or along with it), older people may create instructions for the disposition of prized possessions, make funeral arrangements, provide oral histories, or write their life stories as a legacy for their loved ones. All of these tasks involve the exercise of cognitive competencies within a social and emotional context.

Not everyone goes through these stages within the suggested time frames. Indeed, Schaie's stages of adulthood may apply less widely in an era of varied and rapidly changing choices and paths, when medical and other societal advances

Can you . . .

- ⬥ Differentiate between reflective and postformal thinking?
- ⬥ Tell why postformal thought may be especially suited to solving social problems?
- ⬥ Identify Schaie's seven stages of cognitive development?

keep many people active and engaged in constructive, responsible endeavors into old age.

If adults do go through stages such as these, then traditional psychometric tests, which use the same kinds of tasks to measure intelligence at all periods of life, may be inappropriate for them. Tests developed to measure knowledge and skills in children may not be suitable for measuring cognitive competence in adults, who use knowledge and skills to solve practical problems and achieve self-chosen goals. We may instead need means to assess competence in dealing with real-life challenges, such as balancing a checkbook, reading a railroad timetable, and making informed decisions about medical problems. Robert Sternberg's work has taken this direction.

Sternberg: Insight and Know-How

Alix, Barbara, and Courtney applied to graduate programs at Yale University. Alix had earned almost straight A's in college, scored high on the Graduate Record Examination (GRE), and had excellent recommendations. Barbara's grades were only fair, and her GRE scores were low by Yale's standards, but her letters of recommendation enthusiastically praised her exceptional research and creative ideas. Courtney's grades, GRE scores, and recommendations were good but not among the best.

Alix and Courtney were admitted to the graduate program. Barbara was not admitted but was hired as a research associate and took graduate classes on the side. Alix did very well for the first year or so, but less well after that. Barbara confounded the admissions committee by doing outstanding work. Courtney's performance in graduate school was only fair, but she had the easiest time getting a good job afterward (Trotter, 1986).

According to Sternberg's (1985, 1987) triarchic theory of intelligence (introduced in Chapter 9), Barbara and Courtney were strong in two aspects of intelligence that psychometric tests miss: creative insight (what Sternberg calls the *experiential element*) and practical intelligence (the *contextual element*). Because insight and practical intelligence are important in adult life, psychometric tests are much less useful in gauging adults' intelligence and predicting their life success than in measuring children's intelligence and predicting their school success. As an undergraduate, Alix's analytical ability (the *componential element*) helped her sail through examinations. However, in graduate school, where original thinking is expected, Barbara's superior experiential intelligence—her fresh insights and innovative ideas—began to shine. So did Courtney's practical, contextual intelligence—her street smarts. She knew her way around. She chose hot research topics, submitted papers to the right journals, and knew where and how to apply for jobs.

An important aspect of practical intelligence is *tacit knowledge* (defined in Chapter 9): "inside information," "know-how," or "savvy" that is not formally taught or openly expressed (Sternberg, Grigorenko, & Oh, 2001; Sternberg & Wagner, 1993; Sternberg et al., 1995; Wagner & Sternberg, 1986). Tacit knowledge is commonsense knowledge of how to get ahead—how to win a promotion or cut through red tape. It is not well correlated with measures of general cognitive ability, but it may be a better predictor of managerial success (Sternberg, Grigorenko, & Oh, 2001).

Tacit knowledge may include *self-management* (knowing how to motivate oneself and organize time and energy), *management of tasks* (knowing how to write a term paper or grant proposal), and *management of others* (knowing when and how to reward or criticize subordinates) (E. A. Smith, 2001). Sternberg's method of testing tacit knowledge in adults is to compare a test-taker's chosen course of action in hypothetical, work-related situations (such as how best to angle for a promotion) with the choices of experts in the field and with accepted rules of thumb. Tacit knowledge, measured in this way, seems to be unrelated to IQ and predicts job performance better than do psychometric tests (Herbig, Büssing, & Ewert, 2001; Sternberg et al., 1995).

Of course, tacit knowledge is not all that is needed to succeed; other aspects of intelligence count, too. In studies of business managers, tests of tacit knowledge *together with* IQ and personality tests predicted virtually all of the variance in performance, measured by such criteria as salary, years of management experience, and the company's success (Sternberg et al., 1995). In one study, tacit knowledge was related to the salaries managers earned at a given age and to how high their positions were, independent of family background and education. The most knowledgeable managers were not those who had spent many years with a company or many years as managers, but those who had worked for the most companies, perhaps gaining a greater breadth of experience (Sternberg et al., 2000).

Emotional Intelligence

In 1990, two psychologists, Peter Salovey and John Mayer (Mayer & Salovey, 1997; Salovey & Mayer, 1990), coined the term **emotional intelligence (EI).** It refers to four related skills: the abilities to *perceive, use, understand,* and *manage,* or regulate, emotions—our own and those of others—so as to achieve goals. Emotional intelligence enables a person to harness emotions to deal more effectively with the social environment. It requires awareness of the type of behavior that is appropriate in a given social situation.

To measure emotional intelligence, psychologists use the Mayer-Salovey-Caruso Emotional Intelligence Test (MSCEIT) (Mayer, Salovey, & Caruso, 2002), a 40-minute battery of questions that generates a score for each of the four abilities, as well as a total score. The test includes such questions as, "Tom felt anxious and became a bit stressed when he thought about all the work he needed to do. When his supervisor brought him an additional project, he felt (a) overwhelmed, (b) depressed, (c) ashamed, (d) self-conscious, or (e) jittery." Answers may be scored by a panel of emotion researchers or by a worldwide sample of laypersons; both methods yield similar scores.

Emotional intelligence affects the quality of personal relationships. Studies have found that college students who score high on the MSCEIT are more likely to report positive relationships with parents and friends (Lopes, Salovey, & Straus, 2003), that college-age men who score low on the MSCEIT report engaging in more drug use and consuming more alcohol (Brackett, Mayer, & Warner, 2004), and that close friends of college students who score well on the MSCEIT rate them as more likely to provide emotional support in time of need (Lopes et al., 2004). College-age couples in which both partners scored high on the MSCEIT reported the happiest relationships, whereas couples who scored low were unhappiest (Brackett, Cox, Gaines, & Salovey, 2005).

Emotional intelligence also affects effectiveness at work. Among a sample of employees of a Fortune 500 insurance company, those with higher MSCEIT scores were rated higher by colleagues and supervisors on sociability, interpersonal sensitivity, leadership potential, and ability to handle stress and conflict. High scores also were related to higher salaries and more promotions (Lopes, Grewal, Kadis, Gall, & Salovey, 2006).

Ultimately, acting on emotions often comes down to a value judgment. Is it smarter to obey or disobey authority? To inspire others or exploit them? "Emotional

Checkpoint

Can you . . .

♦ Tell why Sternberg's three kinds of intelligence may be especially applicable to adults?

emotional intelligence (EI) Salovey and Mayer's term for ability to understand and regulate emotions; an important component of effective, intelligent behavior.

What's Your View?

• In what kinds of situations would reflective thought be most useful? Give specific examples. Do the same for postformal thought, tacit knowledge, and emotional intelligence.

• Who is the most intelligent person you know? Why do you consider this person exceptionally intelligent? Would you ask this person for advice about a personal problem? Why or why not?

Checkpoint

Can you . . .

♦ Explain the concept of emotional intelligence and how it is tested?

Guidepost 5

How does moral reasoning develop?

skills, like intellectual ones, are morally neutral. . . . Without a moral compass to guide people in how to employ their gifts, emotional intelligence can be used for good or evil" (Gibbs, 1995, p. 68). Let's look next at the development of that "moral compass" in adulthood.

Moral Reasoning

In Kohlberg's theory, introduced in Chapter 11, moral development of children and adolescents accompanies cognitive maturation. Young people advance in moral judgment as they shed egocentrism and become capable of abstract thought. In adulthood, however, moral judgments become more complex.

According to Kohlberg, advancement to the third level of moral reasoning—fully principled, postconventional morality—is chiefly a function of experience. Most people do not reach this level until their twenties, if ever (Kohlberg, 1973). Two experiences that spur moral reasoning in young adults are encountering conflicting values away from home (as may happen in college or the armed services or in foreign travel) and being responsible for the welfare of others (as in parenthood).

Experience may lead adults to reevaluate their criteria for what is right and fair. Some adults spontaneously offer personal experiences as reasons for their answers to moral dilemmas. For example, people who have had cancer, or whose relatives or friends have had cancer, are more likely to condone a man's stealing an expensive drug to save his dying wife, and to explain this view in terms of their own experience (Bielby & Papalia, 1975). With regard to moral judgments, then, cognitive stages do not tell the whole story. Of course, someone whose thinking is still egocentric is unlikely to make moral decisions at a postconventional level; but even someone who can think abstractly may not reach the highest level of moral development unless experience catches up with cognition.

Shortly before his death in 1987, as we mentioned in Chapter 11, Kohlberg proposed a seventh stage of moral reasoning, which moves beyond considerations of justice. In the seventh stage, adults reflect on the question, *"Why* be moral?" (Kohlberg & Ryncarz, 1990, p. 192; emphasis added). The answer, said Kohlberg, lies in achieving a cosmic perspective: "a sense of unity with the cosmos, nature, or God," which enables a person to see moral issues "from the standpoint of the universe as a whole" (Kohlberg & Ryncarz, 1990, pp. 191, 207). The achievement of such a perspective is so rare that Kohlberg himself had questions about calling it a stage of development. Kohlberg did note that it parallels the most mature stage of faith that the theologian James Fowler (1981) identified (Box 13-2), in which "one experiences a oneness with the ultimate conditions of one's life and being" (Kohlberg & Ryncarz, 1990, p. 202).

Culture and Moral Reasoning

Heinz's dilemma, described in Chapter 11, was revised for use in Taiwan. In the revision, a shopkeeper will not give a man *food* for his sick wife. This version would seem unbelievable to Chinese villagers, who are more accustomed to hearing a shopkeeper in such a situation say, "You have to let people have things whether they have money or not" (Wolf, 1968, p. 21).

Whereas Kohlberg's system is based on justice, the Chinese ethos leans toward conciliation and harmony. In Kohlberg's format, respondents make an either-or decision based on their own value system. In Chinese society, people faced with moral dilemmas are expected to discuss them openly, be guided by community standards, and try to find a way of resolving the problem to please as many parties as possible. In the West, even good people may be harshly punished if, under the force of

BOX **13-2 Research** *in Action*

Development of Faith across the Life Span

What is faith, and how does it develop? James Fowler (1981, 1989) defined *faith* broadly as a way of seeing or knowing the world. To find out how people arrive at this knowledge, Fowler and his students at Harvard Divinity School interviewed more than 400 people of all ages with various ethnic, educational, and socioeconomic backgrounds and various religious or secular identifications and affiliations.

According to Fowler, faith develops—as do other aspects of cognition—through interaction between the maturing person and the environment. As in other stage theories, each of Fowler's stages of faith builds on those that went before. New experiences—crises, problems, or revelations—that challenge or upset a person's equilibrium may prompt a leap from one stage to the next. The ages at which these transitions occur are variable, and some people never leave a particular stage. Fowler's stages correspond roughly to those described by Piaget, Kohlberg, and Erikson.

- *Stage 1: Intuitive-projective faith* (ages 18–24 months to 7 years). The beginnings of faith, says Fowler, come after children have developed what Erikson called *basic trust:* the sense that their needs will be met by powerful others. As young children struggle to understand the forces that control their world, they form powerful, imaginative images of God, heaven, and hell, drawn from the stories adults tell or read to them. Still egocentric, they have difficulty distinguishing God's point of view from their own or their parents'. They think of God mainly in terms of expecting obedience to avoid punishment.
- *Stage 2: Mythic-literal faith* (ages 7 to 12 years). Children begin to develop a more logical, coherent view of the universe. They tend to take religious stories and symbols literally. They can now see God as having a perspective and judgment beyond their own, which takes into account effort and intent. They believe that God is fair and that people get what they deserve.
- *Stage 3: Synthetic-conventional faith* (adolescence or beyond). Adolescents, now capable of abstract thought, begin to adopt belief systems and commitments to ideals. As they search for identity, they may seek a more personal relationship with God, but they look to others (often to peers) for moral authority. Their faith typically is unquestioning and conforms to community standards. About 50 percent of adults may remain at this stage.
- *Stage 4: Individuative-reflective faith* (early to middle twenties or beyond). Adults who reach this stage examine their faith critically and think out their own beliefs, independent of external authority and group norms.
- *Stage 5: Conjunctive faith* (midlife or beyond). Middle-aged people may become more aware of the limits of reason. They recognize life's paradoxes and contradictions, and they

often struggle with conflicts between fulfilling their own needs and sacrificing for others. As they begin to anticipate death, they may achieve a deeper understanding and acceptance through faith.
- *Stage 6: Universalizing faith* (late life). In this rare category Fowler placed such moral and spiritual leaders as Mahatma Gandhi, Martin Luther King Jr., and Mother Teresa, whose vision or commitment profoundly inspires others. Because they threaten the established order, they may become martyrs; and though they love life, they do not cling to it. This stage parallels Kohlberg's proposed seventh stage of moral development.

As one of the first researchers to systematically study how faith develops, Fowler has had great impact; his work has become required reading in many divinity schools. It also has been criticized on several counts (Koenig, 1994). Critics point out that his sample was not random or representative. They say Fowler's concept of faith is at odds with conventional definitions, which involve acceptance, not introspection. They challenge his emphasis on cognitive knowledge and maintain that he underestimates the maturity of a simple, solid, unquestioning faith. Critics also question whether faith develops in stages—at least in those Fowler identified. Fowler himself has cautioned that his advanced stages should not be seen as better or truer than others, though he does portray people at his highest stage as moral and spiritual exemplars.

Some of these criticisms resemble those made against other major models of life-span development. Piaget's, Kohlberg's, and Erikson's initial samples were not randomly selected either, and the validity of their proposed stages has been questioned. More research is needed to confirm, modify, or extend Fowler's theory, especially in non-Western cultures.

What's Your View?

Is faith in God necessary to be a religious person? Do you fit into one of the stages of faith that Fowler described?

Check It Out

For more information on this topic, go to www.psywww.com/psyrelig (a website intended as an introduction to psychology of religion, which describes "what psychologists have learned about how religion influences people's lives").

Table 13-1	Gilligan's Levels of Moral Development in Women
Stage	**Description**
Level 1: Orientation of individual survival	The woman concentrates on herself—on what is practical and what is best for her.
Transition 1: From selfishness to responsibility	The woman realizes her connection to others and thinks about what the responsible choice would be in terms of other people (including her unborn baby), as well as herself.
Level 2: Goodness as self-sacrifice	This conventional feminine wisdom dictates sacrificing the woman's own wishes to what other people want—and will think of her. She considers herself responsible for the actions of others, while holding others, responsible for her own choices. She is in a dependent position, one in which her indirect efforts to exert control often turn into manipulation, sometimes through the use of guilt.
Transition 2: From goodness to truth	The woman assesses her decisions not on the basis of how others will react to them but on her intentions and the consequences of her actions. She develops a new judgment that takes into account her own needs, along with those of others. She wants to be "good" by being responsible to others, but also wants to be "honest" by being responsible to herself. Survival returns as a major concern.
Level 3: Morality of nonviolence	By elevating the injunction against hurting anyone (including herself) to a principle that governs all moral judgment and action, the woman establishes a "moral equality" between herself and others and is then able to assume the responsibility for choice in moral dilemmas.

Source: Reprinted and adapted by permission of the publisher from *In a Different Voice: Psychological Theory and Women's Development* by Carol Gilligan, Cambridge, Mass. Harvard University Press. Copyright © 1982, 1993 by Carol Gilligan.

What's Your View?

• Have you ever observed or had an experience with a person from another culture that revealed cultural differences in moral principles?

circumstances, they break a law. The Chinese are unaccustomed to universally applied laws; they are taught to abide by the decisions of a wise judge (Dien, 1982).

However, we need to be careful to avoid making broad-brush generalizations about cultural attitudes. Concepts of rights, welfare, and justice exist in all cultures, though they may be applied differently. To say that Western cultures are individualistic and Eastern cultures are collectivist ignores individual differences and even diametrically opposed attitudes within each culture, and the specific contextual situations in which moral judgments are applied (Turiel, 1998). For example, the outpouring of relief funds from the United States for survivors of the tsunami in Southeast Asia and of Hurricane Katrina in New Orleans and the Gulf coast showed that compassion may be as strong a part of the American ethos as competition.

Gender and Moral Reasoning

Carol Gilligan suggested that a woman's central moral dilemma is the conflict between her needs and those of others (see Chapter 11). To find out how women make moral choices, Gilligan (1982/1993) interviewed 29 pregnant women about their decisions to continue or end their pregnancies. These women saw morality in terms of selfishness versus responsibility, defined as an obligation to exercise care and avoid hurting others. Gilligan concluded that women think less about abstract justice and fairness than men do and more about their responsibilities to specific people. (Table 13-1 lists Gilligan's proposed levels of moral development in women.)

However, other research has not, on the whole, found significant gender differences in moral reasoning (Brabeck & Shore, 2003). One analysis comparing results from 66 studies found no significant differences in men's and women's responses to Kohlberg's dilemmas across the life span. In the few studies in which men scored slightly higher, the findings were not clearly gender-related, as the men generally were better educated and had better jobs than the women (L. J. Walker, 1984). A more recent analysis of 113 studies reached a slightly more nuanced conclusion. Although women were more likely to think in terms of care, and men in terms of justice, these differences were small, especially among university students. Ages of respondents and the types of dilemmas or questions presented were more significant factors than gender (Jaffee & Hyde, 2000). Thus, the weight of evidence does not appear to back up either of Gilligan's original contentions: a male bias in Kohlberg's theory or a distinct female perspective on morality (L. Walker, 1995).

In her later research, Gilligan has described moral development in *both* men and women as evolving beyond abstract reasoning. In studies using real-life moral dilemmas (such as whether a woman's lover should confess their affair to her husband), rather than hypothetical dilemmas like the ones Kohlberg used, Gilligan and her colleagues found that many people in their twenties become dissatisfied with a narrow moral logic and become more able to live with moral contradictions (Gilligan, Murphy, & Tappan, 1990). It seems, then, that if Gilligan's earlier research reflected an alternative value system, it was not gender-based. At the same time, with the inclusion of his seventh stage, Kohlberg's thinking evolved to a point of greater agreement with Gilligan's. Both theories now place responsibility to others at the highest level of moral thought. Both recognize the importance for both sexes of connections with other people and of compassion and care.

Education and Work

Unlike young people in past generations, who typically could expect to move directly from school to work and financial independence, many emerging adults today do not have a clear career path. Some alternate between education and work; others pursue both at the same time. Most of those who do not enroll in postsecondary education, or do not finish, enter the job market, but many return later for more schooling (Furstenberg et al., 2005; Hamilton & Hamilton, 2006; NCES, 2005b). Some, especially in the United Kingdom, take a year off from formal education or the workplace—a *gap year*—to gain new skills, do volunteer work, travel, or study abroad (Jones, 2004). And some combine college with marriage and child rearing (Fitzpatrick & Turner, 2007). Many emerging adults who are in school or living in their parents' homes are financially dependent (Schoeni & Ross, 2005).

Educational and vocational choices after high school may present opportunities for cognitive growth. Exposure to a new educational or work environment offers the opportunity to hone abilities, question long-held assumptions, and try out new ways of looking at the world. For the increasing number of students of nontraditional age (age 25 and up), college or workplace education is rekindling intellectual curiosity, improving employment opportunities, and enhancing work skills.

The College Transition

College is an increasingly important path to adulthood, though it is only one such path and, until recently, not the most common one (Montgomery & Côté, 2003). Between 1972 and 2005, the proportion of U.S. high school graduates who went

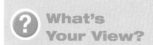

What's Your View?

• Which, if either, do you consider to be higher moral priorities: justice and rights, or compassion and responsibility?

Checkpoint

Can you . . .

♦ Give examples of the roles of experience and culture in adult moral development?

♦ State Gilligan's original position on gender differences in moral development, and summarize research findings on the subject?

Guidepost 6

How do emerging adults make the transitions to higher education and work, and how do these experiences affect cognitive development?

College enrollments in the United States are at an all-time high. More than 2 out of 3 high school graduates go right to college.

right on to a two- or four-year college grew from less than half (49 percent) to more than two-thirds (69 percent), and 58 percent of all 25- to 29-year-olds had completed at least some college work (NCES, 2007a). Six out of ten undergraduate students attend four-year, degree-granting institutions (Knapp, Kelly-Reid, Whitmore, & Miller, 2007), but an increasing proportion attend college part-time or go to two-year, vocationally oriented community colleges (NCES, 2004a; Seftor & Turner, 2002).

College courses and even complete degree or certificate programs are now widely available by *distance learning,* in which courses are delivered via mail, e-mail, the Internet, or other technological means (NCES, 2004a). About 3.5 million students, nearly 20 percent of all U.S. higher education enrollees, took at least one online course during the fall of 2006 (Allen & Seaman, 2007).

Gender, Socioeconomic Status, and Race/Ethnicity   U.S. college enrollment reaches record highs each year, thanks largely to a faster-growing number of female students. In a reversal of the traditional gender gap, women now make up 57 percent of U.S. undergraduate students and 57.4 percent of those earning bachelor's degrees, up from 42 percent in 1970 (NCES, 2007a). This development is due in part to a decline in gender discrimination and in part to women's growing awareness of the need to support themselves (Buchmann & DiPrete, 2006). Similarly, women have higher postsecondary enrollment rates than men in most European countries, as well as Australia, Canada, New Zealand, Japan, and the Russian Federation (Buchmann & DiPrete, 2006; Sen et al., 2005). U.S. women are more likely than men to enroll in graduate school and earn master's degrees (59 percent) and almost as likely to complete doctoral degrees (NCES, 2007a).

Still, gender differences are evident at these highest educational levels (Halpern et al., 2007). In the United States, women, with their stronger verbal facility, remain more likely than men to major in traditionally women's fields, such as education, nursing, English literature, and psychology, and not in math and science (NCES, 2007a). Although women generally do better than men in high school math and science courses, they tend to score lower on standardized college and graduate school entrance tests—a fact that may relate to men's advantage at the upper end of the mathematical, visual, and spatial ability range or perhaps to differences in the way men and women solve novel problems (Halpern et al., 2007). Even so, women have made gains in almost every field (NCES, 2006b). More women than in the past now earn engineering degrees, though at least 80 percent of bachelor's degrees in that field still go to men (Halpern et al., 2007; NCES, 2007a). The percentage of professional degrees (law, medicine, dentistry, and so forth) awarded to women has risen dramatically since 1970 (NCES, 2005c).

Socioeconomic status and race/ethnicity affect access to postsecondary education. In 2005, 81 percent of high school graduates from high-income families, as compared with only 53.5 percent from low-income families, enrolled in college immediately after high school. Minority participation, however, has risen at all levels. More than 50 percent of Hispanics and blacks who finished high school in 2005 went directly to college. Although white students earned about 73 percent of bachelor's degrees, minority students accounted for about half the increase in those degrees (NCES, 2007a).

Adjusting to College   Many freshmen feel overwhelmed by the demands of college. Family support seems to be a key factor in adjustment, both for students commuting from home and for those living on campus. Students who are adaptable, have high aptitude and good problem-solving skills, become actively engaged in their studies and in the academic environment, and enjoy close but autonomous relationships with their parents tend to adjust best and get the most out of college. Also important is being able to build a strong social and academic network among peers and instructors (Montgomery & Côté, 2003).

Cognitive Growth in College   College can be a time of intellectual discovery and personal growth, especially in verbal and quantitative skills, critical thinking, and moral reasoning (Montgomery & Côté, 2003). Students change in response to (1) the curriculum, which offers new insights and new ways of thinking; (2) other students who challenge long-held views and values; (3) the student culture, which is different from the culture of society at large; and (4) faculty members, who provide new role models. In terms of both immediate and long-term benefits, going to college—any college—is more important than which college a person attends (Montgomery & Côté, 2003).

The college experience may lead to fundamental change in the way students think (Fischer & Pruyne, 2003). In a groundbreaking study that foreshadowed more recent research on reflective and postformal thought, William Perry (1970) interviewed 67 Harvard and Radcliffe students throughout their undergraduate years and found that their thinking progressed from *rigidity* to *flexibility* and ultimately to *freely chosen commitments*. Many students come to college with rigid ideas about truth; they cannot conceive of any answer but the "right" one. As students begin to encounter a wide range of ideas and viewpoints, said Perry, they are assailed by uncertainty. They consider this stage temporary, however, and expect to learn the "one right answer" eventually. Next, they come to see all knowledge and values as relative. They recognize that different societies and different individuals have different value systems. They now realize that their opinions on many issues are as valid as anyone else's, even those of a parent or teacher; but they cannot find meaning or value in this maze of systems and beliefs. Chaos has replaced order. Finally, they achieve *commitment within relativism:* They make their own judgments and choose their own beliefs and values despite uncertainty and the recognition of other valid possibilities.

A diverse student body can contribute to cognitive growth. In one experiment, small-group discussions were held among 357 students at three selective universities. Each group consisted of three white students and a fourth student, collaborating with the researchers, who was either white or black. Discussions in which a black collaborator participated produced greater novelty and complexity of ideas than those in which all participants were white. So, to a lesser extent, did discussions in which the collaborator (black or white) disagreed with the other participants (Antonio et al., 2004).

Community College and Occupational Education   About 37 percent of undergraduates are enrolled in two-year community colleges (Knapp, Kelly-Reid, Whitmore, & Miller, 2007). Compared with students in four-year institutions, these students tend to be 24 or older, female, from minority or low-income

What's Your View?

• From your observation, does college students' thinking typically seem to follow the stages Perry outlined?

• Have you found that ethnic diversity increases the intellectual level of a discussion?

The future looks bright for this young woman. Today, more women than men enter college and earn degrees, and many colleges offer support and facilities for students with disabilities. A college education is often the key to a successful career and a healthy, satisfying life.

✔ **Checkpoint**

Can you . . .

◆ Discuss factors affecting who goes to college and who finishes?

◆ Tell how college can affect cognitive development?

families, and independent of their parents. They are likely to attend classes part-time and work full-time (Horn & Nevill, 2006). Many of these students are pursuing occupational rather than academic studies (Hudson, Kienzl, & Diehl, 2007).

As compared with students in four-year colleges, community college students tend to be less likely to complete a degree (Gardenhire-Crooks, Collado, & Ray, 2006; Hamilton & Hamilton, 2006). A significant proportion of these students enroll to enhance job skills or for reasons of personal interest (Horn & Nevill, 2006).

Completing College   Although college entrance has become more common in the United States, *finishing* college has not. Only 1 out of 4 young people who start college (1 out of 2 at four-year institutions) have received a degree after five years (Horn & Berger, 2004; NCES, 2004a). This does not mean that the rest drop out. A growing number of students, especially men, remain in college more than five years or switch from two-year to four-year institutions (Horn & Berger, 2004; Peter & Horn, 2005).

Whether a person completes college may depend, not only on motivation, academic aptitude and preparation, and ability to work independently, but also on social integration and social support: employment opportunities, financial support, suitability of living arrangements, quality of social and academic interactions, and the fit between what the college offers and what the student wants and needs. Intervention programs for at-risk students have improved college attendance rates by creating meaningful bonds between students and teachers, finding opportunities for students to work while in college, providing academic assistance, and helping students see how college can move them toward a better future (Montgomery & Côté, 2003).

Entering the World of Work

By their midtwenties, most emerging adults have moved out of their parents' households and are either working or pursuing advanced education (Hamilton & Hamilton, 2006). Those who enter the workforce face a rapidly changing picture. The nature of work is changing, and work arrangements are becoming more varied and less stable. Manufacturing jobs in the United States have virtually disappeared. More and more adults are self-employed, working at home, telecommuting, on flexible work schedules, or acting as independent contractors. These changes, together with a more competitive job market and the demand for a highly skilled workforce, make education and training more vital than ever before (Corcoran & Matsudaira, 2005).

Higher education expands employment opportunities and earning power (Figure 13-4) and enhances long-term quality of life for adults worldwide (Centre for Educational Research and Innovation, 2004; Montgomery & Côté, 2003). In the United States, adults with advanced degrees earn four times more than those with less than a high school diploma (U.S. Census Bureau, 2007b). For adults without higher education, unemployment rates are high (U.S. Census Bureau, 2006a), and it may be difficult to earn enough to establish an independent household. A cross-national survey in Belgium, Canada, Germany, and Italy found a decline in economic self-sufficiency among 18- to 34-year-old men and among women in their early twenties between the mid-1980s and 1995–2000. Women in their late twenties and early thirties were doing better than before, but still not as well as men their age. North America and, to some extent, the United Kingdom showed more positive trends: improved employment rates and more stable or slightly increased earnings (Bell, Burtless, Gornick, & Smeeding, 2007). Still, workers in their twenties, especially their early twenties, tend to be concentrated in low-wage, low-skilled positions and frequently change jobs (Hamilton & Hamilton, 2006).

Although income differentials between male and female workers exist at all levels of educational attainment, these gaps have narrowed considerably. In 1980, the average young man with a bachelor's degree earned 36 percent more than the average young woman; in 2002 the difference was 23 percent (NCES, 2007a). However, a report by the American Association of University Women (2007) found that the earnings gap increases during the 10 years after graduation, so that women at that point earn only 69 percent of what their male counterparts do. Furthermore, one-fourth of the pay gap is unexplained by such factors as hours, occupations, and parenthood, suggesting that it stems from gender discrimination.

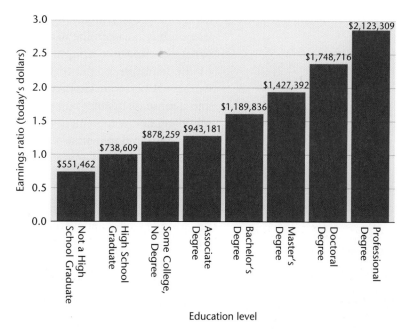

Figure 13-4
Expected lifetime earnings (present value) by educational level: United States, 2007. Even considering the cost of an education, higher educational levels mean more lifetime earnings. *Note:* Based on the sum of median 2005 earnings from ages 25 to 64 for each education level. Future earnings are discounted using a 3 percent annual rate to account for the reality that, because of foregone interest, dollars received in the future are not worth as much as those received today. Data from U.S. Census Bureau. (Source: Adapted from Baum & Ma, 2007, p.10.)

Combining Work and Schooling   Nearly half (49 percent) of full-time U.S. college students were employed, usually part-time, in 2005 (NCES, 2007a). How does juggling work and study affect cognitive development and career preparation? One longitudinal study followed a random sample of incoming freshmen through their first three years of college. During the first two years, on- or off-campus work had little or no effect on reading comprehension, mathematical reasoning, or critical thinking skills. By the third year, part-time work had a positive effect, perhaps because employment forces students to organize their time efficiently and learn better work habits. However, working more than 15 to 20 hours a week tended to have a negative impact (Pascarella, Edison, Nora, Hagedorn, & Terenzini, 1998).

Cognitive Growth at Work   Do people change as a result of the kind of work they do? Some research says yes: People seem to grow in challenging jobs, the kind that are becoming increasingly prevalent today. This research has revealed a reciprocal relationship between the **substantive complexity** of work—the degree of thought and independent judgment it requires—and a person's flexibility in coping with cognitive demands (Kohn, 1980).

Brain research casts light on how people deal with complex work. Full development of the frontal lobes during young adulthood may equip people to handle several tasks at the same time. Magnetic resonance imaging shows that the most frontward part of the frontal lobes has a special function in problem solving and planning. This portion of the brain springs into action when a person needs to put an unfinished task on hold and shift attention to another task. It permits a worker to keep the first task in working memory while attending to the second—for example, to resume reading a report after being interrupted by the telephone (Koechlin, Basso, Pietrini, Panzer, & Grafman, 1999).

Cognitive growth need not stop at the end of the workday. According to the **spillover hypothesis,** cognitive gains from work carry over to nonworking hours. Studies support this hypothesis: Substantive complexity of work strongly influences the intellectual level of leisure activities (Kohn, 1980; K. Miller & Kohn, 1983).

substantive complexity Degree to which a person's work requires thought and independent judgment.

spillover hypothesis Hypothesis that a positive correlation exists between intellectuality of work and of leisure activities because of a carryover of cognitive gains from work to leisure.

Smoothing the Transition to the Workplace Although some emerging adults successfully navigate the worlds of education and work, others flounder or sink. What does it take to achieve a successful transition from school to work? A review of the literature points to four key factors: (1) competence (in general and at work); (2) personal characteristics such as initiative, flexibility, purposefulness, and a sense of urgency; (3) positive personal relationships; and (4) links between schooling and employment (Blustein, Juntunen, & Worthington, 2000).

Some developmental scientists (Furstenberg et al., 2005; Settersten, 2005) suggest measures to strengthen the links between work and educational institutions, especially community colleges.

- Improve dialogue between educators and employers.

- Modify school and work schedules to adapt to the needs of working students.

- Let employers help design work-study programs.

- Increase availability of temporary and part-time work.

- Relate better what students learn at work and in school.

- Improve training of vocational guidance counselors.

- Make better use of study and support groups and tutoring and mentoring programs.

- Provide scholarships, financial aid, and health insurance to part-time as well as full-time students and employees.

Work affects day-to-day life, not only on the job but at home, and it brings both satisfaction and stress. In Chapter 14, we explore the effects of work on relationships as we look at psychosocial development in young adulthood.

Checkpoint

Can you . . .

- Summarize recent changes in the workplace?

- Discuss the impact of combining work and schooling?

- Explain the relationship between substantive complexity of work and cognitive development?

- List proposals for easing the transition to the workplace?

Summary and Key Terms

Emerging Adulthood

Guidepost 1: *What does it mean to be an adult, and what factors affect the timing of entrance to adulthood?*

- For many young people in advanced technological societies, entrance into adulthood is not clearly marked; it takes longer and follows more varied routes than in the past. Some developmental scientists suggest that the late teens through the midtwenties has become a transitional period called *emerging adulthood.*

- Emerging adulthood consists of multiple milestones or transitions, and their order and timing varies. Passage of these milestones, or other culture-specific criteria, may determine when a young person becomes an adult.

emerging adulthood (423)

PHYSICAL DEVELOPMENT

Health and Fitness

Guidepost 2: *In what physical condition is the typical young adult, and what factors affect health and well-being?*

- Physical and sensory abilities are typically excellent in emerging and young adulthood.

- Accidents are the leading cause of death in this age group.

- The mapping of the human genome is enabling the discovery of genetic bases for certain disorders.

- Lifestyle factors such as diet, obesity, exercise, sleep, smoking, and substance use or abuse can affect health and survival.

- Good health is related to higher income and education. African Americans and some other minorities tend to be less healthy than other Americans, in part due to SES.
- Social relationships, especially marriage, tend to be associated with physical and mental health.
- Mental health is generally good in early adulthood, but certain conditions, such as depression, become more prevalent. Alcohol abuse and alcoholism are the most common substance disorders.

alcoholism (430)

Sexual and Reproductive Issues

Guidepost 3: *What are some sexual and reproductive issues at this time of life?*

- Almost all U.S. young adults have sexual relations before marriage.
- Sexually transmitted diseases, menstrual disorders, and infertility can be concerns during young adulthood.
- The highest rates of STDs in the United States are among emerging adults, particularly among young women.
- The most common cause of infertility in men is a low sperm count; the most common cause in women is blockage of the fallopian tubes.
- Infertile couples now have several options for assisted reproduction. These techniques involve ethical and practical issues.

premenstrual syndrome (PMS) (432)

infertility (433)

COGNITIVE DEVELOPMENT

Perspectives on Adult Cognition

Guidepost 4: *What is distinctive about adult thought?*

- Some investigators propose distinctively adult forms of cognition beyond formal operations. Reflective thinking emphasizes complex logic; postformal thought involves intuition and emotion as well.
- Schaie proposed seven stages of age-related cognitive development: acquisitive (childhood and adolescence), achieving (young adulthood), responsible and executive (middle adulthood), and reorganizational, reintegrative, and legacy-creating (late adulthood).
- According to Sternberg's triarchic theory of intelligence, the experiential and contextual elements become particularly important during adulthood. Tests that

measure tacit knowledge can be useful complements to traditional intelligence tests.
- Emotional intelligence may play an important part in life success.

reflective thinking (435)

postformal thought (435)

emotional intelligence (EI) (439)

Moral Reasoning

Guidepost 5: *How does moral reasoning develop?*

- According to Kohlberg, moral development in adulthood depends primarily on experience, though it cannot exceed the limits set by cognitive development. Experience may be interpreted differently in various cultural contexts.
- Gilligan initially proposed that women have an ethic of care, whereas Kohlberg's theory emphasizes justice. However, later research, including her own, has not supported a distinction between men's and women's moral outlook.

Education and Work

Guidepost 6: *How do emerging adults make the transitions to higher education and work, and how do these experiences affect cognitive development?*

- A majority of emerging adults now go to college, either to two-year or four-year institutions. More women than men now go to college, and an increasing percentage pursue advanced degrees even in traditionally male-dominated fields. Minority participation is growing, but more slowly.
- According to Perry, college students' thinking tends to progress from rigidity to flexibility to freely chosen commitments.
- Research has found a relationship between substantive complexity of work and cognitive growth, as well as between complex work and intellectually demanding leisure activities.
- Changes in the workplace call for higher education or training. Higher education greatly expands workplace opportunities and earnings.
- The transition to the workplace could be eased through measures to strengthen vocational education and its links with work.

substantive complexity (447)

spillover hypothesis (447)

Every adult is in need of help, of warmth, of protection . . . in many ways differing [from] and yet in many ways similar to the needs of the child.

—Erich Fromm, *The Sane Society*, 1955

Did You **Know...**

- Emerging adults reportedly are happiest when they are in college, have not yet married, and have no children?

- About half of emerging adults ages 18 to 24 in the United States live at home with one or both parents?

- Historically and across cultures, the most common way of selecting a mate has been through arrangement, either by the parents or by professional matchmakers?

- The proportion of young adults ages 25 to 34 in the United States who have not yet married has approximately tripled since 1970?

- Half of young parents say they have too little time with their children, according to national surveys?

- The U.S. divorce rate in 2006 was at its lowest point since 1970?

These are just a few of the interesting and important topics we will cover in this chapter. Personal choices made in emerging and young adulthood establish a framework for the rest of life. How have paths to adulthood changed in recent decades? How does identity develop in emerging adulthood, and how do emerging adults renegotiate relationships with parents? Does personality stop growing when the body does, or does it keep developing throughout life? In this chapter, we explore questions such as these. We also examine the choices that frame personal and social life: adopting a sexual lifestyle; marrying, cohabiting, or remaining single; having children or not; and establishing and maintaining friendships. After you have read and studied this chapter, you should be able to answer each of the Guidepost questions on the following page.

Guideposts *for Study*

1. What influences today's varied paths to adulthood, and how do emerging adults develop a sense of adult identity and an autonomous relationship with their parents?

2. Does personality change during adulthood, and, if so, how?

3. How is intimacy expressed in friendship and love?

4. When and why do young adults choose to remain single, form gay or lesbian relationships, cohabit, or marry, and how satisfying and stable are those lifestyles?

5. When do most adults become parents, and how does parenthood affect a marriage?

6. What are the trends in divorce rates, and how do young adults adjust to divorce, remarriage, and stepparenthood?

Guidepost 1

What influences today's varied paths to adulthood, and how do emerging adults develop a sense of adult identity and an autonomous relationship with their parents?

Emerging Adulthood: Patterns and Tasks

Mark, Alissa, and Molly grew up in a middle-class family. Their father, as was typical in his generation, had gone straight from high school to college and into a job as an accountant. Their mother, also typically, had stayed home while they were growing up and then had begun a midlife career selling real estate. The three siblings, born near the end of the baby boom, all graduated from high school and went on to college. But from there on, the similarity ends.

Mark, the oldest, was a talented tenor who majored in music but dropped out of college after his freshman year. After exploring various options, from a temporary job as a carpenter's helper to a summer gig as a singing waiter on a cruise ship, in his late twenties he hired a vocal coach and began to get singing engagements. By his early thirties he had established a vocal career. He remained single.

Alissa graduated from college and took a one-year internship as a teaching assistant before applying to graduate school. At 24 she earned a master's degree in special education and found a job teaching students with learning disabilities. At 28, she married and, by age 36, had four children, whom she stayed home and raised.

Molly, the youngest, had a head for figures. After graduating from college, she spent five years as a bookkeeper while living with a man she had met at work. At 29 she earned an M.B.A. and was hired by a major corporation, where she met the man she married at age 32. With three young children in five years, she and her husband juggled the responsibilities of corporate careers and parenthood.

Varied Paths to Adulthood

Paths to adulthood are far more varied than in the past. Before the 1960s, young people in the United States typically finished school, left home, got a job, got married, and had children, in that order. By the 1990s, only 1 in 4 young adults followed that sequence (Mouw, 2005).

For many young people today, emerging adulthood is a time of experimentation before assuming adult roles and responsibilities. A young man or woman may get a job and an apartment and revel in the single life. A young married couple may move in with parents while they finish school or get on their feet or after a job loss. Such traditional developmental tasks as finding stable work and developing long-term romantic relationships may be postponed until the thirties or even later (Roisman, Masten, Coatsworth, & Tellegen, 2004). What influences affect these varied paths to adulthood?

Influences on Paths to Adulthood Individual paths to adulthood are influenced by such factors as gender, academic ability, early attitudes toward education, expectations in late adolescence, and social class. Increasingly, emerging adults of both sexes extend education and delay parenthood (Osgood et al., 2005), and these decisions are usually keys to future success (Sandefur, Eggerling-Boeck, & Park, 2005) as well as to current well-being. In a longitudinal study that followed a nationally representative sample of high school seniors each year since 1975, emerging adults with the highest well-being were those who were not yet married, had no children, attended college, and lived away from their childhood home (Schulenberg et al., 2005). In another study, youth who were downwardly mobile tended to leave home earlier, get less support from parents, forgo higher education, and have children earlier. Early parenthood particularly limited future prospects (Mollenkopf, Waters, Holdaway, & Kasinitz, 2005).

Some emerging adults have more resources—financial and developmental—than others. Much depends on *ego development:* a combination of ability to understand oneself and one's world, to integrate and synthesize what one perceives and knows, and to take charge of planning one's life course. Some emerging adults have more highly developed egos than others and are therefore more ready to learn to stand alone (Tanner, 2006).

Identity Development in Emerging Adulthood

As we discussed in Chapter 12, Erikson saw the search for identity as a lifelong task focused largely on adolescence. Increasingly, in postindustrialized countries today, the active search for identity extends into emerging adulthood (Côté, 2006). Emerging adulthood offers a moratorium, or time out, from developmental pressures and the freedom to experiment with various roles and lifestyles, but it also represents a turning point during which adult role commitments gradually crystallize. By the end of these years, the self "consolidates around a set of roles and beliefs that define a relatively stable adult personality" (Tanner, 2006, p. 24), and young adulthood begins. Until and unless that task is accomplished, however, identity confusion may set in (Côté, 2006).

Recentering **Recentering** is a proposed name for the process that underlies the shift to an adult identity. It is the primary task of emerging adulthood. Recentering is a three-stage process in which power, responsibility, and decision making gradually shift from the family of origin to the independent young adult (Tanner, 2006):

- At *stage 1,* the beginning of emerging adulthood, the individual is still embedded in the family of origin, but expectations for self-reliance and self-directedness begin to increase.

- In *stage 2,* during emerging adulthood, the individual remains connected to (and may be financially dependent on) but no longer embedded within the family of origin. Temporary, exploratory involvements in a variety of college courses, jobs, and intimate partners mark this stage. Toward the end of this stage, the individual is moving toward serious commitments and gaining the resources to support them.

What's Your View?

- What path have you taken, or are you taking, toward adulthood? Do you have friends who took other paths?

Checkpoint

Can you ...

◆ Give examples of various paths to adulthood?

◆ Discuss influences on paths young people take to adulthood?

recentering Process that underlies the shift to an adult identity.

- In *stage 3,* usually by age 30, the individual moves into young adulthood. This stage is marked by independence from the family of origin (while retaining close ties to it) and commitment to a career, a partner, and possibly children.

The Contemporary Moratorium   A fragmented, postindustrial society offers many emerging adults little guidance and less pressure to grow up. As a result, they need to fall back on their own resources (Heinz, 2002). They must construct their life course out of the opportunities and constraints they find around them. Not everyone is equally up to the task (Côté, 2006).

Identity status research has found that only 10 to 30 percent of Western youth seem to go through what Marcia termed the *moratorium* status, a self-conscious crisis that leads to a resolution. Most seem to do little active, conscious deliberation, instead taking a passive (diffused) approach or taking the lead from their parents (foreclosure). For some, an extended moratorium can lead to a dead-end state called *youthhood,* a more or less permanent alternative to adulthood. Nevertheless, about 3 out of 4 settle on some sort of occupational identity by the end of their twenties. Identity confusion persists for 10 to 20 percent, who lack what Erikson called *fidelity:* faith in something larger than themselves (Côté, 2006).

Racial/Ethnic Identity Exploration   Identity exploration is somewhat different for racial/ethnic minorities than for the majority white population. Many minority youth must take on adult responsibilities earlier than their peers. At the same time, they tend to value close and interdependent family relations and may feel obligated to assist their families financially. They may be under pressure to marry and have children at an early age. Thus, for them, emerging adulthood may be curtailed. On the other hand, they must deal with special identity issues regarding their ethnicity, and this process may extend well beyond the twenties (Phinney, 2006).

If they are living in settings different from their culture of origin, they may begin to question the traditional values of their ethnic group. To achieve a secure ethnic identity, they must come to understand themselves both as part of an ethnic group and of the wider, diverse society. Multiracial young people have the added challenge of figuring out where they fit in. Still, many reach a resolution that leads to identity achievement, as in the following:

> "When I was younger I felt I didn't belong anywhere. But now I've just come to the conclusion that . . . that's just the way I am, . . . and my home is inside myself. . . . I no longer feel the compulsion to fit in 'cause if you're just trying to fit in you never do." (Alipuria, 2002, p. 143)

Developing Adult Relationships with Parents

A measure of how successfully emerging adults handle the developmental task of leaving the childhood home is their ability to maintain autonomous but connected relationships with their parents (Aquilino, 2006a; Scharf et al., 2004). As young people leave home, they must complete the negotiation of autonomy begun in adolescence and redefine their relationship with their parents as one between adults. Parents who are unable to acknowledge this change may slow their children's development (Aquilino, 2006a).

Influences on Relationships with Parents   Even though they are no longer children, emerging adults still need parental acceptance, empathy, and support, and attachment to the parents remains a key ingredient of well-being. Financial support from parents, especially for education, enhances emerging adults' chances of success in adult roles (Aquilino, 2006a).

Checkpoint

Can you . . .

◆ Define *recentering* and summarize its three stages?

◆ Discuss identity status research on emerging adults in postindustrial societies?

◆ Explain why identity development of racial/ ethnic minorities is complex?

In a longitudinal study of more than 900 New Zealand families, positive parent-child relationships during early adolescence predicted warmer and less conflicted relationships with both mothers and fathers when the children reached age 26 (Belsky, Jaffee, Hsieh, & Silva, 2001). These relationships were better when the young adult was married but childless, engaging in productive activity (either school, employment, or homemaking), and not living in the childhood home. This finding suggests that parents and young adult children get along best when the young adult is following a normative life course but has deferred the responsibility of parenthood until other adult roles are well established (Belsky, Jaffee, Caspi, Moffitt, & Silva, 2003).

The quality of the parent–adult child relationship may be affected by the relationship between the mother and father (Aquilino, 2006a). If that relationship is conflicted, young adult children may feel caught in the middle (Amato & Afifi, 2006a).

Failure to Launch In the 2006 movie *Failure to Launch,* Matthew McConaughey plays a 30-year-old man who still lives with his parents. This scenario has become increasingly common in the United States. In 2005, 53 percent of young men and 46 percent of young women ages 18 to 24 lived with one or both parents in their home (U.S. Census Bureau, 2007c). Emerging adults from high-income families are more likely to live with parents than those from low-income families (Hill & Holzer, 2007). Reasons include the high cost of college and of housing and difficulties in finding jobs (Matsudaira, 2006).

Adult children who continue to live with parents may have trouble renegotiating their relationship. The process may be a gradual one that takes many years, especially when the adult child still needs parental financial support (Aquilino, 2006a).

The trend for emerging adults to live in the parents' home also exists in some European countries where government benefits to unemployed youth are lacking; in Italy, more than half of young men live with their parents until age 30. Although living with parents has been associated with lower life satisfaction, this is becoming less true as the practice becomes widespread. Indeed, Europeans may be witnessing a new developmental stage, *in-house adulthood,* in which live-in adult children and their parents treat each other as equals (Newman & Aptekar, 2007; Figure 14-1).

Though emerging adults may no longer rely on parents for basic sustenance, they still may benefit from parental companionship and social support.

 **Checkpoint**

Can you . . .

♦ Explain how relationships with parents affect adjustment to adulthood and how emerging adults renegotiate their relationships with their parents?

♦ Discuss the failure-to-launch trend?

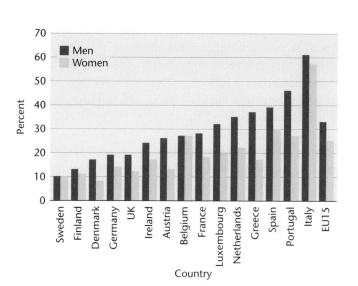

Figure 14-1

Percent of European young adults ages 18 to 34 living with parents without their own partners or children. Many young adults fail to launch from the nest at the expected time or return to it in times of trouble.

(Source: Newman & Aptekar, 2007, Fig. 1.)

Table 14-1	Four Views of Personality Development		
Models	**Questions Asked**	**Methods Used**	**Change or Stability**
Normative-stage models	Does personality change in typical ways at certain periods throughout the life course?	In-depth interviews, biographical materials	Normative personality changes having to do with personal goals, work, and relationships occur in stages.
Timing-of-events model	When do important life events typically occur? What if they occur earlier or later than usual?	Statistical studies, interviews, questionnaires	Nonnormative timing of life events can cause stress and affect personality development.
Trait models	Do personality traits fall into groups, or clusters? Do these clusters of traits change with age?	Personality inventories, questionnaires, factor analysis	Personality changes substantially until age 30, more slowly thereafter.
Typological models	Can basic personality types be identified, and how well do they predict the life course?	Interviews, clinical judgments, Q-sorts, behavior ratings, self-reports	Personality types tend to show continuity from childhood through adulthood, but certain events can change the life course.

Guidepost 2

Does personality change during adulthood, and if so, how?

Personality Development: Four Views

Does personality primarily show stability or change? The answer depends in part on how we study and measure it. Four approaches to adult psychosocial development are represented by *normative-stage models,* the *timing-of-events model, trait models,* and *typological models.* These four approaches ask different questions about adult personality, look at different aspects of its development, and often use different methods (Table 14-1). It is not surprising, then, that researchers within these traditions often come out with results that are difficult to reconcile or even to compare.

Normative-Stage Models

normative-stage models
Theoretical models that describe psychosocial development in terms of a definite sequence of age-related changes.

Normative-stage models hold that adults follow a basic sequence of age-related psychosocial changes. The changes are *normative* in that they seem to be common to most members of a population; and they emerge in successive periods, or *stages,* sometimes marked by emotional crises that pave the way for further development.

intimacy versus isolation
Erikson's sixth stage of psychosocial development, in which young adults either make commitments to others or face a possible sense of isolation and self-absorption.

Erikson: Intimacy versus Isolation   Erikson's sixth stage of psychosocial development, **intimacy versus isolation,** turns on what he saw as the major issue of young adulthood. If young adults cannot make deep personal commitments to others, said Erikson, they risk becoming overly isolated and self-absorbed. However, they do need some isolation to reflect on their lives. As they work to resolve conflicting demands of intimacy, competitiveness, and distance, they develop an ethical sense, which Erikson considered the mark of the adult. Intimate relationships demand sacrifice and compromise. Young adults who have developed a strong sense of self are ready to fuse their identity with that of another person. (As we have discussed, for many people today the process of identity formation extends well into adulthood, and, thus, according to Erikson, the achievement of intimacy also must be postponed.)

Resolution of this stage results in the virtue of *love:* mutual devotion between partners who have chosen to share their lives, have children, and help those children achieve their own healthy development. A decision not to fulfill the natural procreative urge has serious consequences for development, according to Erikson.

His theory has been criticized for excluding single, celibate, homosexual, and childless people from his blueprint for healthy development, as well as for taking the male pattern of developing intimacy after identity as the norm.

Erikson's Heirs: Vaillant and Levinson

Erik Erikson's belief that personality changes throughout life inspired classic studies by George Vaillant and Daniel Levinson. In 1938, Vaillant selected 268 self-reliant and emotionally and physically healthy 18-year-old Harvard undergraduates for the Grant Study. By the time the students reached midlife, Vaillant (1977) saw a typical developmental pattern emerge. At age 20, many men were still dominated by their parents. During their twenties, and sometimes their

Young adults who have a strong sense of self are likely to be ready for the demands of an intimate relationship, according to Erikson.

thirties, they achieved autonomy, married, had children, and deepened friendships. They worked hard at their careers and devoted themselves to their families, rarely questioning whether they had chosen the right woman or the right occupation.

Levinson (1978, 1980, 1986) and his colleagues at Yale University conducted in-depth interviews and personality tests of 40 men ages 35 to 45 and formulated a theory of personality development based on an evolving **life structure:** "the underlying pattern or design of a person's life at a given time" (1986, p. 6). Between about ages 17 and 33, a man builds his first provisional life structure. He leaves his parents' home, perhaps to go to college or into the armed services, and becomes financially and emotionally independent. He chooses an occupation, perhaps a wife, and forms a *dream* about what he hopes to achieve in the future. At about age 30, he reevaluates his first life structure. He then settles down and sets goals (a professorship, for instance, or a certain level of income) and a time for achieving them (say, by age 40). He anchors his life in family, occupation, and community. How he deals with the issues of this phase will affect how well he weathers the transition to midlife.

In a companion study of 45 women, Levinson (1996) found that women go through similar patterns of development. However, because of traditional cultural divisions between masculine and feminine roles, women may face different psychological and environmental constraints in forming their life structures, and their transitions tend to take longer.

life structure In Levinson's theory, the underlying pattern of a person's life at a given time, built on whatever aspects of life the person finds most important.

Evaluating Normative-Stage Models

Both the Grant Study and Levinson's early work were based on small groups of men born in the 1920s or 1930s. Likewise, Levinson's small sample of women born between about 1935 and 1945 was not representative. These men's and women's development was affected by societal events unique to their cohorts, as well as by their socioeconomic status, ethnicity, and gender. Today, young adults follow much more diverse developmental paths and, as a result, may develop differently than did the men and women in these studies. In addition, the findings of normative-stage research may not apply to other cultures, some of which have very different patterns of life course development.

Nevertheless, normative-stage research has had a continuing impact on the field. Psychologists, drawing especially on the work of Erikson, have identified

developmental tasks that need to be accomplished for successful adaptation to each stage of life (Roisman, Masten, Coatsworth, & Tellegen, 2004). Among the developmental tasks of young adulthood are leaving the childhood home for advanced schooling, work, or military service; developing new and more intimate friendships and romantic relationships; and developing a sense of efficacy and *individuation*—a sense of the self as independent and self-reliant (Arnett, 2000, 2004; Scharf, Mayseless, & Kivenson-Baron, 2004). Other developmental tasks of this period, discussed in Chapter 13, include completing education, entering the world of work, and becoming financially independent.

Perhaps the most important message of normative-stage models is that development does not end with attainment of adulthood. Whether or not people follow the specific patterns suggested by these models, normative-stage research supports the idea that human beings do continue to change and develop throughout their lives.

Timing-of-Events Model

Instead of looking at adult personality development purely as a function of age, the **timing-of-events model,** supported by Bernice Neugarten and others (Neugarten, Moore, & Lowe, 1965; Neugarten & Neugarten, 1987), holds that the course of development depends on when certain events occur in people's lives. **Normative life events** (also called *normative age-graded events;* refer to Chapter 1) are those that typically happen at certain times of life—such events as marriage, parenthood, grandparenthood, and retirement. According to this model, people usually are keenly aware of both their timing and the **social clock,** their society's norms or expectations for the appropriate timing of life events.

If events occur on time, development proceeds smoothly. If not, stress can result. Stress may come from an unexpected event (such as losing a job), an event that happens off time (being widowed at age 35 or being forced to retire at 50), or the failure of an expected event to occur at all (never being married, or being unable to have a child). Personality differences influence the way people respond to life events and may even influence their timing. For example, a resilient person is likely to experience an easier transition to adulthood and the tasks and events that lie ahead than an overly anxious person, who may put off relationship or career decisions.

The typical timing of events varies from culture to culture and from generation to generation. The rise in the average age when adults first marry in the United States (U.S. Census Bureau, 2007a) and the trend toward delayed first childbirth (Martin et al., 2007) are two examples of events for which timing has shifted. A timetable that seems right to people in one cohort may not seem so to the next.

Since the mid-twentieth century, many Western societies have become less age-conscious. Today people are more accepting of 40-year-old first-time parents and 40-year-old grandparents, 50-year-old retirees and 75-year-old workers, 60-year-olds in jeans and 30-year-old college presidents. This widened range of age norms undermines the predictability on which the timing-of-events model is based.

The timing-of-events model has made an important contribution to our understanding of adult personality by emphasizing the individual life course and challenging the idea of universal, age-related change. However, its usefulness may well be limited to cultures and historical periods in which norms of behavior are stable and widespread.

Trait Models: Costa and McCrae's Five Factors

Trait models look for stability or change in personality traits. Paul T. Costa and Robert R. McCrae have developed and tested a **five-factor model** (Figure 14-2)

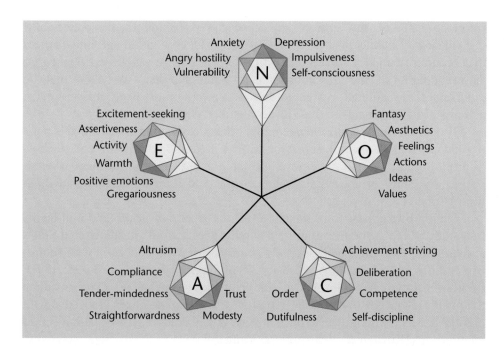

Figure 14-2

Costa and McCrae's five-factor model. Each factor, or dimension, of personality, represents a cluster of related traits, or facets. N = neuroticism, E = extraversion, O = openness to experience, A = agreeableness, C = conscientiousness. (Source: Adapted from Costa & McCrae, 1980.)

consisting of factors, or dimensions, that seem to underlie five groups of associated traits, known as the "Big Five." They are (1) *neuroticism (N)*, (2) *extraversion (E)*, (3) *openness to experience (O)*, (4) *conscientiousness (C)*, and (5) *agreeableness (A)*.

Neuroticism is a cluster of six traits, or facets, indicating emotional instability: anxiety, hostility, depression, self-consciousness, impulsiveness, and vulnerability. *Extraversion* also has six facets: warmth, gregariousness, assertiveness, activity, excitement-seeking, and positive emotions. People who are *open to experience* are willing to try new things and embrace new ideas. *Conscientious* people are achievers: They are competent, orderly, dutiful, deliberate, and disciplined. *Agreeable* people are trusting, straightforward, altruistic, compliant, modest, and easily swayed. Studies in more than 30 cultures, from Zimbabwe to Peru, have found the same five factors, which appear, therefore, to be universal. However, they may not be equally important in every culture, and additional factors may exist in some cultures (McCrae, 2002).

Continuity and Change in the Five-Factor Model   In analyses of large longitudinal and cross-sectional samples of U.S. men and women of all ages, Costa and McCrae (1980, 1988, 1994a, 1994b, 2006; Costa et al., 1986; McCrae, 2002; McCrae & Costa, 1984; McCrae, Costa, & Busch, 1986) found considerable continuity as well as noticeable change in all five domains between adolescence and age 30, with much slower change thereafter. However, the *direction* of change varied for different personality factors. Agreeableness and conscientiousness generally increased, whereas neuroticism, extraversion, and openness to experience declined (McCrae et al., 2000). These patterns of age-related change appeared to be universal across cultures and, thus, according to these authors, maturational (McCrae, 2002). Heritability of the Big Five seemed to be between 40 and 66 percent (Bouchard, 1994).

In partial contradiction, other analyses of many longitudinal and cross-sectional studies found important change in almost *all* personality traits *throughout* adulthood (Roberts, Walton, & Viechtbauer, 2006a, 2006b; Roberts & Mroczek, 2008). True, traits changed more markedly in young adulthood than in any other period, but in a uniformly positive direction, with especially large increases in social dominance (assertiveness, a facet of extraversion), conscientiousness, and emotional stability. Yet, as we discuss in Chapters 16 and 18, personality also showed clear, generally positive change after age 30, even in old age; and changes that occurred tended to be retained. Furthermore, there was little evidence for maturational or genetic causes for the early adult changes: "We believe that life experiences . . . centered in young adulthood are the most likely reason for the patterns of development we see" (Roberts et al., 2006a, p. 18).

Of course, some people change more, others less; and not all change is positive. People with successful, satisfying careers in young adulthood tend to show disproportionate increases in emotional stability and conscientiousness, whereas people who shirk or act aggressively at work tend to show decreases in those traits (Roberts & Mroczek, 2008).

The Big Five appear to be linked to various aspects of health and well-being. In a study of representative samples of adults ages 25 to 65 in the United States and Germany, the Big Five (especially neuroticism) were associated with subjective feelings of health and well-being (Staudinger, Fleeson, & Baltes, 1999). Conscientiousness has been linked with health-related behaviors that contribute to long life (Bogg & Roberts, 2004). Big Five traits also have been associated with marital satisfaction (Gattis, Berns, Simpson, & Christensen, 2004), parent-infant relationships (Kochanska, Friesenborg, Lange, & Martel, 2004), and personality disorders. People high in neuroticism tend to be subject to anxiety and depression; people low in extraversion are prone to social phobia and agoraphobia (fear of open spaces) (Bienvenu et al., 2001).

Evaluating the Five-Factor Model   This body of work originally made a powerful case for continuity of personality, especially after age 30. More recent research has eroded that conclusion to the point where Costa and McCrae now acknowledge that change occurs throughout life.

However, the question of causation needs further study. Do maturational changes impel people to seek out social roles that fit their maturing personalities, or do adults change to meet the demands of their new roles? Or is change bidirectional? In a longitudinal study of 980 people in New Zealand, personality traits at age 18 affected work experiences in emerging adulthood, and these work experiences, in turn, affected changes in personality as measured at age 26. For example, adolescents who were sociable and affable tended to rise faster in their early careers; and, in turn, those who were in higher-status, more satisfying jobs tended to become more sociable and affable (Roberts, Caspi, & Moffitt, 2003). So it seems that personality in adulthood may be more malleable and more complex than previous trait research suggests.

Other criticisms of the five-factor model are methodological. Jack Block (1995a, 1995b) argues that, because the five-factor model is based largely on subjective ratings, it may lack validity unless supplemented by other measures. The selection of factors and their associated facets is arbitrary and perhaps not all-inclusive; other researchers have chosen different factors and have divided up the associated traits differently. (For example, is warmth a facet of extraversion, as in the Big Five model, or is it better classified as an aspect of agreeableness?) Finally, personality is more than a collection of traits. A model that looks only at individual differences in trait groupings offers no theoretical framework for understanding how personality works within the person.

Typological Models

typological approach Theoretical approach that identifies broad personality types, or styles.

Jack Block (1971; Block & Block, 2006b) was a pioneer in the **typological approach.** Typological research seeks to complement and expand trait research by looking at personality as a functioning whole.

Researchers have identified three personality types: *ego-resilient, overcontrolled,* and *undercontrolled.* These three types differ in **ego-resiliency,** or adaptability under stress, and **ego-control,** or self-control. *Ego-resilient* people are well-adjusted: self-confident, independent, articulate, attentive, helpful, cooperative, and task-focused. *Overcontrolled* people are shy, quiet, anxious, and dependable; they tend to keep their thoughts to themselves and to withdraw from conflict, and they are the most subject to depression. *Undercontrolled* people are active, energetic, impulsive, stubborn, and easily distracted. These or similar personality types seem to exist in both sexes, across cultures and ethnic groups, and in children, adolescents, and adults (Caspi, 1998; Hart, Hofmann, Edelstein, & Keller, 1997; Pulkkinen, 1996; Robins, John, Caspi, Moffitt, & Stouthamer-Loeber, 1996; van Lieshout, Haselager, Riksen-Walraven, & van Aken, 1995).

A 30-year longitudinal study of 128 preschoolers, still ongoing when the participants were age 32, demonstrates the predictive power of these personality types. Children who had been overcontrolled as preschoolers, for example, were likely to be relatively conservative politically at age 23, whereas those who had been undercontrolled were more likely to be liberal (Block & Block, 2006a). Ego control and ego resiliency in preschool also predicted such diverse outcomes as drug usage in adolescence and depression in 18-year-olds.

A 19-year longitudinal study in Munich further supports the lasting influence of childhood personality. Teachers and parents assessed 103 children annually between ages 3 and 12, and then again at ages 17 and 23. Children who had been overcontrolled (contained their emotions) between ages 4 and 6 tended to be shy in late adolescence and emerging adulthood, whereas those who had been undercontrolled (emotionally expressive) in early childhood were more aggressive; and these traits became more accentuated between ages 17 and 23. In addition, both overcontrolled and undercontrolled types had more difficulty than more resilient types in assuming adult social roles: leaving the parental home, establishing romantic relationships, and getting part-time jobs (Dennissen, Asendorpt, & van Aken, 2008).

Of course, the finding of a tendency toward continuity of attitudes and behavior does not mean that personalities never change, or that certain people are condemned to a life of maladjustment. Undercontrolled children may get along better in early adulthood if they find niches in which their energy and spontaneity are considered a plus. Overcontrolled youngsters may come out of their shell if they find that their quiet dependability is valued. And, although personality types established in childhood may predict *trajectories,* or long-term patterns of behavior, certain events may change the life course (Caspi, 1998). For young people with adjustment problems, for example, marriage to a supportive person can lead to more positive outcomes.

Foundations of Intimate Relationships

Erikson saw the development of intimate relationships as the crucial task of young adulthood. The need to form strong, stable, close, caring relationships is a powerful motivator of human behavior. An important element of intimacy is *self-disclosure:* "revealing important information about oneself to another" (Collins & Miller, 1994, p. 457). People become intimate—and remain intimate—through shared disclosures, responsiveness to one another's needs, and mutual acceptance and respect (Harvey & Omarzu, 1997; Reis & Patrick, 1996).

Intimate relationships require self-awareness; empathy; the ability to communicate emotions, resolve conflicts, and sustain commitments; and, if the relationship

ego-resiliency Adaptability under potential sources of stress.

ego-control Self-control.

What's Your View?

• Which of the models presented here seems to you to most accurately describe psychosocial development in adulthood?

Checkpoint

Can you . . .

◆ Compare four theoretical approaches to adult psychosocial development?

Guidepost 3

How is intimacy expressed in friendship and love?

Intimate relationships involve self-awareness, empathy, and the ability to communicate. Such skills are pivotal as young adults decide whether to marry or form partnerships.

is potentially a sexual one, sexual decision making. Such skills are pivotal as young adults decide whether to marry or form intimate partnerships and to have or not to have children (Lambeth & Hallett, 2002).

Let's look at two expressions of intimacy in young adulthood: friendship and love.

Friendship

Friendships during emerging adulthood may be less stable than in earlier and later periods because of the frequency with which people this age relocate (Collins & Van Dulmen, 2006). Friendships in young adulthood tend to center on work and parenting activities and the sharing of confidences and advice. Some friendships are extremely intimate and supportive; others are marked by frequent conflict. Some friendships are lifelong; others are fleeting (Hartup & Stevens, 1999). Some "best friendships" are more stable than ties to a lover or spouse.

Young single adults rely more on friendships to fulfill their social needs than young married adults or young parents do (Carbery & Buhrmester, 1998). The number of friends and the amount of time spent with them generally decreases in the course of young adulthood. Still, friendships are important to young adults. People with friends tend to have a sense of well-being; either having friends makes people feel good about themselves, or people who feel good about themselves have an easier time making friends (Hartup & Stevens, 1999; Myers, 2000).

Women typically have more intimate friendships than men do. Men are more likely to share information and activities, not confidences, with friends (Rosenbluth & Steil, 1995). Women are more likely than men to talk with their friends about marital problems and to receive advice and support (Helms, Crouter, & McHale, 2003).

Many young adults incorporate friends into chosen family networks. These close, supportive friends are considered to be **fictive kin.** Among gays and lesbians, fictive kinship relationships are often with straight friends of the other sex. In one study, the relationships that lasted the longest tended to be those in which the straight friend was unmarried or lived an unconventional lifestyle (Muraco, 2006).

On the other hand, an increasing number of young adults today have no intimate confidants, according to a longitudinal study. During a 19-year period the number of people who said that there is no one with whom they discuss important matters nearly tripled. The declines were sharpest among educated, middle-class people, who may keep in touch with friends and family by e-mail or phone but not face-to-face (McPherson, Smith-Lovin, & Brashears, 2006).

Love

Most people like love stories, including their own. According to Robert J. Sternberg's **triangular theory of love** (1995, 1998b, 2006), the way love develops *is* a story. The lovers are its authors, and the story they create reflects their personalities and their conceptions of love.

Thinking of love as a story may help us see how people select and mix the elements of the plot. According to Sternberg (1986, 1998a, 2006), the three elements, or components, of love are intimacy, passion, and commitment. *Intimacy,*

Table 14-2	Patterns of Loving
Type	**Description**
Nonlove	All three components of love—intimacy, passion, and commitment—are absent. This describes most interpersonal relationships, which are simply casual interactions.
Liking	Intimacy is the only component present. There is closeness, understanding, emotional support, affection, bondedness, and warmth. Neither passion nor commitment is present.
Infatuation	Passion is the only component present. This is "love at first sight," a strong physical attraction and sexual arousal, without intimacy or commitment. Infatuation can flare up suddenly and die just as fast—or, given certain circumstances, can sometimes last for a long time.
Empty love	Commitment is the only component present. Empty love is often found in long-term relationships that have lost both intimacy and passion, or in arranged marriages.
Romantic love	Intimacy and passion are both present. Romantic lovers are drawn to each other physically and bonded emotionally. They are not, however, committed to each other.
Companionate love	Intimacy and commitment are both present. This is a long-term, committed friendship, often occurring in marriages in which physical attraction has died down but in which the partners feel close to each other and have made the decision to stay together.
Fatuous love	Passion and commitment are present without intimacy. This is the kind of love that leads to a whirlwind courtship, in which a couple make a commitment on the basis of passion without allowing themselves the time to develop intimacy. This kind of love usually does not last, despite the initial intent to commit.
Consummate love	All three components are present in this "complete" love, which many people strive for, especially in romantic relationships. It is easier to achieve it than to hold on to it. Either partner may change what he or she wants from the relationship. If the other partner changes, too, the relationship may endure in a different form. If the other partner does not change, the relationship may dissolve.

Source: Based on Sternberg, 1986.

the emotional element, involves self-disclosure, which leads to connection, warmth, and trust. *Passion,* the motivational element, is based on inner drives that translate physiological arousal into sexual desire. *Commitment,* the cognitive element, is the decision to love and to stay with the beloved. The degree to which each of the three elements is present determines what type of love people feel (Table 14-2).

Communication is an essential part of intimacy. In a cross-cultural study, 263 young adult couples in Brazil, Italy, Taiwan, and the United States reported on communication and satisfaction in their romantic relationships. In all four places, couples who communicated constructively tended to be more satisfied with their relationships than those who did not (Christensen, Eldridge, Catta-Preta, Lim, & Santagata, 2006).

Checkpoint

Can you ...

♦ List skills that promote and maintain intimacy?

♦ Identify characteristic features of friendship in young adulthood?

♦ Identify the three components of love, according to Sternberg?

Marital and Nonmarital Lifestyles

In many Western countries, today's rules for socially acceptable lifestyles are more flexible than they were during the first half of the twentieth century, and a person's choices may change during the course of adulthood. People marry later, if at all; more people have children outside of marriage, if at all; and more break up their marriages. Many divorce and become single parents; others remain childless; some remarry. Some people remain single; others live with a partner of either sex. Some married couples with separate careers have *commuter marriages,* sometimes called *living apart together* (Adams, 2004).

In this section, we look more closely at marital and nonmarital lifestyles. In the next section we examine parenthood.

Guidepost 4

When and why do young adults choose to remain single, form gay or lesbian relationships, cohabit, or marry, and how satisfying and stable are those lifestyles?

Single Life

The proportion of young adults ages 25 to 34 in the United States who have not yet married approximately tripled between 1970 and 2005. For women, the increase was from 9 percent to 32 percent, and for men, from 15 percent to 43 percent (U.S. Census Bureau, 2007c). The trend is particularly pronounced among African American women, 35 percent of whom are still single in their late thirties (Teachman, Tedrow, & Crowder, 2000). In a study of 300 black, white, and Latina single women in the Los Angeles area (Tucker & Mitchell-Kernan, 1998), members of all three groups had difficulty finding eligible men with similar educational and social backgrounds; but unlike the other two groups, African American women, whose average age was 40, seemed relatively untroubled by the situation. Perhaps, as the timing-of-events model might predict, this is because they saw singlehood as normative in their ethnic group.

Oprah Winfrey is just one of many African American women who remain single through young and middle adulthood.

While some young adults stay single because they have not found the right mates, others are single by choice. More women today are self-supporting, and there is less social pressure to marry. Some people want to be free to move across the country or across the world, pursue careers, further their education, or do creative work without worrying about how their quest for self-fulfillment affects another person. Some enjoy sexual freedom. Some find the lifestyle exciting. Some just like being alone. And some postpone or avoid marriage because of fear that it will end in divorce.

Gay and Lesbian Relationships

Surveys suggest that 40 to 60 percent of gay men and 45 to 80 percent of lesbians in the United States are in romantic relationships, and 8 to 28 percent of these couples have lived together for at least 10 years (Kurdek, 2004).

In some ways, gay and lesbian relationships mirror heterosexual relationships. Gay and lesbian couples tend to be at least as satisfied with their relationships as heterosexual couples, though satisfaction tends to diminish over time. The factors that predict the quality of both homosexual and heterosexual relationships—personality traits, perceptions of the relationship by the partners, ways of communicating and resolving conflicts, and social support—are similar (Kurdek, 2004, 2005, 2006). Indeed, committed same-sex relationships are hardly distinguishable in quality from committed heterosexual relationships (Roisman, Clausell, Holland, Fortuna, & Elieff, 2008). In longitudinal studies of 80 gay and 53 lesbian cohabiting couples, all childless, and 80 married heterosexual couples with children, the homosexual relationships remained at least as healthy as the heterosexual ones (Kurdek, 2004). (The investigator chose to compare childless homosexual couples and heterosexual couples with children because this is the most common family form for each type of relationship.)

Differences between gay and lesbian couples and heterosexual couples also have emerged from research (Kurdek, 2006). First, gay and lesbian couples are more likely than heterosexual couples to negotiate household chores to achieve a balance that works for them and accommodates the interests, skills, and schedules of both partners. Second, they tend to resolve conflicts in a more positive atmosphere than heterosexual couples do. Third, gay and lesbian relationships are less stable than heterosexual relationships, mainly due to the lack of institutional supports. On the basis of such research and in view of the similarities between same-sex and heterosexual relationships, the American Psychological Association (2004a) has declared it unfair and discriminatory to deny same-sex couples legal access to civil (i.e., nonreligious) marriage.

The Netherlands was the first country to legalize same-sex marriage, in 2001; Belgium followed suit in 2003 and Spain and Canada in 2005. By 2005, 16 European countries* had recognized civil unions or domestic partnerships, in which couples have some of the economic and other benefits, rights, and responsibilities of marriage but without the title (Associated Press, 2005; Knox, 2004).

Gays and lesbians in the United States are struggling to obtain legal recognition of their unions and the right to adopt children or raise their own. They argue that same-sex marriage would offer benefits—tangible and intangible—that civil unions would not (Herek, 2006; King & Bartlett, 2006).

As of September 2008, Massachusetts and California were the only states where same-sex marriage was legal. Connecticut, New Hampshire, New Jersey, and Vermont permit civil unions, and Hawaii, Maine, Oregon, and Washington offer registration of domestic partnerships.

What's Your View?

• Should gays and lesbians be allowed to marry? Adopt children? Be covered by a partner's health care plan?

Cohabitation

Cohabitation is an increasingly common lifestyle in which an unmarried couple involved in a sexual relationship live together. Its rise in recent decades reflects the exploratory nature of emerging adulthood and the trend toward postponing marriage.

Types of Cohabitation: International Comparisons Surveys in 14 European countries, Canada, New Zealand, and the United States found wide variations in the probability that a woman will cohabit at least once before age 45, ranging from more than 83 percent in France down to less than 5 percent in Poland. In all countries the overwhelming majority of cohabiting women have never been married (Figure 14-3). Cohabitors who do not marry tend to stay together longer in countries where cohabitation is an *alternative* to or *tantamount to marriage* than in countries where it usually leads to marriage (Heuveline & Timberlake, 2004).

Consensual or *informal unions,* almost indistinguishable from marriage, have long been as accepted as marriage in many Latin American countries, especially for low-SES couples (Phillips & Sweeney, 2005). In such countries, cohabiting couples have practically the same legal rights as married couples (Popenoe & Whitehead, 1999; Seltzer, 2000). In Canada, too, cohabitors have gained legal benefits and obligations close to those of married couples (Cherlin, 2004; Le Bourdais & Lapierre-Adamcyk, 2004). In most Western countries, unmarried couples who cohabit typically intend to, and do, marry; and these cohabitations tend to be relatively short (Heuveline & Timberlake, 2004). Premarital cohabitation in Great Britain and in the United States has accompanied a trend toward delayed marriage (Ford, 2002).

Cohabitation in the United States The United States, according to one analysis, appears to be in transition as cohabitation becomes a lifestyle in itself instead of a transition to marriage (Cherlin, 2004).

*Denmark, Norway, Sweden, Luxembourg, Iceland, Hungary, France, Germany, Portugal, Spain, Switzerland, Finland, Croatia, Poland, Britain, and Scotland. At this writing, the Czech Republic was considering recognition of civil unions.

Figure 14-3

Expected probability (%) of a woman's experiencing at least one adult cohabitation by about age 45, by previous marital status, selected countries. *Note:* Countries sorted in descending order by total percentage expected to cohabit. Estimates derived from single decrement life tables. (Source: Heuveline & Timberlake, 2004. Data come from Family and Fertility Surveys in member countries of the United Nations Economic Commission for Europe and were collected during the early to mid-1990s.)

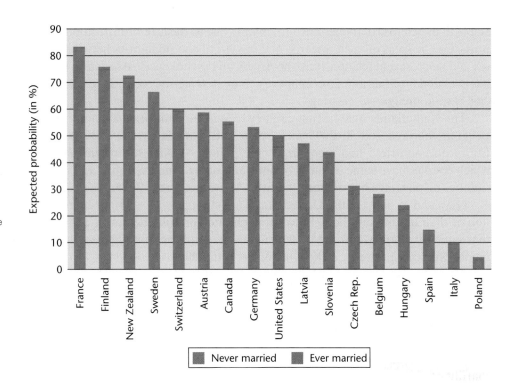

The widespread acceptance of cohabitation is remarkable. In 2003, 4.6 million U.S. households—more than 4 percent of U.S. households—consisted of cohabiting couples, more than 10 times the number in 1960, and 41 percent of these households included children under 18. The increase in cohabitation in the United States has occurred among all racial/ethnic groups and at all educational levels, but people with less education are more likely to cohabit than those with higher education (Fields, 2004; Seltzer, 2004).

More than half of U.S. couples who marry have lived together first, and about half of cohabiting couples eventually marry, though that proportion has been declining (Seltzer, 2000, 2004). Although U.S. family law currently gives cohabitors few of the legal rights and benefits of marriage, this situation is changing, particularly with regard to protection for children of cohabiting couples (Cherlin, 2004; Seltzer, 2004).

Cohabiting relationships tend to be less satisfying and less stable than marriages (Binstock & Thornton, 2003; Bramlett & Mosher, 2002; Heuveline & Timberlake, 2004; Seltzer, 2000, 2004). In particular, cohabiting couples who have divergent expectations about the division of household labor are highly likely to break up (Hohmann-Marriott, 2006). Cohabitors who want to marry tend to put off marriage until they feel their economic circumstances permit it. This means getting out of debt and having enough money for a "real" wedding, home ownership, and financial stability (Smock, Manning, & Porter, 2005). The dissolution of cohabiting relationships is associated with a drop in household income. Some 20 percent of men and 30 percent of women end up in poverty after a cohabiting relationship (Avellar & Smock, 2005).

Some research suggests that cohabiting couples who marry tend to have unhappier marriages and greater likelihood of divorce than those who wait to live together until marriage (Bramlett & Mosher, 2002; Dush, Cohan, & Amato, 2003; Popenoe & Whitehead, 1999; Seltzer, 2000). However, in a nationally representative cross-sectional survey of 6,577 women ages 15 to 45, women who cohabited or had premarital sex *only with their future husbands* had no special risk of marital dissolution (Teachman, 2003).

What's Your View?

• From your experience or observation, is it a good idea to cohabit before marriage? Why or why not? Does it make a difference whether children are involved?

Cohabitation patterns, and the stability of cohabitation, vary among racial/ethnic groups. Perhaps for economic reasons, black and Hispanic couples are less likely than non-Hispanic white couples to regard cohabitation as a trial marriage and more likely to regard it as a substitute for marriage (Phillips & Sweeney, 2005).

The meaning of cohabitation is different for older adults than for younger adults. Older couples are more likely to view their relationship as an alternative to marriage, whereas young couples tend to view cohabitation as a prelude to marriage. Older cohabitors who have no plans to marry report more satisfaction with the relationship and more stability than younger cohabitors do (King & Scott, 2005)

Cohabitation after divorce is more common than premarital cohabitation and may function as a form of remarriage mate selection. However, postdivorce cohabitation, especially with serial partners, greatly delays remarriage and contributes to instability in a new marriage (Xu, Hudspeth, & Bartkowski, 2006).

Checkpoint

Can you . . .

♦ State reasons why people remain single?

♦ Compare gay and lesbian relationships with heterosexual relationships?

♦ Give reasons for the rise in cohabitation, compare types of cohabitation, and cite factors in outcomes?

Marriage

In most societies, the institution of marriage is considered the best way to ensure the protection and raising of children. It allows for a division of labor and a sharing of material goods. Ideally, it offers intimacy, commitment, friendship, affection, sexual fulfillment, companionship, and an opportunity for emotional growth, as well as new sources of identity and self-esteem (Gardiner & Kosmitzki, 2005; Myers, 2000). In certain Eastern philosophical traditions, the harmonious union of male and female is considered essential to spiritual fulfillment and the survival of the species (Gardiner & Kosmitzki, 2005). However, the United States and other postindustrial societies have seen a weakening of the social norms that once made marriage almost universal and its meaning universally understood.

U.S. marriage rates vary by race/ethnicity. In 2005, 56 percent of non-Hispanic whites and 58 percent of Asian Americans ages 15 and older were married, as compared with only 31 percent of African Americans and 46 percent of Hispanic Americans (U.S. Census Bureau, 2007a).

What Marriage Means to Emerging and Young Adults Today   The proportion of emerging and young adults in the United States who choose marriage is not much different from what it was among young adults at the beginning of the twentieth century (Fussell & Furstenberg, 2005), but they seem to think about it differently. This finding comes from in-depth, open-ended interviews with 22- to 38-year-olds in three urban areas and in rural Iowa. These respondents view the traditional marriage with its rigid gender roles as no longer viable in today's world. Instead, they expect greater space for individual interests and pursuits, both within and outside of the marriage. They put more emphasis on friendship and compatibility and less on romantic love (Kefalas, Furstenberg, & Napolitano, 2005).

Instead of seeing marriage as an inevitable step toward adulthood, as in the past, today's young adults tend to believe that, to be married, one should already *be* an adult. Most plan to marry, but only when they feel ready; and they see getting on their feet financially and establishing themselves in stable jobs or careers as formidable obstacles. A minority, typically in rural areas, simply drift into marriage (Kefalas et al., 2005).

Entering Matrimony   For the reasons just mentioned—as well as because of the increasing enrollment in higher education—the typical marrying age has increased

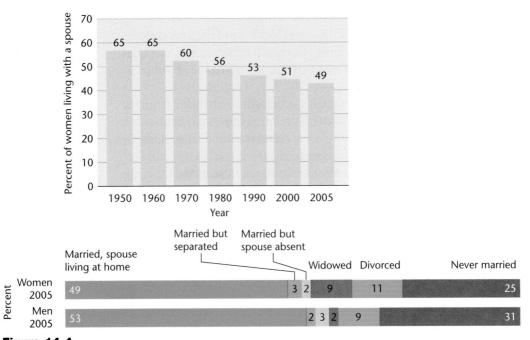

Figure 14-4

Percentage of women age 15 and over living with a spouse, United States, 1950–2005. A little less than half of U.S. women, compared with more than half of U.S. men, are now married and living with a spouse. (Source: U.S. Census Bureau, 2005.)

in industrialized countries. Thirty to 50 years ago, most people married in or before their early twenties. In the United States in 2006 the average age of first-time bridegrooms was 27.5 and of first-time brides, 25.9—a rise of more than four years since the 1970s (U.S. Census Bureau, 2007a). For the first time, slightly more women are living without a spouse than with one (Figure 14-4). In England, France, Germany, and Italy the average marrying age is even higher: 29 or 30 for men and 27 for men (van Dyk, 2005). In Canada, the average age of first marriage for men has risen since 1961 from about 26 to 28, and for women from about 23 to 26 (van Dyk, 2005; Wu, 1999).

Historically and across cultures, the most common way of selecting a mate has been through arrangement, either by the parents or by professional match-makers. Sometimes betrothal takes place in childhood. The bride and groom may not even meet until their wedding day. Only in modern times has free choice of mates on the basis of love become the norm in the Western world (Broude, 1994; Ingoldsby, 1995).

The transition to married life brings major changes in sexual functioning, living arrangements, rights and responsibilities, attachments, and loyalties. Among other tasks, marriage partners need to redefine the connection with their original families, balance intimacy with autonomy, and establish a fulfilling sexual relationship.

Sexual Activity after Marriage Americans apparently have sex less often than media images suggest, and married people have sex more often than singles, though not as often as cohabitors. Face-to-face interviews with a random sample of 3,432 men and women ages 18 to 59 found that only about one-third, including 40 percent of married couples, have intercourse at least twice a week (Laumann et al., 1994; Laumann & Michael, 2000; Michael et al., 1994). However, married couples report more emotional satisfaction from sex than single or cohabiting couples (Waite & Joyner, 2000).

It is hard to know just how common extramarital sex is, because there is no way to tell how truthful people are about their sexual practices, but surveys suggest that it is much less common than is generally assumed. An estimated 3 percent of married people reported having a sexual partner other than their spouse in 2002, and about 18 percent reported having had extramarital relations at some time during their married lives. Current extramarital activity is most prevalent among younger adults and about twice as common among husbands as among wives (4.3 percent versus 1.9 percent) (T. W. Smith, 2003).

Young adults of both sexes have become less permissive in their attitudes toward extramarital sex (T. W. Smith, 2005). In fact, disapproval of extramarital sex is even greater in U.S. society today (94 percent) than disapproval of homosexuality. The pattern of strong disapproval of homosexuality, even stronger disapproval of extramarital sex, and far weaker disapproval of premarital sex also holds true in such European countries as Britain, Ireland, Germany, Sweden, and Poland, though degrees of disapproval differ from one country to another. The United States has more restrictive attitudes than any of these countries except Ireland, where the influence of the Catholic Church is strong (Scott, 1998).

Marital Satisfaction Married people tend to be happier than unmarried people, though those in unhappy marriages are less happy than those who are unmarried or divorced (Myers, 2000). People who marry and stay married, especially women, tend to become better off financially than those who do not marry or

This mass wedding in India, organized by social workers for members of impoverished families, is an example of the variety of marriage customs around the world.

who divorce (Hirschl, Altobelli, & Rank, 2003; Wilmoth & Koso, 2002). However, we do not know that marriage causes wealth; it may be that people who seek wealth and who have characteristics favorable to obtaining it are more likely to marry and to stay married (Hirschl et al., 2003). Nor is it certain that marriage causes happiness; it may be that the greater happiness of married people reflects a greater tendency of happy people to marry (Lucas, Clark, Georgellis, & Diener, 2003).

Marriages, by and large, are just about as happy as they were a quarter-century ago, but husbands and wives spend less time doing things together. Those conclusions come from two national surveys of married persons. Marital happiness was positively affected by increased economic resources, equal decision making, nontraditional gender attitudes, and support for the norm of lifelong marriage but was negatively affected by premarital cohabitation, extramarital affairs, wives' job demands, and wives' longer working hours. Increases in husbands' share of housework appeared to lower marital satisfaction among husbands but improve it among wives (Amato, Johnson, Booth, & Rogers, 2003).

In a study of 197 Israeli couples, a tendency toward emotional instability and negativity in either spouse was a strong predictor of marital unhappiness (Lavee & Ben-Ari, 2004).

One factor underlying marital satisfaction may be a difference in what the man and woman expect from marriage. Women tend to place more importance on emotional expressiveness—their own and their husbands'—than men do (Lavee & Ben-Air, 2004). Wives also tend to prolong discussion of an issue and resent it if their husbands seek to retaliate or avoid responsibility for their role in a quarrel. Husbands, on the other hand, tend to be satisfied if their wives simply want to make up (Fincham, Beach, & Davila, 2004).

At least four theoretical perspectives on women's happiness in marriage have been advanced (Wilcox & Nock, 2006):

- The *companionate model* holds that egalitarian marriages, in which both husband and wife share work and family responsibilities, are likely to be happiest and the most intimate.

- The *institutional model* suggests that women are happier in marriage if they are committed to the traditional institution of marriage.

- The *equity model* claims that a woman's *perception* of fairness in the marriage, and not the actual division of labor, affects marital quality.

- The *gender model* suggests that women are happiest in marriages characterized by gender-typical roles.

Data from a nationally representative survey gave little support to either the companionate model or the gender model. Instead, the study found that most women are happier in a marriage that combines gender equity with a normative commitment to the institution of marriage. Men's efforts to express positive emotion to their wives, to pay attention to the dynamics of the relationship, and to set aside time for activities focused on building the relationship are important to women's perceptions of marital quality (Wilcox & Nock, 2006).

Factors in Marital Success Can the outcome of a marriage be predicted before the couple ties the knot? In one study, researchers followed 100 mostly European American couples for 13 years, starting when they were not yet married. Such factors as premarital income and education levels, whether a couple cohabited before marriage or had premarital sex, and how long they had known each other or dated before marriage had no effect on marital success. What did matter were the partners' happiness with the relationship, their sensitivity to each other, their validation of each other's feelings, and their communication and conflict management skills (Clements, Stanley, & Markman, 2004). Couples who engaged in premarital counseling tend to be more satisfied with and committed to their marriages than couples who did not have such counseling, and their marriages are less likely to end in divorce (Stanley, Amato, Johnson, & Markman, 2006).

The way people describe their marriage can tell much about its likelihood of success. In a nationally representative longitudinal study, 2,034 married people age 55 or younger were asked what held their marriages together. Those who perceived the cohesiveness of their marriage as based on *rewards,* such as love, respect, trust, communication, compatibility, and commitment to the partner, were more likely to be happy in marriage and to remain married after 14 years than people who referred to *barriers* to leaving the marriage, such as children, religious beliefs, financial interdependence, and commitment to the institution of marriage (Previti & Amato, 2003).

Checkpoint

Can you . . .

- Identify several benefits of marriage?

- Discuss differences between traditional views of marriage and the way emerging and young adults view it today?

- Note cultural differences in methods of mate selection and historical changes in marrying age?

- Cite findings on sexual relations in and outside of marriage?

- Identify factors in marital satisfaction and success?

Parenthood

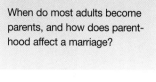

Guidepost 5

When do most adults become parents, and how does parenthood affect a marriage?

People in industrial societies typically have fewer children today than in earlier generations, and they start having them later in life, in many cases because they spend their emerging adult years getting an education and establishing a career. As the average age of first births in the United States has risen (Figure 14-5), the percentage of women who give birth for the first time in their late thirties and even in their forties and fifties has increased dramatically, often with the help of fertility treatments.

A woman's age of first birth varies with ethnic and cultural background. In 2006, Asian American and Pacific Islander women had their first babies at an average age of 28.5, whereas American Indian and Alaska Native women gave birth for the first time, on average, at just under age 22 (Martin et al., 2007). In 2005, 36.9 percent of U.S. births were to unmarried women, and about 40 percent of these women were cohabiting (Martin et al., 2007). The U.S. fertility rate is higher than that in several other developed countries, such as Japan and the United Kingdom, where the average age of first birth is about 29 (Martin, Hamilton, Ventura, Menacker, & Park, 2002; van Dyk, 2005).

At the same time, an increasing proportion of U.S. couples remain childless. The percentage of households with children has fallen from 45 percent in 1970 to about 32 percent today (Fields, 2004). The aging of the population as well as delays in marriage and childbearing may help explain these data, but some couples undoubtedly remain childless by choice. Some see marriage primarily as a way to enhance their intimacy, not as an institution dedicated to the bearing and raising of children (Popenoe & Whitehead, 2003). Others may be discouraged by the financial burdens of parenthood and the difficulty of combining parenthood with employment. Better child care and other support services might help couples make truly voluntary decisions.

Parenthood as a Developmental Experience

A first baby marks a major transition in parents' lives. This totally dependent new person changes a man and woman and changes their relationship. As children develop, parents do, too.

Along with feeling excitement, wonder, and awe, most new parents experience some anxiety about the responsibility of caring for a child, the commitment of time and energy it entails, and the feeling of permanence that parenthood imposes on a marriage. Pregnancy and the recovery from childbirth can affect a couple's relationship, sometimes increasing intimacy and sometimes creating barriers.

Men's and Women's Involvement in Parenthood Most women's expectations about parenthood and its influence on their well-being are matched or exceeded by their experience, according to a survey of 71 first-time mothers before and after giving birth. When the parenting experience did *not* meet expectations, women tended to show signs of depression and a poorer adjustment to parenthood (Harwood, McLean, & Durkin, 2007).

Figure 14-5

Mean age of mother at first birth: United States, 1970–2005. Many women today start families at a later age than in their parents' generation, raising the average age at first birth. (Source: Martin et al., 2007, Fig. 5.)

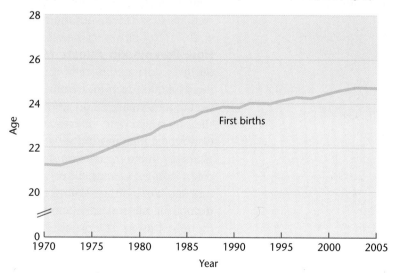

Celebrating a child's birthday is one of the many joys of parenthood. Today most families are smaller than in preindustrial times.

Even though most mothers now work outside the home, women spend more time on child care than their counterparts did in the 1960s, when 60 percent of children lived with a breadwinner father and a stay-at-home mother. Today, only about 30 percent of children live in such families. Yet, married mothers spent 12.9 hours a week on child care in 2000 compared with 10.6 hours in 1965, and single mothers spent 11.8 hours a week on child care as compared with 7.5 hours in 1965 (Bianchi, Robinson, & Milkie, 2006).

How and why do they do it? For one thing, many people delay parenting until a time when they want to spend time with their children. Families are smaller and parents tend to have more financial resources to invest in their children. Also, social norms have changed; today's parents feel more pressure to invest time and energy in child rearing. And they feel a need to keep a closer eye on their children because of concerns about crime, school violence, and other negative influences (Bianchi et al., 2006).

Fathers today are more involved in their children's lives and in child care and housework than ever before. In 2000, married fathers spent 9.7 hours on housework and 6.5 hours on child care each week, more than twice as much as in 1965 (Bianchi et al., 2006). Nonetheless, most fathers are not as involved as mothers are. The time fathers spend with children is more nearly equal to mothers' on weekends and increases as children get older (Yeung, Sandberg, Davis-Kean, & Hofferth, 2001).

Despite these trends, half of parents say they have too little time with their children, according to two national surveys of 2,817 adults. Fathers with long working hours, especially, expressed this feeling (Milkie, Mattingly, Nomaguchi, Bianchi, & Robinson, 2004).

Besides time spent in direct child care, fatherhood may change other aspects of men's lives. Among 5,226 men ages 19 to 65, fathers living with their dependent children were less involved in their own outside social activities than those who had no children but were *more* likely to be engaged in school-related activities, church groups, and community service organizations. The most involved fathers were more satisfied with their lives (Eggebeen & Knoester, 2001).

How Parenthood Affects Marital Satisfaction   Marital satisfaction typically declines during the child-raising years. An analysis of 146 studies including nearly 48,000 men and women found that parents report lower marital satisfaction than nonparents do, and the more children, the less satisfied parents are with their marriage. The difference is most striking among mothers of infants; 38 percent report high marital satisfaction compared with 62 percent of childless wives, probably due to restriction on mothers' freedom and the need to adjust to a new role (Twenge, Campbell, & Foster, 2003). Two prospective longitudinal studies had similar findings: Young couples who had babies reported a small but steady decline in marital satisfaction, while couples who remained childless did not (Schulz, Cowan, & Cowan, 2006; Shapiro & Gottman, 2003).

What accounts for the typical decline in satisfaction? New parents are likely to experience stressors, which may affect their health and state of mind. They may feel isolated and lose sight of the fact that other parents are going through similar problems. The division of household tasks between the man and the woman can become an issue, for example, if the woman was working outside the home before becoming a mother, is now staying home, and the burden of housework and child care falls mostly on her (Cowan & Cowan, 2000; Schulz et al., 2006). Something as simple as a baby's crying, which keeps the parents up at night, can lessen marital satisfaction during the first year of parenthood (Meijer & van den Wittenboer, 2007).

Parents who participate in professionally led couples discussion groups about parenting issues and relationships, beginning in the last trimester of pregnancy, report significantly smaller declines in satisfaction. Such discussions can help new parents take stock of the way the changes in their lives are affecting their relationships with each other and with their babies and can encourage them to search for their own solutions (Schulz et al., 2006).

✓ Checkpoint

Can you . . .

◆ Describe trends in family size and age of parenthood?

◆ Compare men's and women's attitudes toward and exercise of parental responsibilities?

◆ Discuss how parenthood affects marital satisfaction?

How Dual-Income Families Cope

Most families with children in the United States today are dual-income families. Dual-income families take diverse forms (Barnett & Hyde, 2001). In most of these families, traditional gender roles prevail, with the man as the main provider and the woman as secondary provider; but this pattern is changing (Gauthier & Furstenberg, 2005). In 2003, wives' earnings accounted for an average of 35 percent of their families' incomes as compared with only 26 percent in 1973, and 25 percent of working wives earned more than their husbands (Bureau of Labor Statistics, 2005).

In some families, both earners have high-powered careers and high earnings. In other families, one or both partners scale back: Cut back on working hours or refuse overtime or turn down jobs that require excessive travel, so as to increase family time and reduce stress (Barnett & Hyde, 2001; Becker & Moen, 1999; Crouter & Manke, 1994). Or a couple may make trade-offs: trading a career for a job, or trading off whose work takes precedence, depending on shifts in career opportunities and family responsibilities. Women are more likely to do the scaling back, which usually occurs during the early years of child rearing (Becker & Moen, 1999; Gauthier & Furstenberg, 2005).

Combining work and family roles is generally good for both men's and women's mental and physical health and for the strength of their relationship (Barnett & Hyde, 2001). Contributing to family income makes women more independent and gives them a greater share of economic power, and it reduces the pressure on men to be providers. Less tangible benefits may include a more equal relationship between husband and wife, greater self-esteem for the woman, and a closer relationship between a father and his children (Gilbert, 1994).

However, the benefits of multiple roles depend on how many roles each partner carries, the time demands of each role, the success or satisfaction the partners derive from their roles, and the extent to which couples hold traditional or nontraditional attitudes about gender roles (Barnett & Hyde, 2001; Voydanoff, 2004). Working couples may face extra demands on time and energy, conflicts between work and family, possible rivalry between spouses, and anxiety and guilt about meeting children's needs. The family is most demanding, especially for women who are employed full-time, when there are young children (Milkie & Peltola, 1999; Warren & Johnson, 1995). Careers are especially demanding when a worker is getting established or being promoted. Both kinds of demands frequently occur in young adulthood.

In one study, 82 husbands and wives with an oldest child in kindergarten each completed questionnaires at the end of their workday and at bedtime for three days. Daily fluctuations in men's and women's workday pace and in their mood at the end of the workday affected their behavior with their spouses after work, suggesting that the emotions aroused by tension at work spill over to marital relations (Schulz, Cowan, Cowan, & Brennan, 2004).

To lessen the pressures on dual-income families, most countries have adopted workplace protection for such families (Heymann, Siebert, & Wei, 2007). Fathers in 65 countries—but not in the United States—get *paid* paternity leave. (The U.S. Family and Medical Leave Act of 1993 grants 12 weeks of *unpaid* leave.) At least 34 countries—but not the United States—set a maximum length for the work week. Proposals for paid family leave have been introduced in the U.S. Senate and in the New York and Oregon legislatures, but California, New Jersey, and Washington are currently the only states to adopt paid family leave. Washington's law, which is limited to care of newborns or newly adopted children, goes into effect in October 2009.

Checkpoint

Can you ...

♦ Identify benefits and drawbacks of a dual-earner household?

Guidepost 6

What are the trends in divorce rates, and how do young adults adjust to divorce, remarriage, and stepparenthood?

When Marriage Ends

In the United States, the average marriage that ends in divorce does so after seven to eight years (Kreider, 2005). Divorce, more often than not, leads to remarriage with a new partner and the formation of a stepfamily, which includes children born to or adopted by one or both partners before the current marriage.

Divorce

The U.S. divorce rate in 2006 was at its lowest point since 1970—3.6 divorces per 1,000 married women ages 15 and older, according to provisional data (Eldridge & Sutton, 2007). This rate is about twice what it was in 1960 but has fallen gradually since its peak in 1981. About 1 in 5 U.S. adults has been divorced (Kreider, 2005).

The sharpest drop in divorce has occurred among younger cohorts—those born since the mid-1950s (U.S. Census Bureau, 2007c). College-educated women, who previously had the most permissive views about divorce, have become less so, whereas women with lower educational levels have become more permissive and thus more likely to divorce (Martin & Parashar, 2006). Age at marriage is another predictor of whether a union will last. Thus, the decline in divorce may reflect higher educational levels as well as the later age of first marriages, both of which are associated with marital stability (Popenoe & Whitehead, 2004). It also may reflect the rise in cohabitation, which, if it ends, does not end in divorce (A. Cherlin, personal communication, in Lopatto, 2007). Teenagers, high school dropouts, and nonreligious persons have higher divorce rates (Bramlett & Mosher, 2001, 2002; Popenoe & Whitehead, 2004). The rates of marital disruption for black women remain higher than for white women (Sweeney & Phillips, 2004).

Why Do Marriages Fail? Looking back on their marriages, 130 divorced U.S. women who had been married an average of eight years showed remarkable agreement on the reasons for the failure of their marriages. The most frequently cited reasons were incompatibility and lack of emotional support; for more recently divorced, presumably younger, women, this included lack of career support. Spousal abuse was third, suggesting that intimate partner violence may be more frequent than is generally realized (Dolan & Hoffman, 1998; Box 14-1).

BOX 14-1 **Research** *in Action*

Intimate Partner Violence

Intimate partner violence (*IPV*), or *domestic violence,* is the physical, sexual, or psychological maltreatment of a spouse, a former spouse, or an intimate partner. Each year, U.S. women are the victims of about 4.8 million intimate partner–related physical assaults, and U.S. men are the victims of about 2.9 million such assaults (Tjaden & Thoennes, 2000). In 2004, intimate partner violence resulted in 1,544 deaths, 25 percent of them males and 75 percent females (Bureau of Justice Statistics, 2006). The true extent of domestic violence is difficult to ascertain because the victims are often too ashamed or afraid to report what has happened, especially if the victim is male.

Most studies in the United States find that men are far more likely than women to perpetrate intimate partner violence (Tjaden & Thoennes, 2000). Women's violence against men in domestic relationships does happen, but it is typically less injurious, and less likely to be motivated by a desire to dominate or control their partners (Kimmel 2002). Both women and men who have been victimized or threatened by IPV tend to report more chronic health conditions and health risk behaviors than those who have not experienced IPV. However, it is not clear whether these conditions and behaviors are a cause or a result of the violence (Black & Breiding, 2008).

Research on intimate partner violence has identified three types of violence: *situational couple violence, emotional abuse,* and *intimate terrorism* (DeMaris, Benson, Fox, Hill, & Van Wyk, 2003; Frye & Karney, 2006; Leone, Johnson, Cohan, & Lloyd, 2004). *Situational couple violence* refers to physical confrontations that develop in the heat of an argument. This type of violence, in the context of marriage, may reflect poor marital adjustment or acute stress (Frye & Karney, 2006). It may be initiated by either partner and is unlikely to escalate in severity (DeMaris et al., 2003).

Emotional abuse, such as insults and intimidation, may occur either with or without physical violence (Kaukinen, 2004; WHO, 2005). In a survey of 25,876 Canadian men and women, emotional abuse of women tended to occur when a woman's education, occupational status, and income were higher than her partner's. Such behavior may be a man's way of asserting dominance (Kaukinen, 2004).

The most serious type of partner violence is *intimate terrorism*—systematic use of emotional abuse, coercion, and, sometimes, threats and violence to gain or enforce power or control over a partner. This type of abuse tends to become more frequent and more severe as time goes on. Its most important distinguishing characteristic is its underlying control-seeking motivation (DeMaris et al., 2003; Leone et al., 2004). Victims of

intimate terrorism are most likely to be female and to experience physical injuries, time lost from work, poor health, and psychological distress (Leone et al., 2004).

Why do victims stay with partners who abuse or terrorize them? Some blame themselves. Constant ridicule, criticism, threats, punishment, and psychological manipulation destroy their self-confidence and overwhelm them with self-doubt. Some are more concerned about preserving the family than about protecting themselves. Often victims feel trapped in an abusive relationship. Their partners isolate them from family and friends. They may be financially dependent and lack outside social support. Some are afraid to leave—a realistic fear, as some abusive husbands track down, harass, and beat or even kill their estranged wives (Fawcett, Heise, Isita-Espejel, & Pick, 1999; Harvard Medical School, 2004b; Walker, 1999).

The U.S. Violence Against Women Act, adopted in 1994, provides for tougher law enforcement, funding for shelters, a national domestic violence hotline, and educating judges and court personnel, as well as young people, about domestic violence. To be effective, shelters need to offer expanded employment and educational opportunities for abused women who are economically dependent on their partners. Health providers need to question women about suspicious injuries and tell them about the physical and mental health risks of staying with abusive partners (Kaukinen, 2004). Community standards can make a difference. In communities where neighborhood cohesion and informal social control are strong, rates of intimate partner violence and homicide tend to be low, and women are more likely to disclose their problems and seek social support (Browning, 2002).

What's Your View?

What more do you think can or should be done to prevent or stop intimate partner violence?

Check It Out

For more information on this topic, go to www.ncadv.org (the website of the National Coalition Against Domestic Violence, with links to information about the problem, community response, getting help, public policy, and other resources).

According to a randomized telephone survey of 1,704 married people, the greatest likelihood of *either* spouse's bringing up divorce exists when the couple's economic resources are about equal and their financial obligations to each other are relatively small (Rogers, 2004). Instead of staying together "for the sake of the children," many embattled spouses conclude that exposing children to continued parental conflict does greater damage. And, for the increasing number of childless couples, it's easier to return to a single state (Eisenberg, 1995).

Divorce breeds more divorce. Adults with divorced parents are more likely to expect that their marriages will not last (Glenn & Marquardt, 2001) and to become divorced themselves than those whose parents remained together (Shulman, Scharf, Lumer, & Maurer, 2001).

Adjusting to Divorce Ending even an unhappy marriage can be painful for both partners, especially when there are young children in the home. Issues concerning custody and visitation often force divorced parents to maintain contact with each other, and these contacts may be stressful (Williams & Dunne-Bryant, 2006). (Children's adjustment to divorce was discussed in Chapter 10.)

Divorce tends to reduce long-term well-being, especially for the partner who did not initiate the divorce or does not remarry (Amato, 2000). Especially for men, divorce can have negative effects on physical or mental health or both (Wu & Hart, 2002). Women are more likely than men to experience a sharp reduction in economic resources and living standards after separation or divorce (Kreider & Fields, 2002; Williams & Dunne-Bryant, 2006). People who were—or thought they were—happily married tend to react more negatively and adapt more slowly to divorce (Lucas et al., 2003). On the other hand, when a marriage was highly conflicted, its ending may improve well-being (Amato, 2000).

An important factor in adjustment is emotional detachment from the former spouse. People who argue with their ex-mates or who have not found a new partner or spouse experience more distress. An active social life, both at the time of divorce and afterward, helps (Amato, 2000; Thabes, 1997; Tschann, Johnston, & Wallerstein, 1989).

Remarriage and Stepparenthood

Remarriage, said the essayist Samuel Johnson, "is the triumph of hope over experience." Evidence for the truth of that statement is that remarriages are more likely than first marriages to end in divorce (Adams, 2004; Parke & Buriel, 1998).

In the United States and abroad, rates of remarriage are high and rising (Adams, 2004). More than 1 out of 3 U.S. marriages are remarriages for both bride and groom (Kreider, 2005). Half of those who remarry after divorce from a first marriage do so within three to four years (Kreider & Fields, 2002; Kreider, 2005). Men and women living with children from a previous relationship are most likely to form a new union with someone who also has resident children, thus forming a his-and-hers stepfamily (Goldscheider & Sassler, 2006). About one-fourth of stepfamilies in the United States and one-half in Canada are formed by cohabitation (Cherlin, 2004).

The more recent the current marriage and the older the stepchildren, the harder stepparenting seems to be. Women, especially, seem to have more difficulties in raising stepchildren than in raising biological children, perhaps because women generally spend more time with the children than men do (MacDonald & DeMaris, 1996).

Still, the stepfamily has the potential to provide a warm, nurturing atmosphere, as does any family that cares about all its members. One researcher (Papernow, 1993) identified several stages of adjustment: At first, adults expect a smooth, rapid adjustment, while children fantasize that the stepparent will go away and the original parent will return. As conflicts develop, each parent may side with his or her biological children. Eventually, the adults form a strong alliance to meet the needs of all the children. The stepparent gains the role of a significant adult figure, and the family becomes an integrated unit with its own identity.

The bonds forged in young adulthood with friends, lovers, spouses, and children often endure throughout life and influence development in middle and late adulthood. The changes people experience in their more mature years also affect their relationships, as we'll see in upcoming chapters.

Checkpoint

Can you . . .

⬧ Give reasons for the decrease in divorce since 1981?

⬧ Discuss factors in adjustment to divorce?

⬧ Discuss factors in adjustment to remarriage and stepparenthood?

Summary and Key Terms

Emerging Adulthood: Patterns and Tasks

Guidepost 1: *What influences today's varied paths to adulthood, and how do emerging adults develop a sense of adult identity and an autonomous relationship with their parents?*

- Emerging adulthood is often a time of experimentation before assuming adult roles and responsibilities. Such traditional developmental tasks as finding stable work and developing long-term romantic relationships may be postponed until the thirties or even later.

- Paths to adulthood may be influenced by such factors as gender, academic ability, early attitudes toward education, expectations in late adolescence, social class, and ego development.

- Identity development in emerging adulthood may take the form of recentering, the gradual development of a stable adult identity. For racial/ethnic minorities, the task of identity formation may be accelerated.

- Emerging adulthood offers a moratorium, a period in which young people are free from pressure to make lasting commitments. However, some emerging adults remain in a perpetual moratorium, a dead-end status called *youthhood*.

- A measure of how successfully emerging adults handle the developmental task of leaving the childhood home is their ability to maintain close but autonomous relationships with their parents.

- Failure to launch is increasingly common, often for financial reasons, and can complicate the negotiation of an adult relationship with parents.

  recentering (453)

Personality Development: Four Views

Guidepost 2: *Does personality change during adulthood, and, if so, how?*

- Four theoretical perspectives on adult personality development are normative-stage models, the timing-of-events model, trait models, and typological models.

- Normative-stage models hold that age-related social and emotional change emerges in successive periods sometimes marked by crises. In Erikson's theory, the major issue of young adulthood is intimacy versus isolation.

- The timing-of-events model, advocated by Neugarten, proposes that adult psychosocial development is influenced by the occurrence and timing of normative life events. As society becomes less age-conscious, however, the social clock has less meaning.

- The five-factor model of Costa and McCrae is organized around five groupings of related traits: neuroticism, extraversion, openness to experience, conscientiousness, and agreeableness. Current studies find that each of these traits changes during young adulthood and to some extent throughout life.

- Typological research, pioneered by Jack Block, has identified personality types that differ in ego-resiliency and ego-control. These types seem to persist from childhood through adulthood.

  normative-stage models (456)

  intimacy versus isolation (456)

  life structure (457)

  developmental tasks (458)

  timing-of-events model (458)

  normative life events (458)

  social clock (458)

  trait models (458)

  five-factor model (458)

  typological approach (460)

  ego-resiliency (461)

  ego-control (461)

Foundations of Intimate Relationships

Guidepost 3: *How is intimacy expressed in friendship and love?*

- Young adults seek intimacy in relationships with peers and romantic partners. Self-disclosure is an important aspect of intimacy.
- Most young adults have friends but have increasingly limited time to spend with them. Women's friendships tend to be more intimate than men's.
- Many young adults, particularly gays and lesbians, have friends who are considered fictive kin.
- According to Sternberg's triangular theory of love, love has three aspects: intimacy, passion, and commitment.

fictive kin (462)

triangular theory of love (462)

Marital and Nonmarital Lifestyles

Guidepost 4: *When and why do young adults choose to remain single, form gay or lesbian relationships, cohabit, or marry, and how satisfying and stable are those lifestyles?*

- Today, more adults than in the past postpone marriage or never marry. The trend is particularly pronounced among African American women.
- Reasons for staying single include career opportunities, travel, sexual and lifestyle freedom, a desire for self-fulfillment, women's greater self-sufficiency, reduced social pressure to marry, fear of divorce, difficulty in finding a suitable mate, and lack of dating opportunities or of available mates.
- Both gay men and lesbians form enduring sexual and romantic relationships.
- The ingredients of long-term satisfaction are similar in homosexual and heterosexual relationships.
- Gays and lesbians in the United States are fighting for rights other people enjoy, such as the right to marry.
- With the new stage of emerging adulthood and the delay in age of marriage, cohabitation has increased and has become the norm in some countries.
- Cohabitation can be a trial marriage, an alternative to marriage, or, in some places, almost indistinguishable from marriage. Cohabiting relationships in the United States tend to be less stable than marriages.

- Marriage (in a variety of forms) is universal and meets basic economic, emotional, sexual, social, and child-raising needs.
- Mate selection and marrying age vary across cultures. People in industrialized nations now marry later than in past generations.
- Fewer people appear to be having extramarital sexual relationships than in the past.
- Success in marriage may depend on partners' sensitivity to each other, their validation of each other's feelings, and their communication and conflict management skills. Men's and women's differing expectations may be important factors in marital satisfaction.

Parenthood

Guidepost 5: *When do most adults become parents, and how does parenthood affect a marriage?*

- Today women in industrialized societies are having fewer children and having them later in life, and an increasing number choose to remain childless.
- Fathers are usually less involved in child raising than mothers, but more so than in previous generations.
- Marital satisfaction typically declines during the childbearing years.
- In most cases, the burdens of a dual-earner lifestyle fall most heavily on the woman.
- Family-friendly workplace policies may help alleviate marital stress.

When Marriage Ends

Guidepost 6: *What are the trends in divorce rates, and how do young adults adjust to divorce, remarriage, and stepparenthood?*

- Divorce rates in the United States have fallen from their high in 1981. Among the likely reasons are increasing educational levels, the delay in age of marriage, and the rise in cohabitation.
- Adjusting to divorce can be painful. Emotional distance from the ex-spouse is a key to adjustment.
- Many divorced people remarry within a few years, but remarriages tend to be less stable than first marriages.
- Stepfamilies may go through several stages of adjustment.

The primitive, physical, functional pattern of the morning of life, the active years before forty or fifty, is outlived. But there is still the afternoon opening up, which one can spend not in the feverish pace of the morning but in having time at last for those intellectual, cultural, and spiritual activities that were pushed aside in the heat of the race.

—Anne Morrow Lindbergh, *Gift from the Sea,* 1955

Did You **Know...**

- One-third to one-half of Americans in their late sixties and seventies think of themselves as middle-aged?
- During the early nineteenth century in Western cultures, menopause was seen as a disease?
- Physical activity in midlife can increase the chances of remaining mobile in old age?
- Positive emotions and personality traits, such as hope, optimism, and conscientiousness, tend to predict good health and long life?
- Cognitively speaking, many middle-aged people are in their prime?
- Middle-aged people who engage in complex work tend to show stronger cognitive performance than their peers?

These are just a few of the interesting and important topics we will cover in this chapter. In it, we examine physical changes common in middle adulthood. We discuss how health problems may be worsened by poverty, racial discrimination, and other stresses. We consider how intelligence changes, how thought processes mature, and what underlies creative performance. We look at trends in work and early retirement and at participation in educational activities. After you have studied this chapter, you should be able to answer each of the Guidepost questions on the following page.

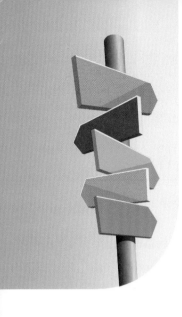

Guideposts *for Study*

1. What are the distinguishing features of middle age?
2. What physical changes generally occur during the middle years, and what is their psychological impact?
3. What factors affect physical and mental health at midlife?
4. What cognitive gains and losses occur during middle age?
5. Do mature adults think differently than younger people do?
6. What accounts for creative achievement, and how does it change with age?
7. How are patterns of work and education changing, and how does work contribute to cognitive development?

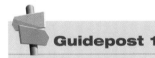

Guidepost 1

What are the distinguishing features of middle age?

What's Your View?

- When would you say middle age begins and ends?
- Think of several people you know who are middle-aged. Do they seem to be in good health? How involved are they in work or other activities?

Middle Age: A Social Construct

The term *midlife* first came into the dictionary in 1895 (Lachman, 2004), as life expectancy began to lengthen. Today, in industrial societies, middle adulthood is considered to be a distinct stage of life with its own societal norms, roles, opportunities, and challenges. However, some traditional societies, such as upper-caste Hindus in rural India (Menon, 2001) and the Gusii in Kenya (see Box 16-1 on page 521), do not recognize a middle stage of adulthood at all. Thus, some scholars describe middle age as a social construct.

In this book, we define *middle adulthood* in chronological terms as the years between ages 40 and 65, but this definition is arbitrary. There is no consensus on when middle age begins and ends or on specific biological or social events that mark its boundaries. With improvements in health and length of life, the subjective upper limits of middle age are rising (Lachman, 2001, 2004). One-third of U.S. adults in their 70s and half of those between 65 and 69, think of themselves as middle-aged (National Council on Aging, 2000). However, people with low socioeconomic status tend to name earlier beginning and endpoints for midlife, perhaps because of poorer health or earlier transitions to retirement and grandparenthood (Lachman, 2004).

As the United States entered the twenty-first century, more than 80 million baby boomers, born between 1946 and 1964, were between ages 54 and 35 and constituted about 30 percent of the total population (U.S. Census Bureau, 2000). On the whole, this is the best educated and most affluent cohort ever to reach middle age anywhere, and it is changing our perspective on that time of life (Eggebeen & Sturgeon, 2006; Willis & Reid, 1999).

The Midlife in the United States (MIDUS) study, a comprehensive survey of a national sample of 7,189 noninstitutionalized adults ages 25 to 75, has enabled researchers to study factors that influence health, well-being, and productivity in midlife and how adults navigate the transition to old age (Brim, Ryff, & Kessler, 2004). According to the MIDUS data, most middle-aged people

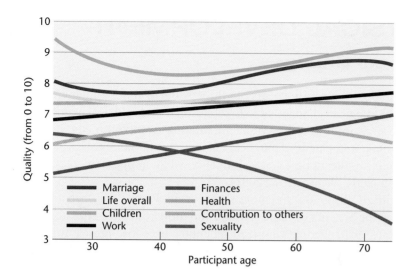

Figure 15-1

How U.S. adults of various ages rate aspects of their quality of life and overall quality of life. (Source: Fleeson, 2004; data from MacArthur Foundation Research Network on Successful Midlife Development [the MIDUS National Survey].)

are in good physical, cognitive, and emotional shape and feel good about the quality of their lives (Fleeson, 2004; Figure 15-1). However, the experience of middle age varies with health, gender, race/ethnicity, socioeconomic status, cohort, and culture, as well as with personality, marital and parental status, and employment (Lachman, 2004). Furthermore, the experiences, roles, and issues of early middle age differ from those of late middle age. (Keegan, Gross, Fisher, & Remez, 2004).

According to the MIDUS research, "aging, at least up until the midseventies, appears to be a positive phenomenon" (Fleeson, 2004, p. 269). At the same time, the middle years are marked by growing individual differences and a multiplicity of life paths (Lachman, 2004). Some middle-aged people can run marathons; others get winded climbing a steep stairway. Some have a sharper memory than ever; others feel their memory beginning to slip. Many adults in the middle years feel a stable sense of control over their lives (Skaff, 2006) as they handle weighty responsibilities and multiple, demanding roles: running households, departments, or enterprises; launching children; and perhaps caring for aging parents or starting new careers. Others, having made their mark and raised their children, have an increased feeling of freedom and independence (Lachman, 2001). Some are at the height of creativity or careers; others have gotten a slow start or have reached dead ends. Still others dust off mothballed dreams or pursue new and more challenging goals. What people do and how they live has much to do with how they age. Middle age can be a time not primarily of decline and loss but also of mastery, competence, and growth—a time of reevaluating goals and aspirations and deciding how best to use the remaining part of the life span.

Checkpoint

Can you . . .

◆ Explain why middle age is considered a social construct?

◆ Cite individual differences in the experience of middle age?

Many middle-aged people are at the peak of their careers, enjoying a sense of freedom, responsibility, and control over their lives and making important contributions to social betterment. Bill Gates, who as a young man founded the software giant Microsoft, at 51 expends most of his efforts on philanthropy through the foundation he and his wife, Melinda, established in 1999. Here they appeal to a forum of scientists and policy makers to join in his goal of eradicating malaria worldwide.

PHYSICAL DEVELOPMENT

Physical Changes

Guidepost 2

What physical changes generally occur during the middle years, and what is their psychological impact?

"Use it or lose it!" Research bears out the wisdom of that popular creed. Although some physiological changes are direct results of biological aging and genetic makeup, behavioral and lifestyle factors dating from youth can affect the likelihood, timing, and extent of physical change. By the same token, health and lifestyle habits in the middle years influence what happens in the years beyond (Lachman, 2004; Whitbourne, 2001).

The more people do, the more they *can* do. People who become active early in life reap the benefits of more stamina and more resilience after age 60 (Spirduso & MacRae, 1990). People who lead sedentary lives lose muscle tone and energy and become even less inclined to exert themselves physically. Still, it is never too late to adopt a healthier lifestyle.

Sensory and Psychomotor Functioning

From young adulthood through the middle years, sensory and motor changes are almost imperceptible—until one day a 45-year-old man realizes that he cannot read the telephone directory without eyeglasses, or a 60-year-old woman has to admit that she is not as quick on her feet as she was.

Age-related visual problems occur mainly in five areas: *near vision, dynamic vision* (reading moving signs), *sensitivity to light, visual search* (for example, locating a sign), and *speed of processing* visual information (Kline et al., 1992; Kline & Scialfa, 1996; Kosnik, Winslow, Kline, Rasinski, & Sekuler, 1988). Also common is a slight loss in *visual acuity,* or sharpness of vision. Because of changes in the pupil of the eye, middle-aged people may need about one-third more brightness to compensate for the loss of light reaching the retina (Belbin, 1967; Troll, 1985).

Because the lens of the eye becomes progressively less flexible, its ability to shift focus diminishes. This change usually becomes noticeable in early middle age and is practically complete by age 60 (Kline & Scialfa, 1996). Many people ages 40 and older need reading glasses for **presbyopia,** a lessened ability to focus on near objects—a condition associated with aging. (The prefix *presby-* means "with age.") The incidence of **myopia** (nearsightedness) also increases through middle age (Merrill & Verbrugge, 1999). Bifocals and trifocals—corrective eyewear in which lenses for reading are combined with lenses for distant vision—aid the eye in adjusting between near and far objects.

A gradual hearing loss, rarely noticed earlier in life, speeds up in the fifties (Merrill & Verbrugge, 1999). This condition, **presbycusis,** normally is limited to higher-pitched sounds than those used in speech (Kline & Scialfa, 1996). Hearing loss proceeds twice as quickly in men as in women (Pearson et al., 1995). Today, a preventable increase in hearing loss is occurring among 45-to 64-year-olds due to continuous or sudden exposure to noise at work, at loud concerts, through earphones, and the like (Wallhagen, Strawbridge, Cohen, & Kaplan, 1997). Hearing losses due to environmental noise can be avoided by wearing hearing protectors, such as earplugs or special earmuffs.

Sensitivity to taste and smell generally begins to decline in midlife (Cain, Reid, & Stevens, 1990; Stevens, Cain, Demarque, & Ruthruff, 1991). As the taste buds become less sensitive and the number of olfactory cells diminishes, foods may seem more bland (Merrill & Verbrugge, 1999; Troll, 1985). Women tend to retain these senses longer than men. There are individual differences, however. One person may become less sensitive to salty foods, another to sweet, bitter, or sour foods. And the

presbyopia Age-related, progressive loss of the eyes' ability to focus on nearby objects due to loss of elasticity in the lens.

myopia Nearsightedness.

presbycusis Age-related, gradual loss of hearing, which accelerates after age 55, especially with regard to sounds at higher frequencies.

Though strength and coordination may decline, many middle-aged people find that their improved ability to use strategies gained by experience outweighs the changes in their physical capabilities.

same person may remain more sensitive to some of these tastes than to others (Stevens, Cruz, Hoffman, & Patterson, 1995; Whitbourne, 1999).

Adults begin to lose sensitivity to touch after age 45, and to pain after age 50. However, pain's protective function remains: Although people feel pain less, they become less able to tolerate it (Katchadourian, 1987).

Strength and coordination decline gradually from their peak during the twenties. Some loss of muscle strength is usually noticeable by age 45; 10 to 15 percent of maximum strength may be gone by 60. The reason is a loss of muscle fiber, which is replaced by fat. Grip strength reflects birth weight and muscle growth earlier in life as well as parents' childhood socioeconomic status and is an important predictor of future disability, functional losses, and mortality (Guralnik, Butterworth, Wadsworth, & Kuh, 2006; Kuh et al., 2006). Still, decline is not inevitable; strength training in middle age can prevent muscle loss and even regain strength (Whitbourne, 2001).

Endurance often holds up much better than strength (Spirduso & MacRae, 1990). Loss of endurance results from a gradual decrease in the rate of **basal metabolism** (use of energy to maintain vital functions) after age 40 (Merrill & Verbrugge, 1999). Often-used skills are more resistant to effects of age than those that are used less; thus athletes show a smaller-than-average loss in endurance (Stones & Kozma, 1996).

basal metabolism Use of energy to maintain vital functions.

Manual dexterity generally becomes less efficient after the midthirties (Vercruyssen, 1997), though some pianists, such as Vladimir Horowitz, have continued to perform brilliantly in their eighties. Simple reaction time (as in pressing a button when a light flashes) slows very little until about age 50, but choice reaction time (as in pressing one of four numbered buttons when the same number appears on a screen) slows gradually throughout adulthood (Der & Deary, 2006). When a vocal rather than a manual response is called for, age differences in simple reaction time are substantially less (S. J. Johnson & Rybash, 1993).

Tasks that involve a choice of responses (such as hitting one button when a light flashes and another button when a tone is heard) and complex motor skills involving many stimuli, responses, and decisions (as in driving a car) decline more; but the decline does not necessarily result in poorer performance. Typically, middle-aged adults are better drivers than younger ones (McFarland, Tune, & Welford, 1964), and 60-year-old typists are as efficient as 20-year-olds (Spirduso & MacRae, 1990; Salthouse, 1984).

In these and other activities, knowledge based on experience may more than make up for physical changes. Skilled industrial workers in their forties and fifties are often more productive than ever, partly because they tend to be more conscientious and careful. Middle-aged workers are less likely than younger workers to suffer disabling injuries on the job (Salthouse & Maurer, 1996)—a likely result of experience and good judgment, which compensate for any lessening of coordination and motor skills.

Structural and Systemic Changes

Changes in appearance may become noticeable during the middle years. By the fifth or sixth decade, the skin may become less taut and smooth as the layer of fat below the surface becomes thinner, collagen molecules more rigid, and elastin fibers more brittle. Hair may become thinner, due to a slowed replacement rate, and grayer as production of melanin, the pigmenting agent, declines. Middle-aged people tend to gain weight as a result of accumulation of body fat and lose height due to shrinkage of the intervertebral disks (Merrill & Verbrugge, 1999; Whitbourne, 2001).

Bone density normally peaks in the twenties or thirties. From then on, people typically experience some bone loss as more calcium is absorbed than replaced, causing bones to become thinner and more brittle. Bone loss accelerates in the fifties and sixties; it occurs twice as rapidly in women as in men, sometimes leading to osteoporosis (discussed later in this chapter) (Merrill & Verbrugge, 1999; Whitbourne, 2001). Smoking, alcohol use, and a poor diet earlier in adulthood tend to speed bone loss; it can be slowed by aerobic exercise, resistance training with weights, increased calcium intake, and vitamin C. Joints may become stiffer as a result of accumulated stress. Exercises that expand range of motion and strengthen the muscles supporting a joint can improve functioning (Whitbourne, 2001).

Large proportions of middle-aged and even older adults show little or no decline in organ functioning (Gallagher, 1993). In some, however, the heart begins to pump more slowly and irregularly in the midfifties; by 65, it may lose up to 40 percent of its aerobic power. Arterial walls may become thicker and more rigid. Heart disease becomes more common beginning in the late forties or early fifties. **Vital capacity**—the maximum volume of air the lungs can draw in and expel—may begin to diminish at about age 40 and may drop by as much as 40 percent by age 70. Temperature regulation and immune response may begin to weaken, and sleep may become less deep (Merrill & Verbrugge, 1999; Whitbourne, 2001).

Sexuality and Reproductive Functioning

Sexuality is not only a hallmark of youth. Although both sexes experience losses in reproductive capacity sometime during middle adulthood—women become unable to bear children and men's fertility begins to decline—sexual enjoyment can continue throughout adult life. (Changes in the male and female reproductive systems are summarized in Table 15-1.) Still, many middle-aged people have concerns related to sexuality and reproductive functioning. Let's look at these.

vital capacity Amount of air that can be drawn in with a deep breath and expelled.

Checkpoint

Can you . . .

♦ Summarize changes in sensory and motor functioning and body structure and systems that may begin during middle age?

♦ Identify factors that contribute to individual differences in physical condition?

Table 15-1	Changes in Human Reproductive Systems during Middle Age	
	Female	**Male**
Hormonal change	Drop in estrogen and progesterone	Drop in testosterone
Symptoms	Hot flashes, vaginal dryness, urinary dysfunction	Undetermined
Sexual changes	Less intense arousal, less frequent and quicker orgasms	Loss of psychological arousal, less frequent erections, slower orgasms, longer recovery between ejaculations, increased risk of erectile dysfunction
Reproductive capacity	Ends	Continues; some decrease in fertility occurs

Menopause and Its Meanings   **Menopause** takes place when a woman permanently stops ovulating and menstruating and can no longer conceive a child; it is generally considered to have occurred one year after the last menstrual period. This happens, on average, at about age 50 to 52 (Avis & Crawford, 2006).

Menopause is not a single event but a process, now called the *menopausal transition* (NIH, 2005; Rossi, 2004). Beginning in her midthirties to midforties, a woman's production of mature ova begins to decline, and the ovaries produce less of the female hormone estrogen. The period of three to five years during which this slowing of hormone production and ovulation occurs, prior to and during the first year after menopause, is called **perimenopause,** also known as the *climacteric,* or "change of life." During perimenopause, menstruation becomes irregular, with less flow than before and a longer time between menstrual periods, before it ceases altogether (Finch, 2001; Whitbourne, 2001). The timing of menopause varies greatly, but most women experience it between ages 45 and 55 (Avis & Crawford, 2006).

Attitudes toward Menopause   During the early nineteenth century in Western cultures, menopause was seen as a disease, a failure of the ovaries to perform their natural function. In the United States today, most women who have gone through menopause view it positively, as a natural process (Avis & Crawford, 2006; Rossi, 2004). Menopause can be seen as a sign of a transition into the second half of adult life—a time of role changes, greater independence, and personal growth.

Symptoms and Myths   Most women experience some symptoms during the menopausal transition, but some have no symptoms at all, and racial/ethnic variations exist. Many symptoms widely attributed to menopause may have other causes, often related to natural aging (Avis & Crawford, 2006; NIH, 2005). Table 15-2 summarizes the current evidence concerning reported symptoms of menopause.

Most commonly reported are hot flashes and night sweats, sudden sensations of heat that flash through the body due to erratic changes in hormone secretion that affect the temperature control centers in the brain. There is strong evidence that the menopausal transition is responsible for these symptoms (NIH, 2005). However, some women never have them, and others have them almost every day (Avis & Crawford, 2006; Rossi, 2004).

menopause   Cessation of menstruation and of ability to bear children.

perimenopause   Period of several years during which a woman experiences physiological changes of menopause; includes first year after end of menstruation; also called *climacteric.*

Table 15-2   Which Symptoms of Menopause Have Research Support?

Symptom	Reported Prevalence	Research Support
Hot flashes, night sweats	Before menopause: 14–51% Perimenopause: 35–50% Postmenopause: 30–80%	Strong support
Vaginal dryness, painful intercourse	Before menopause: 4–22% Perimenopause: 7–39% Postmenopause: 17–30%	Strong support
Sleep disturbances	Before menopause: 16–42% Perimenopause: 39–47% Postmenopause: 35–60%	Moderate support
Mood disturbances (depression, anxiety, irritability)	Before menopause: 8–37% Perimenopause: 11–21% Postmenopause: 8–38%	Limited support
Urinary incontinence	Before menopause: 10–36% Perimenopause: 17–39% Postmenopause: 15–36%	Mixed results, inadequate to show causal connection
Cognitive disturbances (i.e., forgetfulness)	No data	Insufficient evidence to separate aging effects from effects of menopause
Somatic symptoms (back pain, tiredness, stiff or painful joints)	No data	No association with menopausal status shown
Sexual dysfunction	No data	No assocation with menopausal status shown

Source: NIH, 2005.

Declining estrogen levels have not been found to affect sexual desire in women (American Medical Association, 1998; NIH, 2005). However, some women find intercourse painful because of thinning vaginal tissues and inadequate lubrication (NIH, 2005). Water-soluble gels can prevent or relieve this problem (King, 1996; Williams, 1995).

Irritability, nervousness, tension, and depression increase in women of menopausal age, but research does not establish a clear connection between these disturbances and this normal biological change (Lachman, 2004; NIH, 2005; Whitbourne, 2001). Many women at this time are undergoing stressful changes in roles, relationships, and responsibilities, and these changes may affect their mental state (Avis, 1999; Lachman, 2004; NIH, 2005; Rossi, 2004).

All in all, the research suggests that some of the presumed symptoms of menopausal syndrome may be related more to other natural changes of aging than to menopause itself (NIH, 2005). They also may reflect societal views of women and of aging (Box 15-1). In cultures in which women view menopause positively or in which older women acquire social, religious, or political power after menopause, few problems are associated with this natural event (Aldwin & Levenson, 2001; Avis, 1999). However, physical changes in bone density and heart functioning after menopause can affect women's health, as we discuss later in this chapter.

Menopause the Musical, *a hilarious celebration of women going through "the change," epitomizes many contemporary women's attitudes toward this natural biological event.*

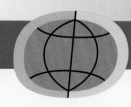

BOX 15-1 **Window** *on the World*

Cultural Differences in Women's Experience of Menopause

Many women accept hot flashes and night sweats as normal, though unwelcome, accompaniments of menopause. Yet, women in some cultures rarely or never experience these symptoms.

In research conducted by Margaret Lock (1994), fewer than 10 percent of Japanese women whose menstruation was becoming irregular reported having had hot flashes during the previous two weeks, compared with about 40 percent of a Canadian sample and 35 percent of a U.S. sample. In fact, fewer than 20 percent of Japanese women had *ever* experienced hot flashes, compared with 65 percent of Canadian women, and most of the Japanese women who had experienced hot flashes reported little or no physical or psychological discomfort. Furthermore, only about 3 percent of the Japanese women said they experienced night sweats, and they were far less likely than Western women to suffer from insomnia, depression, irritability, or lack of energy (Lock, 1994).

In Japan, menopause is not regarded as a medical condition, and the end of menstruation has far less significance than it does for Western women. The closest term for it, *kônenki,* refers not specifically to what Westerners call menopause, but to a considerably longer period comparable to perimenopause (Lock, 1994, 1998). There also is no specific Japanese term for "hot flash," even though the Japanese language makes many subtle distinctions among body states. Aging itself is less feared in Japan than in the West; it brings newfound freedom—as does menopause (Lock, 1998). It has been suggested that because women's diet in Japan is high in plant foods containing *phytoestrogens,* estrogen-like compounds, Japanese women may not experience symptoms of dramatic declines in estrogen levels.

Attitudes toward menopause vary greatly across cultures. In some cultures, such as that of the southwestern Papago Indians, menopause seems to be virtually ignored. In other cultures, such as those of India and South Asia, it is a welcome event; women's status and freedom of movement increase once they are free of taboos connected with menstruation and fertility (Avis, 1999; Lock, 1994).

In the United States, a national study of women's health came up with some paradoxical findings. African American women tended to have more positive feelings about menopause than did Caucasian women, perhaps because in comparison with racism, which many African American women have experienced, menopause is perceived as a minor stressor (Avis & Crawford, 2006; Sommer et al., 1999). Yet, in other studies, African American women have reported more frequent hot flashes than did white women (Avis & Crawford, 2006). In the national women's study, white women agreed that menopause signaled freedom and independence (Sommer et al., 1999). Yet, in a large, community-based study, white women were more likely to experience psychological distress during menopause than women of other racial/ethnic groups (Bromberger et al., 2001). In the national women's study, Japanese American and Chinese American women reported the most negative feelings about menopause, contrary to the findings about Japanese women in Japan (Avis & Crawford, 2006; Sommer et al., 1999).

Clearly, more research is needed. However, these findings show that even such a universal biological event as menopause has major cultural variations, once again affirming the importance of cross-cultural research.

What's Your View?

What do you think might explain cultural differences in women's experience of menopause?

Check It Out

For more information on menopause in Japan, and additional data on Japanese women's health and aging, go to www.gfmer.ch/Books/bookmp/185.htm (a website maintained by members of the Department of Obstetrics and Gynaecology, Kyoto Prefectural University of Medicine in Kyoto, Japan).

Treatment of Menopausal Symptoms Short-term, low-dose administration of artificial estrogen is the most effective way to alleviate hot flashes, but it carries serious risks, as we discuss later in this chapter (Avis & Crawford, 2006; NIH, 2005). Various nonhormonal therapies have been tried. Studies have found some evidence of effectiveness for certain antidepressant drugs as well as for the antihypertensive clonidine and the anticonvulsive drug gabapentin in treating hot flashes in women with severe symptoms, but adverse effects and high costs may limit their usefulness for most women (Nelson et al., 2006). Some women have turned to alternative therapies, such as phytomedicines, St. Johns wort, vitamin E, black cohosh, and other natural or herbal preparations, as well as mind-body therapies, energy therapies, and non-Western medicine, but none have been found effective (Avis & Crawford, 2006; Nedrow et al., 2006; Newton et al., 2006; NIH, 2005). However, most of the studies have been small or poorly designed. Also, there is a placebo effect; women in control groups, who are not given the therapy being tested, improve more than 30 percent (NIH, 2005).

Changes in Male Sexual Functioning   Men have no experience quite comparable to menopause. They do not undergo a sudden drop in hormone production at midlife, as women do, and they can continue to reproduce until late in life. Men do seem to have a biological clock, however. Testosterone levels decrease slowly after the thirties—about 1 percent a year, with wide individual variations (Asthana et al., 2004; Finch, 2001; Lewis, Legato, & Fisch, 2006; Whitbourne, 2001). Men's sperm count declines with age, making conception less likely. The genetic quality of the sperm declines as well; as we discussed in Chapter 3, advancing paternal age may be a source of birth defects and other undesirable conditions (Lewis et al., 2006).

The decline in testosterone has been associated with reductions in bone density and muscle mass (Asthana et al., 2004) as well as decreased energy, lower sex drive, overweight, emotional irritability, and depressed mood. Low testosterone also has been linked to diabetes and cardiovascular disease and may increase mortality (Lewis et al., 2006).

A drop in testosterone levels does not necessarily mean an end to sexual activity. However, some middle-aged and older men experience **erectile dysfunction** (popularly called *impotence*): persistent inability to achieve or maintain an erect enough penis for satisfactory sexual performance. An estimated 39 percent of 40-year-old men and 67 percent of 70-year-old men experience erectile dysfunction at least sometimes (Feldman, Goldstein, Hatzichristou, Krane, & McKinlay, 1994; Goldstein et al., 1998). Diabetes, hypertension, high cholesterol, kidney failure, depression, neurological disorders, and many chronic diseases are associated with erectile dysfunction. Alcohol, drugs, smoking, poor sexual techniques, lack of knowledge, unsatisfying relationships, anxiety, and stress can be contributing factors (Lewis et al., 2006; Utiger, 1998).

Sildenafil (Viagra) and other, similar, testosterone therapies have been found safe and effective (Goldstein et al., 1998; Nurnberg et al., 2003; Utiger, 1998), and their use has mushroomed. However, they should not be prescribed indiscriminately—only for men with known testosterone deficiency (Lewis et al., 2006; Whitbourne, 2001). If there is no apparent physical problem, psychotherapy or sex therapy (with the support and involvement of the partner) may help (NIH, 1992).

Sexual Activity   Myths about sexuality in midlife—for example, the idea that satisfying sex ends at menopause—have sometimes become self-fulfilling prophecies. Now advances in health care and more liberal attitudes toward sex are making people more aware that sex can be a vital part of life during these and even later years.

Frequency of sexual activity and satisfaction with sex life do tend to diminish gradually during the forties and fifties. In the MIDUS study, 61 percent of married or cohabiting premenopausal women but only 41 percent of postmenopausal women reported having sex once a week or more. This decline was related, not to menopause, but to age and physical condition (Rossi, 2004). Possible physical causes include chronic disease, surgery, medications, and too much food or alcohol. Often, however, a decline in frequency has nonphysiological causes: monotony in a relationship, preoccupation with business or financial

erectile dysfunction   Inability of a man to achieve or maintain an erect penis sufficient for satisfactory sexual performance.

Checkpoint

Can you . . .

♦ Contrast men's and women's reproductive changes at midlife?

♦ Identify factors that can affect women's experience of menopause?

♦ Tell which reported symptoms have been found to be related to menopause, and which have not?

♦ Identify changes in male sexual functioning in middle age?

♦ Discuss changes in sexual activity during middle age?

worries, mental or physical fatigue, depression, failure to make sex a high priority, fear of failure to attain an erection, or lack of a partner (King, 1996; Masters & Johnson, 1966; Weg, 1989). Treating these causes may bring renewed vitality to a couple's sex life.

Physical and Mental Health

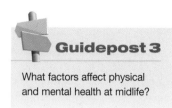

Guidepost 3

What factors affect physical and mental health at midlife?

Most middle-aged Americans, like middle-aged people in other industrialized countries, are quite healthy (Lachman, 2004). All but 12 percent of 45- to 54-year-olds and 18 percent of 55- to 64-year-olds consider themselves in good to excellent health. Only 12.5 percent of 45- to 54-year-olds and 20 percent of 55- to 64-year-olds are limited in activities because of chronic conditions (chiefly arthritis and circulatory conditions), which increase with age (NCHS, 2006; Schiller & Bernadel, 2004).

However, baby boomers may be less healthy than previous generations. In a comparison of three birth cohorts—those born in 1936–1941 (ages 71 to 66), 1942–1947 (ages 65 to 60), and 1948–1953 (ages 59 to 54)—the two youngest cohorts were less likely than the oldest to say that their health was excellent or very good at ages 51 to 56. Also, the youngest cohort reported more pain, chronic health conditions, difficulty getting around, and psychiatric problems than those who had been the same age 12 years earlier (Soldo, Mitchell, & McCabe, 2007). Furthermore, people in the United States, regardless of socioeconomic status (SES), are less healthy than their counterparts in England in late middle age (Banks, Marmot, Oldfield, & Smith, 2006).

Health Trends at Midlife

Despite their generally good health, many people in midlife, especially those with low SES, experience increasing health problems (Lachman, 2004) or are concerned about signs of potential decline. They may have less energy than in their youth and are likely to experience occasional or chronic pains and fatigue. They can no longer stay awake late with ease. They are more likely to contract certain diseases, such as hypertension and diabetes, and they take longer to recover from illness or extreme exertion (Merrill & Verbrugge, 1999; Siegler, 1997).

Hypertension (chronically high blood pressure) is an increasingly important concern from midlife on as a risk factor for cardiovascular disease and kidney disease. The prevalence of hypertension in the United States has increased 30 percent in the past decade to an all-time high (Fields et al., 2004); it now affects nearly 30 percent of adults, and its prevalence increases with age (NCHS, 2006). People who consume more vegetable protein tend to have lower blood pressure (Elliott et al., 2006). Impatience and hostility increase the long-term risk of developing hypertension (Yan et al., 2003). Hypertension can be controlled through blood pressure screening, a low-salt diet, and medication; but only 73.5 percent of middle-aged adults with hypertension are aware of having the condition, only 61 percent are under treatment, and in only 40.5 percent is the condition under control (Glover et al., 2005).

Hypertension is 60 percent more prevalent in Europe than in the United States and Canada (Wolf-Maier et al., 2003). The proportion of the world's population with high blood pressure is expected to increase from one-quarter to one-third by 2025, leading to a predicted epidemic of cardiovascular disease, which already is responsible for 30 percent of all deaths worldwide (Kearney et al., 2005).

hypertension Chronically high blood pressure.

In the United States, cancer has replaced heart disease as the leading cause of death between ages 45 and 64 (Heron & Smith, 2007). Overall, death rates have declined sharply since the 1970s for people in this age bracket, in large part because of improvements in treatment of heart attack patients (Hoyert, Arias, Smith, Murphy, & Kochanek, 2001; Rosamond et al., 1998). Chest pain is the most common symptom of a heart attack in both men and women, but women may experience other symptoms, such as back and jaw pain, nausea and vomiting, indigestion, difficult breathing, or palpitations (Patel, Rosengren, & Ekman, 2004).

The prevalence of **diabetes** doubled in the 1990s (Weinstein et al., 2004), making it the fourth leading cause of death in middle age (NCHS, 2006). The most common type, mature-onset (type II) diabetes, typically develops after age 30 and becomes more prevalent with age. Unlike juvenile-onset (type-I), or insulin-dependent, diabetes, in which the level of blood sugar rises because the body does not produce enough insulin, in mature-onset diabetes glucose levels rise because the cells lose their ability to use the insulin the body produces. As a result, the body may try to compensate by producing too much insulin. People with mature-onset diabetes often do not realize they have it until they develop such serious complications as heart disease, stroke, blindness, kidney disease, or loss of limbs (American Diabetes Association, 1992).

Behavioral Influences on Health

As in young adulthood, nutrition, smoking, alcohol and drug use, and physical activity continue to affect health in middle age (Lachman, 2004) and beyond. People who do not smoke, exercise regularly, drink alcohol only in moderation, and eat plenty of fruits and vegetables have four times less mortality risk in midlife and old age—equivalent to 14 years' difference—than people who do not follow those behaviors (Khaw et al., 2008). In fact, they not only live longer but have shorter periods of disability at the end of life (Vita, Terry, Hubert, & Fries, 1998). Middle-aged men and women who stop smoking lessen their risk of heart disease and stroke (AHA, 1995; Kawachi et al., 1993; Stamler et al., 1993; Wannamethee, Shaper, Whincup, & Walker, 1995). Obesity, lack of exercise, and sedentary behavior such as watching television are associated with heightened risk of diabetes (Hu, Li, Colditz, Willett, & Manson, 2003; Weinstein et al., 2004).

Excess weight in middle age increases the risk of impaired health and death, even in healthy people (Yan et al., 2006) and those who have never smoked (Adams et al., 2006). In a 12-year prospective study of 1,213,829 Korean adults, ages 30 to 95, those who were either overweight or underweight had higher death rates than those of normal weight (Jee et al., 2006). Even small changes in weight can make a big difference (Byers, 2006).

Physical activity in midlife can increase the chances of remaining mobile in old age (Patel et al., 2006). It also helps fend off mortality. Among a nationally representative sample of 9,824 U.S. adults ages 51 to 61 in 1992, those who engaged in regular moderate or vigorous exercise were about 35 percent less likely to die in the next eight years than those with sedentary lifestyles. Those with cardiovascular risk factors, such as smoking, diabetes, high blood pressure, and a history of coronary artery disease, benefited most from being physically active (Richardson, Kriska, Lantz, & Hayward, 2004). As little as 72 minutes of exercise each week can significantly increase fitness in previously sedentary women (Church, Earnest, Skinner, & Blair, 2007).

Indirect influences, such as socioeconomic status, race/ethnicity, and gender, also continue to affect health. So do social relationships (Ryff, Singer, & Palmersheim,

2004). Another important influence is stress, whose cumulative effects on both physical and mental health often begin to appear in middle age (Aldwin & Levenson, 2001).

Socioeconomic Status and Health

Social inequalities continue to affect health in middle age (Marmot & Fuhrer, 2004). People with low socioeconomic status tend to have poorer health, shorter life expectancy, more activity limitations due to chronic disease, lower well-being, and more restricted access to health care than people with higher SES (Spiro, 2001). In the MIDUS study, low SES was linked with self-reported health status, overweight, and psychological well-being (Marmot & Fuhrer, 2004). In a follow-up study of 2,606 stroke patients, SES affected the likelihood of death, independent of the severity of the stroke (Arrich, Lalouschek, & Müllner, 2005).

In part, the reasons for the connection between SES and health may be psychosocial. People with low SES tend to have more negative emotions and thoughts and live in more stressful environments (Gallo & Matthews, 2003). People with higher SES tend to have a greater sense of control over what happens to them as they age; they tend to choose healthier lifestyles and seek medical attention and social support when they need it (Lachman & Firth, 2004; Marmot & Fuhrer, 2004; Whitbourne, 2001). However, there are wide individual differences in health among low-SES adults. Protective influences include the quality of social relationships and the level of religious engagement from childhood on (Ryff, Singer, & Palmersheim, 2004).

As we mentioned in Chapter 13, many poor people lack health insurance. In a prospective national study of 7,577 adults who were 51 to 61 years old in 1992, those without health insurance were 63 percent more likely to show a decline in health during the next four years and 23 percent more likely to develop problems in walking or climbing stairs (Baker, Sudano, Albert, Borawski, & Dor, 2001).

Race/Ethnicity and Health

Racial/ethnic disparities in health have decreased in the United States since 1990, but substantial differences persist (Bach et al., 2002; Keppel, Pearcy, & Wagener, 2002). As in young adulthood, overall death rates in middle age are higher for African Americans than for white, Hispanic, Asian, and Native Americans (Kochanek et al., 2004).

Hypertension is 50 percent more prevalent among African Americans than among white Americans. During 1999–2002, 40.5 percent of U.S. non-Hispanic blacks had hypertension, as compared with 27.4 percent of non-Hispanic whites and 25.1 percent of Mexican Americans. On the other hand, Mexican Americans are less likely to have their blood pressure under control (Glover et al., 2005). Non-Hispanic blacks are more likely than non-Hispanic whites to be obese and to have poor cardiovascular fitness and are less likely to participate in regular, moderate physical activity (Lavie, Kuruvanka, Milani, Prasad, & Ventura, 2004; Office of Minority Health, Centers for Disease Control, 2005).

Probably the largest single underlying factor in African Americans' health problems is poverty, which is related to poor nutrition, substandard housing, and poor access to health care (Otten, Teutsch, Williamson, & Marks, 1990; Smedley & Smedley, 2005). Still, poverty cannot be the sole explanation because the death rate of middle-aged Hispanic Americans, who also are disproportionately poor, is lower than that of white Americans (Kochanek et al., 2004).

✓ **Checkpoint**

Can you . . .

◆ Describe the typical health status in middle age, and identify health concerns that become more prevalent at this time?

◆ Discuss behavioral, socioeconomic, and racial/ethnic factors in health and mortality at middle age?

Hispanic Americans, like African Americans, do have a disproportionate incidence of stroke, liver disease, diabetes, HIV infection, homicide, and cancers of the cervix and stomach (Office of Minority Health, Centers for Disease Control, 2005). They are less likely than non-Hispanic whites to have health insurance and a regular source of health care. They are also less likely to be screened for cholesterol and for breast, cervical, and colorectal cancers or to receive influenza and pneumonia vaccines (Balluz, Okoro, & Strine, 2004).

Research on the human genome has found distinctive variations in the DNA code among people of European, African, and Chinese ancestry (Hinds et al., 2005). These variations are linked to predispositions to certain diseases, from cancer to obesity. This research may ultimately open the way to targeted treatments or preventive measures.

Gender and Health

Which are healthier: women or men? We know that women have a higher life expectancy than men and lower death rates throughout life (Miniño, Heron, Murphy, & Kochanek, 2007; see Chapter 17). Women's greater longevity has been attributed to genetic protection given by the second X chromosome (which men do not have) and, before menopause, to beneficial effects of the female hormone estrogen, particularly on cardiovascular health (Rodin & Ickovics, 1990; USDHHS, 1992). However, psychosocial and cultural factors, such as men's greater propensity for risk taking, also may play a part (Liebman, 1995; Schardt, 1995).

Despite their longer life, women are more likely than men to report being in fair or poor health, and they go to doctors or seek outpatient or emergency room care more often. Men are less likely to seek professional help for health problems, but they have longer hospital stays, and their health problems are more likely to be chronic and life-threatening (Addis & Mahalik, 2003; Kroenke & Spitzer, 1998; NCHS, 2004; Rodin & Ickovics, 1990). According to the MIDUS survey, middle-aged women tend to report more specific symptoms and chronic conditions, and men are more likely to report alcohol or drug problems (Cleary, Zaborski, & Ayanian, 2004).

Women's greater tendency to seek medical care does not necessarily mean that they are in worse health than men, nor that they are imagining ailments or are preoccupied with illness. They may simply be more health-conscious. Women devote more effort to maintaining their health (Cleary, Zaborski, & Ayanian, 2004). Men may feel that admitting illness is not masculine, and seeking help means a loss of control (Addis & Mahalik, 2003). It may well be that the better care women take of themselves helps them live longer than men.

Public awareness of men's health issues has increased. The availability of impotence treatment and of screening tests for prostate cancer is bringing more men into doctor's offices. In a 40-year prospective cohort study of 5,820 middle-aged Japanese American men in Honolulu, 42 percent survived to age 85. Good grip strength together with avoidance of overweight, smoking, hypertension, and

Women's greater longevity has been attributed to genetic protection given by the second X chromosome (which men do not have) and, before menopause, to beneficial effects of the female hormone estrogen, particularly on cardiovascular health.

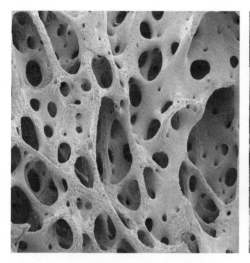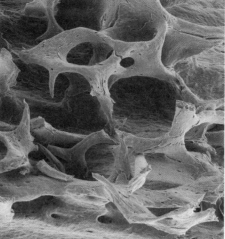

Images of normal (left) *and osteoporotic* (right) *bones.*

high blood sugar (which can lead to diabetes) increased the chances of long and healthy lives.

Meanwhile, as women's lifestyles have become more like men's, so—in some ways—have their health patterns. Fewer people of both sexes are now dying of lung cancer (Espey et al., 2007). The gender gap in deaths from heart disease has reversed, perhaps in part because of the sharper decline in men's smoking and women's greater tendency to overweight and sedentary lifestyles. This trend may help explain why the difference between women's and men's life expectancy shrank from 7.6 years in 1970 to 5.2 years in 2005, according to preliminary data (Kung, Hoyert, Xu, & Murphy, 2007; Kochanek et al., 2004; NCHS, 2004).

Women are at increased risk after menopause, particularly for osteoporosis, breast cancer, and heart disease. With longer life spans, women in many developed countries now can expect to live half their adult lives after menopause. As a result, increasing attention is being paid to women's health issues at this time of life (Barrett-Connor et al., 2002).

Bone Loss and Osteoporosis   In women, bone loss rapidly accelerates in the first five to ten years after menopause as levels of estrogen, which helps in calcium absorption, fall. Extreme bone loss may lead to **osteoporosis** ("porous bones"), a condition in which the bones become thin and brittle as a result of calcium depletion. Common signs of osteoporosis are marked loss in height and a hunchbacked posture that results from compression and collapse of a weakened spinal column. In a national observational study of 200,160 postmenopausal women, almost half had previously undetected low bone mineral density, and 7 percent of these women had osteoporosis (Siris et al., 2001). Osteoporosis is a major cause of broken bones in old age and can greatly affect quality of life and even survival (NIH Consensus Development Panel on Osteoporosis Prevention, Diagnosis, and Therapy, 2001; NIH, 2003; Siris et al., 2001).

Almost 3 out of 4 cases of osteoporosis occur in white women, most often in those with fair skin, small frame, low weight and BMI, and a family history of the condition, and those whose ovaries were surgically removed before menopause (NIA, 1993; NIH Consensus Development Panel, 2001; "Should You Take," 1994; Siris et al., 2001). Other risk factors, besides age, include smoking and lack of exercise (Siris et al., 2001; Table 15-3). A predisposition to osteoporosis seems to have a genetic basis, so measurement of bone density is an especially wise precaution for women with affected family members (Prockop,

osteoporosis Condition in which the bones become thin and brittle as a result of rapid calcium depletion.

Table 15-3	Risk Factors for Osteoporosis

Factors You Cannot Change

Being a woman
Getting older
Being Caucasian or Asian
Having a family history of fractures

Factors You Can Change

Low estrogen levels in women, low testosterone levels in men
Anorexia
Lifetime diet low in calcium and vitamin D
Use of certain medications, such as steroids and some anticonvulsants
Inactive lifestyle or prolonged bed rest
Cigarette smoking
Excessive alcohol use

Source: NIH, 2003.

1998; Uitterlinden et al., 1998). However, good lifestyle habits make a significant difference, especially if started early in life (NIH Consensus Development Panel, 2001).

Even if bone loss has started, it can be slowed or even reversed with proper nutrition, weight-bearing exercise, and avoidance of smoking (Barrett-Connor et al., 2002; Eastell, 1998). High-intensity strength training and resistance training have proven particularly effective (Layne & Nelson, 1999; Nelson et al., 1994). Women over age 40 should get 1,000 to 1,500 milligrams of dietary calcium a day, along with recommended daily amounts of vitamin D, which helps the body absorb calcium (NIA, 1993). Studies have found that calcium and vitamin D supplements improve bone density (Jackson et al., 2006).

Alendronate (Fosamax) and risedronate (Actonel) have been found to reduce hip fractures (Black et al., 2007). Raloxifene, one of a new group of designer estrogens, seems to favorably affect bone density and possibly cholesterol levels and reduce the risk of genetic breast cancer (Barrett-Connor et al., 2002). A once-a-year intravenous infusion of zoledronic acid can reduce the risk of vertebral, hip, and other fractures (Black et al., 2007; Compston, 2007). Other FDA-approved medications for osteoporosis include teriparatide (Forteo) and calcitonin (Miacalcin or Calcimar). However, most of these drugs have side effects, and their long-term effects are unknown (NIH, 2003).

Breast Cancer and Mammography One in 8 American women and 1 in 9 British women develop breast cancer at some point in their lives (American Cancer Society [ACS], 2001; Pearson, 2002). As with other cancers, the chances of developing breast cancer increase with age (Barrett-Connor et al., 2002).

About 5 to 10 percent of breast cancer cases are thought to be hereditary, resulting from inherited mutations. The most common of these are mutations of the *BRCA1* and *BRCA2* genes. Women who have a *BRCA1* or *BRCA2* mutation have as much as an 80 percent chance of developing breast cancer (ACS, 2007).

However, the vast majority of breast cancer cases are environmentally influenced. Once found mostly in affluent countries, breast cancer is becoming a worldwide problem as Western lifestyles move into the developing world (Porter,

2008). Overweight women, those who drink alcohol, those who experienced early menarche and late menopause, those with a family history of breast cancer, and those who have no children or who bore children later in life have a greater risk of breast cancer, whereas those who are moderately physically active and eat low-fat, high-fiber diets are at less risk (ACS, 2007; Barrett-Connor et al., 2002; Clavel-Chapelton et al., 2002; McTiernan et al., 2003; U.S. Preventive Services Task Force, 2002). Weight gain, especially after menopause, increases a woman's risk of breast cancer, and weight loss decreases the risk (Eliassen, Colditz, Rosner, Willett, & Hankinson, 2006).

Advances in diagnosis and treatment have dramatically improved prospects for breast cancer patients. Fully 98 percent of U.S. women with breast cancer now survive at least five years if the cancer is caught before it spreads (Ries et al., 2007). Although benefits of **mammography,** diagnostic X-ray examination of the breasts, appear to be greatest for women over 50, a U.S. Preventive Services Task Force (2002) recommends screening every one or two years for all women beginning at age 40, especially those with a family history of breast cancer before menopause.

Tamoxifen, a drug that blocks the action of estrogen, is used to treat advanced breast cancer. It also can be preventive in women at high risk for the disease. In women who already have breast cancer, it can reduce the risk of recurrence or of a new cancer in the other breast. (National Cancer Institute, 2002).

Getting more exercise and eating a low-fat diet can lower a woman's risk for breast cancer.

mammography   Diagnostic X-ray examination of the breasts.

Hormone Therapy   Because the most troublesome physical effects of menopause are linked to reduced levels of estrogen, **hormone therapy (HT)** in the form of artificial estrogen has been prescribed to relieve hot flashes, night sweats, and other symptoms. Estrogen taken alone increases the risk of uterine cancer, so women whose uterus has not been surgically removed are usually given estrogen in combination with progestin, a form of the female hormone progesterone. Now, however, medical evidence challenges some of HT's presumed benefits and bears out some suspected risks.

On the positive side, HT, when started at menopause and continued for at least five years, can prevent or stop bone loss after menopause (Barrett-Connor et al., 2002; Lindsay, Gallagher, Kleerekoper, & Pickar, 2002) and can prevent hip and other bone fractures (Writing Group for the Women's Health Initiative Investigators, 2002). However, bone loss resumes within three years if and when HT stops (Barrett-Connor et al., 2002; Heiss et al., 2008) and, as we have discussed, can be treated in safer ways.

Contrary to early correlational research, which suggested that HT cut the risk of heart disease (Davidson, 1995; Ettinger, Friedman, Bush, & Quesenberry, 1996; Grodstein, 1996), a large-scale randomized, controlled study found that hormone treatment either provides *no* cardiovascular benefit to high-risk women—those who already have heart disease or related conditions—or actually *increases* the risks (Grady et al., 2002; Hulley et al, 2002; Petitti, 2002). Then, a large-scale randomized, controlled trial of estrogen plus progestin in healthy women was stopped after five years because of evidence that the risks of breast cancer, heart attack, stroke, and blood clots exceeded the benefits (NIH, 2005; Wassertheil-Smoller et al., 2003; Writing Group for the Women's Health Initiative Investigators, 2002). The cardiovascular risks dropped back to normal within three years after the end of the trial (Heiss et al., 2008). However, age may make a difference. The results of the Women's Health Initiative (WHI) study were driven

hormone therapy (HT) Treatment with artificial estrogen, sometimes in combination with the hormone progesterone, to relieve or prevent symptoms caused by decline in estrogen levels after menopause.

mainly by effects on older women (Mendelsohn & Karas, 2007). Estrogen therapy does reduce clogging of the coronary arteries in women in their fifties, who have recently gone through menopause, and may be safer for women that age (Manson et al., 2007).

Still, the American Heart Association now advises *against* HT, though the decision should, of course, be made in consultation with a physician (Mosca et al., 2001). Lifestyle changes such as losing weight and stopping smoking, together with any necessary drugs to lower cholesterol and blood pressure, appear to be wiser courses for heart disease prevention in most women (Manson & Martin, 2001).

Unlike the cardiovascular risks, risks of breast cancer and other cancers *rose* slightly after the WHI treatment ended. In fact, the combined risk of all cancers increased throughout and after the trial (Heiss et al., 2008). Heightened risk of breast cancer seems to occur mainly among current or recent estrogen users, and the risk increases with length of use (Chen, Weiss, Newcomb, Barlow, & White, 2002; Willett, Colditz, & Stampfer, 2000). Long-term estrogen use also has been associated with heightened risk of ovarian cancer (Lacey et al., 2002; Rodriguez, Patel, Calle, Jacob, & Thun, 2001) and gallbladder disease (Cirillo et al., 2005). Yet to be analyzed are WHI data on women with hysterectomies who used only estrogen without progestin (Heiss et al., 2008). Another large-scale study found the breast cancer risk of estrogen alone less than when combined with progestin (Schairer et al., 2000).

Finally, studies have found, contrary to earlier research (Zandi et al., 2002), that estrogen—either alone or with progestin—does not improve cognition or prevent cognitive impairment after age 65. Instead, it *increases* the risk of dementia or cognitive decline (Espeland et al., 2004; Rapp et al., 2003; Shumaker et al., 2003, 2004). However, in a randomized one-year study of 5,692 postmenopausal women in Australia, New Zealand, and the United Kingdom, HT improved health-related quality of life (Welton et al., 2008).

✔ **Checkpoint**

Can you . . .

◆ Discuss changes in women's health risks after menopause, and weigh the risks and benefits of hormone replacement therapy?

stress Response to physical or psychological demands.

stressors Perceived environmental demands that may produce stress.

Stress in Middle Age

Stress is the damage that occurs when perceived environmental demands, or **stressors,** exceed a person's capacity to cope with them (Ray, 2004). The body's capacity to adapt to stress involves the brain, which perceives danger (either real or imagined); the adrenal glands, which mobilize the body to fight it; and the immune system, which provides the defenses.

People early in middle age tend to experience higher and more frequent stress levels and different kinds of stressors than do younger or older adults. According to a nationally representative survey (American Psychological Association, 2007), 39 percent of U.S. 35- to 54-year-olds report extreme stress 1 in 4 days each month. Chief stressors for this age group are family relationships, work, money, and housing. Younger adults, ages 18 to 34, and late middle-aged and older adults, age 55 and up, have somewhat lower stress levels, with 29 percent and 25 percent, respectively, reporting high stress.

Losing a job can be a huge stressor. For these people waiting in line to apply for unemployment compensation, it can result in loss of status, purpose, self-esteem, and control over their lives.

Younger respondents are more stressed by unhealthy behaviors, such as smoking, losing sleep, and skipping meals. For older adults, as we discuss in Chapter 18, stress tends to center on issues related to health and aging.

Similarly, in the MIDUS study, middle-aged adults reported more frequent, multiple, and severe stressors than did older adults and a greater degree of overload and disruption in their daily lives. Stress in middle age tended to come from role changes: career transitions, grown children leaving home, and the renegotiation of family relationships (Almeida & Horn, 2004; Almeida, Serido, & McDonald, 2006). The frequency of interpersonal tensions, such as arguments with spouses, decreased with age, but stressors involving, for example, a sick friend or relative increased. Unique to midlife was a significant increase in stressors posing financial risk or involving children. However, middle-aged people reported fewer stressors over which they had little or no control (Almeida & Horn, 2004).

Middle-aged people may be better equipped to cope with stress than people in other age groups (Lachman, 2004). They have a better sense of what they can do to change stressful circumstances and may be better able to accept what cannot be changed. They also have learned more effective strategies for avoiding or minimizing stress. For example, instead of having to worry about running out of gas on a long trip, they are likely to check to make sure the gas tank is full before starting out (Aldwin & Levenson, 2001).

Women tend to report more extreme stress than men (35 percent compared to 28 percent) and to be more concerned about stress (American Psychological Association 2007). The classic stress response—*fight or flight*—may be primarily masculine, activated in part by testosterone. Women's response pattern is more typically *tend and befriend*—nurturant activities that promote safety, and reliance on social networks to exchange resources and responsibilities. These patterns, activated by oxytocin and other female reproductive hormones, may have evolved through natural selection and may draw on women's involvement in attachment and caregiving (Taylor et al., 2000; Taylor, 2006).

How Stress Affects Health   The more stressful the changes that take place in a person's life, the greater the likelihood of serious illness within the next year or two. Change—even positive change—can be stressful, and some people react to stress by getting sick. That was the finding of a landmark study in which two psychiatrists, on the basis of interviews with 5,000 hospital patients, ranked the stressfulness of important life-changing events, such as divorce, the death of a spouse or other family member, or loss of a job, which had preceded their illness, and then tried the resulting scale on a healthy population (Holmes & Rahe, 1976). About 50 percent the people with between 150 and 300 "life change units" (LCUs) in a single year, and about 70 percent of those with 300 or more LCUs, became ill. This classic study became the basis of the widely used Life Changes Stress Test, or Social Readjustment Rating Scale.

Stress from most life changes is increasing, according to an online survey based on selected items from the Life Changes scale (First 30 Days, 2008; Table 15-4). Rahe found that the stress of adjusting to life events was 45 percent higher in 1997 than in 1967 (Miller & Rahe, 1997).

Daily stressors—irritations, frustrations, and overloads (Figure 15-2)—may be less severe in their impact than life changes, but their buildup also can affect health and emotional adjustment (Almeida et al., 2006; American Psychological Association, 2007). Stress is under increasing scrutiny as a factor in such age-related diseases as hypertension, heart ailments, stroke, diabetes, osteoporosis, peptic ulcers, depression, HIV/AIDS, and cancer (Baum, Cacioppo, Melamed,

Table 15-4	Stress from Life Changes, United States, 1967 and 2007	
	Life Change Units (LCUs)	
	1967	**2007**
Death of spouse	100	80
Death of family member	63	70
Divorce/separation	73/65	66
Job layoff or firing	47	62
Birth of child/pregnancy	40	60
Death of a friend	37	58
Marriage	50	50
Retirement	45	49
Marital reconciliation	45	48
Change job field	36	47
Child leaves home	29	43

Note: A comparison of First 30 Days findings and the Social Readjustment Rating Scale, Thomas H. Holmes and Richard H. Rahe, *Journal of Psychosomatic Research.* Stress levels from many life changes have increased. Because the study methods differ, findings should be interpreted as relative and directional.

Source: First 30 Days, 2008.

Figure 15-2

Significant sources of stress, United States, 2007. Work and money are greater stressors than relationships or health, a national survey found.

(Source: American Psychological Association, 2007.)

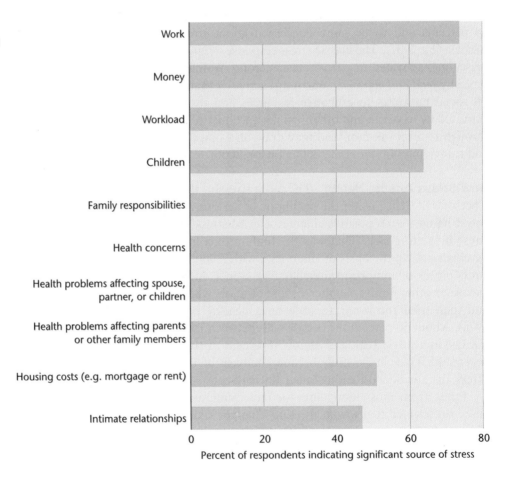

Percent of respondents indicating significant source of stress

Gallant, & Travis, 1995; Cohen, Janicki-Deverts, & Miller, 2007; Levenstein, Ackerman, Kiecolt-Glaser, & Dubois, 1999; Light et al., 1999; Sapolsky, 1992; Wittstein et al., 2005).

How does stress produce illness? And why do some people handle stress better than others? Chronic stressors may activate the immune system, leading to persistent inflammation and disease (Miller & Blackwell, 2006). However, many studies have shown that only a small percentage of persons infected with a pathogen develop symptoms of illness. Illness occurs only when the strength of the infection exceeds the body's ability to cope with it. Genetic factors may be involved. In a longitudinal study of 847 New Zealanders followed from birth, nearly 43 percent of those who experienced multiple stressful events between ages 21 and 26 and who had a stress-sensitive version of the serotonin transponder gene developed depression, compared with only 17 percent of those with a stress-protective version of the gene (Caspi et al., 2003).

Distinct types of stressors affect the immune system differently. Acute, or short-term, stress, such as the challenge of taking a test or speaking before an audience, strengthens the immune system; but intense or prolonged stress, such as results from poverty or disability, can weaken or break it down, increasing susceptibility to illness (Segerstrom & Miller, 2004). Research has found suppressed immune function in breast cancer patients (Compas & Luecken, 2002), abused women, hurricane survivors, and men with a history of post-traumatic stress disorder (PTSD) (Harvard Medical School, 2002). Unsafe neighborhoods with poor-quality housing and few resources can produce or worsen depression (Cutrona, Wallace, & Wesner, 2006). As we will discuss in Chapter 17, severe long-term stress can cause genetic aging (Epel et al., 2004).

Stress may harm health indirectly, through other lifestyle factors. People under stress may sleep less, smoke and drink more, eat poorly, and pay too little attention to their health (American Psychological Association, 2007) even though regular exercise, good nutrition, at least seven hours of sleep a night, and frequent socializing are associated with lower stress (Baum et al., 1995). People who believe they have control over their lives tend to engage in healthier behaviors and have fewer illnesses and better physical functioning (Lachman & Firth, 2004).

How do people deal with a traumatic event? Surprisingly, the most common outcome is resilience. After the 9/11 attacks, more than 65 percent of a random sample of New Yorkers showed resilience. Even among those personally exposed, resilience did not fall below 33 percent (Bonanno, Galea, Bucciarelli, & Vlahov, 2006). Resilient people who sustain a disruption in their normal lives somehow manage to keep functioning as effectively, or almost as effectively, as ever. Supportive relationships, along with a person's own ability to adapt flexibly and pragmatically to challenges, contribute to resilience (Bonanno, 2005).

✔ **Checkpoint**

Can you . . .

◆ Discuss causes and effects of stress and sources of stress in middle age?

◆ Explain how stress affects health?

Emotions and Health

The ancient proverb of Solomon, "A merry heart doeth good like medicine" (Proverbs 17:22), is being borne out by contemporary research. Negative emotions, such as anxiety and despair, are often associated with poor physical and mental health, and positive emotions, such as hope, with good health and longer life (Ray, 2004; Salovey, Rothman, Detweiler, & Steward, 2000; Spiro, 2001). Because the brain interacts with all of the body's biological systems, feelings and beliefs affect bodily functions, including the functioning of the immune system (Ray, 2004; Richman et al., 2005). Negative moods seem to suppress immune functioning and increase susceptibility to illness; positive moods seem to enhance immune functioning (Salovey et al., 2000).

Positive emotion may protect against the development of disease. When adult volunteers were exposed to a virus that can cause colds, those with a positive emotional outlook were less likely to get sick (Cohen, Doyle, Turner, Alper, & Skoner,

A positive outlook may guard against disease and buffer the impact of stress. People with a positive outlook tend to take care of their health.

2003). In a study of patients in a large medical practice, two positive emotions—hope and curiosity—were found to lessen the likelihood of having or developing hypertension, diabetes, or respiratory tract infections (Richman et al., 2005).

However, we can't be sure that outcomes such as this are *caused* by the emotions shown. People with a positive emotional outlook are likely to engage in more healthful practices, such as regular sleep and exercise, and to pay more attention to health-related information. Positive emotions also may affect health indirectly by softening the impact of stressful life events (Cohen & Pressman, 2006; Richman et al., 2005).

Not only specific emotions, but also personality traits seem to be related to health (Ray, 2004; T. W. Smith, 2006: Spiro, 2001). In prospective studies, neuroticism and hostility are consistently associated with serious illness and reduced longevity, whereas optimism and conscientiousness are assocated with better health and longer life. However, the underlying mechanisms have yet to be identified and tested (T. W. Smith, 2006).

Mental Health

Middle-aged adults are more likely than younger or older adults to suffer from serious psychological distress: extreme sadness, nervousness, restlessness, hopelessness, and feelings of worthlessness much of the time. Adults with serious psychological distress are more likely than their peers to be diagnosed with heart disease, diabetes, arthritis, or stroke and to report needing help with activities of daily living, such as bathing and dressing (Pratt, Dey, & Cohen, 2007).

In a large national study of middle-aged women, about 1 in 4 showed depressive symptoms. As in previous studies, prevalence was highest among African American and Hispanic American women and lowest among Chinese American and Japanese American women. Differences in SES and other risk factors may explain these racial/ethnic discrepancies. Women who were less educated and who had difficulty affording basic necessities were more likely to have depressive symptoms. So, too, were those who called their health poor or fair and those who were under stress or lacked social support—and these factors may be more important than the more obvious marker of SES (Bromberger, Harlow, Avis, Kravitz, & Cordal, 2004).

Checkpoint

Can you . . .

♦ Explain how emotions and personality may affect health?

♦ Identify risk factors for psychological distress and depressive symptoms?

Table 15-5	Tests of Primary Mental Abilities Given in Seattle Longitudinal Study of Adult Intelligence		
Test	**Ability Measured**	**Task**	**Type of Intelligence***
Verbal meaning	Recognition and understanding of words	Find synonym by matching stimulus word with another word from multiple-choice list	Crystallized
Word fluency	Retrieving words from long-term memory	Think of as many words as possible beginning with a given letter, in a set time period	Part crystallized, part fluid
Number	Performing computations	Do simple addition problems	Crystallized
Spatial orientation	Manipulating objects mentally in two-dimensional space	Select rotated examples of figure to match stimulus figure	Fluid
Inductive reasoning	Identifying patterns and inferring principles and rules for solving logical problems	Complete a letter series	Fluid
Perceptual speed	Making quick, accurate discriminations between visual stimuli	Identify matching and nonmatching images flashed on a computer screen	Fluid

*Fluid and crystallized intelligence are defined in the next section.

Sources: Schale, 1989; Willis 8 Schaie, 1999.

COGNITIVE DEVELOPMENT

What happens to cognitive abilities in middle age? Do they improve or decline, or both? Do people develop distinctive ways of thinking at this time of life? How does age affect the ability to solve problems, to learn, to create, and to perform on the job?

Measuring Cognitive Abilities in Middle Age

The status of cognitive abilities in middle age has been a subject of debate. Studies using different methodologies and measuring different characteristics have had somewhat different findings. Largely cross-sectional studies based on the Wechsler Adult Intelligence Scale, a psychometric instrument (see Chapter 17), show declines in both verbal and performance abilities beginning in young adulthood. However, two other lines of research, K. Warner Schaie's Seattle Longitudinal Study and Horn and Cattell's studies of fluid and crystallized intelligence, have produced more encouraging findings.

Guidepost 4

What cognitive gains and losses occur during middle age?

Schaie: The Seattle Longitudinal Study

Cognitively speaking, in many respects middle-aged people are in their prime. The Seattle Longitudinal Study of Adult Intelligence, conducted by K. Warner Schaie and his colleagues (Schaie, 1990, 1994, 1996a, 1996b, 2005; Willis & Schaie, 1999, 2006), demonstrates this fact.

Although this ongoing study is called longitudinal, it uses sequential methods by measuring successive cohorts. The study began in 1956 with 500 randomly chosen participants: 25 men and 25 women in each five-year age bracket from 22 to 67. Participants took timed tests of six primary mental abilities. (Table 15-5 gives definitions and sample tasks for each ability.) Every seven years, the existing participants were retested and a new cohort was added.

Figure 15-3

Cohort differences in scores on tests of primary mental abilities. More recent cohorts scored higher on inductive reasoning, word fluency, and spatial orientation. (Source: From K. W. Schaie, *Developmental Influences on Adult Intelligence: The seattle Longitudinal Study* (2005), Fig. 6.1, p. 137. By permission of Oxford University Press, Inc.)

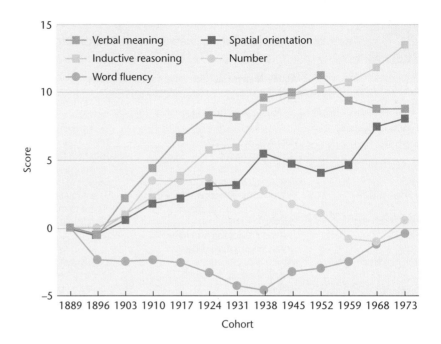

The researchers found no uniform patterns of age-related change, either among individuals or across cognitive abilities (Schaie, 1994, 2005; Willis & Schaie, 2006). Although both gains and losses occurred, several abilities peaked during middle age, and verbal meaning improved into old age. Only 13 to 17 percent of adults declined in number, memory recall, or verbal fluency between ages 39 and 53. Although most participants showed remarkable stability, one might decline early, while another might show great plasticity (Willis & Schaie, 2006).

Despite such wide individual differences, most participants in the Seattle study showed *no* significant reduction in most abilities until after age 60, and then not in most areas. Virtually no one declined on all fronts, and many people improved in some areas (Schaie, 1994, 2005). Possibly because of improvements in education, healthy lifestyles, and other positive environmental influences, successive cohorts have scored progressively higher at the same ages on most abilities. However, numerical ability declined after the cohort born in 1924, except for an uptick for the cohort born in 1973. Verbal meaning, the strongest ability in earlier cohorts, began to decline with the cohort born in 1952. Word fluency, which dropped gradually in earlier cohorts, has increased gradually beginning with the cohort born in 1938 (Willis & Schaie, 2006; Figure 15-3).

Individuals who scored highest tended to have high educational levels, to have flexible personalities, to be in intact families, to pursue cognitively complex occupations and other activities, to be married to someone more cognitively advanced, and to be satisfied with their accomplishments (Schaie, 1994, 2005; Willis & Schaie, 2006). Given the strong cognitive performance of most middle-agers, evidence of substantial cognitive decline in persons younger than 60 may indicate a neurological problem (Schaie, 2005; Willis & Shaie, 1999). In particular, midlife decline in memory recall and verbal fluency, a measure of executive functioning, can predict cognitive impairment in old age (Willis & Schaie, 2006).

In another longitudinal study of 384 Baltimore adults age 50 and above, those with larger social networks better maintained their cognitive functioning 12 years later. It is not clear, however, whether more social contacts produce or merely reflect better cognitive functioning. If the former, the benefit may result from the wider variety of informational and interactional opportunities that a wide circle of friends and families provides (Holtzman et al., 2004).

Our growing knowledge about the brain's genetic aging may shed light on patterns of cognitive decline. Researchers who examined postmortem brain tissue from 30 people ages 26 to 106 identified two groups of genes that tend to become damaged with age. Among these were genes involved in learning and memory. Middle-aged brains showed the greatest variability, some exhibiting gene patterns much like those of young adults and others showing gene patterns more like older adults (Lu et al., 2004). This finding may help account for the wide range of individual differences in cognitive functioning in midlife.

Horn and Cattell: Fluid and Crystallized Intelligence

Another line of research (Cattell, 1965; Horn, 1967, 1968, 1970, 1982a, 1982b; Horn & Hofer, 1992) has distinguished between two aspects of intelligence: *fluid* and *crystallized*. **Fluid intelligence** is the ability to solve novel problems that require little or no previous knowledge, such as discovering the pattern in a sequence of figures. It involves perceiving relations, forming concepts, and drawing inferences, abilities largely determined by neurological status. **Crystallized intelligence** is the ability to remember and use information acquired over a lifetime, such as finding a synonym for a word. It is measured by tests of vocabulary, general information, and responses to social situations and dilemmas, abilities that depend largely on education and cultural experience.

These two types of intelligence follow different paths. Typically, fluid intelligence has been found to peak in young adulthood, whereas crystallized intelligence improves through middle age and often until near the end of life (Horn, 1982a, 1982b; Horn & Donaldson, 1980). However, much of this research is cross-sectional and thus may at least partly reflect generational differences rather than changes with age. The Seattle study's sequential findings were somewhat different. Although fluid abilities did decline earlier than crystallized abilities, losses in certain fluid abilities—inductive reasoning and spatial orientation—did not set in until the mid-fifties (Willis & Schaie, 1999).

One fluid ability that is generally agreed to peak quite early, beginning in the twenties, is perceptual speed. Working memory capacity also begins to decline. However, these changes are gradual and do not necessarily cause functional impairment (Lachman, 2004; Willis & Schaie, 1999). Physical activity seems to improve cognitive functioning, particularly fluid intelligence (Singh-Manoux, Hillsdon, Brunner, & Marmot, 2005).

The Distinctiveness of Adult Cognition

Instead of measuring the same cognitive abilities at different ages, some developmental scientists find distinctive qualities in the thinking of mature adults. Some, working within the psychometric tradition, claim that accumulated knowledge changes the way fluid intelligence operates. Others, as we noted in Chapter 13, maintain that mature thought represents a new stage of cognitive development—a "special form of intelligence" (Sinnott, 1996, p. 361), which may underlie mature interpersonal skills and contribute to practical problem solving.

The Role of Expertise

Two young resident physicians in a hospital radiology laboratory examine a chest X-ray. They study an unusual white blotch on the left side. "Looks like a large tumor," one of them says finally. The other nods. Just then, a longtime

fluid intelligence Type of intelligence, proposed by Horn and Cattell, that is applied to novel problems and is relatively independent of educational and cultural influences.

crystallized intelligence Type of intelligence, proposed by Horn and Cattell, involving the ability to remember and use learned information; it is largely dependent on education and culture.

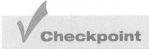

Checkpoint

Can you . . .

♦ Summarize results of the Seattle Longitudinal Study?

♦ Distinguish between fluid and crystallized intelligence, and tell how they are affected by age?

♦ Compare the findings of the Seattle study with those of Horn and Cattell?

Guidepost 5

Do mature adults think differently than younger people do?

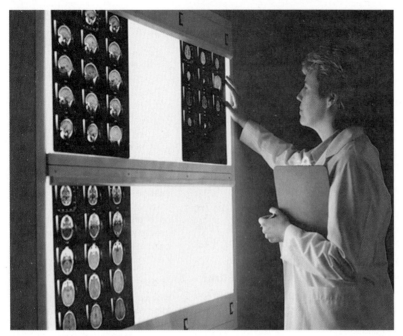

Expertise in interpreting X-rays, as in many other fields, depends on accumulated, specialized knowledge, which continues to increase with age. Experts often appear to be guided by intuition and cannot explain how they arrive at conclusions.

encapsulation In Hoyer's terminology, progressive dedication of information processing and fluid thinking to specific knowledge systems, making knowledge more readily accessible.

staff radiologist walks by and looks over their shoulders at the X-ray. "That patient has a collapsed lung and needs immediate surgery," he declares (Lesgold, 1983; Lesgold et al., 1988).

Why do mature adults show increasing competence in solving problems in their chosen fields? One answer seems to lie in *specialized knowledge,* or *expertise*—a form of crystallized intelligence.

Advances in expertise continue at least through middle adulthood and are relatively independent of general intelligence and of any declines in the brain's information-processing machinery. With experience, it has been suggested, information processing and fluid abilities become *encapsulated,* or dedicated to specific kinds of knowledge, making that knowledge easier to access, add to, and use. In other words, **encapsulation** captures fluid abilities for expert problem solving. Thus, although middle-aged people may take somewhat longer than younger people to process new information, in solving problems in their own fields they more than compensate with judgment developed from experience (Hoyer & Rybash, 1994; Rybash, Hoyer, & Roodin, 1986).

In one classic study (Ceci & Liker, 1986), researchers identified 30 middle-aged and older men who were avid horse-racing fans. On the basis of skill in picking winners, the investigators divided the men into two groups: "expert" and "nonexpert." The experts used a more sophisticated method of reasoning, incorporating interpretations of much interrelated information, whereas nonexperts used simpler, less successful methods. Superior reasoning was not related to IQ; there was no significant difference in average measured intelligence between the two groups, and experts with lower IQs used more complex reasoning than nonexperts with higher IQs.

Studies of people in such diverse occupations as chess players, street vendors, abacus counters, physics experts, hospitality workers, airline counter workers, and airplane pilots illustrate how specific knowledge contributes to superior performance in a particular domain (Billet, 2001) and can help buffer age-related declines in cognitive resources when solving problems in that domain (Morrow, Menard, Stine-Morrow, Teller, & Bryant, 2001).

Experts notice different aspects of a situation than novices do, and they process information and solve problems differently. Their thinking is often more flexible and adaptable. They assimilate and interpret new knowledge more efficiently by referring to a rich, highly organized storehouse of mental representations of what they already know. They sort information on the basis of underlying principles, rather than surface similarities and differences. And they are more aware of what they do *not* know (Charness & Schultetus, 1999; Goldman, Petrosino, & Cognition and Technology Group at Vanderbilt, 1999).

Cognitive performance is not the only ingredient of expertise. Problem solving occurs in a social context. Ability to make expert judgments depends on familiarity with the way things are done—with the expectations and demands of the job and the culture of the community or enterprise. Even concert pianists, who spend hours practicing in isolation, must adapt to various concert halls with different acoustics, to the musical conventions of the time and place, and to the musical tastes of their audiences (Billet, 2001).

Expert thinking often seems automatic and intuitive. Experts generally are not fully aware of the thought processes that lie behind their decisions (Charness & Schultetus, 1999; Dreyfus, 1993–1994; Rybash et al., 1986). They cannot readily explain how they arrive at a conclusion or where a nonexpert has gone wrong: The experienced radiologist could not see why the residents would even consider diagnosing a collapsed lung as a tumor. Such intuitive, experience-based thinking is also characteristic of what has been called postformal thought.

Integrative Thought

Although not limited to any particular period of adulthood, postformal thought (introduced in Chapter 13) seems well suited to the complex tasks, multiple roles, and perplexing choices and challenges of midlife, such as the need to synthesize and balance work and family demands (Sinnott, 1998, 2003). An important feature of postformal thought is its *integrative* nature. Mature adults integrate logic with intuition and emotion; they integrate conflicting facts and ideas; and they integrate new information with what they already know. They interpret what they read, see, or hear in terms of its meaning for them. Instead of accepting something at face value, they filter it through their life experience and previous learning.

In one study (C. Adams, 1991), early and late adolescents and middle-aged and older adults were asked to summarize a Sufi teaching tale. In the story, a stream was unable to cross a desert until a voice told it to let the wind carry it; the stream was dubious but finally agreed and was blown across. Adolescents recalled more details of the story than adults did, but their summaries were largely limited to repeating the story line. Adults, especially women, gave summaries that were rich in interpretation, integrating what was in the text with its psychological and metaphorical meaning for them, as in this response of a 39-year-old:

> I believe what this story was trying to say was that there are times when everyone needs help and must sometimes make changes to reach their goals. Some people may resist change for a long time until they realize that certain things are beyond their control and they need assistance. When this is finally achieved and they can accept help and trust from someone, they can master things even as large as a desert. (p. 333)

Society benefits from this integrative feature of adult thought. Generally, it is mature adults who translate their knowledge about the human condition into inspirational stories to which younger generations can turn for guidance.

Creativity

At about age 40, Frank Lloyd Wright designed Robie House in Chicago, Agnes deMille choreographed the Broadway musical *Carousel,* and Louis Pasteur developed the germ theory of disease. Charles Darwin was 50 when he presented his theory of evolution. Toni Morrison won the Pulitzer Prize for *Beloved,* a

What's Your View?

• If you needed surgery, would you rather go to a middle-aged doctor or one who is considerably older or younger? Why?

Checkpoint

Can you . . .

◆ Discuss the relationship between expertise, knowledge, and intelligence?

◆ Give an example of integrative thinking?

Guidepost 6

What accounts for creative achievement, and how does it change with age?

Helen Mirren, long a highly respected, classically trained British stage, screen, and radio actress, reached the apex of her career in 2006, at the age of 61, when she won the Academy Award for Best Actress for her portrayal of a proud, aging Queen Elizabeth II in the film The Queen.

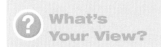

• Think of an adult you know who is a creative achiever. To what combination of personal qualities and environmental forces would you attribute her or his creative performance?

Can you . . .

◆ Discuss prerequisites for creative achievement?

◆ Summarize the relationship between creative performance and age?

novel she wrote at about 55. Many creative people have reached their greatest achievements in middle age.

Characteristics of Creative Achievers

Creativity is not limited to the Darwins and deMilles; we can see it in an inventor who comes up with a better mousetrap or a promoter who finds an innovative way to sell it. Creativity begins with talent, but talent is not enough. Children may show *creative potential;* but in adults, what counts is *creative performance:* what, and how much, a creative mind produces (Sternberg & Lubart, 1995).

Creativity develops in a social context, and not necessarily in nurturing environments. Instead, it seems to emerge from diverse experiences that weaken conventional constraints and from challenging experiences that strengthen the ability to persevere and overcome obstacles (Simonton, 2000).

Extraordinary creative achievement, according to one analysis (Keegan, 1996), results from deep, highly organized knowledge of a subject, intrinsic motivation, and a strong emotional attachment to the work, which spurs the creator to persevere in the face of obstacles. A person must first be thoroughly grounded in a field before she or he can see its limitations, envision radical departures, and develop a new and unique point of view.

General intelligence, or IQ, has little relationship to creative performance (Simonton, 2000). Highly creative people are self-starters and risk takers. They tend to be independent, nonconformist, unconventional, and flexible, and they are open to new ideas and experiences. Their thinking processes are often unconscious, leading to sudden moments of illumination (Simonton, 2000; Torrance, 1988). They look at a problem more deeply than other people do and come up with solutions that do not occur to others (Sternberg & Horvath, 1998).

Creativity and Age

Is there a relationship between creative performance and age? On psychometric tests of divergent thinking (described in Chapter 9), age differences consistently appear. Whether data are cross-sectional or longitudinal, scores peak, on average, around the late thirties. A similar age curve emerges when creativity is measured by variations in output (number of publications, paintings, or compositions). A person in the last decade of a creative career typically produces only about half as much as during the late thirties or early forties, though somewhat more than in the twenties (Simonton, 1990).

However, the age curve varies depending on the field. Poets, mathematicians, and theoretical physicists tend to be most prolific in their late twenties or early thirties. Research psychologists reach a peak around age 40, followed by a moderate decline. Novelists, historians, and philosophers become increasingly productive through their late forties or fifties and then level off. These patterns hold true across cultures and historical periods (Dixon & Hultsch, 1999; Simonton, 1990). Losses in productivity may be offset by gains in quality. A study of the swan songs of 172 composers found that their last works—usually fairly short and melodically simple—were among their richest, most important, and most successful (Simonton, 1989).

Work and Education

Guidepost 7

How are patterns of work and education changing, and how does work contribute to cognitive development?

In industrialized societies, occupational roles typically are based on age. Young people are students; young and middle-aged adults are workers; older adults organize their lives around retirement and leisure. In postindustrial societies, people make multiple transitions throughout their adult lives (Czaja, 2006). College students take work-study programs or stop out for a while before resuming their education. Emerging adults explore various avenues before settling into careers, and even then, their decisions may be open-ended. A person may have several careers in succession, each requiring additional education or training. Mature adults take evening classes or take time off work to pursue a special interest. People retire earlier or later than in the past, or not at all. Retirees devote time to study or to a new line of work, paid or unpaid.

Work versus Early Retirement

Before 1985, people retired earlier and earlier. The average age of retirement moved steadily downward. Since then, the trend has reversed. Before bringing their working lives to a complete stop, people may reduce work hours or days, gradually moving into retirement over a number of years. This practice is called *phased retirement.* Or they may switch to another company or a new line of work, a practice called *bridge employment* (Czaja, 2006). About half of workers ages 55 to 65 take a bridge job before moving to full retirement (Purcell, 2002).

What has brought about this change? People may continue working to maintain their physical and emotional health and their personal and social roles, or simply because they enjoy the stimulation of work, and their reasons may change at different times (Czaja, 2006; Sterns & Huyck, 2001). Others work primarily for financial reasons. Many of today's middle-aged and older workers have inadequate savings or pensions or need continued health insurance. The rise in the Social Security retirement age to 67 for full benefits offers an inducement to keep working. The Age Discrimination in Employment Act, which eliminated mandatory retirement ages for most occupations, and the Americans with Disabilities Act, which requires employers to make reasonable accommodations for workers with disabilities, have helped mature workers to keep their jobs. Furthermore, baby boomers, now nearing retirement age, are better educated than in previous generations, and their options therefore are wider (Czaja, 2006).

Work and Cognitive Development

"Use it or lose it" applies to the mind as well as the body. Work can influence cognitive functioning.

Research (introduced in Chapter 13) suggests that flexible thinkers tend to obtain substantively complex work—work requiring thought and independent judgment. This type of work, in turn, stimulates more flexible thinking; and flexible thinking increases the ability to do complex work (Kohn, 1980). Thus, people who are deeply engaged in complex work tend to show stronger cognitive performance than their peers as they age (Avolio & Sosik, 1999; Kohn & Schooler, 1983; Schaie, 1984; Schooler, 1984, 1990). The same is true of men and women engaged in complex household work, such as planning a budget or a household move or making complicated repairs, such as putting in new plumbing (Caplan & Schooler, 2006). If work—both on the job and at home—could be made meaningful and challenging, more adults might retain or improve their cognitive abilities (Avolio & Sosik, 1999).

This seems to be happening already. The gains in most cognitive abilities found in recent middle-aged and older cohorts may well reflect workplace changes that emphasize self-managed, multifunctional teams and put a premium on adaptability, initiative, and decentralized decision making (Avolio & Sosik, 1999). Unfortunately, older workers are less likely than younger workers to be offered, or to volunteer for, training, education, and challenging job assignments, in the mistaken belief that older people cannot handle such opportunities. Yet the Seattle study found that declines in cognitive ability generally do not occur until very late in life, well after the working years. Indeed, work performance shows greater variability *within* age groups than between them (Avolio & Sosik, 1999).

Adults can actively affect their future cognitive development by the occupational choices they make. Those who constantly seek more stimulating opportunities are likely to remain mentally sharp (Avolio & Sosik, 1999). A study in Frankfurt, Germany, compared 195 patients with dementia, age 55 and up, with 229 nondemented adults age 60 and up. Those who had worked in intellectually demanding jobs that called for a high degree of control and involved wide circles of communication were less likely to have dementia (Seidler et al., 2004; Wilson, 2005).

The Mature Learner

In 2005, 44 percent of U. S. adults, including 48 percent of 45- to 54-year-olds and 40 percent of 55- to 64-year-olds, reported having participated in adult education, 27 percent in work-related courses. About one-third of these adults (32 percent) used distance learning (NCES, 2007a; O'Donnell, 2006).

Why do middle-aged people engage in formal education? Education enables adults to develop their cognitive potential, improve their self-esteem, help their children with homework, or keep up with the changing world of work. Some seek specialized training to update their knowledge and skills. Some train for new occupations. Some want to move up the career ladder or to go into business for themselves. Some women who have devoted their young adult years to homemaking and parenting are taking their first steps toward reentering the job market. People close to retirement often want to expand their minds and skills to make more productive and interesting use of leisure. Some people simply enjoy learning and want to keep doing it throughout life.

College Programs A small minority (5 percent) of adults take part-time college programs leading to diplomas or degrees (NCES, 2007a). Some colleges accommodate the practical needs of students of nontraditional age by granting credit for life experience and previous learning. Many offer part-time matriculation, Saturday and night classes, independent study, child care, financial aid, free or reduced-tuition courses, and distance learning via computers or closed-circuit broadcasts.

Unfortunately, some learning institutions are not structured to meet mature adults' educational and psychological needs or to take advantage of their cognitive strengths. Adult learners have their own motives, goals, developmental tasks, and experiences. They need knowledge they can apply to specific situations. Cooperative study built around self-generated problems or projects is most appropriate to a mature adult (Sinnott, 1998).

Adult Education and Work Skills Changes in the workplace often entail a need for more training or education. Expanding technology and shifting job markets require a life-span approach to learning. Technological skills are increasingly

Checkpoint

Can you ...

◆ Discuss trends in work and retirement in middle age?

◆ Explain how work can affect cognitive functioning?

What's Your View?

● From what you have seen, do students of nontraditional age seem to do better or worse in college than younger students? How would you explain your observation?

necessary for success in the modern world and are a major component of work-related adult education. With experience, middle-aged people can perform computer-based tasks as well as young adults (Czaja, 2006).

About 75 percent of work-related education for 25- to 64-year-olds is employer-supported (NCES, 2003). Employers see benefits of workplace education in improved morale, increased quality of work, better teamwork and problem solving, and greater ability to cope with new technology and other changes in the workplace (Conference Board, 1999).

Literacy Training **Literacy** is a fundamental requisite for participation not only in the workplace but in all facets of a modern, information-driven society. Literate adults can use printed and written information to function in society, achieve their goals, and develop their knowledge and potential. At the turn of the century, a person with a fourth-grade education was considered literate; today, a high school diploma is barely adequate.

In 2003, 14 percent of U.S. adults could not locate clearly identifiable information in brief English prose, 22 percent could not perform simple numerical operations such as addition, and 12 percent could not read documents well enough to succeed in today's economy—all components of basic literacy (NCES, 2006c). Also in 2003, U.S. adults performed worse on an international literacy test than adults in Bermuda, Canada, Norway, and Switzerland but better than those in Italy (Lemke et al., 2005; NCES, 2005b).

Middle-aged and older adults tend to have lower literacy levels than young adults, but the average literacy level of adults ages 50 to 59 has increased since 1992. Adults below basic literacy are less likely to be employed than adults at higher literacy levels (Kutner et al., 2007; NCES, 2006c).

Globally, 774 million adults—about 1 in 5—are illiterate, mostly in sub-Saharan Africa and East and South Asia (UNESCO, 2004, 2007). Illiteracy is especially common among women in developing nations, where education typically is considered unimportant for them. In 1990, the United Nations launched literacy programs in such developing countries as Bangladesh, Nepal, and Somalia (Linder, 1990). More recently, the UN has named 2003 to 2012 the Literacy Decade and is sponsoring conferences and programs to promote literacy development. In the United States, the National Literacy Act requires the states to establish literacy training centers with federal funding assistance.

Research about education and work—as well as about problem solving, creativity, and moral choices—shows that the mind continues to develop during adulthood. Such research illustrates the links between the cognitive side of development and its social and emotional aspects, to which we turn again in Chapter 16.

literacy In an adult, ability to use printed and written information to function in society, achieve goals, and develop knowledge and potential.

Checkpoint

Can you . . .

♦ Give reasons why mature adults return to the classroom, and tell some ways in which educational institutions attempt to meet their needs?

♦ Discuss the need for literacy training in the United States and internationally?

Summary and Key Terms

Middle Age: A Social Construct

Guidepost 1 *What are the distinguishing features of middle age?*

• The concept of middle age is a social construct. It came into use in industrial societies as an increasing life span led to new roles at midlife.

• The span of middle adulthood is often subjective.

• Middle adulthood is a time of both gains and losses.

• Most middle-aged people are in good physical, cognitive, and emotional condition. They have heavy responsibilities and multiple roles and feel competent to handle them.

• Middle age is a time for taking stock and making decisions about the remaining years.

PHYSICAL DEVELOPMENT

Physical Changes

Guidepost 2 *What physical changes generally occur during the middle years, and what is their psychological impact?*

- Although some physiological changes result from aging and genetic makeup, behavior and lifestyle can affect their timing and extent.
- Most middle-aged adults compensate well for gradual, minor declines in sensory and psychomotor abilities. Losses in bone density and vital capacity are common.
- Symptoms of menopause and attitudes toward it may depend on cultural factors and natural changes of aging.
- Although men can continue to father children until late in life, many middle-aged men experience a decline in fertility and in frequency of orgasm.
- A large proportion of middle-aged men experience erectile dysfunction. Erectile dysfunction can have physical causes but also may be related to health, lifestyle, and emotional well-being.
- Sexual activity generally diminishes gradually in middle age.

presbyopia (484)

myopia (484)

presbycusis (484)

basal metabolism (485)

vital capacity (486)

menopause (487)

perimenopause (487)

erectile dysfunction (490)

Physical and Mental Health

Guidepost 3 *What factors affect physical and mental health at midlife?*

- Most middle-aged people are healthy and have no functional limitations; however, baby boomers may be less healthy than previous generations at middle age.
- Hypertension is a major health problem beginning in midlife. Cancer has passed heart disease as the number one killer in midlife. The prevalence of diabetes has doubled, and it is now the fourth leading cause of death in this age group.

- Diet, exercise, alcohol use, and smoking affect present and future health. Preventive care is important.
- Low income is associated with poorer health, in part because of lack of insurance.
- Racial and ethnic disparities in health and health care have decreased but still persist.
- Postmenopausal women become more susceptible to heart disease as well as to bone loss leading to osteoporosis. Chances of developing breast cancer also increase with age, and routine mammography is recommended for women beginning at age 40.
- Mounting evidence suggests that the risks of hormone therapy may outweigh its benefits.
- Stress occurs when the body's ability to cope is not equal to the demands on it. Stress is often greatest in middle age and can be related to a variety of practical problems. Severe stress can affect immune functioning.
- Role and career changes and other experiences typical of middle age can be stressful, but resilience is common.
- Personality and negative emotionality can affect health. Positive emotions tend to be associated with good health.
- Psychological distress becomes more prevalent in middle age.

hypertension (491)

diabetes (492)

osteoporosis (493)

mammography (497)

hormone therapy (HT) (497)

stress (498)

stressors (498)

COGNITIVE DEVELOPMENT

Measuring Cognitive Abilities in Middle Age

Guidepost 4 *What cognitive gains and losses occur during middle age?*

- The Seattle Longitudinal Study found that several of the primary mental abilities remain strong during middle age, but there is great individual variability.
- Fluid intelligence declines earlier than crystallized intelligence.

fluid intelligence (505)

crystallized intelligence (505)

The Distinctiveness of Adult Cognition

Guidepost 5 *Do mature adults think differently than younger people do?*

- Some theorists propose that cognition takes distinctive forms at midlife. Advances in expertise, or specialized knowledge, have been attributed to encapsulation of fluid abilities within a person's chosen field.
- Postformal thought seems especially useful in situations calling for integrative thinking.

  encapsulation (506)

Creativity

Guidepost 6 *What accounts for creative achievement, and how does it change with age?*

- Creative performance depends on personal attributes and environmental forces.
- Creativity is not strongly related to intelligence.
- An age-related decline appears in both psychometric tests of divergent thinking and actual creative output, but peak ages for output vary by occupation. Losses in productivity with age may be offset by gains in quality.

Work and Education

Guidepost 7 *How are patterns of work and education changing, and how does work contribute to cognitive development?*

- A shift away from early retirement and toward more flexible options is occurring.
- Complex work may improve cognitive flexibility.
- Many adults go to college at a nontraditional age or participate in other educational activities, often to improve work-related skills and knowledge.
- Mature adults have special educational needs and strengths.
- Literacy training is an urgent need in the United States and globally.

  literacy (511)

To accept all experience as raw material out of which the human spirits distill meanings and values is a part of the meaning of maturity.

—Howard Thurman, *Meditations of the Heart,* 1953

Did You **Know...**

- The idea of a midlife crisis has been largely discredited, and it is fairly unusual to have one?
- Marital satisfaction generally bottoms in early middle age and peaks when children are grown?
- The number one reason for midlife divorce, given in a major survey, is partner abuse?
- Most women find an "empty nest" liberating?
- With adequate support, caring for an infirm parent can be an opportunity for personal growth?

These are just a few of the interesting and important topics we will cover in this chapter. The middle years are the central years of the adult life span. Middle-aged people are not only in a position to look back and ahead in their own lives; they also bridge older and younger generations. Very often, they are the ones who hold families together and make societal institutions and enterprises work. Much can happen during the 25-year span we call *middle adulthood;* and these experiences affect the way people look, feel, and act as they enter old age.

In this chapter we look at theoretical perspectives and research on psychosocial issues and themes at midlife. We then focus on intimate relationships: marriage, cohabitation, and divorce; gay and lesbian relationships; friendships; and relationships with maturing children, aging parents, siblings, and grandchildren. All these may be woven into the rich texture of the middle years. After you have read and studied this chapter, you should be able to answer each of the Guidepost questions on the following page.

Guideposts *for Study*

1. How do developmental scientists approach the study of psychosocial development in middle adulthood?
2. What do theorists have to say about psychosocial change in middle age?
3. What issues concerning the self come to the fore during middle adulthood?
4. What role do social relationships play in the lives of middle-aged people?
5. How do marriages, cohabitations, gay and lesbian relationships, and friendships fare during the middle years, and how common is divorce at this time of life?
6. How do parent-child relationships change as children approach and reach adulthood?
7. How do middle-aged people get along with parents and siblings?
8. What roles do today's grandparents play?

Guidepost 1

How do developmental scientists approach the study of psychosocial development in middle adulthood?

Checkpoint

Can you ...

♦ Distinguish between objective and subjective views of the life course?

♦ Identify factors that affect the life course in middle age?

Looking at the Life Course in Middle Age

Developmental scientists view the course of midlife psychosocial development in several ways. *Objectively,* they look at trajectories or pathways, such as a once-traditional wife and mother's pursuit of a midlife career. *Subjectively,* they look at how people construct their identity and the structure of their lives (Moen & Wethington, 1999).

Change and continuity in the middle years must be seen in the perspective of the entire life span, but early patterns are not necessarily blueprints for later patterns (Lachman & James, 1997), and there are differences between early and late middle age (Lachman, 2004). Just compare the typical concerns of a 40-year-old with those of a 60-year-old. Today, of course, it is hard to say what life course, if any, is typical. At 40, some people become parents for the first time, while others become grandparents. At 50, some people are starting new careers, while others are taking early retirement.

Furthermore, lives do not progress in isolation. Individual pathways intersect or collide with those of family members, friends, acquaintances, and strangers. Work and personal roles are interdependent, and those roles are affected by trends in the larger society.

Cohort, gender, ethnicity, culture, and socioeconomic status can profoundly affect the life course. The path of a woman with a midlife career may be very different from that of her mother, who made her family her total life's work. This woman's course also may be different from that of an educated young woman today who embarks on a career before marriage and motherhood. Her trajectory most likely would have been different, too, had she been a man, or had she been too poor or poorly educated to aspire to a career, or had she grown up in a highly traditional society. All these factors, and more, enter into the study of psychosocial development in middle adulthood.

Change at Midlife: Theoretical Approaches

Guidepost 2

What do theorists have to say about psychosocial change in middle age?

In psychosocial terms, middle adulthood once was considered a relatively settled period. Freud (1906/1942) saw no point in psychotherapy for people over 50 because he believed personality is permanently formed by that age.

In contrast, humanistic theorists such as Abraham Maslow and Carl Rogers looked on middle age as an opportunity for positive change. According to Maslow (1968), the full realization of human potential, which he called *self-actualization,* can come only with maturity. Rogers (1961) held that full human functioning requires a constant, lifelong process of bringing the self in harmony with experience.

Longitudinal studies show that psychosocial development involves both stability and change (Franz, 1997; Helson, 1997). But what *types* of changes occur and what brings them about? Several theorists have sought to answer that question.

Trait Models

Costa and McCrae's trait research (see, especially, 2006), which originally claimed continuity or consistency of personality after age 30 in the Big Five trait groupings—neuroticism (anxiety, hostility, instability), extraversion, openness to experience, conscientiousness, and agreeableness—has now acknowledged slower change during the middle and older years as well, as we reported in Chapter 14. Other investigators testing a similar trait structure have found more significant positive change during those years (Roberts & Mroczek, 2008).

In middle age, conscientiousness, for example, tends to show remarkable gains apparently attendant on work experience, while emotional stability continues the steady upward climb begun in young adulthood. People tend to become more socially mature—confident, warm, responsible, and calm—as they move through the prime of life, and maturity in turn enables them to be more productive contributors at work and to society and to lead longer and healthier lives. Individual differences based on experience often occur; for example, men who remarry in middle age tend to become less neurotic (Roberts & Mroczek, 2008).

Normative-Stage Models

Two early normative-stage theorists whose work continues to provide a frame of reference for much developmental theory and research on middle adulthood are Carl G. Jung and Erik Erikson.

Carl G. Jung: Individuation and Transcendence   The Swiss psychologist Carl Jung (1933, 1953, 1969, 1971) held that healthy midlife development calls for **individuation,** the emergence of the true self through balancing or integrating conflicting parts of the personality, including those parts that previously have been neglected. Until about age 40, said Jung, adults concentrate on obligations to family and society and develop aspects of personality that will help them reach external goals. Women emphasize expressiveness and nurturance; men are primarily oriented toward achievement. At midlife, people shift their preoccupation to their inner, spiritual, selves. Both men and women seek a *union of opposites* by expressing their previously disowned aspects.

Two necessary but difficult tasks of midlife are giving up the image of youth and acknowledging mortality. According to Jung (1966), the need to acknowledge mortality requires a search for meaning within the self. This inward turn may be unsettling; as people question their commitments, they may temporarily lose their

individuation   Jung's term for emergence of the true self through balancing or integration of conflicting parts of the personality.

moorings. Yet, people who avoid this transition and do not reorient their lives appropriately miss the chance for psychological growth.

Erik Erikson: Generativity versus Stagnation In contrast to Jung, who saw midlife as a time of turning inward, Erikson described an outward turn. Erikson saw the years around age 40 as the time when people enter their seventh normative stage, **generativity versus stagnation. Generativity,** as Erikson defined it, is the concern of mature adults for establishing and guiding the next generation, perpetuating oneself through one's influence on those to follow. People who do not find an outlet for generativity become self-absorbed, self-indulgent, or stagnant (inactive or lifeless). The virtue of this period is *care:* "a widening commitment to *take care of* the persons, the products, and the ideas one has learned *to care for*" (Erikson, 1985, p. 67). Later theory and research has supported and expanded on Erikson's views.

How does generativity arise? According to one model (McAdams, 2001), inner desires for symbolic immortality, or a need to be needed, combine with external demands (increased expectations and responsibilities) to produce a conscious concern for the next generation. This concern, together with what Erikson called "belief in the species," leads to generative commitments and actions. Generativity tends to be associated with prosocial behavior (McAdams, 2006).

Generativity, a concern for guiding the younger generation, can be expressed through coaching or mentoring. Generativity may be a key to well-being in midlife.

generativity versus stagnation Erikson's seventh stage of psychosocial development, in which the middle-aged adult develops a concern with establishing, guiding, and influencing the next generation or else experiences stagnation (a sense of inactivity or lifelessness).

generativity Erikson's term for concern of mature adults for establishing, guiding, and influencing the next generation.

Generativity, Age, and Gender Generativity, according to Erikson, is "a sign of both psychological maturity and psychological health" (McAdams, 2001, p. 425). It typically emerges during midlife because the demands of work and family during this period call for generative responses. Highly generative parents tend to be more involved in their children's schooling than those who are less generative and tend to have authoritative parenting styles (McAdams, 2006).

Using such techniques as behavioral checklists and self-reports (Table 16-1), researchers have found that middle-aged people do tend to score higher on generativity than younger and older ones. However, generativity is not limited to middle age. The age at which individuals achieve generativity varies, as does its strength at any particular time. Furthermore, some people are more generative than others (Keyes & Ryff, 1998; McAdams, 2006; McAdams, de St. Aubin, & Logan, 1993; Stewart & Vandewater, 1998). Women typically report higher levels of generativity than men, but this difference fades in late adulthood (Keyes & Ryff, 1998).

These studies were mostly cross-sectional and so cannot with certainty trace a connection between generativity and age. However, the few longitudinal studies of generativity, such as the Vaillant study discussed in a later section, also support this connection (Stewart & Vandewater, 1998).

Forms of Generativity As the central challenge of the middle years, generativity can be expressed, not only through parenting and grandparenting, but also through teaching or mentorship, productivity or creativity, and *self-generation,* or self-development. It can extend to the world of work, to politics, to religion,

Table 16-1	A Self-Report Test for Generativity

- I try to pass along the knowledge I have gained through my experiences.
- I do not feel that other people need me.
- I think I would like the work of a teacher.
- I feel as though I have made a difference to many people.
- I do not volunteer to work for a charity.
- I have made and created things that have had an impact on other people.
- I try to be creative in most things that I do.
- I think that I will be remembered for a long time after I die.
- I believe that society cannot be responsible for providing food and shelter for all homeless people.
- Others would say that I have made unique contributions to society.
- If I were unable to have children of my own, I would like to adopt children.
- I have important skills that I try to teach others.
- I feel that I have done nothing that will survive after I die.
- In general, my actions do not have a positive effect on others.
- I feel as though I have done nothing of worth to contribute to others.
- I have made many commitments to many different kinds of people, groups, and activities in my life.
- Other people say that I am a very productive person.
- I have a responsibility to improve the neighborhood in which I live.
- People come to me for advice.
- I feel as though my contributions will exist after I die.

Source: Loyola Generativity Scale. Reprinted from McAdams & de St. Aubin, 1992.

to hobbies, to art, music, and other spheres—or to, as Erikson called it, "maintenance of the world."

Volunteering for community service or a political cause is an expression of generativity. In the MIDUS study, volunteering increased between very early and middle adulthood. It then declined slightly after age 55 and rose again after 65 (Hart, Southerland, & Atkins, 2003). Relief from primary family and work responsibilities may free middle-aged and older adults to express generativity on a broader scale (Keyes & Ryff, 1998).

Generativity, then, may derive from involvement in multiple roles (Staudinger & Bluck, 2001). Such involvement has been linked to well-being and satisfaction both in midlife (McAdams, 2001) and in later life (Sheldon & Kasser, 2001; Vandewater, Ostrove, & Stewart, 1997), perhaps through the sense of having contributed meaningfully to society. Again, however, because these findings are correlational, we cannot be sure that generativity *causes* well-being; it may be that people who are happy with their lives are more likely to be generative (McAdams, 2001). Because of the centrality of generativity in middle age, we will return to generativity later in this chapter.

Jung's and Erikson's Legacy: Vaillant and Levinson   Jung's and Erikson's ideas and observations inspired George Vaillant's (1977, 1989) and Daniel Levinson's (1978) longitudinal studies of men (introduced in Chapter 14). Both described major midlife shifts—from occupational striving in the thirties to reevaluation and often drastic restructuring of lives in the forties to mellowing and relative stability in the fifties.*

Vaillant, like Jung, reported a lessening of gender differentiation at midlife and a tendency for men to become more nurturant and expressive. Likewise,

* Levinson's description of the fifties was only projected.

interiority Neugarten's term for a concern with inner life (introversion or introspection), which usually appears in middle age.

Levinson's men at midlife became less obsessed with personal achievement and more concerned with relationships; and they showed generativity by becoming mentors to younger people.

Vaillant echoed Jung's concept of turning inward. In the forties, many of the men in his Grant Study of Harvard graduates abandoned the "compulsive, unreflective busywork of their occupational apprenticeships and once more [became] explorers of the world within" (1977, p. 220). Bernice Neugarten (1977) noted a similar introspective tendency at midlife, which she called **interiority.** For Levinson's men, the transition to middle adulthood was stressful enough to be considered a crisis.

Vaillant (1993) also studied the relationship between generativity, age, and mental health. As his Harvard alumni approached and moved through middle age, an increasing proportion were rated as having achieved generativity: 50 percent at age 40 and 83 percent at 60. In their fifties, the best-adjusted men were the most generative, as measured by their responsibility for other people at work, their gifts to charity, and the accomplishments of their children (Soldz & Vaillant, 1998).

As we pointed out in Chapter 14, Vaillant's and Levinson's studies, insightful as they may have been, had serious weaknesses of sampling and methodology. Despite Levinson's (1996) posthumous publication of a small study of women, his model and, especially, that of Vaillant were built on research on mostly middle-class or upper-middle-class men, whose experiences were taken as norms.

Furthermore, their findings reflected the experiences of members of a particular cohort in a particular culture. They may not apply in a society in which masculinity and femininity no longer have such distinct meanings, and in which career development and life choices for both men and women have become more varied and more flexible. These findings also may not apply to people for whom economic survival is a pressing issue or to cultures that have different patterns of life course development (Box 16-1). Also, these studies dealt exclusively with heterosexuals and may not apply to gays and lesbians. More recent research on midlife psychosocial development is more broadly based, uses more diverse samples and research designs, and covers more dimensions of personality and experience.

• On the basis of your observations, do you believe that adults' personalities change significantly during middle age? If so, do such changes seem related to maturation, or do they accompany important events, such as divorce, occupational change, or grandparenthood?

Timing of Events: The Social Clock

According to the timing-of-events model introduced in Chapter 14, adult personality development hinges less on age than on important life events. Middle age often brings a restructuring of social roles: launching children, becoming grandparents, changing jobs or careers, and eventually, retirement. For the cohorts represented by the early normative-stage studies, the occurrence and timing of such major events were fairly predictable. Today, lifestyles are more diverse, and the boundaries of middle adulthood have blurred, "eras[ing] the old definitions of the 'social clock'" (Josselson, 2003, p. 431).

When occupational patterns were more stable and retirement at age 65 was almost universal, the meaning of work at midlife for both men and women may have been different from its current meaning in a period of frequent job changes, downsizing, and early or delayed retirement. When women's lives revolved around bearing and rearing children, the end of the reproductive years meant something different from what it means now, when so many middle-aged women have entered the workforce. When people died earlier, middle-aged survivors felt old, realizing that they too were nearing the end of their lives. Many middle-aged people now find themselves busier and more involved than ever—some still raising young children while others redefine their roles as parents to adolescents and young

Can you . . .

◆ Summarize important changes that occur at midlife, according to trait and normative-stage theory and research?

◆ Tell how historical and cultural changes have affected the social clock for middle age?

BOX 16-1 **Window** *on the World*

A Society without Middle Age

The Gusii are a rural society of more than 1 million people in southwestern Kenya (Levine, 1980; LeVine & LeVine, 1998). They have a *life plan,* a hierarchy of stages based largely on the achievement of reproductive capacity and its extension through the next generation.

The Gusii have no words for "adolescent," "young adult," or "middle-aged." A boy or girl is circumcised sometime between ages 9 and 11 and becomes an elder when his or her first child marries. Between these two events, a man is in the stage of *omo-mura,* or "warrior." The *omomura* stage may last anywhere from 25 to 40 years, or even longer. Because of the importance of marriage in a woman's life, women have an additional stage: *omosubaati,* or "young married woman."

Childbearing is not confined to early adulthood. As in other preindustrial societies, where many hands are needed to raise crops, and death in infancy or early childhood is common, fertility is highly valued. People continue to reproduce as long as they are physiologically able. The average woman bears 10 children. When a woman reaches menopause, her husband may take a younger wife and create another family.

In Gusii society, then, transitions depend on life events. Status is linked to circumcision, marriage (for women), having children, and, finally, becoming a parent of a married child and thus a prospective grandparent and respected elder. The Gusii have a *social clock,* a set of expectations for the ages at which these events should normally occur. People who marry late or do not marry at all, men who become impotent or sterile, and women who fail to conceive, have their first child late, bear no sons, or have few children are ridiculed and ostracized and may undergo rituals to correct the situation.

Although the Gusii have no recognized midlife transition, some of them do reassess their lives around the time they are old enough to be grandparents. Awareness of mortality and of

waning physical powers, especially among women, may lead to a career as a ritual healer. The quest for spiritual powers has a generative purpose, too: Elders are responsible for ritually protecting their children and grandchildren from death or illness. Many older women who become ritual practitioners or witches seek power either to help people or to harm them, perhaps to compensate for their lack of personal and economic power in a male-dominated society.

Gusii society has undergone change, particularly since the 1970s, as a result of British colonial rule and its aftermath. With infant mortality curtailed, rapid population growth is straining the supply of food and other resources; and a life plan organized around maximizing reproduction is no longer adaptive. Growing acceptance of birth limitation among younger Gusii suggests that "conceptions of adult maturity less centered on fertility will eventually become dominant in the Gusii culture" (LeVine & LeVine, 1998, p. 207).

What's Your View?

Given the current dramatic changes in Gusii society, would you expect shifts in the way the Gusii define life's stages? If so, in what direction?

Check It Out

For more information about the Gusii, go to the website for the Kenya Project, www.societies.cam.ac.uk/kenyap/gusii.html.

---

adults and often as caregivers to aging parents. Yet despite the multiple challenges and variable events of midlife, most middle-aged adults seem well able to handle them (Lachman, 2001, 2004).

The Self at Midlife: Issues and Themes

"I'm a completely different person now from the one I was twenty years ago," said a 47-year-old architect as six friends, all in their forties and fifties, nodded vigorously in agreement. Many people feel and observe personality change occurring at midlife. Whether we look at middle-aged people objectively, in terms of their outward behavior, or subjectively, in terms of how they describe themselves, certain issues and themes emerge. Is there such a thing as a midlife crisis? How does identity develop in middle age? Do men and women change in different ways? What contributes to psychological well-being? All of these questions revolve around the self.

Guidepost 3

What issues concerning the self come to the fore during middle adulthood?

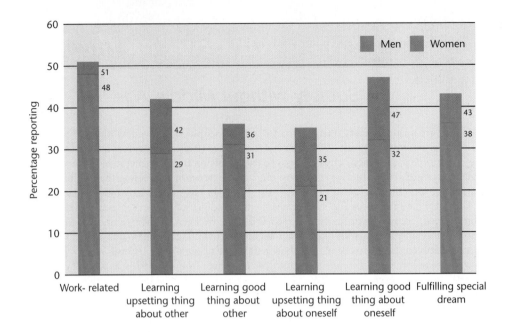

Figure 16-1
Turning points reported by 25- to 74-year-olds as having occurred in the past five years. (Source: Wethington et al., 2004, Fig. 3.)

midlife crisis In some normative-crisis models, stressful life period precipitated by the review and reevaluation of one's past, typically occurring in the early to middle forties.

Is There a Midlife Crisis?

Changes in personality and lifestyle during the early to middle forties are often attributed to the **midlife crisis,** a supposedly stressful period triggered by review and reevaluation of one's life. The midlife crisis was conceptualized as a crisis of identity; indeed, it has been called a second adolescence. What brings it on, said Elliott Jacques (1967), the psychoanalyst who coined the term, is awareness of mortality. Many people now realize that they will not be able to fulfill the dreams of their youth, or that fulfillment of their dreams has not brought the satisfaction they expected. They know that if they want to change direction, they must act quickly. Levinson (1978, 1980, 1986, 1996) maintained that midlife turmoil is inevitable as people struggle with the need to restructure their lives.

However, the term *midlife crisis* is now considered an inaccurate representation of what most people experience in midlife. In fact, its occurrence seems to be fairly unusual (Aldwin & Levenson, 2001; Heckhausen, 2001; Lachman, 2004). Some middle-aged people may experience crisis or turmoil, but others feel at the peak of their powers. Still others may fall somewhere in between—with neither a peak nor a crisis—or may experience both crisis and competence at different times or in different domains of life (Lachman, 2004).

The onset of middle age may be stressful, but no more so than some events of young adulthood (Chiriboga, 1997; Wethington et al., 2004). Indeed, some researchers have proposed the occurrence of a *quarterlife crisis* in the midtwenties to early thirties, as emerging adults seek to settle into satisfying work and relationships (Lachman, 2004; Robbins & Wilner, 2001).

Apparently, midlife is just one of life's *turning points*—psychological transitions that involve significant change or transformation in the perceived meaning, purpose, or direction of a person's life. Turning points may be triggered by major life events, normative changes, or a new understanding of past experience, either positive or negative, and they may be stressful. However, in the MIDUS survey and a follow-up study of Psychological Turning Points (PTP), many respondents reported positive growth from successful resolution of stressful situations (Wethington et al., 2004; Figure 16-1).

Table 16-2	Characteristics of Ego-Resilient Adults

Most Characteristic	Most Uncharacteristic
Has insight into own motives and behavior	Has brittle ego-defense; maladaptive under stress
Has warmth; capacity for close relationships	Is self-defeating
Has social poise and presence	Is uncomfortable with uncertainty and complexities
Is productive; gets things done	Overreacts to minor frustrations; is irritable
Is calm, relaxed in manner	Denies unpleasant thoughts and experiences
Is skilled in social techniques of imaginary play	Does not vary roles; relates to all in same way
Is socially perceptive of interpersonal cues	Is basically anxious
Can see to the heart of important problems	Gives up and withdraws from frustration or adversity
Is genuinely dependable and responsible	Is emotionally bland
Responds to humor	Is vulnerable to real or fancied threat; fearful
Values own independence and autonomy	Tends to ruminate and have preoccupying thoughts
Tends to arouse liking and acceptance	Feels cheated and victimized by life
Initiates humor	Feels a lack of personal meaning in life

Note: These items are used as criteria for rating ego-resiliency, using the California Adult Q-Set.

Source: Adapted from Block, 1991, as reprinted in Klohnen, 1996.

Turning points often involve an introspective review and reappraisal of values and priorities (Helson, 1997; Reid & Willis, 1999; Robinson, Rosenberg, & Farrell, 1999). The **midlife review** can be a time of stocktaking, yielding new insights into the self and spurring midcourse corrections in the design and trajectory of one's life. Along with recognition of the finiteness of life, a midlife review may bring regret over failure to achieve a dream or keener awareness of *developmental deadlines*—time constraints on, say, the ability to have a child or to make up with an estranged friend or family member (Heckhausen, 2001; Heckhausen, Wrosch, & Fleeson, 2001; Wrosch & Heckhausen, 1999).

Whether a turning point becomes a crisis may depend less on age than on individual circumstances and personal resources. People high in neuroticism are more likely to experience midlife crises (Lachman, 2004). People with *ego-resiliency*—the ability to adapt flexibly and resourcefully to potential sources of stress—and those who have a sense of mastery and control are more likely to navigate the midlife crossing successfully (Heckhausen, 2001; Klohnen et al., 1996; Lachman, 2004; Lachman & Firth, 2004). For people with resilient personalities, even negative events, such as an unwanted divorce, can become springboards for positive growth (Klohnen et al., 1996; Moen & Wethington, 1999). Table 16-2 outlines qualities considered most and least characteristic of ego-resilient adults.

midlife review Introspective examination that often occurs in middle age, leading to reappraisal and revision of values and priorities.

A midlife review might inspire a woman who senses her biological clock ticking to move forward on her wish to have a child.

Identity Development

Although Erikson defined identity formation as the main concern of adolescence, he noted that identity continues to develop. Indeed, some developmental scientists view the process of identity formation as the central issue of adulthood (McAdams & de St. Aubin, 1992). Most middle-aged adults have a well-developed sense of self and can cope well with change (Lachman, 2004). Let's look at current theories and research on identity development, particularly in middle age.

Susan Krauss Whitbourne: Identity Processes   According to the **identity process theory (IPT)** of Susan Krauss Whitbourne (1987, 1996; Jones, Whitbourne, & Skultety, 2006; Whitbourne & Connolly, 1999), identity is made up of accumulated perceptions of the self. Perceived physical characteristics, cognitive abilities, and personality traits ("I am sensitive" or "I am stubborn") are incorporated into identity schemas. These self-perceptions are continually confirmed or revised in response to incoming information, which can come from intimate relationships, work-related situations, community activities, and other experiences.

People interpret their interactions with the environment by means of two processes, similar to those Piaget described for children's cognitive development (see Chapter 2): *identity assimilation* and *identity accommodation.* **Identity assimilation** is an attempt to hold on to a consistent sense of self in the face of new experiences that do not fit an existing schema; **identity accommodation** is adjustment of the schema to fit new experiences. Identity assimilation tends to maintain continuity of the self; identity accommodation tends to bring about needed change.

Overuse of either assimilation or accommodation is unhealthy, say Whitbourne and her colleagues. People who constantly *assimilate* are inflexible and do not learn from experience. People who constantly *accommodate* are weak and highly vulnerable to criticism; their identity is easily undermined. Most healthy is **identity balance,** which enables a person to maintain a stable sense of self while adjusting the self-schemas to incorporate new information, such as the effects of aging.

People deal with physical, mental, and emotional changes associated with the onset of aging much as they deal with other experiences that challenge the identity schema. People who overuse assimilation may seek, perhaps unrealistically, to maintain a youthful self-image and ignore what is going on in their bodies. This process of denial may make it harder for them to confront the reality of aging when it can no longer be ignored. People who are overly accommodative may overreact to early signs of aging, such as the first gray hair. They may feel hopeless, and pessimism may hasten their physical and cognitive declines. People who use identity balance can recognize the changes that are occurring and respond flexibly; they seek to control what can be controlled and accept what cannot. A stronger, more stable identity enables them to resist negative self-stereotyping, seek help when needed, and face the future without panic or undue anxiety (Jones et al., 2006).

In questionnaire surveys of middle-aged and older people, midlife adults were more likely to accommodate and less likely to assimilate to age-related changes than were older adults. However, cohort influences the way people respond to signs of aging. The baby boom generation, now in middle age, have set high standards for youthfulness and beauty and may be overly alarmed by the changes they see in their bodies that are beyond their control. Gender also makes a difference. Middle-aged women are more likely than men that age to use identity accommodation, whereas men are more likely to use identity assimilation (Jones et al., 2006).

Generativity, Identity, and Age   Erikson saw generativity as an aspect of identity formation. As he wrote, "I am what survives me" (1968, p. 141). Research supports this connection.

---

identity process theory (IPT) Whitbourne's theory of identity development based on processes of assimilation and accommodation.

identity assimilation Whitbourne's term for effort to fit new experience into an existing self-concept.

identity accommodation Whitbourne's term for adjusting the self-concept to fit new experience.

identity balance   Whitbourne's term for a tendency to balance assimilation and accommodation.

Checkpoint

Can you . . .

♦ Compare the concepts of the midlife crisis and of turning points and discuss their relative prevalence?

♦ State typical concerns of the midlife transition and factors that affect how successfully people come through it?

♦ Summarize Whitbourne's identity process theory and tell how identity assimilation, identity accommodation, and identity balance differ, especially in response to signs of aging?

Among 40 middle-class, female bank employees in their early forties who were mothers of school-age children, the women who had achieved identity were the most psychologically healthy. They also expressed the greatest degree of generativity, bearing out Erikson's view that successful achievement of identity paves the way for other tasks (DeHaan & MacDermid, 1994). In a cross-sectional study of 333 female, mostly white, University of Michigan graduates in their sixties, high levels of generativity went hand in hand with increased certainty about their identity and a sense of confidence in their powers (Zucker, Ostrove, & Stewart, 2002). In the Radcliffe class of 1984, women who had attained generativity at age 43, as measured by a Q-sort instrument, reported greater investment 10 years later in their cross-generational roles as daughter and mother and felt less burdened by the care of aging parents (Peterson, 2002).

The popularity of regular Botox injections to temporarily smooth lines and wrinkles may express what Whitbourne calls an assimilative identity style.

Narrative Psychology: Identity as a Life Story The field of *narrative psychology* views the development of the self as a continuous process of constructing one's life story—a dramatic narrative, or personal myth, to help make sense of one's life and connect the past and present with the future (McAdams, 2006). This evolving story provides a person with a "narrative identity" (Singer, 2004). Indeed, some narrative psychologists view identity itself as this internalized *script* or story. People follow the script they have created as they act out their identity (McAdams, Diamond, de St. Aubin, & Mansfield, 1997). Midlife often is a time for revision of the life story or a break in the continuity and coherence of the story line (McAdams, 1993; Rosenberg et al., 1999).

Studies in narrative psychology are based on a standardized two-hour life-story interview. The participant is asked to think of his or her life as a book, to divide the book into chapters, and to recall eight key scenes, each of which includes a turning point. Research using this technique has found that people's scripts tend to reflect their personalities (McAdams, 2006).

Highly generative adults tend to construct *generativity scripts.* These scripts often feature a theme of *redemption,* or deliverance from suffering, and are associated with psychological well-being. In one such story, a nurse devotes herself to the care of a good friend during a fatal illness. Although devastated by her friend's death, she comes out of the experience with a renewed sense of confidence and determination to help others. A man who was born as a result of his mother's rape goes on to tell of a life of one terrible scene after another, culminating in his recovery from a stab wound. "The doctors brought me back to life," he says. Despite everything he has gone through, his philosophy of life is positive: "If you go with the positive ideas, you'll progress; if you get involved in the negative, you'll drown" (McAdams, 2006, p. 90).

Often the main characters in these redemptive stories enjoyed advantaged childhoods—a special talent, or a privileged home environment—but were deeply troubled by the suffering of others. This moral contrast inspired them to want to give back to society. As children and adolescents, they internalized a stable sense of moral values. As adults, they dedicate their lives to social improvement and do not swerve from that mission despite frustrating obstacles, which eventually have positive resolutions. They anticipate the future with optimism (McAdams, 2006).

These stories are very American, their second-chance themes reminiscent of the Horatio Alger rags-to-riches tales, of escapes from slavery, of immigrants who became millionaires, and of recovery from drug addiction. Generative narratives in other cultures may stress different themes (McAdams, 2006).

Gender Identity and Gender Roles As Erikson observed, identity is closely tied to social roles and commitments ("I am a parent," "I am a teacher," "I am a citizen"). Changing roles and relationships at midlife may affect gender identity (Josselson, 2003).

In many studies during the 1960s, 1970s, and 1980s, middle-aged men were more open about feelings, more interested in intimate relationships, and more nurturing—characteristics traditionally labeled as feminine—than at earlier ages, whereas middle-aged women became more assertive, self-confident, and achievement-oriented, characteristics traditionally labeled as masculine (Cooper & Gutmann, 1987; Cytrynbaum et al., 1980; Helson & Moane, 1987; Huyck, 1990, 1999; Neugarten, 1968). Jung saw these changes as part of the process of individuation, or balancing the personality. The psychologist David Gutmann (1975, 1977, 1985, 1987) offers an explanation that goes further than Jung's.

Traditional gender roles, according to Gutmann, evolved to ensure the well-being of growing children: The mother must be the caregiver, the father the provider. Once active parenting is over, there is not just a balancing but a reversal of roles—a **gender crossover.** Men, now free to explore their previously repressed feminine side, become more passive; women, free to explore their masculine side, become more dominant and independent.

These changes may have been normative in the preliterate, agricultural societies Gutmann studied, which had distinct gender roles, but they are not necessarily universal (Franz, 1997). In U.S. society today, men's and women's roles are becoming less distinct. In an era in which most young women combine employment with child rearing, when many men take an active part in parenting, and when childbearing may not even begin until midlife, gender crossover in middle age seems less likely (Antonucci & Akiyama, 1997; Barnett, 1997; James & Lewkowicz, 1997).

In a longitudinal study of alumnae of Mills College, between the beginning and the end of active parenting the women increased more than their male partners in competence, confidence, and independence, while the men increased more in affiliative traits (Helson, 1997). Again, however, these changes did not amount to a gender crossover (Helson, 1993). Furthermore, an analysis of longitudinal studies of men's and women's personality change during the life course found little support for the crossover hypothesis, or even for the idea that men and women change in different ways, or in ways related to their changing gender roles (Roberts, Walton, & Viechtbauer, 2006a, 2006b).

Psychological Well-Being and Positive Mental Health

Mental health is not just the absence of mental illness. *Positive* mental health involves a sense of psychological well-being, which goes hand in hand with a healthy sense of self (Keyes & Shapiro, 2004; Ryff & Singer, 1998). This subjective sense of well-being, or happiness, is a person's evaluation of his or her life (Diener, 2000). How do developmental scientists measure well-being, and what factors affect well-being at midlife?

Emotionality, Personality, and Age Many studies, including the MIDUS survey, have found a gradual average decline in negative emotions through

What's Your View?

• From what you have observed, do men seem to become less masculine and women less feminine at midlife?

gender crossover Gutmann's term for reversal of gender roles after the end of active parenting.

Checkpoint

Can you . . .

◆ Explain the connection between generativity and identity and discuss research on generativity and age?

◆ Explain the concept of identity as a life story, and how it relates to generativity?

◆ Compare Jung's and Gutmann's concepts of changes in gender identity at midlife, and assess their research support?

midlife and beyond, though women in the MIDUS study reported slightly more negative emotionality (such as anger, fear, and anxiety) at all ages than men (Mroczek, 2004). According to the MIDUS findings, positive emotionality (such as cheerfulness) increases, on average, among men but falls among women in middle age and then rises sharply for both sexes, but especially men, in late adulthood. The general trends in positive and negative emotionality seem to suggest that as people age, they tend to have learned to accept what comes (Carstensen, Pasupathi, Mayr, & Nesselroade, 2000) and to regulate their emotions effectively (Lachman, 2004).

Middle-aged and younger adults in the MIDUS study showed greater individual variation in emotionality than older adults; however, the factors that affected emotionality differed. Only physical health had a consistent impact on emotionality in adults of all ages, but two other factors—marital status and education—had significant impacts in middle age. Married people at midlife tended to report more positive emotion and less negative emotion than unmarried people. People with higher education reported more positive emotion and less negative emotional—but only when stress, which tends to be high at midlife, was controlled (Mroczek, 2004).

Subjective well-being (how happy a person feels) also is known to be related to dimensions of personality identified by the five-factor model. In particular, people who are emotionally stable (low in neuroticism), physically and socially active (high in extraversion), and highly conscientious tend to feel happiest. A study of 973 monozygotic and dizygotic twin pairs has found that a common genetic structure underlies *both* personality traits and well-being and thus may help account for their relative consistency throughout life (Weiss, Bates, & Luciano, 2008).

Life Satisfaction and Age In numerous surveys worldwide using various techniques for assessing subjective well-being, most adults of all ages, both sexes, and all races report being satisfied with their lives, (e.g., Diener, 2000; Myers & Diener, 1995, 1996; Walker, Skowronski, & Thompson, 2003). One reason for this general finding of life satisfaction is that the positive emotions associated with pleasant memories tend to persist, whereas the negative feelings associated with unpleasant memories fade. Most people have good coping skills (Walker et al., 2003). After either especially happy or distressing events, such as marriage or divorce, they generally adapt, and subjective well-being returns to, or close to, its previous level (Lucas et al., 2003; Diener, 2000).

Social support—friends and spouses—and religiosity are important contributors to life satisfaction (Csikszentmihalyi, 1999; Diener, 2000; Myers, 2000). are certain personality dimensions—extraversion and conscientiousness (Mrocz & Spiro, 2005; Siegler & Brummett, 2000)—and the quality of work and leisure (Csikszentmihalyi, 1999; Diener, 2000; Myers, 2000).

Does life satisfaction change with age? In a 22-year longitudinal study of 1,927 men, life satisfaction gradually rose, peaked at age 65, and then slowly declined. However, individual differences were found (Mroczek & Spiro, 2005). In a 17-year longitudinal study of 3,608 Germans, originally ages 16 to 40, about 1 in 4 experienced significant changes in life satisfaction (Fujita & Diener, 2005).

In the Mills College studies, mentioned earlier, life satisfaction tended to peak in the latter part of middle age. Most of the Mills alumnae found their early forties a time of turmoil but by the early fifties rated their quality of life as high (Helson & Wink, 1992). Similarly, among a cross-sectional sample of nearly 700 Mills alumnae ages 26 to 80, women in their early fifties most often described their lives as "first-rate" (Mitchell & Helson, 1990).

The Red Hat Society, whose members go to tea in red hats and purple dresses, began with a few women friends' decision to greet middle age with verve, humor, and élan.

Among a subsample of middle-aged MIDUS respondents, life satisfaction was strongly affected by physical health, a capacity for enjoying life, and positive feelings about the self, as well as serenity in looking at life events. Both the highly educated and the less educated were reasonably satisfied with their lives (Markus, Ryff, Curhan, & Palmersheim, 2004).

Enhanced life satisfaction may be the outcome of a midlife review or revision—a search for balance through the pursuit of previously submerged desires and aspirations (Josselson, 2003). In the Radcliffe study, about two-thirds of the women made major life changes between ages 36 and 43. Women who had midlife regrets—many, about educational or work options they had put aside to assume traditional family roles—and changed their lives accordingly, had greater well-being and better psychological adjustment in the late forties than those who had regrets but did not make the desired changes (Stewart & Ostrove, 1998; Stewart & Vandewater, 1999).

Well-Being at Midlife: Recent International Comparisons Although research on life satisfaction, discussed in the previous section, suggested that middle age is a high point for psychological well-being, a more recent worldwide study of 2 million people in 80 countries found otherwise (Blanchflower & Oswald, 2008). Controlling for cohort effects, the researchers discovered a U-shaped curve. People in most cultures, with some exceptions in developing countries, tend to be happiest early and late in life and unhappiest in early middle age. Well-being generally begins to rise again in the fifties.

What causes the U-shaped pattern? The researchers offered three hypotheses, each of which may in part explain the findings: (1) By midlife, people have learned to maximize their strengths, adapt to their weaknesses, and subdue their impossible dreams. (2) Because cheerful people tend to live longer than discontented ones, the rise in average well-being after midlife may be a selection effect. (3) People who remain physically fit and who see friends and acquaintances their age fall ill and die or suffer disabilities learn to count their blessings during their remaining years.

Unexplained gender differences within the U-shaped pattern occur in some parts of the world. Among Europeans, for example, life satisfaction is lowest for both sexes in the midforties; for British men and women, the likelihood of depression peaks at about age 44. In the United States, too, life satisfaction is lowest for both sexes in the midforties, perhaps due to pressures of work and the rearing of adolescent children. Women tend to be happiest in their late thirties and men in their early fifties (in contrast with the Mills studies, which found the fifties to be a group of educated women's prime of life), but men in recent cohorts have been less and less contented with their lives. Further research may help explain such varying conclusions, which may in part result from the way researchers define terms such as *emotionality, psychological well-being*, and *life satisfaction* and in part from the methods they use to measure these concepts.

Table 16-3   Dimensions of Well-Being Used in Ryff's Scale

Self-Acceptance

High scorer: possesses a positive attitude toward the self, acknowledges and accepts multiple aspects of self including good and bad qualities; feels positive about past life.

Low scorer: feels dissatisfied with self, is disappointed with what has occurred in past life; is troubled about certain personal qualities; wishes to be different [from] what he or she is.

Positive Relations with Others

High scorer: has warm, satisfying, trusting relationships with others; is concerned about the welfare of others; [is] capable of strong empathy, affection, and intimacy; understands give-and-take of human relationships.

Low scorer: has few close, trusting relationships with others; finds it difficult to be warm, open, and concerned about others; is isolated and frustrated in interpersonal relationships; [is] not willing to make compromises to sustain important ties with others.

Autonomy

High scorer: is self-determining and independent; [is] able to resist social pressures to think and act in certain ways; regulates behavior from within; evaluates self by personal standards.

Low scorer: is concerned about the expectations and evaluations of others; relies on judgments of others to make important decisions; conforms to social pressures to think and act in certain ways.

Environmental Mastery

High scorer: has a sense of mastery and competence in managing the environment; controls complex array of external activities; makes effective use of surrounding opportunities; [is] able to choose or create contexts suitable to personal needs and values.

Low scorer: has difficulty managing everyday affairs; feels unable to change or improve surrounding context; is unaware of surrounding opportunities; lacks sense of control over external world.

Purpose in Life

High scorer: has goals in life and a sense of directedness; feels there is meaning to present and past life; holds beliefs that give life purpose; has aims and objectives for living.

Low scorer: lacks a sense of meaning in life; has few goals or aims, lacks sense of direction; does not see purpose in past life; has no outlooks or beliefs that give life meaning.

Personal Growth

High scorer: has a feeling of continued development; sees self as growing and expanding; is open to new experiences; has sense of realizing his or her potential; sees improvement in self and behavior over time; is changing in ways that reflect more self-knowledge and effectiveness.

Low scorer: has a sense of personal stagnation; lacks sense of improvement or expansion over time; feels bored [with] and uninterested [in] life; feels unable to develop new attitudes or behaviors.

Source: Adapted from Keyes & Ryff, 1999, p. 163, Table 1.

Carol Ryff: Multiple Dimensions of Well-Being   Carol Ryff and colleagues (Keyes & Ryff, 1999; Ryff, 1995; Ryff & Singer, 1998) have developed a model that includes six dimensions of well-being and a self-report scale, the Ryff Well-Being Inventory (Ryff & Keyes, 1995), to measure them. The six dimensions are *self-acceptance, positive relations with others, autonomy, environmental mastery, purpose in life,* and *personal growth* (Table 16-3). According to Ryff, psychologically healthy people have positive attitudes toward themselves and others. They make their own decisions and regulate their behavior, and they choose or shape environments compatible with their needs. They have goals that make their lives meaningful, and they strive to explore and develop themselves as fully as possible.

A series of cross-sectional studies using Ryff's scale have shown midlife to be a period of generally positive mental health (Ryff & Singer, 1998). Middle-aged people expressed greater well-being than older and younger adults in some areas, though not in others. They were more autonomous than younger adults but somewhat less purposeful and less focused on personal growth—future-oriented dimensions that declined even more sharply in late adulthood. Environmental mastery, on the other hand, increased between middle and late adulthood. Self-acceptance was relatively stable for all age groups. Of course, since this research was cross-sectional, we do not know whether the differences were due to maturation, aging, or cohort factors. Overall, men's and women's well-being were quite similar, but women had more positive social relationships (Ryff & Singer, 1998).

When Ryff's scale was used to measure the psychological well-being of minority group members, the collective portrait replicated these age-related patterns. Still, black and Hispanic women scored lower than black and Hispanic men in several areas, revealing "a wider expanse of compromised well-being among ethnic/minority women of differing ages" (Ryff, Keyes, & Hughes, 2004, p. 417). However, when employment and marital status were controlled, minority status predicted positive well-being in several areas, even when education and perceived discrimination were accounted for. It may be that such factors as self-regard, mastery, and personal growth are strengthened by meeting the challenges of minority life (Ryff et al., 2004).

Research suggests that immigrants to the United States may be more physically and mentally healthy than those who have been here for two or more generations. Why? One study, which assessed 312 first-generation Mexican American and Puerto Rican immigrants and 242 second-generation Puerto Ricans, found that resistance to assimilation promotes well-being in the immigrant generation, especially in the domains of autonomy, quality of relationships, and purpose in life. The researchers propose the term *ethnic conservatism* for this tendency to resist assimilation and cling to familiar values and practices that give meaning to life. Ethnic conservatism was less effective in promoting well-being among the second generation, who may find it harder or more psychologically conflicting to resist the pull of assimilation (Horton & Schweder, 2004).

Relationships at Midlife

It is hard to generalize about the meaning of relationships in middle age today. Not only does that period cover a quarter-century of development; it also embraces a greater multiplicity of life paths than ever before (S. L. Brown, Bulanda, & Lee, 2005). For most middle-aged people, however, relationships with others are very important—perhaps in a different way than earlier in life.

Theories of Social Contact

According to **social convoy theory,** people move through life surrounded by *social convoys:* circles of close friends and family members of varying degrees of closeness, on whom they can rely for assistance, well-being, and social support, and to whom they in turn also offer care, concern, and support (Antonucci & Akiyama, 1997; Kahn & Antonucci, 1980). Characteristics of the person (gender, race, religion, age, education, and marital status) together with characteristics of that person's situation (role expectations, life events, financial stress, daily hassles, demands,

Checkpoint

Can you . . .

♦ Explain the concept of positive mental health?

♦ Discuss age trends in emotionality, personality, life satisfaction, and psychological well-being?

♦ Explain the importance of a multifaceted measure of well-being, and name and describe the six dimensions in Ryff's model?

What role do social relationships play in the lives of middle-aged people?

social convoy theory Theory, proposed by Kahn and Antonucci, that people move through life surrounded by concentric circles of intimate relationships on which they rely for assistance, well-being, and social support.

and resources) influence the size and composition of the convoy, or support network; the amount and kinds of social support a person receives; and the satisfaction derived from this support. All of these factors contribute to health and well-being (Antonucci, Akiyama, & Merline, 2001).

Although convoys usually show long-term stability, their composition can change. At one time, bonds with siblings may be more significant; at another time, ties with friends (Paul, 1997). Middle-aged people in industrialized countries tend to have the largest convoys because they are likely to be married, to have children, to have living parents, and to be in the workforce unless they have retired early (Antonucci et al., 2001). Women's convoys, particularly the inner circle, tend to be larger than men's (Antonucci & Akiyama, 1997).

Laura Carstensen's (1991, 1995, 1996; Carstensen, Isaacowitz, & Charles, 1999) **socioemotional selectivity theory** offers a life-span perspective on how people choose with whom to spend their time. According to Carstensen, social interaction has three main goals: (1) It is a source of information; (2) it helps people develop and maintain a sense of self; and (3) it is a source of pleasure and comfort, or emotional well-being. In infancy, the third goal, the need for emotional support, is paramount. From childhood through young adulthood, information-seeking comes to the fore. As young people strive to learn about their society and their place in it, strangers may well be the best sources of knowledge. By middle age, although information-seeking remains important (Fung, Carstensen, & Lang, 2001), the original, emotion-regulating function of social contacts begins to reassert itself. In other words, middle-aged people increasingly seek out others who make them feel good (Figure 16-2). In research testing the theory, middle-aged and older adults placed greater emphasis than young adults on emotional affinity in choosing hypothetical social partners (Carstensen et al., 1999).

High

Importance of Motives for Social Contact

Emotion-seeking

Knowledge-seeking

Low

Infancy Adolescence Middle age Old age

Figure 16-2

How motives for social contact change across the life span. According to socioemotional selectivity theory, infants seek social contact primarily for emotional comfort. In adolescence and young adulthood, people tend to be most interested in seeking information from others. From middle age on, emotional needs increasingly predominate. (Source: Adapted from Carstensen, Gross, & Fung, 1997.)

socioemotional selectivity theory Theory, proposed by Carstensen, that people select social contacts on the basis of the changing relative importance of social interaction as a source of information, as an aid in developing and maintaining a self-concept, and as a source of emotional well-being.

Relationships, Gender, and Quality of Life

For most middle-aged adults, relationships are the most important key to well-being (Markus et al., 2004). They can be a major source of health and satisfaction (Lachman, 2004). Indeed, having a partner and being in good health are the biggest factors in well-being for women in their fifties, according to two national surveys. Having or not having children made little difference. Least happy, loneliest, and most depressed were mothers who were single, divorced, or widowed (Koropeckyj-Cox, Pienta, & Brown, 2007).

However, relationships also can present stressful demands (Lachman, 2004), which tend to fall most heavily on women. A sense of responsibility and concern for others may impair a woman's well-being when problems or misfortunes beset her mate, children, parents, friends, or coworkers. This vicarious stress may help explain why middle-aged women are especially susceptible to depression and other mental health problems and why, as we will see, they tend to be unhappier with their marriages than are men (Antonucci & Akiyama, 1997; S. P. Thomas, 1997).

In studying midlife social relationships, then, we need to keep in mind that their effects can be both positive and negative. In the remaining sections of this

Checkpoint

Can you . . .

◆ Summarize two theoretical models of the selection of social contacts?

◆ Discuss how relationships can affect quality of life in middle adulthood?

chapter, we examine how intimate relationships develop during the middle years. We look first at relationships with spouses, cohabiting partners, homosexual partners, and friends; next at bonds with maturing children; and then at ties with aging parents, siblings, and grandchildren.

Consensual Relationships

Marriages, cohabitations, homosexual unions, and friendships typically involve two people of the same generation who mutually choose each other. How do these relationships fare in middle age?

Marriage

Midlife marriage is very different from what it used to be. When life expectancies were shorter, couples who remained together for 25, 30, or 40 years were rare. The most common pattern was for marriages to be broken by death and for survivors to remarry. People had many children and expected them to live at home until they married. It was unusual for a middle-aged husband and wife to be alone together. Today, more marriages end in divorce, but couples who stay together can often look forward to 20 or more years of married life after the last child leaves home.

What happens to the quality of a longtime marriage? An analysis of two surveys of 8,929 men and women in first marriages found a U-shaped curve similar to the pattern found for psychological well-being in recent international comparisons. During the first 20 to 24 years of marriage, the longer a couple have been married, the less satisfied they tend to be. Then the association between marital satisfaction and length of marriage begins to turn positive. At 35 to 44 years of marriage, a couple tend to be even more satisfied than during the first four years (Orbuch et al., 1996).

Marital satisfaction generally hits bottom early in middle age, when many couples have teenage children and are heavily involved in careers. Satisfaction usually reaches a height when children are grown; many people are retired or entering retirement, and a lifetime accumulation of assets helps ease financial worries (Orbuch et al., 1996). On the other hand, these changes may produce new pressures and challenges (Antonucci et al., 2001).

Sexual satisfaction affects marital satisfaction and stability, according to a longitudinal study of 283 married couples. Those who were satisfied with their sex lives tended to be satisfied with their marriages, and better marital quality led to longer marriages for both men and women (Yeh, Lorenz, Wickrama, Conger, & Elder, 2006).

Cohabitation

Although cohabitation has increased greatly in the United States, it is only half as common in midlife as in young adulthood (Blieszner & Roberto, 2006). With the aging of the baby boom generation, however, it is becoming more so (S. L. Brown et al., 2005).

Do cohabitants reap the same rewards as married people? Although there is little research on cohabitation among middle-aged and older people, one study suggests that the answer, at least for men, is no. Among 18,598 Americans over age 50, cohabiting men (but not cohabiting women) were more likely to be depressed than their married counterparts, even when such variables as physical health, social support, and economic resources were controlled. Indeed, cohabiting

Guidepost 5

How do marriages, cohabitations, gay and lesbian relationships, and friendships fare during the middle years, and how common is divorce at this time of life?

What's Your View?

• How many longtime happily married couples do you know? Can you tell whether their marriages followed patterns similar to those mentioned in the text?

men were about as likely to be depressed as men without partners—widowed, divorced, separated, or never married. It may be that men and women view their relationships differently. Women, like men, may want an intimate companion but may be able to enjoy that companionship without the commitment of formal marriage—a commitment that, in middle age, may come to mean the possibility of having to care for an infirm husband. Aging men, by the same token, may need or anticipate needing the kind of care that wives traditionally provide and may worry about not getting it (S. L. Brown et al., 2005).

Divorce

Divorce in midlife is relatively unusual, though it is becoming more common than in the past (Aldwin & Levenson, 2001; Blieszner & Roberto, 2006). Still, for people who go through a divorce at midlife, when they may have assumed their lives were settled, the breakup can be traumatic. In an American Association of Retired Persons (AARP) survey of men and women who had been divorced at least once in their forties, fifties, or sixties, most respondents described the experience as more emotionally devastating than losing a job and about as devastating as a major illness, though less devastating than a spouse's death. Midlife divorce seems especially hard for women, who are more negatively affected by divorce at any age than men are (Marks & Lambert, 1998; Montenegro, 2004).

Long-standing marriages may be less likely to break up than more recent ones because as couples stay together they build **marital capital,** financial and emotional benefits of marriage that become difficult to give up (Becker, 1991; Jones, Tepperman, & Wilson, 1995). College education decreases the risk of separation or divorce after the first decade of marriage, perhaps because educated couples tend to have accumulated marital assets and may have too much to lose financially from divorce (Hiedemann et al., 1998). Middle-aged divorcees, especially women, who do not remarry tend to be less financially secure than those who remain married (Wilmoth & Koso, 2002) and may have to go to work, perhaps for the first time (Huyck, 1999). According to the AARP survey, loss of financial security is a major concern of people in their forties who divorce and need to show they can get on with their lives. However, people in their fifties have the most difficulty with midlife divorce, perhaps because they worry more about their chances of remarriage and, unlike older divorcees, are more concerned about their future (Montenegro, 2004).

Why do middle-aged people divorce? The number one reason given by the AARP respondents was partner abuse—verbal, physical, or emotional. Other frequent reasons were differing values or lifestyles, infidelity, alcohol or drug abuse, and simply falling out of love.

Most middle-aged divorced people bounce back eventually. On average, the AARP respondents rated their outlook on life as highly as does the general over-45 population and higher than that of singles in their age group. Three out of four said that ending their marriage was the right decision. About one out of three (32 percent) had remarried—6 percent to their former spouses—and their outlook was better than that of those who had not remarried (Montenegro, 2004).

Still, stress often remains, for whatever reason. Nearly half (49 percent) of the AARP respondents, especially women, said they suffered greatly from stress and 28 percent from depression. These proportions are similar to the rates among singles the same age (Montenegro, 2004). On the positive side, the stress of divorce may lead to personal growth (Aldwin & Levenson, 2001; Helson & Roberts, 1994).

The sense of violated expectations may be diminishing as midlife divorce becomes more common (Marks & Lambert, 1998; Norton & Moorman, 1987).

marital capital Financial and emotional benefits built up during a long-standing marriage, which tend to hold a couple together.

This change appears to be due largely to women's growing economic independence (Hiedemann et al., 1998). Divorce rates among aging baby boomers now in their fifties, many of whom married later and had fewer children than in previous generations, are projected to continue to rise (Hiedemann et al., 1998; Uhlenberg, Cooney, & Boyd, 1990). Even in long marriages, the increasing number of years that people can expect to live in good health after child rearing ends may make the dissolution of a marginal marriage and the prospect of possible remarriage a more practical and attractive option (Hiedemann et al., 1998).

Indeed, divorce today may be *less* a threat to well-being in middle age than in young adulthood. That conclusion comes from a five-year longitudinal study that compared the reactions of 6,948 young and middle-aged adults taken from a nationally representative sample. The researchers used Ryff's six-dimensional measure of psychological well-being, as well as other criteria. In almost all respects, middle-aged people showed more adaptability than younger people in the face of separation or divorce, despite their more limited prospects for remarriage (Marks & Lambert, 1998).

Marital Status, Well-Being, and Health

As in young adulthood, marriage offers major benefits: social support, encouragement of health-promoting behaviors, socioeconomic resources (Gallo, Troxel, Matthews, & Kuller, 2003), and wealth accumulation (Wilmoth & Koso, 2002). In the MIDUS sample, men's and women's well-being benefited equally from marriage; but the single state seemed emotionally hardest on midlife men, who tended to be more anxious, sad, or restless and less generative than their younger counterparts. Formerly married, noncohabiting women and men reported more negative emotionality than those still in a first marriage. Still, midlife women who were divorced, remarried, or cohabiting experienced more well-being than their younger counterparts, suggesting that life experience is an asset for women in such situations (Marks et al., 2004).

In cross-sectional studies, married people appear to be healthier, both physically and mentally, in middle age and tend to live longer than single, separated, or divorced people (Brown et al., 2005; Kaplan & Kronick, 2006; Zhang, 2006). Those who never married may be at highest risk, primarily from cardiovascular and other chronic (Kaplan & Kronick, 2006). However, marital status alone is not necessarily the key factor. Among 494 mostly white women ages 42 to 50 followed for 13 years those in highly satisfying marital *or* cohabiting relationships had lower risk factors for cardiovascular disease than women who were not currently in such relationships. This was not true of women who were less satisfied with their relationships. Thus, the stress of a bad relationship may cancel out the potential benefits (Gallo et al., 2003).

Other studies also point to the importance of marital quality. In a national longitudinal survey, marital strains increased both men's and women's aging-related declines in health, and this effect was stronger the older a couple grew (Umberson, Williams, Powers, Liu, & Needham, 2006). A review of many studies suggests that marital conflict can contribute to severe health problems, especially in women, who tend to be more affected by the emotional quality of their marriage. For example, a man's hostile behavior to his wife during a quarrel can raise her blood pressure if she has hypertension. Abrasive relationships also are associated with reduced immune function, more depressive symptoms, and poor health practices. Middle-aged and older adults are at greatest risk because the effects of marital stress interact with the vulnerability associated with aging (Kiecolt-Glaser & Newton, 2001).

✓ **Checkpoint**

Can you . . .

◆ Describe the typical age-related pattern of marital satisfaction, and cite factors that may help explain it?

◆ Compare the benefits of marriage and cohabitation in middle age?

◆ Give reasons for the tendency for divorce to occur early in a marriage, and cite factors that may increase the risk of divorce in midlife?

◆ Discuss the effects of marriage, cohabitation, and divorce on well-being and physical and mental health?

Gay and Lesbian Relationships

Gays and lesbians now in middle age grew up at a time when homosexuality was considered a mental illness, and homosexuals tended to be isolated not only from the larger community but from each other. Today this pioneer generation is just beginning to explore the opportunities inherent in the growing acceptance of homosexuality (Kimmel & Sang, 1995).*

The timing of coming out can affect other aspects of development. Some middle-aged gays and lesbians may be associating openly for the first time and establishing relationships. Many are still working out conflicts with parents and other family members (sometimes including spouses) or hiding their homosexuality from them. Some move to cities with large gay populations where they can more easily seek out and form relationships.

This couple proudly display their certificate of civil union recognizing their relationship as partners. Some gay men and women do not come out until well into adulthood and so may develop intimate relationships later in life than their heterosexual counterparts.

Gay men who do not come out until midlife often go through a prolonged search for identity, marked by guilt, secrecy, heterosexual marriage, and conflicted relationships with both sexes. In contrast, those who recognize and accept their sexual orientation early in life often cross racial, socioeconomic, and age barriers within the gay community.

Midlife friendships often have a special importance for homosexuals. Lesbians are more likely to get emotional support from lesbian friends, lovers, and even ex-lovers than from relatives. Gay men, too, rely on friendship networks, or *fictive kin* (refer back to Chapter 14), which they actively create and maintain. Friendship networks provide solidarity and contact with younger people, which middle-aged heterosexuals normally get through family.

Checkpoint

Can you . . .

- Discuss issues regarding gay and lesbian relationships at midlife?

Friendships

As Carstensen's theory predicts, social networks tend to become smaller and more intimate at midlife. Still, friendships persist and are a strong source of emotional support and well-being, especially for women (Adams & Allan, 1998; Antonucci et al., 2001). Midlife baby boomers have as many as seven good friends on average (Blieszner & Roberto, 2006). Friendships often revolve around work and parenting; others are based on neighborhood contacts or on association in volunteer organizations (Antonucci et al., 2001; Hartup & Stevens, 1999).

The quality of midlife friendships often makes up for what they lack in quantity of time spent. Especially during a crisis, such as a divorce or a problem with an aging parent, adults turn to friends for emotional support, practical guidance, comfort, companionship, and talk (Antonucci & Akiyama, 1997; Hartup & Stevens, 1999; Suitor & Pillemer, 1993). Conflicts with friends often center on differences in values, beliefs, and lifestyles; friends usually can talk out these conflicts while maintaining mutual dignity and respect (Hartup & Stevens, 1999).

* Unless otherwise referenced, this section is based on Kimmel & Sang (1995).

Checkpoint

Can you . . .

♦ Summarize the quantity, quality, and importance of friends in middle age?

Guidepost 6

How do parent-child relationships change as children approach and reach adulthood?

The importance of friendships can vary from time to time. In a longitudinal study of 155 mostly white men and women from middle- and lower-class backgrounds, friends were more important to women's well-being in early middle age, but to men's well-being in late middle age (Paul, 1997).

Relationships with Maturing Children

Parenthood is a process of letting go, and this process usually approaches or reaches its climax during the parents' middle age (Marks et al., 2004). It is true that, with contemporary trends toward delayed marriage and parenthood, some middle-aged people now face such issues as finding a good day care or preschool program and screening the content of Saturday morning cartoons. However, most parents in the early part of middle age must cope with a different set of issues, which arise from living with children who will soon be leaving home. Once children become adults and have their own children, the intergenerational family multiplies in number and in connections. It is middle-aged parents, usually women, who tend to be the family *kinkeepers,* maintaining ties among the various branches of the extended family (Putney & Bengtson, 2001).

Families today are diverse and complex. Increasingly, middle-aged parents have to deal with an adult child's continuing to live in the family home or leaving it only to return. One thing, though, has not changed: Parents' well-being tends to hinge on how their children turn out (Allen, Blieszner, & Roberto, 2000). Fortunately, the parent-child relationship often improves with age (Blieszner & Roberto, 2006).

Adolescent Children: Issues for Parents

Ironically, the people at the two times of life popularly linked with emotional crises—adolescence and midlife—often live in the same household. It is usually middle-aged adults who are the parents of adolescent children. While dealing with their own special concerns, parents have to cope daily with young people who are undergoing great physical, emotional, and social changes.

Although research contradicts the stereotype of adolescence as a time of inevitable turmoil and rebellion, some rejection of parental authority is necessary. An important task for parents is to accept maturing children as they are, not as what the parents had hoped they would be.

Theorists from a variety of perspectives have described this period as one of questioning, reappraisal, or diminished well-being for parents. However, this too is not inevitable. In the MIDUS study, being a parent was associated with more psychological distress than being child-free but also brought greater psychological wellness and generativity, especially to men (Marks et al., 2004).

A questionnaire survey of 129 two-parent families with a firstborn son or daughter between ages 10 and 15 illustrates this complexity. For some parents, especially white-collar and professional men with sons, a child's adolescence brought increased satisfaction, well-being, and even pride. For most parents, however, the normative changes of adolescence elicited a mixture of positive and negative emotions. This was particularly true of mothers with early adolescent daughters, whose relationships tend to be both close and conflict-filled (Silverberg, 1996). In a longitudinal study of 191 families with adolescent children, parents tended to compensate for lack of acceptance and warmth in mother-son and father-daughter relationships by increasing their emotional involvement with work and, in the case of fathers, spending more time there (Fortner, Crouter, & McHale. 2004).

When Children Leave: The Empty Nest

Research is challenging popular ideas about the **empty nest**—a supposedly difficult transition, especially for women, that occurs when the youngest child leaves home. Although some women, heavily invested in mothering, do have problems in adjusting to the empty nest, they are far outnumbered by those who find the departure liberating (Antonucci et al., 2001; Antonucci & Akiyama, 1997; Barnett, 1985; Chiriboga, 1997; Helson, 1997; Mitchell & Helson, 1990). For some women, the empty nest may bring relief from what Gutmann called the "chronic emergency of parenthood" (Cooper & Gutmann, 1987, p. 347). They can pursue their own interests as they bask in their grown children's accomplishments. Today, the refilling of the nest by grown children returning home may be far more stressful (Thomas, 1997).

empty nest Transitional phase of parenting following the last child's leaving the parents' home.

The effects of the empty nest on a marriage depend on its quality and length. In a good marriage, the departure of grown children may usher in a second honeymoon (Robinson & Blanton, 1993). The empty nest may be harder on couples whose identity is dependent on the parental role, or who now must face marital problems they had previously pushed aside under the press of parental responsibilities (Antonucci et al., 2001).

The empty nest does not signal the end of parenthood. It is a transition to a new stage: the relationship between parents and adult children.

Parenting Grown Children

Elliott Roosevelt, a son of President Franklin Delano Roosevelt, used to tell this story about his mother, Eleanor Roosevelt: At a state dinner, Eleanor, who was seated next to him, leaned over and whispered in his ear. A friend later asked Elliott, then in his forties, what she had said. "She told me to eat my peas," he answered.

Even after the years of active parenting are over and children have left home for good, parents are still parents. The midlife role of parent to young adults raises new issues and calls for new attitudes and behaviors on the part of both generations (Marks et al., 2004).

Middle-aged parents generally give their children more help and support than they get from them as the young adults establish careers and families (Antonucci et al., 2001). Parents give the most help to children who need it most, typically those who are single or are single parents (Blieszner & Roberto, 2006). At the same time, adult children's problems reduce their parents' well-being (Greenfield & Marks, 2006). Some parents have difficulty treating their offspring as adults, and many young adults have difficulty accepting their parents' continuing concern about them. In a warm, supportive family environment, such conflicts can be managed by an open airing of feelings (Putney & Bengtson, 2001).

Most young adults and their middle-aged parents enjoy each other's company and get along well. However, intergenerational families do not all fit one mold. An estimated 25 percent of intergenerational families are *tight-knit,* both geographically and emotionally; they have frequent contact with mutual help and support. Another 25 percent are *sociable,* but with less emotional affinity or commitment. About 16 percent have *obligatory* relationships, with much interaction but little emotional attachment; and 17 percent are *detached,* both emotionally and geographically. An in-between category consists of those who are *intimate but distant* (16 percent), spending little time together but retaining warm feelings that might lead to a renewal of contact and exchange. Adult children tend to be closer to their mothers than to their fathers (Bengtson, 2001; Silverstein & Bengtson, 1997).

What's Your View?

• Do you think it is a good idea for adult children to live with their parents?

revolving door syndrome
Tendency for young adults who have left home to return to their parents' household in times of financial, marital, or other trouble.

Checkpoint

Can you . . .

♦ Discuss the changes parents of adolescent children go through?

♦ Compare how women and men respond to the empty nest?

♦ Describe typical features of relationships between parents and grown children?

♦ Give reasons for the prolonged parenting phenomenon, and discuss its effects?

Guidepost 7

How do middle-aged people get along with parents and siblings?

Prolonged Parenting: The "Cluttered Nest"

What happens if the nest does not empty when it normally should, or unexpectedly refills? Since the 1980s, in most Western nations, more and more adult children have delayed leaving home until the late twenties or beyond—a phenomenon called *failure to launch,* discussed in Chapter 14 (Mouw, 2005). Furthermore, the **revolving door syndrome,** sometimes called the *boomerang phenomenon,* has become more common: Increasing numbers of young adults, especially men, return to their parents' home, sometimes more than once, and sometimes with their own families (Aquilino, 1996; Blieszner & Roberto, 2006; Putney & Bengtson, 2001).

Prolonged parenting may lead to intergenerational tension when it contradicts parents' normative expectations (Putney & Bengtson, 2001). As children move from adolescence to young adulthood, parents typically expect them to become independent, and children expect to do so. An adult child's autonomy is a sign of parental success. As the timing-of-events model would predict, then, a grown child's delayed departure from the nest or return to it may produce family stress (Antonucci et al., 2001; Aquilino, 1996). As we mentioned in Chapter 14, parents and adult children tend to get along best when the young adults are employed and living on their own (Belsky, Jaffee. Caspi, Moffitt, & Silva, 2003). When adult children live with parents, relations tend to be smoother when the parents see the adult child moving toward autonomy—for instance, by enrolling in college (Antonucci et al., 2001; Aquilino, 1996).

However, the nonnormative experience of parent-child coresidence is becoming less so, especially for parents with more than one child. Rather than an abrupt leave-taking, the empty nest transition is coming to be seen as a more prolonged process of separation, often lasting several years (Aquilino, 1996; Putney & Bengtson, 2001). Coresidence with adult children may be seen as an expression of family solidarity, an extension of the normative expectation of assistance from parents to young adult children. A nationally representative longitudinal survey of 1,365 married couples with grown children, about 1 in 4 of them living in the parental home, suggests that prolonged parenting need not be a disruptive experience. The presence of adult children seemed to have no effect on the parents' marital happiness, on the amount of marital conflict, or on the amount of time couples had with each other (Ward & Spitze, 2004).

Other Kinship Ties

Except in times of need, ties with the family of origin—parents and siblings—tend to recede in importance during young adulthood, when work, spouses or partners, and children take precedence. At midlife, these earliest kinship ties may reassert themselves in a new way, as the responsibility for care and support of aging parents may begin to shift to their middle-aged children. In addition, a new relationship typically begins at this time of life: grandparenthood.

Relationships with Aging Parents

The middle years may bring dramatic, though gradual, changes in parent-child relationships. Many middle-aged people look at their parents more objectively than before, seeing them as individuals with both strengths and weaknesses. Something else may happen during these years: One day a middle-aged adult may look at a mother or father and see an old person, who may need a daughter's or son's care.

Contact and Mutual Help   Even when they do not live close to each other, most middle-aged adults and their parents have warm, affectionate relationships based on frequent contact, mutual help, feelings of attachment, and shared values. Daughters and older mothers tend to be especially close (Bengtson, 2001; Fingerman & Dolbin-MacNab, 2006; Willson, Shuey, & Elder, 2003). Positive relationships with parents contribute to a strong sense of self and to emotional well-being at midlife (Blieszner & Roberto, 2006).

Most middle-aged adults and their aging parents have warm, affectionate relationships.

Bonds are stronger when middle-aged adults and their parents have similar educational levels and similar work experiences or attitudes toward work. This is more often true of baby boomers and their parents than at any earlier time in history, despite the shifts in gender roles, sexual attitudes, and family structures that have occurred between the two generations. However, about one-third of baby boomers report mixed feelings about their parents (Fingerman & Dolbin-MacNab, 2006).

Mostly, help and assistance continue to flow from parents to child, especially in times of crisis, until quite late in life (Bengtson, 2001; Fingerman & Dolbin-MacNab, 2006). But although most older adults are physically fit, vigorous, and independent, some seek their children's assistance in making decisions and may depend on them for daily tasks and financial help. There may even be a role reversal; a parent, especially after the death of a spouse, now becomes the one who needs help from the child (Antonucci et al., 2001). In the MIDUS study, 1 in 5 adults ages 40 to 59 had a sole surviving parent in poor health, usually the mother (Marks et al., 2004).

With the lengthening of the life span, some developmental scientists have proposed a new life stage called **filial maturity,** when middle-aged children "learn to accept and to meet their parents' dependency needs" (Marcoen, 1995, p. 125). This normative development is seen as the healthy outcome of a **filial crisis,** in which adults learn to balance love and duty to their parents with autonomy within a two-way relationship. Most middle-aged people willingly accept their obligations to their parents (Antonucci et al., 2001).

However, family relations in middle and late adulthood can be complex. With increasing longevity, middle-aged couples with limited emotional and financial resources may need to allocate them among two sets of aging parents as well as provide for their own (and possibly their own adult children's) needs. In one study, researchers interviewed 738 middle-aged sons and daughters from 420 close-knit, mostly two-parent, households. More than 25 percent of the relationships between adult children and their aging parents or in-laws were characterized by ambivalence—nearly 8 percent highly so (Willson et al., 2003).

Ambivalence may surface in trying to juggle competing needs. In a national longitudinal survey of 3,622 married couples with at least one surviving parent, the allocation of assistance to aging parents involved tradeoffs and often depended on family lineage. Most couples contributed time or money, but not both, and few assisted both sets of parents. Couples tended to respond more readily to the needs of the wife's parents, presumably because of her greater closeness to them. African American and Hispanic couples were more likely than white couples to provide consistent assistance of all types to parents on each side of the family (Shuey & Hardy, 2003).

Becoming a Caregiver for Aging Parents   The generations typically get along best while parents are healthy and vigorous. When older people become infirm—especially if they undergo mental deterioration or personality changes—the

filial maturity   Stage of life, proposed by Marcoen and others, in which middle-aged children, as the outcome of a filial crisis, learn to accept and meet their parents' need to depend on them.

filial crisis   In Marcoen's terminology, normative development of middle age, in which adults learn to balance love and duty to their parents with autonomy within a two-way relationship.

burden of caring for them may strain the relationship (Antonucci et al., 2001; Marcoen, 1995). Given the high cost of nursing homes and most older people's reluctance to enter and stay in them (see Chapter 18), many dependent elders receive long-term care in their own home or that of a caregiver (Sarkisian & Gerstel, 2004).

The world over, caregiving is typically a female function (Kinsella & Velkoff, 2001). When an ailing mother is widowed or a divorced woman can no longer manage alone, it is most likely that a daughter will take on the caregiving role (Antonucci et al., 2001; Pinquart & Sörensen, 2006; Schulz & Martire, 2004). Sons do contribute to caregiving, especially if they are not employed (Sarkisian & Gerstel, 2004), but they are less likely to provide primary, personal care (Blieszner & Roberto, 2006; Marks, 1996; Matthews, 1995).

Strains of Caregiving Caregiving can be stressful (Schulz & Martire, 2004). Many caregivers find the task a physical, emotional, and financial burden, especially if they work full-time, have limited financial resources, or lack support and assistance (Lund, 1993a; Schulz & Martire, 2004). It is hard for women who work outside the home to assume an added caregiving role (Marks, 1996), and reducing work hours or quitting a job to meet caregiving obligations can increase financial stress (Schulz & Martire, 2004). Flexible work schedules and family and medical leave could help alleviate this problem.

Emotional strain may come not only from caregiving itself but from the need to balance it with the many other responsibilities of midlife (Antonucci et al., 2001; Climo & Stewart, 2003). Elderly parents may become dependent at a time when middle-aged adults need to launch their children or, if parenthood was delayed, to raise them. Members of this generation in the middle, sometimes called the **sandwich generation,** may be caught in a squeeze between these competing needs and their limited resources of time, money, and energy. Also, a middle-aged child, who may be preparing to retire, can ill afford the additional costs of caring for a frail older person or may have health problems of his or her own (Kinsella & Velkoff, 2001).

Caring for a person with physical impairments is hard. It can be even more difficult to care for someone with dementia, who, in addition to being unable to carry on basic functions of daily living, may be incontinent, suspicious, agitated or depressed, subject to hallucinations, likely to wander about at night, dangerous to self and others, and in need of constant supervision (Biegel, 1995; Schultz & Martire, 2004). Spending hours on end with an elderly, demented parent who may not even recognize her caregiver can be agonizingly isolating (Climo & Stewart, 2003), and the relationship between the two may deteriorate. Sometimes the caregiver becomes physically or mentally ill under the strain (Pinquart & Sörensen, 2007; Schultz & Martire, 2004; Vitaliano, Zhang, & Scanlan, 2003). Because women are more likely than men to give personal care, their mental health and well-being may be more likely to suffer (Amirkhanyan & Wolf, 2006; Climo & Stewart, 2003; Pinquart & Sörensen, 2006). Sometimes the stress created by the incessant, heavy demands of caregiving is so great as to lead to abuse, neglect, or even abandonment of the dependent elderly person (see Chapter 18).

A result of these and other strains may be **caregiver burnout,** a physical, mental, and emotional exhaustion that can affect adults who care for aged relatives (Barnhart, 1992). Even the most patient, loving caregiver may become frustrated, anxious, or resentful under the constant strain of meeting an older person's seemingly endless needs. Often families and friends fail to recognize that caregivers have a right to feel discouraged, frustrated, and put upon. Caregivers need a life of their own, beyond the loved one's disability or disease. Sometimes other arrangements,

sandwich generation Middle-aged adults squeezed by competing needs to raise or launch children and to care for elderly parents.

caregiver burnout Condition of physical, mental, and emotional exhaustion affecting adults who provide continuous care for sick or aged persons.

such as institutionalization, assisted living, or a division of responsibilities among siblings, must be made (Shuey & Hardy, 2003).

Community support programs can reduce the strains and burdens of caregiving, prevent burnout, and postpone the need for institutionalization of the dependent person. Support services may include meals and housekeeping; transportation and escort services; and adult day care centers, which provide supervised activities and care while caregivers work or attend to personal needs. *Respite care* (substitute supervised care by visiting nurses or home health aides) gives regular caregivers some time off, whether for a few hours, a day, a weekend, or a week. Temporary admission of the patient to a nursing home is another alternative. Through counseling, support, and self-help groups, caregivers can share problems, gain information about community resources, and improve skills.

Community support may improve caregivers' morale and reduce stress (Gallagher-Thompson, 1995). In one longitudinal study, caregivers given adequate support became more empathic, caring, understanding, patient, and compassionate, closer to the person they were caring for, and more appreciative of their own good health. Others felt good about having fulfilled their responsibilities. Some had "learned to value life more and to take one day at a time" (Lund, 1993a).

More broadly based interventions target both the caregiver and the patient, offering individual or family counseling, case management, skills training, environmental modification, and behavior management strategies. Such a combination of diverse services and supports can reduce caregivers' burdens and improve their skills, satisfaction, and well-being—and even, sometimes, improve the patient's symptoms (Schulz & Martire, 2004).

Some family caregivers, looking back, regard the experience as uniquely rewarding (Climo & Stewart, 2003). Although role conflicts can seem overwhelming, some middle-aged adults flourish in multiple roles. Circumstances and contexts make a difference, as do the attitudes a person brings to the task (Bengtson, 2001). If a caregiver deeply loves an infirm parent, cares about family continuity, looks at caregiving as a challenge, and has adequate personal, family, and community resources to meet that challenge, caregiving can be an opportunity for personal growth in competence, compassion, self-knowledge, and self-transcendence (Bengtson, 2001; Climo & Stewart, 2003; Bengtson, Rosenthal, & Burton, 1996; Biegel, 1995; Lund, 1993a).

Relationships with Siblings

Sibling ties are the longest-lasting relationships in most people's lives (Blieszner & Roberto, 2006). In some cross-sectional research, sibling relationships over the life span look like an hourglass, with the most contact at the two ends—childhood and middle to late adulthood—and the least contact during the child-raising years. After establishing careers and families, siblings may renew their ties (Bedford, 1995; Cicirelli, 1995; Putney & Bengtson, 2001). Other studies indicate a decline in contact throughout adulthood. Sibling conflict tends to diminish with age—perhaps because siblings who do not get along see each other less (Putney & Bengtson, 2001).

Relationships with siblings who remain in contact can be central to psychological well-being in midlife (Antonucci et al., 2001; Spitze & Trent, 2006). As in young adulthood, sisters tend to be closer than brothers (Blieszner & Roberto, 2006; Spitze & Trent, 2006).

Dealing with the care of aging parents can bring siblings closer together but also can cause resentment and conflict (Antonucci et al., 2001; Bengtson et al., 1996; Blieszner & Roberto, 2006; Ingersoll-Dayton, Neal, Ha, & Hammer, 2003). Disagreements may arise over the division of care or over an inheritance, especially if the sibling relationship has not been good.

What's Your View?

• What would you do if one or both of your parents required long-term care? To what extent should children or other relatives be responsible for such care? To what extent, and in what ways, should society help?

Checkpoint

Can you . . .

♦ Describe the change in the balance of filial relationships that often occurs between middle-aged children and elderly parents?

♦ Cite sources of potential strain in caregiving for elderly parents?

♦ Discuss the nature of sibling relationships in middle age?

In Japan, grandmothers traditionally wear red as a sign of their noble status. Grandparenthood is an important milestone in Western societies as well.

Guidepost 8

What roles do today's grandparents play?

Grandparenthood

Often grandparenthood begins before the end of active parenting. Adults in the United States become grandparents, on average, around age 45 (Blieszner & Roberto, 2006). With today's lengthening life spans, many adults spend several decades as grandparents and live to see grandchildren become adults (Reitzes & Mutran, 2004).

Grandparenthood today is different in other ways from grandparenthood in the past. Most U.S. grandparents have fewer grandchildren than their parents or grandparents did (Blieszner & Roberto, 2006). With the rising incidence of midlife divorce, about 1 in 5 grandparents is divorced, widowed, or separated (Davies & Williams, 2002), and many are stepgrandparents. Middle-aged grandparents tend to be married, active in their communities, and employed and thus less available to help out with their grandchildren. They also are likely to be raising one or more children of their own (Blieszner & Roberto, 2006).

On the other hand, early retirement frees some grandparents to spend more time with their grandchildren. Many grandparents still have living parents, whose care they must balance with grandchildren's needs. And grandparents in both developed and developing countries often provide part-time or primary care for grandchildren (Kinsella & Velkoff, 2001; Szinovacz, 1998).

The Grandparent's Role In many developing societies, such as those in Latin America and Asia, extended-family households predominate, and grandparents play an integral role in child raising and family decisions. In such Asian countries as Thailand and Taiwan, about 40 percent of the population ages 50 and over live in the same household with a minor grandchild, and half of those with grandchildren age 10 or younger—usually grandmothers—provide care for the child (Kinsella & Velkoff, 2001).

In the United States, the extended family household is common in some minority communities, but the dominant household pattern is the nuclear family. When children grow up, they typically leave home and establish new, autonomous nuclear families wherever their inclinations, aspirations, and job hunts take them. Although 68 percent of the grandparents in an AARP survey see at least one grandchild every one or two weeks, 45 percent live too far away to see their grandchildren regularly (Davies & Williams, 2002). However, distance does not necessarily affect the quality of relationships with grandchildren (Kivett, 1991, 1993, 1996).

In general, grandmothers have closer, warmer, more affectionate relationships with their grandchildren (especially granddaughters) than grandfathers do, and see them more (Putney & Bengtson, 2001). Grandparents who have frequent contact with their grandchildren, feel good about grandparenthood, attribute importance to the role, and have high self-esteem tend to be more satisfied with being grandparents (Reitzes & Mutran, 2004).

About 15 percent of U.S. grandparents provide child care for working parents (Davies & Williams, 2002). Indeed, grandparents are almost as likely to be child care providers as organized child care centers or preschools; 30 percent of children under age 5 with employed mothers are under a grandparent's care while the mothers are at work (U.S. Census Bureau, 2008b).

Grandparenting after Divorce and Remarriage   One result of the rise in divorce and remarriage is a growing number of grandparents and grandchildren whose relationships are endangered or severed. After a divorce, because the mother usually has custody, her parents tend to have more contact and stronger relationships with their grandchildren, and the paternal grandparents tend to have less (Cherlin & Furstenberg, 1986; Myers & Perrin, 1993). A divorced mother's remarriage typically reduces her need for support from her parents, but not their contact with their grandchildren. For paternal grandparents, however, the new marriage increases the likelihood that they will be displaced or that the family will move away, making contact more difficult (Cherlin & Furstenberg, 1986).

Because ties with grandparents are important to children's development, every state in the Union has given grandparents (and in some states, great-grandparents, siblings, and others) the right to visitation after a divorce or the death of a parent, if a judge finds it in the best interests of the child. However, a few state courts have struck down such laws, and some legislatures have restricted grandparents' visitation rights. The Supreme Court in June 2000 invalidated Washington State's "grandparents' rights" law as too broad an intrusion on parental rights (Greenhouse, 2000).

Raising Grandchildren   Many grandparents are their grandchildren's sole or primary caregivers. One reason, in developing countries, is the migration of rural parents to urban areas to find work. These *skip-generation* families exist in all regions of the world, particularly in Afro-Caribbean countries. In sub-Saharan Africa, the AIDS epidemic has left many orphans whose grandparents step into the parents' place (Kinsella & Velkoff, 2001).

In the United States, about 2.4 million grandparents (and even some great-grandparents) are serving as *parents by default* for children whose parents are unable to care for them—often as a result of teenage pregnancy, substance abuse, illness, divorce, or death (Allen, Blieszner, & Roberto, 2000; Blieszner & Roberto, 2006). Surrogate parenting by grandparents is a well-established pattern in African

What's Your View?

• Have you had a close relationship with a grandmother or grandfather? If so, in what specific ways did that relationship influence your development?

Checkpoint

Can you . . .

◆ Tell how grandparenthood has changed in recent generations?

◆ Describe the roles grandparents play in family life?

American families (Blieszner & Roberto, 2006). Many of these caregiver-grandparents are divorced or widowed and live on fixed incomes (Hudnall, 2001). Four out of five African American caregiver-grandmothers living below the poverty line do not receive public assistance (Minkler & Fuller-Thomson, 2005).

Unexpected surrogate parenthood can be a physical, emotional, and financial drain on middle-aged or older adults (Blieszner & Roberto, 2006). They may have to quit their jobs, shelve their retirement plans, drastically reduce their leisure pursuits and social life, and endanger their health. Most grandparents do not have as much energy, patience, or stamina as they once had and may not be up on current educational and social trends (Hudnall, 2001).

Most grandparents who take on the responsibility to raise their grandchildren do it because they do not want their grandchildren placed in a stranger's foster home. However, the age difference can become a barrier, and both generations may feel cheated out of their traditional roles. At the same time, grandparents often have to deal with a sense of guilt because the adult children they raised have failed their own children, and also with the rancor they feel toward these adult children. For some caregiver couples, the strains produce tension in their relationship. And, if one or both parents resume their normal roles, it may be emotionally wrenching to return the child (Crowley, 1993; Larsen, 1990–1991).

Grandparents providing **kinship care** who do not become foster parents or gain custody have no legal status and no more rights than unpaid babysitters. They may face many practical problems, from enrolling the child in school and gaining access to academic records to obtaining medical insurance for the child. Grandchildren are usually not eligible for coverage under employer-provided health insurance even if the grandparent has custody. Like working parents, working grandparents need good, affordable child care and family-friendly workplace policies, such as time off to care for a sick child. The federal Family and Medical Leave Act of 1993 does cover grandparents who are raising grandchildren, but many do not realize it.

Grandparents can be sources of guidance, companions in play, links to the past, and symbols of family continuity. They express generativity, a longing to transcend mortality by investing themselves in the lives of future generations. Men and women who do not become grandparents may fulfill generative needs by becoming foster grandparents or volunteering in schools or hospitals. By finding ways to develop what Erikson called the virtue of *care,* adults prepare themselves to enter the culminating period of adult development, which we discuss in Chapters 17 and 18.

kinship care Care of children living without parents in the home of grandparents or other relatives, with or without a change of legal custody.

Checkpoint

Can you . . .

◆ Tell how parents' divorce and remarriage can affect grandparents' relationships with grandchildren?

◆ Discuss the challenges involved in raising grandchildren?

Summary and Key Terms

Looking at the Life Course in Middle Age

Guidepost 1 *How do developmental scientists approach the study of psychosocial development in middle adulthood?*

• Developmental scientists view midlife psychosocial development both objectively, in terms of trajectories or pathways, and subjectively, in terms of people's sense of self and the way they actively construct their lives.

• Change and continuity must be seen in context and in terms of the whole life span.

Change at Midlife: Theoretical Approaches

Guidepost 2 *What do theorists have to say about psychosocial change in middle age?*

• Although some theorists held that personality is essentially formed by midlife, there is a growing consensus that midlife development shows change as well as stability.

• Humanistic theorists such as Maslow and Rogers saw middle age as an opportunity for positive change.

- Costa and McCrae's five-factor model shows slowed change after age 30. Other trait research has found more significant positive change with individual differences.
- Jung held that men and women at midlife express previously suppressed aspects of personality. Two necessary tasks are giving up the image of youth and acknowledging mortality.
- Erikson's seventh psychosocial stage is generativity versus stagnation. Generativity can be expressed through parenting and grandparenting, teaching or mentorship, productivity or creativity, self-development, and "maintenance of the world." The virtue of this period is *care*. Current research on generativity finds it most prevalent at middle age but not universally so.
- Vaillant and Levinson found major midlife shifts in lifestyle and personality.
- The greater fluidity of the life cycle today has partly undermined the assumption of a "social clock."

individuation (517)

generativity versus stagnation (518)

generativity (518)

interiority (520)

The Self at Midlife: Issues and Themes

Guidepost 3 *What issues concerning the self come to the fore during middle adulthood?*

- Key psychosocial issues and themes during middle adulthood concern the existence of a midlife crisis, identity development (including gender identity), and psychological well-being.
- Research does not support a normative midlife crisis. It is more accurate to refer to a transition that may be a psychological turning point.
- According to Whitbourne's identity process theory, people continually confirm or revise their perceptions about themselves on the basis of experience and feedback from others. Identity processes typical of an individual can predict adaptation to aging.
- Generativity is an aspect of identity development.
- Narrative psychology describes identity development as a continuous process of constructing a life story. Highly generative people tend to focus on a theme of redemption.
- Some research has found increasing "masculinization" of women and "feminization" of men at midlife, but this may be largely a cohort effect. Research does *not* support Gutmann's proposed gender crossover.
- Emotionality and personality are related to psychological well-being.
- Research based on Ryff's six-dimensional scale has found that midlife is generally a period of positive mental health and well-being, though socioeconomic status is a factor.
- Although surveys find that life satisfaction rises through middle age, international comparisons suggest that

psychological well-being follows a U-shaped curve with lowest happiness levels at midlife.

midlife crisis (522)

midlife review (523)

identity process theory (IPT) (524)

identity assimilation (524)

identity accommodation (524)

identity balance (524)

gender crossover (526)

Relationships at Midlife

Guidepost 4 *What role do social relationships play in the lives of middle-aged people?*

- Two theories of the changing importance of relationships are Kahn and Antonucci's social convoy theory and Carstensen's socioemotional selectivity theory. According to both theories, socioemotional support is an important element in social interaction at midlife and beyond.
- Relationships at midlife are important to physical and mental health but also can present stressful demands.

social convoy theory (530)

socioemotional selectivity theory (531)

Consensual Relationships

Guidepost 5 *How do marriages, cohabitations, gay and lesbian relationships, and friendships fare during the middle years, and how common is divorce at this time of life?*

- Research on the quality of marriage suggests a U-shaped curve: a dip in marital satisfaction during the years of child rearing, followed by an improved relationship after the children leave home.
- Cohabitation in midlife may negatively affect men's but not women's well-being.
- Divorce at midlife is relatively uncommon but is increasing; it can be stressful and life-changing. Marital capital tends to dissuade midlife divorce.
- Divorce today may be less threatening to well-being in middle age than in young adulthood.
- Married people tend to be happier at middle age than people with any other marital status.
- Because some gays and lesbians delayed coming out, at midlife they may be just establishing intimate relationships.
- Middle-aged people tend to invest less time in friendships than younger adults do but depend on friends for emotional support and practical guidance.
- Friendships may have special importance for gays and lesbians.

marital capital (533)

Relationships with Maturing Children

Guidepost 6 *How do parent-child relationships change as children approach and reach adulthood?*

- Parents of adolescents have to come to terms with a loss of control over their children's lives.
- The emptying of the nest is liberating for most women but may be stressful for couples whose identity is dependent on the parental role or those who now must face previously submerged marital problems.
- Middle-aged parents tend to remain involved with their adult children, and most are generally happy with the way their children turned out. Conflict may arise over grown children's need to be treated as adults and parents' continuing concern about them.
- Today, more young adults are delaying departure from their childhood home or are returning to it, sometimes with their own families. Adjustment tends to be smoother if the parents see the adult child as moving toward autonomy.

empty nest (537)
revolving door syndrome (538)

Other Kinship Ties

Guidepost 7 *How do middle-aged people get along with parents and siblings?*

- Relationships between middle-aged adults and their parents are usually characterized by a strong bond of affection. The two generations generally maintain frequent contact and offer and receive assistance. Aid flows mostly from parents to children.

- As life lengthens, more and more aging parents become dependent for care on their middle-aged children. Acceptance of these dependency needs is the mark of filial maturity and may be the outcome of a filial crisis.
- The chances of becoming a caregiver to an aging parent increase in middle age, especially for women.
- Caregiving can be a source of considerable stress but also of satisfaction. Community support programs can help prevent caregiver burnout.
- Although siblings tend to have less contact at midlife than before and after, most middle-aged siblings remain in touch, and their relationships are important to well-being.

filial maturity (539)
filial crisis (539)
sandwich generation (540)
caregiver burnout (540)

Guidepost 8 *What roles do today's grandparents play?*

- Most U.S. adults become grandparents in middle age and have fewer grandchildren than in previous generations.
- Geographic separation does not necessarily affect the quality of grandparenting relationships.
- Divorce and remarriage of an adult child can affect grandparent-grandchild relationships.
- A growing number of grandparents are raising grandchildren whose parents are unable to care for them. Raising grandchildren can create physical, emotional, and financial strains.

kinship care (544)

Why not look at these new years of life in terms of continued or new roles in society, another stage in personal or even spiritual growth and development?

—Betty Friedan, *The Fountain of Age,* 1993

Did You Know...

- A baby born in the United States today can expect to live about 29 years longer than one born in 1900?

- In many parts of the world, the fastest-growing age group consists of people in their eighties and older?

- Older brains can grow new nerve cells—something researchers once thought impossible?

- Educated people and those who engage in cognitively stimulating activities such as Sudoku puzzles have a reduced risk of developing Alzheimer's disease?

- Longitudinal findings suggest that training may enable older adults not only to recover lost competence, but even to *surpass* their previous attainments?

These are just a few of the interesting and important topics we will cover in this chapter. Today a new view of aging challenges the formerly pervasive picture of old age as a time of inevitable physical and mental decline. People today are living longer and better than at any time in history. In the United States, older adults as a group are healthier, more numerous, and younger at heart than ever before. With improved health habits and medical care, it is becoming harder to draw the line between the end of middle adulthood and the beginning of late adulthood, a line we arbitrarily draw at age 65.

In this chapter we begin by sketching demographic trends among today's older population. We look at the increasing length and quality of life in late adulthood and at causes of biological aging. We examine physical changes and health. We then turn to cognitive development: changes in intelligence and memory, the emergence of wisdom, and the prevalence of continuing education in late life. What emerges is a picture not of "the elderly" but of individual human beings—some needy and frail, but most of them independent, healthy, and involved. After you have read and studied this chapter, you should be able to answer each of the Guidepost questions on the following page.

Guideposts *for Study*

1. How is today's older population changing?

2. How has life expectancy changed, what causes aging, and what possibilities exist for extending the life span?

3. What physical changes occur during old age, and how do these changes vary among individuals?

4. What health problems are common in late adulthood, what factors influence health, and what mental and behavioral problems do some older people experience?

5. What gains and losses in cognitive abilities tend to occur in late adulthood, and are there ways to improve older people's cognitive performance?

Guidepost 1

How is today's older population changing?

ageism Prejudice or discrimination against a person (most commonly an older person) based on age.

The growing visibility of such active, healthy older adults as Nelson Mandela is changing the perception of old age. At age 75, Mandela won the Nobel Peace Prize; and, at age 76, he became president of South Africa.

Old Age Today

In Japan, old age is a status symbol; travelers checking into hotels there are often asked their age to ensure that they will receive proper deference. In the United States, in contrast, aging is generally seen as undesirable. Stereotypes about aging, internalized in youth and reinforced for decades by societal attitudes, may become self-stereotypes, unconsciously affecting older people's expectations about their behavior and often acting as self-fulfilling prophecies (Levy, 2003).

Today, efforts to combat **ageism**—prejudice or discrimination based on age—are making headway, thanks to the growing visibility of active, healthy older adults. Reports about aging achievers appear frequently in the media. On television, older people are less often portrayed as doddering and helpless and more often as level-headed, respected, and wise.

We need to look beyond distorted images of age to its true, multi-faceted reality. What does today's older population look like?

The Graying of the Population

The global population is aging. In 2006, nearly 500 million people world-wide were age 65 or older, and the annual net gain is more than 850,000 each month. By 2030, the total population in that age group is projected to reach 1 billion—1 in every 8 of the earth's human inhabitants. The most rapid increases will be in developing countries, where 60 percent of the world's older people now live. These countries are expected to experience a 140 percent jump in their older population (Dobriansky, Suzman, & Hodes, 2007; Kinsella & Phillips, 2005; Figure 17-1).

Aging populations result from declines in fertility accompanied by economic growth, better nutrition, healthier lifestyles, improved control of infectious disease, safer water and sanitation facilities, and advances in science, technology, and medicine (Administration on Aging, 2003; Dobriansky et al., 2007; Kinsella & Velkoff, 2001).

The aged population itself is aging. In many parts of the world, the fastest-growing age group consists of people in their eighties and older (Dobriansky et al., 2007; Kinsella & Phillips, 2005). Now just 7 percent of the world's older adult population, they are projected to increase

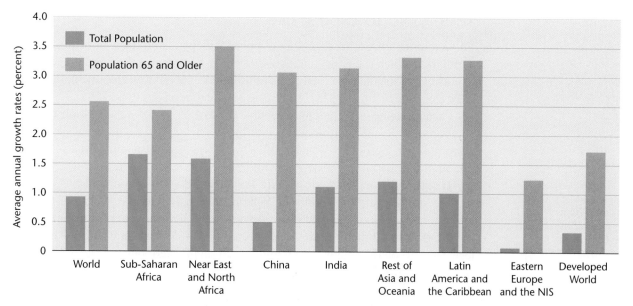

Figure 17-1

Change in the world's older population and total population by region, 2002–2025. The growth of the population age 65 and up is projected to be faster than that of any other segment of the population in all world regions. Growth will be greatest in much of the developing world. (Source: U.S. Census Bureau, 2004; data from U.S. Census Bureau International Programs Center, International Data Base and unpublished tables.)

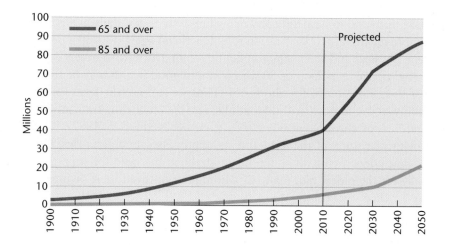

Figure 17-2

United States population age 65 and over, 1900–2000 (selected years) and 2010–2050, projected. (Source: Federal Interagency Forum on Aging-Related Statistics, 2006 p. 2.)

151 percent by 2030 as compared with 104 percent for the older population as a whole and 20 percent for the under-65 population (Dobriansky et al., 2007).

In the United States, the graying of the population has several specific causes, among them high birthrates and high immigration rates during the early to midtwentieth century and a trend toward smaller families, which has reduced the relative size of younger age groups. Since 1900, the proportion of Americans age 65 and up has more than tripled, from 4.1 to 12.4 percent. With the baby boomers turning 65, nearly 20 percent of Americans—71.5 million—are likely to be 65 and older in 2030, almost twice as many as in 2000 (Administration on Aging, 2006; Federal Interagency Forum on Aging-Related Statistics, 2004; Figure 17-2).

Ethnic diversity among older adults is increasing. In 2005, 18.5 percent of older Americans were members of minority groups; by 2050, nearly 39 percent will be. The older Hispanic population is projected to grow most rapidly, from 6 percent of the over-65 population in 2004 to 17.5 percent in 2050, and will become the largest older minority population by 2028 (Federal Interagency Forum on Aging-Related Statistics, 2004, 2006).

What's Your View?

• What stereotypes about aging have you heard in the media and in everyday life?

Young Old to Oldest Old

The economic impact of a graying population depends on the proportion of that population which is healthy and able-bodied. In this regard, the trend is encouraging. Many problems that used to be considered unavoidable are now understood to be due, not to aging itself, but to lifestyle factors or diseases.

Primary aging is a gradual, inevitable process of bodily deterioration that begins early in life and continues through the years, irrespective of what people do to stave it off. **Secondary aging** results from disease, abuse, and disuse—factors that are often within a person's control (Busse, 1987; J. C. Horn & Meer, 1987).

Health and longevity are closely linked to education and other aspects of socioeconomic status (Kinsella & Velkoff, 2001). In George Vaillant's 60-year longitudinal study of 237 Harvard students and 332 disadvantaged urban youth, the disadvantaged men's health deteriorated faster—unless they had finished college. Certain predictors of health and length of life were beyond the individual's control: parents' social class, cohesion of the childhood family, ancestral longevity, and childhood temperament. Other predictors, besides higher education, were at least partly controllable: alcohol abuse, smoking, body mass index, exercise, marital stability, and coping techniques (Vaillant & Mukamal, 2001).

Today, social scientists who specialize in the study of aging refer to three groups of older adults: the "young old," "old old," and "oldest old." Chronologically, *young old* generally refers to people ages 65 to 74, who are usually active, vital, and vigorous. The *old old,* ages 75 to 84, and the *oldest old,* age 85 and above, are more likely to be frail and infirm and to have difficulty managing activities of daily living.

A more meaningful classification is by **functional age:** how well a person functions in a physical and social environment in comparison with others of the same chronological age. A person of 90 who is still in good health may be functionally younger than a person of 65 who is not. Thus we can use the term *young old* for the healthy, active majority of older adults, and *old old* for the frail, infirm minority, regardless of chronological age (Neugarten & Neugarten, 1987). Research in **gerontology,** the study of the aged and aging processes, and **geriatrics,** the branch of medicine concerned with aging, has underlined the need for support services, especially for the oldest old, many of whom have outlived their savings and cannot pay for their own care.

PHYSICAL DEVELOPMENT

Longevity and Aging

How long will you live? Why do you have to grow old? Would you want to live forever? Human beings have been wondering about these questions for thousands of years.

The first question involves several related concepts. **Life expectancy** is the age to which a person born at a certain time and place is statistically likely to live, given his or her current age and health status. Life expectancy is based on the average **longevity,** or actual length of life, of members of a population. Gains in life expectancy reflect declines in *mortality rates,* or death rates (the proportions of a total population or of certain age groups who die in a given year). The human **life span** is the longest period that members of our species can live.

The second question expresses an age-old theme: a yearning for a fountain or potion of youth. Behind this yearning is a fear, not so much of chronological age as of biological aging: loss of health and physical powers. The third question expresses a concern not just with length but with quality of life.

---

primary aging Gradual, inevitable process of bodily deterioration throughout the life span.

secondary aging Aging processes that result from disease and bodily abuse and disuse and are often preventable.

functional age Measure of a person's ability to function effectively in his or her physical and social environment in comparison with others of the same chronological age.

gerontology Study of the aged and the process of aging.

geriatrics Branch of medicine concerned with processes of aging and medical conditions associated with old age.

Checkpoint

Can you . . .

 ◆ Discuss the causes and impact of the aging population?

 ◆ State two criteria for differentiating among the young old, old old, and oldest old?

Guidepost 2

How has life expectancy changed, what causes aging, and what possibilities exist for extending the life span?

life expectancy Age to which a person in a particular cohort is statistically likely to live (given his or her current age and health status), on the basis of average longevity of a population.

longevity Length of an individual's life.

life span The longest period that members of a species can live.

Trends and Factors in Life Expectancy

The graying of the population reflects a rapid rise in life expectancy. A baby born in the United States in 2006 could expect to live 78.1 years, about 29 years longer than a baby born in 1900 (Heron, Hoyert, Xu, Scott, & Tejada-Vera, 2008, NCHS, 2007), according to preliminary data, and more than four times as long as at the dawn of human history (Wilmoth, 2000). Internationally, the average life expectancy in some countries more than doubled in the twentieth century (Kinsella & Phillips, 2005). Such long life is unprecedented in the history of humankind (Figure 17-3). However, some noted gerontologists predict that, in the absence of major lifestyle changes, life expectancy in the United States may halt its upward trend and even decline during coming decades as a rise in obesity-related and infectious diseases offsets gains from medical advances (Olshansky et al., 2005, Preston, 2005).

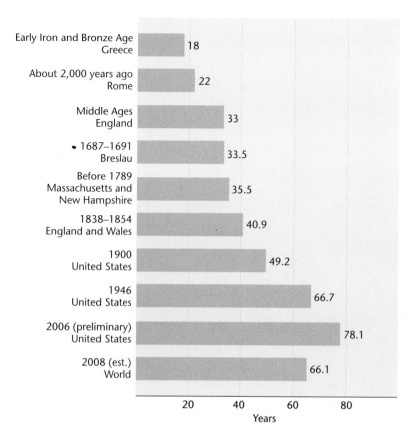

Figure 17-3

Changes in life expectancy from ancient to modern times. (Source: Adapted from Katchadourian, 1987; 2008 estimated world data from Central Intelligence Agency, 2008; preliminary 2006 U.S. data from Heron et al., 2008.)

Gender Differences Nearly all over the world, women of all ages typically live longer than men (Kinsella & Phillips, 2005). The gender gap is widest in high-income industrialized nations, where female mortality dropped sharply with improvements in prenatal and obstetric care. Women's longer lives also have been attributed to their greater tendency to take care of themselves and to seek medical care, the higher level of social support they enjoy, the rise in women's socioeconomic status in recent decades, and men's higher death rates throughout life. Physically, estrogen helps protect women against heart disease and strengthens their immune systems (Gorman & Read, 2007).

In the United States, women's life expectancy in 1900 was only two years longer than men's. The gender gap widened to 7.8 years in the late 1970s, mainly because more men were dying from smoking-related illnesses (heart disease and lung cancer) and fewer women were dying in childbirth. Since then the gap has narrowed to 5.3 years, according to preliminary data (Heron et al., 2008), largely because more women are smoking (Gorman & Read, 2007). Because of the difference in life expectancy, older women in the United States outnumber older men by nearly 3 to 2 (Administration on Aging, 2006), and this disparity increases with advancing age. By age 85, the ratio of women to men is more than 2 to 1 (Gist & Hetzel, 2004).

Regional and Racial/Ethnic Differences The gap in life expectancies between developed and developing countries is vast. More than 6 out of 10 people in developed countries, but only 3 out of 10 in developing countries, live to their 70th birthdays. In the African nation of Sierra Leone, a man born in 2005 could expect to live 37 years, as compared to 80 years for a man in San Marino, a tiny republic surrounded by Italy (WHO, 2003, 2007).

The most dramatic improvements in developing regions have occurred in East Asia, where life expectancy grew from less than 45 years in 1950 to more

Figure 17-4

Life expectancy at birth in years and at age 65, by sex and race: United States, 1970–2004. (Source: NCHS, 2007.)

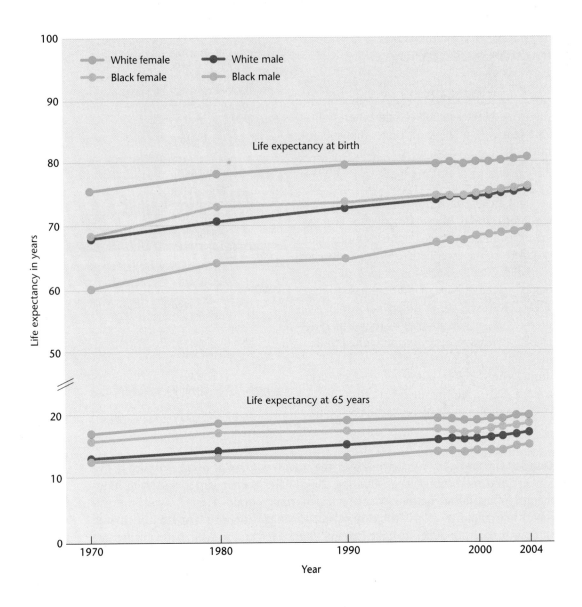

than 72 years today. Almost all nations have shown improvement, however, with some exceptions in Latin America and in Africa, the latter due to the AIDS epidemic (Kinsella & Phillips, 2005).

Wide racial/ethnic, socioeconomic, and geographic disparities in life expectancy exist in the United States. In contrast to the upward national trend, life expectancy has stagnated or even declined since 1983 in many of the nation's poorest counties, mainly in the Deep South, along the Mississippi River, in Appalachia, and in Texas and the southern Plains region (Ezzati, Friedman, Kulkarni, & Murray, 2008). On average, white Americans live about five years longer than African Americans, though this difference has narrowed somewhat with greater reductions in African American death rates from homicide, HIV, accidents, cancer, diabetes, influenza, pneumonia, and, among women, heart disease (Harper, Lynch, Burris, & Smith, 2007; Heron et al., 2008; NCHS, 2007). African Americans, especially men, are more vulnerable than white Americans to illness and death from infancy through middle adulthood. However, the gap begins to close in older adulthood, and by age 85 African Americans can expect slightly more remaining years than white people (Federal Interagency Forum on Aging-Related Statistics, 2004; NCHS, 2007; Figure 17-4).

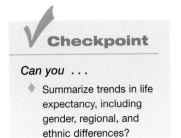

Checkpoint

Can you . . .

♦ Summarize trends in life expectancy, including gender, regional, and ethnic differences?

A new way to look at life expectancy is in terms of the number of years a person can expect to live in good health, free of disabilities. Worldwide, Japan has one of the longest *healthy* life expectancies at birth, 82.2 years. The United States ranks 33rd, with an average healthy life expectancy of 77.9 years. Reasons for this relatively poor showing as compared with other industrialized nations include ill health among the urban poor and some ethnic groups, a relatively large proportion of HIV-related death and disability in young and middle adulthood, high rates of lung disease and coronary heart disease, and fairly high levels of violence (WHO, 2000, 2007).

Why People Age

Hope of further extending healthy life expectancy depends on our growing knowledge of what happens to the human body with the passage of time. What causes **senescence,** a period marked by obvious declines in body functioning associated with aging, and why does its onset vary from one person to another? For that matter, why do people age at all?

Most theories about biological aging fall into two categories (summarized in Table 17-1): *genetic-programming theories* and *variable-rate theories.*

This Japanese woman's active lifestyle has contributed to her long healthy life and to her country's lengthy healthy life expectancy.

Genetic-Programming Theories   **Genetic-programming theories** hold that people's bodies age according to a normal developmental timetable built into the genes. One such theory is that aging results from *programmed senescence:* specific genes "switching off" before age-related losses (for example, in vision, hearing, and motor control) become evident.

senescence   Period of the life span marked by declines in physical functioning usually associated with aging; begins at different ages for different people.

genetic-programming theories   Theories that explain biological aging as resulting from a genetically determined developmental timetable.

Table 17-1	Theories of Biological Aging

Genetic-Programming Theories	Variable-Rate Theories
Programmed senescence theory. Aging is the result of the sequential switching on and off of certain genes. Senescence is the time when the resulting age-associated deficits become evident.	*Wear-and-tear theory.* Cells and tissues have vital parts that wear out.
Endocrine theory. Biological clocks act through hormones to control the pace of aging.	*Free-radical theory.* Accumulated damage from oxygen radicals causes cells and eventually organs to stop functioning.
Immunological theory. A programmed decline in immune system functions leads to increased vulnerability to infectious disease and thus to aging and death.	*Rate-of-living theory.* The greater an organism's rate of metabolism, the shorter its life span.
Evolutionary theory. Aging is an evolved trait enabling members of a species to live only long enough to reproduce.	*Autoimmune theory.* Immune system becomes confused and attacks its own body cells.

Source: Adapted from NIH/NIA, 1993, p. 2.

Twin studies have found that genetic differences account for about one-fourth of the variance in the adult human life span. This genetic influence is minimal before age 60 but increases after that age. It probably involves many rare gene variants, each with small effects (Christensen, Johnson, & Vaupel, 2006; Molofsky et al., 2006). One such gene variant, *APOE2,* is protective against cardiovascular disease and Alzheimer's disease, while another variant of the same gene, *APOE4,* moderately increases the risk of both diseases (Christensen et al., 2006).

Mitochondria, tiny organisms that generate energy for cell processes, play an important role in helping cells survive under stress. A study of worms found that fragmentation of mitochondria prompts cells to self-destruct (Jagasia, Grote, Westermann, & Conradt, 2005), and such defects may be a major cause of aging (Holliday, 2004). Researchers have identified two genes, *SIRT3* and *SIRT4,* that make proteins for mitochondria and thus help keep the body healthy and youthful (Yang et al., 2007). Another protein called NAD activates those genes and thus helps prevent cell death (Yang et al., 2007).

One line of research suggests that aging is regulated by a gradual shrinking of the *telomeres,* the protective tips of chromosomes, which shorten each time cells divide. This programmed erosion may eventually progress to the point where cell division stops (de Lange, 1998). A study of 143 normal, unrelated adults age 60 and up found a link between shorter telomeres and early death, particularly from heart disease and infectious disease (Cawthon, Smith, O'Brien, Sivatchenko, & Kerber, 2003). However, larger studies failed to support this finding when age was controlled (Bischoff et al., 2006) and showed that telomere lengths in blood cells fluctuate from time to time (Martin-Ruiz et al., 2005). Analysis of blood samples from 58 young and middle-aged mothers suggested that stress can affect telomere change (Epel et al., 2004).

According to *endocrine theory,* the biological clock acts through genes that control hormonal changes. Loss of muscle strength, accumulation of fat, and atrophy of organs may be related to declines in hormonal activity (Lamberts, van den Beld, & van der Lely, 1997; Rudman et al., 1990). *Immunological theory* proposes that certain genes may cause problems in the immune system, which declines with age, leaving the body vulnerable to infectious disease (Holliday, 2004; Kiecolt-Glaser & Glaser, 2001).

Still another variant of genetic-programming theory is the *evolutionary theory of aging.* According to this theory, reproductive fitness is the primary aim of natural selection, and no reproductive purpose is served by putting genetic resources into life beyond reproductive age (Baltes, 1997). Thus, aging is an evolved trait enabling members of a species to live only long enough to reproduce. What, then, explains human beings' lengthening life span? One hypothesis is that life span lengthens when adults do not have to compete with their young for available resources (Travis, 2004). Another proposal is that humans continue to serve a reproductive purpose through continuing care of their young (Lee, 2003; Rogers, 2003).

Variable-Rate Theories **Variable-rate theories,** sometimes called *error theories,* view aging as a result of random processes that vary from person to person. In most variable-rate theories, aging involves damage due to chance errors in, or environmental assaults on, biological systems. Other variable-rate theories focus on internal processes such as **metabolism** (the process by which the body turns food and oxygen into energy), which may directly and continuously influence the rate of aging (NIA, 1993; Schneider, 1992).

Wear-and-tear theory holds that the body ages as a result of accumulated damage to the system at the molecular level (Hayflick, 2004; Holliday, 2004). As we mentioned in Chapter 3, the body's cells are constantly multiplying through

variable-rate theories Theories that explain biological aging as a result of processes that vary from person to person and are influenced by both the internal and the external environment; sometimes called *error theories.*

metabolism Conversion of food and oxygen into energy.

cell division; this process is essential to balance the programmed death of useless or potentially dangerous cells and to keep organs and systems functioning properly. As people age, they are less able to repair or replace damaged parts. Internal and external stressors (including the accumulation of harmful materials, such as chemical by-products of metabolism) may aggravate the wearing-down process.

Free-radical theory focuses on harmful effects of **free radicals:** highly unstable oxygen atoms or molecules formed during metabolism, which react with and can damage cell membranes, cell proteins, fats, carbohydrates, and even DNA. Damage from free radicals accumulates with age; it has been associated with arthritis, muscular dystrophy, cataracts, cancer, late-onset diabetes, and neurological disorders such as Parkinson's disease (Stadtman, 1992; Wallace, 1992). Support for free-radical theory comes from research in which fruit flies, given extra copies of genes that eliminate free radicals, lived as much as one-third longer than usual (Orr & Sohal, 1994). Conversely, a strain of mice bred without a gene called *MsrA* that normally protects against free radicals had shorter-than-normal life spans (Moskovitz et al., 2001).

free radicals Unstable, highly reactive atoms or molecules, formed during metabolism, which can cause internal bodily damage.

Rate-of-living theory suggests that the body can do just so much work, and that's all; the faster it works, the more energy it uses, and the faster it wears out. Thus, speed of metabolism, or energy use, determines length of life. Fish whose metabolism is lowered by putting them in cooler water live longer than they would in warm water (Schneider, 1992). (We present additional evidence for rate-of-living theory in the next section.)

Autoimmune theory suggests that an aging immune system can become "confused" and release antibodies that attack the body's own cells. This malfunction, called **autoimmunity,** is thought to be responsible for some aging-related diseases and disorders (Holliday, 2004).

autoimmunity Tendency of an aging body to mistake its own tissues for foreign invaders and to attack and destroy them.

Genetic-programming and variable-rate theories have practical implications. If human beings are programmed to age at a certain rate, they can do little to retard the process except to try to alter the appropriate genes. If, on the other hand, aging is variable, then sound lifestyle and health practices may influence it. However, there is no evidence to support the profusion of commercial "anti-aging" remedies now on the market (International Longevity Center, 2002; Olshansky, Hayflick, & Carnes, 2002a, 2002b; Olshansky, Hayflick, & Perls, 2004). The fundamental assumption of the quest for such remedies is that something is wrong with aging—indeed, that aging is a disease. Actually, it is a natural part of life. Instead of looking for anti-aging remedies, many gerontologists urge that more resources be devoted to research on "longevity medicine"—ways to combat specific diseases and thus prolong life (International Longevity Center, 2002; Olshansky et al., 2002a).

It seems likely that several of these theoretical perspectives offer parts of the truth (Holliday, 2004). Controllable environmental and lifestyle factors may interact with genetic factors to determine how long a person lives and in what condition. In a study of 1,402 adults of various ages, genetic factors explained 57 percent of the variance in biological age of bone tissue. The remaining variance was presumably environmentally influenced (Karasik, Hannan, Cupples, Felson, & Kiel, 2004).

A current theory incorporating both evolutionary and variable-rate theories (Hayflick, 2004) is that natural selection has resulted in energy resources sufficient only to maintain the body until reproduction. After reproduction, there is insufficient energy left to continue to maintain the molecular integrity of body cells and systems. As time goes on, these deteriorate randomly, beyond the body's capacity to repair them, resulting in increased vulnerability to disease and death. Although everyone goes through the same aging process, its rate varies from cell to cell, tissue to tissue, and organ to organ.

Edna Parker holds a rose she was given during her 115th birthday party in Shelbyville, Indiana, April 18, 2008. Parker, who was born April 20, 1893, is the world's oldest known living person, having outlived her two sisters and two sons. She is a participant in the New England Cententarians Study.

survival curves Curves, plotted on a graph, showing percentages of a population that survive at each age level.

Hayflick limit Genetically controlled limit, proposed by Hayflick, on the number of times cells can divide in members of a species.

What's Your View?

• If you could live as long as you wanted to, how long would you choose to live? What factors would affect your answer?

• Which would you rather do: live a long life, or live a shorter life with a higher quality of life?

How Far Can the Life Span Be Extended?

The idea that people can control the length and quality of their lives goes back to Luigi Cornaro, a nobleman of the sixteenth-century Italian Renaissance (Haber, 2004). Cornaro practiced moderation in all things, and he lived to be 98—close to what scientists once considered the upper limit of the human life span. Today that limit has been greatly exceeded by the growing number of centenarians—people who live well past 100 (Box 17-1). Is it possible for human beings to live even longer?

Until recently, **survival curves**—percentages of people or animals who live to various ages—supported the idea of a biological limit to the life span, with more and more members of a species dying each year as they approach it. Although many people were living longer than in the past, the curves still ended around age 100. This observation suggested that, regardless of health and fitness, the maximum life span is not much higher.

Leonard Hayflick (1974) found that human cells will divide in the laboratory no more than 50 times. This is called the **Hayflick limit,** and it has been shown to be genetically controlled (Schneider, 1992). If, as Hayflick (1981) suggested, cells go through the same process in the body as in a laboratory culture, there might be a biological limit to the life span of human cells, and therefore of human life—a limit Hayflick estimated at 110 years.

However, the pattern appears to change at very old ages. In Sweden, for example, the maximum life span increased from about 101 years in the 1860s to 108 years in the 1990s, mainly due to reductions in death rates after age 70 (Wilmoth, Deegan, Lundstrom, & Horiuchi, 2000). Furthermore, death rates actually *decrease* after 100 (Coles, 2004). People at 110 are no more likely to die in a given year than people in their eighties (Vaupel et al., 1998). In other words, people hardy enough to reach a certain age are likely to go on living a while longer. This is why life expectancy at 65, for example, is longer than life expectancy at birth (Administration on Aging, 2006). From this and other demographic evidence, at least one researcher suggests that there is no fixed limit on the human life span (Wilmoth, 2000).

Others believe that genetics plays at least a partial role in human longevity (Coles, 2004) and that the idea of an exponential increase in the human life span is unrealistic (Holliday, 2004). Gains in life expectancy since the 1970s have come from reductions in age-related diseases, such as heart disease, cancer, and stroke, and further gains will be far more difficult to achieve unless scientists find ways to modify the basic processes of aging—a feat some gerontologists consider impossible (Hayflick, 2004; Holliday, 2004).

Animal research, however, challenges the idea of an unalterable biological limit for each species. Scientists have extended the healthy life spans of worms, fruit flies, and mice through slight genetic mutations (Ishii et al., 1998; T. E. Johnson, 1990; Kolata, 1999; Lin, Seroude, & Benzer, 1998; Parkes et al., 1998; Pennisi, 1998). Such research suggests the possibility of delayed senescence and a significant increase in the average and maximum life spans (Arking, Novoseltsev, & Novoseltseva, 2004). In human beings, of course, genetic control of a biological process may be far more complex. Because no single gene or process seems responsible for senescence and the end of life, we are less likely to find genetic quick fixes for human aging (Holliday, 2004; Olshansky et al., 2002a).

BOX 17-1 Research *in Action*

Centenarians

A century ago, most Americans did not live to their 50th birthdays. Today people over 100 are a fast-growing segment of the population. Statistics show an 88 percent increase in the number of centenarians in the United States since 1990 (Administration on Aging, 2006). In Europe's industrialized countries, the centenarian population has doubled each decade since 1950 (Kinsella & Phillips, 2005).

Leading gerontologists worry that a longer life span means an increasing number of people with chronic disease, but that prediction may not necessarily come true. Remarkably, among 424 centenarians in the United States and Canada, about one-half of both men and women were free of heart disease, stroke, and cancer (other than skin cancer), the three most common causes of mortality in old age. The researchers found three alternative patterns in the centenarians' health histories. Nearly 1 in 5 (32 percent of the men and 15 percent of the women) were *escapers*—they were disease-free. *Survivors* (24 percent of the men and 43 percent of the women) had been diagnosed with an age-associated illness such as stroke, heart disease, cancer, hypertension, diabetes, or chronic obstructive pulmonary disease before age 80 but had survived it. The largest category, *delayers* (44 percent of the men and 42 percent of the women), had managed to delay the onset of age-related disease until age 80 or later. Altogether, 87 percent of the men and 83 percent of the women had escaped or delayed these diseases (Evert, Lawler, Bogan, & Perls, 2003).

What might explain this pattern? One possibility is exceptional genes. Centenarians tend to be relatively free of genes linked to age-related fatal diseases such as cancer and Alzheimer's. A region on chromosome 4, shared by many of the centenarians studied, has been linked to exceptionally long life (Perls, Kunkel & Puca, 2002a, 2002b; Puca et al., 2001) and also to healthy aging (Reed, Dick, Uniacke, Foroud, & Nichols, 2004). In other research, a gene variant studied in people of Ashkenazi (Eastern European) Jewish descent age 95 and older seemed to protect memory and the ability to think and learn (Barzilai, Atzmon, Derby, Bauman, & Lipton, 2006).

Centenarians studied in eight New England towns vary widely in educational level, socioeconomic status, religion, ethnicity, and diet patterns. Some are vegetarians, while others eat a lot of saturated fats. Some were athletes and some did no strenuous activity. However, few are obese, and heavy smoking is rare among them. A disproportionate number are never-married women; and, among those who are mothers, a disproportionate number had children after age 40. The only shared personality trait is the ability to manage stress (Perls, Alpert, & Fretts, 1997; Perls, Hutter-Silver, & Lauerman, 1999; Silver, Bubrick, Jilinskaia, & Perls, 1998).

Perhaps this quality was exemplified by Anna Morgan of Rehoboth, Massachusetts. Before her death at 101, she made her own funeral arrangements. "I don't want my children to be burdened with all this," she explained to the researchers. "They're old, you know" (Hilts, 1999, p. D7).

What's Your View?

Have you ever known someone who lived past 100? If so, to what did that person attribute his or her longevity? Did he or she have family members who also were long-lived?

Check It Out

For more information on this topic, go to www.bumc.bu.edu/ Dept/Content.aspx?DepartmentID=361&PageID=5749. This is a page on the website of Boston University School of Medicine, which gives background information on centenarians and links to information about the New England Centenarians Study. Or visit www.grg.org/calment.html. This website contains lists of supercentenarians currently alive, as well as information on past supercentenarians recorded throughout history.

One promising line of research—inspired by rate-of-living theories that view the speed of metabolism, or energy use, as the crucial determinant of aging—is on dietary restriction. Drastic caloric reduction (but still including all necessary nutrients) has been found to greatly extend life in worms, fish, and monkeys—in fact, in nearly all animal species on which it has been tried (Bodkin, Alexander, Ortmeyer, Johnson, & Hansen, 2003; Heilbronn & Ravussin, 2003; Weindruch & Walford, 1988). A review of 15 years of research suggests that calorie restriction can have beneficial effects on human aging and life expectancy (Fontana & Klein, 2007).

The Calorie Restriction Society practices voluntary caloric restriction, avoiding processed foods rich in refined carbohydrates and partially hydrogenated oils.

Checkpoint

Can you . . .

♦ Compare two types of theories of biological aging and discuss their implications and supporting evidence?

♦ Discuss findings of life-extension research and its limitations in human beings?

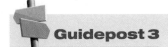

Guidepost 3

What physical changes occur during old age, and how do these changes vary among individuals?

reserve capacity   Ability of body organs and systems to put forth four to ten times as much effort as usual under acute stress; also called *organ reserve.*

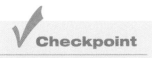

Checkpoint

Can you . . .

♦ Summarize common changes and variations in systemic functioning during late life?

In comparison with control groups eating a typical Western diet, society members show many of the same improvements in metabolic and organ function previously reported in calorie-restricted mice, among them, a low percentage of body fat, low blood pressure, and cardiac function similar to that of persons 16 years younger (Fontana & Klein, 2007).

However, the optimal amount of caloric restriction in humans is not known, and neither are any adverse effects of such extreme restriction. For these reasons, and because a very-low-calorie diet takes great discipline to maintain, there is increasing interest in developing drugs that mimic the effects of caloric restriction (Fontana & Klein, 2007).

If human beings someday realize the age-old dream of a fountain of youth, some gerontologists fear a rise in age-related diseases and disabling infirmities (Banks & Fossel, 1997; Cassel, 1992; Stock & Callahan, 2004; Treas, 1995). Life-extension studies in animals and research on human centenarians, though, suggest that such fears may be unwarranted and that fatal diseases would come very near the end of a longer life (International Longevity Center, 2002).

Physical Changes

Some physical changes typically associated with aging are obvious to a casual observer, though they affect some older people more than others. Older skin tends to become paler and less elastic; and, as fat and muscle shrink, the skin may wrinkle. Varicose veins may appear on the legs. The hair on the head thins and turns gray and then white, and body hair becomes sparser.

Older adults become somewhat shorter as the disks between their spinal vertebrae atrophy. Especially in women with osteoporosis, thinning of the bones may cause *kyphosis,* commonly called a "dowager's hump," an exaggerated curvature of the spine. In addition, the chemical composition of the bones changes, creating a greater risk of fractures. Less visible but equally important changes affect internal organs and body systems; the brain; and sensory, motor, and sexual functioning.

Organic and Systemic Changes

Changes in organic and systemic functioning are highly variable, both among and within individuals. Some body systems decline rapidly, others hardly at all (Figure 17-5). Aging, together with chronic stress, can depress immune function, making older people more susceptible to respiratory infections (Kiecolt-Glaser & Glaser, 2001) and less likely to ward them off (Koivula, Sten, & Makela, 1999). The digestive system, on the other hand, remains relatively efficient. The rhythm of the heart tends to become slower and more irregular. Deposits of fat accumulate around the heart and may interfere with functioning, and blood pressure often rises.

Reserve capacity, or *organ reserve,* is a backup capacity that helps body systems function to their utmost limits in times of stress. With age, reserve levels tend to drop, and many older people cannot respond to extra physical demands as well as they once did. A person who used to be able to shovel snow and then go skiing afterward may now exhaust the heart's capacity just by shoveling or may have to stop shoveling altogether.

Still, many older adults barely notice changes in systemic functioning. Many activities do not require peak performance. By pacing themselves, most older adults can do almost anything they need and want to do.

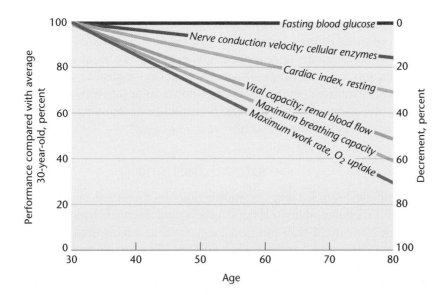

Figure 17-5
Declines in organ functioning.
Differences in functional efficiency
of various internal body systems
are typically slight in young adulthood but widen by old age.
(Source: Katchadourian, 1987.)

The Aging Brain

In normal, healthy people, changes in the aging brain are generally subtle. They make little difference in functioning and vary considerably from one person to another, from one region of the brain to another, and from one type of task to another (Burke & Barnes, 2006; Finch & Zelinski, 2005. Declines in long-term memory tend to begin in the late fifties, whereas the ability to understand unfamiliar words from their context remains strong until the late seventies (Finch & Zelinski, 2005). Furthermore, the brain's plasticity can "reorganize neural circuitry to respond to the challenge of neurobiological aging" (Park & Gutchess, 2006, p. 107).

In late adulthood, the brain gradually diminishes in volume and weight, particularly in the frontal cortex, which controls executive functions (Park & Gutchess, 2006; von Hippel, 2007). This gradual shrinkage was formerly attributed to a loss of neurons (nerve cells). However, most researchers now agree that—except in certain specific brain areas, such as the cerebellum, which coordinates sensory and motor activity—neuronal loss is not substantial and does not affect cognition (Burke & Barnes, 2006; Finch & Zelinski, 2005).

Another typical change is a decrease in the number, or density, of dopamine neurotransmitters due to losses of synapses (neuronal connections). This change generally results in slowed response time—though in some complex tasks such as skilled typing, older adults respond more quickly than younger adults.

Beginning in the midfifties, the myelin sheathing that enables neuronal impulses to travel rapidly between brain regions begins to thin out. This deterioration of the brain's myelin, or white matter, is associated with cognitive and motor declines (Andrews-Hanna et al., 2007; Finch & Zelinski, 2005).

Postmortem examinations of brain tissue collected from 30 people ages 26 to 106 found significant DNA damage in certain genes that affect learning and memory in most very old people and some middle-aged people (Lu et al., 2004). However, such deterioration is *not* inevitable. A postmortem examination of the brain of a Dutch woman who died at 115 found no evidence of dementia. Two to three years before her death, her neurological and cognitive performance tested better than that of the average 60- to 75-year-old (den Dunnen et al., 2008).

Not all changes in the brain are destructive. Researchers have discovered that older brains can grow new nerve cells from stem cells—something once thought impossible. Evidence has been found of cell division in the hippocampus, a portion of the brain involved in learning and memory (Eriksson et al., 1998; Van Praag et al., 2002).

Checkpoint

Can you . . .

♦ Identify several age-related changes in the brain and their effects on cognitive and social functioning?

Changes in the brain can have social as well as cognitive consequences. Loss of executive function in the frontal cortex can lessen the ability to inhibit irrelevant or unwanted thoughts; thus, older adults may talk too much about matters apparently unconnected to the topic of conversation. On the positive side, the amygdala, the seat of emotions, shows lessened response to negative, but not positive, events; thus, older adults tend to be more constructive in resolving conflicts than are younger adults (von Hippel, 2007).

Sensory and Psychomotor Functioning

Individual differences in sensory and motor functioning increase with age. Some older people experience sharp declines; others find their abilities virtually unchanged. One 80-year-old man can hear every word of a whispered conversation; another cannot hear the doorbell. One 70-year-old woman runs five miles a day; another cannot walk around the block. Impairments tend to be more severe among the old old. Visual and hearing problems may deprive them of social relationships and independence (Desai, Pratt, Lentzner, & Robinson, 2001; O'Neill, Summer, & Shirey, 1999), and motor impairments may limit everyday activities.

Vision and Hearing   Older eyes need more light to see, are more sensitive to glare, and may have trouble locating and reading signs. Thus driving may become hazardous, especially at night. Older adults may have difficulty with depth or color perception or with such daily activities as reading, sewing, shopping, and cooking (Desai et al., 2001). Losses in visual contrast sensitivity can cause difficulty reading very small or very light print (Akutsu, Legge, Ross, & Schuebel, 1991; Kline & Scialfa, 1996). Vision problems also can cause accidents and falls. Approximately 1.8 million community-dwelling older adults report difficulty with bathing, dressing, and walking around the house, in part because they are visually impaired (Desai et al., 2001).

People with moderate visual losses often can be helped by corrective lenses or changes in the environment. Still, 17 percent of U.S. older adults and 30 percent of those 85 and older have trouble seeing, even when wearing glasses or contact lenses (Schoenborn, Vickerie, & Powell-Griner, 2006).

cataracts   Cloudy or opaque areas in the lens of the eye, which cause blurred vision.

age-related macular degeneration   Condition in which the center of the retina gradually loses its ability to discern fine details; leading cause of irreversible visual impairment in older adults.

glaucoma   Irreversible damage to the optic nerve caused by increased pressure in the eye.

Cataracts, cloudy or opaque areas in the lens of the eye, are common in older adults and eventually cause blurred vision (Schaumberg et al., 2004). Surgery to remove cataracts is usually successful and is one of the most frequent operations among older Americans. **Age-related macular degeneration,** in which the center of the retina gradually loses the ability to sharply distinguish fine details, is the leading cause of visual impairment in older adults. In some cases, treatments such as laser surgery, photodynamic therapy, and antioxidant and zinc supplements can prevent further vision loss (Foundation Fighting Blindness, 2005).

Glaucoma is irreversible damage to the optic nerve caused by increased pressure in the eye. If left untreated it can cause blindness. Early treatment can lower elevated pressure in the eye and delay the onset of the condition (Heijl et al., 2002). Worldwide, glaucoma is the second leading cause of blindness (Quigley & Broman, 2006).

Hearing impairments increase with age, affecting 31.4 percent of Americans ages 65 to 74 and 58 percent of those 85 and over. Men are more likely to experience hearing loss than women, and white people more than black people (Schoenborn et al., 2006). Hearing loss may contribute to a false perception of older people as distractible, absentminded, and irritable and tends to have a negative impact on the well-being, not only of the impaired person, but of his or her spouse or partner (Wallhagen, Strawbridge, Shema, & Kaplan, 2004). It also may contribute to difficulty remembering what others say (Wingfield et al., 2005). Hearing aids can help but are expensive and may magnify background

In age-related macular degeneration, the leading cause of visual impairment in older adults, the center of the retina gradually loses the ability to distinguish details. In these photos, the left is an image as seen by a person with normal vision and the right is the same image as seen by a person with macular degeneration.

noises as well as the sounds a person wants to hear. Another device for assisting hearing is a built-in telephone amplifier.

Changes in environmental design, such as brighter reading lights and a closed captioning option on television sets can help many older adults with sensory limitations. Table 17-2 lists these and other ways in which inventors are redesigning the physical environment to meet the needs of an aging population.

Table 17-2	Environmental Changes for an Aging Population*

Aids to Vision
Brighter reading lights
Larger-print books
Carpeted or textured (not shiny) floors
Spoken as well as visual signals: "talking" exit signs, appliances that speak up when they get hot, cameras that announce when the light is too low, automobiles that warn of an impending collision

Aids to Hearing
Closed captioning on TV sets
Public address systems and recordings engineered to an older adult's auditory range
Park benches and couches angled or clustered so older adults can communicate face-to-face

Aids to Manual Dexterity
Comb and brush extenders
Stretchable shoelaces
Velcro tabs instead of buttons
Lightweight motorized pot-and-pan scrubbers and garden tools
Tap turners on faucets
Foot mops that eliminate bending
Voice-activated telephone dialers
Long-handled easy-grip zippers
Contoured eating utensils

Aids to Mobility and Safety in the Home
Ramps instead of stairs
Levers instead of knobs

Lower closet shelves
Lower windows for people who sit a lot
Regulators to keep tap water from scalding
"Soft tubs" to prevent slips, add comfort, and keep bath water from cooling too fast
Sensors to monitor the movements of an older person living alone and alert friends or relatives to any unusual activity

Aids to Pedestrian Safety
Street lights that change more slowly
Traffic islands to let slow walkers pause and rest
Lower bus platforms and steps

Aids to Safe Driving
Clearer road signs and pavement markings
Automobiles programmed to operate windows, radio, heater, lights, wipers, and even the ignition by verbal commands
Windshields that automatically adjust their tint to weather and light conditions and are equipped with large, liquid-crystal displays of speed and other information, so that older drivers need not take their eyes off the road and readjust their focus

Temperature Adjustments
Homes and hotels with heated furniture
Thermostats in each room
Heated clothing
Heat-producing foods

*Many of these innovations are already in place; others are likely to occur in the near future.

Sources: Dychtwald & Flower, 1990; Eisenberg, 2001; Staplin, Lococo, Byington, & Harkey, 2001a, 2001b.

Table 17-3	Safety Checklist for Preventing Falls in the Home
Stairways, hallways, and pathways	Free of clutter Good lighting, especially at top of stairs Light switches at top and bottom of stairs Tightly fastened handrails on both sides and full length of stairs Carpets firmly attached and not frayed; rough-textured or abrasive strips to secure footing
Bathrooms	Grab bars conveniently located inside and outside of tubs and showers and near toilets Nonskid mats, abrasive strips, or carpet on all surfaces that may get wet Night lights
Bedrooms	Telephones and night lights or light switches within easy reach of beds
All living areas	Electrical cords and telephone wires out of walking paths Rugs and carpets well secured to floor No exposed nails or loose threshold trim Furniture and other objects in familiar places and not in the way; rounded or padded table edges Couches and chairs proper height to get into and out of easily

Source: Adapted from NIA, 1993.

Strength, Endurance, Balance, and Reaction Time Adults generally lose about 10 to 20 percent of their strength up to age 70 and more after that. Endurance declines more consistently with age, especially among women, than some other aspects of fitness, such as flexibility (Van Heuvelen, Kempen, Ormel, & Rispens, 1998). Declines in muscle strength and power may result from a combination of natural aging, decreased activity, and disease (Barry & Carson, 2004).

These losses seem to be partly reversible. In controlled studies with people in their sixties to nineties, weight training, power training, or resistance training programs lasting eight weeks to two years increased muscle strength, size, and mobility; speed, endurance, and leg muscle power; and spontaneous physical activity (Ades, Ballor, Ashikaga, Utton, & Nair, 1996; Fiatarone et al., 1990, 1994; Fiatarone, O'Neill, & Ryan, 1994; Foldvari et al., 2000; McCartney, Hicks, Martin, & Webber, 1996). Although these gains may result to some extent from improvements in muscle mass, the primary factor in older adults is likely to be a training-induced adaptation in the brain's ability to activate and coordinate muscular activity (Barry & Carson, 2004). This evidence of plasticity in older adults is especially important because people whose muscles have atrophied are more likely to suffer falls and fractures and to need help with tasks of day-to-day living (Agency for Healthcare Research and Quality and CDC, 2002).

Many falls and fractures are preventable by boosting muscle strength, balance, and gait speed and by eliminating hazards commonly found in the home (Agency for Healthcare Research and Quality and CDC, 2002; NIH Consensus Development Panel on Osteoporosis, 2001; Table 17-3). The Korean martial art of *tae kwon do* is effective in improving balance and walking ability (Cromwell, Meyers, Meyers, & Newton, 2007).

Sleep

Older people tend to sleep less and dream less than before. Their hours of deep sleep are more restricted, and they may awaken more easily because of physical problems or exposure to light (Czeisler et al., 1999; Lamberg, 1997). However, the assumption that sleep problems are normal in old age can be dangerous. Chronic *insomnia,* or sleeplessness, can be a symptom of, or, if untreated, a forerunner of, depression.

Cognitive-behavioral therapy (staying in bed only when asleep, getting up at the same time each morning, and learning about false beliefs pertaining to sleep needs) has produced long-term improvement with or without drug treatment (Morin, Colecchi, Stone, Sood, & Brink, 1999; Reynolds, Buysse, & Kupfer, 1999). In a two-week study of 12 older men and women, 90 minutes daily of mild to moderate physical activity interspersed with socializing improved cognitive functioning and self-perceived sleep quality (Benloucif et al., 2004).

Sexual Functioning

The most important factor in maintaining sexual functioning is consistent sexual activity over the years. A healthy man who has been sexually active generally can continue some form of active sexual expression into his seventies or eighties. Women are physiologically able to be sexually active as long as they live. In a national survey, 53 percent of U.S. adults ages 65 to 74 and 26 percent of those ages 75 to 85 reported being sexually active. Men are much more likely than women to remain sexually active in old age, largely because, being less numerous, they are more likely to have a spouse or partner (Lindau et al., 2007).

Sex is different in late adulthood from what it was earlier. Men typically take longer to develop an erection and to ejaculate, may need more manual stimulation, and may experience longer intervals between erections. Women's breast engorgement and other signs of sexual arousal are less intense than before. In the survey just mentioned, about half of both men and women who were sexually active reported sexual problems (Lindau et al., 2007).

Sexual activity can be more satisfying for older people if both young and old recognize it as normal and healthy. Housing arrangements and care providers should consider the sexual needs of elderly people. Physicians should avoid prescribing drugs that interfere with sexual functioning if alternatives are available and, when such a drug must be taken, should alert the patient to its effects.

Checkpoint

Can you . . .

♦ Describe typical changes in sensory and motor functioning and in sleep needs, and tell how they can affect everyday living?

♦ Summarize changes in sexual functioning and possibilities for sexual activity in late life?

Physical and Mental Health

Increasing life expectancy is raising pressing questions about the relationship between longevity and health, both physical and mental. How healthy are older adults today, and how can they stave off declines in health?

Guidepost 4

What health problems are common in late adulthood, what factors influence health, and what mental and behavioral problems do some older people experience?

Health Status

Poor health is *not* an inevitable consequence of aging (Moore, Moir, & Patrick, 2004). Most older adults in the United States are in good general health, though not as good, on average, as younger and middle-aged adults. About 76 percent of U.S. adults age 65 and older consider themselves in good to excellent health. As earlier in life, poverty is strongly related to poor health and to limited access to, and use of, health care (Federal Interagency Forum on Aging-Related Statistics, 2006; Schoenborn et al., 2006).

Chronic Conditions and Disabilities

At least 80 percent of older Americans have at least one chronic condition, and 50 percent have at least two (Moore et al., 2004). A much smaller proportion—but about half of those over 85—are frail: weak and vulnerable to stress, disease, disability and death (Ostir, Ottenbacher, & Markides, 2004).

| Table 17-4 | Warning Signs of Stroke |

- Sudden numbness or weakness of the face, arm, or leg, especially on one side of the body
- Sudden confusion, trouble speaking or understanding
- Sudden trouble seeing in one or both eyes
- Sudden trouble walking, dizziness, loss of balance or coordination
- Sudden, severe headache with no known cause

Source: American Stroke Association, 2005.

Common Chronic Conditions   Six of the seven leading causes of death in old age in the United States are chronic conditions: heart disease, cancer, stroke, chronic lower respiratory disease, diabetes, and influenza/pneumonia (which government health authorities count as a single condition). In fact, heart disease, cancer, and stroke account for about 60 percent of deaths among older Americans (Federal Interagency Forum on Aging-Related Statistics, 2006; NCHS, 2007). However, cancer deaths have declined since the early 1990s due to reductions in smoking, early screening, and more effective treatment (Howe et al., 2006). Worldwide, the leading causes of death at age 60 and above are heart disease, stroke, chronic pulmonary disease, lower respiratory infections, and lung cancer (WHO, 2003). As we will discuss, many of these deaths could be prevented through healthier lifestyles. Almost 95 percent of health care costs for older Americans are for chronic diseases (Moore et al., 2004).

Hypertension and diabetes are increasing in prevalence, affecting about 52 percent and 17 percent of the older population, respectively (Federal Interagency Forum on Aging-Related Statistics, 2006). Hypertension, which can affect blood flow to the brain, is related to declines in attention, learning, memory, executive functions, psychomotor abilities, and visual, perceptual, and spatial skills and is a risk factor for stroke (Waldstein, 2003). Table 17-4 lists warning signs of stroke.

Aside from hypertension and diabetes, the most common chronic conditions are arthritis (50 percent), heart disease (32 percent), and cancer (21 percent). Women are more likely to report hypertension, asthma, chronic bronchitis, and arthritis, whereas men are more likely to have heart disease, stroke, cancer, diabetes, and emphysema (Federal Interagency Forum on Aging-Related Statistics, 2006).

Chronic conditions vary by race/ethnicity. In 2000–2001, 65 percent of older blacks had hypertension, compared with fewer than 50 percent of older whites and Hispanics. Older blacks and Hispanics were almost twice as likely as older whites to have diabetes—25 percent and 23 percent, respectively, as compared with 14 percent. On the other hand, 22 percent of older whites had cancer, compared with 10 percent of older blacks and Hispanics.

Disabilities and Activity Limitations   The proportion of older adults in the United States with chronic physical disabilities or activity limitations has declined since the mid-1980s (Federal Interagency Forum on Aging-Related Statistics, 2004, 2006), perhaps due in part to the increasing number of older people who are educated and knowledgeable about preventive measures. More than 90 percent of U.S. older adults can carry out such essential **activities of daily living (ADLs)** as dressing, bathing, and getting around the house, but more than 20 percent have difficulty with more complex **instrumental activities of daily living (IADLs),** such as going shopping or to a doctor's office alone—indicators of ability to function independently (Gist & Hetzel,

activities of daily living (ADLs) Essential activities that support survival, such as eating, dressing, bathing, and getting around the house.

instrumental activities of daily living (IADLs) Indicators of functional well-being and of the ability to live independently.

The benefits these cross-country skiers gain from this lifelong activity are numerous. Exercise helps them live longer, healthier lives, and the social aspect of their sport helps keep them mentally healthy.

2004). About 40 percent of older adults report some difficulty being on their feet for two hours, and 51 percent have trouble stooping, crouching, or kneeling (Ervin, 2006). These numbers rise sharply with age. About 22 percent of 65- to 74-year-olds, 33 percent of 75- to 84-year-olds, and 53 percent of those 85 and older must limit their *functional activities*—walking, climbing stairs, reaching, lifting, or carrying—because of chronic conditions (Gist & Hetzel, 2004).

When a condition is not severe, it can usually be managed so that it does not interfere with daily life. A person who is arthritic or short of breath may take fewer steps or move items to lower shelves within easy reach. However, in the presence of chronic conditions and loss of reserve capacity, even a minor illness or injury can have serious repercussions. In a longitudinal study of 754 older adults in New Haven, Connecticut, those who had to be hospitalized or had at least one period of restricted activity (for example, due to a fall) were more likely to develop permanent disabilities (Gill, Allore, Holford, & Guo, 2004).

Even older people who say they have no difficulty walking may have trouble rapidly walking a quarter of a mile. In one study, 70- to 79-year-olds who could not complete this test were at greater risk of cardiovascular disease, mobility limitations or disabilities, and death after age 80, and each extra minute necessary to complete the test heightened these risks (Newman et al., 2006).

Checkpoint

Can you . . .

◆ Summarize the health status of older adults, and identify common chronic conditions common in late life?

Lifestyle Influences on Health and Longevity

The chances of remaining healthy and fit in late life often depend on lifestyle, especially exercise and diet (de Groot et al., 2004). Adults who live in poverty are less likely to engage in such healthy behaviors as leisure-time physical activity, avoidance of smoking, and maintenance of appropriate body weight (Schoenborn et al., 2006).

Physical Activity In 2003, when Yuichiro Miura first scaled the summit of Mount Everest, he was 70 years old. Not satisfied, he continued to train with weights and a treadmill, hoping to capture that distinction again. Miura is one of Japan's "old men of the mountain," a small group of aging climbers who seek the title of oldest person to have conquered the world's tallest peak (Watanabe, 2007).

Not every older adult can aspire to climb a mountain, but a lifelong program of exercise may prevent many physical changes once associated with normal aging. Regular exercise can strengthen the heart and lungs and decrease stress. It can protect against hypertension, hardening of the arteries, heart disease, osteoporosis, and diabetes. It helps maintain speed, stamina, strength, and endurance, and such basic functions as circulation and breathing. It reduces the chance of injuries by making joints and muscles stronger and more flexible, and it helps prevent or relieve lower-back pain and symptoms of arthritis. It can enable people with such conditions as lung disease and arthritis to remain independent and can help prevent the development of limitations on mobility. In addition, it may improve mental alertness and cognitive performance, help relieve anxiety and mild depression, and enhance feelings of mastery and well-being (Agency for Healthcare Research and Quality and CDC, 2002; Blumenthal et al., 1991; Butler, Davis, Lewis, Nelson, & Strauss, 1998a, 1998b; Kramer et al., 1999; Kritchevsky et al., 2005; Mazzeo et al., 1998; Netz, Wu, Becker, & Tenenbaum, 2005; NIA, 1995; NIH Consensus Development Panel, 2001; Rall, Meydani, Kehayias, Dawson-Hughes, & Roubenoff, 1996).

*In*activity contributes to heart disease, diabetes, colon cancer, and high blood pressure. It may lead to obesity, which affects the circulatory system, the kidneys, and sugar metabolism; contributes to degenerative disorders; and tends to shorten life (Agency for Healthcare Research and Quality and CDC, 2002). In a longitudinal study of 7,553 white older women, those who increased their activity levels over a six-year period had lower death rates during the following six and a half years (Gregg et al., 2003). In a 12-month randomized, controlled study of 201 adults age 70 and older, a combination of exercise, training in self-management of chronic disease, and peer support improved the ability of those with mild to moderate disabilities to carry out ADLs (Phelan, Williams, Penninx, LoGerfo, & Leveille, 2004). An analysis of many studies found that aerobic activity of moderate intensity was most beneficial to well-being (Netz et al., 2005).

Nutrition   Five out of six Americans age 60 and older have diets that are poor or need improvement, according to a national nutritional survey. Older women tend to have healthier diets than older men (Ervin, 2008).

Nutrition plays a large part in susceptibility to such chronic illnesses as atherosclerosis, heart disease, and diabetes as well as functional and activity limitations (Houston, Stevens, Cai, & Haines, 2005). Excessive body fat, which can come from a diet heavy in red and processed meats and alcohol, has been linked to several types of cancer (World Cancer Research Fund, 2007).

A healthy diet can reduce risks of obesity as well as of high blood pressure and high cholesterol (Federal Interagency Forum on Aging-Related Statistics, 2006). A Mediterranean diet (high in olive oil, whole grains, vegetables, and nuts) has been found to reduce cardiovascular risk (Esposito et al., 2004) and—in combination with physical activity, moderate alcohol use, and refraining from smoking—cut 10-year mortality from all causes in healthy 70- to 90-year-old Europeans by nearly two-thirds (Knoops et al., 2004; Rimm & Stampfer, 2004). Eating fruits and vegetables—especially those rich in vitamin C, citrus fruits and juices, green leafy vegetables, broccoli, cabbage, cauliflower, and brussels sprouts—lowers the risk of stroke (Joshipura et al., 1999). Consuming fish high in omega-3 fatty acids offers cardiovascular benefits and possibly protection against Alzheimer's disease (Weil et al., 2005).

Loss of teeth due to decay or *periodontitis* (gum disease), often attributable to infrequent dental care, can have serious implications for nutrition. Although more

What's Your View?

• Do you engage regularly in physical exercise? How many of the older people you know do so? What types of physical activity do you expect to maintain as you get older?

older Americans are keeping their natural teeth than ever before, in 2003 more than 1 in 4 had lost all of their teeth (Schoenborn et al., 2006).

Checkpoint

Can you . . .

♦ Give evidence of the influences of exercise and nutrition on health and longevity?

Mental and Behavioral Problems

Only 6 percent of older Americans report frequent mental distress (Moore et al., 2004). However, mental and behavioral disturbances that do occur can result in functional impairment in major life activities as well as cognitive decline (van Hooren et al., 2005).

Many older people and their families mistakenly believe that they can do nothing about mental and behavioral problems, even though close to 100 such conditions can be prevented, cured, or alleviated. Among these are drug intoxication, delirium, metabolic or infectious disorders, malnutrition, anemia, low thyroid functioning, minor head injuries, alcoholism, and depression (NIA, 1980, 1993; Wykle & Musil, 1993).

Depression In 2002, 11 percent of older men and 18 percent of older women in the United States reported symptoms of clinical depression (Federal Interagency Forum on Aging-Related Statistics, 2004). Heredity may account for 40 to 50 percent of the risk for major depression (Bouchard, 2004; Harvard Medical School, 2004d). Vulnerability seems to result from the influence of multiple genes interacting with environmental factors, such as stressful events, loneliness, and substance abuse. Special risk factors in late adulthood include chronic illness or disability, cognitive decline, and divorce, separation, or widowhood (Harvard Medical School, 2003b; Mueller et al., 2004; NIMH, 1999b).

Roots of depression may be found early in life. In the MIDUS survey (introduced in Chapters 15 and 16), a reported lack of parental emotional support during childhood was associated with depressive symptoms and chronic health conditions in adulthood and old age (Shaw, Krause, Chatters, Connell, & Ingersoll-Dayton, 2004).

Depression is often coupled with other medical conditions. Some physicians, when treating multiple illnesses, may give depression lower priority than a physical ailment, such as diabetes or arthritis. Yet, in a study of 1,801 older adults with clinically severe depression—each of whom had, on average, four chronic medical illnesses—depression played a more pervasive role in mental functional status, disability, and quality of life than did any of the other conditions (Noël et al., 2004).

Because depression can speed physical declines of aging, accurate diagnosis, prevention, and treatment could help many older people live longer and remain more active (Penninx et al., 1998). Depression can be treated by antidepressant drugs, psychotherapy, or both (Harvard Medical School, 2005). Regular aerobic exercise can reduce symptoms of mild to moderate depression (Dunn, Trivedi, Kampert, Clark, & Chambliss, 2005).

Dementia **Dementia** is the general term for physiologically caused cognitive and behavioral decline sufficient to interfere with daily activities (American Psychiatric Association [APA], 1994). Cognitive decline becomes increasingly common with advanced age, affecting 5 percent of U.S. adults in their seventies, 24 percent in their eighties, and 37.4 percent of those 90 and older (Plassman et al., 2007). Still, cognitive impairment severe enough to be diagnosed as dementia is not inevitable.

dementia Deterioration in cognitive and behavioral functioning due to physiological causes.

Checkpoint

Can you ...

♦ Tell why late-life depression may be more common than is generally realized?

♦ Name the three main causes of dementia in older adults?

Most forms of dementia are irreversible, but about 10 percent of cases can be reversed with early diagnosis and treatment (NIA, 1980, 1993; Wykle & Musil, 1993). About two-thirds of cases of dementia may be caused by **Alzheimer's disease (AD),** a progressive, degenerative brain disorder (Gatz, 2007). **Parkinson's disease,** the second most common disorder involving progressive neurological degeneration, is characterized by tremor, stiffness, slowed movement, and unstable posture (Nussbaum, 1998). These two diseases, together with *multi-infarct dementia (MD),* which is caused by a series of small strokes, account for at least 8 out of 10 cases of dementia, all irreversible.

Certain personality traits are associated with a person's chances of developing dementia. In a 25-year longitudinal study of Swedish twins, those high in neuroticism at midlife were at increased risk of cognitive impairment in old age, whereas those who were moderately extraverted were not (Crowe, Andel, Pederson, Fratiglioni, & Gatz, 2006). In the Nun Study, a longitudinal study of Alzheimer's disease and aging in 678 Roman Catholic nuns, conscientiousness tended to protect against AD (Wilson, Schneider, Arnold, Bienias, & Bennett, 2007). Education also seems to protect against dementia (Mortimer, Snowdon, & Markesbery, 2002), as does a challenging job (Seidler et al., 2004) and lifelong bilingualism (Bialystok, Craik, & Freeman, 2007). Cognitive impairment is more likely in people in poor physical health, especially those who have had strokes or diabetes (Tilvis et al., 2004).

The risk of cognitive impairment may be lessened by walking or by other long-term, regular physical activity (Abbott et al., 2004; van Gelder et al., 2004; Weuve et al., 2004). In one study, older women who drank moderate amounts of alcohol each day had a 40 percent lower risk of cognitive impairment or dementia (Espeland et al., 2005). A longitudinal study of 354 adults age 50 and older found that people who had large social networks or had frequent social contact or could rely on emotional support from family or friends were less likely to show cognitive decline 12 years later (Holtzman et al., 2004).

Alzheimer's Disease Alzheimer's disease (AD) is one of the most common and most feared terminal illnesses among aging persons. It gradually robs patients of intelligence, awareness, and even the ability to control their bodily functions—and finally kills them. The disease affects more than 26 million people throughout the world, nearly half of them in Asia, and its incidence is expected to quadruple by 2050 (Brookmeyer, Johnson, Ziegler-Graham, & Arrighi, 2007).

In the United States, AD was the sixth leading cause of death in 2006, according to preliminary data (Heron, et al., 2008). An estimated 5 million people in the United States—including 1 in 8 people age 65 and older—are living with AD, and by 2050 the incidence could reach 16 million. Furthermore, as many as half a million people under 65 may have an early-onset form of the disease (Alzheimer's Association, 2007). The risk rises dramatically with age; thus, increases in longevity mean that more people will survive to an age when the risk of AD is greatest (Hebert, Scherr, Bienias, Bennett, & Evans, 2003).

Symptoms The classic symptoms of Alzheimer's disease are memory impairment, deterioration of language, and deficits in visual and spatial processing (Cummings, 2004). The most prominent early symptom is inability to recall recent events or take in new information. A person may repeat questions that were just answered or leave an everyday task unfinished. These early signs may be overlooked because they look like ordinary forgetfulness or may be interpreted as signs of normal aging. (Table 17-5 compares early warning signs of Alzheimer's disease with normal mental lapses.)

Table 17-5 Alzheimer's Disease versus Normal Behavior

Symptoms of Disease	Normal Behavior
Permanently forgetting recent events; asking the same questions repeatedly	Temporarily forgetting things
Inability to do routine tasks with many such as making and serving a meal steps,	Inability to do some challenging tasks
Forgetting simple words	Forgetting unusual or complex words
Getting lost on one's own block	Getting lost in a strange city
Forgetting that a child is in one's care and leaving the house	Becoming momentarily distracted and failing to watch a child
Forgetting what the numbers in a checkbook mean and what to do with them	Making mistakes in balancing a checkbook
Putting things in inappropriate places where one cannot usefully retrieve them (e.g., a wristwatch in a fishbowl)	Misplacing everyday items
Rapid, dramatic mood swings and personality changes; loss of initiative	Occasional mood changes

Source: Adapted from Alzheimer's Association, n.d.

Personality changes—most often, rigidity, apathy, egocentricity, and impaired emotional control—tend to occur early in the disease's development and may aid in early detection and diagnosis (Balsis, Carpenter, & Storandt, 2005). More symptoms follow: irritability, anxiety, depression, and, later, delusions, delirium, and wandering. Long-term memory, judgment, concentration, orientation, and speech all become impaired, and patients have trouble handling basic activities of daily life. By the end, the patient cannot understand or use language, does not recognize family members, cannot eat without help, cannot control the bowels and bladder, and loses the ability to walk, sit up, and swallow solid food. Death usually comes within eight to ten years after symptoms appear ("Alzheimer's Disease, Part I," 1998; Cummings, 2004; Hoyert & Rosenberg, 1999; Small et al., 1997).

Causes and Risk Factors   Accumulation of an abnormal protein called *beta amyloid peptide* appears to be the main culprit contributing to the development of Alzheimer's disease (Bird, 2005; Cummings, 2004; Gatz et al., 2006). The brain of a person with AD contains excessive amounts of **neurofibrillary tangles** (twisted masses of dead neurons) and large waxy clumps of **amyloid plaque** (nonfunctioning tissue formed by beta amyloid in the spaces between neurons). Because these plaques are insoluble, the brain cannot clear them away. They may become dense, spread, and destroy surrounding neurons (Harvard Medical School, 2003a). The breakdown of myelin may promote the buildup of plaques (Bartzokis et al., 2007).

Alzheimer's disease, or at least its age of onset, is strongly heritable (Gatz et al., 2006). A variant of the *APOE* gene has been found to contribute to susceptibility to late-onset AD, the most common form, which typically develops after age 65 (Gatz, 2007). A variant of another gene called *SORL1* was found to stimulate the formation of amyloid plaque (Meng, 2007; Rogaeva et al., 2006). However, identified genes are thought to explain no more than half of all AD cases. Epigenetic modifications that determine whether a particular gene is activated may play a part (Gatz, 2007).

Lifestyle factors, such as diet and physical activity, may be especially important for persons who are not at genetic risk (Gatz, 2007). Foods rich in vitamin E, n-3

neurofibrillary tangles Twisted masses of protein fibers found in brains of persons with Alzheimer's disease.

amyloid plaque Waxy chunks of insoluble tissue found in brains of persons with Alzheimer's disease.

Esther Lipman Rosenthal's battle with Alzheimer's disease is evident in her artwork. She created the picture on the left, showing her husband golfing, at age 55 and the picture on the right, showing him on cross-country skis, at age 75, during the early and middle stages of her disease. Photos courtesy of Linda Goldman.

fatty acids, and unhydrogenated unsaturated fats—such as oil-based salad dressings, nuts, seeds, fish, mayonnaise, and eggs—may be protective against AD, whereas foods high in saturated and transunsaturated fats, such as red meats, butter, and ice cream, may be harmful (Morris, 2004). Smokers have increased risk of AD (Launer et al., 1999; Ott et al., 1998). Use of nonsteroidal anti-inflammatory drugs such as aspirin and ibuprofen may cut the risk of AD (Vlad, Miller, Kowall, & Felson, 2008; Zandi et al., 2002).

Education and cognitively stimulating activities have consistently been associated with reduced risk of the disorder (Billings, Green, McGaugh, & LaFerla, 2007; Crowe, Andel, Pedersen, Johansson, & Gatz, 2003; Wilson & Bennett, 2003; Wilson, Scherr, Schneider, Tang, & Bennett, 2007). The protective effect appears to be due, not to education itself, but to the fact that educated people tend to be cognitively active (Wilson & Bennett, 2003). How might cognitive activity protect against AD? One hypothesis is that ongoing cognitive activity may build **cognitive reserve** and thus delay the onset of dementia (Crowe et al., 2003). Cognitive reserve, like organ reserve, may enable a deteriorating brain to continue to function under stress, up to a point, without showing signs of impairment. An analysis of 26 studies worldwide concluded that a mere 5 percent increase in cognitive reserve could prevent one-third of Alzheimer's cases (de la Fuente-Fernandez, 2006).

cognitive reserve Hypothesized fund of energy that may enable a deteriorating brain to continue to function normally.

Diagnosis and Prediction Until recently, AD could be diagnosed definitively only by postmortem examination of brain tissue, but scientists are now developing tools to enable fairly reliable diagnosis in a living person. Neuroimaging is particularly useful in excluding alternative causes of dementia (Cummings, 2004) and in allowing researchers to see brain lesions indicative of AD in a living patient (Shoghi-Jadid et al., 2002). Noninvasive PET (positron emission tomography) scanning has been used to detect the plaques and tangles characteristic of Alzheimer's, and the results were as good as those obtained by autopsy (Mosconi et al., 2008; Small et al., 2006).

Other researchers are seeking ways to predict and perhaps delay the onset of Alzheimer's by identifying mild cognitive impairment, which, if untreated, can lead to AD. A longitudinal study found that reduced metabolic activity in the hippocampus of healthy adults can accurately predict who will get Alzheimer's or a related memory impairment within the next nine years (Mosconi et al., 2005). In what could lead to a definitive test for early AD, researchers have used a new technology to detect amyloid beta-derived diffusible ligands (ADDLs) in cerebral and spinal fluid (Georganopoulou et al., 2005). In addition, certain blood tests and electroencephalogram (EEG) results may predict AD in the early stages (Gandhi, Green, Kounios, Clark, & Polikar, 2006; Ray et al., 2007).

Degenerative changes in brain structure can forecast AD. In one study, brain scans of older adults who were considered cognitively normal found less gray matter in memory processing areas of the brain in those who were diagnosed with AD four years later (C. D. Smith et al., 2007). In another imaging study, shrinkage of the amygdala and hippocampus predicted which apparently healthy older adults would develop AD within the next six years (den Heijer et al., 2006).

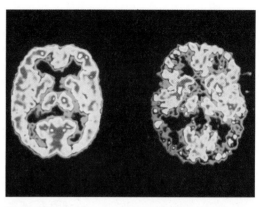

These PET (position emission tomography) scans show dramatic deterioration in the brain of an Alzheimer's patient (right) as compared with a normal brain (left). The red and yellow areas represent high brain activity; the blue and black areas, low activity. The scan on the right shows reduction of both function and blood flow in both sides of the brain.

Cognitive tests alone may distinguish between patients experiencing cognitive changes related to normal aging and those in early stages of dementia. In the Seattle Longitudinal Study of Adult Intelligence (introduced in Chapter 15), results of psychometric tests predicted dementia as much as 14 years prior to diagnosis (Schaie, 2005). In the Nun Study, a research team examined autobiographies the nuns had written in their early twenties. The women whose autobiographies were densely packed with ideas were least likely to become cognitively impaired or to develop Alzheimer's disease later in life (Riley, Snowdon, Desrosiers, & Markesbery, 2005).

Despite the identification of several genes associated with AD, genetic testing so far has a limited role in prediction and diagnosis. Still, it may be useful in combination with cognitive tests, brain scans, and clinical evidence of symptoms.

Treatment   Although no cure has yet been found, early diagnosis and treatment can slow the progress of Alzheimer's disease and improve quality of life. One medication approved by the U.S. Food and Drug Administration is memantine (commercially known as Namenda). In a double-blind, placebo-controlled trial, daily doses of memantine taken for as long as a year reduced deterioration in patients with moderate to severe AD without significant adverse effects (Reisberg et al., 2006).

Cholinesterase inhibitors, such as donepezil, commercially known as Aricept, have become standard treatment for slowing or stabilizing the progress of mild to moderate AD (Cummings, 2004). Reviews of several studies found that Aricept and two similar drugs, Razadyne and Exelon, can lead to small improvements in mental functioning and the ability to carry out daily activities. Aricept was effective as long as one year after treatment began (Birks, 2006; Birks & Harvey, 2006; Loy & Schneider, 2006). However, a five-year trial found no significant difference after the first two years between patients taking Aricept and those given a placebo (AD2000 Collaborative Group, 2004).

A promising experimental approach is immunotherapy. In one study, Alzheimer's patients vaccinated with beta amyloid performed better on memory tests up to a year later than patients injected with a placebo (N. C. Fox et al., 2005; Gilman et al., 2005).

Checkpoint

Can you . . .

♦ Summarize what is known about the prevalence, symptoms, causes, risk factors, diagnosis, and treatment of Alzheimer's disease?

In the absence of a cure, management of the disease is critical. In the early stages, memory training and memory aids may improve cognitive functioning (Camp et al., 1993; Camp & McKitrick, 1992; McKitrick, Camp, & Black, 1992). Behavioral therapies can slow deterioration, improve communication, and reduce disruptive behavior (Barinaga, 1998). Drugs can relieve agitation, lighten depression, and help patients sleep. Proper nourishment and fluid intake together with exercise, physical therapy, and control of other medical conditions are important, and cooperation between the physician and the caregiver is essential (Cummings, 2004).

COGNITIVE DEVELOPMENT

Aspects of Cognitive Development

Guidepost 5

What gains and losses in cognitive abilities tend to occur in late adulthood, and are there ways to improve older people's cognitive performance?

Old age "adds as it takes away," wrote the poet William Carlos Williams in one of three books of verse he produced between his first stroke at the age of 68 and his death at 79. This comment seems to sum up current findings about cognitive functioning in late adulthood. As Baltes's life-span developmental approach suggests, age brings gains as well as losses. Let's look first at intelligence and general processing abilities, then at memory, and then at wisdom, which is popularly associated with the later years.

Intelligence and Processing Abilities

Does intelligence diminish in late adulthood? The answer depends on what abilities are being measured, and how. Some abilities, such as speed of mental processes and abstract reasoning, may decline in later years, but other abilities tend to improve throughout most of adult life. And, although changes in processing abilities may reflect neurological deterioration, there is much individual variation, suggesting that declines in functioning are not inevitable and may be preventable.

The impact of cognitive changes is influenced by earlier cognitive ability, SES, and educational status. Childhood intelligence test scores reliably predict cognitive ability at age 80; and SES and educational level predict cognitive status after age 70 better than do health ratings or the presence or severity of medical conditions (Finch & Zelinski, 2005).

Wechsler Adult Intelligence Scale (WAIS) Intelligence test for adults, which yields verbal and performance scores as well as a combined score.

Measuring Older Adults' Intelligence To measure the intelligence of older adults, researchers often use the **Wechsler Adult Intelligence Scale (WAIS).** Scores on the WAIS subtests yield a verbal IQ, a performance IQ, and a total IQ. Older adults tend not to perform as well as younger adults on the WAIS, but the difference is primarily in nonverbal performance. On the five subtests in the performance scale (such as identifying the missing part of a picture, copying a design, and mastering a maze), scores drop with age; but on the six tests making up the verbal scale—particularly tests of vocabulary, information, and comprehension—scores fall only slightly and very gradually (Figure 17-6). This is called the *classic aging pattern* (Botwinick, 1984).

What might account for this pattern? For one thing, the verbal items that hold up with age are based on knowledge; they do not require the test-taker to figure out or do anything new. The performance tasks involve the processing of new information; they require perceptual speed and motor skills, which can reflect muscular and neurological slowing. The variance in retention of different types of cognitive skills in old age has generated several lines of theory and research.

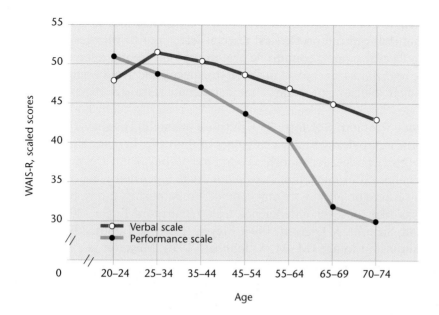

Figure 17-6

Classic aging pattern on the revised version of the Wechsler Adult Intelligence Scale (WAIS-R). Scores on the performance sub-tests decline far more rapidly with age than scores on the verbal subtests. (Source: Botwinick, 1984.)

The Seattle Longitudinal Study: Use It or Lose It   In the Seattle Longitudinal Study of Adult Intelligence, researchers measured six primary mental abilities: verbal meaning, word fluency, number (computational ability), spatial orientation, inductive reasoning, and perceptual speed. Consistent with other studies, perceptual speed tended to decline earliest and most rapidly. Cognitive decline in other respects, however, was slow and not across-the-board. If they live long enough, it seems, most people's functioning will flag at some point; but very few weaken in all or even most abilities, and many improve in some areas. Most fairly healthy older adults show only small losses until the late sixties or seventies. Not until the eighties do they fall below the average performance of younger adults. And even then, declines in verbal abilities and reasoning are modest (Schaie, 2005).

The most striking feature of the Seattle findings is the tremendous variation among individuals. Some participants showed declines during their forties, but a few maintained full functioning very late in life. Even in their late eighties, virtually all participants retained their competence in one or more of the abilities tested (Schaie, 2005). Those most likely to show declines were men who had low educational levels, were dissatisfied with their success in life, and exhibited a significant decrease in flexibility of personality. Participants who engaged in cognitively complex work tended to retain their abilities longer (Schaie, 2005). Engaging in activities that challenge cognitive skills promotes the retention or growth of those skills (Schaie, 1983) and, as we mentioned earlier, appears to protect against dementia.

Older adults can improve their cognitive performance. In training connected with the Seattle study, older people who already had shown declines in intelligence gained significantly in two fluid abilities: spatial orientation and, especially, inductive reasoning. In fact, about 4 out of 10 participants regained levels of proficiency they had shown 14 years earlier. Gains measured in the laboratory showed substantial correlations with objective measures of everyday functioning (Schaie, 1994, 2005; Willis, Jay, Diehl, & Marsiske, 1992).

Longitudinal findings suggest that training may enable older adults not only to recover lost competence but even to surpass their previous attainments (Schaie & Willis, 1996). In the Seattle study, trained participants retained an edge over an untrained control group, even after seven years (Schaie, 1994, 1996a, 1996b; Willis, 1990; Willis & Nesselroade, 1990).

What's Your View?

• What are some ways to sustain a high level of intellectual activity in late life? Do you think you need to develop new or broader interests that you will want to pursue as you age?

Checkpoint

Can you . . .

♦ Compare the classic aging pattern on the WAIS with those of the Seattle Longitudinal Study with regard to cognitive changes in old age?

♦ Cite evidence of the plasticity of cognitive abilities in late adulthood?

♦ Discuss the relationship between practical problem solving and age?

Cognitive deterioration, then, often may be related to disuse. Much as many aging athletes can call on physical reserves, older people who get training, practice, and social support seem to be able to draw on mental reserves. Adults may be able to maintain or expand this reserve capacity and avoid cognitive decline by engaging in a lifelong program of mental exercise (Dixon & Baltes, 1986).

Everyday Problem Solving   The purpose of intelligence, of course, is not to take tests but to deal with the challenges of daily life. In many studies, the quality of practical decisions (such as what car to buy, what treatment to get for breast cancer, how much money to put away in a pension plan, or how to compare insurance policies) bore only a modest relationship, if any, to performance on tasks like those on intelligence tests (Blanchard-Fields, 2007; M. M. S. Johnson, Schmitt, & Everard, 1994; Meyer, Russo, & Talbot, 1995) and, often, no relationship to age (M. M. S. Johnson, 1990; Meyer et al., 1995; Walsh & Hershey, 1993). Similarly, much research on everyday problem solving (such as what to do about a flooded basement) has not found as early a decline as is often seen in measures of fluid intelligence, and some research has found marked improvement (Berg & Klaczynski, 1996; Perlmutter, Kaplan, & Nyquist, 1990; Sternberg, Grigorenko, & Oh, 2001). A review of the literature concluded that the effectiveness of everyday problem solving remains stable from young adulthood until late life and then declines. However, because most studies of everyday problem solving have been cross-sectional, we cannot be sure that the findings actually show *changes* with age (Thornton & Dumke, 2005).

Age differences are reduced in studies that focus on *interpersonal* problems—such as how to deal with a new mother who insists on showing her older, more experienced, mother-in-law how to hold the baby—rather than on *instrumental* problems—such as how to return defective merchandise (Thornton & Dumke, 2005). Older adults are more effective and flexible problem solvers when a problem has emotional relevance for them or when it requires a balancing of strategies. Older adults have more extensive and varied repertoires of strategies to apply to different situations than younger adults do (Berg & Klaczynski, 1996; Blanchard-Fields, 2007; Blanchard-Fields, Chen, & Norris, 1997; Blanchard-Fields, Mienaltowski, & Seay, 2007).

In one study, older adults solved such interpersonal problems as a family quarrel more effectively than younger adults. In dealing with such a problem, older adults tended to "keep their cool" by avoiding the issue whenever possible and letting others solve it. On the other hand, when dealing with an instrumental problem, such as how to protect themselves from a wave of burglaries in the neighborhood, older adults were more likely than younger adults to plan proactively (Blanchard-Fields et al., 2007).

Changes in Processing Abilities   What explains the varied course of cognitive abilities in late adulthood? In many older adults, a general slowdown in central nervous system functioning is a major contributor to losses of efficiency of information processing and changes in cognitive abilities. Speed of processing, one of the first abilities to decline, is related to health status, balance, and gait and to performance of activities of daily living, such as looking up phone numbers and counting out change (Ball, Edwards, & Ross, 2007).

One ability that tends to slow with age is ease in switching attention from one task or function to another (Salthouse, Fristoe, McGuthry, & Hambrick, 1998). This finding may help explain why many older adults have difficulty driving, which requires rapid attentional shifts (Bialystok et al., 2004). Older adults tend to do better on tasks that depend on ingrained habits and knowledge (Bialystok, Craik, Klein, & Viswanathan, 2004; Craik & Salthouse, 2000).

Training can increase older adults' processing speed—their ability to process more, and more complex, information in shorter and shorter periods of time. Training typically involves practice, feedback, and the learning of task-specific strategies. In studies of several training programs, participants who started with the worst performance made the most gains. A method aimed at improving driving ability was the most successful, perhaps because it had a concrete, practical goal. This research underlines the brain's plasticity even with regard to a basic fluid ability, speed of processing (Ball et al., 2007).

Cognitive Abilities and Mortality Psychometric intelligence may be an important predictor of how long and in what condition adults will live. That was the conclusion of a study of 2,230 Scottish adults who had taken an IQ test at age 11. On average, someone who had a childhood IQ 15 points lower than another participant was only 79 percent as likely to live to age 76 (Gottfredson & Deary, 2004). The same IQ differential was associated with a 27 percent increase in cancer deaths among men and a 40 percent increase among women (Deary, Whalley, & Starr, 2003).

However, in another study, reaction time at age 56 more strongly predicted mortality by age 70 than did IQ, suggesting that efficiency of information processing may explain the link between intelligence and timing of death (Deary & Der, 2005). Another possible explanation is that intelligent people learn information and problem-solving skills that help them prevent chronic disease and accidental injury and cooperate in their treatment when they do get sick or hurt (Deary & Der, 2005; Gottfredson & Deary, 2004).

Memory: How Does It Change?

Failing memory is often considered a sign of aging. The man who always kept his schedule in his head now has to write it in a calendar; the woman who takes several medicines now measures out each day's dosages and puts them where she is sure to see them. Loss of memory is the chief worry reported by older Americans (National Council on the Aging, 2002). An estimated 1 in 5 adults over age 70 has some degree of memory impairment short of dementia (Plassman et al., 2008). Yet in memory, as in other cognitive abilities, older people's functioning declines slowly and varies greatly.

To understand age-related memory decline, we need to review the various memory systems introduced in Chapters 7 and 9, which enable the brain to process information for use at a later time (Budson & Price, 2005). These systems are traditionally classified as "short-term" and "long-term."

Short-Term Memory Researchers assess short-term memory by asking a person to repeat a sequence of numbers, either in the order in which they were presented (*digit span forward*) or in reverse order (*digit span backward*). Digit span forward ability holds up well with advancing age (Craik & Jennings, 1992; Poon, 1985; Wingfield & Stine, 1989), but digit span backward performance does not (Craik & Jennings, 1992; Lovelace, 1990). Why? A widely accepted explanation is that immediate forward repetition requires only **sensory memory,** which retains efficiency throughout life, whereas backward repetition requires the manipulation of information in **working memory,** which gradually shrinks in capacity after about age 45 (Swanson, 1999), making it harder to handle more than one task at a time (E. E. Smith et al., 2001).

Checkpoint

Can you . . .

♦ Discuss findings on the slowdown in neural processing and its relationship to cognitive decline?

♦ Discuss the relationship of intelligence to health and mortality?

sensory memory Initial, brief, temporary storage of sensory information.

working memory Short-term storage of information being actively processed.

A key factor is the complexity of the task (Kausler, 1990; Wingfield & Stine, 1989). Tasks that require only *rehearsal,* or repetition, show very little decline. Tasks that require *reorganization* or *elaboration* show greater falloff (Craik & Jennings, 1992). If you are asked to verbally rearrange a series of items (such as "Band-Aid, elephant, newspaper") in order of increasing size ("Band-Aid, newspaper, elephant"), you must call to mind your previous knowledge of Band-Aids, newspapers, and elephants (Cherry & Park, 1993). More mental effort is needed to keep this additional information in mind, using more of the limited capacity of working memory.

Long-Term Memory Information-processing researchers divide long-term memory into three major systems: *episodic memory, semantic memory,* and *procedural memory.*

Do you remember what you had for breakfast this morning? Did you lock your car when you parked it? Such information is stored in **episodic memory,** the long-term memory system most likely to deteriorate with age. The ability to recall newly encountered information, especially, seems to drop off (Poon, 1985; A. D. Smith & Earles, 1996).

Because episodic memory is linked to specific events, you retrieve an item from this mental "diary" by reconstructing the original experience in your mind. Older adults are less able than younger people to do so, perhaps because they focus less on context (where something happened, who was there) and thus have fewer connections to jog their memory (Kausler, 1990; Lovelace, 1990). Also, older people have had many similar experiences that tend to run together. When older people perceive an event as distinctive, they can remember it as well as younger people (Camp, 1989; Cavanaugh, Kramer, Sinnott, Camp, & Markley, 1985; Kausler, 1990).

Semantic memory is like a mental encyclopedia; it holds stored knowledge of historical facts, geographic locations, social customs, meanings of words, and the like. Semantic memory does not depend on remembering when and where something was learned, and it shows little decline with age (Camp, 1989; Horn, 1982b; Lachman & Lachman, 1980). In fact, vocabulary and knowledge of rules of language may even increase (Camp, 1989; Horn, 1982b). In a large-scale, representative sequential study of 829 adults ages 35 to 80, semantic memory showed substantially less decline after age 60 than episodic memory (Rönnlund, Nyberg, Bäckman, & Nilsson, 2005).

Remembering how to ride a bicycle or use a typewriter is an example of **procedural memory** (Squire, 1992, 1994). This includes motor skills, habits, and processes that, once learned, can be activated without conscious effort. Procedural memory is relatively unaffected by age, though older adults may need to compensate for an age-related slowing in responses (Kausler, 1990; Salthouse, 1985).

Speech and Memory: Effects of Aging Have you ever been unable to come up with a word you knew perfectly well? This experience occurs among people of all ages but becomes increasingly common in late adulthood (Burke & Shafto, 2004). On a test that calls for definitions of words, older adults often do better than younger adults, but they have more trouble coming up with a word when given its meaning (A. D. Smith & Earles, 1996). Such tip-of-the-tongue experiences may relate to problems in working memory (Heller & Dobbs, 1993; Light, 1990; Schonfield, 1974; Schonfield & Robertson, 1960, cited in Horn, 1982b). Older adults also make more errors in naming pictures of objects aloud, make more ambiguous references

episodic memory Long-term memory of specific experiences or events, linked to time and place.

semantic memory Long-term memory of general factual knowledge, social customs, and language.

procedural memory Long-term memory of motor skills, habits, and ways of doing things, which can be recalled without conscious effort; sometimes called *implicit memory.*

Riding a bicycle requires procedural memory. Once learned, procedural skills can be activated without conscious effort, even after a long period of disuse.

and slips of the tongue in everyday speech, and more frequently fill in pauses with "um" or "er." Older adults also show an increasing tendency to misspell words (such as *indict*) that are spelled differently than they sound (Burke & Shafto, 2004). These problems reflect a failure of verbal *retrieval,* and not a failure of vocabulary *knowledge*—which, as we have seen, usually remains strong.

What other aspects of speech decline with age? In a longitudinal study, researchers asked 30 healthy older adults, ages 65 to 75, such questions as "Describe the person who most influenced your life" and "Describe an unexpected event that happened to you." Participants' oral answers showed declines between ages 65 and 80—most rapid in the midseventies—in both the complexity of grammar and depth of content (Kemper, Thompson, & Marquis, 2001).

Why Do Some Memory Systems Decline?   What explains older adults' memory losses? Investigators have offered several hypotheses. One approach focuses on the biological structures that make memory work. Another approach looks at problems with the three steps required to process information in memory: *encoding, storage,* and *retrieval.*

Neurological Change   The decline in processing speed described earlier in this chapter seems to be a fundamental contributor to age-related memory loss (Luszcz & Bryan, 1999; Hartley, Speer, Jonides, Reuter-Lorenz, & Smith, 2001). In a number of studies, controlling for perceptual speed eliminated virtually the entire age-related drop in memory performance (A. D. Smith & Earles, 1996).

As discussed in Chapter 5, different memory systems depend on different brain structures. Thus, a disorder that damages a particular brain structure may impair the type of memory associated with it. For example, Alzheimer's disease disrupts working memory (located in the prefrontal cortex at the front of the frontal lobes) as well as semantic and episodic memory (located in the frontal and temporal lobes); Parkinson's disease affects procedural memory, located in the cerebellum, basal ganglia, and other areas (Budson & Price, 2005).

The main structures involved in normal memory processing and storage include the *frontal lobes* and the *hippocampus*. The *frontal lobes* are active in both encoding and retrieval of episodic memories. Dysfunction of the frontal lobes may cause false memories—"remembering" events that never occurred (Budson & Price, 2005). Early decline in the prefrontal cortex may underlie such common problems as inability to concentrate or pay attention and difficulty in performing a task with several steps (Budson & Price, 2005). The *hippocampus,* a small, centrally located structure deep in the temporal lobe, seems critical to the ability to store new information in episodic memory (Budson & Price, 2005; Squire, 1992). Lesions in the hippocampus or other brain structures involved in episodic memory may result in loss of recent memories (Budson & Price, 2005).

The brain often compensates for age-related declines in specialized regions by tapping other regions to help. In one study, when asked to remember sets of letters on a computer screen, college students used only the left hemisphere; when asked to remember the locations of points on the screen, they used only the right hemisphere. Older adults, who did just as well as the students, used *both* the right and left frontal lobes for both tasks (Reuter-Lorenz, Stanczak, & Miller, 1999; Reuter-Lorenz et al., 2000). In another study, educated younger adults performing memory tasks relied more on the medial temporal lobes, whereas educated older adults doing the same tasks relied more on the frontal lobes (Springer, McIntosh, Winocur, & Grady, 2005). The brain's ability to shift functions may help explain why symptoms of Alzheimer's disease often do not appear until the disease is well advanced, and previously unaffected regions of the brain, which have taken over for impaired regions, lose their own working capacity ("Alzheimer's Disease, Part I," 1998; Finch & Zelinski, 2005).

Problems in Encoding, Storage, and Retrieval   Older adults tend to be less efficient and precise than younger adults in *encoding* new information to make it easier to remember—for example, by arranging material alphabetically or creating mental associations (Craik & Byrd, 1982). Most studies have found that older and younger adults are about equally knowledgeable as to effective encoding strategies (Salthouse, 1991). Yet in laboratory experiments, older adults are less likely to *use* such strategies unless trained—or at least prompted or reminded—to do so (Craik & Jennings, 1992; Salthouse, 1991). And even when older adults use the same strategy as younger adults, they may use it less effectively (Dunlosky & Hertzog, 1998).

Another hypothesis is that material in *storage* may deteriorate to the point where retrieval becomes difficult or impossible. Some research suggests that a small increase in "storage failure" may occur with age (Camp & McKitrick, 1989; Giambra & Arenberg, 1993). However, traces of decayed memories are likely to remain, and it may be possible to reconstruct them, or at least to relearn the material speedily (Camp & McKitrick, 1989; Chafetz, 1992).

Older adults have more trouble with recall than younger adults but do about as well with recognition, which puts fewer demands on the *retrieval* system (Hultsch, 1971; Lovelace, 1990). Even in recognition tasks, however, it takes older people longer than younger people to search their memories (Lovelace, 1990).

We should keep in mind that most of the research on encoding, storage, and retrieval has been done in the laboratory. Those functions may operate differently in the real world. In one naturalistic study, when 333 older adults were asked to keep daily diaries, they were more likely to report memory failures on days when they experienced stress, especially from other people (Neupert, Almeida, Mroczek, & Spiro, 2006). On the other hand, studies based on Laura Carstensen's socioemotional selectivity theory (introduced in Chapter 16) have found that older adults are motivated to preserve memories that have positive emotional meaning to them (Carstensen & Mikels, 2005). Thus, emotional factors need to be considered in studying memory changes in old age.

Wisdom

With the graying of the planet, wisdom—long the subject of philosophical speculation—has become an important topic of psychological research (Shedlock & Cornelius, 2003). Personality theorists, such as Jung and Erikson, see wisdom as the culmination of a lifetime of personal growth and ego development. (Erikson's views on wisdom are discussed in Chapter 18.)

Wisdom also has been studied as a cognitive ability. As such, it has been defined as "exceptional breadth and depth of knowledge about the conditions of life and human affairs and reflective judgment about the application of this knowledge." It may involve insight and awareness of the uncertain, paradoxical nature of reality and may lead to *transcendence,* detachment from preoccupation with the self (Kramer, 2003, p. 132). Some theorists define wisdom as an extension of postformal thought, a synthesis of reason and emotion (Labouvie-Vief, 1990a, 1990b).

The most extensive research on wisdom as a cognitive ability has been done by Paul Baltes and his colleagues (Baltes, 1993; Baltes & Staudinger, 2000; Pasupathi, Staudinger, & Baltes, 2001). In a series of studies, Baltes and his associates at the Max Planck Institute in Berlin asked adults of various ages and

Checkpoint

Can you . . .

♦ Identify two aspects of memory that tend to decline with age, and give reasons for this decline?

♦ Discuss neurological changes related to memory?

♦ Explain how problems in encoding, storage, and retrieval may affect memory in late adulthood, and discuss how emotional factors may affect memory?

The average age of the members of the U.S. Supreme Court in 2008 was 68. Does wisdom increase with age? Not necessarily, according to research.

occupations to think aloud about hypothetical dilemmas. Responses were rated according to whether they showed rich factual and procedural knowledge about the human condition and about dealing with life's problems. Other criteria were awareness that contextual circumstances can influence problems, that problems tend to lend themselves to multiple interpretations and solutions, and that choices of solutions depend on individual values, goals, and priorities (Baltes & Staudinger, 2000; Pasupathi et al., 2001).

In one of these studies, 60 well-educated German professionals ages 25 to 81 were given four dilemmas involving such issues as weighing career against family needs and deciding whether to accept early retirement. Of 240 solutions, only 5 percent were rated wise, and these responses were distributed nearly evenly among young, middle-aged, and older adults. Participants showed more wisdom about decisions applicable to their own stage of life. For example, the oldest group gave its best answers to the problem of a 60-year-old widow who, having just started her own business, learns that her son has been left with two young children and wants her to help care for them (J. Smith & Baltes, 1990).

Apparently, then, wisdom is not necessarily a property of old age—or of any age. Instead, it appears to be a relatively rare and complex phenomenon that shows relative stability or slight growth in certain individuals (Staudinger & Baltes, 1996; Staudinger, Smith, & Baltes, 1992). A variety of factors, including personality and life experience—either direct or vicarious—may contribute to it (Shedlock & Cornelius, 2003), and guidance from mentors may help prepare the way (Baltes & Staudinger, 2000; Pasupathi et al., 2001).

Research on physical functioning, cognition, and aging is more encouraging than some might expect. Older adults tend to make the most of their abilities, often exploiting gains in one area to offset declines in another. Research highlights the widely varying paths of physical and cognitive development among individuals. It also points to the importance of emotional well-being in late adulthood, the topic of Chapter 18.

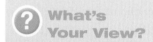

What's Your View?

• Think of the wisest person you know. Which, if any, of the criteria for wisdom mentioned in this chapter seem to describe this person? If none do, how would you define and measure wisdom?

Checkpoint

Can you . . .

◆ Compare various approaches to the study of wisdom?

◆ Discuss findings from Baltes's studies of wisdom?

Summary and Key Terms

Old Age Today

Guidepost 1 *How is today's older population changing?*

- Efforts to combat ageism are making headway, thanks to the visibility of a growing number of active, healthy older adults.

- The proportion of older people in the United States and world populations is greater than ever before and is expected to continue to grow. People over 80 are the fastest-growing age group.

- Although effects of primary aging may be beyond people's control, they often can avoid effects of secondary aging.

- Specialists in the study of aging sometimes refer to people between ages 65 and 74 as the *young old,* those over 75 as the *old old,* and those over 85 as the *oldest old.* However, these terms may be more useful when used to refer to functional age.

ageism (550)

primary aging (552)

secondary aging (552)

functional age (552)

gerontology (552)

geriatrics (552)

PHYSICAL DEVELOPMENT

Longevity and Aging

Guidepost 2 *How has life expectancy changed, what causes aging, and what possibilities exist for extending the life span?*

- Life expectancy has increased dramatically. The longer people live, the longer they are likely to live.

- In general, life expectancy is greater in developed countries than in developing countries, among white Americans than among African Americans, and among women as compared to men.

- Recent gains in life expectancy come largely from progress toward reducing death rates from diseases affecting older people. Further large improvements in life expectancy may depend on whether scientists can learn to modify basic processes of aging.

- Theories of biological aging fall into two categories: genetic-programming theories and variable-rate, or error, theories.

- Research on extension of the life span through genetic manipulation or caloric restriction has challenged the idea of a biological limit to the life span.

life expectancy (552)

longevity (552)

life span (552)

senescence (555)

genetic-programming theories (555)

variable-rate theories (556)

metabolism (556)

free radicals (557)

autoimmunity (557)

survival curves (558)

Hayflick limit (558)

Physical Changes

Guidepost 3 *What physical changes occur during old age, and how do these changes vary among individuals?*

- Changes in body systems and organs are highly variable. Most body systems continue to function fairly well, but the heart becomes more susceptible to disease. Reserve capacity declines.

- Although the brain changes with age, the changes are usually modest. They include loss of volume and weight and a slowing of responses. However, the brain can grow new neurons and build new connections late in life.

- Vision and hearing problems may interfere with daily life but often can be corrected. Irreversible damage may result from age-related macular degeneration or glaucoma. Losses in taste and smell may lead to poor nutrition. Training can improve muscular strength, balance, and reaction time. Older adults tend to be susceptible to accidents and falls.

- Older people tend to sleep less and dream less than before, but chronic insomnia can be an indication of depression.

- Many older adults remain sexually active, though the intensity of sexual experience is generally lower than for younger adults.

reserve capacity (560)

cataracts (562)

age-related macular degeneration (562)

glaucoma (562)

Physical and Mental Health

Guidepost 4 *What health problems are common in late adulthood, what factors influence health, and what mental and behavioral problems do some older people experience?*

- Most older people are reasonably healthy, especially if they follow a healthy lifestyle. Many do have chronic conditions, but these usually do not greatly limit activities or interfere with daily life.

- Exercise and diet are important influences on health. Loss of teeth can seriously affect nutrition.

- Most older people are in good mental health. Depression, alcoholism, and many other conditions can be reversed with treatment; a few, such as Alzheimer's disease, are irreversible.
- Alzheimer's disease becomes more prevalent with age. It is highly heritable, but diet, exercise, and other lifestyle factors may play a part. Cognitive activity may be protective by building up a cognitive reserve that enables the brain to function under stress. Behavioral and drug therapies can slow deterioration. Mild cognitive impairment can be an early sign of the disease, and researchers are developing tools for early diagnosis.

activities of daily living (ADLs) (566)

instrumental activities of daily living (IADLs) (566)

dementia (569)

Alzheimer's disease (570)

Parkinson's disease (570)

neurofibrillary tangles 571)

amyloid plaque (571)

cognitive reserve (572)

COGNITIVE DEVELOPMENT

Aspects of Cognitive Development

Guidepost 5 *What gains and losses in cognitive abilities tend to occur in late adulthood, and are there ways to improve older people's cognitive performance?*

- Older adults do better on the verbal portion of the Wechsler Adult Intelligence Scale than on the performance portion.
- The Seattle Longitudinal Study found that cognitive functioning in late adulthood is highly variable. Few people decline in all or most areas, and many people improve in some. The engagement hypothesis seeks to explain these differences.
- Older adults are more effective in solving practical problems that have emotional relevance for them.
- A general slowdown in central nervous system functioning may affect the speed of information processing.
- Intelligence may be a predictor of longevity.
- Sensory memory, semantic memory, and procedural memory, appear nearly as efficient in older adults as in younger adults. The capacity of working memory and the ability to recall specific events or recently learned information are often less efficient.
- Older adults have more problems with oral word retrieval and spelling than younger adults. Grammatical complexity and content of speech decline.
- Neurological changes and problems in encoding, storage, and retrieval may account for much of the decline in memory functioning in older adults. However, the brain can compensate for some age-related declines.
- Older people show considerable plasticity in cognitive performance and can benefit from training.
- According to Baltes's studies, wisdom is not age-related, but people of all ages give wiser responses to problems affecting their own age group.

Wechsler Adult Intelligence Scale (WAIS) (574)

sensory memory (577)

working memory (577)

episodic memory (578)

semantic memory (578)

procedural memory (578)

There is still today

And tomorrow fresh with dreams:

Life never grows old

—Rita Duskin, "Haiku," *Sound and Light,* 1987

Did You **Know...**

- Research suggests that older adults do not become more rigid with age?

- Productive activity seems to play an important part in successful aging?

- In most developed countries, older women are more likely to live alone than older men?

- As the baby boom generation ages and if current nursing home usage rates continue, the number of U.S. nursing home residents is projected to double by 2030?

- Contrary to stereotype, older workers are often more productive than younger workers?

- People who can confide their feelings and thoughts to friends tend to deal better with the changes and challenges of aging?

These are just a few of the interesting and important topics we will cover in this chapter. In it, we look at theory and research on psychosocial development in late adulthood. We discuss such late-life options as work, retirement, and living arrangements and their impact on society's ability to support an aging population and to care for the frail and infirm. Finally, we look at relationships with families and friends, which greatly affect the quality of these last years. After you have read and studied this chapter, you should be able to answer each of the Guidepost questions on the following page.

Guideposts *for Study*

1. Does personality change in old age, and what special issues and tasks do older people face?

2. What strategies and resources contribute to older adults' well-being and mental health?

3. How do older adults handle work and retirement decisions, financial resources, and living arrangements?

4. How do personal relationships change in old age, and what is their effect on well-being?

5. What are the characteristics of long-term marriages in late life, and what impact do widowhood, divorce, and remarriage have at this time?

6. How do unmarried older adults and those in cohabiting and gay and lesbian relationships fare, and how does friendship change in old age?

7. How do older adults get along with—or without—grown children and with siblings, and how do they adjust to great-grandparenthood?

Guidepost 1

Does personality change in old age, and what special issues and tasks do older people face?

Theory and Research on Personality Development

In the early 1980s, when the writer Betty Friedan was asked to organize a seminar at Harvard University on "Growth in Aging," the distinguished behaviorist B. F. Skinner declined to participate. Age and growth, he said, were "a contradiction in terms" (Friedan, 1993, p. 23). Skinner was far from alone in that belief. Yet almost three decades later, late adulthood is increasingly recognized as a time of potential growth.

The examples of such people as former President Jimmy Carter, who won the Nobel Peace Prize at age 78 for his ongoing work in human rights, education, preventive health research, and conflict resolution worldwide, have led most theorists to view late adulthood as a developmental stage with its own special issues and tasks. It is a time when people can reexamine their lives, complete unfinished business, and decide how best to channel their energies and spend their remaining days, months, or years. Some wish to leave a legacy to their grandchildren or to the world, pass on the fruits of their experience, or validate the meaning of their lives. Others simply want to enjoy favorite pastimes or to do things they never had enough time for when they were younger. "Growth in aging" *is* possible; and many older adults who feel healthy, competent, and in control of their lives experience this last stage of life as a positive one.

Let's see what theory and research can tell us about personality in this final phase of the life span and about the psychosocial challenges and opportunities of aging. In the next section, we will discuss how older adults cope with stress and loss and what constitutes successful aging.

Jimmy Carter, one of the most active ex-presidents in American history, won the Nobel Prize at age 78 for his continuing work in human rights, education, preventive health research, and conflict resolution, much of it in developing countries.

Erik Erikson: Normative Issues and Tasks

What factors contribute to personal growth? According to normative-stage theorists, growth depends on carrying out the psychological tasks of each stage of life in an emotionally healthy way.

For Erikson, the crowning achievement of late adulthood is a sense of *ego integrity,* or integrity of the self, an achievement based on reflection about one's life. In the eighth and final stage of the life span, **ego integrity versus despair,** older adults need to evaluate and accept their lives so as to accept death. Building on the outcomes of the seven previous stages, they struggle to achieve a sense of coherence and wholeness, rather than give way to despair over their inability to relive the past differently (Erikson, Erikson, & Kivnick, 1986).

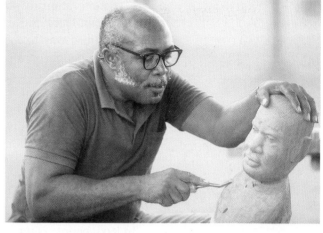

According to Erikson, ego integrity in late adulthood requires continuing stimulation and challenge, which, for this sculptor, come from creative work.

People who succeed in this final, integrative, task gain a sense of the meaning of their lives within the larger social order. The virtue that may develop during this stage is *wisdom,* an "informed and detached concern with life itself in the face of death itself" (Erikson, 1985, p. 61).

Wisdom, said Erikson, means accepting the life one has lived, without major regrets: without dwelling on "should-have-dones" or "might-have-beens." It means accepting imperfection in the self, in parents, in children, and in life. (This definition of *wisdom* as an important psychological resource differs from the largely cognitive definitions explored in Chapter 17.)

Although integrity must outweigh despair if this stage is to be resolved successfully, Erikson maintained that some despair is inevitable. People need to mourn—not only for their own misfortunes and lost chances but for the vulnerability and transience of the human condition.

Yet, Erikson believed, even as the body's functions weaken, people must maintain a "vital involvement" in society. On the basis of studies of life histories of people in their eighties, he concluded that ego integrity comes not just from reflecting on the past but from continued stimulation and challenge—whether through political activity, fitness programs, creative work, or relationships with grandchildren (Erikson et al., 1986).

ego integrity versus despair According to Erikson, the eighth and final stage of psychosocial development, in which people in late adulthood either achieve a sense of integrity of the self by accepting the lives they have lived, and thus accept death, or yield to despair that their lives cannot be relived.

The Five-Factor Model: Personality Traits in Old Age

Does personality change in late life? The answer may depend in part on the way stability and change are measured.

Measuring Stability and Change in Late Adulthood The long-term stability reported by Costa and McCrae and discussed in Chapters 14 and 16 is in *average levels* of various traits within a population. According to the five-factor model and its supporting research, hostile people, on average, are unlikely to mellow much with age unless they get psychotherapeutic treatment, and optimistic people are likely to remain their hopeful selves. However, other longitudinal and cross-sectional studies using a modified version of this model found continued change after age 60: increases in agreeableness and conscientiousness accompanied by declines in social vitality (gregariousness) and openness to experience (Roberts & Mroczek, 2008).

Another way to assess stability or change is *within individuals.* A six-year randomized study of 2,117 people ages 55 to 85 in the Netherlands found little individual change in neuroticism, and what changes did occur were independent of deterioration in physical health or cognitive function (Steunenberg, Twisk, Beekman, Deeg, & Kerkhof, 2005).

A third way to measure stability or change is in *rank-order comparisons* of different people on a given trait. A review of 152 longitudinal studies found that relative differences among individuals become increasingly stable until sometime between ages 50 and 70 and then plateau (Roberts & DelVecchio, 2000). If Elsa is more conscientious than Manuel as a young adult, she is likely to remain the more conscientious of the two in late adulthood.

Early cross-sectional research suggested that personality becomes more rigid in old age. However, McCrae and Costa (1994), in large longitudinal studies using a variety of samples and measures, have shown that this is not true for most people. Likewise, personality tests of 3,442 participants in the Seattle Longitudinal Study found no age-related trends in inflexibility (Schaie, 2005). Indeed, people in more recent cohorts seem to be more flexible (that is, less rigid) than previous cohorts. These findings suggest that increases in rigidity found in the early studies may actually have been tied, not to age, but to the life experience that a particular cohort carried throughout adulthood (Schaie & Willis, 1991). These findings fly in the face of the widespread stereotype that older people become rigid and set in their ways.

Personality as a Predictor of Emotionality, Health, and Well-Being

Personality is a strong predictor of emotionality and subjective well-being—stronger in most respects than social relationships and health (Isaacowitz & Smith, 2003). In a longitudinal study that followed four generations for 23 years, self-reported *negative* emotions such as restlessness, boredom, loneliness, unhappiness, and depression decreased with age (though the rate of decrease slowed after age 60). At the same time, *positive* emotionality—excitement, interest, pride, and a sense of accomplishment—tended to remain stable until late life and then declined only slightly and gradually (Charles, Reynolds, & Gatz, 2001).

A possible explanation for this generally positive picture comes from socioemotional selectivity theory: As people get older, they tend to seek out activities and people that give them emotional gratification. In addition, older adults' greater ability to regulate their emotions may help explain why they tend to be happier and more cheerful than younger adults and to experience negative emotions less often and more fleetingly (Blanchard-Fields, Stein, & Watson, 2004; Carstensen, 1999; Mroczek & Kolarz, 1998).

Two of the Big Five personality traits—extraversion and neuroticism—tend to modify the pattern just described. As Costa and McCrae (1980) predicted, people with *extraverted* personalities (outgoing and socially oriented) tend to report especially high levels of positive emotion initially and are more likely than others to retain their positivity throughout life (Charles et al., 2001; Isaacowitz & Smith, 2003). In a 22-year longitudinal study of 1,927 men, most of them ages 40 to 85, those highest in extraversion were more likely than their peers to maintain a high level of life satisfaction in old age (Mroczek & Spiro, 2005).

People with *neurotic* personalities (moody, touchy, anxious, and restless) tend to report negative and not positive emotions, and they tend to become less positive as they age (Charles et al., 2001; Isaacowitz & Smith, 2003). Neuroticism is a far more powerful predictor of moods and mood disorders than age, race, gender, income, education, and marital status (Costa & McCrae, 1996). Highly neurotic people who become more neurotic as they age have low survival rates, possibly because they are likely to smoke or use alcohol or drugs to help calm their negative emotions and because they are ineffective in managing stress (Mroczek & Spiro, 2007). In contrast, *conscientiousness,* or dependability, has been found to

Checkpoint

Can you . . .

♦ Discuss Erikson's stage of ego integrity versus despair, and tell what Erikson meant by *wisdom*?

♦ Summarize research about stability of personality and its effects on emotionality and well-being in old age?

predict health and longevity, most likely because conscientious people tend to avoid risky behaviors and to engage in activities that promote their health (Baltes, Lindenberger, & Staudinger, 1998; Roberts, Walton, & Bogg, 2005).

Well-Being in Late Adulthood

Their health may not be what it was, they've lost old friends and family members—often spouses—and they probably don't earn the money they once did. Their lives keep changing in countless stressful ways. Yet, in general, older adults have fewer mental disorders and are happier and more satisfied with life than younger adults (Mroczek & Kolarz, 1998; Wykle & Musil, 1993; (Yang, 2008). What accounts for this remarkable ability to cope, and what contributes to successful aging?

In an analysis of 33 years of annual U.S. national surveys from 1972 to 2004, happiness, or subjective well-being, increased overall during the life course, with a dip in middle age (discussed in Chapter 16) followed by rising happiness in old age. This finding may in part reflect the value of a mature outlook, but it also may reflect the selective survival of people who are happier or have more to be happy about. Some cohort variations and social disparities exist. For example, baby boomers report lower levels of happiness than do earlier and later cohorts, perhaps due to the immense size of their generation and the resulting competitive strains for schooling, jobs, and economic security, as well as the turbulent societal events of their formative years. Gender, racial/ethnic, and educational disparities in happiness have narrowed or, in the case of gender, disappeared, especially since the mid-1990s. Furthermore, social disparities may have less impact in old age as biological changes, life events, the ability to cope with stress, and access to social welfare and support services play a more important role (Yang, 2008).

Coping and Mental Health

Coping is adaptive thinking or behavior aimed at reducing or relieving stress that arises from harmful, threatening, or challenging conditions. It is an important aspect of mental health. Let's look at two theoretical approaches to the study of coping: adaptive defenses and the cognitive-appraisal model. Then we'll examine a support system to which many older adults turn: religion.

George Vaillant: Adaptive Defenses   What makes for positive mental health in old age? According to three 50-year prospective studies, an important predictive factor is the use of mature *adaptive defenses* in coping with problems earlier in life.

Vaillant (2000) looked at the survivors of his earlier studies as well as at a subsample of women from Terman's study of gifted California schoolchildren born about 1910. Those who, in old age, showed the best psychosocial adjustment were those who, earlier in adulthood, had used such mature adaptive defenses as altruism, humor, suppression (keeping a stiff upper lip), anticipation (planning for the future), and sublimation (redirecting negative emotions into productive pursuits).

How do adaptive defenses work? According to Vaillant (2000), they can change people's perceptions of realities they are powerless to change. For example, in the studies just mentioned, the use of adaptive defenses predicted *subjective* physical functioning even though it did not predict *objective* physical health as measured by physicians.

Guidepost 2

What strategies and resources contribute to older adults' well-being and mental health?

coping   Adaptive thinking or behavior aimed at reducing or relieving stress that arises from harmful, threatening, or challenging conditions.

Adaptive defenses may be unconscious or intuitive. In contrast, the cognitive-appraisal model, to which we turn now, emphasizes consciously chosen coping strategies.

Cognitive-Appraisal Model   In the **cognitive-appraisal model** (Lazarus & Folkman, 1984), people consciously choose coping strategies on the basis of the way they perceive and analyze a situation. Coping includes anything an individual thinks or does in trying to adapt to stress, regardless of how well it works. Choosing the most appropriate strategy requires continuous reappraisal of the relationship between person and environment.

Coping Strategies: Problem-Focused versus Emotion-Focused   Coping strategies may be either *problem-focused* or *emotion-focused*. **Problem-focused coping** involves the use of *instrumental,* or action-oriented, strategies to eliminate, manage, or improve a stressful condition. This type of coping generally predominates when a person sees a realistic chance of changing the situation. **Emotion-focused coping** is directed toward "feeling better": managing the emotional response to a stressful situation to relieve its physical or psychological impact. This type of coping is likely to predominate when a person concludes that little or nothing can be done about the situation itself.

Problem-focused responses to a series of harsh reprimands from an employer might be to work harder, seek ways to improve one's work skills, or look for another job. Emotion-focused responses might be to refuse to think about the reprimands or to convince oneself that the boss didn't really mean to be so critical. Research has distinguished between two types of emotion-focused coping: *proactive* (confronting or expressing one's emotions or seeking social support) and *passive* (avoidance, denial, suppression of emotions, or acceptance of the situation as it is).

Age Differences in Choice of Coping Styles   Older adults tend to do more emotion-focused coping than younger people (Folkman, Lazarus, Pimley, & Novacek, 1987; Prohaska, Leventhal, Leventhal, & Keller, 1985). Is that because they are less able to focus on problems, or because they are better able to control their emotions? Research suggests that the latter is the answer (Blanchard-Fields, Stein, & Watson, 2004).

In studies in which young, middle-aged, and older adults were asked how they would deal with various kinds of problems, participants, regardless of age, most often picked problem-focused strategies (either direct action or analyzing the problem so as to understand it better). The largest age differences appeared in problems with highly emotional or stressful implications, such as that of a divorced man who is allowed to see his child only on weekends but wants to see the child more often. Adults of all ages were more likely to use emotion-focused coping in such situations, but older adults chose emotion-focused strategies (such as doing nothing, waiting until the child is older, or trying not to worry about it) more often than younger adults did (Blanchard-Fields, Jahnke, & Camp, 1995; Blanchard-Fields et al., 2004).

Apparently, with age, people develop a more flexible repertoire of coping strategies (Blanchard-Fields, Stein, & Watson, 2004). Older adults *can* employ problem-focused strategies but may be more able than younger adults to use emotion regulation when a situation seems to call for it, as when problem-focused action might be futile or counterproductive (Blanchard-Fields & Camp, 1990; Blanchard-Fields, Chen, & Norris, 1997; Blanchard-Fields et al., 1995; Folkman & Lazarus, 1980; Labouvie-Vief, Hakim-Larson, & Hobart, 1987).

Emotion-focused coping can be especially useful in coping with what the family therapist Pauline Boss (1999, 2004) calls **ambiguous loss** (see Box 19-1 on page 625). Boss applies that term to losses that are not clearly defined or do not

cognitive-appraisal model
Model of coping, proposed by Lazarus and Folkman, which holds that, on the basis of continuous appraisal of their relationship with the environment, people choose appropriate coping strategies to deal with situations that tax their normal resources.

problem-focused coping   In the cognitive-appraisal model, coping strategy directed toward eliminating, managing, or improving a stressful situation.

emotion-focused coping   In the cognitive-appraisal model, coping strategy directed toward managing the emotional response to a stressful situation so as to lessen its physical or psychological impact.

What's Your View?

• Which type of coping do you tend to use more: problem-focused or emotion-focused? Which type do your parents use more? Your grandparents? In what kinds of situations does each type of coping seem most effective?

ambiguous loss   A loss that is not clearly defined or does not bring closure.

bring closure, such as the loss of a still-living loved one to Alzheimer's disease or the loss of a homeland, which elderly immigrants may feel as long as they live. In such situations, experience may teach people to accept what they cannot change—a lesson often reinforced by religion.

Does Religion or Spirituality Affect Health and Well-Being? Religion becomes increasingly important to many people as they age. In a nationally representative survey, about 50 percent of U.S. adults in their seventies and eighties said they attend services every week (Cornwell, Laumann, & Schumm, 2008). Religion seems to play a supportive role for many older people. Some possible explanations include social support,

Religious activity seems to help many people cope with stress and loss in later life, and some research suggests that its effect on health and well-being may be real.

encouragement of healthy lifestyles, the perception of a measure of control over life through prayer, fostering of positive emotional states, reduction of stress, and faith in God as a way of interpreting misfortunes (Seybold & Hill, 2001). But does religion actually improve health and well-being?

Many studies suggest a positive link between religion or spirituality and health, though much of this research is not methodologically sound (Miller & Thoresen, 2003; Seeman, Dubin, & Seeman, 2003; Sloan & Bagiella, 2002). A review of studies with relatively sound methodology found a 25 percent reduction in risk of mortality among healthy adults who attended religious services weekly (Powell, Shahabi, & Thoresen, 2003). Another research review found positive associations between religiosity or spirituality and measures of health, well-being, marital satisfaction, and psychological functioning and negative associations with suicide, delinquency, criminality, and drug and alcohol use (Seybold & Hill, 2001).

Relatively little of the research on religion and spirituality has been done with racial/ethnic minorities. In one such study, among 3,050 older Mexican Americans, those who attended church once a week had a 32 percent lower mortality risk than those who never attended. This was true even when sociodemographic characteristics, cardiovascular health, activities of daily living, cognitive functioning, physical functioning, social support, health behaviors, mental health, and perceived health were controlled (Hill, Angel, Ellison, & Angel, 2005). For elderly black people, religion is closely related to life satisfaction and well-being (Coke, 1992; Coke & Twaite, 1995; Krause, 2004a; Walls & Zarit, 1991). A special factor is the belief held by many black people that the church helps sustain them in confronting racial injustice (Krause, 2004a).

> ## ✔ Checkpoint
>
> *Can you . . .*
>
> ◆ Identify five mature adaptive mechanisms identified by Vaillant, and discuss how they work?
>
> ◆ Describe the cognitive-appraisal model of coping, and explain the relationship between age and choice of coping strategies?
>
> ◆ Discuss how religiosity and spirituality relate to mortality risk, health, and well-being in late life?

Models of "Successful," or "Optimal," Aging

With a growing number of active, healthy older adults, the concept of aging has shifted. *Successful,* or *optimal, aging* has largely replaced the idea that aging results from inevitable, intrinsic processes of loss and decline. Given that modifiable factors play a part in rates of aging, as discussed in Chapter 17, it follows that some people may age more successfully than others (Rowe & Kahn, 1997).

A considerable body of work has identified three main components of successful aging: (1) avoidance of disease or disease-related disability, (2) maintenance of high physical and cognitive functioning, and (3) sustained, active engagement in social and productive activities (activities, paid or unpaid, that create social value). Successful agers tend to have social support, both emotional and material, which aids mental health; and as long as they remain active and productive, they do not think of themselves as old (Rowe & Kahn, 1997). Another approach emphasizes subjective well-being and satisfaction with life (Jopp & Smith, 2006).

Yet, all definitions of *successful,* or *optimal, aging* are value-laden—unavoidably so. These terms, critics say, may burden, rather than liberate, older people by putting pressure on them to meet standards they cannot or do not wish to meet (Holstein & Minkler, 2003). The concept of successful aging, according to these critics, does not pay enough attention to the constraints that may limit lifestyle choices. Not all adults have the good genes, education, and favorable circumstances to "construct the kind of life they choose" (p. 792), and the "already marginalized" are most likely to "come up on the wrong side of . . . the either-or divide" (p. 791). An unintended result of labeling older adults as successful or unsuccessful may be to blame the victims and drive them to self-defeating, anti-aging, strategies. It also tends to demean old age itself and to deny the importance of accepting, or adapting to, what cannot be changed.

Keeping these concerns in mind, let's look at some classic and current theories and research about aging well.

Disengagement Theory versus Activity Theory

Who is making a healthier adjustment to old age: a person who tranquilly watches the world go by from a rocking chair or one who keeps busy from morning till night? According to **disengagement theory,** aging normally brings a gradual reduction in social involvement and greater preoccupation with the self. According to **activity theory,** the more active older people remain, the better they age.

Disengagement theory was one of the first influential theories in gerontology. Its proponents (Cumming & Henry, 1961) saw disengagement as a universal condition of aging. They maintained that declines in physical functioning and awareness of the approach of death result in a gradual, inevitable withdrawal from social roles (worker, spouse, parent); and, because society stops providing useful roles for the older adult, the disengagement is mutual. Disengagement is thought to be accompanied by introspection and a quieting of the emotions. However, after more than four decades, disengagement theory has received little independent research support and has "largely disappeared from the empirical literature" (Achenbaum & Bengtson, 1994, p. 756).

Activity theory, in contrast to disengagement theory, links activity with life satisfaction. Because activities tend to be tied in with social roles and connections, the greater the loss of these roles—through retirement, widowhood, distance from children, or infirmity—the less satisfied a person is likely to be. People who are aging well keep up as many activities as possible and find substitutes for lost roles (Neugarten, Havighurst, & Tobin, 1968). Indeed, research has found that the loss of major role identities is a risk factor for declines in well-being and mental health (Greenfield & Marks, 2004).

Nevertheless, activity theory, as originally framed, is now regarded as oversimplistic. In early research (Neugarten et al., 1968), activity generally was associated with satisfaction. However, some disengaged people also were well-adjusted. This finding suggests that although activity may work best for most people, disengagement may be appropriate for some, and that generalizations about a particular pattern of successful aging may be risky (Moen, Dempster-McClain, & Williams, 1992; Musick, Herzog, & House, 1999).

A more specific version of activity theory proposes that it is the *frequency* and social *intimacy* of activities that are important to life satisfaction (Lemon,

Checkpoint

Can you . . .

♦ Tell what is meant by *successful,* or *optimal, aging* and why the concept is controversial.

disengagement theory Theory of aging, proposed by Cumming and Henry, which holds that successful aging is characterized by mutual withdrawal of the older person and society.

activity theory Theory of aging, proposed by Neugarten and others, which holds that in order to age successfully a person must remain as active as possible.

Bengtson, & Peterson, 1972). In several studies, either the number of activities older people engaged in or the frequency with which they engaged in them was positively related to well-being and predicted physical health, functional and cognitive status, incidence of Alzheimer's disease, and survival. According to a nationally representative survey mentioned earlier in this chapter, about 75 percent of late middle-aged and older adults socialize with neighbors, attend religious services, volunteer, or attend meetings at least weekly. Those in their eighties are twice as likely to do so as those in their fifties (Cornwell et al., 2008).

However, inconsistencies in defining *activities* make it difficult to compare studies (Menec, 2003). Furthermore, most of the research on activity theory has been correlational. If a relationship between activity levels and successful aging were found, it would not reveal whether people age well because they are active or whether people remain active because they are aging well (Musick et al., 1999).

Continuity Theory **Continuity theory,** proposed by the gerontologist Robert Atchley (1989), emphasizes people's need to maintain a connection between past and present. In this view, activity is important, not for its own sake, but to the extent that it represents the continuation of a lifestyle. For older adults who always have been active and involved, it may be important to continue a high level of activity. Many retired people are happiest pursuing work or leisure activities similar to those they have enjoyed in the past (J. R.

Older people who feel useful to others, as this grandparent does to his grandson, are more likely to age successfully.

Kelly, 1994). Women who have been involved in multiple roles (such as wife, mother, worker, and volunteer) tend to continue those involvements—and to reap the benefits—as they age (Moen et al., 1992). On the other hand, people who have been less active may do better in the proverbial rocking chair.

In a 34-year longitudinal study of a representative sample of Swedes ages 18 to 75, people who, in old age, participated in a leisure activity such as reading books, pursuing a hobby, or gardening tended to have engaged in that activity in middle age as well, though participation rates decreased and some older adults had to adapt to visual, motor, or cognitive impairments (Agahi, Ahacic, & Parker, 2006).

continuity theory Theory of aging, described by Atchley, which holds that in order to age successfully people must maintain a balance of continuity and change in both the internal and external structures of their lives.

The Role of Productivity Some researchers focus on productive activity, either paid or unpaid, as a key to aging well. Older people who feel useful to others are more likely to remain alive and healthy. Adults in their seventies who do not feel useful to others are more likely than those who frequently feel useful to experience increased disabilities or to die within the next seven years (Gruenewald, Karlamangla, Greendale, Singer, & Seeman, 2007).

Research supports the idea that productive activity plays an important part in successful aging. A six-year longitudinal study of 3,218 older adults in Manitoba, Canada, found that *social* and *productive activities* (such as visiting family or housework and gardening) were related to self-rated happiness, better physical functioning, and less chance of having died six years later. *Solitary activities,* such as reading and handiwork, did not have physical benefits but were related to happiness, perhaps by promoting a sense of engagement with life (Menec, 2003).

However, some research suggests that frequent participation in *leisure activities* can be as beneficial to health and well-being as frequent participation in

Checkpoint

Can you . . .

♦ Compare disengagement theory, activity theory, and continuity theory?

♦ Discuss the importance of productivity in late adulthood?

productive activities. It may be that *any* regular activity that expresses and enhances some aspect of the self can contribute to successful aging (Herzog et al., 1998).

Selective Optimization with Compensation According to Baltes and his colleagues (Baltes, 1997; Baltes & Baltes, 1990; Baltes & Smith, 2004; Riediger, Freund, & Baltes, 2005), successful aging involves **selective optimization with compensation (SOC).** This model describes strategies that enable people to adapt to the changing balance of growth and decline throughout life. In childhood, resources are primarily used for growth, and in early adulthood, to maximize reproductive fitness. In old age, resources are increasingly directed toward maintenance of health and management of loss (Baltes & Smith, 2004; Jopp & Smith, 2006). In late adulthood, SOC can enable adults to conserve resources by *selecting* fewer and more meaningful activities or goals on which to focus their efforts; *optimizing,* or making the most of, the resources they have to achieve their goals; and *compensating* for losses by mobilizing resources in alternative ways to achieve their goals, such as using hearing aids to compensate for hearing loss (Baltes, 1997; Baltes & Smith, 2004; Jopp & Smith, 2006; Lang, Rieckmann, & Baltes, 2002). The celebrated concert pianist Arthur Rubinstein, who gave his farewell concert at age 89, compensated for memory and motor losses by maintaining a smaller repertoire, practicing longer each day, and playing more slowly before fast movements (which he could no longer play at top speed) to heighten the contrast (Baltes & Baltes, 1990).

The same life-management strategies apply to psychosocial development. According to Carstensen's (1991, 1995, 1996) socioemotional selectivity theory, older adults become more selective about social contacts, keeping up with friends and relatives who can best meet their current needs for emotional satisfaction. Such meaningful contacts may compensate for the narrowing of possibilities in old age.

Older people who are rich in resources are more likely to survive, to remain active, and to use SOC strategies to adapt to aging losses than people poorer in resources (Lang et al., 2002). Even in old-old people whose resources are substantially depleted, however, these strategies can buffer losses in life satisfaction and increase well-being. Maintaining a positive attitude toward aging can lengthen life (Jopp & Smith, 2006).

SOC strategies are thought to be universal, according to Baltes and his colleagues, but some people use them more, and more effectively, than others (Baltes & Smith, 2004; Jopp & Smith, 2006). Why? One answer may lie in the amount of control people feel they retain over their lives (Schulz & Heckhausen, 1996). In the face of stress, older adults may select emotion-focusing strategies to compensate for loss of control. In one study, people reported greater feelings of control over their work, finances, and marriages as they aged, but less control over their sex lives and relationships with children (Lachman & Weaver, 1998). Another study found that people tend to live longer if they have a sense of control over the role (such as spouse, parent, provider, or friend) that is most important to them (Krause & Shaw, 2000).

Research has found that use of SOC is associated with positive developmental outcomes, including greater well-being (Baltes & Smith, 2004). Eventually, though, older people may reach the limit of their available resources, and compensatory efforts may no longer seem to work. In a four-year longitudinal study of 762 adults, compensatory efforts increased up to age 70 but then declined. Among young-old and middle-old participants, compensatory activities sufficed to maintain previous levels of performance, but this was no longer true of the

---

selective optimization with compensation (SOC) Enhancing over all cognitive functioning by using stronger abilities to compensate for those that have weakened.

What's Your View?

- Are you satisfied with any of the definitions of successful, or optimal, aging presented in this section? Why or why not?

old old. Adjusting one's personal standards to changes in what is possible to achieve may be essential to maintaining a positive outlook on life (Rothermund & Brandtstädter, 2003).

The argument about what constitutes successful or optimal aging and what contributes to well-being in old age is far from settled, and may never be. One thing is clear: People differ greatly in the ways they can and do live—and want to live—in the later years of life.

Practical and Social Issues Related to Aging

"I—will—never—retire!" wrote the comedian George Burns (1983, p. 138) at age 87. Burns—who continued performing until two years before his death at the age of 100—was one of many late-life achievers who have kept their minds and bodies active doing the work they love.

Whether and when to retire are among the most crucial lifestyle decisions people make as they approach late adulthood. These decisions affect their financial situation and emotional state, as well as the ways they spend their waking hours and the ways they relate to family and friends. The need to provide financial support for large numbers of retired older people also has serious implications for society, especially as the baby boom generation starts to retire. Another social issue is the need for appropriate living arrangements and care for older people who can no longer manage on their own. (Box 18-1 reports on issues related to support of the aging in Asia.)

Work and Retirement

Retirement took hold in many industrialized countries during the late nineteenth and early twentieth centuries as life expectancy increased. In the United States, the creation of the Social Security system in the 1930s, together with company-sponsored pension plans negotiated by labor unions, made it possible for many older workers to retire with financial security. Eventually, mandatory retirement at age 65 became almost universal.

Today, compulsory retirement has been virtually outlawed in the United States as a form of age discrimination (except for certain occupations, such as airline pilots), and the line between work and retirement is not as clear as it used to be. There are no longer norms concerning the timing of retirement, how to plan for it, and what to do afterward. Adults have many choices. The biggest factors in the decision usually are health and financial considerations. For many older adults, retirement is a "phased phenomenon, involving multiple transitions out of and into paid and unpaid 'work'" (Kim & Moen, 2001, p. 489).

Trends in Late-Life Work and Retirement Most adults who *can* retire *do* retire; and, with increasing longevity, they spend more time in retirement than in the past (Dobriansky, Suzman, & Hodes, 2007; Kim & Moen, 2001; Kinsella & Velkoff, 2001).

Proportions of older adults in the labor force generally depend on whether a country is poor or rich. In most of the developing world, it is common for older people to continue to work, mostly on farms. In some developing countries, more than 50 percent of older men are economically active, while in some industrialized countries only 2 percent are active. In developed countries, about 4 percent of older women typically are in the workforce. Women's economic activity in developing countries, mainly in subsistence agriculture and household industries, is generally underreported (Kinsella & Phillips, 2005), but while older men's workforce

✔ Checkpoint

Can you . . .

◆ Explain how selective optimization with compensation helps older adults deal with losses?

Guidepost 3

How do older adults handle work and retirement decisions, financial resources, and living arrangements?

BOX **18-1** *Window on the World*

Aging in Asia

Challenges of an aging population are common to Eastern and Western societies, but differing cultural traditions and economic systems affect the way societies deal with these challenges. In East Asia, in particular, the shifting balance of young and old, together with rapid economic development, has caused societal dislocations and cultural strains, upsetting ancient traditions.

One dramatic result of an aging population is fewer young people to care for the old. By 2030 Japan, for example, is projected to have twice as many older adults, nearly 40 percent of them at least 80 years old, as children. Pension reserves will likely be exhausted, and retirement and health care costs for the elderly may consume nearly three-fourths of the national income (Dobriansky et al., 2007; Kinsella & Phillips, 2005; WuDunn, 1997).

In China, the over-60 population is growing faster than in any other major country. By midcentury, about 430 million Chinese—one-third of the population—will be retirees (United Nations, 2007). In its rapid transition to a market economy, China has not established a fully functioning system of old-age insurance. A steady rise in the number of retirees together with a decline in the ratio of workers to pensioners threatens the stability of the system. One possible solution—raising the currently low retirement age—would make jobs for the 30 percent of recent university graduates who are unemployed even more scarce (Dobriansky et al., 2007; French, 2007).

Throughout Asia, a large proportion of older people still live with their children in the Confucian tradition of spiritual obligation to aid and care for parents. However, this tradition is eroding. In Hong Kong, China, Korea, and Japan, significant numbers of older adults now live alone (Dobriansky et al., 2007; Kinsella & Phillips, 2005; Silverstein, Cong, & Li, 2006).

All of these changes make the tradition of home care of the elderly less feasible. Institutionalization—virtually nonexistent in 1960—is seen as a violation of traditional obligations, but the exploding older Japanese population is outgrowing family-based care. To halt this trend, the government has made it a legal obligation to care for elderly relatives and has provided tax relief to those who give them financial help (Lin et al., 2003; L. G. Martin, 1988; Oshima, 1996).

In urban areas of China, where housing is scarce, older parents continue to live with adult children, usually married sons, following the traditional patriarchal custom (Pimentel & Liu, 2004; Silverstein et al., 2006; Zhang, 2004). In rural areas, however, where many working-age adults have migrated to cities in search of jobs, a decline in multigenerational households undermines Confucian ideals. Still, in the absence of universal public pensions and long-term care programs, older parents remain largely dependent on their children. In one rural province, more than half (51 percent) of older parents live with adult children, grandchildren, or both, and almost all receive material assistance from their children—but for many parents such assistance is less important than maintaining the tradition of a multigenerational household (Silverstein et al., 2006).

Because of China's one-child policy, in force since 1979, singleton adult children, usually daughters-in-law who may be in the workforce, are expected to care for two parents and four grandparents, a task that will become increasingly unworkable. The aging population has increased the prevalence of chronic diseases and disabilities and expanded the need for long-term care. The government has begun to develop disease-prevention programs and long-term care systems, but it is doubtful whether enough funding will be available to cover rising health care costs (Kaneda, 2006).

What's Your View?

In what ways is aging in Asia becoming similar to aging in the United States? In what ways is it different?

Check It Out

For more information on aging in Japan, go to http://spice.stanford.edu/docs/173. This is a list, at the website of the National Clearinghouse for U.S.-Japan Studies, of links to discussions of Japan's aging population.

---

participation has declined, older women's participation in most countries has increased (Dobriansky et al., 2007). In the United States in 2005, about 20 percent of older men and 11.5 percent of older women were in the workforce (Administration on Aging, 2006), but the rates decreased rapidly with age (Federal Interagency Forum on Aging-Related Statistics, 2006).

How Does Age Affect Attitudes toward Work and Job Performance?

People who continue to work after age 65 typically like their work and do not find it unduly stressful. They tend to be better educated and in better health

What's Your View?

• At what age, if ever, do you expect to retire? Why? How would you like to spend your time if and when you retire?

than those who retire earlier (Kiefer, Summer, & Shirey, 2001; Kim & Moen, 2001; Parnes & Sommers, 1994).

Contrary to ageist stereotypes, older workers are often more productive than younger workers. Although they may work more slowly than younger people, they are more accurate (Czaja & Sharit, 1998; Salthouse & Maurer, 1996; Treas, 1995). Although younger workers tend to be better at tasks requiring quick responses, older workers tend to be more capable of work that depends on precision, a steady pace, and mature judgment (Forteza & Prieto, 1994; Warr, 1994). A key factor may be experience rather than age: when older people perform better, it may be because they have been on a job, or have done similar work, longer (Warr, 1994).

In the United States, the Age Discrimination in Employment Act (ADEA), which applies to firms with 20 or more employees, protects workers ages 40 and older from being denied a job, fired, paid less, or forced to retire because of age. A task force commissioned by Congress found that (1) physical fitness and mental abilities vary increasingly with age and differ more *within* age groups than between age groups, and (2) tests of specific psychological, physical, and perceptual-motor abilities can predict job performance far better than age can (Landy, 1992, 1994). Still, many employers exert subtle pressures on older employees (Landy, 1994), and age discrimination cases can be difficult to prove (Carpenter, 2004).

Life after Retirement   Retirement is not a single event but an ongoing process. Personal resources (health, SES, and personality), economic resources, and social-relational resources, such as support from a partner and friends, can affect how well retirees weather this transition (Kim & Moen, 2001, 2002). So can a person's attachment to work. (van Solinge & Henkens, 2005).

In a two-year longitudinal study of 458 relatively healthy married men and women ages 50 to 72, men whose morale at work had been low tended to enjoy a boost during the "honeymoon period" immediately following retirement, but *continuous* retirement was associated with an increase in depressive symptoms. Women's well-being was less influenced by retirement—their own or their husbands'; their morale was more affected by marital quality. A sense of personal control was a key predictor of morale in both men and women (Kim & Moen, 2002).

Socioeconomic status may affect the way retired people use their time. One common pattern, the **family-focused lifestyle,** consists largely of accessible, low-cost activities that revolve around family, home, and companions: conversation, watching television, visiting with family and friends, informal entertaining, playing cards, or just doing "what comes along." Another pattern, **balanced investment,** is typical of more educated people, who allocate their time more equally among family, work, and leisure (J. R. Kelly, 1987, 1994). These patterns may change with age. In one study, the younger retirees who were most satisfied with their quality of life were those who traveled regularly and went to cultural events; but after age 75, family- and home-based activity yielded the most satisfaction (J. R. Kelly, Steinkamp, & Kelly, 1986).

Sunday painters, amateur carpenters, and others who have made the effort to master a craft or pursue an intense interest often make that passion central to their lives during retirement (Mannell, 1993). This lifestyle pattern, **serious leisure,** is dominated by activity that "demands skill, attention, and commitment" (J. R. Kelly, 1994, p. 502). Retirees who engage in this pattern tend to be extraordinarily satisfied with their lives.

family-focused lifestyle Pattern of retirement activity that revolves around family, home, and companions.

balanced investment Pattern of retirement activity allocated among family, work, and leisure.

serious leisure Leisure activity requiring skill, attention, and commitment.

About 500,000 older Americans volunteer through the Senior Corps program. These volunteers are building a home for a low-income family through Habitat for Humanity.

Volunteer work is closely tied to well-being during retirement; it may "help replace the social capital lost when an individual exits the world of work" (Kim & Moen, 2001, p. 510). In a sample of adults ages 65 to 74 from the MIDUS study, volunteering predicted positive emotionality. It also tended to protect against declines in well-being associated with major role-identity losses (Greenfield & Marks, 2004). In Japan, older adults who are healthy and active are encouraged to be volunteers. In a longitudinal study of older Japanese adults, those who rated themselves as useful to others and to society were more likely to survive six years later, even after adjustment for self-rated health (Okamoto & Tanaka, 2004).

The many paths to a meaningful, enjoyable retirement have two things in common: doing satisfying things and having satisfying relationships. For most older people, both "are an extension of histories that have developed throughout the life course" (J. R. Kelly, 1994, p. 501).

How Do Older Adults Fare Financially?

Since the 1960s, Social Security has provided the largest share of older Americans' income. Nine out of ten Americans age 65 and older report income from this source (Administration on Aging, 2006). In 2004, Social Security accounted for 39 percent of older Americans' total income, followed by earnings (26 percent), pensions (19 percent), and asset income (13 percent). Dependence on Social Security and asset income rises dramatically with age and decreases with income level (Federal Interagency Forum on Aging-Related Statistics, 2006).

Social Security and other government programs, such as Medicare, which covers basic health insurance for U.S. residents who are 65 or older or are disabled, have enabled today's older Americans, as a group, to live fairly comfortably. Since 1959 the proportion of older adults living in poverty fell from 35 percent to less than 10 percent in 2004 (Federal Interagency Forum on Aging-Related Statistics, 2004, 2006), and the poverty rate for older adults now is lower than that of the total population (Gist & Hetzel, 2004). However, with a graying population and proportionately fewer workers to contribute to the Social Security system, it seems likely that, unless changes are made, benefits will eventually decline, though the timing and severity of the problem are in dispute (Sawicki, 2005).

Women—especially if they are single, widowed, separated, or divorced or if they were previously poor or worked only part-time in middle age—are more likely than men to live in poverty in old age (Administration on Aging, 2006; Vartanian & McNamara, 2002). Older African Americans and Hispanic Americans are about two and a half times more likely to do so than older white Americans. The highest poverty rates are among older Hispanic women and older African American women who live alone (Administration on Aging, 2006).

Living Arrangements

In developing countries, older adults typically live with adult children and grandchildren in multigenerational households, though this custom is declining. In

Checkpoint

Can you . . .

◆ Describe current trends in late-life work and retirement?

◆ Cite findings on the relationship between aging and work attitudes and skills?

◆ Discuss how retirement can affect well-being, and describe three common lifestyle patterns after retirement?

◆ Discuss the economic status of older adults and issues concerning Social Security and pension plans?

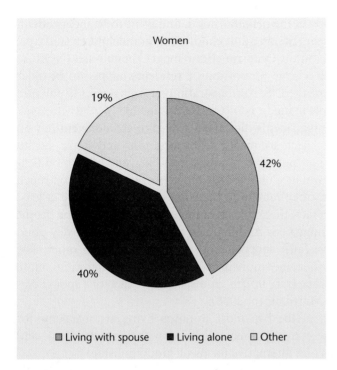
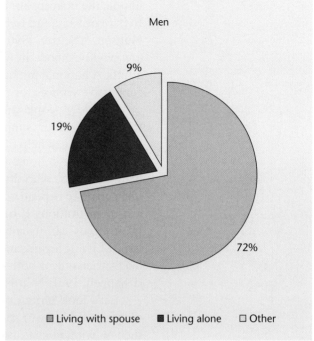

Figure 18-1

Living arrangements of noninstitutionalized men and women age 65 and over, United States, 2005. In part because of women's longer life expectancy, they are more likely to live alone (especially as they get older), while men are more likely to live with a spouse. The "Other" category includes those living with adult children, other relatives, or nonrelatives. (Source: Administration on Aging, 2006.)

developed countries, most older people live alone or with a partner or spouse (Kinsella & Phillips, 2005).

In the United States, in 2005, 95.5 percent of persons age 65 and older lived in the community, 5 percent of them in senior housing of various types, many with supportive services available (Administration on Aging, 2006). Because of women's greater life expectancy, about 72 percent of noninstitutionalized men but only about 42 percent of noninstitutionalized women lived with a spouse. Nearly 19 percent of the men and 40 percent of the women lived alone, while 9 percent of the men and 19 percent of the women lived with other relatives or nonrelatives, including partners and children. With advancing age, the percentages of women, particularly, living with a spouse decreased and the percentage living alone increased. Minority elders, especially Asian and Hispanic Americans, in keeping with their traditions, were more likely than white elders to live in extended-family households (Administration on Aging, 2006; Federal Interagency Forum on Aging-Related Statistics, 2006; Figure 18-1).

Living arrangements alone do not tell us much about older adults' well-being. For example, living alone does not necessarily imply lack of family cohesion and support; instead, it may reflect an older person's good health, economic self-sufficiency, and desire for independence. By the same token, living with adult children tells us nothing about the quality of relationships in the household (Kinsella & Velkoff, 2001).

Aging in Place Most older adults in industrialized countries prefer, if possible, to stay in their own homes and communities (Kinsella & Phillips, 2005). This option, called **aging in place,** makes sense for those who can manage on their own or with minimal help, have an adequate income or a paid-up mortgage, can

aging in place Remaining in one's own home, with or without assistance, in later life.

handle the upkeep, are happy in the neighborhood, and want to be independent, to have privacy, and to be near friends, adult children, or grandchildren (Gonyea, Hudson, & Seltzer, 1990). Naturally Occurring Retirement Communities (NORCs) are neighborhoods in which a large proportion of residents happen to be older adults. A national initiative of the U.S. Administration on Aging seeks to enhance supportive services for people living in NORCs (Bernstein, 2008).

For older people with impairments that make it hard to get along entirely on their own, minor support—such as meals, transportation, and home health aides—often can help them stay put. So can ramps, grab bars, and other modifications within the home (Newman, 2003). Most older people do not need much help; and those who do can often remain in the community if they have at least one person to depend on. In fact, the single most important factor keeping people out of institutions is being married. As long as a couple are in relatively good health, they can usually live fairly independently and care for each other. The issue of living arrangements becomes more pressing and institutionalization more likely when one or both become frail, infirm, or disabled, or when one spouse dies (Chappell, 1991; Nihtilä & Martikainen, 2008).

Let's look more closely at the two most common living arrangements for older adults without spouses—living alone and living with adult children—and then at living in institutions and alternative forms of group housing.

Living Alone Because women live longer than men and are more likely to be widowed, older women in the United States are more than twice as likely as older men to live alone, and the likelihood increases with age. Older people living alone are more likely than older people with spouses to be poor (Administration on Aging, 2006) and to end up in institutions (McFall & Miller, 1992; Steinbach, 1992).

The picture is similar in most developed countries: Older women are more likely to live alone than older men. The growth of elderly single-person households has been spurred by greater longevity, increased benefits and pensions, increased home ownership, more elder-friendly housing, more availability of community support, and reduced public assistance with nursing home costs (Kinsella & Phillips, 2005).

It might seem that older people who live alone, particularly the oldest old, would be lonely. However, such factors as personality, cognitive abilities, physical health, and a depleted social network may play a greater role in loneliness (P. Martin, Hagberg, & Poon, 1997). Social activities, such as going to a senior center or doing volunteer work, can help an older person living alone stay connected to the community (Hendricks & Cutler, 2004; Kim & Moen, 2001).

Living with Adult Children Historically, older people in many African, Asian, and Latin American societies could expect to live and be cared for in their children's or grandchildren's homes, but this pattern is changing rapidly, as Figure 18-2 shows with regard to Japan. Most older people in developed countries, even when in difficult circumstances, prefer not to live with their children (Kinsella & Phillips, 2005). They are reluctant to burden their families and to give up their freedom. It can be inconvenient to absorb an extra person into a household, and everyone's privacy—and relationships—may suffer. The parent may feel useless, bored, and isolated from friends. If the adult child is married and the spouse and parent do not get along well, or caregiving duties become too burdensome, the marriage may be threatened (Lund, 1993a; Shapiro, 1994). (Caregiving for elderly parents is discussed in Chapter 16 and later in this chapter.)

The success of such an arrangement depends largely on the quality of the relationship that has existed in the past and on the ability of both generations to

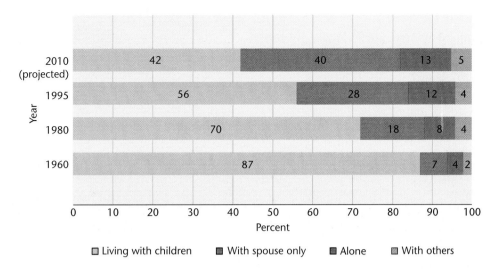

Figure 18-2

Living arrangements of older adults in Japan, 1960 to 2010 (projected). Older people in Japan, as in other relatively developed countries, are much less likely than in the past to live with their children. (Source: Kinsella & Phillips, 2005.)

communicate fully and frankly. The decision to move a parent into an adult child's home should be mutual and needs to be thought through carefully and thoroughly. Parents and children need to respect each other's dignity and autonomy and accept their differences (Shapiro, 1994).

Living in Institutions The use of nonfamily institutions for care of the frail elderly varies greatly around the world. Institutionalization has been rare in developing regions but is becoming less so in Southeast Asia, where declines in fertility have resulted in a rapidly aging population and a shortage of family caregivers (Kinsella & Velkoff, 2001). Comprehensive geriatric home visitation programs in some countries, such as the United Kingdom, Denmark, and Australia have been effective in holding down nursing home admissions (Stuck, Egger, Hammer, Minder, & Beck, 2002).

In all countries, the likelihood of living in a nursing home increases with age—in the United States, from about 1 percent at ages 65 to 74 to 18 percent at age 85 and over (Administration on Aging, 2006; Kinsella & Velkoff, 2001). Most older nursing-home residents worldwide and almost 3 out of 4 in the United States are women (Federal Interagency Forum on Aging-Related Statistics, 2004; Kinsella & Velkoff, 2001). Most likely to be institutionalized are those living alone, those who do not take part in social activities, those whose daily activities are limited by poor health or disability, and those whose informal caregivers are overburdened (McFall & Miller, 1992; Steinbach, 1992).

The number of U.S. nursing home residents has increased considerably since the late 1970s due to growth of the older population, but their proportion of the older population has declined from 5.1 percent in 1990 to 4.5 percent in 2005 (Administration on Aging, 2006; U.S. Census Bureau, 2001). This decline may be attributed in part to a reduction in the proportion of the older population with disabilities. In addition, liberalization of Medicare long-term care coverage and the emergence of widespread private long-term care insurance have spurred a shift from institutionalization to less expensive alternative living options (discussed in the next section) and home health care (Ness, Ahmed, & Aronow, 2004). However, as the baby boom generation ages and if current nursing home usage rates continue, the number of residents is projected to double by 2030 (Sahyoun, Pratt, et al., 2001). Such growth would greatly burden Medicaid, the national health insurance program for low-income persons and the major source of payments for nursing home usage (Ness et al., 2004).

Federal law sets strict requirements for nursing homes and gives residents the right to choose their own doctors, to be fully informed about their care and

Table 18-1	Group Living Arrangements for Older Adults

Facility	Description
Retirement hotel	Hotel or apartment building remodeled to meet the needs of independent older adults. Typical hotel services (switchboard, maid service, message center) are provided.
Retirement community	Large, self-contained development with owned or rental units or both. Support services and recreational facilities are often available as in active adult communities.
Shared housing	Housing can be shared informally by adult parents and children or by friends. Sometimes social agencies match people who need a place to live with people who have houses or apartments with extra rooms. The older person usually has a private room but shares living, eating, and cooking areas and may exchange services such as light housekeeping for rent.
Accessory apartment or ECHO (elder cottage housing opportunity) housing	An independent unit created so that an older person can live in a remodeled single-family home or in a portable unit on the grounds of a single-family home—often, but not necessarlly, that of an adult child. Units offer privacy, proximity to caregivers, and security.
Congregate housing	Private or government-subsidized rental apartment complexes or mobile home parks designed for older adults provide meals, housekeeping, transportation, social and recreational activities, and sometimes health care. One type of congregate housing is a *group home:* A social agency that owns or rents a house brings together a small number of elderly residents and hires helpers to shop, cook, do heavy cleaning, drive, and give counseling. Residents take care of their personal needs and take some responsibility for day-to-day tasks.
Assisted-living facility	Semi-independent living in one's own room or apartment. Similar to congregate housing, but residents receive personal care (bathing, dressing, and grooming) and protective supervision according to their needs and desires. *Board-and-care homes* are similar but smaller and offer more personal care and supervision.
Foster-care home	Owners of a single-family residence take in an unrelated older adult and provide meals, housekeeping, and personal care.
Continuing care retirement community	Long-term housing planned to provide a full range of accommodations and services for affluent elderly people as their needs change. A resident may start out in an independent apartment; then move into congregate housing with such services as cleaning, laundry, and meals; then into an assisted-living facility; and finally into a nursing home. *Life-care communities* are similar but guarantee housing and medical or nursing care for a specified period or for life; they require a substantial entry fee in addition to monthly payments.

Source: Laquatra & Chi, 1998; Porcino, 1993.

treatment, and to be free from physical or mental abuse, corporal punishment, involuntary seclusion, and physical or chemical restraints. Some states train volunteer ombudsmen to act as advocates for nursing home residents, to explain their rights, and to resolve their complaints about such matters as privacy, treatment, food, and financial issues.

An essential element of good care is the opportunity for residents to make decisions and exert some control over their lives. Among 129 intermediate-care nursing home residents, those who had higher self-esteem, less depression, and a greater sense of satisfaction and meaning in life were less likely to die within four years—perhaps because their psychological adjustment motivated them to want to live and to take better care of themselves (O'Connor & Vallerand, 1998).

Alternative Housing Options Some older adults who cannot or do not want to maintain a house, do not need special care, do not have family nearby, prefer a different locale or climate, or want to travel move into maintenance-free or low-maintenance townhouses, condominiums, cooperative or rental apartments, or mobile homes. A relatively new but growing segment of the housing market is in age-qualified active adult communities. In these communities, for people age 55 and older, residents can walk out their front door and find a variety of leisure opportunities—fitness centers, tennis courts, golf courses—close by.

For those who cannot or prefer not to live completely independently, a wide array of group housing options, many of them shown in Table 18-1, have emerged.

What's Your View?

• As you become older and possibly at least partly incapacitated, what type of living arrangement would you prefer?

Older adults in a retirement village with supportive living facilities keep their minds active. These women are taking a computer class in cooperation with a nearby community college.

Some of these newer arrangements enable older people with health problems or disabilities to receive needed services or care without sacrificing autonomy, privacy, and dignity.

One popular option is *assisted living,* the fastest-growing form of housing specifically for older adults in the United States (Hawes, Phillips, Rose, Holan, & Sherman, 2003). Assisted-living facilities enable tenants to live in their own homelike space while giving them easy 24-hour access to needed personal and health care services. In most of these facilities a person can move, when and if necessary, from relative independence (with housekeeping and meals provided) to help with bathing, dressing, managing medications, and using a wheelchair to get around. However, assisted-living facilities vary widely in accommodations, operation, philosophy, and rates, and those offering adequate privacy and services are generally not affordable for moderate- and low-income persons unless they dispose of or spend down their assets to supplement their income (Hawes et al., 2003).

Personal Relationships in Late Life

As people age, they tend to spend less time with others (Carstensen, 1996). Work is often a convenient source of social contact; longtime retirees have fewer social contacts than more recent retirees or those who continue to work. For some older adults, infirmities make it harder to get out and see people. All in all, older adults report only half as many people in their social networks as younger adults do (Lang, 2001). Yet the relationships older adults *do* maintain are more important to their well-being than ever (Antonucci & Akiyama, 1995; Carstensen, 1995; Lansford, Sherman, & Antonucci, 1998) and help keep their minds and memories sharp (Crooks, Lubben, Petitti, Little, & Chiu, 2008; Ertel, Glymour, & Berkman, 2008). In a National Council on Aging (2002) survey, only about 1 out of 5 U.S. older adults reported loneliness as a serious problem, and nearly 9 out of 10 placed the highest importance on family and friends for a meaningful, vital life.

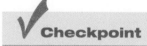

Checkpoint

Can you . . .

♦ Compare various kinds of living arrangements for older adults, their relative prevalence, and their advantages and disadvantages?

Guidepost 4

How do personal relationships change in old age, and what is their effect on well-being?

Theories of Social Contact and Social Support

According to *social convoy theory* (introduced in Chapter 16), aging adults maintain their level of social support by identifying members of their social network who can help them and avoiding those who are not supportive. As former coworkers and casual friends drop away, most older adults retain a stable inner circle of social convoys: close friends and family members on whom they can rely and who strongly affect their well-being (Antonucci, 1991; Antonucci & Akiyama, 1995; Kahn & Antonucci, 1980).

A somewhat different explanation of changes in social contact comes from *socioemotional selectivity theory* (Carstensen, 1991, 1995, 1996). As remaining time becomes short, older adults choose to spend time with people and in activities that meet immediate emotional needs. A college student may put up with a disliked teacher for the sake of gaining needed knowledge; an older adult may be less willing to spend precious time with a friend who gets on her nerves. Young adults with a free half-hour may spend it with someone they would like to get to know better; older adults tend to spend free time with someone they know well.

Thus, even though older adults may have smaller social networks than younger adults do, they tend to have as many very close relationships (Lang & Carstensen, 1994, 1998) and to be more satisfied with those they have (Antonucci & Akiyama, 1995). Their positive feelings toward old friends are as strong as those of young adults, and their positive feelings toward family members are stronger (Charles & Piazza, 2007).

Among a nationally representative sample, older adults tended to see friends less often but family about as frequently as before. This finding, consistent with socioemotional selectivity theory, suggests that as people age, they invest the time and energy they still have in maintaining more intimate relationships. In line with social convoy theory, the researchers also found a shifting balance of tangible, informational, and emotional support; as they age, adults, especially men, give less support to others but receive more. As older adults give up some of the support they formerly received from friends, they gain more emotional support from a smaller network of family ties (Shaw, Krause, Liang, & Bennett, 2007).

The Importance of Social Relationships

Emotional support helps older people maintain life satisfaction in the face of stress and trauma, such as the loss of a spouse or child or a life-threatening illness or accident (Krause, 2004b), and positive ties tend to improve health and well-being. However, conflicted relationships may play an even larger negative role. A longitudinal survey of 515 older adults found that difficult or unpleasant relationships—marred by criticism, rejection, competition, violation of privacy, or lack of reciprocity—can be chronic stressors (Krause & Rook, 2003).

As earlier in life, social relationships go hand in hand with health (Bosworth & Schaie, 1997; Vaillant, Meyer, Mukamal, & Soldz, 1998). Socially isolated people tend to be lonely, and loneliness can speed physical and cognitive decline (Hawkley & Cacioppo, 2007; Holtzman et al., 2004).

Social ties literally can be a lifesaver. In a 10-year longitudinal study of 28,369 men, the most socially isolated men were 53 percent more likely than the most socially connected men to die of cardiovascular disease and more than twice as likely to die from accidents or suicide (Eng, Rimm, Fitzmaurice, & Kawachi, 2002). For older women, who often are widowed and live alone, emotional support is essential. In a 10-year study of Finnish 80-year-olds, women who received the most social support—a sense of being needed and valued, a sense of belonging, and emotional intimacy—were two and a half times less likely to die within the study period than those who received the least such support. Assistance-related support, on the other hand, made no difference in mortality (Lyyra & Heikkinen, 2006).

The Multigenerational Family

The late-life family has special characteristics. Historically, families rarely spanned more than three generations. Today, many families in developed countries include four or even five generations, making it possible for a person to be both a grandparent and a grandchild at the same time (Kinsella & Velkoff, 2001).

The presence of so many family members can be enriching but also can create special pressures. Increasing numbers of families are likely to have at least one member who has lived long enough to have several chronic illnesses and whose care may be physically and emotionally draining (C. L. Johnson, 1995). Now that the fastest-growing group in the population is age 85 and over, many people in their late sixties or beyond, whose own health and energy may be faltering, find themselves serving as caregivers. Indeed, many women spend a bigger part of their lives caring for parents than for children (Abel, 1991).

The ways families deal with these issues often have cultural roots. The nuclear family and the desire of older adults to live apart from their children reflect dominant U.S. values of individualism, autonomy, and self-reliance. Hispanic and Asian American cultures traditionally emphasize *lineal,* or intergenerational, obligations with power and authority lodged in the older generation. However, this pattern is being modified through assimilation into the dominant U.S. culture. African Americans and Irish Americans, whose cultures have been heavily impacted by poverty, stress *collateral,* egalitarian relationships. Household structures may be highly flexible, often taking in siblings, aunts, uncles, cousins, or friends who need a place to stay. These varied cultural patterns affect family relationships and responsibilities toward the older generation (C. L. Johnson, 1995).

In the remainder of this chapter we'll look more closely at older people's relationships with family and friends. We'll also examine the lives of older adults who are divorced, remarried, or widowed, those who have never married, and those who are childless. Finally, we'll consider the importance of a new role: that of great-grandparent.

Marital Relationships

Unlike other family relationships, marriage—at least in contemporary Western cultures—is generally formed by mutual consent. Thus, its effect on well-being has characteristics of both friendship and kinship ties (Antonucci & Akiyama, 1995). It can provide both the highest emotional highs and the lowest lows a person experiences (Carstensen et al., 1996). What happens to marital quality in late life?

Long-Term Marriage

Because women usually marry older men and outlive them and because men are more likely to remarry after divorce or widowhood, many more men than women throughout the world are married in late life (Federal Interagency Forum on Aging-Related Statistics, 2006; Kinsella & Phillips, 2005; Figure 18-3).

Married couples who are still together in late adulthood are more likely than middle-aged couples to report their marriage as satisfying, and many say it has improved (Carstensen et al., 1996; Gilford, 1986). Because divorce has been easier

Have you ever lived in a multigenerational household? Do you think you ever might? What aspects of this lifestyle do or do not appeal to you, and why?

Checkpoint

Can you . . .

♦ Tell how social contact changes in late life, and discuss theoretical explanations of this change?

♦ Explain the importance of positive social contact and social support, and cite evidence for a relationship between social interaction and health?

♦ Discuss issues concerning the new multigenerational family?

Guidepost 5

What are the characteristics of long-term marriages in late life, and what impact do widowhood, divorce, and remarriage have at this time?

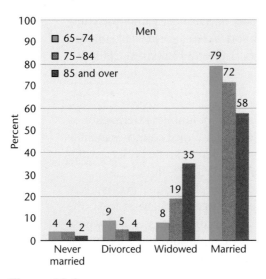

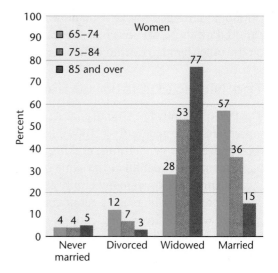

Figure 18-3

Marital status of the U.S. population age 65 and over by age group and sex, 2004. Because of women's greater longevity, they are more likely than men to be widowed in late life, whereas men are more likely to be married or remarried in late life. *Note:* Married includes married, spouse present; married, spouse absent; and separated. These data refer to the civilian noninstitutionalized population. (Source: Federal Interagency Forum on Aging-Related Statistics, 2006.)

to obtain for some years, spouses who remain together are likely to have worked out their differences and to have arrived at mutually satisfying accommodations (Huyck, 1995). With the end of child rearing, children tend to become a source of shared pleasure and pride instead of a source of conflict (Carstensen et al., 1996). Still, according to the MacArthur Successful Aging Study, men receive social support primarily from their wives, whereas women rely more heavily on friends, relatives, and children (Gurung, Taylor, & Seeman, 2003).

The way couples resolve conflicts is a key to marital satisfaction throughout adulthood. Married people with much discord in their marriages tend to be anxious and depressed, whereas those with less discordant marriages tend to have greater life satisfaction and self-esteem (Whisman, Uebelacker, Tolejko, Chatav, & McKelvie, 2006). Patterns of conflict resolution tend to remain fairly constant throughout a marriage, but older couples' greater ability to regulate their emotions may make their conflicts less severe (Carstensen et al., 1996).

Throughout the developed world, married people are healthier and live longer than unmarried people (Kinsella & Phillips, 2005), but the relationship between marriage and health may be different for husbands than for wives. Whereas *being* married seems to have health benefits for older men, older women's health seems to be linked more to the *quality* of the marriage (Carstensen, Graff, Levenson, & Gottman, 1996).

Late-life marriage can be severely tested by advancing age and physical ills, though a close marital relationship can moderate the negative psychological effects of functional disabilities by reducing anxiety and depression and increasing self-esteem (Mancini & Bonanno, 2006). Spouses who must care for disabled partners may feel isolated, angry, and frustrated, especially if they are in poor health themselves. Such

Many couples who are still together late in life say they are happier in marriage than they were in their younger years. Important benefits of marriage include intimacy, sharing, and a sense of belonging to one another.

couples may be caught in a vicious cycle: the illness puts strains on the marriage, and these strains may aggravate the illness, stretching coping capacity to the breaking point (Karney & Bradbury, 1995) and putting the caregiver's life at heightened risk (Kiecolt-Glaser & Glaser, 1999; Schulz & Beach, 1999). Indeed, a study of more than 500,000 couples on Medicare found that when one spouse was hospitalized, the other's risk of death increased (Christakis & Allison, 2006).

A longitudinal study of 818 late-life couples captured the fragile nature of spousal caregiving in late life. Only about one-fourth of the 317 persons who had been caring for spouses at the outset were still doing so five years later; the rest either had died, or their spouses had died or had been placed in long-term care. Furthermore, about half of the 501 persons not caring for spouses at the outset became caregivers in the next five years. Those in both groups who moved into heavy caregiving generally had poorer health and more symptoms of depression (Burton, Zdaniuk, Schulz, Jackson, & Hirsch, 2003).

The quality of the caregiving experience can affect the way caregivers react to the death of the person they have cared for. In one study, spousal caregivers were interviewed before and after bereavement. Those who, prior to the death, had emphasized benefits of caregiving ("makes me feel useful," "enables me to appreciate life more") more than its burdens reported more grief after the death, suggesting that grief was accentuated by the loss not only of the deceased spouse but of the caregiving role (Boerner, Schulz, & Horowitz, 2004).

Widowhood

Just as older men are more likely than women to be married, older women are more likely than men to be widowed, and for similar reasons. Women tend to outlive their husbands and are less likely than men to marry again. As Figure 18-3 shows, U.S. women ages 65 and over are far more likely than men of the same age to be widowed (Federal Interagency Forum on Aging-Related Statistics, 2006). However, as the gender gap in life expectancy narrows, as it has done in the United States since 1990, an increasing proportion of older men will outlive their wives (Hetzel & Smith, 2001). In most countries, more than half of older women are widows (Kinsella & Velkoff, 2001). Issues concerning adjustment to widowhood are discussed in Chapter 19.

Divorce and Remarriage

Divorce in late life is rare; only about 11 percent of U.S. adults age 65 and over were divorced and not remarried in 2005 (Administration on Aging, 2006; see Figure 18-3). However, these numbers have nearly doubled since 1980 and probably will continue to increase as younger cohorts with larger proportions of divorced people reach late adulthood (Administration on Aging, 2006).

Remarriage in late life may have a special character. Among 125 well-educated, fairly affluent men and women, those in late-life remarriages seemed more trusting and accepting and less in need of deep sharing of personal feelings than in earlier marriages. Men, but not women, tended to be more satisfied in late-life remarriages than in midlife remarriages (Bograd & Spilka, 1996).

Remarriage has societal benefits. Older married people are less likely than those living alone to need help from the community. Remarriage could be encouraged by letting people keep pension and Social Security benefits derived from a previous marriage and by greater availability of group housing and other shared living quarters.

Checkpoint

Can you . . .

♦ Compare marital satisfaction in middle and late adulthood?

♦ Explain gender differences in the prevalence of widowhood?

♦ Tell why divorce in late life is rare, and identify the special character of remarriage in late adulthood?

Guidepost 6

How do unmarried older adults and those in cohabiting and gay and lesbian relationships fare, and how does friendship change in old age?

Nonmarital Lifestyles and Relationships

Single Life

In most countries, 5 percent or less of older men and 10 percent or less of older women have never married. In Europe, this gender difference may reflect the toll on marriageable men taken by World War II, when today's older cohort were of marrying age. In some Latin American and Caribbean countries, proportions of never-marrieds are higher, probably due to the prevalence of consensual unions (Kinsella & Phillips, 2005). In the United States, only about 4 percent of men and women 65 years and older have never married (Administration on Aging, 2006; see Figure 18-3). This percentage is likely to increase as today's middle-aged adults grow old because larger proportions of that cohort, especially African Americans, have remained single (U.S. Bureau of the Census, 1991a, 1991b, 1992, 1993).

Older never-married people in the United States are more likely than older divorced or widowed people to prefer single life and less likely to be lonely (Dykstra, 1995), even though they are most likely to live alone and receive the least social support. They are least likely to experience "single strain"—chronic practical and emotional stressors attributed to the lack of an intimate partner. The reasons may be that never-marrieds have never gone through the stress of transitioning out of marriage and have developed earlier in adult life skills and resources such as autonomy and self-reliance that help them cope with single-hood. They also have greater tangible resources: They are in better health and have higher education and income than those who have been married (Pudrovska, Schieman, & Carr, 2006).

White never-married women report more single strain than their male counterparts. Women in older cohorts were socialized to view the roles of wife and mother as normative and may face negative cultural attitudes if they do not marry. Black women show less single strain than white women; with a shortage of marriageable black men, being single is normative and statistically prevalent among black women (Prudrovska et al., 2006).

Previously married older men are much more likely to date than previously married older women, probably because of the greater availability of women in this age group. Most elderly daters are sexually active but do not expect to marry. Among both whites and blacks, men are more interested in romantic involvement than women, who may fear getting locked into traditional gender roles (K. Bulcroft & O'Conner, 1986; R. A. Bulcroft & Bulcroft, 1991; Tucker, Taylor, & Mitchell-Kernan, 1993).

Cohabitation

Older adults are increasingly likely to cohabit, as are younger adults, but for them cohabitation typically comes after a prior marriage, not before marriage. More than 1 million U.S. older adults, 4 percent of the unmarried population, currently cohabit, and 9 out of 10 of them were previously married (S. L. Brown, Lee, & Bulanda, 2006).

Older cohabitors have certain disadvantages as compared with older people who are remarried. Older cohabitors, particularly women, tend to have lower incomes and are less likely to own their homes. In comparison with older adults without partners, on the other hand, they tend to have higher household incomes and are more likely to have full-time jobs. In comparison with *both* the remarried and the unpartnered, they are less likely to be religious and to have friends or relatives living nearby (S. L. Brown et al., 2006).

Women, especially, seem to be disadvantaged by cohabiting. For example, they are three times more likely to have no health insurance than either remarried or unpartnered women. For men there is no such difference. In fact, marital status makes more difference overall for women than for men (S. L. Brown et al., 2006).

Gay and Lesbian Relationships

There is little research on homosexual relationships in old age, largely because the current cohort of older adults grew up at a time when living openly as a homosexual was rare (Huyck, 1995). For aging gays and lesbians who recognized their homosexuality before the rise of the gay liberation movement in the late 1960s, their self-concept tended to be shaped by the then-prevailing stigma against homosexuality. Those who came of age after the liberation movement (and the shift in public discourse it brought about) was in full swing are more likely to view their homosexuality simply as a *status:* a characteristic of the self like any other (Rosenfeld, 1999).

Intimacy is important to older lesbians, as it is to older heterosexual adults. Contrary to stereotype, homosexual relationships in late life are strong and supportive.

Gay and lesbian relationships in late life tend to be strong, supportive, and diverse. Many homosexuals have children from earlier marriages; others have adopted children. Friendship networks or support groups may substitute for the traditional family (Reid, 1995). Those who have maintained close relationships and strong involvement in the homosexual community tend to adapt to aging with relative ease (Friend, 1991; Reid, 1995).

The main problems of many older gays and lesbians grow out of societal attitudes: strained relationships with the family of origin, discrimination in nursing homes and elsewhere, lack of medical or social services and social support, insensitive policies of social agencies, and, when a partner falls ill or dies, dealing with health care providers, bereavement and inheritance issues, and lack of access to a partner's Social Security benefits (Berger & Kelly, 1986; Kimmel, 1990; Reid, 1995).

Friendships

Most older people have close friends, and, as in early and middle adulthood, those with an active circle of friends tend to be healthier and happier (Antonucci & Akiyama, 1995; Babchuk, 1978–1979; Lemon et al., 1972; Steinbach, 1992). People who can confide their feelings and thoughts and can talk about their worries and pain with friends tend to deal better with the changes and crises of aging (Genevay, 1986; Lowenthal & Haven, 1968) and to live longer (Steinbach, 1992). The element of choice in friendship may be especially important to older people, who may feel their control over their lives slipping away (R. G. Adams, 1986). Intimacy is another important benefit of friendship for older adults, who need to know that they are still valued and wanted despite physical and other losses (Essex & Nam, 1987).

Older people enjoy time spent with their friends more than time spent with their families. As earlier in life, friendships revolve around pleasure and leisure, whereas family relationships tend to involve everyday needs and tasks (Antonucci & Akiyama, 1995; Larson, Mannell, & Zuzanek, 1986). Friends are a powerful source of *immediate* enjoyment; the family provides greater emotional security and support. Thus, friendships have the greatest positive effect on older people's well-being; but when family relationships are poor or absent, the negative effects can be profound (Antonucci & Akiyama, 1995). In line with socioemotional selectivity theory, older adults tend to have stronger positive feelings about old friends than about new friends (Charles & Piazza, 2007).

Checkpoint

Can you . . .

♦ Discuss differences between never-married and previously married singles in late life?

♦ Tell why older women who are cohabiting may be at a disadvantage?

♦ Discuss strengths and problems of gay and lesbian relationships in late life?

♦ Identify special characteristics of friendship in old age?

Guidepost 7

How do older adults get along with—or without—grown children and with siblings, and how do they adjust to great-grandparenthood?

People usually rely on neighbors in emergencies and on relatives for long-term commitments, such as caregiving; but friends may, on occasion, fulfill both these functions. Although friends cannot replace a spouse or partner, they can help compensate for the lack of one (Hartup & Stevens, 1999), by playing the role of fictive kin, a psychological family. Among 131 older adults in the Netherlands who were never married or were divorced or widowed, those who received high levels of emotional and practical support from friends were less likely to be lonely (Dykstra, 1995).

In line with social convoy and socioemotional selectivity theories, longtime friendships often persist into very old age (Hartup & Stevens, 1999). Sometimes, however, relocation, illness, or disability make it hard to keep up with old friends. Although many older people do make new friends, even after age 85 (C. L. Johnson & Troll, 1994), older adults are more likely than younger adults to attribute the benefits of friendship (such as affection and loyalty) to specific individuals, who cannot easily be replaced if they die, go into a nursing home, or move away (de Vries, 1996).

Nonmarital Kinship Ties

Some of the most lasting and important relationships in late life come, not from mutual choice (as marriages, cohabitations, homosexual partnerships, and friendships do), but from kinship bonds. Let's look at these.

Relationships with Adult Children

Parent-child bonds remain strong in old age. Children provide a link with other family members, especially grandchildren. Parents who have good relationships with their adult children are less likely to be lonely or depressed than those whose parent-child relationships are not so good (Koropeckyj-Cox, 2002).

Most older people have living children, but, because of global trends toward smaller families, have fewer of them than in previous generations (Dobriansky et al., 2007; Kinsella & Phillips, 2005). In European countries, about one-third of adults in their sixties live with an adult child, and almost half live within 15 miles. These proportions remain fairly stable or increase with age. Coresidence is most common in the more traditional Mediterranean countries (Greece, Italy, and Spain) and least common in the Scandinavian countries (Denmark and Sweden) with their strong welfare services and cultural emphasis on autonomy. About half of older parents below age 80 report contact with a child, most often a daughter, at least once a week (Hank, 2007). In the United States, immigrants who arrived as older adults are most likely to live with adult children and to be dependent on them (Glick & Van Hook, 2002).

The mother-daughter relationship tends to be especially close. In one study, researchers recorded conversations between 48 mostly European American, well-educated, mother-daughter pairs. The mothers were over age 70 and in good health. Each pair was asked to construct a story about a picture of an older and a younger woman. These conversations were characterized by warmth and mutual affection, encouragement, and support, with little criticism or hostility. Both mothers and daughters held their relationship in high regard, reporting that they had many positive feelings and few negative ones toward each other (Lefkowitz & Fingerman, 2003).

The balance of mutual aid between parents and their adult children tends to shift as parents age, with children providing a greater share of support (Bengtson et al., 1990; 1996). Mothers'—but not fathers'—willingness to ask adult children

BOX 18-2 **Research** *in Action*

Mistreatment of the Elderly

A middle-aged woman drives up to a hospital emergency room in a middle-sized U.S. city. She lifts a frail, elderly woman (who appears somewhat confused) out of the car and into a wheelchair, wheels her into the emergency room, and quietly walks out and drives away, leaving no identification (Barnhart, 1992).

"Granny dumping" is an example of *elder abuse:* maltreatment or neglect of dependent older persons or violation of their personal rights. Mistreatment of the elderly may fall into any of six categories: (1) *physical abuse*—physical force that may cause bodily injury, physical pain, or impairment; (2) *sexual abuse*—nonconsensual sexual contact with an elderly person; (3) *emotional or psychological abuse*—infliction of anguish, pain, or distress (such as the threat of abandonment or institutionalization); (4) *financial or material exploitation*—illegal or improper use of an elder's funds, property, or assets; (5) *neglect*—refusal or failure to fulfill any part of one's obligations or duties to an elder; and (6) *self-neglect*—behaviors of a depressed, frail, or mentally incompetent elderly person that threaten his or her health or safety, such as failure to eat or drink adequately or to take prescribed medications (National Center on Elder Abuse & Westat, Inc., 1998). The American Medical Association (1992) has added a seventh category: *violating personal rights*—for example, the older person's right to privacy and to make her or his personal and health decisions.

In almost 9 out of 10 maltreatment cases with a known perpetrator, that person is a family member; and 2 out of 3 of these perpetrators are spouses or adult children (National Center on Elder Abuse & Westat, Inc., 1998). Neglect by family caregivers is usually unintentional. Many do not know how to give proper care or are in poor health themselves. The states of mind of caregivers and the older persons under their care may reinforce each other. When older women receiving informal long-term care feel respected and valued by their caregivers, they are less likely to be depressed (Wolff & Agree, 2004).

Other types of elder abuse should be recognized as forms of domestic violence. Abusers need counseling or treatment to recognize what they are doing and assistance to reduce the stress of caregiving (AARP, 1993). Self-help groups may help victims acknowledge what is happening, recognize that they do not have to put up with mistreatment, and find out how to stop it or get away from it.

What's Your View?

In your opinion, what steps could be taken to reduce mistreatment of the elderly?

Check It Out

For more information on elder abuse, go to http://lisanerenberg.com/blog/2006/10/archstone-foundation-creates-community.html. There you will find an article on community projects of the Archstone Foundation to prevent various forms of elder abuse.

for help reflects their earlier parenting styles. Warm, responsive mothers are more likely to ask for financial help or personal advice than mothers who were more dominant or restrictive during their children's adolescence and young adulthood (Schooler, Revell, & Caplan, 2007). In the United States and other developed countries, institutional supports such as Social Security and Medicare have lifted some responsibilities for older adults from family members; but many adult children do provide significant assistance and direct care, as discussed in Chapter 16. The trend toward smaller families means fewer potential family caregivers for ailing, aging parents (Kinsella & Phillips, 2005), increasing the strains on those who do serve as caregivers—strains that may lead to mistreatment of a "difficult" frail patient (Box 18-2).

Older parents who can do so often continue to provide financial support to children. In less developed countries, older parents contribute through housekeeping, child care, and socialization of grandchildren (Kinsella & Phillips, 2005). Older parents continue to show strong concern about their children (Bengtson et al., 1996). They tend to be distressed if their children have serious problems and may consider such problems a sign of their failure as parents (G. R. Lee et al., 1995; Pillemer & Suitor, 1991; Suitor, Pillemer, Keeton, & Robison, 1995; Troll

& Fingerman, 1996). Many older people whose adult children are mentally ill, retarded, physically disabled, or stricken with serious illnesses serve as primary caregivers for as long as both parent and child live (Brabant, 1994; Greenberg & Becker, 1988; Ryff & Seltzer, 1995).

Furthermore, a growing number of older adults, particularly African Americans, raise or help raise grandchildren or great-grandchildren. As discussed in Chapter 16, these nonnormative caregivers, pressed into active parenting at a time when such a role is unexpected, frequently feel strain. Often ill-prepared physically, emotionally, and financially for the task, they may not know where to turn for help and support (Abramson, 1995).

What about the increasing number of older adults *without* living children? According to questionnaires and interviews with a nationally representative sample of late middle-aged and older adults, the impact of childlessness on well-being is influenced by gender and by a person's feelings about being childless. Childless women who said it would be better to have a child were more likely to be lonely and depressed than women who did not agree with that statement. That was not true of men, probably because of the greater importance of motherhood to women's identity. However, mothers *and* fathers who had poor relationships with their children were more likely to be lonely or depressed. Thus, parenthood does not guarantee well-being in old age, nor does childlessness necessarily harm it. Attitudes and the quality of relationships are what count (Koropeckyj-Cox, 2002).

Relationships with Siblings

When Elizabeth ("Bessie") Delany was 102 and her sister Sarah ("Sadie") was 104, they published a best-selling book, *Having Our Say: The Delany Sisters' First 100 Years* (Delany, Delany, & Hearth, 1993). The daughters of a freed slave, they overcame racial and gender discrimination—Bessie to become a dentist and Sadie a high school teacher. The sisters never married; for three decades they lived together in Mount Vernon, New York. Although their personalities were as different as sugar and spice, the two women were best friends, sharing a sense of fun and the values their parents had instilled in them.

Bessie and Sadie Delany were best friends all their lives. Elderly siblings are an important part of each other's support network, and sisters are especially vital in maintaining family relationships.

Brothers and sisters play important roles in older people's support networks. Siblings, more than other family members, provide companionship, as friends do; but siblings, more than friends do, provide emotional support (Bedford, 1995). Conflict and overt rivalry generally decrease by old age, and some siblings try to resolve earlier conflicts; but underlying feelings of rivalry may remain, especially between brothers (Cicirelli, 1995).

Most older adult siblings say they stand ready to provide tangible help and would turn to a sibling for such help if needed, but relatively few actually do so except in emergencies such as illness (when they may become caregivers) or the death of a spouse (Cicirelli, 1995). Siblings in developing countries are more likely to furnish economic aid (Bedford, 1995). Regardless of how much help they actually give, siblings' *readiness* to help is a source of comfort and security in late life (Cicirelli, 1995).

The nearer older people live to their siblings and the more siblings they have, the more likely they are to confide in them (Connidis & Davies, 1992). Reminiscing about shared early experiences becomes more frequent in old age and may help in reviewing a life and putting the significance of family relationships into perspective (Cicirelli, 1995).

Sisters are especially vital in maintaining family relationships and well-being, perhaps because of women's emotional expressiveness and traditional role as nurturers (Bedford, 1995; Cicirelli, 1989, 1995). Older people who are close to their sisters feel better about life and worry less about aging than those without sisters or without close ties to them (Cicirelli, 1977, 1989).

Although the death of a sibling in old age may be understood as a normative part of that stage of life, survivors may grieve intensely and become lonely or depressed. The loss of a sibling represents, not only a loss of someone to lean on and a shift in the family constellation, but perhaps even a partial loss of identity. To mourn for a sibling is to mourn for the lost completeness of the original family within which one came to know oneself and can bring home one's own nearness to death (Cicirelli, 1995).

Becoming Great-Grandparents

As grandchildren grow up, grandparents generally see them less often (see the discussion of grandparenthood in Chapter 16). Then, when grandchildren become parents, grandparents move into a new role: great-grandparenthood.

Because of age, declining health, and the scattering of families, great-grandparents tend to be less involved than grandparents in a child's life; and, because four- or five-generation families are relatively new, there are few generally accepted guidelines for what great-grandparents are supposed to do (Cherlin & Furstenberg, 1986). Still, most great-grandparents find the role fulfilling (Pruchno & Johnson, 1996). Great-grandparenthood offers a sense of personal and family renewal, a source of diversion, and a mark of longevity. When 40 great-grandfathers and great-grandmothers, ages 71 to 90, were interviewed, 93 percent made such comments as "Life is starting again in my family," "Seeing them grow keeps me young," and "I never thought I'd live to see it" (Doka & Mertz, 1988, pp. 193–194). More than one-third of the sample (mostly women) were close to their great-grandchildren. The ones with the most intimate connections were likely to live nearby and to be close to the children's parents and grandparents as well, often helping out with loans, gifts, and babysitting.

Grandparents and great-grandparents are important to their families. They are sources of wisdom, companions in play, links to the past, and symbols of the continuity of family life. They are engaged in the ultimate generative function: expressing the human longing to transcend mortality by investing themselves in the lives of future generations.

What's Your View?

- Which theories of psychosocial development in late life seem best supported by the information in this chapter on work, retirement, living arrangements, and relationships? Why?

Checkpoint

Can you ...

- Tell how contact and mutual aid between parents and grown children changes during late adulthood, and how childlessness can affect older people?

- Discuss the importance of sibling relationships in late life?

- Identify several values great-grandparents find in their role?

Summary and Key Terms

Theory and Research on Personality Development

Guidepost 1 *Does personality change in old age, and what special issues and tasks do older people face?*

- Erik Erikson's final stage, ego integrity versus despair, culminates in the virtue of *wisdom,* or acceptance of one's life and impending death.

- Erikson maintained that people must maintain a vital involvement in society.

- Personality traits tend to remain fairly stable in late adulthood, depending on how they are measured.

- Older adults in recent cohorts seem to be less rigid in personality than in previous cohorts.

- Emotionality tends to become more positive and less negative in old age, but personality traits can modify this pattern.

  ego integrity versus despair (587)

Well-Being in Late Adulthood

Guidepost 2 *What strategies and resources contribute to older adults' well-being and mental health?*

- George Vaillant found that the use of mature adaptive defenses earlier in adulthood predicts psychosocial adjustment in late life.
- In research based on the cognitive-appraisal model, adults of all ages generally prefer problem-focused coping, but older adults do more emotion-focused coping than younger adults when the situation calls for it.
- Religion is an important source of emotion-focused coping for many older adults. The link between religion or spirituality and health, longevity, or well-being is an important new area of study.
- The concept of successful or optimal aging reflects the growing number of healthy, vital older adults, but there is dispute over how to define and measure it and over the validity of the concept.
- Two contrasting early models of *successful,* or *optimal,* aging are disengagement theory and activity theory. Disengagement theory has little support, and findings on activity theory are mixed. Newer refinements of activity theory include continuity theory and an emphasis on productive activity.
- Baltes and his colleagues suggest that successful aging, in the psychosocial as well as the cognitive realm, may depend on selective optimization with compensation.

coping (589)

cognitive-appraisal model (590)

problem-focused coping (590)

emotion-focused coping (590)

ambiguous loss (590)

disengagement theory (592)

activity theory (592)

continuity theory (593)

selective optimization with compensation (SOC) (594)

Practical and Social Issues Related to Aging

Guidepost 3 *How do older adults handle work and retirement decisions, financial resources, and living arrangements?*

- Some older adults continue to work for pay, but most are retired. However, many retired people start new careers or do part-time paid or volunteer work. Often retirement is a phased process.

- Older adults tend to be more satisfied with their work and often more productive than younger ones. Age has both positive and negative effects on job performance, and individual differences are more significant than age differences.
- Retirement is an ongoing process. Personal, economic, and social resources may affect morale.
- Common lifestyle patterns after retirement include a family-focused lifestyle, balanced investment, and serious leisure.
- The financial situation of older Americans has improved, and fewer live in poverty. Women, Hispanic Americans, and African Americans are most likely to be poor in old age.
- In developing countries, the elderly often live with children or grandchildren. In developed countries, most older people live with a spouse or live alone. Minority elders are more likely than white elders to live with extended family members.
- Most older adults in industrialized nations prefer to age in place. Most can remain in the community if they can depend on a spouse or someone else for help.
- Older women are more likely than older men to live alone.
- Older adults in developed countries typically do not expect to live with adult children and do not wish to do so.
- Institutionalization is rare in developing countries. Its extent varies in developed countries. In the United States, only 4.5 percent of the older population are institutionalized, but the proportion increases greatly with age. Most likely to be institutionalized are older women, older adults who live alone or do not take part in social activities, those who have poor health or disabilities, and those whose informal caregivers are overburdened.
- Fast-growing alternatives to institutionalization include assisted-living facilities and other types of group housing.

family-focused lifestyle (597)

balanced investment (597)

serious leisure (597)

aging in place (599)

Personal Relationships in Late Life

Guidepost 4 *How do personal relationships change in old age, and what is their effect on well-being?*

- Relationships are important to older people, even though frequency of social contact declines in old age.
- According to social convoy theory, reductions or changes in social contact in late life do not impair well-being because a stable inner circle of social support is maintained. According to socioemotional selectivity theory, older people choose to spend time with people who enhance their emotional well-being.

- Social interaction is associated with good health and life satisfaction, and isolation is a risk factor for mortality.
- The way multigenerational late-life families function often has cultural roots.

Marital Relationships

Guidepost 5 *What are the characteristics of long-term marriages in late life, and what impact do widowhood, divorce, and remarriage have at this time?*

- As life expectancy increases, so does the potential longevity of marriage. More men than women are married in late life. Marriages that last into late adulthood tend to be relatively satisfying.
- Although a growing proportion of men are widowed, women tend to outlive their husbands and are less likely to marry again.
- Divorce is uncommon among older people, and most older adults who have been divorced are remarried. Remarriages may be more relaxed in late life.

Nonmarital Lifestyles and Relationships

Guidepost 6 *How do unmarried older adults and those in cohabiting and gay and lesbian relationships fare, and how does friendship change in old age?*

- A small but increasing percentage of adults reach old age without marrying. Never-married adults are less likely to be lonely than divorced or widowed ones.

- Older adults are more likely to cohabit after than before marriage.
- Many gays and lesbians adapt to aging with relative ease. Adjustment may be influenced by coming-out status.
- Most older adults have close friends, and those who do are healthier and happier.
- Older people enjoy time spent with friends more than with family, but the family is the main source of emotional and practical support.

Nonmarital Kinship Ties

Guidepost 7 *How do older adults get along with— or without—grown children and with siblings, and how do they adjust to great-grandparenthood?*

- Older parents and their adult children frequently see or contact each other, are concerned about each other, and offer each other assistance. Many older parents are caregivers for adult children, grandchildren, or great-grandchildren.
- In some respects, childlessness does not seem to be an important disadvantage in old age.
- Often siblings offer each other emotional support, and sometimes more tangible support as well. Sisters, in particular, maintain sibling ties.
- Great-grandparents are usually less involved in children's lives than grandparents are, but most find the role fulfilling.

The key to the question of death unlocks the door of life.

—Elisabeth Kübler-Ross, *Death: The Final Stage of Growth,* 1975

Did You Know...

- A marked cognitive decline, in the absence of known physical illness, can predict death nearly 15 years later?

- "Near-death" experiences may result from biological changes in the brain?

- Research has challenged earlier notions of a single, "normal" pattern of grieving and a "normal" timetable for recovery?

- Children as young as 4 may have some understanding of what happens after death but may not fully understand it until well into the school years?

- The death of a parent can bring about significant changes in an adult child and in his or her relationships with others?

- Although more women than men in the United States attempt suicide, men are four times more likely to succeed?

These are just a few of the interesting and important topics we will cover in this chapter. In it we look at the many interwoven aspects of death (the state) and dying (the process), including societal views and customs surrounding death and mourning. We examine how people of different ages think and feel about dying. We describe various forms grief can take and how people deal with the loss of a spouse, parent, or child.

Death is generally considered to be the cessation of bodily processes. However, criteria for death have become more complex with the development of medical apparatus that can prolong basic signs of life. These medical developments have raised questions about whether or when life supports may be withheld or removed and whose judgment should prevail. In some places, the claim of a *right to die* has led to laws either permitting or forbidding physicians to help a person who is terminally ill end a life that is felt to be a burden. We explore all these issues. Finally, we see how confronting death can give deeper meaning and purpose to life. After you have read and studied this chapter, you should be able to answer each of the Guidepost questions on the following page.

617

Guideposts *for Study*

1. How do attitudes and customs concerning death differ across cultures, and what are the implications of the "mortality revolution" in developed countries?

2. How do people deal with dying, and how do they grieve for a loss?

3. What special challenges are involved in surviving a spouse, a parent, or a child, or in mourning a miscarriage?

4. How are attitudes toward hastening death changing, and what concerns do such practices raise?

5. How can people overcome fear of dying and come to terms with death?

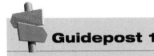

Guidepost 1

How do attitudes and customs concerning death differ across cultures, and what are the implications of the "mortality revolution" in developed countries?

The Many, Changing Meanings of Death and Dying

Death is a *biological* fact; but it also has *social, cultural, historical, religious, legal, psychological, developmental, medical,* and *ethical* aspects, and often these are closely intertwined.

Although death and loss are universal experiences, they have a cultural and historical context. The ways people face death, as well as its meaning and impact, are profoundly influenced by what people feel and do, and people's feelings and behavior are shaped by the time and place in which they live.

Cultural and religious attitudes toward death and dying affect how people deal with their own death and the deaths of those close to them. Death may mean one thing to an elderly Japanese person, imbued with Buddhist teachings of accepting the inevitable, and another to a third-generation Japanese American youth who has grown up with a belief in directing one's own destiny. Death used to come early and frequently in the life of a family and community and was a constant household companion. Today, people in most countries live longer, and death is a less frequent and less visible occurrence.

Let's look more closely at death and mourning in their cultural and historical context.

The Cultural Context

Customs concerning disposal and remembrance of the dead, transfer of possessions, and even expression of grief vary greatly from culture to culture and often are governed by religious or legal prescriptions that reflect a society's view of what death is and what happens afterward. Cultural aspects of death include care of and behavior toward the dying and the dead, the setting where death usually takes place, and mourning customs and rituals—from the all-night Irish wake, at which friends and family toast the memory of the dead person, to the weeklong Jewish *shiva,* at which mourners vent their feelings and share memories of the deceased. Some cultural conventions, such as flying a flag at half-mast after the death of a public figure, are codified in law.

In ancient Greece, bodies of heroes were publicly burned as a sign of honor. Cremation still is widely practiced by Hindus in India and Nepal. In contrast, cremation is prohibited under Orthodox Jewish law in the belief that the dead will rise again for a Last Judgment and the chance for eternal life (Ausubel, 1964).

In Japan, religious rituals encourage survivors to maintain contact with the deceased. Families keep an altar in the home dedicated to their ancestors; they talk to their dead loved ones and offer them food or cigars. In Gambia the dead are considered part of the community; among Native Americans, the Hopi fear the spirits of the dead and try to forget a deceased person as quickly as possible. Muslims in Egypt show grief through expressions of deep sorrow; Muslims in Bali are encouraged to suppress sadness, to laugh, and to be joyful (Stroebe, Gergen, Gergen, & Stroebe, 1992). All these varied customs and practices help people deal with death and bereavement through well-understood cultural meanings that provide a stable anchor amid the turbulence of loss.

Some modern social customs have evolved from ancient ones. Embalming goes back to the ancient practice of mummification common in ancient Egypt and China: preserving a body so the soul can return to it. A traditional Jewish custom is never to leave a dying person alone. Anthropologists suggest that the original reason for this may have been a belief that evil spirits hover around, trying to enter the dying body (Ausubel, 1964). Such rituals give people facing a loss something predictable and important to do at a time when they otherwise might feel confused and helpless.

Checkpoint

Can you . . .

♦ Give examples of cross-cultural differences in customs and attitudes related to death?

The Mortality Revolution

Until the twentieth century, in all societies throughout history, death was a frequent, expected event, sometimes welcomed as a peaceful end to suffering. Caring for a dying loved one at home was a common experience, as it still is in some rural communities.

Great historical changes regarding death and dying have taken place since the late nineteenth century, especially in developed countries. Advances in medicine and sanitation, new treatments for many once-fatal illnesses, and a better-educated, more health-conscious population have brought about a *mortality revolution.* Women today are less likely to die in childbirth, infants are more likely to survive their first year, children are more likely to grow to adulthood, young adults are more likely to reach old age, and older people often can overcome illnesses they grew up regarding as fatal. The top causes of death in the United States in the 1900s were diseases that most often affected children and young people: pneumonia and influenza, tuberculosis, diarrhea, and enteritis. Today, despite recent increases in apparently drug-related deaths of people in their twenties and in early middle age as well as a spike in midlife suicide, nearly three-quarters of deaths in the United States still occur among people age 65 and over; and close to one-half of deaths are from heart disease, cancer, and stroke, the three leading causes of death in late adulthood (Kung et al., 2008; Paulozzi, Crosby, & Ryan, 2007).

Yet, in the course of all this progress in improving health and lengthening life, something important may have been lost. Looking death in the eye, bit by bit, day by day, people growing up in traditional societies absorbed an important truth: Dying is part of living. As death increasingly became a phenomenon of late adulthood, it became "invisible and abstract" (Fulton & Owen, 1987–1988, p. 380). Care of the dying and the dead became largely a task for professionals. Such social conventions as placing the dying person in a hospital or nursing home and refusing to openly discuss his or her condition reflected and perpetuated attitudes of avoidance and denial of death. Death—even of the very old—came to be regarded as a failure of medical treatment rather than as a natural end to life (McCue, 1995).

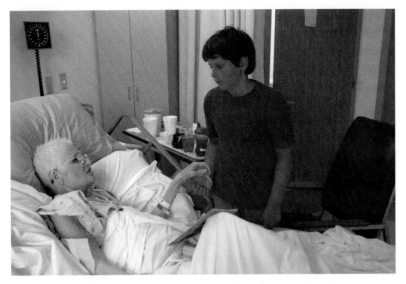

Hospice care seeks to ease patients' pain and treat their symptoms to keep them as comfortable and alert as possible. It also seeks to help families deal with illness and death.

Today, this picture again is changing. **Thanatology,** the study of death and dying, is arousing interest, and educational programs have been established to help people deal with death. Because of the prohibitive cost of extended hospital care that cannot save the terminally ill, many more deaths are now occurring at home, as they once did the world over.

Care of the Dying

Along with a growing tendency to face death more honestly, movements have arisen to make dying more humane. These include hospice care and self-help support groups for dying people and their families.

Hospice care is personal, patient- and family-centered, compassionate care for the terminally ill. Its focus is on **palliative care** (also called *comfort care*): relief of pain and suffering, control of symptoms, maintaining a satisfactory quality of life, and allowing the patient to die in peace and dignity. Hospice care usually takes place at home; but such care can be given in a hospital or another institution, at a hospice center, or through a combination of home and institutional care. Family members often take an active part. Palliative care also can be introduced earlier in an illness that is not yet terminal. In 2005 more than 4,100 hospice programs in the United States provided care to an estimated 1.2 million patients (National Hospice and Palliative Care Organization, n.d.).

What does it mean to preserve the dignity of a patient who is dying? One research team decided to ask patients themselves. From interviews with 50 Canadian patients with advanced terminal cancer, researchers concluded that dignity-conserving care depends, not only on how patients are treated, but on how they are regarded: "When dying patients are seen, and know that they are seen, as being worthy of honor and esteem by those who care for them, dignity is more likely to be maintained" (Chochinov, Hack, McClement, Harlos, & Kristjanson, 2002, p. 2259). Table 19-1 lists suggestions for helping a dying person maintain dignity.

thanatology Study of death and dying.

hospice care Warm, personal, patient- and family-centered care for a person with a terminal illness.

palliative care Care aimed at relieving pain and suffering and allowing the terminally ill to die in peace, comfort, and dignity. Also called *comfort care*.

Checkpoint

Can you . . .

♦ Discuss the mortality revolution in developed countries?

♦ Identity the chief goals of hospice care?

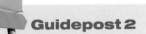

Guidepost 2

How do people deal with dying, and how do they grieve for a loss?

Facing Death and Loss

Death is an important chapter in human development. People change in response to death and dying, whether their own or that of a loved one. What changes do people undergo shortly before death? How do they come to terms with its imminence? How do people handle grief? How do attitudes toward death change across the life span?

Physical and Cognitive Changes Preceding Death

Even without any identifiable illness, people around the age of 100—close to the present limit of the human life span—tend to experience functional declines, lose interest in eating and drinking, and die a natural death (Johansson et al., 2004; McCue, 1995; Rabbitt et al., 2002; Singer, Verhaeghen, Ghisletta,

Factors/Subthemes	Dignity-Related Questions	Therapeutic Interventions
Illness-Related Concerns		
Symptom distress		
Physical distress	"How comfortable are you?" "Is there anything we can do to make you more comfortable?"	Exercise vigilance in symptom management. Do frequent assessments. Apply comfort care.
Psychological distress	"How are you coping with what is happening to you?"	Assume a supportive stance. Be an empathetic listener. Consider referral to counseling.
Medical uncertainty	"Is there anything further about your illness that you would like to know?" "Are you getting all the information you feel you need?"	On request, provide accurate, understandable information and strategies to deal with possible future crises.
Death anxiety	"Are there things about the later stages of your illness that you would like to discuss?"	
Level of independence		
Independence	"Has your illness made you more dependent on others?"	Have patients participate in decision making, regarding both medical and personal issues.
Cognitive acuity	"Are you having any difficulty with your thinking?"	Treat delirium. When possible, avoid sedating medication.
Functional capacity	"How much are you able to do for yourself?"	Use orthotics, physiotherapy, and occupational therapy.
Dignity-Conserving Repertoire		
Dignity-conserving perspectives		
Continuity of self	"Are there things about you that this disease does not affect?"	Acknowledge and take interest in those aspects of the patient's life that he/she most values.
Role preservation	"What things did you do before you were sick that were most important to you?"	See the patient as worthy of honor, respect, and esteem.
Maintenance of pride	"What about yourself or your life are you most proud of?"	Encourage and enable the patient to participate in meaningful or purposeful activities.
Hopefulness	"What is still possible?"	
Autonomy/control	"How in control do you feel?"	Involve patient in treatment and care decisions.
Generativity/legacy	"How do you want to be remembered?"	Suggest life projects (e.g., making audio/videotapes, writing letters, journaling). Provide dignity psychotherapy.
Acceptance	"How at peace are you with what is happening to you?"	Support the patient in his/her outlook.
Resilience/fighting spirit	"What part of you is strongest right now?"	Encourage doing things that enhance his/her sense of well-being (e.g., meditation, light exercise, listening to music, prayer).
Dignity-conserving practices		
Living in the moment	"Are there things that take your mind away from illness, and offer you comfort?"	Allow the patient to participate in normal routines, or take comfort in momentary distractions (e.g., daily outings, light exercise, listening to music).
Maintaining normalcy	"Are there things you still enjoy doing on a regular basis?"	
Finding spiritual comfort	"Is there a religious or spiritual community that you are, or would like to be, connected with?"	Make referrals to chaplain or spiritual leader. Enable the patient to participate in particular spiritual and/or culturally based practices.
Social Dignity Inventory		
Privacy boundaries	"What about your privacy or your body is important to you?"	Ask permission to examine patient. Ensure proper draping to safeguard and respect privacy.
Social support	"Who are the people that are most important to you?" "Who is your closest confidante?"	Adopt liberal policies about visitation, rooming in. Enlist involvement of a wide support network.
Care tenor	"Is there anything in the way you are treated that is undermining your sense of dignity?"	Treat the patient as worthy of honor, esteem, and respect; adopt a stance conveying this.
Burden to others	"Do you worry about being a burden to others?" "If so, to whom and in what ways?"	Encourage explicit discussion about these concerns with those they fear they are burdening.
Aftermath concerns	"What are your biggest concerns for the people you will leave behind?"	Encourage the settling of affairs, preparation of an advanced directive, making a will, funeral planning.

Source: Adapted from Chochinov, Hack, McClement, Harlos, & Kristjanson, 2002, p 2255.

When a brain is deprived of oxygen, certain images arise due to alterations in the visual cortex and can result in the perception of a tunnel, like the images reported by people who have had near-death experiences.

terminal drop A frequently observed decline in cognitive abilities near the end of life. Also called *terminal decline*.

Lindenberger, & Baltes, 2003; B. J. Small, Fratiglioni, von Strauss, & Bäckman, 2003). Such changes also have been noted in younger people whose death is near. In a 22-year longitudinal study of 1,927 men, life satisfaction showed steep declines within one year before death, regardless of self-rated health (Mroczek & Spiro, 2005).

Terminal drop, or *terminal decline,* refers specifically to a widely observed decline in cognitive abilities shortly before death. This effect has been found in longitudinal studies in various countries—not only of the very old (Johansson et al., 2004; T. Singer et al., 2003; B. J. Small et al., 2003), but also of adults of a wide range of ages (Rabbitt et al., 2002; B. J. Small et al., 2003) with no signs of dementia. Losses of perceptual speed have been found to predict death nearly 15 years later (Thorvaldsson et al., 2008). Declines in verbal ability and spatial reasoning are other important markers of terminal drop (Rabbitt et al., 2002; Thorvaldsson et al., 2008).

Some people who have come close to dying have told of *near-death experiences,* often involving a sense of being out of the body or sucked into a tunnel and visions of bright lights or mystical encounters. These reports are highly subjective, and skeptics generally interpret them as resulting from physiological changes that accompany the process of dying. According to one Dutch anesthesiologist, near-death experiences are probably biological events in the brain, and the similarities in individuals' reports about their experiences reflect the common bodily structures affected by the process of dying. When a brain is deprived of oxygen, as happens in 9 out of 10 dying persons, consciousness dims, and certain images arise due to alterations in the visual cortex. A similar effect has been shown to occur from oxygen deprivation due to the drug LSD, which can result in the perception of a tunnel similar to those reported in near-death experiences (Woerlee, 2005).

Some people may be biologically predisposed to near-death experiences. One study found altered functioning of the temporal lobes in people who experience near-death imagery (Britton & Bootzin, 2004). In another study, interviews with 55 Europeans who said they had had such experiences revealed that these experiences also occurred in the transition between wakefulness and sleep. The researchers suggested that such people may have disturbances in the brain's arousal system, which permit an intrusion of REM sleep elements when they are not quite asleep, bringing on temporary visual or auditory hallucinations (Nelson, Mattingly, & Schmitt, 2007).

Confronting One's Own Death

The psychiatrist Elisabeth Kübler-Ross, in her pioneering work with dying people, found that most of them welcomed an opportunity to speak openly about their condition and were aware of being close to death, even when they had not been told. After speaking with some 500 terminally ill patients, Kübler-Ross (1969, 1970) outlined five stages in coming to terms with death: (1) *denial* ("This can't be happening to me!"); (2) *anger* ("Why me?"); (3) *bargaining for extra time* ("If I can only live to see my daughter married, I won't ask for anything more"); (4) *depression;* and ultimately (5) *acceptance.* She also proposed a similar progression in the feelings of people facing imminent bereavement (Kübler-Ross, 1975).

Kübler-Ross's model has been criticized and modified by other professionals who work with dying patients. Although the emotions she described are common, not everyone goes through all five stages and not necessarily in the same sequence.

A person may go back and forth between anger and depression, for example, or may feel both at once. Unfortunately, some health professionals assume that these stages are inevitable and universal, and others feel that they have failed if they cannot bring a patient to the final stage of acceptance.

Dying, like living, is an individual experience. For some people, denial or anger may be a healthier way to face death than calm acceptance. Kübler-Ross's findings, valuable as they are in helping us understand the feelings of those who are facing the end of life, should not be considered the sole model or criterion for a "good death."

Patterns of Grieving

Bereavement—the loss of someone to whom a person feels close and the process of adjusting to it—can affect practically all aspects of a survivor's life. Bereavement often brings a change in status and role (for example, from a wife to a widow or from a son or daughter to an orphan). It may have social and economic consequences—a loss of friends and sometimes of income. But first there is **grief**—the emotional response experienced in the early phases of bereavement.

Grief, like dying, is a highly personal experience. Today, research has challenged earlier notions of a single, "normal" pattern of grieving and a "normal" timetable for recovery. A widow talking to her late husband might once have been considered emotionally disturbed; now this is recognized as a common and helpful behavior (Lund, 1993b). Some people recover fairly quickly after bereavement; others never do.

The Classic Grief Work Model A classic pattern of grief is three-stages in which the bereaved person accepts the painful reality of the loss, gradually lets go of the bond with the dead person, and readjusts to life by developing new interests and relationships. This process of **grief work,** the working out of psychological issues connected with grief, often takes the following path—though, as with Kübler-Ross's stages, it may vary (J. T. Brown & Stoudemire, 1983; R. Schulz, 1978).

1. *Shock and disbelief.* Immediately following a death, survivors often feel lost and confused. As awareness of the loss sinks in, the initial numbness gives way to overwhelming feelings of sadness and frequent crying. This first stage may last several weeks, especially after a sudden or unexpected death.

2. *Preoccupation with the memory of the dead person.* In the second stage, which may last six months to two years or so, the survivor tries to come to terms with the death but cannot yet accept it. A widow may relive her husband's death and their entire relationship. From time to time, she may be seized by a feeling that her dead husband is present. These experiences diminish with time, though they may recur—perhaps for years—on such occasions as the anniversary of the marriage or of the death.

3. *Resolution.* The final stage has arrived when the bereaved person renews interest in everyday activities. Memories of the dead person bring fond feelings mingled with sadness, rather than sharp pain and longing.

Grieving: Multiple Variations Although the pattern of grief work just described is common, grieving does not necessarily follow a straight line from shock to resolution. One team of psychologists (Wortman & Silver, 1989) found three

Some people recover quickly from the loss of a loved one, others never do.

bereavement Loss, due to death, of someone to whom one feels close and the process of adjustment to the loss.

grief Emotional response experienced in the early phases of bereavement.

grief work Working out of psychological issues connected with grief.

What's Your View?

• What advice would you give a friend about what to say— and what *not* to say—to a person in mourning?

Table 19-2	Helping Someone Who Has Lost a Loved One

These suggestions from mental health professionals may enable you to help someone you know through the grieving process:

- *Share the sorrow.* Allow—or encourage—the bereaved person to talk about feelings of loss and share memories of the deceased person.
- *Don't offer false comfort.* Saying such things as "It's all for the best" or "You'll get over it in time" is not helpful. Instead, simply express sorrow—and take time to listen.
- *Offer practical help.* Babysitting, cooking, and running errands are ways to help someone who is grieving.
- *Be patient.* It can take a long time to recover from a significant loss. Be available to talk and listen.
- *Suggest professional help when necessary.* Don't hesitate to recommend professional help when it appears that someone is experiencing too much pain to cope alone.

Source: National Mental Health Association, n.d.

main patterns of grieving. In the *commonly expected* pattern, the mourner goes from high to low distress. In the *absent grief* pattern, the mourner does not experience intense distress immediately or later. In the *chronic grief* pattern, the mourner remains distressed for a long time (Wortman & Silver, 1989). Chronic grief may be especially painful and acceptance most difficult when a loss is *ambiguous,* as when a loved one is missing and presumed dead (Box 19-1).

In another study, researchers interviewed 1,532 married older adults and then did follow-up interviews with 185 (161 women and 24 men) whose spouses had died. The interviews took place six months after and again up to four years after the loss (Boerner, Wortman, & Bonanno, 2005; Bonanno, Wortman, & Nesse, 2004; Bonanno et al., 2002). By far the most prevalent pattern (shown by 46 percent of the sample) was *resilience:* a low and gradually diminishing level of distress. The resilient mourners expressed acceptance of death as a natural process. After their loss, they spent relatively little time thinking and talking about it or searching for meaning in it, though the majority did report some yearning and emotional pangs during the first six months. These findings challenge the assumption that something is wrong if a bereaved person shows only mild distress. They demonstrate that " 'doing well' after a loss is not necessarily a cause for concern but rather a normal response for many older adults" (Boerner et al., 2005, p. P72).

The knowledge that grief takes varied forms and patterns has important implications for helping people deal with loss (Boerner et al., 2004, 2005; Bonanno et al., 2002; Table 19-2 lists suggestions). It may be unnecessary and even harmful to urge or lead mourners to work through a loss or to expect them to follow a set pattern of emotional reactions—just as it may be unnecessary and harmful to expect all dying patients to experience Kübler-Ross's stages. Respect for different ways of showing grief can help the bereaved deal with loss without making them feel that their reactions are abnormal.

Attitudes about Death and Dying across the Life Span

There is no single way of viewing death at any age; people's attitudes toward it reflect their personality and experience, as well as how close they believe they are to dying. Still, broad developmental differences apply. As the timing-of-events

Checkpoint

Can you ...

- Summarize changes that may occur in a person close to death?
- Cite possible explanations for near-death experiences?
- Name Kübler-Ross's five stages of confronting death, and tell why her work is controversial?
- Identify the three stages commonly described as *grief work,* and discuss newer findings of variations in the grieving process?

BOX 19-1 Research *in Action*

Ambiguous Loss

A woman whose husband was in the World Trade Center at the time of the terrorist attack on September 11, 2001, did not truly believe he was dead until months later, when cleanup workers turned up a shard of one of his bones. Victims of the tsunami in Southeast Asia in 2005 continue to grieve for partners, children, and parents swept away without a trace by the massive waves. Middle-aged women and men fly to Vietnam and Cambodia to search for the remains of husbands and fathers whose planes were shot down decades ago.

Dealing with the death of a loved one is difficult enough under normal circumstances. But when there is no body—no clear evidence of death—it can be harder to face the finality of loss. This is especially true in U.S. culture, with its tendency to deny the reality of death. "People yearn for a body," says the family therapist Pauline Boss (2002, p. 15), "because, paradoxically, *having* the body enables them to let go of it." Viewing the body overcomes confusion, "provides cognitive certainty of death," and thus enables the bereaved to begin mourning. Without a body, survivors feel cheated out of the chance to say goodbye and to honor the loved one properly.

Boss (1999, 2002, 2004, 2006, 2007; Boss, Beaulieu, Wieling, Turner, & LaCruz, 2003) applies the term *ambiguous loss* (introduced in Chapter 18) to situations in which loss is not clearly defined and therefore is confusing and difficult to resolve. Ambiguous loss is not a psychological disorder but a relational disorder in which grief remains frozen and resolution cannot occur. It is not an illness but a source of debilitating stress. When loss lacks tangible confirmation, people are denied ritual and emotional closure and may be immobilized—unable to go on with the necessary task of reorganizing family roles and relationships. The loss goes on and on, creating physical and emotional exhaustion, and the support of friends and family may drop away. Boss also has applied the concept of ambiguous loss to situations in which the loved one is physically present but psychologically absent, as in Alzheimer's disease, drug addiction, and other chronic mental illnesses.

People who can best tolerate ambiguous loss tend to have certain characteristics: (1) They are deeply spiritual and do not expect to understand what happens in the world—they have faith and trust in the unknown. (2) They are optimistic by nature. (3) They can hold two opposite ideas at one time ("I need to reorganize my life but keep hope alive") and thus can live with uncertainty. (4) Often they grew up in a family or culture where mastery, control, and finding answers to questions was less important than learning to live with what is.

Therapy can help people to "understand, cope, and move on after the loss, even if it remains unclear" (Boss, 1999, p. 7). Telling and hearing stories about the missing person may begin the healing process. Reconstructing family rituals can affirm that family life goes on.

Therapists working with people suffering from ambiguous loss need to be able to tolerate ambiguity themselves. They must recognize that the classic stages of grief work (described in this chapter) do not apply. Pressing for closure will bring resistance. Families can learn to manage the stress of ambiguous loss at their own pace and in their own way.

Sources: Boss, 1999, 2002, 2004, 2006, 2007; Boss et al., 2003.

What's Your View?

Have you ever experienced an ambiguous loss, or do you know someone who has? If so, what coping strategies seemed most effective?

Check It Out

For more information related to this topic, go to www .nytimes.com/pages/national/portraits to see "Portraits of Grief," a way of remembering the missing and dead from the World Trade Center attack.

---

model suggests, death probably does not mean the same thing to an 85-year-old man with excruciatingly painful arthritis, a 56-year-old woman at the height of a brilliant legal career who discovers she has breast cancer, and a 15-year-old who dies of an overdose of drugs. Typical changes in attitudes toward death across the life span depend both on cognitive development and on the normative or non-normative timing of the event.

Childhood and Adolescence According to early neo-Piagetian research (Speece & Brent, 1984), sometime between ages 5 and 7 most children come to understand that death is *irreversible*—that a dead person, animal, or flower cannot come to life again. At about the same age, children realize two other important concepts about death: first, that it is *universal* (all living things die) and therefore *inevitable;* and

Example of Questions and Statements about Dying at Approximate Age	Thoughts That Guide Behavior	Developmental Understanding of Dying	Strategies and Responses to Questions and Statements about Dying
1–3 years "Mommy, after I die, how long will it be before I'm alive again?" "Daddy, will you still tickle me while I'm dead?"	Limited understanding of accidental events, of future and past time, and of the difference between living and nonliving	Death is often viewed as continuous with life. Life and death are often considered alternate states, like being awake and being asleep, or coming and going.	Maximize physical comfort, familiar persons, and favorite toys. Be consistent. Use simple physical contact and communication to satisfy child's need for sense of self-worth and love. "I will always love you." "You are my wonderful child and I will always find a way to tickle you."
3–5 years "I've been a bad boy, so I have to die." "I hope the food is good in heaven."	Concepts are crude and irreversible. The child may not distinguish between reality and fantasy. Perceptions dominate judgment.	The child sees death as temporary and reversible and not necessarily universal (only old people die). Because of egocentricity, the child often believes that he or she somehow caused the death, or views it as a punishment. Death is like an external force that can get you and may be personified (e.g., the bogeyman).	Correct the child's perception of illness as a punishment. Maximize the child's presence with his or her parents. Children at this age may be concerned about how the family will function without them. Help parents accept and appreciate the openness of these discussions. Reassure the child and help parents lessen the guilt that the child may feel about leaving by using honest and precise language. "When you die, we will always miss you, but we will know you are with us and that you are in a safe, wonderful place [perhaps with another loved one who has died]."
5–10 years "How will I die? Will it hurt? Is dying scary?"	The child begins to demonstrate organized, logical thought. Thinking becomes less egocentric. The child begins to problem-solve concretely, reason logically, and organize thoughts coherently. However, he or she has limited abstract reasoning.	The child begins to understand death as real and permanent. Death means that your heart stops, your blood does not circulate, and you do not breathe. It may be viewed as a violent event. The child may not accept that death could happen to himself or herself or anyone he or she knows but starts to realize that people he or she knows will die.	Be honest and provide specific details if they are requested. Help and support the child's need for control. Permit and encourage the child's participation in decision making. "We will work together to help you feel comfortable. It is very important that you let us know how you are feeling and what you need. We will always be with you so that you do not need to feel afraid."

second, that a dead person is *nonfunctional* (all life functions end at death). Before then, children may believe that certain groups of people (say, teachers, parents, and children) do not die, that a person who is smart enough or lucky enough can avoid death, and that they themselves will be able to live forever. They also may believe that a dead person still can think and feel. The concepts of irreversibility, universality, and cessation of functions, these studies suggest, usually develop during the shift from preoperational to concrete operational thinking, when concepts of causation become more mature.

More recent research suggests that children may acquire a partial understanding of what happens after death as early as age 4, but that understanding may not be complete until well into the school years. In a series of studies at two suburban, university-affiliated schools, most preschoolers and kindergartners expressed knowledge

Example of Questions and Statements about Dying at Approximate Age	Thoughts That Guide Behavior	Developmental Understanding of Dying	Strategies and Responses to Questions and Statements about Dying
Adolescents 10–13 years "I'm afraid If I die my mom will just break down. I'm worried that when I die, I'll miss my family, or forget them or something."	Thinking becomes more abstract, incorporating the principles of formal logic. The ability to generate abstract propositions, multiple hypotheses, and their possible outcomes becomes apparent.	The preteen begins to understand death as real, final, and universal. It could happen to him or her or family members. The biological aspects of illness and death and details of the funeral may begin to interest the preadolescent. He or she may see death as a punishment for poor behavior and may worry about who will care for him or her if a parent or caregiver dies. He or she needs reassurance that he or she will continue to be cared for and loved.	Help reinforce the adolescent's self-esteem, sense of worth, and self-respect. Allow and respect the adolescent's need for privacy but maintain his or her access to friends and peers. Tolerate the teenager's need to express strong emotions and feelings. Support the need for independence, and permit and encourage participation in decision making. "Though I will miss you, you will always be with me and I will rely on your presence in me to give me strength."
14–18 years "This is so unfair! I can't believe how awful this cancer made me look." "I just need to be alone!" "I can't believe I'm dying. . . . What did I do wrong?"	Thinking becomes more abstract. Adolescence is marked by risk-taking behavior that seems to deny the teenager's own mortality. At this age, the teenager needs someone to use as a sounding board for his or her emotions.	A more mature and adult understanding of death develops. Death may be viewed as an enemy that can be fought against. Thus, dying may be viewed by the teenager as a failure, as giving up.	"I can't imagine how you must be feeling. You need to know that despite it all, you are doing an incredible job handling all of this. I'd like to hear more about what you are hoping for and what you are worrying about."

Source: Hurwitz, Duncan, & Wolfe, 2004.

that a dead mouse will never be alive again or grow up to be an old mouse, but 54 percent said the mouse might still need to eat. By age 7, 91 percent of the children were consistent in their knowledge that such biological processes as eating and drinking cease at death. Yet, when similar questions were put in psychological terms ("Is he still hungry?"), children this age and younger were less consistent. Only 21 percent of kindergartners and 55 percent of early elementary students knew, for example, that a dead mouse would no longer feel sick, compared with 75 percent of late elementary students ages 11 to 12. The understanding that cognitive states cease at death lagged even further; only 30 percent of the late elementary group consistently answered questions about whether thoughts, feelings, and desires persist after death (Bering & Bjorklund, 2004). Table 19-3 summarizes the developmental sequence in understanding of death. It gives examples of questions dying children of various ages typically ask and how caregivers can respond.

Children can better understand death if they are introduced to the concept at an early age and are encouraged to talk about it. The death of a pet may provide a natural opportunity. If another child dies, teachers and parents need to try

Table 19-4	Manifestations of Grief in Children		
Under 3 Years	**3 to 5 Years**	**School-Age Children**	**Adolescents**
Regression	Increased activity	Deterioration of school	Depression
Sadness	Constipation	performance caused	Somatic complaints
Fearfulness	Soiling	by loss of concentration,	Delinquent behavior
Loss of appetite	Bed-wetting	lack of interest, lack of	Promiscuity
Failure to thrive	Anger and temper	motivation, failure to com-	Suicide attempts
Sleep disturbance	tantrums	plete assignments, and	Dropping out
Social withdrawal	Out-of-control	daydreaming in class	of school
Developmental	behavior	Resistance to attending	
delay	Nightmares	school	
Irritability	Crying spells	Crying spells	
Excessive crying		Lying	
Increased		Stealing	
dependency		Nervousness	
Loss of speech		Abdominal pain	
		Headaches	
		Listlessness	
		Fatigue	

Source: Adapted from AAP Committee on Psychosocial Aspects of Child and Family Health, 1992.

to allay the surviving children's anxieties. For children with terminal illnesses, the need to understand death may be more pressing and more concrete. Yet parents may avoid bringing up the subject, whether because of their own difficulty in accepting the prospect of loss or because they are trying to protect their child. In so doing, they may miss an opportunity for the child and family to prepare emotionally for what is to come (Wolfe, 2004).

Like their understanding of death, the way children show grief depends on cognitive and emotional development (Table 19-4). Children sometimes express grief through anger, acting out, or refusal to acknowledge a death, as if the pretense that a person is still alive will make it so. They may be confused by adults' euphemisms: that someone "expired" or that the family "lost" someone or that someone is "asleep" and will never awaken.

Adjusting to loss is more difficult if a child had a troubled relationship with the person who died; if a surviving parent depends too much on the child; if the death was unexpected, especially if it was a murder or suicide; if the child has had previous behavioral or emotional problems; or if family and community support are lacking (AAP Committee on Psychosocial Aspects of Child and Family Health, 1992). More than half (56.8 percent) of children who lost a parent during the September 11, 2001, World Trade Center attacks developed anxiety disorders, including post-traumatic stress disorder, in the three years after the event—more than twice as many as in a control group who had not been bereaved (Pfeffer, Altemus, Heo, & Jiang, 2007)

Parents and other adult caregivers can help children deal with bereavement by explaining that death is final and inevitable and that they did not cause the death by their misbehavior or thoughts. Children need reassurance that they will continue to receive care from loving adults. It is usually advisable to make as few changes as possible in a child's environment, relationships, and daily activities; to answer questions simply and honestly; and to encourage the child to talk about his or her feelings and about the person who died (AAP Committee on Psychosocial Aspects of Child and Family Health, 2000).

For adolescents, death is not something they normally think much about unless they are directly faced with it—as they are in some urban communities. Many of them take unnecessary risks. They hitchhike, drive recklessly, or experiment with drugs and sex—often with tragic results. In their urge to discover and express their identity, they tend to focus more on *how* they live than on how *long* they are likely to live.

Adulthood Young adults who have finished their education and have embarked on careers, marriage, or parenthood are generally eager to live the lives they have been preparing for. If they are suddenly struck by a potentially fatal illness or injury, they are likely to be extremely frustrated and angry. People who develop terminal illnesses in their twenties or thirties must face issues of death and dying at an age when they normally would be dealing with such issues of young adulthood as establishing an intimate relationship. Rather than having a long lifetime of losses as gradual preparation for the final loss of life, they find their entire world collapsing at once.

In middle age, most adults understand that they are indeed going to die. Their bodies send them signals that they are not as young, agile, and hearty as they once were. More and more they think about how many years they may have left and how to make the most of those years (Neugarten, 1967). Often—especially after the death of both parents—there is a new awareness of being the older generation or the next in line to die (Scharlach & Fredriksen, 1993). Middle-aged and older adults may prepare for death emotionally as well as in practical ways by making a will, planning their funerals, and discussing their wishes with family and friends.

Older adults may have mixed feelings about the prospect of dying. Physical losses and other problems and losses of old age may diminish their pleasure in living and their will to live (McCue, 1995). Some older adults, especially after age 70, give up on achieving unfulfilled goals. Others push harder to do what they can with life in the time they have left. Many try to extend their remaining time by adopting healthier lifestyles or struggle to live even when they are profoundly ill (Cicirelli, 2002).

When they think or talk of their impending death, some older adults express fear. Others, especially the devoutly religious, compare death to falling asleep, an easy and painless transition to an afterlife. They do not talk about the process of dying itself or the declines that may precede it. For them, this approach may mute fear of dying (Cicirelli, 2002).

According to Erikson, older adults who resolve the final critical alternative of *integrity versus despair* (see Chapter 18) achieve acceptance both of what they have done with their lives and of their impending death. One way to accomplish this resolution is through a *life review,* discussed later in this chapter. People who feel that their lives have been meaningful and who have adjusted to their losses may be better able to face death.

Significant Losses

Especially difficult losses that may occur during adulthood are the deaths of a spouse, a parent, and a child. The loss of a potential offspring through miscarriage or stillbirth can also be painful but usually draws less social support.

The unnecessary risks adolescents sometimes take can have tragic results.

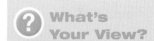

What's Your View?

• Try to imagine that you are terminally ill. What do you imagine your feelings would be? Would they be similar to or different from those described in the text with reference to your age group?

Checkpoint

Can you . . .

♦ Discuss how people of different ages understand and cope with death and bereavement?

Guidepost 3

What special challenges are involved in surviving a spouse, a parent, or a child, or in mourning a miscarriage?

Surviving a Spouse

Because women tend to live longer than men and to be younger than their husbands, they are more likely to be widowed. They also tend to be widowed at an earlier age. Some 28 percent of U.S. women, but less than 9 percent of U.S. men, lose their spouses by age 65 (Federal Interagency Forum on Aging-Related Statistics, 2006).

The stress of widowhood often affects physical and mental health. Bereavement can impair the immune system, resulting in headaches, dizziness, indigestion, or chest pain. It also entails higher risks of disability, drug use, hospitalization, and even death (Stroebe, Schut, & Stroebe, 2007). In a large-scale Finnish study, men who lost their wives within the five-year period of the study were 21 percent more likely to die within the same period than men who remained married, and widowed women were 10 percent more likely to die than nonwidowed women (Martikainen & Valkonen, 1996). The risk of either natural death or suicide is greatest in the early months after a loss and is higher for younger adults. Bereavement also can lead to memory problems, loss of appetite, and difficulty with concentration and heightens the risks of anxiety, depression, insomnia, and social dysfunction. These reactions may range from fairly short and mild to extreme and long lasting, sometimes even for years (Stroebe et al., 2007).

Social relationships, as discussed in earlier chapters, are related to good health. Thus, the loss of companionship may help explain the strong likelihood that a widowed person, especially a widower, will soon follow the spouse to the grave (Ray, 2004). However, a more practical explanation also may apply; after the death of a spouse, there may be no one to remind an older widow to take her pills or to make sure a widowed man adheres to a special diet. Those who receive such reminders (say, from children or health workers) tend to improve in health habits and reported health (Williams, 2004).

The quality of the marital relationship that has been lost may affect the degree to which widowhood affects mental health. In one study, widowed persons who had been especially close to, or highly dependent on, their spouses tended to become more anxious and yearned more for their partners six months after the death than did widowed persons who had not been so close or dependent (Carr et al., 2000). The loss of a husband may be especially hard for a woman who has structured her life and her identity around pleasing or caring for him (Marks & Lambert, 1998). Such a woman has lost not only a companion but an important, perhaps central, role (Lucas, Clark, Georgellis, & Diener, 2003).

Widowhood can create practical problems, too. Widows whose husbands were chief breadwinners may experience economic hardship or fall into poverty (Hungerford, 2001). Widowed husbands may have to buy household services a homemaker wife provided. When both spouses were employed, the loss of one income can be hard. For women, the main consequences of widowhood are more likely to be economic strain, whereas for men the chief consequences are

Older widows are more likely than older widowers to stay in touch with friends and benefit from the support of a social network.

Table 19-5

Table 19-5 Self-Reported Psychological Impacts of a Parent's Death on Adult Children

Impacts	Death of Mother (percent)	Death of Father (percent)
Self-concept		
More "adult"	29	43
More self-confident	19	20
More responsible	11	4
Less mature	14	3
Other	8	17
No impact	19	12
Feelings about mortality		
Increased awareness of own mortality	30	29
More accepting of own death	19	10
Made concrete plans regarding own death	10	4
Increased fear of own death	10	18
Other	14	16
No impact	17	23
Religiosity		
More religious	26	29
Less religious	11	2
Other	3	10
No impact	60	59
Personal priorities		
Personal relationships more important	35	28
Simple pleasures more important	16	13
Personal happiness more important	10	7
Material possessions less important	5	8
Other	20	8
No impact	14	36
Work or career plans		
Left job	29	16
Adjusted goals	15	10
Changed plans due to family needs	5	6
Moved	4	10
Other	13	19
No impact	34	39

Source: Schartach & Fredriksen, 1993, p. 311, Table 1.

more likely to be social isolation and loss of emotional intimacy (Pudrovska et al., 2006). Older widows are more likely than older widowers to stay in touch with friends from whom they receive social support (Kinsella & Velkoff, 2001).

Ultimately, the distress of loss can be a catalyst for introspection and growth—for discovering submerged aspects of oneself and learning to stand on one's own feet (Lieberman, 1996). In one study, widows continued to talk and think about their deceased husbands decades after the loss, but these thoughts rarely upset them. Instead, these women said they had become stronger and more self-confident as a result of their loss (Carnelley et al., 2006).

Losing a Parent in Adulthood

The loss of a parent at any time is difficult, even in adulthood. In-depth interviews with 83 volunteers ages 35 to 60 found a majority of bereaved adult children still experiencing emotional distress—ranging from sadness and crying to depression and thoughts of suicide—after one to five years, especially following loss of a mother (Scharlach & Fredriksen, 1993). Still, the death of a parent can be a maturing experience. It can push adults into resolving important developmental issues: achieving a stronger sense of self and a more pressing, realistic awareness of their own mortality, along with a greater sense of responsibility, commitment, and attachment to others (M. S. Moss & Moss, 1989; Scharlach & Fredriksen, 1993).

The death of a parent often brings changes in other relationships. A bereaved adult child may assume more responsibility for the surviving parent and for keeping the family together (Aldwin & Levenson, 2001). The intense emotions of bereavement may draw siblings closer, or they may become alienated over differences that arose during the parent's final illness. A parent's death may free an adult child to spend more time and energy on relationships that were temporarily neglected to meet demands of caregiving. Or the death may free an adult child to shed a relationship that was being maintained to meet the parent's expectations (M. S. Moss & Moss, 1989; Scharlach & Fredriksen, 1993).

The death of a second parent can have especially great impact. The adult child may feel a sharpened sense of mortality now that the buffer of the older generation is gone (Aldwin & Levenson, 2001). This awareness can be an opportunity for growth, leading to a more mature outlook on life and a greater appreciation of the value of personal relationships (Scharlach & Frederiksen, 1993). Recognition of the finality of death and of the impossibility of saying anything more to the deceased parent motivates some people to resolve disturbances in their ties to the living while there is still time. Some people are moved to reconcile with their adult children. Sometimes estranged siblings, realizing that the parent who provided a link between them is no longer there, try to mend the rift.

Losing a Child

In earlier times, it was not unusual for a parent to bury a child. Today, with medical advances and the increase in life expectancy in industrialized countries, infant mortality has reached record lows, and a child who survives the first year of life is far more likely to live to old age.

A parent is rarely prepared emotionally for the death of a child. Such a death, no matter at what age, comes as a cruel, unnatural shock, an untimely event that, in the normal course of things, should never happen. The parents may feel they have failed, no matter how much they loved and cared for the child, and they may find it hard to let go. If a marriage is strong, the couple may draw closer together, supporting each other in their shared loss. In other cases, the loss weakens and eventually destroys the marriage (Brandt, 1989). Parents, especially mothers, who have lost a child are at heightened risk of being hospitalized for mental illness (Li, Laursen, Precht, Olsen, & Mortensen, 2005). The stress of a child's loss may even hasten a parent's death (Li, Precht, Mortensen, & Olsen, 2003).

Many parents hesitate to discuss a terminally ill child's impending death with the child, but those who do so tend to achieve a sense of closure that helps them cope after the loss. In 2001, a Swedish research team surveyed 449 Swedish parents who had lost a child to cancer four to nine years earlier. About one-third of the parents said they had talked with their children about their impending death, and none of these parents regretted having done so, whereas 27 percent of those who had not brought up the subject regretted it. Most likely to have regrets were parents who had sensed that their child was aware of his or her imminent death but who had not spoken to the child about it, and a disproportionate number of these parents were still suffering from depression and anxiety (Kreicbergs, Valdimarsdóttir, Onelöv, Henter, & Steineck, 2004).

The impact of parental bereavement may vary depending on such factors as the age of the child, the cause of death, and the number of remaining children a couple has. In a longitudinal study, 219 Dutch couples who had lost a child were followed for 20 months after the death. Grief was greater the older the child (up to age 17). Parents whose child had died a traumatic death grieved more than those whose child had died of an illness or disorder or those who experienced a stillbirth or neonatal death. Parents who had expected the death and those who had other children expressed the least grief. Mothers tended to grieve more than fathers, but parents of either sex who had higher education or worked more hours reported less grief than those with less education or fewer working hours. As time went by, grief tended to diminish, especially among couples who became pregnant again (Wijngaards-de Meij et al., 2005).

Although each bereaved parent must cope with grief in his or her own way, some have found that plunging into work, interests, and other relationships or joining a support group eases the pain. Some well-meaning friends tell parents not to dwell on their loss, but remembering the child in a meaningful way may be exactly what they need to do. When asked what most helped them cope with the end of their child's life, 73 percent of parents whose children died in intensive-care units gave religious or spiritual responses. They mentioned prayer, faith, discussions with clergy, or a belief that the parent-child relationship endures beyond death. Parents also said they were guided by insight and wisdom, inner values, and spiritual virtues such as hope, trust, and love (Robinson, Thiel, Backus, & Meyer, 2006).

Mourning a Miscarriage

At a Buddhist temple in Tokyo, small statues of infants accompanied by toys and gifts are left as offerings to Jizo, an enlightened being who is believed to watch over miscarried and aborted fetuses and eventually, through reincarnation, to guide them into a new life. The ritual of *mizuko kuyo,* a rite of apology and remembrance, is observed as a means of making amends to the aborted life (Orenstein, 2002).

The Japanese word *mizuko* means "water child." Japanese Buddhists believe that life flows into an organism gradually, like water, and a mizuko is somewhere on the continuum between life and death (Orenstein, 2002). In English, in contrast, there is no special word for a miscarried or aborted fetus and, in American life, no customary ritual for mourning the loss. Families, friends, and health professionals tend to avoid talking about such losses, which often are considered insignificant compared with the loss of a living child (Van, 2001). Grief can be more wrenching without social support.

How do prospective parents cope with the loss of a child they never knew? Each person's or couple's experience of loss is unique (Van, 2001). In one small study, 11 men whose child had died in utero reported being overcome with frustration and helplessness during and after the delivery, but several found relief in supporting their partners (Samuelsson, Radestad, & Segesten, 2001). In another study, grieving parents perceived their spouses and extended families as most helpful and their doctors as least helpful. Some bereaved parents benefited from a support group, and some not (DiMarco, Menke, & McNamara, 2001). Differences in the ways men and women grieve may be a source of tension and divisiveness in a couple's relationship (Caelli, Downie, & Letendre, 2002). Couples who have gone through the loss of a pregnancy may need extra-compassionate care during a later pregnancy (Caelli et al., 2002).

In response to the wishes of many parents who have experienced stillbirth, at least 19 states have enacted laws providing birth certificates for stillborn babies to recognize and validate the births (Lewin, 2007).

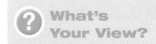

What's Your View?

- Have you lost a parent, a sibling, a spouse, a child, or a friend? If not, which of these losses do you imagine would be hardest to bear, and why? If you have experienced more than one of these types of loss, how did your reactions differ?

Checkpoint

Can you . . .

- Identify specific challenges involved in losing a spouse?
- Discuss ways in which an adult's loss of a spouse or parent can be a maturing experience?
- Explain why parents are rarely prepared emotionally for the death of a child?
- Suggest ways to help expectant parents cope with the loss of a pregnancy?

Guidepost 4

How are attitudes toward hastening death changing, and what concerns do such practices raise?

Medical, Legal, and Ethical Issues: The "Right to Die"

Do people have a right to die? If so, under what circumstances? Should a terminally ill person who wants to commit suicide be allowed or helped to do so? Should a doctor prescribe medicine that will relieve pain but may shorten the patient's life? What about giving a lethal injection to end a patient's suffering? Who decides that a life is not worth prolonging? These are some of the thorny moral, ethical, and legal questions that face individuals, families, physicians, and society—questions involving the quality of life and the nature and circumstances of death.

Suicide

Although suicide is no longer a crime in modern societies, there is still a stigma against it, based in part on religious prohibitions and in part on society's interest in preserving life. A person who expresses suicidal thoughts may be considered mentally ill. On the other hand, a growing number of people consider a mature adult's deliberate choice of a time to end his or her life a rational decision and a right to be defended.

Suicide rates in the United States began declining in the late 1990s after a 25 percent rise from 1981 to 1997 (Sahyoun, Lentzner, Hoyert, & Robinson, 2001). Still, more than 32,000 people took their own lives in 2006, according to preliminary data, making suicide the 11th leading cause of death. The suicide rate in the United States—10.7 deaths per 100,000 population (Heron et al., 2008)—is lower than in many other industrialized countries (Kinsella & Velkoff, 2001). Worldwide, suicide is the 13th leading cause of death (WHO, 2003).

Statistics probably understate the number of suicides; many go unreported and some (such as traffic "accidents" and "accidental" medicinal overdoses) are not recognized as such. Also, the figures on suicides often do not include suicide *attempts;* an estimated 20 to 60 percent of people in the United States who commit suicide have tried before, and about 10 percent of people who attempt suicide will kill themselves within 10 years (Harvard Medical School, 2003b).

In most nations, suicide rates rise with age and are higher among men than among women (Kinsella & Velkoff, 2001; Nock et al., 2008), though more women consider or attempt suicide. Young, unmarried women with little education and those who are unusually impulsive, anxious, or depressed are most at risk for suicidal thoughts and behavior (Nock et al., 2008). In the United States, men are four times as likely as women to succeed in taking their own life—though this gap has greatly diminished in recent years. Men's suicide rates are higher mainly because they are far more likely to use reliable methods, such as firearms, whereas women are more likely to choose other means, such as poisoning or hanging. More than half of completed suicides are by gunshot (CDC, 2007b; Kung et al., 2008; Miniño et al., 2007).

Among racial/ethnic groups, white and Native American men have the highest suicide rates. Older blacks are only about one-third as likely to commit suicide as older whites (NCHS, 2006), perhaps because of religious commitment and because they may be accustomed to hard knocks (NCHS, 1998; NIMH, 1999a). However, suicide rates among black people, especially those who are younger and less educated, have increased significantly since the mid-1980s (Joe, Baser, Breeden, Neighbors, & Jackson, 2006).

What's Your View?

• In your opinion, is the intentional ending of one's own life ever justified? Would you ever consider this option? If so, under what circumstances?

| Table 19-6 | Changes in Suicide Rates by Age, United States, 1999–2004 |

Suicide rates rose the most among middle-aged people while decreasing for the elderly, whose risk nevertheless remains the highest.

	SUICIDE RATE, PER 100,000 PEOPLE		
Age Group	Rate in 1999	Rate in 2004	Percentage Change from 1999 to 2004
15 to 24	10.1	10.3	+2
25 to 34	12.7	12.7	0
35 to 44	14.3	15.0	+ 4.9
45 to 54	**13.9**	**16.6**	**+19.4%**
55 to 64	**12.2**	**13.8**	**+13.1%**
65 to 74	13.4	12.3	− 8.2
75 to 84	18.1	16.3	− 9.9
85 and over	19.3	16.4	−15

Sources: Based on data from CDC, 2008; Cohen, 2008; Paulozzi et al., 2007.

Due to a recent unexplained jump in midlife suicide (Table 19-6), U.S. suicide rates now reach a high for adults in their forties and early fifties and then subside and rise again after age 75 (Bergen, Chen, Warner, & Fingerhut, 2008). Very old people are more likely than younger people to be depressed and socially isolated, and if they try to commit suicide, they are more likely to succeed the first time (CDC, 2002). Divorced and widowed men have high suicide rates at all ages. Suicide in older adults is associated with physical illness, family conflict, and financial troubles (Harvard Medical School, 2003b). (Teenage suicide is discussed in Chapter 11.)

A family history of suicide or suicide attempts greatly raises the risk of completing suicide. An apparent hereditary vulnerability may be related to low activity of the mood- and impulse-regulating brain chemical serotonin in the prefrontal cortex, the seat of judgment, planning, and inhibition (Harvard Medical School, 2003b).

Although some people intent on suicide carefully conceal their plans, most give warning signs. These may include talking about death or suicide; giving away prized possessions; abusing drugs or alcohol; and personality changes, such as unusual anger, sadness, boredom, or apathy. People who are about to kill themselves may neglect their appearance and sleep or eat much more or less than usual. They often show signs of depression, such as unusual difficulty concentrating, loss of self-esteem, and feelings of helplessness, hopelessness, or panic (American College of Emergency Physicians, 2008; Harvard Medical School, 2003b).

Survivors of people who take their own lives have been called "suicide's other victims." Many blame themselves for failing to recognize the signs. They "obsessively replay the events leading up to the death, imagining how they could have prevented it and berating themselves for their failure to do so" (Goldman & Rothschild, n.d.). Because of the stigma attached to suicide, these survivors often struggle with their emotions alone rather than share them with others who might understand. (Table 19-7 lists warning signs of suicide and steps to take if someone threatens suicide.)

The highest rate of suicide is among white men age 75 and over, the risk rises among men 85 and older. Older people are more likely than younger people to be depressed and socially isolated.

Table 19-7 Preventing Suicide

Warning signs of suicide:

- Feeling depressed, down, or excessively sad.
- Feelings of hopelessness, worthlessness, or having no purpose in life, along with a loss of interest or pleasure in doing things.
- Preoccupation with death, dying, or violence, or talking about wanting to die.
- Seeking access to medications, weapons, or other means of committing suicide.
- Wide mood swings—feeling extremely up one day and terribly down the next.
- Feelings of great agitation, rage, or uncontrolled anger, or wanting to get revenge.
- Changes in eating and sleeping habits, appearance, behavior, or personality.
- Risky or self-destructive behavior, such as driving recklessly or taking illegal drugs.
- Sudden calmness (a sign that a person has made the decision to attempt suicide).
- Life crises, trauma, or setbacks, including school, work, or relationship problems, job loss, divorce, death of a loved one, financial difficulties, diagnosis of a terminal illness.
- Putting one's affairs in order, including giving away belongings, visiting family members and friends, drawing up a will, or writing a suicide note.

If someone threatens suicide:

- Stay calm.
- Take the threat seriously.
- Don't leave the person alone. Prevent access to firearms, knives, medications, or any other item the person may use to commit suicide.
- Don't try to handle the situation alone. Call 911 or the local emergency response number. Phone the person's doctor, the police, a local crisis intervention team, or others who are trained to help.
- While waiting for help, listen closely to the person. Let the person know you're listening by maintaining eye contact, moving closer, or holding his or her hand, if appropriate.
- Ask questions to determine what method of suicide the person is considering and whether he or she has an organized plan.
- Remind the person that help is available.
- If the person does attempt suicide, immediately call for emergency medical assistance and administer first aid, if necessary.

Source: Adapted from American College of Emergency Physicians, 2008.

Hastening Death

In February 1990, at the age of 26, Terri Schiavo suddenly collapsed. With oxygen cut off to her brain, she went into what doctors diagnosed as a persistent vegetative state. (In such a state, a person, although technically alive, has no awareness and only rudimentary brain functioning.) Schiavo's husband, Michael, insisted that Terri would not have wanted to live in that condition and, in 1998, sought to turn off the machinery that was keeping her alive. Her parents bitterly disagreed as to what Terri's wishes would have been and questioned whether her condition was truly irreversible. A seven-year legal battle erupted, which, because of intense public controversy over the issue of hastening death, was marked by an unprecedented congressional intervention in the judicial process. Finally, the U.S. Supreme Court let stand the decision of the lower courts that Terri had no hope of recovery. In March 2005, Terri's feeding tube was removed, and she died less than two weeks later (Annas, 2005).

Until recent decades, the idea of helping a suffering loved one hasten death was virtually unheard of. Changing attitudes toward hastening death can be attributed largely to revulsion against technologies that keep patients alive against their will despite intense suffering, and sometimes even after the brain has, for all practical purposes, stopped functioning.

Terri Shiavo's death was an example of **passive euthanasia:** withholding or discontinuing treatment that might extend the life of a terminally ill patient, such as medication, life-support systems, or feeding tubes. In contrast, in **active euthanasia** (sometimes called *mercy killing*), action is taken directly and deliberately to shorten a life. *Euthanasia* means "good death"; both types of euthanasia are intended to end suffering or allow a terminally ill person to die with dignity. However, active euthanasia is generally illegal; passive euthanasia, in some circumstances, is not. An important question regarding either form of euthanasia is whether it is *voluntary;* that is, whether it is done at the direct request, or to carry out the expressed wishes, of the person whose death results.

Advance Directives Terri Schiavo's case might have been very different had she left written instructions as to her wishes. The U.S. Supreme Court held, in the case of Nancy Cruzan, that a person whose wishes are clearly known has a constitutional right to refuse or discontinue life-sustaining treatment (*Cruzan v. Director, Missouri Department of Health,* 1990). A mentally competent person's wishes can be spelled out in advance in a document called an **advance directive (living will),** which contains instructions for when and how to discontinue futile medical care. All 50 states have since legalized some form of advance directive or adopted other provisions governing the making of end-of-life decisions (APA Working Group on Assisted Suicide and End-of-Life Decisions, 2005).

A *living will* may contain specific provisions with regard to circumstances in which treatment should be discontinued, what extraordinary measures—if any—should be taken to prolong life, and what kind of pain management is desired. A person also may specify, through a donor card or a signature on the back of his or her driver's license, that his or her organs be donated to someone in need of an organ transplant (Box 19-2).

Some living will legislation applies only to terminally ill patients, not to those who are incapacitated by illness or injury but may live many years in severe pain. Nor do advance directives help many patients in comas or in persistent vegetative states. Such situations can be covered by a **durable power of attorney,** which appoints another person to make decisions if the maker of the document becomes incompetent to do so. A number of states have adopted a simple form known as a *medical durable power of attorney* expressly for decisions about health care. However, even with advance directives, many patients have undergone protracted, fruitless treatment against their expressed wishes (SUPPORT Principal Investigators, 1995).

Such situations led the American Medical Association to form a Task Force on Quality Care at the End of Life. Many hospitals now have ethics committees that create guidelines, review cases, and help doctors, patients, and their families with decisions about end-of-life care (Simpson, 1996); and some hospitals employ full-time ethics consultants.

Assisted Suicide: Pros and Cons Assisted suicide—in which a physician or someone else helps a person bring about a self-inflicted death by, for example, prescribing or obtaining drugs or enabling a patient to inhale a deadly gas—commonly refers to situations in which people with incurable, terminal illnesses request help in ending their lives. Assisted suicide is still illegal in most places but in recent years has come to the forefront of public debate. It may be similar in principle to voluntary active euthanasia, in which, for example, a patient asks for, and receives, a lethal injection; but in assisted suicide the person who wants to die performs the actual deed.

passive euthanasia Deliberate withholding or discontinuation of life-prolonging treatment of a terminally ill person in order to end suffering or allow death with dignity.

active euthanasia Deliberate action taken to shorten the life of a terminally ill person in order to end suffering or to allow death with dignity; also called *mercy killing*.

advance directive (living will) Document specifying the type of care wanted by the maker in the event of an incapacitating or terminal illness.

durable power of attorney Legal instrument that appoints an individual to make decisions in the event of another person's incapacitation.

assisted suicide Suicide in which a physician or someone else helps a person take his or her own life.

BOX **19-2** **Window** *on the World*

Organ Donation: The Gift of Life

Snowboarder Chris Klug won a bronze medal in the Men's Parallel Giant Slalom event at the winter Olympics in Salt Lake City in February 2002—just 18 months after receiving a lifesaving liver transplant.

In 2006, 28,923 lifesaving transplants of donated organs and tissue—a record high—took place in the United States (Health Resources and Services Administration [HRSA], 2007). In a 2005 Gallup poll, 78 percent of respondents said they would be likely or very likely to donate their organs, and nearly 53 percent had given permission on a driver's license or organ donor card (Gallup Organization, 2005).

Deceased donors can give multiple organs that improve or save the lives of several people (USDHHS, 2005). Organs are less likely to be rejected by the body of the recipient if they come from a donor of the same race or ethnicity; and some diseases of the kidney, heart, lung, pancreas, and liver are more common in certain racial and ethnic minorities than in the general population (USDHHS, 2002).

Despite the positive outcomes of organ donation, there is a worldwide shortage of organs (West & Burr, 2002). In the United States about 16 people die every day—close to 6,000 each year—while waiting for transplants (Scientific Registry of Transplant Recipients, 2004). More than 99,000 are on the waiting list (Organ Procurement and Transplantation Network, 2008).

The shortage of organs for transplantation would be more severe were it not for a rise in "living donations": donations of a single organ, usually a kidney, by a living person. In 2006, nearly 22 percent of all donors were living (HRSA, 2007), thanks to medical advances that make such donation safer and more likely to succeed (USDHHS, 2002). Nearly two-thirds of living donors are related to the recipients by blood, and most of the others have personal relationships with the recipients, but some are complete strangers (Steinbrook, 2005).

Organ donation by living donors, however, can pose ethical issues. Donors have been openly solicited on the Internet and through advertising, raising questions about the potential for financial exploitation, inequitable allocation of organs, and possible violations of standards for donation (Steinbrook, 2005). Medical ethicists say that living donation should occur only when the likelihood of success is high, the risk to the donor

is low, and voluntary consent is obtained. Donors need to be informed about the risks of the surgery and about possible long-term effects (Ingelfinger, 2005). The process for evaluating potential donors needs to be standardized, with independent counselors to help donors make an informed choice (Truog, 2005).

The decision to be a donor—either living or after death—or to allow a deceased loved one to be a donor may not be an easy one. Among the factors influencing denial of consent are misunderstanding of brain death, the timing and setting of the request, and the approach of the person making the request. Cultural attitudes play a part (West & Burr, 2002). Some objections to donation among rural African Americans are related to religious beliefs (Wittig, 2001). Asians in the Glasgow, Scotland, region are unsympathetic to organ transplantation, especially after death (Baines, Joseph, & Jindal, 2002). In India, too, there are moral, religious, and emotional compunctions against donating organs of a dead person, so most donations are by living donors (Chandra & Singh, 2001).

Culturally sensitive education may make a difference. An educational program among Native American communities in the Southwest showed a need to change not only attitudes of potential donors, but also stereotypes about Native Americans commonly held by health care providers who ask for the donations (Thomas, 2002).

What's Your View?

Would you donate an organ to a friend or family member who needed it? To a stranger? On your death? Why or why not?

Check It Out

For more information on this topic, go to www.organdonor.gov (a website of the U.S. Department of Health and Human Services, which gives basic facts and statistics about organ donation).

In the United States, assisted suicide is illegal in almost all states but often goes on covertly, without regulation. The American Medical Association opposes physician aid in dying as contrary to a practitioner's oath to "do no harm." Doctors are permitted to give drugs that may shorten a life if the purpose is to relieve pain (Gostin, 1997; Quill, Lo, & Brock, 1997), but some physicians refuse for reasons of personal or medical ethics (APA, 2001).

The *ethical arguments for* assisted suicide are based on the principles of autonomy and self-determination: that mentally competent persons should have the right to control the quality of their own lives and the timing and nature of their death. Proponents of assisted suicide place a high value on preserving the dignity and personhood of the dying human being. *Medical arguments* hold that a doctor is obligated to take all measures necessary to relieve suffering. Besides, in assisted suicide the patient is the one who takes the actual step to end life. A *legal argument* is that legalizing assisted suicide would permit the regulation of practices that now occur anyway out of compassion for suffering patients. It is argued that adequate safeguards against abuse can be put in place through a combination of legislation and professional regulation (APA, 2001).

Some ethical and legal scholars go further: They favor legalizing all forms of *voluntary euthanasia* with safeguards against involuntary euthanasia. The key issue, according to these scholars, is not how death occurs but who makes the decision. They see no difference in principle between pulling the plug on a respirator, pulling out feeding tubes, giving a lethal injection, and prescribing an overdose of pills at the patient's request. They maintain that aid in dying, if openly available, would reduce fear and helplessness by enabling patients to control their own fate (APA, 2001; Brock, 1992; Epstein, 1989; Orentlicher, 1996).

Ethical arguments against assisted suicide center on two principles: (1) the belief that taking a life, even with consent, is wrong and (2) concern for protection of the disadvantaged. Opponents of aid-in-dying point out that autonomy is often limited by poverty or disability or membership in a stigmatized social group, and they fear that persons in these categories may be subtly pressured into choosing suicide with cost containment as an underlying factor. *Medical arguments* against assisted suicide include the possibility of misdiagnosis, the potential future availability of new treatments, the likelihood of incorrect prognosis, and the belief that helping someone die is incompatible with a physician's role as healer and that adequate safeguards are not possible. *Legal arguments* against assisted suicide include concerns about enforceability of safeguards and about lawsuits when family members disagree about the propriety of terminating a life (APA, 2001).

Because self-administered pills do not always succeed, some opponents contend that physician-assisted suicide would lead to voluntary active euthanasia (Groenewoud et al., 2000). The next step on the slippery slope, some warn, would be involuntary euthanasia—not only for the terminally ill but for others, such as people with disabilities, whose quality of life is perceived as diminished. The opponents claim that people who want to die are often temporarily depressed and might change their minds with treatment or palliative care (APA, 2005; Butler, 1996; Hendin, 1994; Latimer, 1992; Quill et al., 1997; Simpson, 1996; P. A. Singer, 1988; P. A. Singer & Siegler, 1990).

Legalizing Physician Aid in Dying   In September, 1996, a 66-year-old Australian man with advanced prostate cancer was the first person to die legally by assisted suicide. Under a law passed in the Northern Territory, he pressed a computer key that administered a lethal dose of barbiturates. In 1997, the law was repealed ("Australian Man," 1996; Voluntary Euthanasia Society, 2002).

Since 1997, when a unanimous U.S. Supreme Court left regulation of physician aid in dying up to the states, measures to legalize assisted suicide for the terminally ill have been introduced in several states, but so far Oregon is the only state to pass such a law, the Death with Dignity Act. In 1994, Oregonians voted to let mentally competent patients, who have been told by two doctors that they have less than six months to live, request a lethal prescription with strong safeguards to make sure that the request is serious and voluntary and that all other alternatives have been considered. In January 2006 the Supreme Court upheld the Oregon law (Gostin, 2006; Greenhouse, 2005).

What has been the experience under the Oregon law? In its first eight years of operation, 292 terminally ill patients were reported to state health officials to have taken their lives under the act, 46 of them in 2006. The concerns most frequently mentioned by patients who requested and used lethal prescriptions were loss of autonomy (96 percent), loss of ability to participate in activities that make life enjoyable (96 percent), and loss of dignity (76 percent). Only 48 percent were concerned about inadequate pain control (Summary of Oregon's Death with Dignity Act, 2006).

Active euthanasia remains illegal in the United States, even in Oregon, but not in the Netherlands, where in 2002 a law permitting voluntary euthanasia for patients in a state of continuous, unbearable, and incurable suffering went into effect. In such cases, doctors can now inject a lethal dose of medication. Belgium also legalized voluntary euthanasia in 2002 (Agence France-Presse, 2005). In 2005, a reported 1.8 percent of deaths in the Netherlands resulted from euthanasia or assisted suicide (Van der Heide et al., 2007).

Before 2002, both assisted suicide and active euthanasia were technically illegal in the Netherlands, but physicians who engaged in these practices could avoid prosecution under strict conditions of reporting and government oversight (Simons, 1993). A similar situation still exists in Switzerland. In France, a law effective in February 2006 authorizes doctors to withhold unnecessary medical treatment or to intensify pain relief, even if these decisions unintentionally hasten death.

End-of-Life Decisions and Cultural Attitudes It is hard to compare the experience of the Netherlands, which has a homogeneous population and universal national health coverage, with that of such a large, diverse country as the United States. Nevertheless, with increasing numbers of Americans—3 out of 4 in a 2005 Gallup poll (Moore, 2005)—favoring euthanasia for a patient who is incurably ill and wants to die, some U.S. doctors have agreed to help patients requesting assistance in hastening death. A nationwide survey of 1,902 physicians whose specialties involve care of dying patients found that, of those who had received requests for help with suicide (18 percent) or lethal injections (11 percent), about 7 percent had complied at least once (Meier et al., 1998). On the other hand, in a survey in the United Kingdom, 80 percent of geriatric physicians—but only 52 percent of intensive care physicians—considered active voluntary euthanasia *never* ethically justified (Dickinson, Lancaster, Clark, Ahmedzai, & Noble, 2002).

The first representative study of end-of-life decisions in six European countries (Belgium, Denmark, Italy, the Netherlands, Sweden, and Switzerland) found important cultural differences. In all six countries, physicians reported withholding or withdrawing life-prolonging treatment—most typically medication, followed by hydration or nutrition—but the frequency varied greatly, from 41 percent of deaths in Switzerland to 6 percent in Italy (Bosshard et al., 2005). Active forms of physician-assisted death were most prevalent in the Netherlands and Belgium (van der Heide et al., 2003). In a later survey of physicians in the same six countries, direct physician-assisted deaths were rare; but in one-quarter to one-half of all deaths (23 percent in Italy, 51 percent in Switzerland), physicians made death-hastening decisions, such as deep sedation, sometimes accompanied by withdrawal of artificial nutrition and hydration (Bilsen, Cohen, & Deliens, 2007).

Special end-of-life issues concern treatment of newborns with incurable conditions or very poor prognoses for quality of life. Forgoing or withdrawing life-prolonging treatment for newborns with no chance of survival and those born with severe brain abnormalities or extensive organ damage is now widely accepted medical practice (Verhagen & Sauer, 2005). Yet, here, too, cultural differences appear. In a study of physicians' self-reported practices in France, Germany, Italy, the Netherlands, Spain, Sweden, and the United Kingdom, the vast majority of neonatal practitioners in all seven countries had been involved at least once in decisions to withhold or not institute treatment (Cuttini et al., 2000).

End-of-Life Options and Diversity Concerns   One beneficial result of the aid-in-dying controversy has been to call attention to the need for better palliative care and closer attention to patients' motivation and state of mind. When doctors talk openly with patients about their physical and mental symptoms, their expectations, their fears and goals, their options for end-of-life care, their family concerns, and their need for meaning and quality of life, ways may be found to diminish these concerns without the taking of life (Bascom & Tolle, 2002). In terminally ill patients, the will to live can fluctuate greatly, so if aid in dying is contemplated, it is essential to ensure that the request is not just a passing one (Chochinov, Tataryn, Clinch, & Dudgeon, 1999).

In the United States, with its ethnically diverse population, issues of social and cultural diversity need to be addressed in end-of-life decision making. Planning for death is inconsistent with traditional Navajo values, which avoid negative thinking and talk. Chinese families may seek to protect a dying person from unfavorable information, including knowledge of his or her impending death. Recent Mexican or Korean immigrants may believe less in individual autonomy than is customary in the dominant U.S. culture. Among some ethnic minorities, the value of longevity may take priority over health. Both African Americans and Hispanic Americans, for example, are more likely than European Americans to prefer life-sustaining treatment regardless of the state of the disease and of their educational level (APA Working Group on Assisted Suicide, 2005).

Issues of hastening death will become more pressing as the population ages. In years to come, both the courts and the public will be forced to come to terms with these issues as increasing numbers of people claim a right to die with dignity and with help.

Finding Meaning and Purpose in Life and Death

The struggle to find meaning in life and in death—often dramatized in books and movies—has been borne out by research. In one study of 39 women whose average age was 76, those who saw the most purpose in life had the least fear of death (Durlak, 1973). Conversely, according to Kübler-Ross (1975), facing the reality of death is a key to living a meaningful life:

> It is the denial of death that is partially responsible for [people's] living empty, purposeless lives; for when you live as if you'll live forever, it becomes too easy to postpone the things you know that you must do. In contrast, when you fully understand that each day you awaken could be the last you have, you take the time that day to grow, to become more of who you really are, to reach out to other human beings. (p. 164)

Reviewing a Life

In Charles Dickens's *A Christmas Carol,* Scrooge changes his greedy, heartless ways after seeing ghostly visions of his past, his present, and his future death.

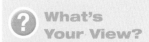
What's Your View?

• Do you think assisted suicide should be legalized? If so, what safeguards should be provided? Would your answers be the same or different for voluntary active euthanasia? Do you see an ethical distinction between euthanasia and oversedation of the terminally ill?

Checkpoint

Can you . . .

◆ Explain why intent to commit suicide is sometimes not recognized, and list warning signs?

◆ Discuss the ethical, practical, and legal issues involved in advance directives, euthanasia, and assisted suicide?

Guidepost 5

How can people overcome fear of dying and come to terms with death?

Sharing memories evoked by a photo album is one way to review a life. Life review can help people recall important events and can motivate them to rebuild damaged relationships or complete unfinished tasks.

life review Reminiscence about one's life in order to see its significance.

In the movie *It's a Wonderful Life,* when an angel helps George Bailey (played by Jimmy Stewart) to see the world without himself in it, he realizes how meaningful his life is. These fictional characters make their remaining time more purposeful through **life review,** a process of reminiscence that enables a person to see the significance of his or her life.

Life review can, of course, occur at any time. However, it may have special meaning in old age, when it can foster ego integrity—according to Erikson, the final critical task of the life span. As the end of their journey approaches, people may look back over their accomplishments and failures and ask themselves what their lives have meant. Awareness of mortality may be an impetus for reexamining values and seeing one's experiences and actions in a new light. Some people find the will to complete unfinished tasks, such as reconciling with estranged family members or friends, and thus to achieve a satisfying sense of closure.

Not all memories are equally conducive to mental health and growth. Older people who use reminiscence for self-understanding show the strongest ego integrity, while those who entertain only pleasurable memories show less. Most poorly adjusted are those who keep recalling negative events and are obsessed with regret, hopelessness, and fear of death; their ego integrity has given way to despair (Sherman, 1993; Walasky, Whitbourne, & Nehrke, 1983–1984).

Life-review therapy can help focus the natural process of life review and make it more conscious, purposeful, and efficient (Butler, 1961; M. I. Lewis & Butler, 1974). Methods often used for uncovering memories in life-review therapy (which also may be used by individuals on their own) include recording an autobiography; constructing a family tree; spending time with scrapbooks, photo albums, old letters, and other memorabilia; making a trip back to scenes of childhood and young adulthood; reuniting with former classmates or colleagues or distant family members; describing ethnic traditions; and summing up one's life's work.

Development: A Lifelong Process

In his late seventies, the artist Pierre-Auguste Renoir had crippling arthritis and chronic bronchitis and had lost his wife. He spent his days in a wheelchair, and his pain was so great that he could not sleep through the night. He was unable to hold a palette or grip a brush: his brush had to be tied to his right hand. Yet he continued to produce brilliant paintings, full of color and vibrant life. Finally, stricken by pneumonia, he lay in bed, gazing at some anemones his attendant had picked. He gathered enough strength to sketch the form of these beautiful flowers, and then—just before he died—lay back and whispered, "I think I am beginning to understand something about it" (L. Hanson, 1968).

Even dying can be a developmental experience. As one health practitioner put it, ". . . there are things to be gained, accomplished in dying. Time with and for those whom we are close to, achieving a final and enduring sense of self-worth, and a readiness to let go are priceless elements of a good death" (Weinberger, 1999).

✔ Checkpoint

Can you . . .

◆ Explain why life review can be especially helpful in old age and how it can help overcome fear of death?

◆ Tell what types of memories are most conducive to a life review?

◆ List several activities used in life review therapy?

◆ Explain how dying can be a developmental experience?

Within a limited life span, no person can realize all capabilities, gratify all desires, explore all interests, or experience all the richness that life has to offer. The tension between possibilities for growth and a finite time in which to do the growing defines human life. By choosing which possibilities to pursue and by continuing to follow them as far as possible, even up to the very end, each person contributes to the unfinished story of human development.

Summary and Key Terms

The Many, Changing Meanings of Death and Dying

Guidepost 1: *How do attitudes and customs concerning death differ across cultures, and what are the implications of the "mortality revolution" in developed countries?*

- Death has biological, social, cultural, historical, religious, legal, psychological, developmental, medical, and ethical aspects.

- Customs surrounding death and mourning vary greatly from one culture to another, depending on the society's view of the nature and consequences of death. Some modern customs have evolved from ancient beliefs and practices.

- Death rates dropped drastically during the twentieth century, especially in developed countries.

- Nearly three-quarters of deaths in the United States occur among the elderly, and the top causes of death are diseases that primarily affect older adults.

- As death became primarily a phenomenon of late adulthood, it became largely "invisible," and care of the dying took place in isolation, by professionals.

- There is now an upsurge of interest in understanding and dealing realistically and compassionately with death. Examples of this tendency are a growing interest in thanatology and increasing emphasis on hospice care and palliative, or comfort, care.

  thanatology (620)

  hospice care (620)

  palliative care (620)

Facing Death and Loss

Guidepost 2: *How do people deal with dying, and how do they grieve for a loss?*

- People often undergo cognitive and functional declines shortly before death.

- Some people who come close to dying have "near-death" experiences that may result from physiological changes.

- Elisabeth Kübler-Ross proposed five stages in coming to terms with dying: denial, anger, bargaining, depression,

and acceptance. These stages, and their sequence, are not universal.

- There is no universal pattern of grief. The most widely studied pattern moves from shock and disbelief to preoccupation with the memory of the dead person and finally to resolution. However, research has found wide variations and a prevalence of resilience.

- Children's understanding of death develops gradually. Young children can better understand death if it is part of their own experience. Children show grief in age-related ways based on cognitive and emotional development.

- Although adolescents generally do not think much about death, violence and the threat of death are part of some adolescents' daily life. Adolescents tend to take needless risks.

- Realization and acceptance of the inevitability of death increases throughout adulthood.

  terminal drop (622)

  bereavement (623)

  grief (623)

  grief work (623)

Significant Losses

Guidepost 3: *What special challenges are involved in surviving a spouse, a parent, or a child, or in mourning a miscarriage?*

- Women are more likely to be widowed, and widowed younger, than men, and may experience widowhood somewhat differently. Physical and mental health tend to decline after widowhood, but for some people widowhood can ultimately become a positive developmental experience.

- Death of a parent can precipitate changes in the self and in relationships with others.

- The loss of a child can be especially difficult because it is no longer normative.

- Because miscarriage and stillbirth are not generally considered significant losses in U.S. society, those who experience such losses are often left to deal with them with little social support.

Medical, Legal, and Ethical Issues: The "Right to Die"

Guidepost 4: *How are attitudes toward hastening death changing, and what concerns do such practices raise?*

- Although suicide is no longer illegal in modern societies, there is still a stigma attached to it. Some people maintain a "right to die," especially for people with long-term degenerative illness.

- Suicide is the 11th leading cause of death in the United States and 13th worldwide. The number of suicides is probably underestimated.

- Suicide rates tend to rise with age and are more common among men than among women, though women are more likely to attempt suicide. The highest rate of suicide in the United States is among elderly white men. It is often related to depression, isolation, family conflict, financial troubles, and debilitating ailments.

- Euthanasia and assisted suicide involve controversial ethical, medical, and legal issues.

- To avoid unnecessary suffering through artificial prolongation of life, passive euthanasia is generally permitted with the patient's consent or with advance directives. However, such directives are not consistently followed. Most hospitals now have ethics committees to deal with decisions about end-of-life care.

- Active euthanasia and assisted suicide are generally illegal, but public support for physician aid in dying has increased. The state of Oregon has a law permitting physician-assisted suicide for the terminally ill. The Netherlands and Belgium have legalized both euthanasia and assisted suicide.

- Forgoing or withdrawing treatment of newborns who cannot survive or who can do so only with extremely poor quality of life is becoming a more widely accepted practice than in the past, especially in some European countries.

- The aid-in-dying controversy has focused more attention on the need for better palliative care and understanding of patients' state of mind. Issues of social and cultural diversity need to be considered.

passive euthanasia (637)

active euthanasia (637)

advance directive (living will) (637)

durable power of attorney (637)

assisted suicide (637)

Finding Meaning and Purpose in Life and Death

Guidepost 5: *How can people overcome fear of dying and come to terms with death?*

- The more meaning and purpose people find in their lives, the less they tend to fear death.

- Life review can help people prepare for death and give them a last chance to complete unfinished tasks.

- Even dying can be a developmental experience.

life review (642)

Glossary

acceleration programs Programs for educating the gifted that move them through the curriculum at an unusually rapid pace. (317)

accommodation Piaget's term for changes in a cognitive structure to include new information. (31)

acquired immune deficiency syndrome (AIDS) Viral disease that undermines effective functioning of the immune system. (85)

active engagement Personal involvement in schooling, work, family, or other activity. (384)

active euthanasia Deliberate action taken to shorten the life of a terminally ill person in order to end suffering or to allow death with dignity; also called *mercy killing*. (637)

activities of daily living (ADLs) Essential activities that support survival, such as eating, dressing, bathing, and getting around the house. (566)

activity theory Theory of aging, proposed by Neugarten and others, which holds that in order to age successfully a person must remain as active as possible. (592)

acute medical conditions Illnesses that last a short time. (291)

adaptation Piaget's term for adjustment to new information about the environment, achieved through processes of assimilation and accommodation. (31)

adolescence Developmental transition between childhood and adulthood entailing major physical, cognitive, and psychosocial changes. (354)

adolescent growth spurt Sharp increase in height and weight that precedes sexual maturity. (358)

adolescent rebellion Pattern of emotional turmoil, characteristic of a minority of adolescents, which may involve conflict with family, alienation from adult society, reckless behavior, and rejection of adult values. (405)

adrenarche Maturation of adrenal glands. (356)

advance directive (living will) Document specifying the type of care wanted by the maker in the event of an incapacitating or terminal illness. (637)

ageism Prejudice or discrimination against a person (most commonly an older person) based on age. (550)

age-related macular degeneration Condition in which the center of the retina gradually loses its ability to discern fine details; leading cause of irreversible visual impairment in older adults. (562)

aging in place Remaining in one's own home, with or without assistance, in later life. (599)

alcoholism Chronic disease involving dependence on use of alcohol, causing interference with normal functioning and fulfillment of obligations. (430)

alleles Two or more alternative forms of a gene that occupy the same position on paired chromosomes and affect the same trait. (59)

altruism Behavior intended to help others out of inner concern and without expectation of external reward; may involve self-denial or self-sacrifice. (274)

Alzheimer's disease Progressive, irreversible, degenerative brain disorder characterized by cognitive deterioration and loss of control of bodily functions, leading to death. (570)

ambiguous loss A loss that is not clearly defined or does not bring closure. (590)

ambivalent (resistant) attachment Pattern in which an infant becomes anxious before the primary caregiver leaves, is extremely upset during his or her absence, and both seeks and resists contact on his or her return. (190)

amyloid plaque Waxy chunks of insoluble tissue found in brains of persons with Alzheimer's disease. (571)

animism Tendency to attribute life to objects that are not alive. (230)

anorexia nervosa Eating disorder characterized by self-starvation. (364)

anoxia Lack of oxygen, which may cause brain damage. (102)

Apgar scale Standard measurement of a newborn's condition; it assesses appearance, pulse, grimace, activity, and respiration. (103)

art therapy Therapeutic approach that allows a person to express troubled feelings without words, using a variety of art materials and media. (345)

assimilation Piaget's term for incorporation of new information into an existing cognitive structure. (31)

assisted suicide Suicide in which a physician or someone else helps a person take his or her own life. (637)

asthma A chronic respiratory disease characterized by sudden attacks of coughing, wheezing, and difficulty in breathing. (291)

attachment Reciprocal, enduring tie between two people—especially between infant and caregiver—each of whom contributes to the quality of the relationship. (189)

attention-deficit/hyperactivity disorder (ADHD) Syndrome characterized by persistent inattention and distractibility, impulsivity, low tolerance for frustration, and inappropriate overactivity. (314)

authoritarian parenting In Baumrind's terminology, parenting style emphasizing control and obedience. (272)

authoritative parenting In Baumrind's terminology, parenting style blending respect for a child's individuality with an effort to instill social values. (272)

autobiographical memory Memory of specific events in one's life. (238)

autoimmunity Tendency of an aging body to mistake its own tissues for foreign invaders and to attack and destroy them. (557)

autonomy versus shame and doubt Erikson's second stage in psychosocial development, in which children achieve a balance between self-determination and control by others. (198)

autosomes In humans, the 22 pairs of chromosomes not related to sexual expression. (57)

avoidant attachment Pattern in which an infant rarely cries when separated from the primary caregiver and avoids contact on his or her return. (190)

balanced investment Pattern of retirement activity allocated among family, work, and leisure. (597)

basal metabolism Use of energy to maintain vital functions. (485)

basic trust versus basic mistrust Erikson's first crisis in psychosocial development, in which infants develop a sense of the reliability of people and objects. (188)

Bayley Scales of Infant and Toddler Development Standardized test of infants' and toddlers' mental and motor development. (143)

behavioral genetics Quantitative study of relative hereditary and environmental influences on behavior. (66)

behaviorism Learning theory that emphasizes the predictable role of environment in causing observable behavior. (28)

behaviorist approach Approach to the study of cognitive development that is concerned with basic mechanics of learning. (140)

behavior therapy Therapeutic approach using principles of learning theory to encourage desired behaviors or eliminate undesired ones; also called *behavior modification*. (345)

bereavement Loss, due to death, of someone to whom one feels close and the process of adjustment to the loss. (623)

bilingual Fluent in two languages. (307)

bilingual education System of teaching non-English-speaking children in their native language while they learn English, and later switching to all-English instruction. (307)

bioecological theory Bronfenbrenner's approach to understanding processes and contexts of human development that identifies five levels of environmental influence. (34)

body image Descriptive and evaluative beliefs about one's appearance. (288, 364)

Brazelton Neonatal Behavioral Assessment Scale (NBAS) Neurological and behavioral test to measure neonate's responses to the environment. (103)

bulimia nervosa Eating disorder in which a person regularly eats huge quantities of food and then purges the body by laxatives, induced vomiting, fasting, or excessive exercise. (365)

bullying Aggression deliberately and persistently directed against a particular target, or victim, typically one who is weak, vulnerable, and defenseless. (341)

canalization Limitation on variance of expression of certain inherited characteristics. (70)

caregiver burnout Condition of physical, mental, and emotional exhaustion affecting adults who provide continuous care for sick or aged persons. (540)

case study Study of a single subject, such as an individual or family. (40)

cataracts Cloudy or opaque areas in the lens of the eye, which cause blurred vision. (562)

cell death In brain development, normal elimination of excess brain cells to achieve more efficient functioning. (121)

central executive In Baddeley's model, element of working memory that controls the processing of information. (237)

central nervous system Brain and spinal cord. (118)

centration In Piaget's theory, the tendency of preoperational children to focus on one aspect of a situation and neglect others. (231)

cephalocaudal principle Principle that development proceeds in a head-to-tail direction, that is, that upper parts of the body develop before lower parts of the trunk. (114)

cesarean delivery Delivery of a baby by surgical removal from the uterus. (99)

child-directed speech (CDS) Form of speech often used in talking to babies or toddlers; includes slow, simplified speech, a high-pitched tone, exaggerated vowel sounds, short words and sentences, and much repetition; also called *parentese* or *motherese*. (172)

childhood depression Mood disorder characterized by such symptoms as a prolonged sense of friendlessness, inability to have fun or concentrate, fatigue, extreme activity or apathy, feelings of worthlessness, weight change, physical complaints, and thoughts of death or suicide. (344)

chromosomes Coils of DNA that consist of genes. (56)

chronic medical conditions Illnesses or impairments that persist for at least three months. (291)

circular reactions Piaget's term for processes by which an infant learns to reproduce desired occurrences originally discovered by chance. (147)

classical conditioning Learning based on associating a stimulus that does not ordinarily elicit a response with another stimulus that does elicit the response. (29, 141)

class inclusion Understanding of the relationship between a whole and its parts. (293)

code mixing Use of elements of two languages, sometimes in the same utterance, by young children in households where both languages are spoken. (172)

code switching Changing one's speech to match the situation, as in people who are bilingual. (172)

cognitive-appraisal model Model of coping, proposed by Lazarus and Folkman, which holds that, on the basis of continuous appraisal of their relationship with the environment, people choose appropriate coping strategies to deal with situations that tax their normal resources. (590)

cognitive development Pattern of change in mental abilities, such as learning, attention, memory, language, thinking, reasoning, and creativity. (6)

cognitive neuroscience Study of links between neural processes and cognitive abilities. (40)

cognitive neuroscience approach Approach to the study of cognitive development that links brain processes with cognitive ones. (140)

cognitive perspective View that thought processes are central to development. (30)

cognitive reserve Hypothesized fund of energy that may enable a deteriorating brain to continue to function normally. (572)

cognitive-stage theory Piaget's theory that children's cognitive development advances in a series of four stages involving qualitatively distinct types of mental operations. (31)

cohort A group of people born at about the same time. (14)

commitment Marcia's term for personal investment in an occupation or system of beliefs. (392)

committed compliance Kochanska's term for wholehearted obedience of a parent's orders without reminders or lapses. (201)

componential element Sternberg's term for the analytic aspect of intelligence. (303)

conceptual knowledge Acquired interpretive understandings stored in long-term memory. (374)

concordant Term describing tendency of twins to share the same trait or disorder. (68)

concrete operations Third stage of Piagetian cognitive development (approximately ages 7 to 12), during which children develop logical but not abstract thinking. (292)

conduct disorder (CD) Repetitive, persistent pattern of aggressive, antisocial behavior violating societal norms or the rights of others. (343)

conscience Internal standards of behavior, which usually control one's conduct and produce emotional discomfort when violated. (201)

conservation Piaget's term for awareness that two objects that are equal according to a certain measure remain equal in the face of perceptual alteration so long as nothing has been added to or taken away from either object. (232)

constructive play Play involving use of objects or materials to make something. (265)

contextual element Sternberg's term for the practical aspect of intelligence. (304)

contextual perspective View of human development that sees the individual as inseparable from the social context. (34)

continuity theory Theory of aging, described by Atchley, which holds that in order to age successfully people must maintain a balance of continuity and change in both the internal and external structures of their lives. (593)

control group In an experiment, a group of people, similar to those in the experimental group, who do not receive the treatment under study. (43)

conventional morality (or morality of conventional role conformity) Second level in Kohlberg's theory of moral reasoning in which standards of authority figures are internalized. (375)

convergent thinking Thinking aimed at finding the one right answer to a problem. (317)

coping Adaptive thinking or behavior aimed at reducing or relieving stress that arises from harmful, threatening, or challenging conditions. (589)

coregulation Transitional stage in the control of behavior in which parents exercise general supervision and children exercise moment-to-moment self-regulation. (325)

corporal punishment Use of physical force with the intention of causing pain but not injury so as to correct or control behavior. (270)

correlational study Research design intended to discover whether a statistical relationship between variables exists. (41)

creativity Ability to see situations in a new way, to produce innovations, or to discern previously unidentified problems and find novel solutions. (316)

crisis Marcia's term for period of conscious decision making related to identity formation. (392)

critical period Specific time when a given event or its absence has a specific impact on development. (16)

cross-modal transfer Ability to use information gained by one sense to guide another. (156)

cross-sectional study Study designed to assess age-related differences, in which people of different ages are assessed on one occasion. (46)

crystallized intelligence Type of intelligence, proposed by Horn and Cattell, involving the ability to remember and use learned information; it is largely dependent on education and culture. (505)

cultural bias Tendency of intelligence tests to include items calling for knowledge or skills more familiar or meaningful to some cultural groups than to others. (302)

cultural socialization Parental practices that teach children about their racial/ethnic heritage and promote cultural practices and cultural pride. (395)

culture A society's or group's total way of life, including customs, traditions, beliefs, values, language, and physical products—all learned behavior, passed on from parents to children. (12)

culture-fair tests Intelligence tests that deal with experiences common to various cultures, in an attempt to avoid cultural bias. (302)

culture-free tests Intelligence tests that, if they were possible to design, would have no culturally linked content. (302)

culture-relevant tests Intelligence tests that would draw on and adjust for culturally related content. (303)

decenter In Piaget's terminology, to think simultaneously about several aspects of a situation. (231)

declarative knowledge Acquired factual knowledge stored in long-term memory. (374)

decoding Process of phonetic analysis by which a printed word is converted to spoken form before retrieval from long-term memory. (308)

deductive reasoning Type of logical reasoning that moves from a general premise about a class to a conclusion about a particular member or members of the class. (294)

deferred imitation Piaget's term for reproduction of an observed behavior after the passage of time by calling up a stored symbol of it. (150)

dementia Deterioration in cognitive and behavioral functioning due to physiological causes. (569)

Denver Developmental Screening Test Screening test given to children 1 month to 6 years old to determine whether they are developing normally. (130)

deoxyribonucleic acid (DNA) Chemical that carries inherited instructions for the development of all cellular forms of life. (56)

dependent variable In an experiment, the condition that may or may not change as a result of changes in the independent variable. (44)

depth perception Ability to perceive objects and surfaces three-dimensionally. (132)

developmental tasks In normative-stage theories, typical challenges that need to be mastered for successful adaptation to each stage of life. (458)

developmental tests Psychometric tests that compare a baby's performance on a series of tasks with standardized norms for particular ages. (143)

diabetes Disease in which the body does not produce or properly use insulin, a hormone that converts sugar, starches, and other foods into energy needed for daily life. (492)

differentiation Process by which cells acquire specialized structures and functions. (121)

"difficult" children Children with irritable temperament, irregular biological rhythms, and intense emotional responses. (183)

discipline Methods of molding children's character and of teaching them to exercise self-control and engage in acceptable behavior. (270)

disengagement theory Theory of aging, proposed by Cumming and Henry, which holds that successful aging is characterized by mutual withdrawal of the older person and society. (592)

dishabituation Increase in responsiveness after presentation of a new stimulus. (155)

disorganized-disoriented attachment Pattern in which an infant, after separation from the primary caregiver, shows contradictory, repetitious, or misdirected behaviors on his or her return. (190)

divergent thinking Thinking that produces a variety of fresh, diverse possibilities. (317)

dizygotic twins Twins conceived by the union of two different ova (or a single ovum that has split) with two different sperm cells; also called *fraternal twins;* they are no more alike genetically than any other siblings. (55)

dominant inheritance Pattern of inheritance in which, when a child receives different alleles, only the dominant one is expressed. (59)

Down syndrome Chromosomal disorder characterized by moderate-to-severe mental retardation and by such physical signs as a downward-sloping skin fold at the inner corners of the eyes. (65)

dramatic play Play involving imaginary people or situations; also called *pretend play, fantasy play,* or *imaginative play.* (265)

drug therapy Administration of drugs to treat emotional disorders. (346)

dual representation hypothesis Proposal that children under age 3 have difficulty grasping spatial relationships because of the need to keep more than one mental representation in mind at the same time. (153)

durable power of attorney Legal instrument that appoints an individual to make decisions in the event of another person's incapacitation. (637)

dynamic systems theory (DST) Esther Thelen's theory, which holds that motor development is a dynamic process of active coordination of multiple systems within the infant in relation to the environment. (134)

dyslexia Developmental disorder in which reading achievement is substantially lower than predicted by IQ or age. (313)

early intervention Systematic process of providing services to help families meet young children's developmental needs. (145)

"easy" children Children with a generally happy temperament, regular biological rhythms, and a readiness to accept new experiences. (183)

ecological theory of perception Theory developed by Eleanor and James Gibson, which describes developing motor and perceptual abilities as interdependent parts of a functional system that guides behavior in varying contexts. (133)

egocentrism Piaget's term for inability to consider another person's point of view; a characteristic of young children's thought. (231)

ego-control Self-control. (461)

ego integrity versus despair According to Erikson, the eighth and final stage of psychosocial development, in which people in late adulthood either achieve a sense of integrity of the self by accepting the lives they have lived, and thus accept death, or yield to despair that their lives cannot be relived. (587)

ego-resiliency Adaptability under potential sources of stress. (461)

elaboration Mnemonic strategy of making mental associations involving items to be remembered. (298)

electronic fetal monitoring Mechanical monitoring of fetal heartbeat during labor and delivery. (98)

elicited imitation Research method in which infants or toddlers are induced to imitate a specific series of actions they have seen but not necessarily done before. (150)

embryonic stage Second stage of gestation (2 to 8 weeks), characterized by rapid growth and development of major body systems and organs. (79)

emergent literacy Preschoolers' development of skills, knowledge, and attitudes that underlie reading and writing. (244)

emerging adulthood Proposed transitional period between adolescence and adulthood. (423)

emotional intelligence (EI) Salovey and Mayer's term for ability to understand and regulate emotions; an important component of effective, intelligent behavior. (439)

emotional maltreatment Rejection, terrorization, isolation, exploitation, degradation, ridicule, or failure to provide emotional support, love, and affection; or other action or inaction that may cause behavioral, cognitive, emotional, or mental disorders. (207)

emotion-focused coping In the cognitive-appraisal model, coping strategy directed toward managing the emotional response to a stressful situation so as to lessen its physical or psychological impact. (590)

emotions Subjective reactions to experience that are associated with physiological and behavioral changes. (178)

empathy Ability to put oneself in another person's place and feel what the other person feels. (181)

empty nest Transitional phase of parenting following the last child's leaving the parents' home. (537)

encapsulation In Hoyer's terminology, progressive dedication of information processing and fluid thinking to specific knowledge systems, making knowledge more readily accessible. (506)

encoding Process by which information is prepared for long-term storage and later retrieval. (236)

English-immersion approach Approach to teaching English as a second language in which instruction is presented only in English. (307)

enrichment programs Programs for educating the gifted that broaden and deepen knowledge and skills through extra activities, projects, field trips, or mentoring. (317)

enuresis Repeated urination in clothing or in bed. (219)

environment Totality of nonhereditary, or experiential, influences on development. (10)

epigenesis Mechanism that turns genes on or off and determines functions of body cells. (60)

episodic memory Long-term memory of specific experiences or events, linked to time and place. (238, 578)

equilibration Piaget's term for the tendency to seek a stable balance among cognitive elements; achieved through a balance between assimilation and accommodation. (31)

erectile dysfunction Inability of a man to achieve or maintain an erect penis sufficient for satisfactory sexual performance. (490)

ethnic gloss Overgeneralization about an ethnic or cultural group that obscures differences within the group. (14)

ethnic group A group united by ancestry, race, religion, language, and/or national origins, which contribute to a sense of shared identity. (12)

ethnographic study In-depth study of a culture, which uses a combination of methods including participant observation. (41)

ethology Study of distinctive adaptive behaviors of species of animals that have evolved to increase survival of the species. (35)

evolutionary psychology Application of Darwinian principles of natural selection and survival of the fittest to individual behavior. (35)

evolutionary/sociobiological perspective View of human development that focuses on evolutionary and biological bases of behavior. (35)

executive function Conscious control of thoughts, emotions, and actions to accomplish goals or solve problems. (237, 297)

experiential element Sternberg's term for the insightful or creative aspect of intelligence. (303)

experiment Rigorously controlled, replicable procedure in which the researcher manipulates variables to assess the effect of one on the other. (42)

experimental group In an experiment, the group receiving the treatment under study. (43)

explicit memory Intentional and conscious memory, generally of facts, names, and events. (161)

extended family Multigenerational kinship network of parents, children, and other relatives, sometimes living together in an extended-family household. (11)

externalizing behaviors Behaviors by which a child acts out emotional difficulties; for example, aggression or hostility. (325)

external memory aids Mnemonic strategies using something outside the person. (298)

failure to thrive An apparently healthy, well-fed baby's failure to grow, often as a result of emotional neglect. (208)

family-focused lifestyle Pattern of retirement activity that revolves around family, home, and companions. (597)

family therapy Psychological treatment in which a therapist sees the whole family together to analyze patterns of family functioning. (345)

fast mapping Process by which a child absorbs the meaning of a new word after hearing it once or twice in conversation. (241)

fertilization Union of sperm and ovum to produce a zygote; also called *conception*. (54)

fetal alcohol syndrome (FAS) Combination of mental, motor, and developmental abnormalities affecting the offspring of some women who drink heavily during pregnancy. (83)

fetal stage Final stage of gestation (from 8 weeks to birth), characterized by increased differentiation of body parts and greatly enlarged body size. (80)

fictive kin Friends who are considered and behave like family members. (462)

filial crisis In Marcoen's terminology, normative development of middle age, in which adults learn to balance love and duty to their parents with autonomy within a two-way relationship. (539)

filial maturity Stage of life, proposed by Marcoen and others, in which middle-aged children, as the outcome of a filial crisis, learn to accept and meet their parents' need to depend on them. (539)

fine motor skills Physical skills that involve the small muscles and eye-hand coordination. (130, 221)

five-factor model Theoretical model of personality, developed and tested by Costa and McCrae, based on the "Big Five" factors underlying clusters of related personality traits: neuroticism, extraversion, openness to experience, conscientiousness, and agreeableness. (458)

fluid intelligence Type of intelligence, proposed by Horn and Cattell, that is applied to novel problems and is relatively independent of educational and cultural influences. (505)

foreclosure Identity status, described by Marcia, in which a person who has not spent time considering alternatives (that is, has not been in crisis) is committed to other people's plans for his or her life. (392)

formal games with rules Organized games with known procedures and penalties. (266)

formal operations Piaget's final stage of cognitive development, characterized by the ability to think abstractly. (371)

free radicals Unstable, highly reactive atoms or molecules, formed during metabolism, which can cause internal bodily damage. (557)

functional age Measure of a person's ability to function effectively in his or her physical and social environment in comparison with others of the same chronological age. (552)

functional play Play involving repetitive large muscular movements. (265)

gender Significance of being male or female. (187)

gender constancy Awareness that one will always be male or female; also called *sex-category constancy*. (261)

gender crossover Gutmann's term for reversal of gender roles after the end of active parenting. (526)

gender identity Awareness, developed in early childhood, that one is male or female. (256)

gender roles Behaviors, interests, attitudes, skills, and traits that a culture considers appropriate for each sex; differ for males and females. (257)

gender-schema theory Theory, proposed by Bem, that children socialize themselves in their gender roles by developing a mentally organized network of information about what it means to be male or female in a particular culture. (261)

gender stereotypes Preconceived generalizations about male or female role behavior. (258)

gender-typing Socialization process by which children, at an early age, learn appropriate gender roles. (188, 257)

generalized anxiety disorder Anxiety not focused on any single target. (344)

generativity Erikson's term for concern of mature adults for establishing, guiding, and influencing the next generation. (518)

generativity versus stagnation Erikson's seventh stage of psychosocial development, in which the middle-aged adult develops a concern with establishing, guiding, and influencing the next generation or else experiences stagnation (a sense of inactivity or lifelessness). (518)

generic memory Memory that produces scripts of familiar routines to guide behavior. (238)

genes Small segments of DNA located in definite positions on particular chromosomes; functional units of heredity. (56)

genetic code Sequence of bases within the DNA molecule; governs the formation of proteins that determine the structure and functions of living cells. (56)

genetic counseling Clinical service that advises prospective parents of their probable risk of having children with hereditary defects. (65)

genetic-programming theories Theories that explain biological aging as resulting from a genetically determined developmental timetable. (555)

genotype Genetic makeup of a person, containing both expressed and unexpressed characteristics. (60)

genotype-environment correlation Tendency of certain genetic and environmental influences to reinforce each other; may be passive, reactive (evocative), or active. Also called *genotype-environment covariance*. (71)

genotype-environment interaction The portion of phenotypic variation that results from the reactions of genetically different individuals to similar environmental conditions. (70)

geriatrics Branch of medicine concerned with processes of aging and medical conditions associated with old age. (552)

germinal stage First 2 weeks of pre-natal development, characterized by rapid cell division, blastocyst formation, and implantation in the wall of the uterus. (75)

gerontology Study of the aged and the process of aging. (552)

gestation Period of development between conception and birth. (74)

gestational age Age of an unborn baby, usually dated from the first day of an expectant mother's last menstrual cycle. (75)

glaucoma Irreversible damage to the optic nerve caused by increased pressure in the eye. (562)

gonadarche Maturation of testes or ovaries. (356)

goodness of fit Appropriateness of environmental demands and constraints to a child's temperament. (184)

grief Emotional response experienced in the early phases of bereavement. (623)

grief work Working out of psychological issues connected with grief. (623)

gross motor skills Physical skills that involve the large muscles. (130, 220)

guided participation Adult's participation in a child's activity that helps to structure it and bring the child's understanding of it closer to the adult's. (162)

habituation Type of learning in which familiarity with a stimulus reduces, slows, or stops a response. (154)

handedness Preference for using a particular hand. (221)

haptic perception Ability to acquire information about properties of objects, such as size, weight, and texture, by handling them. (132)

Hayflick limit Genetically controlled limit, proposed by Hayflick, on the number of times cells can divide in members of a species. (558)

heredity Inborn traits or characteristics inherited from the biological parents. (9)

heritability Statistical estimate of contribution of heredity to individual differences in a specific trait within a given population. (68)

heterozygous Possessing differing alleles for a trait. (59)

historical generation A group of people strongly influenced by a major historical event during their formative period. (14)

holophrase Single word that conveys a complete thought. (166)

Home Observation for Measurement of the Environment (HOME) Instrument to measure the influence of the home environment on children's cognitive growth. (144)

homozygous Possessing two identical alleles for a trait. (59)

hormone therapy (HT) Treatment with artificial estrogen, sometimes in combination with the hormone progesterone, to relieve or prevent symptoms caused by decline in estrogen levels after menopause. (497)

hospice care Warm, personal, patient- and family-centered care for a person with a terminal illness. (620)

hostile attribution bias Tendency to perceive others as trying to hurt one and to strike out in retaliation or self-defense. (339)

human development Scientific study of processes of change and stability throughout the human life span. (4)

human genome Complete sequence of genes in the human body. (56)

hypertension Chronically high blood pressure. (290, 491)

hypotheses Possible explanations for phenomena, used to predict the outcome of research. (22)

hypothetical-deductive reasoning Ability, believed by Piaget to accompany the stage of formal operations, to develop, consider, and test hypotheses. (372)

ideal self The self one would like to be. (253)

identification In Freudian theory, the process by which a young child adopts characteristics, beliefs, attitudes, values, and behaviors of the parent of the same sex. (260)

identity According to Erikson, a coherent conception of the self, made up of goals, values, and beliefs to which a person is solidly committed. (390)

identity accommodation Whitbourne's term for adjusting the self-concept to fit new experience. (524)

identity achievement Identity status, described by Marcia, that is characterized by commitment to choices made following a crisis, a period spent in exploring alternatives. (392)

identity assimilation Whitbourne's term for effort to fit new experience into an existing self-concept. (524)

identity balance Whitbourne's term for a tendency to balance assimilation and accommodation. (524)

identity diffusion Identity status, described by Marcia, that is characterized by absence of commitment and lack of serious consideration of alternatives. (393)

identity process theory (IPT) Whitbourne's theory of identity development based on processes of assimilation and accommodation. (524)

identity statuses Marcia's term for states of ego development that depend on the presence or absence of crisis and commitment. (391)

identity versus identity confusion Erikson's fifth stage of psychosocial development, in which an adolescent seeks to develop a coherent sense of self, including the role she or he is to play in society. Also called *identity versus role confusion*. (390)

implicit memory Unconscious recall, generally of habits and skills; sometimes called *procedural memory*. (161)

imprinting Instinctive form of learning in which, during a critical period in early development, a young animal forms an attachment to the first moving object it sees, usually the mother. (15)

incomplete dominance Pattern of inheritance in which a child receives two different alleles, resulting in partial expression of a trait. (63)

independent variable In an experiment, the condition over which the experimenter has direct control. (44)

individual differences Differences in characteristics, influences, or developmental outcomes. (9)

individual psychotherapy Psychological treatment in which a therapist sees a troubled person one-on-one. (345)

individuation (1) Adolescents' struggle for autonomy and personal identity. (407) (2) Jung's term for emergence of the true self through balancing or integration of conflicting parts of the personality. (517)

inductive reasoning Type of logical reasoning that moves from particular observations about members of a class to a general conclusion about that class. (294)

inductive techniques Disciplinary techniques designed to induce desirable behavior by appealing to a child's sense of reason and fairness. (271)

industry versus inferiority Erikson's fourth stage of psychosocial development, in which children must learn the productive skills their culture requires or else face feelings of inferiority. (323)

infant mortality rate Proportion of babies born alive who die within the first year. (110)

infertility Inability to conceive after 12 months of trying. (433)

information-processing approach Approach to the study of cognitive development that analyzes processes involved in perceiving and handling information. (33, 140)

initiative versus guilt Erikson's third stage in psychosocial development, in which children balance the urge to pursue goals with reservations about doing so. (256)

instrumental activities of daily living (IADLs) Indicators of functional well-being and of the ability to live independently. (566)

instrumental aggression Aggressive behavior used as a means of achieving a goal. (275)

integration Process by which neurons coordinate the activities of muscle groups. (121)

intelligent behavior Behavior that is goal oriented and adaptive to circumstances and conditions of life. (143)

interiority Neugarten's term for a concern with inner life (introversion or introspection), which usually appears in middle age. (520)

internalization During socialization, process by which children accept societal standards of conduct as their own. (199)

internalizing behaviors Behaviors by which emotional problems are turned inward; for example, anxiety or depression. (325)

intimacy versus isolation Erikson's sixth stage of psychosocial development, in which young adults either make commitments to others or face a possible sense of isolation and self-absorption. (456)

invisible imitation Imitation with parts of one's body that one cannot see. (150)

IQ (intelligence quotient) tests Psychometric tests that seek to measure intelligence by comparing a test-taker's performance with standardized norms. (143)

irreversibility Piaget's term for a preoperational child's failure to understand that an operation can go in two or more directions. (232)

kangaroo care Method of skin-to-skin contact in which a newborn is laid face down between the mother's breasts for an hour or so at a time after birth. (107)

Kaufman Assessment Battery for Children (K-ABC-II) Nontraditional individual intelligence test designed to provide fair

assessments of minority children and children with disabilities. (305)

kinship care Care of children living without parents in the home of grandparents or other relatives, with or without a change of legal custody. (544)

laboratory observation Research method in which all participants are observed under the same controlled conditions. (39)

language Communication system based on words and grammar. (163)

language acquisition device (LAD) In Chomsky's terminology, an inborn mechanism that enables children to infer linguistic rules from the language they hear. (169)

lateralization Tendency of each of the brain's hemispheres to have specialized functions. (119)

learning disabilities (LDs) Disorders that interfere with specific aspects of learning and school achievement. (314)

learning perspective View of human development which holds that changes in behavior result from experience or from adaptation to the environment. (28)

life expectancy Age to which a person in a particular cohort is statistically likely to live (given his or her current age and health status), on the basis of average longevity of a population. (552)

life review Reminiscence about one's life in order to see its significance. (642)

life span The longest period that members of a species can live. (552)

life-span development Concept of human development as a lifelong process, which can be studied scientifically. (4)

life structure In Levinson's theory, the underlying pattern of a person's life at a given time, built on whatever aspects of life the person finds most important. (457)

linguistic speech Verbal expression designed to convey meaning. (166)

literacy (1) Ability to read and write. (172) (2) In an adult, ability to use printed and written information to function in society, achieve goals, and develop knowledge and potential. (511)

longevity Length of an individual's life. (552)

longitudinal study Study designed to assess age changes in a sample over time. (46)

long-term memory Storage of virtually unlimited capacity that holds information for long periods. (237)

low birth weight Weight of less than 5½ pounds (2,500 grams) at birth because of prematurity or being small for date. (106)

mammography Diagnostic X-ray examination of the breasts. (497)

marital capital Financial and emotional benefits built up during a long-standing marriage, which tend to hold a couple together. (533)

maturation Unfolding of a natural sequence of physical and behavioral changes. (10)

mechanistic model Model that views human development as a series of predictable responses to stimuli. (23)

menarche Girl's first menstruation. (359)

menopause Cessation of menstruation and of ability to bear children. (487)

mental retardation Significantly subnormal cognitive functioning. (313)

metabolism Conversion of food and oxygen into energy. (556)

metacognition Awareness of a person's own mental processes. (309)

metamemory Understanding of processes of memory. (298)

midlife crisis In some normative-crisis models, stressful life period precipitated by the review and reevaluation of one's past, typically occurring in the early to middle forties. (522)

midlife review Introspective examination that often occurs in middle age, leading to reappraisal and revision of values and priorities. (523)

mnemonic strategies Techniques to aid memory. (298)

monozygotic twins Twins resulting from the division of a single zygote after fertilization; also called *identical twins;* they are genetically similar. (55)

moratorium Identity status, described by Marcia, in which a person is currently considering alternatives (in crisis) and seems headed for commitment. (393)

multifactorial transmission Combination of genetic and environmental factors to produce certain complex traits. (60)

mutations Permanent alterations in genes or chromosomes that may produce harmful characteristics. (59)

mutual regulation Process by which infant and caregiver communicate emotional states to each other and respond appropriately. (195)

myelination Process of coating neural pathways with a fatty substance, myelin, that enables faster communication between cells. (122)

myopia Nearsightedness. (484)

nativism Theory that human beings have an inborn capacity for language acquisition. (169)

natural childbirth Method of childbirth that seeks to prevent pain by eliminating the mother's fear through education about the physiology of reproduction and training in breathing and relaxation during delivery. (99)

naturalistic observation Research method in which behavior is studied in natural settings without intervention or manipulation. (39)

neglect Failure to meet a dependent's basic needs. (207)

neonatal jaundice Condition, in many newborn babies, caused by immaturity of liver and evidenced by yellowish appearance; can cause brain damage if not treated promptly. (102)

neonatal period First 4 weeks of life, a time of transition from intrauterine dependency to independent existence. (101)

neonate Newborn baby, up to 4 weeks old. (101)

neurofibrillary tangles Twisted masses of protein fibers found in brains of persons with Alzheimer's disease. (571)

neurons Nerve cells. (120)

niche-picking Tendency of a person, especially after early childhood, to seek out environments compatible with his or her genotype. (71)

nonnormative Characteristic of an unusual event that happens to a particular person or a typical event that happens at an unusual time of life. (15)

nonshared environmental effects The unique environment in which each child grows up, consisting of distinctive influences or influences that affect one child differently than another. (72)

normative Characteristic of an event that occurs in a similar way for most people in a group. (14)

normative life events In the timing-of-events model, commonly expected life experiences that occur at customary times. (458)

normative-stage models Theoretical models that describe psychosocial development in terms of a definite sequence of age-related changes. (456)

nuclear family Two-generational kinship, economic, and household unit consisting of one or two parents and their biological children, adopted children, or stepchildren. (10)

obesity Extreme overweight in relation to age, sex, height, and body type. (73)

object permanence Piaget's term for the understanding that a person or object still exists when out of sight. (151)

observational learning Learning through watching the behavior of others. (30)

obsessive-compulsive disorder (OCD) Anxiety aroused by repetitive, intrusive thoughts, images, or impulses, often leading to compulsive ritual behaviors. (344)

operant conditioning (1) Learning based on association of behavior with its consequences. (29) (2) Learning based on reinforcement or punishment. (141)

operational definition Definition stated solely in terms of the operations or procedures used to produce or measure a phenomenon. (40)

oppositional defiant disorder (ODD) Pattern of behavior, persisting into middle childhood, marked by negativity, hostility, and defiance. (343)

organismic model Model that views human development as internally initiated by an active organism and as occurring in a sequence of qualitatively different stages. (23)

organization (1) Piaget's term for the creation of categories or systems of knowledge. (31) Mnemonic strategy of categorizing material to be remembered. (298)

osteoporosis Condition in which the bones become thin and brittle as a result of rapid calcium depletion. (495)

Otis-Lennon School Ability Test (OLSAT8) Group intelligence test for kindergarten through twelfth grade. (300)

overt aggression Aggression that is openly directed at its target. (275)

palliative care Care aimed at relieving pain and suffering and allowing the terminally ill to die in peace, comfort, and dignity. Also called *comfort care*. (620)

Parkinson's disease Progressive, irreversible, degenerative neurological disorder characterized by tremor, stiffness, slowed movement, and unstable posture. (570)

participant observation Research method in which the observer lives with the people or participates in the activity being observed. (41)

parturition Process of uterine, cervical, and other changes, usually lasting about two weeks, preceding childbirth. (97)

passive euthanasia Deliberate withholding or discontinuation of life-prolonging treatment of a terminally ill person in order to end suffering or allow death with dignity. (637)

perimenopause Period of several years during which a woman experiences physiological changes of menopause; includes first year after end of menstruation; also called *climacteric*. (487)

permissive parenting In Baumrind's terminology, parenting style emphasizing self-expression and self-regulation. (272)

personality The relatively consistent blend of emotions, temperament, thought, and behavior that makes a person unique. (178)

phenotype Observable characteristics of a person. (60)

phonetic (code-emphasis) approach Approach to teaching reading that emphasizes decoding of unfamiliar words. (308)

physical abuse Action taken deliberately to endanger another person, involving potential bodily injury. (207)

physical development Growth of body and brain, including patterns of change in sensory capacities, motor skills, and health. (5)

Piagetian approach Approach to the study of cognitive development that describes qualitative stages in cognitive functioning. (140)

plasticity (1) Range of modifiability of performance. (17) (2) Modifiability, or "molding," of the brain through experience. (127)

play therapy Therapeutic approach that uses play to help a child cope with emotional distress. (346)

polygenic inheritance Pattern of inheritance in which multiple genes at different sites on chromosomes affect a complex trait. (59)

postconventional morality (or morality of autonomous moral principles) Third level of Kohlberg's theory of moral reasoning, in which people follow internally held moral principles and can decide among conflicting moral standards. (375)

postformal thought Mature type of thinking that relies on subjective experience and intuition as well as logic and is useful in dealing with ambiguity, uncertainty, inconsistency, contradiction, imperfection, and compromise. (435)

postmature Referring to a fetus not yet born as of 2 weeks after the due date or 42 weeks after the mother's last menstrual period. (108)

power assertion Disciplinary strategy designed to discourage undesirable behavior through physical or verbal enforcement of parental control. (271)

pragmatics (1) The practical knowledge needed to use language for communicative purposes. (243) (2) Set of linguistic rules that govern the use of language for communication. (306)

preconventional morality First level of Kohlberg's theory of moral reasoning, in which control is external and rules are obeyed in order to gain rewards or avoid punishment or out of self-interest. (375)

prejudice Unfavorable attitude toward members of certain groups outside one's own, especially racial or ethnic groups. (335)

prelinguistic speech Forerunner of linguistic speech; utterance of sounds that are not words. Includes crying, cooing, babbling, and accidental and deliberate imitation of sounds without understanding their meaning. (163)

premenstrual syndrome (PMS) Disorder producing symptoms of physical discomfort and emotional tension for up to two weeks before a menstrual period. (432)

preoperational stage In Piaget's theory, the second major stage of cognitive development, in which symbolic thought expands but children cannot yet use logic. (228)

prepared childbirth Method of childbirth that uses instruction, breathing exercises, and social support to induce controlled physical responses to uterine contractions and reduce fear and pain. (99)

presbycusis Age-related, gradual loss of hearing, which accelerates after age 55, especially with regard to sounds at higher frequencies. (484)

presbyopia Age-related, progressive loss of the eyes' ability to focus on nearby objects due to loss of elasticity in the lens. (484)

pretend play Play involving imaginary people and situations; also called *fantasy play, dramatic play,* or *imaginative play.* (229)

preterm (premature) infants Infants born before completing the 37th week of gestation. (105)

primary aging Gradual, inevitable process of bodily deterioration throughout the life span. (552)

primary sex characteristics Organs directly related to reproduction, which enlarge and mature during adolescence. (357)

private speech Talking aloud to oneself with no intent to communicate with others. (243)

problem-focused coping In the cognitive-appraisal model, coping strategy directed toward eliminating, managing, or improving a stressful situation. (590)

procedural knowledge Acquired skills stored in long-term memory. (374)

procedural memory Long-term memory of motor skills, habits, and ways of doing things, which can be recalled without conscious awareness; sometimes called *implicit memory.* (578)

prosocial behavior Any voluntary behavior intended to help others. (274)

protective factors Influences that reduce the impact of potentially negative influences, such as stress, and tend to predict positive outcomes. (110, 349)

proximodistal principle Principle that development proceeds from within to without, that is, that parts of the body near the center develop before the extremities. (114)

psychoanalytic perspective View of human development as being shaped by unconscious forces. (25)

psychological aggression Verbal attacks on a child by a parent that may result in psychological harm. (271)

psychometric approach Approach to the study of cognitive development that seeks to measure the quantity of intelligence a person possesses. (140)

psychosexual development In Freudian theory, an unvarying sequence of stages of childhood personality development in which gratification shifts from the mouth to the anus and then to the genitals. (26)

psychosocial development (1) Pattern of change in emotions, personality, and social relationships. (6) (2) In Erikson's eight-stage theory, the socially and culturally influenced process of development of the ego, or self. (28)

puberty Process by which a person attains sexual maturity and the ability to reproduce. (354)

punishment In operant conditioning, a process that weakens and discourages repetition of a behavior. (29)

qualitative change Change in kind, structure, or organization, such as the change from nonverbal to verbal communication. (24)

qualitative research Research that focuses on nonnumerical data, such as subjective experiences, feelings, or beliefs. (37)

quantitative change Change in number or amount, such as in height, weight, or the size of vocabulary. (24)

quantitative research Research that deals with objectively measurable data. (37)

random assignment Assignment of participants in an experiment to groups in such a way that each person has an equal chance of being placed in any group. (44)

random selection Selection of a sample in such a way that each person in a population has an equal and independent chance of being chosen. (37)

reaction range Potential variability, depending on environmental conditions, in the expression of a hereditary trait. (69)

real self The self one actually is. (253)

recall Ability to reproduce material from memory. (237)

recentering Process that underlies the shift to an adult identity. (453)

receptive cooperation Kochanska's term for eager willingness to cooperate harmoniously with a parent in daily interactions, including routines, chores, hygiene, and play. (201)

recessive inheritance Pattern of inheritance in which a child receives identical recessive alleles, resulting in expression of a nondominant trait. (59)

reciprocal determinism Bandura's term for bidirectional forces that affect development. (30)

recognition Ability to identify a previously encountered stimulus. (237)

reflective thinking Type of logical thinking that may emerge in adulthood, involving continuous, active evaluation of information and beliefs in the light of evidence and implications. (435)

reflex behaviors Automatic, involuntary, innate responses to stimulation. (124)

rehearsal Mnemonic strategy to keep an item in working memory through conscious repetition. (298)

reinforcement In operant conditioning, a process that strengthens and encourages repetition of a desired behavior. (29)

relational (social) aggression Aggression aimed at damaging or interfering with another person's relationships, reputation, or psychological well-being. (275)

representational ability Piaget's term for capacity to store mental images or symbols of objects and events. (149)

representational mappings In neo-Piagetian terminology, second stage in development of self-definition, in which a child makes logical connections between aspects of the self but still sees these characteristics in all-or-nothing terms. (253)

representational systems   In neo-Piagetian terminology, the third stage in development of self-definition, characterized by breadth, balance, and the integration and assessment of various aspects of the self. (322)

reserve capacity   Ability of body organs and systems to put forth four to ten times as much effort as usual under acute stress; also called *organ reserve*. (560)

resilient children   Children who weather adverse circumstances, function well despite challenges or threats, or bounce back from traumatic events. (349)

retrieval   Process by which information is accessed or recalled from memory storage. (236)

revolving door syndrome   Tendency for young adults who have left home to return to their parents' household in times of financial, marital, or other trouble. (538)

risk factors   Conditions that increase the likelihood of a negative developmental outcome. (12)

rough-and-tumble play   Vigorous play involving wrestling, hitting, and chasing, often accompanied by laughing and screaming. (287)

sample   Group of participants chosen to represent the entire population under study. (37)

sandwich generation   Middle-aged adults squeezed by competing needs to raise or launch children and to care for elderly parents. (540)

scaffolding   Temporary support to help a child master a task. (33, 241)

schemes   Piaget's term for organized patterns of thought and behavior used in particular situations. (31, 147)

schizophrenia   Mental disorder marked by loss of contact with reality; symptoms include hallucinations and delusions. (74)

school phobia   Unrealistic fear of going to school; may be a form of *separation anxiety disorder* or *social phobia*. (344)

scientific method   System of established principles and processes of scientific inquiry, which includes identifying a problem to be studied, formulating a hypothesis to be tested by research, collecting data, analyzing the data, forming tentative conclusions, and disseminating findings. (37)

script   General remembered outline of a familiar, repeated event, used to guide behavior. (238)

secondary aging   Aging processes that result from disease and bodily abuse and disuse and are often preventable. (552)

secondary sex characteristics   Physiological signs of sexual maturation (such as breast development and growth of body hair) that do not involve the sex organs. (357)

secular trend   Trend that can be seen only by observing several generations, such as the trend toward earlier attainment of adult height and sexual maturity, which began a century ago in some countries. (359)

secure attachment   Pattern in which an infant cries or protests when the primary caregiver leaves and actively seeks out the caregiver on his or her return. (190)

selective optimization with compensation (SOC)   Enhancing overall cognitive functioning by using stronger abilities to compensate for those that have weakened. (594)

self-awareness   Realization that one's existence and functioning are separate from those of other people and things. (180)

self-concept   Sense of self; descriptive and evaluative mental picture of one's abilities and traits. (197, 252)

self-conscious emotions   Emotions, such as embarrassment, empathy, and envy, that depend on self-awareness. (180)

self-definition   Cluster of characteristics used to describe oneself. (252)

self-efficacy   Sense of one's capability to master challenges and achieve goals. (30)

self-esteem   The judgment a person makes about his or her self-worth. (253)

self-evaluative emotions   Emotions, such as pride, shame, and guilt, that depend on both self-awareness and knowledge of socially accepted standards of behavior. (180)

self-regulation   A child's independent control of behavior to conform to understood social expectations. (199)

semantic memory   Long-term memory of general factual knowledge, social customs, and language. (578)

senescence   Period of the life span marked by declines in physical functioning usually associated with aging; begins at varying ages. (555)

sensitive periods   Times in development when a person is particularly open to certain kinds of experiences. (17)

sensorimotor stage   Piaget's first stage of cognitive development, in which infants learn through senses and motor activity. (146)

sensory memory   Initial, brief, temporary storage of sensory information. (237, 577)

separation anxiety   Distress shown by someone, typically an infant, when a familiar caregiver leaves. (192)

separation anxiety disorder   Condition involving excessive, prolonged anxiety concerning separation from home or from people to whom a person is attached. (344)

sequential study   Study design that combines cross-sectional and longitudinal techniques. (47)

seriation   Ability to order items along a dimension. (293)

serious leisure   Leisure activity requiring skill, attention, and commitment. (597)

sex chromosomes   Pair of chromosomes that determines sex: XX in the normal human female, XY in the normal human male. (57)

sex-linked inheritance   Pattern of inheritance in which certain characteristics carried on the X chromosome inherited from the mother are transmitted differently to her male and female offspring. (63)

sexual abuse   Physically or psychologically harmful sexual activity or any sexual activity involving a child and an older person. (207)

sexually transmitted diseases (STDs)   Diseases spread by sexual contact. (399)

sexual orientation   Focus of consistent sexual, romantic, and affectionate interest, either heterosexual, homosexual, or bisexual. (396)

shaken baby syndrome (SBS)   Form of maltreatment in which shaking an infant or toddler can cause brain damage, paralysis, or death. (208)

single representations   In neo-Piagetian terminology, first stage in development of self-definition, in which children describe themselves in terms of individual, unconnected characteristics and in all-or-nothing terms. (253)

situational compliance   Kochanska's term for obedience of a parent's orders only in the presence of signs of ongoing parental control. (201)

"slow-to-warm-up" children   Children whose temperament is generally mild but who are hesitant about accepting new experiences. (183)

small-for-date (small-for-gestational-age) infants   Infants whose birth weight is less than that of 90 percent of babies of the same gestational age, as a result of slow fetal growth. (105)

social capital Family and community resources on which a person can draw. (311)

social clock Set of cultural norms or expectations for the times of life when certain important events, such as marriage, parenthood, entry into work, and retirement, should occur. (458)

social cognitive theory Albert Bandura's expansion of social learning theory; holds that children learn gender roles through socialization. (262)

social construction A concept or practice that may appear natural and obvious to those who accept it, but that in reality is an invention of a particular culture or society. (6)

social-contextual approach Approach to the study of cognitive development that focuses on environmental influences, particularly parents and other caregivers. (140)

social convoy theory Theory, proposed by Kahn and Antonucci, that people move through life surrounded by concentric circles of intimate relationships on which they rely for assistance, well-being, and social support. (530)

social interaction model Model, based on Vygotsky's sociocultural theory, which proposes that children construct autobiographical memories through conversation with adults about shared events. (238)

socialization Development of habits, skills, values, and motives shared by responsible, productive members of a society. (199)

social learning theory Theory that behaviors are learned by observing and imitating models. Also called *social cognitive theory.* (30)

social phobia Extreme fear and/or avoidance of social situations. (344)

social referencing Understanding an ambiguous situation by seeking another person's perception of it. (195)

social speech Speech intended to be understood by a listener. (243)

sociocultural theory Vygotsky's theory of how contextual factors affect children's development. (32)

socioeconomic status (SES) Combination of economic and social factors describing an individual or family, including income, education, and occupation. (11)

socioemotional selectivity theory Theory, proposed by Carstensen, that

people select social contacts on the basis of the changing relative importance of social interaction as a source of information, as an aid in developing and maintaining a self-concept, and as a source of emotional well-being. (531)

spermarche Boy's first ejaculation. (359)

spillover hypothesis Hypothesis that a positive correlation exists between intellectuality of work and of leisure activities because of a carryover of cognitive gains from work to leisure. (447)

spontaneous abortion Natural expulsion from the uterus of an embryo that cannot survive outside the womb; also called *miscarriage.* (80)

Stanford-Binet Intelligence Scales Individual intelligence tests for age 2 and up used to measure fluid reasoning, knowledge, quantitative reasoning, visual-spatial processing, and working memory. (240)

state of arousal An infant's physiological and behavioral status at a given moment in the periodic daily cycle of wakefulness, sleep, and activity. (104)

Sternberg Triarchic Abilities Test (STAT) Test that seeks to measure componential, experiential, and contextual intelligence. (304)

stillbirth Death of a fetus at or after the 20th week of gestation. (108)

storage Retention of information in memory for future use. (236)

stranger anxiety Wariness of strange people and places, shown by some infants during the second half of the first year. (192)

Strange Situation Laboratory technique used to study infant attachment. (189)

stress Response to physical or psychological demands on a person or organism. (87, 498)

stressors Perceived environmental demands that may produce stress. (498)

substance abuse Repeated, harmful use of a substance, usually alcohol or other drugs. (366)

substance dependence Addiction (physical, or psychological, or both) to a harmful substance. (366)

substantive complexity Degree to which a person's work requires thought and independent judgment. (447)

sudden infant death syndrome (SIDS) Sudden and unexplained death of an apparently healthy infant. (112)

survival curves Curves, plotted on a graph, showing percentages of a population that survive at each age level. (558)

symbolic function Piaget's term for ability to use mental representations (words, numbers, or images) to which a child has attached meaning. (229)

syntax Rules for forming sentences in a particular language. (167)

systems of action Increasingly complex combinations of motor skills, which permit a wider or more precise range of movement and more control of the environment. (130, 221)

tacit knowledge Sternberg's term for information that is not formally taught or openly expressed but is necessary to get ahead. (304)

telegraphic speech Early form of sentence use consisting of only a few essential words. (167)

temperament Characteristic disposition, or style of approaching and reacting to situations. (74, 182)

teratogenic Capable of causing birth defects. (82)

terminal drop A frequently observed decline in cognitive abilities near the end of life. Also called *terminal decline.* (622)

thanatology Study of death and dying. (620)

theory Coherent set of logically related concepts that seeks to organize, explain, and predict data. (22)

theory of mind Awareness and understanding of mental processes. (233)

theory of multiple intelligences Gardner's theory that each person has several distinct forms of intelligence. (303)

theory of sexual selection Darwin's theory that gender roles developed in response to men's and women's differing reproductive needs. (259)

timing-of-events model Theoretical model of personality development that describes adult psychosocial development as a response to the expected or unexpected occurrence and timing of important life events. (458)

trait models Theoretical models of personality development that focus on mental, emotional, temperamental, and behavioral traits, or attributes. (458)

transduction Piaget's term for a preoperational child's tendency to mentally link particular phenomena, whether or not there is logically a causal relationship. (230)

transitive inference Understanding of the relationship between two objects by knowing the relationship of each to a third object. (293)

triangular theory of love Sternberg's theory that patterns of love hinge on the balance among three elements: intimacy, passion, and commitment. (462)

triarchic theory of intelligence Sternberg's theory describing three elements of intelligence: componential, experiential, and contextual. (303)

two-way (dual-language) learning Approach to second-language education in which English speakers and non-English speakers learn together in their own and each other's languages. (307)

typological approach Theoretical approach that identifies broad personality types, or styles. (460)

ultrasound Prenatal medical procedure using high-frequency sound waves to detect the outline of a fetus and its movements, so as to determine whether a pregnancy is progressing normally. (80)

variable-rate theories Theories that explain biological aging as a result of processes that vary from person to person and are influenced by both the internal and the external environment; sometimes called *error theories.* (556)

violation-of-expectations Research method in which dishabituation to a stimulus that conflicts with experience is taken as evidence that an infant recognizes the new stimulus as surprising. (160)

visible imitation Imitation with parts of one's body that one can see. (150)

visual cliff Apparatus designed to give an illusion of depth and used to assess depth perception in infants. (133)

visual guidance Use of the eyes to guide movements of the hands or other parts of the body. (132)

visually based retrieval Process of retrieving the sound of a printed word when seeing the word as a whole. (308)

visual preference Tendency of infants to spend more time looking at one sight than another. (155)

visual recognition memory Ability to distinguish a familiar visual stimulus from an unfamiliar one when shown both at the same time. (155)

vital capacity Amount of air that can be drawn in with a deep breath and expelled. (486)

Wechsler Adult Intelligence Scale (WAIS) Intelligence test for adults, which yields verbal and performance scores as well as a combined score. (574)

Wechsler Intelligence Scale for Children (WISC-III) Individual intelligence test for school-age children, which yields verbal and performance scores as well as a combined score. (300)

Wechsler Preschool and Primary Scale of Intelligence, Revised (WPPSI-III) Individual intelligence test for children ages 2½ to 7 that yields verbal and performance scores as well as a combined score. (240)

whole-language approach Approach to teaching reading that emphasizes visual retrieval and use of contextual clues. (308)

withdrawal of love Disciplinary strategy that involves ignoring, isolating, or showing dislike for a child. (271)

working memory Short-term storage of information being actively processed. (161, 237, 577)

zone of proximal development (ZPD) Vygotsky's term for the difference between what a child can do alone and what the child can do with help. (32, 241)

zygote One-celled organism resulting from fertilization. (54)

Bibliography

Aaron, V., Parker, K. D., Ortega, S., & Calhoun, T. (1999). The extended family as a source of support among African Americans. *Challenge: A Journal of Research on African American Men, 10*(2), 23–36.

Abbott, R. D., White, L. R., Ross, G. W., Masaki, K. H., Curb, J. D., & Petrovitch, H. (2004). Walking and dementia in physically capable elderly men. *Journal of the American Medical Association, 292,* 1447–1453.

Abel, E. K. (1991). *Who cares for the elderly?* Philadelphia: Temple University Press.

Aber, J. L., Brown, J. L., & Jones, S. M. (2003). Developmental trajectories toward violence in middle childhood: Course, demographic differences, and response to school-based intervention. *Developmental Psychology, 39,* 324–348.

Abma, J. C., Chandra, A., Mosher, W. D., Peterson, L., & Piccinino, L. (1997). Fertility, family planning, and women's health: New data from the 1995 National Survey of Family Growth. *Vital Health Statistics, 23*(19), Washington, DC: National Center for Health Statistics.

Abma, J. C., Martinez, G. M., Mosher, W. D., & Dawson, B. S. (2004). Teenagers in the United States: Sexual activity, contraceptive use, and childbearing, 2002. *Vital Health Statistics, 23*(24). Washington, DC: National Center for Health Statistics.

Aboa-Eboulé, C., Brisson, C., Maunsell, E., Mâsse, B., Bourbonnais, R., Vézina, M., Milot, A., Théroux, P., & Dagenais, G. R. (2007). Job strain and risk of acute recurrent coronary heart disease events. *Journal of the American Medical Association, 298,* 1652–1660.

Abramovitch, R., Corter, C., & Lando, B. (1979). Sibling interaction in the home. *Child Development, 50,* 997–1003.

Abramovitch, R., Corter, C., Pepler, D., & Stanhope, L. (1986). Sibling and peer interactions: A final follow-up and comparison. *Child Development, 57,* 217–229.

Abramovitch, R., Pepler, D., & Corter, C. (1982). Patterns of sibling interaction among preschool-age children. In M. E. Lamb (Ed.), *Sibling relationships: Their nature and significance across the lifespan.* Hillsdale, NJ: Erlbaum.

Abramson, T. A. (1995, Fall). From non-normative to normative caregiving. *Dimensions: Newsletter of American Society on Aging,* pp. 1–2.

Achenbaum, W. A., & Bengtson, V. L. (1994). Re-engaging the disengagement theory of aging: On the history and assessment of theory development in gerontology. *Gerontologist, 34,* 756–763.

Achter, J. A., & Lubinski, D. (2003). Fostering exceptional development in intellectually talented populations. In W. B. Walsh (Ed.), *Counseling psychology and optimal human functioning* (pp. 279–296). Mahwah, NJ: Erlbaum.

Ackerman, B. P., Kogos, J., Youngstrom, E., Schoff, K., & Izard, C. (1999). Family instability and the problem behaviors of children from economically disadvantaged families. *Developmental Psychology, 35*(1), 258–268.

Ackerman, M. J., Siu, B. L., Sturner, W. Q., Tester D. J., Valdivia, C. R., Makielski, J. C., & Towbin, J. A. (2001). Postmortem molecular analysis of SCN5A defects in sudden infant death syndrome. *Journal of the American Medical Association, 286,* 2264–2269.

Acosta, M. T., Arcos-Burgos, M., & Muenke, M. (2004). Attention deficit/hyperactivity disorder (ADHD): Complex phenotype, simple genotype? *Genetics in Medicine, 6,* 1–15.

ACT for Youth Upstate Center of Excellence. (2002). Adolescent brain development. Research facts and findings. [A collaboration of Cornell University, University of Rochester, and the NYS Center for School Safety.] Retrieved March 23, 2004, from www.human.cornell.edu/actforyouth.

AD2000 Collaborative Group. (2004). Long-term donepezil treatment in 565 patients with Alzheimer's disease (AD2000): Randomized double-blind trial. *Lancet, 363,* 2105–2115.

Adam, E. K., Gunnar, M. R., & Tanaka, A. (2004). Adult attachment, parent emotion, and observed parenting behavior: Mediator and moderator models. *Child Development, 75,* 110–122.

Adams, B. N. (2004). Families and family study in international perspective. *Journal of Marriage and Family, 66,* 1076–1088.

Adams, C. (1991). Qualitative age differences in memory for text: A life-span developmental perspective. *Psychology and Aging, 6,* 323–336.

Adams, K. F., Schatzkin, A., Harris, T. B., Kipnis, V., Mouw, T., Ballard-Barbash, R., Hollenbeck, A., & Leitzmann, M. F. (2006). Overweight, obesity, and mortality in a large prospective cohort of persons 50 to 71 years old. *New England Journal of Medicine, 355,* 763–778.

Adams, L. A., & Rickert, V. I. (1989). Reducing bedtime tantrums: Comparison between positive routines and graduated extinction. *Pediatrics, 84,* 756–761.

Adams, R., & Laursen, B. (2001). The organization and dynamics of adolescent conflict with parents and friends. *Journal of Marriage and the Family, 63,* 97–110.

Adams, R. G. (1986). Friendship and aging. *Generations, 10*(4), 40–43.

Adams, R. G., & Allan, G. (1998). *Placing friendship in context.* Cambridge, MA: Cambridge University Press.

Addis, M. E., & Mahalik, J. R. (2003). Men, masculinity, and the contexts of help seeking. *American Psychologist, 58,* 5–14.

Ades, P. A., Ballor, D. L., Ashikaga, T., Utton, J. L., & Nair, K. S. (1996). Weight training improves walking endurance in healthy elderly persons. *Annals of Internal Medicine, 124,* 568–572.

Administration for Children and Families. (2006a). *FACES 2003 Research Brief and Program Quality in Head Start.* Washington, DC: Author.

Administration for Children and Families. (2006b). *FACES findings: New research on Head Start outcomes and program quality.* Washington, DC: Author.

Administration on Aging. (2003, August 27). *Challenges of global aging* [Fact sheet]. Washington, DC: U.S. Department of Health and Human Services.

Adminstration on Aging. (2006). *A profile of older Americans: 2006.* Washington, DC: U.S. Department of Health and Human Services.

Adolph, K. E. (1997). Learning in the development of infant locomotion. *Monographs of the Society for Research in Child Development, 62*(3), Serial No. 251.

Adolph, K. E. (2000). Specificity of learning: Why infants fall over a veritable cliff. *Psychological Science, 11,* 290–295.

Adolph, K. E., & Eppler, M. A. (2002). Flexibility and specificity in infant motor skill acquisition. In J. Fagen & H. Hayne (Eds.), *Progress in infancy research* (Vol. 2, pp. 121–167). Mahwah, NJ: Erlbaum.

Adolph, K. E., Vereijken, B., & Shrout, P. E. (2003). What changes in infant walking and why. *Child Development, 74,* 475–497.

Agahi, N., Ahacic, K., & Parker, M. G. (2006). Continuity of leisure participation from middle age to old age. *Journal of Gerontology: Social Sciences, 61*B, S340–S346.

Agence France-Presse. (2005, March 21). Euthanasia in Europe: How it works. *Free New Mexican.* Retrieved June 26, 2007, from www.freenewmexican.com/story_print.php?storyid=11769.

Agency for Healthcare Research and Quality and the Centers for Disease Control. (2002). *Physical activity and older Americans: Benefits and strategies.* Retrieved from www.ahrq.gov/ppip/activity.htm.

Agoda, L. (1995). Minorities and ESRD. Review: African American study of kidney disease and hypertension clinical trials. *Nephrology News & Issues, 9,* 18–19.

Ahnert, L., Gunnar, M. R., Lamb, M. E., & Barthel, M. (2004). Transition to child care: Associations with infant-mother attachment, infant negative emotion and corticol elevation. *Child Development, 75,* 639–650.

Ahnert, L., & Lamb, M. E. (2003). Shared care: Establishing a balance between home and child care settings. *Child Development, 74,* 1044–1049.

Ahrons, C. R., & Tanner, J. L. (2003). Adult children and their fathers: Relationship changes 20 years after parental divorce. *Family Relations, 52,* 340–351.

Ainsworth, M. D. S. (1967). *Infancy in Uganda: Infant care and the growth of love.* Baltimore: Johns Hopkins University Press.

Ainsworth, M. D. S., Blehar, M. C., Waters, E., & Wall, S. (1978). *Patterns of attachment: A psychological study of the strange situation.* Hillsdale, NJ: Erlbaum.

Akinbami, L. (2006). The state of childhood asthma, United States, 1980–2005. *Advance Data from Vital and Health Statistics, 381.* Hyattsville, MD: National Center for Health Statistics.

Akutsu, H., Legge, G. E., Ross, J. A., & Schuebel, K. J. (1991). Psychophysics of reading: Effects of age-related changes in vision. *Journal of Gerontology: Psychological Sciences, 46*(6), P325–P331.

Alaimo, K., Olson, C. M., & Frongillo, E. A. (2001). Food insufficiency and American school-aged children's cognitive, academic, and psychosocial development. *Pediatrics, 108,* 44–53.

Alan Guttmacher Institute (AGI). (1994). *Sex & America's teenagers.* New York: Author.

Alan Guttmacher Institute (AGI). (1999). *Facts in brief: Teen sex and pregnancy.* Retrieved January 31, 2000, from www.agi_usa.org/pubs/fb_teen_sex.html#sfd.

Alati, R., Al Mamun, A., Williams, G. M., O'Callaghan, M., Najman, J. M., & Bor, W. (2006). In utero alcohol exposure and prediction of alcohol disorders in early adulthood: A birth cohort study. *Archives of General Psychiatry, 63*(9), 1009–1016.

Aldwin, C. M., & Levenson, M. R. (2001). Stress, coping, and health at midlife: A developmental perspective. In M. E. Lachman (Ed.), *Handbook of midlife development* (pp. 188–214). New York: Wiley.

Alexander, K. L., Entwisle, D. R., & Dauber, S. L. (1993). First-grade classroom behavior: Its short- and long-term consequences for school performance. *Child Development, 64,* 801–814.

Alexander, K. L., Entwisle, D. R., & Olson, L. S. (2007). Lasting consequences of the summer learning gap. *American Sociological Review, 72,* 167–180.

Alfred, Lord Tennyson. (1850). "In Memoriam A. H. H., Canto 54."

Alipuria, L. (2002). Ethnic, racial, and cultural identity/self: An integrated theory of identity/self in relation to large-scale social cleavages. *Dissertation Abstracts International, 63B,* 583. (UMI No. 3039092).

Allen, G. L., & Ondracek, P. J. (1995). Age-sensitive cognitive abilities related to children's acquisition of spatial knowledge. *Developmental Psychology, 31,* 934–945.

Allen, J. E., & Seaman, J. (2007). *Online nation: Five years of growth in online learning.* Needham, MA: Sloan Consortium.

Allen, J. P., McElhaney, K. B., Land, D. J., Kuperminc, G. P., Moore, C. W., O'Beirner-Kelly, H., & Kilmer, S. L. (2003). A secure base in adolescence: Markers of attachment security in the mother-adolescent relationship. *Child Development, 74,* 292–307.

Allen, J. P., & Philliber, S. (2001). Who benefits most from a broadly targeted prevention program? Differential efficacy across populations in the Teen Outreach Program. *Journal of Community Psychology, 29,* 637–655.

Allen, J. P., Porter, M. R., McFarland, F. C., Marsh, P., & McElhaney, K. B. (2005). The two faces of adolescents' success with peers: Adolescent popularity, social adaptation, and deviant behavior. *Child Development, 76*(3), 747–760.

Allen, K. R., Blieszner, R., & Roberto, K. A. (2000). Families in the middle and later years: A review and critique of research in the 1990s. *Journal of Marriage and Family, 62,* 911–926.

Alliance for a Healthier Generation. (2007). *Facts and figures.* Retrieved December 13, 2007, from www.healthiergeneration.org/about.aspx?id=316&ekmensel=1ef02451_48_52_btnlink.

Almeida, D. M., & Horn, M. C. (2004). Is daily life more stressful during adulthood? In O. G. Brim, C. D. Riff, & R. C. Kessler (Eds.). *How healthy are we? A national study of well-being at midlife.* Chicago: University of Chicago Press.

Almeida, D. M., Serido, J., & McDonald, D. (2006). Daily life stressors of early and late baby boomers. In S. K. Whitbourne & S. L. Willis (Eds.), *The baby boomers grow up: Contemporary perspectives on midlife* (pp. 165–183). Mahwah, NJ: Erlbaum.

Als, H., Duffy, F. H., McAnulty, G. B., Rivkin, M. J., Vajapeyam, S., Mulkern, R. V., Warfield, S. K., Huppi, P. S., Butler, S. C., Conneman, N., Fischer, C., and Eichenwald, E. C. (2004). Early experience alters brain function and structure. *Pediatrics, 113,* 846–857.

Altarac, M., & Saroha, E. (2007). Lifetime prevalence of learning disabilities among U.S. children. *Pediatrics, 119*(Suppl. 1), S77–S83.

Altschul, I., Oyserman, D., & Bybee, D. (2006). Racial-ethnic identity in mid-adolescence: Content and change as predictors of academic achievement. *Child Development, 77,* 1155–1169.

Alzheimer's Association. (2007). *Alzheimer's disease: Facts and Figures.* Chicago: Author.

Alzheimer's Association. (n.d.). *Is it Alzheimer's? Warning signs you should know.* Chicago: Author.

Alzheimer's Disease: The search for causes and treatments—Part I. (1998, August). *Harvard Mental Health Letter, 15*(2).

Amato, P. R. (2000). The consequences of divorce for adults and children. *Journal of Marriage and Family, 62,* 1269–1287.

Amato, P. R. (2003). Reconciling divergent perspectives: Judith Wallerstein, quantitative family research, and children of divorce. *Family Relations, 52,* 332–339.

Amato, P. R. (2005). The impact of family formation change on the cognitive, social, and emotional well-being of the next generation. *Future of Children, 15,* 75–96.

Amato, P. R., & Afifi, T. D. (2006). Feeling caught between parents: Adult children's relations with parents and subjective well-being. *Journal of Marriage and Family, 68,* 222–235.

Amato, P. R., & Booth, A. (1997). *A generation at risk: Growing up in an era of family upheaval.* Cambridge, MA: Harvard University Press.

Amato, P. R., & Gilbreth, J. G. (1999). Nonresident fathers and children's well-being: A meta-analysis. *Journal of Marriage and Family, 61,* 557–573.

Amato, P. R., Johnson, D. R., Booth, A., & Rogers, S. J. (2003). Continuity and change in marital quality between 1980 and 2000. *Journal of Marriage and Family, 65,* 1–22.

American Academy of Child & Adolescent Psychiatry (AACAP). (1997). *Children's sleep problems* [Fact Sheet No. 34].

American Academy of Child & Adolescent Psychiatry. (2003). Talking to children about terrorism and war. *Facts for Families* #87. Retrieved April 22, 2005, from www.aacap.org/publications/factsfam/87.htm.

American Academy of Pediatrics (AAP). (1986). *Positive approaches to day care dilemmas: How to make it work.* Elk Grove Village, IL: Author.

American Academy of Pediatrics (AAP). (1992, Spring). Bedtime doesn't have to be a struggle. *Healthy Kids,* pp. 4–10.

American Academy of Pediatrics (AAP). (2000). *Shaken baby syndrome.* Retrieved February 17, 2007, from www.medem.com/search/article_display.cfm?path=\\TANQUERAY\M_ContentItem&mstr=/M_ContentItem/ZZZM8JMMH4C.html&soc=AAP&srch_typ=NAV_SERCH.

American Academy of Pediatrics (AAP). (2004, September 30). American Academy of Pediatrics (AAP) supports Institute of Medicine's (IOM) childhood obesity recommendation [Press release].

American Academy of Pediatrics (AAP) and Canadian Paediatric Society. (2000). Prevention and management of pain and stress in the neonate. *Pediatrics, 105*(2), 454–461.

American Academy of Pediatrics (AAP) Committee on Accident and Poison Prevention. (1988). Snowmobile statement. *Pediatrics, 82,* 798–799.

American Academy of Pediatrics (AAP) Committee on Adolescence. (1994). Sexually transmitted diseases. *Pediatrics, 94,* 568–572.

American Academy of Pediatrics (AAP) Committee on Adolescence. (1999). Adolescent pregnancy—Current trends and issues: 1998. *Pediatrics, 103,* 516–520.

American Academy of Pediatrics (AAP) Committee on Adolescence. (2000). Suicide and suicide attempts in adolescents. *Pediatrics, 105*(4), 871–874.

American Academy of Pediatrics (AAP) Committee on Adolescence. (2001). Condom use by adolescents. *Pediatrics, 107*(6), 1463–1469.

American Academy of Pediatrics (AAP) Committee on Adolescence. (2003). Policy statement: Identifying and treating eating disorders. *Pediatrics, 111,* 204–211.

American Academy of Pediatrics (AAP) Committee on Adolescence and Committee on Early Childhood, Adoption, and Dependent Care. (2001). Care of adolescent parents and their children. *Pediatrics, 107,* 429–434.

American Academy of Pediatrics (AAP) Committee on Bioethics. (1992, July). Ethical issues in surrogate motherhood. *AAP News,* 14–15.

American Academy of Pediatrics (AAP) Committee on Bioethics. (2001). Ethical issues with genetic testing in pediatrics. *Pediatrics, 107*(6), 1451–1455.

American Academy of Pediatrics (AAP) Committee on Child Abuse and Neglect. (2001). Shaken baby syndrome: Rotational cranial injuries—technical report. *Pediatrics, 108,* 206–210.

American Academy of Pediatrics (AAP) Committee on Children with Disabilities and Committee on Drugs. (1996). Medication for children with attentional disorders. *Pediatrics, 98,* 301–304.

American Academy of Pediatrics (AAP) Committee on Drugs. (1994). The transfer of drugs and other chemicals into human milk. *Pediatrics, 93,* 137–150.

American Academy of Pediatrics (AAP) Committee on Drugs. (2000). Use of psychoactive medication during pregnancy and possible effects on the fetus and newborn. *Pediatrics, 105,* 880–887.

American Academy of Pediatrics (AAP) Committee on Environmental Health. (2005). Lead exposure in children: Prevention, detection, and management. *Pediatrics, 116,* 1036–1046.

American Academy of Pediatrics (AAP) Committee on Fetus and Newborn & American College of Obstetricians and Gynecologists (ACOG) Committee on Obstetric Practice. (1996). Use and abuse of the Apgar score. *Pediatrics, 98,* 141–142.

American Academy of Pediatrics (AAP) Committee on Genetics. (1996). Newborn screening fact sheet. *Pediatrics, 98,* 1–29.

American Academy of Pediatrics (AAP) Committee on Infectious Diseases. (2000).

Recommended childhood immunization schedule—United States, January-December, 2000 (pp. 105, 148).

American Academy of Pediatrics (AAP) Committee on Injury and Poison Prevention. (2000). Firearm-related injuries affecting the pediatric population. *Pediatrics, 105*(4), 888–895.

American Academy of Pediatrics (AAP) Committee on Injury and Poison Prevention. (2001). Bicycle helmets. *Pediatrics, 108*(4), 1030–1032.

American Academy of Pediatrics (AAP) Committee on Injury and Poison Prevention and Committee on Sports Medicine and Fitness. (1999). Policy statement: Trampolines at home, school, and recreational centers. *Pediatrics, 103,* 1053–1056.

American Academy of Pediatrics (AAP) Committee on Nutrition. (1992). Statement on cholesterol. *Pediatrics, 90,* 469–473.

American Academy of Pediatrics (AAP) Committee on Nutrition. (2003). Prevention of pediatric overweight and obesity. *Pediatrics, 112,* 424–430.

American Academy of Pediatrics (AAP) Committee on Practice and Ambulatory Medicine and Section on Ophthalmology. (1996). Eye examination and vision screening in infants, children, and young adults. *Pediatrics, 98,* 153–157.

American Academy of Pediatrics (AAP) Committee on Practice and Ambulatory Medicine and Section on Ophthalmology. (2002). Use of photoscreening for children's vision screening. *Pediatrics, 109,* 524–525.

American Academy of Pediatrics (AAP) Committee on Psychosocial Aspects of Child and Family Health. (1992). The pediatrician and childhood bereavement. *Pediatrics, 89*(3), 516–518.

American Academy of Pediatrics (AAP) Committee on Psychosocial Aspects of Child and Family Health. (1998). Guidance for effective discipline. *Pediatrics, 101,* 723–728.

American Academy of Pediatrics (AAP) Committee on Psychosocial Aspects of Child and Family Health. (2000). The pediatrician and childhood bereavement. *Pediatrics, 105,* 445–447.

American Academy of Pediatrics (AAP) Committee on Psychosocial Aspects of Child and Family Health. (2002). Coparent or second-parent adoption by same-sex parents. *Pediatrics, 109*(2), 339–340.

American Academy of Pediatrics (AAP) Committee on Psychosocial Aspects of Child and Family Health and Committee on Adolescence. (2001). Sexuality education for children and adolescent. *Pediatrics, 108*(2), 498–502.

American Academy of Pediatrics (AAP) Committee on Public Education (2001). Policy statement: Children, adolescents, and television. *Pediatrics, 107,* 423–426.

American Academy of Pediatrics (AAP) Committee on Quality Improvement.

(2002). Making Advances against Jaundice in Infant Care (MAJIC). Retrieved October 25, 2002, from www/aap.org/visit/majic .htm.

American Academy of Pediatrics (AAP) Committee on Sports Medicine and Fitness. (1992). Fitness, activity, and sports participation in the preschool child. *Pediatrics, 90,* 1002–1004.

American Academy of Pediatrics (AAP) Committee on Sports Medicine and Fitness. (2000). Injuries in youth soccer: A subject review. *Pediatrics, 105*(3), 659–660.

American Academy of Pediatrics (AAP) Committee on Sports Medicine and Fitness. (2001). Risk of injury from baseball and softball in children. *Pediatrics, 107*(4), 782–784.

American Academy of Pediatrics (AAP) Committee on Substance Abuse. (2001). Tobacco's toll: Implications for the pediatrician. *Pediatrics, 107,* 794–798.

American Academy of Pediatrics (AAP) Committee on Substance Abuse and Committee on Children with Disabilities. (1993). Fetal alcohol syndrome and fetal alcohol effects. *Pediatrics, 91,* 1004–1006.

American Academy of Pediatrics (AAP) Section on Breastfeeding. (2005). Breastfeeding and the use of human milk. *Pediatrics, 115,* 496–506.

American Academy of Pediatrics (AAP) Task Force on Infant Sleep Position and Sudden Infant Death Syndrome. (2000). Changing concepts of sudden infant death syndrome: Implications for infant sleeping environment and sleep position. *Pediatrics, 105,* 650–656.

American Academy of Pediatrics (AAP) Task Force on Sudden Infant Death Syndrome. (2005). The changing concept of sudden infant death syndrome: Diagnostic coding shifts, controversies regarding sleeping environment, and new variables to consider in reducing risk. *Pediatrics, 116,* 1245–1255.

American Association of Retired Persons (AARP). (1993). *Abused elders or battered women?* Washington, DC: Author.

American Association of University Women. (2007). *Behind the pay gap.* Washington, DC: AAUW Educational Foundation.

American Cancer Society. (2001). *Cancer facts and figures.* Atlanta: Author.

American Cancer Society. (2007). What are the risk factors for breast cancer? *Cancer Reference Information.* Oklahoma City, Oklahoma: Author.

American College of Emergency Physicians. (2008, March 10). *Know suicide's warning sign* [Press release]. Irving, TX: Author.

American College of Obstetricians and Gynecologists (ACOG). (2000). Premenstrual syndrome. *ACOG Practice Bulletin,* No. 15. Washington, DC: Author.

American College of Obstetricians and Gynecologists (ACOG). (2002). *Early pregnancy loss: Miscarriage and molar pregnancy.* Washington, DC: Author.

American Diabetes Association. (1992). *Diabetes facts.* Alexandria, VA: Author.

American Heart Association (AHA). (1995). *Silent epidemic: The truth about women and heart disease.* Dallas: Author.

American Heart Association, Gidding, S. S., Dennison, B. A., Birch, L. L., Daniels, S. R., Gilman, M. W., Lichtenstein, A. H., Rattay, K. T., Steinberger, J., Stettler, N., & Van Horn, L. (2006). Dietary recommendations for children and adolescents: A guide for practitioners. *Pediatrics, 117,* 544–559.

American Medical Association (AMA). (1992). *Diagnosis and treatment guidelines on elder abuse and neglect.* Chicago: Author.

American Medical Association (AMA). (1998). *Essential guide to menopause.* New York: Simon & Schuster.

American Psychiatric Association. (1994). *Diagnostic and statistical manual of mental disorders* (4th ed.). Washington, DC: Author.

American Psychiatric Association. (2000). *Diagnostic and Statistical Manual of Mental Disorders* (4th ed., Text Revision). Washington, DC: Author.

American Psychological Association (APA). (2002). Ethical principles of psychologists and code of conduct. *American Psychologist, 57,* 1060–1073.

American Psychological Association (APA). (2004a). *Resolution on sexual orientation and marriage.* Retrieved November 14, 2004, from www.apa.org/pi/lgbc/policy/marriage.pdf.

American Psychological Association (APA). (2004b, July). *Resolution on sexual orientation, parents, and children.* Retrieved January 23, 2007, from www.apa.org/pi/lgbc/policy/parents.html.

American Psychological Association (APA). (2007). *Stress in America.* Washington, DC: Author.

American Psychological Association (APA). (n.d.). *Answers to your questions about sexual orientation and homosexuality* [Brochure]. Washington, DC: Author.

American Psychological Association (APA) and American Academy of Pediatrics (AAP). (1996). *Raising children to resist violence: What you can do* [Brochure]. Retrieved from www.apa.org/pubinfo/apaaap.html.

American Psychological Association (APA) Online. (2001). *End-of-life issues and care.* Retrieved March 11, 2005, from www.apa.org/pi/eol/arguments.html.

American Psychological Association (APA) Working Group on Assisted Suicide and End-of-Life Decisions. (2005). *Orientation to end-of-life decision-making.* Retrieved February 7, 2005, from www.apa.org/pi/aseol/section1.html.

American Public Health Association. (2004). *Disparities in infant mortality* [Fact sheet]. Retrieved April 18, 2004, from www.medscape.com/viewarticle/472721.

American Stroke Association. (2005). Learn to recognize a stroke. Retrieved May 23, 2005, from www.strokeassociation.org/presenter.jhtml?identifier=1020.

Ames, E. W. (1997). *The development of Romanian orphanage children adopted to Canada: Final report* (National Welfare Grants Program, Human Resources Development, Canada). Burnaby, BC, Canada: Fraser University, Psychology Department.

Amirkhanyan, A. A., & Wolf, D. A. (2006). Parent care and the stress process: Findings from panel data. *Journal of Gerontology: Social Sciences, 61B,* S248–S255.

Amsel, E., Goodman, G., Savoie, D., & Clark, M. (1996). The development of reasoning about causal and noncausal influences on levers. *Child Development, 67,* 1624–1646.

Amso, D., & Casey, B. J. (2006). Beyond what develops when: Neuroimaging may inform how cognition changes with development. *Current Directions in Psychological Science, 15,* 24–29.

Anastasi, A. (1988). *Psychological testing* (6th ed.). New York: Macmillan.

Anastasi, A., & Schaefer, C. E. (1971). Note on concepts of creativity and intelligence. *Journal of Creative Behavior, 3,* 113–116.

Anderson, A. H., Clark, A., & Mullin, J. (1994). Interactive communication between children: Learning how to make language work in dialog. *Journal of Child Language, 21,* 439–463.

Anderson, C. (2000). *The impact of interactive violence on children.* Statement before the Senate Committee on Commerce, Science, and Transportation, 106th Congress, 1st session.

Anderson, C. A., Berkowitz, L., Donnerstein, E., Huesmann, L. R., Johnson, J. D., Linz, D., Malamuth, N. M., & Wartella, E. (2003). The influence of media violence on youth. *Psychological Science in the Public Interest, 4,* 81–110.

Anderson, D., & Anderson, R. (1999). The cost-effectiveness of home birth. *Journal of Nurse Mid-Wifery, 44*(11), 30–35.

Anderson, D. A., & Hamilton, M. (2005). Gender role stereotyping of parents in children's picture books: The invisible father. *Sex Roles, 52,* 145–151.

Anderson, D. R., Huston, A. C., Schmitt, K. L., Linebarger, D. L., & Wright, J. C. (2001). Early childhood television viewing and adolescent behavior. *Monographs of the Society for Research in Child Development, 66* (1, Serial No. 264).

Anderson, D. R., & Pempek, T. A. (2005). Television and very young children. *American Behavioral Scientist, 48*(5), 505–522.

Anderson, J. E., Mosher, W. D., & Chandra, A. (2006). Measuring HIV risk in the U.S. population ages 15–44: Results from Cycle 6 of the National Survey of Family Growth. *Advance Data from Vital and Health Statistics,* No. 337. Hyattsville, MD: National Center for Health Statistics.

Anderson, M., Kaufman, J., Simon, T. R., Barrios, L., Paulozzi, L., Ryan, G., Hammond, R., Modzeleski, W., Feucht, T., Potter, L., & the School-Associated Violent Deaths Study Group. (2001). School-associated violent deaths in the United States, 1994–1999. *Journal of the American Medical Association, 286*(21), 2695–2702.

Anderson, P., Doyle, L. W., & the Victorian Infant Collaborative Study Group (2003). *Journal of the American Medical Association, 289,* 3264–3272.

Anderson, R. N., & Smith, B. L. (2005). Deaths: Leading causes for 2002. *National Vital Statistics Reports, 53*(17). Hyattsville, MD: National Center for Health Statistics.

Anderson, S. E., Dallal, G. E., & Must, A. (2003). Relative weight and race influence average age at menarche: Results from two nationally representative surveys of U.S. girls studied 25 years apart. *Pediatrics 2003, 111,* 844–850.

Anderson, W. F. (1998). Human gene therapy. *Nature, 392*(Suppl.), 25–30.

Anderssen, N., Amlie, C., & Ytteroy, E. A. (2002). Outcomes for children with lesbian or gay parents: A review of studies from 1978 to 2000. *Scandinavian Journal of Psychology, 43*(4), 335–351.

Andrews-Hanna, J. R., Snyder, A. Z., Vincent, J. L., Lustig, C., Head, D., Raichie, M. E., & Buckner, R. L. (2007). Disruption of large-scale brain systems in advanced aging. *Neuron, 56,* 924–935.

Annas, G. J. (2005). "Culture of life" politics at the bedside—The case of Terri Shiavo. *New England Journal of Medicine, 352,* 1710–1715. Retrieved March 23, 2005, from www.nejm.org.

Antonarakis, S. E., & Down Syndrome Collaborative Group. (1991). Parental origin of the extra chromosome in trisomy 21 as indicated by analysis of DNA polymorphisms. *New England Journal of Medicine, 324,* 872–876.

Antonio, A. L., Chang, M. J., Hakuta, K., Kenny, D. A., Levin, S., & Milem, J. F. (2004). Effects of racial diversity on complex thinking in college students. *Psychological Science, 15,* 507–510.

Antonucci, T., & Akiyama, H. (1997). Concern with others at midlife: Care, comfort, or compromise? In M. E. Lachman & J. B. James (Eds.), *Multiple paths of midlife development* (pp. 145–169). Chicago: University of Chicago Press.

Antonucci, T. C. (1991). Attachment, social support, and coping with negative life events in mature adulthood. In E. M. Cummings, A. L. Greene & K. H. Karraker (Eds.), *Life-span developmental psychology: Perspectives on stress and coping* (pp. 261–276). Hillsdale, NJ: Erlbaum.

Antonucci, T. C., & Akiyama, H. (1995). Convoys of social relations: Family and friendships within a life-span context. In R. Blieszner & V. Hilkevitch (Eds.), *Handbook of aging and the family* (pp. 355–371). Westport, CT: Greenwood Press.

Antonucci, T. C., Akiyama, H., & Merline, A. (2001). Dynamics of social relationships in midlife. In M. E. Lachman (Ed.), *Handbook of midlife development* (pp. 571–598). New York: Wiley.

Apgar, V. (1953). A proposal for a new method of evaluation of the newborn infant. *Current Research in Anesthesia and Analgesia, 32,* 260–267.

Aquilino, W. S. (1996). The returning adult child and parental experience at midlife. In C. Ryff & M. M. Seltzer (Eds.), *The parental experience in midlife* (pp. 423–458). Chicago: University of Chicago Press.

Aquilino, W. S. (2006a). Family relationships and support systems in emerging adulthood. In J. J. Arnett & J. L. Tanner (Eds.), *Emerging adults in America: Coming of age in the 21st century* (pp. 193–217). Washington, DC: American Psychological Association.

Aquilino, W. S. (2006b). The noncustodial father-child relationship from adolescence into young adulthood. *Journal of Marriage and Family, 68,* 929–946.

Archer, J. (2004). Sex differences in aggression in real-world settings: A meta-analytic review. *Review of General Psychology, 8,* 291–322.

Archer, S. L. (1993). Identity in relational contexts: A methodological proposal. In J. Kroger (Ed.), *Discussions on ego identity* (pp. 75–99). Hillsdale, NJ: Erlbaum.

Arcus, D., & Kagan, J. (1995). Temperament and craniofacial variation in the first two years. *Child Development, 66,* 1529–1540.

Arend, R., Gove, F., & Sroufe, L. A. (1979). Continuity of individual adaptation from infancy to kindergarten: A predictive study of ego-resiliency and curiosity in preschoolers. *Child Development, 50*(4), 950–959.

Arias, E., MacDorman, M. F., Strobino, D. M., & Guyer, B. (2003). Annual summary of vital statistics—2002. *Pediatrics, 112,* 1215–1230.

Ariès, P. (1962). *Centuries of childhood.* New York: Random House.

Arking, R., Novoseltsev, V., & Novoseltseva, J. (2004). The human life span is not that limited: The effect of multiple longevity phenotypes. *Journal of Gerontology: Biological Sciences, 59A,* 697–704.

Arnestad, M., Crotti, L., Rognum, T. O., Insolia, R., Pedrazzini, M., Ferrandi, C., Vege, A., Wang, D. W., Rhodes, T. E., George, A. L., & Schwartz, P. J. (2007). Prevalence of long-qt syndrome gene variants in sudden infant death syndrome. *Circulation, 115,* 361–367.

Arnett, J. J. (1999). Adolescent storm and stress, reconsidered. *American Psychologist, 54,* 317–326.

Arnett, J. J. (2000). Emerging adulthood: A theory of development from the late teens through the twenties. *American Psychologist, 55,* 469–480.

Arnett, J. J. (2004). *Emerging adulthood.* New York: Oxford University Press.

Arnett, J. J. (2006). Emerging adulthood: Understanding the new way of coming of age. In J. J. Arnett & J. L. Tanner (Eds.), *Emerging adults in America: Coming of age in the 21st century* (pp. 3–19). Washington, DC: American Psychological Association.

Arrich, J., Lalouschek, W., & Müllner, M. (2005). Influence of socioeconomic status on mortality after stroke: Retrospective cohort study. *Stroke, 36,* 310–314.

Asher, M. I., Montefort, S., Björkstén, B., Lai, C. K., Strachan, D. P., Weiland, S. K., Williams, H., & the ISAAC Phase Three Study Group. (2006). Worldwide time trends in the prevalence of symptoms of asthma, allergic rhinoconjunctivitis, and eczema in childhood: ISAAC phases one and three repeat multicountry cross-sectional surveys. *Lancet, 368*(9537), 733–743.

Ashman, S. B., & Dawson, G. (2002). Maternal depression, infant psychobiological development, and risk for depression. In S. H. Goodman, & I. H. Gotlib (Eds.), *Children of depressed parents: Mechanisms of risk and implications for treatment* (pp. 37–58). Washington, DC: American Psychological Association.

Associated Press. (2004, April 29). *Mom in C-section case received probation: Woman originally charged with murder for delaying operation.* Retrieved June 8, 2004, from www.msnbc.msn.com/id/4863415/.

Associated Press. (2005, February 22). Britain starts gay civil unions this year, predicts 42,000. *Chicago Sun-Times,* p. 39.

Asthana, S., Bhasin, S., Butler, R. N., Fillit, H., Finkelstein, J., Harman, S. M., Holstein, L., Korenman, S. G., Matsumoto, A. M., Morley, J. E., Tsitouras, P., & Urban, R. (2004). Masculine vitality: Pros and cons of testosterone in treating the andropause. *Journal of Gerontology: Medical Sciences, 59A,* 461–466.

Astington, J. W. (1993). *The child's discovery of the mind.* Cambridge, MA: Harvard University Press.

Atchley, R. C. (1989). A continuity theory of normal aging. *Gerontologist, 29,* 183–190.

Athansiou, M. S. (2001). Using consultation with a grandmother as an adjunct to play therapy. *Family Journal—Consulting and Therapy for Couples and Families, 9,* 445–449.

Austin, E. W., Pinkleton, B. E., & Fujioka, Y. (2000). The role of interpretation processes and parental discussion in the media's effects on adolescents' use of alcohol. *Pediatrics, 105*(2), 343–349.

Australian man first in world to die with legal euthanasia. (1996, September 26). *New York Times* (International ed.), p. A5.

Ausubel, N. (1964). *The book of Jewish knowledge.* New York: Crown.

Autism Society of American (2008). *Frequently asked questions.* Retrieved April 3, 2008, from www.autism-society.org/site/PageServer?pagename=about_FAQ.

Avellar, S., & Smock, P. J. (2005). The economic consequences of the dissolution of cohabiting unions. *Journal of Marriage and Family, 67,* 315–327.

Avis, N. E. (1999). Women's health at midlife. In S. L. Willis & J. D. Reid (Eds.), *Life in the middle: Psychological and social development in middle age* (pp. 105–146). San Diego: Academic Press.

Avis, N. E., & Crawford, S. (2006). Menopause: Recent research findings. In S. K. Whitbourne & S. L. Willis (Eds.), *The baby boomers grow up: Contemporary perspectives on midlife* (pp. 75–109). Mahwah, NJ: Erlbaum.

Avolio, B. J., & Sosik, J. J. (1999). A life-span framework for assessing the impact of work on white-collar workers. In S. L. Willis & J. D. Reid (Eds.), *Life in the middle: Psychological and social development in middle age.* San Diego: Academic Press.

Babchuk, N. (1978–1979). Aging and primary relations. *International Journal of Aging and Human Development, 9*(2), 137–151.

Babu, A., & Hirschhorn, K. (1992). A guide to human chromosome defects (Birth Defects: Original Article Series, 28[2]). White Plains, NY: March of Dimes Birth Defects Foundation.

Bach, P. B., Schrag, D., Brawley, O. W., Galaznik, A., Yakren, S., & Begg, C. B. (2002). Survival of blacks and whites after a cancer diagnosis. *Journal of the American Medical Association, 287,* 2106–2113.

Bada, H. S., Das, A., Bauer, C. R., Shankaran, S., Lester, B., LaGasse, L., Hammond, J., Wright, L. L., & Higgins, R. (2007). Impact of prenatal cocaine exposure on child behavior problems through school age. *Pediatrics, 119,* 348–359.

Baddeley, A. (1996). Exploring the central executive. *Quarterly Journal of Experimental Psychology: Human Experimental Psychology* (Special Issue: Working Memory), *49A,* 5–28.

Baddeley, A. (1998). Recent developments in working memory. *Current Opinion in Neurobiology, 8,* 234–238.

Baddeley, A. D. (1981). The concept of working memory: A view of its current state and probable future development. *Cognition, 10,* 17–23.

Baddeley, A. D. (1986). *Working memory.* London: Oxford University Press.

Baddeley, A. D. (1992). Working memory. *Science, 255,* 556–559.

Baer, J. S., Sampson, P. D., Barr, H. M., Connor, P. D., & Streissguth, A. P. (2003). A 21-year longitudinal analysis of the effects of prenatal alcohol exposure on young adult drinking. *Archives of General Psychiatry, 60,* 377–385.

Bagwell, C. L., Newcomb, A. F., & Bukowski, W. M. (1998). Preadolescent friendship and peer rejection as predictors of adult adjustment. *Child Development, 69,* 140–153.

Baillargeon, R. (1994). How do infants learn about the physical world? *Current Directions in Psychological Science, 3,* 133–140.

Baillargeon, R. (1999). Young infants' expectations about hidden objects. *Developmental Science, 2,* 115–132.

Baillargeon, R., & DeVos, J. (1991). Object permanence in young infants: Further evidence. *Child Development, 62,* 1227–1246.

Baillargeon, R. H., Zoccolillo, M., Keenan, K., Côté, S., Pérusse, D., Wu, H.-X., Boivin, M., & Tremblay, R. E. (2007). Gender differences in physical aggression: A prospective population-based survey of children before and after 2 years of age. *Developmental Psychology, 43,* 13–26.

Bainbridge, J. W. B., Smith, A. J., Barker, S. S., Robbie, S., Henderson, R., Balaggan, K., Viswanathan, A., Holder, G. E., Stockman, A., Tyler, N., Petersen-Jones, S., Bhattacharya, S. S., Thrasher, A. J., Fitzke, F. W., Carter, B. J., Rubin, G. S., Moore, A. T., & Ali, R. R. (2008). Effect of gene therapy on visual function in Leber's congenital amaurosis. *New England Journal of Medicine, 358,* 2231–2239.

Baines, L. S., Joseph, J. T., & Jindal, R. M. (2002). A public forum to promote organ donation amongst Asians: The Scottish initiative. *Transplant International, 15,* 124–131.

Baird, A. A., Gruber, S. A., Fein, D. A., Maas, L. C., Steingard, R. J., Renshaw, P. F., Cohen, B. M., & Yurgelon-Todd, D. A. (1999). Functional magnetic resonance imaging of facial affect recognition in children and adolescents. *Journal of the American Academy of Child and Adolescent Psychiatry, 38,* 195–199.

Baird, G., Pickles, A., Simonoff, E., Charman, T., Sullivan, P., Chandler, S., Loucas, T., Meldrum, D., Afzal, M., Thomas, B., Li, J., & Brown, D. (2008). Measles vaccination and antibody response in autism spectrum disorders. *Archives of Disease in Childhood.* (Published online first Feburary 5, 2008, DOI: 10.1136/adc.2007.122937).

Baker, D. W., Sudano, J. J., Albert, J. M., Borawski, E. A., & Dor, A. (2001). Lack of health insurance and decline in overall health in late middle age. *New England Journal of Medicine, 345,* 1106–1112.

Baker, J. L., Olsen, L. W., & Sorensen, T. I.A. (2007). Childhood body-mass index and the risk of coronary heart disease in adulthood. *New England Journal of Medicine, 357,* 2329–2336.

Baldi, S., Jin, Y., Skemer, M., Green, P. J., & Herget, D. (2007). *Highlights from PISA 2006: Performance of U.S. 15-year-old students in science and mathematics literacy in an international context* (NCES 2008-016). Washington, DC: U.S. Department of Education, National Center for Education Statistics.

Balercia, G., Mosca, F., Mantero, F., Boscaro, M., Mancini, A., Ricciardo-Lamonica, G., & Littarru, G. (2004). Coenzyme q(10) supplementation in infertile men with idiopathic asthenozoospermia: An open, uncontrolled pilot study. *Fertility and Sterility, 81,* 93–98.

Ball, K., Edwards, J. D., & Ross, L. A. (2007). The impact of speed of processing training on cognitive and everyday functions. *Journal of Gerontology: Psychological Sciences* (Special Issue I), *62B,* 19–31.

Balluz, L. S., Okoro, C. A., & Strine, T. W. (2004). Access to health-care preventive services among Hispanics and non-Hispanics—United States, 2001–2002. *Morbidity and Mortality Weekly Report, 53,* 937–941.

Balsis, S., Carpenter, B. D., & Storandt, M. (2005). Personality change precedes clinical diagnosis of dementia of the Alzheimer type. *Journal of Gerontology: Psychological Sciences, 60B,* P98–P101.

Baltes, P. B. (1987). Theoretical propositions of life-span development psychology: On the dynamics between growth and decline. *Developmental Psychology 23*(5), 611–626.

Baltes, P. B. (1993). The aging mind: Potential and limits. *Gerontologist, 33,* 580–594.

Baltes, P. B. (1997). On the incomplete architecture of human ontogeny: Selection, optimization, and compensation as foundation of developmental theory. *American Psychologist, 52,* 366–380.

Baltes, P. B., & Baltes, M. M. (1990). Psychological perspectives on successful aging: The model of selective optimization with compensation. In P. B. Baltes & M. M. Baltes (Eds.), *Successful aging: Perspectives from the behavioral sciences* (pp. 1–34). New York: Cambridge University Press.

Baltes, P. B., Lindenberger, U., & Staudinger, U. M. (1998). Life-span theory in developmental psychology. In R. M. Lerner (Ed.), *Handbook of child psychology: Vol. 1. Theoretical models of human development* (pp. 1029–1143). New York: Wiley.

Baltes, P. B., & Smith, J. (2004). Lifespan psychology: From developmental contextualism to developmental biocultural co-constructivism. *Research in Human Development, 1,* 123–144.

Baltes, P. B., & Staudinger, U. M. (2000). Wisdom: A metaheuristic (pragmatic) to orchestrate mind and virtue toward excellence. *American Psychologist, 55,* 122–136.

Bandura, A. (1977). *Social learning theory.* Englewood Cliffs, NJ: Prentice-Hall.

Bandura, A. (1989). Social cognitive theory. In R. Vasta (Ed.), *Annals of child development: Vol. 6. Six theories of child development.* (pp. 1–60). Greenwich, CT: JAI.

Bandura, A. (1994). Self-efficacy. In V. S. Ramachaudran (Ed.), *Encyclopedia of human behavior* (Vol. 4, pp. 71–81). New York: Academic Press.

Bandura, A., Barbaranelli, C., Caprara, G. V., & Pastorelli, C. (1996). Multifaceted impact of self-efficacy beliefs on academic functioning. *Child Development, 67,* 1206–1222.

Bandura, A., Barbaranelli, C., Caprara, G. V., & Pastorelli, C. (2001). Self-efficacy beliefs as shapers of children's aspirations and career trajectories. *Child Development 72*(1), 187–206.

Bandura, A., Ross, D., & Ross, S. A. (1961). Transmission of aggression through imitation of aggressive models. *Journal of Abnormal and Social Psychology, 63,* 575–582.

Bandura, A., Ross, D., & Ross, S. A. (1963). Imitation of film-mediated aggressive models. *Journal of Abnormal and Social Psychology, 66,* 3–11.

Bandura, A., & Walters, R. H. (1963). *Social learning and personality development.* New York: Holt, Rinehart & Winston.

Banks, D. A., & Fossel, M. (1997). Telomeres, cancer, and aging: Altering the human life span. *Journal of the American Medical Association, 278,* 1345–1348.

Banks, E. (1989). Temperament and individuality: A study of Malay children. *American Journal of Orthopsychiatry, 59,* 390–397.

Banks, J., Marmot, M., Oldfield, Z., & Smith, J. P. (2006). Disease and disadvantage in the United States and in England. *Journal of the American Medical Association, 295,* 2037–2045.

Barinaga, M. (1998). Alzheimer's treatments that work now. *Science, 282,* 1030–1032.

Barkley, R. A. (1998a, February). How should attention deficit disorder be described? *Harvard Mental Health Letter,* p. 8.

Barkley, R. A. (1998b, September). Attention-deficit hyperactivity disorder. *Scientific American,* pp. 66–71.

Barnes, G. M., Hoffman, J. H., & Welte, J. W. (2006). Effects of parental monitoring and peer deviance in substance abuse and delinquency. *Journal of Marriage and Family, 68,* 1084–1104.

Barnes, P. M., & Schoenborn, C. A. (2003). Physical activity among adults: United States, 2000. *Advance Data from Vital and Health Statistics,* No. 133. Hyattsville, MD: National Center for Health Statistics.

Barnett, R. (1985, March). *We've come a long way—but where are we and what are the rewards?* Paper presented at the conference on Women in Transition, New York University School of Continuing Education, Center for Career and Life Planning, New York.

Barnett, R. C. (1997). Gender, employment, and psychological well-being: Historical and life-course perspectives. In M. E. Lachman & J. B. James (Eds.), *Multiple paths of midlife development* (pp. 325–343). Chicago: University of Chicago Press.

Barnett, R. C., & Hyde, J. S. (2001). Women, men, work, and family. *American Psychologist, 56,* 781–796.

Barnhart, M. A. (1992, Fall). Coping with the Methuselah syndrome. *Free Inquiry,* pp. 19–22.

Baron-Cohen, S. (2005). The essential difference: The male and female brain. *Phi Kappa Phi Forum, 85*(1), 23–26.

Barrett-Connor, E., Hendrix, S., Ettinger, B., Wenger, N. K., Paoletti, R., Lenfant, C. J. M., & Pinn, V. W. (2002). Best clinical practices: Chapter 13. *International position paper on women's health and menopause: A comprehensive approach.* Washington, DC: National Heart, Lung, and Blood Institute.

Barry, B. K., & Carson, R. G. (2004). The consequences of resistance training for movement control in older adults. *Journal of Gerontology: Medical Sciences, 59A,* 730–754.

Barry, C. M., & Wentzel, K. R. (2006). Friend influence on prosocial behavior: The role of motivational factors and friendship characteristics. *Developmental Psychology, 42,* 153–163.

Bartoshuk, L. M., & Beauchamp, G. K. (1994). Chemical senses. *Annual Review of Psychology, 45,* 419–449.

Bartzokis, G., Lu, P. H., Tishler, T. A., Fong, S. M., Oluwadara, B., Finn, J. P., Huange, D., Bordelon, Y., Mintz, J., & Perlman, S. (2007). Myelin breakdown and iron changes in Huntington's Disease: Pathogenesis and treatment implications. *Neurochemical Research, 32*(10), 1655–1664.

Barzilai, N., Atzmon, G., Derby, C. A., Bauman, J. M., & Lipton, R. B. (2006). A genotype of exceptional longevity is associated with preservation of cognitive function. *Neurology, 67,* 2170–2175.

Bascom, P. B., & Tolle, S. W. (2002). Responding to requests for physician-assisted suicide: "These are uncharted waters for both of us. . . ." *Journal of the American Medical Association, 288,* 91–98.

Bates, E., O'Connell, B., & Shore, C. (1987). Language and communication in infancy. In J. D. Osofsky (Ed.), *Handbook of infant development* (2nd ed.). New York: Wiley.

Bauer, P. J. (1993). Memory for gender-consistent and gender-inconsistent event sequences by twenty-five-month-old children. *Child Development, 64,* 285–297.

Bauer, P. J. (1996). What do infants recall of their lives? Memory for specific events by 1- to 2-year-olds. *American Psychologist, 51,* 29–41.

Bauer, P. J. (2002). Long-term recall memory: Behavioral and neurodevelopmental changes in the first 2 years of life. *Current Directions in Psychological Science, 11,* 137–141.

Bauer, P. J., Wenner, J. A., Dropik, P. L., & Wewerka, S. S. (2000). Parameters of remembering and forgetting in the transition from infancy to early childhood. *Monographs of the Society for Research in Child Development, 65*(4, Serial No. 263). Malden, MA: Blackwell.

Bauer, P. J., Wiebe, S. A., Carver, L. J., Waters, J. M., & Nelson, C. A. (2003). Developments in long-term explicit memory late in the first year of life: Behavioral and electrophysiological indices. *Psychological Science, 14,* 629–635.

Baum, A., Cacioppo, J. T., Melamed, B. G., Gallant, S. J., & Travis, C. (1995). *Doing the right thing: A research plan for healthy living.* Washington, DC: American Psychological Association Science Directorate.

Baum, S., & Ma, J. (2007). *Education pays 2007: The benefits of higher education for individuals and society* (Trends in Higher Education Series 070342217). Washington, DC: College Board.

Baumer, E. P., & South, S. J. (2001). Community effects on youth sexual activity. *Journal of Marriage and Family, 63,* 540–554.

Baumrind, D. (1971). Harmonious parents and their preschool children. *Developmental Psychology, 41,* 92–102.

Baumrind, D. (1989). Rearing competent children. In W. Damon (Ed.), *Child development today and tomorrow* (pp. 349–378). San Francisco: Jossey-Bass.

Baumrind, D. (1991). Parenting styles and adolescent development. In J. Brooks-Gunn, R. Lerner, & A. C. Peterson (Eds.), *The encyclopedia of adolescence* (pp. 746–758). New York: Garland.

Baumrind, D. (1996a). A blanket injunction against disciplinary use of spanking is not warranted by the data. *Pediatrics, 88,* 828–831.

Baumrind, D. (1996b). The discipline controversy revisited. *Family Relations, 45,* 405–414.

Baumrind, D. (2005). Patterns of parental authority and adolescent autonomy. In J. Smetana (Ed.), *Changing boundaries of parental authority during adolescence* (New Directions for Child and Adolescent Development, No. 108, pp. 61–70). San Francisco: Jossey-Bass.

Baumrind, D., & Black, A. E. (1967). Socialization practices associated with dimensions of competence in preschool boys and girls. *Child Development, 38,* 291–327.

Bauserman, R. (2002). Child adjustment in joint-custody versus sole-custody arrangements: A meta-analytic review. *Journal of Family Psychology, 16,* 91–102.

Bayley, N. (1969). *Bayley Scales of Infant Development.* New York: Psychological Corporation.

Bayley, N. (1993). *Bayley Scales of Infant Development: II.* New York: Psychological Corporation.

Bayley, N. (2005). *Bayley Scales of Infant Development, Third Ed.* (Bayley-III). New York: Harcourt Brace.

Bayliss, D. M., Jarrold, C., Baddeley, A. D., Gunn, D. M., & Leigh, E. (2005). Mapping the developmental constraints on working memory span performance. *Developmental Psychology, 41*(4), 579–597.

Bearman, P. S., & Bruckner, H. (2001). Promising the future: Virginity pledges and first intercourse. *American Journal of Sociology, 106,* 859–913.

Becker, G. S. (1991). *A treatise on the family* (Enlarged ed.). Cambridge, MA: Harvard University Press.

Becker, P. E., & Moen, P. (1999). Scaling back: Dual-earner couples' work-family strategies. *Journal of Marriage and Family, 61,* 995–1007.

Beckett, C., Maughan, B., Rutter, M., Castle, J., Colvert, E., Groothues, C., Kreppner, J., Stevens, S., O'Connor, T. G., & Sonuga-Barke, E. J. S. (2006). Do the effects of severe early deprivation on cognition persist into early adolescence? Findings from the English and Romanian adoptees study. *Child Development, 77,* 696–711.

Bedford, V. H. (1995). Sibling relationships in middle and old age. In R. Blieszner & V. Hilkevitch (Eds.), *Handbook of aging and the family* (pp. 201–222). Westport, CT: Greenwood Press.

Behrman, R. E. (1992). *Nelson textbook of pediatrics* (13th ed.). Philadelphia: Saunders.

Beidel, D. C., & Turner, S. M. (1998). *Shy children, phobic adults: Nature and treatment of social phobia.* Washington, DC: American Psychological Association.

Bekedam, D. J., Engelsbel, S., Mol, B. W., Buitendijk, S. E., & van der Pal-de Bruin, K. M. (2002). Male predominance in fetal distress during labor. *American Journal of Obstetrics and Gynecology, 187,* 1605–1607.

Belbin, R. M. (1967). Middle age: What happens to ability? In R. Owen (Ed.), *Middle age.* London: BBC.

Belizzi, M. (2002, May). *Obesity in children—What kind of future are we creating?* Presentation at the 55th World Health Assembly Technical Briefing, Geneva.

Bell, L., Burtless, G., Gornick, J., & Smeedling, T. M. (2007). A cross-national survey of trends in the transition to economic independence. In S. Danzinger & C. Rouse (Eds.), *The price of independence: The economics of early adulthood* (pp. 27–55). New York: Russell Sage Foundation.

Bell, L. G., & Bell, D. C. (2005). Family dynamics in adolescence affect midlife well-being. *Journal of Family Psychology, 19,* 198–207.

Bell, M. A., & Fox, N. A. (1992). The relations between frontal brain electrical activity and cognitive development during infancy. *Child Development, 63,* 1142–1163.

Bellinger, D. (2004). Lead. *Pediatrics, 113,* 1016–1022.

Belsky, J. (1984). Two waves of day care research: Developmental effects and conditions of quality. In R. Ainslie (Ed.), *The child and the day care setting.* New York: Praeger.

Belsky, J., Fish, M., & Isabella, R. (1991). Continuity and discontinuity in infant negative and positive emotionality: Family antecedents and attachment consequences. *Developmental Psychology, 27,* 421–431.

Belsky, J., Jaffee, S., Hsieh, K., & Silva, P. A. (2001). Childrearing antecedents of intergenerational relations in young adulthood: A prospective study. *Developmental Psychology, 37,* 801–814.

Belsky, J., Jaffee, S. R., Caspi, A., Moffitt, T., & Silva, P. A. (2003). Intergenerational relationships in young adulthood and their life course, mental health, and personality correlates. *Journal of Family Psychology, 17,* 460–471.

Belsky, J., Steinberg, L. D., Houts, R. M., Friedman, S. L., DeHart, G., Cauffman, E., Roisman, G. I., Halpern-Felsher, B. L., Susman, E., & the NICHD Early Child Care Research Network. (2007). Family rearing antecedents of pubertal timing. *Child Development, 78*(4), 1302–1321.

Belsky, J., Vandell, D. L., Burchinal, M., Clarke-Stewart, K. A., McCartney, K., Owen, M. T., & the NICHD Early Child Care Research Network (2007). Are there long-term effects of early child care? *Child Development, 78,* 681–701.

Bem, S. L. (1983). Gender schema theory and its implications for child development: Raising gender-aschematic children in a gender-schematic society. *Signs, 8,* 598–616.

Bem, S. L. (1985). Androgyny and gender schema theory: A conceptual and empirical integration. In T. B. Sondregger (Ed.), *Nebraska symposium on motivation, 1984: Psychology and gender.* Lincoln: University of Nebraska Press.

Bem, S. L. (1993). *The lenses of gender: Transforming the debate on sexual inequality.* New Haven, CT: Yale University Press.

Bendersky, M., Bennett, D., & Lewis, M. (2006). Aggression at age 5 as a function of prenatal exposure to cocaine, gender, and environmental risk. *Journal of Pediatric Psychology, 31,* 71–84.

Benenson, J. F. (1993). Greater preference among females than males for dyadic interaction in early childhood. *Child Development, 64,* 544–555.

Benes, F. M., Turtle, M., Khan, Y., & Farol, P. (1994). Myelination of a key relay zone in the hippocampal formation occurs in the human brain during childhood, adolescence, and adulthood. *Archives of General Psychiatry, 51,* 447–484.

Bengtson, V. L. (2001). Beyond the nuclear family: The increasing importance of multigenerational bonds. *Journal of Marriage and Family, 63,* 1–16.

Bengtson, V. L., Rosenthal, C., & Burton, L. (1996). Paradoxes of families and aging. In R. H. Binstock & L. K. George (Eds.), *Handbook of aging and the social sciences* (4th ed., pp. 253–282). San Diego: Academic Press.

Bengtson, V. L., Rosenthal, C. J., & Burton, L. M. (1990). Families and aging: Diversity and heterogeneity. In R. Binstock & L. George (Eds.), *Handbook of aging and the social sciences* (3rd ed., pp. 263–287). San Diego: Academic Press.

Benloucif, S., Orbeta, L., Ortiz, R., Janssen, I., Finkel, S. I., Bleiberg, J., & Zee, P. C. (2004). Morning or evening activity improves neuropsychological performance and subjective sleep quality in older adults. *Sleep, 27,* 1542–1551.

Benson, E. (2003). Intelligent intelligence testing. *Monitor on Psychology, 43*(2), 48–51.

Berg, C. A., & Klaczynski, P. A. (1996). Practical intelligence and problem solving: Search for perspectives. In F. Blanchard-Fields & T. M. Hess (Eds.), *Perspectives on cognitive change in adulthood and aging* (pp. 323–357). New York: McGraw-Hill.

Bergeman, C. S., & Plomin, R. (1989). Genotype-environment interaction. In M. Bornstein & J. Bruner (Eds.), *Interaction in human development* (pp. 157–171). Hillsdale, NJ: Erlbaum.

Bergen, D. (2002). The role of pretend play in children's cognitive development. *Early Childhood Research & Practice, 4*(1). Retrieved from http:// ecrp.uiuc.edu/v4n1/ bergen.html.

Bergen, D., Reid, R., & Torelli, L. (2000). *Educating and caring for very young children: The infant-toddler curriculum.* Washington, DC: National Association for the Education of Young Children.

Bergen, G., Chen, L. H., Warner, M., & Fingerhut, L. A. (2008). *Injury in the United States: 2007 Chartbook.* Hyattsville, MD: National Center for Education Statistics.

Berger, A., Tzur, G., & Posner, M. I. (2006). Infant brains detect arithmetic errors. *Proceedings of the National Academy of Sciences (PNAS), 103,* 12649–12653.

Berger, K. S. (2007). Update on bullying at school: Science forgotten? *Developmental Review, 27,* 91–92.

Berger, R. M., & Kelly, J. J. (1986). Working with homosexuals of the older population. *Social Casework, 67,* 203–210.

Bering, J. M., & Bjorklund, D. F. (2004). The natural emergence of reasoning ability about the afterlife as a developmental regularity. *Developmental Psychology, 40,* 217–233.

Berk, L. E. (1986a). Development of private speech among preschool children. *Early Child Development and Care, 24,* 113–136.

Berk, L. E. (1986b). Private speech: Learning out loud. *Psychology Today, 20*(5), 34–42.

Berk, L. E. (1992). Children's private speech: An overview of theory and the status of research. In R. M. Diaz & L. E. Berk (Eds.), *Private speech: From social interaction to self-regulation* (pp. 17–53). Hillsdale, NJ: Erlbaum.

Berk, L. E., & Garvin, R. A. (1984). Development of private speech among low income Appalachian children. *Developmental Psychology, 20,* 271–286.

Berkman, L. F., & Glass, T. (2000). Social integration, social networks, social support, and health. In L. F. Berkman & I. Kawachi (Eds.), *Social epidemiology* (pp. 137–173). New York: Oxford University Press.

Berkowitz, G. S., Skovron, M. L., Lapinski, R. H., & Berkowitz, R. L. (1990). Delayed childbearing and the outcome of pregnancy. *New England Journal of Medicine, 322,* 659–664.

Berkowitz, R. I., Stallings, V. A., Maislin, G., & Stunkard, A. J. (2005). Growth of children at high risk of obesity during the first 6 y of life: Implications for prevention. *American Journal of Clinical Nutrition, 81,* 140–146.

Bernard, S. J., Paulozzi, L. J., & Wallace, L. J. D. (2007). Fatal injuries among children by race and ethnicity—United States, 1999–2002. *Morbidity and Mortality Weekly Report, 56*(SS05), 1–16.

Berndt, T. J., & Perry, T. B. (1990). Distinctive features and effects of early adolescent friendships. In R. Montemayor, G. R. Adams, & T. P. Gullotta (Eds.), *From childhood to adolescence: A transitional period?* (Vol. 2, pp. 269–287). Newbury Park, CA: Sage.

Bernert, R. A., Merrill, K. A., Braithwaite, S. R., Van Orden, K. A., & Joiner, T. E. (2007). Family life stress and insomnia symptoms in a prospective evaluation of young adults. *Journal of Family Psychology, 21,* 58–66.

Bernstein, L., Patel A. V., Sullivan-Halley, J., Press, M. F., Deapen, D., Berlin, J. A., Daling, J. R., McDonald, J. A., Norman, S. A., Malone, K. E., Strom, B. L., Liff, J., Folger, S. G., Simon, M. S., Burkman, R. T., Marchbanks, P. A., Weiss, L. K., & Spirtas, R. (2005). Lifetime recreational exercise activity and breast cancer risk among black women and white women. *Journal of the National Cancer Institute, 97,* 1671–1679.

Bernstein, N. (2008). *"Aging in place" communities offer seniors independence and support.* Retrieved July 24, 2008, from www.caring .com/articles/aging-in-place.

Bernstein, P. S. (2003). Achieving equity in women's and perinatal health. *Medscape Ob/ Gyn & Women's Health, 8.* (Posted 12/12/03).

Berrick, J. D. (1998). When children cannot remain home: Foster family care and kinship care. *Future of Children, 8,* 72–87.

Berrueta-Clement, J. R., Schweinhart, L. J., Barnett, W. S., Epstein, A. S., & Weikart, D. P. (1985). *Changed lives: The effects of the Perry Preschool Program on youths through age 19.* Ypsilanti, MI: High/Scope.

Berrueta-Clement, J. R., Schweinhart, L. J., Barnett, W. S., & Weikart, D. P. (1987). The effects of early educational intervention on crime and delinquency in adolescence and early adulthood. In J. D. Burchard & S. N. Burchard (Eds.), *Primary prevention of psychopathology: Vol. 10. Prevention of delinquent behavior* (pp. 220–240). Newbury Park, CA: Sage.

Berry, M., Dylla, D. J., Barth, R. P., & Needell, B. (1998). The role of open adoption in the adjustment of adopted children and their families. *Children and Youth Services Review, 20,* 151–171.

Berry, N., Jobanputra, V., & Pal, H. (2003). Molecular genetics of schizophrenia: A critical review. *Journal of Psychiatry and Neuroscience, 28,* 415–429.

Berry, R. J., Li, Z., Erickson, J. D., Li, S., Moore, C. A., Wang, H., Mulinare, J., Zhao, P., Wong, L.-Y. C., Gindler, J., Hong, S.-X., & Correa, A. for the China-U.S. Collaborative Project for Neural Tube Defect Prevention. (1999). Prevention of neural-tube defects with folic acid in China. *New England Journal of Medicine, 341,* 1485–1490.

Bertenthal, B. I., & Campos, J. J. (1987). New directions in the study of early experience. *Child Development, 58,* 560–567.

Bertenthal, B. I., Campos, J. J., & Barrett, K. C. (1984). Self-produced locomotion: An organizer of emotional, cognitive, and social development in infancy. In R. N. Emde & R. J. Harmon (Eds.), *Continuities and discontinuities in development.* New York: Plenum Press.

Bertenthal, B. I., Campos, J. J., & Kermoian, R. (1994). An epigenetic perspective on the development of self-produced locomotion and its consequences. *Current Directions in Psychological Science, 3*(5), 140–145.

Bertenthal, B. I., & Clifton, R. K. (1998). Perception and action. In W. Damon (Series Ed.), D. Kuhn, & R. S. Siegler (Vol. Eds.), *Handbook of child psychology: Vol. 2. Cognition, perception, and language* (pp. 51–102). New York: Wiley.

Berz, J. B., Murdock, K. K., & Mitchell, D. K. (2005). Children's asthma, internalizing problems, and social functioning: An urban perspective. *Journal of Child and Adolescent Psychiatric Nursing, 18*(4), 181–197.

Bethell, C. D., Read, D., & Blumberg, S. J. (2005). Mental health in the United States: Health care and well-being of children with chronic emotional, behavioral, or developmental problem—United States, 2001. *Morbidity and Mortality Weekly Report, 54,* 985–989.

Beumont, P. J. V., Russell, J. D., & Touyz, S. W. (1993). Treatment of anorexia nervosa. *Lancet, 341,* 1635–1640.

Beversdorf, D. Q., Manning, S. E., Anderson, S. L., Nordgren, R. E., Walters, S. E., Cooley, W. C., Gaelic, S. E., & Bauman, M. L. (2001, November 10–15). *Timing of prenatal stressors and autism.* Presentation at the 31st annual meeting of the Society for Neuroscience, San Diego.

Bhaskaran, K., Hamouda, O., Sannesa, M., Boufassa, F., Johnson, A. M., Lambert, P. C., & Porter, K., for the CASCADE Collaboration. (2008). Changes in the risk of death after HIV seroconversion compared with mortality in the general population. *Journal of the American Medical Association, 300,* 51–59.

Bialystok, E., & Senman, L. (2004). Executive processes in appearance-reality tasks: The role of inhibition of attention and symbolic representation. *Child Development, 75,* 562–579.

Bialystok, E., Craik, F. I.M., & Freeman, M. (2007). Bilingualism as a protection against the onset of symptoms of dementia. *Neuropsychologia, 45*(2), 459–464.

Bialystok, E., Craik, F. I.M., Klein, R., & Viswanathan, M. (2004). Bilingualism, aging, and cognitive control: Evidence from the Simon task. *Psychology and Aging, 19,* 290–303.

Bianchi, S., Robinson, J., & Milkie, M. (2006). *The changing rhythms of American family life.* New York: Russell Sage Foundation.

Biason-Lauber, A., Konrad, D., Navratil, F., & Schoenle, E. J. (2004). A WNT4 mutation associated with Mullerian-duct regression and virilization in a 46,XX woman. *New England Journal of Medicine, 351,* 792–798.

Bibbins-Domingo, K., Coxson, P., Pletcher, M. J., Lightwood, J., & Goldman, L.

(2007). Adolescent overweight and future adult coronary heart disease. *New England Journal of Medicine, 357,* 2371–2379.

Bickham, D., & Rich, M. (2006). Is television viewing associated with social isolation?: Roles of exposure time, viewing context, and violent content. *Archives of Pediatrics and Adolescent Medicine, 160,* 387–392.

Biegel, D. E. (1995). Caregiver burden. In G. E. Maddox (Ed.), *The encyclopedia of aging* (2nd ed., pp. 138–141). New York: Springer.

Bielby, D., & Papalia, D. (1975). Moral development and perceptual role-taking egocentrism: Their development and interrelationship across the lifespan. *International Journal of Aging and Human Development, 6*(4), 293–308.

Bienvenu, O. J., Nestadt, G., Samuels, J. F., Costa, P. T., Howard, W. T., & Eaton, W. W. (2001). Phobic, panic, and major depressive disorders and the five-factor model of personality. *Journal of Mental Diseases, 189,* 154–161.

Bierman, K. L., Smoot, D. L., & Aumiller, K. (1993). Characteristics of aggressive rejected, aggressive (nonrejected), and rejected (non-aggressive) boys. *Child Development, 64,* 139–151.

Billet, S. (2001). Knowing in practice: Reconceptualising vocational expertise. *Learning and Instruction, 11,* 431–452.

Billings, L. M., Green, K. N., McGaugh, J. L., & LaFerla, F. M. (2007). Learning decreases A beta*56 and tau pathology and ameliorates behavioral decline in 3xTg-AD mice. *Journal of Neuroscience, 27*(4), 751–761.

Bilsen, J., Cohen, J., & Deliens, L. (2007). End of life in Europe: An overview of medical practices. *Populations and Societies.* No. 430. Paris: INED.

Binstock, G., & Thornton, A. (2003). Separations, reconciliations, and living apart in cohabiting and marital units. *Journal of Marriage and Family, 65,* 432–443.

Bird, T. D. (2005). Genetic factors in Alzheimer's disease. *New England Journal of Medicine, 352,* 862–864.

Birks, J. (2006). Cholinesterase inhibitors for Alzheimer's disease. *Cochrane Database of Systematic Reviews,* Issue 1, Art. No. CD005593. (DOI: 10.1002/14651858. CD005593).

Birks, J., & Harvey R. J. (2006). Donepezil for dementia due to Alzheimer's disease. *Cochrane Database of Systematic Reviews,* Issue 1, Art. No. CD001190. (DOI: 10.1002/14651858.CD001190.pub2).

Birmaher, B. (1998). Should we use antidepressant medications for children and adolescents with depressive disorders? *Psychopharmacology Bulletin, 34,* 35–39.

Birmaher, B., Ryan, N. D., Williamson, D. E., Brent, D. A., Kaufman, J., Dahl, R. E., Perel, J., & Nelson, B. (1996). Childhood and adolescent depression: A review of the past 10 years. *Journal of the American Academy of Child and Adolescent Psychiatry, 35,* 1427–1440.

Bischoff, C., Petersen, H. C., Graakjaer, J., Andersen-Ranberg, K., Vaupel, J. W., Bohr, V. A., Steen, K., & Christensen, K. (2006). No association between telomere length and survival among the elderly and the oldest old. *Epidemiology, 17,* 190–194.

Bjork, J. M., Knutson, B., Fong, G. W., Caggiano, D. M., Bennett, S. M., & Hommer, D. W. (2004). Incentive-elicited brain activities in adolescents: Similarities and differences from young adults. *Journal of Neuroscience, 24,* 1793–1802.

Bjorklund, D. F. (1997). The role of immaturity in human development. *Psychological Bulletin, 122,* 153–169.

Bjorklund, D. F., & Harnishfeger, K. K. (1990). The resources construct in cognitive development: Diverse sources of evidence and a theory of inefficient inhibition. *Developmental Review, 10,* 48–71.

Bjorklund, D. F., & Pellegrini, A. D. (2000). Child development and evolutionary psychology. *Child Development, 71,* 1687–1708.

Bjorklund, D. F., & Pellegrini, A. D. (2002). *The origins of human nature: Evolutionary developmental psychology.* Washington, DC: American Psychological Association.

Black, D. M., Delmas, P. D., Eastell, R., Reid, I. R., Boonen, S., Cauley, J. A., Cosman, F., Lakatos, P., Leung, P. C., Man, Z., Mautalen, C., Mesenbrink, P., Hu, H., Caminis, J., Tong, K., Rosario-Jansen, T., Krasnow, J., Hue, T. F., Sellmeyer, D., Eriksen, E. F., Cummings, S. R., & the HORIZON Pivotal Fracture Trial. (2007). Once-yearly Zoledronic acid for treatment of postmenopausal osteoporosis. *New England Journal of Medicine, 356,* 1809–1822.

Black, J. E. (1998). How a child builds its brain: Some lessons from animal studies of neural plasticity. *Preventive Medicine, 27,* 168–171.

Black, M. C., & Breiding, M. J. (2008). Adverse health conditions and health risk behaviors associated with intimate partner violence—United States, 2005. *Morbidity and Mortality Weekly Report, 57,* 113–117.

Black, M. M., & Krishnakumar, A. (1998). Children in low-income, urban settings: Interventions to promote mental health and well-being. *American Psychologist, 53,* 636–646.

Black, R. E., Morris, S. S., & Bryce, J. (2003). Where and why are 10 million children dying each year? *Lancet, 361,* 2226–2234.

Blagrove, M., Alexander, C., & Horne, J. A. (1995). The effects of chronic sleep reduction on the performance of cognitive tasks sensitive to sleep deprivation. *Applied Cognitive Psychology, 9,* 21–40.

Blair, C. (2002). School readiness: Integrating cognition and emotion in a neurobiological conceptualization of children's functioning at school entry. *American Psychologist, 57,* 111–127.

Blakemore, S., & Choudhury, S. (2006). Development of the adolescent brain: Implications for executive function and social cognition. *Journal of Child Psychology and Psychiatry, 47*(3), 296–312.

Blakeslee, S. (1997, April 17). Studies show talking with infants shapes basis of ability to think. *New York Times*, p. D21.

Blanchard-Fields, F. (2007). Everyday problem solving and emotion: An adult developmental perspective. *Current Directions in Psychological Science, 16*(1), 26–31.

Blanchard-Fields, F., Chen, Y., & Norris, L. (1997). Everyday problem solving across the adult life span: Influence of domain specificity and cognitive appraisal. *Psychology and Aging, 12*, 684–693.

Blanchard-Fields, F., & Irion, J. C. (1988). Coping strategies from the perspective of two developmental markers: Age and social reasoning. *Journal of Genetic Psychology 149*(2), 141–151.

Blanchard-Fields, F., Jahnke, H. C., & Camp, C. J. (1995). Age differences in problem solving style: The role of emotional salience. *Psychology and Aging, 10*, 173–180.

Blanchard-Fields, F., Mienaltowski, A., & Seay, R. B. (2007). Age differences in everyday problem-solving effectiveness: Older adults select more effective strategies for interpersonal problems. *Journal of Gerontology: Psychological Sciences, 62B*, P61–P64.

Blanchard-Fields, F., & Norris, L. (1994). Causal attributions from adolescence through adulthood: Age differences, ego level, and generalized response style. *Aging and Cognition, 1*, 67–86.

Blanchard-Fields, F., Stein, R., & Watson, T. L. (2004). Age differences in emotion-regulation strategies in handling everyday problems. *Journal of Gerontology: Psychological Sciences, 59B*, P261–P269.

Blanchflower, D. G., & Oswald, A. J. (2008). Is well-being U-shaped over the life cycle? *Social Science and Medicine, 66*(8), 1733–1749.

Bleske-Rechek, A., Lubinski, D., & Benbow, C. P. (2004). Meeting the educational needs of special populations. Advanced placement's role in developing exceptional human capital. *Psychological Sciences, 15*, 217–224.

Blieszner, R., & Roberto, K. (2006). Perspectives on close relationships among the baby boomers. In S. K. Whitbourne & S. L. Willis (Eds.), *The baby boomers grow up: Contemporary perspectives on midlife* (pp. 261–279). Mahwah, NJ: Erlbaum.

Block, J. (1971). *Lives through time.* Berkeley, CA: Bancroft.

Block, J. (1991). *Prototypes for the California Adult Q-set.* Berkeley: University of California, Department of Psychology.

Block, J. (1995a). A contrarian view of the Five-Factor approach to personality description. *Psychological Bulletin, 117*, 187–215.

Block, J. (1995b). Going beyond the five factors given: Rejoinder to Costa and McCrae (1995) and Goldberg and Saucier (1995). *Psychological Bulletin, 117*, 226–229.

Block, J., & Block, J. H. (2006a). Nursery school personality and political orientation two decades later. *Journal of Research in Personality, 40*(5), 734–749.

Block, J., & Block, J. H. (2006b). Venturing a 30-year longitudinal study. *American Psychologist, 61*, 315–327.

Block, R. W., Krebs, N. F., Committee on Child Abuse and Neglect, & Committee on Nutrition. (2005). Failure to Thrive as a Manifestation of Child Neglect. *Pediatrics, 116*(5), 1234–1237.

Bloom, B. (1985). *Developing talent in young people.* New York: Ballantine.

Blumenthal, J. A., Emery, C. F., Madden, D. J., Schniebolk, S., Walsh-Riddle, M., George, L. K., McKee, D. C., Higginbotham, M. B., Cobb, F. R., & Coleman, R. E. (1991). Long-term effects of exercise on psychological functioning in older men and women. *Journal of Gerontology, 46*(6), P352–P361.

Blustein, D. L., Juntunen, C. L., & Worthington, R. L. (2000). The school-to-work transition: Adjustment challenge for the forgotten half. In S. D. Brown & R. W. Lent (Eds.), *Handbook of counseling psychology* (pp. 435–470). New York: Wiley.

Boatman, D., Freeman, J., Vining, E., Pulsifer, M., Miglioretti, D., Minahan, R., Carson, B., Brandt, J., & McKhann, G. (1999). Language recovery after left hemispherectomy in children with late onset seizures. *Annals of Neurology, 46*(4), 579–586.

Bocskay, K. A., Tang, D., Orjuela, M. A., Liu, X., Warburton, D. P., & Perera, F. P. (2005). Chromosomal aberrations in cord blood are associated with prenatal exposure to carcinogenic polycyclic aromatic hydrocarbons. *Cancer Epidemiology Biomarkers and Prevention, 14*, 506–511.

Bodkin, N. L., Alexander, T. M., Ortmeyer, H. K., Johnson, E., & Hansen, B. C. (2003). Mortality and morbidity in laboratory-maintained rhesus monkeys and effects of long-term dietary restriction. *Journal of Gerontology: Biological Sciences, 58A*, 212–219.

Bodrova, E., & Leong, D. J. (1998). Adult influences on play: The Vygotskian approach. In D. P. Fromberg & D. Bergen (Eds.), *Play from birth to twelve and beyond: Contexts, perspectives, and meanings* (pp. 277–282). New York: Garland.

Boerner, K., Schulz, R., & Horowitz, A. (2004). Positive aspects of caregiving and adaptation to bereavement. *Psychology and Aging, 19*, 668–675.

Boerner, K., Wortman, C. B., & Bonanno, G. A. (2005). Resilient or at risk? A 4-year study of older adults who initially showed high or low distress following conjugal loss. *Journal of Gerontology: Psychological Sciences, 60B*, P67–P73.

Bogaert, A. F. (2006). Biological versus nonbiological older brothers and men's sexual orientation. *Proceedings of the National Academy of Sciences, 103*, 10771–10774.

Bogg, T., & Roberts, B. W. (2004). Conscientiousness and health-related behaviors: A meta-analysis of the leading behavioral contributors to mortality. *Psychological Bulletin, 130*, 887–919.

Bograd, R., & Spilka, B. (1996). Self-disclosure and marital satisfaction in mid-life and late-life remarriages. *International Journal of Aging and Human Development, 42*(3), 161–172.

Bojczyk, K. E., & Corbetta, D. (2004). Object retrieval in the 1st year of life: Learning effects of task exposure and box transparency. *Developmental Psychology, 40*, 54–66.

Bollinger, M. B. (2003). Involuntary smoking and asthma severity in children: Data from the Third National Health and Nutrition Examination Survey (NHANES III). *Pediatrics, 112*, 471.

Bonanno, G. A. (2005). Resilience in the face of potential trauma. *Current Directions in Psychological Science, 14*, 135–138.

Bonanno, G. A., Galea, S., Bucciarelli, A., & Vlahov, D. (2006). Psychological resilience after disaster. *Current Directions in Psychological Science, 17*, 181–186.

Bonanno, G. A., Wortman, C. B., Lehman, D. R., Tweed, R. G., Haring, M., Sonnega, J., Carr, D., & Nesse, R. M. (2002). Resilience to loss and chronic grief: A prospective study from preloss to 18-month postloss. *Journal of Personality and Social Psychology,* 1150–1164.

Bonanno, G. A., Wortman, C. B., & Nesse, R. M. (2004). Prospective patterns of resilience and maladjustment during widowhood. *Psychology and Aging, 19*, 260–271.

Bonham, V. L., Warshauer-Baker, E., & Collins, F. S. (2005). Race and ethnicity in the genome era. *American Psychologist, 60*, 9–15.

Booth, A. E., & Waxman, S. (2002). Object names and object functions serve as cues to categories for infants. *Developmental Psychology, 38*, 948–957.

Booth, J. L., & Siegler, R. S. (2006). Developmental and individual differences in pure numerical estimation. *Developmental Psychology, 41*, 189–201.

Booth, J. R., Perfetti, C. A., MacWhinney, B. (1999). Quick, automatic, and general activation of orthographic and phonological representations in young readers. *Developmental Psychology, 35*(1), 3–19.

Booth-Kewley, S., Minagawa, R. Y., Shaffer, R. A., & Brodine, S. K. (2002). A behavioral intervention to prevent sexually transmitted diseases/human immunodeficiency virus in a Marine Corps sample. *Military Medicine, 167*, 145–150.

Bornstein, M., Kessen, W., & Weiskopf, S. (1976). The categories of hue in infancy. *Science, 191*, 201–202.

Bornstein, M. H., & Cote, L. R., with Maital, S., Painter, K., Park, S. Y., Pascual, L., Pecheux, M. G., Ruel, J., Venuti, P., and Vyt, A. (2004). Cross-linguistic analysis of vocabulary in young children: Spanish, Dutch, French, Hebrew, Italian, Korean, and American English. *Child Development, 75*, 1115–1139.

Bornstein, M. H., Haynes, O. M., O'Reilly, A. W., & Painter, K. (1996). Solitary and collaborative pretense play in early childhood: Sources of individual variation in the development of representational competence. *Child Development, 67,* 2910–2929.

Bornstein, M. H., & Sigman, M. D. (1986). Continuity in mental development from infancy. *Child Development, 57,* 251–274.

Bornstein, M. H., & Tamis-LeMonda, C. S. (1994). Antecedents of information processing skills in infants: Habituation, novelty responsiveness, and cross-modal transfer. *Infant Behavior and Development, 17,* 371–380.

Borowsky, I. A., Ireland, M., & Resnick, M. D. (2001). Adolescent suicide attempts: Risks and protectors. *Pediatrics, 107*(3), 485–493.

Bosch, J., Sullivan, S., Van Dyke, D. C., Su, H., Klockau, L., Nissen, K., Blewer, K., Weber, E., & Eberly, S. S. (2003). Promoting a healthy tomorrow here for children adopted from abroad. *Contemporary Pediatrics, 20*(2), 69–86.

Bosma, H., Peter, R., Siegrist, J., & Marmot, M. (1998). Two alternative job stress models and the risk of coronary heart disease. *American Journal of Public Health, 88,* 68–74.

Boss, P. (1999). *Ambiguous loss.* Cambridge, MA: Harvard University Press.

Boss, P. (2002). Ambiguous loss: Working with the families of the missing. *Family Process, 41,* 14–17.

Boss, P. (2004). Ambiguous loss research, theory, and practice: Reflections after 9/11. *Journal of Marriage and Family, 66*(3), 551–566.

Boss, P. (2006). *Loss, trauma, and resilience: Therapeutic work with ambiguous loss.* New York: Norton.

Boss, P. (2007). Ambiguous loss theory: Challenges for scholars and practitioners. *Family Relations, 56*(2), 105–111.

Boss, P., Beaulieu, L., Wieling, E., Turner, W., & LaCruz, S. (2003). Healing loss, ambiguity, and trauma: A community-based intervention with families of union workers missing after the 9/11 attack in New York City. *Journal of Marital and Family Therapy, 29*(4), 455–467.

Bosshard, G., Nilstun, T., Bilsen, J., Norup, M., Miccinesi, G., vanDelden, J. J. M, Faisst, K., & van der Heide, A., for the European End-of-Life (EURELD) Consortium. (2005). Forgoing treatment at the end of life in 6 European countries. *Archives of Internal Medicine, 165,* 401–407.

Bosworth, H. B., & Schaie, K. W. (1997). The relationship of social environment, social networks, and health outcomes in the Seattle Longitudinal Study: Two analytical approaches. *Journal of Gerontology: Psychological Sciences, 52B,* P197–P205.

Botwinick, J. (1984). *Aging and behavior* (3rd ed.). New York: Springer.

Bouchard, T. J. (1994). Genes, environment, and personality. *Science, 264,* 1700–1701.

Bouchard, T. J. (2004). Genetic influence on human psychological traits: A survey.

Current Directions in Psychological Science, 13, 148–154.

Bouchey, H. A., & Furman, W. (2003). Dating and romantic experiences in adolescence. In G. R. Adams and M. D. Berzonsky, (Eds.). *Blackwell handbook of adolescence* (pp. 313–329). Oxford, UK: Blackwell.

Boulé, N. G., Haddad, E., Kenny, G. P., Wells, G. A., & Sigal, R. J. (2001). Effects of exercise on glycemic control and body mass in type 2 diabetes mellitus: A meta-analysis of controlled clinical trials. *Journal of the American Medical Association, 286,* 1218–1227.

Boulton, M. J. (1995). Playground behaviour and peer interaction patterns of primary school boys classified as bullies, victims and not involved. *British Journal of Educational Psychology, 65,* 165–177.

Boulton, M. J., & Smith, P. K. (1994). Bully/victim problems in middle school children: Stability, self-perceived competence, peer perception, and peer acceptance. *British Journal of Developmental Psychology, 12,* 315–329.

Boutin, P., Dina, C., Vasseur, F., Dubois, S. S., Corset, L., Seron, K., Bekris, L., Cabellon, J., Neve, B., Vasseur-Delannoy, V., Chikri, M., Charles, M. A., Clement, K., Lernmark, A., & Froguel, P. (2003). GAD2 on chromosome 10p12 is a candidate gene for human obesity. *Public Library of Science Biology, 1*(3), E68.

Bower, B. (1993). A child's theory of mind. *Science News, 144,* 40–42.

Bowlby, J. (1951). Maternal care and mental health. *Bulletin of the World Health Organization, 3,* 355–534.

Bowlby, J. (1969). *Attachment and loss: Vol. I. Attachment.* London: Hogarth Press & the Institute of Psychoanalysis.

Boyles, S. (2002, January 27). Toxic landfills may boost birth defects. *WebMD Medical News.* Retrieved February 5, 2007, from www.webmd.com/content/article/25/3606_1181.htm.

Brabant, S. (1994). An overlooked AIDS affected population: The elderly parent as caregiver. *Journal of Gerontological Social Work, 22,* 131–145.

Brabeck, M. M., & Shore, E. L. (2003). Gender differences in intellectual and moral development? The evidence refutes the claims. In J. Demick and C. Andreoletti (Eds.), *Handbook of adult development* (pp. 351–368). New York: Plenum Press.

Bracher, G., & Santow, M. (1999). Explaining trends in teenage childbearing in Sweden. *Studies in Family Planning, 30,* 169–182.

Brackett, M. A., Cox, A., Gaines, S. O., & Salovey, P. (2005). *Emotional intelligence and relationship quality among heterosexual couples.* Manuscript submitted for publication.

Brackett, M. A., Mayer, J. D., & Warner, R. M. (2004). Emotional intelligence and the prediction of behavior. *Personality and Individual Differences, 36,* 1387–1402.

Bradley, R., & Caldwell, B. (1982). The consistency of the home environment and its

relation to child development. *International Journal of Behavioral Development, 5,* 445–465.

Bradley, R., Caldwell, B., & Rock, S. (1988). Home environment and school performance: A ten-year follow-up and examination of three models of environmental action. *Child Development, 59,* 852–867.

Bradley, R. H. (1989). Home measurement of maternal responsiveness. In M. H. Bornstein (Ed.), *Maternal responsiveness: Characteristics and consequences* (New Directions for Child Development, No. 43). San Francisco: Jossey-Bass.

Bradley, R. H., Caldwell, B. M., Rock, S. L., Ramey, C. T., Barnard, K. E., Gray, C., Hammond, M. A., Mitchell, S., Gottfried, A. W., Siegel, L., & Johnson, D. L. (1989). Home environment and cognitive development in the first 3 years of life: A collaborative study involving six sites and three ethnic groups in North America. *Developmental Psychology, 25,* 217–235.

Bradley, R. H., Corwyn, R. F., Burchinal, M., McAdoo, H. P., & Coll, C. G. (2001). The home environment of children in the United States: Part II: Relations with behavioral development through age thirteen. *Child Development, 72*(6), 1868–1886.

Bradley, R. H., Corwyn, R. F., McAdoo, H. P., & Coll, C. G. (2001). The home environment of children in the United States: Part I: Variation by age, ethnicity, and poverty status. *Child Development, 72*(6), 1844–1867.

Braine, M. (1976). Children's first word combinations. *Monographs of the Society for Research in Child Development, 41*(1, Serial No. 164).

Bramlett, M. D., & Mosher, W. D. (2001). *First marriage dissolution, divorce, and remarriage: United States.* Advance Data from Vital and Health Statistics, No. 323. Hyattsville, MD: National Center for Health Statistics.

Bramlett, M. D., & Mosher, W. D. (2002). Cohabitation, marriage, divorce, and remarriage in the United States. *Vital Health Statistics, 23*(22). Hyattsville, MD: National Center for Health Statistics.

Brandt, B. (1989). A place for her death. *Humanistic Judaism, 17*(3), 83–85.

Brass, L. M., Isaacsohn, J. L., Merikangas, K. R., & Robinette, C. D. (1992). A study of twins and stroke. *Stroke, 23*(2), 221–223.

Braswell, G. S. (2006). Sociocultural contexts for the early development of semiotic production. *Psychological Bulletin, 132,* 877–894.

Braswell, G. S., & Callanan, M. A. (2003). Learning to draw recognizable graphic representations during mother-child interactions. *Merrill-Palmer Quarterly, 49,* 471–494.

Bratton, S. C., & Ray, D. (2002). Humanistic play therapy. In D. J. Cain (Ed.), *Humanistic psychotherapies: Handbook of research and practice* (pp. 369–402.). Washington, DC: American Psychological Association.

Braun, H., Jenkins, F., & Grigg, W. (2006). *A closer look at charter schools using hierarchical linear modeling* (NCES 2006-460). Washington, DC: U.S. Government Printing Office.

Braungart, J. M., Plomin, R., DeFries, J. C., & Fulker, D. W. (1992). Genetic influence on tester-rated infant temperament as assessed by Bayley's Infant Behavior Record: Nonadoptive and adoptive siblings and twins. *Developmental Psychology, 28,* 40–47.

Bray, J. H., & Hetherington, E. M. (1993). Families in transition: Introduction and overview. *Journal of Family Psychology, 7,* 3–8.

Brazelton, T. B. (1973). *Neonatal behavioral assessment scale.* Philadelphia: Lippincott.

Brazelton, T. B. (1984). *Neonatal behavioral assessment scale* (2nd ed.). Philadelphia: Lippincott.

Brazelton, T. B., & Nugent, J. K. (1995). *Neonatal behavioral assessment scale* (3rd ed.). Cambridge, England: Cambridge University Press.

Breastfeeding and HIV International Transmission Study Group. (2004). Late postnatal transmission of HIV-1 in breast-fed children: An individual patient data meta-analysis. *Journal of Infectious Diseases, 189,* 2154–2166.

Brendgen, M., Dionne, G., Girard, A., Boivin, M., Vitaro, F., & Perusse, D. (2005). Examining genetic and environmental effects on social aggression: A study of 6-year-old twins. *Child Development, 76,* 930–946.

Brenneman, K., Massey, C., Machado, S. F., & Gelman, R. (1996). Young children's plans differ for writing and drawing. *Cognitive Development, 11,* 397–419.

Brenner, M. H. (1991). Health, productivity, and the economic environment: Dynamic role of socio-economic status. In G. Green & F. Baker (Eds.), *Work, health, and productivity* (pp. 241–255). New York: Oxford University Press.

Brent, D. A., & Birmaher, B. (2002). Adolescent depression. *New England Journal of Medicine, 347,* 667–671.

Brent, D. A., & Mann, J. J. (2006). Familial pathways to suicidal behavior—Understanding and preventing suicide among adolescents. *New England Journal of Medicine, 355,* 2719–2721.

Bretherton, I. (1990). Communication patterns, internal working models, and the intergenerational transmission of attachment relationships. *Infant Mental Health Journal, 11*(3), 237–252.

Brewaeys, A., Ponjaert, I., Van Hall, V. E., & Golombok, S. (1997). Donor insemination: Child development and family functioning in lesbian mother families. *Human Reproduction, 12,* 1349–1359.

Brezina, T. (1999). Teenage violence toward parents as an adaptation to family strain: Evidence from a national survey of male adolescents. *Youth and Society, 30,* 416–444.

Bridge, J. A., Iyengar, S., Salary, C. B., Barbe, R. P., Birmaher, B., Pincus, H. A., Ren, L., & Brent, D. A. (2007). Clinical response and risk for reported suicidal ideation and suicide attempts in pediatric antidepressant treatment: A meta-analysis of randomized controlled trials. *Journal of the American Medical Association, 297,* 1683–1696.

Brim, O. G., Ryff, C. D., & Kessler, R. C. (2004). The MIDUS National Survey: An overview. In O. G. Brim, C. D. Ryff, & R. C. Kessler (Eds.), *How healthy are we? A national study of well-being at midlife.* Chicago: University of Chicago Press.

Britton, W. B., & Bootzin, R. R. (2004). Near-death experiences and the temporal lobe. *Psychological Science, 15,* 254–258.

Brock, D. W. (1992, March–April). Voluntary active euthanasia. *Hastings Center Report,* pp. 10–22.

Brody, G. H. (1998). Sibling relationship quality: Its causes and consequences. *Annual Review of Psychology, 49,* 1–24.

Brody, G. H. (2004). Siblings' direct and indirect contributions to child development. *Current Directions in Psychological Science, 13,* 124–126.

Brody, G. H., Chen, Y.-F., Murry, V. M., Ge, X., Simons, R. L., Gibbons, F. X., Gerrard, M., & Cutrona, C. E. (2006). Perceived discrimination and the adjustment of African American youths: A five-year longitudinal analysis with contextual moderation effects. *Child Development, 77*(5), 1170–1189.

Brody, G. H., Ge., X., Conger, R., Gibbons, F. X., Murry, V. M., Gerrard, M., & Simons, R. L. (2001). The influence of neighborhood disadvantage, collective socialization, and parenting on African American children's affiliation with deviant peers. *Child Development, 72*(4), 1231–1246.

Brody, G. H., Kim, S., Murry, V. M., & Brown, A. C. (2004). Protective longitudinal paths linking child competence to behavioral problems among African American siblings. *Child Development, 75,* 455–467.

Brody, J. E. (1995, June 28). Preventing birth defects even before pregnancy. *New York Times,* p. C10.

Brody, L. R., Zelazo, P. R., & Chaika, H. (1984). Habituation-dishabituation to speech in the neonate. *Developmental Psychology, 20,* 114–119.

Brodzinsky, D. (1997). Infertility and adoption adjustment: Considerations and clinical issues. In S. R. Leiblum (Ed.), *Infertility: Psychological issues and counseling strategies* (pp. 246–262). New York: Wiley.

Broidy, L. M., Tremblay, R. E., Brame, B., Fergusson, D., Horwood, J. L., Laird, R., Moffitt, T. E., Nagin, D. S., Bates, J. E., Dodge, K. A., Loeber, R., Lyam, D. R., Pettit, G. S., & Vitaro, F. (2003). Developmental trajectories of childhood disruptive behaviors and adolescent delinquency: A six-site cross-national study. *Developmental Psychology, 39,* 222–245.

Bromberger, J. T., Harlow, S., Avis, N., Kravitz, H. M., & Cordal, A. (2004). Racial/ethnic differences in the prevalence of depressive symptoms among middle-aged women: The study of women's health across the nation (SWAN). *American Journal of Public Health, 94,* 1378–1385.

Bromberger. J. T., Meyer, P. M., Kravitz, H. M., Sommer, B., Cordal, A., Powell, L., Ganz, P. A., & Sutton-Tyrell, K. (2001). Psychologic distress and natural menopause: A multiethnic community study. *American Journal of Public Health, 91,* 1435–1442.

Bronfenbrenner, U. (1979). *The ecology of human development.* Cambridge, MA: Harvard University Press.

Bronfenbrenner, U. (1986). Ecology of the family as a context for human development: Research perspectives. *Developmental Psychology, 22,* 723–742.

Bronfenbrenner, U. (1994). Ecological models of human development. In T. Husen & T. N. Postlethwaite (Eds.), *International encyclopedia of education* (2nd ed., Vol. 3, pp. 1643–1647). Oxford: Pergamon Press/ Elsevier Science.

Bronfenbrenner, U., & Morris, P. A. (1998). The ecology of developmental processes. In W. Damon (Series Ed.) & R. Lerner (Vol. Ed.), *Handbook of child psychology: Vol. 1. Theoretical models of human development* (5th ed., pp. 993–1028). New York: Wiley.

Bronstein, P. (1988). Father-child interaction: Implications for gender role socialization. In P. Bronstein & C. P. Cowan (Eds.), *Fatherhood today: Men's changing role in the family.* New York: Wiley.

Bronstein, P., Clauson, J., Stoll, M. F., & Abrams, C. L. (1993). Parenting behavior and children's social, psychological, and academic adjustment in diverse family structures. *Family Relations, 42,* 268–276.

Brookmeyer, K. A., Henrich, C. C., & Schwab-Stone, M. (2005). Adolescents who witness community violence: Can parent support and prosocial cognitions protect them from committing violence? *Child Development, 76,* 917–929.

Brookmeyer, R., Johnson, E., Ziegler-Graham, K., & Arrighi, H. M. (2007). Forecasting the global burden of Alzheimer's disease. *Alzheimer's and Dementia, 3*(3), 186–191. Paper also presented in June 2007 at the meeting of the second Alzheimer's Association International Conference on Prevention of Dementia, Washington, DC.

Brooks, R., & Meltzoff, A. N. (2002). The importance of eyes: How infants interpret adult looking behavior. *Developmental Psychology, 38,* 958–966.

Brooks, R., & Meltzoff, A. N. (2005). The development of gaze following and its relation to language. *Developmental Science, 8,* 535–543.

Brooks-Gunn, J. (2003). Do you believe in magic? What can we expect from early childhood intervention programs? *SRCD Social Policy Report, 17*(1).

Brooks-Gunn, J., Britto, P. R., & Brady, C. (1998). Struggling to make ends meet: Poverty and child development. In M. E. Lamb (Ed.), *Parenting and child development in "non-traditional" families* (pp. 279–304). Mahwah, NJ: Erlbaum.

Brooks-Gunn, J., & Duncan, G. J. (1997). The effects of poverty on children. *The Future of Children, 7,* 55–71.

Brooks-Gunn, J., Han, W.-J., & Waldfogel, J. (2002). Maternal employment and child cognitive outcomes in the first three years of life: The NICHD study of early child care. *Child Development, 73,* 1052–1072.

Broude, G. J. (1994). *Marriage, family, and relationships: A cross-cultural encyclopedia.* Santa Barbara, CA: ABC-CLIO.

Broude, G. J. (1995). *Growing up: A cross-cultural encyclopedia.* Santa Barbara, CA: ABC-CLIO.

Brousseau, E. (2006, May). *The effect of maternal body mass index on efficacy of dinoprostone vaginal insert for cervical ripening.* Paper presented at the annual meeting of the American College of Obstetricians and Gynecologists, Washington, DC.

Brown, A. L., Metz, K. E., & Campione, J. C. (1996). Social interaction and individual understanding in a community of learners: The influence of Piaget and Vygotsky. In A. Tryphon & J. Voneche (Eds.), *Piaget-Vygotsky: The social genesis of thought* (pp. 145–170). Hove, UK: Psychology Press.

Brown, A. S., Begg, M. D., Gravenstein, S., Schaefer, C. A., Wyatt, R. J., Bresnahan, M., Babulas, V. P., & Susser, E. S. (2004). Serologic evidence of prenatal influence in the etiology of schizophrenia. *Archives of General Psychiatry, 61,* 774–780.

Brown, A. S., Tapert, S. F., Granholm, E., & Delis, D. C. (2000) Neurocognitive functioning of adolescents: Effects of protracted alcohol use. *Alcoholism: Clinical and Experimental Research, 24,* 64–171.

Brown, B. B., & Klute, C. (2003). Friendships, cliques, and crowds. In G. R. Adams & M. D. Berzonsky. (Eds.), *Blackwell handbook of adolescence* (pp. 330–348). Malden, MA: Blackwell.

Brown, B. B., Mounts, N., Lamborn, S. D., & Steinberg, L. (1993). *Parenting practices and peer group affiliation in adolescence* (pp. 245–270). Cambridge, UK; Cambridge University Press.

Brown, J. D., L'Engle, K. L., Pardun, C. J., Guo, G., Kenneavy, K., & Jackson, C. (2006). Sexy media matter: Exposure to sexual content in music, movies, television, and magazines predicts black and white adolescents' sexual behavior. *Pediatrics, 117,* 1018–1027.

Brown, J. L. (1987). Hunger in the U.S. *Scientific American, 256*(2), 37–41.

Brown, J. R., & Dunn, J. (1996). Continuities in emotion understanding from three to six years. *Child Development, 67,* 789–802.

Brown, J. T., & Stoudemire, A. (1983). Normal and pathological grief. *Journal of the American Medical Association, 250,* 378–382.

Brown, L. M., & Gilligan, C. (1990, April). *The psychology of women and the development of girls.* Paper presented at the Laurel-Harvard Conference on the Psychology of Women and the Education of Girls, Cleveland, OH.

Brown, N. M. (1990). Age and children in the Kalahari. *Health and Human Development Research, 1,* 26–30.

Brown, P. (1993, April 17). Motherhood past midnight. *New Scientist,* pp. 4–8.

Brown, S. L. (2004). Family structure and child well-being: The significance of parental cohabitation. *Journal of Marriage and Family, 66,* 351–367.

Brown, S. L., Bulanda, J. R., & Lee, G. R. (2005). The significance of nonmarital cohabitation: Marital status and mental health benefits among middle-aged and older adults. *Journal of Gerontology: Social Sciences, 60B,* S21–S29.

Brown, S. L., Lee, G. R., & Bulanda, J. R. (2006). Cohabitation among older adults: A national portrait. *Journal of Gerontology: Social Sciences, 61B,* S71–S79.

Browne, A., & Finkelhor, D. (1986). Impact of child sexual abuse: A review of research. *Psychological Bulletin, 99*(1), 66–77.

Brownell, C. A., Ramani, G. B., & Zerwas, S. (2006). Becoming a social partner with peers: Cooperation and social understanding in one- and two-year-olds. *Child Development, 77,* 803–821.

Browning, C. R. (2002). The span of collective efficacy: Extending social disorganization theory to partner violence. *Journal of Marriage and Family, 64,* 833–850.

Bruder, C. E. G., Piotrowski, A., Gijsbers, A. A. C. J., Andersson, R., Erickson, S., de Stahl, T. D., Menzel, U., Sandgren, J., von Tell, D., Poplawski, A., Crowley, M., Crasto, C., Partridge, E. C., Tiwari, H., Allison, D. B., Komorowski, J., van Ommen, G.-J. B., Boomsma, D. I., Pedersen, N. L., den Dunnen, J. T., Wirdefeldt, K., & Dumanski, J. P. (2008). Phenotypically concordant and discordant monozygotic twins display different DNA copy-number-variation profiles. *American Journal of Human Genetics, 82*(3), 763–771.

Bruer, J. T. (2001). A critical and sensitive period primer. In D. B. Bailey, J. T. Bruer, F. J. Symons, & J. W. Lichtman (Eds.), *Critical thinking about critical periods: A series from the National Center for Early Development and Learning* (pp. 289–292). Baltimore, MD: Paul Brooks Publishing.

Bruner, A. B., Joffe, A., Duggan, A. K., Casella, J. F., & Brandt, J. (1996). Randomised study of cognitive effects of iron supplementation in non-anaemic iron-deficient adolescent girls. *Lancet, 348,* 992–996.

Brunson, K. L., Kramar, E., Lin, B., Chen, Y., Colgin, L. L., Yanagihara, T. K., Lynch, G., & Baram, T. Z. (2005). Mechanisms of late-onset cognitive decline after early-life stress. *Journal of Neurosicence, 25*(41), 9328–9338.

Bryant, B. K. (1987). Mental health, temperment, family, and friends: Perspectives on children's empathy and social perspective taking. In N. Eisenberg & J. Strayer (Eds.), Empathy and its development of competence in adolescence. *Child Development, 66,* 129–138.

Bryce, J., Boschi-Pinto, C., Shibuya, K., Black, R. E., & the WHO Child Health Epidemiology Reference Group. (2005). WHO estimates of the causes of death in children. *Lancet, 365,* 1147–1152.

Buchanan, C. M., Eccles, J. S., & Becker, J. B. (1992). Are adolescents the victims of raging hormones? Evidence for activational effects of hormones on moods and behavior at adolescence. *Psychological Bulletin, 111*(1), 62–107.

Büchel, C., & Sommer, M. (2004). Unsolved mystery: What causes stuttering? *PLoS Biology, 2,* 0159–0163.

Buchmann, C., & DiPrete, T. A. (2006). The growing female advantage in college completion: The role of family background and academic achievement. *American Sociological Review, 71,* 515–541.

Buckner, J. C., Bassuk, E. L., Weinreb, L. F., & Brooks, M. G. (1999). Homelessness and its relation to the mental health and behavior of low-income school-age children. *Developmental Psychology, 35*(1), 246–257.

Budson, A. E., & Price, B. H. (2005). Memory dysfunction. *New England Journal of Medicine, 352,* 692–699.

Buehler, C. (2006). Parents and peers in relation to early adolescent problem behavior. *Journal of Marriage and Family, 68,* 109–124.

Buhrmester, D. (1990). Intimacy of friendship, interpersonal competence, and adjustment during preadolescence and adolescence. *Child Development, 61,* 1101–1111.

Buhrmester, D. (1996). Need fulfillment, interpersonal competence, and the developmental contexts of early adolescent friendship. In W. M. Bukowski, A. F. Newcomb, & W. W. Hartup (Eds.), *The company they keep: Friendship in childhood and adolescence* (pp. 158–185). New York: Cambridge University Press.

Buhrmester, D., & Furman, W. (1990). Perceptions of sibling relationships during middle childhood and adolescence. *Child Development, 61,* 138–139.

Bulcroft, K., & O'Conner, M. (1986). The importance of dating relationships on quality of life for older persons. *Family Relations, 35,* 397–401.

Bulcroft, R. A., & Bulcroft, K. A. (1991). The nature and function of dating in later life. *Research on Aging, 13,* 244–260.

Bulkley, K., & Fisler, J. (2002). *A decade of charter schools: From theory to practice.* Philadelphia: Consortium for Policy Research in Education, Graduate School of Education, University of Pennsylvania.

Bunikowski, R., Grimmer, I., Heiser, A., Metze, B., Schafer, A., & Obladen, M. (1998). Neurodevelopmental outcome after prenatal exposure to opiates. *European Journal of Pediatrics, 157,* 724–730.

Burchinal, M. R., Campbell, F. A., Bryant, D. M., Wasik, B. H., & Ramey, C. T. (1997). Early intervention and mediating processes in cognitive performance of children of low-income African American families. *Child Development, 68,* 935–954.

Burchinal, M. R., Roberts, J. E., Nabors, L. A., & Bryant, D. M. (1996). Quality of center child care and infant cognitive and language development. *Child Development, 67,* 606–620.

Bureau of Justice Statistics. (2006). *Homicide trends in the United States.* Retrieved August 28, 2006, from www.ojp.usdoj.gov/bjs/homicide/intimates.htm.

Bureau of Labor Statistics. (2005). Data on unemployment rate. Retrieved February 16, 2005, from www.bls.gov/cps/home.htm.

Bureau of Labor Statistics. (2006, April 27). Employment characteristics of families in 2005 (News release). Washington, DC: Author.

Burhans, K. K., & Dweck, C. S. (1995). Helplessness in early childhood: The role of contingent worth. *Child Development, 66,* 1719–1738.

Burke, D. M., & Shafto, M. A. (2004). Aging and language production. *Current Directions in Psychological Science, 13,* 81–84.

Burke, S. N., & Barnes, C. A. (2006). Neural plasticity in the ageing brain. *Nature Review Neuroscience, 7,* 30–40.

Burns, B. J., Phillips, S. D., Wagner, H. R., Barth, R. P., Kolko, D. J., Campbell, Y., & Landsverk, J. (2004). Mental health need and access to mental health services by youths involved with child welfare: A national survey. *Journal of the American Academy of Child & Adolescent Psychiatry, 43,* 960–970.

Burns, G. (1983). *How to live to be 100—or more: The ultimate diet, sex, and exercise book.* New York: Putnam.

Burt, A., Annest, J. L., Ballesteros, M. F., & Budnitz, D. S. (2006). Nonfatal, unintentional medication exposures among young children—United States, 2001–2003. *Morbidity and Mortality Weekly Report, 55,* 1–5.

Burton, L. C., Zdaniuk, B., Schulz, R., Jackson, S., & Hirsch, C. (2003). Transitions in spousal caregiving. *Gerontologist, 43,* 230–241.

Bushnell, E. W., & Boudreau, J. P. (1993). Motor development and the mind: The potential role of motor abilities as a determinant of aspects of perceptual development. *Child Development, 64,* 1005–1021.

Busse, E. W. (1987). Primary and secondary aging. In G. L. Maddox (Ed.), *The encyclopedia of aging* (p. 534). New York: Springer.

Bussey, K., & Bandura, A. (1992). Self-regulatory mechanisms governing gender development. *Child Development, 63,* 1236–1250.

Bussey, K., & Bandura, A. (1999). Social cognitive theory of gender development and differentiation. *Psychological Review, 106,* 676–713.

Butler, R. (1961). Re-awakening interests. *Nursing Homes: Journal of the American Nursing Home Association, 10,* 8–19.

Butler, R. (1996). The dangers of physician-assisted suicide. *Geriatrics, 51,* 7.

Butler, R. N., Davis, R., Lewis, C. B., Nelson, M. E., & Strauss, E. (1998a). Physical fitness: Benefits of exercise for the older patient. 2. *Geriatrics 53,* 46, 49–52, 61–62.

Butler, R. N., Davis, R., Lewis, C. B., Nelson, M. E., & Strauss, E. (1998b). Physical fitness: How to help older patients live stronger and longer. 1. *Geriatrics, 53,* 26–28, 31–32, 39–40.

Byers, T. (2006). Overweight and mortality among baby boomers—now we're getting personal. *New England Journal of Medicine, 355,* 758–760.

Byrne, M., Agerbo, E., Ewald, H., Eaton, W. W., & Mortensen, P. B. (2003). Parental age and risk of schizophrenia. *Archives of General Psychiatry, 60,* 673–678.

Byrnes, J. P., & Fox, N. A. (1998). The educational relevance of research in cognitive neuroscience. *Educational Psychology Review, 10,* 297–342.

Bystron, I., Rakic, P., Molnar, Z., & Blakemore, C. (2006). The first neurons of the human cerebral cortex. *Nature Neuroscience, 9*(7), 880–886.

Cabrera, N. J., Tamis-LeMonda, C. S., Bradley, R. H., Hofferth, S., & Lamb, M. E. (2000). Fatherhood in the twenty-first century. *Child Development, 71,* 127–136.

Caelli, K., Downie, J., & Letendre, A. (2002). Parents' experiences of midwife-managed care following the loss of a baby in a previous pregnancy. *Journal of Advanced Nursing, 39,* 127–136.

Cain, W. S., Reid, F., & Stevens, J. C. (1990). Missing ingredients: Aging and the discrimination of flavor. *Journal of Nutrition for the Elderly, 9,* 3–15.

Caldwell, B. M., & Bradley, R. H. (1984). *Home observation for measurement of the environment.* Unpublished manuscript, University of Arkansas at Little Rock.

Calkins, S. D., & Fox, N. A. (1992). The relations among infant temperament, security of attachment, and behavioral inhibition at twenty-four months. *Child Development, 63,* 1456–1472.

Callahan, S. T., & Cooper, W. O. (2005). Uninsurance and health care access among young adults in the United States. *Pediatrics, 116,* 88–95.

Camarata, S., & Woodcock, R. (2006). Sex differences in processing speed: Developmental effects in males and females. *Intelligence, 34*(3), 231–252.

Cameron, L., Rutland, A., Brown, R., & Douch, R. (2006). Changing children's intergroup attitudes towards refugees: Testing different models of extended contact. *Child Development, 77,* 1208–1219.

Camp, C. J. (1989). World-knowledge systems. In L. W. Poon, D. C. Rubin, & B. A. Wilson (Eds.), *Everyday cognition in adulthood and late life.* Cambridge, England: Cambridge University Press.

Camp, C. J., Foss, J. W., Stevens, A. B., Reichard, C. C., McKitrick, L. A., & O'Hanlon, A. M. (1993). Memory training in normal and demented populations: The E-I-E-I-O model. *Experimental Aging Research, 19,* 277–290.

Camp, C. J., & McKitrick, L. A. (1989). The dialectics of remembering and forgetting across the adult lifespan. In D. Kramer & M. Bopp (Eds.), *Dialectics and contextualism in clinical and developmental psychology: Change, transformation, and the social context* (pp. 169–187). New York: Springer.

Camp, C. J., & McKitrick, L. A. (1992). Memory interventions in Alzheimer's-type dementia populations: Methodological and theoretical issues. In R. L. West & J. D. Sinnott (Eds.), *Everyday memory and aging: Current research and methodology* (pp. 155–172). New York: Springer-Verlag.

Campa, M. J., & Eckenrode, J. J. (2006). Pathways to intergenerational adolescent childbearing in a high-risk sample. *Journal of Marriage and Family, 68,* 558–572.

Campbell, A., Shirley, L., & Candy, J. (2004). A longitudinal study of gender-related cognition and behaviour. *Developmental Science, 7,* 1–9.

Campbell, A., Shirley, L., Heywood, C., & Crook, C. (2000). Infants' visual preference for sex-congruent babies, children, toys, and activities: A longitudinal study. *British Journal of Developmental Psychology, 18,* 479–498.

Campbell, F. A., Pungello, E. P., Miller-Johnson, S., Burchinal, M., & Ramey, C. T. (2001). The development of cognitive and academic abilities: Growth curves from an early childhood education experiment. *Developmental Psychology, 37*(2), 231–242.

Campos, J., Bertenthal, B., & Benson, N. (1980, April). *Self-produced locomotion and the extraction of form invariance.* Paper presented at the meeting of the International Conference on Infant Studies, New Haven, CT.

Canli, T., Qui, M., Omura, K., Congdon, E., Haas, B., Amin, Z., Herrmann, M. J., Constable, R. T., & Lesch, K. P. (2006). *Proceedings of the National Academy of Sciences, USA, 103,* 16033–16038.

Cannon, T. D., Hennah, W., van Erp, T. G. M., Thompson, P. M., Lonnqvistt, J., Huttenen, M., Gasperoni, T., Tuulio-Henriksson, A., Pirkola, T., Toga, A. W., Kaprio, J., Mazziotta, J., & Peltonen, L. (2005). Association of DISC1/TRAX haplotypes with schizophrenia, reduced prefrontal gray matter, and impaired short- and long-term memory. *Archives of General Psychiatry, 62,* 1205–1213.

Cantor, J. (1994). Confronting children's fright responses to mass media. In D. Zillman, J. Bryant, & A. C. Huston (Eds.), *Media, children, and the family: Social scientific, psychoanalytic, and clinical perspectives* (pp. 139–150). Hillsdale, NJ: Erlbaum.

Cao, A., Saba, L., Galanello, R., & Rosatelli, M. C. (1997). Molecular diagnosis and carrier screening for thalassemia. *Journal of the American Medical Association, 278,* 1273–1277.

Capaldi, D. M., Stoolmiller, M., Clark, S., & Owen, L. D. (2002). Heterosexual risk behaviors in at-risk young men from early adolescence to young adulthood: Prevalence, prediction, and STD contraction. *Developmental Psychology, 38,* 394–406.

Caplan, L. J., & Schooler, C. (2006). Household work complexity, intellectual functioning, and self-esteem in men and women. *Journal of Marriage and Family, 68,* 883–900.

Caplan, M., Vespo, J., Pedersen, J., & Hay, D. F. (1991). Conflict and its resolution in small groups of one- and two-year olds. *Child Development, 62,* 1513–1524.

Capute, A. J., Shapiro, B. K., & Palmer, F. B. (1987). Marking the milestones of language development. *Contemporary Pediatrics, 4*(4), 24.

Caraballo, R. S., Giovino, G. A., Pechacek, T. F., Mowery, P. D., Richter, P. A., Strauss, W. J., Sharp, D. J., Eriksen, M. P., Pirkle, J. L., & Maurer, K. R. (1998). Racial and ethnic differences in serum cotinine levels of cigarette smokers. *Journal of the American Medical Association, 280,* 135–139.

Carbery, J., & Buhrmester, D. (1998). Friendship and need fulfillment during three phases of young adulthood. *Journal of Social & Personal Relationships, 15,* 393–409.

Carlson, E. A. (1998). A prospective longitudinal study of attachment disorganization/ disorientation. *Child Development, 69*(4), 1107–1128.

Carlson, E. A., Sroufe, L. A., & Egeland, B. (2004). The construction of experience: A longitudinal study of representation and behavior. *Child Development, 75,* 66–83.

Carlson, M. J. (2006). Family structure, father involvement, and adolescent behavioral outcomes. *Journal of Marriage and Family, 68,* 137–154.

Carlson, S. M., Moses, L. J., & Hix, H. R. (1998). The role of inhibitory processes in young children's difficulties with deception and false belief. *Child Development, 69*(3), 672–691.

Carlson, S. M., & Taylor, M. (2005). Imaginary companions and impersonated characters: Sex differences in children's fantasy play. *Merrill-Palmer Quarterly, 51*(1), 93–118.

Carlson, S. M., Wong, A., Lemke, M., & Cosser, C. (2005). Gesture as a window in children's beginning understanding of false belief. *Child Development, 76,* 73–86.

Carnelley, K. B., Wortman, C. B., Bolger, N., & Burke, C. T. (2006). The time course of grief reactions to spousal loss: Evidence from a national probability sample. *Journal of Personality and Social Psychology, 91,* 476–492.

Carnethon, M. R., Gulati, M., & Greenland, P. (2005). Prevalence and cardiovascular disease correlates of low cardiorespiratory fitness in adolescents and adults. *Journal of the American Medical Association, 294,* 2981–2988.

Carothers, S. S., Borkowski, J. G., Lefever, J. B., & Whitman, T. L. (2005). Religiosity and the socioemotional adjustment of adolescent mothers and their children. *Journal of Family Psychology, 19,* 263–275.

Carpenter, D. (2004, May 16). An age-old issue: Some expect more lawsuits with half the work force 40 or older. *Chicago Sun-Times,* p. 45A.

Carr, D., House, J. S., Kessler, R. C., Nesse, R. M., Sonnega, J., & Wortman, C. (2000). Marital quality and psychological adjustment to widowhood among older adults: A longitudinal analysis. *Journal of Gerontology: Social Sciences, 55B,* S197–S207.

Carraher, T. N., Schliemann, A. D., & Carraher, D. W. (1988). Mathematical concepts in everyday life. In G. B. Saxe and M. Gearhart (Eds.), *Children's mathematics.* (New Directions in Child Development, No. 41, pp. 71–87). San Francisco: Jossey-Bass.

Carrel, L., & Willard, B. F. (2005). X-inactivation profile reveals extensive variability in X-linked gene expression in females. *Nature, 434,* 400–404.

Carskadon, M. A., Acebo, C., Richardson, G. S., Tate, B. A., & Seifer, R. (1997). Long nights protocol: Access to circadian parameters in adolescents. *Journal of Biological Rhythms, 12,* 278–289.

Carstensen, L. L. (1991). Selectivity theory: Social activity in life-span context. In *Annual review of gerontology and geriatrics* (Vol. 11, pp. 195–217). New York: Springer.

Carstensen, L. L. (1995). Evidence for a life-span theory of socioemotional selectivity. *Current Directions in Psychological Science, 4,* 150–156.

Carstensen, L. L. (1996). Socioemotional selectivity: A life-span developmental account of social behavior. In M. R. Merrens & G. G. Brannigan (Eds.), *The developmental psychologists: Research adventures across the life span* (pp. 251–272). New York: McGraw-Hill.

Carstensen, L. L. (1999). Elderly show their emotional know-how. (Cited in *Science News, 155,* p. 374). Paper presented at the meeting of the American Psychological Society, Denver, CO.

Carstensen, L. L., Graff, J., Levenson, R. W., & Gottman, J. M. (1996). Affect in intimate relationships: The development course of marriage. In C. Magai & S. H. McFadden (Eds.), *Handbook of emotion, adult development, and aging* (pp. 227–247). San Diego: Academic Press.

Carstensen, L. L., Gross, J., & Fung, H. (1997). The social context of emotion. *Annual Review of Geriatrics and Gerontology, 17,* 331.

Carstensen, L. L., Isaacowitz, D. M., & Charles, S. T. (1999). Taking time seriously: A theory of socioemotional selectivity. *American Psychologist, 54,* 165–181.

Carstensen, L. L., & Mikels, J. A. (2005). At the intersection of emotion and cognition: Aging and the positivity effect. *Current Directions in Psychological Science, 14,* 117–122.

Carstensen, L. L., Pasupathi, M., Mayr, U., & Nesselroade, J. (2000). Emotional experience in everyday life across the adult life span. *Journal of Personality and Social Psychology, 79,* 644–655.

Carter, R. C., Jacobson, S. W., Molteno, C. D., Chiodo, L. M., Viljoen, D., & Jacobson, J. L. (2005). Effects of prenatal alcohol exposure on infant visual acuity. *Journal of Pediatrics, 147*(4), 473–479.

Carver, P. R., & Iruka, I. U. (2006). *After-school programs and activities: 2005* (NCES 2006-076). Washington, DC: National Center for Education Statistics.

Casaer, P. (1993). Old and new facts about perinatal brain development. *Journal of Child Psychology and Psychiatry, 34*(1), 101–109.

Case, R. (1985). *Intellectual development: Birth to adulthood.* Orlando, FL: Academic Press.

Case, R. (1992). Neo-Piagetian theories of child development. In R. Sternberg & C. Berg (Eds.), *Intellectual development* (pp. 161–196). New York: Cambridge University Press.

Case, R., & Okamoto, Y. (1996). The role of central conceptual structures in the development of children's thought. *Monographs of the Society for Research in Child Development, 61*(1–2, Serial No. 246).

Casey, B. M., McIntire, D. D., & Leveno, K. J. (2001). The continuing value of the Apgar score for the assessment of newborn infants. *New England Journal of Medicine, 344,* 467–471.

Casper, L. M. (1997). My daddy takes care of me: Fathers as care providers. *Current Population Reports* (P70–59). Washington, DC: U.S. Bureau of the Census.

Caspi, A. (1998). Personality development across the life course. In W. Damon (Series Ed.) & N. Eisenberg (Vol. Ed.), *Handbook of child psychology: Vol. 3. Social, emotional, and personality development* (5th ed., pp. 311–388). New York: Wiley.

Caspi, A. (2000). The child is father of the man: Personality continuity from childhood to adulthood. *Journal of Personality and Social Psychology, 78,* 158–172.

Caspi, A., Lynam, D., Moffitt, T. E., & Silva, P. A. (1993). Unraveling girls' delinquency: Biological, dispositional, and contextual contributions to adolescent misbehavior. *Developmental Psychology, 29*(1), 19–30.

Caspi, A., McClay, J., Moffitt, T. E., Mill, J., Martin, J., Craig, I. W., Taylor, A., & Poulton, R. (2002). Role of genotype in the cycle of violence in maltreated children. *Science, 297,* 851–854.

Caspi, A., Moffitt, T. E., Cannon, M., McClay, J., Murray, R., Harrington, H., Taylor, A., Arseneault, L., Williams, B., Braithwaite, A., Poulton, R., & Craig, I. W. (2005). Moderation of the effect of adolescent-onset cannabis use on adult psychosis by a functional polymorphism in the COMT gene: Longitudinal evidence of a gene x environment interaction. *Biological Psychiatry, 57,* 1117–112.

Caspi, A., & Silva, P. (1995). Temperamental qualities at age 3 predict personality traits in young adulthood: Longitudinal evidence from a birth cohort. *Child Development, 66,* 486–498.

Caspi, A., Sugden, K., Moffitt, T. E., Taylor, A., Craig, I. W., Harrington, H., McClay, J., Mill, J., Martin, J., Braithwaite, A., & Poulton, R. (2003). Influence of life stress on depression: Moderation by a polymorphism in the 5-HTT gene. *Science, 301,* 386–389.

Cassel, C. (1992). Ethics and the future of aging research: Promises and problems. *Generations, 16*(4), 61–65.

Cassidy, K. W., Werner, R. S., Rourke, M., Zubernis, L. S., & Balaraman, G. (2003). The relationship between psychological understanding and positive social behaviors. *Social Development, 12,* 198–221.

Cates, K. (2007, August 17). Mom delivers rare identical quadruplets. *Associated Press.*

Cattell, R. B. (1965). *The scientific analysis of personality.* Baltimore: Penguin Books.

Caughey, A. B., Hopkins, L. M., & Norton, M. E. (2006). Chorionic villus sampling compared with amniocentesis and the difference in the rate of pregnancy loss. *Obstetrics and Gynecology, 108,* 612–616.

Cavanaugh, J. C., Kramer, D. A., Sinnott, J. D., Camp, C. J., & Markley, R. P. (1985). On missing links and such: Interfaces between cognitive research and everyday problem solving. *Human Development, 28,* 146–168.

Cavazzana-Calvo, M., & Fischer, A. (2007). Gene therapy for severe combined immunodeficiency: Are we there yet? *Journal of Clinical Investigation, 117,* 1456–1465.

Cavazzana-Calvo, M., Hacein-Bey, S., de Saint Basile, G., Gross, F., Yvon, E., Nusbaum, P., Selz, F., Hue, C., Certain, S., Casanova, J. L., Bousso, P., Deist, F. L., & Fischer, A. (2000). Gene therapy of human severe combined immunodeficiency (SCID)-X1 disease. *Science, 288,* 669–672.

Cawthon, R. M., Smith, K. R., O'Brien, E., Sivatchenko, A., & Kerber, R. A. (2003). Association between telomere length in blood and mortality in people aged 60 years or older. *Lancet, 361,* 393–394.

CBS News. (2004, August 6). *48 Hours.* Retrieved April 11, 2008, from www .cbsnews.com/stories/2004/07/29/48hours/ main632909.shtml.

Ceci, S., & Liker, J. (1986). A day at the races: A study of IQ, expertise, and cognitive complexity. *Journal of Experimental Psychology: General, 114,* 255–266.

Ceci, S. J. (1991). How much does schooling influence general intelligence and its cognitive components? A reassessment of the evidence. *Developmental Psychology, 27,* 703–722.

Ceci, S. J., & Williams, W. M. (1997). Schooling, intelligence, and income. *American Psychologist, 52*(10), 1051–1058.

Celis, W. (1990). More states are laying school paddle to rest. *New York Times,* pp. A1, B12.

Center for Autism Research. (n.d.). *MRI research.* Retrieved May 10, 2006, from www.courchesneautismlab.org/mri.html.

Center for Education Reform. (2004, August 17). Comprehensive data discounts *New York Times* account; reveals charter schools performing at or above traditional schools [Press release]. Retrieved September 17, 2004, from http://edreform.com/index .cfm?fuseAction=document&documentID =1806.

Center for Education Reform. (2008). *Just the FAQs–charter schools.* Retrieved April 8, 2008, from www.edreform.com/index .cfm?fuseAction=document&documentID= 60&sectionID=67&NEWSYEAR=2008.

Center for Weight and Health (2001). *Pediatric overweight: A review of the literature: Executive summary.* Berkeley: University of California at Berkeley.

Center on Addiction and Substance Abuse at Columbia University (CASA). (1996, June). *Substance abuse and the American woman.* New York: Author.

Centers for Disease Control and Prevention (CDC). (2000a). *CDC's guidelines for school and community programs: Promoting lifelong physical activity.* Retrieved May 26, 2000, from www.cdc.gov/nccdphp/dash/ phactaag.htm.

Centers for Disease Control and Prevention (CDC). (2000b). *Tracking the hidden epidemic: Trends in STDs in the U.S., 2000.* Washington, DC: Author.

Centers for Disease Control and Prevention (CDC). (2002). Youth risk behavior surveillance—United States, 2001. *Morbidity and Mortality Weekly Report, 5I*(4). Atlanta, GA: Author.

Centers for Disease Control and Prevention (CDC). (2004). National, state, and urban area vaccination coverage among children aged 19–36 months—United States, 2003. *Morbidity and Mortality Weekly Report, 53,* 658–661.

Centers for Disease Control and Prevention (CDC). (2005). *Assisted reproductive technology: Home.* Retrieved January 25, 2006, from www.cdc.gov/ART/

Centers for Disease Control and Prevention (CDC). (2006a). Achievements in public health: Reduction in perinatal transmission of HIV infection—United States, 1985–2005. *Morbidity and Mortality Weekly Report, 55*(21), 592–597.

Centers for Disease Control and Prevention (CDC). (2006b). Improved national prevalence estimates for 18 selected major birth defects—United States, 1999–2001. *Morbidity and Mortality Weekly Report, 54*(51 & 52), 1301–1305.

Centers for Disease Control and Prevention (CDC). (2006c). National, state, and urban area vaccination coverage among children aged 19–35 months—United States, 2005. *Morbidity and Mortality Weekly Report, 55*(36), 988–993.

Centers for Disease Control and Prevention (CDC). (2006d). Youth risk behavior surveillance—United States, 2005. *Morbidity and Mortality Weekly Report, 55*(SS-5).

Centers for Disease Control and Prevention (CDC). (2007a). Cases of HIV infection and AIDS in the United States and dependent areas, 2005. *HIV/AIDS Surveillance Report, 17* (Rev. ed., June 2007).

Centers for Disease Control and Prevention (CDC). (2007b, Summer). *Suicide: Facts at a Glance.* Retrieved May 18, 2008 from www.cdc.gov/ncipc/dvp/Suicide/ SuicideDataSheet.pdf.

Centers for Disease Control and Prevention (CDC). (2007c). *Web-based Injury Statistics Query and Reporting System.* Retrieved June 2007 from www.cdc.gov/ncipc/wisqars/ default.htm.

Centers for Disease Control and Prevention (CDC). (2008). *WISQARS database.* Retrieved May 19, 2008 from www.cdc.gov/ ncipc/wisqars/default.htm.

Centers for Disease Control and Prevention (CDC) Office of Media Relations. (2006, June 29). *CDC's advisory committee recommends human papillomavirus virus vaccination* [Press release]. Atlanta, GA: Author.

Central Intelligence Agency. (2008). *The world factbook.* Retrieved June 23, 2008, from www.cia.gov/library/publications/the-world-factbook/geos/xx.html.

Centre for Educational Research and Innovation. (2004). Education at a Glance: OECD indicators—2004. *Education and Skills, 2004*(14), 1–456.

Cepeda-Benito, A., Reynoso, J. T., & Erath, S. (2004). Meta-analysis of the efficacy of nicotine replacement therapy for smoking cessation: Differences between men and women. *Journal of Consulting and Clinical Psychology, 72,* 712–722.

Chafetz, M. D. (1992). *Smart for life.* New York: Penguin Books.

Chambers, R. A., Taylor, J. R., & Potenza, M. N. (2003). Developmental neurocircuitry of motivation in adolescence: A critical period of addiction vulnerability. *American Journal of Psychiatry, 160,* 1041–1052.

Chan, R. W., Raboy, B., & Patterson, C. J. (1998). Psychosocial adjustment among children conceived via donor insemination by lesbian and heterosexual mothers. *Child Development, 69,* 443–457.

Chandra, H., & Singh, P. (2001). Organ transplantation: Present scenario and future strategies for transplant programme (specially cadaveric) in India: Socioadministrative respects. *Journal of the Indian Medical Association, 99,* 374–377.

Chao, R. (1996). Chinese and European American mothers' beliefs about the role of parenting in children's school success. *Journal of Cross-Cultural Psychology, 27,* 403–423.

Chao, R. K. (1994). Beyond parental control and authoritarian parenting style: Understanding Chinese parenting through the cultural notion of training. *Child Development, 65,* 1111–1119.

Chao, R. K. (2001). Extending research on the consequences of parenting style for Chinese Americans and European Americans. *Child Development, 72,* 1832–1843.

Chapman, M., & Lindenberger, U. (1988). Functions, operations, and décalage in the development of transitivity. *Developmental Psychology, 24,* 542–551.

Chappell, N. L. (1991). Living arrangements and sources of caregiving. *Journal of Gerontology: Social Sciences, 46*(1), S1–S8.

Charles, S. T., & Piazza, J. R. (2007). Memories of social interactions: Age differences in emotional intensity. *Psychology and Aging, 22,* 300–309.

Charles, S. T., Reynolds, C. A., & Gatz, M. (2001). Age-related differences and change in positive and negative affect over 23 years. *Journal of Personality and Social Psychology, 80,* 136–151.

Charlesworth, A., & Glantz, S. A. (2005). Smoking in the movies increases adolescent smoking: A review. *Pediatrics, 116,* 1516–1528.

Charness, N., & Schultetus, R. S. (1999). Knowledge and expertise. In F. T. Durso (Ed.), *Handbook of applied cognition* (pp. 57–81). Chichester, England: Wiley.

Chehab, F. F., Mounzih, K., Lu, R., & Lim, M. E. (1997, January 3). Early onset of reproductive function in normal female mice treated with leptin. *Science, 275,* 88–90.

Chen, A., & Rogan, W. J. (2004). Breast-feeding and the risk of postneonatal death in the United States. *Pediatrics, 113,* e435–e439.

Chen, C., & Stevenson, H. W. (1995). Motivation and mathematics achievement: A comparative study of Asian-American, Caucasian-American, and East Asian high school students. *Child Development, 66,* 1215–1234.

Chen, C. L., Weiss, N. S., Newcomb, P., Barlow, W., & White, E. (2002). Hormone replacement therapy in relation to breast cancer. *Journal of the American Medical Association, 287,* 734–741.

Chen, E., Matthews, K. A., & Boyce, W. T. (2002). Socioeconomic differences in children's health: How and why do these relationships change with age? *Psychological Bulletin, 128,* 295–329.

Chen, L., Baker, S. B., Braver, E. R., & Li, G. (2000). Carrying passengers as a risk factor for crashes fatal to 16- and 17-year-old drivers. *Journal of the American Medical Association, 283*(12), 1578–1582.

Chen, W., Li, S., Cook, N. R., Rosner, B. A., Srinivasan, S. R., Boerwinkle, E., & Berenson, G. S. (2004). An autosomal genome scan for loci influencing longitudinal burden of body mass index from childhood to young adulthood in white sibships. The Bogalusa Heart Study. *International Journal of Obesity, 28,* 462–469.

Chen, X., Cen, G., Li, D., & He, Y. (2005). Social functioning and adjustment in Chinese children: The imprint of historical time. *Child Development, 76,* 182–195.

Chen, X. K., Wen, S. W., Krewski, D., Fleming, N., Yang, Q., & Walker, M. C. (2008). Paternal age and adverse birth outcomes: Teenager or 40+, who is at risk? *Human Reproduction.* (Advance Access published February 6, 2008, DOI: 10.1093/humrep/dem403).

Cherlin, A. (2004). The deinstitutionalization of American marriage. *Journal of Marriage and Family, 66,* 848–861.

Cherlin, A., & Furstenberg, F. F. (1986). *The new American grandparent.* New York: Basic Books.

Cherry, K. E., & Park, D. C. (1993). Individual differences and contextual variables influence spatial memory in younger and older adults. *Psychology and Aging, 8,* 517–526.

Cheruku, S. R., Montgomery-Downs, H. E., Farkas, S. L., Thoman, E. B., & Lammi-Keefe, C. J. (2002). Higher maternal plasma docosahexaenoic acid during pregnancy is associated with more mature neonatal sleep-state patterning. *American Journal of Clinical Nutrition, 76,* 608–613.

Chia, S. E., Shi, L. M., Chan, O. Y., Chew, S. K., & Foong, B. H. (2004). A population-based study on the association between parental occupations and some common birth defects in Singapore (1994–1998). *Journal of Occupational and Environmental Medicine, 46*(9), 916–923.

Children's Defense Fund (CDF). (1998). *The state of America's children yearbook, 1998.* Washington, DC: Author.

Children's Defense Fund (CDF). (2004). *The state of America's children, 2004.* Washington, DC: Author.

Chiriboga, C. A., Brust, J. C.M., Bateman, D., & Hauser, W. A. (1999). Dose-response effect of fetal cocaine exposure on newborn neurologic function. *Pediatrics, 103,* 79–85.

Chiriboga, D. A. (1997). Crisis, challenge, and stability in the middle years. In M. E. Lachman & J. B. James (Eds.), *Multiple paths of midlife development* (pp. 293–322). Chicago: University of Chicago Press.

Chochinov, H. M., Hack, T., McClement, S., Harlos, M., & Kristjanson, L. (2002). Dignity in the terminally ill: A developing empirical model. *Social Science Medicine, 54,* 433–443.

Chochinov, H. M., Tataryn, D., Clinch, J. J., & Dudgeon, D. (1999). Will to live in the terminally ill. *Lancet, 354,* 816–819.

Chodirker, B. N., Cadrin, C., Davies, G. A.L., Summers, A. M., Wilson, R. D., Winsor, E. J. T., & Young, D. (2001, July). Canadian guidelines for prenatal diagnosis: Techniques of prenatal diagnosis. *JOGC Clinical Practice Guidelines,* No. 105.

Chomitz, V. R., Cheung, L. W. Y., & Lieberman, E. (1995). The role of lifestyle in preventing low birth weight. *Future of Children, 5*(1), 121–138.

Chomsky, C. S. (1969). *The acquisition of syntax in children from five to ten.* Cambridge, MA: MIT Press.

Chomsky, N. (1957). *Syntactic structures.* The Hague: Mouton.

Chomsky, N. (1972). *Language and mind* (2nd ed.). New York: Harcourt Brace Jovanovich.

Chomsky, N. (1995). *The minimalist program.* Cambridge, MA: MIT Press.

Chorpita, B. P., & Barlow, D. H. (1998). The development of anxiety: The role of control in the early environment. *Psychological Bulletin, 124,* 3–21.

Christakis, D. A., Zimmerman, F. J., DiGiuseppe, D. L., & McCarty, C. A. (2004). Early television exposure and subsequent attentional problems in children. *Pediatrics, 113,* 708–713.

Christakis, N. A., & Allison, P. D. (2006). Mortality after the hospitalization of a spouse. *New England Journal of Medicine, 354,* 719–730.

Christakis, N. A., & Fowler, J. H. (2007). The spread of obesity in a large social network over 32 years. *New England Journal of Medicine, 357,* 370–379.

Christensen, A., Eldridge, K., Catta-Preta, A. B., Lim, V. R., & Santagata, R. (2006). Cross-cultural consistency of the demand/withdraw interaction pattern in couples. *Journal of Marriage and Family, 68,* 1029–1044.

Christensen, K., Johnson, T. E., & Vaupel, J. W. (2006). The quest for genetic determinants of human longevity: Challenges and insights. *Nature Reviews Genetics, 7,* 436–448.

Christian, M. S., & Brent, R. L. (2001). Teratogen update: Evaluation of the reproductive and developmental risks of caffeine. *Teratology, 64*(1), 51–78.

Christie, J. F. (1991). *Psychological research on play: Connections with early literacy development.* Albany: State University of New York Press.

Christie, J. F. (1998). Play as a medium for literacy development. In D. P. Fromberg & D. Bergen (Eds.), *Play from birth to 12 and beyond: Contexts, perspectives, and meanings* (pp. 50–55). New York: Garland.

Chung, H. L., & Steinberg, L. (2006). Relations between neighborhood factors, parenting behaviors, peer deviance, and delinquency among serious juvenile offenders. *Developmental Psychology, 42,* 319–331.

Church, T. S., Earnest, C. P. Skinner, J. S., & Blair, S. N. (2007). Effects of different doses of physical activity on cardiorespiratory fitness among sedentary, overweight or obese postmenopausal women with elevated blood pressure. *Journal of the American Medical Association, 297,* 2081–2091.

Cicchetti, D., & Toth, S. L. (1998). The development of depression in children and adolescents. *American Psychologist, 53,* 221–241.

Cicero, S., Curcio, P., Papageorghiou, A., Sonek, J., & Nicolaides, K. (2001). Absence of nasal bone in fetuses with trisomy 21 at 11–14 weeks of gestation: An observational study. *Lancet, 358,* 1665–1667.

Cicirelli, V. G. (1976). Family structure and interaction: Sibling effects on socialization. In M. F. McMillan & S. Henao (Eds.), *Child psychiatry: Treatment and research.* New York: Brunner/Mazel.

Cicirelli, V. G. (1977). Relationship of siblings to the elderly person's feelings and concerns. *Journal of Gerontology, 12*(3), 317–322.

Cicirelli, V. G. (1989). Feelings of attachment to siblings and well-being in later life. *Psychology and Aging, 4*(2), 211–216.

Cicirelli, V. G. (1994). Sibling relationships in cross-cultural perspective. *Journal of Marriage and Family, 56,* 7–20.

Cicirelli, V. G. (1995). *Sibling relationships across the life span.* New York: Plenum Press.

Cicirelli, V. G. (Ed.). (2002). *Older adults' views on death.* New York: Springer.

Cillessen, A. H.N., & Mayeux, L. (2004). From censure to reinforcement: Developmental changes in the association between aggression and social status. *Child Development, 75,* 147–163.

Cirillo, D. J., Wallace, R. B., Rodabough, R. J., Greenland, P., LaCroix, A. Z., Limacher, M. C., & Larson, J. C. (2005). Effect of estrogen therapy on gallbladder disease. *Journal of the American Medical Association, 293,* 330–339.

Clark, A. G., Glanowski, S., Nielsen, R., Thomas, P. D., Kejariwal, A., Todd, M. A., Tanenbaum, D. M., Civello, D., Lu, F., Murphy, B., Ferriera, S., Wang, G., Zheng, X., White, T. J., Sninsky, J. J., Adams, M. D., & Cargill, M. (2003). Inferring non-neutral evolution from human-chimpmouse orthologous gene trios. *Science, 302,* 1960–1963.

Clark-Plaskie, M., & Lachman, M. E. (1999). The sense of control in midlife. In S. L. Willis & J. D. Reid (Eds.), *Life in the middle* (pp. 181–208). San Diego: Academic Press.

Clarke-Stewart, K. A. (1987). Predicting child development from day care forms and features: The Chicago study. In D. A. Phillips (Ed.), *Quality in child care: What does the research tell us?* (Research Monographs of the National Association for the Education of Young Children). Washington, DC: National Association for the Education of Young Children.

Clavel-Chapelon, G., and the E3N-EPIC Group. (2002). Differential effects of reproductive factors on the risk of pre- and post-menopausal breast cancer: Results from a large cohort of French women. *British Journal of Cancer, 86,* 723–727. (DOI 10.1038/sj/bjc/6600124).

Clayton, E. W. (2003). Ethical, legal, and social implications of genomic medicine. *New England Journal of Medicine, 349,* 562–569.

Clearfield, M. W., & Mix, K. S. (1999). Number versus contour length in infants' discrimination of small visual sets. *Current Directions in Psychological Science, 10,* 408–411.

Cleary, P. D., Zaborski, L. B., & Ayanian, J. Z. (2004). Sex differences in health over the course of midlife. In O. G. Brim, C. E. Ryff, & R. C. Kessler (Eds.), *How healthy are we? A national study of well-being at midlife.* Chicago: University of Chicago Press.

Clément, K., Vaisse, C., Lahlou, N., Cabrol, S., Pelloux, V., Cassuto, D., Gourmelen, M., Dina, C., Chambaz, J., Lacorte, J.-M., Basdevant, A., Bougnères, P., Lebouc, Y., Froguel, P., & Guy-Grand, B. (1998). A mutation in the human leptin receptor gene causes obesity and pituitary dysfunction. *Nature, 392,* 398–401.

Clements, M. L., Stanley, S. M., & Markman, H. J. (2004). Before they said "I do": Discriminating among marital outcomes over 13 years. *Journal of Marriage and Family, 66,* 613–626.

Cleveland, E., & Resse, E. (2005). Maternal structure and autonomy support in conversations about the past: Contributions to children's autobiographical memory. *Development Psychology, 41,* 376–388.

Cleveland, H. H., & Wiebe, R. P. (2003). The moderation of adolescent-to-peer similarity in tobacco and alcohol use by school level of substance use. *Child Development, 74,* 279–291.

Clifton, R. K., Muir, D. W., Ashmead, D. H., & Clarkson, M. G. (1993). Is visually guided reaching in early infancy a myth? *Child Development, 64,* 1099–1110.

Climo, A. H., & Stewart, A. J. (2003). Eldercare and personality development in middle age. In J. Demick & C. Andreoletti (Eds.), *Handbook of adult development.* New York: Plenum Press.

Cnattingius, S., Bergström, R., Lipworth, L., & Kramer, M. S. (1998). Prepregnancy weight and the risk of adverse pregnancy outcomes. *New England Journal of Medicine, 338,* 147–152.

Cnattingius, S., Signorello, L. B., Anneré, G., Clausson, B., Ekbom, A., Ljunger, E., Blot, W. J., McLaughlin, J. K., Petersson, G., Rane, A., & Granath, F. (2000). Caffeine intake and the risk of first-trimester spontaneous abortion. *New England Journal of Medicine, 343*(25), 1839–1845.

Cohen, D. A., Nsuami, M., Martin, D. H., & Farley, T. A. (1999). Repeated school-based screening for sexually transmitted diseases: A feasible strategy for reaching adolescents. *Pediatrics, 104*(6), 1281–1285.

Cohen, L. B., & Amsel, L. B. (1998). Precursors to infants' perception of the causality of a simple event. *Infant Behavior and Development, 21,* 713–732.

Cohen, L. B., & Oakes, L. M. (1993). How infants perceive a simple causal event. *Developmental Psychology, 29,* 421–433.

Cohen, L. B., Rundell, L. J., Spellman, B. A., & Cashon, C. H. (1999). Infants' perception of causal chains. *Current Directions in Psychological Science, 10,* 412–418.

Cohen, P. (2008, February 19). Midlife suicide rises, puzzling researchers. *New York Times.* Retrieved May 19. 2008, from www.nytimes.com/2008/02/19/us/19suicide.html?sq=Patricia%20Cohen%20AND%20midlife%20Suicide%20Rises&st=nyt&adxnnl=&scp=1&adxnnlx=1211123393-GTNahP64215qoaC+qMQ8Ug.

Cohen, S. (2004). Social relationships and health. *American Psychologist, 59,* 676–684.

Cohen, S., Doyle, W. J., Skoner, D. P., Rabin, B. S., & Gwaltney, J. M., Jr. (1997). Social ties and susceptibility to the common cold. *Journal of the American Medical Association, 277,* 1940–1944.

Cohen, S., Doyle, W. J., Turner, R. B., Alper, C. M., & Skoner, D. P. (2003). Emotional style and susceptibility to the common cold. *Psychosomatic Medicine, 65,* 652–657.

Cohen, S., Gottlieb, B., & Underwood, L. (2000). Social relationships and health. In S. Cohen, L. Underwood, & B. Gottlieb (Eds.), *Measuring and intervening in social support* (pp. 3–25). New York: Oxford University Press.

Cohen, S., Janicki-Deverts, D., & Miller, G. E. (2007). Psychological stress and disease. *Journal of the American Medical Association, 298,* 1685–1687.

Cohen, S., & Pressman, S. D. (2006). Positive affect and health. *Current Directions in Psychological Science, 15,* 122–125.

Coie, J. D., & Dodge, K. A. (1998). Aggression and antisocial behavior. In W. Damon (Series Ed.) & N. Eisenberg (Vol. Ed.), *Handbook of child psychology: Vol. 3. Social, emotional, and personality development* (5th ed., pp. 780–862). New York: Wiley.

Coke, M. M. (1992). Correlates of life satisfaction among elderly African-Americans. *Journal of Gerontology: Psychological Sciences, 47*(5), P316–P320.

Coke, M. M., & Twaite, J. A. (1995). *The black elderly: Satisfaction and quality of later life.* New York: Haworth.

Colby, A., & Damon, W. (1992). *Some do care: Contemporary lives of moral commitment.* New York: Free Press.

Colby, A., Kohlberg, L., Gibbs, J., & Lieberman, M. (1983). A longitudinal study of moral development. *Monographs of the Society for Research in Child Development, 48*(1–2, Serial No. 200).

Cole, M. (1998). *Cultural psychology: A once and future discipline.* Cambridge, MA: Belknap.

Cole, P. M., Barrett, K. C., & Zahn-Waxler, C. (1992). Emotion displays in two-year-olds during mishaps. *Child Development, 63,* 314–324.

Cole, P. M., Bruschi, C. J., & Tamang, B. L. (2002). Cultural differences in children's emotional reactions to difficult situations. *Child Development, 73*(3), 983–996.

Cole, T. B. (1999). Ebbing epidemic: Youth homicide rate at a 14-year low. *Journal of the American Medical Association, 281,* 25–26.

Coleman, J. S. (1988). Social capital in the creation of human capital. *American Journal of Sociology, 94*(Suppl. 95), S95–S120.

Coles, L. S. (2004). Demography of human supercentenarians. *Journal of Gerontology: Biological Sciences, 59A,* 579–586.

Coley, R. L., Morris, J. E., & Hernandez, D. (2004). Out-of-school care and problem behavior trajectories among low-income adolescents: Individual, family, and neighborhood characteristics as added risks. *Child Development, 75,* 948–965.

Collier, V. P. (1995). Acquiring a second language for school. *Directions in Language and Education, 1*(4), 1–11.

Collins, N. L., & Miller, L. C. (1994). Self-disclosure and liking: A meta-analytic review. *Psychological Bulletin, 116,* 457–475.

Collins, W. A., Maccoby, E. E., Steinberg, L., Hetherington, E. M., & Bornstein, M. H. (2000). Contemporary research in parenting: The case for nature and nurture. *American Psychologist, 55,* 218–232.

Collins, W. A., & van Dulmen, M. (2006). Friendships and romance in emerging adulthood: Assessing the distinctiveness in close relationships. In J. J. Arnett & J. L. Tanner (Eds.), *Emerging adults in America: Coming of age in the 21st century* (pp. 219–234). Washington DC: American Psychological Association.

Colliver, J. D., Kroutil, L. A., Dai, L., & Gfroerer, J. C. (2006). *Misuse of prescription drugs: Data from the 2002, 2003, and 2004 National Surveys on Drug Use and Health* (DHHS Publication No. SMA 06-4192, Analytic Series A-28). Rockville, MD: Substance Abuse and Mental Health Services Administration, Office of Applied Studies.

Colombo, J. (2002). Infant attention grows up: The emergence of a developmental cognitive neuroscience perspective. *Current Directions in Psychological Science, 11,* 196–200.

Colombo, J., Kannass, K. N., Shaddy, J., Kundurthi, S., Maikranz, J. M., Anderson, C. J., Bkaga, O. M., & Carlson, S. E. (2004). Maternal DHA and the development of attention in infancy and toddlerhood. *Child Development, 75,* 1254–1267.

Coltrane, S., & Adams, M. (1997). Work-family imagery and gender stereotypes: Television and the reproduction of difference. *Journal of Vocational Behavior, 50,* 323–347.

Commissioner's Office of Research and Evaluation and Head Start Bureau, Department of Health and Human Services. (2001). *Building their futures: How Early Head Start programs are enhancing the lives of infants and toddlers in low-income families. Summary report.* Washington, DC: Author.

Community Paediatrics Committee, Canadian Paediatrics Society. (2005). Management of primary nocturnal enuresis. *Paediatrics and Child Health, 10,* 611–614.

Compas, B. E., & Luecken, L. (2002). Psychological adjustment to breast cancer. *Current Directions in Psychological Science, 11,* 111–114.

Compston, J. (2007). Treatments for osteoporosis—Looking beyond the HORIZON. *New England Journal of Medicine, 356,* 1878–1880.

Comuzzie, A. G., & Allison, D. B. (1998). The search for human obesity genes. *Science, 280,* 1374–1377.

Conde-Agudelo, A., Rosas-Bermúdez, A., & Kafury-Goeta, A. C. (2006). Birth spacing and risk of adverse perinatal outcomes: A meta-analysis. *Journal of the American Medical Association, 295,* 1809–1823.

Conel, J. L. (1959). *The postnatal development of the human cerebral cortex.* Cambridge, MA: Harvard University Press.

Conference Board. (1999, June 25). *Workplace education programs are benefiting U.S. corporations and workers* [Press release]. Retrieved from www.newswise.com/articles/1999/6/WEP.TCB.html.

Connidis, I. A., & Davies, L. (1992). Confidants and companions: Choices in later life. *Journal of Gerontology: Social Sciences, 47*(30), S115–S122.

Constantino, J. N. (2003). Autistic traits in the general population: A twin study. *Archives of General Psychiatry, 60,* 524–530.

Constantino, J. N., Grosz, D., Saenger, P., Chandler, D. W., Nandi, R., & Earls, F. J. (1993). Testosterone and aggression in children. *Journal of the Academy of Child and Adolescent Psychiatry, 32,* 1217–1222.

Cooper, K. L., & Gutmann, D. L. (1987). Gender identity and ego mastery style in middle-aged, pre- and post-empty nest women. *Gerontologist, 27*(3), 347–352.

Cooper, R. P., & Aslin, R. N. (1990). Preference for infant-directed speech in the first month after birth. *Child Development, 61,* 1584–1595.

Cooper, W. O., Hernandez-Diaz, S., Arbogast, P. G., Dudley, J. A., Dyer, S., Gideon, P. S., Hall, K., & Ray, W. A. (2006). Major congenital formations after first-trimester exposure to ACE inhibitors. *New England Journal of Medicine, 354,* 2443–2451.

Coplan, R. J., Prakash, K., O'Neil, K., & Armer, M. (2004). Do you "want" to play? Distinguishing between conflicted-shyness and social disinterest in early childhood. *Developmental Psychology, 40,* 244–258.

Corbet, A., Long, W., Schumacher, R., Gerdes, J., Cotton, R., & the American Exosurf Neonatal Study Group 1. (1995). Double-blind developmental evaluation at 1-year corrected age of 597 premature infants with birth weight from 500 to 1,350 grams enrolled in three placebo-controlled trials of prophylactic synthetic surfactant. *Journal of Pediatrics, 126,* S5–S12.

Corbin, C. (1973). *A textbook of motor development.* Dubuque, IA: Wm. C. Brown.

Corcoran, M., & Matsudaira, J. (2005). Is it getting harder to get ahead? Economic attainment in early adulthood for two cohorts. In R. A. Settersten, Jr., F. F. Furstenberg, Jr., & R. G. Rumbaut (Eds.), *On the frontier of adulthood: Theory, research,*

and public policy (pp. 356–395). (John D. and Catherine T. MacArthur Foundation Series on Mental Health and Development, Research Network on Transitions to Adulthood and Public Policy.) Chicago: University of Chicago Press.

Cornwell, B., Laumann, E. O., & Schumm, L. P. (2008). The social connectedness of older adults: A national profile. *American Sociological Review, 73,* 185–203.

Correa, A., Botto, L., Liu, V., Mulinare, J., & Erickson, J. D. (2003). Do multivitamin supplements attenuate the risk for diabetes-associated birth defects? *Pediatrics, 111,* 1146–1151.

Costa, P. T., Jr., & McCrae, R. R. (1980). Still stable after all these years: Personality as a key to some issues in adulthood and old age. In P. B. Baltes, Jr., & O. G. Brim (Eds.), *Lifespan development and behavior* (Vol. 3, pp. 65–102). New York: Academic Press.

Costa, P. T., Jr., & McCrae, R. R. (1988). Personality in adulthood: A six-year longitudinal study of self-reports and spouse ratings on the NEO Personality Inventory. *Journal of Personality and Social Psychology, 54,* 853–863.

Costa, P. T., Jr., & McCrae, R. R. (1994a). Set like plaster? Evidence for the stability of adult personality. In T. F. Heatherton & J. L. Weinberger (Eds.), *Can personality change?* (pp. 21–41). Washington, DC: American Psychological Association.

Costa, P. T., Jr., & McCrae, R. R. (1994b). Stability and change in personality from adolescence through adulthood. In C. F. Halverson, G. A. Kohnstamm, & R. P. Martin (Eds.), *The developing structure of temperament and personality from infancy to adulthood.* Hillsdale, NJ: Erlbaum.

Costa, P. T., Jr., & McCrae, R. R. (1996). Mood and personality in adulthood. In C. Magai & S. H. McFadden (Eds.), *Handbook of emotion, adult development, and aging* (pp. 369–383). San Diego: Academic Press.

Costa, P. T., Jr., & McCrae, R. R. (2006). Age changes in personality and their origins: Comments on Roberts, Walton, and Viechtbauer (2006). *Psychological Bulletin, 1,* 26–28.

Costa, P. T., Jr., McCrae, R. R., Zonderman, A. B., Barbano, H. E., Lebowitz, B., & Larson, D. M. (1986). Cross-sectional studies of personality in a national sample: 2. Stability in neuroticism, extraversion, and openness. *Psychology and Aging, 1,* 144–149.

Costello, E. J., Compton, S. N., Keeler, G., & Angold, A. (2003). Relationship between poverty and psychopathology: A natural experiment. *Journal of the American Medical Association, 290,* 2023–2029.

Côté, J. E. (2006). Emerging adulthood as an institutionalized moratorium: Risks and benefits to identity formation. In J. J. Arnett & J. L. Tanner (Eds.), *Emerging adults in America: Coming of age in the 21st century* (pp. 85–116). Washington, DC: American Psychological Association.

Council on Sports Medicine and Fitness & Council on School Health. (2006). Active healthy living: Prevention of childhood obesity through increased physical activity. *Pediatrics, 117,* 1834–1842.

Courage, M. L., & Howe, M. L. (2002). From infant to child: The dynamics of cognitive change in the second year of life. *Psychological Bulletin, 128,* 250–277.

Cowan, C. P., & Cowan, P. A. (2000). *When partners become parents: The big life change for couples.* Mahwah, NJ; Erlbaum.

Craik, F. I.M., & Byrd, M. (1982). Aging and cognitive deficits: The role of attentional resources. In F. I.M. Craik & S. Trehub (Eds.), *Aging and cognitive processes* (pp. 191–221). New York: Plenum Press.

Craik, F. I.M., & Jennings, J. M. (1992). Human memory. In F. I.M. Craik & T. A. Salthouse (Eds.), *Handbook of aging and cognition* (pp. 51–110). Hillsdale, NJ: Erlbaum.

Craik, F. I.M., & Salthouse, T. A. (Eds.). (2000). *The handbook of aging and cognition* (2nd ed.). Mahwah, NJ: Erlbaum.

Crain-Thoreson, C., & Dale, P. S. (1992). Do early talkers become early readers? Linguistic precocity, preschool language, and emergent literacy. *Developmental Psychology, 28,* 421–429.

Cratty, B. J. (1986). *Perceptual and motor development in infants and children* (3rd ed.). Englewood Cliffs, NJ: Prentice-Hall.

Crawford, C. (1998). Environments and adaptations: Then and now. In C. Crawford & D. L. Krebs (Eds.), *Handbook of evolutionary psychology: Ideas, issues, and applications* (pp. 275–302). Mahwah, NJ: Erlbaum.

Crawford, J. (2002). Obituary: The Bilingual Ed Act, 1968–2002. *Rethinking Schools Online.* Retrieved August 26, 2006, from www.rethinkingschool.org/specialreports/bilingual/Bill64.shtml.

Crawford, J. (2007). The decline of bilingual education: How to reverse a troubling trend? *International Multilingual Research Journal, 1*(1), 33–38.

Creed, P. A., & Macintyre, S. R. (2001). The relative effects of deprivation of the latent and manifest benefits of employment on the well-being of unemployed people. *Journal of Occupational Health Psychology, 6,* 324–331.

Crick, N. R., Casas, J. F., & Nelson, D. A. (2002). Toward a more comprehensive understanding of peer maltreatment: Studies of relational victimization. *Current Directions in Psychological Science, 11*(3), 98–101.

Crick, N. R., & Dodge, K. A. (1994). A review and reformulation of social information-processing mechanisms in children's social adjustment. *Psychological Bulletin, 115,* 74–101.

Crick, N. R., & Dodge, K. A. (1996). Social information-processing mechanisms in reactive and proactive aggression. *Child Development, 67,* 993–1002.

Crick, N. R., & Grotpeter, J. K. (1995). Relational aggression, gender, and social psychological adjustment. *Child Development, 66,* 710–722

Crisp, J., Ungerer, J. A., & Goodnow, J. J. (1996). The impact of experience on children's understanding of illness. *Journal of Pediatric Psychology, 21,* 57–72.

Crockenberg, S. C. (2003). Rescuing the baby from the bathwater: How gender and temperament influence how child care affects child development. *Child Development, 74,* 1034–1038.

Cromwell, R. L., Meyers, P. M., Meyers, P. E., & Newton, R. A. (2007). Tae kwon do: An effective exercise for improving balance and walking ability in older adults. *Journal of Gerontology: Biological and Medical Sciences, 62,* 641–646.

Cronk, L. B., Ye, B., Tester, D. J., Vatta, M., Makielski, J. C., & Ackerman, M. J. (2006, May). *Identification of CAV3-encoded caveolin-3 mutations in sudden infant death syndrome.* Presentation at Heart Rhythm 2006, the 27th annual Scientific Sessions of the Heart Rhythm Society, Boston.

Crooks, V. C., Lubben, J., Petitti, D. B., Little, D., & Chiu, V. (2008). Social network, cognitive function, and dementia incidence among elderly women. *American Journal of Public Health, 98,* 1221–1227.

Crouter, A., & Larson, R. (Eds.). (1998). *Temporal rhythms in adolescence: Clocks, calendars, and the coordination of daily life* (New Directions in Child and Adolescent Development, No. 82). San Francisco: Jossey-Bass.

Crouter, A. C., MacDermid, S. M., McHale, S. M., & Perry-Jenkins, M. (1990). Parental monitoring and perception of children's school performance and conduct in dual- and single-earner families. *Developmental Psychology, 26,* 649–657.

Crouter, A. C., & Manke, B. (1994). The changing American workplace: Implications for individuals and families. *Family Relations, 43,* 117–124.

Crowe, M., Andel, R., Pedersen, N. L., Fratiglioni, L., & Gatz, M. (2006). Personality and risk of cognitive impairment 25 years later. *Psychology and Aging, 21,* 573–580.

Crowe, M., Andel, R., Pedersen, N. L., Johansson, B., & Gatz, M. (2003). Does participation in leisure activities lead to reduced risk of Alzheimer's Disease? A prospective study of Swedish twins. *Journal of Gerontology: Psychological Sciences, 58B,* P249–P255.

Crowley, S. L. (1993, October). Grandparents to the rescue. *AARP Bulletin,* pp. 1, 16–17.

Cruzan v. Director, Missouri Department of Health, 110 S. Ct. 2841 (1990).

Csikszentmihalyi, M. (1996). *Creativity: Flow and the psychology of discovery and invention.* New York: HarperCollins.

Csikszentmihalyi, M. (1999). If we are so rich, why aren't we happy? *American Psychologist, 54,* 821–827.

Cui, M., Conger, R. D., & Lorenz, F. O. (2005). Predicting change in adolescent adjustment from change in marital problems. *Developmental Psychology, 41,* 812–823.

Cumming, E., & Henry, W. (1961). *Growing old.* New York: Basic Books.

Cummings, J. L. (2004). Alzheimer's disease. *New England Journal of Medicine, 351,* 56–67.

Cunniff, C., & Committee on Genetics. (2004). Prenatal screening and diagnosis for pediatricians. *Pediatrics, 114,* 889–894.

Cunningham, F. G., & Leveno, K. J. (1995). Childbearing among older women: The message is cautiously optimistic. *New England Journal of Medicine, 333,* 1002–1004.

Currie, C., Roberts, C., Morgan, A., Smith, R., Settertobulte, W., & Samdal, O. (Eds.). (2004). *Young people's health in context.* Geneva: World Health Organization.

Curtiss, S. (1977). *Genie.* New York: Academic Press.

Cutrona, C. E., Wallace, G., & Wesner, K. A. (2006). Neighborhood characteristics and depressions: An examination of stress processes. *Current Directions in Psychological Science, 15,* 188–192.

Cuttini, M., Nadai, M., Kaminski, M., Hansen, G., de Leeuw, R., Lenoir, S., Persson, J., Rabagliato, M., Reid, M., de Vonderweid, U., Lenard, H. G., Orzalesi, M., & Saracci, R., for the EURONIC Study Group. (2000). End-of-life decisions in neonatal intensive care: Physicians' self-reported practices in seven European countries. *Lancet, 355,* 2112–2118.

Cytrynbaum, S., Bluum, L., Patrick, R., Stein, J., Wadner, D., & Wilk, C. (1980). Midlife development: A personality and social systems perspective. In L. Poon (Ed.), *Aging in the 1980s.* Washington, DC: American Psychological Association.

Czaja, A. J., & Sharit, J. (1998). Ability-performance relationships as a function of age and task experience for a data entry task. *Journal of Experimental Psychology— Applied, 4,* 332–351.

Czaja, S. J. (2006). Employment and the baby boomers: What can we expect in the future? In S. K. Whitbourne & S. L. Willis (Eds.), *The baby boomers grow up: Contemporary perspectives on midlife* (pp. 283–298). Mahwah, NJ: Erlbaum.

Czeisler, C. A., Duffy, J. F., Shanahan, T. L., Brown, E. N., Mitchell, J. F., Rimmer, D. W., Ronda, J. M., Silva, E. J., Allan, J. S., Emens, J. S., Dijk, D., & Kronauer, R. E. (1999). Stability, precision, and near 24-hour period of the human circadian pacemaker. *Science, 284,* 2177–2181.

da Vinci, L. *The notebooks of Leonardo da Vinci* (E. MacCurdy, Trans.). London: Cape, 1938.

Dale, P. S., Price, T. S., Bishop, D. V. M., & Plomin, R. (2003). Outcomes of early language delay: I. Predicting persistent and transient language difficulties at 3 and 4 years. *Journal of Speech, Language, and Hearing Research, 46,* 544–560.

Dale, P. S., Simonoff, E., Bishop, D. V. M., Eley, T. C., Oliver, B., Price, T. S., Purcell, S., Stevenson, J., & Plomin, R. (1998). Genetic influence on language delay in two-year-old children. *Nature Neuroscience, 1,* 324–328.

Daly, R., (2005). Drop in youth antidepressant use prompts call for FDA monitoring. *Psychiatric News, 40*(19), 18.

Danesi, M. (1994). *Cool: The signs and meanings of adolescence.* Toronto: University of Toronto Press.

Darling, N., & Steinberg, L. (1993). Parenting style as context: An integrative model. *Psychological Bulletin, 113,* 487–496.

Darroch, J. E., Singh, S., Frost, J. J., & the Study Team. (2001). Differences in teenage pregnancy rates among five developed countries: The roles of sexual activity and contraceptive use. *Family Planning Perspectives, 33,* 244–250, 281.

Datar, A., & Sturm, R. (2004a). Childhood overweight and parent- and teacher-reported behavior problems. *Archives of Pediatric and Adolescent Medicine, 158,* 804–810.

Datar, A., & Sturm, R. (2004b). Duke physical education in elementary school and body mass index: Evidence from the Early Childhood Longitudinal Study. *American Journal of Public Health, 94,* 1501–1507.

David and Lucile Packard Foundation. (2004). Children, families, and foster care: Executive summary. *Future of Children, 14*(1). Retrieved from www.futureofchildren.org.

Davidson, J. I.F. (1998). Language and play: Natural partners. In D. P. Fromberg & D. Bergen (Eds.), *Play from birth to 12 and beyond: Contexts, perspectives, and meanings* (pp. 175–183). New York: Garland.

Davidson, N. E. (1995). Hormone-replacement therapy—breast versus heart versus bone. *New England Journal of Medicine, 332,* 1638–1639.

Davidson, R. J., & Fox, N. A. (1989). Frontal brain asymmetry predicts infants' response to maternal separation. *Journal of Abnormal Psychology, 948*(2), 58–64.

Davies, C., & Williams, D. (2002). *The grandparent study 2002 report.* Washington, DC: American Association of Retired Persons.

Davis, M., & Emory, E. (1995). Sex differences in neonatal stress reactivity. *Child Development, 66,* 14–27.

Davis-Kean, P. E. (2005). The influence of parent education and family income on child achievement: The indirect role of parental expectation and the home environment. *Journal of Family Psychology, 19,* 294–304.

Davison, K. K., & Birch, L. L. (2001). Weight status, parent reaction, and self-concept in 5-year-old girls. *Pediatrics, 107,* 46–53.

Davison, K. K., Susman, E. J., & Birch, L. L. (2003). Percent body fat at age 5 predicts earlier pubertal development among girls at age 9. *Pediatrics, 111,* 815–821.

Dawson, D. A. (1991). Family structure and children's health and well-being. Data from the 1988 National Health Interview Survey on child health. *Journal of Marriage and Family, 53,* 573–584.

Dawson, G. (2007). Despite major challenges, autism research continues to offer hope. *Archives of Pediatric and Adolescent Medicine, 161,* 411–412.

Dawson, G., Frey, K., Panagiotides, H., Yamada, E., Hessl, D. and Osterling, J. (1999). Infants of depressed mothers exhibit atypical frontal electrical brain activity during interactions with mother and with a familiar nondepressed adult. *Child Development, 70,* 1058–1066.

Dawson, G., Klinger, L. G., Panagiotides, H., Hill, D., & Spieker, S. (1992). Frontal lobe activity and affective behavior of infants of mothers with depressive symptoms. *Child Development, 63,* 725–737.

Day, J. C., Janus, A., & Davis, J. (2005). Computer and Internet use in the United States: 2003. *Current Population Reports* (P23–P208). Washington, DC: U.S. Census Bureau.

Day, S. (1993, May). Why genes have a gender. *New Scientist, 138*(1874), 34–38.

de Castro, B. O., Veerman, J. W., Koops, W., Bosch, J. D., & Monshouwer, H. J. (2002). Hostile attribution of intent and aggressive behavior: A meta-analysis. *Child Development, 73,* 916–934.

de Groot, L. C. P. M. G., Verheijden, M. W., de Henauw, S., Schroll, M., & van Staveren, W. A. for the SENECA Investigators. (2004). Lifestyle, nutritional status, health, and mortality in elderly people across Europe: A review of the longitudinal results of the SENECA study. *Journal of Gerontology: Medical Sciences, 59A,* 1277–1284.

de la Fuente-Fernandez, R. (2006). Impact of neuroprotection on incidence of Alzheimer's Disease. *PLoS ONE, 1*(1), e52. Retrieved March 5, 2008, from www.pubmedcentral.nih.gov/articlerender.fcgi?artid=1762379. (DOI: 10.1371/journal.pone.0000052)

de Lange, T. (1998). Telomeres and senescence: Ending the debate. *Science, 279,* 334–335.

De Schipper, E., Riksen-Walraven, M., & Geurts, S. (2006). Effects of child-caregiver ratio on the interactions between caregivers and children in child-care centers: An experimental study. *Child Development, 77*(4), 861–874.

de Vries, B. (1996). The understanding of friendship: An adult life course perspective. In C. Magai & S. H. McFadden (Eds.), *Handbook of emotion, adult development, and aging* (pp. 249–269). San Diego: Academic Press.

De Wolff, M. S., & van IJzendoorn, M. H. (1997). Sensitivity and attachment: A meta-analysis on parental antecedents of infant attachment. *Child Development, 68,* 571–591.

Deary, I. J., & Der, G. (2005). Reaction time explains IQ's association with death. *Psychological Science, 16,* 64–69.

Deary, I. J., Whalley, L. J., & Starr, J. M. (2003). IQ at age 11 and longevity: Results from a follow-up of the Scottish Mental Survey 1932. In C. D. Finch, J.-M. Robine, & Y. Christen (Eds.), *Brain and longevity: Perspectives in longevity* (pp. 153–164). Berlin: Springer.

DeBell, M., & Chapman, C. (2006). *Computer and Internet use by students in 2003: Statistical analysis report* (NCES 2006-065). Washington, DC: National Center for Education Statistics.

DeCasper, A. J., & Fifer, W. P. (1980). Of human bonding: Newborns prefer their mothers' voices. *Science, 208,* 1174–1176.

DeCasper, A. J., Lecanuet, J. P., Busnel, M. C., Granier-Deferre, C., & Maugeais, R. (1994). Fetal reactions to recurrent maternal speech. *Infant Behavior and Development, 17,* 159–164.

DeCasper, A. J., & Spence, M. J. (1986). Prenatal maternal speech influences newborns' perceptions of speech sounds. *Infant Behavior and Development, 9,* 133–150.

Dee, D. L., Li, R., Lee, L., & Grummer-Strawn, L. M. (2007). Association between breastfeeding practices and young children's language and motor development. *Pediatrics, 119*(Suppl. 1), 592–598.

DeHaan, L. G., & MacDermid, S. M. (1994). Is women's identity achievement associated with the expression of generativity? Examining identity and generativity in multiple roles. *Journal of Adult Development, 1,* 235–247.

Dekovic, M., & Janssens, J. (1992). Parents' child-rearing style and child's sociometric status. *Developmental Psychology, 28,* 925–932.

Del Carmen, R. D., Pedersen, F. A., Huffman, L. C., & Bryan, V. E. (1993). Dyadic distress management predicts subsequent security of attachment. *Infant Behavior and Development, 16,* 131–147.

Delany, E., Delany, S., & Hearth, A. H. (1993). *The Delany sisters' first 100 years.* New York: Kodansha America.

DeLoache, J. S. (2000). Dual representation and young children's use of scale models. *Child Development, 71,* 329–338.

DeLoache, J. S. (2004). Becoming symbol-minded. *Trends in Cognitive Science, 8,* 66–70.

DeLoache, J. S. (2006). Mindful of symbols. *Scientific American Mind, 17,* 70–75.

DeLoache, J., & Gottlieb, A. (2000). If Dr. Spock were born in Bali: Raising a world of babies. In J. DeLoache & A. Gottlieb (Eds.), *A world of babies: Imagined childcare guides for seven societies* (pp. 1–27). New York: Cambridge University Press.

DeLoache, J. S., Miller, K. F., & Pierroutsakos, S. L. (1998). Reasoning and problem solving. In D. Kuhn & R. S. Siegler (Eds.), *Handbook of child psychology: Vol. 2. Cognition, perception, and language* (5th ed., pp. 801–850). New York: Wiley.

DeLoache, J. S., Miller, K. F., & Rosengren, K. S. (1997). The credible shrinking room: Very young children's performance with symbolic and nonsymbolic relations. *Psychological Science, 8,* 308–313.

DeLoache, J. S., Pierroutsakos, S. L., & Uttal, D. H. (2003). The origins of pictorial competence. *Current Directions in Psychological Science, 12,* 114–118.

DeLoache, J. S., Pierroutsakos, S. L., Uttal, D. H., Rosengren, K. S., & Gottlieb, A. (1998). Grasping the nature of pictures. *Psychological Science, 9,* 205–210.

DeLoache, J. S., Uttal, D. H., & Rosengren, K. S. (2004). Scale errors offer evidence for a perception-action dissociation early in life. *Science, 304,* 1027–1029.

DeMaris, A., Benson, M. L., Fox, G. L, Hill, T., & Van Wyk, J. (2003). Distal and proximal factors in domestic violence: A test of an integrated model. *Journal of Marriage and Family, 65,* 652–667.

den Dunnen, W. F.A., Bouwer, W. H., Bijlard, E., Kamphuis, J., van Linschoten, K., Eggens-Meijer, E., & Holstege, G. (2008). No disease in the brain of a 115-year-old woman. *Neurobiology of Aging, 29,* 1127–1132.

den Heijer, T. Geerlings, M. I., Hoebeek, F. E., Hofman, A., Koudstaal, P. J., & Breteler, M. M. B. (2006). Use of hippocampal and amygdalar volumes on magnetic resonance imaging to predict dementia in cognitively intact elderly people. *Archives of General Psychiatry, 63,* 57–62.

DeNavas-Walt, C., Proctor, B. D., & Smith, J. (2007). Income, poverty, and health insurance in the United States: 2006. *Current Population Reports* (P60-P233). Washington, DC: U.S. Census Bureau.

Denham, S. A., Blair, K. A., DeMulder, E., Levitas, J., Sawyer, K., Auerbach-Major, S., & Queenan, P. (2003). Preschool emotional competence: Pathway to social competence? *Child Development, 74,* 238–256.

Dennis, T. (2006). Emotional self-regulation in preschoolers: The interplay of child approach reactivity, parenting, and control capacities. *Developmental Psychology, 42,* 84–97.

Dennissen, J. J. A., Asendorpt, J. B., & van Aken, M. A. G. (2008). Childhood personality predicts long-term trajectories of shyness and aggressiveness in the context of demographic transitions in emerging adulthood. *Journal of Personality, 76,* 67–99.

Denton, K., West, J., and Walston, J. (2003). *Reading—young children's achievement and classroom experiences: Findings from* The Condition of Education 2003. Washington, DC: National Center for Education Statistics.

Department of Immunization, Vaccines, and Biologicals, World Health Organization; United Nations Children's Fund; Global Immunization Division, National Center for Immunization and Respiratory Diseases (proposed); & McMorrow, M. (2006). Vaccine preventable deaths and the global immunization vision and strategy, 2006–2015. *Morbidity and Mortality Weekly Report, 55,* 511–515.

Der, G., & Deary, I. J. (2006). Age and sex differences in reaction time in adulthood: Results from the United Kingdom Health and Lifestyle Study. *Psychology and Aging, 21,* 62–73.

Desai, M., Pratt, L. A., Lentzner, H., & Robinson, K. N. (2001). Trends in vision and hearing among older Americans. *Aging Trends,* No. 2. Hyattsville, MD: National Center for Health Statistics.

Detrich, R., Phillips, R., & Durett, D. (2002). *Critical issue: Dynamic debate— determining the evolving impact of charter schools.* North Central Regional Educational Laboratory. Retrieved from www.ncrel.org/sdrs/areas/issues/envrnmnt/go/go800.htm.

Devaney, B., Johnson, A., Maynard, R., & Trenholm, C. (2002). *The evaluation of abstinence education programs funded under Title V, Section 510: Interim report.* Washington, DC: U.S. Department of Health and Human Services.

DeVoe, J. F., Peter, K., Kaufman, P., Miller, A., Noonan, M., Snyder, T. D., & Baum, K. (2004). *Indicators of school crime and safety: 2004* (NCES 2005-002/NCJ 205290). Washington, DC: U.S. Departments of Education and Justice.

Dewey, J. (1910/1991). *How we think.* Amherst, NY: Prometheus Books.

Dewing, P., Shi, T., Horvath, S., & Vilain, E. (2003). Sexually dimorphic gene expression in mouse brain precedes gonadal differentiation. *Molecular Brain Research, 118,* 82–90.

Dey, A. N., Schiller, J. S., & Tai, D. A. (2004). Summary health statistics for U.S. children: National Health Interview Survey, 2002. *Vital Health Statistics 10* (221). Bethesda, MD: National Center for Health Statistics.

Diamond, A. (1991). Neuropsychological insights into the meaning of object concept development. In S. Carey & R. Gelman (Eds.), *Epigensis of mind* (pp. 67–110). Hillsdale, NJ: Erlbaum.

Diamond, A. (2007). Interrelated and interdependent. *Developmental Science, 10,* 152–158.

Diamond, L. M., & Savin-Williams, R. C. (2003). The intimate relationships of sexual-minority youths. In G. R. Adams & M. D. Berzonsky (Eds.), *Blackwell handbook of adolescence* (pp. 393–412). Malden, MA: Blackwell.

Diamond, M., & Sigmundson, H. K. (1997). Sex reassignment at birth: Longterm review and clinical implications. *Archives of Pediatric and Adolescent Medicine, 151,* 298–304.

Dick, D. M., Alieve, F., Kramer, J., Wang, J., Anthony, H., Bertelsen, S., Kuperman, S., Schuckit, M., Nurnberger, J., Jr., Edenberg, H., Porjesz, B., Begleiter, H., Hesselbrock, V., Goate, A., & Bierut, L. (2007). Association of CHRM2 with IQ: Converging evidence for a gene influencing intelligence. *Behavior Genetics, 37*(2), 265–272.

Dick, D. M., Rose, R. J., Kaprio, J., & Viken, R. (2000). Pubertal timing and substance use: Associations between and within families across late adolescence. *Developmental Psychology, 36,* 180–189.

Dickens, W. T., & Flynn, J. R. (2006). Black Americans reduce the racial IQ gap: Evidence from standardization samples. *Psychological Science, 17*(10), 913–920.

Dickinson, G. E., Lancaster, C. J., Clark, D., Ahmedzai, S. H., & Noble, W. (2002). U.K. physicians' attitudes toward active voluntary euthanasia and physician-assisted suicide. *Death Studies, 26,* 479–490.

Dien, D. S. F. (1982). A Chinese perspective on Kohlberg's theory of moral development. *Developmental Review, 2,* 331–341.

Diener, E. (2000). Subjective well-being: The science of happiness and a proposal for a national index. *American Psychologist, 55,* 34–43.

Dietert, R. R. (2005). Developmental immunotoxicology (DIT): Is DIT testing necessary to ensure safety? *Proceedings of the 14th Immunotoxicology Summer School, Lyon, France, October 2005,* 246–257.

DiFranza, J. R., Aligne, C. A., & Weitzman, M. (2004). Prenatal and postnatal environmental tobacco smoke exposure and children's health. *Pediatrics, 113,* 1007–1015.

Dilworth-Bart, J. E., & Moore., C. F. (2006). Mercy mercy me: Social injustice and the prevention of environmental pollutant exposures among ethnic minority and poor children. *Child Development, 77*(2), 247–265.

DiMarco, M. A., Menke, E. M., & McNamara, T. (2001). Evaluating a support group for perinatal loss. *MCN American Journal of Maternal and Child Nursing, 26,* 135–140.

Dingfelder, S. (2004). Programmed for psychopathology? Stress during pregnancy may increase children's risk for mental illness, researchers say. *Monitor on Psychology, 35*(2), 56–57.

DiPietro, J. A. (2004). The role of prenatal maternal stress in child development. *Current Directions in Psychological Science, 13*(2), 71–74.

DiPietro, J. A., Hodgson, D. M., Costigan, K. A., Hilton, S. C., & Johnson, T. R. B. (1996). Development of fetal movement— fetal heart rate coupling from 20 weeks through term. *Early Human Development, 44,* 139–151.

DiPietro, J. A., Novak, M. F. S. X., Costigan, K. A., Atella, L. D., & Reusing, S. P. (2006). Maternal psychological distress during pregnancy in relation to child development at age 2. *Child Development, 77*(3), 573–587.

Dishion, T. J., McCord, J., & Poulin, F. (1999). When intervention harms. *American Psychologist, 54,* 755–764.

Dittmar, H., Halliwell, E., & Ive, S. (2006). Does Barbie make girls want to be thin? The effect of experimental exposure to images of dolls on the body image of 5- to

8-year-old girls. *Developmental Psychology, 42,* 283–292.

Dixon, R. A., & Baltes, P. B. (1986). Toward lifespan research on the functions and pragmatics of intelligence. In R. J. Sternberg & R. K. Wagner (Eds.), *Practical intelligence: Nature and origins of competence in the everyday world* (pp. 203–235). New York: Cambridge University Press.

Dixon, R. A., & Hultsch, D. F. (1999). Intelligence and cognitive potential in late life. In J. C. Cavanaugh & S. K. Whitbourne (Eds.), *Gerontology: An interdisciplinary perspective.* New York: Oxford University Press.

Dixon, S. V., Graber, J. A., & Brooks-Gunn, J. (2008). The roles of respect for authority and parenting practices in parent-child conflict among African American, Latino, and European American families. *Journal of Family Psychology, 22,* 1–10.

Dobriansky, P. J., Suzman, R. M., & Hodes, R. J. (2007). *Why population aging matters: A global perspective.* Washington, DC: U.S. Department of State and Department of Health and Human Services, National Institute on Aging, & National Institutes of Health.

Dodge, K. A., Coie, J. D., Pettit, G. S., & Price, J. M. (1990). Peer status and aggression in boys' groups: Developmental and contextual analysis. *Child Development, 61,* 1289–1309.

Dodge, K. A., Dishion, T. J., & Lansford, J. E. (2006). Deviant peer influences in intervention and public policy for youth. *Social Policy Report, XX,* 3–19.

Dodge, K. A., Pettit, G. S., & Bates, J. E. (1994). Socialization mediators of the relation between socioeconomic status and child conduct problems. *Child Development, 65,* 649–665.

Doherty, W. J., Kouneski, E. F., & Erickson, M. F. (1998). Responsible fathering: An overview and conceptual framework. *Journal of Marriage and Family, 60,* 277–292.

Doka, K. J., & Mertz, M. E. (1988). The meaning and significance of great-grandparenthood. *Gerontologist, 28*(2), 192–197.

Dolan, M. A., & Hoffman, C. D. (1998). Determinants of divorce among women: A reexamination of critical influences. *Journal of Divorce and Remarriage, 28,* 97–106.

D'Onofrio, B. M., Turkheimer, E., Emery, R. E., Slutske, W. S., Heath, A. C., Madden, P. A., & Martin, N. G. (2006). A genetically informed study of the processes underlying the association between parental marital instability and offspring adjustment. *Developmental Psychology, 42,* 486–499.

Donovan, W. L., Leavitt, L. A., & Walsh, R. O. (1998). Conflict and depression predict maternal sensitivity to infant cries. *Infant Behavior and Development, 21,* 505–517.

Dorsey, M. J., and Schneider, L. C. (2003). Improving asthma outcomes and self-management behaviors of inner-city children. *Pediatrics, 112,* 474.

Dougherty, T. M., & Haith, M. M. (1997). Infant expectations and reaction time as predictors of childhood speed of processing and IQ. *Developmental Psychology, 33,* 146–155.

Dowshen, S., Crowley, J., & Palusci, V. J. (2004). *Shaken baby/shaken impact syndrome.* Retrieved February 17, 2007, from www.kidshealth.org/parent/medical/brain/shaken.html.

Dozier, M., Stovall, K. C., Albus, K. E., & Bates, B. (2001). Attachment for infants in foster care: The role of caregiver state of mind. *Child Development, 72,* 1467–1477.

Dreyfus, H. L. (1993–1994, Winter). What computers still can't do. *Key Reporter,* pp. 4–9.

Dubé, E. M., & Savin-Williams, R. C. (1999). Sexual identity development among ethnic sexual-minority youths. *Developmental Psychology, 35*(6), 1389–1398.

Dube, S. R., Anda, R. F., Felitti, V. J., Chapman, D. P., Williamson, D. F., & Giles, W. H. (2001). Childhood abuse, household dysfunction, and the risk of attempted suicide throughout the life span: Findings from the Adverse Childhood Experiences Study. *Journal of the American Medical Association, 286*(24), 3089–3096.

Dube, S. R., Felitti, V. J., Dong, M., Chapman, D. P., Giles, W. H., & Anda, R. F. (2003, March). Childhood abuse, neglect, and household dysfunction and the risk of illicit drug use: The Adverse Childhood Experiences Study. *Pediatrics, 111*(3), 564–572.

Dubowitz, H. (1999). The families of neglected children. In M. E. Lamb (Ed.), *Parenting and child development in "nontraditional" families* (pp. 327–345). Mahwah, NJ: Erlbaum.

Duckworth, A., & Seligman, M. E. P. (2005). Self-discipline outdoes IQ in predicting academic performance of adolescents. *Psychological Science, 26,* 939–944.

Duenwald, M. (2003, July 15). After 25 years, new ideas in the prenatal test tube. *New York Times.* Retrieved from www.nytimes.com/2003/07/15/health/15IVF.html?ex.

Duke, J., Huhman, M., & Heitzler, C. (2003). Physical activity levels among children aged 9–13 years—United States, 2002. *Morbidity and Mortality Weekly Report, 52,* 785–788.

Duncan, G. J., & Brooks-Gunn, J. (1997). Income effects across the life span: Integration and interpretation. In G. J. Duncan & J. Brooks-Gunn (Eds.), *Consequences of growing up poor* (pp. 596–610). New York: Russell Sage Foundation.

Duncan, G. J., Dowsett, C. J., Claessens, A., Magnuson, K., Huston, A. C., Klebanov, P., Pagani, L. S., Feinstein, L., Engel, M., Brooks-Gunn, J., Sexton, H., Duckworth, K., & Japel, C. (2007). School readiness and later achievement. *Developmental Psychology, 43*(6), 1428–1446.

Dunlosky, J., & Hertzog, C. (1998). Aging and deficits in associative memory: What is the role of strategy production? *Psychology and Aging, 13,* 597–607.

Dunn, A. L., Trivedi, M. H., Kampert, J. B., Clark, C. G., & Chambliss, H. O. (2005). Exercise treatment for depression: Efficacy and dose response. *American Journal of Preventive Medicine, 28,* 1–8.

Dunn, J. (1991). Young children's understanding of other people: Evidence from observations within the family. In D. Frye & C. Moore (Eds.), *Children's theories of mind: Mental states and social understanding.* Hillsdale, NJ: Erlbaum.

Dunn, J. (1996). Sibling relationships and perceived self-competence: Patterns of stability between childhood and early adolescence. In A. J. Sameroff & M. M. Haith (Eds.), *The five to seven year shift: The age of reason and responsibility* (pp. 253–269). Chicago: University of Chicago Press.

Dunn, J., Brown, J., Slomkowski, C., Tesla, C., & Youngblade, L. (1991). Young children's understanding of other people's feelings and beliefs: Individual differences and antecedents. *Child Development, 62,* 1352–1366.

Dunn, J., & Hughes, C. (2001). "I got some swords and you're dead!": Violent fantasy, antisocial behavior, friendship, and moral sensibility in young children. *Child Development, 72,* 491–505.

Dunn, J., & Munn, P. (1985). Becoming a family member: Family conflict and the development of social understanding in the second year. *Child Development, 56,* 480–492.

Dunson, D. (2002). *Late breaking research session. Increasing infertility with increasing age: Good news and bad news for older couples.* Paper presented at 18th annual meeting of the European Society of Human Reproduction and Embryology, Vienna.

Dunson, D. B., Colombo, B., & Baird, D. D. (2002). Changes with age in the level and duration of fertility in the menstrual cycle. *Human Reproduction, 17,* 1399–1403.

DuPont, R. L. (1983). Phobias in children. *Journal of Pediatrics, 102,* 999–1002.

Durand, A. M. (1992). The safety of home birth: The Farm Study. *American Journal of Public Health, 82,* 450–452.

DuRant, R. H., Smith, J. A., Kreiter, S. R., & Krowchuk, D. P. (1999). The relationship between early age of onset of initial substance use and engaging in multiple health risk behaviors among young adolescents. *Archives of Pediatrics & Adolescent Medicine, 153,* 286–291.

Durlak, J. A. (1973). Relationship between attitudes toward life and death among elderly women. *Developmental Psychology, 8*(1), 146.

Dush, C. M. K., Cohan, C. L., & Amato, P. R. (2003). The relationship between cohabitation and marital quality and stability: Change across cohorts? *Journal of Marriage and Family, 65,* 539–549.

Duskin, Rita. (1987). Haiku. In C. Spelius (Ed.), *Sound and Light.* Deerfield, IL: Lakeshore Publishing.

Dwyer, T., Ponsonby, A. L., Blizzard, L., Newman, N. M., & Cochrane, J. A. (1995). The contribution of changes in the prevalence of prone sleeping position to the decline in sudden infant death syndrome in Tasmania. *Journal of the American Medical Association, 273,* 783–789.

Dychtwald, K., & Flower, J. (1990). *Age wave: How the most important trend of our time will change your future.* New York: Bantam Books.

Dykstra, P. A. (1995). Loneliness among the never and formerly married: The importance of supportive friendships and a desire for independence. *Journal of Gerontology: Social Sciences, 50B,* S321–S329.

Early College High School Initiative. (n.d). Retrieved March 31, 2004, from www .earlycolleges.org.

East, P. L., & Khoo, S. T. (2005). Longitudinal pathways linking family factors and sibling relationship qualities to adolescent substance use and sexual risk behaviors. *Journal of Family Psychology, 19,* 571–580.

Eastell, R. (1998). Treatment of postmenopausal osteoporosis. *New England Journal of Medicine, 338,* 736–746.

Eating disorders—Part I. (1997, October). *Harvard Mental Health Letter,* pp. 1–5.

Eaton, D. K., Kann, L., Kinchen, S., Ross, J., Hawkins, J., Harris, W. A., Lowry, R., McManus, T., Chyen, D., Shanklin, S., Lim, C., Grunbaum, J. A., & Wechsler, H. (2006). Youth risk behavior surveillance—United States, 2005. *Morbidity and Mortality Weekly Report, 55*(SS-5).

Eaton, D. K., Kann, L., Kinchen, S., Shanklin, S., Ross, J., Hawkins, J., Harris, W. A., Lowry, R., McManus, T., Chyen, D., Lim, C., Brener, N. D., & Wechsler, H. (2008). Youth risk behavior surveillance—United States, 2007. *Morbidity and Mortality Weekly Report, 57*(SS-4), 1–131.

Eccles, A. (1982). *Obstetrics and gynaecology in Tudor and Stuart England.* Kent, OH: Kent State University Press.

Eccles, J. S. (2004). Schools, academic motivation, and stage-environment fit. In R. M. Lerner & L. Steinberg (Eds), *Handbook of adolescent development* (2nd ed., pp. 125–153). Hoboken, NJ: Wiley.

Eccles, J. S., Wigfield, A., & Byrnes, J. (2003). Cognitive development in adolescence. In I. B. Weiner, (Series Ed.), R. M. Lerner, M. A. Easterbrooks, & J. Mistry (Vol. Eds.), *Handbook of psychology: Vol. 6. Developmental psychology.* New York: Wiley.

Ecker, J. L., & Frigoletto, F. D., Jr. (2007). Cesarean delivery and the risk-benefit calculus. *New England Journal of Medicine, 356,* 885–888.

Eckerman, C. O., Davis, C. C., & Didow, S. M. (1989). Toddlers' emerging ways of achieving social coordination with a peer. *Child Development, 60,* 440–453.

Eckerman, C. O., & Didow, S. M. (1996). Nonverbal imitation and toddlers' mastery of verbal means of achieving coordinated action. *Developmental Psychology, 32,* 141–152.

Eckerman, C. O., & Stein, M. R. (1982). The toddler's emerging interactive skills. In K. H. Rubin & H. S. Ross (Eds.), *Peer relationships and social skills in childhood.* New York: Springer-Verlag.

Eddleman, K. A., Malone, F. D., Sullivan, L., Dukes, K., Berkowitz, R. L., Kharbutli, Y., Porter, T. F., Luthy, D. A., Comstock, C. H., Saade, G. R., Klugman, S., Dugoff, L., Craigo, S. D., Timor-Tritsch, I. E., Carr, S. R., Wolfe, H. M., & D'Alton, M. E. (2006). Pregnancy loss rates after midtrimester amniocentesis. *Obstetrics and Gynecology, 108*(5), 1067–1072.

Eden, G. F., Jones, K. M., Cappell, K., Gareau, L., Wood, F. B., Zeffiro, T. A., Dietz, N. A. E., Agnew, J. A., & Flowers, D. L. (2004). Neural changes following remediation in adult developmental dyslexia. *Neuron, 44,* 411–422.

Eder, W., Ege, M. J., & von Mutius, E. (2006). The asthma epidemic. *New England Journal of Medicine, 355,* 2226–2235.

Edwards, C. P. (1981). The comparative study of the development of moral judgment and reasoning. In R. Monroe, R. Monroe, & B. B. Whiting (Eds.), *Handbook of cross-cultural human development.* New York: Garland.

Edwards, C. P. (1994, April). *Cultural relativity meets best practice, or, anthropology and early education, a promising friendship.* Paper presented at the meeting of the American Educational Research Association, New Orleans.

Egan, M. F., Straub, R. E., Goldberg, T. E., Yakub I., Callicott, J. H., Hariri, A. R., Mattay, V. S., Bertolino, A., Hyde, T. M., Shannon-Weickert, C., Akil, M., Crook, J., Vakkalanka, R. K., Balkissoon, R., Gibbs, R. A., Kleinman, J. E., & Weinberger, D. R. (2004). Variation in GRM3 affects cognition, prefrontal glutamate, and risk for schizophrenia. *Proceedings of the National Academy of Sciences (USA), 101*(34), 12604–12609.

Eggebeen, D. J., & Knoester, C. (2001). Does fatherhood matter for men? *Journal of Marriage and Family, 63,* 381–393.

Eggebeen, D. J., & Sturgeon, S. (2006). Demography of the baby boomers. In S. K. Whitbourne & S. L. Willis (Eds.), *The baby boomers grow up: Contemporary perspectives on midlife* (pp. 3–21). Mahwah, Erlbaum.

Eichler, E. E., & Zimmerman, A. W. (2008). A hot spot of genetic instability in autism. *New England Journal of Medicine, 358,* 737–739.

Eimas, P., Siqueland, E., Jusczyk, P., & Vigorito, J. (1971). Speech perception in infants. *Science, 171,* 303–306.

Eisenberg, A. (April 5, 2001). A "smart" home, to avoid the nursing home. *New York Times,* pp. G1, G6.

Eisenberg, A. R. (1996). The conflict talk of mothers and children: Patterns related to culture, SES, and gender of child. *Merrill-Palmer Quarterly, 42,* 438–452.

Eisenberg, L. (1995, Spring). Is the family obsolete? *Key Reporter,* pp. 1–5.

Eisenberg, N. (1992). *The caring child.* Cambridge, MA: Harvard University Press.

Eisenberg, N. (2000). Emotion, regulation, and moral development. *Annual Review of Psychology, 51,* 665–697.

Eisenberg, N., & Fabes, R. A. (1998). Prosocial development. In W. Damon (Series Ed.) & N. Eisenberg (Vol. Ed.), *Handbook of child psychology: Vol. 3. Social, emotional, and personality development* (5th ed., pp. 701–778). New York: Wiley.

Eisenberg, N., Fabes, R. A., Guthrie, I. K., & Reiser, M. (2000). Dispositional emotionality and regulation: Their role in predicting quality of social functioning. *Journal of Personality and Social Psychology, 78,* 136–157.

Eisenberg, N., Fabes, R. A., & Murphy, B. C. (1996). Parents' reactions to children's negative emotions: Relations to children's social competence and comforting behavior. *Child Development, 67,* 2227–2247.

Eisenberg, N., Fabes, R. A., Nyman, M., Bernzweig, J., & Pinuelas, A. (1994). The relations of emotionality and regulation to children's anger-related reactions. *Child Development, 65,* 109–128.

Eisenberg, N., Fabes, R. A., Shepard, S. A., Guthrie, I. K., Murphy, B. C., & Reiser, M. (1999). Parental reactions to children's negative emotions: Longitudinal relations to quality of children's social functioning. *Child Development, 70*(2), 513–534.

Eisenberg, N., Guthrie, I. K., Fabes, R. A., Reiser, M., Murphy, B. C., Holgren, R., Maszk, P., & Losoya, S. (1997). The relations of regulation and emotionality to resiliency and competent social functioning in elementary school children. *Child Development, 68,* 295–311.

Eisenberg, N., & Morris, A. D. (2004). Moral cognitions and prosocial responding in adolescence. In R. M. Lerner & L. Steinberg (Eds.), *Handbook of adolescent psychology* (2nd ed., pp. 155–188). Hoboken, NJ: Wiley.

Eisenberg, N., Spinrad, T. L., Fabes, R. A., Reiser, M., Cumberland, A., Shepard, S. A., Valiente, C., Losoya, S. H., Guthrie, I. K., & Thompson, M. (2004). The relations of effortful control and impulsivity to children's resiliency and adjustment. *Child Development, 75,* 25–46.

Elder, G. H., Jr. (1974). *Children of the Great Depression: Social change in life experience.* Chicago: University of Chicago Press.

Eldridge, R. I., & Sutton, P. D. (2007). Births, marriages, divorces, and deaths: Provisional data for 2006. *National Vital Statistics Reports, 55*(20). Hyattsville, MD: National Center for Health Statistics.

Elia, J., Ambrosini, P. J., & Rapoport, J. L. (1999). Treatment of attention-deficit hyperactivity disorder. *New England Journal of Medicine, 340,* 780–788.

Eliassen, H., Colditz, G. A., Rosner, B., Willett, W. C., & Hankinson, S. E. (2006). Adult weight change and risk of post-menopausal breast cancer. *Journal of the American Medical Association, 296,* 193–201.

Elicker, J., Englund, M., & Sroufe, L. A. (1992). Predicting peer competence and peer relationships in childhood from early parent-child relationships. In R. Parke & G. Ladd (Eds.), *Family peer relationships: Modes of linkage* (pp. 77–106). Hillsdale, NJ: Erlbaum.

Elkind, D. (1981). *The hurried child.* Reading, MA: Addison-Wesley.

Elkind, D. (1984). *All grown up and no place to go.* Reading, MA: Addison-Wesley.

Elkind, D. (1986). *The miseducation of children: Superkids at risk.* New York: Knopf.

Elkind, D. (1997). *Reinventing childhood: Raising and educating children in a changing world.* Rosemont, NJ: Modern Learning Press.

Elkind, D. (1998). *Teenagers in crisis: All grown up and no place to go.* Reading, MA: Perseus Books.

Elliott, D. S. (1993). Health enhancing and health compromising lifestyles. In S. G. Millstein, A. C. Petersen, & E. O. Nightingale (Eds.), *Promoting the health of adolescents: New directions for the twenty-first century* (pp. 119–145). New York: Oxford University Press.

Elliott, P., Stamler, J., Dyer, A. R., Appel, L., Dennis, B., Kesteloot, H., Ueshima, H., Okayama, A., Chan, Q., Garside, D. B., & Zhou, B. for the INTERMAP Cooperative Research Group. (2006). Association between protein intake and blood pressure. *Annals of Internal Medicine 166,* 79–87.

Elliott, V. S. (2000, November 20). Doctors caught in middle of ADHD treatment controversy: Critics charge that medications are being both under- and overprescribed. *AMNews.* Retrieved April 21, 2005, from www.ama-assn.org/amednews/2000/11/20/hlsb1120.htm.

Ellis, A. & Oakes, L. M. (2006). Infants flexibly use different dimensions to categorize objects. *Developmental Psychology, 42,* 1000–1011.

Ellis, B. J., Bates, J. E., Dodge, K. A., Fergusson, D. M., Horwood, L. J., Pettit, G. S., & Woodward, L. (2003). Does father-absence place daughters at special risk for early sexual activity and teenage pregnancy? *Child Development, 74,* 801–821.

Ellis, B. J., McFadyen-Ketchum, S., Dodge, K. A., Pettit, G. S., & Bates, J. E. (1999). Quality of early family relationships and individual differences in the timing of pubertal maturation in girls: A longitudinal test of an evolutionary model. *Journal of Personality and Social Psychology, 77,* 387–401.

Ellis, K. J., Abrams, S. A., & Wong, W. W. (1997). Body composition of a young,

multiethnic female population. *American Journal of Clinical Nutrition, 65,* 724–731.

Else-Quest, N. M., Hyde, J. S., Goldsmith, H. H., & Van Hulle, C. A. (2006). Gender differences in temperament: A meta-analysis. *Psychological Bulletin, 132,* 33–72.

Eltzschig, H. K., Lieberman, E. S., & Camann, W. R. (2003). Regional anesthesia and analgesia for labor and delivery. *New England Journal of Medicine, 348,* 319–332.

Emde, R. N., Plomin, R., Robinson, J., Corley, R., DeFries, J., Fulker, D. W., Reznick, J. S., Campos, J., Kagan, J., & Zahn-Waxler, C. (1992). Temperament, emotion, and cognition at 14 months: The MacArthur longitudinal twin study. *Child Development, 63,* 1437–1455.

Eng, P. M., Rimm, E. B., Fitzmaurice, G., & Kawachi, I. (2002). Social ties and change in social ties in relation to subsequent total and cause-specific mortality and coronary heart disease incidence in men. *American Journal of Epidemiology, 155,* 700–709.

Engle, P. L., & Breaux, C. (1998). Fathers' involvement with children: Perspectives from developing countries. *Social Policy Report, 12*(1), 1–21.

Eogan, M. A., Geary, M. P., O'Connell, M. P., & Keane, D. P. (2003). Effect of fetal sex on labour and delivery: Retrospective review. *British Medical Journal, 326,* 137.

Epel, E. S., Blackburn, E. H., Lin, J., Dhabhar, F. S., Adler, N. E., Morrow, J. D., & Cawthon, R. M. (2004). Accelerated telomere shortening in response to life stress. *Proceedings of the National Academy of Sciences, 101,* 17312–17315.

Epstein, R. A. (1989, Spring). Voluntary euthanasia. *Law School Record* (University of Chicago), pp. 8–13.

Erdley, C. A., Cain, K. M., Loomis, C. C., Dumas-Hines, F., & Dweck, C. S. (1997). Relations among children's social goals, implicit personality theories, and responses to social failure. *Developmental Psychology, 33,* 263–272.

Erikson, E. H. (1950). *The life cycle completed.* New York: Norton.

Erikson, E. H. (1968). *Identity: Youth and crisis.* New York: Norton.

Erikson, E. H. (1973). The wider identity. In K. Erikson (Ed.), *In search of common ground: Conversations with Erik H. Erikson and Huey P. Newton.* New York: Norton.

Erikson, E. H. (1982). *The life cycle completed.* New York: Norton.

Erikson, E. H. (1985). *The life cycle completed* (Paperback reprint ed.). New York: Norton.

Erikson, E. H., Erikson, J. M., & Kivnick, H. Q. (1986). *Vital involvement in old age: The experience of old age in our time.* New York: Norton.

Eriksson, P. S., Perfilieva, E., Björk-Eriksson, T., Alborn, A., Nordborg, C., Peterson, D. A., & Gage, F. H. (1998). Neurogenesis

in the adult human hippocampus. *Nature Medicine, 4,* 1313–1317.

Eron, L. D. (1980). Prescription for reduction of aggression. *American Psychologist, 35,* 244–252.

Eron, L. D. (1982). Parent-child interaction, television violence, and aggression in children. *American Psychologist, 37,* 197–211.

Eron, L. D., & Huesmann, L. R. (1986). The role of television in the development of prosocial and antisocial behavior. In D. Olweus, J. Block, & M. Radke-Yarrow (Eds.), *The development of antisocial and prosocial behavior: Research, theories, and issues.* New York: Academic Press.

Ertel, K. A., Glymour, M. M., & Berkman, L. F. (2008). Effects of social integration on preserving memory function in a nationally representative elderly population. *American Journal of Public Health, 98,* 1215–1220.

Ervin, R. B. (2006). Prevalence of functional limitations among adults 60 years of age and over: United States, 1999–2002. *Advance Data from Vital and Health Statistics,* No. 375. Hyattsville, MD: National Center for Health Statistics.

Ervin, R. B. (2008). Healthy Index Eating scores among adults, 60 years of age and over, by sociodemographic and health characteristics: United States, 1999–2002. *Advance Data from Vital and Health Statistics,* No. 395. Hyattsville, MD: National Center for Health Statistics.

Ervin, R. B., Wright, J. D., Wang, C.-Y., & Kennedy-Stephenson, J. (2004). Dietary intake of fats and fatty acids for the United States Population: 1999–2000. *Advance Data from Vital and Health Statistics,* No. 348. Hyattsville, MD: National Center for Health Statistics.

Espeland, M. A., Gu, L., Masaki, K. H., Langer, R. D., Coker, L. H., Stefanick, M. L., Ockene, J., & Rapp, S. R., for the Women's Health Initiative Memory Study. (2005). Association between reported alcohol intake and cognition: Results from the Women's Health Initiative Memory Study. *American Journal of Epidemiology, 161,* 228–238.

Espeland, M. A., Rapp, S. R., Shumaker, S. A., Brunner, R., Manson, J. E., Sherwin, B. B., Hsia, J., Margolis, K. L., Hogan, P. E., Wallace, R., Dailey, M., Freeman, R., Hays, J., for the Women's Health Initiative Memory Study Investigators. (2004). Conjugated equine estrogens and global cognitive function in postmenopausal women: Women's Health Initiative Memory Study. *Journal of the American Medical Association, 21,* 2959–2968.

Espey, D. K., Wu, X.-C., Swan, J., Wiggins, C., Jim, M. A., Ward, E., Wingo, P. A., Howe, H. L., Ries, L. A. G., Miller, B. A., Jemal., A., Ahmed, F., Cobb, N., Kaur, J. S., & Edwards, B. K. (2007). Commentary: Annual report to the nation on the status of cancer, 1975–2004, featuring cancer in American Indians and Alaska Natives. *Cancer, 110,* 2119–2152.

Esposito, K., Marfella, R., Ciotola, M., DiPalo, C., Giugliano, F., Giugliano, G., D'Armiento, M., D'Andrea, F., & Giugliano, D. (2004). Effects of a Mediterranean-style diet on endothelial dysfunction and markers of vascular inflammation in the metabolic syndrome: A randomized trial. *Journal of the American Medical Association, 292,* 1440–1446.

Essex, M. J., & Nam, S. (1987). Marital status and loneliness among older women: The differential importance of close family and friends. *Journal of Marriage and Family, 49,* 93–106.

Ettinger, B., Friedman, G. D., Bush, T., & Quesenberry, C. P. (1996). Reduced mortality associated with long-term post-menopausal estrogen therapy. *Obstetrics & Gynecology, 87,* 6–12.

Etzel, R. A. (2003). How environmental exposures influence the development and exacerbation of asthma. *Pediatrics, 112*(1): 233–239.

Evans, G. W. (2004). The environment of childhood poverty. *American Psychologist, 59,* 77–92.

Evans, G. W., & English, K. (2002). The environment of poverty: Multiple stressor exposure, psychophysiological stress and socioemotional adjustment. *Child Development, 73*(4), 1238–1248.

Evert, J., Lawler, E., Bogan, H., & Perls, T. (2003). Morbidity profiles of centenarians: Survivors, delayers, and escapers. *Journal of Gerontology: Medical Sciences, 58A,* 232–237.

Ezzati, M., Friedman, A. B., Kulkarni, S. C., & Murray, C. J. L. (2008). The reversal of fortunes: Trends in country mortality and cross-country mortality disparities in the United States. *PloS Medicine, 5*(4), e66. (DOI: 10:1371/journal.pmed.0050066).

Ezzati, M., & Lopez, A. D. (2004). Regional, disease specific patterns of smoking-attributable mortality in 2000. *Tobacco Control, 13,* 388–395.

Fabes, R. A., Carlo, G., Kupanoff, K., & Laible, D. (1999). Early adolescence and prosocial/moral behavior: I. The role of individual processes. *Journal of Early Adolescence, 19,* 5–16.

Fabes, R. A., & Eisenberg, N. (1992). Young children's coping with interpersonal anger. *Child Development, 63,* 116–128.

Fabes, R. A., Leonard, S. A., Kupanoff, K., & Martin, C. L. (2001). Parental coping with children's negative emotions: Relations with children's emotional and social responding. *Child Development, 72,* 907–920.

Fabes, R. A., Martin, C. L., & Hanish, L. D. (2003). Young children's play qualities in same-, other-, and mixed-gender peer groups. *Child Development, 74*(3), 921–932.

Fabricius, W. V. (2003). Listening to children of divorce: New findings that diverge from Wallerstein, Lewis, and Blakeslee. *Family Relations, 52,* 385–394.

Faden, V. B. (2006). Trends in initiation of alcohol use in the United States: 1975–2003.

Alcoholism: Clinical and Experimental Research, 30(6), 1011–1022.

Fagot, B. I. (1997). Attachment, parenting, and peer interactions of toddler children. *Developmental Psychology, 33,* 489–499.

Fagot, B. I., & Leinbach, M. D. (1995). Gender knowledge in egalitarian and traditional families. *Sex Roles, 32,* 513–526.

Falbo, T. (2006). *Your one and only: Educational psychologist dispels myths surrounding only children.* Retrieved July 20, 2006, from www.utexas.edu/features/archive/2004/single.htm.

Falbo, T., & Polit, D. F. (1986). Quantitative review of the only child literature: Research evidence and theory development. *Psychological Bulletin, 100*(2), 176–189.

Falbo, T., & Poston, D. L. (1993). The academic, personality, and physical outcomes of only children in China. *Child Development, 64,* 18–35.

Fantz, R. L. (1963). Pattern vision in newborn infants. *Science, 140,* 296–297.

Fantz, R. L. (1964). Visual experience in infants: Decreased attention to familiar patterns relative to novel ones. *Science, 146,* 668–670.

Fantz, R. L. (1965). Visual perception from birth as shown by pattern selectivity. In H. E. Whipple (Ed.), New issues in infant development. *Annals of the New York Academy of Science, 118,* 793–814.

Fantz, R. L., Fagen, J., & Miranda, S. B. (1975). Early visual selectivity. In L. Cohen & P. Salapatek (Eds.), *Infant perception: From sensation to cognition: Vol. 1. Basic visual processes* (pp. 249–341). New York: Academic Press.

Fantz, R. L., & Nevis, S. (1967). Pattern preferences and perceptual-cognitive development in early infancy. *Merrill-Palmer Quarterly, 13,* 77–108.

Farver, J. A. M., Kim, Y. K., & Lee, Y. (1995). Cultural differences in Korean and Anglo-American preschoolers' social interaction and play behavior. *Child Development, 66,* 1088–1099.

Farver, J. A. M., Xu, Y., Eppe, S., Fernandez, A., & Schwartz, D. (2005). Community violence, family conflict, and preschoolers' socioemotional functioning. *Developmental Psychology, 41,* 160–170.

Fawcett, G. M., Heise, L. L., Isita-Espejel, L., & Pick, S. (1999). Change community responses to wife abuse: A research and demonstration project in Iztacalco, Mexico. *American Psychologist, 54,* 41–49.

Fawzi, W. W., Msamanga, G. I., Urassa, W., Hertzmark, E., Petraro, P., Willett, W. C., & Spiegelman, D. (2007). Vitamins and perinatal outcomes among HIV-negative women in Tanzania. *New England Journal of Medicine, 356,* 1423–1431.

Fearon, P., O'Connell, P., Frangou, S., Aquino, P., Nosarti, C., Allin, M., Taylor, M., Stewart, A., Rifkin, L., & Murray, R. (2004). Brain volume in adult survivors of very low birth weight: A sibling-controlled study. *Pediatrics, 114,* 367–371.

Federal Bureau of Investigation (FBI). (2007). *Crime in the United States, 2005.* Retrieved June 2007 from www.fbi.gov/ucr/05cius.

Federal Interagency Forum on Aging-Related Statistics. (2004). *Older Americans 2004: Key indicators of well-being.* Washington, DC: U.S. Government Printing Office.

Federal Interagency Forum on Aging-Related Statistics. (2006). *Older Americans update 2006: Key indicators of well-being.* Washington, DC: U.S. Government Printing Office.

Federal Interagency Forum on Child and Family Statistics. (2005). *America's children: Key national indicators of well-being, 2005.* Washington, DC: U.S. Government Printing Office.

Federal Interagency Forum on Child and Family Statistics. (2006). *America's children in brief: Key national indicators of well-being, 2006.* Washington, DC: U.S. Government Printing Office.

Federal Interagency Forum on Child and Family Statistics. (2007). *America's children: Key indicators of well-being, 2007.* Washington, DC: U.S. Government Printing Office.

Feingold, A., & Mazzella, R. (1998). Gender differences in body image are increasing. *Psychological Science, 9*(3), 190–195.

Feldman, H. A., Goldstein, I., Hatzichristou, D. G., Krane, R. J., & McKinlay, J. B. (1994). Impotence and its medical and psychosocial correlates: Results of the Massachusetts Male Aging Study. *Journal of Urology, 151,* 54–61.

Ferber, R. (1985). *Solve your child's sleep problems.* New York: Simon & Schuster.

Ferber, S. G., & Makhoul, I. R. (2004). The effect of skin-to-skin contact (Kangaroo Care) shortly after birth on the neuro-behavioral responses of the term newborn: A randomized, controlled trial. *Pediatrics, 113,* 858–865.

Fergusson, D. M., Horwood, L. J., Ridder, E. M., & Beautrais, A. L. (2005). Subthreshold depression in adolescence and mental health outcomes in adulthood. *Archives of General Psychiatry, 62*(1), 66–72.

Fernald, A., & O'Neill, D. K. (1993). Peekaboo across cultures: How mothers and infants play with voices, faces, and expectations. In K. MacDonald (Ed.), *Parent-child play* (pp. 259–285). Albany, NY: State University of New York Press.

Fernald, A., Perfors, A., & Marchman, V. A. (2006). Picking up speed in understanding: Speech processing efficiency and vocabulary growth across the second year. *Developmental Psychology, 42,* 98–116.

Fernald, A., Pinto, J. P., Swingley, D., Weinberg, A., & McRoberts, G. W. (1998). Rapid gains in speed of verbal processing by infants in the 2nd year. *Psychological Science, 9*(3), 228–231.

Fernald, A., Swingley, D., and Pinto, J. P. (2001). When half a word is enough: Infants can recognize spoken words using partial phonetic information. *Child Development, 72,* 1003–1015.

Fiatarone, M. A., Marks, E. C., Ryan, N. D., Meredith, C. N., Lipsitz, L. A., & Evans, W. J. (1990). High-intensity strength training in nonagenarians: Effects on skeletal muscles. *Journal of the American Medical Association, 263,* 3029–3034.

Fiatarone, M. A., O'Neill, E. F., Ryan, N. D., Clements, K. M., Solares, G. R., Nelson, M. E., Roberts, S. B., Kehayias, J. J., Lipsitz, L. A., & Evans, W. J. (1994). Exercise training and nutritional supplementation for physical frailty in very elderly people. *New England Journal of Medicine, 330,* 1769–1775.

Field, A. E., Camargo, C. A., Taylor, B., Berkey, C. S., Roberts, S. B., & Colditz, G. A. (2001). Peer, parent, and media influence on the development of weight concerns and frequent dieting among preadolescent and adolescent girls and boys. *Pediatrics, 107*(1), 54–60.

Field, T. (1995). Infants of depressed mothers. *Infant Behavior and Development, 18,* 1–13.

Field, T. (1998a). Emotional care of the at-risk infant: Early interventions for infants of depressed mothers. *Pediatrics, 102,* 1305–1310.

Field, T. (1998b). Massage therapy effects. *American Psychologist, 53,* 1270–1281.

Field, T. (1998c). Maternal depression effects on infants and early intervention. *Preventive Medicine, 27,* 200–203.

Field, T., Diego, M., & Hernandez-Reif, M. (2007). Massage therapy research. *Developmental Review, 27,* 75–89.

Field, T., Diego, M., Hernandez-Reif, M., Schanberg, S., & Kuhn, C. (2003). Depressed mothers who are "good interaction" partners versus those who are withdrawn or intrusive. *Infant Behavior & Development, 26,* 238–252.

Field, T., Fox, N. A., Pickens, J., Nawrocki, T., & Soutollo, D. (1995). Right frontal EEG activation in 3- to 6-month-old infants of depressed mothers. *Developmental Psychology, 31,* 358–363.

Field, T., Grizzle, N., Scafidi, F., Abrams, S., Richardson, S., Kuhn, C., & Schanberg, S. (1996). Massage therapy for infants of depressed mothers. *Infant Behavior and Development, 19,* 107–112.

Field, T. M. (1978). Interaction behaviors of primary versus secondary caretaker fathers. *Developmental Psychology, 14,* 183–184.

Field, T. M., & Roopnarine, J. L. (1982). Infant-peer interaction. In T. M. Field, A. Huston, H. C. Quay, L. Troll, & G. Finley (Eds.), *Review of human development.* New York: Wiley.

Field, T. M., Sandberg, D., Garcia, R., Vega-Lahr, N., Goldstein, S., & Guy, L. (1985). Pregnancy problems, postpartum depression, and early infant-mother interactions. *Developmental Psychology, 21,* 1152–1156.

Fields, J. (2003). Children's living arrangements and characteristics: March 2002. *Current Population Reports* (P20-547). Washington, DC: U.S. Bureau of the Census.

Fields, J. (2004). America's families and living arrangements: 2003. *Current Population Reports* (P20-553). Washington, DC: U.S. Census Bureau.

Fields, J. M., & Smith, K. E. (1998, April). *Poverty, family structure, and child well-being: Indicators from the SIPP* (Population Division Working Paper No. 23, U.S. Bureau of the Census). Paper presented at the annual meeting of the Population Association of America, Chicago.

Fields, L. E., Burt, V. L., Cutler, J. A., Hughes, J., Roccella, E. J., & Sorlie, P. (2004). The burden of adult hypertension in the United States 1999 to 2000: A rising tide. *Hypertension, 44,* 398.

Fifer, W. P., & Moon, C. M. (1995). The effects of fetal experience with sound. In J. P. Lecanuet, W. P. Fifer, N. A. Krasnegor, & W. P. Smotherman (Eds.), *Fetal development. A psychobiological perspective* (pp. 351–366). Hillsdale, NJ: Erlbaum.

Finch, C. E. (2001). Toward a biology of middle age. In M. E. Lachman (Ed.), *Handbook of midlife development* (pp. 77–108). New York: Wiley.

Finch, C. E., & Zelinski, E. M. (2005). Normal aging of brain structure and cognition: Evolutionary perspectives. *Research in Human Development, 2,* 69–82.

Fincham, F. D., Beach, S. H., & Davila, J. (2004). Forgiveness and conflict resolution in marriage. *Journal of Family Psychology, 18,* 72–81.

Finer, L. B. (2007). Trends in premarital sex in the United States, 1954–2003. *Public Health Reports, 122,* 73–78.

Fingerman, K., & Dolbin-MacNab, M. (2006). The baby boomers and their parents: Cohort influences and intergenerational ties. In S. K. Whitbourne & S. L. Willis (Eds.), *The baby boomers grow up: Contemporary perspectives on midlife* (pp. 237–259). Mahwah, NJ: Erlbaum.

Finn, J. D. (2006). *The adult lives of at-risk students: The roles of attainment and engagement in high school* (NCES 2006-328). Washington, DC: U. S. Department of Education, National Center for Education Statistics.

Finn, J. D., Gerber, S. B., & Boyd-Zaharias, J. (2005). Small classes in the early grades, academic achievement, and graduating from high school. *Journal of Educational Psychology, 97,* 214–223.

Finn, J. D., & Rock, D. A. (1997). Academic success among students at risk for dropout. *Journal of Applied Psychology, 82,* 221–234.

First 30 Days. (2008). *The change report.* Research conducted by Southeastern Institute of Research, Retrieved May 7, 2008, from www.first30days.com/pages/the_change_report.html.

Fiscella, K., Kitzman, H. J., Cole, R. E., Sidora, K. J., & Olds, D. (1998). Does child abuse predict adolescent pregnancy? *Pediatrics, 101,* 620–624.

Fischer, K. (1980). A theory of cognitive development: The control and construction of hierarchies of skills. *Psychological Review, 87,* 477–531.

Fischer, K. W., & Pruyne, E. (2003). Reflective thinking in adulthood. In J. Demick & C. Andreoletti (Eds.), *Handbook of adult development.* New York: Plenum Press.

Fischer, K. W., & Rose, S. P. (1994). Dynamic development of coordination of components in brain and behavior: A framework for theory and research. In G. Dawson & K. W. Fischer (Eds.), *Human behavior and the developing brain* (pp. 3–66). New York: Guilford Press.

Fischer, K. W., & Rose, S. P. (1995, Fall). Concurrent cycles in the dynamic development of brain and behavior. *SRCD Newsletter,* pp. 3–4, 15–16.

Fitzpatrick, M. D., & Turner, S. E. (2007). Blurring the boundary: Changes in the transition from college participation to adulthood. In S. Danziger & C. Rouse (Eds.)., *The price of independence: The economics of early adulthood* (pp. 107–137). New York: Russell Sage Foundation.

Fivush, R., & Haden, C. A. (2006). Elaborating on elaborations: Role of maternal reminiscing style in cognitive and socioemotional development. *Child Development, 77,* 1568–1588.

Fivush, R., & Nelson, K. (2004). Culture and language in the emergence of autobiographical memory. *Psychological Science, 15,* 573–577.

Flannagan, C. A., Bowes, J. M., Jonsson, B., Csapo, B., & Sheblanova, E. (1998). Ties that bind: Correlates of adolescents' civic commitment in seven countries. *Journal of Social Issues, 54,* 457–475.

Flavell, J. (1963). *The developmental psychology of Jean Piaget.* New York: Van Nostrand.

Flavell, J. H. (1970). Developmental studies of mediated memory. In H. W. Reese & L. P. Lipsitt (Eds.), *Advances in child development and behavior* (Vol. 5, pp. 181–211). New York: Academic Press.

Flavell, J. H. (1993). Young children's understanding of thinking and consciousness. *Current Directions in Psychological Science, 2,* 40–43.

Flavell, J. H., Green, F. L., & Flavell, E. R. (1986). Development of knowledge about the appearance-reality distinction. *Monographs of the Society for Research in Child Development, 51*(1, Serial No. 212).

Flavell, J. H., Green, F. L., & Flavell, E. R. (1995). Young children's knowledge about thinking. *Monographs of the Society for Research in Child Development, 60*(1, Serial No. 243).

Flavell, J. H., Green, F. L., Flavell, E. R., & Grossman, J. B. (1997). The development of children's knowledge about inner speech. *Child Development, 68,* 39–47.

Flavell, J. H., Miller, P. H., & Miller, S. A. (1993). *Cognitive development.* Englewood Cliffs, NJ: Prentice-Hall.

Flavell, J. H., Miller, P. H., & Miller, S. A. (2002). *Cognitive development.* Englewood Cliffs, NJ: Prentice-Hall.

Fleeson, W. (2004). The quality of American life at the end of the century. In O. G. Brim, C. D. Ryff, & R. C. Kessler (Eds.), *How healthy are we? A national study of well-being at midlife* (pp. 252–272). Chicago: University of Chicago Press.

Flegal, K. M., Graubard, B. I., Williamson, D. F., & Gail, M. H. (2005). Excess deaths associated with underweight, overweight, and obesity. *Journal of the American Medical Association, 293,* 1861–1867.

Flook, L., Repetti, R. L., & Ullman, J. B. (2005). Classroom social experiences as predictors of academic performance. *Developmental Psychology, 41,* 319–327.

Flores, G., Olson, L, & Tomany-Korman, S. C. (2005). Racial and ethnic disparities in early childhood health and health care. *Pediatrics, 115,* e183–e193.

Flynn, J. R. (1984). The mean IQ of Americans: Massive gains 1932 to 1978. *Psychological Bulletin, 95,* 29–51.

Flynn, J. R. (1987). Massive IQ gains in 14 nations: What IQ tests really measure. *Psychological Bulletin, 101,* 171–191.

Foldvari, M., Clark, M., Laviolette, L. C., Bernstein, M. A., Kaliton, D., Castaneda, C., Pu, C. T., Hausdorff, J. M., Fielding, R. A., & Singh, M. A. (2000). Association of muscle power with functional status in community-dwelling elderly women. *Journal of Gerontology: Biological and Medical Sciences, 55,* M192–M199.

Folkman, S., Lazarus, R. S., Pimley, S., & Novacek, J. (1987). Age differences in stress and coping processes. *Psychology and Aging, 2,* 171–184.

Fomby, P., & Cherlin, A. J. (2007). Family instability and child well-being. *American Sociological Review, 72*(2), 181–204.

Fontana, L., & Klein, S. (2007). Aging, adiposity, and calorie restriction. *Journal of the American Medical Association, 297,* 986–994.

Fontanel, B., & d'Harcourt, C. (1997). *Babies, history, art and folklore.* New York: Abrams.

Ford, P. (April 10, 2002). In Europe, marriage is back. *Christian Science Monitor,* p. l.

Ford, R. P., Schluter, P. J., Mitchell, E. A., Taylor, B. J., Scragg, R., & Stewart, A. W. (1998). Heavy caffeine intake in pregnancy and sudden infant death syndrome (New Zealand Cot Death Study Group). *Archives of Disease in Childhood, 78*(1), 9–13.

Forhan, S. E., Gottlieb, S. L., Sternberg, M. R., Xu, F., Datta, D., Berman, S., & Markowitz, L. E. (2008, March 13). *Prevalence of sexually transmitted infections and bacterial vaginosis among female adolescents in the United States: Data from the National Health and Nutritional Examination Survey (NHANES) 2003–2004.* Oral presentation at the meeting of the 2008 National STD Prevention Conference, Chicago.

Forteza, J. A., & Prieto, J. M. (1994). Aging and work behavior. In H. C. Triandis, M. D. Dunnette, & L. M. Hough (Eds.), *Handbook of industrial and organizational psychology* (pp. 447–483). Palo Alto, CA: Consulting Psychologists Press.

Fortner, M. R., Crouter, A. C., & McHale, S. M. (2004). Is parents' work involvement responsive to the quality of relationships with adolescent offspring? *Journal of Family Psychology, 18,* 530–538.

Foundation Fighting Blindness. (2005). *Macular Degeneration—Treatments.* Retrieved May 21, 2005, from www .blindness.org/disease/treatmentdetail .asp?typed=2&id=6.

Fowler, J. (1981). *Stages of faith: The psychology of human development and the quest for meaning.* New York: Harper & Row.

Fowler, J. W. (1989). Strength for the journey: Early childhood development in selfhood and faith. In D. A. Blazer, J. W. Fowler, K. J. Swick, A. S. Honig, P. J. Boone, B. M. Caldwell, R. A. Boone, & L. W. Barber (Eds.), *Faith development in early childhood* (pp. 1–63). New York: Sheed & Ward.

Fox, M. K., Pac, S., Devaney, B., & Jankowski, L. (2004). Feeding Infants and Toddlers Study: What foods are infants and toddlers eating? *Journal of the American Dietetic Association, 104,* 22–30.

Fox, N., Nelson, C. A., Zeanah, C., & Johnson, D. (2006, February 17). *Effects of social deprivation: The Bucharest early intervention project.* Presentation at the annual meeting of the American Association for the Advancement of Science, St. Louis, MO.

Fox, N. A., Hane, A. A., & Pine, D. S. (2007). Plasticity for affective neurocircuitry: How the environment affects gene expression. *Current Directions in Psychological Science, 16*(1), 1–5.

Fox, N. A., Kimmerly, N. L., & Schafer, W. D. (1991). Attachment to mother/ attachment to father: A meta-analysis. *Child Development, 62,* 210–225.

Fox, N. C., Black, R. S., Gilman, S., Rossor, M. N., Griffith, S. G., Jenkins, L., & Koller, M., for the AN1792(QS-21)-201 Study Team. (2005). Effects of Aβ immunization (AN1792) on MRI measures of cerebral volume in Alzheimer disease. *Neurology, 64,* 1563–1572.

Fraga, M., F., Ballestar, E., Paz, M. F., Ropero, S., Setien, F., Ballestar, M. L., Heine-Suñer, D., Cigudosa, J. C., Urioste, M., Benitez, J., Boix-Chornet, M., Sanchez-Aguilera, A., Ling, C., Carlsson, E., Poulsen, P., Vaag, A., Zarko, S., Spector, T. D., Yue-Zhong, W., Plass, C., & Esteller, M. (2005). Epigenetic differences arise during the lifetime of monozygotic twins. *Proceedings of the National Academy of Sciences, USA, 102,* 10604–10609.

Fraiberg, S. (1959). *The magic years.* New York: Scribners.

Frank, D. A., Augustyn, M., Knight, W. G., Pell, T., & Zuckerman, B. (2001). Growth, development, and behavior in early childhood following prenatal cocaine exposure. *Journal of the American Medical Association, 285,* 1613–1625.

Frankenburg, W. K., Dodds, J., Archer, P., Bresnick, B., Maschka. P., Edelman, N., & Shapiro, H. (1992). *Denver II training manual.* Denver: Denver Developmental Materials.

Frankenburg, W. K., Dodds, J. B., Fandal, A. W., Kazuk, E., & Cohrs, M. (1975). *The Denver Developmental Screening Test: Reference manual.* Denver: University of Colorado Medical Center.

Franz, C. E. (1997). Stability and change in the transition to midlife: A longitudinal study of midlife adults. In M. E. Lachman & J. B. James (Eds.), *Multiple paths of midlife development* (pp. 45–66). Chicago: University of Chicago Press.

Fraser, A. M., Brockert, J. F., & Ward, R. H. (1995). Association of young maternal age with adverse reproductive outcomes. *New England Journal of Medicine, 332*(17), 1113–1117.

Fredricks, J. A., & Eccles, J. S. (2002). Children's competence and value beliefs from childhood through adolescence: Growth trajectories in two male-sex-typed domains. *Developmental Psychology, 38,* 519–533.

Freeark, K., Rosenberg, E. B., Bornstein, J., Jozefowicz-Simbeni, D., Linkevich, M., & Lohnes, K. (2005). Gender differences and dynamics shaping the adoption life cycle: Review of the literature and recommendations. *American Journal of Orthopsychiatry, 75,* 86–101.

Freeman, C. (2004). *Trends in educational equity of girls & women: 2004* (NCES 2005-016). Washington, DC: National Center for Education Statistics.

Freeman, D. (1983). *Margaret Mead and Samoa: The making and unmaking of an anthropological myth.* Cambridge, MA: Harvard University Press.

French, H. W. (2007, March 22). China scrambles for stability as its workers age. *New York Times,* p. A1.

French, S. E., Seidman, E., Allen, L., & Aber, J. L. (2006). The development of ethnic identity during adolescence. *Developmental Psychology, 42,* 1–10.

Freud, A. (1946). *The ego and the mechanisms of defense.* New York: International Universities Press.

Freud, S. (1942). On psychotherapy. In E. Jones (Ed.), *Collected papers. London:* Hogarth. (Original work published 1906)

Freud, S. (1953). *A general introduction to psychoanalysis* (J. Rivière, Trans.). New York: Permabooks. (Original work published 1935)

Freud, S. (1964a). New introductory lectures on psychoanalysis. In J. Strachey (Ed. & Trans.), *The standard edition of the complete psychological works of Sigmund Freud* (Vol. 22). London: Hogarth. (Original work published 1933)

Freud, S. (1964b). An outline of psycho-analysis. In J. Strachey (Ed. & Trans.), *The standard edition of the complete psychological works of Sigmund Freud* (Vol. 23). London: Hogarth. (Original work published 1940)

Frey, K. S., Hirschstein, M. K., Snell, J. L., Edstrom, L. V. S., MacKenzie, E. P., & Broderick, C. J. (2005). Reducing playground bullying and supporting beliefs: An experimental trial of the Steps to Respect program. *Developmental Psychology, 41,* 479–491.

Fried, P. A., & Smith, A. M. (2001). A literature review of the consequences of prenatal marijuana exposure: An emerging theme of a deficiency in aspects of executive function. *Neurotoxicology and Teratology, 23,* 1–11.

Friedan, B. (1993). *The fountain of age.* New York: Simon & Schuster.

Friedman, L. J. (1999). *Identity's architect.* New York: Scribner.

Friedmann, P. D., Saitz, R., & Samet, J. H. (1998). Management of adults recovering from alcohol or other drug problems. *Journal of the American Medical Association, 279,* 1227–1231.

Friend, M., & Davis, T. L. (1993). Appearance-reality distinction: Children's understanding of the physical and affective domains. *Developmental Psychology, 29,* 907–914.

Friend, R. A. (1991). Older lesbian and gay people: A theory of successful aging. In J. A. Lee (Ed.), *Gay midlife and maturity* (pp. 99–118). New York: Haworth.

Fries, A. B. W., Ziegler, T. E., Kurian, J. R., Jacoris, S., & Pollak, S. D. (2005). Early experiences in humans is associated with changes in neuropeptides critical for regulating social behavior. *Proceedings of the National Academy of Sciences, USA, 102,* 17237–17240.

Fromkin, V., Krashen, S., Curtiss, S., Rigler, D., & Rigler, M. (1974). The development of language in Genie: Acquisition beyond the "critical period." *Brain and Language, 15*(9), 28–34.

Fromm, Erich. (1995). *The Sane Society.* New York: Rinehart.

Frydman, O., & Bryant, P. (1988). Sharing and the understanding of number equivalence by young children. *Cognitive Development, 3,* 323–339.

Frye, N. E., & Karney, B. R. (2006). The context of aggressive behavior in marriage: A longitudinal study of newlyweds. *Journal of Family Psychology, 20,* 12–20.

Fuchs, C. S., Stampfer, M. J., Colditz, G. A., Giovannucci, E. L., Manson, J. E., Kawachi, I., Hunter, D. J., Hankinson, S. E., Hennekens, C. H., Rosner, B., Speizer, F. E., & Willett, W. C. (1995). Alcohol consumption and mortality among women. *New England Journal of Medicine, 332,* 1245–1250.

Fujita, F., & Diener, E. (2005). Life satisfaction set point: Stability and change. *Journal of Personality and Social Psychology, 88,* 158–164.

Fuligni, A. J. (1997). The academic achievement of adolescents from immigrant families: The roles of family background, attitudes, and behavior. *Child Development, 68,* 351–363.

Fuligni, A. J., & Eccles, J. S. (1993). Perceived parent-child relationships and early adolescents' orientation toward peers. *Developmental Psychology, 29,* 622–632.

Fuligni, A. J., Eccles, J. S., Barber, B. L., & Clements, P. (2001). Early adolescent peer orientation and adjustment during high school. *Developmental Psychology, 37*(1), 28–36.

Fuligni, A. J., & Stevenson, H. W. (1995). Time use and mathematics achievement among American, Chinese, and Japanese high school students. *Child Development, 66,* 830–842.

Fuligni, A. J., Yip, T., & Tseng, V. (2002). The impact of family obligation on the daily activities and psychological well-being of Chinese American adolescents. *Child Development, 73*(1), 302–314.

Fulton, R., & Owen, G. (1987–1988). Death and society in twentieth-century America. *Omega: Journal of Death and Dying, 18*(4), 379–395.

Fung, H. H., Carstensen, L. L., & Lang, F. R. (2001). Age-related patterns in social networks among European-Americans and African-Americans: Implications for socioemotional selectivity across the life span. *International Journal of Aging and Human Development, 52,* 185–206.

Furman, L. (2005). What is attention-deficit hyperactivity disorder (ADHD)? *Journal of Child Neurology, 20,* 994–1003.

Furman, L., Taylor, G., Minich, N., & Hack, M. (2003). The effect of maternal milk on neonatal morbidity of very low birth-weight infants. *Archives of Pediatrics and Adolescent Medicine, 157,* 66–71.

Furman, W. (1982). Children's friendships. In T. M. Field, A. Huston, H. C. Quay, L. Troll, & G. E. Finley (Eds.), *Review of human development.* New York: Wiley.

Furman, W., & Bierman, K. L. (1983). Developmental changes in young children's conception of friendship. *Child Development, 54,* 549–556.

Furman, W., & Buhrmester, D. (1985). Children's perceptions of the personal relationships in their social networks. *Developmental Psychology, 21,* 1016–1024.

Furman, W., & Wehner, E. A. (1997). Adolescent romantic relationships: A developmental perspective. In S. Shulman & A. Collins (Eds.). *Romantic relationships in adolescence: Developmental perspectives* (New Directions for Child and Adolescent Development, No. 78, pp. 21–36). San Francisco: Jossey-Bass.

Furrow, D. (1984). Social and private speech at two years. *Child Development, 55,* 355–362.

Furstenberg, F. F., Jr., Rumbaut, R. G., & Setterstein, R. A., Jr., (2005). On the frontier of adulthood: Emerging themes and new directions. In R. A. Settersten Jr., F. F. Furstenberg Jr., & R. G. Rumbaut (Eds.), *On the frontier of adulthood: Theory, research, and public policy* (pp. 3–25). (John D. and Catherine T. MacArthur Foundation Series on Mental Health and Development, Research Network on Transitions to Adulthood and Public Policy.) Chicago: University of Chicago Press.

Fussell, E., & Furstenberg, F. (2005). The transition to adulthood during the twentieth century: Race, nativity, and gender. In R. A. Settersten Jr., F. F. Furstenberg Jr., & R. G. Rumbaut (Eds.), *On the frontier of adulthood: Theory, research, and public policy* (pp. 29–75). (John D. and Catherine T. MacArthur Foundation Series on Mental Health and Development, Research Network on Transitions to Adulthood and Public Policy.) Chicago: University of Chicago Press.

Gabbard, C. P. (1996). *Lifelong motor development* (2nd ed.). Madison, WI: Brown & Benchmark.

Gabhainn, S., & François, Y. (2000). Substance use. In C. Currie, K. Hurrelmann, W. Settertobulte, R. Smith, & J. Todd (Eds.), *Health behaviour in school-aged children: A WHO cross-national study (HBSC) international report* (pp. 97–114). WHO Policy Series: Healthy Policy for Children and Adolescents, Series No. 1. Copenhagen, Denmark: World Health Organization Regional Office for Europe.

Gabriel, T. (1996, January 7). High-tech pregnancies test hope's limit. *New York Times,* pp. A1, A18–19.

Gaffney, M., Gamble, M., Costa, P., Holstrum, J., & Boyle, C. (2003). Infants tested for hearing loss—United States, 1999–2001. *Morbidity and Mortality Weekly Report, 51,* 981–984.

Galinsky, E., Kim, S. S., & Bond, J. T. (2001). *Feeling overworked: When work becomes too much.* New York: Families and Work Institute.

Gallagher, W. (1993, May). Midlife myths. *Atlantic Monthly,* pp. 51–68.

Gallagher-Thompson, D. (1995). Caregivers of chronically ill elders. In G. E. Maddox (Ed.), *The encyclopedia of aging* (pp. 141–144). New York: Springer.

Gallo, L. C., & Matthews, K. A. (2003). Understanding the association between socioeconomic status and physical health: Do negative emotions play a role? *Psychological Bulletin, 129,* 10–51.

Gallo, L. C., Troxel, W. M., Matthews, K. A., & Kuller, L. H. (2003). Marital status and quality in middle-aged women: Associations with levels and trajectories of cardiovascular risk factors. *Health Psychology, 22,* 453–463.

Gallup Organization. (2005). *2005 national survey of organ and tissue donation attitudes and behaviors.* Washington, DC: Author. Retrieved May 18, 2008, from www .organdonor.gov/survey2005/.

Galobardes, B., Smith, G. D., & Lynch, J. W. (2006). Systematic review of the influence of childhood socioeconomic circumstances on risk for cardiovascular disease in adulthood. *Annals of Epidemiology, 16,* 91–104.

Galotti, K. M., Komatsu, L. K., & Voelz, S. (1997). Children's differential performance on deductive and inductive syllogisms. *Developmental Psychology, 33,* 70–78.

Gandhi, H., Green, D., Kounios. J., Clark., C. M., & Polikar, R., (2006, September). *Stacked generalization for early diagnosis of Alzheimer's Disease.* Paper presented at the meeting of the 28th International Conference of the IEEE Engineering in Medicine and Biology Society (EMBC 2006), New York.

Ganger, J., & Brent, M. R. (2004). Reexamining the vocabulary spurt. *Developmental Psychology, 40,* 621–632.

Gannon, P. J., Holloway, R. L., Broadfield, D. C., & Braun, A. R. (1998). Asymmetry of chimpanzee planum temporale: Human-like pattern of Wernicke's brain language homolog. *Science, 279,* 22–222.

Gans, J. E. (1990). *America's adolescents: How healthy are they?* Chicago: American Medical Association.

Garbarino, J., Dubrow, N., Kostelny, K., & Pardo, C. (1992). *Children in danger: Coping with the consequences of community violence.* San Francisco: Jossey-Bass.

Garbarino, J., Dubrow, N., Kostelny, K., & Pardo, C. (1998). *Children in danger: Coping with the consequences of community violence.* San Francisco: Jossey-Bass.

Garbarino, J., & Kostelny, K. (1993). Neighborhood and community influences on parenting. In T. Luster & L. Okagaki (Eds.), *Parenting: An ecological perspective* (pp. 203–226). Hillsdale, NJ: Erlbaum.

Gardenhire-Crooks, A., Collado, H., & Ray, B. (2006). *A whole 'nother world: Students navigating community college.* New York: MDRC.

Gardiner, H. W., & Kosmitzki, C. (2005). *Lives across cultures: Cross-cultural human development.* Boston: Allyn & Bacon.

Gardner, H. (1993). *Frames of mind: The theory of multiple intelligences.* New York: Basic Books. (Original work published 1983)

Gardner, H. (1995). Reflections on multiple intelligences: Myths and messages. *Phi Delta Kappan,* pp. 200–209.

Gardner, H. (1998). Are there additional intelligences? In J. Kane (Ed.), *Education, information, and transformation: Essays on learning and thinking.* Englewood Cliffs, NJ: Prentice-Hall.

Gardner, M., & Steinberg, L. (2005). Peer influence on risk taking, risk preference, and risky decision making in adolescence and adulthood: An experimental study. *Developmental Psychology, 41,* 625–635.

Garland, A. F., & Zigler, E. (1993). Adolescent suicide prevention: Current research and social policy implications. *American Psychologist, 48*(2), 169–182.

Garlick, D. (2003). Integrating brain science research with intelligence research. *Current Directions in Psychological Science, 12,* 185–192.

Garmon, L. C., Basinger, K. S., Gregg, V. R., & Gibbs, J. C. (1996). Gender differences in stage and expression of moral judgment. *Merrill-Palmer Quarterly, 42,* 418–437.

Garner, P. W., & Power, T. G. (1996). Preschoolers' emotional control in the disappointment paradigm and its relation to temperament, emotional knowledge, and family expressiveness. *Child Development, 67,* 1406–1419.

Gartrell, N., Deck, A., Rodas, C., Peyser, H., & Banks, A. (2005). The National Lesbian Family Study: Interviews with the 10-year-old children. *American Journal of Orthopsychiatry, 75,* 518–524.

Gatewood, J. D., Wills, A., Shetty, S., Xu, J., Arnold, A. P., Burgoyne, P. S., & Rissman, E. F. (2006). Sex chromosome complement and gonadal sex influence aggressive and parental behaviors in mice. *Journal of Neuroscience, 26,* 2335–2342.

Gattis, K. S., Berns, S., Simpson, L. E., & Christensen, A. (2004). Birds of a feather or strange birds? Ties among personality dimensions, similarity, and marital quality. *Journal of Family Psychology, 18,* 564–574.

Gatz, M. (2007). Genetics, dementia, and the elderly. *Current Directions in Psychological Science, 16,* 123–127.

Gatz, M., Reynolds, C. A., Fratiglioni, L., Johansson, B., Mortimer, J. A., Berg, S., Fiske, A., & Pederson, N. L. (2006). Role of genes and environments for explaining Alzheimer disease. *Archives of General Psychiatry, 63,* 168–174.

Gauthier, A. H., & Furstenberg, F. F., Jr., (2005). Historical trends in patterns of time use among young adults in developed countries. In R. A. Settersten Jr., F. F. Furstenberg Jr., & R. G. Rumbaut (Eds.), *On the frontier of adulthood: Theory, research, and public policy* (pp. 150–176). (John D. and Catherine T. MacArthur Foundation Series on Mental Health and Development, Research Network on Transitions to Adulthood and Public Policy.) Chicago: University of Chicago Press.

Gauvain, M. (1993). The development of spatial thinking in everyday activity. *Developmental Review, 13,* 92–121.

Gauvain, M., & Perez, S. M. (2005). Parent-child participation in planning children's activities outside of school in European American and Latino families. *Child Development, 76,* 371–383.

Ge, X., Brody, G. H., Conger, R. D., Simons, R. L., & Murry, V. (2002). Contextual amplification of pubertal transitional effect on African American children's problem behaviors. *Developmental Psychology, 38,* 42–54.

Ge, X., Conger, R. D., & Elder, G. H. (2001). Pubertal transition, stressful life events, and the emergence of gender differences in adolescent depressive symptoms. *Developmental Psychology, 37*(3), 404–417.

Geary, D. C. (1993). Mathematical disabilities: Cognitive, neuropsychological, and genetic components. *Psychological Bulletin, 114,* 345–362.

Geary, D. C. (1999). Evolution and developmental sex differences. *Current Directions in Psychological Science, 8*(4), 115–120.

Geen, R. (2004). The evolution of kinship care: Policy and practice. In David and Lucile Packard Foundation, Children, families, and foster care. *Future of Children, 14*(1). Retrieved from www.futureofchildren.org.

Geier, D. A., & Geier, M. R. (2006). Early downward trends in neurodevelopmental disorders following removal of thimerosal-containing vaccines. *Journal of American Physicians and Surgeons, 11*(1), 8–13.

Gelfand, D. M., & Teti, D. M. (1995, November). How does maternal depression affect children? *Harvard Mental Health Letter,* p. 8.

Gélis, J. (1991). *History of childbirth: Fertility, pregnancy, and birth in early modern Europe.* Boston: Northeastern University Press.

Gelman, R. (2006). Young natural-number mathematicians. *Current Directions in Psychological Science, 15,* 193–197.

Gelman, R., Spelke, E. S., & Meck, E. (1983). What preschoolers know about animate and inanimate objects. In D. R. Rogers & J. S. Sloboda (Eds.), *The acquisition of symbolic skills* (pp. 297–326). New York: Plenum Press.

Genesee, F., Nicoladis, E., & Paradis, J. (1995). Language differentiation in early bilingual development. *Journal of Child Language, 22,* 611–631.

Genevay, B. (1986). Intimacy as we age. *Generations, 10*(4), 12–15.

Georganopoulou, D. G., Chang, L., Nam, J.-M., Thaxton, C. S., Mufson, E. J., Klein, W. L., & Mirkin, C. A. (2005). Nanoparticle-based detection in cerebral spinal fluid of a soluble pathogenic biomarker for Alzheimer's disease. *Proceedings of the National Academy of Sciences, 102,* 2273–2276.

George, C., Kaplan, N., & Main, M. (1985). *The Berkeley Adult Attachment Interview.* Unpublished protocol, Department of Psychology, University of California, Berkeley.

George, T. P., & Hartmann, D. P. (1996). Friendship networks of unpopular, average, and popular children. *Child Development, 67,* 2301–2316.

Gershoff, E. T. (2002). Corporal punishment by parents and associated child behaviors and experiences: A meta-analytic and theoretical review. *Psychological Bulletin, 128,* 539–579.

Gershoff, E. T., Aber, J. L., Raver, C. C., & Lennon, M. C. (2007). Income is not enough: Incorporating material hardship into models of income associations with parenting and child development. *Child Development, 78,* 70–95.

Getzels, J. W. (1964). Creative thinking, problem-solving, and instruction. In *Yearbook of the National Society for the Study of Education* (Pt. 1, pp. 240–267). Chicago: University of Chicago Press.

Getzels, J. W. (1984, March). *Problem finding in creativity in higher education.* The Fifth Rev. Charles F. Donovan, S. J., Lecture, Boston College, School of Education, Boston, MA.

Getzels, J. W., & Jackson, P. W. (1962). *Creativity and intelligence: Explorations with gifted students.* New York: Wiley.

Getzels, J. W., & Jackson, P. W. (1963). The highly intelligent and the highly creative adolescent: A summary of some research findings. In C. W. Taylor & F. Baron (Eds.), *Scientific creativity; Its recognition and development* (pp. 161–172). New York: Wiley.

Giambra, L. M., & Arenberg, D. (1993). Adult age differences in forgetting sentences. *Psychology and Aging, 8,* 451–462.

Gibbs, J. C. (1991). Toward an integration of Kohlberg's and Hoffman's theories of moral development. In W. M. Kurtines & J. L. Gewirtz (Eds.), *Handbook of moral behavior and development: Advances in theory, research, and application* (Vol. 1). Hillsdale, NJ: Erlbaum.

Gibbs, J. C. (1995). The cognitive developmental perspective. In W. M. Kurtines & J. L. Gewirtz (Eds.), *Moral development: An introduction.* Boston: Allyn & Bacon.

Gibbs, J. C., & Schnell, S. V. (1985). Moral development "versus" socialization. *American Psychologist, 40*(10), 1071–1080.

Gibson, E. J. (1969). *Principles of perceptual learning and development.* New York: Appleton-Century-Crofts.

Gibson, E. J., & Pick, A. D. (2000). *An ecological approach to perceptual learning and development.* New York: Oxford University Press.

Gibson, E. J., & Walk, R. D. (1960). The "visual cliff." *Scientific American, 202,* 64–71.

Gibson, E. J., & Walker, A. S. (1984). Development of knowledge of visual tactual affordances of substance. *Child Development, 55,* 453–460.

Gibson, J. J. (1979). *The ecological approach to visual perception.* Boston: Houghton-Mifflin.

Giedd, J. N., Blumenthal, J., Jeffries, N. O., Castellanos, F. X., Zijdenbos, A., Paus, T., Evans, A. C., & Rapoport, J. L. (1999). Brain development during childhood and adolescence: A longitudinal MRI study. *Nature Neuroscience, 2,* 861–863.

Gilbert, L. A. (1994). Current perspectives in dual-career families. *Current Directions in Psychological Science, 3,* 101–105.

Gilford, R. (1986). Marriages in later life. *Generations, 10*(4), 16–20.

Gill, T. M., Allore, H. G., Holford, T. R, & Guo, Z. (2004). Hospitalization, restricted activity, and the development of disability among older persons. *Journal of the American Medical Association, 292,* 2115–2124.

Gilligan, C. (1982/1993). *In a different voice: Psychological theory and women's development.* Cambridge, MA: Harvard University Press.

Gilligan, C. (1987a). Adolescent development reconsidered. In E. E. Irwin (Ed.), *Adolescent social behavior and health.* San Francisco: Jossey-Bass.

Gilligan, C. (1987b). Moral orientation and moral development. In E. F. Kittay & D. T. Meyers (Eds.), *Women and moral theory* (pp. 19–33). Totowa, NJ: Rowman & Littlefield.

Gilligan, C., Murphy, J. M., & Tappan, M. B. (1990). Moral development beyond adolescence. In C. N. Alexander & E. J. Langer (Eds.), *Higher stages of human development* (pp. 208–228). New York: Oxford University Press.

Gilman, S., Koller, M., Black., R. S., Jenkins, L., Griffith, S. G., Fox, N. C., Eisner, L., Kirby, L., Rovira, B., Forette, F., & Orgogozo, J.-M. for the AN1792(QS-21)-201 Study Team. (2005). Clinical effects of Aβ immunization (AN1792) in patients with AD in an interrupted trial. *Neurology, 64,* 1553–1562.

Gilmore, J., Lin, W., Prastawa, M. W., Looney, C. B., Vetsa, Y. S. K., Knickmeyer, R. C., Evans, D. D., Smith, J. K., Hamer, R. M., Lieberman, J. A., & Gerig, G. (2007). Regional gray matter growth, sexual dimorphism, and cerebral asymmetry in the neonatal brain. *Journal of Neuroscience, 27*(6), 1255–1260.

Ginsburg, G. S., & Bronstein, P. (1993). Family factors related to children's intrinsic/extrinsic motivational orientation and academic performance. *Child Development, 64,* 1461–1474.

Ginsburg, H., & Opper, S. (1979). *Piaget's theory of intellectual development* (2nd ed.). Englewood Cliffs, NJ: Prentice-Hall.

Ginsburg, H. P. (1997). Mathematics learning disabilities: A view from developmental psychology. *Journal of Learning Disabilities, 30,* 20–33.

Ginsburg, K., & Committee on Communications and Committee on Psychosocial Aspects of Child and Family Health, American Academy of Pediatrics (AAP). (2007). *Pediatrics, 119,* 182–191.

Ginzburg, N. (1985). *The Little Virtues.* (D. Davis, Trans.). Manchester, England: Carcanet.

Giordano, P. C., Cernkovich, S. A., & DeMaris, A. (1993). The family and peer relations of black adolescents. *Journal of Marriage and Family, 55,* 277–287.

Giscombé, C. L., & Lobel, M. (2005). Explaining disproportionately high rates of adverse birth outcomes among African Americans: The impact of stress, racism, and related factors in pregnancy. *Psychological Bulletin, 131,* 662–683.

Gist, Y. J., & Hetzel, L. I. (2004). We the people: Aging in the United States. *Census 2000 Special Reports.* Washington, DC: U.S. Census Bureau.

Gjerdingen, D. (2003). The effectiveness of various postpartum depression treatments and the impact of antidepressant drugs on nursing infants. *Journal of American Board of Family Practice, 16,* 372–382.

Glaser, D. (2000). Child abuse and neglect and the brain: A review. *Journal of Child Psychiatry, 41,* 97–116.

Glasgow, K. L., Dornbusch, S. M., Troyer, L., Steinberg, L., & Ritter, P. L. (1997). Parenting styles, adolescents' attributions, and educational outcomes in nine heterogeneous high schools. *Child Development, 68,* 507–529.

Glasson, E. J., Bower, C., Petterson, B., de Klerk, N., Chaney, G., & Hallmayer, J. F. (2004). Perinatal factors and the development of autism: A population study. *Archives of General Psychiatry, 61,* 618–627.

Gleason, T. R., Sebanc, A. M., & Hartup, W. W. (2000). Imaginary companions of preschool children. *Developmental Psychology, 36,* 419–428.

Glenn, N., & Marquardt, E. (2001). *Hooking up, hanging out, and hoping for Mr. Right: College women on dating and mating today.* New York: Institute for American Values.

Glick, J. E., & Van Hook, J. (2002). Parents' coresidence with adult children: Can immigration explain racial and ethnic variation? *Journal of Marriage and Family, 64,* 240–253.

Glover, M. J., Greenlund, K. J., Ayala, C., & Croft, J. B. (2005). Racial/ethnic disparities in prevalence, treatment, and control of hypertension—United States, 1999–2002. *Morbidity and Mortality Weekly Report, 54,* 7–9.

Goetz, P. J. (2003). The effects of bilingualism on theory of mind development. *Bilingualism: Language and Cognition, 6,* 1–15.

Gogtay, N., Giedd, J. N., Lusk, L., Hayashi, K. M., Greenstein, D., Vaituzis, A. C., Nugent, T. F., III, Herman, D. H., Clasen, L. S., Toga, A. W., Rapoport, J. L., & Thompson, P. M. (2004). Dynamic mapping of human cortical development during childhood through early adulthood. *Proceedings of the National Academy of Sciences, USA, 101,* 8174–8179.

Goldberg, W. A., Prause, J. A., Lucas-Thompson, R., & Himsel, A. (2008). Maternal employment and children's achievement in context: A meta-analysis of four decades of research. *Psychological Bulletin, 134,* 77–108.

Goldenberg, R. L., & Rouse, D. J. (1998). Prevention of premature labor. *New England Journal of Medicine, 339,* 313–320.

Goldenberg, R. L., Tamura, T., Neggers, Y., Copper, R. L., Johnston, K. E., DuBard, M. B., & Hauth, J. C. (1995). The effect of zinc supplementation on pregnancy outcome. *Journal of the American Medical Association, 274,* 463–468.

Goldin-Meadow, S. (2007). Pointing sets the stage for learning language—and creating language. *Child Development, 78*(3), 741–745.

Goldin-Meadow, S., & Mylander, C. (1998). Spontaneous sign systems created by deaf children in two cultures. *Nature, 391,* 279–281.

Goldman, L., Falk, H., Landrigan, P. J., Balk, S. J., Reigart, J. R., and Etzel, R. A. (2004). Environmental pediatrics and its impact on government health policy. *Pediatrics, 113,* 1146–1157.

Goldman, L. L., & Rothschild, J. (n.d.). *Healing the wounded with art therapy.* Unpublished manuscript.

Goldman, S. R., Petrosino, A. J., & Cognition and Technology Group at Vanderbilt. (1999). Design principles for instruction in content domains: Lessons from research on expertise and learning. In F. T. Durso (Ed.), *Handbook of applied cognition* (pp. 595–627). Chichester, England: Wiley.

Goldscheider, F., & Sassler, S. (2006). Creating stepfamilies: Integrating children into the study of union formation. *Journal of Marriage and Family, 68,* 275–291.

Goldstein, I., Padma-Nathan, H., Rosen, R. C., Steers, W. D., & Wicker, P. A., for the Sildenafil Study Group. (1998). Oral sildenafil in the treatment of erectile dysfunction. *New England Journal of Medicine, 338,* 1397–1404.

Goldstein, M., King, A., & West, M. (2003). Social interaction shapes babbling: Testing parallels between birdsong and speech. *Proceedings of the National Academy of Sciences, USA, 100,* 8030–8035.

Goldstein, S. E., Davis-Kean, P. E., & Eccles, J. E. (2005). Parents, peers, and problem behavior: A longitudinal investigation of the impact of relationship perceptions and characteristics on the development of adolescent problem behavior. *Developmental Psychology, 2,* 401–413.

Golinkoff, R. M., & Hirsch-Pasek, K. (2006). Baby wordsmith. *Current Directions in Psychological Science, 15,* 30–33.

Golinkoff, R. M., Jacquet, R. C., Hirsh-Pasek, K., & Nandakumar, R. (1996). Lexical principles may underlie the learning of verbs. *Child Development, 67,* 3101–3119.

Golomb, C., & Galasso, L. (1995). Make believe and reality: Explorations of the imaginary realm. *Developmental Psychology, 31,* 800–810.

Golombok, S., Perry B., Burston, A., Murray, C., Mooney-Summers, J., Stevens, M., & Golding, J. (2003). Children with lesbian parents: A community study. *Developmental Psychology, 39,* 20–33.

Gonyea, J. G., Hudson, R. B., & Seltzer, G. B. (1990). Housing preferences of vulnerable elders in suburbia. *Journal of Housing for the Elderly, 7,* 79–95.

Gonzalez, E., Kulkarni, H., Bolivar, H., Mangano, A., Sanchez, R., Catano, G., Nibbs, R. J., Freedman, B. I., Quinones, M. P., Bamshad, M. J., Murthy, K. K., Rovin, B. H., Bradley, W., Clark, R. A., Anderson, S. A., O'Connell, R. J., Agan, B. K., Ahuja, S. S., Bologna, R., Sen, L., Dolan, M. J., & Ahuja, S. K. (2005). The influence of *CCL3L1* gene-containing segmental duplications on HIV-1/AIDS susceptibility. *Science, 307*(5714), 1434–1440. (DOI: 10.1126/science.1101160).

Gonzales, N. A., Cauce, A. M., & Mason, C. A. (1996). Interobserver agreement in the assessment of parental behavior and parent-adolescent conflict: African American mothers, daughters, and independent observers. *Child Development, 67,* 1483–1498.

Gooden, A. M. (2001). Gender representation in Notable Children's picture books: 1995–1999. *Sex Roles: A Journal of Research.* Retrieved April 20, 2005, from www.findarticles.com/p/articles/mim2294/is_2001_July/ai_81478076.

Goodman, G. S., Emery, R. E., & Haugaard, J. J. (1998). Developmental psychology and law: Divorce, child maltreatment, foster care, and adoption. In W. Damon (Series Ed.), I. E. Sigel, & K. A. Renninger (Vol. Eds.), *Handbook of child psychology* (Vol. 4, pp. 775–874). New York: Wiley.

Goodwyn, S. W., & Acredolo, L. P. (1998). Encouraging symbolic gestures: A new perspective on the relationship between gesture and speech. In J. M. Iverson & S. Goldin-Meadow (Eds.), *The nature and functions of gesture in children's communication* (pp. 61–73). San Francisco: Jossey-Bass.

Gootman, E. (2007, January 22). Taking middle schoolers out of the middle. *New York Times,* p. A1.

Gopnik, A., Sobel, D. M., Schulz, L. E., & Glymour, C. (2001). Causal learning mechanisms in very young children: Two-, three-, and four-year-olds infer causal relations from patterns of variation and covariation. *Developmental Psychology, 37*(5), 620–629.

Gorman, B. K., & Read, J. G. (2007). Why men die younger than women. *Geriatrics and Aging, 10,* 182–191.

Gorman, M. (1993). Help and self-help for older adults in developing countries. *Generations, 17*(4), 73–76.

Gortmaker, S. L., Must, A., Perrin, J. M., Sobol, A. M., & Dietz, W. H. (1993). Social and economic consequences of overweight in adolescence and young adulthood. *New England Journal of Medicine, 329,* 1008–1012.

Gosden, R. G., & Feinberg, A. P. (2007). Genetics and epigenetics—nature's pen-and-pencil set. *New England Journal of Medicine, 356,* 731–733.

Gostin, L. O. (1997). Deciding life and death in the courtroom: From Quinlan to Cruzan, Glucksberg, and Vacco—a brief history and analysis of constitutional protection of the "right to die." *Journal of the American Medical Association, 278,* 1523–1528.

Gostin, L. O. (2006). Physician-assisted suicide. *Journal of the American Medical Association, 295,* 1941–1943.

Gottfredson, L. S., & Deary, I. J. (2004). Intelligence predicts health and longevity, but why? *Current Directions in Psychological Science, 13,* 1–4.

Gottfried, A., E., Fleming, J. S., & Gottfried, A. W. (1998). Role of cognitively stimulating home environment in children's academic intrinsic motivation: A longitudinal study. *Child Development, 69,* 1448–1460.

Gottlieb, G. (1991). Experiential canalization of behavioral development theory. *Developmental Psychology, 27*(1), 4–13.

Gottlieb, G. (1997). *Synthesizing nature-nurture: Prenatal roots of instinctive behavior.* Mahwah, NJ: Erlbaum.

Gottlieb, G. (2007). Probabilistic epigenesis. *Developmental Science, 10,* 1–11.

Gottman, J. M., & Notarius, C. I. (2000). Decade review: Observing marital interaction. *Journal of Marriage and Family, 62,* 927–947.

Goubet, N., & Clifton, R. K. (1998). Object and event representation in 6½-month-old infants. *Developmental Psychology, 34,* 63–76.

Gould, E., Reeves, A. J., Graziano, M. S. A., & Gross, C. G. (1999). Neurogenesis in the neocortex of adult primates. *Science, 286,* 548–552.

Graber, J. A., Brooks-Gunn, J., & Warren, M. P. (1995). The antecedents of menarcheal age: Heredity, family environment, and stressful life events. *Child Development, 66,* 346–359.

Grady, D., Herrington, D., Bittner, V., Blumenthal, R., Davidson, M., Hlatky, M., Hsia, J., Hulley, S., Herd, A., Khan, S., Newby, L. K., Waters, D., Vittinghoff, E., & Wenger, N. (2002). Cardiovascular disease outcomes during 6.8 years of hormone therapy: Heart and Estrogen/Progestin Replacement Study follow-up (HERS II). *Journal of the American Medical Association, 288,* 49–57.

Grant, B. F., Stinson, F. S., Dawson, D. A., Chou, S. P., Dufour, M. C., Compton, W., Pickering, R. P., & Kaplan, K. (2004). Prevalence and co-occurrence of substance use disorders and independent mood and anxiety disorders: Results from the National Epidemiologic Survey on Alcohol and Related Conditions. *Archives of General Psychiatry, 61,* 807–816.

Grantham-McGregor, S., Powell, C., Walker, S., Chang, S., & Fletcher, P. (1994). The long-term follow-up of severely malnourished children who participated in an intervention program. *Child Development, 65,* 428–439.

Gray, J. R., & Thompson, P. M. (2004). Neurobiology of intelligence: Science and ethics. *Neuroscience, 5,* 471–492.

Gray, M. R., & Steinberg, L. (1999). Unpacking authoritative parenting: Reassessing a multidimensional construct. *Journal of Marriage and Family, 61,* 574–587.

Graziano, A. M., & Mooney, K. C. (1982). Behavioral treatment of "nightfears" in children: Maintenance and improvement at 2½- to 3-year follow-up. *Journal of Counseling and Clinical Psychology, 50,* 598–599.

Greenberg, J., & Becker, M. (1988). Aging parents as family resources. *Gerontologist, 28*(6), 786–790.

Greene, M. F. (2002). Outcomes of very low birth weight in young adults. *New England Journal of Medicine, 346*(3), 146–148.

Greene, M. L., & Way, N. (2005). Self-esteem trajectories among ethnic minority adolescents: A growth curve analysis of the patterns and predictors of change. *Journal of Research on Adolescence, 15,* 151–178.

Greenfield, E. A., & Marks, N. F. (2004). Formal volunteering as a protective factor for older adults' psychological well-being. *Journal of Gerontology: Social Sciences, 59B,* S258–S264.

Greenfield, E. A., & Marks, N. F. (2006). Linked lives: Adult children's problems and their parents' psychological and relational well-being. *Journal of Marriage and Family, 68,* 442–454.

Greenfield, P. M., & Childs, C. P. (1978). Understanding sibling concepts: A developmental study of kin terms in Zinacanten. In P. R. Dasen (Ed.), *Piagetian psychology* (pp. 335–358). New York: Gardner.

Greenhouse, L. (2000, June 6). Justices reject visiting rights in divided case: Ruling favors mother over grandparents. *New York Times* (National ed.), pp. A1, A15.

Greenhouse, L. (2005, February 23). Justices accept Oregon case weighing assisted suicide. *New York Times,* p. A1.

Greenstone, M., & Chay, K. (2003). The impact of air pollution on infant mortality: Evidence from geographic variation in pollution shocks induced by a recession. *Quarterly Journal of Economics, 118,* 1121–1167.

Gregg, E. W., Cauley, J. A., Stone, K., Tompson, T. J., Bauer, D. C., Cummings, S. R., & Ensrud, K. E., for the Study of Osteoporotic Fractures Research Group. (2003). Relationship of changes in physical activity and mortality among older women. *Journal of the American Medical Association, 289,* 2379–2386.

Gregg, E. W., Cheng, Y. J., Cadwell, B. L., Imperatore, G., Williams, D. E., Flegal, K. M., Narayan, K. M.V., & Williamson, D. F. (2005). Secular trends in cardiovascular disease risk factors according to body mass index in U.S. adults. *Journal of the American Medical Association, 293,* 1868–1874.

Grigorenko, E. L., Meier, E., Lipka, J., Mohatt, G., Yanez, E., & Sternberg, R. J. (2004). Academic and practical intelligence: A case study of the Yup'ik in Alaska. *Learning and Individual Differences, 14*(4), 183–207.

Grigorenko, E. L., & Sternberg, R. J. (1998). Dynamic testing. *Psychological Bulletin, 124,* 75–111.

Grodstein, F. (1996). Postmenopausal estrogen and progestin use and the risk of cardiovascular disease. *New England Journal of Medicine, 335,* 453.

Groenewoud, J. H., van der Heide, A., Onwuteaka-Philipsen, B. D., Willems, D. L., van der Maas, P. J., & van der Wal, G. (2000). Clinical problems with the performance of euthanasia and physician-assisted suicide in the Netherlands. *New England Journal of Medicine, 342,* 551–556.

Grotevant, H. D., McRoy, R. G., Eide, C. L., & Fravel, D. L. (1994). Adoptive family system dynamics: Variations by level of openness in the adoption. *Family Process, 33*(2), 125–146.

Gruber, H. (1981). *Darwin on man: A psychological study of scientific creativity* (2nd ed.). Chicago: University of Chicago Press.

Gruenewald, T. L., Karlamangla, A. S., Greendale, G. A., Singer, B. H., & Seeman, T. E. (2007). Feelings of usefulness to others, disability, and mortality in older adults: The MacArthur Study of Successful Aging. *Journal of Gerontology: Psychological Sciences, 62B,* P28–P37.

Grusec, J. E., & Goodnow, J. J. (1994). Impact of parental discipline methods on the child's internalization of values: A reconceptualization of current points of view. *Developmental Psychology, 30,* 4–19.

Guberman, S. R. (1996). The development of everyday mathematics in Brazilian children with limited formal education. *Child Development, 67,* 1609–1623.

Guerino, P., Hurwitz, M. D, Noonan, M. E., & Kaffenberger, S. M. (2006). *Crime, violence, discipline, and safety In U.S. public schools: Findings from the School Survey on Crime and Safety: 2003–2004* (NCES 2007-303). Washington, DC: National Center for Education Statistics.

Guilford, J. P. (1956). Structure of intellect. *Psychological Bulletin, 53,* 267–293.

Guilford, J. P. (1959). Three faces of intellect. *American Psychologist, 14,* 469–479.

Guilford, J. P. (1960). Basic conceptual problems of the psychology of thinking. *Proceedings of the New York Academy of Sciences, 91,* 6–21.

Guilford, J. P. (1967). *The nature of human intelligence.* New York: McGraw-Hill.

Guilford, J. P. (1986). *Creative talents: Their nature, uses and development.* Buffalo, NY: Bearly.

Guilleminault, C., Palombini, L., Pelayo, R., & Chervin, R. D. (2003). Sleeping and sleep terrors in prepubertal children: What triggers them? *Pediatrics, 111,* pp. e17–e25.

Gullone, E. (2000). The development of normal fear: A century of research. *Clinical Psychology Review, 20,* 429–451.

Gunnar, M. R., Larson, M. C., Hertsgaard, L., Harris, M. L., & Brodersen, L. (1992). The stressfulness of separation among 9-month-old infants: Effects of social context variables and infant temperament. *Child Development, 63,* 290–303.

Gunnoe, M. L., & Mariner, C. L. (1997). Toward a developmental-contextual model of the effects of parental spanking on children's aggression. *Archives of Pediatric and Adolescent Medicine, 151,* 768–775.

Guralnik, J. M., Butterworth, S., Wadsworth, M. E. J., & Kuh, D. (2006). Childhood socioeconomic status predicts physical functioning a half century later. *Journal of Gerontology: Medical Sciences, 61A,* 694–701.

Gurung, R. A. R., Taylor, S. E., & Seeman, T. E. (2003). Accounting for changes in social support among married older adults: Insights from the MacArthur studies of successful aging. *Psychology and Aging, 18,* 487–496.

Gutman, L. M., & Eccles, J. S. (2007). Stage-environment fit during adolescence: Trajectories of family relations and adolescent outcomes. *Developmental Psychology, 43,* 522–537.

Gutmann, D. (1975). Parenting: A key to the comparative study of the life cycle. In N. Datan & L. H. Ginsberg (Eds.), *Life-span developmental psychology: Normative life crises.* New York: Academic Press.

Gutmann, D. (1977). The cross-cultural perspective: Notes toward a comparative psychology of aging. In J. E. Birren & K. W. Schaie (Eds.), *Handbook of the psychology of aging* (pp. 302–326). New York: Van Nostrand Reinhold.

Gutmann, D. (1985). The parental imperative revisited. In J. Meacham (Ed.), *Family and individual development.* Basel, Switzerland: Karger.

Gutmann, D. L. (1987). *Reclaimed powers; Toward a new psychology of men and women in later life.* New York: Basic Books.

Guyer, B., Strobino, D. M., Ventura, S. J., & Singh, G. K. (1995). Annual summary of vital statistics—1994. *Pediatrics, 96,* 1029–1039.

Guzick, D. S., Carson, S. A., Coutifaris, C., Overstreet, J. W., Factor-Litvak, P., Steinkampf, M. P., Hill, J. A., Mastroianni, L., Buster, J. E., Nakajima, S. T., Vogel, D. L., & Canfield, R. E. (1999). Efficacy of superovulation and intrauterine insemination in the treatment of infertility. *New England Journal of Medicine, 340,* 177–183.

Haber, C. (2004). Life extension and history: The continual search for the Fountain of Youth. *Journal of Gerontology: Biological Sciences, 59A,* 515–522.

Hack, M., Flannery, D. J., Schluchter, M., Cartar, L., Borawski, E., & Klein, N. (2002). Outcomes in young adulthood for very low-birth-weight infants. *New England Journal of Medicine, 346*(3), 149–157.

Hack, M., Youngstrom, E. A., Cartar, L., Schluchter, M., Taylor, H. G., Flannery, D., Klein, N., & Borawski, E. (2004). Behavioral outcomes and evidence of psychopathology among very low birth weight infants at age 20 years. *Pediatrics, 114,* 932–940.

Hagan, J. F., Committee on Psychosocial Aspects of Child and Family Health, & Task Force on Terrorism. (2005). Psychosocial implications of disaster or terrorism on children: A guide for pediatricians. *Pediatrics, 116,* 787–796.

Hahn, R., Fuqua-Whitley, D., Wethington, H., Lowy, J., Liberman, A., Crosby, A., Fullilove, M., Johnson, R., Moscicki, E., Price, L., Snyder, S. R., Tuma, F., Cory, S., Stone, G., Mukhopadhaya, K., Chattopadhayay, S., & Dahlberg, L. (2007). The effectiveness of universal school-based programs for the prevention of violent and aggressive behavior: A report on recommendations of the Task Force on Community Preventive Services. *Morbidity and Mortality Weekly Report, 56*(RR07), 1–12.

Haith, M. M. (1986). Sensory and perceptual processes in early infancy. *Journal of Pediatrics, 109*(1), 158–171.

Haith, M. M. (1998). Who put the cog in infant cognition? Is rich interpretation too costly? *Infant Behavior and Development, 21*(2), 167–179.

Haith, M. M., & Benson, J. B. (1998). Infant cognition. In D. Kuhn & R. S. Siegler (Eds.), *Handbook of Child Psychology: Vol. 2. Cognition, perception, and language* (5th ed., pp. 199–254). New York: Wiley.

Halgunseth, L. C., Ispa, J. M., & Rudy, D. (2006). Parental control in Latino families: An integrated review of the literature. *Child Development, 77,* 1282–1297.

Hall, D. G., & Graham, S. A. (1999). Lexical form class information guides word-to-object mapping in preschoolers. *Child Development, 70,* 78–91.

Hall, G. S. (1916). *Adolescence.* New York: Appleton. (Original work published 1904)

Hallfors, D. D., Waller, M. W., Bauer, D., Ford, C. A., & Halpern, C. T. (2005). Which comes first in adolescence—sex and drugs or depression? *American Journal of Preventive Medicine, 29,* 1163–1170.

Halpern, D. F. (1997). Sex differences in intelligence: Implications for education. *American Psychologist, 52*(10), 1091–1102.

Halpern, D. F., Benbow, C. P., Geary, D. C., Gur, R. C., Hyde, J. S., & Gernsbacher, M. A. (2007). The science of sex differences in science and mathematics. *Psychological Science in the Public Interest, 8,* 1–51.

Halterman, J. S., Aligne, A., Auinger, P., McBride, J. T., & Szilagyi, P. G. (2000). Inadequate therapy for asthma among children in the United States. *Pediatrics, 105*(1), 272–276.

Hamilton, B. E., Martin, J. A., & Ventura, S. J. (2007). Births: Preliminary data for 2006. *National Vital Statistics Reports, 56*(7). Hyattsville, MD: National Center for Health Statistics.

Hamilton, B. E., Miniño, A. M., Martin, J. A., Kochanek, K. D., Strobino, D. M., & Guyer, B. (2007). Annual summary of vital statistics, 2005. *Pediatrics, 119,* 345–360.

Hamilton, L., Cheng, S., & Powell, B. (2007). Adoptive parents, adaptive parents: Evaluating the importance of biological ties for parental involvement. *American Sociological Review, 72,* 95–116.

Hamilton, S. F., & Hamilton, M. A. (2006). School, work, and emerging adulthood. In J. J. Arnett & J. L. Tanner (Eds.), *Emerging adults in America: Coming of age in the 21st century* (pp. 257–277). Washington, DC: American Psychological Association.

Hamm, J. V. (2000). Do birds of a feather flock together? The variable bases for African American, Asian American, and European American adolescents' selection of similar friends. *Developmental Psychology, 36*(2), 209–219.

Hammad, T. A., Laughren, T., & Racoosin, J. (2006). Suicidality in pediatric patients treated with antidepressant drugs. *Archives of General Psychiatry, 63,* 332–339.

Hampden-Thompson, G., & Johnston, J. S. (2006). *Variation in the relationship between nonschool factors and student achievement on international assessments* (NCES 2006-014). Washington, DC: U.S. Department of Education, National Center for Education Statistics.

Hamre, B. K., & Pianta, R. C. (2005). Can instructional and emotional support in the first-grade classroom make a difference for children at risk of school failure? *Child Development, 76,* 949–967.

Handmaker, N. S., Rayburn, W. F., Meng, C., Bell, J. B., Rayburn, B. B., & Rappaport, V. J. (2006). Impact of alcohol exposure after pregnancy recognition on ultrasonographic fetal growth measures. *Alcoholism: Clinical and Experimental Research, 30,* 892–898.

Hank, K. (2007). Proximity and contacts between older parents and their children: A European comparison. *Journal of Marriage and Family, 69,* 157–173.

Hankin, B. L., Mermelstein, R., & Roesch, L. (2007). Sex differences in adolescent depression: Exposure and reactivity models. *Child Development, 78,* 279–295.

Hansen, D., Lou, H. C., & Olsen, J. (2000). Serious life events and congenital malformations: A national study with complete follow-up. *Lancet, 356,* 875–880.

Hansen, M., Janssen, I., Schiff, A., Zee, P. C., & Dubocovich, M. L. (2005). The impact of school daily schedule on adolescent sleep. *Pediatrics, 115,* 1555–1561.

Hanson, L. (1968). *Renoir: The man, the painter, and his world.* New York: Dodd, Mead.

Hara, H. (2002). Justifications for bullying among Japanese school children. *Asian Journal of Social Psychology, 5,* 197–204.

Hardway, C., & Fuligni, A. J. (2006). Dimensions of family connectedness among adolescents with Mexican, Chinese, and European backgrounds. *Developmental Psychology, 42,* 1246–1258.

Hardy, R., Kuh, D., Langenberg, C., & Wadsworth, M. E. (2003). Birth weight, childhood social class, and change in adult blood pressure in the 1946 British birth cohort. *Lancet, 362,* 1178–1183.

Hardy-Brown, K., & Plomin, R. (1985). Infant communicative development: Evidence from adoptive and biological families for genetic and environmental influences on rate differences. *Developmental Psychology, 21,* 378–385.

Hardy-Brown, K., Plomin, R., & DeFries, J. C. (1981). Genetic and environmental influences on rate of communicative development in the first year of life. *Developmental Psychology, 17,* 704–717.

Harlaar, N., Dale, P. S., & Plomin, R. (2007). From learning to read to reading to learn: Substantial and stable genetic influences. *Child Development, 78,* 116–131.

Harlow, H. F., & Harlow, M. K (1962). The effect of rearing conditions on behavior. *Bulletin of the Menninger Clinic, 26,* 213–224.

Harlow, H. F., & Zimmerman, R. R. (1959). Affectional responses in the infant monkey. *Science, 130,* 421–432.

Harnishfeger, K. K., & Bjorklund, D. F. (1993). The ontogeny of inhibition mechanisms: A renewed approach to cognitive development. In M. L. Howe & R. P. Pasnak (Eds.), *Emerging themes in cognitive development* (Vol. 1, pp. 28–49). New York: Springer-Verlag.

Harnishfeger, K. K., & Pope, R. S. (1996). Intending to forget: The development of cognitive inhibition in directed forgetting. *Journal of Experimental Psychology, 62,* 292–315.

Harper, S., Lynch, J., Burris, S., & Smith, G. D. (2007). Trends in the black-white life expectancy gap in the United States, 1983–2003. *Journal of the American Medical Association, 297,* 1224–1232.

Harris, G. (1997). Development of taste perception and appetite regulation. In G. Bremner, A. Slater, & G. Butterworth (Eds.), *Infant development: Recent advances* (pp. 9–30). East Sussex, UK: Psychology Press.

Harris, G. (2005, March 3). Gene therapy is facing a crucial hearing. *New York Times.* Retrieved March 3, 2005, from www.nytimes.com/2005/03/03/politics/03gene.html.

Harris, K. M., Gordon-Larsen, P., Chantala, K., Udry, J. R. (2006). Longitudinal trends in race/ethnic disparities in leading health indicators from adolescence to young adulthood. *Archives of Pediatric and Adolescent Medicine, 160,* 74–81.

Harris, P. L., Brown, E., Marriott, C., Whittall, S., & Harmer, S. (1991). Monsters, ghosts, and witches: Testing the limits of the fantasy-reality distinction in young children. In G. E. Butterworth, P. L. Harris, A. M. Leslie, & H. M. Wellman (Eds.), *Perspective on the child's theory of mind.* Oxford: Oxford University Press.

Harris, P. L., Olthof, T., Meerum Terwogt, M., & Hardman, C. (1987). Children's knowledge of situations that provoke emotion. *International Journal of Behavioral Development, 10,* 319–343.

Harrison, Y., & Horne, J. A. (1997). Sleep deprivation affects speech. *Sleep, 20,* 871–877.

Harrison, Y., & Horne, J. A. (2000a). Impact of sleep deprivation on decision making: A review. *Journal of Experimental Psychology, 6,* 236–249.

Harrison, Y., & Horne, J. A. (2000b). Sleep loss and temporal memory. *Quarterly Journal of Experimental Psychology: Human Experimental Psychology, 53A,* 271–279.

Harrist, A. W., & Waugh, R. M. (2002). Dyadic synchrony: Its structure and function in children's development. *Developmental Review, 22,* 555–592.

Harrist, A. W., Zain, A. F., Bates, J. E., Dodge, K. A., & Pettit, G. S. (1997). Subtypes of social withdrawal in early childhood: Sociometric status and social-cognitive differences across four years. *Child Development, 68,* 278–294.

Hart, C. H., DeWolf, M., Wozniak, P., & Burts, D. C. (1992). Maternal and paternal disciplinary styles: Relations with pre-schoolers' playground behavioral orientation and peer status. *Child Development, 63,* 879–892.

Hart, C. H., Ladd, G. W., & Burleson, B. R. (1990). Children's expectations of the outcome of social strategies: Relations with sociometric status and maternal disciplinary style. *Child Development, 61,* 127–137.

Hart, D., Hofmann, V., Edelstein, W., & Keller, M. (1997). The relation of childhood personality types to adolescent behavior and development: A longitudinal study of Icelandic children. *Developmental Psychology, 33,* 195–205.

Hart, D., Southerland, N., & Atkins, R. (2003). Community service and adult development. In J. Demick & C. Andreoletti (Eds.), *Handbook of adult development* (pp. 585–597). New York: Plenum Press.

Harter, S. (1990). Causes, correlates, and the functional role of global self-worth: A life-span perspective. In J. Kolligan & R. Sternberg (Eds.), *Competence considered: Perceptions of competence and incompetence across the life-span* (pp. 67–97). New Haven, CT: Yale University Press.

Harter, S. (1993). Developmental changes in self-understanding across the 5 to 7 shift. In A. Sameroff & M. Haith (Eds.), *Reason and responsibility: The passage through childhood* (pp. 207–236). Chicago: University of Chicago Press.

Harter, S. (1996). Developmental changes in self-understanding across the 5 to 7 shift. In A. J. Sameroff & M. M. Haith (Eds.), *The five to seven year shift: The age of reason and responsibility* (pp. 207–235). Chicago: University of Chicago Press.

Harter, S. (1998). The development of self-representations. In W. Damon (Series Ed.) & N. Eisenberg (Vol. Ed.), *Handbook of child psychology: Vol. 3. Social, emotional, and personality development* (5th ed., pp. 553–617). New York: Wiley.

Hartford, J. (1971). *Life prayer.*

Hartley, A. A., Speer, N. K., Jonides, J., Reuter-Lorenz, P. A., & Smith, E. E. (2001). Is the dissociability of working memory systems for name identity, visual-object identity, and spatial location maintained in old age? *Neuropsychology, 15,* 3–17.

Hartshorn, K., Rovee-Collier, C., Gerhardstein, P., Bhatt, R. S., Wondoloski, R. L., Klein, P., Gilch, J., Wurtzel, N., & Campos-de-Carvalho, M. (1998). The ontogeny of long-term memory over the first year-and-a-half of life. *Developmental Psychobiology, 32,* 69–89.

Hartup, W. W. (1992). Peer relations in early and middle childhood. In V. B. Van Hasselt & M. Hersen (Eds.), *Handbook of social development: A lifespan perspective* (pp. 257–281). New York: Plenum Press.

Hartup, W. W. (1996a). The company they keep: Friendships and their developmental significance. *Child Development, 67,* 1–13.

Hartup, W. W. (1996b). Cooperation, close relationships, and cognitive development. In W. M. Bukowski, A. F. Newcomb, & W. W. Hartup (Eds.), *The company they keep: Friendship in childhood and adolescence* (pp. 213–237). New York: Cambridge University Press.

Hartup, W. W., & Stevens, N. (1999). Friendships and adaptation across the life span. *Current Directions in Psychological Science, 8,* 76–79.

Harvard Medical School. (2002). The mind and the immune system—Part I. *Harvard Mental Health Letter, 18*(10), pp. 1–3.

Harvard Medical School. (2003a, November). Alzheimer's disease: A progress report. *Harvard Mental Health Letter, 20*(5), 1–4.

Harvard Medical School. (2003b, May). Confronting suicide—Part I. *Harvard Mental Health Letter, 19*(11), 1–4.

Harvard Medical School. (2004a, December). Children's fears and anxieties. *Harvard Mental Health Letter, 21*(6), 1–3.

Harvard Medical School. (2004b, April). Countering domestic violence. *Harvard Mental Health Letter, 20*(10), pp. 1–5.

Harvard Medical School. (2004c, October). Is obesity a mental health issue? *Harvard Mental Health Letter, 21*(4).

Harvard Medical School. (2004d, May). Women and depression: How biology and society may make women more vulnerable to mood disorders. *Harvard Mental Health Letter, 20*(11), 1–4.

Harvard Medical School. (2005, February). Dysthymia: Psychotherapists and patients confront the high cost of "low-grade" depression. *Harvard Mental Health Letter, 21*(8), 1–3.

Harvey, J. H., & Omarzu, J. (1997). Minding the close relationship. *Personality and Psychology Review, 1,* 224–240.

Harvey, J. H., & Pauwels, B. G. (1999). Recent developments in close relationships theory. *Current Directions in Psychological Science, 8*(3), 93–95.

Harwood, K. McLean, N., & Durkin, K. (2007). First-time mothers' expectations of parenthood: What happens when optimistic expectations are not matched by later experiences? *Developmental Psychology, 43,* 1–12.

Harwood, R. L., Schoelmerich, A., Ventura-Cook, E., Schulze, P. A., & Wilson, S. P. (1996). Culture and class influences on Anglo and Puerto Rican mothers' beliefs regarding long-term socialization goals and child behavior. *Child Development, 67,* 2446–2461.

Haswell, K., Hock, E., & Wenar, C. (1981). Oppositional behavior of preschool children: Theory and prevention, *Family Relations, 30,* 440–446.

Hatcher, P. J., Hulme, C., & Ellis, A. W. (1994). Ameliorating early reading failure by integrating the teaching of reading and phonological skills: The phonological linkage hypotheses. *Child Development, 65,* 41–57.

Hauck, F. R., Herman, S. M., Donovan, M., Iyasu, S., Moore, C. M., Donoghue, E., Kirschner, R. H., & Willinger, M. (2003). Sleep environment and the risk of sudden infant death syndrome in an urban population: The Chicago Infant Mortality Study. *Pediatrics, 111,* 1207–1214.

Hauck, F. R., Omojokun, O. O., & Siadaty, M. S. (2005). Do pacifiers reduce the risk of sudden infant death syndrome? A meta-analysis. *Pediatrics, 116,* e716–e723.

Haugaard, J. J. (1998). Is adoption a risk factor for the development of adjustment problems? *Clinical Psychology Review, 18,* 47–69.

Hawes, A. (1996). Jungle gyms: The evolution of animal play. *ZooGoer, 25*(1). Retrieved July 18, 2006, from http:// nationalzoo .si.edu/Publications/ZooGoer.1996/1/junglegyms.cfm.

Hawes, C., Phillips, C. D., Rose, M., Holan, S., & Sherman, M. (2003). A national survey of assisted living facilities. *Gerontologist, 43,* 875–882.

Hawkins, J. D., Catalano, R. F., Kosterman, R., Abbott, R., & Hill, K. G. (1999). Preventing adolescent health-risk behaviors by strengthening protection during childhood. *Archives of Pediatrics and Adolescent Medicine, 153,* 226–234.

Hawkins, J. D., Catalano, R. F., & Miller, J. Y. (1992). Risk and protective factors for alcohol and other drug problems in adolescence and early adulthood: Implications for substance abuse programs. *Psychological Bulletin, 112*(1), 64–105.

Hawkley, L. C., & Cacioppo, J. T. (2007). Aging and loneliness: Downhill quickly? *Current Directions in Psychological Science, 16,* 187–191.

Hay, D. (2003). Pathways to violence in the children of mothers who were depressed post partum. *Developmental Psychology, 39,* 1083–1094.

Hay, D. F., Pedersen, J., & Nash, A. (1982). Dyadic interaction in the first year of life. In K. H. Rubin & H. S. Ross (Eds.), *Peer relationships and social skills in children.* New York: Springer.

Hayes, A., & Batshaw, M. L. (1993). Down syndrome. *Pediatric Clinics of North America, 40,* 523–535.

Hayflick, L. (1974). The strategy of senescence. *Gerontologist, 14*(1), 37–45.

Hayflick, L. (1981). Intracellular determinants of aging. *Mechanisms of Aging and Development, 28,* 177.

Hayflick, L. (2004). "Anti-aging" is an oxymoron. *Journal of Gerontology: Biological Sciences, 59A,* 573–578.

Hays, J., Ockene, J. K., Brunner, R. L., Kotchen, J. M., Manson, J. A. E., Patterson, R. E., Aragaki, A. K., Schumaker, S. A., Brzyski, R. G., LaCroix, A. Z., Granek, I. A., & Valanis, B. G., for the Women's Health Initiative Investigators. (2003). Effects of estrogen plus progestin on health-related quality of life. *New England Journal of Medicine, 348.* Retrieved March 20, 2003, from www.nejm.org. (DOI: 10.1056/NEJMoa030311).

Health Resources and Services Administration (HRSA). (2007). *HRSA Transplant Center Growth and Management Collaborative: Best practices evaluation: Final report: Executive summary.* Retrieved May 5, 2008, from http://organdonor.gov/research/best_practices/exec_summary.htm.

Healy, A. J., Malone, F. D., Sullivan, L. M., Porter, T. F., Luthy, D. A., Comstock, C. H., Saade, G., Berkowitz, R., Klugman, S., Dugoff, L., Craigo, S. D., Timor-Tritsch, I., Carr, S. R., Wolfe, H. M., Bianchi, D. W., & D'Alton, M. E. (2006). Early access to prenatal care: Implications for racial disparity in perinatal mortality. *Obstetrics and Gynecology, 107,* 625–631.

Heath, S. B. (1989). Oral and literate tradition among black Americans living in poverty. *American Psychologist, 44,* 367–373.

Hebert, L. E., Scherr, P. A., Bienias, J. L., Bennett, D. A., & Evans, D. A. (2003). Alzheimer disease in the U.S. population: Prevalence estimates using the 2000 census. *Archives of Neurology, 60,* 1119–1122.

Heckhausen, J. (2001). Adaptation and resilience in midlife. In M. E. Lachman (Ed.), *Handbook of midlife development* (pp. 345–394). New York: Wiley.

Heckhausen, J., Wrosch, C., & Fleeson, W. (2001). Developmental regulation before and after a developmental deadline: The sample case of biological clock for childbearing. *Psychology and Aging, 16,* 400–413.

Heffner, L. J. (2004). Advanced maternal age—how old is too old? *New England Journal of Medicine, 351,* 1927–1929.

Heijl, A., Leske, M. C., Bengtsson, B., Hyman, L., Bengtsson, B., & Hussein, M., for the Early Manifest Glaucoma Trial Group. (2002). Reduction of intraocular pressure and glaucoma progression: Results from the Early Manifest Glaucoma Trial. *Archives of Ophthalmology, 120,* 1268–1279.

Heilbronn, L. K., & Ravussin, E. (2003). Calorie restriction and aging: Review of the literature and implications for studies in humans. *American Journal of Clinical Nutrition, 78,* 361–369.

Heinz, W. (2002). Self-socialization and post-traditional society. *Advances in Life Course Research, 7,* 41–64.

Heiss, G., Wallace, R., Anderson, G. L., Aragaki, A., Beresford, S. A. A., Brzyski, R., Chlebowski, R. T., Gass, M., LaCroix, A., Manson, J. A. E., Prentice, R. L., Rossouw, J., & Stefanick, M. L., for the WHI Investigators. (2008). Health risks and benefits 3 years after stopping randomized treatment with estrogen and progestin. *Journal of the American Medical Association, 299,* 1036–1045.

Heller, R. B., & Dobbs, A. R. (1993). Age differences in word finding in discourse and nondiscourse situations. *Psychology and Aging, 8,* 443–450.

Helms, H. M., Crouter, A. C., & McHale, S. M. (2003). Marital quality and spouses' marriage work with close friends and each other. *Journal of Marriage and Family, 65,* 963–977.

Helms, J. E. (1992). Why is there no study of cultural equivalence in standardized cognitive ability testing? *American Psychologist, 47,* 1083–1101.

Helms, J. E., Jernigan, M., & Mascher, J. (2005). The meaning of race in psychology and how to change it: A methodological perspective. *American Psychologist, 60,* 27–36.

Helson, R. (1993). Comparing longitudinal studies of adult development: Toward a paradigm of tension between stability and change. In D. C. Funder, R. D. Parke, C. Tomlinson-Keasey, & K. Widaman (Eds.), *Studying lives through time: Personality and development* (pp. 93–120). Washington, DC: American Psychological Association.

Helson, R. (1997). The self in middle age. In M. E. Lachman & J. B. James (Eds.), *Multiple paths of midlife development* (pp. 21–43). Chicago: University of Chicago Press.

Helson, R., & Moane, G. (1987). Personality change in women from college to midlife. *Journal of Personality and Social Psychology, 53,* 176–186.

Helson, R., & Roberts, B. W. (1994). Ego development and personality change in adulthood. *Journal of Personality and Social Psychology, 66,* 911–920.

Helson, R., & Wink, P. (1992). Personality change in women from the early 40s to the early 50s. *Psychology and Aging, 7*(1), 46–55.

Helwig, C. C., & Jasiobedzka, U. (2001). The relation between law and morality: Children's reasoning about socially beneficial and unjust laws. *Child Development, 72,* 1382–1393.

Henderson, H. A., Marshall, P. J., Fox, N. A., & Rubin, K. H. (2004). Psychophysiological and behavioral evidence for varying forms and functions of nonsocial behavior in preschoolers. *Child Development, 75,* 251–263.

Hendin, H. (1994, December 16). Scared to death of dying. *New York Times,* p. A39.

Hendricks, J., & Cutler, S. J. (2004). Volunteerism and socioemotional selectivity in later life. *Journal of Gerontology: Social Sciences, 59B,* S251–S257.

Heraclitus, fragment (sixth century B.C.).

Herbig, B., Büssing, A., & Ewert, T. (2001). The role of tacit knowledge in the work context of nursing. *Journal of Advanced Nursing, 34,* 687–695.

Herek, G. M. (2006). Legal recognition of same-sex unions in the United States: A social science perspective. *American Psychologist, 61,* 607–621.

Hernandez, D. J. (1997). Child development and the social demography of childhood. *Child Development, 68,* 149–169.

Hernandez, D. J. (2004, Summer). Demographic change and the life circumstances of immigrant families. In R. E. Behrman (Ed.), Children of immigrant families (pp. 17–48). *Future of Children, 14*(2). Retrieved October 7, 2004, from www.futureofchildren.org.

Hernandez, D. J., Denton, N. A., & Macartney, S. E. (2007). *Children in immigrant families—the U.S. and 50 states: National origins, language, and early education* (Child Trends and the Center for Social and Demographic Analysis, University at Albany, SUNY: 2007 Research Brief Series).

Hernandez, D. J., & Macartney, S. E. (2008, January). *Racial-ethnic inequality in child well-being from 1985–2004: Gaps narrowing, but persist* (No. 9). New York: Foundation for Child Development.

Heron, M. P., Hoyert, D. L., Xu, J., Scott, C., & Tejada-Vera, B. (2008). Deaths: Preliminary data for 2006. *National Vital Statistics Reports, 56*(16). Hyattsville, MD: National Center for Health Statistics.

Heron, M. P., & Smith, B. L. (2007). Deaths: Leading causes for 2003. *National Vital Statistics Reports, 55*(10). Hyattsville, MD: National Center for Health Statistics.

Herrnstein, R. J., & Murray, C. (1994). *The bell curve: Intelligence and class structure in American life.* New York: Free Press.

Hertenstein, M. J., & Campos, J. J. (2004). The retention effects of an adult's emotional displays on infant behavior. *Child Development, 75,* 595–613.

Hertz-Pannier, L., Chiron, C., Jambaque, I., Renaux-Kieffer, V., Van de Moortele, P., Delalande, O., Fohlen, M., Brunelle, F., & Le Bihan, D. (2002). Late plasticity for language in a child's non-dominant hemisphere. A pre- and post-surgery fMRI study. *Brain, 125*(2), 361–372.

Herzog, A. R., Franks, M. M., Markus, H. R., & Holmberg, D. (1998). Activities and well-being in older age: Effects of self-concept and educational attainment. *Psychology and Aging, 13*(2), 179–185.

Hesketh, T., Lu, L., & Xing, Z. W. (2005). The effect of China's one-child policy after

25 years. *New England Journal of Medicine, 353,* 1171–1176.

Hesso, N. A., & Fuentes, E. (2005). Ethnic differences in neonatal and postneonatal mortality. *Pediatrics, 115,* e44–e51.

Hetherington, E. M. (1987). Family relations six years after divorce. In K. Pasley & M. Ihinger-Tallman (Eds.), *Remarriage and parenting today: Research and theory.* New York: Guilford Press.

Hetherington, E. M., Bridges, M., & Insabella, G. M. (1998). What matters? What does not? Five perspectives on the association between marital transitions and children's adjustment. *American Psychologist, 53,* 167–184.

Hetherington, E. M., & Kelly, J. (2002). *For better or worse: Divorce reconsidered.* New York: Norton.

Hetherington, E. M., Stanley-Hagan, M., & Anderson, E. (1989). Marital transitions: Child's perspective. *American Psychologist, 44,* 303–312.

Hetzel, L., & Smith, A. (2001). The 65 years and over population: 2000 (Census 2000 Brief C2KBR/01-10). Washington, DC: U.S. Census Bureau.

Heuveline, P., & Timberlake, J. M. (2004). The role of cohabitation in family formation: The United States in comparative perspective. *Journal of Marriage and Family, 66,* 1214–1230.

Hewlett, B. S. (1987). Intimate fathers: Patterns of paternal holding among Aka pygmies. In M. E. Lamb (Ed.), *The father's role: Cross-cultural perspectives* (pp. 295–330). Hillsdale, NJ: Erlbaum.

Hewlett, B. S. (1992). Husband-wife reciprocity and the father-infant relationship among Aka pygmies. In B. S. Hewlett (Ed.), *Father-child relations: Cultural and biosocial contexts* (pp. 153–176). New York: de Gruyter.

Hewlett, B. S., Lamb, M. E., Shannon, D., Leyendecker, B., & Schölmerich, A. (1998). Culture and early infancy among central African foragers and farmers. *Developmental Psychology, 34*(4), 653–661.

Heymann, J., Siebert, W. S., & Wei, X. (2007). The implicit wage costs of family friendly work practices. *Oxford Economic Papers, 59*(2), 275–300.

Hickling, A. K., & Wellman, H. M. (2001). The emergence of children's causal explanations and theories: Evidence from everyday conversations. *Developmental Psychology, 37*(5), 668–683.

Hickman, M., Roberts, C., & de Matos, M. G. (2000). Exercise and leisure time activities. In C. Currie, K. Hurrelmann, W. Settertobulte, R. Smith, & J. Todd (Eds.), *Health and health behaviour among young people: A WHO cross-national study (HBSC) international report* (pp. 73–82.). WHO Policy Series: Health Policy for Children and Adolescents, Series No. 1. Copenhagen, Denmark: World Health Organization Regional Office for Europe.

Hiedemann, B., Suhomilinova, O., & O'Rand, A. M. (1998). Economic independence, economic status, and empty nest in midlife marital disruption. *Journal of Marriage and Family, 60,* 219–231.

Hill, A. L., Degan, K. A., Calkins, S. D., & Keane, S. P. (2006). Profiles of externalizing behavior problems for boys and girls across preschool: The roles of emotional regulation and inattention. *Developmental Psychology, 42,* 913–928.

Hill, C., & Holzer, H. (2007). Labor market experiences and the transition to adulthood. In S. Danziger & C. Rouse (Eds.), *The price of independence: The economics of early adulthood* (pp. 141–169). New York: Russell Sage Foundation.

Hill, D. A., Gridley, G., Cnattingius, S., Mellemkjaer, L., Linet, M., Adami, H.-O., Olsen, J. H., Nyren, O., & Fraumeni, J. F. (2003). Mortality and cancer incidence among individuals with Down syndrome. *Archives of Internal Medicine, 163,* 705–711.

Hill, J. L., Waldfogel, J., Brooks-Gunn, J., & Han, W.-J. (2005). Maternal employment and child development: A fresh look using newer methods. *Developmental Psychology, 41,* 833–850.

Hill, N. E., & Taylor, L. C. (2004). Parental school involvement and children's academic achievement: Pragmatics and issues. *Current Directions in Psychological Science, 13,* 161–168.

Hill, T. D., Angel, J. L., Ellison, C. G., & Angel, R. J. (2005). Religious attendance and mortality: An 8-year follow-up of older Mexican Americans. *Journal of Gerontology: Social Sciences, 60B,* S102–S109.

Hillier, L. (2002). "It's a catch-22": Same-sex-attracted young people on coming out to parents. In S. S. Feldman & D. A. Rosenthal, (Eds.), *Talking sexuality. (New Directions for Child and Adolescent Development,* No. *97,* pp. 75–91). San Francisco: Jossey-Bass.

Hillis, S. D., Anda, R. F., Dubé, S. R., Felitti, V. J., Marchbanks, P. A., & Marks, J. S. (2004). The association between adverse childhood experiences and adolescent pregnancy, long-term psychosocial consequences, and fetal death. *Pediatrics, 113,* 320–327.

Hilts, P. J. (1999, June 1). Life at age 100 is surprisingly healthy. *New York Times,* p. D7.

Hinckley, A. F., Bachand, A. M., & Reif, J. S. (2005). Late pregnancy exposures to disinfection by-products and growth-related birth outcomes. *Environmental Health Perspectives, 113,* 1808–1813.

Hinds, D. A., Stuve, L. L., Nilsen, G. B., Halperin, E., Eskin, E., Ballinger, D. G., Frazer, K. A., & Cox, D. R. (2005). Whole-genome patterns of common DNA variation in three human populations. *Science, 307,* 1072–1079.

Hines, A. M. (1997). Divorce-related transitions, adolescent development, and the role of the parent-child relationship: A review

of the literature. *Journal of Marriage and Family, 59,* 375–388.

Hines, M., Chiu, L., McAdams, L. A., Bentler, M. P., & Lipcamon, J. (1992). Cognition and the corpus callosum: Verbal fluency, visual-spatial ability, language lateralization related to midsagittal surface areas of the corpus callosum. *Behavioral Neuroscience, 106,* 3–14.

Hingson, R., Heeren, T., Winter, M., & Wechsler, H. (2005). Magnitude of alcohol-related mortality and morbidity among U.S. college students ages 18–24: Changes from 1998–2001. *Annual Reviews, 26,* 259–279.

Hirschl, T. A., Altobelli, J., & Rank, M. R. (2003). Does marriage increase the odds of affluence? Exploring the life course probabilities. *Journal of Marriage and Family, 65,* 927–938.

Hitchins, M. P., & Moore, G. E. (2002, May 9). Genomic imprinting in fetal growth and development. *Expert Reviews in Molecular Medicine.* Retrieved November 21, 2006, from www.expertreviews.org/0200457Xh .htm.

Hitlin, S., Brown, J. S., & Elder, G. H. (2006). Racial self-categorization in adolescence: Multiracial development and social pathways. *Child Development, 77,* 1298–1308.

Hoban, T. F. (2004). Sleep and its disorders in children. *Seminars in Neurology, 24,* 327–340.

Hobson, J. A., & Silvestri, L. (1999, February). Parasomnias. *Harvard Mental Health Letter,* pp. 3–5.

Hodges, E. V. E., Boivin, M., Vitaro, F., & Bukowski, W. M. (1999). The power of friendship: Protection against an escalating cycle of peer victimization. *Developmental Psychology, 35,* 94–101.

Hoff, E. (2003). The specificity of environmental influence: Socioeconomic status affects early vocabulary development via maternal speech. *Child Development, 74,* 1368–1378.

Hoff, E. (2006). How social contexts support and shape language development. *Developmental Review, 26,* 55–88.

Hofferth, S. L., & Jankuniene, Z. (2000, April 2). *Children's after-school activities.* Paper presented at biennial meeting of the Society for Research on Adolescence, Chicago, IL.

Hoffman, M. L. (1970a). Conscience, personality, and socialization techniques. *Human Development, 13,* 90–126.

Hoffman, M. L. (1970b). Moral development. In P. H. Mussen (Ed.), *Carmichael's manual of child psychology* (Vol. 2, 3rd ed., pp. 261–360). New York: Wiley.

Hofman, P. L., Regan, F., Jackson, W. E., Jefferies, C., Knight, D. B., Robinson, E. M., & Cutfield, W. S. (2004). Premature birth and later insulin resistance. *New England Journal of Medicine, 351,* 2179–2186.

Hogge, W. A. (2003). The clinical use of karyotyping spontaneous abortions. *American Journal of Obstetrics and Gynecology, 189,* 397–402.

Hohmann-Marriott, B. E. (2006). Shared beliefs and the union stability of married and cohabiting couples. *Journal of Marriage and Family, 68,* 1015–1028.

Holden, G. W., & Miller, P. C. (1999). Enduring and different: A meta-analysis of the similarity in parents' child rearing. *Psychological Bulletin, 125,* 223–254.

Holliday, R. (2004). The multiple and irreversible causes of aging. *Journal of Gerontology: Biological Sciences, 59A,* 568–572.

Holmes, T. H., & Rahe, R. H. (1976). The social readjustment rating scale. *Journal of Psychosomatic Research, 11,* 213.

Holowka, S., & Petitto, L. A. (2002). Left hemisphere cerebral specialization for babies while babbling. *Science, 297,* 1515.

Holstein, M. B., & Minkler, M. (2003). Self, society, and the "New Gerontology." *Gerontologist, 43,* 787–796.

Holtzman, N. A., Murphy, P. D., Watson, M. S., & Barr, P. A. (1997). Predictive genetic testing: From basic research to clinical practice. *Science, 278,* 602–605.

Holtzman, R. E., Rebok, G. W., Saczynski, J. S., Kouzis, A. C., Doyle, K. W., & Eaton, W. W. (2004). Social network characteristics and cognition in middle-aged and older adults. *Journal of Gerontology: Psychological Sciences, 59B,* 278–284.

Honein, M. A., Paulozzi, L. J., Mathews, T. J., Erickson, J. D., & Wong, L.-Y. C. (2001). Impact of folic acid fortification of the U.S. food supply on the occurrence of neural tube defects. *Journal of the American Medical Association, 285,* 2981–2986.

Hopkins, B., & Westra, T. (1988). Maternal handling and motor development: An intracultural study. *Genetic, Social and General Psychology Monographs, 14,* 377–420.

Hopkins, B., & Westra, T. (1990). Motor development, maternal expectations and the role of handling. *Infant Behavior and Development, 13,* 117–122.

Horbar, J. D., Wright, E. C., Onstad, L., & the Members of the National Institute of Child Health and Human Development Neonatal Research Network. (1993). Decreasing mortality associated with the introduction of surfactant therapy: An observational study of neonates weighing 601 to 1300 grams at birth. *Pediatrics, 92,* 191–196.

Horn, J. C., & Meer, J. (1987, May). The vintage years. *Psychology Today,* pp. 76–90.

Horn, J. L. (1967). Intelligence—Why it grows, why it declines. *Transaction, 5*(1), 23–31.

Horn, J. L. (1968). Organization of abilities and the development of intelligence. *Psychological Review, 75,* 242–259.

Horn, J. L. (1970). Organization of data on lifespan development of human abilities. In L. R. Goulet & P. B. Baltes (Eds.), *Life-span developmental psychology: Theory and research* (pp. 424–466). New York: Academic Press.

Horn, J. L. (1982a). The aging of human abilities. In B. B. Wolman (Ed.), *Handbook of developmental psychology* (pp. 847–870). Englewood Cliffs, NJ: Prentice-Hall.

Horn, J. L. (1982b). The theory of fluid and crystallized intelligence in relation to concepts of cognitive psychology and aging in adulthood. In F. I.M. Craik & S. Trehub (Eds.), *Aging and cognitive processes* (pp. 237–278). New York: Plenum Press.

Horn, J. L., & Donaldson, G. (1980). Cognitive development: 2. Adulthood development of human abilities. In O. G. Brim & J. Kagan (Eds.), *Constancy and change in human development.* Cambridge, MA: Harvard University Press.

Horn, J. L., & Hofer, S. M. (1992). Major abilities and development in the adult. In R. J. Sternberg & C. A. Berg (Eds.), *Intellectual development.* New York Cambridge University Press.

Horn, L., & Berger, R. (2004). *College persistence on the rise? Changes in 5-year completion and postsecondary persistence rates between 1994 and 2000* (NCES 2005-156). Washington, DC: U.S. Department of Education, National Center for Education Statistics.

Horn, L., & Nevill, S. (2006). Profile of undergraduates in U.S. postsecondary education institutions: 2003–04: With a special analysis of community college students (NCES 2006–184). Washington, DC: U.S. Department of Education, National Center for Education Statistics.

Horne, J. (2000). Neuroscience: Images of lost sleep. *Nature, 403,* 605–606.

Horton, R., & Shweder, R. A. (2004). Ethnic conservatism, psychological well-being, and the downside of mainstreaming: Generational differences. In O. G. Brim, C. D. Ryff, & R. C. Kessler (Eds.), *How healthy are we? A national study of well-being at midlife* (pp. 373–397). Chicago: University of Chicago Press.

Hossain, P., Kawar, B., & Nahas, M. E. (2007). Obesity and diabetes in the developing world— a growing challenge. *New England Journal of Medicine, 356,* 213–215.

Houston, D. K., Stevens, J., Cai, J., & Haines, P. S. (2005). Dairy, fruit, and vegetable intakes and functional limitations and disability in a biracial cohort: The Atherosclerosis Risk in Communities Study. *American Journal of Clinical Nutrition, 81,* 515–522.

How to raise HDL. (2001, December). *University of California, Berkeley Wellness Letter, 18*(3), p. 3.

Howard, K. S., Lefever, J. B., Borkowski, J. G., & Whitman, T. L. (2006). Fathers' influence in the lives of children with adolescent mothers. *Journal of Family Psychology, 20,* 468–476.

Howe, H. L., Wu, X., Ries, L. A., Cokkinides, V., Ahmed, F., Jemal, A., Miller, B., Williams, M., Ward, E., Wingo, P. A., Ramirez, A., & Edwards, B. K. (2006). Annual report to the nation on the status of cancer, 1975–2003, Featuring cancer among U.S. Hispanic/Latino population. *Cancer, 107*(8), 1711–1742.

Howe, M. L. (2003). Memories from the cradle. *Current Directions in Psychological Science, 12,* 62–65.

Howe, M. L., & Courage, M. L. (1993). On resolving the enigma of infantile amnesia. *Psychological Bulletin, 113,* 305–326.

Howe, M. L., & Courage, M. L. (1997). The emergence and early development of autobiographical memory. *Psychological Review, 104,* 499–523.

Howe, N., Petrakos, H., Rinaldi, C. M., & LeFebvre, R. (2005). "This is a bad dog, you know . . ." : Constructing shared meanings during sibling pretend play. *Child Development, 76,* 783–794.

Howell, R. R. (2006). We need expanded newborn screening. *Pediatrics, 117,* 1800–1805.

Hoxby, C. M. (2004). *Achievement in charter schools and regular public schools in the United States: Understanding the differences.* Cambridge, MA: Department of Economics, Harvard University.

Hoyer, W. J., & Rybash, J. M. (1994). Characterizing adult cognitive development. *Journal of Adult Development, 1*(1), 7–12.

Hoyert, D., Olshansky, S. J., & Katz, D. (2007). Deaths: Preliminary Data for 2005. Bethesda, MD: National Center for Health Statistics.

Hoyert, D. L., Arias, E., Smith, B. L., Murphy, S. L., & Kochanek, K. D. (2001). Deaths: Final data for 1999. *National Vital Statistics Reports, 49*(8). Hyattsville, MD: National Center for Health Statistics.

Hoyert, D. L., Heron, M. P., Murphy, S. L., & Kung, H. C. (2006). Deaths: Final data for 2003. *National Vital Statistics Reports, 54*(13). Hyattsville, MD: National Center for Health Statistics.

Hoyert, D. L., Kochanek, K. D., & Murphy, S. L. (1999). Deaths: Final data for 1997. *National Vital Statistics Reports, 47*(19). Hyattsville, MD: National Center for Health Statistics.

Hoyert, D. L., Mathews, T. J., Menacker, F., Strobino, D. M., & Guyer, B. (2006). Annual summary of vital statistics: 2004. *Pediatrics, 117,* 168–183.

Hoyert, D. L., & Rosenberg, H. M. (1999). Mortality from Alzheimer's disease: An update. *National Vital Statistics Reports, 47*(20). Hyattsville, MD: National Center for Health Statistics.

Hu, F. B., Li, T. Y., Colditz, G. A., Willett, W. C., & Manson, J. E. (2003). Television watching and other sedentary behaviors in relation to risk of obesity and type 2 diabetes mellitus in women. *Journal of the American Medical Association, 289,* 1785–1791.

Hu, F. B., Manson, J. E., Stampfer, M. J., Colditz, G., Liu, S., Solomon, C. G., & Willett, W. C. (2001). Diet, lifestyle, and the risk of type 2 diabetes mellitus in women. *New England Journal of Medicine, 345,* 790–797.

Hu, F. B., Willett, W. C., Li, T., Stampfer, M. J., Colditz, G. A., & Manson, J. E. (2004). Adiposity as compared with physical activity in predicting mortality among women. *New England Journal of Medicine, 351,* 2694–2703.

Hubbard, F. O. A., & van IJzendoorn, M. H. (1991). Maternal unresponsiveness and infant crying across the first 9 months: A naturalistic longitudinal study. *Infant Behavior and Development, 14,* 299–312.

Hudnall, C. E. (2001, November). "Grand" parents get help: Programs aid aging caregivers and youngsters. *AARP Bulletin,* pp. 9, 12–13.

Hudson, L., Kienzl, G., & Diehl, J. (2007). *Students entering and leaving postsecondary occupational education: 1995–2001* (NCES 2007-041). Washington, DC: U.S. Department of Education, National Center for Education Statistics.

Huebner, C. E., & Meltzoff, A. N. (2005). Intervention to change parent-child reading style: A comparison of instructional methods. *Applied Developmental Psychology, 26,* 296–313.

Huesmann, L. R. (1986). Psychological processes promoting the relation between exposure to media violence and aggressive behavior by the viewer. *Journal of Social Issues, 42,* 125–139.

Huesmann, L. R., & Eron, L. D. (1984). Cognitive processes and the persistence of aggressive behavior. *Aggressive Behavior, 10,* 243–251.

Huesmann, L. R., Moise-Titus, J., Podolski, C. L., & Eron, L. (2003). Longitudinal relations between children's exposure to TV violence and their aggressive and violent behavior in young adulthood: 1977–1992. *Developmental Psychology, 39,* 201–221.

Hughes, D., Rodriguez, J., Smith, E. P., Johnson, D. J., Stevenson, H. C., & Spicer, P. (2006). Parents' ethnic-racial socialization practices: A review of research and directions for future study. *Developmental Psychology, 42,* 747–770.

Hughes, I. A. (2004). Female development—all by default? *New England Journal of Medicine, 351,* 748–750.

Hughes, K. L., Bailey, T. R., & Mechur, M. J. (2001). *School-to-work: Making a difference in education: A research report to America.* New York: Columbia University, Teachers College, Institute on Education and the Economy.

Hughes, M. (1975). *Egocentrism in preschool children.* Unpublished doctoral dissertation, Edinburgh University, Edinburgh, Scotland.

Huizink, A., Robles de Medina, P., Mulder, E., Visser, G., & Buitelaar, J. (2002). Psychological measures of prenatal stress as predictors of infant temperament. *Journal of the American Academy of Child and Adolescent Psychiatry, 41,* 1078–1085.

Huizink, A. C., Mulder, E. J. H., & Buitelaar, J. K. (2004). Prenatal stress and risk for psychopathology: Specific effects or induc-

tion of general susceptibility? *Psychological Bulletin 130,* 80–114.

Hujoel, P. P., Bollen, A.-M., Noonan, C. J., & del Aguila, M. A. (2004). Antepartum dental radiography and infant low birth weight. *Journal of the American Medical Association, 291,* 1987–1993.

Hulley, S., Furberg, C., Barrett-Connor, E., Cauley, J., Grady, D., Haskell, W., Knopp, R., Lowery, M., Satterfield, S., Schrott, H., Vittinghoff, E., & Hunninghake, D. (2002). Non-cardiovascular disease outcomes during 6.8 years of hormone therapy. *Journal of the American Medical Association, 288,* 58–66.

Hultsch, D. F. (1971). Organization and memory in adulthood. *Human Development, 14,* 16–29.

Humphreys, A. P., & Smith, P. K. (1984). Rough-and-tumble in preschool and playground. In P. K. Smith (Ed.), *Play in animals and humans.* Oxford: Blackwell.

Hungerford, T. L. (2001). The economic consequences of widowhood on elderly women in the United States and Germany. *Gerontologist, 41,* 103–110.

Hunt, C. E. (1996). Prone sleeping in healthy infants and victims of sudden infant death syndrome. *Journal of Pediatrics, 128,* 594–596.

Huntsinger, C. S., & Jose, P. E. (1995). Chinese American and Caucasian American family interaction patterns in spatial rotation puzzle solutions. *Merrill-Palmer Quarterly, 41,* 471–496.

Hurwitz, C. A., Duncan, J., & Wolfe, J. (2004). Caring for the child with cancer at the close of life. *Journal of the American Medical Association, 292*(17), 2141–2149.

Huston, A. C., & Aronson, S. R. (2005). Mothers' time with infant and time in employment as predictors of mother-child relationships and children's early development. *Child Development, 76,* 467–482.

Huston, A. C., Duncan, G. J., McLoyd, V. C., Crosby, D. A., Ripke, M. N., Weisner, T. S., & Eldred, C. A. (2005). Impacts on children of a policy to promote employment and reduce poverty for low-income parents: New hope after 5 years. *Developmental Psychology, 41,* 902–918.

Huston, H. C., Duncan, G. J., Granger, R., Bos, J., McLoyd, V., Mistry, R., Crosby, D., Gibson, C., Magnuson, K., Romich, J., and Ventura, A. (2001). Work-based antipoverty programs for parents can enhance the performance and social behavior of children. *Child Development, 72*(1), 318–336.

Huttenlocher, J. (1998). Language input and language growth. *Preventive Medicine, 27,* 195–199.

Huttenlocher, J., Haight, W., Bryk, A., Seltzer, M., & Lyons, T. (1991). Early vocabulary growth: Relation to language input and gender. *Developmental Psychology, 27,* 236–248.

Huttenlocher, J., Levine, S., & Vevea, J. (1998). Environmental input and cognitive growth: A study using time period comparisons. *Child Development, 69,* 1012–1029.

Huttenlocher, J., Vasilyeva, M., Cymerman, E., & Levine, S. (2002). Language input and child syntax. *Cognitive Psychology, 45,* 337–374.

Huyck, M. H. (1990). Gender differences in aging. In J. E. Birren & K. W. Schaie (Eds.), *Handbook of the psychology of aging* (3rd ed., pp. 124–132). San Diego: Academic Press.

Huyck, M. H. (1995). Marriage and close relationships of the marital kind. In R. Blieszner & V. Hilkevitch (Eds.), *Handbook of aging and the family* (pp. 181–200). Westport, CT: Greenwood Press.

Huyck, M. H. (1999). Gender roles and gender identity in midlife. In S. L. Willis & J. D. Reid (Eds.), *Life in the middle: Psychological and social development in middle age* (pp. 209–232). New York: Academic Press.

Hwang, S. J., Beaty, T. H., Panny, S. R., Street, N. A., Joseph, J. M., Gordon, S., McIntosh, I., & Francomano, C. A. (1995). Association study of transforming growth factor alpha (TGFa) TaqI polymorphism and oral clefts: Indication of gene-environment interaction in a population-based sample of infants with birth defects. *American Journal of Epidemiology, 141,* 629–636.

Hyde, J. S. (2005). The gender similarity hypothesis. *American Psychologist, 60,* 581–592.

Ialongo, N. S., Edelsohn, G., & Kellam, S. G. (2001). A further look at the prognostic power of young children's reports of depressed mood and feelings. *Child Development, 72,* 736–747.

Iervolino, A. C., Hines, M., Golombok, S. E., Rust, J., & Plomin, R. (2005). Genetic and environmental influences on sex-types behavior during the preschool years. *Child Development, 76,* 826–840.

Iervolino, A. C., Pike, A., Manke, B., Reiss, D., Hetherington, E. M., & Plomin, R. (2002). Genetic and environmental influences in adolescent peer socialization: Evidence from two genetically sensitive designs. *Child Development, 73*(1), 162–174.

Iglehart, J. K. (2007). The fate of SCHIP—Surrogate marker for health care ideology? *New England Journal of Medicine, 357,* 2104–2107.

Iglowstein, I., Jenni, O. G., Molinari, L., & Largo, R. H. (2003). Sleep duration from infancy to adolescence: Reference values and generational trends. *Pediatrics, 111,* 302–307.

Imada, T., Zhang, Y., Cheour, M., Taulu, S., Ahonen, A., & Kuhl, P. (2006). Infant speech perception activates Broca's area: A developmental magnetoencephalography study. *NeuroReport, 17,* 957–962.

Impagnatiello, F., Guidotti, A. R., Pesold, C., Dwivedi, Y., Caruncho, H., Pisu, M. G., Uzonov, D. P., Smalheiser, N. R., Davis, J. M., Pandey, G. N., Pappas, G. D., Tueting, P., Sharma, R. P., & Costa, E. (1998). A decrease of reelin expression as a putative vulnerability factor in schizophrenia. *Proceedings of the National Academy of Sciences, 95,* 15718–15723.

Ingelfinger, J. R. (2005). Risks and benefits to the living donor. *New England Journal of Medicine, 353,* 447–449.

Ingersoll, E. W., & Thoman, E. B. (1999). Sleep/wake states of preterm infants: Stability, developmental change, diurnal variation, and relation with care giving activity. *Child Development, 70,* 1–10.

Ingersoll-Dayton, B., Neal, M. B., Ha, J., & Hammer, L. B. (2003). Redressing inequity in parent care among siblings. *Journal of Marriage and Family, 65,* 201–212.

Ingoldsby, B. B. (1995). Mate selection and marriage. In B. B. Ingoldsby & S. Smith (Eds.), *Families in multicultural perspective* (pp. 143–160). New York: Guilford Press.

Ingram, J. L., Stodgell, C. S., Hyman, S. L., Figlewicz, D. A., Weitkamp, L. R., & Rodier, P. M. (2000). Discovery of allelic variants of HOXA1 and HOXB1: Genetic suscepibility to autism spectrum disorders. *Teratology, 62,* 393–406.

Institute of Medicine (IOM) National Academy of Sciences. (1993, November). *Assessing genetic risks: Implications for health and social policy.* Washington, DC: National Academy of Sciences.

Institute of Medicine (IOM) of the National Academies. (2005). *Preventing childhood obesity: Health in the balance.* Washington, DC: Author.

International Cesarean Awareness Network. (2003, March 5). Statistics: International cesarean and VBAC rates. Retrieved January 20, 2004, from www.icanonline.org/resources.statistics3.htm.

International Committee for Monitoring Assisted Reproductive Technologies (ICMART). (2006, June). *2002 World report on ART.* Report released at meeting of the European Society of Human Reproduction and Embryology, Prague.

International Human Genome Sequencing Consortium. (2004). Finishing the euchromatic sequence of the human genome. *Nature, 431,* 931–945.

International Longevity Center-USA. (2002). *Is there an anti-aging medicine? ILC Workshop Report.* Retrieved from www.ilcusa.org.

Iruka, I. U., & Carver, P. R. (2006). *Initial results from the 2005 NHDS Early Childhood Program Participation Survey* (NCES 2006-075). Washington, DC: National Center for Education Statistics.

Isaacowitz, D. M., & Smith, J. (2003). Positive and negative affect in very old age. *Journal of Gerontology: Psychological Sciences, 58B,* P143–P152.

Ishii, N., Fujii, M., Hartman, P. S., Tsuda, M., Yasuda, K., Senoo-Matsuda, N., Yanase, S., Ayusawa, D., & Suzuki, K. (1998). A mutation in succinate dehydrogenase cytochrome b causes oxidative stress and ageing in nematodes. *Nature, 394,* 694–697.

ISLAT Working Group. (1998). ART into science: Regulation of fertility techniques. *Science, 281,* 651–652.

Izard, C. E., Porges, S. W., Simons, R. F., Haynes, O. M., & Cohen, B. (1991). Infant cardiac activity: Developmental changes and relations with attachment. *Developmental Psychology, 27,* 432–439.

Jaccard, J., & Dittus, P. J. (2000). Adolescent perceptions of maternal approval of birth control and sexual risk behavior. *American Journal of Public Health, 90,* 1426–1430.

Jackson, R. D., LaCroix, A. Z., Gass, M., Wallace, R. B., Robbins, J., Lewis, C. E., Bassford, T., Beresford, S. A., Black, H. R., Blanchette, P., Bonds, D. E., Brunner, R. L., Brzyski, R. G., Caan, B., Cauley, J. A., Chlebowski, R. T., Cummings, S. R., Granek, I., Hays, J., Heiss, G., Hendrix, S. L., Howard, B. V., Hsai, J., Hubbell, F. A., Johnson, K. C., Judd, H., Kotchen, J. M., Kuller, L. H., Langer, R. D., Lasser, N. L., Limacher, M. C., Ludlam, S., Manson, J. E., Margolis, K. L., McGowan, J., Ockene, J. K., O'Sullivan, M. J., Phillips, L., Prentice, R. L. Sarto, G. E., Stefanick, M. L., Van Horn, L., Wactawski-Wende, J., Whitlock, E., Anderson, G. L., Assaf, A. R., & Barad, D., & Women's Health Initiative Invesigators. (2006). Calcium plus Vitamin D supplementation and the risk of fractures. *New England Journal of Medicine, 354,* 669–683.

Jacobsen, T., & Hofmann, V. (1997). Children's attachment representations: Longitudinal relations to school behavior and academic competency in middle childhood and adolescence. *Developmental Psychology, 33,* 703–710.

Jacobson, J. L., & Wille, D. E. (1986). The influence of attachment pattern on developmental changes in peer interaction from the toddler to the preschool period. *Child Development, 57,* 338–347.

Jacques, E. (1967). The midlife crisis. In R. Owen (Ed.), *Middle age.* London: BBC.

Jaffari-Bimmel, N., Juffer, F., van IJzendoorn, M. H., Bakermans-Kranenburg, M. J., & Mooijaart, A. (2006). Social development from infancy to adolescence: Longitudinal and concurrent factors in an adoption sample. *Developmental Psychology, 42,* 1143–1153.

Jaffee, S., & Hyde, J. S. (2000). Gender differences in moral orientation: A meta-analysis. *Psychological Bulletin, 126,* 703–726.

Jaffee, S. R., Caspi, A., Moffitt, T. E., Dodge, K. A., Rutter, M., Taylor, A., & Tully, L. A. (2005). Nature x nature: Genetic vulnerabilities interact with physical maltreatment to promote conduct problems. *Developmental Psychopathology, 17,* 67–84.

Jaffee, S. R., Caspi, A., Moffitt, T. E., Polo-Tomas, M., Price, T. S., & Taylor, A. (2004). The limits of child effects: Evidence for genetically mediated child effects on corporal punishment but not on physical maltreatment. *Developmental Psychology, 40,* 1047–1058.

Jagasia, R., Grote, P., Westermann, B., & Conradt, B. (2005). DRP-1-mediated mitochondrial fragmentation during EGL-1-induced cell death in *C. elegans. Nature, 433,* 754–760.

Jagers, R. J., Bingham, K., & Hans, S. L. (1996). Socialization and social judgments among inner-city African-American kindergartners. *Child Development, 67,* 140–150.

Jain, T., Missmer, S. A., & Hornstein, M. D. (2004). Trends in embryo-transfer practice and in outcomes of the use of assisted reproductive technology in the United States. *New England Journal of Medicine, 350,* 1639–1645.

Jakicic, J. M., Marcus, B. H., Gallagher, K. I., Napolitano, M., & Lang, W. (2003). Effect of exercise duration and intensity on weight loss in overweight sedentary women: A randomized trial. *Journal of the American Medical Association, 290,* 1323–1330.

James, J. B., & Lewkowicz, C. J. (1997). Themes of power and affiliation across time. In M. E. Lachman & J. B. James (Eds.), *Multiple paths of midlife development* (pp. 109–143). Chicago: University of Chicago Press.

Jankowiak, W. (1992). Father-child relations in urban China. In B. S. Hewlett (Ed.), *Father-child relations: Cultural and bisocial contexts* (pp. 345–363). New York: de Gruyter.

Jankowski, J. J., Rose, S. A., & Feldman, J. F. (2001). Modifying the distribution of attention in infants. *Child Development, 72,* 339–351.

Janowsky, J. S., & Carper, R. (1996). Is there a neural basis for cognitive transitions in school-age children? In A. J. Sameroff & M. M. Haith (Eds.), *The five to seven year shift: The age of reason and responsibility* (pp. 33–56). Chicago: University of Chicago Press.

Janssen, I., Craig, W. M., Boyce, W. F., & Pickett, W. (2004). Associations between overweight and obesity with bullying behaviors in school-aged children. *Pediatrics, 113,* 1187–1194.

Jarvis, M. J. (2004). Why people smoke. In J. Britton (Ed.), *ABC of smoking cessation* (pp. 4–6). Malden, MA: Blackwell.

Javaid, M. K., Crozier, S. R., Harvey, N. C., Gale, C. R., Dennison, E. M., Boucher, B. J., Arden, N. K., Godfrey, K. M., Cooper, C., & Princess Anne Hospital Study Group. (2006). Maternal vitamin D status during pregnancy and childhood bone mass at age 9 years: A longitudinal study. *Lancet, 367(9504),* 36–43.

Jee, S. H., Sull, J. W., Park, J., Lee, S., Ohrr, H., Guallar, E., & Samet, J. M. (2006). Body-mass index and mortality in Korean men and women. *New England Journal of Medicine, 355,* 779–787.

Jeffery, H. E., Megevand, M., & Page, M. (1999). Why the prone position is a risk factor for sudden infant death syndrome. *Pediatrics, 104,* 263–269.

Jensen, A. R. (1969). How much can we boost IQ and scholastic achievement? *Harvard Educational Review, 39,* 1–123.

Jeynes, W. H., & Littell, S. W. (2000). A meta-analysis of studies examining the effect of whole language instruction on the literacy of low-SES students. *Elementary School Journal, 101*(1), 21–33.

Ji, B. T., Shu, X. O., Linet, M. S., Zheng, W., Wacholder, S., Gao, Y. T., Ying, D. M., & Jin, F. (1997). Paternal cigarette smoking and the risk of childhood cancer among offspring of nonsmoking mothers. *Journal of the National Cancer Institute, 89,* 238–244.

Jiao, S., Ji, G., & Jing, Q. (1996). Cognitive development of Chinese urban only children and children with siblings. *Child Development, 67,* 387–395.

Jodl, K. M., Michael, A., Malanchuk, O., Eccles, J. S., & Sameroff, A. (2001). Parents' roles in shaping early adolescents' occupational aspirations. *Child Development 72*(4), 1247–1265.

Joe, S., Baser, R. E., Breeden, G., Neighbors, H. W., & Jackson, J. S. (2006). Prevalence of and risk factors for lifetime suicide attempts among blacks in the United States. *Journal of the American Medical Association, 296,* 2112–2123.

Johansson, B., Hofer, S. M., Allaire, J. C., Maldonado-Molina, M. M., Piccinin, A. M., Berg, S., Pedersen, N. L., & McClearn, G. E. (2004). Change in cognitive capabilities in the oldest old: The effects of proximity to death in genetically related individuals over a 6-year period. *Psychology and Aging, 19,* 145–156.

Johansson, G., Evans, G. W., Rydstedt, L. W., & Carrere, S. (1998). Job hassles and cardiovascular reaction patterns among urban bus drivers. *International Journal of Behavioral Medicine, 5,* 267–280.

Johnson, C. L. (1995). Cultural diversity in the late-life family. In R. Blieszner & V. Hilkevitch (Eds.), *Handbook of aging and the family* (pp. 307–331). Westport, CT: Greenwood Press.

Johnson, C. L., & Troll, L. E. (1994). Constraints and facilitators to friendships in late late life. *Gerontologist, 34,* 79–87.

Johnson, C. P., Myers, S. M., & the Council on Children with Disabilities. (2007). Identification and evaluation of children with autism spectrum disorders. *Pediatrics, 120,* 1183–1215.

Johnson, D. J., Jaeger, E., Randolph, S. M., Cauce, A. M., Ward, J., & National Institute of Child Health and Human Development Early Child Care Research Network (2003). Studying the effects of early child care experiences on the development of children of color in the United States: Toward a more inclusive research agenda. *Child Development, 74,* 1227–1244.

Johnson, J., Stewart, W., Hall, E., Fredlund, P., & Theorell, T. (1996). Long-term psychosocial work environment and cardiovascular mortality among Swedish men. *American Journal of Public Health, 86,* 324–331.

Johnson, J. E. (1998). Play development from ages four to eight. In D. P. Fromberg & D. Bergen (Eds.), *Play from birth to twelve and beyond: Contexts, perspectives, and meanings* (pp. 145–153). New York: Garland.

Johnson, J. G., Cohen, P., Gould, M. S., Kasen, S., Brown, J., & Brook, J. S. (2002). Childhood adversities, interpersonal difficulties, and risk for suicide attempts during late adolescence and early adulthood. *Archives of General Psychiatry, 59,* 741–749.

Johnson, J. O. (2005). Who's minding the kids? Child care arrangements: Winter 2002. *Current Population Reports* (P70-101). Washington, DC: U.S. Census Bureau.

Johnson, K. E., Scott, P., & Mervis, C. B. (1997). Development of children's understanding of basic-subordinate inclusion relations. *Developmental Psychology, 33,* 745–763.

Johnson, M. H. (1998). The neural basis of cognitive development. In D. Kuhn & R. S. Siegler (Eds.), *Handbook of child psychology: Vol. 2. Cognition, perception, and language* (5th ed., pp. 1–49). New York: Wiley.

Johnson, M. M. S. (1990). Age differences in decision making: A process methodology for examining strategic information processing. *Journal of Gerontology: Psychological Sciences, 45,* P75–P78.

Johnson, M. M. S., Schmitt, F. A., & Everard, K. (1994). *Task driven strategies: The impact of age and information on decision-making performance.* Unpublished manuscript, University of Kentucky, Lexington.

Johnson, R. A., Hoffmann, J. P., & Gerstein, D. R. (1996). *The relationship between family structure and adolescent substance use* (DHHS Publication No. SMA 96–3086). Washington, DC: U.S. Department of Health and Human Services.

Johnson, S. J., & Rybash, J. M. (1993). A cognitive neuroscience perspective on age-related slowing: Developmental changes in the functional architecture. In J. Cerella, J. M. Rybash, W. J. Hoyer, & M. L. Commons (Eds.), *Adult information processing: Limits on loss* (pp. 143–175). San Diego: Academic Press.

Johnson, T. E. (1990). Age-1 mutants of *Caenorhabditis elegans* prolong life by modifying the Gompertz rate of aging. *Science, 229,* 908–912.

Johnston, L. D., O'Malley, P. M., Bachman, J. G., & Schulenberg, J. E. (2006). *Monitoring the Future national results on adolescent drug use: Overview of key findings, 2005* (NIH Publication No. 06-5882). Bethesda, MD: National Institute on Drug Abuse.

Johnston, L. D., O'Malley, P. M., Bachman, J. G., & Schulenberg, J. E. (2007). *Monitoring the Future national results on adolescent drug use: Overview of key findings, 2006* (NIH Publication No. 07-6202). Bethesda, MD: National Institute on Drug Abuse.

Johnston, L. D., O'Malley, P. M., Bachman, J. G., & Schulenberg, J. E. (2008). *Monitoring the Future national results on adolescent drug use: Overview of key findings, 2007* (NIH Publication No. 08-6418). Bethesda, MD: National Institute on Drug Abuse.

Jones, A. M. (2004). *Review of gap year provisions.* London: Department of Education and Skills.

Jones, C. L., Tepperman, L., & Wilson, S. J. (1995). *The future of the family.* Englewood Cliffs, NJ: Prentice-Hall.

Jones, K. M., Whitbourne, S. K., & Skultety, K. M. (2006). Identity processes and the transition to midlife amog baby boomers. In S. K. Whitbourne & S. L. Willis (Eds.), *The baby boomers grow up: Contemporary perspectives on midlife* (pp. 149–164). Mahwah, NJ: Erlbaum.

Jones, N. A., Field, T., Fox, N. A., Davalos, M., Lundy, B., & Hart, S. (1998). Newborns of mothers with depressive symptoms are physiologically less developed. *Infant Behavior & Development, 21*(3), 537–541.

Jones, N. A., Field, T., Fox, N. A., Lundy, B., & Davalos, M. (1997). EEG activation in one-month-old infants of depressed mothers. *Development and Psychopathology, 9,* 491–505.

Jones, S. S. (1996). Imitation or exploration? Young infants' matching of adults' oral gestures. *Child Development, 67,* 1952–1969.

Jopp, D., & Smith, J. (2006). Resources and life management strategies as determinants of successful aging: On the protective effect of selection, optimization, and compensation. *Psychology and Aging, 21,* 253–265.

Jordan, N. C., Kaplan, D., Oláh, L. N., & Locuniak, M. N. (2006). Number sense growth in kindergarten: A longitudinal investigation of children at risk for mathematics difficulties. *Child Development, 77,* 153–175.

Joshipura, K. J., Ascherio, A., Manson, J. E., Stampfer, M. H., Rim, E. B., Speizer, F. E., Hennekens, C. H., Spiegleman, D., & Willett, W. C. (1999). Fruit and vegetable intake in relation to risk of ischemic stroke. *Journal of the American Medical Association, 282,* 1233–1239.

Josselson, R. (2003). Revisions: Processes of development in midlife women. In J. Demick and C. Andreoletti (Eds.), *Handbook of adult development.* New York: Plenum Press.

Jung, C. G. (1933). *Modern man in search of a soul.* New York: Harcourt Brace.

Jung, C. G. (1953). The stages of life. In H. Read, M. Fordham, & G. Adler (Eds.), *Collected works* (Vol. 2). Princeton, NJ: Princeton University Press. (Original work published 1931)

Jung, C. G. (1966). Two essays on analytic psychology. In *Collected works* (Vol. 7). Princeton, NJ: Princeton University Press.

Jung, C. G. (1969). *The structure and dynamics of the psyche.* Princeton, NJ: Princeton University Press.

Jung, C. G. (1971). Aion: Phenomenology of the self (the ego, the shadow, the syzgy: Anima/animus). In J. Campbell (Ed.), *The portable Jung.* New York: Viking Penguin.

Jusczyk, P. W. (2003). The role of speech perception capacities in early language acquisition. In M. T. Banich & M. Mack (Eds.), *Mind, brain, and language: Multidisciplinary perspectives.* Mahwah, NJ: Erlbaum.

Jusczyk, P. W., & Hohne, E. A. (1997). Infants' memory for spoken words. *Science, 277,* 1984–1986.

Just, M. A., Cherkassky, V. L., Keller, T. A., Kana, R. K., & Minshew, N. J. (2007). Functional and anatomical cortical underconnectivity in autism: Evidence from an fMRI study of an executive function task and corpus callosum morphometry. *Cerebral Cortex, 17*(4), 951–961.

Juster, F. T., Ono, H., & Stafford, F. P. (2004). *Changing times of American youth: 1981–2003* (Child Development Supplement). Ann Arbor, MI: University of Michigan Institute for Social Research.

Juul-Dam, N., Townsend, J. & Courchesne, E. (2001). Prenatal, perinatal, and neonatal factors in autism, pervasive developmental disorder—not otherwise specified, and the general population. *Pediatrics, 107*(4), p. e63.

Kaczynski, K. J., Lindahl, K. M., Malik, N. M., & Laurenceau, J. (2006). Marital conflict, maternal and paternal parenting, and child adjustment: A test of mediation and moderation. *Journal of Family Psychology, 20,* 199–208.

Kagan, J. (1997). Temperament and the reactions to unfamiliarity. *Child Development, 68,* 139–143.

Kagan, J., & Snidman, N. (1991a). Infant predictors of inhibited and uninhibited behavioral profiles. *Psychological Science, 2,* 40–44.

Kagan, J., & Snidman, N. (1991b). Temperamental factors in human development. *American Psychologist, 46,* 856–862.

Kagan, J., & Snidman, N. (2004). *The long shadow of temperament.* Cambridge, MA: Belknap Press.

Kagan, J., Snidman, N., Kahn, V., & Towsley, S. (2007). The preservation of two infant temperaments into adolescence. *Monograph of Society for Research in Child Development, 92* (2, Serial No. 287).

Kahn, R. L., & Antonucci, T. C. (1980). Convoys over the life course: Attachment, roles, and social support. In P. B. Baltes & O. G. Brim Jr. (Eds.), *Life-span development and behavior* (pp. 253–286). New York: Academic Press.

Kaiser Family Foundation, Hoff, T., Greene, L., & Davis, J. (2003). *National survey of adolescents and young adults: Sexual health knowledge, attitudes and experiences.* Menlo Park, CA: Henry J. Kaiser Foundation.

Kalil, A., & Ziol-Guest, K. M. (2005). Single mothers' employment dynamics and adolescent well-being. *Child Development, 76,* 196–211.

Kalish, C. W. (1998). Young children's predictions of illness: Failure to recognize probabilistic cause. *Developmental Psychology, 34*(5), 1046–1058.

Kanaya, T., Scullin, M. H., & Ceci, S. J. (2003). The Flynn effect and U.S. policies: The impact of rising IQ scores on American society via mental retardation diagnoses. *American Psychologist, 58,* 778–790.

Kaneda, T. (2006). *China's concern over population aging and health.* Washington, DC: Population Reference Bureau. Retrieved March 8, 2008, from www.prb.org/Articles/2006/ChinasConcernOverPopulationAgingandHealth.aspx.

Kanetsuna, T., & Smith, P. K. (2002). Pupil insight into bullying and coping with bullying: A bi-national study in Japan and England. *Journal of School Violence, 1,* 5–29.

Kaplan, H., & Dove, H. (1987). Infant development among the Ache of East Paraguay. *Developmental Psychology, 23,* 190–198.

Kaplan, R. M., & Kronick, R. G. (2006). Marital status and longevity in the United States population. *Journal of Epidemiological Community Health, 60,* 760–765.

Kaplowitz, P. B., Oberfield, S. E., & the Drug and Therapeutics and Executive Committees of the Lawson Wilkins Pediatric Endocrine Society. (1999). Reexamination of the age limit for defining when puberty is precocious in girls in the United States: Implications for evaluation and treatment. *Pediatrics, 104,* 936–941.

Karafantis, D. M., & Levy, S. R. (2004). The role of children's lay theories about the malleability of human attributes in beliefs about and volunteering for disadvantaged groups. *Child Development, 75,* 236–250.

Karasik, D., Hannan, M. T., Cupples, L. A., Felson, D. T., & Kiel, D. P. (2004). Genetic contribution to biological aging: The Framingham study. *Journal of Gerontology: Biological Sciences, 59A,* 218–226.

Karney, B. R., & Bradbury, T. N. (1995). The longitudinal course of marital quality and stability: A review of theory, method, and research. *Psychological Bulletin, 118,* 3–34.

Katchadourian, H. (1987). *Fifty: Midlife in perspective.* New York: Freeman.

Katzman, R. (1993). Education and prevalence of Alzheimer's disease. *Neurology, 43,* 13–20.

Kaufman, A. S., & Kaufman, N. L. (1983). *Kaufman Assessment Battery for Children: Administration and scoring manual.* Circle Pines, MN: American Guidance Service.

Kaufman, A. S., & Kaufman, N. L. (2003). *Kaufman Assessment Battery for Children* (2nd ed.). Circle Pines, MN: American Guidance Service.

Kaukinen, C. (2004). Status compatibility, physical violence, and emotional abuse in intimate relationships. *Journal of Marriage and Family, 66,* 452–471.

Kausler, D. H. (1990). Automaticity of encoding and episodic memory-processes. In E. A. Lovelace (Ed.), *Aging and cognition: Mental processes, self-awareness, and interventions* (pp. 29–67). Amsterdam: North-Holland, Elsevier.

Kawachi, I., Colditz, G. A., Stampfer, M. J., Willett, W. C., Manson, J. E., Rosner, B., Speizer, F. E., & Hennekens, C. H. (1993). Smoking cessation and decreased risk of stroke in women. *Journal of the American Medical Association, 269,* 232–236.

Kazdin, A. E., & Benjet, C. (2003). Spanking children: Evidence and issues. *Current Directions in Psychological Science, 12,* 99–103.

Kearney, P. M., Whelton, M., Reynolds, K., Muntner, P., Whelton, P. K., & He, J. (2005). Global burden of hypertension: Analysis of worldwide data. *Lancet, 365,* 217–223.

Keegan, C., Gross, S., Fisher, L., & Remez, S. (2004). *Boomers at midlife: The AARP Life Stage Study: Executive summary.* Wave 3. Washington, DC: American Association of Retired Persons.

Keegan, R. T. (1996). *Creativity from childhood to adulthood: A difference of degree and not of kind (New Directions for Child Development, No. 72,* pp. 57–66). San Francisco: Jossey-Bass.

Keel, P. K., & Klump, K. L. (2003). Are eating disorders culture-bound syndromes? Implications for conceptualizing their etiology. *Psychological Bulletin, 129,* 747–769.

Keenan, K., & Shaw, D. (1997). Developmental and social influences on young girls' early problem behavior. *Psychological Bulletin, 121*(1), 95–113.

Kefalas, M., Furstenberg, F., & Napolitano, L. (2005, September). *Marriage is more than being together: The meaning of marriage among young adults in the United States.* Network on Transitions to Adulthood Research Network Working Paper.

Keller, B. (1999, February 24). A time and place for teenagers. *Education Week on the WEB.* Retrieved March 11, 2004, from www.edweek.org/ew/vol-18/24studen.h18.

Kelley, M. L., Smith, T. S., Green, A. P., Berndt, A. E., & Rogers, M. C. (1998). Importance of fathers' parenting to African-American toddlers' social and cognitive development. *Infant Behavior & Development, 21,* 733–744.

Kellman, P. J., & Arterberry, M. E. (1998). *The cradle of knowledge: Development of perception in infancy.* Cambridge, MA: MIT Press.

Kellman, P. J., & Banks, M. S. (1998). Infant visual perception. In W. Damon (Series Ed.), D. Kuhn, & R. S. Siegler (Vol. Eds.), *Handbook of child psychology: Vol. 2. Cognition, perception, and language* (5th ed., pp. 103–146). New York: Wiley.

Kellogg, N., & the Committee on Child Abuse and Neglect. (2005). The evaluation of sexual abuse in children. *Pediatrics, 116*(2), 506–512.

Kellogg, R. (1970). Understanding children's art. In P. Cramer (Ed.), *Readings in developmental psychology today.* Delmar, CA: CRM.

Kelly, A. M., Wall, M., Eisenberg, M., Story, M., & Neumark-Sztainer, D. (2004). High body satisfaction in adolescent girls: Association with demographic, socioenvironmental, personal, and behavioral factors. *Journal of Adolescent Health, 34,* 129.

Kelly, J. B., & Emery, R. E. (2003). Children's adjustment following divorce: Risk and resiliency perspectives. *Family Relations, 52,* 352–362.

Kelly, J. R. (1987). *Peoria winter: Styles and resources in later life.* Lexington, MA: Lexington.

Kelly, J. R. (1994). Recreation and leisure. In A. Monk (Ed.), *The Columbia retirement handbook* (pp. 489–508). New York: Columbia University Press.

Kelly, J. R., Steinkamp, M., & Kelly, J. (1986). Later life leisure: How they play in Peoria. *Gerontologist, 26,* 531–537.

Kemper, S., Thompson, M., & Marquis, J. (2001). Longitudinal change in language production: Effects of aging and dementia on grammatical complexity and propositional content. *Psychology and Aging, 16,* 600–614.

Keppel, K. G., Pearcy, J. N., & Wagener, D. K. (2002). Trends in racial and ethnic-specific rates for the health status indicators: United States, 1990–1998. *Statistical Notes,* No. 23. Hyattsville, MD: National Center for Health Statistics.

Kere, J., Hannula-Jouppi, K., Kaminen-Ahola, N., Taipale, M., Eklund, R., Nopola-Hemmi, J., & Kaariainen, H. (2005, October). *Identification of the dyslexia susceptibility gene for DYX5 on chromosone 3.* Paper presented at the meeting of the American Society of Human Genetics, Salt Lake City, UT.

Kerns, K. A., Don, A., Mateer, C. A., & Streissguth, A. P. (1997). Cognitive deficits in nonretarded adults with fetal alcohol syndrome. *Journal of Learning Disabilities, 30,* 685–693.

Kessler, R. C., Berglund, P., Demler, O., Jin, R., Merikangas, K. R., & Walters, E. E. (2005). Lifetime prevalence and age-of-onset distributions of *DSM-IV* disorders in the National Comorbidity Survey Replication. *Archives of General Psychiatry, 62,* 593–602.

Kessler, R. C., Gilman, S. E., Thornton, L. M., & Kendler, K. S. (2004). Health, well-being, and social responsibility in the MIDUS twin and sibling subsamples. In O. G. Brim, C. D. Ryff, & R. Kessler (Eds.), *How healthy are we? A national study of well-being in midlife* (pp. 124–152). Chicago: University of Chicago Press.

Kestenbaum, R., & Gelman, S. A. (1995). Preschool children's identification and understanding of mixed emotions. *Cognitive Development, 10,* 443–458.

KewalRamani, A., Gilbertson, L., Fox, M. A., & Provasnik, S. (2007). *Status and trends in the education of racial and ethnic minorities* (NCES-2007039). Washington, DC: National Center for Education Statistics.

Keyes, C. L. M., & Ryff, C. D. (1998). Generativity in adult lives: Social structural contours and quality of life consequences. In D. P. McAdams & E. de St. Aubin (Eds.), *Generativity and adult development*

(pp. 227–263). Washington, DC: American Psychological Association.

Keyes, C. L. M., & Ryff, C. D. (1999). Psychological well-being in midlife. In S. L. Willis & J. D. Reid (Eds.), *Life in the middle* (pp. 161–180). San Diego: Academic Press.

Khaw, K. T., Wareham, N., Bingham, S., Welch, A., Luben, R., & Day, N. (2008). Combined impact of health behaviours and mortality in men and women: The EPIC-Norfolk Prospective Population Study. *PLoS Medicine, 5*(1), e12. (DOI: 10.1371/journal.pmed.0050012).

Khoury, M. J., McCabe, L. L., & McCabe, E. R. B. (2003). Population screening in the age of genomic medicine. *New England Journal of Medicine, 348,* 50–58.

Kiecolt-Glaser, J. K., & Glaser, R. (1999). Chronic stress and mortality among older adults. *Journal of the American Medical Association, 282,* 2259–2260.

Kiecolt-Glaser, J. K., & Glaser, R. (2001). Stress and immunity: Age enhances the risks. *Current Directions in Psychological Science, 10,* 18–21.

Kiecolt-Glaser, J. K., & Newton, T. L. (2001). Marriage and health: His and hers. *Psychological Bulletin, 127,* 472–503.

Kiefe, C. I., Williams, O. D., Weissman, N. W., Schreiner, P. J., Sidney, S., & Wallace, D. D. (2000). Changes in U.S. health care access in the 90s: Race and income differences from the CARDIA study. Coronary Artery Risk Development in Young Adults. *Ethnicity and Disease, 10,* 418–431.

Kiefer, K. M., Summer, L., & Shirey, L. (2001). What are the attitudes of young retirees and older workers? *Data Profiles: Young Retirees and Older Workers, 5.*

Kier, C., & Lewis, C. (1998). Preschool sibling interaction in separated and married families: Are same-sex pairs or older sisters more sociable? *Journal of Child Psychology and Psychiatry, 39,* 191–201.

Killen, J. D., Robinson, T. N., Ammerman, S., Hayward, C., Rogers, J., Stone, C., Samuels, D., Levin, S. K., Green, S., & Schatzberg, A. F. (2004). Randomized clinical trial of the efficacy of bupropion combined with nicotine patch in the treatment of adolescent smokers. *Journal of Consulting and Clinical Psychology, 72,* 729–735.

Kim, J., McHale, S. M., Osgood, D. W., & Crouter, A. C. (2006). Longitudinal course and family correlates of sibling relationships from childhood through adolescence. *Child Development, 77,* 1746–1761.

Kim, J., Peterson, K. E., Scanlon, K. S., Fitzmaurice, G. M., Must, A., Oken, E., Rifas-Shiman, S. L., Rich-Edwards, J. W., & Gillman, M. W. (2006). Trends in overweight from 1980 through 2001 among preschool-aged children enrolled in a health maintenance organization. *Obesity, 14*(7), 1107–1112.

Kim, J. E., & Moen, P. (2001). Moving into retirement: Preparation and transitions in late midlife. In M. E. Lachman (Ed.),

Handbook of midlife development (pp. 487–527). New York: Wiley.

Kim, J. E., & Moen, P. (2002). Retirement transitions, gender, and psychological well-being: A life-course, ecological model. *Journal of Gerontology: Psychological Sciences, 57B,* P212–P222.

Kim, Y., S., Koh, Y.-J., & Leventhal, B. (2005). School bullying and suicidal risk in Korean middle school students. *Pediatrics, 115,* 357–363.

Kimball, M. M. (1986). Television and sex-role attitudes. In T. M. Williams (Ed.), *The impact of television: A natural experiment in three communities* (pp. 265–301). Orlando, FL: Academic Press.

Kim-Cohen, J., Caspi, A., Moffitt, T. E., Harrington, H., Milne, B. J., & Poulton, R. (2003). Prior juvenile diagnoses in adults with mental disorder: Developmental follow-back of a prospective-longitudinal cohort. *Archives of General Psychiatry, 60,* 709–717.

Kim-Cohen, J., Moffitt, T. E., Caspi, A., & Taylor, A. (2004). Genetic and environmental processes in young children's resilience and vulnerability to socioeconomic deprivation. *Child Development, 75,* 651–668.

Kimmel, D. (1990). *Adulthood and aging: An interdisciplinary, developmental view.* New York: Wiley.

Kimmel, D. C., & Sang, B. E. (1995). Lesbians and gay men in midlife. In A. R. D'Augelli & C. J. Patterson (Eds.), *Lesbian, gay, and bisexual identities over the lifespan: Psychological perspectives* (pp. 190–214). New York: Oxford University Press.

Kimmel, M. S. (2002). "Gender symmetry" in domestic violence: A substantive and methodological research review. *Violence Against Women, 8,* 1332–1363.

King, B. M. (1996). *Human sexuality today.* Englewood Cliffs, NJ: Prentice-Hall.

King, M., & Bartlett, A. (2006). What same sex civil partnerships may mean for health. *Journal of Epidemiology and Community Health, 60,* 188–191.

King, V. (2006). The antecedents and consequences of adolescents' relationships with stepfathers and nonresident fathers. *Journal of Marriage and Family, 68,* 910–928.

King, V., & Scott, M. E. (2005). A comparison of cohabiting rerlationships among older and younger adults. *Journal of Marriage and Family, 67,* 271–285.

King, V., & Sobolewski, J. M. (2006). Nonresident fathers' contributions to adolescent well-being. *Journal of Marriage and Family, 68,* 537–557.

King, W. J., MacKay, M., Sirnick, A., & The Canadian Shaken Baby Study Group. (2003). Shaken baby syndrome in Canada: Clinical characteristics and outcomes of hospital cases. *CMAJ (Canadian Medical Association Journal), 168,* 155–159.

Kinsella, K., & Phillips, P. (2005, March). Global aging: The challenges of success. *Population Bulletin,* No. 1. Washington, DC: Population Reference Bureau.

Kinsella, K., & Velkoff, V. A. (2001). An aging world: 2001 (U.S. Census Bureau, Series P95/01-1). Washington, DC: U.S. Government Printing Office.

Kirby, D. (1997). *No easy answers: Research findings on programs to reduce teen pregnancy.* Washington, DC: National Campaign to Prevent Teen Pregnancy.

Kisilevsky, B. S., Hains, S. M. J., Lee, K., Muir, D. W., Xu, F., Fu, G., Zhao, Z. Y., & Yang, R. L. (1998). The still-face effect in Chinese and Canadian 3- to 6-month-old infants. *Developmental Psychology, 34*(4), 629–639.

Kisilevsky, B. S., Hains, S. M J., Lee, K., Xie, X., Huang, H., Ye, H. H., Zhang, K., & Wang, Z. (2003). Effects of experience on fetal voice recognition. *Psychological Science, 14,* 220–224.

Kisilevsky, B. S., Muir, D. W., & Low, J. A. (1992). Maturation of human fetal responses to vibroacoustic stimulation. *Child Development, 63,* 1497–1508.

Kitzmann, K. M., & Beech, B. (2006). Family-based interventions for pediatric obesity: Methodological and conceptual challenges from family psychology. *Journal of Family Psychology, 20,* 175–189.

Kivett, V. R. (1991). Centrality of the grandfather role among older rural black and white men. *Journal of Gerontology: Social Sciences, 46*(5), S250–S258.

Kivett, V. R. (1993). Racial comparisons of the grandmother role: Implications for strengthening the family support system of older black women. *Family Relations, 42,* 165–172.

Kivett, V. R. (1996). The saliency of the grandmother-granddaughter relationship: Predictors of association. *Journal of Women and Aging, 8,* 25–39.

Klar, A. J. S. (1996). A single locus, RGHT, specifies preference for hand utilization in humans. *Cold Spring Harbor Symposia on Quantitative Biology 61,* 59–65. Cold Spring Harbor, NY: Cold Spring Harbor Laboratory Press.

Klaus, M. H., & Kennell, J. H. (1997). The doula: An essential ingredient of childbirth rediscovered. *Acta Paediatrica, 86,* 1034–1036.

Klebanoff, M. A., Levine, R. J., DerSimonian, R., Clemens, J. D., & Wilkins, D. G. (1999). Maternal serum paraxanthine, a caffeine metabolite, and the risk of spontaneous abortion. *New England Journal of Medicine, 341,* 1639–1644.

Klein, J. D., & the American Academy of Pediatrics Committee on Adolescence. (2005). Adolescent pregnancy: Current trends and issues. *Pediatrics, 116,* 281–286.

Kleinman, R., Hall, S., Green, H., Korzec-Ramirez, D., Patton, K., Pagano, M. and Murphy, J. (2002). Diet, breakfast and academic performance in children. *Annals of Nutrition and Metabolism, 46,* 24–30.

Klein-Velderman, M., Bakermans-Kranenburg, M. J., Juffer, F., & van IJzendoorn, M. H. (2006). Effects of attachment-based interventions on maternal sensitivity and infant attachment: Differential susceptibility of highly reactive infants. *Journal of Family Psychology, 20,* 266–274.

Klibanoff, R. S., Levine, S. C., Huttenlocher, J., Vasilyeva, M., & Hedges, L. V. (2006). Preschool children's mathematical knowledge: The effect of teacher "math talk." *Developmental Psychology, 42,* 59–69.

Kline, D. W., Kline, T. J. B., Fozard, J. L., Kosnik, W., Schieber, F., & Sekuler, R. (1992). Vision, aging, and driving: The problems of older drivers. *Journal of Gerontology: Psychological Sciences, 47*(1), P27–P34.

Kline, D. W., & Scialfa, C. T. (1996). Visual and auditory aging. In J. E. Birren & K. W. Schaie (Eds.), *Handbook of the psychology of aging* (pp. 191–208). San Diego: Academic Press.

Klohnen, E. C. (1996). Conceptual analysis and measurement of the construct of ego-resiliency. *Journal of Personality and Social Psychology, 70,* 1067–1079.

Klohnen, E. C., Vandewater, E., & Young, A. (1996). Negotiating the middle years: Ego-resiliency and successful midlife adjustment in women. *Psychology and Aging, 11,* 431–442.

Klump, K. L., & Culbert, K. M. (2007). Molecular genetic studies of eating disorders: Current status and future directions. *Current Directions in Psychological Science, 16,* 37–41.

Knafo, A., & Plomin, R. (2006). Parental discipline and affection and children's prosocial behavior: Genetic and environmental links. *Journal of Personality and Social Psychology, 90,* 147–164.

Knapp, L. G., Kelly-Reid, J. E., Whitmore, R. W., & Miller, E. (2007). *Enrollment in postsecondary institutions, Fall 2005; graduation rates, 1999 and 2002 cohorts; and financial statistics, fiscal year, 2005* (NCES 2007-154). Washington, DC: U.S. Department of Education, National Center for Education Statistics. Retrieved July 16, 2007, from http://nces.ed.gov/pubresearch/pubinfo.asp?pubid=2007154.

Knickmeyer, R., Baron-Cohen, S., Raggatt, P., & Taylor, K. (2005). Foetal testosterone, social relationships, and restricted interests in children. *Journal of Child Psychology and Psychiatry, 46,* 198–210.

Knoester, C., Haynie, D. L., & Stephens, C. M. (2006). Parenting practices and adolescents' friendship networks. *Journal of Marriage and Family, 68,* 1247–1260.

Knoop, R. (1994). Relieving stress through value-rich work. *Journal of Social Psychology, 134,* 829–836.

Knoops, K. T. B., deGroot, L. C. P. G. M., Kromhout, D., Perrin, E., Moreiras-Varela, O., Menotti, A., & van Staveren, W. A. (2004). Mediterranean diet, lifestyle factors, and 10-year mortality in elderly European men and women. *Journal of the American Medical Association, 292,* 1433–1439.

Knox, N. (2004, July 14). European gay-union trends influence U.S. debate: Lawmakers look to other nations. *USA Today.* Retrieved January 2, 2005, from www.keepmedia.com/pubs/USATODAY/2004/07/14/506463.

Kochanek, K. D., Murphy, S. L., Anderson, R. N., & Scott, C. (2004). Deaths: Final data for 2002. *National Vital Statistics Reports, 53*(5). Hyattsville, MD: National Center for Health Statistics.

Kochanek, K. D., & Smith, B. L. (2004). Deaths: Preliminary data for 2002. *National Vital Statistics Reports, 52*(13). Hyattsville, MD: National Center for Health Statistics.

Kochanska, G. (1993). Toward a synthesis of parental socialization and child temperament in early development of conscience. *Child Development, 64,* 325–347.

Kochanska, G. (1995). Children's temperament, mothers' discipline, and security of attachment: Multiple pathways to emerging internalization. *Child Development, 66,* 597–615.

Kochanska, G. (1997a). Multiple pathways to conscience for children with different temperaments: From toddlerhood to age 5. *Developmental Psychology, 33,* 228–240.

Kochanska, G. (1997b). Mutually responsive orientation between mothers and their young children: Implications for early socialization. *Child Development, 68,* 94–112.

Kochanska, G. (2001). Emotional development in children with different attachment histories: The first three years. *Child Development, 72,* 474–490.

Kochanska, G. (2002). Mutually responsive orientation between mothers and their young children: A context for the early development of conscience. *Current Directions in Psychological Science, 11,* 191–195.

Kochanska, G., & Aksan, N. (1995). Mother-child positive affect, the quality of child compliance to requests and prohibitions, and maternal control as correlates of early internalization. *Child Development, 66,* 236–254.

Kochanska, G., Aksan, N., & Carlson, J. J. (2005). Temperament, relationships, and young children's receptive cooperation with their parents. *Developmental Psychology, 41,* 648–660.

Kochanska, G., Aksan, N., & Joy, M. E. (2007). Children's fearfulness as a moderator of parenting in early socialization: Two longitudinal studies. *Developmental Psychology, 43,* 222–237.

Kochanska, G., Aksan, N., Knaack, A., & Rhines, H. M. (2004). Maternal parenting and children's conscience: Early security as moderator. *Child Development, 75,* 1229–1242.

Kochanska, G., Coy, K. C., & Murray, K. T. (2001). The development of self-regulation in the first four years of life. *Child Development, 72*(4), 1091–1111.

Kochanska, G., Friesenborg, A. E., Lange, L. A., & Martel, M. M. (2004). Parents' personality and infants' temperament as contibutors to their emerging relationship. *Journal of Personality and Social Psychology, 86,* 744–759.

Kochanska, G., Tjebkes, T. L., & Forman, D. R. (1998). Children's emerging regulation of conduct: Restraint, compliance, and internalization from infancy to the second year. *Child Development, 69*(5), 1378–1389.

Koechlin, E., Basso, G., Pietrini, P., Panzer, S., & Grafman, J. (1999). The role of the anterior prefrontal cortex in human cognition. *Nature, 399,* 148–151.

Koenig, H. G. (1994). *Aging and God.* New York: Haworth.

Kogan, M. D., Newacheck, P. W., Honberg, L., & Strickland, B. (2005). Association between underinsurance and access to care among children with special health care needs in the United States. *Pediatrics, 116,* 1162–1169.

Kohlberg, L. (1966). A cognitive-developmental analysis of children's sex role concepts and attitudes. In E. E. Maccoby (Ed.), *The development of sex differences.* Stanford, CA: Stanford University Press.

Kohlberg, L. (1969). Stage and sequence: The cognitive-developmental approach to socialization. In D. A. Goslin (Ed.), *Handbook of socialization theory and research.* Chicago: Rand McNally.

Kohlberg, L. (1973). Continuities in childhood and adult moral development revisited. In P. Baltes & K. W. Schaie (Eds.), *Lifespan developmental psychology: Personality and socialization* (pp. 180–207). New York: Academic Press.

Kohlberg, L. (1981). *Essays on moral development.* San Francisco: Harper & Row.

Kohlberg, L., & Gilligan, C. (1971, Fall). The adolescent as a philosopher: The discovery of the self in a postconventional world. *Daedalus,* pp. 1051–1086.

Kohlberg, L., & Ryncarz, R. A. (1990). Beyond justice reasoning: Moral development and consideration of a seventh stage. In C. N. Alexander & E. J. Langer (Eds.), *Higher stages of human development* (pp. 191–207). New York: Oxford University Press.

Kohlberg, L., Yaeger, J., & Hjertholm, E. (1968). Private speech: Four studies and a review of theories. *Child Development, 39,* 691–736.

Kohn, M. L. (1980). Job complexity and adult personality. In N. J. Smelser & E. H. Erikson (Eds.), *Themes of work and love in adulthood.* Cambridge, MA: Harvard University Press.

Kohn, M. L., & Schooler, C. (1983). The cross-national universality of the interpretive model. In M. L. Kohn & C. Schooler (Eds.), *Work and personality: An inquiry into the impact of social stratification* (pp. 281–295). Norwood, NJ: Ablex.

Koivula, I., Sten, M., & Makela, P. H. (1999). Prognosis after community-acquired pneumonia in the elderly. *Archives of Internal Medicine, 159,* 1550–1555.

Kolata, G. (1999, March 9). Pushing limits of the human life span. *New York Times.* Retrieved from www.nytimes.com/library/national/science/030999sci-aging.html.

Kolata, G. (2003, February 18). Using genetic tests, Ashkenazi Jews vanquish a disease. *New York Times,* pp. D1, D6.

Kolbert, E. (1994, January 11). Canadians curbing TV violence. *New York Times,* pp. C15, C19.

Kopp, C. B. (1982). Antecedents of self-regulation. *Developmental Psychology, 18,* 199–214.

Koren, G., Pastuszak, A., & Ito, S. (1998). Drugs in pregnancy. *New England Journal of Medicine, 338,* 1128–1137.

Korner, A. (1996). Reliable individual differences in preterm infants' excitation management. *Child Development, 67,* 1793–1805.

Korner, A. F., Zeanah, C. H., Linden, J., Berkowitz, R. I., Kraemer, H. C., & Agras, W. S. (1985). The relationship between neonatal and later activity and temperament. *Child Development, 56,* 38–42.

Koropeckyj-Cox, T. (2002). Beyond parental status: Psychological well-being in middle and old age. *Journal of Marriage and Family, 64,* 957–971.

Koropeckyj-Cox, T., Pienta, A. M., & Brown, T. H. (2007). Women of the 1950s and the "normative" life course: The implications of childlessness, fertility timing, and marital status for psychological well-being in late midlife. *International Journal of Aging and Human Development, 64*(4), 299–330.

Korte, D., & Scaer, R. (1984). *A good birth, a safe birth.* New York: Bantam Books.

Kosnik, W., Winslow, L., Kline, D., Rasinski, K., & Sekuler, R. (1988). Visual changes in daily life throughout adulthood. *Journal of Gerontology: Psychological Sciences, 43*(3), P63–P70.

Kosterman, R., Graham, J. W., Hawkins, J. D., Catalano, R. F., & Herrenkohl, T. I. (2001). Childhood risk factors for persistence of violence in the transition to adulthood: A social development perspective. *Violence & Victims. Special Issue: Developmental Perspectives on Violence and Victimization, 16*(4), 355–369.

Kovas, Y., Hayiou-Thomas, M. E., Dale, P. S., Bishop, D. V. M., & Plomin, R. (2005). Genetic influences in different aspects of language development: The etiology of language skills in 4.5-year-old twins. *Child Development, 76,* 632–651.

Kowal, A. K., & Pike, L. B. (2004). Sibling influences on adolescents' attitudes toward safe sex practices. *Family Relations, 53,* 377–384.

Kozlowska, K., & Hanney, L. (1999). Family assessment and intervention using an interactive art exercise. *Australia and New Zealand Journal of Family Therapy, 20*(2), 61–69.

Kramer, A. F., Hahn, S., McAuley, E., Cohen, N. J., Banich, M. T., Harrison, C., Chason, J., Boileau, R. A., Bardell, L., Colcombe, A., & Vakil, E. (1999). Ageing, fitness and neurocognitive function. *Nature, 400,* 418–419.

Kramer, D. A. (2003). The ontogeny of wisdom in its variations. In J. Demick & C. Andreolett (Eds.), *Handbook of adult development* (pp. 131–151). New York: Plenum Press.

Kramer, L., & Kowal, A. K. (2005). Sibling relationship quality from birth to adolescence: The enduring contributions of friends. *Journal of Family Psychology, 19,* 503–511.

Kramer, M. S., Aboud, F., Mironova, E., Vanilovich, I., Platt, R. W., Matush, L., Igumnov, S., Fombonne, E., Bogdanovich, N., Ducruet, T., Collet, J-P., Chalmers, B., Hodnett, E., Davidovsky, S., Skugarevsky, O., Trofimovich, O., Kozlova, L., & Shaprio, S., for the Promotion of Breastfeeding Intervention Trial (PROBIT) Study Group. (2008). Breastfeeding and child cognitive development: New evidence from a large randomized trial. *Archives of General Psychiatry, 65*(5), 578–584.

Kramer, M. S., Chalmers, B., Hodnett, E. D., Sevkovskaya, Z., Dzikovich, I., Shapiro, S., Collet, J.-P., Vanilovich, I., Ducruet, T., Shishko, G., Zubovich, V., Mknuik, D., Gluchanina, E., Dombrovskiy, V., Ustinovich, N., Ovchinikova, L., & Helsing, E., for the PROBIT Study Group. (2001). Promotion of Breastfeeding Intervention Trial (PROBIT): A randomized trial in the Republic of Belarus. *Journal of the American Medical Association, 285,* 413–420.

Krashen, S., & McField, G. 2005. What works? Reviewing the latest evidence on bilingual education. *Language Learner 1*(2): 7–10, 34.

Krause, N. (2004a). Common facets of religion, unique facets of religion, and life satisfaction among older African Americans. *Journal of Gerontology: Social Sciences, 59B,* S109–S117.

Krause, N. (2004b). Lifetime trauma, emotional support, and life satisfaction among older adults. *Gerontologist, 44,* 615–623.

Krause, N., & Rook, K. S. (2003). Negative interaction in late life: Issues in the stability and generalizability of conflict across relationships. *Journal of Gerontology: Psychological Sciences, 58B,* P88–P99.

Krause, N., & Shaw, B. A. (2000). Role-specific feelings of control and mortality. *Psychology and Aging, 15,* 617–626.

Kreicbergs, U., Valdimarsdóttir, U., Onelov, E., Henter, J., & Steineck, G. (2004). Talking about death with children who have severe malignant disease. *New England Journal of Medicine, 351,* 1175–1253.

Kreider, R. M. (2003). Adopted children and stepchildren: 2000. *Census 2000 Special Reports.* Washington, DC: U.S. Bureau of the Census.

Kreider, R. M. (2005). Number, timing, and duration of marriages and divorces: 2001. *Household Economic Studies* (P70-97). Washington, DC: U.S. Census Bureau.

Kreider, R. M., & Fields, J. (2005). Living arrangements of children: 2001. *Current Population Reports* (P70-104). Washington, DC: U.S. Census Bureau.

Kreider, R. M., & Fields, J. M. (2002). Number, timing, and duration of marriages and divorces: Fall 1996. *Current Population Reports* (P70-80). Washington, DC: U.S. Census Bureau.

Kreutzer, M., Leonard, C., & Flavell, J. (1975). An interview study of children's knowledge about memory. *Monographs of the Society for Research in Child Development, 40*(1, Serial No. 159).

Krevans, J., & Gibbs, J. C. (1996). Parents' use of inductive discipline: Relations to children's empathy and prosocial behavior. *Child Development, 67,* 3263–3277.

Kringelbach, M. L., Lehtonen A., Squire, S., Harvey, A. G., Crashke, M.G., Holliday, I. E., Green, A. L., Aziz, T. Z., Hansen, P. C., Cornelissen, P. L., & Stein, A. (2008). A specific and rapid neural signature for parental instinct. *PLoS ONE, 3*(2), e1664. (DOI: journal.pone.0001664).

Krishnamoorthy, J. S., Hart, C., & Jelalian, E. (2006). The epidemic of childhood obesity: Review of research and implications for public policy. *Society for Research in Child Development (SRCD) Social Policy Report, 20*(2).

Kritchevsky, S. B., Nicklas, B. J., Visser, M., Simonsick, E. M., Newman, A. B., Harris, T. B., Lange, E. M., Penninx, B. W., Goodpaster, B. H., Satterfield, S., Colbert, L. H., Rubin, S. M., & Pahor, M. (2005). Angiotensin-converting enzyme insertion/deletion genotype, exercise, and physical decline. *Journal of the American Medical Association, 294,* 691–698.

Kroenke, K., & Spitzer, R. L. (1998). Gender differences in the reporting of physical and somatoform symptoms. *Psychosomatic Medicine, 60,* 50–155.

Kroger, J. (1993). Ego identity: An overview. In J. Kroger (Ed.), *Discussions on ego identity* (pp. 1–20). Hillsdale, NJ: Erlbaum.

Kroger, J. (2003). Identity development during adolescence. In G. R. Adams & M. D. Berzonsky (Eds.), *Blackwell handbook of adolescence* (pp. 205–226). Malden, MA: Blackwell.

Kroger, J., & Haslett, S. J. (1991). A comparison of ego identity status transition pathways and change rates across five identity domains. *International Journal of Aging and Human Development, 32,* 303–330.

Krueger, A. B. (2003, February). Economic considerations and class size. *Economic Journal, 113,* F34–F63.

Krueger, A. B., & Whitmore, D. M. (April 2000). The effect of attending a small class in the early grades on college-test taking and middle school test results: Evidence from Project STAR (NBER Working Paper No. W7656).

Kübler-Ross, E. (1969). *On death and dying.* New York: Macmillan.

Kübler-Ross, E. (1970). *On death and dying* [Paperback]. New York: Macmillan.

Kübler-Ross, E. (Ed.). (1975). *Death: The final stage of growth.* Englewood Cliffs, NJ: Prentice-Hall.

Kuczmarski, R. J., Ogden, C. L., Grummer-Strawn, L. M., Flegal, K. M., Guo, S. S., Wei, R., Mei, Z., Curtin, L. R., Roche, A. F., & Johnson, C. L. (2000). CDC growth charts: United States. *Advance Data,* No. 314. Centers for Disease Control and Prevention, U.S. Department of Health and Human Services.

Kuczynski, L., & Kochanska, G. (1995). Function and content of maternal demands: Developmental significance of early demands for competent action. *Child Development, 66,* 616–628.

Kuh, D., Hardy, R., Butterworth, S., Okell, L., Wadsworth, M., Cooper, C., & Sayer, A. A. (2006). Developmental origins of midlife grip strength: Findings from a birth cohort study. *Journal of Gerontology: Medical Sciences, 61A,* 702–706.

Kuhl, P. K. (2004). Early language acquisition: Cracking the speech code. *Nature Reviews Neuroscience, 5,* 831–843.

Kuhl, P. K., Andruski, J. E., Chistovich, I. A., Chistovich, L. A., Kozhevnikova, E. V., Ryskina, V. L., Stolyarova, E. I., Sundberg, U., & Lacerda, F. (1997). Cross-language analysis of phonetic units in language addressed to infants. *Science, 277,* 684–686.

Kuhl, P. K., Conboy, B. T., Padden, D., Nelson, T., & Pruitt, J. (2005). Early speech perception and later language development: Implications for the "critical period." *Language Learning and Development, 1,* 237–264.

Kuhl, P. K., Williams, K. A., Lacerda, F., Stevens, K. N., & Lindblom, B. (1992). Linguistic experience alters phonetic perception in infants by 6 months of age. *Science, 255,* 606–608.

Kuhn, D. (2006). Do cognitive changes accompany developments in the adolescent brain? *Perspectives on Psychological Science, 1,* 59–67.

Kuhn, D., & Dean, D. (2005). Is developing scientific thinking all about learning to control variables? *Psychological Science, 16,* 866–870.

Kung, H.-C., Hoyert, D. L., Xu, J., & Murphy, S. L. (2007, September). Deaths: Preliminary data for 2005. *Health E-Stats.* Retrieved February 22, 2008, from www.cdc.gov/nchs/products/pubs/pubd/hestats/prelimdeaths05/prelimdeaths05.htm.

Kung, H.-C., Hoyert, D. L., Xu, J., & Murphy, S. L. (2008). Deaths: Final data for 2005. *National Vital Statistics Reports, 56*(10). Hyattsville, MD: National Center for Health Statistics.

Kuperman, S., Chan, G., Kramer, J. R., Bierut, L., Buckholz, K. K., Fox, L., Hesslebrock, V., Numberger, V. I., Jr., Reich, T., Reich, W., & Schuckit, M. A. (2005). Relationship of age of first drink to child behavioral problems and family psychopathology. *Alcoholism: Clinical and Experimental Research, 29*(10), 1869–1876.

Kupersmidt, J. B., & Coie, J. D. (1990). Preadolescent peer status, aggression, and school adjustment as predictors of externalizing problems in adolescence. *Child Development, 61,* 1350–1362.

Kurdek, L. A. (2004). Are gay and lesbian cohabiting couples really different from heterosexual married couples? *Journal of Marriage and Family, 66,* 880–900.

Kurdek, L. A. (2005). What do we know about gay and lesbian couples? *Current Directions in Psychological Science, 5,* 251–254.

Kurdek, L. A. (2006). Differences between partners from heterosexual, gay, and lesbian cohabiting couples. *Journal of Marriage and Family, 68,* 509–528.

Kuther, T., & McDonald, E. (2004). Early adolescents' experiences with, and views of, Barbie. *Adolescence, 39,* 39–51.

Kutner, M., Greenberg, E., Jin, Y., Boyle, B., Hsu, Y., & Dunleavy, E. (2007). *Literacy in everyday life: Results from the 2003 National Assessment of Adult Literacy* (NCES 2007-480). Washington, DC: U.S. Department of Education, National Center for Education Statistics.

Kye, C., & Ryan, N. (1995). Pharmacologic treatment of child and adolescent depression. *Child and Adolescent Psychiatric Clinics of North America, 4,* 261–281.

Labarere, J., Gelbert-Baudino, N., Ayral, A. S., Duc, C., Berchotteau, M., Bouchon, N., Schelstraete, C., Vittoz, J.-P., Francois, P., & Pons, J.-C. (2005). Efficacy of breast-feeding support provided by trained clinicians during an early, routine, preventive visit: A prospective, randomized, open trial of 226 mother-infant pairs. *Pediatrics, 115,* e139–e146.

Laberge, L., Tremblay, R. E., Vitaro, F., & Montplaisir, J. (2000). Development of parasomnias from childhood to early adolescence. *Pediatrics, 106,* 67–74.

Labouvie-Vief, G. (1990a). Modes of knowledge and the organization of development. In M. L. Commons, C. Armon, L. Kohlberg, F. Richards, T. Grotzer, & J. Sinnott (Eds.), *Adult development: Vol. 2. Models and methods in the study of adult and adolescent thought* (pp. 43–62). New York: Praeger.

Labouvie-Vief, G. (1990b). Wisdom as integrated thought: Historical and development perspectives. In R. J. Sternberg (Ed.), *Wisdom: Its nature, origins, and development* (pp. 52–83). Cambridge, England: Cambridge University Press.

Labouvie-Vief, G. (2006). Emerging structures of adult thought. In J. J. Arnett & J. L. Tanner (Eds.), *Emerging adults in America: Coming of age in the 21st century* (pp. 59–84). Washington, DC: American Psychological Association.

Labov, T. (1992). Social and language boundaries among adolescents. *American Speech, 67,* 339–366.

Lacey, J. V., Jr., Mink, P. J., Lubin, J. H., Sherman, M. E., Troisi, R., Hartge, P.,

Schatzkin, A., & Schairer, C. (2002). Menopausal hormone replacement therapy and risk of ovarian cancer. *Journal of the American Medical Association, 288,* 334–341.

Lachman, J. L., & Lachman, R. (1980). Age and the actualization of knowledge. In L. W. Poon, J. L. Fozard, L. S. Cermak, D. Arenberg, & L. W. Thompson (Eds.), *New directions in memory and aging* (pp. 313–343). Hillsdale, NJ: Erlbaum.

Lachman, M. E. (2001). Introduction. In M. E. Lachman (Ed.), *Handbook of midlife development.* New York: Wiley.

Lachman, M. E. (2004). Development in midlife. *Annual Review of Psychology, 55,* 305–331.

Lachman, M. E., & Firth, K. M. P. (2004). The adaptive value of feeling in control during midlife. In O. G. Brim, C. D. Ryff, & R. C. Kessler (Eds.), *How healthy are we? A national study of well-being at midlife.* (pp. 320–349). Chicago: University of Chicago Press.

Lachman, M. E., & James, J. B. (1997). Charting the course of midlife development: An overview. In M. E. Lachman & J. B. James (Eds.), *Multiple paths of midlife development* (pp. 1–17). Chicago: University of Chicago Press.

Lachman, M. E., & Weaver, S. L. (1998). Sociodemographic variations in the sense of control by domain: Findings from the MacArthur Studies of Midlife. *Psychology and Aging, 13,* 553–562.

LaFontana, K. M., & Cillessen, A. H. N. (2002). Children's perceptions of popular and unpopular peers: A multi-method assessment. *Developmental Psychology, 38,* 635–647.

Lagattuta, K. H. (2005). When you shouldn't do what you want to do: Young children's understanding of desires, rules, and emotions. *Child Development, 76,* 713–733.

Lagercrantz, H., & Slotkin, T. A. (1986). The "stress" of being born. *Scientific American, 254*(4), 100–107.

Laible, D. J., & Thompson, R. A. (1998). Attachment and emotional understanding in preschool children. *Developmental Psychology, 34*(5), 1038–1045.

Laible, D. J., & Thompson, R. A. (2002). Mother-child conflict in the toddler years: Lessons in emotion, morality, and relationships. *Child Development, 73,* 1187–1203.

Laird, J., DeBell, M., Kienzl, G., & Chapman, C. (2007). *Dropout rates in the United States: 2005* (NCES 2007-059). Retrieved June 28, 2007, from http://nces.ed.gov/pubsearch/pubsinfo.asp?pubid=2007059.

Laird, J., Lew, S., DeBell, M., & Chapman, C. (2006). *Dropout rates in the United States: 2002 and 2003* (NCES 2006-062). Washington, DC: U. S. Department of Education, National Center for Education Statistics.

Laird, R. D., Pettit, G. S., Bates, J. E., & Dodge, K. A. (2003). Parents' monitoring relevant knowledge and adolescents' delinquent behavior: Evidence of correlated developmental changes and reciprocal influences. *Child Development, 74,* 752–768.

Lalonde, C. E., & Werker, J. F. (1995). Cognitive influences on cross-language speech perception in infancy. *Infant Behavior and Development, 18,* 459–475.

Lamason, R. L., Mohideen, M. A. P. K., Mest, J. R., Wong, A. C., Norton, H. L., Arcs, M. C., et al. (2005). SLC24A5, a putative cation exchanger, affects pigmentation in zebrafish and humans. *Science, 310,* 1782–1786.

Lamb, M. E. (1981). The development of father-infant relationships. In M. E. Lamb (Ed.), *The role of the father in child development* (2nd ed.). New York: Wiley.

Lamb, M. E., Frodi, A. M., Frodi, M., & Hwang, C. P. (1982). Characteristics of maternal and paternal behavior in traditional and non-traditional Swedish families. *International Journal of Behavior Development, 5,* 131–151.

Lamberg, L. (1997). "Old and gray and full of sleep"? Not always. *Journal of the American Medical Association, 278,* 1302–1304.

Lamberts, S. W. J., van den Beld, A. W., & van der Lely, A. (1997). The endocrinology of aging. *Science, 278,* 419–424.

Lambeth, G. S., & Hallett, M. (2002). Promoting healthy decision making in relationships: Developmental interventions with young adults on college and university campuses. In C. L. & D. R. Atkinson (Eds.), *Counseling across the lifespan: Prevention and treatment* (pp. 209–226). Thousand Oaks, CA: Sage.

Lamborn, S. D., Mounts, N. S., Steinberg, L., & Dornbusch, S. M. (1991). Patterns of competence and adjustment among adolescents from authoritative, authoritarian, indulgent, and neglectful families. *Child Development, 62,* 1049–1065.

Lamm, C., Zelazo, P. D., & Lewis, M. D. (2006) Neural correlates of cognitive control in childhood and adolescence: Disentangling the contributions of age and executive function. *Neuropsychologia, 44,* 2139–2148.

Landon, M. B., Hauth, J. C., Leveno, K. J., Spong, C. Y., Leindecker, S., Varner, M. W., Moawad, A. H., Caritis, S. N., Harper, M., Wapner, R. J., Sorokin, Y., Miodovnik, M., Carpenter, M., Peaceman, A. M., O'Sullivan, M. J., Sibai, B., Langer, O., Thorp, J. M., Ramin, S. M., Mercer, B. M., & Gabbe, S. G., for the National Institute of Child Health and Human Development Maternal-Fetal Medicine Units Network. (2004). Maternal and perinatal outcomes associated with a trial of labor after prior cesarean delivery. *New England Journal of Medicine, 351,* 2581–2589.

Landry, S. H., Smith, K. E., & Swank, P. R. (2006). Responsive parenting: Establishing early foundations for social, communication and independent problem-solving skills. *Developmental Psychology, 42,* 627–642.

Landy, F. J. (1992, February). *Research on the use of fitness tests for police and fire fighting jobs.* Paper presented at the second annual Scientific Psychology Forum of the American Psychological Association, Washington, DC.

Landy, F. J. (1994, July–August). Mandatory retirement age: Serving the public welfare? *Psychological Science Agenda* (Science Directorate, American Psychological Association), pp. 10–11, 20.

Lang, F. R. (2001). Regulation of social relationships in later adulthood. *Journal of Gerontology: Psychological and Social Sciences, 56B,* P321–P326.

Lang, F. R., & Carstensen, L. L. (1994). Close emotional relationships in late life: Further support for proactive aging in the social domain. *Psychology and Aging, 9,* 315–324.

Lang, F. R., & Carstensen, L. L. (1998). Social relationships and adaptation in later life. In A. S. Bellack & M. Hersen (Eds.), *Comprehensive clinical psychology* (pp. 55–72). Oxford: Pergamon Press.

Lang, F. R., Rieckmann, N., & Baltes, M. M. (2002). Adapting to aging losses: Do resources facilitate strategies of selection, compensation, and optimization in everyday functioning? *Journal of Gerontology: Psychological Sciences, 57B,* P501–P509.

Lange, G., MacKinnon, C. E., & Nida, R. E. (1989). Knowledge, strategy, and motivational contributions to preschool children's object recall. *Developmental Psychology, 25,* 772–779.

Långström, N., Rahman, Q., Carlström, E., & Lichtenstein, P. (2008). Genetic and environmental effects on same-sex sexual behavior: A population study of twins in Sweden. *Archives of Sexual Behavior.* Retrieved June 7, 2008, from https://commerce.metapress.com/content/2263646523551487/resource-secured/?target=fulltext.pdf&sid=ur4ndr55ssgnkk550wsdrbuz&sh=www.springerlink.-com. (DOI: 10.1007/s10508-008-9386-1)

Lanphear, B. P., Aligne, C. A., Auinger, P., Weitzman, M., & Byrd, R. S. (2001). Residential exposure associated with asthma in U.S. children. *Pediatrics, 107,* 505–511.

Lansford, J. E., Chang, L., Dodge, K. A., Malone, P. S., Oburu, P., Palmérus, K., Bacchini, D., Pastorelli, C., Bombi, A. S., Zelli, A., Tapanya, S., Chaudhary, N., Deater-Deckard, K., Manke, B., & Quinn, N. (2005). Physical discipline and children's adjustment: Cultural normativeness as a moderator. *Child Development, 76,* 1234–1246.

Lansford, J. E., Dodge, K. A., Pettit, G. S., Bates, J. E., Crozier, J., & Kaplow, J. (2002). A 12-year prospective study of the long-term effects of early child physical maltreatment on psychological, behavioral, and academic problems in adolescence. *Archives of Pediatric and Adolescent Medicine, 156*(8), 824–830.

Lansford, J. E., Malone, P. S., Castellino, D. R., Dodge, K. A., Pettit, G. S., & Bates, J. E. (2006). Trajectories of internalizing, externalizing, and grades for children who have and have not experienced their parents' divorce or separation. *Journal of Family Psychology, 20,* 292–301.

Lansford, J. E., Sherman, A. M., & Antonucci, T. C. (1998). Satisfaction with social networks: An examination of socioemotional selectivity. *Psychology and Aging, 13*(4), 544–552.

Lanting, C. I., Fidler, V., Huisman, M., Touwen, B. C. L., & Boersma, E. R. (1994). Neurological differences between 9-year-old children fed breastmilk or formula-milk as babies. *Lancet, 334,* 1319–1322.

Lapham, E. V., Kozma, C., & Weiss, J. O. (1996). Genetic discrimination: Perspectives of consumers. *Science, 274,* 621–624.

Laquatra, J., & Chi, P. S. K. (1998, September). *Housing for an aging-in-place society.* Paper presented at the European Network for Housing Research Conference, Cardiff, Wales.

Larsen, D. (1990, December–1991, January). Unplanned parenthood. *Modern Maturity,* pp. 32–36.

Larson, R., Mannell, R., & Zuzanek, J. (1986). Daily well-being of older adults with friends and family. *Psychology and Aging, 1*(2), 117–126.

Larson, R., & Seepersad, S. (2003). Adolescents' leisure time in the United States: Partying, sports, and the American experiment. In S. Verma and R. Larson (Eds.), *Examining adolescent leisure time across cultures: Developmental opportunities and risks.* (New Directions for Child and Adolescent Development, No. 99, pp. 53–64). San Francisco: Jossey-Bass.

Larson, R., & Wilson, S. (2004). Adolescents across place and time: Globalization and the changing pathways to adulthood. In R. M. Lerner & L. Steinberg (Eds.), *Handbook of adolescent psychology* (2nd ed., pp. 299–331). Hoboken, NJ: Wiley.

Larson, R. W. (1997). The emergence of solitude as a constructive domain of experience in early adolescence. *Child Development, 68,* 80–93.

Larson, R. W., Moneta, G., Richards, M. H., & Wilson, S. (2002). Continuity, stability, and change in daily emotional experience across adolescence. *Child Development, 73,* 1151–1165.

Larson, R. W., Richards, M. H., Moneta, G., Holmbeck, G., & Duckett, E. (1996). Changes in adolescents' daily interactions with their families from ages 10 to 18: Disengagement and transformation. *Developmental Psychology, 32,* 744–754.

Larson, R. W., & Verma, S. (1999). How children and adolescents spend time across the world: Work, play, and developmental opportunities. *Psychological Bulletin, 125,* 701–736.

Larzalere, R. E. (2000). Child outcomes of nonabusive and customary physical punishment by parents: An updated literature review. *Clinical Child and Family Psychology Review, 3,* 199–221.

Latimer, E. J. (1992, February). Euthanasia: A physician's reflections. *Ontario Medical Review,* pp. 21–29.

Laumann, E. O., Gagnon, J. H., Michael, R. T., & Michaels, S. (1994). *The social organization of sexuality: Sexual practices in the United States.* Chicago: University of Chicago Press.

Laumann, E. O., & Michael, R. T. (Eds.). (2000). *Sex, love, and health in America: Private choices and public policies.* Chicago: University of Chicago Press.

Launer, L. J., Andersen, K., Dewey, M. E., Letenneur, L., Ott, A., Amaducci, L. A., Brayne, C., Copeland, J. R.M., Dartigues, J.-F., Kragh-Sorensen, P., Lobo, A., Martinez-Lage, J. M., Stijnen, T., & Hofman, A. (1999). Rates and risk factors for dementia and Alzheimer's disease: Results from EURODEM pooled analyses. *Neurology, 52,* 78–84.

Laursen, B. (1996). Closeness and conflict in adolescent peer relationships: Interdependence with friends and romantic partners. In W. M. Bukowski, A. F. Newcomb, & W. W. Hartup (Eds.), *The company they keep: Friendship in childhood and adolescence* (pp. 186–210). New York: Cambridge University Press.

Lavee, Y., & Ben-Ari, A. (2004). Emotional expressiveness and neuroticism: Do they predict marital quality? *Journal of Marriage and Family, 18,* 620–627.

Lavelli, M., & Fogel, A. (2005). Developmental changes in the relationship between the infant's attention and emotion during early face-to-face communication: The 2-month transition. *Developmental Psychology, 41,* 265–280.

Lavie, C. J., Kuruvanka, T., Milani, R. V., Prasad, A., & Ventura, H. O. (2004). Exercise capacity in adult African-Americans referred for exercise stress testing: Is fitness affected by race? *Chest, 126,* 1962–1968.

Lawn, J. E., Cousens, S., & Zupan, J., for the Lancet Neonatal Survival Steering Team. (2005). 4 million neonatal deaths: When? Where? Why? *Lancet, 365,* 891–900.

Layne, J. E., & Nelson, M. E. (1999). The effects of progressive resistance training on bone density: A review. *Medicine and Science in Sports and Exercise, 31,* 25–30.

Lazarus, R. S., & Folkman, S. (1984). *Stress, appraisal, and coping.* New York: Springer.

Le Bourdais, C., & LaPierre-Adamcyk, E. (2004). Changes in conjugal life in Canada: Is cohabitation progressively replacing marriage? *Journal of Marriage and Family, 66,* 929–942.

Leaper, C., Anderson, K. J., & Sanders, P. (1998). Moderators of gender effects on parents' talk to their children: A meta-analysis. *Developmental Psychology, 34*(1), 3–27.

Leaper, C., & Smith, T. E. (2004). A meta-analytic review of gender variations in children's language use: Talkativeness, affiliative speech, and assertive speech. *Developmental Psychology, 40,* 993–1027.

Leblanc, M., & Ritchie, M. (2001). A meta-analysis of play therapy outcomes. *Counseling Psychology Quarterly, 14,* 149–163.

Lecanuet, J. P., Granier-Deferre, C., & Busnel, M.-C. (1995). Human fetal auditory perception. In J. P. Lecanuet, W. P. Fifer, N. A. Krasnegor, & W. P. Smotherman (Eds.), *Fetal development: A psychobiological perspective* (pp. 239–262). Hillsdale, NJ: Erlbaum.

Lee, G. M., Gortmaker, S. L., McIntosh, K., Hughes, M. D., Oleske, J. M., & Pediatric AIDS Clinical Trials Group Protocol 219C Team. (2006). Quality of life for children and adolescents: Impact of HIV infection and antiretroviral treatment. *Pediatrics, 117,* 273–283.

Lee, G. R., Netzer, J. K., & Coward, R. T. (1995). Depression among older parents: The role of intergenerational exchange. *Journal of Marriage and Family, 57,* 823–833.

Lee, J. M., Appugliese, D., Kaciroti, N., Corwyn, R. F., Bradley, R., & Lumeng, J. C. (2007). Weight status in young girls and the onset of puberty. *Pediatrics, 119,* e624–e630.

Lee, R. D. (2003). Rethinking the evolutionary theory of aging: Transfers, not births, shape senescence in social species. *Proceedings of the National Academy of Sciences, 100,* 9637–9642.

Lee, S. J., Ralston, H. J. P., Drey, E. A., Partridge, J. C., & Rosen, M. A. (2005). Fetal pain: A systematic multidisciplinary review of the evidence. *Journal of the American Medical Association, 294,* 947–954.

Lefkowitz, E. S., & Fingerman, K. L. (2003). Positive and negative emotional feelings and behaviors in mother-daughter ties in late life. *Journal of Family Psychology, 17,* 607–617.

Lefkowitz, E. S., & Gillen, M. M. (2006). "Sex is just a normal part of life": Sexuality in emerging adulthood. In J. J. Arnett & J. L. Tanner (Eds.), *Emerging adults in America: Coming of age in the 21st century* (pp. 235–255). Washington, DC: American Psychological Association.

Legerstee, M., & Varghese, J. (2001). The role of maternal affect mirroring on social expectancies in three-month-old infants. *Child Development, 72,* 1301–1313.

Leibel, R. L. (1997). And finally, genes for human obesity. *Nature Genetics, 16,* 218–220.

Leigh, B. C. (1999). Peril, chance, adventure: Concepts of risk, alcohol use, and risky behavior in young adults. *Addiction, 94*(3), 371–383.

Leman, P. J., Ahmed, S., & Ozarow, L. (2005). Gender, gender relations, and the social dynamics of children's conversations. *Developmental Psychology, 41,* 64–74.

Lemke, M., Miller, D., Johnson, J., Krenze, T., Alvarez-Rojas, L., Kastberg, D., & Jocelyn, L. (2005). *Highlights from the 2003 International Adult Literacy and Lifeskills Survey (ALL) Revised* (NCES 2005-117). Washington, DC: National Center for Education Statistics.

Lemke, M., Sen, A., Pahlke, E., Partelow, L., Miller, D., Williams, T., Kastberg, D., & Jocelyn, L. (2004). *International outomes of learning in mathematics literacy and problem solving: PISA 2003. Results from the U.S. Perspective* (NCES 2005-003). Washington, DC: National Center for Education Statistics.

Lemon, B., Bengtson, V., & Peterson, J. (1972). An exploration of the activity theory of aging: Activity types and life satisfaction among in-movers to a retirement community. *Journal of Gerontology, 27*(4), 511–523.

Lenneberg, E. H. (1967). *Biological functions of language.* New York: Wiley.

Lenneberg, E. H. (1969). On explaining language. *Science, 164*(3880), 635–643.

Lenroot, R. K., & Giedd, J. N. (2006). Brain development in children and adolescents: Insights from anatomical magnetic resonance imaging. *Neuroscience and Biobehavioral Reviews, 30*(6), 718–729.

Leone, J. M., Johnson, M. P., Cohan, C. L., & Lloyd, S. E. (2004). Consequences of male partner violence for low-income minority women. *Journal of Marriage and Family, 66*, 472–490.

Lerman, C., Caporaso, N. E., Audrain, J., Main, D., Bowman, E. D., Lockshin, B., Boyd, N. R., & Shields, P. G. (1999). Evidence suggesting the role of specific genetic factors in cigarette smoking. *Health Psychology, 18*, 14–20.

Lesch, K. P., Bengel, D., Heils, A., Sabol, S. Z., Greenberg, B. D., Petri, S., Benjamin, J., Müller, C. R., Hamer, D. H., & Murphy, D. L. (1996). Association of anxiety-related traits with a polymorphism in the serotonin transporter gene regulatory region. *Science, 274*, 1527–1531.

Lesgold, A., Glaser, R., Rubinson, H., Klopfer, D., Feltovich, P., & Wang, Y. (1988). Expertise in a complex skill: Diagnosing X-ray pictures. In M. T. H. Chi, R. Glaser, & M. J. Farr (Eds.), *The Nature of Expertise* (pp. 311–342). Hillsdale, NJ: Erlbaum.

Lesgold, A. M. (1983). *Expert systems.* Paper represented at the Cognitive Science Meetings, Rochester, NY.

Leslie, A. M. (1982). The perception of causality in infants. *Perception, 11*, 173–186.

Leslie, A. M. (1984). Spatiotemporal continuity and the perception of causality in infants. *Perception, 13*, 287–305.

Leslie, L. K., Newman, T. B., Chesney, J., & Perrin, J. M. (2005). The Food and Drug Administration's deliberations on antidepressant use in pediatric patients. *Pediatrics, 116*, 195–204.

Lester, B. M., & Boukydis, C. F. Z. (1985). *Infant crying: Theoretical and research perspectives.* New York: Plenum Press.

LeVay, S. (1991). A difference in hypothalamic structure between heterosexual and homosexual men. *Science, 253*, 1034–1037.

Levenstein, S., Ackerman, S., Kiecolt-Glaser, J. K., & Dubois, A. (1999). Stress and peptic ulcer disease. *Journal of the American Medical Association, 281*, 10–11.

Levine, J. A., Emery, C. R., & Pollack, H. (2007). The well-being of children born to teen mothers. *Journal of Marriage and Family, 69*, 105–122.

Levine, R. (1980). Adulthood among the Gusii of Kenya. In N. J. Smelser & E. H. Erikson (Eds.), *Themes of work and love in adulthood* (pp. 77–104). Cambridge, MA: Harvard University Press.

LeVine, R. A. (1974). Parental goals: A cross-cultural view. *Teachers College Record, 76*, 226–239.

LeVine, R. A. (1989). Human parental care: Universal goals, cultural strategies, individual behavior. In R. A. LeVine, P. M. Miller, & M. M. West (Eds.), *Parental behavior in diverse societies* (pp. 3–12). San Francisco: Jossey-Bass.

LeVine, R. A. (1994). *Child care and culture: Lessons from Africa.* Cambridge, England: Cambridge University Press.

LeVine, R. A., & LeVine, S. (1998). Fertility and maturity in Africa: Gusii parents in middle adulthood. In R. A. Schweder (Ed.), *Welcome to middle age! (and other cultural fictions)* (189–207). Chicago: University of Chicago Press.

Levine, S. C., Vasilyeva, M., Lourenco, S. E., Newcombe, N. S., & Huttenlocher, J. (2005). Socioeconimic status modifies the sex differences in spatial skills. *Psychological Science, 16*, 841–845.

Levinson, D. (1978). *The seasons of a man's life.* New York: Knopf.

Levinson, D. (1980). Toward a conception of the adult life course. In N. J. Smelser & E. H. Erikson (Eds.), *Themes of work and love in adulthood* (pp. 265–290). Cambridge, MA: Harvard University Press.

Levinson, D. (1986). A conception of adult development. *American Psychologist, 41*, 3–13.

Levinson, D. (1996). *The seasons of a woman's life.* New York: Knopf.

Leviton, A., & Cowan, L. (2002). A review of the literature relating caffeine consumption by women to their risk of reproductive hazards. *Food and Chemical Toxicology, 40*(9), 1271–1310.

Levron, J., Aviram, A., Madgar, I., Livshits, A., Raviv, G., Bider, D., Hourwitz, A., Barkai, G., Goldman, B., & Mashiach, S. (1998, October). *High rate of chromosomal aneupoloidies in testicular spermatozoa retrieved from azoospermic patients undergoing testicular sperm extraction for in vitro fertilization.* Paper presented at the 16th World Congress on Fertility and Sterility and the 54th annual meeting of the American Society for Reproductive Medicine, San Francisco.

Levy, B. R. (2003). Mind matters: Cognitive and physical effects of aging self-stereotypes. *Journal of Gerontology: Psychological Sciences, 58B*, P203–P211.

Levy-Shiff, R., Zoran, N., & Shulman, S. (1997). International and domestic adoption: Child, parents, and family adjustment. *International Journal of Behavioral Development, 20*, 109–129.

Lewin, T. (2007, May 22). Out of grief grows desire for birth certificates for stillborn babies. *New York Times,* p. A16.

Lewinsohn, P. M., Gotlib, I. H., Lewinsohn, M., Seeley, J. R., & Allen, N. B. (1998). Gender differences in anxiety disorders and anxiety symptoms in adolescence. *Journal of Abnormal Psychology, 107*, 109–117.

Lewis, B. H., Legato, M., & Fisch, H. (2006). Medical implications of the male biological clock. *Journal of the American Medical Association, 19*, 2369–2371.

Lewis, M. (1995). Self-conscious emotions. *American Scientist, 83*, 68–78.

Lewis, M. (1997). The self in self-conscious emotions. In S. G. Snodgrass & R. L. Thompson (Eds.), *The self across psychology: Self-recognition, self-awareness, and the self-concept: Vol. 818. Annals of the New York Academy of Sciences.* New York: New York Academy of Sciences.

Lewis, M. (1998). Emotional competence and development. In D. Pushkar, W. Bukowski, A. E. Schwartzman, D. M. Stack, & D. R. White (Eds.), *Improving competence across the lifespan* (pp. 27–36). New York: Plenum Press.

Lewis, M., & Brooks, J. (1974). Self, other, and fear: Infants' reaction to people. In H. Lewis & L. Rosenblum (Eds.), *The origins of fear: The origins of behavior* (Vol. 2). New York: Wiley.

Lewis, M. I., & Butler, R. N. (1974). Life-review therapy: Putting memories to work in individual and group psychotherapy. *Geriatrics, 29*, 165–173.

Lewit, E., & Kerrebrock, N. (1997). Population-based growth stunting. *Future of Children, 7*(2), 149–156.

Li, J., Laursen, T. M., Precht, D. H., Olsen, J., & Mortensen, P. B. (2005). Hospitalization for mental illness among parents after the death of a child. *New England Journal of Medicine, 352*, 1190–1196.

Li, J., Precht, D. H., Mortensen, P. B., & Olsen, J. (2003). Mortality in parents after death of a child in Denmark: A nationwide follow-up study. *Lancet, 361*, 363–367.

Li, R., Chase, M., Jung, S., Smith, P. J. S., & Loeken, M. R. (2005). Hypoxic stress in diabetic pregnancy contributes to impaired embryo gene expression and defective development by inducing oxidative stress. *American Journal of Physiology: Endocrinology and Metabolism, 289*, 591–599.

Li, X., Li, S., Ulusoy, E., Chen, W., Srinivasan, S. R., & Berenson, G. S. (2004). Childhood adiposity as a predictor of cardiac mass in adulthood. *Circulation, 110*, 3488–3492.

Liberman, I. Y., & Liberman, A. M. (1990). Whole language vs. code emphasis: Underlying assumptions and their implications for reading instruction. *Annals of Dyslexia, 40,* 51–76.

Lickliter, R., & Honeycutt, H. (2003). Developmental dynamics: Toward a biologically plausible evolutionary psychology. *Psychological Bulletin, 129,* 819–835.

Lickona, T. (Ed.). (1976). *Moral development and behavior.* New York: Holt.

Lieberman, M. (1996). *Doors close, doors open: Widows, grieving and growing.* New York: Putnam.

Liebman, B. (1995, June). A meat & potatoes man. *Nutrition Action Health Letter, 22*(5), 6–7.

Light, K. C., Girdler, S. S., Sherwood, A., Bragdon, E. E., Brownley, K. A., West, S. G., & Hinderliter, A. L. (1999). High stress responsivity predicts later blood pressure only in combination with positive family history and high life stress. *Hypertension, 33,* 1458–1464.

Light, L. L. (1990). Interactions between memory and language in old age. In J. E. Birren & K. W. Schaie (Eds.), *Handbook of the psychology of aging* (pp. 275–290). San Diego: Academic Press.

Lillard, A., & Curenton, S. (1999). Do young children understand what others feel, want, and know? *Young Children, 54*(5), 52–57.

Lin, I., Goldman, N., Weinstein, M., Lin, Y., Gorrindo, T., & Seeman, T. (2003). Gender differences in adult childrens' support of their parents in Taiwan. *Journal of Marriage and Family, 65,* 184–200.

Lin, S., Hwang, S. A., Marshall, E. G., & Marion, D. (1998). Does paternal occupational lead exposure increase the risks of low birth weight or prematurity? *American Journal of Epidemiology, 148,* 173–181.

Lin, S. S., & Kelsey, J. L. (2000). Use of race and ethnicity in epidemiological research: Concepts, methodological issues, and suggestions for research. *Epidemiologic Reviews, 22*(2), 187–202.

Lin, Y., Seroude, L., & Benzer, S. (1998). Extended life-span and stress resistance in the Drosophila mutant methuselah. *Science, 282,* 943–946.

Lindau, S. T., Schumm, P., Laumann, E. O., Levinson, W., O'Muircheartaigh, C. A., & Waite, L. J. (2007). A study of sexuality and health among older adults in the United States. *New England Journal of Medicine, 357,* 762–774.

Lindbergh, Anne Morrow (1955). *Gift from the sea.* New York: Pantheon Books.

Linder, K. (1990). *Functional literacy projects and project proposals: Selected examples.* Paris: United Nations Educational, Scientific, and Cultural Organization.

Lindsay, R., Gallagher, J. C., Kleerekoper, M., & Pickar, J. H. (2002). Effect of lower doses of conjugated equine estrogens with and without medroxyprogesterone acetate on bone in early postmenopausal women. *Journal of the American Medical Association, 287,* 2668–2676.

Linnet, K. M., Wisborg, K., Obel, C., Secher, N. J., Thomsen, P. H., Agerbo, E., & Henriksen, T. B. (2005). Smoking during pregnancy and the risk of hyperkinetic disorder in offspring. *Pediatrics, 116,* 462–467.

Lissau, I., Overpeck, M. D., Ruan, J., Due, P., Holstein, B. E., Hediger, M. L., & Health Behaviours in School-Aged Children Obesity Working Group. (2004). Body mass index and overweight in adolescents in 13 European countries, Israel, and the United States. *Archives of Pediatric and Adolescent Medicine, 158,* 27–33.

Liszkowski, U., Carpenter, M., Striano, T., & Tomasello, M. (2006). 12- and 18-month-olds point to provide information for others. *Journal of Cognition and Development, 7,* 173–187.

Littleton, H., Breitkopf, C., & Berenson, A. (2006, August 13). *Correlates of anxiety symptoms during pregnancy and association with perinatal outcomes: A meta-analysis.* Presentation at the 114th annual convention of the American Psychological Association, New Orleans.

Liu, J., Raine, A., Venables, P. H., Dalais, C., and Mednick, S. A. (2003). Malnutrition at age 3 years and lower cognitive ability at age 11 years. *Archives of Pediatric and Adolescent Medicine, 157,* 593–600.

Lloyd, J. J., & Anthony, J. C. (2003). Hanging out with the wrong crowd: How much difference can parents make in an urban environment? *Journal of Urban Health, 80,* 383–399.

Lloyd, T., Andon, M. B., Rollings, N., Martel, J. K., Landis, J. R., Demers, L. M., Eggli, D. F., Kieselhorst, K., & Kulin, H. E. (1993). Calcium supplementation and bone mineral density in adolescent girls. *Journal of the American Medical Association, 270,* 841–844.

Lock, A., Young, A., Service, V., & Chandler, P. (1990). Some observations on the origin of the pointing gesture. In V. Volterra & C. J. Erting (Eds.), *From gesture to language in hearing and deaf children.* New York: Springer.

Lock, M. (1994). Menopause in cultural context. *Experimental Gerontology, 29,* 307–317.

Lock, M. (1998). Deconstructing the change: Female maturation in Japan and North America. In R. A. Shweder (Ed.), *Welcome to middle age! (and other cultural fictions)* (pp. 45–74). Chicago: University of Chicago Press.

Lockwood, C. J. (2002). Predicting premature delivery—no easy task. *New England Journal of Medicine, 346,* 282–284.

Lohse, N., Hansen, A. E., Pedersen, G., Kronborg, G., Gerstoft, J., Sørensen, H. T., Væth, M., & Obel, N. (2007). Survival of persons with and without HIV infection in Denmark, 1995–2005. *Annals of Internal Medicine, 146,* 87–95.

Lonczak, H. S., Abbott, R. D., Hawkins, J. D., Kosterman, R., & Catalano, R. F. (2002). Effects of the Seattle Social Development Project on sexual behavior, pregnancy, birth, and sexually transmitted disease. *Archives of Pediatric and Adolescent Medicine, 156,* 438–447.

Longnecker, M. P., Klebanoff, M. A., Zhou, H., & Brock, J. W. (2001). Association between maternal serum concentration of the DDT metabolite DDE and preterm and small-for-gestational-age babies at birth. *Lancet, 358,* 110–114.

Lonigan, C. J., Burgess, S. R., & Anthony, J. L. (2000). Development of emergent literacy and early reading skills in preschool children: Evidence from a latent-variable longitudinal study. *Developmental Psychology, 36,* 593–613.

Lopatto, E. (2007, May 12). *Marrying smarter, later leading to decline in US divorce rate: Survey shows figure is lowest since 1970.* Retrieved May 13, 2007, from www.boston.com/news/nation/articles/2007/05/12/marrying_smarter_later_leading_to_decline_in_us_divorce_rate/.

Lopes, P. N., Brackett, M. A., Nezlek, J. B., Schütz, A., Sellin, L., & Salovey, P. (2004). Emotional intelligence and social interaction. *Personality and Social Psychology Bulletin, 30,* 1018–1034.

Lopes, P. N., Grewal, D., Kadis, J., Gall, M., & Salovey, P. (2006). Evidence that emotional intelligence is related to job performance and affect and attitudes at work. *Psicothema, 18*(Suppl. 1), 132–138.

Lopes, P. N., Salovey, P., & Straus, R. (2003). Emotional intelligence, personality, and the perceived quality of social relationships. *Personality and Individual Differences, 35,* 641–658.

Lorenz, K. (1957). Comparative study of behavior. In C. H. Schiller (Ed.), *Instinctive behavior.* New York: International Universities Press.

Lorsbach, T. C., & Reimer, J. F. (1997). Developmental changes in the inhibition of previously relevant information. *Journal of Experimental Child Psychology, 64,* 317–342.

Love, J. M., Kisker, E. E., Ross, C., Raikes, H., Constantine, J., Boller, K., Brooks-Gunn, J., Chazan-Cohen, R., Tarullo, L. B., Brady-Smith, C., Fuligni, A. S., Schochet, P. Z., Paulsell, D., & Vogel, C. (2005). The effectiveness of Early Head Start for 3-year-old children and their parents: Lessons for policy and programs. *Developmental Psychology, 41,* 885–901.

Love, J. M., Kisker, E. E., Ross, C. M., Schochet, P. Z., Brooks-Gunn, J., Paulsell, D., Boller, K., Constantine, J., Vogel, C., Fuligni, A. S., & Brady-Smith, C. (2002). *Making a difference in the lives of infants and toddlers and their families: The impacts of Early Head Start: Executive summary.* Washington, DC: U.S. Department of Health and Human Services.

Love, K. M., & Murdock, B. (2004). Attachment to parents and psychological well-being: An examination of young adult college students in intact families and stepfamilies. *Journal of Family Psychology, 18,* 600–608.

Lovelace, E. A. (1990). Basic concepts in cognition and aging. In E. A. Lovelace (Ed.), *Aging and cognition: Mental processes, self-awareness, and interventions* (pp. 1–28). Amsterdam: North-Holland, Elsevier.

Lowenthal, M., & Haven, C. (1968). Interaction and adaptation: Intimacy as a critical variable. *American Sociological Review, 33,* 20–30.

Loy, C., & Schneider L. (2006). Galantamine for Alzheimer's disease and mild cognitive impairment. *Cochrane Database of Systematic Reviews,* Issue 1, Art. No. CD001747. (DOI: 10.1002/14651858. CD001747.pub3).

Lu, T., Pan, Y., Kao, S.-Y., Li, C., Cohane, I., Chan, J., & Yankner, B. A. (2004). Gene regulation and DNA damage in the ageing human brain. *Nature, 429,* 883–891.

Lubell, K. M., Kegler, S. R., Crosby, A. E., & Karch, M. D. (2007). Suicide trends among youths and young adults aged 10–24 years—United States, 1990–2004. *Morbidity and Mortality Weekly Report, 56*(35), 905–908.

Lubell, K. M., Swahn, M. H., Crosby, A. E., & Kegler, S. R. (2004). Methods of suicide among persons aged 10–19 years—United States, 1992–2001. *Morbidity and Mortality Weekly Report, 53,* 471–474.

Lucas, R. E., Clark, A. E., Georgellis, Y., & Diener, E. (2003). Reexamining adaptation and the set point model of happiness: Reactions to changes in marital status. *Journal of Personality and Social Psychology, 84,* 527–539.

Ludwig, D. S. (2007). Childhood obesity—The shape of things to come. *New England Journal of Medicine, 357,* 2325–2327.

Ludwig, J., & Phillips, D. (2007). The benefits and costs of Head Start. *Social Policy Report, 21,* 3–20.

Lugaila, T. A. (2003). A child's day: 2000 (Selected indicators of child well-being). *Current Population Reports* (P70-89). Washington, DC: U.S. Census Bureau.

Luke, B., & Brown, M. B. (2006). The changing risk of infant mortality by gestation, plurality, and race: 1989–1991 versus 1999–2001. *Pediatrics, 118,* 2488–2497.

Luna, B., Garver, K. E., Urban, T. A., Lazar, N. A., & Sweeney, J. A. (2004). Maturation of cognitive processes from late childhood to adulthood. *Child Development, 75,* 1357–1372.

Lund, D. A. (1993a). Caregiving. In R. Kastenbaum (Ed.), *Encyclopedia of adult development* (pp. 57–63). Phoenix, AZ: Oryx Press.

Lund, D. A. (1993b). Widowhood: The coping response. In R. Kastenbaum (Ed.), *Encyclopedia of adult development* (pp. 537–541). Phoenix, AZ: Oryx Press.

Lundy, B. L. (2003). Father- and mother-infant face-to-face interactions: Differences in mind-related comments and infant attachment? *Infant Behavior and Development, 26,* 200–212.

Lundy, B. L., Jones, N. A., Field, T., Nearing, G., Davalos, M., Pietro, P. A., Schanberg, S., & Kuhn, C. (1999). Prenatal depression effects on neonates. *Infant Behavior and Development, 22,* 119–129.

Luszcz, M. A., & Bryan, J. (1999). Toward understanding age-related memory loss in late adulthood. *Gerontology, 45,* 2–9.

Luthar, S. S., & Latendresse, S. J. (2005). Children of the affluent: Challenges to well-being. *Current Directions in Psychological Science, 14,* 49–53.

Lyons-Ruth, K., Alpern, L., & Repacholi, B. (1993). Disorganized infant attachment classification and maternal psychosocial problems as predictors of hostile-aggressive behavior in the preschool classroom. *Child Development, 64,* 572–585.

Lytton, H., & Romney, D. M. (1991). Parents' differential socialization of boys and girls: A meta-analysis. *Psychological Bulletin, 109*(2), 267–296.

Lyyra, T., & Heikkinen, R. (2006). Perceived social support and mortality in older people. *Journal of Gerontology: Social Sciences, 61B,* S147–S152.

Lyytinen, P., Poikkeus, A., Laakso, M., Eklund, K., & Lyytinen, H. (2001). Language development and symbolic play in children with and without familial risk for dyslexia. *Journal of Speech, Language, and Hearing Research, 44,* 873–885.

Maccoby, E. (1980). *Social development.* New York: Harcourt Brace Jovanovich.

Maccoby, E. E. (1984). Middle childhood in the context of the family. In W. A. Collins (Ed.), *Development during middle childhood.* Washington, DC: National Academy.

Maccoby, E. E. (1992). The role of parents in the socialization of children: An historical overview. *Developmental Psychology, 28,* 1006–1017.

Maccoby, E. E. (2002). Gender and group process: A developmental perspective. *Current Directions in Psychological Science, 11,* 54–58.

Maccoby, E. E., & Lewis, C. C. (2003). Less day care or different day care? *Child Development, 74,* 1069–1075.

Maccoby, E. E., & Martin, J. A. (1983). Socialization in the context of the family: Parent-child interaction. In P. H. Mussen (Series Ed.) & E. M. Hetherington (Vol. Ed.), *Handbook of child psychology: Vol. 4. Socialization, personality, and social development* (pp. 1–101). New York: Wiley.

MacDonald, K. (1988). The interfaces between developmental psychology and evolutionary biology. In K. MacDonald (Ed.), *Sociobiological perspectives on human development* (pp. 3–23). New York: Springer-Verlag.

MacDonald, K. (1998). Evolution and development. In A. Campbell & S. Muncer (Eds.), *Social development* (pp. 21–49). London: UCL Press.

MacDonald, W. L., & DeMaris, A. (1996). Parenting stepchildren and biological children. *Journal of Family Issues, 17,* 5–25.

MacDorman, M. F., Hoyert, D. L., Martin, J. A., Munson, M. L., & Hamilton, B. E. (2007). Fetal and perinatal mortality, United States, 2003. *National Vital Statistics Reports, 55*(6). Hyattsville, MD: National Center for Health Statistics.

MacDorman, M. F., Munson, M. L., & Kirmeyer, S. (2007). Fetal and perinatal mortality, United States, 2004. *National Vital Statistics Reports, 56*(3). Hyattsville, MD: National Center for Health Statistics.

MacKinnon-Lewis, C., Starnes, R., Volling, B., & Johnson, S. (1997). Perceptions of parenting as predictors of boys' sibling and peer relations. *Developmental Psychology, 33,* 1024–1031.

Macmillan, C., Magder, L. S., Brouwers, P., Chase, C., Hittelman, J., Lasky, T., Malee, K., Mellins, C. A., & Velez-Borras, J. (2001). Head growth and neurodevelopment of infants born to HIV-1–infected drug-using women. *Neurology, 57,* 1402–1411.

MacMillan, H. M., Boyle, M. H., Wong, M.Y.-Y., Duku, E. K., Fleming, J. E., & Walsh, C. A. (1999). Slapping and spanking in childhood and its association with lifetime prevalence of psychiatric disorders in a general population sample. *Canadian Medical Association Journal, 161,* 805–809.

Macmillan, R., McMorris, B. J., & Kruttschnitt, C. (2004). Linked lives: Stability and change in maternal circumstances and trajectories of antisocial behavior in children. *Child Development, 75,* 205–220.

Madsen, A. M., Frenkel, K., Garduno, E. R., Mooney, L. A., Orjuela, M. A., Powell, J., Tang, D., & Perera, F. P. (2006, November). *The relationship between dietary antioxidants and oxidative damage in smokers: Evidence of effect modification by lifestyle and genetic factors.* Paper presented at the fifth American Association for Cancer Research International Conference on Frontiers in Cancer Prevention Research, Boston.

Maestripieri, D., Higley, J., Lindell, S., Newman, T., McCormack, K., & Sanchez, M. (2006). Early maternal rejection affects the development of monoaminergic systems and adult abusive parenting in Rhesus Macaques (Macaca mulatta). *Behavioral Neuroscience, 120*(5), 1017–1024.

Mahoney, J. L. (2000). School extracurricular activity participation as a moderator in the development of antisocial patterns. *Child Development, 71*(2), 502–516.

Main, M. (1995). Recent studies in attachment: Overview, with selected implications for clinical work. In S. Goldberg, R. Muir, & J. Kerr (Eds.), *Attachment theory: Social, developmental, and clinical perspectives* (pp. 407–470). Hillsdale, NJ: Analytic Press.

Main, M., Kaplan, N., & Cassidy, J. (1985). Security in infancy, childhood and adulthood: A move to the level of representation. In I. Bretherton & E. Waters (Eds.), Growing points in attachment. *Monographs of the Society for Research in Child Development, 50*(1–20), 66–104.

Main, M., & Solomon, J. (1986). Discovery of an insecure, disorganized/disoriented attachment pattern: Procedures, findings, and implications for the classification of behavior. In M. Yogman & T. B. Brazelton (Eds.), *Affective development in infancy.* Norwood, NJ: Ablex.

Makino, M., Tsuboi, K., and Dennerstein, L. (2004). Prevalence of eating disorders: A comparison of Western and non-Western countries. *Medscape General Medicine, 6*(3). Retrieved September 27, 2004, from www .medscape.com/viewarticle/487413.

Malaspina, D., Harlap, S., Fennig, S., Heiman, D., Nahon, D., Feldman, D., & Susser, E. S. (2001). Advancing paternal age and the risk of schizophrenia. *Archives of General Psychiatry, 58,* 361–371.

Malone, F. D., Canick, J. A., Ball, R. H., Nyberg, D. A., Comstock, C. H., Bukowski, R., Berkowitz, R. L., Gross, S. J., Dugoff, L., Craigo, S. D., Timor-Tritsch, I. E., Carr, S. R., Wolfe, H. M., Dukes, K., Bianchi, D. W., Rudnicka, A. R., Hackshaw, A. K., Lambert-Messerlian, G., Wald, N. J., & D'Alton, M. E. (2005). First-trimester or second-trimester screening, or both, for Down's syndrome. *New England Journal of Medicine, 353,* 2001–2011.

Mancini, A. D., & Bonanno, G. A. (2006). Marital closeness, functional disability, and adjustment in late life. *Psychology and Aging, 21,* 600–610.

Mandler, J. M. (1998). Representation. In D. Kuhn & R. S. Siegler (Eds.), *Handbook of child psychology: Vol. 2. Cognition, perception, and language* (5th ed., pp. 255–308). New York: Wiley.

Mandler, J. M. (2007). On the origins of the conceptual system. *American Psychologist, 62,* 741–751.

Mandler, J. M., & McDonough, L. (1993). Concept formation in infancy. *Cognitive Development, 8,* 291–318.

Mandler, J. M., & McDonough, L. (1996). Drinking and driving don't mix: Inductive generalization in infancy. *Cognition, 59,* 307–335.

Mandler, J. M., & McDonough, L. (1998). Cognition across the life span: On developing a knowledge base in infancy. *Developmental Psychology, 34,* 1274–1288.

Manlove, J., Ryan, S., & Franzetta, K. (2003). Patterns of contraceptive use within teenagers' first sexual relationships. *Perspectives on Sexual and Reproductive Health, 35,* 246–255.

Mannell, R. (1993). High investment activity and life satisfaction: Commitment, serious leisure, and flow in the daily lives of older adults. In J. Kelly (Ed.), *Activity and aging.* Newbury Park, CA: Sage.

Manson, J. E., Allison, M. A., Rossouw, J. E., Carr, J. J., Langer, R. D., Hsia, J., Kuller, L. H., Cochrane, B. B., Hunt, J. R., Ludlam, S. E., Pettinger, M. B., Gass, M., Margolis, K. L., Nathan, L., Ockene, J. K., Prentice, R. L., Robbins, J., Stefanick, M. L., & the WHI and WHI-CACS Investigators. (2007). Estrogen therapy and coronary-artery calcification. *New England Journal of Medicine, 356,* 2591–2602.

Manson, J. E., & Martin, K. A. (2001). Postmenopausal hormone-replacement therapy. *New England Journal of Medicine, 345,* 34–40.

March, J., & the TADS Team. (2007). The Treatment for Adolescents with Depression Study (TADS): Long-term effectiveness and safety outcomes. *Archives of General Psychiatry, 64,* 1132–1143.

March of Dimes Birth Defects Foundation. (1987). *Genetic counseling: A public health information booklet* (Rev. ed.). White Plains, NY: Author.

March of Dimes Birth Defects Foundation. (2004a). *Cocaine use during pregnancy* [Fact sheet]. Retrieved October 29, 2004, from www.marchofdimes.com/professionals/ 681_1169.asp.

March of Dimes Birth Defects Foundation. (2004b). *Marijuana: What you need to know.* Retrieved October 29, 2004, from www .marchofdimes.com/pnhec/159_4427.asp.

March of Dimes Foundation. (2002). *Toxoplasmosis* [Fact sheet]. Wilkes-Barre, PA: Author.

Marcia, J. E. (1966). Development and validation of ego identity status. *Journal of Personality and Social Psychology, 3*(5), 551–558.

Marcia, J. E. (1979, June). *Identity status in late adolescence: Description and some clinical implications.* Address given at symposium on identity development, Rijksuniversitat Groningen, Netherlands.

Marcia, J. E. (1980). Identity in adolescence. In J. Adelson (Ed.), *Handbook of adolescent psychology.* New York: Wiley.

Marcia, J. E. (1993). The relational roots of identity. In J. Kroger (Ed.), *Discussions on ego identity* (pp. 101–120). Hillsdale, NJ: Erlbaum.

Marcoen, A. (1995). Filial maturity of middle-aged adult children in the context of parent care: Model and measures. *Journal of Adult Development, 2,* 125–136.

Marcon, R. A. (1999). Differential impact of preschool models on development and early learning of inner-city children: A three-cohort study. *Developmental Psychology, 35*(2), 358–375.

Marcus, G. F., Vijayan, S., Rao, S. B., & Vishton, P. M. (1999). Rule learning by seven-month-old infants. *Science, 283,* 77–80.

Markel, H. (2007). Is there an autism epidemic? *Medscape Pediatrics.* Retrieved February 14, 2007, from www.medscape .com/viewarticle/551540.

Markoff, J. (1992, October 12). Miscarriages tied to chip factories. *New York Times,* pp. A1, D2.

Markowitz, S., Friedman, M. A., & Arent, S. M. (2008). Understanding the relation between obesity and depression: Causal mechanisms and duplications for treatment. *Clinical Psychology: Science and Practice, 15,* 1–20.

Marks, H. (2000). Student engagement in instructional activity: Patterns in the elemen-

tary, middle, and high school years. *American Education Research Journal, 37,* 153–184.

Marks, N. F. (1996). Caregiving across the lifespan: National prevalence and predictors. *Family Relations, 45,* 27–36.

Marks, N. F., Bumpass, L. L., & Jun, H. (2004). Family roles and well-being during the middle life course. In O. G. Brim, C. D. Ryff, & R. C. Kessler (Eds.), *How healthy are we? A national study of well-being at midlife* (pp. 514–549). Chicago: University of Chicago Press.

Marks, N. F., & Lambert, J. D. (1998). Marital status continuity and change among young and midlife adults. *Journal of Family Issues, 19,* 652–686.

Markus, H. R., Ryff, C. D., Curhan, K. B., & Palmersheim, K. A. (2004). In their own words: Well-being at midlife among high school-educated and college-educated adults. In O. G. Brim, C. D. Ryff & R. C. Kessler (Eds.), *How healthy are we? A national study of well-being at midlife* (pp. 273–319). Chicago: University of Chicago Press.

Marlier, L., & Schaal, B. (2005). Human newborns prefer human milk: Conspecific milk odor is attractive without postnatal exposure. *Child Development, 76,* 155–168.

Marlow, N., Wolke, D., Bracewell, M. A., & Samara, M., for the EPICure Study Group. (2005). Neurologic and developmental disability at six years of age after extremely preterm birth. *New England Journal of Medicine, 352,* 9–19.

Marmot, M. G., & Fuhrer, R. (2004). Socioeconomic position and health across midlife. In O. G. Brim, C. D. Ryff, & R. C. Kessler (Eds.), *How healthy are we? A national study of well-being at midlife.* Chicago: University of Chicago Press.

Marshall, N. L. (2004). The quality of early child care and children's development. *Current Directions in Psychological Science, 13,* 165–168.

Martikainen, P., & Valkonen, T. (1996). Mortality after the death of a spouse: Rates and causes of death in a large Finnish cohort. *American Journal of Public Health, 86,* 1087–1093.

Martin, C. L., Eisenbud, L., & Rose, H. (1995). Children's gender-based reasoning about toys. *Child Development, 66,* 1453–1471.

Martin, C. L., & Fabes, R. A. (2001). The stability and consequences of young children's same-sex peer interactions. *Developmental Psychology, 37,* 431–446.

Martin, C. L., & Halverson, C. F. (1981). A schematic processing model of sex typing and stereotyping in children. *Child Development, 52,* 1119–1134.

Martin, C. L., & Ruble, D. (2004). Children's search for gender cues: Cognitive perspectives on gender development. *Current Directions in Psychological Science, 13,* 67–70.

Martin, C. L., Ruble, D. N., & Szkrybalo, J. (2002). Cognitive theories of early gender development. *Psychological Bulletin, 128,* 903–933.

Martin, J. A., Hamilton, B. E., Sutton, P. D., Ventura, S. J., Menacker, F., & Kirmeyer, S. (2006). Births: Final data for 2004. *National Vital Statistics Reports, 55*(1). Hyattsville, MD: National Center for Health Statistics.

Martin, J. A., Hamilton, B. E., Sutton, P. D., Ventura, S. J., Menacker, F., Kirmeyer, S., & Munson, M. (2007). Births: Final data for 2005. *National Vital Statistics Reports, 56*(6). Hyattsville, MD: National Center for Health Statistics.

Martin, J. A., Hamilton, B. E., Sutton, P. D., Ventura, S. J., Menacker, F., & Munson, M. L. (2003). Births: Final data for 2002. *National Vital Statistics Reports, 52*(10). Hyattsville, MD: National Center for Health Statistics.

Martin, J. A., Hamilton, B. E., Sutton, P. D., Ventura, S. J., Menacker, F., & Munson, M. L. (2005). Births: Final data for 2003. *National Vital Statistics Reports, 54*(2). Hyattsville, MD: National Center for Health Statistics.

Martin, J. A., Hamilton, B. E., Ventura, S. J., Menacker, F., & Park, M. M. (2002). Births: Final Data for 2000. *National Vital Statistics Reports, 50*(5). Hyattsville, MD: National Center for Health Statistics.

Martin, J. A., Kochanek, K. D., Strobino, D. M., Guyer, B., & MacDorman, M. F. (2005). Annual summary of vital statistics—2003. *Pediatrics, 115,* 619–634.

Martin, L. G. (1988). The aging of Asia. *Journal of Gerontology: Social Sciences, 43*(4), S99–S113.

Martin, N., & Montgomery, G. (2002, March 18). *Is having twins, either identical or fraternal, in someone's genes? Is there a way to increase your chances of twins or is having twins just luck?* Retrieved March 7, 2006, from http://genepi.qimr.edu.au/Scientific American Twins.html.

Martin, P., Hagberg, B., & Poon, L. W. (1997). Predictors of loneliness in centenarians: A parallel study. *Journal of Cross-Cultural Gerontology, 12,* 203–224.

Martin, R., Noyes, J., Wisenbaker, J., & Huttunen, M. (2000). Prediction of early childhood negative emotionality and inhibition from maternal distress during pregnancy. *Merrill-Palmer Quarterly, 45,* 370–391.

Martin, S. P., & Parashar, S. (2006). Women's changing attitudes toward divorce, 1974–2002: Evidence for an educational crossover. *Journal of Marriage and Family, 68,* 29–40.

Martin-Ruiz, C. M., Gussekloo, J., van Heemst, D., von Zglinicki, T., & Westendorp, R. G. J. (2005). Telomere length in white blood cells is not associated with morbidity or mortality in the oldest old: A population-based study. *Aging Cell, 4,* 287–290.

Martínez-González, M. A., Gual, P., Lahortiga, F., Alonso, Y., de Irala-Estévez, J., & Cervera, S. (2003). Parental factors, mass media influences, and the onset of eating disorders in a prospective population-based cohort. *Pediatrics, 111,* 315–320.

Maslach, C. (2003). Job burnout: New directions in research and intervention. *Current Directions in Psychological Science, 12*(5), 189–192.

Maslow, A. (1968). *Toward a psychology of living.* Princeton, NJ: Van Nostrand Reinhold.

Masse, L. C., & Tremblay, R. E. (1997). Behavior of boys in kindergarten and the onset of substance use during adolescence. *Archives of General Psychiatry, 54,* 62–68.

Masten, A., Best, K., & Garmezy, N. (1990). Resilience and development: Contributions from the study of children who overcome adversity. *Development and Psychopathology, 2,* 425–444.

Masten, A. S. (2001). Ordinary magic: Resilience processes in development. *American Psychologist, 56,* 227–238.

Masten, A. S., & Coatsworth, J. D. (1998). The development of competence in favorable and unfavorable environments: Lessons from research on successful children. *American Psychologist, 53,* 205–220.

Masters, W. H., & Johnson, V. E. (1966). *Human sexual response.* Boston: Little, Brown.

Mathews, T. J., & MacDorman, M. F. (2006). Infant mortality statistics from the 2003 period linked birth/infant death data set. *National Vital Statistics Reports, 54*(16). Hyattsville, MD: National Center for Health Statistics.

Mathews, T. J., & MacDorman, M. F. (2007). Infant mortality statistics from the 2004 period linked birth/infant death data set. *National Vital Statistics Reports, 53*(15). Hyattsville, MD: National Center for Health Statistics.

Matsudaira, J. (2006, November). *Jobs, wages, and leaving the nest* (Policy Brief Issue No. 35). Philadelphia: Network on Transitions to Adulthood, MacArthur Foundation Research Network on Transitions to Adulthood and Public Policy, University of Pennsylvania. Retrieved March 28, 2008, from www.transad.pop.upenn.edu/downloads/matsudaira-formatted.pdf.

Matthews, S. H. (1995). Gender and the division of filial responsibility between lone sisters and their brothers. *Journal of Gerontology: Social Sciences, 50B,* S312–S320.

Maurer, D., & Lewis, T. L. (1979). Peripheral discrimination by three-month-old infants. *Child Development, 50,* 276–279.

Mayer, J. D., & Salovey, P. (1997). What is emotional intelligence? In P. Salovey & D. Sluyter (Eds.), *Emotional development and emotional intelligence: Educational implications* (pp. 3–31). New York: Basic Books.

Mayer, J. D., Salovey, P., & Caruso, D. (2002). *The Mayer-Salovey-Caruso Emotional Intelligence Test (MSCEIT).* Toronto, Ontario: Multi-Health Systems.

Mayo Clinic. (2005, December 7). *Infertility.* Retrieved May 5, 2006, from www.mayoclinic.com/health/infertility/DS00310.

Mazzeo, R. S., Cavanaugh, P., Evans, W. J., Fiatarone, M., Hagberg, J., McAuley, E., & Startzell, J. (1998). ACSM position stand on exercise and physical activity for older adults. *Medicine and Science in Sports and Exercise, 30,* 992–1008.

McAdams, D. (1993). *The stories we live by.* New York: Morrow.

McAdams, D. P. (2001). Generativity in midlife. In M. E. Lachman (Ed.), *Handbook of midlife development* (pp. 395–443). New York: Wiley.

McAdams, D. P. (2006). The redemptive self: Generativity and the stories Americans live by. *Research in Human Development, 3,* 81–100.

McAdams, D. P., & de St. Aubin, E. (1992). A theory of generativity and its assessment through self-report, behavioral acts, and narrative themes in autobiography. *Journal of Personality and Social Psychology, 62,* 1003–1015.

McAdams, D. P., de St. Aubin, E., & Logan, R. L. (1993). Generativity among young, midlife, and older adults. *Psychology and Aging, 8,* 221–230.

McAdams, D. P., Diamond, A., de St. Aubin, E., & Mansfield, E. (1997). Stories of commitment: The psychosocial construction of generative lives. *Journal of Personality and Social Psychology, 72,* 678–694.

McCall, R. B., & Carriger, M. S. (1993). A meta-analysis of infant habituation and recognition memory performance as predictors of later IQ. *Child Development, 64,* 57–79.

McCallum, K. E., & Bruton, J. R. (2003). The continuum of care in the treatment of eating disorders. *Primary Psychiatry, 10*(6), 48–54.

McCartney, N., Hicks, A. L., Martin, J., & Webber, C. E. (1996). A longitudinal trial of weight training in the elderly: Continued improvements in year 2. *Journal of Gerontology: Biological and Medical Sciences, 51,* B425–B433.

McCartt, A. T. (2001). Graduated driver licensing systems: Reducing crashes among teenage drivers. *Journal of the American Medical Association, 286,* 1631–1632.

McCarty, M. E., Clifton, R. K., Ashmead, D. H., Lee, P., & Goubet, N. (2001). How infants use vision for grasping objects. *Child Development, 72,* 973–987.

McClearn, G. E., Johansson, B., Berg, S., Pedersen, N. L., Ahern, F., Petrill, S. A., & Plomin, R. (1997). Substantial genetic influence on cognitive abilities in twins 80 or more years old. *Science, 276,* 1560–1563.

McClintock, M. K., & Herdt, G. (1996). Rethinking puberty: The development of sexual attraction. *Current Directions in Psychological Science, 5*(6), 178–183.

McCord, J. (1996). Unintended consequences of punishment. *Pediatrics, 98,* 832–834.

McCoy, A. R., & Reynolds, A. J. (1999). Grade retention and school performance: An extended investigation. *Journal of School Psychology, 37,* 273–298.

McCrae, R. R. (2002). Cross-cultural research on the five-factor model of personality. In W. J. Lonner, D. L. Dinnel, S. A. Hayes, & D. N. Sattler (Eds.), *Online readings in psychology and culture* (Unit 6, Chapter 1).

Bellingham, WA: Center for Cross-Cultural Research, Western Washington University.

McCrae, R. R., & Costa, P. T., Jr. (1984). *Emerging lives, enduring dispositions.* Boston: Little, Brown.

McCrae, R. R., & Costa, P. T., Jr. (1994). The stability of personality: Observations and evaluations. *Current Directions in Psychological Science, 3*(6), 173–175.

McCrae, R. R., Costa, P. T., Jr., & Busch, C. M. (1986). Evaluating comprehensiveness in personality systems: The California Q-set and the five-factor model. *Journal of Personality, 54,* 430–446.

McCrae, R. R., Costa, P. T., Jr., Ostendorf, F., Angleitner, A., Hebríckóva, M., Avia, M. D., Sanz, J., Sánchez-Bernardos, M. L., Kusdil, M. E., Woodfield, R., Saunders, P. R., & Smith, P. B. (2000). Nature over nurture: Temperament, personality, and lifespan development. *Journal of Personality and Social Psychology, 78,* 173–186.

McCrink, K., & Wynn, K. (2004). Large-number addition and subtraction by 9-month-old infants. *Psychological Science, 15,* 776–781.

McCue, J. D. (1995). The naturalness of dying. *Journal of the American Medical Association, 273,* 1039–1043.

McDaniel, M., Paxson, C., & Waldfogel, J. (2006). Racial disparities in childhood asthma in the United States: Evidence from the National Health Interview Survey, 1997 to 2003. *Pediatrics, 117,* 868–877.

McDowell, M. M., Wang, C.-Y., & Kennedy-Stephenson, J. (2008). *Breastfeeding in the United States: Findings from the National Health and Nutrition Examination Surveys, 1999–2006* (NCHS Data Briefs, No. 5). Hyattsville, MD: National Center for Health Statistics.

McElwain, N. L., & Booth-LaForce, C. (2006). Maternal sensitivity to infant distress and nondistress as predictors of infant-mother attachment security. *Journal of Family Psychology, 20,* 247–255.

McElwain, N. L., & Volling, B. L. (2005). Preschool children's interactions with friends and older siblings: Relationship specificity and joint contributions to problem behavior. *Journal of Family Psychology, 19,* 486–496.

McFall, S., & Miller, B. H. (1992). Caregiver burden and nursing home admission of frail elderly patients. *Journal of Gerontology: Social Sciences, 47,* S73–S79.

McFarland, R. A., Tune, G. B., & Welford, A. (1964). On the driving of automobiles by older people. *Journal of Gerontology, 19,* 190–197.

McGue, M. (1997). The democracy of the genes. *Nature, 388,* 417–418.

McGuffin, P., Owen, M. J., & Farmer, A. E. (1995). Genetic basis of schizophrenia. *Lancet, 346,* 678–682.

McGuffin, P., Riley, B., & Plomin, R. (2001). Toward behavioral genomics. *Science, 291,* 1232–1249.

McGuigan, F., & Salmon, K. (2004). The time to talk: The influence of the timing of adult-child talk on children's event memory. *Child Development, 75,* 669–686.

McHale, S. M., Updegraff, K. A., Helms-Erikson, H., & Crouter, A. C. (2001). Sibling influences on gender development in middle childhood and early adolescence: A longitudinal study. *Developmental Psychology, 37,* 115–125.

McKitrick, L. A., Camp, C. J., & Black, F. W. (1992). Prospective memory intervention in Alzheimer's disease. *Journal of Gerontology: Psychological Sciences, 47*(5), P337–P343.

McKusick, V. A. (2001). The anatomy of the human genome. *Journal of the American Medical Association, 286*(18), 2289–2295.

McLanahan, S., & Sandefur, G. (1994). *Growing up with a single parent.* Cambridge, MA: Harvard University Press.

McLeod, R., Boyer, K., Karrison, T., Kasza, K., Swisher, C., Roizen, N., Jalbrzikowski, J., Remington, J., Heydemann, P., Noble, A. J., Mets, M., Holfels, E., Withers, S., Latkany, P., Meier, P., & Toxoplamosis Study Group. (2006). Outcome of treatment for congenital toxoplasmosis, 1981–2004: The national collaborative Chicago-based, congenital toxoplasmosis study. *Clinical Infectious Diseases: An Official Publication of the Infectious Diseases Society of America, 42*(10), 1383–1394.

McLeskey, J., Lancaster, M., & Grizzle, K. L. (1995). Learning disabilities and grade retention: A review of issues with recommendations for practice. *Learning Disabilities Research and Practice, 10,* 120–128.

McLoyd, V. C. (1990). The impact of economic hardship on black families and children: Psychological distress, parenting, and socioemotional development. *Child Development, 61,* 311–346.

McLoyd, V. C. (1998). Socioeconomic disadvantage and child development. *American Psychologist, 53,* 185–204.

McLoyd, V. C., & Smith, J. (2002). Physical discipline and behavior problems in African American, European American, and Hispanic children: Emotional support as a moderator. *Journal of Marriage and Family, 64,* 40–53.

McNeilly-Choque, M. K., Hart, C. H., Robinson, C. C., Nelson, L. J., & Olsen, S. F. (1996). Overt and relational aggression on the playground. Correspondence among different informants. *Journal of Research in Childhood Education, 11,* 47–67.

McPherson, M., Smith-Lovin, L., & Brashears, M. E. (2006). Social isolation in America: Changes in core discussion networks over two decades. *American Sociological Review, 71,* 353–375.

McQuillan, J., Greil, A. L., White, L., & Jacob, M. C. (2003). Frustrated fertility: Infertility and psychological distress among women. *Journal of Marriage and Family, 65,* 1007–1018.

McTiernan, A., Kooperberg, C., White, E., Wilcox, S., Coates, R., Adams-Campbell, L. L., Woods, N., & Ockene, J. (2003). Recreational physical activity and the risk of breast cancer in postmenopausal women: The Women's Health Initiative Cohort Study. *Journal of the American Medical Association, 290,* 1331–1336.

Mead, M. (1928). *Coming of age in Samoa.* New York: Morrow.

Mead, M. (1935). *Sex and temperament in three primitive societies.* New York: Morrow.

Mears, B. (2005, March 1). *High court: Juvenile death penalty unconstitutional: Slim majority cites "evolving standards" in American society.* CNN.com. Retrieved March 30, 2005, from http://cnn.com./2005/LAW/03/01/scotus.death.penalty.

Mednick, S. C., Nakayama, K., Cantero, J. L., Atienza, M., Levin, A. A., Pathak, N., & Stickgold, R. (2002). The restorative effect of naps on perceptual deterioration. *Nature Neuroscience, 5,* 677–681.

Meeks, J. J., Weiss, J., & Jameson, J. L. (2003, May). Dax1 is required for testis formation. *Nature Genetics, 34,* 32–33.

Meezan, W., & Rauch, J. (2005). Gay marriage, same-sex parenting, and America's children. *Future of Children, 15,* 97–115.

Meier, D. (1995). *The power of their ideas.* Boston: Beacon Press.

Meier, D. E., Emmons, C.-A., Wallenstein, S., Quill, T., Morrison, R. S., & Cassel, C. (1998). A national survey of physician-assisted suicide and euthanasia in the United States. *New England Journal of Medicine, 338,* 1193–1201.

Meier, R. (1991, January–February). Language acquisition by deaf children. *American Scientist, 79,* 60–70.

Meijer, A. M., & van den Wittenboer, G. L. H. (2007). Contributions of infants' sleep and crying to marital relationship of first-time parent couples in the 1st year after childbirth. *Journal of Family Psychology, 21,* 49–57.

Meins, E. (1998). The effects of security of attachment and maternal attribution of meaning on children's linguistic acquisitional style. *Infant Behavior and Development, 21,* 237–252.

Meis, P. J., Klebanoff, M., Thom, E., Dombrowski, M. P., Sibai, B., Moawad, A. H., Spong, C. Y., Hauth, J. C., Miodovnik, M., Varner, M. W., Leveno, K. J., Caritis, S. N., Iams, J. D., Wapner, R. J., Conway, D., O'Sullivan, M. J., Carpenter, M., Mercer, B., Ramin, S. M., Thorp, J. M., Peaceman, A. M., Gabbe, S., & National Institute of Child Health and Human Development Maternal-Fetal Medicine Units Network. (2003). Prevention of recurrent preterm delivery by 17 alpha-hydroxyprogesterone caproate. *New England Journal of Medicine, 348,* 2379–2385.

Meltzoff, A., & Gopnik, A. (1993). The role of imitation in understanding persons and developing a theory of mind. In S. Baron-Cohen, H. Tager-Flusberg, & D. J. Cohen (Eds.), *Understanding other minds: Perspectives from autism* (pp. 335–366). Oxford: Oxford University Press.

Meltzoff, A. N. (2007). "Like me": A foundation for social cognition. *Developmental Science, 10,* 126–134.

Meltzoff, A. N., & Moore, M. K. (1983). Newborn infants imitate adult facial gestures. *Child Development, 54,* 702–709.

Meltzoff, A. N., & Moore, M. K. (1989). Imitation in newborn infants: Exploring the range of gestures imitated and the underlying mechanisms. *Developmental Psychology, 25,* 954–962.

Meltzoff, A. N., & Moore, M. K. (1994). Imitation, memory, and the representation of persons. *Infant Behavior and Development, 17,* 83–99.

Meltzoff, A. N., & Moore, M. K. (1998). Object representation, identity, and the paradox of early permanence: Steps toward a new framework. *Infant Behavior and Development, 21,* 201–235.

Menacker, F., Martin, J. A., MacDorman, M. F., & Ventura, S. J. (2004). Births to 10–14 year-old mothers, 1990–2002: Trends and health outcomes. *National Vital Statistics Reports, 53*(7). Hyattsville, MD: National Center for Health Statistics.

Mendelsohn, M. E., & Karas, R. H. (2007). HRT and the young at heart. *New England Journal of Medicine, 356,* 2639–2643.

Mendle, J., Turkheimer, E., D'Onofrio, B. M., Lynch, S. K., Emery, R. E., Slutske, W. S., & Martin, N. G. (2006). Family structure and age at menarche: A children-of-twins approach. *Developmental Psychology, 42,* 533–542.

Menec, V. H. (2003). The relation between everyday activities and successful aging: A 6-year longitudinal study. *Journal of Gerontology: Social Sciences, 58B,* S74–S82.

Menegaux, F., Baruchel, A., Bertrand, Y., Lescoeur, B., Leverger, G., Nelken, B., Sommelet, D., Hemon, D., & Clavel, J. (2006). Household exposure to pesticides and risk of childhood acute leukaemia. *Occupational and Environmental Medicine, 63*(2), 131–134.

Meng, H., Smith, S. D., Hager, K., Held, M., Liu, J., Olson, R. K., Pennington, B. F., Defires, J. C., Gelernter, J., O'Reilly-Pol, T., Somlo, S., Skudlarski, P., Shaywitz, S., Shaywitz, B., Marchione, K., Page, G. P., & Gruen, J. R. (2005, October). *A deletion in DCDC2 on 6p22 is associated with reading disability.* Paper presented at the American Society of Human Genetics meeting, Salt Lake City, UT.

Meng, Y., Lee, J. H., Cheng, R., St. George-Hyslop, P., Mayeux, R., & Farrer, L. A. (2007). Association between SORL1 and Alzheimer's disease in a genome-wide study. *NeuroReport, 18*(17), 1761–1764.

Mennella, J. A., & Beauchamp, G. K. (1996a). The early development of human flavor preferences. In E. D. Capaldi (Ed.), *Why we eat what we eat: The psychology of eating* (pp. 83–112). Washington DC: American Psychological Association.

Mennella, J. A., & Beauchamp, G. K. (1996b). The human infants' response to vanilla flavors in mother's milk and formula. *Infant Behavior and Development, 19,* 13–19.

Mennella, J. A., & Beauchamp, G. K. (2002). Flavor experiences during formula feeding are related to preferences during childhood. *Early Human Development, 68,* 71–82.

Menon, U. (2001). Middle adulthood in cultural perspective: The imagined and the experienced in three cultures. In M. E. Lachman (Ed.), *Handbook of midlife development* (pp. 40–74). New York: Wiley.

Ment, L. R., Vohr, B., Allan, W., Katz, K. H., Schneider, K. C., Westerveld, M., Duncan, C. C., & Makuch, R. W. (2003). Changes in cognitive function over time in very low-birth-weight infants. *Journal of the American Medical Association, 289,* 705–711.

Merewood, A., Mehta, S. D., Chamberlain, L. B., Philipp, B. L., & Bauchner, H. (2005). Breastfeeding rates in US baby-friendly hospitals: Results of a national survey. *Pediatrics, 116,* 628–634.

Merriam, E. (1964). Conversation with myself. In *Halloween abc.* Tappan, NJ: Simon & Schuster, 1987.

Merrill, S. S., & Verbrugge, L. M. (1999). Health and disease in midlife. In S. L. Willis & J. D. Reid (Eds.), *Life in the middle: Psychological and social development in middle age* (pp. 78–103). San Diego: Academic Press.

Merva, M., & Fowles, R. (1992). *Effects of diminished economic opportunities on social stress: Heart attacks, strokes, and crime* [Briefing paper]. Washington, DC: Economic Policy Institute.

Messinger, D. S., Bauer, C. R., Das, A., Seifer, R., Lester, B. M., Lagasse, L. L., Wright, L. L., Shankaran, S., Bada, H. S., Smeriglio, V. L., Langer, J. C., Beeghly, M., & Poole, W. K. (2004). The maternal lifestyle study: Cognitive, motor, and behavioral outcomes of cocaine-exposed and opiate-exposed infants through three years of age. *Pediatrics, 113,* 1677–1685.

Messinis, L., Krypianidou, A., Maletaki, S., & Papathanasopoulos, P. (2006). Neuropsychological deficits in long-term cannabis users. *Neurology, 66,* 737–739.

Meyer, B. J. F., Russo, C., & Talbot, A. (1995). Discourse comprehension and problem solving: Decisions about the treatment of breast cancer by women across the lifespan. *Psychology in Aging, 10,* 84–103.

Miech, R. A., Kumanyika, S. K., Stettler, N., Link, B., Phelan, J. C., & Chang, V. W. (2006). Trends in the association of poverty with overweight among US adolescents, 1971–2004. *Journal of the American Medical Association, 295,* 2385–2393.

Miedzian, M. (1991). *Boys will be boys: Breaking the link between masculinity and violence.* New York: Doubleday.

Migeon, B. R. (2006). The role of X inactivation and cellular mosaicism in women's health and sex-specific disorders. *Journal of the American Medical Association, 295,* 1428–1433.

Mikkola, K., Ritari, N., Tommiska, V., Salokorpi, T., Lehtonen, L., Tammela, O., Paakkonen, L., Olsen, P., Korkman, M., & Fellman, V., for the Finnish ELBW Cohort Study Group. (2005). Neurodevelopmental outcome at 5 years of age of a national cohort of extremely low birth weight infants who were born in 1996–1997. *Pediatrics, 116,* 1391–1400.

Milkie, M. A., Mattingly, M. J., Nomaguchi, S. M., Bianchi, S. M., & Robinson, J. P. (2004). The time squeeze: Parental statuses and feelings about time with children. *Journal of Marriage and Family, 66,* 739–761.

Milkie, M. A, & Peltola, P. (1999). Playing all the roles: Gender and the work-family balancing act. *Journal of Marriage and Family, 61,* 476–490.

Miller, G. E., & Blackwell, E. (2006). Turning up the heat. *Current Directions in Psychological Science, 15,* 269–272.

Miller, J. W., Naimi, T. S., Brewer, R. D., & Jones, S. E. (2007). Binge drinking and associated health risk behaviors among high school students. *Pediatrics, 119,* 76–85.

Miller, K., & Kohn, M. (1983). The reciprocal effects of job condition and the intellectuality of leisure-time activities. In M. L. Kohn & C. Schooler (Eds.), *Work and personality: An inquiry into the impact of social stratification* (pp. 217–241). Norwood, NJ: Ablex.

Miller, M. A., & Rahe, R. H. (1997). Life changes scaling for the 1990s. *Journal of Psychosomatic Research, 43,* 279–292.

Miller, W. R., & Thoresen, C. E. (2003). Spirituality, religion, and health. *American Psychologist, 58,* 24–35.

Miller-Kovach, K. (2003). Childhood and adolescent obesity: A review of the scientific literature. Weight Watchers International: Unpublished manuscript.

Millman, R. P., Working Group on Sleepiness in Adolescents/Young Adults, & AAP Committee on Adolescents. (2005). Excessive sleepiness in adolescents and young adults: Causes, consequences, and treatment strategies. *Pediatrics, 115,* 1774–1786.

Milunsky, A. (1992). *Heredity and your family's health.* Baltimore: Johns Hopkins University Press.

Miniño, A. M., Anderson, R. N., Fingerhut, L. A., Boudreault, M. A., & Warner, M. (2006). Deaths: Injuries, 2002. *National Vital Statistics Reports, 54*(10). Hyattsville, MD: National Center for Health Statistics.

Miniño, A. M., Heron, M. P., Murphy, S. L., & Kochanek, K. D. (2007). Deaths: Final data for 2004. *National Vital Statistics Reports, 55*(19). Hyattsville, MD: National Center for Health Statistics.

Minkler, M., & Fuller-Thomson, E. (2005). African American grandparents raising grandchildren: A national study using the Census 2000 American Community Survey. *Journal of Gerontology: Social Sciences, 60B,* S82–S92.

Mintz, T. H. (2005). Linguistic and conceptual influences on adjective acquisition in 24- to 36-month-olds. *Developmental Psychology, 41,* 17–29.

Mistry, R. S., Vandewater, E. A., Huston, A. C., & McLoyd, V. (2002). Economic well-being and children's social adjustment: The role of family process in an ethnically diverse low income sample. *Child Development, 73,* 935–951.

Mitchell, E. A., Blair, P. S., & L'Hoir, M. P. (2006). Should pacifiers be recommended to prevent sudden infant death syndrome? *Pediatrics, 117,* 1755–1758.

Mitchell, V., & Helson, R. (1990). Women's prime of life: Is it the 50s? *Psychology of Women Quarterly, 16,* 331–347.

Mix, K. S., Huttenlocher, J., & Levine, S. C. (2002). Multiple cues for quantification in infancy: Is number one of them? *Psychological Bulletin, 128,* 278–294.

Mix, K. S., Levine, S. C., & Huttenlocher, J. (1999). Early fraction calculation ability. *Developmental Psychology, 35,* 164–174.

Miyake, K., Chen, S., & Campos, J. (1985). Infants' temperament, mothers' mode of interaction and attachment in Japan: An interim report. In I. Bretherton & E. Waters (Eds.), Growing points of attachment theory and research. *Monographs of the Society for Research in Child Development, 50*(1–2, Serial No. 109), 276–297.

Mlot, C. (1998). Probing the biology of emotion. *Science, 280,* 1005–1007.

Modzeleski, W., Feucht, T., Rand, M., Hall, J. E., Simon, T. R., Butler, L., Taylor, A., Hunter, M., Anderson, M. A., Barrios, L., & Hertz, M. (2008). School-associated student homicides—United States, 1992-2006. *Morbidity and Mortality Weekly Report, 57*(02), 33–36.

Moen, P., Dempster-McClain, D., & Williams, R. M., Jr. (1992). Successful aging: Life-course perspective on women's multiple roles and health. *American Journal of Sociology, 97,* 1612–1638.

Moen, P., & Wethington, E. (1999). Midlife development in a life course context. In S. L. Willis & J. D. Reid (Eds.), *Life in the middle: Psychological and social development in middle age* (pp. 1–23). San Diego: Academic Press.

Moffitt, T. E. (1993). Adolescent-limited and life-course-persistent antisocial behavior: A developmental taxonomy. *Psychological Review, 100,* 674–701.

Mokdad, A. H., Bowman, B. A., Ford, E. S., Vinicor, F., Marks, J. S., & Koplan, J. P. (2001). The continuing epidemics of obesity and diabetes in the United States. *Journal of the American Medical Association, 286,* 1195–1200.

Mokdad, A. H., Ford, E. S., Bowman, B. A., Dietz, W. H., Vinicor, F., Bales, V. S., & Marks, J. S. (2003). Prevalence of obesity, diabetes, and obesity-related health risk factors, 2001. *Journal of the American Medical Association, 289,* 76–79.

Mokdad, A. H., Marks, J. S., Stroup, D. F., & Gerberding, J. L. (2005). Correction: Actual causes of death in the United States, 2000.

Journal of the American Medical Association, 293, 293–294.

Moline, M. L., & Zendell, S. M. (2000). Evaluating and managing premenstrual syndrome. *Medscape General Medicine, 2.* Retrieved December 27, 2004, from www.medscape.com/viewarticle/408913_print.

Mollenkopf, J., Waters, M. C., Holdaway, J., & Kasinitz, P. (2005). The ever-winding path: Ethnic and racial diversity in the transition to adulthood. In R. A. Settersten Jr., F. F. Furstenberg Jr., & R. G. Rumbaut (Eds.), *On the frontier of adulthood: Theory, research, and public policy* (pp. 454–497). (John D. and Catherine T. MacArthur Foundation Series on Mental Health and Development, Research Network on Transitions to Adulthood and Public Policy.) Chicago: University of Chicago Press.

Molofsky, A. V., Slutsky, S. G., Joseph, N. M., He, S., Pardal, R., Krishnamurthy, J., Sharpless, N. E., & Morrison, S. J. (2006). Increasing p16INK4a expression decreases forebrain progenitors and neurogenesis during ageing. *Nature, 443,* 448–452.

Mondschein, E. R., Adolph, K. E., & Tamis-LeMonda, C. S. (2000). Gender bias in mothers' expectations about infant crawling. *Journal of Experimental Child Psychology* (Special Issue on Gender), *77,* 304–316.

Money, J., Hampson, J. G., & Hampson, J. L. (1955). Hermaphroditism: Recommendations concerning assignment of sex, change of sex and psychologic management. *Bulletin of the Johns Hopkins Hospital, 97*(4), 284–300.

Monk, T. H. (2000). What can the chronobiologist do to help the shift worker? *Journal of Biological Rhythms, 15,* 86–94.

Montague, D. P. F., & Walker-Andrews, A. S. (2001). Peekaboo: A new look at infants' perception of emotion expressions. *Developmental Psychology, 37,* 826–838.

Montenegro, X. P. (2004). *The divorce experience: A study of divorce at midlife and beyond.* Washington, DC: American Association of Retired Persons.

Montgomery, M. J., & Côté, J. E. (2003). College as a transition to adulthood. In G. R. Adams & M. D. Berzonsky (Eds.), *Blackwell handbook of adolescence.* Malden, MA: Blackwell.

Moolchan, E. T., Franken, F. H., & Jaszyna-Gasior, M. (2006). Adolescent nicotine metabolism: Ethnoracial differences among dependent smokers. *Ethnicity and Disease, 16*(1), 239–243.

Moon, C., Cooper, R. P., & Fifer, W. P. (1993). Two-day-olds prefer their native language. *Infant Behavior and Development, 16,* 495–500.

Moon, C., & Fifer, W. P. (1990, April). *Newborns prefer a prenatal version of mother's voice.* Paper presented at the biannual meeting of the International Society of Infant Studies, Montreal, Canada.

Mooney-Somers, J., & Golombok, S. (2000). Children of lesbian mothers: From the

1970s to the new millennium. *Sexual and Relationship Therapy, 15*(2), 121–126.

Moore, D. W. (2005, May 17). *Three in four Americans support euthanasia: Significantly less support for doctor-assisted suicide.* The Gallup Organization. Retrieved May 24, 2005, from www.gallup.com/poll/content/login.aspx?ci=16333.

Moore, M. J., Moir, P., & Patrick, M. M. (2004). *The state of aging and health in America 2004.* Washington, DC: Centers for Disease Control and Prevention and Merck Institute of Aging & Health.

Moore, S. E., Cole, T. J., Poskitt, E. M. E., Sonko, B. J., Whitehead, R. G., McGregor, I. A., & Prentice, A. M. (1997). Season of birth predicts mortality in rural Gambia. *Nature, 388,* 434.

Morgan, W. J., Crain, E. F., Gruchalla, R. S., O'Connor, G. T., Kattan, M., Evans, R., Stout, J., Malindzak, G., Smartt, E., Plaut, M., Walter, M., Vaughan, B., & Mitchell, H., for the Inner-City Asthma Study Group. (2004). Results of a home-based environmental intervention among urban children with asthma. *New England Journal of Medicine, 351,* 1068–1080.

Morin, C. M., Colecchi, C., Stone, J., Sood, R., & Brink, D. (1999). Behavioral and pharmacological therapies for late-life insomnia: A randomized controlled trial. *Journal of the American Medical Association, 281,* 991–999.

Morison, P., & Masten, A. S. (1991). Peer reputation in middle childhood as a predictor of adaptation in adolescence: A seven-year follow-up. *Child Development, 62,* 991–1007.

Morris, M. C. (2004). Diet and Alzheimer's Disease: What the evidence shows. *Medscape General Medicine, 6,* 1–5.

Morris, R., & Kratochwill, T. (1983). *Treating children's fears and phobias: A behavioral approach.* Elmsford, NY: Pergamon.

Morrison, J. A., Friedman, L. A., Harlan, W. R., Harlan, L. C., Barton, B. A., Schreiber, G. B., & Klein, D. J. (2005). Development of the metabolic syndrome in black and white adolescent girls. *Pediatrics, 116,* 1178–1182.

Morrow, D. G., Menard, W. W. E., Stine-Morrow, E. A. L., Teller, T., & Bryant, D. (2001). The influence of expertise and task factors on age differences in pilot communication. *Psychology and Aging, 16,* 31–46.

Mortensen, E. L., Michaelson, K. F., Sanders, S. A., & Reinisch, J. M. (2002). The association between duration of breast-feeding and adult intelligence. *Journal of the American Medical Association, 287,* 2365–2371.

Mortimer, J. A., Snowdon, D. A., & Markesbery, W. R. (2002). Head circumference, education, and risk of dementia: Findings from the Nun Study. *Journal of Clinical and Experimental Neuropsychology, 25,* 671–679.

Mosca, L., Collins, P., Harrington, D. M., Mendelsohn, M. E., Pasternak, R. C., Robertson, R. M., Schenck-Gustafsson, K.,

Smith, S. C., Jr., Taubert, K. A., & Wenger, N. K., (2001). Hormone therapy and cardiovascular disease: A statement for healthcare professionals from the American Heart Association. *Circulation, 104,* 499–503.

Mosconi, L., Tsui, W.-H., De Santi, S., Li, J., Rusinek, H., Convit, A., Li, Y., Boppana, M., & de Leon, M. J. (2005). Reduced hippocampal metabolism in MCI and ADO Automated FDG-PET image analysis. *Neurology, 64,* 1860–1867.

Mosconi, L., Tsui, W. H., Herholz, K., Pupi, A., Drzezga, A., Lucignani, G., Reiman, E. M., Holthoff, V., Kalbe, E., Sorbi, S., Diehl-Schmid, J., Perneczky, R., Clerici, F., Caselli, R., Beuthien-Baumann, B., Kurz, A., Minoshima, S., & de Leon, M. J. (2008). Multicenter standardized ^{18}F-FDG PET diagnosis of mild cognitive impairment, Alzheimer's disease, and other dementias. *Journal of Nuclear Medicine, 49,* 390–398.

Moses, L. J., Baldwin, D. A., Rosicky, J. G., & Tidball, G. (2001). Evidence for referential understanding in the emotions domain at twelve and eighteen months. *Child Development, 72,* 718–735.

Mosher, W. D., Chandra, A., & Jones, J. (2005). Sexual behavior and selected health measures: Men and women 15–44 years of age, United States, 2002. *Advance Data from Vital and Health Statistics,* No. 362. Hyattsville, MD: Centers for Disease Control and Prevention, National Center for Health Statistics.

Mosier, C. E., & Rogoff, B. (2003). Privileged treatment of toddlers: Cultural aspects of individual choice and responsibility. *Developmental Psychology, 39,* 1047–1060.

Moskovitz, J., Bar-Noy, S., Williams, W. M., Requena, J., Berlett, B. S., & Stadtman, E. R. (2001). Methionine sulfoxide reductase (MsrA) is a regulator of antioxidant defense and lifespan in mammals. *Proceedings of the National Academy of Sciences, 98,* 12920–12925.

Moss, E., & St-Laurent, D. (2001). Attachment at school age and academic performance. *Developmental Psychology, 37,* 863–874.

Moss, M. S., & Moss, S. Z. (1989). The death of a parent. In R. A. Kalish (Ed.), *Midlife loss: Coping strategies.* Newbury Park, CA: Sage.

Mounts, N. S., & Steinberg, L. (1995). An ecological analysis of peer influence on adolescent grade point average and drug use. *Developmental Psychology, 31,* 915–922.

Mouw, T. (2005). Sequences of early adult transition: A look at variability and consequences. In R. A. Settersten Jr., F. F. Furstenberg Jr., & R. G. Rumbaut (Eds.), *On the frontier of adulthood: Theory, research, and public policy* (pp. 256–291). (John D. and Catherine T. MacArthur Foundation Series on Mental Health and Development, Research Network on Transitions to Adulthood and Public Policy.) Chicago: University of Chicago Press.

Mroczek, D. K. (2004). Positive and negative affect at midlife. In O. G. Brim, C. D. Ryff,

and R. C. Kessler (Eds.), *How healthy are we? A national study of well-being at midlife* (pp. 205–226). Chicago: University of Chicago Press.

Mroczek, D. K., & Kolarz, C. M. (1998). The effect of age on positive and negative affect: A developmental perspective on happiness. *Journal of Personality and Social Psychology, 75*(5), 1333–1349.

Mroczek, D. K., & Spiro, A. (2005). Change in life satisfaction during adulthood: Findings from the Veterans Affairs Normative Aging Study. *Journal of Personality and Social Psychology, 88,* 189–202.

Mroczek, D. K., & Spiro, A., III. (2007). Personality change influences mortality in older men. *Psychological Science, 18*(5), 371–376.

Msall, M. S. E. (2004). Developmental vulnerability and resilience in extremely preterm infants. *Journal of the American Medical Association, 292,* 2399–2401.

MTA Cooperative Group. (1999). A 14-month randomized clinical trial of treatment strategies for attention-deficit/hyperactivity disorder. *Archives of General Psychiatry, 56,* 1073–1986.

MTA Cooperative Group. (2004a). National Institute of Mental Health multimodal treatment study of ADHD follow-up: Changes in effectiveness and growth after the end of treatment. *Pediatrics, 113,* 762–769.

MTA Cooperative Group. (2004b). National Institute of Mental Health multimodal treatment study of ADHD follow-up: 24-month outcomes of treatment strategies for attention-deficit/hyperactivity disorder. *Pediatrics, 113,* 754–769.

Mueller, T. I., Kohn, R., Leventhal, N., Leon, A. C., Solomon, D., Coryell, W., Endicott, J., Alexopoulos, G. S., & Keller, M. B. (2004). The course of depression in elderly patients. *American Journal of Psychiatry, 12,* 22–29.

Mullan, D., & Currie, C. (2000). Socioeconomic equalities in adolescent health. In C. Currie, K. Hurrelmann, W. Settertobulte, R. Smith, & J. Todd (Eds.), *Health and health behaviour among young people: A WHO cross-national study (HBSC) international report* (pp. 65–72). WHO Policy Series: Healthy Policy for Children and Adolescents, Series No. 1. Copenhagen, Denmark: World Health Organization Regional Office for Europe.

Mulrine, A. (2004, February 2). Coming of age in ancient times. *U.S. News & World Report.* Retrieved March 31, 2004, from www.usnews.com/usnews/culture/articles/040202/2child.htm.

Mumme, D. L., & Fernald, A. (2003). The infant as onlooker: Learning from emotional reactions observed in a television scenario. *Child Development, 74,* 221–237.

Munakata, Y. (2001). Task-dependency in infant behavior: Toward an understanding of the processes underlying cognitive development. In F. Lacerda, C. von Hofsten, &

M. Heimann (Eds.), *Emerging cognitive abilities in early infancy.* Hillsdale, NJ: Erlbaum.

Munakata, Y., McClelland, J. L., Johnson, M. J., & Siegler, R. S. (1997). Rethinking infant knowledge: Toward an adaptive process account of successes and failures in object permanence tasks. *Psychological Review, 104,* 686–714.

Munk-Olsen, T., Laursen, T. M., Pedersen, C. B., Mors, O., & Mortensen, P. B. (2006). New parents and mental disorders: A population-based register study. *Journal of the American Medical Association, 296,* 2582–2589.

Munson, M. L., & Sutton, P. D. (2004). Births, marriages, divorces, and deaths: Provisional data for November 2003. *National Vital Statistics Reports, 52*(20). Hyattsville, MD: National Center for Health Statistics.

Muntner, P., He, J., Cutler, J. A., Wildman, R. P., & Whelton, P. K. (2004, May 5). Trends in blood pressure among children and adolescents. *Journal of the American Medical Association, 291,* 2107–2113.

Murachver, T., Pipe, M., Gordon, R., Owens, J. L., & Fivush, R. (1996). Do, show, and tell: Children's event memories acquired through direct experience, observation, and stories. *Child Development, 67,* 3029–3044.

Muraco, A. (2006). Intentional families: Fictive kin ties between cross-gender, different sexual orientation friends. *Journal of Marriage and Family, 68,* 1313–1325.

Muris, P., Merckelbach, H., & Collaris, R. (1997). Common childhood fears and their origins. *Behaviour Research and Therapy, 35,* 929–937.

Murphy, J. M., Pagano, M. E., Nachmani, J., Sperling, P., Kane, S., & Kleinman, R. E. (1998). The relationship of school breakfast to psychosocial and academic functioning: Cross-sectional and longitudinal observations in an inner-city school sample. *Archives of Pediatric and Adolescent Medicine, 152,* 899–907.

Murray, M. L., de Vries, C. S., and Wong, I. C. K. (2004). A drug utilisation study of anti-depressants in children and adolescents using the General Practice Research data base. *Archives of the Diseases of Children, 89,* 1098–1102.

Musick, M. A., Herzog, A. R., & House, J. S. (1999). Volunteering and mortality among older adults: Findings from a national sample. *Journal of Gerontology: Psychological Sciences, 54B,* S173–S180.

Mustanski, B. S., DuPree, M. G., Nievergelt, C. M., Bocklandt, S., Schork, N. J., & Hamer, D. H. (2005). A genomewide scan of male sexual orientation. *Human Genetics, 116,* 272–278.

Mustillo, S., Worthman, C., Erkanli, A., Keeler, G., Angold, A., & Costello, E. J. (2003). Obesity and psychiatric disorder: Developmental trajectories. *Pediatrics, 111,* 851–859.

Muter, V., Hulme, C., Snowling, M. J., & Stevenson, J. (2004). Phonemes, rimes, vocabulary, and grammatical skill as foundations of early reading development: Evidence from a longitudinal study. *Developmental Psychology, 40,* 665–681.

Myers, D., & Diener, E. (1995). Who is happy? *Psychological Science, 6,* 10–19.

Myers, D. G. (2000). The funds, friends, and faith of happy people. *American Psychologist, 55,* 56–67.

Myers, D. G., & Diener, E. (1996). The pursuit of happiness. *Scientific American, 274,* 54–56.

Myers, J. E., & Perrin, N. (1993). Grandparents affected by parental divorce: A population at risk? *Journal of Counseling and Development, 72,* 62–66.

Myers, S. M., Johnson, C. P., & Council on Children with Disabilities. (2007). Management of children with autism spectrum disorders. *Pediatrics, 120*(5), 1162–1182.

Nadig, A. S., Ozonoff, S., Young, G. S., Rozga, A., Sigman, M., & Rogers, S. J. (2007). A prospective study of response to name in infants at risk for autism. *Archives of Pediatric and Adolescent Medicine, 161,* 378–383.

Nagaoka, J., & Roderick, M. (2004, April). *Ending social promotion: The effects of retention.* Chicago: Consortium on Chicago School Research.

Nagaraja, J., Menkedick, J., Phelan, K. J., Ashley, P., Zhang, X., & Lanphear, B. P. (2005). Deaths from residential injuries in US children and adolescents, 1985–1997. *Pediatrics, 116,* 454–461.

Naito, M., & Miura, H. (2001). Japanese childrens' numerical competencies: Age and school-related influences on the development of number concepts and addition skills. *Developmental Psychology, 37,* 217–230.

Nansel, T. R., Overpeck, M., Pilla, R. S., Ruan, W. J., Simons-Morton, B., & Scheidt, P. (2001). Bullying behaviors among U.S. youth: Prevalence and association with psychosocial adjustment. *Journal of the American Medical Association, 285,* 2094–2100.

Nash, J. M. (1997, February 3). Fertile minds. *Time,* pp. 49–56.

Natenshon, A. (2006). *Parental influence takes precedence over Barbie and the media.* Retrieved December 15, 2007, from www.empoweredparents.com/1prevention/prevention_09.htm.

Nathanielsz, P. W. (1995). The role of basic science in preventing low birth weight. *Future of Our Children, 5*(1), 57–70.

National Assessment of Educational Progress: The Nation's Report Card. (2004). *America's charter schools: Results from the NAEP 2003 Pilot Study* (NCES 2005-456). Jessup, MD: U.S. Department of Education.

National Association for Gifted Children (NAGC). (n.d.). *Frequently asked questions.* Retrieved April 22, 2006, from www.nagc.org/index.aspx?id=548.

National Association of State Boards of Education. (2000). *Fit, healthy, and ready to learn: A school health policy guide.* Alexandria, VA: Author.

National Cancer Institute. (2002). *Fact sheet: Tamoxifen questions and answers.* Retrieved January 22, 2008, from www.cancer.gov/cancertopics/factsheet/Therapy/tamoxifen.

National Center for Biotechnology Information (NCBI). (2002). *Genes and disease.* Retrieved from www.ncbi.nlm.nih.gov/disease.

National Center for Education Statistics (NCES). (2001). *The condition of education 2001* (NCES 2001-072). Washington, DC: U.S. Government Printing Office.

National Center for Education Statistics (NCES). (2003). *The condition of education, 2003* (NCES 2003-067). Washington, DC: Author.

National Center for Education Statistics (NCES). (2004a). *The condition of education 2004* (NCES 2004-077). Washington, DC: U.S. Government Printing Office.

National Center for Education Statistics (NCES). (2004b). *National assessment of educational progress: The nation's report card. Mathematics highlights 2003* (NCES 2004-451). Washington, DC: U.S. Department of Education.

National Center for Education Statistics (NCES). (2005a). *Children born in 2001—First results from the base year of Early Childhood Longitudinal Study, Birth Cohort* (ECLS-B). Retrieved November 19, 2004, from http://nces.ed.gov/pubs2005/children/index.asp.

National Center for Education Statistics (NCES). (2005b). *The condition of education 2005* (NCES 2005-094). Washington, DC: U.S. Government Printing Office.

National Center for Education Statistics (NCES). (2005c). *Trends in educational equity of girls & women 2004.* Retrieved May 8, 2008, from http://nces.ed.gov/pubsearch/pubsinfo.asp?pubid=2005016.

National Center for Education Statistics. (NCES). (2006a). *Calories in, calories out: Food and exercise in public elementary schools, 2005* (NCES 2006-057). Washington, DC: Author.

National Center for Education Statistics. (NCES). (2006b). *The condition of education 2006* (NCES 2006-071). Washington, DC: U.S. Government Printing Office.

National Center for Education Statistics (NCES). (2006c). *National Assessment of Adult Literacy (NAAL): A first look at the literacy of America's adults in the 21st century* (NCES 2006-470). Washington, DC: Author.

National Center for Education Statistics (NCES). (2007a). *The condition of education 2007* (NCES 2007-064). Washington, DC: Author.

National Center for Education Statistics (NCES). (2007b). *The Nation's Report Card: Mathematics 2007* (NCES 2007-494). Washington, DC: Author.

National Center for Education Statistics (NCES). (2007c). *The Nation's Report Card: Reading 2007* (NCES 2007-496). Washington, DC: Author.

National Center for Education Statistics (NCES). (2007d). *The reading literacy of U.S. fourth-grade students in an international context: Results from the 2001 and 2006 Progress in International Reading Literacy Study (PIRLS)* (NCES 2008-017). Washington, DC: Author.

National Center for Health Statistics (NCHS). (1998). *Health, United States, 1998 with socioeconomic status and health chartbook.* Hyattsville, MD: Author.

National Center for Health Statistics (NCHS). (1999). Abstract adapted from *Births: Final data for 1999* by Mid Atlantic Parents of Multiples. Retrieved March 7, 2006, from www.orgsites.com/va/mapom/_pgg1.php3.

National Center for Health Statistics (NCHS). (2004). *Health, United States, 2004 with chartbook on trends in the health of Americans* (DHHS Publication No. 2004-1232). Hyattsville, MD: National Center for Health Statistics.

National Center for Health Statistics (NCHS). (2005). *Health, United States, 2005* (DHHS Publication No. 2005-1232). Hyattsville, MD: Author.

National Center for Health Statistics. (NCHS). (2006). *Health, United States, 2006.* Hyattsville, MD: Author.

National Center for Health Statistics. (NCHS). (2007). *Health, United States, 2007 with chartbook on trends in the health of Americans.* Hyattsville, MD: Author.

National Center for Injury Prevention and Control (NCIPC). (2004). *Fact sheet: Teen drivers.* Retrieved May 7, 2004, from www.cdc.gov/ncip.

National Center for Learning Disabilities. (2004a). *Dyslexia: Learning disabilities in reading* [Fact sheet]. Retrieved May 30, 2004, from www.ld.org/LDInfoZone/InfoZone_ FactSheet_Dyslexia.cfm.

National Center for Learning Disabilities (2004b). *LD at a glance* [Fact sheet]. Retrieved May 30, 2004, from www.ld.org/LDInfoZone/InfoZone_FactSheet_LD.cfm.

National Center on Elder Abuse & Westat, Inc. (1998). *National Elder Abuse Incidence Study: Executive summary.* Washington, DC: American Public Human Services Association.

National Center on Shaken Baby Syndrome. (2000). *SBS questions.* Retrieved from www.dontshake.com/sbsquestions.html.

National Children's Study. (2004, November 16). *National Children's Study releases study plan and locations.* Retrieved April 3, 2005, from www.nationalchildrensstudy.gov/research/study plan/index.cfm.

National Clearinghouse on Child Abuse and Neglect Information (NCCANI). (2004). Long-term consequences of child abuse and neglect. Washington, DC: Retrieved October, 5, 2004, from http://nccanch.acf.hhs.gov/pubs/factsheets/longtermconsequences.cfm.

National Coalition for the Homeless. (2006a). *Education of homeless children and youth*

(NCH Fact Sheet No. 10). Washington, DC: Author.

National Coalition for the Homeless. (2006b). *Homeless families with children* (NCH Fact Sheet No. 12). Washington, DC: Author.

National Coalition for the Homeless. (2006c). *How many people experience homelessness?* (NCH Fact Sheet No. 2). Washington, DC: Author.

National Coalition for the Homeless. (2006d). *Who is homeless?* (NCH Fact Sheet No. 3). Washington, DC: Author.

National Coalition for the Homeless. (2006e). *Why are people homeless?* (NCH Fact Sheet No. 1). Washington, DC: Author.

National Council on Aging. (2000, March). *Myths and Realities: 2000 survey results.* Washington, DC: Author.

National Council on Aging. (2002). American perceptions of aging in the 21st century: The NCOA's Continuing Study of the Myths and Realities of Aging (2002 update). Washington, DC: Author.

National Highway Traffic Safety Administration. (2003). *Traffic safety facts 2002: Young drivers.* Washington, DC: Author.

National Hospice and Palliative Care Organization. (n.d.). *What is hospice and palliative care?* Retrieved June 25, 2007, from www.nhpco.org/i4a/pages/Index.cfm?pageid=3253&openpage=3253.

National Institute of Mental Health (NIMH). (1999a, April). *Suicide facts.* Washington, DC: Author. Retrieved from www.nimh.nih.gov/research/suifact.htm.

National Institute of Mental Health (NIMH). (1999b, June 1). *Older adults: Depression and suicide facts.* Washington, DC: Author. Retrieved from www.nimh.hin.gov/publicat/elderlydepsuicide.htm.

National Institute of Mental Health (NIMH). (2001a). *Helping children and adolescents cope with violence and disasters: Fact sheet* (NIH Publication No. 01-3518). Bethesda, MD: Author.

National Institute of Mental Health (NIMH). (2001b). *Teenage brain: A work in progress.* Retrieved March 11, 2004, from www.nimh.gov/publicat/teenbrain.cfm.

National Institute of Neurological Disorders and Stroke (NINDS). (2006, January 25). *NINDS Shaken baby syndrome information page.* Retrieved June 20, 2006, from www.ninds.nih.gov/disorders/shakenbaby/shakenbaby.htm.

National Institute of Neurological Disorders and Stroke (NINDS). (2007). *NINDS Asperger syndrome information page.* Retrieved April 3, 2008, from www.ninds.nih.gov/disorders/asperger/asperger.htm.

National Institute on Aging (NIA). (1980). *Senility: Myth or madness.* Washington, DC: U.S. Government Printing Office.

National Institute on Aging (NIA). (1993). *Bound for good health: A collection of Age Pages.* Washington, DC: U.S. Government Printing Office.

National Institute on Aging (NIA). (1995). *Don't take it easy—exercise.* Washington, DC: U.S. Government Printing Office.

National Institute on Alcohol Abuse and Alcoholism (NIAAA). (1996, July). *Alcohol alert* (No. 33-1996 [PH 366]). Bethesda, MD: Author.

National Institute on Drug Abuse (NIDA). (1996). *Monitoring the future.* Washington, DC: National Institutes of Health.

National Institute on Drug Abuse (NIDA). (2008). Quarterly Report: Potency Monitoring Project (Report 100). December 16, 2007 thru March 15, 2008. Conducted by National Center for Natural Products Research, University of Mississippi.

National Institutes of Health (NIH). (1992, December 7–9). Impotence. *NIH Consensus Statement, 10*(4). Washington, DC: U.S. Government Printing Office.

National Institutes of Health (NIH). (2003). The low-down on osteoporosis: What we know and what we don't. *Word on health.* Bethesda, MD: Author.

National Institutes of Health (NIH) Consensus Development Panel. (2001). National Institutes of Health Consensus Development conference statement: Phenylketonuria screening and management. October 16–18, 2000. *Pediatrics, 108*(4), 972–982.

National Institutes of Health (NIH) Consensus Development Panel on Osteoporosis Prevention, Diagnosis, and Therapy. (2001). Osteoporosis prevention, diagnosis, and therapy. *Journal of the American Medical Association, 285,* 785–794.

National Institutes of Health/National Institute on Aging. (1993, May). *In search of the secrets of aging* (NIH Publication No. 93-2756). Washington, DC: National Institutes of Health.

National Institutes of Health (NIH) State-of-the-Science Conference Statement. (2005). NIH state-of-the-science conference statement: Management of menopause-related symptoms. *Annals of Internal Medicine, 142* (12, Pt.1), 1003–1013.

National Law Center on Homelessness and Poverty. (2004). *Homelessness in the United States and the human right to housing.* Retrieved June 21, 2007, from www.nlchp.org/view_report.cfm?id-123.

National Library of Medicine. (2003). *Medical Encyclopedia: Conduct disorder.* Retrieved April 23, 2005, from www.nlm.nih.gov/medlineplus/ency/article/000919.htm.

National Library of Medicine. (2004). *Medical Encyclopedia: Oppositional defiant disorder.* Retrieved April 23, 2005, from www.nlm.nih.gov/medlineplus/ency/article/001537.htm.

National Mental Health Association. (n.d.). *Coping with loss—bereavement and grief* [Fact sheet]. Alexandria, VA: Author.

National Parents' Resource Institute for Drug Education. (1999, September 8). *PRIDE surveys, 1998–99 national summary: Grades 6–12.* Bowling Green, KY: Author.

National Reading Panel. (2000). *Report of the National Reading Panel. Teaching children to read: An evidence-based assessment of the scientific research literature on reading and its implications for reading instruction: Reports of the subgroups.* Washington, DC: National Institute of Child Health and Human Development.

National Research Council (NRC). (1993a). *Losing generations: Adolescents in high risk settings.* Washington, DC: National Academy Press.

National Research Council (NRC). (1993b). *Understanding child abuse and neglect.* Washington, DC: National Academy Press.

National Sleep Foundation. (2001). *2001 Sleep in America poll.* Retrieved October 18, 2002, from www.sleepfoundation.org/publications/2001poll.html.

National Sleep Foundation. (2004). *Sleep in America.* Washington, DC: Author.

Nedrow, A., Miller, J., Walker, M., Nygren, P., Huffman, L. H., & Nelson, H. D. (2006). Complementary and alternative therapies for the management of menopause-related symptoms. *Archives of Internal Medicine, 166,* 1453–1465.

Nef, S., Verma-Kurvari, S., Merenmies, J., Vassallt, J.-D., Efstratiadis, A., Accili, D., & Parada, L. F. (2003). Testis determination requires insulin receptor family function in mice. *Nature, 426,* 291–295.

Neisser, U., Boodoo, G., Bouchard, T. J., Jr., Boykin, A. W., Brody, N., Ceci, S. J., Halpern, D. F., Loehlin, J. C., Perloff, R., Sternberg, R. J., & Urbina, S. (1996). Intelligence: Knowns and unknowns. *American Psychologist, 51*(2), 77–101.

Neitzel, C., & Stright, A. D. (2003). Relations between parents' scaffolding and children's academic self-regulation: Establishing a foundation of self-regulatory competence. *Journal of Family Psychology, 17,* 147–159.

Nelson, C. A. (1995). The ontogeny of human memory: A cognitive neuroscience perspective. *Developmental Psychology, 31,* 723–738.

Nelson, C. A., Monk, C. S., Lin, J., Carver, L. J., Thomas, K. M., & Truwit, C. L. (2000). Functional neuroanatomy of spatial working memory in children. *Developmental Psychology, 36,* 109–116.

Nelson, H. D., Vescon, K. K., Haney, E., Fu, R., Nedrow, A., Miller, J., Nicolaidis, C., Walker, M., & Humphrey, L. (2006). Nonhormonal therapies for menopausal hot flashes: Systematic review and meta-analysis. *Journal of the American Medical Association, 295,* 2057–2071.

Nelson, K. (1992). Emergence of autobiographical memory at age 4. *Human Development, 35,* 172–177.

Nelson, K. (1993). The psychological and social origins of autobiographical memory. *Psychological Science, 47,* 7–14.

Nelson, K. (2005). Evolution and development of human memory systems. In B. J. Ellis & D. F. Bjorklund (Eds.), *Origins of the social mind: Evolutionary psychology and child development* (pp. 319–345). New York: Guilford Press.

Nelson, K., & Fivush, R. (2004). The emergence of autobiographical memory: A social cultural developmental theory. *Psychological Bulletin, 111,* 486–511.

Nelson, K., Mattingly, M., & Schmitt, F. A. (2007). Out-of-body experience and arousal. *Neurology, 68,* 94–795.

Nelson, K. B., Dambrosia, J. M., Ting, T. Y., & Grether, J. K. (1996). Uncertain value of electronic fetal monitoring in predicting cerebral palsy. *New England Journal of Medicine, 334,* 613–618.

Nelson, M. C., & Gordon-Larsen, P. (2006). Physical activity and sedentary behavior patterns are associated with selected adolescent risk behaviors. *Pediatrics, 117,* 1281–1290.

Nelson, M. E., Fiatarone, M. A., Morganti, C. M., Trice, I., Greenberg, R. A., & Evans, W. J. (1994). Effects of high-intensity strength training on multiple risk factors for osteoporotic fractures: A randomized controlled trial. *Journal of the American Medical Association, 272,* 1909–1914.

Ness, J., Ahmed, A., & Aronow, W. S. (2004). Demographics and payment characteristics of nursing home residents in the United States: A 23-year trend. *Journal of Gerontology: Medical Sciences, 59A,* 1213–1217.

Netz, Y., Wu, M., Becker, B. J., & Tenenbaum, G. (2005). Physical activity and psychological well-being in advanced age: A meta-analysis of intervention studies. *Psychology and Aging, 20,* 272–284.

Neugarten, B. L. (1967). The awareness of middle age. In R. Owen (Ed.), *Middle age.* London: BBC.

Neugarten, B. L. (1968). Adult personality: Toward a psychology of the life cycle. In B. Neugarten (Ed.), *Middle age and aging.* Chicago: University of Chicago Press.

Neugarten, B. L. (1977). Personality and aging. In J. E. Birren & K. W. Schaie (Eds.), *Handbook of the psychology of aging and the social sciences.* New York: Van Nostrand Reinhold.

Neugarten, B. L., Havighurst, R., & Tobin, S. (1968). Personality and patterns of aging. In B. Neugarten (Ed.), *Middle age and aging.* Chicago: University of Chicago Press.

Neugarten, B. L., Moore, J. W., & Lowe, J. C. (1965). Age norms, age constraints, and adult socialization. *American Journal of Sociology, 70,* 710–717.

Neugarten, B. L., & Neugarten, D. A. (1987, May). The changing meanings of age. *Psychology Today,* pp. 29–33.

Neupert, S. D., Almeida, D. M., Mroczek, D. K., & Spiro, A. (2006). Daily stressors and memory failures in a naturalistic setting: Findings from the VA Normative Aging Study. *Psychology and Aging, 21,* 424–429.

Neville, A. (n.d.). *The emotional and psychological effects of miscarriage.* Retrieved April 9, 2006, from www.opendoors.com.au/EffectsMiscarriage/EffectsMiscarriage.htm.

Neville, H. J., & Bavelier, D. (1998). Neural organization and plasticity of language. *Current Opinion in Neurobiology, 8*(2), 254–258.

Newcomb, A. F., & Bagwell, C. L. (1995). Children's friendship relations: A meta-analytic review. *Psychological Bulletin, 117*(2), 306–347.

Newcomb, A. F., Bukowski, W. M., & Pattee, L. (1993). Children's peer relations: A meta-analytic review of popular, rejected, neglected, controversial, and average sociometric status. *Psychological Bulletin, 113,* 99–128.

Newman, A. B., Simonsick, E. M., Naydeck, B. L., Boudreau, R. M., Kritchevsky, S. B., Nevitt, M. C., Pahor, M., Satterfield, S., Brach, J. S., Studenski, S. A., & Harris, T. B. (2006). Association of long-distance corridor walk performance with mortality, cardiovascular disease, mobility limitation, and disability. *Journal of the American Medical Association, 295,* 2018–2026.

Newman, D. L., Caspi, A., Moffitt, T. E., & Silva, P. A. (1997). Antecedents of adult interpersonal functioning: Effects of individual differences in age 3 temperament. *Developmental Psychology, 33,* 206–217.

Newman, K., & Aptekar, S. (2007). Sticking around: Delayed departure from the parental nest in Western Europe. In S. Danziger & C. Rouse (Eds.), *The price of independence: The economics of early adulthood.* (pp. 207–230). New York: Russell Sage Foundation.

Newman, R. S. (2005). The cocktail party effect in infants revisited: Listening to one's name in noise. *Developmental Psychology, 41,* 352–362.

Newman, S. (2003). The living conditions of elderly Americans. *Gerontologist, 43,* 99–109.

Newport, E., & Meier, R. (1985). The acquisition of American Sign Language. In D. Slobin (Ed.), *The cross-linguistic study of language acquisition* (Vol. 1, pp. 881–938). Hillsdale, NJ: Erlbaum.

Newport, E. L. (1991). Contrasting conceptions of the critical period for language. In S. Carey & R. Gelman (Eds.), *The epigenesis of mind: Essays on biology and cognition.* Hillsdale, NJ: Erlbaum.

Newport, E. L., Bavelier, D., & Neville, H. J. (2001). Critical thinking about critical periods: Perspectives on a critical period for language acquisition. In E. Dupoux (Ed.), *Language, brain, and cognitive development: Essays in honor of Jacques Mehler* (pp. 481–502). Cambridge, MA: MIT Press.

Newschaffer, C. J., Falb, M. D., & Gurney, J. G. (2005). National autism prevalence trends from United States special education data. *Pediatrics, 115,* e277–e282.

Newswise. (2004, November 16). *High stress doubles risk of painful periods.* Retrieved November 18, 2004, from www.newswise.com/p/articles/view/508336.

Newton, K. M., Reed, S. D., LaCroix, A. Z., Grothaus, L. C., Ehrlich, K., & Guiltinan, J. (2006). Treatment of vasomotor symptoms of menopause with black cohosh, multibotanicals, soy, hormone therapy, or placebo: A randomized trial. *Annals of Internal Medicine, 145*(12), 869–879.

NICHD Early Child Care Research Network. (1996). Characteristics of infant child care: Factors contributing to positive caregiving. *Early Childhood Research Quarterly, 11,* 269–306.

NICHD Early Child Care Research Network. (1997). The effects of infant child care on infant-mother attachment security: Results of the NICHD study of early child care. *Child Development, 68,* 860–879.

NICHD Early Child Care Research Network. (1998a). Early child care and self-control, compliance and problem behavior at 24 and 36 months. *Child Development, 69,* 1145–1170.

NICHD Early Child Care Research Network. (1998b). Relations between family predictors and child outcomes: Are they weaker for children in child care? *Developmental Psychology, 34,* 1119–1127.

NICHD Early Child Care Research Network. (1998c, November). *When child care classrooms meet recommended guidelines for quality.* Paper presented at the meeting of the National Association for the Education of Young People.

NICHD Early Child Care Research Network. (1999a). Child outcomes when child care center classes meet recommended standards for quality. *American Journal of Public Health, 89,* 1072–1077.

NICHD Early Child Care Research Network. (1999b). Chronicity of maternal depressive symptoms, maternal sensitivity, and child functioning at 36 months. *Developmental Psychology, 35,* 1297–1310.

NICHD Early Child Care Research Network. (2000). The relation of child care to cognitive and language development. *Child Development, 71,* 960–980.

NICHD Early Child Care Research Network. (2001a). Child care and children's peer interaction at 24 and 36 months: The NICHD Study of Early Child Care. *Child Development, 72,* 1478–1500.

NICHD Early Child Care Research Network. (2001b). Child-care and family predictors of preschool attachment and stability from infancy. *Developmental Psychology, 37,* 847–862.

NICHD Early Child Care Research Network. (2002). Child-care structure, process, and outcome: Direct and indirect effects of child-care quality on young children's development. *Psychological Science, 13,* 199–206.

NICHD Early Child Care Research Network. (2003). Does amount of time spent in child care predict socioemotional adjustment during the transition to kindergarten? *Child Development, 74,* 976–1005.

NICHD Early Child Care Research Network. (2004a). Are child developmental outcomes related to before- and afterschool care arrangement? Results from the NICHD Study of Early Child Care. *Child Development 75,* 280–295.

NICHD Early Child Care Research Network. (2004b). Does class size in first grade relate to children's academic and social performance or observed classroom processes? *Developmental Psychology, 40,* 651–664.

NICHD Early Child Care Research Network. (2005a). Duration and developmental timing of poverty and children's cognitive and social development from birth through third grade. *Child Development, 76,* 795–810.

NICHD Early Child Care Research Network. (2005b). Pathways to reading: The role of oral language in the transition to reading. *Developmental Psychology, 41,* 428–442.

NICHD Early Child Care Research Network. (2005c). Predicting individual differences in attention, memory, and planning in first graders from experiences at home, child care, and school. *Developmental Psychology, 41,* 99–114.

NICHD Early Child Care Research Network. (2006). Infant-mother attachment classification: Risk and protection in relation to changing maternal caregiving quality. *Developmental Psychology, 42,* 38–58.

NICHD Early Child Care Research Network & Duncan, G. J. (2003). Modeling the impacts of child care quality on children's preschool cognitive development. *Child Development, 74,* 1454–1475.

Nielsen, M., Dissanayake, C., & Kashima, Y. (2003). A longitudinal investigation of self-other discrimination and the emergence of mirror self-recognition. *Infant Behavior & Development, 26,* 213–226.

Nielsen, M., Suddendorf, T., & Slaughter, V. (2006). Mirror self-recognition beyond the face. *Child Development, 77,* 176–185.

Nihtilä, E., & Martikainen, P. (2008). Why older people living with a spouse are less likely to be institutionalized: The role of socioeconomic factors and health characteristics. *Scandinavian Journal of Public Health, 36,* 35–43.

Nin, A. (1966). *The diaries of Anaïs Nin* (Vol. I). New York: Harcourt Brace Jovanovich.

Nin, A. (1971). *The diaries of Anaïs Nin* (Vol. IV). New York: Harcourt Brace Jovanovich.

Nisan, M., & Kohlberg, L. (1982). Universality and variation in moral judgment: A longitudinal and cross-sectional study in Turkey. *Child Development, 53,* 865–876.

Nisbett, R. E. (1998). Race, genetics, and IQ. In C. Jencks & M. Phillips (Eds.), *The Black-White test score gap* (pp. 86–102). Washington, DC: Brookings Institution.

Nisbett, R. E. (2005). Heredity, environment, and race differences in IQ: A commentary on Rushton and Jensen (2005). *Psychology, Public Policy, and Law, 11,* 302–310.

Nix, R. L., Pinderhughes, E. E., Dodge, K. A., Bates, J. E., Pettit, G. S., & McFadyen-Ketchum, S. A. (1999). The relation between mothers' hostile attribution tendencies and children's externalizing behavior problems: The mediating role of mothers' harsh discipline practices. *Child Development, 70*(4), 896–909.

Nobre, A. C., & Plunkett, K. (1997). The neural system of language: Structure and development. *Current Opinion in Neurobiology, 7,* 262–268.

Nock, M. K., Borges, G., Bromet, E. J., Alonso, J., Angermeyer, M., Beautrais, A., Bruffaerts, R., Chiu, W. T., de Girolamo, G., Gluzman, S., de Graaf, R., Gureje, O., Haro, J. M., Huang, Y., Karam, E., Kessler, R. C., Lepine, J. P., Levinson, D., Medina-Mora, M. E., Ono, Y., Posada-Villa, J., & Williams, D. (2008). Cross-national prevalence and risk factors for suicidal ideation, plans and attempts. *British Journal of Psychiatry, 192,* 98–105.

Noël, P. H., Williams, J. W., Unutzer, J., Worchel, J., Lee, S., Cornell, J., Katon, W., Harpole, L. H., & Hunkeler, E. (2004). Depression and comorbid illness in elderly primary care patients: Impact on multiple domains of health status and well-being. *Annals of Family Medicine, 2,* 555–562.

Noirot, E., & Algeria, J. (1983). Neonate orientation towards human voice differs with type of feeding. *Behavioral Processes, 8,* 65–71.

Noriuchi, M., Kikuchi, Y., & Senoo, A. (2008). The functional neuroanatomy of maternal love: Mother's response to infant's attachment behaviors. *Biological Psychiatry, 63,* 415–423.

Norton, A. J., & Moorman, J. E. (1987). Current trends in marriage and divorce among American women. *Journal of Marriage and the Family, 49*(1), 3–14.

Nourot, P. M. (1998). Sociodramatic play: Pretending together. In D. P. Fromberg & D. Bergen (Eds.), *Play from birth to twelve and beyond: Contexts, perspectives, and meanings* (pp. 378–391). New York: Garland.

Nucci, L., Hasebe, Y., & Lins-Dyer, M. T. (2005). Adolescent psychological well-being and parental control. In J. Smetana (Ed.), *Changing boundaries of parental authority during adolescence* (New Directions for Child and Adolescent Development, No. 108, pp. 17–30). San Francisco: Jossey-Bass.

Nugent, J. K., Lester, B. M., Greene, S. M., Wieczorek-Deering, D., & O'Mahony, P. (1996). The effects of maternal alcohol consumption and cigarette smoking during pregnancy on acoustic cry analysis. *Child Development, 67,* 1806–1815.

Nurnberg, H. G., Hensley, P. L., Gelenberg, A. J., Fava, M., Lauriello, J., & Paine, S. (2003). Treatment of antidepressant-associated sexual dysfunction with sildenafil. *Journal of the American Medical Association, 289,* 56–64.

Nussbaum, R. L. (1998). Putting the parkin into Parkinson's. *Nature, 392,* 544–545.

Oakes, L. M. (1994). Development of infants' use of continuity cues in their perception of causality. *Developmental Psychology, 30,* 869–879.

Oakes, L. M., Coppage, D. J., & Dingel, A. (1997). By land or by sea: The role of perceptual similarity in infants' categorization of animals. *Developmental Psychology, 33,* 396–407.

Ober, C., Tan, Z., Sun, Y., Possick, J. D., Pan, L., Nicolae, R., Radford, S., Parry, R. R., Heinzmann, A., Deichmann, K. A., Lester, L. A., Gern, J. E., Lemanske, R. F., Jr., Nicolae, D. L., Elias, J. A., & Chupp, G. L. (2008). Effect of variation in *CH13L1* on serum YKL-40 level, risk of asthma, and lung function. *New England Journal of Medicine, 358,* 1682–1691.

O'Brien, C. M., & Jeffery, H. E. (2002). Sleep deprivation, disorganization and fragmentation during opiate withdrawal in newborns. *Pediatric Child Health, 38,* 66–71.

O'Connor, B. P., & Vallerand, R. J. (1998). Psychological adjustment variables as predictors of mortality among nursing home residents. *Psychology and Aging, 13*(3), 368–374.

O'Connor, T., Heron, J., Golding, J., Beveridge, M., & Glover, V. (2002). Maternal antenatal anxiety and children's behavioural/emotional problems at 4 years. *British Journal of Psychiatry, 180,* 502–508.

O'Donnell, K. (2006). *Adult education participation in 2004–06* (NCES 2006-077). Washington, DC: National Center for Education Statistics.

Oehlenschlager, A. G. (1857). *Aladdin, or the wonderful lamp* (T. Martin, Trans.).

Offer, D., & Church, R. B. (1991). Generation gap. In R. M. Lerner, A. C. Petersen, & J. Brooks-Gunn (Eds.), *Encyclopedia of adolescence* (pp. 397–399). New York: Garland.

Offer, D., Kaiz, M., Ostrov, E., & Albert, D. B. (2002). Continuity in family constellation. *Adolescent and Family Health, 3,* 3–8.

Offer, D., Offer, M. K., & Ostrov, E. (2004). *Regular guys: 34 years beyond adolescence.* Dordrecht, Netherlands: Kluwer-Academic.

Offer, D., Ostrov, E., & Howard, K. I. (1989). Adolescence: What is normal? *American Journal of Diseases of Children, 143,* 731–736.

Offer, D., Ostrov, E., Howard, K. I., & Atkinson, R. (1988). *The teenage world: Adolescents' self-image in ten countries.* New York: Plenum Press.

Offer, D., & Schonert-Reichl, K. A. (1992). Debunking the myths of adolescence: Findings from recent research. *Journal of the American Academy of Child and Adolescent Psychiatry, 31,* 1003–1014.

Office of Minority Health, Centers for Disease Control and Prevention. (2005). Health disparities experienced by Black or African Americans—United States. *Morbidity and Mortality Weekly Report, 54,* 1–3.

Office of National Drug Control Policy. (2008). *Teen marijuana use worsens depression: An analysis of recent data shows "self-medicating" could actually make things worse.* Washington, DC: Executive Office of the President.

Office on Smoking and Health, Centers for Disease Control and Prevention. (2006). *The health consequences of involuntary exposure to tobacco smoke: A report of the surgeon-general* (No. 017-024-01685-3). U.S. Department of Health and Human Services.

Offit, P. A., Quarles, J., Gerber, M. A., Hackett, C. J., Marcuse, E. K., Kollman, T. R., Gellin, B. G., & Landry, S. (2002). Addressing parents' concerns: Do multiple vaccines overwhelm or weaken the infant's immune system? *Pediatrics, 109*, 124–129.

Ofori, B., Oraichi, D., Blais, L., Rey, E., & Berard, A. (2006). Risk of congenital anomalies in pregnant users of non-steroidal anti-inflammatory drugs: A nested case-control study. *Birth Defects Research Part B: Developmental and Reproductive Toxicology, 77*(4), 268–279.

Ogden, C. L., Carroll, M. D., Curtin, L. R., McDowell, M. A., Tabak, C. J., & Flegal, K. M. (2006). Prevalence of overweight and obesity in the United States, 1999–2004. *Journal of the American Medical Association, 295*, 1549–1555.

Ogden, C. L., Carroll, M. D., & Flegal, K. M. (2008). High body mass index for age among US children and adolescents, 2003–2006. *Journal of the American Medical Association, 299*, 2401–2405.

Ogden, C. L., Carroll, M. D., McDowell, M. A., & Flegal, K. M. (2007). Obesity among adults in the United States: No change since 2003–2004. *NCHS Data Brief*. Hyattsville, MD: National Center for Health Statistics.

Ogden, C. L., Fryar, C. D., Carroll, M. D., & Flegal, K. M. (2004). Mean body weight, height, and body mass index, United States 1960–2002. *Advance Data from Vital and Health Statistics*, No. 347. Hyattsville, MD: National Center for Health Statistics.

Okamoto, K., & Tanaka, Y. (2004). Subjective usefulness and 6-year mortality risks among elderly persons in Japan. *Journal of Gerontology: Psychological Sciences, 59B*, P246–P249.

Olds, S. W. (1989). *The working parents' survival guide*. Rocklin, CA: Prima.

Olfson, M., Blanco, C., Liu, L., Moreno, C., & Laje, G. (2006). National trends in the outpatient treatment of children and adolescents with antipsychotic drugs. *Archives of General Psychiatry, 63*, 679–685.

Ollendick, T. H., Yang, B., King, N. J., Dong, Q., & Akande, A. (1996). Fears in American, Australian, Chinese, and Nigerian children and adolescents: A cross-cultural study. *Journal of Child Psychology and Psychiatry, 37*, 213–220.

Olshansky, S. J., Hayflick, L., & Carnes, B. A. (2002a). No truth to the fountain of youth. *Scientific American, 286*, 92–95.

Olshansky, S. J., Hayflick, L., & Carnes, B. A. (2002b). The truth about human aging. *Scientific American*. Retrieved August 23, 2002, from www.sciam.com/explorations/2002/051302aging.

Olshansky, S. J., Hayflick, L., & Perls, T. T. (2004). Anti-aging medicine: The hype and the reality—Part I. *Journal of Gerontology: Biological Sciences, 59A*, 513–514.

Olshansky, S. J., Passaro, D. J., Hershow, R. C., Layden, J., Carnes, B. A., Brody, J., Hayflick, L., Butler, R. N., Allison, D. B., & Ludwig, D. S. (2005). A potential decline in life expectancy in the United States in the 21st century. *New England Journal of Medicine, 352*, 1138–1145.

Olthof, T., Schouten, A., Kuiper, H., Stegge, H., & Jennekens-Schinkel, A. (2000). Shame and guilt in children: Differential situational antecedents and experiential correlates. *British Journal of Developmental Psychology, 18*, 51–64.

Olweus, D. (1995). Bullying or peer abuse at school: Facts and intervention. *Current Directions in Psychological Science, 4*, 196–200.

O'Neill, G., Summer, L, & Shirey, L. (1999). Hearing loss: A growing problem that affects quality of life. Washington, DC: National Academy on an Aging Society.

O'Rahilly, S. (1998). Life without leptin. *Nature, 392*, 330–331.

Orbuch, T. L., House, J. S., Mero, R. P., & Webster, P. S. (1996). Marital quality over the life course. *Social Psychology Quarterly, 59*, 162–171.

Orenstein, P. (2002, April 21). Mourning my miscarriage. *New York Times*. Retrieved from www.NYTimes.com.

Orentlicher, D. (1996). The legalization of physician-assisted suicide. *New England Journal of Medicine, 335*, 663–667.

Organ Procurement and Transplantation Network (OPTN). (2008). *Uniting People and information to help save lives: Data*. Retrieved May 5, 2008, from http://optn.org.

Organization for Economic Cooperation and Development (OCED). (2004). Education at a glance: OECD indicators—2004. *Education & Skills, 2004*(14), 1–456.

Orr, W. C., & Sohal, R. S. (1994). Extension of life-span by overexpression of superoxide dimutase and catylase in *Drosphila melanogaster*. *Science, 263*, 1128–1130.

Osgood, D. W., Ruth, G., Eccles, J., Jacobs, J., & Barber, B. (2005). Six paths to adulthood: Fast starters, parents without careers, educated partners, educated singles, working singles, and slow starters. In R. A. Settersten Jr., F. F. Furstenberg Jr., & R. G. Rumbaut (Eds.), *On the frontier of adulthood: Theory, research, and public policy* (pp. 320–355). (John D. and Catherine T. MacArthur Foundation Series on Mental Health and Development, Research Network on Transitions to Adulthood and Public Policy.) Chicago: University of Chicago Press.

Oshima, S. (1996, July 5). Japan: Feeling the strains of an aging population. *Science*, pp. 44–45.

Oshima-Takane, Y., Goodz, E., & Derevensky, J. L. (1996). Birth order effects on early language development: Do secondborn children learn from overheard speech? *Child Development, 67*, 621–634.

Ossorio, P., & Duster, T. (2005). Race and genetics: Controversies in biomedical, behavioral, and forensic sciences. *American Psychologist, 60*, 115–128.

Ostir, G. V., Ottenbacher, K. J., & Markides, K. S. (2004). Onset of frailty in older adults and the protective role of positive affect. *Psychology and Aging, 19*, 402–408.

Otsuka, R., Watanabe, H., Hirata, K., Tokai, K., Muro, T., Yoshiyama, M., Takeuchi, K., & Yoshikawa, J. (2001). Acute effects of passive smoking on the coronary circulation in healthy young adults. *Journal of the American Medical Association, 286*, 436–441.

Ott, A., Slooter, A. J. C., Hofman, A., Van Harskamp, F., Witteman, J. C. M., Van Broeckhoven, C., Van Duijn, C. M., & Breteler, M. M. B. (1998). Smoking and risk of dementia and Alzheimer's disease in a population-based cohort study. *Lancet, 351*, 1840–1843.

Otten, M. W., Teutsch, S. M., Williamson, D. F., & Marks, J. S. (1990). The effect of known risk factors on the excess mortality of black adults in the United States. *Journal of the American Medical Association, 263*(6), 845–850.

Overbeek, G., Stattin, H., Vermulst, A., Ha, T., & Engels, R. C. M. E. (2007). Parent-child relationships, partner relationships, and emotional adjustment: A birth-to-maturity prospective study. *Developmental Psychology, 43*, 429–437.

Owen, C. G., Whincup, P. H., Odoki, K., Gilg, J. A., & Cook, D. G. (2002). Infant feeding and blood cholesterol: A study in adolescents and a systematic review. *Pediatrics, 110*, 597–608.

Owens, R. E. (1996). *Language development* (4th ed.). Boston: Allyn & Bacon.

Padden, C. A. (1996). Early bilingual lives of deaf children. In I. Parasnis (Ed.), *Cultural and language diversity and the deaf experience* (pp. 99–116). New York: Cambridge University Press.

Padilla, A. M., Lindholm, K. J., Chen, A., Duran, R., Hakuta, K., Lambert, W., & Tucker, G. R. (1991). The English-only movement: Myths, reality, and implications for psychology. *American Psychologist, 46*(2), 120–130.

Palella, F. J., Delaney, K. M., Moorman, A. C., Loveless, M. O., Fuhrer, J., Satten, G. A., Aschman, D. J., Holmberg, S. D., & HIV Outpatient Study investigators. (1998). Declining morbidity and mortality among patients with advanced human immunodeficiency virus infection. *New England Journal of Medicine, 358*, 853–860.

Pamuk, E., Makuc, D., Heck, K., Reuben, C., & Lochner, K. (1998). Socioeconomic status and health chartbook. In *Health, United States, 1998*. Hyattsville, MD: National Center for Health Statistics.

Pan, B. A., Rowe, M. L., Singer, J. D., & Snow, C. E. (2005). Maternal correlates of growth in toddler vocabulary production in low-income families. *Child Development, 76*, 763–782.

Pan, S. Y., Ugnat, A. M., Mao, Y., & Canadian Cancer Registries Epidemiology Research Group (2005). Physical activity and the risk of ovarian cancer: A case-control study in Canada. *International Journal of Cancer, 117,* 300–307.

Panigrahy, A., Filiano, J., Sleeper, L. A., Mandell, F., Valdes-Dapena, M., Krous, H. F., Rava, L. A., Foley, E., White, W. F., & Kinney, H. C. (2000). Decreased serotonergic receptor binding in rhombic lip-derived regions of the medulla oblongata in the sudden infant death syndrome. *Journal of Neuropathology and Experimental Neurology, 59,* 377–384.

Papalia, D. (1972). The status of several conservation abilities across the lifespan. *Human Development, 15,* 229–243.

Papernow, P. (1993). *Becoming a stepfamily: Patterns of development in remarried families.* San Francisco: Jossey-Bass.

Park, D., & Gutchess, A. (2006). The cognitive neuroscience of aging and culture. *Current Directions in Psychological Science, 15,* 105–108.

Park, M. J., Mulye, T. P., Adams, S. H., Brindis, C. D., & Irwin, C. E. (2006). The health status of young adults in the United States. *Journal of Adolescent Health, 39,* 305–317.

Park, S., Belsky, J., Putnam, S., & Crnic, K. (1997). Infant emotionality, parenting, and 3-year inhibition: Exploring stability and lawful discontinuity in a male sample. *Developmental Psychology, 33,* 218–227.

Parke, R. D. (2004). The Society for Research in Child Development at 70: Progress and promise. *Child Development, 75,* 1–24.

Parke, R. D., & Buriel, R. (1998). Socialization in the family: Ethnic and ecological perspectives. In W. Damon (Series Ed.) & N. Eisenberg (Vol. Ed.), *Handbook of child psychology: Vol. 3. Social, emotional, and personality development* (5th ed., pp. 463–552). New York: Wiley.

Parke, R. D., Grossman, K., & Tinsley, R. (1981). Father-mother-infant interaction in the newborn period: A German-American comparison. In T. M. Field, A. M. Sostek, P. Viete, & P. H. Leideman (Eds.), *Culture and early interaction.* Hillsdale, NJ: Erlbaum.

Parke, R. D., Ornstein, P. A., Rieser, J. J., & Zahn-Waxler, C. (1994). The past as prologue: An overview of a century of developmental psychology. In R. D. Parke, P. A. Ornstein, J. J. Rieser, & C. Zahn-Waxler (Eds.), *A century of developmental psychology* (pp. 1–70). Washington, DC: American Psychological Association.

Parker, J. D., Woodruff, T. J., Basu, R., & Schoendorf, K. C. (2005). Air pollution and birth weight among term infants in California. *Pediatrics, 115,* 121–128.

Parker, J. G., & Asher, S. R. (1987). Peer relations and later personal adjustment: Are low-accepted children at risk? *Psychological Bulletin, 102,* 357–389.

Parker, L., Pearce, M. S., Dickinson, H. O., Aitkin, M., & Craft, A. W. (1999).

Stillbirths among offspring of male radiation workers at Sellafield Nuclear Reprocessing Plant. *Lancet, 354,* 1407–1414.

Parkes, T. L., Elia, A. J., Dickinson, D., Hilliker, A. J., Phillips, J. P., & Boulianne, G. L. (1998). Extension of Drosophila lifespan by overexpression of human SOD1 in motorneurons. *Nature Genetics, 19,* 171–174.

Parnes, H. S., & Sommers, D. G. (1994). Shunning retirement: Work experience of men in their seventies and early eighties. *Journal of Gerontology: Social Sciences, 49,* S117–S124.

Parten, M. B. (1932). Social play among preschool children. *Journal of Abnormal and Social Psychology, 27,* 243–269.

Pascarella, E. T., Edison, M. I., Nora, A., Hagedorn, L. S., & Terenzini, P. T. (1998). Does work inhibit cognitive development during college? *Educational Evaluation and Policy Analysis, 20,* 75–93.

Pascual-Leone, A., Amedi, A., Fregni, F., & Merabet, L. B. (2005). The plastic human brain cortex. *Annual Review of Neuroscience, 28,* 377–401.

Pastor, P. N., Makuc, D. M., Reuben, C., & Xia, H. (2002). Chartbook on trends in the health of Americans. In *Health, United States, 2002.* Hyattsville, MD: National Center for Health Statistics.

Pasupathi, M., Staudinger, U. M., & Baltes, P. B. (2001). Seeds of wisdom: Adolescents' knowledge and judgment about difficult life problems. *Developmental Psychology, 37*(3), 351–361.

Patel, H., Rosengren, A., & Ekman, I. (2004). Symptoms in acute coronary syndromes: Does sex make a difference? *American Heart Journal, 148,* 27–33.

Patel, K. V., Coppin, A. K., Manini, T. M., Lauretani, F., Bandinelli, S., Ferrucci, L., & Guralnik, J. M. (2006). Midlife physical activity and mobility in older age: The InCHIANTI Study, 10 August 2006. *American Journal of Preventive Medicine, 31*(3), 217–224.

Patenaude, A. F., Guttmacher, A. E., & Collins, F. S. (2002). Genetic testing and psychology: New roles, new responsibilities. *American Psychologist, 57,* 271–282.

Paterson, D. S., Trachtenberg, F. L., Thompson, E. G., Belliveau, R. A., Beggs, A. H., Darnell, R., Chadwick, A. E., Krous, H. F., & Kinney, H. C. (2006). Multiple serotogenic brainstem abnormalities in sudden infant death syndrome. *Journal of the American Medical Association, 296,* 2124–2132.

Patrick, K., Norman, G. J., Calfas, K. J., Sallis, J. F., Zabinski, M. F., Rupp, J., & Cella, J. (2004). Diet, physical activity, and sedentary behaviors as risk factors for overweight in adolescence. *Archives of Pediatric Adolescent Medicine, 158,* 385–390.

Patterson, C. J. (1992). Children of lesbian and gay parents. *Child Development, 63,* 1025–1042.

Patterson, C. J. (1995a). Lesbian mothers, gay fathers, and their children. In A. R. D'Augelli & C. J. Patterson (Eds.), *Lesbian, gay, and bisexual identities over the lifespan: Psychological perspectives* (pp. 293–320). New York: Oxford University Press.

Patterson, C. J. (1995b). Sexual orientation and human development: An overview. *Developmental Psychology, 31,* 3–11.

Patterson, G. R., DeBaryshe, B. D., & Ramsey, E. (1989). A developmental perspective on antisocial behavior. *American Psychologist, 44*(2), 329–335.

Pauen, S. (2002). Evidence for knowledge-based category discrimination in infancy. *Child Development, 73,* 1016–1033.

Paul, E. L. (1997). A longitudinal analysis of midlife interpersonal relationships and well-being. In M. E. Lachman & J. B. James (Eds.), *Multiple paths of midlife development* (pp. 171–206). Chicago: University of Chicago Press.

Paulozzi, L., Crosby, A., & Ryan, G. (2007). Increase in age-group-specific injury mortality—United States, 1999–2004. *Morbidity and Mortality Weekly Report, 56*(49), 1281–1284

Paus, T., Zijdenbos, A., Worsley, K., Collins, D. L., Blumenthal, J., Giedd, J. N., Rapoport, J. L., & Evans, A. C. (1999). Structural maturation of neural pathways in children and adolescents: In vivo study. *Science, 283,* 1908–1911.

Pawelski, J. G., Perrin, E. C., Foy, J. M., Allen, C. E., Crawford, J. E., Del Monte, M., Kaufman, M., Klein, J. D., Smith, K., Springer, S., Tanner, J. L., & Vickers, D. L. (2006). The effects of marriage, civil union, and domestic partnership laws on the health and well-being of children. *Pediatrics, 118,* 349–364.

Pearce, M. J., Jones, S. M., Schwab-Stone, M. E., & Ruchkin, V. (2003). The protective effects of religiousness and parent involvement on the development of conduct problems among youth exposed to violence. *Child Development, 74,* 1682–1696.

Pears, K. C., Pierce, S., Kim, H. K., Capaldi, D. M., & Owen, L. D. (2005). The timing of entry into fatherhood in young, at-risk men. *Journal of Marriage and Family, 67,* 429–447.

Pearson, J. D., Morell, C. H., Gordon-Salant, S., Brant, L. J., Metter, E. J., Klein, L., & Fozard, J. L. (1995). Gender differences in a longitudinal study of age-associated hearing loss. *Journal of the Acoustical Society of America, 97,* 1196–1205.

Pearson, H. (2002, February 12). Study refines breast cancer risks. *Nature Science Update.* Retrieved February 19, 2002, from www.nature.com/nsu/020211/020211 –8.html.

Pearson Education. (2007). *A time-line of recent worldwide school shootings.* Retrieved December 30, 2007, from www.infoplease .com/ipa/A0777958.html.

Peeters, A., Barendregt, J. J., Willekens, F., Mackenbach, J. P., Al Mamun, A., &

Bonneux, L., for NEDCOM, the Netherlands Epidemiology and Demography Compression of Morbidity Research Group (2003). Obesity in adulthood and its consequences for life expectancy. *Annals of Internal Medicine, 138,* 24–32.

Peirce, C. S. (1931). In C. Hartshorne, P. Weiss, & A. Burks (Eds.), *The collected papers of Charles Sanders Peirce.* Cambridge, MA: Harvard University Press.

Pellegrini, A. D., & Archer, J. (2005). Sex differences in competitive and aggressive behavior: A view from sexual selection theory. In B. J. Ellis & D. F. Bjorklund (Eds.), *Origins of the social mind: Evolutionary psychology and child development* (pp. 219–244). New York: Guilford Press.

Pellegrini, A. D., Kato, K., Blatchford, P., & Baines E. (2002). A short-term longitudinal study of children's playground games across the first year of school: Implications for social competence and adjustment to school. *American Educational Research Journal, 39,* 991–1015.

Pellegrini, A. D., & Long, J. D. (2002). A longitudinal study of bullying, dominance, and victimization during the transition from primary school through secondary school. *British Journal of Developmental Psychology, 20,* 259–280.

Pennington, B. F., Moon, J., Edgin, J., Stedron, J., & Nadel, L. (2003). The neuropsychology of Down syndrome: Evidence for hippocampal dysfunction. *Child Development, 74,* 75–93.

Penninx, B. W. J. H., Guralnik, J. M., Ferrucci, L., Simonsick, E. M., Deeg, D. J. H., & Wallace, R. B. (1998). Depressive symptoms and physical decline in community-dwelling older persons. *Journal of the American Medical Association, 279,* 1720–1726.

Pennisi, E. (1998). Single gene controls fruit fly life-span. *Science, 282,* 856.

Pepper, S. C. (1942). *World hypotheses.* Berkeley: University of California Press.

Pepper, S. C. (1961). *World hypotheses.* Berkeley: University of California Press.

Pereira, M. A., Kartashov, A. I., Ebbeling, C. B., Van Horn, L., Slattery, M. L., Jacobs, D. R., Jr., & Ludwig, D. S. (2005). Fast-food habits, weight gain, and insulin resistance (the CARDIA study): 15-year prospective analysis. *Lancet, 365,* 36–42.

Perera, F. P., Rauh, V., Whyatt, R. M., Tsai, W.-Y., Bernert, J. T., Tu, Y.-H., Andrews, H., Ramirez, J., Qu, L., & Tang, D. (2004). Molecular evidence of an interaction between prenatal environmental exposures and birth outcomes in a multiethnic population. *Environmental Health Perspectives, 112,* 626–630.

Pérez-Stable, E. J., Herrera, B., Jacob, P., III, & Benowitz, N. L. (1998). Nicotine metabolism and intake in black and white smokers. *Journal of the American Medical Association, 280,* 152–156.

Perlmutter, M., Kaplan, M., & Nyquist, L. (1990). Development of adaptive competence in adulthood. *Human Development, 33,* 185–197.

Perls, T., Kunkel, L. M., & Puca, A. (2002a). The genetics of aging. *Current Opinion in Genetics and Development, 12,* 362–369.

Perls, T., Kunkel, L. M., & Puca, A. A. (2002b). The genetics of exceptional human longevity. *Journal of the American Geriatric Society, 50,* 359–368.

Perls, T. T., Alpert, L., & Fretts, R. C. (1997). Middle-aged mothers live longer. *Nature, 389,* 133.

Perls, T. T., Hutter-Silver, M., & Lauerman, J. F. (1999). *Living to 100: Lessons in living to your maximum potential at any age.* New York: Basic Books.

Perrin, E. C., and AAP Committee on Psychosocial Aspects of Child and Family Health. (2002). Technical report: Coparent or second-parent adoption by same-sex parents. *Pediatrics, 109*(2), 341–344.

Perrucci, C. C., Perrucci, R., & Targ, D. B. (1988). *Plant closings.* New York: Aldine.

Perry, W. G. (1970). *Forms of intellectual and ethical development in the college years.* New York: Holt.

Pérusse, L., Chagnon, Y. C., Weisnagel, J., & Bouchard, C. (1999). The human obesity gene map: The 1998 update. *Obesity Research, 7,* 111–129.

Pesonen, A., Raïkkönen, K., Keltikangas-Järvinen, L., Strandberg, T., & Järvenpää, A. (2003). Parental perception of infant temperament: Does parents' joint attachment matter? *Infant Behavior and Development, 26,* 167–182.

Peter, K., & Horn, L. (2005). *Gender differences in participation and completion of undergraduate education and how they have changed over time* (NCES 2005-169). Washington, DC: U.S. Government Printing Office.

Peters, R. D., Kloeppel, A. E., Fox, E., Thomas, M. L., Thorne, D. R., Sing, H. C., & Balwinski, S. M. (1994). *Effects of partial and total sleep deprivation on driving performance.* Washington, DC: Federal Highway Administration.

Petersen, A. C. (1993). Presidential address: Creating adolescents: The role of context and process in developmental transitions. *Journal of Research on Adolescents, 3*(1), 1–18.

Petersen, A. C., Compas, B. E., Brooks-Gunn, J., Stemmler, M., Ey, S., & Grant, K. E. (1993). Depression in adolescence. *American Psychologist, 48*(2), 155–168.

Peterson, B. E. (2002). Longitudinal analysis of midlife generativity, intergenerational roles, and caregiving. *Psychology and Aging, 17,* 161–168.

Petit, D., Touchette, E., Tremblay, R. E., Boivin, M., & Montplaisir, J. (2007). Dyssomnias and parasomnias in early childhoold. *Pediatrics, 119*(5), e1016–e1025.

Petitti, D. B. (2002). Hormone replacement therapy for prevention: More evidence, more pessimism. *Journal of the American Medical Association, 288,* 99–101.

Petitto, L. A., Holowka, S., Sergio, L., & Ostry, D. (2001). Language rhythms in babies' hand movements. *Nature, 413,* 35–36.

Petitto, L. A., Katerelos, M., Levy, B., Gauna, K., Tetrault, K., & Ferraro, V. (2001). Bilingual signed and spoken language acquisition from birth: Implications for mechanisms underlying bilingual language acquisition. *Journal of Child Language, 28,* 1–44.

Petitto, L. A., & Kovelman, I. (2003). The bilingual paradox: How signing-speaking bilingual children help us to resolve it and teach us about the brain's mechanisms underlying all language acquisition. *Learning Languages, 8,* 5–18.

Petitto, L. A., & Marentette, P. F. (1991). Babbling in the manual mode: Evidence for the ontogeny of language. *Science, 251,* 1493–1495.

Petrill, S. A., Lipton, P. A., Hewitt, J. K., Plomin, R., Cherny, S. S., Corley, R., & DeFries, J. C. (2004). Genetic and environmental contributions to general cognitive ability through the first 16 years of life. *Developmental Psychology, 40,* 805–812.

Pettit, G. S., Bates, J. E., & Dodge, K. A. (1997). Supportive parenting, ecological context, and children's adjustment: A seven-year longitudinal study. *Child Development, 68,* 908–923.

Pfeffer, C. R., Altemus, M., Heo, M., & Jiang, H. (2007). Salivary cortisol and psychopathology in children bereaved by the September 11, 2001 terror attacks. *Biological Psychiatry, 61*(8), 957–965.

Pharaoh, P. D. P., Antoniou, A., Bobrow, M., Zimmern, R. L., Easton, D. F., & Ponder, B. A. J. (2002). Polygenic susceptibility to breast cancer and implications for prevention. *Nature Genetics, 31,* 33–36.

Phelan, E. A., Williams, B., Penninx, B. W. J. H., LoGerfo, J. P., & Leveille, S. G. (2004). Activities of daily living function and disability in older adults in a randomized trial of the Health Enhancement Program. *Journal of Geronotology: Medical Sciences, 59A,* 838–843.

Phillips, D. F. (1998). Reproductive medicine experts till an increasingly fertile field. *Journal of the American Medical Association, 280,* 1893–1895.

Phillips, J. A., & Sweeney, M. M. (2005). Premarital cohabitation and marital disruption among white, black, and Mexican American women. *Journal of Marriage and Family, 67,* 296–314.

Phinney, J. S. (1998). Stages of ethnic identity development in minority group adolescents. In R. E. Muuss & H. D. Porton (Eds.), *Adolescent behavior and society: A book of readings* (pp. 271–280). Boston: McGraw-Hill.

Phinney, J. S. (2006). Ethnic identity exploration in emerging adulthood. In J. J. Arnett & J. L. Tanner (Eds.), *Emerging adults in America: Coming of age in the 21st century* (pp. 117–134). Washington, DC: American Psychological Association.

Piaget, J. (1929). *The child's conception of the world.* New York: Harcourt Brace.

Piaget, J. (1932). *The moral judgment of the child.* New York: Harcourt Brace

Piaget, J. (1952). *The origins of intelligence in children.* New York: International Universities Press. (Original work published 1936)

Piaget, J. (1962). *The language and thought of the child* (M. Gabain, Trans.). Cleveland, OH: Meridian. (Original work published 1923)

Piaget, J. (1964). *Six psychological studies.* New York: Vintage Books.

Piaget, J. (1969). *The child's conception of time* (A. J. Pomerans, Trans.). London: Routledge & Kegan Paul.

Piaget, J. (1972). Intellectual evolution from adolescence to adulthood. *Human Development, 15,* 1–12.

Piaget, J., & Inhelder, B. (1967). *The child's conception of space.* New York: Norton.

Piaget, J., & Inhelder, B. (1969). *The psychology of the child.* New York: Basic Books.

Pianezza, M. L., Sellers, E. M., & Tyndale, R. F. (1998). Nicotine metabolism defect reduces smoking. *Nature, 393,* 750.

Picker, J. (2005). The role of genetic and environmental factors in the development of schizophrenia. *Psychiatric Times, 22,* 1–9.

Pierce, K. M., Hamm, J. V., & Vandell, D. L. (1999). Experiences in afterschool programs and children's adjustment in first-grade classrooms. *Child Development, 70*(3), 756–767.

Pierroutsakos, S. L., & DeLoache, J. S. (2003). Infants' manual exploration of pictorial objects varying in realism. *Infancy, 4,* 141–156.

Pike, A., Coldwell, J., & Dunn, J. F. (2005). Sibling relationships in early/middle childhood: Links with individual adjustment. *Journal of Family Psychology, 19,* 523–532.

Pillemer, K., & Suitor, J. J. (1991). "Will I ever escape my child's problems?" Effects of adult children's problems on elderly parents. *Journal of Marriage and Family, 53,* 585–594.

Pillow, B. H., & Henrichon, A. J. (1996). There's more to the picture than meets the eye: Young children's difficulty understanding biased interpretation. *Child Development, 67,* 803–819.

Pimentel, E. E., & Liu, J. (2004). Exploring nonnormative coresidence in urban China: Living with wives' parents. *Journal of Marriage and Family, 66,* 821–836.

Pines, M. (1981). The civilizing of Genie. *Psychology Today, 15*(9), 28–34.

Pinquart, M., & Sörensen, S. (2006). Gender differences in caregiver stressors, social resources, and health: An updated meta-analysis. *Journal of Gerontology: Psychological and Social Sciences, 61B,* P33–P45.

Pinquart, M., & Sörensen, S. (2007) Correlates of physical health of informal caregivers: A meta-analysis. *Journal of Gerontology: Psychological and Social Sciences, 62B,* P126–P137.

Piper, M. F., Piasecki, T. M., Federman, E. B., Bolt, D. M., Smith, S. S., Fiore, M. C., & Baker, T. B. (2004). A multiple motives approach to tobacco dependence: The Wisconsin Inventory of Smoking Dependence Motives (WISDM-68). *Journal of Counseling and Clinical Psychology, 72,* 139–154.

Plant, L. D., Bowers, P. N., Liu, Q., Morgan, T., Zhang, T., State, M. W., Chen, W., Kittles, R. A., & Goldstein, S. A. (2006). A common cardiac sodium channel variant associated with sudden infant death in African Americans, SCN5A S1103Y. *Journal of Clinical Investigation, 116*(2), 430–435.

Plassman, B. L., Langa, K. M., Fisher, G. G., Heeringa, S. G., Weir, D. R., Ofstedal, M. B., Burke, J. R., Hurd, M. D., Potter, G. G., Rodgers, W. L., Steffens, D. C., Willis, R. J., & Wallace, R. B. (2007). Prevalence of dementia in the United States: The Aging, Demographics, and Memory Study. *Neuroepidemiology, 29,* 125–132.

Plassman, B. L., Langa, K. M., Fisher, G. G., Heeringa, S. G., Weir, D. R., Ofstedal, M. B., Burke, J. R., Hurd, M. D., Potter, G. G., Rodgers, W. L., Steffens, D. C., McArdle, J. J., Willis, R. J., & Wallace, R. B. (2008). Prevalence of cognitive impairment without dementia in the United States. *Annals of Internal Medicine, 14*(6), 427–434.

Pleck, J. H. (1997). Paternal involvement: Levels, sources, and consequences. In M. E. Lamb (Ed.), *The role of the father in child development* (3rd ed., pp. 66–103). New York: Wiley.

Plomin, R. (1989). Environment and genes: Determinants of behavior. *American Psychologist, 44*(2), 105–111.

Plomin, R. (1990). The role of inheritance in behavior. *Science, 248,* 183–188.

Plomin, R. (1996). Nature and nurture. In M. R. Merrens & G. G. Brannigan (Eds.), *The developmental psychologist: Research adventures across the life span* (pp. 3–19). New York: McGraw-Hill.

Plomin, R., & Daniels, D. (1987). Why are children in the same family so different from one another? *Behavioral and Brain Sciences, 10,* 1–16.

Plomin, R., & DeFries, J. C. (1999). The genetics of cognitive abilities and disabilities. In S. J. Ceci & W. M. Williams (Eds.), *The nature-nurture debate: The essential readings* (pp. 178–195). Malden, MA: Blackwell.

Plomin, R., & Kovas, Y. (2005). Generalist genes and learning disabilities. *Psychological Bulletin, 131,* 592–617.

Plomin, R., Owen, M. J., & McGuffin, P. (1994). The genetic bases of behavior. *Science, 264,* 1733–1739.

Plomin, R., & Rutter, M. (1998). Child development, molecular genetics, and what to do with genes once they are found. *Child Development, 69*(4), 1223–1242.

Plomin, R., & Spinath, F. M. (2004). Intelligence: Genetics, genes, and genomics. *Journal of Personality and Social Psychology, 86,* 112–129.

Plotkin, S. A., Katz, M., & Cordero, J. F. (1999). The eradication of rubella. *Journal of the American Medical Association, 281,* 561–562.

Pogarsky, G., Thornberry, T. P., & Lizotte, A. J. (2006). Developmental outcomes for children of young mothers. *Journal of Marriage and Family, 68,* 332–344.

Polit, D. F., & Falbo, T. (1987). Only children and personality development: A quantitative review. *Journal of Marriage and Family, 49,* 309–325.

Pollock, L. A. (1983). *Forgotten children.* Cambridge, England: Cambridge University Press.

Pomerantz, E. M., & Saxon, J. L. (2001). Conceptions of ability as stable and self-evaluative processes: A longitudinal examination. *Child Development, 72,* 152–173.

Pomery, E. A., Gibbons, F. X., Gerrard, M., Cleveland, M. J., Brody, G. H., & Wills, T. A. (2005). Families and risk: Prospective analyses of familial and social influences on adolescent substance use. *Journal of Family Psychology, 19,* 560–570.

Pong, S., Dronkers, J., & Hampden-Thompson, G. (2003). Family policies and children's school achievement in single-versus two-parent families. *Journal of Marriage and the Family, 65,* 681–699.

Poon, L. W. (1985). Differences in human memory with aging: Nature, causes, and clinical implications. In J. E. Birren & K. W. Schaie (Eds.), *Handbook of the psychology of aging* (pp. 427–462). New York: Van Nostrand Reinhold.

Pope, A. W., Bierman, K. L., & Mumma, G. H. (1991). Aggression, hyperactivity, and inattention-immaturity: Behavior dimensions associated with peer rejection in elementary school boys. *Developmental Psychology, 27,* 663–671.

Popenoe, D., & Whitehead, B. D. (1999). *Should we live together? What young adults need to know about cohabitation before marriage.* New Brunswick: National Marriage Project at Rutgers, State University of New Jersey.

Popenoe, D., & Whitehead, B. D. (2003). *The state of our unions 2003: The social health of marriage in America.* Piscataway, NJ: National Marriage Project.

Popenoe, D., & Whitehead, B. D. (Eds.). (2004). *The state of our unions 2004: The social health of marriage in America.* Piscataway, NJ: National Marriage Project, Rutgers University.

Population Reference Bureau. (2005). Human population: Fundamentals of growth; World health. Retrieved April 11, 2005, from www .prb.org/Content/NavigationMenu/PRB/ Educators/HumanPopulation/Health2/ WorldHealth1.htm.

Population Reference Bureau. (2006). *2006 world population data sheet.* Washington, DC: Author.

Porcino, J. (1993, April–May). Designs for living. *Modern Maturity,* pp. 24–33.

Porter, P. (2008). "Westernizing" women's risks? Breast cancer in lower-income countries. *New England Journal of Medicine, 358,* 213–216.

Posada, G., Gao, Y., Wu, F., Posada, R., Tascon, M., Schoelmerich, A., Sagi, A., Kondo-Ikemura, K., Haaland, W., & Synnevaag, B. (1995). The secure-base phenomenon across cultures: Children's behavior, mothers' preferences, and experts' concepts. In E. Waters, B. E. Vaughn, G. Posada, & K. Kondo-Ikemura (Eds.), Caregiving, cultural, and cognitive perspectives on secure-base behavior and working models: New growing points of attachment theory and research (pp. 27–48). *Monographs of the Society for Research in Child Development, 60*(2–3, Serial No. 244).

Posner, J. K., & Vandell, D. L. (1999). After-school activities and the development of low-income urban children: A longitudinal study. *Developmental Psychology, 35*(3), 868–879.

Posthuma, D., & de Geus, E. J. C. (2006). Progress in the molecular-genetic study of intelligence. *Current Directions in Psychological Science, 15*(4), 151–155.

Povinelli, D. J., & Giambrone, S. (2001). Reasoning about beliefs: A human specialization? *Child Development, 72*, 691–695.

Powell, L. H., Calvin, J. E., III, & Calvin, J. E., Jr. (2007). Effective obesity treatments. *American Psychologist, 62*, 234–246.

Powell, L. H., Shahabi, L., & Thoresen, C. E. (2003). Religion and spirituality: Linkages to physical health. *American Psychologist, 58*, 36–52.

Powell, M. B., & Thomson, D. M. (1996). Children's memory of an occurrence of a repeated event: Effects of age, repetition, and retention interval across three question types. *Child Development, 67*, 1988–2004.

Power, T. G., & Chapieski, M. L. (1986). Childrearing and impulse control in toddlers: A naturalistic investigation. *Developmental Psychology, 22*, 271–275.

Powlishta, K. K., Serbin, L. A., Doyle, A. B., & White, D. R. (1994). Gender, ethnic, and body type biases: The generality of prejudice in childhood. *Developmental Psychology, 30*, 526–536.

Pratt, L. A., Dey, A. N., & Cohen, A. J. (2007). Characteristics of adults with serious psychological distress as measured by the K6 Scale: United States, 2001–04. *Advance Data from Health and Vital Statistics,* No. 382. Hyattsville, MD: National Center for Health Statistics (NCHS).

Pratt, M. (1999). Benefits of lifestyle activity vs. structured exercise. *Journal of the American Medical Association, 281*, 375–376.

Prechtl, H. F. R., & Beintema, D. J. (1964). The neurological examination of the full-term newborn infant. *Clinics in Developmental Medicine* (No. 12). London: Heinemann.

Preissler, M., & Bloom, P. (2007). Two-year-olds appreciate the dual nature of pictures. *Psychological Science, 18*(1), 1–2.

Pressley, J. C., Barlow, B., Kendig, T., & Paneth-Pollak, R. (2007). Twenty-year trends in fatal injuries to very young children: The persistence of racial disparities. *Pediatrics, 119*, 875–884.

Preston, S. H. (2005). Deadweight? The influence of obesity on longevity. *New England Journal of Medicine, 352*, 1135–1137.

Previti, D., & Amato, P. R. (2003). Why stay married? Rewards, barriers, and marital stability. *Journal of Marriage and Family, 65*, 561–573.

Price, T. S., Simonoff, E., Waldman, I., Asherson, P., & Plomin, R. (2001). Hyperactivity in preschool children is highly heritable. *Journal of the American Academy of Child and Adolescent Psychiatry, 40*(12), 1362–1364.

Princiotta, D., Bielick, S., & Chapman, C. (2004). *1.1 million home-schooled students in the United States in 2003* (NCES 2004-115). Washington, DC: National Center for Education Statistics.

Princiotta, D., & Chapman, C. (2006). *Homeschooling in the United States: 2003* (NCES 2006-042). Washington, DC: U.S. Department of Education, National Center for Education Statistics.

Prockop, D. J. (1998). The genetic trail of osteoporosis. *New England Journal of Medicine, 338*, 1061–1062.

Prohaska, T. R., Leventhal, E. A., Leventhal, H., & Keller, M. L. (1985). Health practices and illness cognition in young, middle-aged, and elderly adults. *Journal of Gerontology, 40*, 569–578.

Pruchno, R., & Johnson, K. W. (1996). Research on grandparenting: Current studies and future needs. *Generations, 20*(1), 65–70.

Pruden, S. M., Hirsh-Pasek, K., Golinkoff, R. M., & Hennon, E. A. (2006). The birth of words: Ten-month-olds learn words through perceptual salience. *Child Development, 77*, 266–280.

Puca, A. A., Daly, M. J., Brewster, S. J., Matise, T. C., Barrett, J., Shea-Drinkwater, M., Kang, S., Joyce, E., Nicoli, J., Benson, E., Kunkel, L. M., & Perls, T. (2001). A genomewide scan for linkage to human exceptional longevity identifies a locus on chromosome 4. *Proceedings of the National Academy of Science, 28*, 10505–10508.

Pudrovska, T. Schieman, S., & Carr, D. (2006). Strains of singlehood in later life: Do race and gender matter? *Journal of Gerontology: Social Sciences, 61B*, S315–S322.

Pulkkinen, L. (1996). Female and male personality styles: A typological and developmental analysis. *Journal of Personality and Social Psychology, 70*, 1288–1306.

Purcell, P. J. (2002). *Older workers: Employment and retirement trends.* Congressional Research Service Report for Congress. Washington, DC: Congressional Research Service.

Putallaz, M., & Bierman, K. L. (Eds.). (2004). *Aggression, antisocial behavior, and violence among girls: A developmental perspective.* New York: Guilford Press.

Putney, N. M., & Bengtson, V. L. (2001). Families, intergenerational relationships, and kin-keeping in midlife. In M. E. Lachman (Ed.), *Handbook of midlife development* (pp. 528–570). New York: Wiley.

Quadrel, M. J., Fischoff, B., & Davis, W. (1993). Adolescent (in)vulnerability. *American Psychologist, 48*, 102–116.

Quattrin, T., Liu, E., Shaw, N., Shine, B., & Chiang, E. (2005). Obese children who are referred to the pediatric oncologist: Characteristics and outcome. *Pediatrics, 115*, 348–351.

Quigley, H. A., & Broman, A. T. (2006). The number of people with glaucoma worldwide in 2010 and 2020. *British Journal of Opthlmology, 90*, 262–267.

Quill, T. E., Lo, B., & Brock, D. W. (1997). Palliative options of the last resort. *Journal of the American Medical Association, 278*, 2099–2104.

Quinn, P. C., Eimas, P. D., & Rosenkrantz, S. L. (1993). Evidence for representations of perceptually similar natural categories by 3-month-old and 4-month-old infants. *Perception, 22*, 463–475.

Quinn, P. C., Westerlund, A., & Nelson, C. A. (2006). Neural markers of categorization in 6-month-old infants. *Psychological Science, 17*, 59–66.

Rabbitt, P., Watson, P., Donlan, C., McInnes, L., Horan, M., Pendleton, N., & Clague, J. (2002). Effects of death within 11 years on cognitive performance in old age. *Psychology and Aging, 17*, 468–481.

Rabiner, D., & Coie, J. (1989). Effect of expectancy induction on rejected peers' acceptance by unfamiliar peers. *Developmental Psychology, 25*, 450–457.

Raikes, H., Pan, B. A., Luze, G., Tamis-LeMonda, C. S., Brooks-Gunn, J., Constantine, J., Tarullo, L. B., Raikes, H. A., & Rodriguez, E. T. (2006). Mother-child bookreading in low-income families: Correlates and outcomes during three years of life. *Child Development, 77*, 924–953.

Raine, A., Mellingen, K., Liu, J., Venables, P., & Mednick, S. (2003). Effects of environmental enrichment at ages 3–5 years in schizotypal personality and antisocial behavior at ages 17 and 23 years. *American Journal of Psychiatry, 160*, 1627–1635.

Rakison, D. H. (2005). Infant perception and cognition. In B. J. Ellis & D. F. Bjorklund (Eds.), *Origins of the social mind* (pp. 317–353). New York: Guilford Press.

Rakoczy, H., Tomasello, M., and Striano, T. (2004). Young children know that trying is not pretending: A test of the "behaving-as-if" construal of children's early concept of pretense. *Developmental Psychology, 40*, 388–399.

Rakyan, V., & Beck., S. (2006). Epigenetic inheritance and variation in mammals. *Current Opinion in Genetics and Development, 16*(6), 573–577.

Rall, L. C., Meydani, S. N., Kehayias, B. D. H., Dawson-Hughes, B., & Roubenoff, R. (1996). The effect of progressive resistance training in rheumatoid arthritis. *Arthritis and Rheumatism, 39*, 415–426.

Ram, A., & Ross, H. S. (2001). Problem solving, contention, and struggle: How siblings resolve a conflict of interests. *Child Development, 72,* 1710–1722.

Ramey, C. T., & Campbell, F. A. (1991). Poverty, early childhood education, and academic competence. In A. Huston (Ed.), *Children reared in poverty* (pp. 190–221). Cambridge, England: Cambridge University Press.

Ramey, C. T., Campbell, F. A., Burchinal, M., Skinner, M. L., Gardner, D. M., & Ramey, S. L. (2000). Persistent effects of early childhood education on high-risk children and their mothers. *Applied Development Science, 4*(1), 2–14.

Ramey, C. T., & Ramey, S. L. (1996). Early intervention: Optimizing development for children with disabilities and risk conditions. In M. Wolraich (Ed.), *Disorders of development and learning: A practical guide to assessment and management* (2nd ed., pp. 141–158). Philadelphia: Mosby.

Ramey, C. T., & Ramey, S. L. (1998a). Early intervention and early experience. *American Psychologist, 53,* 109–120.

Ramey, C. T., & Ramey, S. L. (1998b). Prevention of intellectual disabilities: Early interventions to improve cognitive development. *Preventive Medicine, 21,* 224–232.

Ramey, C. T., & Ramey, S. L. (2003, May). *Preparing America's children for success in school.* Paper prepared for an invited address at the White House Early Childhood Summit on Ready to Read, Ready to Learn, Denver, CO.

Ramey, S. L., & Ramey, C. T. (1992). Early educational intervention with disadvantaged children—To what effect? *Applied and Preventive Psychology, 1,* 131–140.

Ramoz, N., Reichert, J. G., Smith, C. J., Silverman, J. M., Bespalova, I. N., Davis, K. L., & Buxbaum, J. D. (2004). Linkage and association of the mitochondrial aspartate/glutamate carrier SLC25A12 gene with autism. *American Journal of Psychiatry, 161,* 662–669.

Ramsey, P. G., & Lasquade, C. (1996). Preschool children's entry attempts. *Journal of Applied Developmental Psychology, 17,* 135–150.

Randall, D. (2005). *Corporal punishment in school.* FamilyEducation.com. Retrieved April 20, 2005, from www.familyeducation.com/article/0,1120,1-3980,00.html.

Rapoport, J. L., Addington, A. M., & Frangou, S. (2005). The neurodevelopmental model of schizophrenia: Update 2005. *Molecular Psychiatry, 10,* 434–449.

Rapp, S. R., Espeland, M. A., Shumaker, S. A., Henderson, V. W., Brunner, R. L., Manson, J. E., Gass, M. L. S., Stefanisk, M. L., Lane, D. S., Hays, J., Johnson, K. C., Coker, L. H., Dailey, M., Bowen, D., for the WHIMIS Investigators. (2003). Effects of estrogen plus progestin on global cognitive function in postmenopausal women: The Women's Health Initiative Memory Study: A randomized controlled trial. *Journal of the American Medical Association, 289*(20), 2663–2672.

Rask-Nissilä, L., Jokinen, E., Terho, P., Tammi, A., Lapinleimu, H., Ronnemaa, T., Viikari, J., Seppanen, R., Korhonen, T., Tuominen, J., Valimaki, I., & Simell, O. (2000). Neurological development of 5-year-old children receiving a low saturated fat, low cholesterol diet since infancy. *Journal of the American Medical Association, 284*(8), 993–1000.

Rathbun, A., West, J., & Germino-Hausken, E. (2004). *From kindergarten through third grade: Children's beginning school experiences* (NCES 2004-007). Washington, DC: National Center for Education Statistics.

Rauh, V. A., Whyatt, R. M., Garfinkel, R., Andrews, H., Hoepner, L., Reyes, A., Diaz, D., Camann, D., & Perera, F. P. (2004). Developmental effects of exposure to environmental tobacco smoke and material hardship among inner-city children. *Neurotoxicology and Teratology, 26,* 373–385.

Raver, C. C. (2002). Emotions matter: Making the case for the role of young children's emotional development for early school readiness. *Social Policy Report, 16*(3).

Ray, O. (2004). How the mind hurts and heals the body. *American Psychologist, 59,* 29–40.

Ray, S., Brischgi, M., Herbert, C., Takeda-Uchimura, Y., Boxer, A., Blennow, K., Friedman, L. F., Galasko, D. R., Jutel, M., Karydas, A., Kaye, J. A., Leszek, J., Miller, B. L., Minthon, L., Quinn, J. F., Rabinovici, G. D., Robinson, W. H., Sabbagh, M. N., So, Y. T., Sparks, D. L., Tabaton, M., Tinklenberg, J., Yesavage, J. A., Tibshirani, R., & Coray-Wyss, T. (2007). Classification and prediction of clinical Alzheimer's diagnosis based on plasma signaling proteins. *Nature Medicine, 13,* 1359–1362.

Reaney, P. (2006, June 21). Three million babies born after fertility treatment. *Medscape.* Retrieved January 29, 2007, from www.medscape.com/viewarticle/537128.

Reed, T., Dick, D. M., Uniacke, S. K., Foroud, T., & Nichols, W. C. (2004). Genomewide scan for a healthy aging phenotype provides support for a locus near D4S1564 promoting healthy aging. *Journal of Gerontology: Biological Sciences, 59A,* 227–232.

Reese, E. (1995). Predicting children's literacy from mother-child conversations. *Cognitive Development, 10,* 381–405.

Reese, E., & Cox, A. (1999). Quality of adult book reading affects children's emergent literacy. *Developmental Psychology, 35,* 20–28.

Reese, E., & Newcombe, R. (2007). Training mothers in elaborative reminiscing enhances children's autobiographical memory and narrative. *Child Development, 78*(4), 1153–1170.

Reichenberg, A., Gross, R., Weiser, M., Bresnahan, M., Silverman, J., Harlap, S., Rabinowitz, J., Shulman, G., Malaspina, D., Lubin, G., Knobler, H. Y., Davidson, M., & Susser, E. (2006). Advancing paternal age and autism. *Archives of General Psychiatry, 63*(9), 1026–1032.

Reid, J. D. (1995). Development in late life: Older lesbian and gay life. In A. R. D'Augelli & C. J. Patterson (Eds.), *Lesbian, gay, and bi-sexual identities over the lifespan: Psychological perspectives* (pp. 215–240). New York: Oxford University Press.

Reid, J. D., & Willis, S. K. (1999). Middle age: New thoughts, new directions. In S. L. Willis & J. D. Reid (Eds.), *Life in the middle* (pp. 272–289). San Diego: Academic Press.

Reijo, R., Alagappan, R. K., Patrizio, P., & Page, D. C. (1996). Severe oligozoospermia resulting from deletions of azoospermia factor gene on Y chromosome. *Lancet, 347,* 1290–1293.

Reiner, W. (2000, May 12). *Cloacal exstrophy: A happenstance model for androgen imprinting.* Presentation at the meeting of the Pediatric Endocrine Society, Boston.

Reiner, W. G., & Gearhart, J. P. (2004). Discordant sexual identity in some genetic males with cloacal exstrophy assigned to female sex at birth. *New England Journal of Medicine, 350*(4), 333–341.

Reis, H. T., & Patrick, B. C. (1996). Attachment and intimacy: Component processes. In E. T. Higgins & A. Kruglanski (Eds.), *Social psychology: Handbook of basic principles* (pp. 523–563). New York: Guilford Press.

Reisberg, B., Doody, R., Stöffler, A., Schmitt, F., Ferris, S., & Möbius, H. J. (2006). A 24-week open-label extension study of memantine in moderate to severe Alzheimer disease. *Archives of Neurology, 63,* 49–54.

Reiss, A. L., Abrams, M. T., Singer, H. S., Ross, J. L., & Denckla, M. B. (1996). Brain development, gender and IQ in children: A volumetric imaging study. *Brain, 119,* 1763–1774.

Reitzes, D. C., & Mutran, E. J. (2004). Grandparenthood: Factors influencing frequency of grandparent-grandchildren contact and role satisfaction. *Journal of Gerontology: Social Sciences, 59,* S9–S16.

Remafedi, G., French, S., Story, M., Resnick, M. D., & Blum, R. (1998). The relationship between suicide risk and sexual orientation: Results of a population-based study. *American Journal of Public Health, 88,* 57–60.

Remez, L. (2000). Oral sex among adolescents: Is it sex or is it abstinence? *Family Planning Perspectives, 32,* 298–304.

Rende, R., Slomkowski, C., Lloyd-Richardson, E., & Niaura, R. (2005). Sibling effects on substance use in adolescence: Social contagion and genetic relatedness. *Journal of Family Psychology, 19,* 611–618.

Repetti, R. L., Taylor, S. E., & Seeman, T. S. (2002). Risky families: Family social environments and the mental and physical health of the offspring. *Psychological Bulletin, 128*(2), 330–366.

Resnick, L. B. (1989). Developing mathematical knowledge. *American Psychologist, 44,* 162–169.

Resnick, M. D., Bearman, P. S., Blum, R. W., Bauman, K. E., Harris, K. M., Jones, J., Tabor, J., Beuhring, T., Sieving, R. E., Shew, M., Ireland, M., Bearinger, L. H., & Udry, J. R. (1997). Protecting adolescents from harm: Findings from the National Longitudinal Study on Adolescent Health. *Journal of the American Medical Association, 278,* 823–832.

Restak, R. (1984). *The brain.* New York: Bantam Books.

Reuter-Lorenz, P. A., Jonides, J., Smith, E. E., Hartley, A., Miller, A., Marshuetz, C., & Koeppe, R. A. (2000). Age differences in the frontal lateralization of verbal and spatial working memory revealed by PET. *Journal of Cognitive Neuroscience, 12,* 174–187.

Reuter-Lorenz, P. A., Stanczak, L., & Miller, A. (1999). Neural recruitment and cognitive aging: Two hemispheres are better than one especially as you age. *Psychological Science, 10,* 494–500.

Reynolds, A. J., & Temple, J. A. (1998). Extended early childhood intervention and school achievement: Age thirteen findings from the Chicago Longitudinal Study. *Child Development, 69,* 231–246.

Reynolds, A. J., Temple, J. A., Robertson, D. L., & Mann, E. A. (2001). Long-term effects of an early childhood intervention on educational achievement and juvenile arrest: A 15-year follow-up of low-income children in public schools. *Journal of the American Medical Association, 285*(18), 2339–2346.

Reynolds, C. F., III, Buysse, D. J., & Kupfer, D. J. (1999). Treating insomnia in older adults: Taking a long-term view. *Journal of the American Medical Association, 281,* 1034–1035.

Rhee, S. H., & Waldman, I. D. (2002). Genetic and environmental influences on antisocial behavior: A meta-analysis of twin and adoption studies. *Psychological Bulletin, 128,* 490–529.

Ricciuti, H. N. (1999). Single parenthood and school readiness in white, black, and Hispanic 6- and 7-year-olds. *Journal of Family Psychology, 13,* 450–465.

Ricciuti, H. N. (2004). Single parenthood, achievement, and problem behavior in white, black, and Hispanic children. *Journal of Educational Research, 97,* 196–206.

Rice, C., Koinis, D., Sullivan, K., Tager-Flusberg, H., & Winner, E. (1997). When 3-year-olds pass the appearance-reality test. *Developmental Psychology, 33,* 54–61.

Rice, M., Oetting, J. B., Marquis, J., Bode, J., & Pae, S. (1994). Frequency of input effects on SLI children's word comprehension. *Journal of Speech and Hearing Research, 37,* 106–122.

Rice, M. L. (1989). Children's language acquisition. *American Psychologist, 44*(2), 149–156.

Rice, M. L., Huston, A. C., Truglio, R., & Wright, J. (1990). Words from "Sesame Street": Learning vocabulary while viewing. *Developmental Psychology, 26,* 421–428.

Richardson, C. R., Kriska, A. M., Lantz, P. M., & Hayward, R. A. (2004). Physical activity and mortality across cardiovascular disease risk groups. *Medicine and Science in Sports and Exercise, 36,* 1923–1929.

Richardson, J. (1995). *Achieving gender equality in families: The role of males* (Innocenti Global Seminar, Summary Report). Florence, Italy: UNICEF International Child Development Centre, Spedale degli Innocenti.

Richman, L. S., Kubzansky, L., Maselko, J., Kawachi, I., Choo, P., & Bauer, M. (2005). Positive emotion and health: Going beyond the negative. *Health Psychology, 24,* 422–429.

Rideout, V. J., Vandewater, E. A., & Wartella, E. A. (2003). *Zero to six: Electronic media in the lives of infants, toddlers and preschoolers.* A Kaiser Family Foundation Report.

Riediger, M., Freund, A. M., & Baltes, P. B. (2005). Managing life through personal goals: Intergoal facilitation and intensity of goal pursuit in younger and older adults. *Journal of Gerontology: Psychological Sciences, 60B,* P84–P91.

Ries, L. A. G., Melbert, D., Krapcho, M., Mariotto, A., Miller, B. A., Feuer, E. J., Clegg, I., Homer, M. J., Howlader, N., Eisner, M. P., Reichman, M., & Edwards, B. K. (Eds.). (2007). *SEER cancer statistics review,* 1975–2004. Bethesda, MD: National Cancer Institute.

Rifkin, J. (1998, May 5). Creating the "perfect" human. *Chicago Sun-Times,* p. 29.

Riley, K. P., Snowdon, D. A., Desrosiers, M. F., & Markesbery, W. R. (2005). Early life linguistic ability, late life cognitive function, and neuropathology: Findings from the Nun Study. *Neurobiology of Aging, 26,* 341–347.

Rimm, E. B., & Stampfer, M. J. (2004). Diet, lifestyle, and longevity—the next steps? *Journal of the American Medical Association, 292,* 1490–1492.

Rios-Ellis, B., Bellamy, L., & Shoji, J. (2000). An examination of specific types of *ijime* within Japanese schools. *School Psychology International, 21,* 227–241.

Ritchie, L., Crawford, P., Woodward-Lopez, G., Ivey, S., Masch, M., & Ikeda, J. (2001). *Prevention of childhood overweight: What should be done?* Berkeley: Center for Weight and Health, University of California, Berkeley.

Ritter, J. (1999, November 23). Scientists close in on DNA code. *Chicago Sun-Times,* p. 7.

Rivera, J. A., Sotres-Alvarez, D., Habicht, J.-P., Shamah, T., & Villalpando, S. (2004). Impact of the Mexican Program for Education, Health and Nutrition (Progresa) on rates of growth and anemia in infants and young children. *Journal of the American Medical Association, 291,* 2563–2570.

Rivera, S. M., Wakeley, A., & Langer, J. (1999). The drawbridge phenomenon: Representational reasoning or perceptual preference? *Developmental Psychology, 35*(2), 427–435.

Robbins, A., & Wilner, A. (Eds.). (2001). *Quarterlife crisis: The unique challenges of life in your twenties.* New York: Putnam.

Roberts, B. W., Caspi, A., & Moffitt, T. E. (2003). Work experiences and personality development in young adulthood. *Journal of Personality and Social Psychology, 84,* 582–593.

Roberts, B. W., & Del Vecchio, W. F. (2000). The rank-order consistency of personality traits from childhood to old age: A quantitative review of longitudinal studies. *Psychological Bulletin, 126,* 3–25.

Roberts, B. W., & Mroczek, D. (2008). Personality trait change in adulthood. *Current Directions in Psychological Science, 17,* 31–35.

Roberts, B. W., Walton, K. E., & Bogg, T. (2005). Conscientiousness and health across the life course. *Review of General Psychology, 9,* 156–168.

Roberts, B. W., Walton, K. E., & Viechtbauer, W. (2006a). Patterns of mean-level change in personality traits across the life course: A meta-analysis of longitudinal studies. *Psychological Bulletin, 132,* 1–25.

Roberts, B. W., Walton, K. E., & Viechtbauer, W. (2006b). Personality traits change in adulthood: Reply to Costa and McCrae (2006). *Psychological Bulletin, 132,* 29–32.

Roberts, G. C., Block, J. H., & Block, J. (1984). Continuity and change in parents' child-rearing practices. *Child Development, 55,* 586–597.

Robin, D. J., Berthier, N. E., & Clifton, R. K. (1996). Infants' predictive reaching for moving objects in the dark. *Developmental Psychology, 32,* 824–835.

Robins, R. W., John, O. P., Caspi, A., Moffitt, T. E., & Stouthamer-Loeber, M. (1996). Resilient, overcontrolled, and undercontrolled boys: Three replicable personality types. *Journal of Personality and Social Psychology, 70,* 157–171.

Robins, R. W., & Trzesniewski, K. H. (2005). Self-esteem development across the lifespan. *Current Directions in Psychological Science, 14*(3), 158–162.

Robinson, L. C., & Blanton, P. W. (1993). Marital strengths in enduring marriages. *Family Relations, 42,* 38–45.

Robinson M., Thiel, M. M., Backus, M. M., & Meyer, E. C. (2006). Matters of spirituality at the end of life in the pediatric intensive care unit. *Pediatrics, 118,* 719–729.

Robinson, S. D., Rosenberg, H. J., & Farrell, M. P. (1999). The midlife crisis revisited. In S. L. Willis & J. D. Reid (Eds.), *Life in the middle: Psychological and social development in middle age* (pp. 47–77). San Diego: Academic Press.

Robinson, T. N., Wilde, M. L., Navacruz, L. C., Haydel, K. F., and Varady, A. (2001). Effects of reducing children's television and video game use on aggressive behavior: A randomized controlled trial. *Archives of Pediatric and Adolescent Medicine, 155,* 17–23.

Rochat, P., Querido, J. G., & Striano, T. (1999). Emerging sensitivity to the timing and structure of proto conversations in early infancy. *Developmental Psychology, 35,* 950–957.

Rochat, P., & Striano, T. (2002). Who's in the mirror? Self-other discrimination in specular images by 4- and 9-month-old infants. *Child Development, 73,* 35–46.

Roderick, M., Engel, M., & Nagaoka, J. (2003). *Ending social promotion: Results from Summer Bridge.* Chicago: Consortium on Chicago School Research.

Rodier, P. M. (2000, February). The early origins of autism. *Scientific American,* pp. 56–63.

Rodin, J., & Ickovics, J. (1990). Women's health: Review and research agenda as we approach the 21st century. *American Psychologist, 45,* 1018–1034.

Rodkin, P. C., Farmer, T. W., Pearl, R., & Van Acker, R. (2000). Heterogeneity of popular boys: Antisocial and prosocial configurations. *Developmental Psychology, 36*(1), 14–24.

Rodriguez, C., Patel, A. V., Calle, E. E., Jacob, E. J., & Thun, M. J. (2001). Estrogen replacement therapy and ovarian cancer mortality in a large prospective study of U.S. women. *Journal of the American Medical Association, 285,* 1460–1465.

Rogaeva, E., Meng, Y., Lee, J. H., Gu, Y., Kawarai, T., Zou, F., Katayama, T., Baldwin, C. T., Cheng, R., Hasegawa, H., Chen, F., Shibata, N., Lunetta, K. L., Pardossi-Piquard, R., Bohm, C., Wakutani, Y., Cupples, L. A., Cuenco, K. T., Green, R. C., Pinessi, L., Rainero, I., Sorbi, S., Bruni, A., Duara, R., Friedland, R. P., Inzelberg, R., Hampe, W., Bujo, H., Song, Y-K., Andersen, O. M., Willnow, T. E., Graff-Radford, N., Petersen, R. C., Dickson, D., Der, S. D., Fraser, P. E., Schmitt-Ulms, G., Younkin, S., Mayeux, R., Farrer, L. A., & St George-Hyslop, P. (2006.) The neuronal sortilin-related receptor SORL1 is genetically associated with Alzheimer disease. *Nature Genetics, 39,* 168–177.

Rogers, A. R. (2003). Economics and the evolution of life histories. *Proceedings of the National Academy of Sciences, 100,* 9114–9115.

Rogers, C. R. (1961). *On becoming a person.* Boston: Houghton Mifflin.

Rogers, F. (1983). *Mister Rogers talk with parents.* New York: Berkley Books.

Rogers, S. J. (2004). Dollars, dependency, and divorce: Four perspectives on the role of wives' income. *Journal of Marriage and Family, 66,* 59–74.

Rogler, L. H. (2002). Historical generations and psychology: The case of the Great Depression and World War II. *American Psychologist, 57*(12), 1013–1023.

Rogoff, B., Mistry, J., Göncü, A., & Mosier, C. (1993). Guided participation in cultural activity by toddlers and caregivers. *Monographs of the Society for Research in Child Development, 58*(8, Serial No. 236).

Rogoff, B., & Morelli, G. (1989). Perspectives on children's development from cultural psychology. *American Psychologist, 44,* 343–348.

Roisman, G. I., Clausell, E., Holland, A., Fortuna, K., & Elieff, C. (2008). Adult romantic relationships as contexts of human development: A multimethod comparison of same-sex couples with opposite-sex dating, engaged, and married dyads. *Developmental Psychology, 44,* 91–101.

Roisman, G. I., Masten, A. S., Coatsworth, J. D., & Tellegen, A. (2004). Salient and emerging developmental tasks in the transition to adulthood. *Child Development, 75,* 123–133.

Rolls, B. J., Engell, D., & Birch, L. L. (2000). Serving portion size influences 5-year-old but not 3-year-old children's food intake. *Journal of the American Dietetic Association, 100,* 232–234.

Rome-Flanders, T., Cronk, C., & Gourde, C. (1995). Maternal scaffolding in mother-infant games and its relationship to language development: A longitudinal study. *First Language, 15,* 339–355.

Ronca, A. E., & Alberts, J. R. (1995). Maternal contributions to fetal experience and the transition from prenatal to postnatal life. In J. P. Lecanuet, W. P. Fifer, N. A. Krasnegor, & W. P. Smotherman (Eds.), *Fetal development: A psychobiological perspective* (pp. 331–350). Hillsdale, NJ: Erlbaum.

Rönnlund, M., Nyberg, L., Bäckman, L., & Nilsson, L.-G. (2005). Stability, growth, and decline in adult life span development of declarative memory: Cross-sectional and longitudinal data from a population-based study. *Psychology and Aging, 20,* 3–18.

Roopnarine, J., & Honig, A. S. (1985, September). The unpopular child. *Young Children,* 59–64.

Roopnarine, J. L., Hooper, F. H., Ahmeduzzaman, M., & Pollack, B. (1993). Gentle play partners: Mother-child and father-child play in New Delhi, India. In K. MacDonald (Ed.), *Parent-child play* (pp. 287–304). Albany: State University of New York Press.

Roopnarine, J. L., Talokder, E., Jain, D., Josh, P., & Srivastav, P. (1992). Personal well-being, kinship ties, and mother-infant and father-infant interactions in single-wage and dual-wage families in New Delhi, India. *Journal of Marriage and Family, 54,* 293–301.

Roosa, M. W., Deng, S., Ryu, E., Burrell, G. L., Tein, J., Jones, S., Lopez, V., & Crowder, S. (2005). Family and child characteristics linking neighborhood context and child externalizing behavior. *Journal of Marriage and Family, 667,* 515–529.

Rosamond, W. D., Chambless, L. E., Folsom, A. R., Cooper, L. S., Conwill, D. E., Clegg, L., Wang, C.-H., & Heiss, G. (1998). Trends in the incidence of myocardial infarction and in mortality due to coronary heart disease, 1987 to 1994. *New England Journal of Medicine, 339,* 861–867.

Rose, S. A. (1994). Relation between physical growth and information processing in infants born in India. *Child Development, 65,* 889–902.

Rose, S. A., & Feldman, J. F. (1995). Prediction of IQ and specific cognitive abilities at 11 years from infancy measures. *Developmental Psychology, 31,* 685–696.

Rose, S. A., & Feldman, J. F. (1997). Memory and speed: Their role in the relation of infant information processing to later IQ. *Child Development, 68,* 630–641.

Rose, S. A., & Feldman, J. F. (2000). The relation of very low birth weight to basic cognitive skills in infancy and childhood. In C. A. Nelson (Ed.), *The effects of early adversity on neurobehavioral development. The Minnesota Symposia on Child Psychology* (Vol. 31, pp. 31–59). Mahwah, NJ: Erlbaum.

Rose, S. A., Feldman, J. F., & Jankowski, J. J. (2001). Attention and recognition memory in the 1st year of life: A longitudinal study of preterm and full-term infants. *Developmental Psychology, 37,* 135–151.

Rose, S. A., Feldman, J. F., & Jankowski, J. J. (2002). Processing speed in the 1st year of life: A longitudinal study of preterm and full-term infants. *Developmental Psychology, 38,* 895–902.

Rosenberg, S. D., Rosenberg, H. J., & Farrell, M. P. (1999). The midlife crisis revisited. In S. L. Willis & J. D. Reid (Eds.), *Life in the middle* (pp. 47–73). San Diego: Academic Press.

Rosenblum, G. D., & Lewis, M. (1999). The relations among body image, physical attractiveness, and body mass in adolescence. *Child Development, 70,* 50–64.

Rosenbluth, S. C., & Steil, J. M. (1995). Predictors of intimacy for women in heterosexual and homosexual couples. *Journal of Social and Personal Relationships, 12*(2), 163–175.

Rosenfeld, D. (1999). Identity work among lesbian and gay elderly. *Journal of Aging Studies, 13,* 121–144.

Ross, H. S. (1996). Negotiating principles of entitlement in sibling property disputes. *Developmental Psychology, 32,* 90–101.

Rossi, A. S. (2004). The menopausal transition and aging process. In O. G. Brim, C. D. Ryff, & R. C. Kessler (Eds.), *How healthy are we? A national study of well-being at midlife.* Chicago: University of Chicago Press.

Rossi, R. (1996, August 30). Small schools under microscope. *Chicago Sun-Times,* p. 24.

Rothbart, M. K., Ahadi, S. A., & Evans, D. E. (2000). Temperament and personality: Origins and outcomes. *Journal of Personality and Social Psychology, 78,* 122–135.

Rotheram-Borus, M. J., & Futterman, D. (2000). Promoting early detection of human immunodeficiency virus infection among adolescents. *Archives of Pediatric and Adolescent Medicine, 154,* 435–439.

Rothermund, K., & Brandtstädter, J. (2003). Coping with deficits and losses in later life: From compensatory action to accommodation. *Psychology and Aging, 18,* 896–905.

Rouse, C., Brooks-Gunn, J., & McLanahan, S. (2005). Introducing the issue. *Future of Children, 15*(1), 5–14.

Roush, S. W., Murphy, T. V., & the Vaccine-Preventable Disease Table Working Group. (2007). Historical comparisons of morbidity and mortality for vaccine-preventable diseases in the United States. *Journal of the American Medical Association, 298,* 2155–2163.

Roush, W. (1995). Arguing over why Johnny can't read. *Science, 267,* 1896–1898.

Rovee-Collier, C. (1996). Shifting the focus from what to why. *Infant Behavior and Development, 19,* 385–400.

Rovee-Collier, C. (1999). The development of infant memory. *Current Directions in Psychological Science, 8,* 80–85.

Rowe, J. W., & Kahn, R. L. (1997). Successful aging. *Gerontologist, 37,* 433–440.

Rowland, A. S., Umbach, D. M., Stallone, L., Naftel, J., Bohlig, E. M., & Sandler, D. P. (2002). Prevalence of medication treatment for attention-deficit hyperactivity disorder among elementary school children in Johnston County, North Carolina. *American Journal of Public Health, 92,* 231–234.

Rubin, D. H., Krasilnikoff, P. A., Leventhal, J. M., Weile, B., & Berget, A. (1986, August 23). Effect of passive smoking on birth weight. *Lancet,* pp. 415–417.

Rubin, K. (1982). Nonsocial play in preschoolers: Necessary evil? *Child Development, 53,* 651–657.

Rubin, K. H., Bukowski, W., & Parker, J. G. (1998). Peer interactions, relationships, and groups. In W. Damon (Series Ed.) & N. Eisenberg (Vol. Ed.), *Handbook of child psychology: Vol. 3. Social, emotional, and personality development* (5th ed., pp. 619–700). New York: Wiley.

Ruble, D. N., & Dweck, C. S. (1995). Self-conceptions, person conceptions, and their development. In N. Eisenberg (Ed.), *Social development: Review of personality and social psychology* (pp. 109–139). Thousand Oaks, CA: Sage.

Ruble, D. N., & Martin, C. L. (1998). Gender development. In W. Damon (Series Ed.) & N. Eisenberg (Vol. Ed.), *Handbook of child psychology: Vol. 3. Social, emotional, and personality development* (5th ed., pp. 933–1016). New York: Wiley

Rudman, D., Axel, G. F., Hoskote, S. N., Gergans, G. A., Lalitha, P. Y., Goldberg, A. F., Schlenker, R. A., Cohn, L., Rudman, I. W., & Mattson, D. E. (1990). Effects of human growth hormone in men over 60 years old. *New England Journal of Medicine, 323*(1), 1–6.

Rudolph, K. D., Lambert, S. F., Clark, A. G., & Kurlakowsky, K. D. (2001). Negotiating the transition to middle school: The role of self-regulatory processes. *Child Development, 72*(3), 929–946.

Rudy, D., & Grusec, J. E. (2006). Authoritarian parenting in individualistic and collectivistic groups: Associations with maternal emotion and cognition and children's self-esteem. *Journal of Family Psychology, 20,* 68–78.

Rueter, M. A., & Conger, R. D. (1995). Antecedents of parent-adolescent disagreements. *Journal of Marriage and Family, 57,* 435–448.

Ruffman, T., Slade, L., & Crowe, E. (2002). The relation between children's and mothers' mental state language and theory-of-mind understanding. *Child Development, 73,* 734–751.

Ruitenberg, A., van Swieten, J. C., Witteman, J. C., Mehta, K. M., van Duijn, C. M., Hofman, A., & Breteler, M. M. (2002). Alcohol consumption and risk of dementia: The Rotterdam Study. *Lancet, 359,* 281–286.

Ruiz, F., & Tanaka, K. (2001). The *ijime* phenomenon and Japan: Overarching consideration for cross-cultural studies. *Psychologia: An International Journal of Psychology in the Orient, 44,* 128–138.

Rushton, J. P., & Jensen, A. R. (2005). Thirty years of research on race differences in cognitive ability. *Psychology, Public Policy, and Law, 11,* 235–294.

Rutland, A. F., & Campbell, R. N. (1996). The relevance of Vygotsky's theory of the "zone of proximal development" to the assessment of children with intellectual disabilities. *Journal of Intellectual Disability Research, 40,* 151–158.

Rutledge, T., Reis, S. T., Olson, M., Owens, J., Kelsey, S. F., Pepine, C. J., Mankad, S., Rogers, W. J., Merz, C. N. B., Sopko, G., Cornell, C. E., Sharaf, B., & Matthews, K. A. (2004). Social networks are associated with lower mortality rates among women with suspected coronary disease: The National Heart, Lung, and Blood Institute-sponsored Women's Ischemia Syndrome Evaluation Study. *Psychosomatic Medicine, 66,* 882–888.

Rutter, M. (2002). Nature, nurture, and development: From evangelism through science toward policy and practice. *Child Development, 73,* 1–21.

Rutter, M. (2007). Gene-environment interdependence. *Developmental Science, 10,* 12–18.

Rutter, M., & English and Romanian Adoptees (ERA) Study Team. (1998). Developmental catch-up, and deficit, following adoption after severe global early privation. *Journal of Child Psychology and Psychiatry, 39,* 465–476.

Rutter, M., O'Connor, T. G., and English and Romanian Adoptees (ERA) Study Team. (2004). Are there biological programming effects for psychological development? Findings from a study of Romanian adoptees. *Developmental Psychology, 40,* 81–94.

Ryan, A. S. (1997). The resurgence of breast-feeding in the United States. *Pediatrics, 99.* Retrieved from www.pediatrics.org/cgi/content/full/99/4/e12.

Ryan, A. S., Wenjun, Z., & Acosta, A. (2002). Breastfeeding continues to increase into the new millennium. *Pediatrics, 110,* 1103–1109.

Ryan, V., & Needham, C. (2001). Nondirective play therapy with children experiencing psychic trauma. *Clinical Child Psychology and Psychiatry* (Special issue), 6, 437–453.

Rybash, J. M., Hoyer, W. J., & Roodin, P. A. (1986). *Adult cognition and aging: Developmental changes in processing, knowing, and thinking.* New York: Pergamon.

Ryff, C. D. (1995). Psychological well-being in adult life. *Current Directions in Psychological Science, 4,* 99–104.

Ryff, C. D., & Keyes, C. L. M. (1995). The structure of psychological well-being revisited. *Journal of Personality and Social Psychology, 69,* 719–727.

Ryff, C. D., Keyes, C. L., & Hughes, D. L. (2004). Psychological well-being in MIDUS: Profiles of ethnic/racial diversity and life-course uniformity. In O. G. Brim, C. D. Ryff, & R. C. Kessler (Eds.), *How healthy are we? A national study of well-being at midlife* (pp. 398–424). Chicago: University of Chicago Press.

Ryff, C. D., & Seltzer, M. M. (1995). Family relations and individual development in adulthood and aging. In R. Blieszner & V. Hilkevitch (Eds.), *Handbook of aging and the family* (pp. 95–113). Westport, CT: Greenwood Press.

Ryff, C. D., & Singer, B. (1998). Middle age and well-being. *Encyclopedia of Mental Health, 2,* 707–719.

Ryff, C. D, Singer, B. H., & Palmersheim, K. A. (2004). Social inequalities in health and well-being: The role of relational and religious protective factors. In O. G. Brim, C. D. Ryff, & R. C. Kessler (Eds.), *How healthy are we? A national study of well-being at midlife.* Chicago: University of Chicago Press.

Rymer, R. (1993). *An abused child: Flight from silence.* New York: HarperCollins.

Saarni, C., Mumme, D. L., & Campos, J. J. (1998). Emotional development: Action, communication, and understanding. In W. Damon (Series Ed.) & N. Eisenberg (Vol. Ed.), *Handbook of child psychology: Vol. 3. Social, emotional, and personality development* (5th ed., pp. 237–309). New York: Wiley.

Sabol, S. Z., Nelson, M. L., Fisher, C., Gunzerath, L., Brody, C. L., Hu, S., Sirota, L. A., Marcus, S. E., Greenberg, B. D., Lucas, F. R., IV, Benjamin, J., Murphy, D. L., & Hamer, D. H. (1999). A genetic association for cigarette smoking behavior. *Health Psychology, 18,* 7–13.

Sadeh, A., Raviv, A., & Gruber, R. (2000). Sleep patterns and sleep disruptions in school age children. *Developmental Psychology, 36*(3), 291–301.

Sahyoun, N. R., Lentzner, H., Hoyert, D., & Robinson, K. N. (2001). Trends in causes of death among the elderly. *Aging Trends,* No.

1. Hyattsville, MD: National Center for Health Statistics.

Sahyoun, N. R., Pratt, L. A., Lentzner, H., Dey, A., & Robinson, K. N. (2001). The changing profile of nursing home residents: 1985–1997. *Aging Trends,* No. 4.

Saigal, S., Hoult, L. A., Streiner, D. L., Stoskopf, B. L., & Rosenbaum, P. L. (2000). School difficulties at adolescence in a regional cohort of children who were extremely low birth weight. *Pediatrics, 105,* 325–331.

Saigal, S., Stoskopf, B., Streiner, D., Boyle, M., Pinelli, J., Paneth, N., & Goddeeris, J. (2006). Transition of extremely low-birth-weight infants from adolescence to young adulthood: Comparison with normal birth-weight controls. *Journal of the American Medical Association, 295,* 667–675.

Saigal, S., Stoskopf, B. L., Streiner, D. L., & Burrows, E. (2001). Physical growth and current health status of infants who were of extremely low birth weight and controls at adolescence. *Pediatrics, 108*(2), 407–415.

Salovey, P., & Mayer, J. D. (1990). Emotional intelligence. *Imagination, Cognition, and Personality, 9,* 185–211.

Salovey, P., Rothman, A. J., Detweiler, J. B., & Steward, W. T. (2000). Emotional states and physical health. *American Psychologist, 55,* 110–121.

Salthouse, T. A. (1984). Effects of age and typing skill. *Journal of Experimental Psychology: General, 113,* 345–371.

Salthouse, T. A. (1985). Anticipatory processing in transcription typing. *Journal of Applied Psychology, 70,* 264–271.

Salthouse, T. A. (1991). *Theoretical perspectives on cognitive aging.* Hillsdale, NJ: Erlbaum.

Salthouse, T. A., Fristoe, N., McGuthry, K. E., & Hambrick, D. Z. (1998). Relation of task switching to speed, age, and fluid intelligence. *Psychology and Aging, 13,* 445–461.

Salthouse, T. A., & Maurer, T. J. (1996). Aging, job performance, and career development. In J. E. Birren & K. W. Schaie (Eds.), *Handbook of the psychology of aging* (pp. 353–364). San Diego: Academic Press.

Samdal, O., & Dür, W. (2000). The school environment and the health of adolescents. In C. Currie, K. Hurrelmann, W. Settertobulte, R. Smith, & J. Todd (Eds.), *Health and health behaviour among young people: A WHO cross-national study (HBSC) international report* (pp. 49–64). WHO Policy Series: Health Policy for Children and Adolescents, Series No. 1. Copenhagen, Denmark: World Health Organization Regional Office for Europe.

Sampson, R. J. (1997). The embeddedness of child and adolescent development: A community-level perspective on urban violence. In J. McCord (Ed.), *Violence and childhood in the inner city* (pp. 31–77). Cambridge, England: Cambridge University Press.

Samuelsson, M., Radestad, I., & Segesten, K. (2001). A waste of life: Fathers' experience of losing a child before birth. *Birth, 28,* 124–130.

Sandberg, S., Järvenpää, S., Penttinen, A., Paton, J. Y., & McCann, D. C. (2004). Asthma exacerbations in children immediately following stressful life events: A Cox's hierarchical regression. *Thorax, 59,* 1046–1051.

Sandefur, G., Eggerling-Boeck, J., & Park, H. (2005). Off to a good start? Postsecondary education and early adult life. In R. A. Settersten Jr., F. F. Furstenberg Jr., & R. G. Rumbaut (Eds.), *On the frontier of adulthood: Theory, research, and public policy* (pp. 292–319). (John D. and Catherine T. MacArthur Foundation Series on Mental Health and Development, Research Network on Transitions to Adulthood and Public Policy.) Chicago: University of Chicago Press.

Sandler, D. P., Everson, R. B., Wilcox, A. J., & Browder, J. P. (1985). Cancer risk in adulthood from early life exposure to parents' smoking. *American Journal of Public Health, 75,* 487–492.

Sandler, W., Meir, I., Padden, C., & Aronoff, M. (2005). The emergence of grammar: Systematic structure in a new language. *Proceedings of the National Academy of Sciences, 102,* 2661–2665.

Sandnabba, H. K., & Ahlberg, C. (1999). Parents' attitudes and expectations about children's cross-gender behavior. *Sex Roles, 40,* 249–263.

Sandstrom, M. J., & Coie, J. D. (1999). A developmental perspective on peer rejection: Mechanisms of stability and change. *Child Development* 70(4), 955–966.

Santos, I. S., Victora, C. G., Huttly, S., & Carvalhal, J. B. (1998). Caffeine intake and low birthweight: A population-based case-control study. *American Journal of Epidemiology, 147,* 620–627.

Sapienza, C. (1990, October). Parental imprinting of genes. *Scientific American,* pp. 52–60.

Sapolsky, R. M. (1992). Stress and neuroendocrine changes during aging. *Generations, 16*(4), 35–38.

Sapp, F., Lee, K., & Muir, D. (2000). Three-year-olds' difficulty with the appearance-reality distinction: Is it real or apparent? *Developmental Psychology, 36,* 547–560.

Sargent, J. D., & Dalton, M. (2001). Does parental disapproval of smoking prevent adolescents from becoming established smokers? *Pediatrics, 108*(6), 1256–1262.

Sarkisian, N., & Gerstel, N. (2004). Explaining the gender gap in help to parents: The importance of employment. *Journal of Marriage and Family, 66,* 431–451.

Satcher, D. (2001). *Women and smoking: A report of the Surgeon General.* Washington, DC: Department of Health and Human Services.

Saudino, K. J., Wertz, A. E., Gagne, J. R., & Chawla, S. (2004). Night and day: Are siblings as different in temperament as parents say they are? *Journal of Personality and Social Psychology, 87,* 698–706.

Savage, S. L., & Au, T. K. (1996). What word learners do when input contradicts the mutual exclusivity assumption. *Child Development, 67,* 3120–3134.

Savic, I., Berglund, H., & Lindström, P. (2005). Brain response to putative pheromones in homosexual men. *Proceedings of the National Academy of Sciences, 102,* 7356–7361.

Savic, I., Berglund, H., Lindström, P. (2006). Brain response to putative pheromones. *Proceedings of the National Academy of Sciences, 102*(20), 7356–7361.

Savic, I., & Lindström, P. (2008). PET and MRI show differences in cerebral asymmetry and functional connectivity between homo- and heterosexual subjects. *Proceedings of the National Academy of Sciences, USA, 105,* 9403–9408. (DOI: 10.1073/pnas.0801566105).

Savin-Williams, R. C. (2006). Who's gay? Does it matter? *Current Directions in Psychological Science, 15,* 40–44.

Sawicki, M. B. (2005, March 16). *Collision course: The Bush budget and Social Security* (EPI Briefing Paper No. 156). Retrieved April 28, 2005, from www.epinet.org/content.cfm/bp156.

Saxe, R., Tenenbaum, J. B., & Carey, S. (2005). Secret agents: Inferences about hidden causes by 10- and 12-month old infants. *Psychological Science, 16,* 995–1001.

Saxe, R., Tzelnic, T., & Carey, S. (2007). Knowing who dunnit: Infants identify the causal agent in an unseen causal interaction. *Developmental Psychology, 43,* 149–158.

Scandinavian Simvastatin Survival Study Group. (1994). Randomized trial of cholesterol lowering in 4444 patients with coronary heart disease: The Scandinavian Simvastatin Survival Study (4S). *Lancet, 344,* 1383–1389.

Scarr, S. (1992). Developmental theories for the 1990s: Development and individual differences. *Child Development, 63,* 1–19.

Scarr, S. (1998). American child care today. *American Psychologist, 53,* 95–108.

Scarr, S., & McCartney, K. (1983). How people make their own environments: A theory of genotype-environment effects. *Child Development, 54,* 424–435.

Schacter, D. L. (1999). The seven sins of memory: Insights from psychology and cognitive neuroscience. *American Psychologist, 54,* 182–203.

Schaie, K. W. (1977–1978). Toward a stage theory of adult cognitive development. *Journal of Aging and Human Development, 8*(2), 129–138.

Schaie, K. W. (1983). The Seattle Longitudinal Study: A twenty-one-year investigation of psychometric intelligence. In K. W. Schaie (Ed.), *Longitudinal studies of adult personality development* (pp. 64–155). New York: Guilford Press.

Schaie, K. W. (1984). Midlife influences upon intellectual functioning in old age. *International Journal of Behavioral Development, 7,* 463–478.

Schaie, K. W. (1989). The hazards of cognitive aging. *Gerontologist, 29,* 484–493.

Schaie, K. W. (1990). Intellectual development in adulthood. In J. E. Birren & K. W. Schaie (Eds.), *Handbook of the psychology of aging* (pp. 291–309). San Diego: Academic Press.

Schaie, K. W. (1994). The course of adult intellectual development. *American Psychologist, 49*(4), 304–313.

Schaie, K. W. (1996a). Intellectual development in adulthood. In J. E. Birren & K. W. Schaie (Eds.), *Handbook of the psychology of aging* (4th ed., pp. 266–286). San Diego: Academic Press.

Schaie, K. W. (1996b). *Intellectual development in adulthood: The Seattle Longitudinal Study.* Cambridge, England: Cambridge University Press.

Schaie, K. W. (2005). *Developmental influences on adult intelligence: The Seattle Longitudinal Study.* New York: Oxford University Press.

Schaie, K. W., & Willis, S. L. (1991). Adult personality and psychomotor performance: Cross-sectional and longitudinal analysis. *Journal of Gerontology, 46*(6), P275–P284.

Schaie, K. W., & Willis, S. L. (1996). Psychometric intelligence and aging. In F. Blanchard-Fields & T. M. Hess (Eds.), *Perspectives on cognitive change in adulthood and aging* (pp. 293–322). New York: McGraw-Hill.

Schaie, K. W., & Willis, S. L. (2000). A stage theory model of adult cognitive development revisited. In B. Rubinstein, M. Moss, & M. Kleban (Eds.), *The many dimensions of aging: Essays in honor of M. Powell Lawton* (pp. 173–191). New York: Springer.

Schairer, C., Lubin, J., Troisi, R., Sturgeon, S., Brinton, L., & Hoover, R. (2000). Menopausal estrogen and estrogen-progestin replacement therapy and breast cancer risk. *Journal of the American Medical Association, 283,* 485–491.

Schardt, D. (1995, June). For men only. *Nutrition Action Health Letter, 22*(5), 4–7.

Scharf, M., Mayseless, O., & Kivenson-Baron, I. (2004). Adolescents' attachment representations and developmental tasks in emerging adulthood. *Developmental Psychology, 40,* 430–444.

Scharlach, A. E., & Fredriksen, K. I. (1993). Reactions to the death of a parent during midlife. *Omega, 27,* 307–319.

Schaubroeck, J., Jones, J. R., & Xie, J. L. (2001). Individual differences in utilizing control to cope with job demands: Effects on susceptibility to infectious disease. *Journal of Applied Psychology, 86,* 265–278.

Schaumberg, D. A., Mendes, F., Balaram, M., Dana, M. R., Sparrow, D., & Hu, H. (2004). Accumulated lead exposure and risk of age-related cataract in men. *Journal of the American Medical Association, 292,* 2750–2754.

Scheers, N. J., Rutherford, G. W., & Kemp, J. S. (2003). Where should infants sleep? A comparison of risk for suffocation of infants sleeping in cribs, adult beds, and other sleeping locations. *Pediatrics, 112,* 883–889.

Scheidt, P., Overpeck, M. D., Whatt, W., & Aszmann, A. (2000). In C. Currie, K. Hurrelmann, W. Settertobulte, R. Smith, & J. Todd (Eds.), *Health and health behaviour among young people: A WHO cross-national study (HBSC) international report* (pp. 24–38). WHO Policy Series: Healthy Policy for Children and Adolescents, Series No. 1. Copenhagen, Denmark: World Health Organization Regional Office for Europe.

Schemo, D. J. (2004, August 19). Charter schools lagging behind, test scores show. *New York Times,* pp. A1, A16.

Scher, M. S., Richardson, G. A., & Day, N. L. (2000). Effects of prenatal crack/cocaine and other drug exposure on electroencephalographic sleep studies at birth and one year. *Pediatrics, 105,* 39–48.

Schieve, L. A., Meikle, S. F., Ferre, C., Peterson, H. B., Jeng, G., & Wilcox, L. S. (2002). Low and very low birth weight in infants conceived with use of assisted reproductive technology. *New England Journal of Medicine, 346,* 731–737.

Schieve, L. A., Rice, C., Boyle, C., Visser, M. S., & Blumberg, S. J. (2006). Mental health in the United States: Parental report of diagnosed autism in children aged 4–17 years—United States, 2003–2004. *Morbidity and Mortality Weekly Report, 55*(17), 481–486.

Schiller, J. S., & Bernadel, L. (2004). Summary health statistics for the U.S. population: National Health Interview Survey, 2002. *Vital and Health Statistics, 10*(220). Hyattsville, MD: National Center for Health Statistics.

Schlegel, A., & Barry, H. (1991). *Adolescence: An anthropological inquiry.* New York: Free Press.

Schmidt, P. J., Nieman, L. K., Danaceau, M. A., Adams, L. F., & Rubinow, D. R. (1998). Differential behavioral effects of gonadal steroids in women with and in those without premenstrual syndrome. *New England Journal of Medicine, 338,* 209–216.

Schmitz, S., Saudino, K. J., Plomin, R., Fulker, D. W., & DeFries, J. C. (1996). Genetic and environmental influences on temperament in middle childhood: Analyses of teacher and tester ratings. *Child Development, 67,* 409–422.

Schnaas, L., Rothenberg, S. J., Flores, M., Martinez, S., Hernandez, C., Osorio, E., Velasco, S. R., & Perroni, E. (2006). Reduced intellectual development in children with prenatal lead exposure. *Environmental Health Perspectives, 114*(5), 791–797.

Schneider, B. H., Atkinson, L., & Tardif, C. (2001). Child-parent attachment and children's peer relations: A quantitative review. *Developmental Psychology, 37,* 86–100.

Schneider, E. L. (1992). Biological theories of aging. *Generations, 16*(4), 7–10.

Schneider, H., & Eisenberg, D. (2006). Who receives a diagnosis of attention-deficit hyperactivity disorder in the United States elementary school population? *Pediatrics, 117,* 601–609.

Schneider, M. (2002). *Do school facilities affect academic outcomes?* Washington, DC: National Clearinghouse for Educational Facilities.

Schoenborn, C. A. (2004). Marital status and health: United States, 1999–2002. *Advance Data from Vital and Health Statistics,* No. 351. Hyattsville, MD: National Center for Health Statistics.

Schoenborn, C. A., Vickerie, J. L., & Powell-Griner, E. (2006). Health characteristics of adults 55 years of age and over: United States, 2000–2003. *Advance Data from Vital and Health Statistics,* No. 370. Hyattsville, MD: National Center for Health Statistics.

Schoeni, R., & Ross, K. (2005). Maternal assistance from families during the transition to adulthood. In R. A. Settersten Jr., F. F. Furstenberg Jr., & R. G. Rumbaut (Eds.), *On the frontier of adulthood: Theory, research, and public policy* (pp. 396–416). (John D. and Catherine T. MacArthur Foundation Series on Mental Health and Development, Research Network on Transitions to Adulthood and Public Policy.) Chicago: University of Chicago Press.

Scholten, C. M. (1985). *Childbearing in American society: 1650–1850.* New York: New York University Press.

Schöner, G., & Thelen, E. (2006). Using dynamic field theory to rethink infant habituation. *Psychological Review, 113,* 273–299.

Schonfield, D. (1974). Translations in gerontology—From lab to life: Utilizing information. *American Psychologist, 29,* 228–236.

Schooler, C. (1984). Psychological effects of complex environments during the life-span: A review and theory. *Intelligence, 8,* 259–281.

Schooler, C. (1990). Psychosocial factors and effective cognitive functioning in adulthood. In J. E. Burren & K. W. Schaie (Eds.), *The handbook of aging* (pp. 347–358). San Diego: Academic Press.

Schooler, C., Revell, A. J., & Caplan, L. J. (2007). Parental practices and willingness to ask for children's help later in life. *Journal of Gerontology Psychological and Social Sciences, 57B,* S3–S13.

Schore, A. N. (1994). *Affect regulation and the origin of the self: The neurobiology of emotional development.* Hillsdale, NJ: Erlbaum.

Schreiber, J. B., Robins, M., Striegel-Moore, R., Obarzanek, E., Morrison, J. A., & Wright, D. J. (1996). Weight modification efforts reported by preadolescent girls. *Pediatrics, 96,* 63–70.

Schulenberg, J., O'Malley, P., Backman, J., & Johnston, L. (2005). Early adult transitions and their relation to well-being and substance use. In R. A. Settersten Jr., F. F. Furstenberg Jr., & R. G. Rumbaut (Eds.), *On the frontier of adulthood: Theory, research, and public policy* (pp. 417–453).

(John D. and Catherine T. MacArthur Foundation Series on Mental Health and Development, Research Network on Transitions to Adulthood and Public Policy.) Chicago: University of Chicago Press.

Schulenberg, J. E., & Zarrett, N. R. (2006). Mental health during emerging adulthood: Continuity and discontinuity in courses, causes, and functions. In J. J. Arnett & J. L. Tanner (Eds.), *Emerging adults in America: Coming of age in the 21st century* (pp. 135–172). Washington, DC: American Psychological Association.

Schulting, A. B., Malone, P. S., & Dodge, K. A. (2005). The effect of school-based kindergarten transition policies and practices on child academic outcomes. *Developmental Psychology, 41,* 860–871.

Schulz, M. S., Cowan, C. P., & Cowan, P. A. (2006). Promoting healthy beginnings: A randomized controlled trial of a preventive intervention to preserve marital quality during the transition to parenthood. *Journal of Consulting and Clinical Psychology, 74,* 20–31.

Schulz, M. S., Cowan, P. A., Cowan, C. P., & Brennan, R. T. (2004). Coming home upset: Gender, marital satisfaction, and the daily spillover of workday experience into couple interactions. *Journal of Family Psychology, 18,* 250–263.

Schulz, R. (1978). *A psychology of death, dying, and bereavement.* Reading, MA: Addison-Wesley.

Schulz, R., & Beach, S. R. (1999). Caregiving as a risk factor for mortality: The Caregiver Health Effects Study. *Journal of the American Medical Association, 282,* 2215–2219.

Schulz, R., & Heckhausen, J. (1996). A life-span model of successful aging. *American Psychologist, 51,* 702–714.

Schulz, R, & Martire, L. M. (2004). Family caregiving of persons with dementia: Prevalence, health effects, and support strategies. *American Journal of Geriatric Psychiatry, 12,* 240–249.

Schumann, C. M., & Amaral, D. G. (2006). Stereological analysis of amygdala neuron number in autism. *Journal of Neuroscience, 26*(29), 7674–7679.

Schumann, J. (1997). The view from elsewhere: Why there can be no best method for teaching a second language. *Clarion: Magazine of the European Second Language Acquisition, 3*(1), 23–24.

Schwartz, D., Chang, L., & Farver, J. M. (2001). Correlates of victimization in Chinese children's peer groups. *Developmental Psychology, 37*(4), 520–532.

Schwartz, D., Dodge, K. A., Pettit, G. S., Bates, J. E., & Conduct Problems Prevention Research Group. (2000). Friendship as a moderating factor in the pathway between early harsh home environment and later victimization in the peer group. *Developmental Psychology, 36,* 646–662.

Schwartz, D., McFadyen-Ketchum, S. A., Dodge, K. A., Pettit, G. S., & Bates, J. E. (1998). Peer group victimization as a predictor of children's behavior problems at home and in school. *Development and Psychopathology, 10,* 87–99.

Schwartz, L. L. (2003). A nightmare for King Solomon: The new reproductive technologies. *Journal of Family Psychology, 17,* 229–237.

Schweinhart, L. J., Barnes, H. V., & Weikart, D. P. (1993). *Significant benefits: The High/Scope Perry Preschool Study through age 27* (Monographs of the High/Scope Educational Research Foundation No. 10). Ypsilanti, MI: High/Scope.

Scientific Registry of Transplant Recipients. (2004). *Fast facts about transplants, July 1, 2003–June 30, 2004.* Retrieved March 15, 2005, from www.ustransplant.org/csr0105/facts.php.

Scott, J. (1998). Changing attitudes to sexual morality: A cross-national comparison. *Sociology, 32,* 815–845.

Sedlak, A. J., & Broadhurst, D. D. (1996). *Executive summary of the third national incidence study of child abuse and neglect* (NIS-3). Washington, DC: U.S. Department of Health and Human Services.

Seeman, E. Dubin, L. F., & Seeman, M. (2003). Religiosity/spirituality and health: A critical review of the evidence for biological pathways. *American Psychologist, 58,* 53–63.

Seftor, N. S., & Turner, S. E. (2002). Back to school: Federal student aid policy and adult college enrollment. *Journal of Human Resources, 37,* 336–352.

Segerstrom, S. C., & Miller, G. E. (2004). Psychological stress and the human immune system: A meta-analytic study of 30 years of inquiry. *Psychological Bulletin, 130,* 601–630.

Seidler, A., Neinhaus, A., Bernhardt, T., Kauppinen, T., Elo, A. L., & Frolich, L. (2004). Psychosocial work factors and dementia. *Occupational and Environmental Medicine, 61,* 962–971.

Seifer, R., Schiller, M., Sameroff, A. J., Resnick, S., & Riordan, K. (1996). Attachment, maternal sensitivity, and infant temperament during the first year of life. *Developmental Psychology, 32,* 12–25.

Seiner, S. H., & Gelfand, D. M. (1995). Effects of mother's simulated withdrawal and depressed affect on mother-toddler interactions. *Child Development, 60,* 1519–1528.

Seitz, V. (1990). Intervention programs for impoverished children: A comparison of educational and family support models. *Annals of Child Development, 7,* 73–103.

Sellers, E. M. (1998). Pharmacogenetics and ethnoracial differences in smoking. *Journal of the American Medical Association, 280,* 179–180.

Selman, R. L. (1980). *The growth of interpersonal understanding: Developmental and clinical analyses.* New York: Academic Press.

Selman, R. L., & Selman, A. P. (1979, April). Children's ideas about friendship: A new theory. *Psychology Today,* pp. 71–80.

Seltzer, J. A. (2000). Families formed outside of marriage. *Journal of Marriage and Family, 62,* 1247–1268.

Seltzer, J. A. (2004). Cohabitation in the United States and Britain: Demography, kinship, and the future. *Journal of Marriage and Family, 66,* 921–928.

Seminara, S. B., Messager, S., Chatzidaki, E. E., Thresher, R. R., Acierno, J. S., Jr., Shagoury, J. K., Bo-Abbas, Y., Kuohung, W., Schwinof, K. M., Hendrick, A. G., Zahn, D., Dixon, J., Kaiser, U. B., Slaugenhaupt, S. A., Gusella, J. F., O'Rahilly, S., Carlton, M. B. L., Crowley W. F., Jr., Aparicio, S. A. J. R., & Colledge, W. H. (2003). The GPR54 gene as a regulator of puberty. *New England Journal of Medicine, 349,* 1614–1627.

Sen, A., Partelow, L., & Miller, D. C. (2005). *Comparative indicators of education in the United States and other G8 countries: 2004* (NCES 2005–021). Washington, DC: National Center for Education Statistics.

Senghas, A., & Coppola, M. (2001). Children creating language: How Nicaraguan sign language acquired a spatial grammar. *Psychological Science, 12,* 323–328.

Senghas, A., Kita, S., & Ozyürek, A. (2004). Children creating core properties of language: Evidence from an emerging sign language in Nicaragua. *Science, 305,* 1779–1782.

Serbin, L., Poulin-Dubois, D., Colburne, K. A., Sen, M., & Eichstedt, J. A. (2001). Gender stereotyping in infancy: Visual preferences for knowledge of gender-stereotyped toys in the second year. *International Journal of Behavioral Development, 25,* 7–15.

Serbin, L. A., Moller, L. C., Gulko, J., Powlishta, K. K., & Colburne, K. A. (1994). The emergence of gender segregation in toddler playgroups. In C. Leaper (Ed.), *Childhood gender segregation: Causes and consequences* (New Directions for Child Development, No. 65, pp. 7–17). San Francisco: Jossey-Bass.

Serres, L. (2001). Morphological changes of the human hippocampal formation from midgestation to early childhood. In C. A. Nelson & M. Luciana (Eds.), *Handbook of developmental cognitive neuroscience* (pp. 45–58). Cambridge, MA: MIT Press.

Sethi, A., Mischel, W., Aber, J. L., Shoda, Y., & Rodriguez, M. L. (2000). The role of strategic attention deployment in development of self-regulation: Predicting preschoolers' delay of gratification from mother-toddler interactions. *Developmental Psychology, 36,* 767–777.

Settersten, R. A., Jr. (2005). Social policy and the transition to adulthood: Toward stronger institutions and individual capacities. In R. A. Settersten Jr., F. F. Furstenberg Jr., & R. G. Rumbaut (Eds.), *On the frontier of adulthood: Theory, research, and public policy* (534–560). Chicago: University of Chicago Press.

Sexton, A. (1966). Little girl, my string bean, my lovely woman. *The complete poems:*

Anne Sexton. New York: Houghton Mifflin, 1981.

Seybold, K. S., & Hill, P. C. (2001). The role of religion and spirituality in mental and physical health. *Current Directions in Psychological Science, 10,* 21–24.

Shah, T., Sullivan, K., & Carter, J. (2006). Sudden infant death syndrome and reported maternal smoking during pregnancy. *American Journal of Public Health, 96*(10), 1757–1759.

Shanahan, M., Porfeli, E., & Mortimer, J. (2005). Subjective age identity and the transition to adulthood: When do adolescents become adults? In R. A. Settersten Jr., F. F. Furstenberg Jr., & R. G. Rumbaut (Eds.), *On the frontier of adulthood: Theory, research, and public policy* (pp. 225–255). (John D. and Catherine T. MacArthur Foundation Series on Mental Health and Development, Research Network on Transitions to Adulthood and Public Policy.) Chicago: University of Chicago Press.

Shankaran, S., Das, A., Bauer, C. R., Bada, H. S., Lester, B., Wright, L. L., & Smeriglio, V. (2004). Association between patterns of maternal substance use and infant birth weight, length, and head circumference. *Pediatrics, 114,* e226–e234.

Shannon, J. D., Tamis-LeMonda, C. S., London, K., & Cabrera, N. (2002). Beyond rough and tumble: Low income fathers' interactions and children's cognitive development at 24 months. *Parenting: Science & Practice, 2*(2), 77–104.

Shapiro, A. F., & Gottman, J. M. (2003, September). Bringing baby home: Effects on marriage of a psycho-education intervention with couples undergoing the transition to parenthood, evaluation at 1-year post intervention. In A. J. Hawkins (Chair), *Early family interventions.* Symposium conducted at the meeting of the National Council on Family Relations, Vancouver, British Columbia.

Shapiro, P. (1994, November). My house is your house: Advance planning can ease the way when parents move in with adult kids. *AARP Bulletin,* p. 2.

Sharma, A. R., McGue, M. K., & Benson, P. L. (1996a). The emotional and behavioral adjustment of United States adopted adolescents, Part I: An overview. *Children and Youth Services Review, 18,* 83–100.

Sharma, A. R., McGue, M. K., & Benson, P. L. (1996b). The emotional and behavioral adjustment of United States adopted adolescents, Part II: Age at adoption. *Children and Youth Services Review, 18,* 101–114.

Shatz, M., & Gelman, R. (1973). The development of communication skills: Modifications in the speech of young children as a function of listener. *Monographs of the Society for Research in Child Development, 38*(5, Serial No. 152).

Shaw, B. A., Krause, N., Chatters, L. M., Connell, C. M., & Ingersoll-Dayton, B. (2004). Emotional support from parents early in life, aging, and health. *Psychology and Aging, 19,* 4–12.

Shaw, B. A., Krause, N., Liang, J., & Bennett, J. (2007). Tracking changes in social relations throughout late life. *Journal of Gerontology: Social Sciences, 62B,* S90–S99.

Shaw, P., Eckstrand, K., Sharp, W., Blumenthal, J., Lerch, J. P., Greenstein, D., Clasen, L., Evans, A., Giedd, J., & Rapoport, J. L. (2007). Attention-deficit/hyperactivity disorder is characterized by a delay in cortical maturation. *Proceedings of the National Academy of Sciences, 104,* 19649–19654.

Shaw, P., Gornick, M., Lerch, J., Addington, A., Seal, J., Greenstein, D., Sharp, W., Evans, A., Giedd, J. N., Castellanos, F. X., & Rapoport, J. L. (2007). Polymorphisms of the dopamine D$_4$ receptor, clinical outcome, and cortical structure in attention-deficit/hyperactivity disorder. *Archives of General Psychiatry, 64,* 921–931.

Shaw, P., Greenstein, D., Lerch, J., Clasen, L., Lenroot, R., Gogtay, N., Evans, A., Rapoport, J., & Giedd, J. (2006). Intellectual ability and cortical development in children and adolescents. *Nature, 440,* 676–679.

Shayer, M., Ginsburg, D., & Coe, R. (2007). Thirty years on—a large anti-Flynn effect? The Piagetian Test Volume & Heaviness norms 1975–2003. *British Journal of Educational Psychology, 77*(1), 25–41.

Shaywitz, S. (2003). *Overcoming dyslexia: A new and complete science-based program for overcoming reading problems at any level.* New York: Knopf.

Shaywitz, S. E. (1998). Current concepts: Dyslexia. *New England Journal of Medicine, 338,* 307–312.

Shaywitz, S. E., Mody, M., & Shaywitz, B. A. (2006). Neural mechanisms in dyslexia. *Current Directions in Psychological Science, 15,* 278–281.

Shea, K. M., Little, R. E., & the ALSPAC Study Team (1997). Is there an association between preconceptual paternal X-ray exposure and birth outcome? *American Journal of Epidemiology, 145,* 546–551.

Shea, S., Basch, C. E., Stein, A. D., Contento, I. R., Irigoyen, M., & Zybert, P. (1993). Is there a relationship between dietary fat and stature or growth in children 3 to 5 years of age? *Pediatrics, 92,* 579–586.

Shedlock, D. J., & Cornelius, S. W. (2003). Psychological approaches to wisdom and its development. In J. Demick & C. Andreoletti (Eds.), *Handbook of adult development* (pp. 153–167). New York: Plenum Press.

Sheldon, K. M., & Kasser, T. (2001). Getting older, getting better? Personal strivings and psychological maturity across the life span. *Developmental Psychology, 37,* 491–501.

Shepherd, J., Cobbe, S. M., Ford, I., Isles, C. G., Lorimer, A. R., MacFarlane, P. W., McKillop, J. H., & Packard, C. J. (1995). Prevention of coronary heart disease with pravastatin in men with hypercholesterolemia. *New England Journal of Medicine, 333,* 1301–1307.

Sherman, E. (1993). Mental health and successful adaptation in late life. *Generations, 17*(1), 43–46.

Shields, A. E., Comstock, C., & Weiss, K. B. (2004). Variations in asthma by race/ethnicity among children enrolled in a state Medicaid program. *Pediatrics, 113,* 496–504.

Shields, M. K., & Behrman, R. E. (2004). Children of immigrant families: Analysis and recommendations. *Future of Children, 14*(2), 4–15. Retrieved October 8, 2004, from www.futureofchildren.org.

Shiono, P. H., & Behrman, R. E. (1995). Low birth weight: Analysis and recommendations. *Future of Children, 5*(1), 4–18.

Shoghi-Jadid, K., Small, G. W., Agdeppa, E. D., Kepe, V., Ercoli, L. M., Siddarth, P., Read, S., Satyamurthy, N., Petric, A., Huang, S. C., & Barrio, J. R. (2002). Localization of neurofibrillary tangles and beta-amyloid plaques in the brains of living patients with Alzheimer disease. *American Journal of Geriatric Psychiatry, 10,* 24–35.

Shonkoff, J., & Phillips, D. (2000). Growing up in child care. In I. Shonkoff & D. Phillips (Eds.), *From neurons to neighborhoods* (pp. 297–327). Washington, DC: National Research Council/Institute of Medicine.

Should you take estrogen to prevent osteoporosis? (1994, August). *Johns Hopkins Medical Letter: Health after 50,* pp. 4–5.

Shuey, K., & Hardy, M. A. (2003). Assistance to aging parents and parents-in-law: Does lineage affect family allocation decisions? *Journal of Marriage and Family, 65,* 418–431.

Shulman, S., Scharf, M., Lumer, D., & Maurer, O. (2001). Parental divorce and young adult children's romantic relationships: Resolution of the divorce experience. *American Journal of Orthopsychiatry, 71,* 473–478.

Shumaker, S. A., Legault, C., Kuller, L., Rapp, S. R., Thal, L., Lane, D. S., Fillit, H., Stefanick, M. L., Hendrix, S. L., Lewis, C. E., Masaki, K. & Coker, L. H., for the Women's Health Initiative Memory Study Investigators. (2004). Conjugated equine estrogens and incidence of probable dementia and mild cognitive impairment in postmenopausal women: Women's Health Initiative Memory Study. *Journal of the American Medical Association, 291,* 2947–2958.

Shumaker, S. A., Legault, C., Rapp, S. R., Thal, L., Wallace, R. B., Ockene, J. K., Hendrix, S. L., Jones, B. N., Assaf, A. R., Jackson, R. D., Kotchen, J. M., Wassertheil-Smoller, S., & Wactawski-Wende, J., for the Women's Health Initiative Memory Study Investigators. (2003). Estrogen plus progestin and the incidence of dementia and mild cognitive impairment in postmenopausal women: The Women's Health Initiative Memory Study: A randomized controlled trial. *Journal of the American Medical Association, 289,* 2651–2662.

Shwe, H. I., & Markman, E. M. (1997). Young children's appreciation of the mental impact of their communicative signals. *Developmental Psychology, 33*(4), 630–636.

Siegal, M., & Peterson, C. C. (1998). Preschoolers' understanding of lies and innocent and negligent mistakes. *Developmental Psychology, 34*(2), 332–341.

Siegler, I. C. (1997). Promoting health and minimizing stress in midlife. In M. E. Lachman & J. B. James (Eds.), *Multiple paths of midlife development* (pp. 241–255). Chicago: University of Chicago Press.

Siegler, I. C., & Brummett, B. H. (2000). Associations among NEO personality assessments and well-being at midlife: Facet-level analyses. *Psychology and Aging, 15,* 710–714.

Siegler, R. S. (1998). *Children's thinking* (3rd ed.). Upper Saddle River, NJ: Prentice Hall.

Siegler, R. S., & Booth, J. L. (2004). Development of numerical estimation in young children. *Child Development, 75,* 428–444.

Siegler, R. S., & Richards, D. (1982). The development of intelligence. In R. Sternberg (Ed.), *Handbook of human intelligence.* London: Cambridge University Press.

Sieving, R. E., McNeely, C. S., & Blum, R. W. (2000). Maternal expectations, mother-child connectedness, and adolescent sexual debut. *Archives of Pediatric & Adolescent Medicine, 154,* 809–816.

Sieving, R. E., Oliphant, J. A., & Blum, R. W. (2002). Adolescent sexual behavior and sexual health. *Pediatrics in Review, 23,* 407–416.

Sigman, M., Cohen, S. E., & Beckwith, L. (1997). Why does infant attention predict adolescent intelligence? *Infant Behavior and Development, 20,* 133–140.

Signorello, L. B., Nordmark, A., Granath, F., Blot, W. J., McLaughlin, J. K., Anneren, G., Lundgren, S., Exbom, A., Rane, A., & Cnattingius, S. (2001). Caffeine metabolism and the risk of spontaneous abortion of normal karyotype fetuses. *Obstetrics and Gynecology, 98*(6), 1059–1066.

Silver, M. H., Bubrick, E., Jilinskaia, E., & Perls, T. T. (1998, August). Is there a centenarian personality? Paper presented at the annual meeting of the American Psychological Association, San Francisco.

Silverberg, S. B. (1996). Parents' well-being as their children transition to adolescence. In C. Ryff & M. M. Seltzer (Eds.), *The parental experience in midlife* (pp. 215–254). Chicago: University of Chicago Press.

Silverman, W. K., La Greca, A. M., & Wasserstein, S. (1995). What do children worry about? Worries and their relation to anxiety. *Child Development, 66,* 671–686.

Silverstein, M., & Bengtson, V. L. (1997). Intergenerational solidarity and the structure of adult child-parent relationships in American families. *American Journal of Sociology, 103,* 429–460.

Silverstein, M., Cong, Z., & Li, S. (2006). Intergenerational transfers and living arrangements of older people in rural China: Consequences for psychological well-being. *Journal of Gerontology: Social Sciences, 61B,* S256–S266.

Simmons, R. G., Blyth, D. A., & McKinney, K. L. (1983). The social and psychological effect of puberty on white females. In J. Brooks-Gunn & A. C. Petersen (Eds.), *Girls at puberty: Biological and psychological perspectives.* New York: Plenum Press.

Simon, G. E. (2006). The antidepressant quandary—considering suicide risk when treating adolescent depression. *New England Journal of Medicine, 355,* 2722–2723.

Simon, G. E., Savarino, J., Operskalski, B. & Wang, P. S. (2006). Suicide risk during antidepressant treatment. *American Journal of Psychiatry, 163,* 41–47.

Simons, M. (1993, February 10). Dutch parliament approves law permitting euthanasia. *New York Times,* p. A10.

Simons, R. L., Chao, W., Conger, R. D., B., & Elder, G. H. (2001). Quality of parenting as mediator of the effect of childhood defiance on adolescent friendship choices and delinquency: A growth curve analysis. *Journal of Marriage and Family, 63,* 63–79.

Simons, R. L., Lin, K.-H., & Gordon, L. C. (1998). Socialization in the family of origin and male dating violence: A prospective study. *Journal of Marriage and Family, 60,* 467–478.

Simonton, D. K. (1989). The swan-song phenomenon: Last-works effects for 172 classical composers. *Psychology and Aging, 4,* 42–47.

Simonton, D. K. (1990). Creativity and wisdom in aging. In J. E. Birren & K. W. Schaie (Eds.), *Handbook of the psychology of aging* (pp. 320–329). New York: Academic Press.

Simonton, D. K. (2000). Creativity: Cognitive, personal, developmental, and social aspects. *American Psychologist, 55,* 151–158.

Simpson, J. A., Collins, A., Tran, S., & Haydon, K. C. (2007). Attachment and the experience and expression of emotions in romantic relationships: A developmental perspective. *Journal of Personality and Social Psychology, 92,* 355–367.

Simpson, K. (2001). The role of testosterone in aggression. *McGill Journal of Medicine, 6,* 32–40.

Simpson, K. H. (1996). Alternatives to physician-assisted suicide. *Humanistic Judaism, 24*(4), 21–23.

Sines, E., Syed, U., Wall, S., & Worley, H. (2007). Postnatal care: A critical opportunity to save mothers and newborns. *Policy Perspectives on Newborn Health.* Washington, DC: Save the Children and Population Reference Bureau.

Singer, D. G., & Singer, J. L. (1990). *The house of make-believe: Play and the developing imagination.* Cambridge, MA: Harvard University Press.

Singer, J. L. (2004). Narrative identity and meaning-making across the adult lifespan. *Journal of Personality, 72,* 437–459.

Singer, J. L., & Singer, D. G. (1981). *Television, imagination, and aggression: A study of preschoolers.* Hillsdale, NJ: Erlbaum.

Singer, J. L., & Singer, D. G. (1998). *Barney & Friends* as entertainment and education: Evaluating the quality and effectiveness of a television series for preschool children. In J. K. Asamen & G. L. Berry (Eds.), *Research paradigms, television, and social behavior* (pp. 305–367). Thousand Oaks, CA: Sage.

Singer, L. T., Minnes, S., Short, E., Arendt, K., Farkas, K., Lewis, B., Klein, N., Russ, S., Min, M. O., & Kirchner, H. L. (2004). Cognitive outcomes of preschool children with prenatal cocaine exposure. *Journal of the American Medical Association, 291,* 2448–2456.

Singer, P. A. (1988, June 1). Should doctors kill patients? *Canadian Medical Association Journal, 138,* 1000–1001.

Singer, P. A., & Siegler, M. (1990). Euthanasia—a critique. *New England Journal of Medicine, 322,* 1881–1883.

Singer, T., Lindenberger, U., & Baltes, P. B. (2003). Plasticity of memory for new learning in very old age: A story of major loss? *Psychology and Aging, 18,* 306–317.

Singer, T., Verhaeghen, P., Ghisletta, P., Lindenberger, U., & Baltes, P. B. (2003). The fate of cognition in very old age: Six-year longitudinal findings in the Berlin Aging Study (BASE). *Psychology and Aging, 18,* 318–331.

Singh, G. K., Kogan, M. D., & Dee, D. L. (2007). Nativity/immigrant status, race/ethnicity, and socioeconomic determinants of breastfeeding initiation and duration in the United States, 2003. *Pediatrics, 119* (Suppl. 1), 538–547.

Singh-Manoux, A., Hillsdon, M., Brunner, E., & Marmot, M. (2005). Effects of physical activity on cognitive functioning in middle age: Evidence from the Whitehall II Prospective Cohort Study. *American Journal of Public Health, 95,* 2252–2258.

Singhal, A., Cole, T. J., Fewtrell, M., & Lucas, A. (2004). Breastmilk feeding and lipoprotein profile in adolescents born preterm: Follow-up of a prospective randomised study. *Lancet, 363,* 1571–1578.

Sinnott, J. (1996). The developmental approach: Postformal thought as adaptive intelligence. In F. Blanchard-Fields & T. M. Hess (Eds.), *Perspectives on cognitive change in adulthood and aging* (pp. 358–386). New York: McGraw-Hill.

Sinnott, J. D. (1984). Postformal reasoning: The relativistic stage. In M. L. Commons, F. A. Richards, & C. Armon (Eds.), *Beyond formal operations: Late adolescence and adult cognitive development* (pp. 357–380). New York: Praeger.

Sinnott, J. D. (1998). *The development of logic in adulthood: Postformal thought and its applications.* New York: Plenum Press.

Sinnott, J. D. (2003). Postformal thought and adult development. In J. Demick and C. Andreoletti (Eds.). Handbook of adult development. New York: Plenum Press.

Sipos, A., Rasmussen, F., Harrison, G., Tynelius, P., Lewis, G., Leon, D. A., et al. (2004). Paternal age and schizophrenia: A population based cohort study. *British Medical Journal, 329,* 1070–1073.

Siris, E. S., Miller, P. D., Barrett-Connor, E., Faulkner, K. G., Wehren, L. E., Abbott, T. A., Berger, M. L., Santora, A. C., & Sherwood, L. M. (2001). Identification and fracture outcomes of undiagnosed low bone mineral density in postmenopausal women: Results from the National Osteoporosis Risk Assessment. *Journal of the American Medical Association, 286,* 2815–2822.

Skadberg, B. T., Morild, I., & Markestad, T. (1998). Abandoning prone sleeping: Effects on the risk of sudden infant death syndrome. *Journal of Pediatrics, 132,* 234–239.

Skaff, M. M. (2006). The view from the driver's seat: Sense of control in the baby boomers at midlife. In S. K. Whitbourne & S. L. Willis (Eds.), *The baby boomers grow up: Contemporary perspectives on midlife* (pp. 185–204). Mahwah, NJ: Erlbaum.

Skinner, B. F. (1938). *The behavior of organisms: An experimental approach.* New York: Appleton-Century.

Skinner, B. F. (1957). *Verbal behavior.* New York: Appleton-Century-Crofts.

Skinner, D. (1989). The socialization of gender identity: Observations from Nepal. In J. Valsiner (Ed.), *Child development in cultural context* (pp. 181–192). Toronto: Hogrefe & Huber.

Skoe, E. E., & Diessner, R. E. (1994). Ethic of care, justice, identity, and gender: An extension and replication. *Merrill-Palmer Quarterly, 40,* 272–289.

Slade, A., Belsky, J., Aber, J. L., & Phelps, J. L. (1999). Mothers' representation of their relationships with their toddlers: Links to adult attachment and observed mothering. *Developmental Psychology, 35,* 611–619.

Sloan, R. P., & Bagiella, E. (2002). Claims about religious involvement and health outcomes. *Annals of Behavioral Medicine, 24,* 14–21.

Slobin, D. (1971). Universals of grammatical development in children. In W. Levitt & G. B. Flores d' Arcais (Eds.), *Advances in psycholinguistic research.* Amsterdam: New Holland.

Slobin, D. (1973). Cognitive prerequisites for the acquisition of language. In C. Ferguson & D. Slobin (Eds.), *Studies of child language development.* New York: Holt, Rinehart & Winston.

Slobin, D. (1983). Universal and particular in the acquisition of grammar. In E. Wanner & L. Gleitman (Eds.), *Language acquisition: The state of the art.* Cambridge, England: Cambridge University Press.

Sly, R. M. (2000). Decreases in asthma mortality in the United States. *Annals of Allergy, Asthma, and Immunology, 85,* 121–127.

Slyper, A. H. (2006). The pubertal timing controversy in the USA, and a review of possible causative factors for the advance in timing of onset of puberty. *Clinical Endocrinology, 65,* 1–8.

Small, B. J., Fratiglioni, L., von Strauss, E., & Bäckman, L. (2003). Terminal decline and cognitive performance in very old age: Does cause of death matter? *Psychology and Aging, 18,* 193–202.

Small, G. W., Kepe, V., Ercoli, L. M., Siddarth, P., Bookheimer, S. Y., Miller, K. J., Lavretsky, H., Burggren, A. C., Cole, G. M., Vinters, H. V., Thompson, P. M., Huang, S.-C., Satyamurthy, N., Phelps, M. E., & Barrio, J. R. (2006). PET of brain amyloid and tau in mild cognitive impairment. *New England Journal of Medicine, 355,* 2652–2663.

Small, G. W., Rabins, P. V., Barry, P. P., Buckholtz, N. S., DeKosky, S. T., Ferris, S. H., Finkel, S. I., Gwyther, L. P., Khachaturian, Z. S., Lebowitz, B. D., McRae, T. D., Morris, J. C., Oakley, F., Schneider, L. S., Streim, J. E., Sunderland, T., Teri, L. A., & Tune, L. E. (1997). Diagnosis and treatment of Alzheimer's Disease and related disorders: Consensus statement of the American Association for Geriatric Psychiatry, the Alzheimer's Association, and the American Geriatrics Society. *Journal of the American Medical Association, 278,* 1363–1371.

Small, M. Y. (1990). *Cognitive development.* New York: Harcourt Brace.

Smedley, A., & Smedley, B. D. (2005). Race as biology is fiction, racism as a social problem is real: Anthropological and historical perspectives on the social construction of race. *American Psychologist, 60,* 16–26.

Smedley, B. D., Stith, A. Y., & Nelson, A. R. (Eds.). (2002). *Unequal treatment: Confronting racial and ethnic disparities in health care.* Washington, DC: National Academy Press.

Smetana, J., Crean, H., & Campione-Barr, N. (2005). Adolescents' and parents' changing conceptions of parental authority. In J. Smetana (Ed.), *Changing boundaries of parental authority during adolescence* (New Directions for Child and Adolescent Development, No. 108, pp. 31–46). San Francisco: Jossey-Bass.

Smetana, J. G., Metzger, A., Gettman, D. C., & Campione-Barr, N. (2006). Disclosure and secrecy in adolescent-parent relationships. *Child Development, 77,* 201–217.

Smilansky, S. (1968). *The effects of sociodramatic play on disadvantaged preschool children.* New York: Wiley.

Smith, A. D., & Earles, J. L. (1996). Memory changes in normal aging. In F. Blanchard-Fields & T. M. Hess (Eds.), *Perspectives on cognitive change in adulthood and aging* (pp. 165–191). New York: McGraw-Hill.

Smith, B. A., & Blass, E. M. (1996). Taste mediated calming in premature, preterm, and full-term human infants. *Developmental Psychology, 32,* 1084–1089.

Smith, C. D., Chebrolu, H., Wekstein, D. R., Schmitt, F. A., Jicha, G. A., Cooper, G., & Markesbery, W. R. (2007). Brain structural alterations before mild cognitive impairment. *Neurology, 68,* 1268–1273.

Smith, E. A. (2001). The role of tacit and explicit knowledge in the workplace. *Journal of Knowledge Management, 5,* 311–321.

Smith, E. E., Geva, A., Jonides, J., Miller, A., Reuter-Lorenz, P., & Koeppe, R. A. (2001). The neural basis of task-switching in working memory: Effects of performance and aging. *Proceedings of the National Academy of Science USA, 98,* 2095–2100.

Smith, G. C. S., Pell, J. P., Cameron, A. D., & Dobbie, R. (2002). Risk of perinatal death associated with labor after previous cesarean delivery in uncomplicated term pregnancies. *Journal of the American Medical Association, 287,* 2684–2690.

Smith, J., & Baltes, P. B. (1990). Wisdom-related knowledge: Age/cohort differences in response to life planning problems. *Developmental Psychology, 26*(3), 494–505.

Smith, L. B., & Thelen, E. (2003). Development as a dynamic system. *Trends in Cognitive Sciences, 7,* 343–348.

Smith, L. M., LaGasse, L. L., Derauf, C., Grant, P., Shah, R., Arria, A., Huestis, M., Haning, W., Strauss, A., Grotta, S. D., Liu, J., & Lester, B. M. (2006). The infant development, environment, and lifestyle study: Effects of prenatal methamphetamine exposure, polydrug exposure, and poverty on intrauterine growth. *Pediatrics, 118,* 1149–1156.

Smith, P. K. (2005a). Play: Types and functions in human development. In A. D. Pellegrini & P. K. Smith (Eds.), *The nature of play* (pp. 271–291). New York: Guilford Press.

Smith, P. K. (2005b). Social and pretend play in children. In A. D. Pellegrini & P. K. Smith (Eds.), *The nature of play* (pp. 173–209). New York: Guilford.

Smith, P. K., & Levan, S. (1995). Perceptions and experiences of bullying in younger pupils. *British Journal of Educational Psychology, 65,* 489–500.

Smith, T. W. (2003). *American sexual behavior: Trends, socio-demographic differences, and risk behavior* (GSS Topical Report No. 25). Chicago: National Opinion Research Center, University of Chicago.

Smith, T. W. (2005). Generation gaps in attitudes and values from the 1970s to the 1990s. In R. A. Settersten Jr., F. F. Furstenberg Jr., & R. G. Rumbaut (Eds.), *On the frontier of adulthood: Theory, research, and public policy* (pp. 177–221). (John D. and Catherine T. MacArthur Foundation Series on Mental Health and Development, Research Network on Transitions to Adulthood and Public Policy.) Chicago: University of Chicago Press.

Smith, T. W. (2006). Personality as risk and resilience in physical health. *Current Directions in Psychological Science, 15,* 227–231.

Smith, V. K., & Rousseau, D. M. (2005). *SCHIP enrollment in 50 states.* Washington, DC: Kaiser Commission on Medicaid and the Uninsured.

Smith-Khuri, E., Iachan, R., Scheidt, P. C., Overpeck, M. D., Gabhainn, S. N., Pickett, W., & Harel, Y. (2004). A cross-national study of violence-related behaviors in adolescents. *Archives of Pediatrics and Adolescent Medicine, 158,* 539–544.

Smock, P. J., Manning, W. D., & Porter, M. (2005). "Everything's there except money"; How money shapes decisions to marry among cohabitors. *Journal of Marriage and Family, 67,* 680–696.

Smotherman, W. P., & Robinson, S. R. (1995). Tracing developmental trajectories into the prenatal period. In J. P. Lecanuet, W. P. Fifer, N. A. Krasnegor, & W. P. Smotherman (Eds.), *Fetal development. A psychobiological perspective* (pp. 15–32). Hillsdale, NJ: Erlbaum.

Smotherman, W. P., & Robinson, S. R. (1996). The development of behavior before birth. *Developmental Psychology, 32,* 425–434.

Snarey, J. R. (1985). Cross-cultural universality of social-moral development: A critical review of Kohlbergian research. *Psychological Bulletin, 97,* 202–232.

Snow, C. E. (1990). The development of definitional skill. *Journal of Child Language, 17,* 697–710.

Snow, C. E. (1993). Families as social contexts for literacy development. In C. Daiute (Ed.), *The development of literacy through social interaction* (New Directions for Child Development, No. 61, pp. 11–24). San Francisco: Jossey-Bass.

Snow, M. E., Jacklin, C. N., & Maccoby, E. E. (1983). Sex-of-child differences in father-child interaction at one year of age. *Child Development, 54,* 227–232.

Snyder, J., Bank, L., & Burraston, B. (2005). The consequences of antisocial behavior in older male siblings for younger brothers and sisters. *Journal of Family Psychology, 19,* 643–653.

Snyder, J., Cramer, A., Afrank, J., & Patterson, G. R. (2005). The contributions of ineffective discipline and parental hostile attributions of child misbehavior to the development of conduct problems at home and school. *Developmental Psychology, 41,* 30–41

Snyder, J., West, L., Stockemer, V., Gibbons, S., & Almquist-Parks, L. (1996). A social learning model of peer choice in the natural environment. *Journal of Applied Developmental Psychology, 17,* 215–237.

Snyder, T. D., Dillow, S. A., & Hoffman, C. M. (2007). *Digest of education statistics 2006* (NCES 2007-017). Washington, DC: National Center for Education Statistics.

Snyder, T. D., & Hoffman, C. M. (2001). *Digest of Education Statistics, 2000.* Washington, DC: National Center for Education Statistics.

Sobel, D. M., & Kirkham, N. Z. (2006). Blickets and babies: The development of causal reasoning in toddlers. *Developmental Psychology, 42,* 1103–1115.

Sobel, D. M., Tenenbaum, J. B., & Gopnik, A. (2004). Children's causal inferences from indirect evidence: Backwards blocking and Bayesian reasoning in preschoolers. *Cognitive Science, 28,* 303–333.

Sobolewski, J. M., & Amato, P. J. (2005). Economic hardship in the family of origin and children's psychological well-being in adulthood. *Journal of Marriage and Family, 67,* 141–156.

Sobolewski, J. M., & King, V. (2005). The importance of the coparental relationship for nonresident fathers' ties to children. *Journal of Marriage and Family, 67,* 1196–1212.

Society for Assisted Reproductive Technology & American Fertility Society. (1993). Assisted reproductive technology in the United States and Canada: 1991 results from the Society for Assisted Reproductive Technology generated from the American Fertility Society Registry. *Fertility and Sterility, 59,* 956–962.

Society for Assisted Reproductive Technology & American Society for Reproductive Medicine. (2002). Assisted reproductive technology in the United States: 1998 results generated from the American Society for Reproductive Medicine/Society for Assisted Reproductive Technology Registry. *Fertility & Sterility, 77*(1), 18–31.

Society for Neuroscience. (2005). *Brain facts: A primer on the brain and nervous system.* Washington, DC: Author.

Society for Research in Child Development (SRCD). (2007). *Ethical standards for research with children. Updated by SRCD Governing Council, March 2007.* Retrieved May 20, 2008, from www.srcd.org/ethicalstandards.html.

Soenens, B., Vansteenkiste, M., Luyckx, K., & Goossens, L. (2006). Parenting and adolescent problem behavior: An integrated model with adolescent self-disclosure and perceived parental knowledge as intervening variables. *Developmental Psychology, 42,* 305–318.

Sokol, R. J., Delaney-Black, V., & Nordstrom, B. (2003). Fetal alcohol spectrum disorder. *Journal of the American Medical Association, 209,* 2996–2999.

Sokol, R. Z., Kraft, P., Fowler, I. M., Mamet, R., Kim, E., & Berhane, K. T. (2006). Exposure to environmental ozone alters semen quality. *Environmental Health Perspectives, 114*(3), 360–365.

Soldo, B. J., Mitchell, O., and McCabe, J. (2007). Cross-cohort differences in health on the verge of retirement. *National Bureau of Economic Research Working Paper 12762.* Cambridge, MA; National Bureau of Economic Research.

Soldz, S., & Vaillant, G. E. (1998). A 50-year longitudinal study of defense use among inner city men: A validation of the DSM-IV defense axis. *Journal of Nervous and Mental Disease, 186,* 104–111.

Solowij, N., Stephens, R. S., Roffman, R. A., Babor, T., Kadden, R., Miller, M., Christiansen, K., McRee, B., & Vendetti, J., for the Marijuana Treatment Research Group. (2002). Cognitive functioning of long-term heavy cannabis users seeking treatment. *Journal of the American Medical Association, 287,* 1123–1131.

Sommer, B., Avis, N., Meyer, P., Ory, M., Madden, T., Kagawa-Singer, M., Mouton, C., Rasor, N. O., & Adler, S. (1999). Attitudes toward menopause and aging across ethnic/racial groups. *Psychosomatic Medicine, 61,* 868–875.

Sondergaard, C., Henriksen, T. B., Obel, C., & Wisborg, K. (2001). Smoking during pregnancy and infantile colic. *Pediatrics, 108*(2), 342–346.

Sood, B., Delaney-Black, V., Covington, C., Nordstrom-Klee, B., Ager, J., Templin, T., Janisse, J., Martier, S., & Sokol, R. J. (2001). Prenatal alcohol exposure and childhood behavior at age 6 to 7 years: I. Dose-response effect. *Pediatrics, 108*(8), e461–e462.

Sophian, C., Garyantes, D., & Chang, C. (1997). When three is less than two: Early developments in children's understanding of fractional quantities. *Developmental Psychology, 33,* 731–744.

Sophian, C., & Wood, A. (1997). Proportional reasoning in young children: The parts and the whole of it. *Journal of Educational Psychology, 89,* 309–317.

Sophian, C., Wood, A., & Vong, K. I. (1995). Making numbers count: The early development of numerical inferences. *Developmental Psychology, 31,* 263–273.

Sorensen, T., Nielsen, G., Andersen, P., & Teasdale, T. (1988). Genetic and environmental influence of premature death in adult adoptees. *New England Journal of Medicine, 318,* 727–732.

Sorof, J. M., Lai, D., Turner, J., Poffenbarger, T., & Portman, R. J. (2004). Overweight, ethnicity, and the prevalence of hypertension in school-aged children. *Pediatrics, 113,* 475–482.

Sossin, W. S., Lacaille, J.-C., Castellucci, V. F., & Belleville, S. (Eds.). (2008). *Progress in brain research* (Vol. 169). Amsterdam: Elsevier B. V.

Souter, V. L., Parisi, M. A., Nyholt, D. R., Kapur, R. P., Henders, A. K., Opheim, K. E., Gunther, D. F., Mitchell, M. E., Glass, I. A., & Montgomery, G. W. (2007). A case of true hermaphroditism reveals an unusual mechanism of twinning. *Human Genetics Journal, 121*(2), 179–185.

Spady, D. W., Saunders. D. L., Schopflocher, D. P., & Svenson, L. W. (2004). Patterns for injury in childhood: A population-based approach. *Pediatrics, 113,* 522–529.

Speece, M. W., & Brent, S. B. (1984). Children's understanding of death: A review of three components of a death concept. *Child Development, 55,* 1671–1686.

Spelke, E. (1994). Initial knowledge: Six suggestions. *Cognition, 50,* 431–445.

Spelke, E. S. (1998). Nativism, empiricism, and the origins of knowledge. *Infant Behavior and Development, 21*(2), 181–200.

Spelke, E. S. (2005). Sex differences in intrinsic aptitude for mathematics and science? A critical review. *American Psychologist, 60,* 950–958.

Spencer, J. P., Clearfield, M., Corbetta, D., Ulrich, B., Buchanan, P., & Schöner, G. (2006). Moving toward a grand theory of development: In memory of Esther Thelen. *Child Development, 77,* 1521–1538.

Spencer, J. P., Smith, L. B., & Thelen, E. (2001). Tests of a dynamic systems account of the A-not-B error: The influence of prior experience on the spatial memory abilities of two-year-olds. *Child Development, 72,* 1327–1346.

Sperling, M. A. (2004). Prematurity—A window of opportunity? *New England Journal of Medicine, 351,* 2229–2231.

Spinath, F. M., Price, T. S., Dale, P. S., & Plomin, R. (2004). The genetic and environmental origins of language disability and ability. *Child Development, 75,* 445–454.

Spinrad, T. L., Eisenberg, N., Harris, E., Hanish, L., Fabes, R. A., Kupanoff, K., Ringwald, S., & Holmes, J. (2004). The relation of children's everyday nonsocial peer play behavior to their emotionality, regulation, and social functioning. *Developmental Psychology, 40,* 67–80.

Spira, E. G., Brachen, S. S., & Fischel, J. E. (2005). Predicting improvement after first-grade reading difficulties: The effects of oral language, emergent literacy, and behavior skills. *Developmental Psychology, 41,* 225–234.

Spirduso, W. W., & MacRae, P. G. (1990). Motor performance and aging. In J. E. Birren & K. W. Schaie (Eds.), *Psychology of aging* (3rd ed., pp. 183–200). New York: Academic Press.

Spiro, A., III. (2001). Health in midlife: Toward a life-span view. In M. E. Lachman (Ed.), *Handbook of midlife development* (pp. 156–187). New York: Wiley.

Spitz, R. A. (1945). Hospitalism: An inquiry into the genesis of psychiatric conditioning in early childhood. In D. Fenschel et al. (Eds.), *Psychoanalytic studies of the child* (Vol. 1, pp. 53–74). New York: International Universities Press.

Spitz, R. A. (1946). Hospitalism: A follow-up report. In D. Fenschel et al. (Eds.), *Psychoanalytic studies of the child* (Vol. 1, pp. 113–117). New York: International Universities Press.

Spitze, G., & Trent, K. (2006). Gender differences in adult sibling relations in two-child families. *Journal of Marriage and Family, 68,* 977–992.

Spohr, H. L., Willms, J., & Steinhausen, H.-C. (1993). Prenatal alcohol exposure and long-term developmental consequences. *Lancet, 341,* 907–910.

Spraggins, C. E. (2003). Women and men in the United States: March 2002. *Current Population Reports* (P20-544). Washington, DC: U.S. Census Bureau.

Springer, M. V., McIntosh, A. R., Winocur, G., & Grady, C. L. (2005). The relation between brain activity during memory tasks and years of education in young and older adults. *Neuropsychology, 19,* 181–192.

Squire, L. R. (1992). Memory and the hippocampus: A synthesis of findings with rats, monkeys, and humans. *Psychological Review, 99,* 195–231.

Squire, L. R. (1994). Declarative and nondeclarative memory: Multiple brain systems supporting learning and memory. In D. L. Schacter & E. Tulving (Eds.), *Memory systems 1994* (pp. 203–232). Cambridge, MA: MIT Press.

Sroufe, L. A. (1979). Socioemotional development. In J. Osofsky (Ed.), *Handbook of infant development* (pp. 462–516). New York: Wiley.

Sroufe, L. A. (1997). *Emotional development.* Cambridge, England: Cambridge University Press.

Sroufe, L. A., Bennett, C., Englund, M., Urban, J., & Shulman, S. (1993). The significance of gender boundaries in preadolescence: Contemporary correlates and antecedents of boundary violation and maintenance. *Child Development, 64,* 455–466.

Sroufe, L. A., Carlson, E., & Shulman, S. (1993). Individuals in relationships: Devel-opment from infancy through adolescence. In D. C. Funder, R. D. Parke, C. Tomlinson-Keasey, & K. Widaman (Eds.), *Studying lives through time: Personality and development* (pp. 315–342). Washington, DC: American Psychological Association.

St. Clair, D., Xu, M., Wang, P., Yu, Y., Fang, Y., Zhang, F., Zheng, X., Gu, N., Feng, G., Sham, P., & He, L. (2005). Rates of adult schizophrenia following prenatal exposure to the Chinese famine of 1959–1961. *Journal of the American Medical Association, 294,* 557–562.

Stadtman, E. R. (1992). Protein oxidation and aging. *Science, 257,* 1220–1224.

Staff, J., Mortimer, J. T., & Uggen, C. (2004). Work and leisure in adolescence. In R. M. Lerner & L. Steinberg (Eds.). *Handbook of adolescent development* (2nd ed., pp. 429–450). Hoboken, NJ: Wiley.

Stahl, S. A., McKenna, M. C., & Pagnucco, J. R. (1994). The effects of whole-language instruction: An update and a reappraisal. *Educational Psychologist, 29,* 175–185.

Stamler, J., Dyer, A. R., Shekelle, R. B., Neaton, J., & Stamler, R. (1993). Relationship of baseline major risk factors to coronary and all-cause mortality, and to longevity: Findings from long-term follow-up of Chicago cohorts. *Cardiology, 82*(2–3), 191–222.

Stanley, S. M., Amato, P. R., Johnson, C. A., & Markman, H. J. (2006). Premarital education, marital quality, and marital stability: Findings from a large, random household survey. *Journal of Family Psychology, 20,* 117–126.

Staplin, L., Lococo, K., Byington, S., & Harkey, D. (2001a). *Guidelines and recommendations to accommodate older drivers and pedestrians.* McLean, VA: Office of Safety and Traffic Operations, Federal Highway Administration.

Staplin, L., Lococo, K., Byington, S., & Harkey, D. (2001b). *Highway design handbook for older drivers and pedestrians.* McLean, VA: Office of Safety and Traffic Operations, Federal Highway Administration.

Starr, J. M., Deary, I. J., Lemmon, H., & Whalley, L. J. (2000). Mental ability age 11 years and health status age 77 years. *Age and Ageing, 29,* 523–528.

Staub, E. (1996). Cultural-societal roots of violence: The examples of genocidal violence and of contemporary youth violence in the United States. *American Psychologist, 51,* 117–132

Stauder, J. E. A., Molenaar, P. C.M., & Van der Molen, M. W. (1993). Scalp topography of event-related brain potentials and cognitive transition during childhood. *Child Development, 64,* 769–788.

Staudinger, U. M., & Baltes, P. B. (1996). Interactive minds: A facilitative setting for wisdom-related performance? *Journal of Personality and Social Psychology, 71,* 746–762.

Staudinger, U. M., & Bluck, S. (2001). A view of midlife development from life-span theory. In M. E. Lachman (Ed.), *Handbook of midlife development* (pp. 3–39). New York: Wiley.

Staudinger, U. M., Fleeson, W., & Baltes, P. B. (1999). Predictors of subjective physical health and global well-being: Similarities and differences between the United States and Germany. *Journal of Personality and Social Psychology, 76,* 305–319.

Staudinger, U. M., Smith, J., & Baltes, P. B. (1992). Wisdom-related knowledge in a life review task: Age differences and the role of professional specialization. *Psychology and Aging, 7,* 271–281.

Steffen, L. M., Kroenke, C. H., Yu, X., Pereira, M. A., Slattery, M. L., Van Horn, L., Gross, M. D., & Jacobs, D. R., Jr., (2005). Associations of plant food, dairy product, and meat intakes with 15-y incidence of elevated blood pressure in young black and white adults: The Coronary Artery Risk Development in Young Adults (CARDIA) Study. *American Journal of Clinical Nutrition, 82,* 1169–1177.

Steinbach, U. (1992). Social networks, institutionalization, and mortality among elderly people in the United States. *Journal of Gerontology: Social Sciences, 47*(4), S183–S190.

Steinberg, L. (2000, January 19). *Should juvenile offenders be tried as adults? A developmental perspective on changing legal policies.* Paper presented as part of a Congressional Research Briefing entitled "Juvenile Crime: Causes and Consequences," Washington, DC.

Steinberg, L. (2005). Psychological control: Style or substance? In J. Smetana (Ed.), *Changing boundaries of parental authority during adolescence* (New Directions for Child and Adolescent Development, No. 108, pp. 71–78). San Francisco: Jossey-Bass.

Steinberg, L. (2007). Risk taking in adolescence: New perspectives from brain and behavioral science. *Current Directions in Psychological Science, 16,* 55–59.

Steinberg, L., & Darling, N. (1994). The broader context of social influence in adolescence. In R. Silberstein & E. Todt

(Eds.), *Adolescence in context.* New York: Springer.

Steinberg, L., Dornbusch, S. M., & Brown, B. B. (1992). Ethnic differences in adolescent achievement: An ecological perspective. *American Psychologist, 47,* 723–729.

Steinberg, L., & Scott, E. S. (2003). Less guilty by reason of adolescence: Developmental immaturity, diminished responsibility, and the juvenile death penalty. *American Psychologist, 58,* 1009–1018.

Steinbrook, R. (2005). Public solicitation of organ donors. *New England Journal of Medicine, 353,* 441–444.

Steinhausen, H. C. (2002). The outcome of anorexia nervosa in the 20th century. *American Journal of Psychiatry, 159,* 1284–1293.

Stennes, L. M., Burch, M. M., Sen, M. G., & Bauer, P. J. (2005). A longitudinal study of gendered vocabulary and communicative action in young children. *Developmental Psychology, 41,* 75–88.

Sternberg, R. J. (1985). *Beyond IQ: A triarchic theory of human intelligence.* New York: Cambridge University Press.

Sternberg, R. J. (1986). A triangular theory of love. *Psychological Review, 93,* 119–135.

Sternberg, R. J. (1987, September 23). The use and misuse of intelligence testing: Misunderstanding meaning, users over-rely on scores. *Education Week,* pp. 22, 28.

Sternberg, R. J. (1993). *Sternberg Triarchic Abilities Test.* Unpublished manuscript.

Sternberg, R. J. (1995). Love as a story. *Journal of Social and Personal Relationships, 12*(4), 541–546.

Sternberg, R. J. (1997). The concept of intelligence and its role in lifelong learning and success. *American Psychologist, 52,* 1030–1037.

Sternberg, R. J. (1998a). *Cupid's arrow.* New York: Cambridge University Press.

Sternberg, R. J. (1998b). *Love is a story: A new theory of relationships.* New York: Oxford University Press.

Sternberg, R. J. (2004). Culture and intelligence. *American Psychologist, 59,* 325–338.

Sternberg, R. J. (2005). There are no public policy implications: A reply to Rushton and Jensen (2005). *Psychology, Public Policy, and Law, 11,* 295–301.

Sternberg, R. J. (2006). A duplex theory of love. In R. J. Sternberg & K. Weis (Eds.), *The new psychology of love* (pp. 184–199). New Haven, CT: Yale University Press.

Sternberg, R. J., & Clinkenbeard, P. (1995). A triarchic view of identifying, teaching, and assessing gifted children. *Roeper Review, 17,* 255–260.

Sternberg, R. J., Forsythe, G. B., Hedlund, J., Horvath, J. A., Wagner, R. K., Williams, W. M., Snook, S. A., & Grigorenko, E. L. (2000). *Practical intelligence in everyday life.* New York: Cambridge University Press.

Sternberg, R. J., Grigorenko, E. L., & Kidd, K. K. (2005). Intelligence, race, and genetics. *American Psychologist, 60,* 46–59.

Sternberg, R. J., Grigorenko, E. L., & Oh, S. (2001). The development of intelligence at midlife. In M. E. Lachman (Ed.), *Handbook of midlife development* (pp. 217–247). New York: Wiley.

Sternberg, R. J., & Horvath, J. A. (1998). Cognitive conceptions of expertise and their relations to giftedness. In R. C. Friedman & K. B. Rogers (Eds.), *Talent in context: Historical and social perspectives on giftedness* (pp. 177–191). Washington, DC: American Psychological Association.

Sternberg, R. J., & Lubart, T. I. (1995). *Defying the crowd: Cultivating creativity in a culture of conformity.* New York: Free Press.

Sternberg, R. J., Torff, B., & Grigorenko, E. L. (1998). Teaching triarchically improves school achievement. *Journal of Educational Psychology, 90*(3), 374–384.

Sternberg, R. J., & Wagner, R. K. (1993). The g-ocentric view of intelligence and job performance is wrong. *Current Directions in Psychological Science, 2*(1), 1–4.

Sternberg, R. J., Wagner, R. K., Williams, W. M., & Horvath, J. A. (1995). Testing common sense. *American Psychologist, 50,* 912–927.

Sterns, H. L., & Huyck, M. H. (2001). The role of work in midlife. In M. E. Lachman (Ed.), *Handbook of midlife development* (pp. 447–486). New York: Wiley.

Steunenberg, B., Twisk, J. W. R., Beekman, A. T. F., Deeg, D. J. H., & Kerkhof, A. J. F. M. (2005). Stability and change of neuroticism in aging. *Journal of Gerontology: Psychological Sciences, 60B,* P27–P33.

Stevens, J. C., Cain, W. S., Demarque, A., & Ruthruff, A. M. (1991). On the discrimination of missing ingredients: Aging and salt flavor. *Appetite, 16,* 129–140.

Stevens, J. C., Cruz, L. A., Hoffman, J. M., & Patterson, M. Q. (1995). Taste sensitivity and aging: High incidence of decline revealed by repeated threshold measures. *Chemical Senses, 20,* 451–459.

Stevens, J. H., & Bakeman, R. (1985). A factor analytic study of the HOME scale for infants. *Developmental Psychology, 21,* 1106–1203.

Stevenson, H. W. (1995). Mathematics achievement of American students: First in the world by the year 2000? In C. A. Nelson (Ed.), *The Minnesota Symposia on Child Psychology: Vol. 28. Basic and applied perspectives on learning, cognition, and development* (pp. 131–149). Mahwah, NJ: Erlbaum.

Stevenson, H. W., Chen, C., & Lee, S. Y. (1993). Mathematics achievement of Chinese, Japanese, and American children: Ten years later. *Science, 258*(5081), 53–58.

Stevenson, H. W., Lee, S., Chen, C., & Lummis, M. (1990). Mathematics achievement of children in China and the United States. *Child Development, 61,* 1053–1066.

Stevenson, H. W., Lee, S. Y., Chen, C., Stigler, J. W., Hsu, C. C., & Kitamura, S. (1990). Contexts of achievement: A study of American, Chinese, and Japanese children.

Monographs of the Society for Research in Child Development, 55(1–2, Serial No. 221).

Stevenson-Hinde, J., & Shouldice, A. (1996). Fearfulness: Developmental consistency. In A. J. Sameroff & M. M. Haith (Eds.), *The five- to seven-year shift: The age of reason and responsibility* (pp. 237–252). Chicago: University of Chicago Press.

Stewart, A. J., & Ostrove, J. M. (1998). Women's personality in middle age: Gender, history, and midcourse correction. *American Psychologist, 53,* 1185–1194.

Stewart, A. J., & Vandewater, E. A. (1998). The course of generativity. In D. P. McAdams & D. de St. Aubin (Eds.), *Generativity and adult development: How and why we care for the next generation.* Washington, DC: American Psychological Association.

Stewart, A. J., & Vandewater, E. A. (1999). "If I had to do it over again": Midlife review, midlife corrections, and women's well-being in midlife. *Journal of Personality and Social Psychology, 76,* 270–283.

Stewart, I. C. (1994, January 29). Two part message [Letter to the editor]. *New York Times,* p. A18.

Stice, E., & Bearman, K. (2001). Body image and eating disturbances prospectively predict increases in depressive symptoms in adolescent girls: A growth curve analysis. *Developmental Psychology, 37*(5), 597–607.

Stice, E., Presnell, K., & Bearman, S. K. (2001). Relation of early menarche to depression, eating disorders, substance abuse, and comorbid psychopathology among adolescent girls. *Developmental Psychology, 37,* 608–619.

Stice, E., Presnell, K., Shaw, H., & Rohde, P. (2005). Psychological and behavioral risk factors for obesity onset in adolescent girls: A prospective study. *Journal of Consulting and Clinical Psychology, 73,* 195–202.

Stipek, D. J., Gralinski, H., & Kopp, C. B. (1990). Self-concept development in the toddler years. *Developmental Psychology, 26,* 972–977.

Stock, G., & Callahan, D. (2004). Point-counterpoint: Would doubling the human life span be a net positive or negative for us either as individuals or as a society? *Journal of Gerontology: Biological Sciences, 59A,* 554–559.

Stoecker, J. J., Colombo, J., Frick, J. E., & Allen, J. R. (1998). Long- and short-looking infants' recognition of symmetrical and asymmetrical forms. *Journal of Experimental Child Psychology, 71,* 63–78.

Stoelhorst, M. S. J., Rijken, M., Martens, S. E., Brand, R., den Ouden, A. L., Wit, J.-M., & Veen, S., on behalf of the Leiden Follow-up Project on Prematurity. (2005). Changes in neonatology: Comparison of two cohorts of very preterm infants (gestational age <32 weeks): The Project on Preterm and Small for Gestational Age Infants 1983 and the Leiden Follow-up Project on Prematurity 1996–1997. *Pediatrics, 115,* 396–405.

Stoll, B. J., Hansen, N. I., Adams-Chapman, I., Fanaroff, A. A., Hintz, S. R., Vohr, B.,

& Higgins, R. D., for the National Institute of Child Health and Human Development Neonatal Research Network. (2004). Neurodevelopmental and growth impairment among extremely low-birth-weight infants with neonatal infection. *Journal of the American Medical Association, 292,* 2357–2365.

Stone, W. L., McMahon, C. R., Yoder, P. J., & Walden, T. A. (2007). Early social-communicative and cognitive development of younger siblings of children with autism spectrum disorders. *Archives of Pediatric and Adolescent Medicine, 161,* 384–390.

Stones, M. J., & Kozma, A. (1996). Activity, exercise, and behavior. In J. E. Birren & K. W. Schaie (Eds.), *Handbook of the psychology of aging* (4th ed., pp. 338–352). San Diego: Academic Press.

Strassberg, Z., Dodge, K. A., Pettit, G. S., & Bates, J. E. (1994). Spanking in the home and children's subsequent aggression toward kindergarten peers. *Development and Psychopathology, 6,* 445–461.

Straus, M. A. (1994a). *Beating the devil out of them: Corporal punishment in American families.* San Francisco: Jossey-Bass.

Straus, M. A. (1994b). Should the use of corporal punishment by parents be considered child abuse? In M. A. Mason & E. Gambrill (Eds.), *Debating children's lives: Current controversies on children and adolescents* (pp. 196–222). Newbury Park, CA: Sage.

Straus, M. A. (1999). The benefits of avoiding corporal punishment: New and more definitive evidence. Submitted for publication in K. C. Blaine (Ed.), *Raising America's Children.*

Straus, M. A., & Field, C. J. (2003). Psychological aggression by American parents: National data on prevalence, chronicity, and severity. *Journal of Marriage and Family, 65,* 795–808.

Straus, M. A., & Paschall, M. J. (1999, July). *Corporal punishment by mothers and children's cognitive development: A longitudinal study of two age cohorts.* Paper presented at the sixth International Family Violence Research Conference, University of New Hampshire, Durham, NH.

Straus, M. A., & Stewart, J. H. (1999). Corporal punishment by American parents: National data on prevalence, chronicity, severity, and duration, in relation to child and family characteristics. *Clinical Child and Family Psychology Review, 2*(21), 55–70.

Straus, M. A., Sugarman, D. B., & Giles-Sims, J. (1997). Spanking by parents and subsequent antisocial behavior of children. *Archives of Pediatric and Adolescent Medicine, 151,* 761–767.

Streissguth, A. P., Aase, J. M., Clarren, S. K., Randels, S. P., LaDue, R. A., & Smith, D. F. (1991). Fetal alcohol syndrome in adolescents and adults. *Journal of the American Medical Association, 265,* 1961–1967.

Streissguth, A. P., Bookstein, F. L., Barr, H. M., Sampson, P. D., O'Malley, K.,

Young, J. K. (2004). Risk factors for adverse life outcomes in fetal alcohol syndrome and fetal alcohol effects. *Journal of Developmental and Behavioral Pediatrics, 25,* 228–238.

Striano, T. (2004). Direction of regard and the still-face effect in the first year: Does intention matter? *Child Development, 75,* 468–479.

Striegel-Moore, R. H., & Bulik, C. (2007). Risk factors for eating disorders. *American Psychologist, 62,* 181–198.

Strobel, A., Camoin, T. I. L., Ozata, M., & Strosberg, A. D. (1998). A leptin missense mutation associated with hypogonadism and morbid obesity. *Nature Genetics, 18,* 213–215.

Stroebe, M., Gergen, M. M., Gergen, K. J., & Stroebe, W. (1992). Broken hearts or broken bonds: Love and death in historical perspective. *American Psychologist, 47*(10), 1205–1212.

Stroebe, M., Schut, H., & Stroebe, W. (2007). Health outcomes of bereavement. *Lancet, 370,* 1960–1973.

Strohschein, L. (2005). Parental divorce and child mental health trajectories. *Journal of Marriage and Family, 67,* 1286–1300.

Strömland, K., & Hellström, A. (1996). Fetal alcohol syndrome—an ophthalmological and socioeducational prospective study. *Pediatrics, 97,* 845–850.

Stuck, A. E., Egger, M., Hammer, A., Minder, C. E., & Beck, J. C. (2002). Home visits to prevent nursing home admission and functional decline in elderly people: Systematic review and meta-regression analysis. *Journal of the American Medical Association, 287,* 1022–1028.

Sturm, R. (2002). The effects of obesity, smoking, and drinking on medical problems and costs. *Health Affairs, 21,* 245–253.

Stuttering Foundation. (2006). *Stuttering: Straight talk for teachers* (Publication No. 0125). Memphis, TN: Author.

Substance Abuse and Mental Health Services Administration (SAMHSA). (2004a, October 22). Alcohol dependence or abuse and age at first use. *The NSDUH Report.* Retrieved December 18, 2004, from http://oas.samhsa.gov/2k4/ageDependence/ageDependence.htm.

Substance Abuse and Mental Health Services Administration (SAMHSA). (2004b). *Results from the 2003 National Survey on Drug Use & Health: National findings* (Office of Applied Studies, NSDUH Series H-25, DHHS Publication No. SMA 04-3964). Rockville, MD: U.S. Department of Health and Human Services.

Substance Abuse and Mental Health Services Administration (SAMHSA), Office of Applied Studies. (2005, December 30). Depression among adolscents. *NSDUH Report.* Rockville, MD: Author.

Substance Abuse and Mental Health Services Administration (SAMHSA), Office of Applied Studies. (2006a). Academic performance and substance use among stu-

dents aged 12 to 17: 2002, 2003, and 2004. *NSDUH Report* (Issue 18). Rockville, MD: Author.

Substance Abuse and Mental Health Services Administration (SAMHSA), Office of Applied Studies. (2006b). Substance use treatment need among adolescents: 2003–2004. *NSDUH Report* (Issue 24). Rockville, MD: Author.

Substance Abuse and Mental Health Services Administration (SAMHSA), Office of Applied Studies. (2006c). Underage alcohol use among full-time college students. *NSDUH Report* (Issue 31). Rockville, MD: Author.

Substance Abuse and Mental Health Services Administration (SAMHSA), Office of Applied Studies. (2007a). *Results from the 2006 National Survey on Drug Use and Health: National Findings* (NSDUH Series H-32, DHHS Publication No. SMA 07-4293). Rockville, MD: Author.

Substance Abuse and Mental Health Services Administration (SAMHSA), Office of Applied Studies. (2007b, March 30). Sexually transmitted diseases and substance use. *NSDUH Report.* Rockville, MD: Author.

Substance Abuse and Mental Health Services Administration, Office of Applied Studies. (2008, April 18). State estimates of persons aged 18 or older driving under the influence of alcohol or illicit drugs. *NSDUH Report.* Rockville, MD: Author.

Suddendorf, T. (2003). Early representational insight: 24-month-olds can use a photo to find an object in the world. *Child Development, 74,* 896–904.

Sue, S., & Okazaki, S. (1990). Asian-American educational achievements: A phenomenon in search of an explanation. *American Psychologist 45*(8), 913–920.

Suicide—Part I. (1996, November). *Harvard Mental Health Letter,* pp. 1–5.

Suitor, J. J., & Pillemer, K. (1993). Support and interpersonal stress in the social networks of married daughters caring for parents with dementia. *Journal of Gerontology: Social Sciences, 41*(1), S1–S8.

Suitor, J. J., Pillemer, K., Keeton, S., & Robison, J. (1995). Aged parents and aging children: Determinants of relationship quality. In R. Blieszner & V. Hilkevitch (Eds.), *Handbook of aging and the family* (pp. 223–242). Westport, CT: Greenwood Press.

Sullivan, M. W., Bennett, D. S., Carpenter, K., & Lewis, M. (2007). *Emotion knowledge in young maltreated children.* Manuscript submitted for publication.

Summary of Oregon's Death with Dignity Act. (2006). Retrieved June 26, 2007, from http://oregon.gov/CHS/ph/pas/index.shtml.

Sun, Y. (2001). Family environment and adolescents' well-being before and after parents' marital disruption. *Journal of Marriage and Family, 63,* 697–713.

Sundet, J., Barlaug, D., & Torjussen, T. (2004). The end of the Flynn Effect? A study of secular trends in mean intelligence test scores of Norwegian conscripts during half a century. *Intelligence, 32,* 349–362.

Suomi, S., & Harlow, H. (1972). Social rehabilitation of isolate-reared monkeys. *Developmental Psychology, 6,* 487–496.

SUPPORT Principal Investigators. (1995). A controlled trial to improve care for seriously ill hospitalized patients: The Study to Understand Prognoses and Preferences for Outcomes and Risks of Treatments (SUPPORT). *Journal of the American Medical Association, 274,* 1591–1598.

Surkan, P. J., Stephansson, O., Dickman, P. W., & Cnattingius, S. (2004). Previous preterm and small-for-gestational-age births and the subsequent risk of stillbirth. *New England Journal of Medicine, 350,* 777–785.

Susman, E. J., & Rogol, A. (2004). Puberty and psychological development. In R. M. Lerner & L. Steinberg (Eds.), *Handbook of adolescent psychology* (2nd ed. pp. 15–44). Hoboken, NJ: Wiley.

Susman-Stillman, A., Kalkoske, M., Egeland, B., & Waldman, I. (1996). Infant temperament and maternal sensitivity as predictors of attachment security. *Infant Behavior and Development, 19,* 33–47.

Susser, E. S., & Lin, S. P. (1992). Schizophrenia after prenatal exposure to the Dutch hunger winter of 1944–1945. *Archives of General Psychiatry, 49,* 983–988.

Swain, I. U., Zelazo, P. R., & Clifton, R. K. (1993). Newborn infants' memory for speech sounds retained over 24 hours. *Developmental Psychology, 29,* 312–323.

Swallen, K. C., Reither, E. N., Haas, S. A., & Meier, A. M. (2005). Overweight, obesity, and health-related quality of life among adolescents: The National Longitudinal Study of Adolescent Health. *Pediatrics, 115,* 340–347.

Swan, S. H., Kruse, R. L., Liu, F., Barr, D. B., Drobnis, E. Z., Redmon, J. B., Wang, C., Brazil, C., Overstreet, J. W., & Study for Future Families Research Group. (2003). Semen quality in relation to biomarkers of pesticide exposure. *Environmental Health Perspectives, 111,* 1478–1484.

Swanson, H. L. (1999). What develops in working memory? *Developmental Psychology, 35,* 986–1000.

Swanston, H. Y., Tebbutt, J. S., O'Toole, B. I., & Oates, R. K. (1997). Sexually abused children 5 years after presentation: A case-control study. *Pediatrics, 100,* 600–608.

Swarr, A. E., & Richards, M. H. (1996). Longitudinal effects of adolescent girls' pubertal development, perceptions of pubertal timing, and parental relations on eating problems. *Developmental Psychology, 32,* 636–646.

Swedo, S., Rettew, D. C., Kuppenheimer, M., Lum, D., Dolan, S., & Goldberger, E. (1991). Can adolescent suicide attemptors be distinguished from at-risk adolescents? *Pediatrics, 88*(3), 620–629.

Sweeney, M. M., & Phillips, J. A. (2004). Understanding racial differences in marital disruption: Recent trends and explanations. *Journal of Marriage and Family, 66,* 639–650.

Swingley, D., & Fernald, A. (2002). Recognition of words referring to present and absent objects by 24-month-olds. *Journal of Memory and Language, 46,* 39–56.

Szaflarski, J. P., Holland, S. K., Schmithorst, V. J., & Weber-Byars, A. (2004). *An fMRI study of cerebral language lateralization in 121 children and adults.* Paper presented at the 56th annual meeting of the American Academy of Neurology, San Francisco.

Szatmari, P., Paterson, A. D., Zwaigenbaum, L., Roberts, W., Brian, J., Liu, X.-Q., Vincent, J. B., Skaug, J. L., Thompson, A. P., Senman, L., Feuk, L., Qian, C., Bryson, S. E., Jones, M. B., Marshall, C. R., Scherer, S. W., Vieland, V. J., Bartlett, C., Mangin, L. V., Goedken, R., Segre, A., Pericak-Vance, M. A., Cuccaro, M. L., Gilbert, J. R., Wright, H. H., Abramson, R. K., Betancur, C., Bourgeron, T., Gillberg, C., Leboyer, M., Buxbaum, J. D., Davis, K. L., Hollander, E., Silverman, J. M., Hallmayer, J., Lotspeich, L., Sutcliffe, J. S., Haines, J. L., Folstein, S. E., Piven, J., Wassink, T. H., Sheffield, V., Geschwind, D. H., Bucan, M., Brown, W. T., Cantor, R. M., Constantino, J. N., Gilliam, T. C., Herbert, M., Lajonchere, C., Ledbetter, D. H., Lese-Martin, C., Miller, J., Nelson, S., Samango-Sprouse, C. A., Spence, S., State, M., Tanzi, R. E., Coon, H., Dawson, G., Devlin, B., Estes, A., Flodman, P., Klei, L., McMahon, W. M., Minshew, N., Munson, J., Korvatska, E., Rodier, P. M., Schellenberg, G. D., Smith, M., Spence, M. A., Stodgell, C., Tepper, P. G., Wijsman, E. M., Yu, C.-E., Rogé, B., Mantoulan, C., Wittemeyer, K., Poustka, A., Felder, B., Klauck, S., Schuster, C., Poustka, F., Bölte, S., Feineis-Matthews, S., Herbrecht, E., Schmötzer, G., Tsiantis, J., Papanikolaou, K., Maestrini, E., Bacchelli, E., Blasi, F., Carone, S., Toma, C., Van Engeland, H., de Jonge, M., Kemner, C., Koop, F., Langemeijer, M., Hijimans, C., Staal, W. G., Baird, G., Bolton, P. F., Rutter, M. L., Weisblatt, E., Green, J., Aldred, C., Wilkinson, J.-A., Pickles, A., Le Couteur, A., Berney, T., McConachie, H., Bailey, A. J., Francis, K., Honeyman, G., Hutchinson, A., Parr, J. R., Wallace, S., Monaco, A. P., Barnby, G., Kobayashi, K., Lamb, J. A., Sousa, I., Sykes, N., Cook, E. H., Guter, S. J., Leventhal, B. L., Salt, J., Lord, C., Corsello, C., Hus, V., Weeks, D. E., Volkmar, F., Tauber, M., Fombonne, E., & Shih, A. (2007). Mapping autism risk loci using genetic linkage and chromosomal rearrangements. *Nature Genetics, 39,* 319–328.

Szinovacz, M. E. (1998). Grandparents today: A demographic profile. *Gerontologist, 38,* 37–52.

Szkrybalo, J., & Ruble, D. N. (1999). God made me a girl: Sex category constancy judgments and explanations revisited. *Developmental Psychology, 35,* 392–403.

Tackett, J. L., Krueger, R. F., Iacono, W. G., & McGue, M. (2005). Symptom-based subfactors of DSM-defined conduct disorder: Evidence for etiologic distinctions. *Journal of Abnormal Psychology, 114,* 483–487.

Tamburro, R. F., Gordon, P. L., D'Apolito, J. P., & Howard, S. C. (2004). Unsafe and violent behavior in commercials aired during televised major sporting events. *Pediatrics, 114,* 694–698.

Tamis-LeMonda, C. S., Bornstein, M. H., & Baumwell, L. (2001). Maternal responsiveness and children's achievement of language milestones. *Child Development, 72*(3), 748–767.

Tamis-LeMonda, C. S., Shannon, J. D., Cabrera, N. J., & Lamb, M. E. (2004). Fathers and mothers at play with their 2- and 3-year-olds: Contributions to language and cognitive development. *Child Development, 75,* 1806–1820.

Tanda, G., Pontieri, F. E., & DiChiara, G. (1997). Cannabinoid and heroin activation of mesolimbic dopamine transmission by a common N1 opiod receptor mechanism. *Science, 276,* 2048–2050.

Tanner, J. L. (2006). Recentering during emerging adulthood: A critical turning point in life span human development. In J. J. Arnett & J. L. Tanner (Eds.), *Emerging adults in America: Coming of age in the 21st century* (pp. 21–55). Washington DC: American Psychological Association.

Tao, K.-T. (1998). An overview of only child family mental health in China. *Psychiatry and Clinical Neurosciences, 52*(Suppl.), S206–S211.

Taubes, G. (1998). As obesity rates rise, experts struggle to explain why. *Science, 280,* 1367–1368.

Taveras, E. M., Capra, A. M., Braveman, P. A., Jensvold, N. G., Escobar, G. J., & Lieu, T. A. (2003). Clinician support and psychosocial risk factors associated with breastfeeding discontinuation. *Pediatrics, 112,* 108–115.

Taylor, M. (1997). The role of creative control and culture in children's fantasy/reality judgments. *Child Development, 68,* 1015–1017.

Taylor, M., & Carlson, S. M. (1997). The relation between individual differences in fantasy and theory of mind. *Child Development, 68,* 436–455.

Taylor, M., Cartwright, B. S., & Carlson, S. M. (1993). A developmental investigation of children's imaginary companions. *Developmental Psychology, 28,* 276–285.

Taylor, M. G. (1996). The development of children's beliefs about social and biological aspects of gender differences. *Child Development, 67,* 1555–1571.

Taylor, R. D., & Roberts, D. (1995). Kinship support in maternal and adolescent well-being in economically disadvantaged African-American families. *Child Development, 66,* 1585–1597.

Taylor, S. E. (2006). Tend and befriend: Biobehavioral bases of affiliation under stress. *Current Directions in Psychological Science, 15,* 273–276.

Taylor, S. E., Klein, L. C., Lewis, B. P., Gruenewald, T. L., Gurung, R., & Updegraff, J. A. (2000). Biobehavioral responses to stress in females: Tend-and-befriend, not fight-or-flight. *Psychological Review, 107,* 411–429.

Taylor, S. E., Lehman, B. J., Kiefe, C. I., & Seeman, T. E. (2006). Relationship of early life stress and psychological functioning to adult c-reactive protein in the coronary artery risk development in young adults study. *Biological Psychiatry, 60*(8), 819–824.

Teachman, J. (2003). Premarital sex, premarital cohabitation, and the risk of subsequent marital dissolution among women. *Journal of Marriage and Family, 65,* 444–455.

Teachman, J. D., Tedrow, L. M., & Crowder, K. D. (2000). The changing demography of America's families. *Journal of Marriage and Family, 62,* 1234–1246.

Teasdale, T. W., & Owen, D. R. (2008). Secular declines in cognitive test scores: A reversal of the Flynn effect. *Intelligence, 36,* 121–126.

Teller, D. Y., & Bornstein, M. H. (1987). Infant color vision and color perception. In P. Salapatek & L. B. Cohen (Eds.), *Handbook of infant perception: Vol. 1. From sensation to perception* (pp. 185–236). Orlando, FL: Academic Press.

Temple, J. A., Reynolds, A. J., & Miedel, W. T. (2000). Can early intervention prevent high school dropout? Evidence from the Chicago Child-Parent Centers. *Urban Education, 35*(1), 31–57.

Termine, N. T., & Izard, C. E. (1988). Infants' responses to their mothers' expressions of joy and sadness. *Developmental Psychology, 24,* 223–229.

Tester, D. J., Carturan, E., Dura, M., Reiken, S., Wronska, A., Marks, A. R., & Ackerman, M. J. (2006, May). *Molecular and functional characterization of novel RyR2-encoded cardiac ryanodine receptor/calcium release channel mutations in sudden infant death syndrome.* Presentation at Heart Rhythm 2006, the 27th Annual Scientific Sessions of the Heart Rhythm Society, Boston.

Teti, D. M., & Ablard, K. E. (1989). Security of attachment and infant-sibling relationships: A laboratory study. *Child Development, 60,* 1519–1528.

Teti, D. M., Gelfand, D. M., Messinger, D. S., & Isabella, R. (1995). Maternal depression and the quality of early attachment: An examination of infants, preschoolers, and their mothers. *Developmental Psychology, 31,* 364–376.

Thabes, V. (1997). A survey analysis of women's long-term, postdivorce adjustment. *Journal of Divorce & Remarriage, 27,* 163–175.

Thal, D., Tobias, S., & Morrison, D. (1991). Language and gesture in late talkers: A one-year follow-up. *Journal of Speech and Hearing Research, 34,* 604–612.

Thapar, A., Fowler, T., Rice, F., Scourfield, J., van den Bree, M., Thomas, H., Harold, G., & Hay, D. (2003). Maternal smoking during pregnancy and attention deficit hyperactivity disorder symptoms in offspring. *American Journal of Psychiatry, 160,* 1985–1989.

Thapar, A., Langley, K., Fowler, T., Rice, F., Turic, D., Whittinger, N., Aggleton, J., Van den Bree, M., Owen, M., & O'Donovan, M. (2005). Catechol O-methyltransferase gene variant and birth weight predict early-onset antisocial behavior in children with attention-deficit/hyperactivity disorder. *Archives of General Psychiatry, 62,* 1275–1278.

Thelen, E. (1995). Motor development: A new synthesis. *American Psychologist, 50*(2), 79–95.

Thelen, E., & Fisher, D. M. (1982). Newborn stepping: An explanation for a "disappearing" reflex. *Developmental Psychology, 18,* 760–775.

Thelen, E., & Fisher, D. M. (1983). The organization of spontaneous leg movements in newborn infants. *Journal of Motor Behavior, 15,* 353–377.

Theodore, A. D., Chang, J. J., Runyan, D. K., Hunter, W. M., Bangdiwala, S. I., & Agans, R. (2005). Epidemiological features of the physical and sexual maltreatment of children in the Carolinas. *Pediatrics, 115,* 331–337.

Thoma, S. J., & Rest, J. R. (1999). The relationship between moral decision making and patterns of consolidation and transition in moral judgment development. *Developmental Psychology, 35,* 323–334.

Thomas, A., & Chess, S. (1977). *Temperament and development.* New York: Brunner/Mazel.

Thomas, A., & Chess, S. (1984). Genesis and evolution of behavioral disorders: From infancy to early adult life. *American Journal of Orthopsychiatry, 141*(1), 1–9.

Thomas, A., Chess, S., & Birch, H. G. (1968). *Temperament and behavior disorders in children.* New York: New York University Press.

Thomas, C. (2002). Development of a culturally sensitive, locality-based program to increase kidney donation. *Advances in Renal Replacement Therapy, 9,* 54–56.

Thomas, S. P. (1997). Psychosocial correlates of women's self-rated physical health in middle adulthood. In M. E. Lachman & J. B. James (Eds.), *Multiple paths of midlife development* (pp. 257–291). Chicago: University of Chicago Press.

Thomas, W. P., & Collier, V. P. (1997). *School effectiveness for language minority students.* Washington, DC: National Clearinghouse for Bilingual Education.

Thomas, W. P., & Collier, V. P. (1998). Two languages are better than one. *Educational Leadership, 55*(4), 23–28.

Thompson, L. A., Goodman, D. C., Chang, C-H., and Stukel, T. A. (2005). Regional variation in rates of low birth weight. *Pediatrics, 116,* 1114–1121.

Thompson, P. M., Cannon, T. D., Narr, K. L., van Erp, T., Poutanen, V., Huttunen, M., Lonnqvist, J., Standertskjold-Nordenstam, C., Kaprio, J., Khaledy, M., Dail, R.,

Zoumalan, C. I., & Toga, A. W. (2001). Genetic influences on brain structure. *Nature Neuroscience, 4,* 1253–1258.

Thompson, P. M., Giedd, J. N., Woods, R. P., MacDonald, D., Evans, A. C., & Toga, A. W. (2000). Growth patterns in the developing brain detected by using continuum mechanical tensor maps. *Nature, 404,* 190–193.

Thompson, R. A. (1991). Emotional regulation and emotional development. *Educational Psychology Review, 3,* 269–307.

Thompson, R. A. (1998). Early sociopersonality development. In W. Damon (Series Ed.) & N. Eisenberg (Vol. Ed.), *Handbook of child psychology: Vol. 3. Social, emotional, and personality development* (4th ed., pp. 25–104). New York: Wiley.

Thompson, S. L. (2001). The social skills of previously institutionalized children adopted from Romania. *Dissertation Abstracts International: Section B: The Sciences and Engineering, 61*(7-B), 3906.

Thompson, W. W., Price, C., Goodson, B., Shay, D. K., Benson, P., Hinrichsen, V. L., Lewis, E., Eriksen, E., Ray, P., Marcy, S. M., Dunn, J., Jackson, L. A., Lieu, T. A., Black, S., Stewart, G., Weintraub, E. S., Davis, R. L., & DeStefano, F., for the Vaccine Safety Datalink Team. (2007). Early thimerosal exposure and neuropsychological outcomes at 7 to 10 years. *New England Journal of Medicine, 357,* 1281–1292.

Thomson, E., Mosley, J., Hanson, T. L., & McLanahan, S. S. (2001). Remarriage, cohabitation, and changes in mothering behavior. *Journal of Marriage and Family, 63,* 370–380.

Thorne, A., & Michaelieu, Q. (1996). Situating adolescent gender and self-esteem with personal memories. *Child Development, 67,* 1374–1390.

Thornton, W. J. L., & Dumke, H. A. (2005). Age differences in everyday problem-solving and decision-making effectiveness: A meta-analytic review. *Psychology and Aging, 20,* 85–99.

Thorvaldsson, V., Hofer, S. M., Berg, S., Skoog, I., Sacuiu, S., & Johansson, B. (2008). Onset of terminal decline in cognitive abilities in individuals without dementia. *Neurology.* (Published online first August 27, 2008, DOI: 10.1212/01.wnl.0000312379.02302.ba).

Thurman, H. (1953). *Meditations of the heart.* New York: Harper.

Tilvis, R. S., Kahonen-Vare, M. H., Jolkkonen, J., Valvanne, J., Pitkala, K. H., & Stradnberg, T. E. (2004). Predictors of cognitive decline and mortality of aged people over a 10-year period. *Journal of Gerontology: Medical Sciences, 59A,* 268–274.

Tincoff, R., & Jusczyk, P. W. (1999). Some beginnings of word comprehension in 6-month-olds. *Psychological Science, 10,* 172–177.

Tisdale, S. (1988). The mother. *Hippocrates, 2*(3) 64–72.

Tjaden, P., & Thoennes, N. (2000). *Extent, nature, and consequences of intimate partner* violence: *Findings from the National Violence Against Women Survey.* Washington, DC: National Institute of Justice and Centers for Disease Control and Prevention.

Toga, A., & Thompson, P. M. (2005). Genetics of brain structure and intelligence. *Annual Review of Neurology, 28,* 1–23.

Toga, A. W., Thompson, P. M., & Sowell, E. R. (2006). Mapping brain maturation. *Trends in Neurosciences, 29*(3), 148–159.

Tolan, P. H., Gorman-Smith, D., & Henry, D. B. (2003). The developmental ecology of urban males' youth violence. *Developmental Psychology, 39,* 274–291.

Tomasello, M., Carpenter, M., & Liszkowski, U. (2007). A new look at infant pointing. *Child Development, 78,* 705–722.

Tomashek, K. M., Hsia, J., & Iyasu, S. (2003). Trends in postneonatal mortality attributable to injury, United States, 1988–1998. *Pediatrics, 111,* 1215–1218.

Tomlinson, M., Cooper, P., & Murray, L. (2005). The mother-infant relationship and infant attachment in a South African peri-urban settlement. *Child Development, 76,* 1044–1054.

Torrance, E. P. (1966). *The Torrance Tests of Creative Thinking: Norms-technical manual* (Research ed.). Princeton, NJ: Personnel Press.

Torrance, E. P. (1974). *The Torrance Tests of Creative Thinking: Technical norms manual.* Bensonville, IL: Scholastic Testing Service.

Torrance, E. P. (1988). The nature of creativity as manifest in its testing. In R. J. Sternberg (Ed.), *The nature of creativity: Contemporary psychological perspectives* (pp. 43–75). Cambridge, UK: Cambridge University Press.

Torrance, E. P., & Ball, O. E. (1984). *Torrance Tests of Creative Thinking: Streamlined (revised) manual, Figural A and B.* Bensonville, IL: Scholastic Testing Service.

Totsika, V., & Sylva, K. (2004). The Home Observation for Measurement of the Environment revisited. *Child and Adolescent Mental Health, 9,* 25–35.

Townsend, N. W. (1997). Men, migration, and households in Botswana: An exploration of connections over time and space. *Journal of Southern African Studies, 23,* 405–420.

Trautner, H. M., Ruble, D. N., Cyphers, L., Kirsten, B., Behrendt, R., & Hartmann, P. (2005). Rigidity and flexibility of gender stereotypes in childhood: Developmental or differential? *Infant and Child Development, 14*(4), 365–381.

Travis, J. M. J. (2004). The evolution of programmed death in a spatially structured population. *Journal of Gerontology: Biological Sciences, 59A,* 301–305.

Treas, J. (1995, May). Older Americans in the 1990s and beyond. *Population Bulletin, 50*(2). Washington, DC: Population Reference Bureau.

Trenholm, C., Devaney, B., Fortson, K., Quay, L., Wheeler, J., & Clark, M. (2007). *Impacts of four Title V, Section 510 abstinence education programs: Final Report.* Princeton, NJ: Mathematica Policy Research, Inc.

Trimble, C. L., Genkinger, J. M., Burke, A. E., Helzlsouer, K. J., Diener-West, M., Com-stock, G. W., & Alberg, A. J. (2005). Active and passive cigarette smoking and the risk of cervical neoplasia. *Obstetrics & Gynecology, 105,* 174–181.

Trimble, J. E., & Dickson, R. (2005). Ethnic gloss. In C. B. Fisher & R. M. Lerner (Eds.), *Encyclopedia of applied developmental science* (Vol. I, pp. 412–415). Thousand Oaks, CA: Sage.

Troiano, R. P. (2002). Physical inactivity among young people. *New England Journal of Medicine, 347,* 706–707.

Troll, L. E. (1985). *Early and middle adulthood* (2nd ed.). Monterey, CA: Brooks/Cole.

Troll, L. E., & Fingerman, K. L. (1996). Connections between parents and their adult children. In C. Magai & S. H. McFadden (Eds.), *Handbook of emotion, adult development, and aging* (pp. 185–205). San Diego: Academic Press.

Tronick, E. (1972). Stimulus control and the growth of the infant's visual field. *Perception and Psychophysics, 11,* 373–375.

Tronick, E. Z. (1989). Emotions and emotional communication in infants. *American Psychologist, 44*(2), 112–119.

Tronick, E. Z., Morelli, G. A., & Ivey, P. (1992). The Efe forager infant and toddler's pattern of social relationships: Multiple and simultaneous. *Developmental Psychology, 28,* 568–577.

Troseth, G. L., & DeLoache, J. S. (1998). The medium can obscure the message: Young children's understanding of video. *Child Development, 69,* 950–965.

Troseth, G. L., Saylor, M. M., & Archer, A. H. (2006). Young children's use of video as a source of socially relevant information. *Child Development, 77,* 786–799.

Trotter, R. J. (1986, August). Profile: Robert J. Sternberg: Three heads are better than one. *Psychology Today,* pp. 56–62.

True, M. M., Pisani, L., & Oumar, F. (2001). Infant-mother attachment among the Dogon of Mali. *Child Development, 72,* 1451–1466.

Truog, R. D. (2005). The ethics of organ donation by living donors. *New England Journal of Medicine, 353,* 444–446.

Tsao, F. M., Liu, H. M., and Kuhl, P. K. (2004). Speech perception in infancy predicts language development in the second year of life: A longitudinal study. *Child Development, 75,* 1067–1084.

Tschann, J., Johnston, J. R., & Wallerstein, J. S. (1989). Resources, stressors, and attachment as predictors of adult adjustment after divorce: A longitudinal study. *Journal of Marriage and Family Therapy, 51,* 1033–1046.

Tucker, M. B., & Mitchell-Kernan, C. (1998). Psychological well-being and perceived marital opportunity among single African American, Latina and White women. *Journal of Comparative Family Studies, 29,* 57–72.

Tucker, M. B., Taylor, R. J., & Mitchell-Kernan, C. (1993). Marriage and romantic involvement among aged African Americans.

Journal of Gerontology: Social Sciences, 48, S123–S132.

Turati, C., Simion, F., Milani, I., & Umilta, C. (2002). Newborns' preference for faces: What is crucial? *Developmental Psychology, 38,* 875–882.

Turiel, E. (1998). The development of morality. In W. Damon (Series Ed.) & N. Eisenberg (Vol. Ed.), *Handbook of child psychology: Vol. 3. Social, emotional, and personality development* (4th ed., pp. 863–932). New York: Wiley.

Turkheimer, E., Haley, A., Waldron, J., D'Onofrio, B., & Gottesman, I. I. (2003). Socioeconomic status modifies heritability of IQ in young children. *Psychological Science, 14,* 623–628.

Turner, C. F., Ku, L., Rogers, S. M., Lindberg, L. D., Pleck, J. H., & Sonenstein, F. L. (1998). Adolescent sexual behavior, drug use, and violence: Increased reporting with computer survey technology. *Science, 280,* 867–873.

Turner, P. J., & Gervai, J. (1995). A multi-dimensional study of gender typing in preschool children and their parents: Personality, attitudes, preferences, behavior, and cultural differences. *Developmental Psychology, 31,* 759–772.

Turrisi, R., Wiersman, K. A., & Hughes, K. K. (2000). Binge-drinking-related consequences in college students: Role of drinking beliefs and mother-teen communication. *Psychology of Addictive Behaviors, 14*(4), 342–345.

Tuulio-Henriksson, A., Haukka, J., Partonen, T., Varilo, T., Paunio, T., Ekelund, J., Cannon, T. D., Meyer, J. M., & Lonnqvist, J. (2002). Heritability and number of quantitative trait loci of neurocognitive functions in families with schizophrenia. *American Journal of Medical Genetics, 114*(5), 483–490.

Twenge, J. M. (2000). The age of anxiety? Birth cohort change in anxiety and neuroticism, 1952–1993. *Journal of Personality and Social Psychology, 79,* 1007–1021.

Twenge, J. M., Campbell, W. K., & Foster, C. A. (2003). Parenthood and marital satisfaction: A meta-analytic review. *Journal of Marriage and Family, 65,* 574–583.

Uhlenberg, P., Cooney, T., & Boyd, R. (1990). Divorce for women after midlife. *Journal of Gerontology, 45*(1), 53–61.

Umberson, D., Williams, K., Powers, D. A., Liu, H., & Needham, B. (2006). You make me sick: Marital quality and health over the life course. *Journal of Health and Social Behavior, 47,* 1–16.

UNAIDS. (2006). *2006 report on the global AIDS epidemic: Executive summary/UNAIDS.* Geneva, Switzerland: Author.

UNAIDS/WHO Joint United Nations Programme on HIV/AIDS and World Health Organization (2004). *AIDS epidemic update* (Publication No. UNAIDS/04.45E). Geneva: Author.

UNICEF. (2002). *Official summary of The State of the World's Children 2002.* Retrieved September 19, 2002, from www.unicef.org/pubsgen/sowc02summary/index.html.

UNICEF. (2003). *Social monitor 2003.* Florence, Italy: Innocenti Social Monitor, UNICEF Innocenti Research Centre.

UNICEF Press Centre. (2007, September 13). *Child deaths fall below 10 million for the first time: UNICEF reports solid progress on child survival.* New York: Author.

United Nations (2007, April). An ageing world poses new challenges for development strategists. *DESA (Department of Economic and Social Affairs) News, 11*(4). Retrieved March 8, 2008, from www.un.org/esa/desa/desaNews/v11n04/feature.html.

United Nations Children's Fund and World Health Organization (WHO). (2004). *Low birthweight: Country, regional and global estimates.* New York: UNICEF.

United Nations Educational, Scientific, and Cultural Organization (UNESCO). (2004). *Education for All Global Monitoring Report 2005—The quality imperative.* Retrieved November 10, 2004 from www.unesco.org/education/GMR2005/press.

United Nations Educational, Scientific, and Cultural Organization (UNESCO). (2007). *Literacy portal: United Nations Literacy Decade: Why the Literacy Decade?* Retrieved November 26, 2007, from http://portal.unesco.org/education/en/ev.php-URL_ID=53899&URL_DO=DO_TOPIC&URL_SECTION=201.htm.

United Nations High Commissioner for Human Rights. (1989, November 20). *Convention on the Rights of the Child.* General Assembly Resolution 44/25.

United Nations International Labor Organization (UNILO). (1993). *Job stress: The 20th-century disease.* New York: United Nations.

United Nations Statistics Division. (2007). *Population and vital statistics report: Series A.* Table 3: Live births, deaths, and infant deaths, latest available year. Retrieved November 26, 2007, from http://unstats.un.org/unsd/demographic/products/vitstats/seriesa2.htm.

United States Breastfeeding Committee. (2002). *Benefits of breastfeeding.* Raleigh, NC: Author.

U.S. Bureau of the Census. (1991a). *Household and family characteristics, March 1991* (Publication No. AP-20–458). Washington, DC: U.S. Government Printing Office.

U.S. Bureau of the Census. (1991b). *1990 census of population and housing.* Washington, DC: Data User Service Division.

U.S. Bureau of the Census. (1992). *Marital status and living arrangements: March 1991* (Current Population Reports, Series P-20-461). Washington, DC: U.S. Government Printing Office.

U.S. Bureau of the Census. (1993). *Sixty-five plus in America.* Washington, DC: U.S. Government Printing Office.

U.S. Census Bureau. (2000, November). Resident population estimates of the United States by age and sex. Washington, DC: Author.

U.S. Census Bureau. (2001). *The 65 years and over population: 2000.* Washington, DC: Author.

U.S. Census Bureau. (2003). *Population in the United States: Population characteristics, June 2002.* Washington, DC: U.S. Government Printing Office.

U.S. Census Bureau. (2004). *Global Population Profile, 2002.* International Population Reports WP/02. Washington, DC: U.S. Government Printing Office.

U.S. Census Bureau (2005). *Table A1: Marital status of people 15 years and over, by age, sex, personal earnings, race, and Hispanic origin.* Washington, DC: Author.

U.S. Census Bureau. (2006a). *Educational attainment in the United States, 2006.* Data from 2006 Current Population Survey's Social and Economic Supplement. Washington, DC: Author.

U.S. Census Bureau. (2006b, August 9). Facts for features: Special edition: 300 million. *U.S. Census Bureau News.* Washington, DC: U.S. Department of Commerce.

U.S. Census Bureau (2007a). American *FactFinder: 2006 American Community Survey.* Retrieved July 10, 2008, from http://factfinder.census.gov/servlet/DatasetMainPageServlet?_program=ACS&_submenuId=&_lang=en&_ts=.

U.S Census Bureau. (2007b, March15). *Earnings gap highlighted by Census Bureau data on educational attainment* [Press release]. Retrieved February 14, 2008, from www.census.gov/Press-Release/www/releases/archives/education/009749.html.

U.S. Census Bureau. (2007c). *The population profile of the United States: Dynamic version.* Retrieved May 13, 2007, from www.census.gov/population/www/pop-profile/profiledynamic.html.

U.S. Census Bureau. (2008a). *Population profile of the United States.* Retrieved February 12, 2008, from www.census.gov/population/www/pop-profile/profiledynamic.html.

U.S. Census Bureau. (2008b). *Who's minding the kids? Child care arrangements: Spring 2005.* Washington, DC: U.S. Census Bureau, Housing and Household Economic Statistics Division, Fertility & Family Statistics Branch.

U.S. Department of Agriculture & U.S. Department of Health and Human Services (USDHHS). (2000). *Dietary guidelines for Americans,* 5th ed. (USDA Home and Garden Bulletin No. 232). Washington, DC: Author.

U.S. Department of Health and Human Services (USDHHS). (1992). *Health, United States, 1991, and Prevention Profile* (DHHS Publication No. PHS 92–1232). Washington, DC: U.S. Government Printing Office.

U.S. Department of Health and Human Services (USDHHS). (1996a). *Health, United States, 1995* (DHHS Publication No. PHS 96-1232). Washington, DC: U.S. Government Printing Office.

U.S. Department of Health and Human Services (USDHHS). (1996b). *HHS releases study of relationship between family structure and adolescent substance abuse* [Press release]. Retrieved from www.hhs.gov.

U.S. Department of Health and Human Services (USDHHS). (1999a). *Blending perspectives and building common ground: A report to Congress on substance abuse and child protection.* Washington, DC: U.S. Government Printing Office.

U.S. Department of Health and Human Services (USDHHS). (1999b). *Mental health: A report of the Surgeon General.* Rockville, MD: U.S. Department of Health and Human Services, Substance Abuse and Mental Health Services Administration, National Institutes of Health, National Institute of Mental Health.

U.S. Department of Health and Human Services (USDHHS). (2002). "Gift of life" donation initiative fact sheet. Retrieved from www.organdonor.gov.

U.S. Department of Health and Human Services (USDHHS). (2003a). *State funded pre-kindergarten: What the evidence shows.* Retrieved from http://aspe.hhs.gov/hsp/statefunded-k/index.htm.

U.S. Department of Health and Human Services (USDHHS). (2003b). *Strengthening Head Start: What the evidence shows.* Retrieved from http://aspe.hhs.gov/hsp/StrengthenHeadStart03/index.htm.

U.S. Department of Health and Human Services (USDHHS). (2004). *Child maltreatment 2002.* Retrieved from www.acf.hhs.gov/programs/cb/publications/cm02/index.htm.

U.S. Department of Health and Human Services (USDHHS). (2005, March 29). New high set for organ transplants: Nearly 27,000 individuals received transplants last year (News release). Retrieved May 17, 2008, from www.hhs.gov/news/press/2005pres/20050329.html.

U.S. Department of Health and Human Services (USDHHS), Administration on Children, Youth, and Families. (2006). *Child maltreatment 2004.* Washington, DC: U.S. Government Printing Office.

U.S. Preventive Services Task Force. (2002). *Screening for breast cancer: Recommendations and rationale.* Rockville, MD: Agency for Healthcare Research and Quality. Retrieved from www.ahrq.gov/clinic/3rduspstf/breast-cancer/brcanrr.htm.

U.S. Preventive Services Task Force. (2006). Screening for speech and language delay in preschool children: Recommendation statement. *Pediatrics, 117,* 497–501.

Uitterlinden, A. G., Burger, H., Huang, Q., Yue, F., McGuigan, F. E. A., Grant, S. F. A., van Leeuwen, J. P. T., Pols, H. A. P., & Ralston, S. H. (1998). Relation of alleles of the collagen type Ia1 gene to bone density and the risk of osteoporitic fractures in postmenopausal women. *New England Journal of Medicine, 33,* 1016–1021.

Utiger, R. D. (1998). A pill for impotence. *New England Journal of Medicine, 338,* 1458–1459.

Vaillant, G., & Mukamal, K. (2001). Successful aging. *American Journal of Psychiatry, 158,* 839–847.

Vaillant, G. E. (1977). *Adaptation to life.* Boston: Little, Brown.

Vaillant, G. E. (1989). The evolution of defense mechanisms during the middle years. In J. M. Oldman & R. S. Liebert (Eds.), *The middle years.* New Haven: Yale University Press.

Vaillant, G. E. (1993). *The wisdom of the ego.* Cambridge, MA: Harvard University Press.

Vaillant, G. E. (2000). Adaptive mental mechanisms: Their role in a positive psychology. *American Psychologist, 55,* 89–98.

Vaillant, G. E., Meyer, S. E., Mukamal, K., & Soldz, S. (1998). Are social supports in late midlife a cause or a result of successful physical aging? *Psychological Medicine, 28*(5), 1159–1168.

Vainio, S., Heikkiia, M., Kispert, A., Chin, N., & McMahon, A. P. (1999). Female development in mammals is regulated by Wnt-4 signaling. *Nature, 397,* 405–409.

Valadez-Meltzer, A., Silber, T. J., Meltzer, A. A., & D'Angelo, L. J. (2005). Will I be alive in 2005? Adolescent level of involvement in risk behaviors and belief in near-future death. *Pediatrics, 116,* 24–31.

Van, P. (2001). Breaking the silence of African American women: Healing after pregnancy loss. *Health Care Women International, 22,* 229–243.

Van den Boom, D. C. (1989). Neonatal irritability and the development of attachment. In G. A. Kohnstamm, J. E. Bates, & M. K. Rothbart (Eds.), *Temperament in childhood* (pp. 299–318). Chichester, England: Wiley.

Van den Boom, D. C. (1994). The influence of temperament and mothering on attachment and exploration: An experimental manipulation of sensitive responsiveness among lower-class mothers with irritable infants. *Child Development, 65,* 1457–1477.

van der Heide, A., Deliens, L., Faisst, K., Nilstun, T., Norup, M., Paci, E., van der Wei, G., & van der Maas, P. J., on behalf of the EURELD consortium. (2003). End-of-life decision making in six European countries: Descriptive study. *Lancet, 362,* 345–350.

van der Heide, A., Onwuteaka-Philipsen, B. D., Rurup, M. L., Buiting, H. M., van Delden, J. J. M., Hanssen-de Wolf, J. E., Janssen, A. G. J. M., Pasman, H. R. W., Rietjens, J. A. C., Prins, C. J. M., Deerrenberg, I. M., Gevers, J. K.M., van der Maas, P. J., & van der Wal, G. (2007). End-of-life practices in the Netherlands under the Euthanasia Act. *New England Journal of Medicine, 356,* 1957–1965.

Van Dongen, H. P. A., Maislin, G., Mullington, J. M., & Dinges, D. F. (2003). The cumulative cost of additional wakefulness: Dose-response effects on neurobehavioral functions and sleep physiology from chronic sleep restriction and total sleep deprivation. *Sleep, 26,* 117–126.

van Dyk, D. (2005, January 24). Parlez-vous twixter? *Time,* p. 50.

van Gelder, B. M., Tijhuis, M. A. R., Kalmijn, S., Giampaoli, S., Nissinen, A., & Krombout, D. (2004). Physical activity in relation to cognitive decline in elderly men. *American Academy of Neurology, 63,* 2316–2321.

van Goozen, S., Fairchild, G., Snoek, H., & Harold, G. (2007). The evidence for a neurobiological model of childhood antisocial behavior. *Psychological Bulletin, 133,* 149–82.

Van Heuvelen, M. J., Kempen, G. I., Ormel, J., & Rispens, P. (1998). Physical fitness related to age and physical activity in older persons. *Medicine and Science in Sports and Exercise, 30,* 434–441.

van Hooren, S. A. H., Valentijn, S. A. M., Bosma, H., Ponds, R. W. H. M., van Boxtel, M. P. J., & Jolles, J. (2005). Relation between health status and cognitive functioning: A 6-year follow-up of the Maastricht Aging Study. *Journal of Gerontology: Psychological Sciences, 60B,* P57–P60.

van IJzendoorn, M. H. (1995). Adult attachment representations, parental responsiveness, and infant attachment: A meta-analysis on the predictive validity of the Adult Attachment Interview. *Psychological Bulletin, 117*(3), 387–403.

van IJzendoorn, M. H., & Kroonenberg, P. M. (1988). Cross-cultural patterns of attachment: A meta-analysis of the Strange Situation. *Child Development, 59,* 147–156.

van IJzendoorn, M. H., & Sagi, A. (1999). Cross-cultural patterns of attachment: Universal and contextual dimensions. In J. Cassidy & P. R. Shaver (Eds.), *Handbook of attachment: Theory, research, and clinical applications* (pp. 713–734). New York: Guilford Press.

van IJzendoorn, M. H., Schuengel, C., & Bakermans-Kranenburg, M. J. (1999). Disorganized attachment in early childhood: Meta-analysis of precursors, concomitants, and sequelae. *Development and Psychopathology, 11,* 225–250.

van Lieshout, C. F. M., Haselager, G. J. T., Riksen-Walraven, J. M., & van Aken, M. A.G. (1995, April). Personality development in middle childhood. In D. Hart (Chair), *The contribution of childhood personality to adolescent competence: Insights from longitudinal studies from three societies.* Symposium conducted at the biennial meeting of the Society for Research in Child Development, Indianapolis, IN.

van Noord-Zaadstra, B. M., Looman, C. W., Alsbach, H., Habbema, J. D., te Velde, E. R., & Karbaat, J. (1991). Delayed childbearing: Effect of age on fecundity and outcome of pregnancy. *British Medical Journal, 302,* 1361–1365.

van Praag, H., Schinder, A. F., Christie, B. R., Toni, N., Palmer, T. D., & Gage, F. H. (2002). Functional neurogenesis in the adult hippocampus. *Nature, 415,* 1030–1034.

van Solinge, H., & Henkens, K. (2005). Couples' adjustment to retirement: A multi-actor panel study. *Journal of Gerontology: Social Sciences, 60B,* S11–S20.

Van Voorhis, B. J. (2007). In vitro fertilization. *New England Journal of Medicine, 356,* 379–386.

Vandell, D. L. (2000). Parents, peer groups, and other socializing influences. *Developmental Psychology, 36,* 699–710.

Vandell, D. L., & Bailey, M. D. (1992). Conflicts between siblings. In C. U. Shantz & W. W. Hartup (Eds.), *Conflict in child and adolescent development* (pp. 242–269). New York: Cambridge University Press.

Vandewater, E. A., Ostrove, J. M., & Stewart, A. J. (1997). Predicting women's well-being in midlife: The importance of personality development and social role involvements. *Journal of Personality and Social Psychology, 72,* 1147–1160.

Vandewater, E. A., Rideout, V. J., Wartella, E. A., Huang, X., Lee, J. H., & Shim, M.-s. (2007). Digital childhood: Electronic media and technology use among infants, toddlers, and preschoolers. *Pediatrics, 119,* e1006–e1015.

Vargha-Khadem, F., Gadian, D. G., Watkins, K. E., Connelly, A., Van Paesschen, W., & Mishkin, M. (1997). Differential effects of early hippocampal pathology on episodic and semantic memory. *Science, 277,* 376–380.

Vartanian, T. P., & McNamara, J. M. (2002). Older women in poverty: The impact of midlife factors. *Journal of Marriage and Family, 64,* 532–548.

Vasilyeva, M. & Huttenlocher, J. (2004). Early development of scaling ability. *Developmental Psychology, 40,* 682–690.

Vasilyeva, M., Huttenlocher, J., & Waterfall, H. (2006). Effects of language intervention on syntactic skill levels in preschoolers. *Developmental Psychology, 42,* 164–174.

Vaswani, M., & Kapur, S. (2001). Genetic basis of schizophrenia: Trinucleotide repeats: An update. *Progress in Neuro-Psychopharmacology & Biological Psychiatry, 25*(6), 1187–1201.

Vaughn, B. E., Stevenson-Hinde, J., Waters, E., Kotsaftis, A., Lefever, G. B., Shouldice, A., Trudel, M., & Belsky, J. (1992). Attachment security and temperament in infancy and early childhood: Some conceptual clarifications. *Developmental Psychology, 28,* 463–473.

Vaupel, J. W., Carey, J. R., Christensen, K., Johnson, T. E., Yashin, A. I., Holm, N. V., Iachine, I. A., Kannisto, V., Khazaeli, A. A., Liedo, P., Longo, V. D., Zeng, Y., Manton, K. G., & Curtsinger, J. W. (1998). Biodemographic trajectories of longevity. *Science, 280,* 855–860.

Vecchiotti, S. (2003). Kindergarten: An overlooked educational policy priority. *SRCD Social Policy Report, 17*(2), 1–19.

Veenstra, R., Lindenberg, S., Oldehinkel, A. J., De Winter, A. F., Verhulst, F. C., & Ormel, J. (2005). Bullying and victimization in elementary schools: A comparison of bullies, victims, bully/victims, and uninvolved preadolescents. *Developmental Psychology, 41,* 672–682.

Ventura, S. J., Abma, J. C., Mosher, W. D., & Henshaw, S. K. (2008). Estimated pregnancy rates by outcome for the United States, 1990–2004. *National Vital Statistics*

Reports, 56(15). Hyattsville, MD: National Center for Health Statistics.

Ventura, S. J., Mathews, T. J., & Hamilton, B. E. (2001). Births to teenagers in the United States, 1940–2000. *National Vital Statistics Reports, 49*(10). Hyattsville, MD: National Center for Health Statistics.

Vercruyssen, M. (1997). Movement control and speed of behavior. In A. D. Fisk & W. A. Rogers (Eds.), *Handbook of human factors and the older adult* (pp. 55–86). San Diego: Academic Press.

Vereecken, C., & Maes, L. (2000). Eating habits, dental care and dieting. In C. Currie, K. Hurrelmann, W. Settertobulte, R. Smith, & J. Todd (Eds.). *Health and health behaviour among young people: A WHO cross-national Study (HBSC) international report* (pp. 83–96). WHO Policy Series: Healthy Policy for Children and Adolescents, Series No. 1. Copenhagen, Denmark: World Health Organization Regional Office for Europe.

Verhagen, E., & Sauer, P. J. J. (2005). The Groningen Protocol—euthanasia in severely ill newborns. *New England Journal of Medicine, 352,* 959–962.

Verlinsky, Y., Rechitsky, S., Verlinsky, O., Masciangelo, C., Lederer, K., & Kuliev, A. (2002). Preimplantation diagnosis for early-onset Alzheimer disease caused by V717L mutation. *Journal of the American Medical Association, 287,* 1018–1021.

Verma, S., & Larson, R. (2003). Editors' notes. In S. Verma and R. Larson (Eds.)., (2002). Chromosomal congenital anomalies and residence near hazardous waste landfill sites. *Lancet, 359,* 320–322.

Verschueren, K., Buyck, P., & Marcoen, A. (2001). Self-representations and socioemotional competence in young children: A 3-year longitudinal study. *Developmental Psychology, 37,* 126–134.

Verschueren, K., Marcoen, A., & Schoefs, V. (1996). The internal working model of the self, attachment, and competence in five-year-olds. *Child Development, 67,* 2493–2511.

Verschuren, W. M. M., Jacobs, D. R., Bloemberg, B. P. M., Kromhout, D., Menotti, A., Aravanis, C., Blackburn, H., Buzina, R., Dontas, A. S., Fidanza, F., Karvonen, M. J., Nedeljkovic, S., Nissinen, A., & Toshima, H. (1995). Serum total cholesterol and long-term coronary heart disease mortality in different cultures. *Journal of the American Medical Association, 274,* 131–136.

Vgontzas, A. N., & Kales, A. (1999). Sleep and its disorders. *Annual Review of Medicine, 50,* 387–400.

Viner, R. M., & Cole, T. J. (2005). Television viewing in early childhood predicts adult body mass index. *Journal of Pediatrics, 147,* 429–435.

Vinokur, A. D., Schul, Y., Vuori, J., & Price, R. H. (2000). Two years after a job loss: Long-term impact of the JOBS program on reemployment and mental health. *Journal of Occupational Health Psychology, 5,* 32–47.

Vita, A. J., Terry, R. B., Hubert, H. B., & Fries, J. F. (1998). Aging, health risk, and cumulative disability. *New England Journal of Medicine, 338,* 1035–1041.

Vitalian., P. P., Zhang, J., & Scanlan, J. M. (2003). Is caregiving hazardous to one's physical health? *A meta-analysis. Psychological Bulletin, 129,* 946–972.

Vitaro, F., Tremblay, R. E., Kerr, M., Pagani, L., & Bukowski, W. M. (1997). Disruptiveness, friends' characteristics, and delinquency in early adolescence: A test of two competing models of development. *Child Development, 68,* 676–689.

Vlad, S. C., Miller, D. R., Kowall, N. W., & Felson, D. T. (2008). Protective effects of NSAIDs on the development of Alzheimer disease. *Neurology, 70,* 1672–1677.

Vohr, B. R., Wright, L. L., Poole, K., & McDonald, S. A., for the NICHD Neonatal Research Network Follow-up Study. (2005). Neurodevelopmental outcomes of extremely low birth weight infants <30 weeks' gestation between 1993 and 1998. *Pediatrics, 116,* 635–643.

Volkow, N., Wang, G.-J., Newcorn, J., Telang, F., Solanto, M. V., Fowler, J. S., Logan, J., Yeming, M., Schulz, K., Pradhan, K., Wong, C., & Swanson, J. M. (2007). Depressed dopamine activity in caudate and preliminary evidence of limbic involvement in adults with attention-deficit/hyperactivity disorder. *Archives of General Psychiatry, 64,* 932–940.

Voluntary Euthanasia Society. (2002). In depth: Factsheets. Australia. Retrieved from www.ves.org.uk/DpFS_Aust.html.

von Hippel, W. (2007). Aging, executive functioning, and social control. *Current Directions in Psychological Science, 16*(5), 240–244.

Von Korff, L., Grotevant, H. D., & McRoy, R. G. (2006). Openness arrangements and psychological adjustment in adolescent adoptees. *Journal of Family Psychology, 20,* 531–534.

Vondra, J. I., & Barnett, D. (1999). A typical attachment in infancy and early childhood among children at developmental risk. *Monographs of the Society for Research in Child Development, 64*(3, Serial No. 258).

Vosniadou, S. (1987). Children and metaphors. *Child Development, 58,* 870–885.

Voydanoff, P. (1987). *Work and family life.* Newbury Park, CA: Sage.

Voydanoff, P. (1990). Economic distress and family relations: A review of the eighties. *Journal of Marriage and Family, 52,* 1099–1115.

Voydanoff, P. (2004). The effects of work demands and resources on work-to-family conflict and facilitation. *Journal of Marriage and Family, 66,* 398–412.

Vrijheld, M., Dolk, H., Armstrong, B., Abramsky, L., Bianchi, F., Fazarinc, I., Garne, E., Ide, R., Nelen, V., Robert, E., Scott, J. E. S., Stone, D., & Tenconi, R. (2002). Chromosomal congenital anomalies and residence near hazardous waste landfill sites. *Lancet, 359*(9303), 320–322.

Vuchinich, S., Angelelli, J., & Gatherum, A. (1996). Context and development in family problem solving with preadolescent children. *Child Development, 67,* 1276–1288.

Vuori, L., Christiansen, N., Clement, J., Mora, J., Wagner, M., & Herrera, M. (1979). Nutritional supplementation and the outcome of pregnancy: 2. Visual habitation at 15 days. *Journal of Clinical Nutrition, 32,* 463–469.

Vygotsky, L. S. (1962). *Thought and language.* Cambridge, MA: MIT Press. (Original work published 1934)

Vygotsky, L. S. (1978). *Mind in society: The development of higher psychological processes.* Cambridge, MA: Harvard University Press.

Waber, D. P., De Moor, C., Forbes, P. W., Almli, C. R., Botteron, K. N., Leonard, G., Milovan, D., Paus, T., Rumsey, J., & Brain Development Cooperative Group. (2007). The NIH MRI study of normal brain development: Performance of a population based sample of healthy children aged 6 to 18 years on a neuropsychological battery. *Journal of the International Neuropsychological Society, 13*(5), 729–746.

Wade, N. (2001, October 4). Researchers say gene is linked to language. *New York Times,* p. Al.

Wahlbeck, K., Forsen, T., Osmond, C., Barker, D. J. P., & Erikkson, J. G. (2001). Association of schizophrenia with low maternal body mass index, small size at birth, and thinness during childhood. *Archives of General Psychiatry, 58,* 48–55.

Wainright, J. L., Russell, S. T., & Patterson, C. J. (2004). Psychosocial adjustment, school outcomes, and romantic relationships of adolescents with same-sex parents. *Child Development, 75,* 1886–1898.

Waisbren, S. E., Albers, S., Amato, S., Ampola, M., Brewster, T. G., Demmer, L., Eaton, R. B., Greenstein, R., Korson, M., Larson, C., Marsden, D., Msall, M., Naylor, E. W., Pueschel, S., Seashore, M., Shih, V. E., & Levy, H. L. (2003). Effect of expanded newborn screening for biochemical disorders on child outcomes and parental stress. *Journal of the American Medical Association, 290,* 2564–2572.

Waite, L. J., & Joyner, K. (2000). Emotional and physical satisfaction with sex in married, cohabiting, and dating sexual unions: Do men and women differ? In E. O. Laumann, & R. T. Michael (Eds.), *Sex, love, and health in America: Private choices and public policies* (pp. 239–269). Chicago: University of Chicago Press.

Wakefield, M., Reid, Y., Roberts, L., Mullins, R., & Gillies, P. (1998). Smoking and smoking cessation among men whose partners are pregnant: A qualitative study. *Social Science and Medicine, 47,* 657–664.

Waknine, Y. (2006). Highlights from MMWR: Prevalence of U.S. birth defects and more. *Medscape.* Retrieved January 9, 2006, from www.medscape.com/viewarticle/521056.

Walasky, M., Whitbourne, S. K., & Nehrke, M. F. (1983–1984). Construction and validation of an ego-integrity status interview. *International Journal of Aging and Human Development, 81,* 61–72.

Wald, N. J. (2004). Folic acid and the prevention of neural-tube defects. *New England Journal of Medicine, 350,* 101–103.

Waldman, I. D. (1996). Aggressive boys' hostile perceptual and response biases: The role of attention and impulsivity. *Child Development, 67,* 1015–1033.

Waldstein, S. R. (2003). The relation of hypertension to cognitive function. *Current Directions in Psychological Sciences, 12,* 9–12.

Walk, R. D., & Gibson, E. J. (1961). A comparative and analytical study of visual depth perception. *Psychology Monographs, 75*(15).

Walker, L. (1995). Sexism in Kohlberg's moral psychology? In W. M. Kurtines & J. L. Gewirtz (Eds.), *Moral development: An introduction* (pp. 83–107). Boston: Allyn & Bacon.

Walker, L. E. (1999). Psychology and domestic violence around the world. *American Psychologist, 54,* 21–29.

Walker, L. J. (1984). Sex differences in the development of moral reasoning: A critical review. *Child Development, 55,* 677–691.

Walker, M. P., Brakefield, T., Morgan, A., Hobson, J. A., & Stickgold, R. (2002). Practice with sleep makes perfect: Sleep-dependent motor skill learning. *Neuron, 35,* 205–211.

Walker, W. R., Skowronski, J. J., & Thompson, C. P. (2003). Life is pleasant—and memory helps to keep it that way! *Review of General Psychology, 7,* 203–210.

Wallace, D. C. (1992). Mitochondrial genetics: A paradigm for aging and degenerative diseases? *Science, 256,* 628–632.

Waller, M. W., Hallfors, D. D., Halpern, C. T., Iritani, B., Ford, C. A., & Guo, G. (2006). Gender differences in associations between depressive symptoms and patterns of substance use and risky sexual behavior among a nationally representative sample of U.S. adolescents. *Archives of Women's Mental Health, 9,* 139–150.

Wallerstein, J., & Corbin, S. B. (1999). The child and the vicissitudes of divorce. In R. M. Galatzer-Levy & L. Kraus (Eds.), *The scientific basis of child custody decisions* (pp. 73–95). New York: Wiley.

Wallerstein, J. S., Lewis, J. M., & Blakeslee, S. (2000). *The unexpected legacy of divorce: A 25-year landmark study.* New York: Hyperion.

Wallhagen, M. I., Strawbridge, W. J., Cohen, R. D., & Kaplan, G. A. (1997). An increasing prevalence of hearing impairment and associated risk factors over three decades of the Alameda County Study. *American Journal of Public Health, 87,* 440–442.

Wallhagen, M. I., Strawbridge, W. J., Shema, S. J., & Kaplan, G. A. (2004). Impact of self-assessed hearing loss on a spouse: A longitudinal analysis of couples. *Journal*

of *Gerontology: Social Sciences, 59,* S190–S196.

Walls, C., & Zarit, S. (1991). Informal support from black churches and well-being of elderly blacks. *Gerontologist, 31,* 490–495.

Walma van der Molen, J. (2004). Violence and suffering in television news: Toward a broader conception of harmful television content for children. *Pediatrics, 113,* 1771–1775.

Walsh, D. A., & Hershey, D. A. (1993). Mental models and the maintenance of complex problem solving skills into old age. In J. Cerella & W. Hoyer (Eds.), *Adult information processing: Limits on loss* (pp. 553–584). New York: Academic Press.

Walston, J. T., & West, J. (2004). *Full-day and half-day kindergarten in the United States: Findings from the Early Childhood Longitudinal Study, Kindergarten Class of 1998–99* (NCES 2004-078). Washington, DC: National Center for Education Statistics.

Wang, D. W., Desai, R. R., Crotti, L., Arnestad, M., Insolia, R., Pedrazzini, M., Ferrandi, C., Vege, A., Rognum, T., Schwartz, P. J., & George, A. L. (2007). Cardiac sodium channel dysfunction in sudden infant death syndrome. *Circulation, 115,* 368–376.

Wang, H., Parry, S., Macones, G., Sammel, M. D., Kuivaniemi, H., Tromp, G., Argyropoulous, G., Halder, I., Shriver, M. D., Romero, R., & Strauss, J. F., III. (2006). A functional SNP in the promoter of the SERPINH1 gene increases risk of preterm premature rupture of membranes in African Americans. *Proceedings of the National Academy of Sciences, USA, 103,* 13463–13467.

Wang, L., Wang, X., Wang, W., Chen, C., Ronnennberg, A. G., Guang, W., Huang, A., Fang, Z., Zang, T., Wang, L., & Xu, X. (2004). Stress and dysmenorrhea: A population-based prospective study. *Occupational and Environmental Medicine, 61,* 1021–1026.

Wang, Q. (2004). The emergence of cultural self-constructs: Autobiographical memory and self-description in European American and Chinese children. *Developmental Psychology, 40,* 3–15.

Wang, Y., & Lobstein, T. (2006). Worldwide trends in childhood overweight and obesity. *International Journal of Obesity, 1*(1), 11–25.

Wannamethee, S. G., Shaper, A. G., Whincup, P. H., & Walker, M. (1995). Smoking cessation and the risk of stroke in middle-aged men. *Journal of the American Medical Association, 274,* 155–160.

Ward, R. A., & Spitze, G. D. (2004). Marital implications of parent-adult child coresidence: A longitudinal view. *Journal of Gerontology: Social Sciences, 59B,* S2–S8.

Wardle, J., Robb, K. A., Johnson, F., Griffith, J., Brunner, E., Power, C., & TovÈe, M. (2004). Socioeconomic variation in attitudes to eating and weight in female adolescents. *Health Psychology, 23,* 275–282.

Warneken, F., & Tomasello, M. (2006). Altruistic helping in human infants and young chimpanzees. *Science, 311,* 1301–1303.

Warner, J. (2008, January 3). Domestic disturbances. *New York Times.* Retrieved February 11, 2008, from http://warner.blogs.nytimes.com/2008/01/03/outsourced-wombs/.

Warr, P. (1994). Age and employment. In H. C. Triandis, M. D. Dunnette, & L. M. Hough (Eds.), *Handbook of industrial and organizational psychology* (Vol. 4, pp. 485–550). Palo Alto, CA: Consulting Psychologists Press.

Warren, J. A., & Johnson, P. J. (1995). The impact of workplace support on work-family role strain. *Family Relations, 44,* 163–169.

Wasik, B. H., Ramey, C. T., Bryant, D. M., & Sparling, J. J. (1990). A longitudinal study of two early intervention strategies: Project CARE. *Child Development, 61,* 1682–1696.

Wassertheil-Smoller, S., Hendrix, S. L., Limacher, M., Heiss, G., Kooperberg, C., Baird, A., Kotchen, T., Curb, J. D., Black, H., Rosssouw, J. E., Aragaki, A., Safford, M., Stein, E., Laowattana, S., Mysiw, W. J., for the WHI Investigators. (2003). Effects of estrogen plus progestin on stroke in postmenopausal women: The Women's Health Initiative: A randomized trial. *Journal of the American Medical Association, 289,* 2673–2684.

Watamura, S. E., Donzella, B., Alwin, J., & Gunnar, M. R. (2003). Morning-to-afternoon increases in cortisol concentrations for infants and toddlers at child care: Age differences and behavioral correlates. *Child Development, 74,* 1006–1020.

Watanabe, C. (2007, October 15). Land of the rising sons: Number of elderly Japanese climbing Everest mounts. *Chicago Sun-Times,* p. 28.

Waters, E., & Deane, K. E. (1985). Defining and assessing individual differences in attachment relationships: Q-methodology and the organization of behavior in infancy and early childhood. *Monographs of the Society for Research in Child Development, 50,* 41–65.

Waters, E., Wippman, J., & Sroufe, L. A. (1979). Attachment, positive affect, and competence in the peer group: Two studies in construct validation. *Child Development, 50,* 821–829.

Watkins, M., Rasmussen, S. A., Honein, M. A., Botto, L. D., & Moore, C. A. (2003). Maternal obesity and risk for birth defects. *Pediatrics, 111,* 1152–1158.

Watson, A. C., Nixon, C. L., Wilson, A., & Capage, L. (1999). Social interaction skills and theory of mind in young children. *Developmental Psychology, 35*(2), 386–391.

Watson, J. B., & Rayner, R. (1920). Conditioned emotional reactions. *Journal of Experimental Psychology, 3,* 1–14.

Weese-Mayer, D. E., Berry-Kravis, E. M., Zhou, L., Maher, B. S., Curran, M. E., Silvestri, J. M., & Marazita, M. L. (2004).

Sudden infant death syndrome: Case-control frequency differences at genes pertinent to autonomic nervous system embryological development. *Pediatric Research, 56,* 391–395.

Weg, R. B. (1989). Sensuality/sexuality of the middle years. In S. Hunter & M. Sundel (Eds.), *Midlife myths*. Newbury Park, CA: Sage.

Weil, M., Bressler, J., Parsons, P., Bolla, K., Glass, T., & Schwartz, B. (2005). Blood mercury levels and neurobehavioral function. *Journal of the American Medical Assocation, 293,* 1875–1882.

Weinberger, B., Anwar, M., Hegyi, T., Hiatt, M., Koons, A., & Paneth, N. (2000). Antecedents and neonatal consequences of low Apgar scores in preterm newborns. *Archives of Pediatric and Adolescent Medicine, 154,* 294–300.

Weinberger, D. R. (2001, March 10). A brain too young for good judgment. *New York Times.* Retrieved from www.nytimes.com/2001/03/10/opinion/10WEIN.html?ex_985250309&ei_1&en_995bc03f7a8c7207.

Weinberger, J. (1999, May 18). Enlightening conversation [Letter to the editor]. *New York Times,* p. F3.

Weindruch, R., & Walford, R. L. (1988). *The retardation of aging and disease by dietary restriction.* Springfield, IL: Thomas.

Weinreb, L., Wehler, C., Perloff, J., Scott, R., Hosmer, D., Sagor, L., and Gundersen, C. (2002). Hunger: Its impact on children's health and mental health. *Pediatrics, 110,* 816.

Weinstein, A. R., Sesso, H. D., Lee, I. M., Cook, N. R., Manson, J. E., Buring, J. E., & Gaziano, J. M. (2004). Relationship of physical activity vs body mass index with type 2 diabetes in women. *Journal of the American Medical Association, 292,* 1188–1194.

Weinstock, H., Berman, S., & Cates, W., Jr., (2004). Sexually transmitted diseases among American youth: Incidence and prevalence estimates, 2000. *Perspectives on Sexual and Reproductive Health, 36,* 6–10.

Weisner, T. S. (1993). Ethnographic and ecocultural perspectives on sibling relationships. In Z. Stoneman & P. W. Berman (Eds.), *The effects of mental retardation, visibility, and illness on sibling relationships* (pp. 51–83). Baltimore, MD: Brooks.

Weiss, A., Bates, T. C., & Luciano, M. (2008). Happiness is a personal(ity) thing. The genetics of personality and well-being in a representative sample. *Psychological Science, 19,* 205–210.

Weiss, B., Amler, S., & Amler, R. W. (2004). Pesticides. *Pediatrics, 113,* 1030–1036.

Weiss, B., Dodge, K. A., Bates, J. E., & Pettit, G. S. (1992). Some consequences of early harsh discipline: Child aggression and a maladaptive social information processing style. *Child Development, 63,* 1321–1335.

Weiss, L. A., Shen, Y., Korn, J. M., Arking, D. E., Miller, D. T., Fossdal, R.,

Saemundsen, E., Stefansson, H., Ferreira, M. A. R., Green, T., Platt, O. S., Ruderfer, D. M., Walsh, C. A., Altshuler, D., Chakravarti, A., Tanzi, R. E., Stefansson, K., Santangelo, S. L., Gusella, J. F., Sklar, P., Wu, B.-L., Daly, M. J., & the Autism Consortium. (2008). Association between microdeletion and microduplication at 16p11.2 and autism. *New England Journal of Medicine, 358,* 667–675.

Weiss, R. (2007, July 28). Patient in gene-therapy trial dies. *Washington Post.* Retrieved August 5, 2007, from www.philly.com/philly/health_and science/20070728_Patient_in_gene-therapy_trial_dies.html.

Weissman, M. M., Warner, V., Wickramaratne, P. J., & Kandel, D. B. (1999). Maternal smoking during pregnancy and psychopathology in offspring followed to adulthood. *Journal of the American Academy of Child and Adolescent Psychiatry, 38,* 892–899.

Weisz, J. R., McCarty, C. A., & Valeri, S. M. (2006). Effects of psychotherapy for depression in children and adolescents: A meta-analysis. *Psychological Bulletin, 132,* 132–149.

Weisz, J. R., Weiss, B., Han, S. S., Granger, D. A., & Morton, T. (1995). Effects of psychotherapy with children and adolescents revisited: A meta-analysis of treatment outcome studies. *Psychological Bulletin, 117*(3), 450–468.

Welch-Ross, M. K., & Schmidt, C. R. (1996). Gender-schema development and children's story memory: Evidence for a developmental model. *Child Development, 67,* 820–835.

Wellman, H. M., & Cross, D. (2001). Theory of mind and conceptual change. *Child Development, 72,* 702–707.

Wellman, H. M., Cross, D., & Watson, J. (2001). Meta-analysis of theory-of-mind development: The truth about false belief. *Child Development, 72,* 655–684.

Wellman, H. M., & Woolley, J. D. (1990). From simple desires to ordinary beliefs: The early development of everyday psychology. *Cognition, 35,* 245–275.

Wells, G. (1985). Preschool literacy-related activities and success in school. In D. R. Olson, N. Torrence, & A. Hilyard (Eds.), *Literacy, language, and learning* (pp. 229–255). New York: Cambridge University Press.

Welton, A. J., Vickers, M. R., Kim, J., Ford, D., Lawton, B. A., MacLennan, A. H., Meredith, S. K., Martin, J., & Meade, T. W. for the WISDOM team. (2008). Health related quality of life after combined hormone replacement therapy: Randomised controlled trial. *British Medical Journal, 337,* a1190.

Weng, X., Odouli, R., & Li, D.-K. (2008). Maternal caffeine consumption during pregnancy and the risk of miscarriage: A prospective cohort study. *American Journal of Obstetrics and Gynecology, 198*(3), 279.e1–279.e8.

Wentworth, N., Benson, J. B., & Haith, M. M. (2000). The development of infants' reaches for stationary and moving targets. *Child Development, 71,* 576–601.

Wentzel, K. R. (2002). Are effective teachers like good parents? Teaching styles and student adjustment in early adolescence. *Child Development, 73,* 287–301.

Werker, J. F. (1989). Becoming a native listener. *American Scientist, 77,* 54–59.

Werker, J. F., Pegg, J. E., & McLeod, P. J. (1994). A cross-language investigation of infant preference for infant-directed communication. *Infant Behavior and Development, 17,* 323–333.

Werner, E., Bierman, L., French, F. E., Simonian, K., Connor, A., Smith, R., & Campbell, M. (1968). Reproductive and environmental casualties: A report on the 10-year follow-up of the children of the Kauai pregnancy study. *Pediatrics, 42,* 112–127.

Werner, E., & Smith, R. S. (2001). *Journeys from childhood to midlife.* Ithaca, NY: Cornell University Press.

Werner, E. E. (1985). Stress and protective factors in children's lives. In A. R. Nichol (Ed.), *Longitudinal studies in child psychology and psychiatry.* New York: Wiley.

Werner, E. E. (1987, July 15). *Vulnerability and resiliency: A longitudinal study of Asian Americans from birth to age 30.* Invited address at the ninth biennial meeting of the International Society for the Study of Behavioral Development, Tokyo, Japan.

Werner, E. E. (1989). Children of the garden island. *Scientific American, 260*(4), 106–111.

Werner, E. E. (1993). Risk and resilience in individuals with learning disabilities: Lessons learned from the Kauai longitudinal study. *Learning Disabilities Research and Practice, 8,* 28–34.

Werner, E. E. (1995). Resilience in development. *Current Directions in Psychological Science, 4*(3), 81–85.

West, R., & Burr, G. (2002). Why families deny consent to organ donation. *Australian Critical Care, 15,* 27–32.

Westen, D. (1998). The scientific legacy of Sigmund Freud: Toward a psychodynamically informed psychological science. *Psychological Bulletin, 124,* 333–371.

Wethington, E., Kessler, R. C., & Pixley, J. E. (2004). Turning points in adulthood. In O. G. Brim, C. D. Ryff, and R. C. Kessler (Eds.), *How healthy are we? A national study of well-being at midlife* (pp. 586–613). Chicago: University of Chicago Press.

Weuve, J., Kang, J. H., Manson, J. E., Breteler, M. M. B., Ware, J. H., & Grodstein, F. (2004). Physical activity, including walking, and cognitive function in older women. *Journal of the American Medical Association, 292,* 1454–1461.

Wexler, I. D., Branski, D., & Kerem, E. (2006). War and children. *Journal of the American Medical Association, 296,* 579–581.

Whalley, L. J., & Deary, I. J. (2001). Longitudinal cohort study of childhood IQ and survival up to age 76. *British Medical Journal, 322,* 819.

Whalley, L. J., Starr, J. M., Athawes, R., Hunter, D., Pattie, A., & Deary, I. J. (2000). Childhood mental ability and dementia. *Neurology, 55,* 1455–1459.

Whisman, M. A., Uebelacker, L. A., Tolejko, N., Chatav, Y., & McKelvie, M. (2006). Marital discord and well-being in older adults: Is the association confounded by personality? *Psychology and Aging, 21,* 626–631.

Whitaker, R. C., Wright, J. A., Pepe, M. S., Seidel, K. D., & Dietz, W. H. (1997). Predicting obesity in young adulthood from childhood and parental obesity. *New England Journal of Medicine, 337,* 869–873.

Whitbourne, S. K. (1987). Personality development in adulthood and old age: Relationships among identity style, health, and well-being. In K. W. Schaie (Ed.), *Annual review of gerontology and geriatrics* (pp. 189–216). New York: Springer.

Whitbourne, S. K. (1996). *The aging individual: Physical and psychological perspectives.* New York: Springer.

Whitbourne, S. K. (1999). Physical changes. In J. C. Cavanaugh & S. K. Whitbourne (Eds.). *Gerontology: An interdisciplinary perspective* (pp. 91–122). New York: Oxford University Press.

Whitbourne, S. K. (2001). The physical aging process in midlife: Interactions with psychological and sociocultural factors. In M. E. Lachman (Ed.), *Handbook of midlife development* (pp. 109–155). New York: Wiley.

Whitbourne, S. K., & Connolly, L. A. (1999). The developing self in midlife. In S. L. Willis & J. D. Reid (Eds.), *Life in the middle: Psychological and social development in middle age* (pp. 25–45). San Diego: Academic Press.

White, A. (2001). *Alcohol and adolescent brain development.* Retrieved from www.duke.edu/~amwhite/alc_adik_pf. html.

White, B. L. (1971, October). *Fundamental early environmental influences on the development of competence.* Paper presented at the third Western Symposium on Learning: Cognitive Learning, Western Washington State College, Bellingham, WA.

White, B. L., Kaban, B., & Attanucci, J. (1979). *The origins of human competence.* Lexington, MA: Heath.

Whitehurst, G. J., Falco, F. L., Lonigan, C. J., Fischel, J. E., DeBaryshe, B. D., Valdez-Menchaca, M. D., & Caulfield, M. (1988). Accelerating language development through picture book reading. *Developmental Psychology, 24,* 552–559.

Whitehurst, G. J., & Lonigan, C. J. (1998). Child development and emergent literacy. *Child Development, 69,* 848–872.

Whyatt, R. M., Rauh, V., Barr, D. B., Camann, D. E., Andrews, H. F., Garfinkel, R., Hoepner, L. A., Diaz, D., Dietrich, J., Reyes, A., Tang, D., Kinney, P. L., & Perera, F. P. (2004). Prenatal insecticide exposures and birth weight and length among an urban minority cohort. *Environmental Health Perspectives, 112*(110), 1125–1132.

Wijngaards-de Meij, L., Stroebe, M., Schut, H., Stroebe, W., van den Bout, J., van der Heijden, P., & Dijkstra, I. (2005). Couples at risk following the death of their child: Predictors of grief versus depression. *Journal of Consulting and Clinical Psychology, 73,* 617–623.

Wilcox, A. J., Dunson, D., & Baird, D. D. (2000). The timing of the "fertile window" in the menstrual cycle: Day specific estimates from a prospective study. *British Medical Journal, 321,* 1259–1262.

Wilcox, W. B., & Nock, S. L. (2006). What's love got to do with it? Equality, equity, commitment and women's marital quality. *Social Forces, 84,* 1321–1345.

Willett, W. C., Colditz, G., & Stampfer, M. (2000). Postmenopausal estrogens—opposed, unopposed, or none of the above. *Journal of the American Medical Association, 283,* 534–535.

Williams, D. L., Goldstein, G., & Minshew, N. J. (2006). Neuropsychologic functioning in children with autism: Further evidence for disordered complex information-processing. *Child Neuropsychology: A Journal on Normal and Abnormal Development in Childhood and Adolescence, 12*(4–5), 279–298.

Williams, E. R., & Caliendo, M. A. (1984). *Nutrition: Principles, issues, and applications.* New York: McGraw-Hill.

Williams, G. (1991, October–November). Flaming out on the job: How to recognize when it's all too much. *Modern Maturity,* pp. 26–29.

Williams, J., Wake, M., Hesketh, K., Maher, E., & Waters, E. (2005). Health-related quality of life of overweight and obese children. *Journal of the American Medical Association, 293,* 70–76.

Williams, K. (2004). The transition to widowhood and the social regulation of health: Consequences for health and health risk behavior. *Journal of Gerontology: Social Sciences, 59B,* S343–S349.

Williams, K., & Dunne-Bryant, A. (2006). Divorce and adult psychological well-being: Clarifying the role of gender and child age. *Journal of Marriage and Family, 68,* 1178–1196.

Williams, M. E. (1995). *The American Geriatric Society's complete guide to aging and health.* New York: Harmony.

Willinger, M., Hoffman, H. T., & Hartford, R. B. (1994). Infant sleep position and risk for sudden infant death syndrome: Report of meeting held January 13 and 14, 1994. *Pediatrics, 93,* 814–819.

Willis, S. L. (1990). Current issues in cognitive training research. In E. A. Lovelace (Ed.), *Aging and cognition: Mental processes, self-awareness, and intervention* (pp. 263–280). Amsterdam: North-Holland, Elsevier.

Willis, S. L., Jay, G. M., Diehl, M., & Marsiske, M. (1992). Longitudinal change and prediction of everyday task competence in the elderly. *Research on Aging, 14,* 68–91.

Willis, S. L., & Nesselroade, C. S. (1990). Long-term effects of fluid ability training in old-old age. *Developmental Psychology, 26,* 905–910.

Willis, S. L., & Reid, J. D. (1999). *Life in the middle.* San Diego: Academic Press.

Willis, S. L., & Schaie, K. W. (1999). Intellectual functioning in midlife. In S. L. Willis & J. D. Reid (Eds.), *Life in the middle: Psychological and social development in middle age* (pp. 233–247). San Diego: Academic Press.

Willis, S. L., & Schaie, K. W. (2006). Cognitive functioning in the baby boomers: Longitudinal and cohort effects. In S. K. Whitbourne & S. L. Willis (Eds.), *The baby boomers grow up: Contemporary perspectives on midlife* (pp. 205–234). Mahwah, NJ: Erlbaum.

Willson, A. E., Shuey, K. M., & Elder, G. H. (2003). Ambivalence in the relationship of adult children to aging parents and in-laws. *Journal of Marriage and Family, 65,* 1055–1072.

Wilmoth, J., & Koso, G. (2002). Does marital history count? Marital status and wealth outcomes among preretirement adults. *Journal of Marriage and Family, 64,* 254–268.

Wilmoth, J. R. (2000). Demography of longevity: Past, present, and future trends. *Experimental Gerontology, 35,* 1111–1129.

Wilmoth, J. R., Deegan, L. J., Lundstrom, H., & Horiuchi, S. (2000). Increase of maximum life-span in Sweden, 1861–1999. *Science, 289,* 2366–2368.

Wilson, E. O. (1975). *Sociobiology: The new synthesis.* Cambridge, MA: Belknap Press of Harvard University Press.

Wilson, G. T., Grilo, C. M., & Vitousek, K. M. (2007). Psychological treatment of eating disorders. *American Psychologist, 62,* 199–216.

Wilson, K., & Ryan, V. (2001). Helping parents by working with their children in individual child therapy. *Child and Family Social Work* (Special issue), *6,* 209–217.

Wilson, R. S. (2005). Mental challenge in the workplace and risk of dementia in old age: Is there a connection? *Occupational and Environmental Medicine, 62,* 72–73.

Wilson, R. S., & Bennett, D. A. (2003). Cognitive activity and risk of Alzheimer's Disease. *Current Directions in Psychological Science, 12,* 87–91.

Wilson, R. S., Scherr, P. A., Schneider, J. A., Tang, Y., & Bennett, D. A. (2007). Relation of cognitive ability to risk of developing Alzheimer disease. *Neurology, 69,* 1911–1920.

Wilson, R. S., Schneider, J. A., Arnold, S. E., Bienias, J. L., & Bennett, D. A. (2007). Conscientiousness and the incidence of Alzheimer disease and mild cognitive impairment. *Archives of General Psychiatry, 64,* 1204–1212.

Wilson-Costello, D., Friedman, H., Minich, N., Siner, B., Taylor, G., Schluchter, M., & Hack, M. (2007). Improved neurodevelopmental outcomes for extremely low birth weight infants in 2000–2002. *Pediatrics, 119,* 37–45.

Wingfield, A., & Stine, E. A. L. (1989). Modeling memory processes: Research and theory on memory and aging. In G. C. Gilmore, P. J. Whitehouse, & M. L. Wykle (Eds.), *Memory, aging, and dementia: Theory, assessment, and treatment* (pp. 4–40). New York: Springer.

Wingfield, A., Tun, P. A., & McCoy, S. L. (2005). Hearing loss in older adulthood: What it is and how it interacts with cognitive performance. *Current Directions in Psychological Science, 14,* 144–148.

Winner, E. (1997). Exceptionally high intelligence and schooling. *American Psychologist, 52*(10), 1070–1081.

Winner, E. (2000). The origins and ends of giftedness. *American Psychologist, 55,* 159–169.

Wisner, K. L., Chambers, C., & Sit, D. K. Y. (2006). Postpartum depression: A major public health problem. *Journal of the American Medical Association, 296,* 2616–2618.

Wittig, D. R. (2001). Organ donation beliefs of African American women residing in a small southern community. *Journal of Transcultural Nursing, 12,* 203–210.

Wittstein, I. S., Thiemann, D. R., Lima, J. A. C., Baughman, K. L., Schulman, S. P., Gerstenblith, G., Wu, K. C., Rade, J. J., Bivalacqua, T. J., & Champion, H. C. (2005). Neurohumoral features of myocardial stunning due to sudden emotional stress. *New England Journal of Medicine, 352,* 539–548.

Woerlee, G. M. (2005). *Mortal minds: The biology of the near-death experience.* New York: Prometheus Books.

Woese, C. (1998). Evolution: The universal ancestor. *Proceedings of the National Academy of Sciences, 95,* 6854–6859.

Wolchik, S. A., Sandler, I. N., Millsap, R. E., Plummer, B. A., Greene, S. M., Anderson, E. R., Dawson-McClure, S. R., Hipke, K., & Haine, R. A. (2002). Six-year follow-up of a randomized, controlled trial of preventive interventions for children of divorce. *Journal of the American Medical Association, 288,* 1874–1881.

Wolf, M. (1968). *The house of Lim.* Englewood Cliffs, NJ: Prentice-Hall.

Wolfe, L. (2004). Should parents speak with a dying child about impending death? *New England Journal of Medicine, 351,* 1251–1253.

Wolff, J. L., & Agree, E. M. (2004). Depression among recipients of informal care: The effects of reciprocity, respect, and adequacy of support. *Journal of Gerontology: Psychological Sciences, 59B,* S173–S180.

Wolff, P. H. (1963). Observations on the early development of smiling. In B. M. Foss (Ed.), *Determinants of infant behavior* (Vol. 2). London: Methuen.

Wolff, P. H. (1966). The causes, controls, and organizations of behavior in the newborn. *Psychological Issues, 5*(1, Whole No. 17), 1–105.

Wolff, P. H. (1969). The natural history of crying and other vocalizations in early infancy. In B. M. Foss (Ed.), *Determinants of infant behavior* (Vol. 4). London: Methuen.

Wolf-Maier, K., Cooper, R. S., Banegas, J. R., Giampaoli, S., Hense, H., Joffres, M., Kastarinen, M., Poulter, N., Primatesta, P., Rodriguez-Artalejo, F., Steggmayr, B., Thamm, M., Tuomilehto, J., Vanuzzo, D., & Vescio, F. (2003). Hypertension prevalence and blood pressure levels in 6 European countries, Canada, and the United States. *Journal of the American Medical Association, 289,* 2363–2369.

Wolraich, M. L., Wibbelsman, C. J., Brown, T. E., Evans, S. W., Gotlieb, E. M., Knight, J. R., Ross, C., Shubiner, H. H., Wender, E. H., & Wilens, T. (2005). Attention-deficit/hyperactivity disorder among adolescents: A review of the diagnosis, treatment, and clinical implications. *Pediatrics, 115,* 1734–1746.

Wong, C. A., Scavone, B. M., Peaceman, A. M., McCarthy, R. J., Sullivan, J. T., Diaz, N. T., Yaghmour, E., Marcus, R.-J. L., Sherwani, S. S., Sproviero, M. T., Yilmaz, M., Patel, R., Robles, C., & Grouper, S. (2005). The risk of cesarean delivery with neuraxial analgesia given early versus late in labor. *New England Journal of Medicine, 352,* 655–665.

Wong, C. K., Murray, M. L., Camilleri-Novak, D., & Stephens, P. (2004). Increased prescribing trends of paediatric psychotropic medications. *Archives of the Diseases of Children, 89,* 1131–1132.

Wong, H., Gottesman, I., & Petronis, A. (2005). Phenotypic differences in genetically identical organisms: The epigenetic perspective. *Human Molecular Genetics, 14*(Review Issue 1), R11–R18.

Wong, M. M., Nigg, J. T., Zucker, R. A., Puttler, L. I., Fitzgerald, H. E., Jester, J. M., Glass, J. M., & Adams, K. (2006). Behavioral control and resiliency in the onset of alcohol and illicit drug use: A prospective study from preschool to adolescence. *Child Development, 77,* 1016–1033.

Wood, D. (1980). Teaching the young child: Some relationships between social interaction, language, and thought. In D. Olson (Ed.), *The social foundations of language and thought* (pp. 280–296). New York: Norton.

Wood, D., Bruner, J., & Ross, G. (1976). The role of tutoring in problem solving. *Journal of Child Psychiatry and Psychology, 17,* 89–100.

Wood, R. M., & Gustafson, G. E. (2001). Infant crying and adults' anticipated caregiving responses: Acoustic and contextual influences. *Child Development, 72,* 1287–1300.

Wood, W., & Eagly, A. (2002). A cross-cultural analysis of the behavior of women and men: Implications for the origins of sex differences. *Psychological Bulletin, 128,* 699–727.

Woodruff, T. J., Axelrad, D. A., Kyle, A. D., Nweke, O., Miller, G. G., & Hurley, B. J. (2004). Trends in environmentally related childhood illnesses. *Pediatrics, 113,* 1133–1140.

Woodward, A. L., Markman, E. M., & Fitzsimmons, C. M. (1994). Rapid word learning in 13- and 18-month olds. *Development Psychology, 30,* 553–566.

Woolley, J. D. (1997). Thinking about fantasy: Are children fundamentally different thinkers and believers from adults? *Child Development, 68*(6), 991–1011.

Woolley, J. D., & Boerger, E. A. (2002). Development of beliefs about the origins and controllability of dreams. *Developmental Psychology, 38*(1), 24–41.

Wooley, J. D., Phelps, K. E., Davis, D. L., and Mandell, D. J. (1999). Where theories of mind meet magic: The development of children's beliefs about wishing. *Child Development, 70,* 571–587.

World Bank. (2006). *Repositioning nutrition as central to development.* Washington, DC: Author.

World Cancer Research Fund. (2007, November). *Food, nutrition, physical activity, and the prevention of cancer: A global perspective.* London: Author.

World Health Organization (WHO). (1998). *Obesity: Preventing and managing the global epidemic.* Geneva: Author.

World Health Organization (WHO). (2000, June 4). *WHO issues new healthy life expectancy rankings: Japan number one in new "healthy life" system* [Press release]. Washington, DC: Author.

World Health Organization (WHO). (2002). *Move for Health.* Geneva: Author.

World Health Organization (WHO). (2003). *The world health report—shaping the future.* Retrieved February 14, 2004, from www.who .int/wrh/2003/chapter1en/index2.html.

World Health Organization (WHO). (2005). *WHO multi-country study on women's health and domestic violence against women: Summary report of initial results of prevalence, health outcomes and women's responses.* Geneva: Author.

World Health Organization. (WHO). (2007). *World Health Statistics 2007.* Geneva: Author.

Wortman, C. B., & Silver, R. C. (1989). The myths of coping with loss. *Journal of Consulting and Clinical Psychology, 57*(3), 349–357.

Wright, J. C., Huston, A. C., Murphy, K. C., St. Peters, M., Pinon, M., Scantlin, R., & Kotler, J. (2001). The relations of early television viewing to school readiness and vocabulary of children from low-income families: The Early Window Project. *Child Development, 72*(5), 1347–1366.

Wright, V. C., Chang, J., Jeng, G., & Macaluso, M. (2006). Assisted reproduction technology surveillance—United States, 2003. *Morbidity and Mortality Weekly Report (Surveillance Summaries), 55*(SS04), 1–22.

Wright, V. C., Chang, J., Jeng, G., & Macaluso, M. (2008, June 20). Assisted reproductive technology surveillance—United States,

2005. *Morbidity and Mortality Weekly Report, 57*(SS05), 1–23.

Wright, V. C., Schieve, L. A., Reynolds, M. A., & Jeng, G. (2003). Assisted Reproductive Technology Surveillance— United States, 2000. Division of Reproductive Health, National Center for Chronic Disease Prevention and Health Promotion. Retrieved from www.cdc.gov/reprod.

Writing Group for the Women's Health Initiative Investigators. (2002). Risks and benefits of estrogen plus progestin in healthy postmenopausal women: Principal results from the Women's Health Initiative randomized controlled trial. *Journal of the American Medical Association, 288,* 321–333.

Wrosch, C., & Heckhausen, J. (1999). Control processes before and after passing a developmental deadline: Activation and deactivation of intimate relationship goals. *Journal of Personality and Social Psychology, 77,* 415–427.

Wu, T., Mendola, P., & Buck, G. M. (2002). Ethnic differences in the presence of secondary sex characteristics and menarche among U.S. girls: The Third National Health and Nutrition Survey, 1988–1994. *Pediatrics, 11,* 752–757.

Wu, Z. (1999). Premarital cohabitation and the timing of first marriage. *Canadian Review of Sociology and Anthropology, 36,* 109–127.

Wu, Z., & Hart, R. (2002). The effects of marital and nonmarital union transition on health. *Journal of Marriage and Family, 64,* 420–432.

WuDunn, S. (1997, January 14). Korean women still feel demands to bear a son. *New York Times* (International ed.), p. A3.

Wulczyn, F. (2004). Family reunification. In David and Lucile Packard Foundation, Children, families, and foster care. *Future of Children, 14*(1). Retrieved from www .futureofchildren.org.

Wykle, M. L., & Musil, C. M. (1993). Mental health of older persons: Social and cultural factors. *Generations, 17*(1), 7–12.

Wynn, K. (1990). Children's understanding of counting. *Cognition, 36,* 155–193.

Wynn, K. (1992). Evidence against empiricist accounts of the origins of numerical knowledge. *Mind and Language, 7,* 315–332.

Wyrobek, A. J., Eskenazi, B., Young, S., Arnheim, N., Tiemann-Boege, I., Jabs, E. W., Glaser, R. L., Pearson, F. G., & Evenson, D. (2006). Advancing age has differential effects on DNA damage, chromatin integrity, gene mutations, and aneuploidies in sperm. *Proceedings of the National Academy of Sciences of the United States of America, 103*(25), 9601–9606.

Xie, H., Li, Y., Boucher, S. M., Hutchins, R. C., & Cairns, B. D. (2006). What makes a girl (or a boy) popular (or unpopular)? African American children's perceptions and developmental differences. *Developmental Psychology, 42,* 599–612.

Xu, B., Wratten, N., Charych, E. I., Buyske, S., Firestein, B. L., & Brzustowicz, L. M. (2005). Increased expression in dorsolateral prefrontal cortex of CAPON in schizophrenia and bipolar disorder. *PLoS Medicine, 2*(10), 999–1007.

Xu, X., Hudspeth, C. D., & Bartkowski, J. P. (2006). The role of cohabitation in remarriage. *Journal of Marriage and Family, 68,* 261–274.

Yamada, H. (2004). Japanese mothers' views of young children's areas of personal discretion. *Child Development, 75,* 164–179.

Yamazaki, J. N., & Schull, W. J. (1990). Perinatal loss and neurological abnormalities among children of the atomic bomb. *Journal of the American Medical Association, 264,* 605–609.

Yan, L. L., Daviglus, M. L., Liu, K., Stamler, J., Wang, R., Pirzada, A., Garside, D. B., Dyer, A. R., Van Horn, L., Laio, Y., Fries, J. F., & Greenland, P. (2006). Midlife body mass index and hospitalization and mortality in older age. *Journal of the American Medical Association, 295,* 190–198.

Yan, L. L., Liu, K., Matthews, K. A., Daviglus, M. L., Ferguson, T. F., & Kiefe, C. I. (2003). Psychosocial factors and risk of hypertension: The Coronary Artery Risk Development in Young Adults (CARDIA) study. *Journal of the American Medical Association, 290,* 2138.

Yang, B., Ollendick, T. H., Dong, Q., Xia, Y., & Lin, L. (1995). Only children and children with siblings in the People's Republic of China: Levels of fear, anxiety, and depression. *Child Development, 66,* 1301–1311.

Yang, H., Yang, T., Baur, J. A., Perez, E., Matsui, T., Carmona, J. J., Lamming, D. W., Souza-Pinto, N. C., Bohr, V. A., Rosenzweig, A., de Cabo, R., Sauve, A. A., & Sinclair, D. (2007). Nutrient-sensitive mitochondrial NAD⁺ levels dictate cell survival. *Cell, 130,* 1095–1107.

Yang, Y. (2008). Social inequalities in happiness in the United States, 1972 to 2004: An age-period-cohort analysis. *American Sociological Review, 73,* 204–226.

Yeh, H., Lorenz, F. O., Wickrama, K. A. S., Conger, R. D., & Elder, G. H. (2006). Relationships among sexual satisfaction, marital quality, and marital instability at midlife. *Journal of Family Psychology, 20,* 339–343.

Yeung, W. J., Sandberg, J. F., Davis-Kean, P. E., & Hofferth, S. L. (2001). Children's time with fathers in intact families. *Journal of Marriage and Family, 63,* 136–154.

Yingling, C. D. (2001). Neural mechanisms of unconscious cognitive processing. *Clinical Neurophysiology, 112*(1), 157–158.

Yip, T., Seaton, E. K., & Sellers, R. M. (2006). African American racial identity across the lifespan: Identity status, identity content, and depressive symptoms. *Child Development, 77,* 1504–1517.

Yokota, F., & Thompson, K. M. (2000). Violence in G-rated animated films. *Journal of the American Medical Association, 283,* 2716–2720.

Yoshikawa, H. (1994). Prevention as cumulative protection: Effects of early family support and education on chronic delinquency and its risks. *Psychological Bulletin, 115*(1), 28–54.

Young, K. A., Holcomb, L. A., Bonkale, W. L., Hicks, P. B., Yazdani, U., & German, D. C. (2007). 5HTTLPR polymorphism and enlargement of the pulvinar: Unlocking the backdoor to the limbic system. *Biological Psychiatry, 61*(1), 813–818.

Young, L. R., & Nestle, M. (2002). The contribution of expanding portion sizes to the US obesity epidemic. *American Journal of Public Health, 92,* 246–249.

Youngblade, L. M., & Belsky, J. (1992). Parent-child antecedents of 5-year-olds' close friendships: A longitudinal analysis. *Developmental Psychology, 28,* 700–713.

Youngblade, L. M., Theokas, C., Schulenberg, J., Curry, L., Huang, I-C., & Novak, M. (2007). Risk and promotive factors in families, schools, and communities: A contextual model of positive youth development in adolescence. *Pediatrics, 119,* 47–53.

Youth violence: A report of the Surgeon General (2001, January). Retrieved from www.surgeongeneral.gov/library/ youthviolence/default.htm.

Yunger, J. L., Carver, P. R., & Perry, D. G. (2004). Does gender identity influence children's psychological well-being? *Developmental Psychology, 40,* 572–582.

Yurgelun-Todd, D. (2002). Inside the Teen Brain. Retrieved from www.pbs.org/wgbh/ pages/frontline/shows/teenbrain/interviews/ todd.html.

Zahn-Waxler, C., Friedman, R. J., Cole, P. M., Mizuta, I., & Hiruma, N. (1996). Japanese and U.S. preschool children's responses to conflict and distress. *Child Development, 67,* 2462–2477.

Zahn-Waxler, C., Radke-Yarrow, M., Wagner, E., & Chapman, M. (1992). Development of concern for others. *Developmental Psychology, 28,* 126–136.

Zametkin, A. J., & Ernst, M. (1999). Problems in the management of attention-deficit-hyperactivity disorder. *New England Journal of Medicine, 340,* 40–46.

Zandi, P. P., Anthony, J. C., Hayden, K. M., Mehta, K., Mayer, L., & Breitner, J. C. S. (2002). Reduced incidence of AD with NSAID but no H₂ receptor antagonists. *Neurology, 59,* 880–886.

Zandi, P. P., Carlson, M. C., Plassman, B. L., Welsh-Bohmer, K. A., Mayer, L. S., Steffens, D. C., & Breitner, J. C. S., for the Cache County Memory Study Investigators. (2002). Hormone replacement therapy and incidence of Alzheimer disease in older women: The Cache County Study. *Journal of the American Medical Association, 288,* 2123–2129.

Zeanah, C. H., Smyke, A. T., Koga, S. F., & Carlson, E. (2005). Attachment in institutionalized and community children in Romania. *Child Development, 76,* 1015–1028.

Zelazo, P. D., & Müller, U. (2002). Executive function in typical and atypical development. In U. Goswami (Ed.), *Handbook of childhood cognitive development* (pp. 445–469). Oxford: Blackwell.

Zelazo, P. D., Müller, U., Frye, D., & Marcovitch, S. (2003). The development of executive function in early childhood. *Monographs of the Society for Research in Child Development, 68*(3, Serial No. 274).

Zelazo, P. R., Kearsley, R. B., & Stack, D. M. (1995). Mental representations for visual sequences: Increased speed of central processing from 22 to 32 months. *Intelligence, 20,* 41–63.

Zhang, Q. F. (2004). Economic transition and new patterns of parent-adult child coresidence in China. *Journal of Marriage and Family, 66,* 1232–1245.

Zhang, Z. (2006). Marital history and the burden of cardiovascular disease in midlife. *Gerontologist, 46,* 266–270.

Zhao, Y. (2002, May 29). Cultural divide over parental discipline. *New York Times.* Retrieved from www.nytimes.com/2002/05/29/nyregion/29DISC.html?ex.

Zigler, E. (1998). School should begin at age 3 years for American children. *Journal of Developmental and Behavioral Pediatrics, 19,* 37–38.

Zigler, E., & Styfco, S. J. (1993). Using research and theory to justify and inform Head Start expansion. *Social Policy Report of the Society for Research in Child Development, 7*(2).

Zigler, E., & Styfco, S. J. (1994). Head Start: Criticisms in a constructive context. *American Psychologist, 49*(2), 127–132.

Zigler, E., & Styfco, S. J. (2001). Extended childhood intervention prepares children for school and beyond. *Journal of the American Medical Association, 285,* 2378–2380.

Zigler, E., Taussig, C., & Black, K. (1992). Early childhood intervention: A promising preventative for juvenile delinquency. *American Psychologist, 47,* 997–1006.

Zigler, E. F. (1987). Formal schooling for four-year-olds? *North American Psychologist, 42*(3), 254–260.

Zimmerman, B. J., Bandura, A., & Martinez-Pons, M. (1992). Self-motivation for academic attainment: The role of self-efficacy beliefs and personal goal setting. *American Educational Research Journal, 29,* 663–676.

Zimmerman, F. J., & Christakis, D. A. (2005). Children's television viewing and cognitive outcomes: A longitudinal analysis of national data. *Archives of Pediatrics & Adolescent Medicine, 159*(7), 619–625.

Zimmerman, F. J., Christakis, D. A., & Meltzoff, A. N. (2007). Associations between media viewing and language development in children under age 2 years. *Journal of Pediatrics, 151*(4), 364–368.

Zito, J. M., Safer, D. J., dosReis, S., Gardner, J. F., Magder, L., Soeken, K., Boles, M., Lynch, F., & Riddle, M. A. (2003). Psychotropic practice patterns for youth: A 10-year perspective. *Archives of Pediatrics and Adolescent Medicine* 57(1), 17–25.

Zizza, C., Siega-Riz, A. M., & Popkin, B. M. (2001). Significant increase in young adults' snacking between 1977–1978 and 1994–1996 represents a cause for concern! *Preventive Medicine, 32,* 303–310.

Zubenko, G. S., Maher, B., Hughes, H. B., III, Zubenko, W. N., Stiffler, J. S., Kaplan, B. B., & Marazita, M. L. (2003). Genome-wide linkage survey for genetic loci that influence the development of depressive disorders in families with recurrent, early-onset, major depression. *American Journal of Medical Genetics Part B: Neuropsychiatric Genetics, 123*(1), 1–18.

Zucker, A. N., Ostrove, J. M., & Stewart, A. J. (2002). College-educated women's personality development in adulthood: Perceptions and age differences. *Psychology and Aging, 17,* 236–244.

Zuckerman, B. S., & Beardslee, W. R. (1987). Maternal depression: A concern for pediatricians. *Pediatrics, 79,* 110–117.

Credits

Name Index

Berget, A., 88
Berglund, H., 397
Bergström, R., 82
Bering, J. M., 626
Berkman, L. F., 429, 603
Berkowitz, G. S., 87
Berkowitz, L., 340, 341
Berkowitz, R. I., 118
Berkowitz, R. L., 87
Berman, S., 401
Bernadel, L., 491
Bernard, S. J., 113
Berndt, A. E., 188
Berndt, T. J., 412
Bernert, R. A., 426
Berns, S., 460
Bernstein, L., 426
Bernstein, P. S., 106
Bernzweig, J., 275
Berrick, J. D., 210
Berrueta-Clement, J. R., 246, 417
Berry, M., 333
Berry, N., 74
Berry, R. J., 82
Bertenthal, B., 131
Bertenthal, B. I., 131, 132
Berthier, N. E., 132
Bethell, C. D., 343
Beumont, P. J. V., 366
Beveridge, M., 87
Beversdorf, D. Q., 87
Bhaskaran, K., 432
Bialystok, E., 236, 570, 576, 577
Bianchi, S., 472
Bianchi, S. M., 472
Biason-Lauber, A., 57
Bibbins-Domingo, K., 363
Bickham, D., 340
Biegel, D. E., 540, 541
Bielby, D., 440
Bienias, J. L., 570
Bienvenu, O. J., 460
Bierman, K. L., 275, 279, 336
Billet, S., 506, 507
Billings, L. M., 572
Bilsen, J., 640
Binet, A., 143
Bingham, K., 271
Binstock, G., 466
Birch, H. G., 74, 183
Birch, L. L., 217, 356, 364
Bird, T. D., 571
Birks, J., 573
Birmaher, B., 345, 369, 370
Bischoff, C., 556
Bishop, D. V. M., 243
Bjork, J. M., 360
Bjorklund, D. F., 35, 36, 150, 259, 260,
    264, 265, 266, 267, 268, 269, 287,
    288, 297, 315, 626
Black, A. E., 272
Black, D. M., 496

Black, J. E., 127
Black, K., 417
Black, M. M., 12
Black, R. E., 224
Blackwell, E., 501
Blagrove, M., 426
Blair, C., 247
Blair, P. S., 113
Blair, S. N., 492
Blais, L., 83
Blakemore, C., 121
Blakemore, S., 285, 360, 361, 374
Blakeslee, S., 145, 330
Blanchard-Fields, F., 437, 576, 588, 590
Blanco, C., 346
Blanton, P. W., 537
Blass, E. M., 128
Blatchford, P., 287
Blehar, M. C., 189
Bleske-Rechek, A., 317
Bliesszner, R., 532, 533, 535, 536, 537,
    538, 539, 540, 541, 542, 543, 544
Blizzard, L., 113
Block, J., 325, 460, 461, 523
Block, J. H., 325, 460, 461
Block, R. W., 207
Bloom, B., 316
Bloom, P., 153
Bluck, S., 17, 519
Blum, R., 371
Blum, R. W., 397, 398
Blumberg, S. J.., 343
Blumenthal, J. A., 568
Blustein, D. L., 448
Blyth, D. A., 360
Boatman, D., 16
Bocskay, K. A., 87
Bode, J., 243
Bodkin, N. L., 559
Bodrova, E., 268, 269
Boerger, E. A., 234
Boerner, K., 607, 624
Boersma, E. R., 116
Bogaert, A. F., 397
Bogan, H., 559
Bogg, T., 460, 584
Bograd, R., 607
Boivin, M., 218, 219, 342
Bojczyk, K. E., 151
Bollen, A.-M., 88
Bollinger, M. B., 291
Bonanno, G. A., 501, 606, 624
Bonham, V. L., 13, 14
Booth, A., 328, 470
Booth, A. E., 158
Booth, J. R., 308
Booth-Kewley, S., 432
Booth-LaForce, C., 191
Bootzin, R. R., 622
Boppana, M., 573
Borawski, E. A., 493
Borkowski, J. G., 403

Bornstein, M., 129
Bornstein, M. H., 129, 149, 155, 158,
    167, 171, 239, 415
Borowsky, I. A., 371
Bosch, J., 333
Bosch, J. D., 339
Boschi-Pinto, C., 110, 224
Boss, P., 590, 625
Bosshard, G., 640
Bosworth, H. B., 604
Botto, L., 86
Botto, L. D., 82
Botwinick, J., 574
Bouchard, C., 73
Bouchard, T. J., 72, 73, 74, 430, 459, 569
Boucher, S. M., 336
Bouchey, H. A., 397, 413
Boudreau, J. P., 17, 129, 132
Boudreault, M. A., 370
Boukydis, C. F. Z., 164
Boulé, N. G., 426
Boulton, M. J., 341, 342
Boutin, P., 73
Bower, B., 233
Bowes, J. M., 379
Bowlby, J., 35, 189, 190
Bowman, B. A., 425
Boyce, W. F., 342
Boyce, W. T., 225
Boyd, R., 534
Boyd-Zaharias, J., 312
Boyle, M., 108
Boyles, S., 88
Brabant, S., 612
Brabeck, M. M., 378, 443
Bracewell, M. A., 108
Brachen, S. S., 309
Bracher, G., 404
Brackett, M. A., 439
Bradbury, T. N., 607
Bradley, R., 145
Bradley, R. H., 144, 145, 187, 328
Brady, C., 327
Braine, M., 167
Brakefield, T., 426
Bramlett, M. D., 466, 477
Brandt, B., 632
Brandt, J., 363
Brandtstadter, J., 595
Branski, D., 347
Brashear, M. E., 462
Brass, L. M., 72
Braswell, G. S., 222
Bratton, S. C., 346
Braun, A. R., 169
Braun, H., 312
Braungart, J. M., 184
Braver, E. R., 370
Bray, J. H., 328, 331
Brazelton, T. B., 103
Breaux, C., 186, 187
Breeden, G., 634

Cohen, S. E., 158
Cohrs, M., 130
Coie, J., 336
Coie, J. D., 275, 276, 336, 338, 339, 340, 343, 414
Coke, M. M., 591
Colburne, K. A., 269
Colby, A., 377, 378
Colditz, G., 498
Colditz, G. A., 492, 497
Coldwell, J., 278
Cole, M., 302
Cole, P. M., 178, 196, 324
Cole, R. E., 210
Cole, T. B., 371
Cole, T. J., 116, 223
Colecchi, C., 565
Coleman, J. S., 311
Coles, L. S., 558
Coley, R. L., 410
Coll, C. G., 144
Collado, H., 446
Collaris, R., 277
Collier, V. P., 307
Collins, A., 194
Collins, F. S., 13, 67
Collins, N. L., 461
Collins, W. A., 415, 416, 462
Colliver, J. D., 367
Colombo, B., 433
Colombo, J., 82, 155, 156
Coltrane, S., 264
Compas, B. E., 501
Compston, J., 496
Compton, S. N., 45
Comuzzie, A. G., 425
Conboy, B. T., 165
Conde-Agudelo, A., 107
Conel, J. L., 124
Cong, Z., 596
Conger, R. D., 369, 408, 409, 416, 532
Connidis, I. A., 612
Connolly, L. A., 524
Connor, P. D., 84
Conradt, B., 556
Constantino, J. N., 122, 259
Convit, A., 573
Cooney, T., 534
Cooper, K. L., 526, 527
Cooper, P., 191
Cooper, R. P., 81, 172
Cooper, W. O., 423
Coplan, R. J., 267
Coppage, D. J., 158
Coppola, M., 169
Corbet, A., 107
Corbetta, D., 151
Corbin, C., 220
Corbin, S. B., 330
Corcoran, M., 446
Cordal, A., 502
Cordero, J. F., 86

Cornelius, S. W., 580, 581
Correa, A., 86
Corter, C., 277
Corwyn, R. F., 144
Cosser, C., 234
Costa, P. T., 588
Costa, P. T., Jr., 458, 459, 517, 587, 588
Costello, E. J., 45, 344
Costigan, K. A., 80, 86
Côté, J. E., 443, 445, 446, 453, 454
Cote, L. R., 167
Courage, M. L., 36, 156, 167, 197, 238
Courchesne, E., 123
Cowan, C. P., 472, 473
Cowan, P. A., 472, 473
Cox, A., 173, 439
Coxson, P., 363
Coy, K. C., 201
Craft, A. W., 88
Craig, W. M., 342
Craik, F. I. M., 570, 577, 578, 580
Crain-Thoreson, C., 173
Cramer, A., 414
Cratty, B. J., 287
Crawford, C., 260
Crawford, J., 307
Crawford, S., 488, 489, 490
Crean, H., 409
Crick, N. R., 275, 339
Crisp, J., 291
Crnic, K., 185
Crockenberg, S. C., 205
Cromwell, R. L., 564
Cronk, C., 152
Cronk, L. B., 112
Crook, C., 187
Crooks, V. C., 603
Crosby, A. E., 371
Cross, D., 233, 234
Crouter, A., 363
Crouter, A. C., 263, 326, 411, 462, 473, 536
Crowder, K. D., 11, 464
Crowe, E., 236
Crowe, M., 570, 572
Crowley, S. L., 544
Cruz, L. A., 485
Cruzan, N., 637
Csapo, B., 379
Csikszentmihalyi, M., 316, 527
Cui, M., 409
Culbert, K. M., 364
Cumming, E., 592
Cummings, J. L., 570, 571, 572, 573, 574
Cunniff, C., 89
Cunningham, F. G., 87
Cupples, L. A., 557
Curcio, P., 89
Curenton, S., 234, 236
Curhan, K. B., 528
Currie, C., 341, 362
Curtiss, S., 16

Cutler, J. A., 290
Cutler, S. J., 600
Cutrona, C. E., 501
Cuttini, M., 641
Cymerman, E., 242
Cytrynbaum, S., 526
Czaja, A. J., 597
Czaja, S. J., 509, 511
Czeisler, C. A., 564

da Vinci, L., 617
Dai, L., 367
Dalais, C., 224
Dale, P. S., 173, 243, 309
Dallal, G. E., 359
Dalton, M., 369
Daly, R., 346
Dambrosia, J. M., 99
Damon, W., 378
Danaceau, M. A., 432
D'Andrea, F., 568
Danesi, M., 375
Daniels, D., 72
D'Apolito, J. P., 340
Darling, N., 272, 273, 408
D'Armiento, M., 568
Darroch, J. E., 403
Darwin, C., 22, 35, 258, 259, 507
Datar, A., 290
Dauber, S. L., 308
Davalos, M., 196
Davidson, J. I. F., 268
Davidson, N. E., 497
Davidson, R. J., 192
Davies, C., 542, 543
Davies, L., 612
Davila, J., 470
Davis, C. C., 203
Davis, D. L., 235
Davis, J., 313, 398
Davis, M., 187
Davis, R., 568
Davis, T. L., 235
Davis-Kean, P. E., 310, 407, 472
Davison, K. K., 356, 364
Dawson, B. S., 398
Dawson, D. A., 328
Dawson, G., 196
Dawson-Hughes, B., 568
Day, J. C., 313
Day, N. L., 85
Day, S., 61
de Castro, B. O., 339
de Groot, L. C. P. M. G., 567
de Gues, E. J. C., 73
de Henauw, S., 567
de la Fuente-Fernandez, R., 572
de Lange, T., 556
de Leon, M. J., 573
de Matos, M. G., 362
De Santi, S., 573
De Schipper, E., 205

Glover, V., 87
Glymour, C., 159
Glymour, M. M., 603
Goddeeris, J., 108
Goetz, P. J., 236
Gogtay, N., 286
Goldenberg, R. L., 83, 106, 107, 109
Golding, J., 87
Goldin-Meadow, S., 166, 169
Goldman, L., 227, 363, 572
Goldman, L. L., 635
Goldman, S. R., 506
Goldscheider, F., 476
Goldsmith, H. H., 257
Goldstein, G., 122
Goldstein, I., 490
Goldstein, M., 171
Goldstein, S. E., 407
Golinkoff, R. M., 167, 242
Golomb, C., 235
Golombok, S., 332
Golombok, S. E., 257
Göncü, A., 163
Gonyea, J. G., 600
Gonzales, N. A., 43
Gonzalez, E., 424
Gooden, A. M., 264
Goodman, D. C., 106
Goodman, G., 292
Goodman, G. S., 333
Goodnow, J. J., 199, 270, 271, 273, 276, 291
Goodwyn, S. W., 166
Goodz, E., 172
Goossens, L., 409
Gootman, E., 383
Gopnik, A., 150, 159
Gordon, P. L., 340
Gordon, R., 238
Gordon-Larsen, P., 362, 424
Gorman, B. K., 553
Gorman, M., 11
Gorman-Smith, D., 414
Gornick, J., 447
Gortmaker, S. L., 363
Gosden, R. G., 60, 61
Gostin, L. O., 638, 639
Gotlib, I. H., 344
Gottesman, I., 61
Gottesman, I. I., 301
Gottfredson, L. S., 577
Gottfried, A. E., 310
Gottfried, A. W., 310
Gottlieb, A., 153, 185
Gottlieb, B., 429
Gottlieb, G., 60, 69, 70
Gottman, J. M., 39, 472, 606
Goubet, N., 132, 152, 160
Gould, E., 122
Gourde, C., 152
Gove, F., 193
Graber, J. A., 359

Grady, C. L., 579
Grady, D., 497
Graff, J., 606
Grafman, J., 448
Graham, J. W., 416
Graham, S. A., 242
Gralinski, H., 198
Granger, D. A., 345
Granholm, E., 368
Granier-Deferre, C., 81, 165
Grant, B. F., 430
Grantham-McGregor, S., 224
Graubard, B. I., 425
Gray, J. R., 301
Gray, M. R., 408
Graziano, A. M., 219
Graziano, M. S. A., 122
Green, A. P., 188
Green, D., 573
Green, F. L., 46, 234, 235
Green, K. N., 572
Greenberg, J., 612
Greendale, G. A., 593
Greene, L., 398
Greene, M. F., 108
Greene, S. M., 84
Greenfield, E. A., 592, 597, 598
Greenfield, P. M., 43
Greenhouse, L., 543, 639
Greenland, P., 362
Greenstone, M., 111
Gregg, E. W., 425, 568
Gregg, V. R., 379
Greil, A. L., 433
Grether, J. K., 99
Grewal, D., 439
Grigg, W., 312
Grigorenko, E. L., 13, 304, 305, 311, 438, 576
Grilo, C. M., 365
Grizzle, K. L., 312
Grodstein, F., 497
Gross, C. G., 122
Gross, J., 531
Gross, S., 483
Grossman, J. B., 234
Grossman, K., 188
Grote, P., 556
Grotevant, H. D., 333
Grotpeter, J. K., 339
Gruber, H., 316
Gruber, R., 362
Gruenewald, T. L., 593
Grummer-Strawn, L. M., 116
Grusec, J. E., 199, 270, 271, 273, 276, 325
Guberman, S. R., 295
Guerino, P., 341, 347
Guilleminault, C., 218
Gulati, M., 362
Gulko, J., 269
Gullone, E., 347

Gunn, D. M., 298
Gunnar, M. R., 193, 194, 205
Guo, Z., 567
Guralnik, J. M., 485
Gurney, J. G., 122
Gurung, R. A. R., 606
Gustafson, G. E., 179
Gutchess, A., 561
Gutman, L. M., 407, 408
Gutmann, D., 526
Gutmann, D. L., 526, 527
Guttmacher, A. E., 67
Guyer, B., 56, 97, 106
Guzick, D. S., 434
Gwaltney, J. M., Jr., 429

Ha, J., 541
Ha, T., 407
Haaland, W., 192
Haas, S. A., 363
Habicht, J.-P., 83, 118
Hack, M., 107, 108
Hack, T., 620, 621
Haddad, E., 426
Haden, C. A., 238, 239
Hagan, J. F., 347, 348
Hagberg, B., 600
Hagedorn, L. S., 447
Hahn, R., 415
Haight, W., 171
Haines, P. S., 568
Haith, M. M., 128, 132, 157, 160, 161, 162
Haley, A., 301
Halgunseth, L. C., 324, 325
Hall, D. G., 242
Hall, G. S., 405
Hallett, M., 462
Hallfors, D. D., 370
Halliwell, E., 289
Halpern, C. T., 370
Halpern, D. F., 257, 258, 309, 310, 381, 444
Halverson, C. F., 261
Hambrick, D. Z., 576
Hamilton, B. E., 55, 56, 80, 82, 84, 87, 88, 97, 98, 99, 103, 105, 106, 107, 108, 109, 110, 111, 402, 403, 471
Hamilton, L., 333
Hamilton, M., 264
Hamilton, M. A., 443, 446, 447
Hamilton, S. F., 443, 446, 447
Hamm, J. V., 326, 412
Hammad, T. A., 346
Hammer, A., 601
Hammer, L. B., 541
Hampden-Thompson, G., 381
Hampson, J. G., 259
Hampson, J. L., 259
Hamre, B. K., 308
Han, S. S., 345
Han, W.-J., 204

Saroha, E., 314
Sassler, S., 476
Satcher, D., 399, 404
Saudino, K. J., 74
Sauer, P. J. J., 641
Saunders, D. L., 292
Savage, S. L., 242
Savarino, J., 346
Savic, I., 397
Savin-Williams, R. C., 298, 396, 397
Savoie, D., 292
Sawicki, M. B., 598
Saxe, R., 159
Saxon, J. L., 255
Saylor, M. M., 153
Scaer, R., 97
Scanlan, J. M., 540
Scarr, S., 71, 72, 207
Schaal, B., 128
Schacter, D. L., 33
Schafer, W. D., 190
Schaie, K. W., 427, 437, 503, 504, 509, 573, 575, 588, 604
Schairer, C., 498
Schanberg, S., 196
Schardt, D., 454, 458
Scharf, M., 330, 458, 476
Scharlach, A. E., 629, 631, 632
Schaumberg, D. A., 562
Scheers, N. J., 113
Scheidt, P., 361, 362
Schemo, D. J., 312
Scher, M. S., 85
Scherr, P. A., 570, 578
Schiavo, M., 636
Schiavo, T., 636, 637
Schieman, S., 608
Schieve, L. A., 56, 122, 434
Schiller, J. S., 491
Schiller, M., 192
Schlegel, A., 405
Schliemann, A. D., 295
Schmidt, C. R., 262
Schmidt, P. J., 432
Schmithorst, V. J., 170
Schmitt, F. A., 576, 622
Schmitt, K. L., 340
Schmitz, S., 74, 184
Schnaas, L., 88
Schneider, B. H., 194
Schneider, E. L., 554, 557, 558
Schneider, H., 315
Schneider, J. A., 578
Schneider, L., 573
Schneider, M., 312
Schnell, S. V., 378
Schoefs, V., 193
Schoelmerich, A., 192, 202
Schoenborn, C. A., 426, 429, 562, 565, 567, 569
Schoendorf, K. C., 87
Schoeni, R., 443

Schoenle, E. J., 57
Schoff, K., 349
Schölmerich, A., 185
Scholten, C. M., 96
Schöner, G., 161
Schonert-Reichl, K. A., 405
Schonfield, D., 578
Schooler, C., 509, 611
Schopflocher, D. P., 292
Schore, A. N., 181
Schouten, A., 323
Schreiber, J. B., 364
Schroll, M., 567
Schuebel, K. J., 562
Schuengel, C., 190
Schulenberg, J., 422, 428, 453
Schulenberg, J. E., 366, 367, 414, 416, 430, 431
Schull, W. J., 88
Schultetus, R. S., 506, 507
Schulting, A . B., 247
Schulz, L. E., 159
Schulz, M. S., 472, 473
Schulz, R., 540, 541, 594, 607, 623
Schulze, P. A., 202
Schumann, C. M., 122
Schumann, J., 16
Schut, H., 630
Schwab-Stone, M., 415
Schwab-Stone, M. E., 415
Schwartz, D., 276, 342
Schwartz, L. L., 434
Schweinhart, L. J., 246, 404, 417
Scialfa, C. T., 484, 562
Scott, C., 110, 423, 553
Scott, E. S., 360, 416
Scott, J., 469
Scott, M. E., 467
Scott, P., 293
Scullin, M. H., 313
Seaman, J., 444
Seaton, E. K., 394
Seay, R. B., 576
Sebanc, A. M., 268
Sedlak, A. J., 208
Seeley, J. R., 344
Seeman, E., 591
Seeman, M., 591
Seeman, T. E., 424, 593, 606
Seeman, T. S., 327
Seepersad, S., 406
Seftor, N. S., 444
Segerstrom, S. C., 501
Segesten, K., 633
Seidler, A., 510, 570
Seifer, R., 192, 363
Seiner, S. H., 196
Sekuler, R., 484
Seligman, M. E. P., 380
Sellers, E. M., 428
Sellers, R. M., 394
Selman, A. P., 337, 338

Selman, R. L., 337, 338
Seltzer, G. B., 600
Seltzer, J. A., 331, 465, 466
Seltzer, M., 171
Seltzer, M. M., 612
Seminara, S. B., 356
Sen, A., 381, 444
Sen, M. G., 187
Senghas, A., 169
Senman, L., 236
Serbin, L., 187
Serbin, L. A., 269, 335
Serido, J., 499
Seroude, L., 558
Serres, L., 161
Service, V., 166
Sethi, A., 201
Settersten, R. A., Jr., 422, 448
Sexton, A., 53
Seybold, K. S., 591
Shaffer, R. A., 432
Shafto, M. A., 579
Shah, T., 84
Shahabi, L., 591
Shamah, T., 83, 118
Shanahan, M., 422
Shankaran, S., 84, 85
Shannon, D., 185
Shannon, J. D., 187, 328
Shaper, A. G., 427, 492
Shapiro, A. D., 526
Shapiro, A. F., 472
Shapiro, B. K., 164
Shapiro, P., 600, 601
Sharit, J., 597
Sharma, A. R., 333, 334
Shatz, M., 243
Shaw, B. A., 569, 594, 604
Shaw, D., 187, 257
Shaw, H., 363
Shaw, N., 223
Shaw, P., 286, 315
Shayer, M., 296
Shaywitz, B. A., 314
Shaywitz, S., 314
Shaywitz, S. E., 314
Shea, K. M., 88
Shea, S., 290
Sheblanova, E., 379
Shedlock, D. J., 580, 581
Sheldon, K. M., 519
Shema, S. J., 562
Shepherd, J., 424
Sherman, A. M., 603
Sherman, E., 642
Sherman, M., 603
Shi, T., 258
Shibuya, K., 110, 224
Shields, B., 196
Shields, M. K., 12
Shine, B., 223
Shiono, P. H., 90, 106

Subject Index

Canada, 13, 55, 108, 291
  centenarians in, 559
  cohabitation in, 465
  economic self-sufficiency in, 446
  literacy in, 511
  marriage in, 468
  obesity in, 425
  older adults in, 593
  same-sex marriage in, 465
  stepparenthood, 476–477
Canadian Cancer Registries
    Epidemiology Research
    Group, 426
Canadian Pediatrics Society, 219, 220
canalization, 70, **70**
cancer, 426, 568
  breast, 496–497
  in US, 492
caregivers, 539–540
  burnout, 540, **540**
  emotional communication with, 195
  language development role of, 170–172
  spouse as, 607
  strains of, 540–541
Carousel, 507
CASA. *See* Center on Addiction and
    Substance Abuse at Columbia
    University
case studies, **40,** 40–41
casual sex, 432
cataracts, 562, **562**
categorization, 149*t,* 158, 230, 293
causality, 149*t,* 159, 230, 292
CD. *See* conduct disorder
CDC. *See* Centers for Disease Control
    and Prevention
CDF. *See* Children's Defense Fund
CDS. *See* child-directed speech
cell death, 121, **121**
centenarians, 559
Center for Autism Research, 122
Center for Education Reform, 312
Center for Weight and Health, 223, 290
Center on Addiction and Substance
    Abuse at Columbia University
    (CASA), 269
Centers for Disease Control and
    Prevention (CDC), 61, 86, 91,
    114, 356, 362, 401, 413, 414, 433,
    434, 564, 568, 634, 635
  Office of Minority Health, 227,
    493, 494
central executive, 237, **237**
central nervous system, 118, **118**
centration, 231, **231**
Centre for Educational Research and
    Innovation, 446
cephalocaudal principle, 114, **114,** 130
cerebellum, 119
cerebrum, 119
cesarean delivery, 99, **99**
change of life, 487, 587–588

child care
  choosing good, 206*t*
  early, 205–207
  factors impacting, 205
  grandparents for, 543
  NICHD study, 206–207
childbirth
  birth process, 97–101
  cesarean delivery, 99, **99**
  complications, 105–110
  culture and, 96–97
  low birth weight, 105–108
  medicalization of, 97
  natural, **99,** 99–101
  postmaturity, 108, **108**
  stages of, 98, 98*f*
  stillbirth, **108,** 108–109, 633
  survival and health, 110–114
child-directed speech (CDS), 172, **172**
childhood. *See also* early
    childhood; middle childhood
  death understanding in, 625–626,
    627*t,* 628–629
  depression, **344,** 344–345
  poverty influencing, 11–12, 11*t*
childlessness, 612
children, 245. *See also* grandchildren
  adult, 454–455
  air pollution influences on, 226–228
  contact with other, 202–203
  cultural influences on, 324
  death of, 632–633
  "difficult," 183, **183,** 183*t*
  divorce influencing, 328–330
  "easy," 183, **183,** 183*t*
  elderly relationships with adult,
    610–612
  ethnicity influencing health of, 226
  in family, 324–335
  genetic testing of, 67
  gifted, 316–317
  grief manifestations in, 628, 628*t*
  leaving, 537
  living arrangements of, 331*f*
  living with adult, 600–601
  mortality comparisons, 226
  nonsibling sociability, 203
  of one-parent families, 330–331
  only, 278–279
  overweight, 118
  parent-, bond, 610
  parent death of adult, 631–632, 631*t*
  parenting grown, 537
  percentages by race/ethnicity, 13*f*
  relationships of, 277–279
  relationships with maturing, 536–538
  resilience in, 349, **349,** 349*t*
  sibling contact, 202–203
  "slow-to-warm-up," 183, **183,** 183*t*
  special needs, 313–317
  stress and functioning of, 349
  of working parents, 204–207

Children's Defense Fund (CDF), 12,
    226, 402, 404
China
  aging in, 596
  birth defects in, 82
Chinese Americans, 489
  adolescent relationships of, 406–407
  infant mortality of, 111
  mental health of, 502
  parenting styles of, 273
Chippewa Indians, 7
chlamydia, 400*t,* 401
cholesterol, 424
cholinesterase inhibitors, 573
chorion, 78, 79*f*
chorionic villus sampling (CVS), 89*t*
A Christmas Carol (Dickens), 641
chromosomal abnormalities, 63, 64*t,* 65
chromosomes, 56, **56**
chronic conditions, 565–566
  common, 566, **566**
chronic emergency of parenthood, 537
chronic grief, 624
chronic medical conditions, 291, **291**
chronosystem, 34–35, 34*f*
circular reactions, 147, **147,** 148*f*
class inclusion, 293, **293**
class size, 312
classical conditioning, 28, 29, **29,** 141,
    141, 142*f*
climacteric, 487
cliques, 411
cluttered nest, 538
code mixing, 172, **172**
code switching, 172, **172**
code-emphasis approach. *See* phonetic
    (code-emphasis) approach
Cognition and Technology Group at
    Vanderbilt, 506
cognitive behavioral therapy, 345
cognitive changes, before death, 620, 622
cognitive complexity, of play, 265
cognitive development, 6, **6,** 8*t,* 24*t*–25*t,*
    30–33, 228–247, 258*t,* 371–386
  achieving stage of, 437
  cognitive-stage theory, of Piaget,
    30–32, **31**
  in emerging and young adult-
    hood, 435–448
  ethic of care, of Gilligan, 378–379
  formal operations, of Piaget, 372–373
  fostering competence of, 145*t*
  in infancy and toddlerhood, 139–175
  information-processing approach, 33,
    33, 154–161
  Kohlberg's, 260–261
  in late adulthood, 574–581
  in middle adulthood, 503–511
  in middle childhood, 292–317
  moral reasoning of Kohlberg, 375,
    377–378
  neo-Piagetian theories, 33

cognitive development—*Cont.*
 Piagetian approach, 140, **140,**
  146–154, 228–236
 preoperational stage, **228,** 228–236,
  228*t*
 psychometric approaches, 143–146,
  239–241
 reintegrative stage of, 437
 reorganizational stage of, 437
 self-concept and, 252–253
 social-contextual approach to, 140,
  140, 162–13
 sociocultural theory of Vygotsky, **32,**
  32–33
cognitive neuroscience, 40, **40**
cognitive neuroscience approach, to cognitive development, 140, **140**
cognitive reserve, 572, **572**
cognitive-appraisal model, 590, **590**
cognitive-stage theory, of Piaget,
  24*t*–25*t*, 27*t*, 30–32, **31**
cohabitation, 465, 466*f*
 in emerging and young adulthood, 465–467
 of family, 331
 international comparisons, 465
 in late adulthood, 608–609
 in middle adulthood, 532–533
cohort, 14, **14, 15**
collective efficacy, 416
college, 443–446
 adjusting to, 445
 cognitive growth in, 445
 finishing, 446
 in middle adulthood, 510
color blindness, 63
Columbine High School, 414–415
Commissioner's Office of Research
  and Evaluation and Head Start
  Bureau, 246
commitment, 392, **392,** 463
committed compliance, **201,** 201–202
communication
 emotional, with caregivers, 195
 knowledge about, 306
community
 college, 445–446
 juvenile delinquency influenced
  by, 414–417
 maltreatment from, 209
 support for caregiving, 541
companionate love, 463*t*
companionate model, of marriage, 470
compliance, 201–202
componential element, 303, **303,** 438
computers, school achievement relating
  to, 312–313
conceptual knowledge, 374, **374**
concordant, 68, **68**
concrete operations, of Piaget, **292,**
  292–296
condoms, 432

conduct disorder (CD), 343, **343**
Conduct Problems Prevention Research
  Group, 342
Conference Board, 511
congenital adrenal hyperplasia
  (CAH), 259
conjunctive faith, 442
connectedness, 394
conscience, **201,** 201–202
conscientious, 459
consensual relationships
 cohabitation, 532–533
 divorce, 533–534
 friendships, 535–536
 health, well-being and marital
  status, 534
 homosexuality, 535
 marriage, 532–536
 in middle adulthood, 532–536
conservation, 232, **232,** 233*t*, 294–295
constructive play, 265, **265**
consummate love, 463*t*
contextual element, 304, **304,** 438
contextual perspective, of
  development, 24*t*–25*t*, **34,** 34–35
contingent self-esteem, 254–255
continuity theory, 593, **593**
continuous development, 24–25
contraceptives, 399, 403–404
control group, 43, **43**
conventional morality, 376*t*, 377, **377**
co-parenting, 328–330
coping, 589, **589**
 age differences in styles of, 590–591
 emotional-focused, 590, **590**
 problem-faced, 590, **590**
 strategies, 349–350, 590
cordocentesis, 89*t*
coregulation, 325, **325**
corporal punishment, **270,** 270–271
corpus callosum, 119
correlational study, **41,** 41–42, 41*t*
Council on Children with
  Disabilities, 122, 123
Council on Sports Medicine and
  Fitness, 288
Council on School Health, 288
creative achievers, 508
creativity, in middle adulthood, 507–508
cremation, 618–619
crisis, 392, **392**
 filial, 539, **539**
 midlife, **522,** 522–523
 in personality, 28
critical period, 16, **16**
cross-cultural research, 42–43
cross-modal transfer, 156, **156**
cross-sectional study, **45,** 45–46, 45*f,* 47*t*
crowd, 411
Cruzan vs. Director, Missouri
  Department of Health, 1990, 637
crying, 164, 179–180, *180*

crystallized intelligence, 505, **505**
cultural bias, 302, **302**
cultural influences
 on adolescent relationships, 406
 aggression and, 276
 on childbirth, 96–97
 on children in family, 324
 on death meanings, 618–620
 on end-of-life decisions, 640–641
 on gender development, 264
 on guided participation, 163
 on intelligence, 302–303
 maltreatment, 209
 on memory, 239
 menopause and, 489
 in middle childhood, 295–296
 on moral reasoning, 440
 on motor development, 134
 in parental authority, 408
 on parenting, 273–274
 on play, 269
 on popularity, 336–337
 on self-definition, 253
 on shyness and boldness, 184–185
cultural socialization, 395, **395**
culture, 12, **12**
 development influenced by, 12–14
 -fair tests, 302, **302**
 -free tests, 302, **302**
 moral development influenced
  by, 378
 -relevant test, 303, **303**
custody issues, 328–330
CVS. *See* chorionic villus sampling
cyberbullying, 341
cytosine, 56, 56*f*

data collection
 basic research designs, 41–43, 41*t*
 behavioral and performance
  measures, 38*t*, 39–40
 forms for research methods, 38–45
 laboratory observation, 38*t*, 39
 naturalistic observation, 38*t*, 39
 self-reports, 38–39, 38*t*
David and Lucile Packard
  Foundation, 209, 210
deafness, 169
death. *See also* bereavement; suicide
 AD related to, 571
 in adolescence, 370
 adolescence understanding of,
  625–626, 627*t*, 628–629
 from AIDS, 432
 attitudes toward, 624–626, 628–629
 in Buddhism, 618, 633
 care for grieving, 624, 624*t*
 cell, 121, **121**
 child understanding of, 223–225,
  625–626, 626*t*–627*t*, 628–629
 of children, 226, 227, 632–633
 cognitive changes before, 620, 622

confronting one's own, 622–623

cultural context, 618–620

dignity-conserving interventions, 621*t*

emerging and young adulthood understanding of, 627*t*

facing loss from, 620, 622–629

of father, 631–632, 631*t*

grieving patterns, 623–624

hastening, 636–641

from heart disease, 492

during infancy, 110–113

in infancy, 110–113

from maltreatment, 208*f*

in marriage, 630

meanings of, 618–620, 641–643

medical and legal issues, 634–640

miscarriage mourning, 633

mortality revolution, 619–620

of mothers, 631–632, 631*t*

near, experience, 622

of parent, 631–632, 631*t*

physical changes before, 620, 622

of sibling, 613

significant losses, 629–633

smoking, obesity, and alcohol related to, 424

social relationships and, 630

surviving spouse, 629–631

toddlerhood understanding of, 626*t*–627*t*

Death with Dignity Act, 639

decenter, 231, **231**

declarative knowledge, 374, **374**

decoding, 308, **308**

deductive reasoning, 294, **294**

defects

birth, 62*t,* 79*f,* 82, 86, 111

sex-linked inheritance, 63, **63**

deferred imitation, 150, **150,** 229

dehydroepiandrosterone (DHEA), 356

dementia, **569,** 569–570

dendrites, 121

Denmark, 111*f,* 610

end-of-life decisions in, 640

institutional living of elderly in, 601

Denver Developmental Screening Test, 130, **130**

deoxyribonucleic acid (DNA), 56, **56,** 56*f,* 121

Department of Health and Human Services, 246

dependent variable, 44, **44**

depression

in adolescence, 369–370

childhood, **344,** 344–345

in emerging and young adulthood, 431

genes related to, 423

in late adulthood, 569

postpartum, 196

depth perception, 132, **132**

detachment, 580

determinism

genetic, 67

reciprocal, 30

development, 22–25. *See also* cognitive development; human development; psychosexual development, of Freud, S.; psychosocial development

active or reactive, 23–24

cognitive perspective, 30–33

context of, 10–14

continuous or discontinuous, 24–25

culture, 12–14

domains of, 5–6

environment influencing, 9–10

evolutionary/sociobiological perspective of, 24*t*–25*t,* **35,** 35–36

family context of, 10–11

heredity influencing, 9–10

historical context, 14

human, 4, **4**

individual differences, **8,** 8–9, **9**

in infancy, 188–195

influences of, 8–17

lifelong process of, 642–643

life-span, **4,** 4–5

maturation influencing, 9–10

mechanistic model of, 23, **23**

nonnormative influences, 14–15, **15**

normative influences, **14,** 14–15

organismic model of, **23,** 23–24

race/ethnicity, 12–14

SES influencing, 11–12

timing of influences on, 15–17

developmental quotients (DQs), 144

developmental research designs, 45–48, 45*f*

cross-sectional study, **45,** 45–46, 45*f,* 47*t*

longitudinal study, 45–47, 45*f,* **46,** 47*t*

sequential study, **47,** 47–48, 47*f,* 47*t*

developmental tasks, 458, **458**

developmental tests, **143,** 143–146

devotion, 456

DHEA. *See* dehydroepiandrosterone

diabetes, 86, 492, **492,** 566

diaries, 38–39, 38*t*

differentiation, 121, **121**

"difficult" children, 183, **183,** 183*t*

digital technology, 5, *5*

direct aggression. *See* overt (direct) aggression

disabilities

activity limitations and, 566–567

education of children with, 316

disbelief, 623

discontinuous development, 24–25

disengagement theory, **592,** 592–593

dishabituation, 155, **155**

disorganized-disoriented attachment, 190, **190**

disruptive conduct disorders, 343

divorce, 328–330, 474, 476

adjusting to, 476

cause of, 474, 476

grandparenting after, 543

in late adulthood, 606*f,* 607

in middle adulthood, 533–534

dizygotic twins, 55, **55**

DNA. *See* deoxyribonucleic acid

"do no harm," 638

dominant inheritance, 59, **59,** 59*f,* 63

dominant inheritance of defects, 63

donor egg, 434

Down syndrome, 65, **65**

Down Syndrome Collaborative Group, 65

DQs. *See* developmental quotients

dramatic play, 265, **265,** 266–267

drug therapy, 346, **346**

drugs

adolescent use and abuse of, 366–369, 367*t*

cocaine during prenatal development, 85

in emerging and young adulthood, 430

illicit use of, 430*f*

paternal exposure to, 88

prenatal intake of, 83

teenage, abuse risk factors, 366–369, 367*t*

trends in use of, 366–367, 367*f*

DST. *See* dynamic systems theory

dual representation hypothesis, 153, **153**

dual-income families, 473–474

dual-language learning. *See* two-way (dual-language) learning

durable power of attorney, 637, **637**

dwarfism, 88

dying, 618–620. *See also* death

care of, 620

dignity of, 620

legalized physician aid in, 639–640

understanding, 626*t*–627*t*

dynamic systems theory (DST), 133–134, **134**

dyslexia, 313, **313**

dysmenorrhea, 433

early childhood, 7, 8*t*

air pollution exposure, 226–228

bodily growth and change in, 216–217, 217*t*

brain development in, 220

cognitive development in, 228–247, 228*t*

death understanding in, 626*t*–627*t*

deaths, 223–225

discipline in, **270,** 270–272

eating habits in, 217*t*

education in, 244–247

environmental influences, 225–228

friendships in, 279

gene expression influenced by, 60–61
heredity and, 66, 68–69
prenatal development hazards, 87–88
epidural injection, 100
epigenesis, **60**, 60–61
episodic memory, 238, 578, **578**
equilibration, 31, **31**
ERA. *See* English and Romanian Adoptees
erectile dysfunction, 490, **490**
error theories, 556
estrogens, 259, 488, 489
ethics
of care, 378–379
of research, 48
ethnic gloss, 14, **14**
ethnic group, 12, **12**
ethnicity, 13*f*
adolescence education influenced by, 382–383
adolescent relationships influenced by, 406, 411
aging related to, 551
children's health influenced by, 226
chronic conditions related to, 566
cohabitation relating to, 466–467
college influenced by, 444–445
development influenced by, 12–14
end-of-life decisions related to, 641
friendships in adolescence and, 412
health in middle adulthood influenced by, 493–494
health in young adulthood influenced by, 428
identity development influenced by, 394–395, 395*t*
identity exploration and, 454
infant mortality rate and, 111–113, 112*f*
intelligence influenced by, 301–302
life expectancy related to, 553–555
marriage related to, 467
suicide and, 634
well-being and, 529
ethnographic study, 41, **41**, 41*t*
ethology, 35
European Americans, 42–43, 200, 326
education of, 383
end-of-life decisions of, 641
executive skill development of, 297
family relations of adolescent, 407
identity development of, 394
maternal employment of, 204
physical development of, 284
self-definition of, 253
euthanasia, 637, 639, 640
evolutionary psychology, 35–36
executive function, 237, **237**, **296**, 296–297, **297**
executive stage, of cognitive development, 437
Exelon, 573

exercise, 567–569
exosystem, 34, 34*f*
experiential element, 303, **303**, 438
experimental group, 43, **43**
experiments, 41*t*, **42**, 42–43
laboratory, field, and natural, 44–45
random assignment, 44, **44**
expertise, 505–507
explicit memory, 161, **161**
extended family, 11, **11**, 542–544
external memory aids, 298, **298**, 299*t*
externalizing behaviors, 325, **325**
extramarital relations, 468
extraversion, 459, 588

failure to launch, 538
Failure to Launch, 455
failure to thrive, 207, **207**
faith, developing, 442
family. *See also* extended family; nuclear family
abusive and neglectful, 208–209
adolescence education influenced by, 381
adolescent relationships with, 404–413
adolescent sensitivity to, 409–410
antisocial behavior running in, 413–414
atmosphere, 325
caregivers, 540–541
children within, 324–335
cohabitation of, 331
conflict and individuation, 407
development influences by, 10–11
dual-income, 473–474
-focused lifestyle, 597, **597**
gender development influence of, 263
help for maltreatment in, 209–210
infancy influenced by, 185–187
juvenile delinquency influencing, 414–417
multigenerational, 605
one-parent, 330–331
sibling relationships, 334–335
skip-generation, 543–544
step, 331–332
stress of children and, 349
structure of, 327–328
therapy, 345, **345**
Family and Medical Leave Act, of 1993, 544
fantasy play, 265
fantasy vs. reality, 235
FAS. *See* fetal alcohol syndrome
fast mapping, 242, **242**
fathers, 186–187. *See also* parents
adolescents influenced by, 409
child development influenced by, 328
death of, 631–632, 631*t*
fatuous love, 463*t*
FBI. *See* Federal Bureau of Investigation

fearfulness, 276
Federal Bureau of Investigation (FBI), 414
Federal Interagency Forum on Aging-Related Statistics, 551, 554, 565, 566, 568, 569, 590, 596, 598, 601, 605, 606, 607, 630
Federal Interagency Forum on Child and Family Statistics, 224, 225, 227, 228, 291, 306, 326, 327
fertilization, **54**, 54–55. *See also* in vitro fertilization
fetal alcohol syndrome (FAS), 83–84, **84**
fetal blood sampling, 89*t*
fetal monitoring, 98–99
fetal stage, of development, **80**, 80–81
fetoscopy, 89*t*
fictive kin, 462, **462**, 610
fidelity, 391
field experiments, 44–45
fight or flight, 499
filial crisis, 539, **539**
filial maturity, 539, **539**
finances, in late adulthood, 598
fine motor skills, 130, **130**, 221, **221**
Finland, 604
firearms, 370–371
first grade, 307–308
first sentences, 167–168
first words, 166–167
fitness, in young adulthood, 424–427
five-factor model, **458**, 458–460, 459*f*
continuity and change in, 459–460
evaluating, 460
in late adulthood, 587–589
fixation, 26
flexibility, in thinking, 509–510
fluid intelligence, 505, **505**
FMRI. *See* functional magnetic resonance imaging
foreclosure, 392, **392**, 393*t*
formal games with rules, 266, **266**
formal operations, **372**, 372–373
formula feeding, 116–117, 116*t*
Forteo, 496
Fosamax, 496
Foundation Fighting Blindness, 562
fountain of youth, 552, 560
France
cohabitation in, 465
end-of-life decisions in, 641
fraternal twins, 55
free radicals, 557, **557**
friendships. *See also* social relationships
in adolescence, 412
in early childhood, 279
in emerging and young adulthood, 462
in late adulthood, 609–610
in middle adulthood, 535–536
in middle childhood, 337–338
stages of, 338*t*

information-processing approach,
  24*t*–25*t*, 33, **33**, 154–161, 236–239
  in adolescence, 373–374
  categorization, 158
  causality, 159
  to cognitive development, 140, **140**
  habituation, **154**, 154–155
  as intelligence predictor, 156–158
  memory retention, 237–239
  in middle childhood, 296–299
  object permanence, 160–161
  Piagetian ability development related
    to, 158–161
  Piagetian tasks and, 299
  processes and capacities, 236–237
  recall, 237, **237**
  recognition, 237, **237**
initiative vs. guilt, 256
Institute of Medicine (IOM), 67, 289
instrumental activities of daily living
  (IADLs), 566, **566**
instrumental aggression, 274, **274,**
  338, 339
integration, 121, **121**
integrative thought, 507
integrity vs. despair, 629
intelligence, 239–241
  crystallized, 505, **505**
  eight, of Gardner, 304*t*
  fluid, 505, **505**
  heredity and, 73
  influences on, 300–303
  information processing as predictor
    of, 156–158
  in late adulthood, 574–577
  measured, 240–241
  measuring older adults, 574
  multiple, 303–305
  reaction range and, 70*f*
  testing, 143–146, 303–305
  theory of multiple, 303, **303**
  triarchic theory of, **303,** 303–305,
    438–439
intelligence quotient. *See* IQ
intelligent behavior, 143, **143**
interactive learning, of Vygotsky,
  239, 241
interiority, 520, **520**
internalization, 199, **199**
internalizing behaviors, 325, **325**
International Cesarean Awareness
  Network, 99
International Committee for Monitoring
  Assisted Reproductive
  Technologies (ICMART), 434
International Human Genome
  Sequencing Consortium, 67
International Longevity Center-
  USA, 557, 560
internet, school achievement relating to
  use of, 312–313
interviews, 38–39, 38*t*

intimacy, 463
  in emerging and young adult-
    hood, 461–463
  friendships and, 412
  isolation vs., of Erikson, **456,** 456–
    457, 456*t*
  sibling relationships and, 411
intimate partner violence (IPV), 475
intimate terrorism, 475
Intuitive-projective faith, 442
invisible imitation, 150, **150**
IOM. *See* Institute of Medicine
IPT. *See* identity process theory
IPV. *See* intimate partner violence
IQ
  controversy, 300, 439
  creativity and, 508
  in older adults, 574
  tests, 143, **143**
Ireland, 111, 469
Irish Americans, multigenerational
  families, 605
irreversibility, 232, **232**
ISLAT Working Group, 434
Italy
  economic self-sufficiency in, 446
  end-of-life decisions in, 640, 641
It's a Wonderful Life, 642
IVF. *See* in vitro fertilization
IVM. *See* in vitro maturation

Japan
  aging in, 596
  authority in, 408
  death rituals in, 619, 633
  infants in, 165
  life expectancy in, 555
  living with adult children in,
    600, 601*f*
  menopause in, 489
Japanese Americans, 489, 618
jaundice, neonatal, 102, **102**
Javanese, of Indonesia, 218
joint custody, 329–330
Judaism, cremation in, 619
justice, 48
juvenile delinquency
  in adolescence, 413–417
  long-term prospects, 416
  preventing, 417

K-ABC-II. *See* Kaufman Assessment
  Battery for Children
Kaiser Family Foundation, 398,
  399, 401
kangaroo care, 107, **107**
karyotype, 66, 66*f*
Kaufman Assessment Battery for
  Children (K-ABC-II), 305, **305**
kindergarten, 246–247
kinship care, 544, **544**
Klinefelter syndrome, 63

knowledge
  about communication, 306
  about objects and space, 151–154
  conceptual, 374, **374**
  declarative, 374, **374**
  procedural, 374, **374**
  tacit, 04, 304, **304,** 438

labor, 97–98
laboratory
  experiments, 44–45
  observation, 38*t*, 39
LAD. *See* language acquisition device
Lamaze method, of childbirth, 100
language, **163**
  acquisition, 16
  in adolescence, 374–375
  to communicate, 229
  delayed development of, 243
  early childhood development of,
    241–244
  early speech characteristics, 168
  early vocalization, 164
  first sentences, 167–168
  first words, 166–167
  gestures, 165–166
  grammar and syntax, 242–243,
    305–306
  in infancy and toddlerhood, 163–173
  influences on development of,
    170–172
  literacy preparation, 244
  in middle childhood, 305–307
  milestones from birth to 3 years, 164*t*
  nature-nurture debate, 168–170
  pragmatics and social speech, 243, **243**
  second-, learning, 306–307
  sound and structure perception, 165
  vocabulary, 241–242, 305–306
language acquisition device (LAD),
  169, **169**
late adulthood, 9*t*
  adult children relationships in,
    610–612
  aging brain in, 561–562
  balance in, 564
  cognitive development in, 574–581
  cohabitation in, 608–609
  depression in, 569
  divorce in, 606*f*, 607
  encoding in, 580
  finances in, 598
  homosexual relationships in, 609
  lifestyle influences on health and
    longevity, 567–569
  living arrangements in, 599–603, 602*t*
  longevity and aging, 552–560
  marital relationships in, 605–607
  memory in, 577–580
  mental and behavioral problems
    in, 569–574
  mistreatment in, 611

models of successful or optimal aging, 591–595

neurological changes in, 579

nonmarital kinship ties in, 610–613

nonmarital lifestyles and relationships, 608–610

organic and systemic changes, 560

parents in, 610–612

personal relationships in, 603–605

personality traits in, 587–589

physical changes in, 560–565

physical health in, 565–574

practical and social issues related to aging, 595–603

problem solving, 576

processing abilities in, 574–577

productivity in, 597

psychomotor functioning in, 563–565

psychosocial development in, 585–615

reaction time in, 564

relationships in, 608

remarriage in, 607

retirement trends, 595–596

retrieval in, 580

sensory and psychomotor functioning, 562–565

sexuality, 565

sibling relationships in, 612–613

single life in, 608

sleep in, 564–565

social relationships in, 604–605

social support in, 604

socioemotional selectivity theory in, 609, 610

stability in, 587–588

storage in, 580

strength in, 564

vision in, 562

well-being in, 589–596

wisdom in, 580–581

lateralization, 119, **119**

Latino Americans

cognitive development of, 297

family values of, 324

identity development of, 394

intelligence and, 301, 311

living with adult children, 600

parenting of, 382

poverty of, 225

sexual activity of, 398

sibling relationships of, 411

socioeconomic status of, 225

laughing, 180

LCUs. *See* life changing units

LDs. *See* learning disabilities

lead, 226–228

learning disabilities (LDs), 313–314, **314**

learning perspective, of development, 24*t*–25*t*, **28**, 28–30

behaviorism, 28, **28**

classical conditioning, 28, 29, **29**, 141, **141**, 142*f*

operant conditioning, 28, **29**, 29–30, 141, **141**

social cognitive theory, 30, **30**, 258*t*, 262, **262**

learning problems, 313–317

learning theory, traditional, 24*t*–25*t*

LeBoyer method, of childbirth, 100

legacy-creating stage, of cognitive development, 437

lesbian relationships. *See* homosexuality

life

meaning of, 641–643

review, 629, 642, **642**

satisfaction, 527–528

span, 552, **552**

-span development, **4**, 4–5, 6–8, 17–18, 437–438

structure, 457, **457**

Life Changes Stress Test, 499

life changing units (LCUs), 499, 501

life expectancy, 552, **552**

trends and factors in, 553–555, 553*f*

lifestyle influences

on AD, 572

on health and longevity, 567–569

liking, 463*t*

linguistic speech, 166, **166**

literacy, **172**, 172–173, 244, 308–313, 511, **511**

Little Albert case study, 29, 48

living arrangements, in late adulthood, 599–603, 599*f*

with adult children, 600–601

aging in place, **599**, 599–600

alone, 600

alternate housing arrangements, 602–603, 602*t*

in institutions, 601–602

living will, 637

locomotion, 131–132

locomotor reflexes, 124

longevity, **552**

aging and, 552–560

animal research on, 558

lifestyle influences on health and, 567–569

longitudinal study, 45–47, 45*f*, **46**, 47*t*

long-term marriage, 605–607

long-term memory, 237, **237**, 578

love, 456

in emerging and young adulthood, 462–463

patterns of, 463*t*

romantic, 463*t*

triangular theory of, 462, **462**

withdrawal of, 271, **271**

low birth weight, 105–108, **106**

likelihood of, 106–107

long-term outcomes, 107–108

treatment and outcomes, 107

MacArthur Successful Aging Study, 606

macrosystem, 34, 34*f*

magical thinking, 235

magnetic resonance imaging (MRI), *40*

male sexual functioning, 490

maltreatment

of children, 207–210

deaths from, 208*f*

ecological view, 208–210

emotional, 208, **208**

help for families in trouble, 209–210

long-term effects of, 210

mammography, 496–497, **497**

manual dexterity, 485, 563*t*

March of Dimes Birth Defects Foundation, 66, 85

March of Dimes Foundation, 79, 86

marijuana

in adolescence, 367–369

during prenatal development, 85

marital capital, 533, **533**

marriage, 429. *See also* cohabitation

companionate model of, 470

death during, 630

in emerging and young adulthood, 463–470

ending, 474, 476

equity model, 470

happiness in, 469–470

institutional model of, 470

in late adulthood, 605–607

long-term, 605–607

in middle adulthood, 532–536

parenthood related to, 472–473

same-sex, 465

satisfaction in, 469–470

sexuality after, 468–469

success factors, 470

in US, 468*f*

well-being and health related to, 534

maternal blood test, 89*t*

maternal employment, 205–207

math

advancement, 231

in middle childhood, 295

maturation, 10, **10**

of children in middle adulthood, 536–538

cognitive, 422

maturity

filial, 539, **539**

post, 108, **108**

sexual, 357–360, 422

Max Planck Institute, 580–581

Mayer-Salovey-Caruso Emotional Intelligence Test (MSCEIT), 439

MD. *See* multi-infarct dementia

mechanistic model, of development, 23, **23**, 24

media violence, 340–341

Medicare, 598, 611

medicated delivery, 99–101

morality of conventional role conformity, 376t, 377, **377**

moratorium, 393, **393**, 393t

mortality, and cognitive abilities, 577

mortality revolution, 619–620

motherese, 172

mothers, 185. *See also* parents
    age at first birth in US, 471f
    death of, 631–632, 631t
    employment of, impacting adolescence, 410
    siblings influenced by, 411
    surrogate, 434
    teenage, 402–404

motor development
    in infancy and toddlerhood, 129–134
    in middle childhood, 286–288, 287t
    milestones, 130–132, 131t

motor skills, 220–222, 220t
    artistic development, 222, 222f
    handedness, 221, **221**

Mount Everest, 567

MRI. *See* magnetic resonance imaging

MSCEIT. *See* Mayer-Salovey-Caruso Emotional Intelligence Test

MTA Cooperative Group, 315, 316

multifactorial transmission, 60, **60**

multigenerational family, 605

multi-infarct dementia (MD), 570

multiple births, 55–56

multiple dimensions in well-being, 528–529, 529t

multiple intelligence theory, of Gardner, 303
    eight intelligences, 304t

multiple solutions, 436

Muslims, death rituals of, 619

mutations, 59, **59**

mutual regulation, 195, **195**

myelination, 122, **122**

myopia, 484, **484**

myth-literal faith, 442

NAEP. *See* National Assessment of Educational Progress

NAGC. *See* National Association for Gifted Children

Namenda, 573

narrative psychology, 525–526

National Assessment of Educational Progress (NAEP), 311, 312

National Association for Gifted Children (NAGC), 316

National Association of State Boards of Education, 289

National Cancer Institute, 497

National Center for Biotechnology Information (NCBI), 425

National Center for Education Statistics (NCES), 205, 244, 246, 290, 307, 311, 312, 316, 328, 354, 380, 415, 443, 444, 445, 447, 510, 511

National Center for Health Statistics (NCHS), 55, 90, 111, 225, 290, 313, 315, 344, 363, 371, 423, 425, 426, 428, 491, 492, 494, 495, 553, 554, 566, 634

National Center for Immunization and Respiratory Diseases, 114

National Center for Injury Prevention and Control (NCIPC), 370

National Center for Learning Disabilities, 314

National Center on Elder Abuse, 611

National Children's Study, 47

National Clearinghouse on Child Abuse and Neglect Information (NCCANI), 210

National Coalition for the Homeless, 225, 226

National Council on Aging, 482, 577, 603

National Highway Traffic Safety Administration, 370

National Hospice and Palliative Care Organization, 620

National Institute of Child Health and Human Development (NICHD)
    child care study, 206–207
    Early Child Care Research Network, 194, 196, 204, 205, 207, 240, 244, 296, 297, 312, 326

National Institute of Mental Health (NIMH), 16, 285, 347, 348, 361, 371, 569, 634

National Institute of Neurological Disorders and Stroke (NINDS), 122

National Institute on Aging (NIA), 427, 495, 496, 556, 564, 568, 569, 570

National Institute on Alcohol Abuse and Alcoholism (NIAAA), 430

National Institute on Drug Abuse (NIDA), 368

National Institutes of Health (NIH), 62, 464, 468, 487, 488, 489, 490, 495, 496, 497
    Consensus Development Panel on Osteoporosis Prevention, Diagnosis, and Therapy, 495

National Institutes of Health Consensus Development Panel, 103

National Law Center on Homelessness and Poverty, 225

National Library of Medicine, 343

National Literacy Act, 511

National Mental Health Association, 624

National Parents' Resource Institute for Drug Education, 368

National Reading Panel, 308, 309

National Research Council (NRC), 209, 210, 330, 385

National Sleep Foundation, 218, 285, 426

Native Americans, 13, 111, 371
    death rituals of, 619
    health in middle adulthood of, 493
    organ donation of, 638
    suicide and, 634

nativism, 169, **169**

natural childbirth, 99, 99–101

natural experiments, 44–45

naturalistic observation, 38t, 39

Naturally Occurring Retirement Communities (NORCs), 600

nature/nurture, 10
    canalization, 70, **70**
    debate, 168–170
    genotype-environmental correlation, 71, **71**
    genotype-environmental interaction, **70**, 70–71
    heredity and environment, 66, 68–74
    reaction range, 69, **69**
    siblings in nonshared environment, 71–72

NBAS. *See* Brazelton Neonatal Behavioral Assessment Scale

NCBI. *See* National Center for Biotechnology Information

NCCANI. *See* National Clearinghouse on Child Abuse and Neglect Information

NCES. *See* National Center for Education Statistics

NCHS. *See* National Center for Health Statistics

NCIPC. *See* National Center for Injury Prevention and Control

NCLB. *See* No Child Left Behind Act, of 2001

near death experience, 622

negativism, 198

neglect, 207–210, **208**

neonatal jaundice, 102, **102**

neonatal period, 101, **101**

neonatal screening, 103–104

neonate, 101, **101**

neo-Piagetian theories, 33

Netherlands, 465, 640, 641

neural connections
    before and after birth, 125f
    growth during first 2 years, 124f

neurofibrillary tangles, 571, **571**

neurons, 120, **120**

neuroticism, 459, 588

neurotransmitters, 121

New York Longitudinal Study (NYLS), 182–183, 183t

New Zealand, 460
    adult relationships with parents in, 455
    cohabitation in, 465
    reading to children in, 173
    stress and health in, 501

passive euthanasia, 637, **637**
passive vocabulary, 167
Pearson Education, 414
pedestrian safety, 563*t*
pedunal block, 100
peekaboo, 152
peers
    adolescence education influenced
        by, 382–383
    adolescence emotional support
        and, 411–413
    aggression and bullying, 338–342
    antisocial, 415
    friendships, 337–338, 338*t*
    gender development influence
        of, 263–264
    influences of, 335
    juvenile delinquency influenced
        by, 414–417
    in middle childhood, 335–342
    moral development influenced
        by, 378
    popularity, 336–337
    positive and negative influences
        of, 335
    school achievement relating to, 311
    sexual information from, 399
penis envy, 26
perceptions, 154–161, 234
    depth, 132, **132**
    haptic, 132, **132**
    motor development and, 132
    visual and auditory, 155–156
perimenopause, 487, **487**
periodontitis, 569
permissive parenting, 272, **272**, 382
personality, 178, **178**
personality development, 28
    in emerging and young adulthood,
        456–461
    heredity and, 73–74
    in middle adulthood, 527
    normative issues and tasks, of
        Erikson, 587
    normative-stage models, 456, **456**, 456*t*
    theory and research, 586–589
    traits in old age, 587–589
Peru, 459
pesticides, 226–228
PET. *See* positron emission tomography
phallic stage, 26, 27*t*
phenotypes, 60, **60**
phenylketonuria (PKU), 103–104
phobia, school, 344, **344**
phonetic (code-emphasis) approach,
    308, **308**
physical abuse, 207, **207**
physical activity
    in adolescence, 362
    dementia aided by, 570
    in emerging and young adulthood,
        425–426

health influenced by, 567–568
    in middle adulthood, 492
    sleep and, 565
physical changes
    before death, 620, 622
    in late adulthood, 560–565
    in middle adulthood, 484–491
physical development, **5**, 8*t*
    in adolescence, 356–371
    in infancy and toddlerhood, 95–136
    in late adulthood, 552–574
    in middle adulthood, 484–502
    in middle childhood, 284–292
    in young adulthood, 423–434
physician aid in dying, legalized, 639–640
Piagetian approach, to cognitive
    development, **140**
pictorial competence, 152–154
PKU. *See* phenylketonuria
placenta, 78, 79*f*
plasticity, 17, **17**, 127, **127**
play, 229
    cognitive levels of, 265–267
    culture influencing, 269
    dramatic, 265, **265**, 266–267
    in early childhood, 264–269
    evolutionary basis of, 266
    gender influencing, 269
    in middle childhood, 286–287
    of Parten, 267, 268*t*
    pretend, 229, **229**, 265, 268
    recess-time, 287–288
    rough-and-tumble, 287, **288**
    social dimension of, 267–269
    therapy, 346, **346**
pleasure principle, 26
PMS. *See* premenstrual syndrome
Poland, 465
polygenic inheritance, 59, **59**
popularity, 336–337
Population Reference Bureau, 110
positron emission tomography
    (PET), 40, 573, *573*
postconventional morality, 376*t*,
    377, **377**
postformal thought, **435**, 435–437
postmaturity, 108, **108**
postpartum depression, 196
postural reflexes, 124
poverty, 25, 225, 493
    development influenced by,
        11–12, 11*t*
    parenting and, 326–327
power assertion, 271, **271**
pragmatics, 243, **243**, 306, **306**, 436
preconception care, 91
preconventional morality, 375, **375**, 376*t*
pregnancy. *See also* miscarriage
    symptoms of, 75*t*
    teenage, 402–404, 403*f*
preimplantation genetic diagnosis, 89*t*
prejudice, 335, **335**

prelinguistic period, 171
prelinguistic speech, 163, **163**
premenstrual syndrome (PMS), **432**,
    432–433
prenatal development, 8*t*, 75–88,
    76*t*–77*t*, 78*f*
    alcohol taken during, 83–84
    assessment techniques, 89*t*
    caffeine during, 84–85
    care disparities, 90
    drugs taken during, 83
    embryonic stage, **79**, 79–80
    fetal stage, **80**, 80–81
    germinal stage, 75, **75**, 78–79
    maternal age, 87
    maternal diseases influencing, 85–86
    maternal factors influencing, 82–88
    maternal malnutrition, 83
    maternal nutrition and weight, 82–83
    maternal stress and anxiety, 86–87
    medical drugs taken during, 83
    monitoring and promoting, 89–91
    nicotine during, 84
    no care during, 91*f*
    non-prescription drugs, 85
    outside environmental hazards, 87–88
    paternal factors, 88
    sperm influencing, 88
preoperational stage, of development,
    228, 228–236, 228*t*, 229*t*
    advances in, 229–231
    causality understanding, 230
    conservation, 232, **232**, 233*t*
    egocentrism, **231**, 231–232
    identities and categorization, 230
    immature aspects of, 231–232
    numbers, 231
    objects in space, 230
    symbolic function, 229, **229**
    theories of mind, **233**, 233–236
prepared childbirth, **99**, 99–101
presbycusis, 484, **484**
presbyopia, 484, **484**
preschools, 245–246. *See also* early
    childhood
pretend play, 229, **229**, 265, 268
preterm (premature) infants, **105**,
    105–106
primary aging, 552, **552**
primary sex characteristics, 357, **357**
primitive reflexes, 124
private speech, 243, **243**
problem definition, 436
problem solving, 576
problem-faced coping, 590, **590**
procedural knowledge, 374, **374**
procedural memory, 578, **578**
process-product shift, 436
productivity
    in late adulthood, 597
    and well-being, 593–594
Project CARE, 145

Age	Physical Developments	Neurological Developments	Cognitive Developments	Language Developments	Emotional Developments	Social Developments	Self/Gender/ Identity Developments	Moral Developments
7–8 years	Balance and control of body improve. Speed and throwing ability improve.	Elimination of unneeded synapses occurs.	Stage of concrete operations begins. Child understands cause and effect, seriation, transitive inference, class inclusion, inductive reasoning, and conservation. Processing of more than one task at a time becomes easier.	Pragmatic skills improve.	Child is aware of own pride or shame.	Rough-and-tumble play is common in boys, as a way to jockey for dominance.	Self-concept is more balanced and realistic. Sense of self-worth becomes explicit.	Moral reasoning is increasingly flexible. Empathic and prosocial behavior increase. Aggression, especially hostile type, declines.
9–11 years	Average girl begins to show pubertal changes, then begins adolescent growth spurt.	Elimination of unneeded synapses continues into adolescence.	Ability to consider multiple perspectives increases. Memory strategies improve.	Understanding of syntax and sentence structure is more sophisticated. Private speech tapers off. Main growth is in pragmatic skills.	Understanding and regulation of emotions increases. Child better understands difference between guilt and shame.	Parent and child share regulation of conduct. Sibling conflicts aid in development of skills for conflict resolution. Friendships become more intimate.	Body image becomes increasingly important, especially for girls.	Moral reasoning is increasingly guided by sense of justice. Child wants to be "good" to maintain social order. Aggression shifts to relational.
12–15 years	Average boy enters puberty, shows adolescent growth spurt.	Frontal lobes are not yet fully developed; processing of information may occur in temporal lobe areas involved with emotional and instinctual reactions.	Adolescent may achieve stage of formal operations; use of abstractions and hypothetical-deductive reasoning. Memory span extends to six digits.	Main growth continues to be in pragmatic skills. Teenage slang is a marker of identity development.	Mood swings may become increasingly frequent; may include feelings of embarrassment, self-consciousness, loneliness, and depression.	Growing desire for autonomy coexists with need for parental intimacy and support. Parent-child conflicts peak.	Identity development becomes central issue. Sexual identity becomes a primary concern.	Moral reasoning reflects increasing awareness of equity and cooperative rule-making.
16–20 years	Following puberty, circadian timing system and biological rhythms shift, affecting sleep-wake cycles. Boys and girls reach virtually full height.	Connections among cortical cells continue to improve, even into adulthood. Parts of the cortex controlling attention and memory are nearly completely myelinated. Myelination of parts of the hippocampus continues to increase during adulthood.	Ability to use hypothetical-deductive reasoning increases. Knowledge base continues to grow.	Adolescent understands about 80,000 words.	Mood swings become less frequent and intense. Adolescent is increasingly able to express own emotions and understand feelings of others.	Independence from parents increases. Sibling relationships become more equal, less intense, and less close. Friendships are more intimate than at any other period. Intimacy may shift to romantic relationships.	Most adolescents have engaged in sexual activity.	Relativism may play a key role in moral reasoning.